THE LOWEST EBB

THE LOWEST EBB

Norman Thomas & America's Minor Parties in 1944

Darcy G. Richardson

Sevierville Publishing

The Lowest Ebb
Norman Thomas & America's Minor Parties in 1944

Copyright © 2019 by Darcy G. Richardson

All rights reserved. No part of this book may be used or reproduced by any means, graphic, electronic, or mechanical, including photocopying, recording, taping or by any information storage retrieval system without the written permission of the publisher and the author except in the case of brief quotations embodied in critical articles and reviews.

Sevierville Publishing

ISBN: 9780692316801

Printed in the United States of America

Dedicated to longtime ballot access champion Richard Winger and other unsung heroes, both living and dead, who have labored tirelessly for the cause of fair and open politics in the United States

Contents

Introduction		i
Chapter I	A Reluctant Rebel	13
Chapter II	The Country's Conscience	34
Chapter III	Keeping the Faith	63
Chapter IV	Long Distance Runner	93
Chapter V	"Such a Little Man, So Big a Depression"	125
Chapter VI	Factionalism & Fascism	151
Chapter VII	Battling a Radio Priest	186
Chapter VIII	Keep America Out of War	204
Chapter IX	Flirting with America First	247
Chapter X	The Loneliest Quest	279
Chapter XI	"A Grim Experience"	303
Chapter XII	The "Great Jasper" Returns	333
Chapter XIII	A New Party with Big Dreams	368
Chapter XIV	A Colorful Dry Crusader	407
Chapter XV	Slim Pickings	436
Chapter XVI	"The Noblest Spartan Band in the Land"	465
Chapter XVII	A Steelworker for President	490
Chapter XVIII	Rumbling on the Right	515
Chapter XIX	"The Great Flop of 1944"	546
Chapter XX	The Draft Byrd Movement	579
Chapter XXI	A Minor Southern Revolt	613
Chapter XXII	The Texas Regulars	632
Chapter XXIII	A Couple of Last Hurrahs	672
Chapter XXIV	The Indispensable Man	703
Appendices		722
Bibliography		755
Index		763

Introduction

While sitting next to a young soldier in a crowded club car as their train sped across the Kansas plains, the Socialist Party's Norman M. Thomas was mildly startled by a question innocently posed by his young traveling companion who had just returned from active duty in the United Kingdom. "Sir, if I may ask you — and, of course, you don't have to answer, who are you going to vote for in the next election? I've been away so long I don't rightly know the score."

The soldier, who was on leave and returning to Texas to visit his mother, had no idea that Thomas was a presidential candidate. "Well," replied Thomas with a slight grin, "this may surprise you, but I'm going to vote for myself." Thomas then introduced himself and explained that he was the Socialist Party's candidate for president. Though obviously taken aback by Thomas's unexpected reply, the soldier hesitated for a moment and then asked, "But sir, suppose you weren't a candidate, or didn't think you could be elected, which of the others would you vote for?"

That brief exchange pretty much summed up life on the campaign trail not only for Thomas, but for each of the minor-party candidates seeking the nation's highest office in 1944. For those challenging the duopoly in wartime America, it was an uphill struggle so steep that it was almost a vertical climb.

Throughout our nation's history, the American people have been more receptive to dissenting voices during tumultuous periods, especially moments of profound economic or social crisis, than in more tranquil times. Occasionally given expression through the country's nationally-organized minor parties, those usually faint yet frequently prophetic voices — the chorus of angels from the antislavery movement during the antebellum era to the relatively short-lived Populist and Progressive movements of the late nineteenth and early twentieth centuries — have often gained popular support, profoundly influencing the course of American history.

That was particularly true during the early years of the Great Depression, a devastating and destructive global economic crisis caused by the reckless policies of a small clique of leading central bankers acting on behalf of the world's financial oligarchy led by the Bank of England's manipulative and mysterious Montagu C. Norman and his willing accomplices on J.P. Morgan-dominated Wall Street, when spontaneous and vibrant third-party movements took hold in New York City, Minnesota, Wisconsin and elsewhere.

Moreover, the once-robust Socialist Party of the late Eugene V. Debs, increasingly viewed as a viable alternative in an atmosphere of widespread joblessness, hunger, and needless suffering engendered by the stock market crash of 1929 and the ensuing and seemingly never-ending economic depression, was again showing signs of life in the early thirties.

A dozen years later, things were quite different for the nation's alternative parties. With more than eleven million American men and women in uniform and relentless around-the-clock Allied bombing of Berlin as a backdrop, the presidential campaign of 1944 — conducted during a deadly conflict that claimed the lives of nearly 417,000 U.S. soldiers and more than 60 million people across the globe, including more than 23 million citizens of the Soviet Union who not only endured the largest and bloodiest theater of war in history, but made the greatest sacrifice in thwarting the Axis Powers and ultimately defeating fascism — war-weary Americans paid precious little attention to the minor-party candidates running for president that year.

Anticipating victory against Nazi Germany and Japan while anxiously prepared for a post-war nation that might or might not resemble the United States prior to December 7, 1941, the much-heralded "Greatest Generation," clinging fiercely to the same tired yet familiar duopoly that never adequately pulled the country out of the deepest economic depression in the nation's history prior to the war, could have cared less about any of the minor-party candidates seeking the highest office in the land or what their visions of post-war America might look like.

Sadly, a majority of the American people were insufferably indifferent to what anybody other than President Franklin D. Roosevelt, who — against seemingly impossible odds — had performed

INTRODUCTION

an extraordinarily heroic task in alleviating much of the country's economic misery during the darkest days of the depression, and Republican challenger Tom Dewey, a young former prosecutor making his second bid for the White House, had to say about the postwar nation that had become the world's "arsenal of democracy."

Completely ignoring the country's alternative voices at the close of war, the vast majority of Americans just wanted life in the United States to return to normal, or as close to normal as possible in a world famously described by Life magazine's Henry Luce some ten months before Pearl Harbor as the "the first great American century."

Coupled with the merger of Minnesota's once-powerful Farmer-Labor Party and that state's Democratic Party earlier that year and the virtual collapse of the once-potent Progressive Party in neighboring Wisconsin, the 1944 presidential election proved to be an unusually lean year for the nation's minor parties — "that phantom," to borrow a particularly perceptive phrase from early twentieth century historian James A. Woodburn, "which makes the two-party system workable."

To the extent there was any such threat to Roosevelt's reelection that year from outside the duopoly it came from former Secretary of War and ex-Kansas Gov. Harry Woodring's aborted attempt to launch a nationally-organized Commonwealth Party of America and later by the creation of the deceptively-named "American Democratic National Committee" (ADNC), an organization briefly chaired by the conservative Kansan, but later headed by Gleason Archer, Sr., the founder of Suffolk University in Boston. Former Democratic congressman John J. O'Connor of New York, who had been famously purged by FDR in 1938 and was still nursing a grudge of gargantuan proportions, emerged as one of the group's leading spokesmen.

Despite their futile efforts to recruit a well-known challenger to oppose Roosevelt for the Democratic nomination — more than a dozen prominent Democrats were approached that winter and spring, including Joseph B. Ely, a fiscally conservative former governor of Massachusetts who waged a forlorn favorite-son candidacy against FDR in the Bay State's Democratic presidential primary in late April — the anti-New Deal Democrats later flirted with the idea of mounting a national third-party effort led by the colorful Sen. W. Lee "Pappy" O'Daniel, but the junior senator from Texas, one of the New Deal's most outspoken critics, decided against mounting what almost certainly would have been a fruitless candidacy.

They also briefly floated a trial balloon promoting a potential bipartisan "coalition" ticket comprised of Republican Gov. John W. Bricker of Ohio, a prewar isolationist who campaigned tirelessly as Thomas Dewey's vice-presidential running mate later that year, and Virginia Sen. Harry F. Byrd, Sr., an ultraconservative states' rights Democrat highly critical of the New Deal.

Failing in those objectives, but still determined to deny Roosevelt a fourth term, the Roosevelt haters then focused on a scheme to deny the president an Electoral College majority by fielding southern-based unpledged electoral tickets friendly to the reluctant Byrd — a favorite of southern white supremacists — in the general election, and by organizing and actively promoting "Democrats for Dewey" organizations throughout the rest of the country. Their stated purpose was to throw the election into the House of Representatives, where the South would potentially hold the balance of power in determining the next president.

While little of this panned out for them, there were a few promising developments for the anti-Roosevelt Democrats in the summer and fall of 1944, the most intriguing and potentially puissant of which involved the amply-financed Texas Regulars, a short-lived reactionary movement that attracted the support of an interesting cavalcade of leading Democratic Lone Star politicians troubled by the administration's friendliness to organized labor and deeply distressed by the demise of white supremacy, particularly the landmark *Smith v. Allwright* U.S. Supreme Court decision outlawing the party's all-white primary earlier that spring.

In addition to the anti-Roosevelt uprising in Texas, which was lavishly funded by deep-pocketed oil and gas interests opposed to federal rationing policies during the war, there was also plenty of speculation that spring and summer about the possibility of fielding independent electoral slates in numerous other southern states.

Despite those occasional glimmers of hope, the ADNC's determined attempt to reclaim the Democratic Party from the New Dealers and restore conservative, constitutional government to the United States by denying FDR a fourth term turned out to be "The Great Flop of 1944." A once-promising movement closely watched by an increasingly worried White House and by the president's anxious supporters on Capitol Hill had been rendered virtually impotent by the almost inexplicable hesitancy of those who might have led its cause.

As the conservative Democratic rebellion fizzled, Roosevelt's reelection was all but assured. That might not have been the case if the immensely popular O'Daniel, who personally raised a relatively impressive $313,000 — the equivalent of more than $4.3 million today — while barnstorming the country in an effort to defeat Roosevelt that year, had agreed to mount an insurgent third-party candidacy from the right.

The conservative Texan, after all, had won four straight statewide elections in a span of only four years, defeating some of the state's most prominent and powerful Democratic politicians in twice gaining the governorship and later winning his Senate seat in 1941 by narrowly defeating New Deal congressman Lyndon B. Johnson and several others in a highly controversial special election. Despite spirited opposition from former governors James Allred and Dan Moody, "Pass-the-biscuits, Pappy" was elected to a full six-year term in the U.S. Senate the following year.

Though O'Daniel's political fortunes would change dramatically a few years later, the former flour salesman — a household name throughout the state for more than a decade — was virtually invincible in Texas during this period.

Few could have tapped into the anti-New Deal, anti-fourth term sentiment prevalent in the South that year like O'Daniel, a folksy political outsider who had famously remarked a few years earlier that "Washington is the only insane asylum in the world run by its own inmates" and had once called Roosevelt a greater menace than Hitler. His candidacy certainly would have received some serious national attention.

As a third-party candidate with an impresario's flair for generating publicity, the former hillbilly music radio host might have been a genuine factor in the November election and — at a minimum — presumably would have given FDR all kinds of fits in one-party Texas, possibly even putting that state's 23 presidential electors in doubt.

The same thing might have been true if Virginia's Harry F. Byrd, throwing caution to the wind, had enthusiastically consented to an independent electoral strategy designed to deny FDR the support of the "Solid South," thereby forcing the increasingly preoccupied and fatigued president to fight for that region's support — something he clearly never had to worry about during his three previous campaigns for the presidency.

As the state's chief executive, Byrd significantly cut government spending, leaving the Old Dominion with a huge surplus, and was later credited with eliminating nearly $2 billion in wasteful federal spending as a U.S. Senator during the New Deal — both of which made him a hero to fiscal conservatives in both parties.

Concerned that his seniority on the Hill would be seriously jeopardized if he decided to formally break with the Democratic Party — a hesitancy that haunted the cherry-cheeked Shenandoah Valley apple grower throughout much of his Senate career — the congenial former newspaper publisher was flattered by the attention, but shrewdly resisted the spirited "Draft Byrd" movement spearheaded by New Orleans industrialist John U. Barr that year.

An unapologetic segregationist who later urged "massive resistance" to the racial integration of public schools throughout the South following the historic 1954 U.S. Supreme Court ruling in *Brown v. Board of Education*, the frugal Virginian was widely respected by southern Democrats and could have potentially altered the dynamics of the 1944 presidential election not only in Virginia, where his own political machine was dominant, but also in South Carolina, Alabama, Mississippi and Louisiana — the latter four states carried by Dixiecrat Strom Thurmond in 1948 — and possibly in Georgia and elsewhere.

Relieved that a southern insurrection never materialized, Roosevelt obviously wasn't the least bit concerned about the minor-party candidates who actually entered the race that year, none of whom stood a puncher's chance against the popular wartime chief executive.

Though his minor-party rivals, particularly the Socialist Party's Norman M. Thomas, often had far more profound and substantive things to say than FDR's youthful and energetic Republican opponent, a "me-too candidate" almost single-mindedly focused on the "tired old men" in Washington, meaning — without ever quite saying it — the president himself, in the minds of most Americans the 1944 presidential election was strictly a contest between President Roosevelt and GOP challenger Thomas E. Dewey.

Demonstrating its awesome power and military might around the globe, America had little time for any "doubting Thomas" in its midst. Having swung noticeably to the right during the 1942 mid-term elections, a year when the GOP picked up 47 House seats and added nine members to the Senate, the United States didn't appear to be a particularly friendly or inviting place for somebody such as Norman Thomas, the dignified, urbane and principled wartime dove and "Conscience of America" who once again answered the fire bell — for the fifth consecutive time — reluctantly agreeing to carry his left-wing party's tattered banner in that year's extraordinarily difficult campaign.

With a combination of weariness and optimism, the 59-year-

INTRODUCTION

old Thomas, who gave up his preacher's pulpit to spend a lifetime fighting for democratic socialism, knew it would be a tremendously difficult campaign, but was determined to keep his party's flame burning. A general without an army that year, the lanky, white-haired Socialist, in an unusually lugubrious mood following the election, described it as a "grim" experience, but later maintained that he was perhaps more proud of his 1944 effort than any of his other five campaigns for the presidency.

Attorney Darlington Hoopes, a Quaker and former state legislator from Reading, Pennsylvania, who would later lead the increasingly inconsequential Socialist ticket in two national campaigns during some of the party's bleakest years in the 1950s, proudly galloped along with Thomas that year.

While FDR regarded the 1944 presidential election as "the meanest campaign of his life," the same thing might have been doubly true for the battle-scarred Thomas, who repeatedly reminded his audiences that the United States was "winning the war, but losing the peace."

Running on a platform opposed to any appeasement of Nazi Germany, fascist Italy, and the Japanese Empire, yet highly critical of Roosevelt's insistence on an "unconditional surrender" — an idea initially proposed by Wall Street's Council on Foreign Relations — the dovish Socialist candidate argued that based on the president's handling of pre-war issues, there was "no reason to accept the indispensability of the Roosevelt administration for handling the peace." Until Pearl Harbor, of course, Thomas had vigorously opposed U.S. entry in World War II.

Partitioning Germany and turning much of Europe over to Stalin — inexorably setting the stage for the ensuing Cold War — coupled with a restoration of the imperialist British, French and Dutch colonial empires in the Far East, was the last thing Thomas, one of the American Left's most prescient and rigorously discerning anti-communists, wanted to see happen at the conclusion of the war. Pricking at the nation's conscience, its inherent sense of fairness, the former Presbyterian minister also favored far more reasonable and less punitive peace terms — except, obviously, for those involved in war crimes — which he firmly believed would lead to an earlier end to hostilities while guaranteeing a more lasting peace.

As a consequence of his courageous and unyielding criticism of the wartime president — a man he personally knew and respected and had frequently visited at the White House — the avuncular Thomas, inarguably the nation's most consistent civil libertarian, was subjected to almost unimaginable abuse during the 1944 campaign.

Despite a longstanding record of demanding asylum for Jewish refugees and others displaced by the atrocities inflicted by the fascist powers, Thomas found himself vilified by a number of leading Jewish newspapers during the campaign, one of which depicted him as a Quisling. Even the *Jewish Daily Forward*, a paper once friendly to the perpetual Socialist standard-bearer, charged that the Socialist Party's platform was offering peace to Hitler on a silver platter.

The five-time presidential candidate was also viciously libeled by the International Brotherhood of Teamsters, which published an article in its magazine accusing the former Presbyterian minister of "fawning on the German and Japs while they were killing Thomas' fellow countrymen." Completely ignoring the fact that Thomas had been one of this country's earliest and most consistent critics of both fascism and Nazism, the Teamsters' publication also breathtakingly maintained that the Socialist nominee's postwar plans fit in perfectly with Hitler's plans for future world conquest, as though Thomas was some sort of spineless appeaser, or worse — an outright pro-Nazi collaborator. In their distorted view, Hitler and Thomas were virtually indistinguishable, "just a couple of socialist boys looking at the world through blood-smeared glasses."

The campaign's ugliness aside, Thomas somehow managed to enjoy some lighter moments on the campaign trail that year. As in his previous bids for the presidency, the good-natured and fast-talking veteran campaigner frequently used humor to make his point, telling a radio audience that he had to speak quickly because he only had a few minutes of air time to discuss what Roosevelt and Dewey would normally take hours to evade.

The Prohibition Party, the nation's third oldest party and oldest third party, also buoyantly entered the fray, arguing that repeal of national prohibition had actually prolonged World War II. The Prohibitionists promised the nation's voters that a dry post-war America would bring both prosperity and happiness.

Fielding more than seventy gubernatorial and congressional candidates, as well as hundreds of local candidates — more than any other nationally-organized minor party that autumn — the venerable Prohibition Party was led by colorful dry crusader Claude A. Watson, a little-known Los Angeles attorney who firmly believed that the nation's once-powerful dry forces still wielded enough political clout to elect a Prohibitionist to the presidency.

Promising to eliminate the "crushing curse" of bureaucracy

INTRODUCTION

while winning World War II as quickly as possible, the pink-cheeked Prohibitionist had been the first candidate to officially enter the 1944 presidential sweepstakes. "If the old adage is true that the early bird catches the worm," Watson joked in early February, "then I will be the next president." While that obviously didn't happen, it certainly wasn't for lack of trying.

Though severely restricted in his ability to freely roam the country that year due to wartime rationing, the plump and pleasant third-party aspirant — railing against a product that "makes a man see double and think half" — had already logged more than 35,000 miles by the time President Roosevelt, running for an unprecedented fourth term, became fully engaged in the autumn campaign.

An ordained Free Methodist minister, the 58-year-old Watson was confident that he would poll the largest popular vote for president in the party's 75-year history, surpassing the 271,000 votes garnered by California's populist-leaning pioneer John Bidwell in 1892. One particularly witty columnist thought he might even have a fighting chance in 1944, not because of his charisma or personality, but because so "many citizens who wouldn't ordinarily vote a dry ticket remember so well that, during prohibition, whiskey was easier to get."

Watson, who campaigned more extensively in the Solid South than any other presidential aspirant that year, believed many southern voters were going to support the Republican and Prohibition tickets for the first time in their lives. "They are no longer slaves of tradition," he asserted shortly after completing a ten-state swing through that region.

With the determination of a prizefighter willing to take one brutal pounding after another in search of the elusive heavyweight crown, the tiny Socialist Labor Party also entered the ring that year. It was the fourteenth consecutive time that the doctrinaire SLP, throbbing to give birth to its long-awaited Socialist Industrial Union, had fielded its own ticket in a presidential election.

Hoping to rekindle the party's ever-so-faint dream of ushering in a socialist revolution by landing a lucky left hook against the twin parties of capitalism — a completely unexpected knockout blow against the entrenched Democratic and Republican parties — the punch-drunk disciples of Daniel De Leon convened at the Cornish Arms Hotel in New York City in late April and enthusiastically nominated Edward A. Teichert, a relatively obscure steelworker from western Pennsylvania, for the presidency.

"The present global war, the greatest crisis ever to face civilized man," explained the little-known Socialist Labor candidate, "grew out of the prewar struggle among the capitalist powers for the markets and resources of the world. The chaos it has wrought is evidence of the breakdown of the capitalist system, of its inability to manage for the benefit of society, the immensely productive machinery created under it." Socialism and only socialism, he declared, offered the only hope for sustained economic security and a lasting peace.

Billed as "the greatest political campaign in the history of the Socialist Labor Party," the small De Leonist party, claiming fewer than 3,000 members nationally, raised more than $100,000 during the 1944 presidential campaign — a figure easily dwarfing the relatively meager war chests amassed by the Socialist and Prohibition parties — almost all of which was spent on radio and newspaper advertising, as well as the printing and distribution of literally millions of leaflets.

Ignored by almost every historian and chronicler of U.S. presidential elections — most books written about the 1944 presidential election, including a couple published in the past few years, don't even mention Teichert's candidacy — the little-remembered Greensburg steelworker and his equally obscure vice-presidential running mate, a young photoengraver from Ohio who remained loyal to the SLP until his death nearly sixty years later, outhustled each of their major and minor-party opponents during that campaign, traveling across the country by automobile and giving the tiny Socialist Labor Party a fighting chance at finishing third in a presidential election for the first time in the party's long and neglected history.

Meanwhile, the Communist Party, which then boasted more than 80,000 dues-paying members and had fielded a ticket in every presidential election since 1924, formally disbanded in the spring of 1944, reconstituted itself as the Communist Political Association, and enthusiastically backed Franklin D. Roosevelt's bid for a fourth term — an uneasy alliance that the president's opponents exploited for all it was worth.

While the Communists formally dissolved as a political party, the nascent Liberal Party of New York — one of the most enduring statewide third parties in U.S. history — made its triumphant debut during the 1944 presidential campaign, the result of a particularly bitter internal skirmish within the older American Labor Party, a left-wing party founded eight years earlier.

Though most pundits believed that Wendell Willkie's presidential ambitions had ended in the snows of Wisconsin earlier that year, the leaders of New York's newly-formed Liberal Party had other plans for the highly intelligent, charisma-filled hustling Hoosier who had seemingly come out of nowhere to capture the GOP's presidential nomination four years earlier. As a possible springboard for a national effort in 1948, the Liberals planned to nominate Willkie for mayor of New York City in 1945, possibly on a fusion ticket with the GOP.

Willkie, still eyeing a prominent role in national politics, was more than a little intrigued by the idea. So, too, was the man in the White House who had defeated him in 1940. As implausible as it might seem today, in the spring of 1944 Roosevelt was already thinking beyond a fourth term while carefully contemplating a major realignment of America's political parties in the years ahead. His health permitting, a fifth term wasn't completely beyond the realm of possibility.

Deeply troubled that his own party had virtually surrendered to the rapacious and predatory forces of Wall Street and increasingly anxious to unite progressives in both major parties under a single banner, Roosevelt — a particularly shrewd and deft politician who had worked closely with various third-party leaders across the country throughout the Great Depression — had privately discussed the possibility of forming a new nationally-organized liberal party once the war was over.

Willkie and the newly-formed Liberal Party of New York both figured prominently in the president's future plans. It was no coincidence, moreover, that First Lady Eleanor Roosevelt had been the featured speaker at the party's gala dinner kicking off the 1944 campaign in early August, urging the party to take a lesson from Tammany and begin organizing at the precinct level while telling the overflow crowd of more than 1,800 that they were "the most hopeful group in the country and perhaps the whole world."

If fate hadn't intervened — tragically striking down the 52-year-old Willkie a month before the 1944 presidential election and claiming FDR's life six months later — could an unlikely pairing of the two men on a forward-looking third-party ticket have been in the offing in 1948, a robust challenge capable of seriously threatening the hegemony of the entrenched "two-party system" in the United States? It's an enormously intriguing question, but one that will forever remain unanswered.

While the party's dream of occupying the White House vanished with the passing of Willkie and Roosevelt, the Liberal Party — a party that sent Roosevelt's son and namesake to Congress against Democratic and Republican opposition in a special election in the spring of 1949 and catapulted the charismatic John V. Lindsay to a second term as mayor of America's largest city twenty years later — persisted for nearly six decades, not as a national entity as the party's founders had initially envisioned, but as an important fixture in New York politics.

Like the leaders of the newly-created Liberal Party in New York, Thomas and the biographically-neglected Watson and Teichert also lived to fight another day. Facing impossibly long odds, all three men ran for the nation's highest office again in 1948, but the desperately lonely and widely ignored campaigns they waged in wartime America in 1944 was nothing less than heroic, a remarkable tribute to those who have consistently labored outside the country's traditional two-party establishment.

Chapter I

A Reluctant Rebel

In the first wartime presidential campaign since Abraham Lincoln's 1864 reelection during the Civil War, few Americans doubted that President Franklin D. Roosevelt would seek a fourth term in 1944. Since he had already shattered the country's longstanding "two-term tradition" in defeating Republican rival Wendell Willkie four years earlier, there was little reason to believe the commander-in-chief, whose bold and programmatic New Deal alleviated much of the pain and suffering experienced during the deepest depression in the nation's history while laying the foundation for future economic growth and prosperity, would step aside while U.S. soldiers were engaged in the deadliest and most destructive war in history.

A kind of modern version of the Hamiltonian "American System," Roosevelt's robust New Deal arguably accomplished more in terms of promoting the nation's general welfare in its first hundred days than during any administration in the eight decades since. It also interrupted a sixty-year trend from roughly the 1870s to the early 1930s in which Wall Street and other private interests — the "investor class" or "kept classes" identified by economist Thorstein Veblen — dominated the U.S. government and shaped the country's economic life.[1]

Roosevelt, perhaps more than any of his contemporaries, realized precisely what he had accomplished during his first three months in office. It was nothing short of extraordinary. By the time Congress adjourned in June of 1933, lawmakers had codified the

---

[1] Donald Gibson, *Wealth, Power, and the Crisis of Laissez Faire Capitalism* (New York, 2011), pp. 95-97.

most sweeping economic reforms in American history, vastly expanding the government's role in the economy, including — most importantly — the financial regulation of Wall Street, whose speculative frenzy was largely responsible for the 1929 stock market crash and the ensuing Great Depression. "More history is being made today than in [any] one day in our national life," remarked the president as he began signing the first of fifteen comprehensive legislative measures approved by Congress.[2]

No longer left to the whims and inadequacies of the vaunted "free market," the American people finally had a chief executive who understood that government had a profoundly important role to play in the economy, particularly during a period when the private sector clearly wasn't up to the task.

While Roosevelt's economic initiatives succeeded in bringing the nation's unemployment rate down for four consecutive years from its high of 24.9 percent in 1933, at the height of the depression, to 14.3 percent in 1937, joblessness surged again in 1938, largely the result of what Assistant Attorney General Robert Jackson and Harold L. Ickes, the longest-serving Secretary of the Interior in the country's history, believed to be a deliberate "capital strike" on the part of big business.[3] Not surprisingly, the nation's jobless rate was still hovering at nearly ten percent when the U.S. entered the war three years later.

Responding to decade-long criticism from the Socialist Party's Norman Thomas and others who argued that the New Deal had never adequately dealt with the country's persistent unemployment problem, FDR hoped to remedy the situation, once and for all, during his fourth term.

Declaring that it was "our duty now to begin to lay the plans and determine the strategy for the winning of a lasting peace and the establishment of an American standard of living higher than ever before known," Roosevelt unveiled his "Economic Bill of Rights," also known as the "Second Bill of Rights" (see Appendix A), during his 1944 State of the Union address — a fireside chat appropriately described by Harvard law professor Cass Sunstein as "the speech of the century."[4]

Hoping to guarantee some of the rights that other industrial

---

[2] William E. Leuchtenburg, *Franklin D. Roosevelt and the New Deal, 1932-1940* (New York, 1963), p. 61.
[3] Conrad Black, *Franklin Delano Roosevelt: Champion of Freedom* (New York, 2003), p. 431.
[4] Cass R. Sunstein, *The Second Bill of Rights: FDR's Unfinished Revolution and Why We Need It More Than Ever* (New York, 2004), p. 12.

democracies had already inscribed in their constitutions, Roosevelt's economic bill of rights included the right to a job, including a decent income to provide for the basic necessities of life — food, shelter, clothing and recreation — adequate medical care, a quality education, the right of every family to a decent home, and the right to protection from the economic ravages of old age, illness, and unemployment. Moreover, farmers were entitled to sell their products at a price high enough to guarantee a decent standard of living and businesses had a right to compete in an atmosphere free from unfair competition.[5]

The United States, declared Roosevelt, anxiously looking forward to implementing his bold and imaginative proposal, "cannot be content, no matter how high that general standard of living may be, if some fraction of our people — whether it be one-third or one-fifth or one-tenth — is ill-fed, ill-clothed, ill-housed, and insecure."[6]

Having effectively ended America's longstanding love affair with laissez-faire capitalism by battering President Hoover at the ballot box a dozen years earlier and barely breaking a sweat four years later against the GOP's Alf Landon — another firm believer in the mythical magic of the "free market" — Roosevelt realized that the 1944 campaign would probably be as difficult as the one he experienced four years earlier. The president faced a formidable challenge that year from disheveled, tousle-haired ex-Democrat Wendell Willkie, a genial, plain-speaking Midwesterner whose boundless energy and exuberance momentarily caught the nation's fancy. FDR prevailed that time, too, but his reelection to an unprecedented third term, largely the result of his opponent's strenuous campaigning, appeared for a time to be in some doubt. Roosevelt eventually won that race by nearly five million votes.

As in 1940, when he faced at least some token opposition within his own party — mostly from supporters of Vice President John N. Garner of Texas and Postmaster General and Democratic National Committee chairman James A. Farley, the latter of whom had managed FDR's first two presidential campaigns — the Democratic president was again denied a unanimous first-ballot nomination when 89 delegates, mostly Dixie dissidents, voted for a reluctant Harry F. Byrd of Virginia while two recalcitrant delegates from New York, each entitled to half a vote, opted for Jim Farley at the party's national convention in Chicago.[7]

---

[5] "'Bill of Rights' Seen as FDR's 1944 Platform,'" *Eugene Register-Guard*, Jan. 12, 1944.
[6] Sunstein, *The Second Bill of Rights*, p. 12.
[7] "Roosevelt Nominated for Fourth Term," *New York Times*, July 21, 1944; "Delegates Name Roosevelt; Wallace, Truman in Hot Race," *Springfield Republican*, July 21, 1944. As

Moreover, there had been several other Democrats anxiously waiting in the wings in the event Roosevelt decided against seeking a fourth term, not the least of whom was Indiana's Paul V. McNutt, a nationally-ambitious and somewhat arrogant former governor who was once described as "Huey Long in Warren G. Harding clothing." He had also been described as a "Hoosier Hitler" by some of his critics while Norman Thomas, never at a loss for a pithy description, denounced the ex-governor as a "two-by-four fascist."[8]

The white-haired McNutt, a former High Commissioner to the Philippines and ex-chairman of the War Manpower Commission who was serving as administrator of the Federal Security Agency during the 1944 presidential campaign, believed that he had a rendezvous with destiny and had been itching to run for president since 1940, if not earlier.[9] In the months leading up to the 1944 campaign, there was even a concerted effort by Oscar Ewing, vice chairman of the Democratic National Committee and counsel for the Aluminum Company of America (ALCOA), to turn the DNC into a McNutt-for-President operation — a bold and audacious move vigorously opposed by New Dealers who were offended by McNutt's atrocious labor record.[10]

In addition to drafting a concise 1,360-word platform, a document less than one-third the length of the verbose platform adopted by the Republicans that year — a vague and needlessly wordy bromide that contained little in the way of substance typical of the GOP — the convention's only real drama occurred in the balloting for vice president when Missouri Sen. Harry S. Truman, supported by a combination of southern conservatives, northern big city bosses, corporate and predatory Wall Street interests and other malefactors of great wealth with a little British hostility and intrigue thrown in for good measure — all of whom desperately wanted Vice President Henry A. Wallace removed from the Democratic ticket — defeated the vice president on the second ballot.[11]

Wallace deserved better. Unlike four years earlier when the

---

a delegate from New York, Farley personally cast his lot with Byrd and favored Kentucky's Alben W. Barkley for vice president.

[8] Jack Alexander, "Paul McNutt: "It Would Be Kind of Nice to Be President, Wouldn't It?," *Life*, Jan. 29, 1940, pp. 65-73; "Norman Thomas Says M'Nutt is 'Two-By-Four Fascist,'" *St. Louis Post-Dispatch*, Sep. 7, 1935.

[9] Ibid.

[10] Drew Pearson and Robert S. Allen, "The Washington Merry-Go-Round," *Pittsburgh Press*, May 11, 1942. McNutt had deeply angered organized labor by using the state militia to break up a general strike in Terre Haute in 1935.

[11] "Democrats Name Truman; Stampede on 2d Ballot Defeats Vice President," *Chicago Tribune*, July 22, 1944.

Democratic president appeared willing to risk it all for the enigmatic Iowan, Roosevelt, while indicating that he would personally vote for Wallace if given the opportunity as a delegate, had effectively sealed his vice president's fate a few weeks prior to the convention by saying that he didn't "wish to appear to be in any way dictating to the convention" and would allow the delegates to choose his running mate.[12] The forward-looking yet much-maligned vice president, in effect, had been left to fend for himself.

Wallace, meanwhile, felt that his removal had been orchestrated in part by British Tories, including the brutishly imperialistic windbag Winston Churchill, who — clearly acting on behalf of his country's financial oligarchy — were committed to continuing the kind of quasi-feudalism inherent in British colonialism through their long-established "free trade" policies designed to loot and pillage struggling Third World economies while protecting and further enhancing the fortunes of England's traditional ruling class following the war.

Churchill, the Scotch and soda sipping, cigar-chomping Bulldog of Britain who once authorized the use of poison gas against "uncivilized tribes" in an attempt "spread a lively terror" in the Middle East, was reportedly livid over Wallace's pamphlet, *Our Job in the Pacific*, a document dealing with U.S. postwar aims in which the vice president drew a sharp distinction between a "free Asia" and an Asia subject to foreign rule, a sharp repudiation of British colonialism and its plundering "free trade" imperialism.[13]

The megalomaniacal prime minister had made his own war aims abundantly clear a few years earlier. In Churchill's eyes, the war was as much about preserving his country's empire, if not expanding it, as it was about defeating the Rome-Berlin-Tokyo Axis. "We mean to hold our own," he famously told the parliament in the autumn of 1942, shortly after a series of Allied victories in North Africa. "I have not become the King's First Minister in order to preside over the liquidation of the British Empire."[14]

Wallace's pamphlet, moreover, had been entirely consistent with FDR's personal opposition to the perpetuation of the British Empire in the postwar period. According to Elliott Roosevelt, the

---

[12] "Wallace Left to Delegates by Roosevelt," *New York Times*, July 18, 1944; Samuel I. Rosenman, *Working with Roosevelt* (New York, 1952), p. 449.

[13] Graham White and John Maze, *Henry A. Wallace: His Search for a New World Order* (Chapel Hill, 1995), pp. 206-207; Patrick J. Buchanan, *Churchill, Hitler, and the Unnecessary War: How Britain Lost Its Empire and the West Lost the World* (New York, 2008), p. 391; Noam Chomsky, *Deterring Democracy* (New York, 1992), p. 182.

[14] Peter Clarke, *The Last Thousand Days of the British Empire: Churchill, Roosevelt, and the Birth of the Pax Americana* (New York, 2008), xvii.

president's second son and traveling companion during five historic wartime summits, President Roosevelt was strongly opposed to British and French colonialism and wanted to see all of the colonial empires dismantled at the close of the war, thereby putting an end to the longstanding British practice of exploiting weaker, developing countries for their raw materials.[15]

Moreover, as historian Donald Gibson astutely noted, Roosevelt didn't view what later became known as free trade imperialism — the free trade policies, adopted in the 1850s, by which the financial oligarchy expanded its vast reach and control of the global economy without having to bother with the expense and trouble of maintaining an increasingly unpopular formal empire — as a desirable substitute for colonialism. Unlike Churchill, FDR strongly believed that developing nations in Asia and elsewhere should be free to pursue their own economic development and trade policies.[16]

Like Wallace, Roosevelt was also deeply concerned that Great Britain had somehow managed to inconspicuously maintain the "same reactionary grip on the peoples of the world and markets of the world, through every war they've ever been in." Roosevelt told his son that the United States, which was then standing shoulder to shoulder with England against a common enemy, hadn't entered the war merely to help the British hang on to their "archaic, medieval Empire ideas." The president, wrote Elliott in his 1946 bestselling book *As He Saw It*, wasn't about "to sit by, after we've won, and watch their system stultify the growth of every country in Asia and half the countries in Europe" following the war.[17]

Backed by Sidney Hillman and Philip Murray, the Scottish-born steelworker who succeeded the powerful John L. Lewis as president of the Congress of Industrial Organizations (CIO), Vice President Wallace amassed a large plurality on the convention's first ballot, garnering 429 ½ votes to Truman's 319 ½ and briefly led in the second round of balloting before Alabama and Indiana switched their votes from favorite-son candidates to Truman, setting off a stampede for the mediocre Missouri senator, an unimpressive and largely unaccomplished product of one of the most corrupt political machines in American history.[18]

---

[15] Gibson, *Wealth, Power, and the Crisis of Laissez Faire Capitalism*, p. 116.
[16] Ibid.
[17] Elliott Roosevelt, *As He Saw It* (New York, 1946), pp. 121-122.
[18] "CIO Leaders Back Wallace for 2nd Place," *Milwaukee Sentinel*, July 14, 1944; "Truman Nominated for Vice Presidency," *New York Times*, July 22, 1944; Eugene H. Roseboom, *A History of Presidential Elections: From George Washington to Richard M. Nixon* (New York, 1970), pp. 485-486.

A RELUCTANT REBEL

While Roosevelt barely broke a sweat in winning a fourth straight nomination, the Republican contest — believe it or not — was even less suspenseful, largely due to the fact that Ohio's Robert A. Taft, the son of President and Chief Justice William Howard Taft and a serious contender for his party's nomination in 1940, refused to run in 1944, focusing instead on his own reelection to the U.S. Senate — a race in which he narrowly escaped defeat.

A profoundly principled conservative who lived and loved politics and whose dogged determination in opposing the New Deal affectionately earned him the nickname "Mr. Republican," Taft gave his blessing to fellow Ohioan John W. Bricker, but the overly cautious, three-term governor's low-key presidential candidacy never caught fire. That was partly because Bricker really didn't have anything to say — veteran journalist John Gunther once described his intellectual prowess as "a vast vacuum occasionally crossed by homeless, wandering clichés" — and partly because the party's conservatives, including those in his home state of Ohio, preferred Taft, the genuine article. Even Taft, it turns out, expressed some serious qualms about Bricker's competence as a presidential candidate, later confiding in a friend that the Ohio governor didn't have "the ability to speak and say anything and is almost certain to make a lot of mistakes."[19]

The impeccably-groomed Bricker, who always looked like he just stepped straight out of central casting, wasn't the darkest horse in the stable. That dubious distinction belonged to six-term congressman Everett M. Dirksen of Illinois — "The Wizard of Ooze," as John F. Kennedy once described him — who had been urged to run by 36 House colleagues.[20]

With Gen. Douglas MacArthur and Minnesota's Harold E. Stassen, the 37-year-old "boy wonder" of American politics, both serving in the South Pacific, the Republican nomination was virtually decided in early April when former lifelong Democrat Wendell Willkie — an unwelcome interloper hoping to repeat his improbable 1940 "Miracle in Philadelphia" — was mercilessly buried in the Wisconsin primary. Willkie's withdrawal from the race on the heels of that stunning disaster left frontrunner Thomas E. Dewey of New York free to pursue the party's nomination in a field virtually bereft of competition.

---

[19] "Taft Launches Bricker Boom for Presidency," *Sarasota Herald-Tribune*, Dec. 6, 1942; Drew Pearson, "Ohio Members of Congress Back Bricker But Privately Want Taft," *St. Petersburg Times*, Nov. 29, 1943; "Bricker Launches 1944 Campaign," *Eugene Register-Guard*, Jan. 8, 1944; Robert A. Taft, Clarence E. Wunderlin, Jr., ed., *The Papers of Robert A. Taft, Volume 3, 1945-1948* (Kent, Ohio, 2003), p. 170.
[20] "Dirksen Enters Presidential Race," *Reading Eagle*, Dec, 2, 1943.

Dewey, who was then waging the second of three consecutive bids for the White House, was something of a prohibitive favorite to win the Republican nomination long before the 1944 campaign got underway, earning the coveted front-runner status by virtue of his lopsided victory in New York's 1942 gubernatorial election — a race in which he demolished his hapless Democratic opponent by nearly 650,000 votes.[21]

In a display of naked ambition arguably as audacious as that of relatively inexperienced Illinois Sen. Barack Obama in 2008 — a restive Wall Street-funded yet largely unaccomplished and untested lawmaker who had only served in the U.S. Senate for a couple of years before launching a seemingly improbable bid for the nation's highest office — the racket-busting prosecutor came remarkably close to capturing his party's presidential nomination in 1940.

Basking in the glow of a much closer-than-expected challenge to Gov. Herbert Lehman, Roosevelt's four-term successor, the previous autumn — losing to the popular incumbent Democrat by fewer than 65,000 votes out of more than 4.7 million votes cast — Dewey, throwing caution to the wind, boldly entered the contest for the Republican nomination in December 1939, barely a year after losing the governor's race.[22]

Unlike Senator Obama in 2008 or his inept and inarticulate predecessor George W. Bush, who famously traded on his vastly-inflated family name in creating what Kevin Phillips described as a modern dynastic presidency, a "not-quite-royal family," Dewey entered the 1940 presidential campaign with some significant public achievements under his belt, including the successful prosecution of Sicilian-born mobster "Lucky" Luciano, head of the modern Genovese crime family, for running a prostitution ring in New York City.[23]

Though Dewey, as governor, later commuted the mobster's sentence — virtually assuring his safe return to Italy — the Luciano prosecution was by far Dewey's most celebrated case and forever cemented his reputation as one of the nation's leading organized-

---

[21] David M. Jordan, *FDR, Dewey, and the Election of 1944* (Bloomington, IN, 2011), p. 16; "20-Year Rule Ends; Democrats Lose State with Bennett Defeat by 600,000 Margin," *New York Times*, Nov. 4, 1942; "Dewey Now in Position for Presidential Coup," *New York Times*, Nov. 8, 1942.
[22] "Dewey Opens Drive for Presidency on Recovery Issue," *New York Times*, Dec. 2, 1939.
[23] Kevin Phillips, *American Dynasty: Aristocracy, Fortune, and the Politics of Deceit in the House of Bush* (New York, 2004), pp. 15-19.

crime fighters.[24] In a little more than two years as a Lehman-appointed special prosecutor, Dewey obtained 72 convictions, including nearly a dozen of the city's most vile and notorious racketeers. Incredibly, only one defendant targeted by the young prosecutor during this period was found not guilty.

Parlaying his success as a special prosecutor into elected office, Dewey — the son of a small-town Michigan newspaper publisher — was easily elected District Attorney for New York County in 1937. Nominated by the Republican, American Labor and City Fusion parties and running on a ticket headed by immensely popular Mayor Fiorello H. La Guardia, Dewey vanquished his Tammany-backed Democratic opponent by more than 108,000 votes.[25]

As district attorney, Dewey continued blazing a racket-busting path, indicting and convicting an assortment of underworld figures, one of the most significant of which was the arrest and conviction of notorious mobster and vicious labor racketeer Louis "Lepke" Buchalter, head of the Mafia's notorious "Murder, Inc." Buchalter, who had been described by the FBI's J. Edgar Hoover as "the most dangerous criminal in the United States," was sentenced to death along with two of his underlings after being found guilty of first-degree murder.

Dewey's office also vigorously pursued a wide array of corrupt public figures, including powerful Tammany "fix-it man" Jimmy Hines for using his considerable political influence to protect local racketeers. In other widely-publicized cases, Dewey also convicted Richard Whitney, a former president of the New York Stock Exchange with close ties to the House of Morgan, and controversial American Nazi leader Fritz Kuhn.

Dewey's youth — he had just turned thirty-seven the previous March — was seen as his biggest impediment in seeking the 1940 Republican presidential nomination, prompting the irascible Harold Ickes, the longtime Secretary of the Interior who had performed a yeoman's task in implementing much of FDR's New Deal program, to famously quip that Dewey had thrown his "diaper into the ring."[26]

A veteran of Teddy Roosevelt's Bull Moose Party whose biting wit was known to draw blood, Ickes had a lot of fun at Dewey's expense that year. Referring to the young Republican's rather

---

[24] Mary M. Stolberg, *Fighting Organized Crime: Politics, Justice, and the Legacy of Thomas E. Dewey* (Boston, 1995), pp. 116-117.
[25] "Fusion Tide Kills Tammany; A.L.P. Has Balance of Power," *New York Evening Post*, Nov. 3, 1937; "Dewey is Winner by 108,823 Margin," *New York Times*, Nov. 3, 1937.
[26] Herbert S. Parmet and Marie B. Hecht, *Never Again: A President Runs for a Third Term* (New York, 1968), p.72.

bland speech in Minneapolis kicking off his campaign in early December 1939, Ickes said that it was nothing more than babbling "baby talk." According to Ickes, the New York Republican had nothing new or significant to say. "He did, however, prove his qualifications as a candidate," asserted the quick-witted curmudgeon. "He talked for 45 minutes without saying anything."[27]

Others were equally unkind to the young prosecutor. "How can you vote for a man who looks like the bridegroom on a wedding cake?" asked the always witty Alice Roosevelt Longworth during the 1944 presidential campaign.[28] While Theodore Roosevelt's daughter readily admitted that she hadn't coined the phrase — it was variously attributed to Democratic operative Helen Murphy, actress Ethel Barrymore, novelist Grace Flandrau, gossip columnist Walter Winchell and even Ickes himself — the grande dame of Washington society, who found Dewey "a frightful bore," peppered the Republican nominee with a few delightful jabs of her own. "You can't make a soufflé rise twice," she said famously of the New Yorker during the 1948 campaign.[29]

Despite his youth and inexperience, the young crusading prosecutor was nevertheless a major contender for the Republican presidential nomination as early as 1940, running neck and neck throughout the primary season with Ohio's Bob Taft, a conservative yet pragmatic lawmaker who had embraced an unyielding noninterventionist stance throughout the neutrality period of 1939-1941. Carefully distinguishing between a policy of preparedness, which he generally supported, and a policy of aggressive militarism, which he adamantly refused to embrace, Taft vigorously opposed peacetime conscription, arguing that it would establish — for the first time in American history — permanent militarism in the United States, a large standing army under the command of an arbitrary executive.[30]

Waging the first of three campaigns for his party's presidential nomination, the 50-year-old Taft, a staunch defender of tariffs designed to protect U.S. manufacturing, had been one of Roosevelt's most vociferous critics in the U.S. Senate, steadfastly opposing most of the president's New Deal policies and lambasting Secre-

---

[27] "Ickes Ridicules Dewey's Address," *Tuscaloosa News*, Dec. 7, 1939.
[28] Steven G. O'Brien and Paula McGuire, *American Political Leaders: From Colonial Times to the Present* (Santa Barbara, 1991), p. 108.
[29] William Safire, *Safire's Political Dictionary* (New York, 2008), p. 415.
[30] Clarence E. Wunderlin, *Robert A. Taft: Ideas, Tradition, and Party in U.S. Foreign Policy* (Lanham, Maryland, 2005), pp. 208-209. Taft was one of ten Republican senators who opposed the Selective Training and Service Act of 1940.

tary of State Cordell Hull for pursuing international free trade policies that he believed would ultimately undermine the country's fragile industrial base and erode the nation's relatively high standard of living.[31]

Beginning with the 1940 campaign, Dewey and Taft bitterly battled for their party's soul over the next dozen years or so, twice competing directly against each other for the Republican presidential nomination. "By 1952," wrote political science professor Jeff Taylor, "Dewey was an arch-enemy who helped lead the stop-Taft effort through the instrumentality of General Eisenhower."[32]

During their initial face-off in 1940, Dewey benefited immensely from the Ohioan's refusal to neglect his Senate duties in Washington by limiting his presidential campaign activities to something of a "weekend warrior." With his chief competitor largely preoccupied in the nation's capital, Dewey — campaigning on an almost full-time basis — ran unopposed in delegate-rich Illinois and swept important primary contests in Wisconsin, Nebraska, Pennsylvania, Maryland and New Jersey.

The nomination seemed within Dewey's grasp and the polished yet somewhat aloof New Yorker actually led on the first three ballots at the party's suspense-filled national convention in Philadelphia that summer before dark horse candidate Wendell Willkie, the dynamic Indiana-born president of the Commonwealth Southern Corporation, seemingly coming out of nowhere, spectacularly surged ahead on the fourth ballot and eventually captured the nomination two ballots later.[33]

There was no such drama in 1944 as Dewey swept to a nearly unanimous victory on the convention's first and only ballot, receiving the votes of all but three of the 1,059 delegates in attendance at the party's national convention at Chicago Stadium. In a show of

---

[31] Ibid., p. 208.
[32] Jeff Taylor, *Politics on a Human Scale: The American Tradition of Decentralism* (Lanham, Maryland, 2013), p. 305.
[33] Charles Peters, *Five Days in Philadelphia* (New York, 2005), pp. 100-108; Steve Neal, *Dark Horse: A Biography of Wendell Willkie* (New York, 1984), pp. 109-116; "Rivals Worn Down," *New York Times*, June 28, 1940; "GOP Nominates Willkie-McNary Ticket," *Milwaukee Journal*, June 28, 1940; "GOP Nominates Willkie; Ex-Democrat Wins on Sixth in Stampede," *St. Petersburg Times*, June 28, 1940; "Summary of the Ballots," *New York Times*, June 28, 1940. Dewey's high-water mark occurred on the first ballot when he garnered 360 votes — 141 shy of the magic number of 501 — to Taft's 189. Willkie, who had only recently joined the GOP, was a distant third with 105. Hoping that lightning would strike, former President Herbert Hoover was one of ten other candidates who received votes on the first ballot, garnering a modest 17 votes on the initial ballot before reaching a high of 32 on the third ballot.

unity, Ohio's John Bricker, who was also seeking the party's nomination, was chosen as Dewey's vice-presidential running mate.[34]

As in three of the four previous presidential elections, Socialist Norman M. Thomas, barely running ahead of the Prohibition Party's Claude A. Watson, was arguably the leading third-party contender for the presidency in 1944. But that wasn't saying much given the fact that fewer than 250,000 votes, or less than one-half of one percent of the total, had been cast for all of the minor-party aspirants for president in 1940 out of nearly fifty million votes nationally.

As in 1940, Thomas again had serious qualms about mounting what would surely be another forlorn bid for the White House. Smaller crowds, a moribund organization, dwindling resources and ever longer odds were finally taking its toll on the good-natured former Presbyterian pastor some had described as the "nation's conscience." Thomas knew that it would be an extraordinarily difficult undertaking and didn't relish the prospect of waging another lonely and largely ignored campaign for an office he would never occupy. "I would like to step aside," he said, "and be considered as the elder statesman."[35]

In February of 1943 — some sixteen months before the party's national convention — the discouraged four-time candidate, dreading the burden of yet another national campaign, told reporters while visiting Chicago that he strongly doubted there would even be a Socialist Party ticket in 1944 unless a larger coalition of progressive elements similar to the Canadian Commonwealth Cooperative Federation was organized in the United States.[36]

A year later, of course, no such broad coalition existed. Sadly, the Socialist Party was as isolated as ever, barely a shell of its former self. Wartime attrition, sapping the party of what little strength it still possessed, had left the Socialists with fewer than 1,000 dues-

---

[34] "Dewey, If Elected, Would Be Youngest President," *Chicago Tribune*, June 29, 1944; "Dewey-Bricker G.O.P. Ticket," *St. Petersburg Evening Independent*, June 28, 1944. Dewey's first-ballot nomination wasn't quite unanimous as one Wisconsin delegate voted for Gen. Douglas MacArthur and two others abstained.

[35] "Norman Thomas Declines to Run Again," *Knickerbocker News* (Albany, N.Y.), Dec. 10, 1943.

[36] "Thomas May Not be Candidate for Presidency in '44," *New Castle News*, Nov. 12, 1943. Emerging from the prairie dust of Canada's devastated western provinces during the Great Depression, the Commonwealth Cooperative Federation of Canada (CCF) was a left-wing party that called for the nationalization of the country's banking, credit, and financial system and public ownership of the nation's transportation, communication, and natural resources. Modeled after the British Labour Party, the CCF had considerable electoral success, particularly in Saskatchewan, and later merged with other socialist and labor groups in founding the New Democratic Party in 1961.

paying members nationally and fewer active locals than ever before. With Thomas unlikely to mount another national campaign, some even wondered whether the party would survive beyond its national convention that year.[37]

But those deeply troubling facts apparently didn't deter the party's young and naively enthusiastic activists. Harry Fleischman, the party's 30-year-old national secretary, announced in early March that the party's National Executive Committee (NEC) had voted to recommend to the national convention in Reading that — come hell or high water — the Socialist Party should wage a vigorous presidential campaign in 1944.[38] That was probably the last thing Thomas wanted to hear.

In the months leading up to his party's national convention, the avuncular Socialist leader had tried in vain to convince University of Chicago economist Maynard Krueger — the man he had painstakingly groomed for the role — to accept the party's presidential nomination, but the 39-year-old educator was apparently more interested in running for Congress that year, possibly as a candidate of the newly-created American Commonwealth Party — a new leftist party headed by famous civil rights attorney Francis Heisler — than undertaking a long-shot quest for the presidency on the fading Socialist Party ticket. Heisler, whose new party never really got off the ground, was the national counsel for the Workers Defense League and had personally defended countless conscientious objectors and draft resisters during WWII.[39]

Krueger (pronounced Krieger) had replaced Thomas as the party's national chairman in 1942. Declining to seek the chairmanship again after a strenuous six-year stint, Thomas was delighted when the Chicago professor was unanimously chosen as his successor at the party's national convention in Milwaukee that year, saying that it was a welcome sign that "the party has more than one man to put in this important position." That same convention, incidentally, overwhelmingly adopted a measure asserting that the Socialist Party "does not give its blessing to this war or any war" and that "a social order that is producing fascism cannot destroy it."[40]

Having carried his party's torch in four consecutive national campaigns, Thomas couldn't have been any more serious about not running in 1944, but few took him at his word. In fact, reporters

---

[37] "Socialist Party Faces Convention Fight for Survival," *Washington Post*, May 26, 1944.
[38] "Socialist Party Plans Convention," *Altoona Mirror*, Mar. 6, 1944.
[39] W. A. Swanberg, *Norman Thomas: The Last Idealist* (New York, 1976), pp. 286-287.
[40] "Socialists Pick Krueger," *New York Times*, June 2, 1942.

laughed when he told them that he wasn't a candidate. They joked that he sounded just like Roosevelt.[41]

When reminded shortly after arriving at the party's national convention that both President Roosevelt and Thomas Dewey — his likely major-party opponents — had made similar statements earlier that year, Thomas was as unflappable as ever. "The President has not named anyone he would like to see get the Democratic nomination and Mr. Dewey would seem not to know that there is an election this year," Thomas pithily retorted. "I at least have named the man I would like to see get the Socialist nomination — Maynard C. Krueger of Chicago."[42]

Krueger, who would have been an ideal candidate to replace Thomas at the top of the ticket, had been the party's vice-presidential candidate in 1940 and performed a yeoman's effort in rallying the party's bedraggled troops during that exceedingly difficult campaign. With his wire-rimmed glasses, the pipe-smoking Krueger looked every bit the intellectual he was. Having studied history and international politics before specializing in economics, the scholarly-looking professor had emerged as a leading spokesman for campus opposition to the war in Europe during the pre-Pearl Harbor period, frequently assailing the nation's seeming fascination with Adolf Hitler, a fixation that nearly bordered on a psychotic disorder.

Krueger was also a popular and witty lecturer and regular guest on the University of Chicago's widely-respected "Round Table" radio program — a forum from which he and political science professor Charles E. Merriam, a former vice chair of the National Resources Planning Board, once shred Vienna-born economist Friedrich von Hayek to pieces. A Nobel Prize-winning economist admired by reactionary ideologues such as Ronald Reagan and Britain's Margaret Thatcher, Hayek was a longtime London School of Economics lecturer and author of *The Road to Serfdom* — an explosively controversial work that was given wide currency in the United States through a condensed version that appeared in *Reader's Digest*. In his widely-read book, the Austrian economist argued rather unconvincingly that the abandonment of classical liberalism and the growing trend toward democratic socialism would eventually lead to totalitarianism.[43]

Krueger, of course, enthusiastically shared Thomas's view of

---

[41] Raymond F. Gregory, *Norman Thomas: The Great Dissenter* (New York, 2008), pp. 199-200.
[42] "Draft," *TIME Magazine*, June 12, 1944.
[43] "Round Table of the Air," University of Chicago, Apr. 22, 1945.

the mythical free market championed by Hayek. "The uncompromising laissez-faire liberalism, the economic system so dear to a Hayek or a von Mises, never really existed, and its reign was limited," Thomas wrote in *A Socialist's Faith*, published a few years later. "Its tenets were worked out of the great misery of the Industrial Revolution; its golden age was short."[44] Krueger, agreeing entirely with Thomas, said that the American people shouldn't listen to the National Association of Manufacturers or Mr. Hayek tell you that a planned economy has to be totalitarian just because the Russians did it that way. We can do it with cooperatives and public corporations in a democratic way," he insisted.[45]

Krueger, who had waged an unsuccessful campaign for alderman in Chicago's sixth ward as an independent candidate the previous year, resisted Thomas's overtures to head the Socialist ticket in 1944, but agreed to remain at the helm as the party's national chair — a post to which he was easily reelected.

Though making it clear that he believed the party would benefit tremendously by nominating a younger candidate, Thomas reluctantly agreed to mount a fifth campaign for the presidency once Krueger firmly took his name out of consideration.[46] He did so, wrote biographer Bernard Johnpoll, not only because he believed there was no significant difference between the two major parties on policy matters, but also because he felt that it was imperative to "keep the ballot open to a new party which someday will do what the Republican Party did in 1856 and 1860."[47]

Convening at the Berkshire Hotel in Reading, Pennsylvania, in early June, the Socialists nominated Thomas by acclamation. Darlington Hoopes, a 47-year-old Reading attorney and former Socialist member of the Pennsylvania legislature, was nominated for vice president after A. Philip Randolph, president of the Brotherhood of Sleeping Car Porters, had wired the convention expressing his deep regret that he couldn't accept the party's nomination because of his union responsibilities.[48]

Thomas and other party leaders never realistically expected Randolph to accept the party's vice-presidential nomination in

---

[44] Wilson Clark, Jr., "Best System — Laissez-Faire," *The Daily Tar Heel* (Chapel Hill, N.C.), Dec. 9, 1965.
[45] Maynard C. Krueger, "Will it be Boom and Bust in America?" *Socialist Call*, June 10, 1946.
[46] "Thomas is Retiring as Socialist Leader," *New York Times*, June 2, 1944.
[47] Bernard K. Johnpoll, *Pacifist's Progress: Norman Thomas and the Decline of American Socialism* (Chicago, 1970), pp. 244-245.
[48] "Socialist Ticket Headed By Thomas," *New York Times*, June 5, 1944; "Thomas Named as Nominee by Socialist Party," *Washington Post*, June 5, 1944.

what was certainly destined to be a doomed national effort, especially since he had recently turned down an opportunity to run for Congress — a race in which many New Yorkers believed he stood a realistic chance of winning.[49]

Keenly aware that the 55-year-old civil rights and labor leader, riding a wave of popularity after convincing President Roosevelt to sign Executive Order 8802, prohibiting racial discrimination in the defense industry, had rejected serious bipartisan support, including overtures from powerful Harlem Democratic leader Herbert L. Bruce and others, to be their candidate against Adam Clayton Powell in New York's newly-created twenty-second congressional district only six weeks earlier, it was highly unlikely that Randolph would now agree to wage a completely hopeless race for vice president.[50] In an interview with biographer Jervis Anderson years later, Randolph said that he "probably would have beaten Powell," but couldn't bring himself to abandon the Brotherhood of Sleeping Car Porters during that crucial period. "It would have appeared that as if I was simply using the porters as a steppingstone to power," he said, almost wistfully.[51]

Since nobody seriously expected Randolph to accept the vice-presidential nomination, several other names had been considered as the convention got underway, including no fewer than three prominent Socialists from Reading, the convention's blue-collar host city in the heart of "Pennsylvania Dutch Country."

In addition to Hoopes, Mayor J. Henry Stump and longtime labor publisher Raymond S. Hofses were both seriously considered as possible running mates, but gracefully stepped aside when Hoopes expressed an interest in seeking the nomination. Stump, a cigar maker and former president of the Federated Trades Council, had been elected mayor of Pennsylvania's fifth-largest city for the third time in sixteen years the previous autumn by defeating a Democratic incumbent. Other names floated for the party's second spot on the eve of the convention included Chester A. Graham of Lansing, Michigan, a leader in the National Farmers' Union, New York's Coleman B. Cheney, the Socialist Party's nominee for governor in 1942, and longtime pacifist and economics professor Tucker P. Smith of Detroit, a former director of the Brookwood Labor College.[52]

---

[49] "Randolph Declines Race," *New York Times*, Apr. 19, 1944.
[50] "Powell Opposed for House as Red," *New York Times*, Apr. 13, 1944; A. Philip Randolph, "Why I Can't Run for Congress on the Old Party Tickets," *Socialist Call*, Apr. 28, 1944.
[51] Jervis Anderson, *A. Philip Randolph: A Biographical Portrait* (Berkeley, 1972; 1986), p. 377.
[52] "Socialist Elected Reading Mayor," *New York Times*, Nov. 3, 1943; "Socialists Gather

Nominating Hoopes for the vice presidency was a particularly shrewd and significant development given the fact that the Berks County Socialists had voted unanimously to re-affiliate with the Socialist Party the previous November, followed shortly thereafter by the entire state organization.[53]

Hoopes, who was elected state chairman at the party's "unity convention" in January 1944, had worked tirelessly to convince the Socialist Party of Pennsylvania to sever its longstanding ties with the increasingly insignificant Social Democratic Federation (SDF) and re-affiliate with the Socialist Party for the first time since the party's devastating split eight years earlier — a development that angered the usually jovial August Claessens and other members of the SDF, most of whom resided in New York City.[54]

Never sharing Claessens' personal hostility toward Thomas, the Reading attorney had always been sort of an odd-man-out in the Social Democratic Federation, never completely agreeing with the organization's affinity for the Democratic Party, whose candidates the majority of the SDF frequently supported. Hoopes and Claessens, moreover, had often sparred, particularly over the question of unity between the SDF and the SP. Hoopes, who had long advocated a speedy reunification of the warring groups and firmly believed that it could be accomplished "in the not too distant future," was deeply disappointed when the New Yorker, in his role as SDF's acting national secretary and later as national chairman, dismissed the idea of unity as "absolutely impossible."[55]

The Reading Socialists, representing one of the party's three municipal strongholds prior to and during the early years of the Great Depression, had been part of the SDF since the party's devastating schism in the mid-1930s — one of the most damaging splits in the party's history. By 1944, most of the major issues that divided the local and national party eight years earlier were no longer relevant, the most significant being the expulsion of the Trotskyists from the national party in August 1937.[56]

Nominated by acclamation once A. Philip Randolph withdrew from the race, Hoopes had been placed in nomination by

---

Here; Delegates Arriving for Party's 24th National Convention," *Reading Eagle*, June 1, 1944. Tucker P. Smith, who headed the economics department at Olivet College, later served as Thomas's vice-presidential running mate in the 1948 campaign.

[53] "Reading Votes Re-affiliation with Socialist Party, U.S.A.," *Socialist Call*, Dec. 10, 1943.

[54] "Pennsylvania Socialists, Reunited, Plan Vigorous State and National Drive," *Socialist Call*, Jan. 21, 1944.

[55] J. Paul Henderson, *Darlington Hoopes: The Political Biography of an American Socialist* (Glasgow, Scotland, U.K., 2005), pp. 100-101.

[56] Ibid., pp. 108-109.

New York's Samuel H. Friedman, a former high school science teacher, social worker and editor of the *Socialist Call*, a weekly newspaper founded by party militants in opposition to *The New Leader* in 1935. Friedman, who was later frequently arrested during the civil rights protests of the 1960s and had initially planned to join slain civil rights worker Michael Schwerner in Mississippi during his fateful voter registration drive in 1964, served as the party's vice-presidential candidate on the Hoopes-led tickets in 1952 and 1956.[57]

An ebullient Hoopes, who was running for a seat on the Pennsylvania Supreme Court at the time of his nomination, accepted the party's nod with great élan.[58] "This is not merely a campaign," he told the cheering delegates, "it's a crusade."[59]

Born on a farm in Bel Air, Maryland, Hoopes was educated at the George School, a Quaker preparatory school outside of Philadelphia, and later attended the University of Wisconsin for a year where he majored in agriculture. He later studied law at night in the office of a Norristown lawyer and was admitted to the Pennsylvania Bar in 1921.

Hoopes had served three terms in the Pennsylvania legislature as a Socialist where he led the fight for passage of the federal child labor amendment and was once voted the state's most outstanding legislator by the Association of Pennsylvania Newspaper Reporters. A brilliant and particularly shrewd parliamentarian, the young Hoopes frequently outmaneuvered the Republicans in the GOP-dominated House during his three terms in the state legislature, winning him accolades from reporters across the state. "When it comes to tying the Republican-controlled House into a knot, Darlington Hoopes, fiery Berks Socialist, seems to be an expert," wrote an Associated Press writer in December 1933.[60]

Long considered the "power behind the throne" during Socialist Mayor J. Henry Stump's second administration, Hoopes also served as Reading's city solicitor from 1936-40 and had nearly been elected president judge of the Court of Common Pleas in Berks County, losing narrowly to a Democratic and Republican fusion candidate whose campaign was largely funded by local bank directors, steel executives and utility magnates looking for the court's protection.[61]

---

[57] "Socialist Ticket Headed by Thomas," *New York Times*, June 5, 1944; "Samuel H. Friedman, 93, Editor and Ex-Socialist Party Candidate," *New York Times*, Mar. 19, 1990.
[58] "Pa. Socialists Active," *Socialist Call*, Feb. 18, 1944.
[59] "The Crusade," *Socialist Call*, June 16, 1944.
[60] "They're in the Limelight: Darlington Hoopes," *Reading Eagle*, Aug. 31, 1934.
[61] Henderson, *Darlington Hoopes.*, pp. 46, 87.

Positioned perfectly for his party's presidential nomination if he was willing to pursue it, Maynard C. Krueger gave the convention's keynote speech, which was broadcast nationally over the CBS radio network. (The national media, it seems, respected the country's established minor parties in those days and even included some of their convention proceedings in their news coverage.)

Declaring that World War II was the only thing that had eased the nation's dire unemployment crisis during the Great Depression, Krueger urged a postwar nationalization of the war industry to "create jobs and maintain security" and criticized both major parties for uniting behind a policy of returning the defense industry to private hands following the war. In marshaling industry for wartime production, the pipe-smoking professor said that the U.S. government had proven that a country weaned on the myth of the free market could indeed plan for production if it so desired — a position long advocated by the Socialists.[62]

"In this process," Krueger continued, "history has confirmed the position advanced by Socialists through the years. It is not a visionary dream that the nation's natural resources, its factories and facilities and its labor power can be combined to produce a greatly increased national income and industrial output. Turning the government's holdings over to the private enterprise system, he said, would be a tragic mistake, a return to the prewar days with all the horrors one could imagine, including "bread lines and apple selling, cobwebbed factories and foreclosed farms."[63]

The New Deal was long dead, he concluded, and even when it was alive it was "merely the same old capitalism with some relief and social insurance for which we Socialists did the political spadework." In calling for a new political alignment in the United States, Krueger said it was time for timid labor leaders to realize that their interminably long honeymoon with Roosevelt and the Democrats was over.[64]

The Socialist Party's platform of 1944 called for "(1) the winning of the earliest possible peace that will last; (2) the provision of economic security for every American, with the preservation and increase of liberty; (3) the establishment of fraternity among all races, with equality of rights and obligations; and (4) the improvement of the techniques of democratic political action."[65]

---

[62] "Krueger Says War Ended Job Crisis," *New York Times*, June 3, 1944.
[63] Ibid.
[64] Ibid.
[65] Bertram Benedict, "The Socialist Vote," *Pittsburgh Press*, Oct. 4, 1944.

The platform, drafted primarily by Thomas, also strongly condemned the Allied demand for an unconditional surrender by Germany and Japan. "By shouting that slogan," the platform stated, "the Roosevelt Administration is prolonging this war and inviting the next by underwriting with the lives of our sons the restoration and maintenance of the British, Dutch, and French Empires in the Far East, and the Balkanization of Europe between Moscow and London."[66]

While rejecting an "America First or isolationist imperialism" as "dangerous to democracy and peace," the party's platform also warned that a new war would not be averted by any "triple alliance" of the world's superpowers and urged the postwar United Nations "to follow the disarmament of the enemy countries by ending their own competitive armaments and military conscription and working out international guarantees of national security."[67]

The party's traditional opposition to racial discrimination and the usual planks calling for the nationalization of industry and the adoption of a full employment program were also expressed in the platform, as was a resolution calling for an end to burdensome and discriminatory state ballot access restrictions for minor parties. In a separate resolution, the party specifically called for the liberalization of California's ballot access law to make it easier for the Socialist and other minor parties to qualify for the ballot.[68] For the first time in his five campaigns for the presidency, Thomas and his running mate had to rely exclusively on a write-in effort in the Golden State that year.

In addition to nominating a presidential ticket and adopting a platform, the delegates also elected Thomas and Hoopes to two-year terms on the party's National Executive Committee (NEC). They were joined on that committee by campaign manager Harry Fleischman, the brilliant Thomas biographer who remained in his role as national secretary. Others elected or re-elected to the NEC in 1944 included Wisconsin's Walter Uphoff, Lawrence Piercey of Michigan, William Becker of New Jersey, Albert Hamilton of Washington, D.C., Morris Milgrim, Ben Horowitz, former national secretary Travers Clement and Robin Myers — the last four from New York.[69]

---

[66] Ibid.
[67] Harry Fleischman, *Norman Thomas: A Biography* (New York, 1964), pp. 210-211.
[68] "Socialists Demand a Peace Offensive," *New York Times*, June 4, 1944.
[69] "Socialist Ticket Headed by Thomas," *New York Times*, June 5, 1944.

As in 1940, money was again a serious problem for the Socialists, whose dues-paying membership had fallen to fewer than 1,000 members nationally. Hoping to raise $100,000 for the national campaign — an unrealistically ambitious figure the party never came close to raising — the cash-strapped Socialists nevertheless received $8,000 in contributions and pledges from the delegates during the convention's closing session, a festive finale in which the cheering delegates enthusiastically named Thomas and Hoopes as their national candidates amid the singing of party songs and the playing of a piano and bass fiddle.[70]

The celebratory mood didn't last long. Like the country's two other nationally-organized minor parties — one that had been around for 75 years and another that had survived for more than half a century — the Socialists were about to embark on one of the most grueling and unrewarding campaigns imaginable.

---

[70] "Socialists Seek $100,000," *Berkshire Eagle* (Pittsfield, MA) June 6, 1944.

Chapter II

The Country's Conscience

The 59-year-old Thomas, who peddled the Marion Star — Warren G. Harding's newspaper — as a young boy growing up in Ohio, was fairly well known as an editor for *The Nation*, the country's most popular liberal magazine, and *The World Tomorrow*, a monthly published by the pacifist Fellowship of Reconciliation, and in later years for his frequent bids for the presidency. Many Americans considered him the "nation's conscience."

A man of considerable charm and persuasiveness, Thomas was an American original. While he never held an elective office, nearly two-and-a-half million votes were cast for him during his lifetime — and several times that number, including more than a few prominent citizens, had seriously considered voting for him at one time or another during his long career. When a White House staff member once confided to Eleanor Roosevelt that he had voted for Thomas in 1932, the First Lady responded by saying, "If I hadn't been married to Franklin, I would have too."[1]

He was, as an upstate New York newspaper described him in 1959, "a Socialist, a radical, a conservative and a liberal at one and the same time," exemplifying "the radical's tendency in his economic outlook although remaining a conservative in constitutional principles." In their view, Thomas had been a constructive critic of his times and, while frequently playing the role of gadfly, had "contributed much to the country's progress."[2]

A graduate of Princeton University and a one-time settlement worker in New York City, Thomas possessed considerable literary

---

[1] Dwight Steward, *Mr. Socialism, Norman Thomas: His Life and Times* (Secaucus, N.J., 1974), p. 9.
[2] "Norman Thomas at 75," *Lockport Union-Sun & Journal*, Dec. 1, 1959.

powers — he authored more than two dozen books — and had a reservoir of personal magnetism. Like his predecessor Eugene V. Debs, the former minister and social worker was a spellbinding public speaker. But unlike Debs, who frequently engaged in demagoguery, the stately Thomas was also a formidable socialist theoretician.

Though he regarded evangelism as his primary calling, or vocation, the young preacher never hesitated to join a picket line — often at great personal risk. He had taken part in the famous textile workers' strike in Passaic, New Jersey, in 1919. Seven years later, he again participated in a Passaic labor dispute and was arrested and jailed until his bail could be raised. The charges against him were later dropped.

In 1922, Thomas assumed the duties of co-director of the League for Industrial Democracy, the educational arm of the Socialist Party. He shared that post with the group's founder, Harry W. Laidler, a prolific author and one of the party's most durable functionaries. An offspring of the Intercollegiate Socialist Society, an organization founded in 1905 to convert college students to the socialist cause and whose members included Paul H. Douglas, who later became a U.S. Senator, W.E.B. Du Bois and poet Babette Deutsch, the League for Industrial Democracy sponsored literally thousands of speeches given by Thomas across the country, making him the undisputed heir to Gene Debs' legacy.

The son and grandson of Presbyterian ministers, Norman Mattoon Thomas decided on the ministry shortly after graduating as class valedictorian from Princeton in 1905. Shortly after his ordination from Union Theological Seminary about six years later, Thomas left Christ Church and gave up his cushy post as associate minister of the swanky Brick Presbyterian Church. He then became pastor of New York's East Harlem Presbyterian Church, an old, dilapidated church on the verge of shutting its doors for lack of members. Thomas served as minister there from 1911 to 1918.

Simultaneously, Thomas also became chairman of the American Parish, a loosely-organized federation of Presbyterian churches and social welfare organizations that included various houses of worship from East 106th Street in Manhattan to East 153rd Street in the Bronx. Largely inhabited by Italians, Poles, Hungarians and Russian Jews, Thomas called the larger parish his "little League of Nations."

It was in this capacity that Thomas witnessed firsthand the squalid living quarters and horrible working conditions of so many of New York's desperately poor immigrants and gradually began to embrace the ideals of socialism.

"What is our democracy worth?" the young minister asked his former Princeton classmates in 1915. "How shall we apply it to our social, industrial and political problems? Are we preparing well for national safety in peace or war when so many of our workers cannot, even under favorable conditions, make the proper living wage?"[3]

Already a confirmed pacifist, Thomas signed on with the Socialist Party just as the United States prepared to enter World War I, only a few years after the party's high-water mark of 1911-12 — a period when nearly 1,200 Socialists were swept into office across the country. Idealistic rather than ideological, Thomas expressed his "profound fear of the undue exultation of the state and a profound faith that the new world we desire must depend upon freedom and fellowship, rather than any sort of coercion whatsoever" in his application to the party.[4]

Thomas abhorred Marxist jargon and shunned violence and deception as acceptable tactics in furthering the cause of socialism. While the idea of class conflict was always secondary to his basic ethical precepts, he nevertheless believed that socialism was democracy's brightest hope.

Having emerged as the Socialist Party's foremost spokesman at a time when many others were leaving the party, Norman Thomas devoted almost every waking hour to the socialist cause, organizing, speaking and writing on behalf of a number of radical and liberal organizations. He was able to become a full-time agitator and social crusader due, in no small measure, to his wife's substantial inheritance.

Describing it as the happiest day in his life, Thomas married Frances Violet Stewart in 1910. Financially comfortable but certainly not wealthy, Violet had come from an old New York family. Her father had been a Wall Street financier. Violet was working in a tuberculosis clinic in the city's slums when she and Norman first met. They eventually had three daughters and three sons, one of whom — Tommy (Norman, Jr.), their oldest child — died at an early age, tragically succumbing to meningitis stemming from an ear infection when he was ten.

The tall and lanky Thomas, a man who enjoyed sailing and tennis but could never remember his shoe size, was an unlikely Socialist. Unlike most of his comrades, many of whom came from

---

[3] Swanberg, *Norman Thomas: The Last Idealist*, p. 40.
[4] "Memory of Norman Thomas Lifts Gathering of American Socialists," *Ottawa Citizen*, Nov. 22, 1984.

working-class backgrounds, including some who barely escaped poverty, Thomas enjoyed a relatively comfortable upbringing.

Born in a two-story parsonage next to his father's Presbyterian Church, he was raised in a solidly middle-class household. "I wasn't born in a log cabin and I'm not likely to live in the White House," he once cautioned a reporter who was planning to write a glowing Lincolnesque story about the Socialist clergyman's humble beginnings. "My folks had to count the pennies pretty carefully," said Thomas, "but I was never hungry."[5]

Despite some childhood ailments, Thomas enjoyed a secure and happy upbringing, never wanting for creature comforts. Though far from privileged, he was nevertheless blessed by the generosity of relatives. A wealthy uncle living in Paris, in fact, provided the financial help that enabled the young Thomas — stifled by the lack of an intellectual atmosphere — to transfer from Bucknell University, a private college in Lewisburg, Pennsylvania, to Princeton University in his sophomore year. Once at Princeton, where he honed his debating skills while excelling in politics and history, Thomas supported himself by tutoring and working at a variety of odd jobs.[6]

Thomas, moreover, had little in common with his predecessor Eugene V. Debs, a man who rose to prominence from the ranks of poverty-stricken toilers. In fact, the urbane and witty Thomas didn't even join the party until he was thirty-three years old. Happily married and by then a father of five, he officially joined the party in 1918, some six years after the party's heyday and just prior to the infamous Palmer Raids and "Red Scare" that swept the country during the First World War.

Like many others opposed to the war, Thomas's name appeared on a list submitted by military intelligence to a Senate committee investigating individuals who had opposed U.S. involvement in World War I. He was in good company. The list of "subversives," among thousands of others, included historian Charles A. Beard, Eugene V. Debs, IWW organizer Elizabeth Gurley Flynn and *Nation* publisher Oswald Garrison Villard. During this period, government agents regularly followed Thomas as he moved about the country.

Mistakenly believing that Thomas was "more insidious than Debs," Postmaster General Albert S. Burleson, a conservative Texas Democrat who came as close to censoring the press as any

---

[5] "Norman Thomas: An American Rebel," *Washington Post*, Dec. 20, 1968.
[6] Swanberg, *Norman Thomas: The Last Idealist*, p. 11; James C. Durham, *Norman Thomas* (New York, 1974), pp. 17-18.

official in American history, refused to deliver three issues of Thomas's *The World Tomorrow* during the summer of 1918 and had even threatened to throw the activist minister in prison as a result of an article he wrote criticizing the U.S. invasion of the Soviet Union in Siberia and at Archangel. Though the initiator of U.S. intervention in the Russian civil war, President Wilson — the man who appointed Burleson as a reward for his help in securing the Democratic presidential nomination in 1912 — decided that his former student's periodical was not seditious and ordered Burleson to back off.

The plight of the nation's nearly 4,000 conscientious objectors during World War I, including that of his brother Evan, had been Thomas's most cherished cause during the war. It was an issue near and dear to his heart. Often finding it more difficult to approach church leaders than military officials in discussing the shabby treatment of the nation's conscientious objectors, Thomas began growing increasingly disillusioned with organized Christianity. "The church," he wrote bitterly a few years earlier, "which has steadily supported the state in its policy of coercing war's heretics is a church which has denied its own right to speak with the voice of God to the hearts of men." In his view, organized Christianity was "committing suicide by the neglect of the things which pertain to her salvation."[7]

Thomas addressed many of those issues in his first book, *The Conscientious Objector in America*, in 1923 — the first of many books he would author over the next forty-five years.[8]

In 1920, Thomas created the American Civil Liberties Bureau, which, in its formative days, included such luminaries as Clarence Darrow, Felix Frankfurter, Helen Keller and John Dewey. The Bureau was renamed the American Civil Liberties League and later became the American Civil Liberties Union (ACLU).

During this period, the intrepid Thomas — a relentless champion of unpopular causes — also argued for U.S. recognition of the Soviet Union and actively promoted the cause of Irish freedom. He also spent countless hours immersed in labor disputes and ideological debates with others across the political spectrum.

A pied piper to thousands of political activists during the Great Depression and thereafter, the anti-Communist leftist lived and breathed politics. He talked about politics incessantly. A fellow bird watcher and friend once observed that Thomas even insisted on caucusing in the quiet of the woods.

---

[7] Murray B. Seidler, *Norman Thomas, Respectable Rebel* (Syracuse, 1967), pp. 71-72.
[8] Ibid., p. 71.

In 1924, Thomas was nominated as the Socialist Party's candidate for governor of New York.[9] The Socialist Party was supporting Wisconsin's "Fighting Bob" La Follette's third-party bid for the White House that year. Buoyed by the Labour Party's success in Great Britain a year earlier, Thomas and other leading Socialists believed that the time was ripe for a similar progressive movement in the United States. The Socialist Party's resurgence, they argued, could play a vital role in making that happen.

Thomas agreed wholeheartedly with Morris Hillquit, who predicted in late October that the La Follette movement would lead to a permanent new progressive party in the United States. "If the forces of political progress in American politics are to assert themselves effectively and lastingly they must be organized into a party of their own," asserted Hillquit in late October of that year. "The La Follette-Wheeler campaign," he continued, "is a definite break-up of the traditional alignment in American politics and will inevitably lead to the formation of a permanent new party. The strength and character of the new party will be very largely determined by the size of the vote cast against both old parties in the coming election."[10]

"If British labor can do it, why can't we?" asked Thomas, while attending the February 1924 Conference for Progressive Political Action meeting in St. Louis as a special correspondent for the *Nation* magazine. Like many Socialists that year, Thomas believed that La Follette's insurgent candidacy represented "the most hopeful event in American politics in our generation."[11]

Not everyone shared Thomas's optimism, however. David Karsner, the former managing editor of *The New York Call* — the country's leading Socialist newspaper before it collapsed in 1923 — believed the Socialist Party's balmiest days had long since passed. Describing the party during that period as "a political ghost stalking in the graveyard," Karsner believed that the organization inherited by Thomas was nothing more than "a debating society."[12]

There was undoubtedly plenty of truth in what Karsner observed, but Thomas wasn't the least bit discouraged and remained determined to revitalize the once-proud party.

---

[9] "Socialists Name Thomas as Head of State Ticket," *New York Times*, July 28, 1924.
[10] "Urges Progressives to Back State Ticket," *New York Times*, Oct. 22, 1924.
[11] Steward, *Mr. Socialism*, pp. 127-128
[12] Ibid., p. 126; David Karsner, "The Passing of the Socialist Party," *Current History* (June 1924), p. 402.

THE LOWEST EBB

During his maiden campaign — one of more than a dozen unsuccessful tries for public office on the Socialist ticket — Thomas doubled as a spokesman for La Follette's presidential campaign. Though stumping more for La Follette and his fledgling Progressive movement than for himself that year, Thomas polled a respectable 99,854 votes against Democrat Alfred E. Smith and Republican Theodore Roosevelt, Jr., son of the late president, in a race narrowly won by the "Happy Warrior."

The following year, Thomas garnered 39,574 votes as the Socialist Party's candidate for mayor of New York City against popular Democrat Jimmy Walker, the colorful song-writing, wise-cracking politician, and his hapless Republican rival Frank Waterman, the fountainpen king. Delving into ever-present Tammany corruption and the myriad problems plaguing America's largest city, Thomas called for city-owned housing for the poor and public ownership of the city's mass transit system during his 1925 mayoral campaign, earning him a national reputation as an urban expert.[13] During the course of the campaign, he also gained the enthusiastic support of Republican congressman Fiorello H. La Guardia, the colorful future mayor who described the tall and lanky Socialist as the most qualified candidate in the race and the only one who had a "platform that is constructive and means something."[14]

Barely pausing to catch his breath, Thomas quickly became a perennial candidate, running unsuccessfully for the State Senate in 1926 and for a seat on New York City's board of aldermen in 1927.

While running for the State Senate in 1926 — his third bid for public office in as many years — Thomas took time out from his campaign to visit the Terre Haute home of Eugene V. Debs, who died in October of that year following a lengthy illness. Debs' death, though not entirely unexpected, shocked and saddened thousands in the Socialist movement.

"There may have been a cloud over Gene Debs's citizenship in the country," Thomas told a crowd that had gathered on the front porch of Debs' home, "but there is no cloud over his citizenship in the great immortals…The secret of his greatness was that he loved people. We cannot say that we love Debs if we go back to the lack of faith and petty compromises. He lives in us. We have kindled our little torches at his great fire — and we must carry on."[15]

---

[13] Steward, *Mr. Socialism*, p. 130.
[14] "La Guardia Backs Thomas," *New York Times*, Oct. 19, 1925.
[15] Charles Gorham, *Leader at Large: The Long and Fighting Life of Norman Thomas* (New York, 1970), p. 89.

And carry on, he certainly did. There was no stopping the hurry-for-a-train Thomas.

The saint-like Thomas, a six-foot-two inch, 185-pound man with cheery pale blue eyes, unbounded energy and a seemingly endless reservoir of vitality, frequently put himself in harm's way during his lifelong crusade for social justice and political reform. Refusing to be intimidated or silenced by threats or the possibility of physical danger, Thomas, a consistent and courageous voice for America's dispossessed, would join almost any picket line, take part in any demonstration or address any potentially hostile audience.

When the one-time Presbyterian minister, at great personal risk, courageously spoke out on behalf of destitute African-American sharecroppers in the small rural hamlet of Birdsong, Arkansas, in March 1935, he was promptly dragged from the podium and manhandled by a mob of inebriated shotgun-wielding whites who pursued Thomas and his small entourage in a harrowing, high-speed chase across the county line. "We don't need no Gawddamn Yankee bastard to tell us what to do with our niggers," yelled one belligerent drunk.[16]

Maintaining his sense of humor even under the most dangerous and dire of circumstances, Thomas later said he would have enjoyed the ride more if there had been shatterproof glass in the rear window. Barely escaping with his life, the Socialist Party leader faced similar racist vigilantes when he spoke for the multiracial Southern Tenant Farmers' Union in other parts of the state during his tour of the South.[17]

One of the most dignified men in public life, the tall and lean Thomas traveled across the Hudson River a few years later to speak out against Jersey City's corrupt machine led by longtime Mayor Frank "I AM THE LAW" Hague. Hague, whose administration was once described as "the best disciplined machine this side of Moscow," was probably the closest thing to a municipal dictator in American history. Candidates for statewide office were rarely elected without his support.

Coining the slogan "Hoover fed the Belgians and starved the Americans," Hague's machine rolled up an impressive 118,000-vote majority for Roosevelt in Hudson County in 1932, enabling FDR to carry New Jersey by a narrow margin. It was the first time a Democrat had carried the state in twenty years. Even Democratic President Woodrow Wilson, a native of New Jersey, failed to carry

---

[16] Fleischman, *Norman Thomas: A Biography*, pp. 148-149.
[17] Ibid.

the Garden State during his campaign for re-election in 1916.

With what appeared to be a free flowing pipeline from the U.S. Treasury, Hague's powerful machine dispensed a seemingly endless number of federal jobs in New Jersey. Hague, who was amply rewarded by the Roosevelt administration for swinging the state's sixteen electoral votes into the Democratic column, later built one of the largest police forces, per capita, in the nation. An unusually large number of policemen lined the city's streets and corners, prompting one frequent visitor to Jersey City to observe that the city "always looks as if there were about to be a parade or riot."[18] It was the closest thing to a police state in America.

A man of modest means, Hague, who usually dressed in expensively tailored clothing, lived a most lavish lifestyle. He somehow always managed to obtain high-priced seats at championship prizefights and box seats at World Series games. He owned a duplex in Jersey City, leased a suite in an exclusive Manhattan hotel, a summer home at the South Jersey shore, a villa in Miami Beach and took frequent vacations to Europe and Hawaii — all on a modest $8,000 annual salary.[19]

When Thomas, who had been forbidden by the mayor from addressing a rally in his city, tried to address a crowd there, Hague's burly police officers punched him and, warning him not to return, escorted him back to New York City. When the Socialist leader returned an hour later, Hague's cops again mauled the gentle preacher and later threw him, bleeding, onto a Manhattan sidewalk.

Undaunted, the patrician rebel, refusing to buckle under to Hague's heavy-handed tactics, went to federal court where a judge immediately issued an injunction against the mayor and his thugs. The bandaged Thomas then proceeded to eloquently denounce Hague's "den of thieves" to a large throng in Jersey City's Journal Square.[20]

"I guess one of the reasons I'm a Socialist instead of a Communist," Thomas remarked later, "is that Stalin acts too much like Hague, and Hague like Hitler."[21]

A tireless crusader for economic and social justice who railed against "income inequality" long before that phrase was popularized by the short-lived Occupy Wall Street movement, "Comrade

---

[18] Reinhard H. Luthin, *American Demagogues* (Gloucester, MA, 1959), p. 143.
[19] Ibid., pp. 141-142.
[20] William Manchester, *The Glory and the Dream: A Narrative History of America 1932-1972* (New York, 1974), p. 207.
[21] "Socialism's Champion Norman Thomas Dies," *Madison Capital Times*, Dec. 19, 1968.

Thomas," as his supporters affectionately called him, was particularly active in the early civil rights movement, working closely with A. Philip Randolph, head of the Brotherhood of Sleeping Car Porters, the nation's first predominantly black labor union. Randolph, who grew up in Jacksonville, Florida, was then in the vanguard of the struggle to improve the lives of African-Americans and later led the 1963 March on Washington in which Martin Luther King, Jr., delivered his immortal "I Have a Dream" speech.

A civil libertarian primarily concerned with individual freedom and justice, it was the moral issues of the day that really seemed to light Thomas's fire, sparking his indignation and prompting him to speak out when almost nobody else would.

During World War II, for example, the ethereal ex-preacher stood virtually alone in condemning the internment of more than a hundred thousand Japanese-Americans in prison camps on the West Coast.[22] Recognizing that a Nazi victory would be "the lowest circle of hell," the Socialist gadfly also sharply criticized President Roosevelt's demand for an unconditional surrender, believing that a statement of democratic peace terms would have been more reasonable and acceptable to the defeated parties. He also strongly condemned the use of atomic bombs on the Japanese cities of Hiroshima and Nagasaki: "We shall pay for this in a horrible hatred of millions of people which goes deeper and farther than we think."[23]

In February 1945, shortly after the Yalta Conference, which took place in a Russian resort town in the Crimea — the second of three meetings between the Big Three — Thomas bitterly condemned the plans adopted by Roosevelt, Churchill and Stalin for Europe's postwar reorganization. "A war began ostensibly to guarantee the integrity of Poland," Thomas sardonically observed, "and entered presumably by the United States on the basis of the principles of the Atlantic Charter, which condemns 'territorial changes that do not accord with the freely-expressed wishes of the peoples concerned,' ends with Stalin in possession of the territory that he took forcibly from Poland in alliance with the Nazi aggressor and with a government in charge which is his creation."[24]

Two months later Roosevelt was dead. Thomas, who had frequently corresponded with the president, occasionally even visiting him in the White House, was profoundly saddened by the president's sudden death. Though it was something he could

---

[22] Manchester, *The Glory and the Dream*, p. 208.
[23] Ibid.
[24] Gorham, *Leader at Large*, p. 162.

never admit during the difficult years of the Great Depression, the period when — for all intents and purposes — he stood as FDR's most consistent adversary on the Left, Thomas realized that Roosevelt had imbued the American people with a renewed sense of hope and confidence during the country's darkest hour. "It is hard to appraise his significance in history in the passions of this hour," he wrote shortly after Roosevelt's passing, "but I do not think there will be much dispute that in the crisis of 1933 he magnificently restored confidence, that in his first term he caught America up in the field of social legislation, and that he appreciably revived faith in the ballot among the masses."[25]

Joining millions of his fellow citizens in mourning the fallen president, Thomas said that the public's sense of loss was more personal, more acute, than what might ordinarily have been expected because of Roosevelt's personal qualities, including his immense charm, his great courage, and his profound and heartfelt sympathy for the downtrodden.[26]

Thomas certainly didn't feel the same way about FDR's successor. President Truman, he said shortly after Roosevelt's death, was "a political accident" who had never shown the slightest "grasp of great political issues." Writing in the *Socialist Call*, the party's weekly newspaper, Thomas described the new president as "a personally honest but completely blind and insensitive henchman of one of the worst bosses in recent American history." If Truman's political career was a lesson for America's youth, added Thomas, "it is a bad and cynical lesson."[27]

When Germany surrendered later that spring, ending the horrific war in Europe, Thomas was profoundly relieved but, too much a humanitarian, found little reason to rejoice, particularly since the war in the Pacific theater was still raging.

In a letter to the *New York Times* shortly after V-E Day, the five-time presidential candidate again questioned the policy of unconditional surrender as the only terms for ending the bloodshed in Asia, a conflict then marked by atrocities on both sides. Declaring that he had diligently sought explanations for what he termed a "costly war of annihilation," Thomas questioned the usual justification for prolonging the war, the emotional argument involving the sneak attack on Pearl Harbor. "The truth about Pearl Harbor has by no means all been told and cannot of itself justify continuing

---

[25] Fleischman, *Norman Thomas: A Biography*, p. 214.
[26] Ibid.
[27] Norman Thomas, "The Political and Economic Legacy of the Roosevelt Administration," *Socialist Call*, Apr. 23, 1945.

this war of annihilation," wrote Thomas.[28]

Rejecting that rationale, Thomas said he had come to two conclusions regarding the reasons for prolonging the war with Japan, neither of which reflected well on the United States. "One of them is an ignoble racism — our enemies are 'rats' and less than human," he said. "Another is a panicky fear of the economic consequences of immediate peace in Asia — a fear shared by Washington, Wall Street and workers who bitterly remember that under our economic system war is the great job provider."[29]

Like many others, Thomas was deeply appalled and saddened by the catastrophic way in which the war in Asia was abruptly ended. "As an American," wrote Thomas, "I cannot rejoice over this inestimable boon of the ending of a victorious war without a sense of shame for the horror which the atomic bomb released upon the earth. I shall be told that it was the bomb which ended the war. As things were, that is probably true, but I shall always believe that the war might have been ended before the first atomic bomb was dropped on Hiroshima bringing death to at least a hundred thousand men, women and children…Certainly that bomb should not have been dropped on a crowded city without warning. It is a tragedy which may be an omen of the eventual destruction of our civilization that we human beings, especially we Americans, are so bold in dealing with things and so unimaginative in the realm of ideas.[30]

"At the very least it would have been within our power to direct the world's attention to the destructive capacity of an atomic bomb at some designated point not crowded with human beings," continued Thomas. "It was wholly inexcusable to drop the second bomb on Nagasaki. Proof of the power of atomic energy did not require the slaughter of hundreds of thousands of human guinea pigs."[31]

As biographer Raymond F. Gregory poignantly noted, Thomas was outraged by both bombings, but was inconsolably incensed by the bombing of Nagasaki only three days after the United States, demonstrating little or no patience, dropped an atomic bomb on Hiroshima — a breathtakingly cruel and devastating blast that instantaneously incinerated tens of thousands and eventually killed as many as 166,000 men, women and children —

---

[28] "Unconditional Surrender: Mr. Thomas Says Hard Terms on Japan Prolong War," *New York Times*, May 21, 1945.
[29] Ibid.
[30] Gorham, *Leader at Large*, p. 166.
[31] Ibid.

without waiting to see if Japan was willing to surrender. His country had let him down again, this time in the most unimaginable and horrific way possible. Thomas was rightfully outraged that the U.S. was unwilling to demonstrate any patience in determining whether its desired psychological objectives had been achieved before callously dropping a second atom bomb.[32] The use of a plutonium implosion-type bomb on Nagasaki, a seaport with a population of about 263,000, claimed between 40,000-80,000 lives, almost all of them civilians.

In July 1945, Thomas testified before the Senate Foreign Relations Committee on the final day of hearings on the ratification of the United Nations Charter. In a prepared statement he told the committee that the Senate should ratify the charter "not because I believe it an adequate basis for lasting peace, but because I believe that the United States will be in a better position to lead in the establishment of such a basis if it should ratify the charter and in good faith use its constructive provisions for an increase in world cooperation."[33]

Thomas was also deeply worried about the growing Soviet threat in the immediate postwar period, telling delegates to the Socialist Party's 1946 annual convention in Chicago that the threat of Nazi global domination during World War II had been replaced by "an equally ruthless drive for power" by the Soviet Union — a dictatorship "with far greater latent strength behind it" than the Nazis ever possessed.[34]

In what might have been an opening salvo to the 1948 presidential campaign, Thomas attacked former Vice President Henry A. Wallace a few months later, accusing the Secretary of Commerce of peddling a policy of appeasement toward the Soviet Union. In a joint statement issued by Thomas and Harry Fleishman, the party's young national secretary, the former presidential candidate described Wallace as heir to the same policy of appeasement pursued by Neville Chamberlain at Munich and later by Roosevelt and Truman at Cairo, Teheran, Yalta and Potsdam. It was absolutely shocking, said Thomas, that Wallace, who had argued so vigorously in favor of going to war against Hitler to preserve Eastern Europe, was now "content to leave so much of Eu-

---

[32] Gregory, *Norman Thomas: The Great Dissenter*, p. 217.
[33] "Pact Hearing Nearing End: Green, Dulles, Thomas and Murray Support It," *Tuscaloosa News*, July 13, 1945.
[34] "Thomas Predicts Threat in Soviet," *New York Times*, June 1, 1946.

rope and Asia to the tender mercies of a dictatorship which practices the same sort of tyranny."[35]

Though Thomas insisted that his 1944 presidential candidacy would be his final campaign for public office, it pained him deeply to watch the party to which he had devoted so much of his life continue to deteriorate.[36] Every new setback experienced by his once-robust party troubled him immensely. When the Socialist Party's statewide candidates — Coleman B. Cheney for governor and labor leader Walter O'Hagan for the U.S. Senate — were arbitrarily removed from New York ballot in 1946 along with the nominees of the smaller Socialist Labor and Socialist Workers parties, Thomas spoke out sharply, criticizing Gov. Herbert Lehman and U.S. Sen. James M. Mead for allowing a Democratic challenge to the minor-party nominating petitions on flimsy technicalities. The lawsuit challenging the state's minor-party petitions had been filed by the Democratic candidate for state controller.[37]

In an angry telegram to Mead, Thomas said that he was holding both men "personally responsible for the unprecedented and outrageous action" of removing the minor parties from the New York ballot. Asserting that the heavy-handed tactics used by their party made a mockery of their stated belief in democracy and liberalism, Thomas excoriated both men for setting "a dangerous precedent" in denying the three minor parties fair access to the ballot, describing it as "one of the most serious offenses against freedom of the ballot in America."[38] Thomas, who received little to no satisfaction in bringing the matter to the attention of the state's two leading Democrats, was relegated to casting write-in votes for his party's nominees in November.[39]

Thomas's latest book, *Appeal to the Nations*, an in-depth analysis of a half-dozen leading proposals for world peace, was published by Henry Holt in March 1947.[40]

---

[35] "Socialist Leaders Criticize Wallace," *New York Times*, Sep. 22, 1946.
[36] "Norman Thomas Won't Run," *New York Times*, Nov. 9, 1946.
[37] "Socialists Oppose Young's Suit," *New York Times*, Sep. 21, 1946; "Fights Minor-Party Ban; Norman Thomas Asks Lehman to Help Balk Suit by Young," *New York Times*, "Minor Parties Ruled Off Ballot in State," *New York Times*, Oct. 26, 1946. The state Supreme Court invalidated the Socialist and Socialist Labor petitions on the grounds that two petition witnesses had allegedly listed erroneous election precincts on the petitions while the Socialist Workers Party was removed because a notary public had failed to sign 13 petition sheets in Steuben County, although the notary had clearly stamped each of the pages.
[38] "Thomas Hits Democrats; Says Mead, Lehman Had Minor Parties Put Off Ballot," *New York Times*, Oct. 23, 1946; "Thomas Raps Democrats as 'Purgers,'" *Knickerbocker News*, Oct. 23, 1946.
[39] "Socialist Asks Write-In Vote," *New York Times*, Nov. 4, 1946.
[40] "Books-Authors," *New York Times*, Mar. 3, 1947.

Hoping to take advantage of his considerable radio experience, Thomas wrote to Edward R. Murrow of CBS in the spring of 1947 to inquire about the possibility of having his own weekly or bi-weekly radio program. He was hoping that landing such a job would enable him to curtail some of the extensive and exhausting travel involved in maintaining his hectic speaking schedule while providing an effective medium for his views. The iconic broadcast journalist responded politely, inviting Thomas to lunch and telling him that his proposal raised both "possibilities and problems." In the end, it was obvious to both Murrow and Thomas that most corporate advertisers would probably object to a Socialist commentator.[41]

Three months later while attending a meeting of the Socialist Party's national executive in Reading, Pennsylvania, Thomas received word that his beloved wife of thirty-four years had died suddenly of a heart attack at their summer home in Cold Spring Harbor, Long Island. Thomas, who had refused to travel far from home during that period due to Violet's heart condition, was devastated by her death.[42]

"The wrong man lost," proclaimed a prominent New York Democrat the day after the 1948 presidential election. "Dewey?" asked a friend. "No," replied the Democrat. "Thomas." That's precisely how William Manchester, one of our country's most gifted historians, summed up the long-distance runner's final campaign for the White House in *The Glory and the Dream*, a magisterial history of the United States covering the period from 1932 to 1972.[43]

Motivated by former Vice President Henry A. Wallace's candidacy on the Communist-tainted Progressive Party ticket, the principled champion of collectivism decided to take one more fling at the White House in 1948. Thomas, who only reluctantly agreed to run after failing to persuade A. Philip Randolph and Maynard Krueger to carry the party's torch that year, didn't think too highly of the former vice president. Describing his Progressive rival as "an amateur mystic," Thomas believed that if by some miracle Wallace was elected president, the country would have "a Messianic, if you prefer a diabolical, idea of destiny in a man with a mind completely disorganized. It is frightful to wonder," he said.[44]

---

[41] Swanberg, *Norman Thomas: The Last Idealist*, p. 305.
[42] "Norman Thomas' Wife Dies Suddenly," *New York Post*, Aug. 1, 1947; "Norman Thomas' Wife Dies in New York City," *Reading Eagle*, Aug. 1, 1947.
[43] Manchester, *The Glory and the Dream*, p. 208.
[44] "Thomas Astonished by Wallaceites' Gains," *Los Angeles Times*, Aug. 17, 1948.

Thomas, who had proposed that the United States should "extend material aid for immediate relief and reconstruction of devastated countries, without using such aid as a weapon" some three years before President Truman unveiled the much-heralded Marshall Plan, objected strongly to Wallace's opposition to the U.S.-led European recovery program.[45] The former vice president, who denounced the Marshall Plan as "a plan based on world division and conflict," had proposed his own seven-point plan, including the placing of Germany's industrial heartland, the Ruhr Valley, under the international control of the victorious Big Four — Britain, France, the United States and the Soviet Union.[46]

Thomas's sixth and final campaign for the presidency was welcomed by a number of leading newspapers, including the *New York Times* and the *Washington Post*. "We suspect he's really more interested in issues than in office," observed the *Baltimore Sun*. "Campaign years just give him an opportunity to make sense as he sees it. More often than not, the sense is pretty good."[47] Asserting that his candidacy would have a "politically hygienic effect" on the campaign, the *Cleveland Plain Dealer* predicted that Thomas would expose the Wallace-led Progressive Party for all of its "fuzzy-mindedness" and "cheap, Communist-abetted, demagogic exploitation of prejudices and political ignorance." Bemoaning the fact that the country's two major parties lacked candidates of Thomas's "integrity and unselfishness," the *Ithaca Journal* also heaped praise on the Socialist standard-bearer, as did the Portland-based *Oregonian*, the latter of which noted that Thomas's platform was far superior to that offered by Wallace and the Progressives. "A strange era it is when so-called liberals demonstrate their boasted liberalism by fawning upon communism," wrote its editorial writers.[48]

"All genuine liberals and radicals, outside of New York, who will want to express their protest against both old parties, will have an opportunity to do this by voting for Norman Thomas, rather than for the confused 'totalitarian liberal" Henry Wallace," observed the usually hostile *Jewish Daily Forward*, a paper that had been highly critical of Thomas four years earlier.[49] Even a Texas newspaper — the *Amarillo Daily News* — had some kind things to say about Thomas's latest candidacy, suggesting that it would be

---

[45] Gorham, *Leader at Large*, p. 161; "Thomas Opposes Wallace," *New York Times*, Mar. 21, 1948.
[46] "Wallace Offers Own Plan to Help Europe Recovery," *New York Times*, Dec. 31, 1947.
[47] Fleischman, *Norman Thomas: A Biography*, pp. 226-227.
[48] "Press Comment on Thomas' Candidacy," *Socialist Call*, June 4, 1948.
[49] Fleischman, *Norman Thomas: A Biography*, pp. 226-227.

"a far healthier sign for the future of the nation if he ran ahead of Henry Wallace." It continued:

> It is not a difficult matter for a good American to agree with Norman Thomas on a number of things. First, he rejects Henry Wallace as 'the apologist for the Russian slave state and the preacher of peace by blind appeasement.' He favors the Baruch plan for control of atomic energy. Any changes in the industrial or social structure of the nation he would make by processes authorized by the laws of the land, as laid down by the constitutions of the nation and the states. If it came to a choice between socialism as understood in Europe and democracy as followed in America, Mr. Thomas would choose American democracy.
>
> No Democrat or Republican will wish to see Mr. Thomas get far in the election next November; but a strong following of his moderate 'left wing' would indicate a healthier sign than heavier support of Wallace's extreme left.[50]

Decrying the frenzied attempt by Wallace's supporters to link the former vice president's candidacy to the late "Fighting Bob" La Follette's progressive legacy of 1924, *The Progressive* magazine endorsed Thomas in its September issue. Condemning Wallace for failing to repudiate Communist support — something the Wisconsin progressive did in no uncertain terms twenty-four years earlier — while citing the inadequacies of the two major party candidates on both domestic and foreign policy issues, the Madison-based magazine asserted that Thomas was "the most meaningful choice for progressives in 1948." Declaring that a vote for the Socialist candidate would speed the development of a long-overdue political realignment in the United States, the magazine's editor urged readers to ignore the wasted vote syndrome. "It seems to us damnable and dangerous nonsense to argue that one should refuse to vote for a man in whom we believe — solely because he hasn't a chance of winning. It seems to us just as preposterous to vote for a man in whom one doesn't believe — solely because he has a chance of winning. Democracy doesn't mean voting for a winner. It means voting for what you want."[51]

Thomas tried repeatedly to engage his Progressive Party rival in a one-on-one debate that year, but Wallace adamantly refused.

---

[50] "Norman Thomas," *Amarillo Daily News*, May 18, 1948.
[51] "Progressive Magazine Supports Norman Thomas for President," *Socialist Call*, Sep. 3, 1948.

The *Progressive* magazine and longtime Socialist Mayor Jasper McLevy of Bridgeport, Connecticut — the working-class city where Wallace launched his candidacy — both offered to host such a debate and the Mutual Broadcasting System, which carried the famous debate between Harold Stassen and Thomas Dewey earlier that year, even offered coast-to-coast radio coverage of such an event — but Wallace steadfastly refused to mix it up with his Socialist rival.[52]

While his 1948 campaign was a far more enjoyable experience than the lonely quest he waged four years earlier, Thomas was nevertheless subjected to the usual slights, one of the most personally painful of which involved theologian Reinhold Niebuhr. Once one of his dearest friends, Niebuhr wrote a full-length article on the presidential campaign for the November 1 issue of *Christianity and Crisis* without once mentioning Thomas's candidacy.[53]

Paired with Tucker Smith, a former labor organizer and head of the economics department at Michigan's Olivet College, as his vice-presidential running mate and a campaign budget of barely $60,000 — a tiny fraction of the $1,133,863 raised by Wallace and the $163,442 reportedly spent by States' Rights candidate Strom Thurmond — Thomas made the most of his extremely limited resources.[54]

Vastly overshadowed by Wallace's candidacy throughout the campaign, Thomas nevertheless stumped vigorously that year, accusing Republican Tom Dewey of "dealing in platitudes" while charging that President Truman was "dealing in invectives." Wallace, he said, was "dealing in exaggerated demagogism."[55] Thomas also accused both of his major-party rivals of stealing from his Socialist platform.[56]

Thomas picked up quite a few individual endorsements during the campaign, including those of novelist James T. Farrell and foreign correspondent Vincent Sheean, the latter of whom had provided some of the most in-depth coverage of the Spanish Civil War as a reporter for the *New York Herald Tribune*.

---

[52] "Commies Refuse to Debate Thomas," *Socialist Call*, May 28, 1948; "Thomas Challenges Wallace — Again," *Socialist Call*, June 4, 1948; "McLevy Invites Truman, Dewey, Wallace to Debate Thomas Here," *Bridgeport Telegram*, Aug. 16, 1948; "Thomas Backers Picket Wallace to Urge Debate," *Socialist Call*, Sep. 17, 1948; "Progressive Editor Raps Wallace for Dodging Debates With Thomas," *Socialist Call*, Oct. 22, 1948.
[53] Daniel F. Rice, *Reinhold Niebuhr and His Circle of Influence* (New York, 2013), p. 105.
[54] Steven J. Rosenstone, Roy L. Behr and Edward H. Lazarus, *Third Parties in America: Citizen Response to Major Party Failure* (Princeton, 1984), p. 28.
[55] "Thomas Hits 3 Opponents," *Wisconsin Rapids Daily Tribune*, Oct. 15, 1948.
[56] Norman Thomas, "Republicans and Democrats are Stealing from My Socialist Platform," *Look*, Aug. 17, 1948, pp. 34, 36, 38.

"A vote for Norman Thomas is the only vote which will not be wasted," wrote Farrell in endorsing Thomas's candidacy. "Norman Thomas is called the 'conscience of America' because he challenges the powers of privilege, opportunism, greed and totalitarianism. He has dedicated his life to the democratic way of life, demonstrating in words and deeds his devotion to the needs and aspirations of all Americans."

Declaring that he was "fit for the presidency," Sheean maintained that Thomas was "the only candidate whose views on international relations during the present period have been governed by principle throughout and owe nothing to expediency. In the dominant question of war and peace," wrote Sheean, "he is to be trusted because he means what he says and has clung to the truth no matter how much it might run counter to temporary waves of feeling."[57]

Journalist Max Lerner, who voted for FDR in each of the four previous presidential elections, also came out in support of Thomas, but the most surprising endorsement came from none other than Thomas's longtime adversary Dorothy Thompson, a prewar interventionist who had sparred vigorously with her Socialist counterpart prior to U.S. entry in World War II. Thompson, one of the most influential woman in America — arguably second only to former First Lady Eleanor Roosevelt — asserted that Thomas was "the only candidate for president who can stand on a record of foresight and principle."

In announcing her support for Thomas, Thompson stated that "'Unconditional Surrender' prolonged the war, dealt a death blow to the anti-Nazi movement within Germany, prevented any possibility of a general mutiny, accelerated the massacre of Jews, and brought about the execution of those Germans who could best have reconstructed a peaceful Germany contributing to the rebirth of Europe."[58] In essence, it was the same argument Thomas had made repeatedly throughout the 1944 campaign — a year when few listened to anything he had to say.

Winding up his sixth consecutive bid for the White House with a speech at New York's City Center on West 55th Street, Thomas promised to devote his energy and remaining years to the formation of a new party committed to economic and political democracy. "Obviously, this is my last campaign for the presidency," he told a crowd of a thousand supporters, "but it is not the end of

---

[57] "We Choose Norman Thomas Because," *Socialist Call*, Oct. 29, 1948.
[58] Dorothy Thompson, "Thomas Held Only Candidate with Foresight," *Pittsburgh Post-Gazette*, Oct. 18, 1948.

my campaign for the great body of Americans devoted to economic democracy, peace and freedom, for it is upon a fellowship of free people that peace depends."[59]

Hoping for a large protest vote — a *Chicago Tribune* poll predicted that he would garner 600,000 votes nationally — the balding, silver-haired veteran of lost causes campaigned mightily that year, but polled a disappointing 139,570 votes.[60]

Despite his relatively poor showing in the 1948 campaign, the accolades kept coming, including one from the *New York Times*, which paid an unexpected tribute to Thomas on his sixty-fifth birthday in November 1949.

> There are not many men in American public life today who command greater esteem or fewer votes than Norman Thomas. The influence which Mr. Thomas has exercised as a Socialist leader is difficult to assess; but at least he has the satisfaction of knowing that a good deal of the early Socialist program has found its way — though under other auspices — into the law of the land. And there is not much of it that would be repealed, no matter which of the two major parties was in power. Today on his sixty-fifth birthday, we extend our congratulations to this great dissenter...whose sincerity, eloquence, perseverance and faith have earned him an honored place in America's political annals.[61]

The following February, some fifteen months after he waged his sixth and final campaign for the White House, the long-distance runner for democratic socialism was honored again by 1,000 guests at a $5-a-plate testimonial luncheon in New York. Many of those in attendance were political figures with whom he had done battle over the previous three decades, including James A. Farley, the former DNC chairman who had managed two of Roosevelt's presidential campaigns and had been personally instrumental in pulling together much of the New Deal coalition. Bernard Baruch, one of the country's leading financial oligarchs and advisor to several U.S. presidents, was also one of the guests that afternoon.[62]

One of those paying homage to Thomas was former Congresswoman Ruth Bryan Owen, the eldest daughter of three-time Democratic presidential nominee William Jennings Bryan and an alternate delegate to the U.N. General Assembly. "In our family," she

---

[59] "Thomas Sees Need for a New Party," *New York Times*, Nov. 1, 1948.
[60] "Wallace Fears Swing to Thomas, Says Fleischman," *Socialist Call*, Oct. 22, 1948.
[61] Gregory, *Norman Thomas: The Great Dissenter*, p. 227.
[62] "Norman Thomas is Honored by Former Political Foes," *Reading Eagle*, Feb. 5, 1950.

cracked, "we have some experience in presidential campaigns which are run, but not won." Another tribute was given by Daniel J. Tobin, whom Thomas had sued for libel six years earlier. The Teamsters president, who served as vice chair of the luncheon, said that he regarded Thomas "not only as an outstanding brilliant human being, but a gentleman, a scholar and a great American in every sense of the word."[63]

Thomas, obviously enjoying every minute of the celebratory event, was in rare form that day. "I'm not particularly anxious to have my tombstone read 'the most defeated man in the United States,'" he sighed. "That's a dubious honor. And in view of the recent flare up against socialism, this remarkable turnout may be accounted for by the fact that I'm not going to run for office again, and if I did, I wouldn't be elected anyway." In his closing remarks, the long-distance runner for socialism said to laughter that he was withdrawing from politics because it had "fallen into the hands of a lot of old men. If you teach, you retire at 65," he chuckled. "But in politics you're just ripe to be chairman of a Senate committee."[64]

His frequent and futile bids for the presidency had nevertheless provided Thomas with a kind of "permanent floating counter pulpit, to the president's bully pulpit," as one writer put it.[65] He obviously enjoyed campaigning, too. "In all the times I've run," he told a reporter during the 1948 campaign, "I've never had any unpleasant episodes. Oh, once a long time ago, an egg was thrown in a hall, but that was just done by a bad little boy." But other candidates, including the late Wendell Willkie and former Vice President Henry Wallace, had it worse, he said. The '48 campaign — his "last hurrah" — turned out be quite a pleasant experience, said Thomas. "Much better than I expected."[66]

On the contrary, the 1944 campaign — the subject of this narrative — was the worst he had ever experienced. "It was grim. That's the only word for it," sighed Thomas. "I felt I was saying very important things; I knew they were important things, and people just wouldn't listen to me."[67]

Leaning back and smiling reminiscently, Thomas said that his 1934 campaign for the U.S. Senate — a year when he and his late wife Violet traveled throughout New York state in an old jalopy —

---

[63] Ibid.
[64] Ibid.
[65] Richard R. Lingeman, "New Biography Details Life of Norman Thomas," *Eugene Register-Guard*, Nov. 27, 1976.
[66] "Norman Thomas Never Wins, But Usually Enjoys Running," *Washington Post*, Oct. 17, 1948.
[67] Ibid.

was the most enjoyable experience of all. "It was beautiful, the fall colors, and we'd just stop in each town we came to and I'd stand up and make a speech," recalled Thomas. "Yes, I think I enjoyed that campaign more than any other."[68]

But Thomas had made it clear shortly after the 1948 campaign that he had no plans to run for office again.[69] The veteran campaigner not only closed the door on the possibility of a seventh bid for the Oval Office, but told a reporter in Seattle that he seriously doubted the Socialist Party would nominate a national ticket in 1952.[70] Believing that another presidential campaign might prove fatal to the party in which he had devoted almost his entire adult life, Thomas had been working quietly to convince party leaders that the party should no longer field a presidential ticket.

Discouraged by the party's relatively poor showing in the 1949 off-year elections — a dismal campaign in which the Socialist Party's Joseph G. Glass, a labor lawyer waging the second of three campaigns for mayor of New York, polled a paltry 3,396 votes while the once-promising mayoral candidacy of Alfred E. Tong in New Haven, Connecticut, crashed and burned, failing to produce even a third of the 11,377 votes (nearly twenty percent) cast for the little-remembered industrial engineer only two years earlier — Thomas recommended that the Socialist Party should abandon electoral activity altogether and focus its limited resources and energy on purely educational activities.

It was with a heavy heart that Thomas initially suggested the party should abandon electoral politics entirely while placing a greater emphasis on education for socialism. Though a majority of the party's NEC supported Thomas's resolution, delegates to the party's 1950 mid-term convention in Detroit overwhelmingly rejected his proposal and, in breaking with the party's six-time presidential standard-bearer, adopted a compromise resolution — an overwhelming repudiation that led to the resignation of the party's longtime national secretary Harry Fleischman, who had faithfully served in that capacity for eight years.[71]

Though Thomas remained active in the party following the Detroit setback, Fleischman, who served as Thomas's campaign manager during the 1944 and 1948 campaigns, chose to work outside the party for the remainder of his long life — he lived to the

---

[68] Ibid.
[69] "Norman Thomas Quits Running for Office," *Washington Post*, Dec. 15, 1949.
[70] "Thomas Will Not Run in '52" *New York Times*, Mar. 5, 1950.
[71] "Socialists Reject Thomas' Program," *New York Times*, June 4, 1950; Swanberg, *Norman Thomas: The Last Idealist*, pp. 332-333.

age of ninety — serving as the longtime chairman of the New York-based Workers Defense League until shortly before his death in late 2004. He had previously served as director of the American Jewish Committee's National Labor Service from 1953 to 1979 and, for a period, was also a labor editor at the Voice of America.[72]

Preferring to continue the ritual of running a presidential ticket in the face of increasingly insurmountable odds, delegates to the Socialist Party's 1952 national convention in Cleveland — a convention in which Thomas was conspicuously absent — enthusiastically nominated Reading attorney and former Pennsylvania legislator Darlington Hoopes for the presidency and named New York's Samuel Friedman as his vice-presidential running mate. Hoopes had been Thomas's vice-presidential co-star in 1944.[73]

When Maynard Krueger, speaking in Los Angeles during the summer of 1952, suggested that he was leaving the party and that Thomas was likewise planning to do so shortly, the six-time presidential candidate immediately — and emphatically — denied that he intended to resign from the party. Saying that while he respected his former vice-presidential running mate's reasons for making such a statement, Thomas said that he was "staying with the Socialist Party." In denying the reports, he also reminded the party faithful that he had already spoken for Darlington Hoopes and the national ticket on several occasions.

In fact, Thomas had pledged his support to Hoopes earlier that spring, joking with reporters in Garden City, New York, in early April that while he liked Ike and thought the general would probably win, he personally planned to support his own party's nominee. Eisenhower, he quipped, "has spent all his life in uniform, but that doesn't mean all generals have brass above the neck."[74]

Thomas reaffirmed his support for the Socialist ticket immediately following his lengthy tour of the Far East — a trip that concluded less than a week after the party's national convention — telling reporters in New York that he fully intended to support the ticket nominated in Cleveland.[75]

He had also made it abundantly clear that he didn't intend to be a candidate for the nation's highest office ever again. "Six times I ran for president and six times I lost. I think that's enough," he told reporters while in Manila shortly before the party's national

---

[72] "Harry Fleischman, 90, Writer of Norman Thomas Biography," *New York Times*, Nov. 7, 2004.
[73] "Lawyer to Head Socialist Ticket," *Cleveland Plain Dealer*, June 2, 1952.
[74] "Norman Thomas Likes Ike, Will Vote Socialist," *Baltimore Sun*, Apr. 3, 1952.
[75] "Norman Thomas Ends Long Tour," *Daily Argus-Leader* (Sioux Falls, S.D.), June 8, 1952.

convention.[76]

Thomas, moreover, bristled at the suggestion that he wasn't actively supporting the party's ticket that year. "It is well known that for some two years I have been urging that we could do more for the Socialist cause under present conditions, given our energy and resources, by other means than running a national ticket," said Thomas, responding to critics. "However, the majority of the party decided otherwise by nominating a ticket, and I am supporting that ticket in the present campaign."[77] He strongly reiterated his support for the Hoopes-Friedman ticket in a July 18 letter-to-the-editor of the *Los Angeles Times*, writing that "support of the ticket seems to me at present much the best way to spread an understanding of democratic socialism."[78]

Contrary to claims that Thomas had personally voted for Democratic nominee Adlai Stevenson that year — an erroneous assertion repeated most recently by Brooklyn writer Jack Ross in his otherwise magnificent and exceptional history of the Socialist Party of America — the former six-time Socialist candidate for the presidency kept his word and actively supported the Hoopes-Friedman ticket in 1952.[79]

Unlike Maynard Krueger, who severed his ties with the party over the decision to field a presidential ticket that year, Thomas stuck with his party.[80] "In this election," wrote Thomas in early August, "we are committed to advance socialist education by support of our own excellent ticket." Thomas even went so far as to strongly urge U.S. Rep. Adam Clayton Powell to support the Socialist ticket. Minister of one of the largest Baptist congregations in the country, Powell was deeply distressed by the evasiveness of both major parties on the issue of civil rights and had famously called on African-American voters to boycott the presidential election unless Stevenson and his running mate, Alabama Sen. John J. Sparkman, took a firm stand on civil rights.[81]

While Thomas deeply admired and clearly sympathized with the sagacious Stevenson, as revealed in his personal correspondence with the Illinois Democrat during this period, he just couldn't

---

[76] "Norman Thomas Says Six Defeats Enough," *Arizona Republic*, May 31, 1952.
[77] "Krueger to Quit Socialist Party," *Los Angeles Times*, July 8, 1952; "Thomas Denies Story He'll Quit Socialists," *New York Times*, July 9, 1952.
[78] "Support by Thomas," *Los Angeles Times*, July 18, 1952.
[79] Jack Ross, *The Socialist Party of America: A Complete History* (Lincoln, NE), p. 459.
[80] "Socialists Still Go It Alone with 'Protest' Ticket," *Rochester Democrat and Chronicle* (Rochester, NY), Aug. 29, 1952.
[81] "Powell Threatens a Boycott of Both Parties by Negroes," *New York Times*, Aug. 4, 1952; Norman Thomas, "Liberals and Democrats," *Socialist Call*, Aug. 8, 1952.

bring himself to publicly support a major-party nominee as long as the Socialist Party was running its own ticket — a point made by several of his more meticulous biographers. Thomas himself intimated as much in his unpublished autobiography, a book written primarily for his children. "He was sympathetic to Adlai Stevenson in the 1952 and 1956 elections," wrote Raymond Gregory, who relied heavily on Thomas's never-published memoir in writing his own biography, "but he could not strongly support him since the Socialist Party was still fielding presidential candidates."[82]

While Stevenson and Eisenhower were both decent men, there were many voters and journalists across the country who longed for one more Thomas campaign. It was a view shared by many others that fall, as eloquently expressed by *Cleveland Press* columnist Joseph S. Newman:

> General Ike is a man I like,
>   And a very good man he'd be,
> But there's Capehart, Dirksen, Jenner and Bricker
>   And Joe McCarthy...see?
>
> I'm longing madly to vote for Adlai,
>   But it's difficult to forget
> There's Byrd, McKellar, McCarran and Smathers
>   And Herman Talmadge yet.
>
> Oh, to return to the naïve past
>   And a world of hope and promise,
> When a man in doubt had a happy out
>   And could vote for Norman Thomas.[83]

Acknowledging that he hadn't campaigned as vigorously for his party's ticket as he had done repeatedly when he was the Socialist Party's standard-bearer, the six-time presidential candidate nevertheless made it clear that he intended to cast his ballot for Hoopes and Friedman that autumn. "Contrary to widely circulated rumors," he wrote in October, "I have not left the party, and have every expectation of voting for the ticket in New York," adding that he deeply admired "the real devotion of the comrades in New York and other states who managed to get us on the ballot."[84]

Thomas, moreover, was genuinely fond of Darlington

---

[82] Gregory, *Norman Thomas: The Great Dissenter*, p. 251.
[83] "Dilemma Dissolved," *Socialist Call*, Sept. 5, 1952.
[84] Norman Thomas, "Forum and Agin 'Em," *Socialist Call*, Oct. 17, 1952.

Hoopes. Among other things, the genial, snow-haired Socialist even made a joint nationwide television appearance with his party's nominee, appearing with Hoopes on the CBS network during a fifteen-minute broadcast in early July.[85] He later joined the Reading attorney and his vice-presidential running mate as a featured speaker at the Socialist Party's annual Debs Day Dinner at New York City's Fifth Avenue Hotel in late October.[86]

Though his heart was never really in it, Thomas did what he could to promote his party's little-known presidential standard-bearer in what proved to be one of the most difficult campaigns in the party's long and storied history.

When Gen. Dwight Eisenhower, bracing for a dogfight against Ohio's Bob Taft at the Republican national convention in Chicago — a convention less than a month away — suggested during a press conference in Abilene, Kansas, in early June that "beyond pure socialism lies dictatorship," Thomas immediately responded, challenging what he described as Ike's "summary dismissal of socialism and socialized medicine" and demanding air time for the Socialist Party's Darlington Hoopes to rebut Eisenhower's statement.[87]

"Do you believe that beyond the socialism professed and practiced in the Scandinavian countries and Britain lies dictatorship?" Thomas asked the former Supreme Allied Commander in Europe in a letter sent to all of the major radio and television networks. "Would you exclude from the definition of Western Europe the democratic socialist parties? Do you think you will get their aid in defense of Western Europe or of the world by the kind of blanket affirmation that you made in Abilene?"[88] Several radio and television stations subsequently granted time to Thomas and Hoopes to present the Socialist Party's rebuttal.

Though with noticeably less enthusiasm than in his own campaigns for the Oval Office, Thomas was nevertheless fully engaged in the campaign. Shortly after Robert Taft, barnstorming for the Republican national ticket, asserted in September that the real issue in the 1952 presidential election was one of "liberty against socialism," Thomas quickly challenged the conservative Ohioan to prove his statement in a public debate on the topic.

---

[85] "The Socialist Campaign on Television," *Socialist Call*, June 27, 1952.
[86] "Socialist Presidential Candidates to Speak at Debs Day Dinner," *Socialist Call*, Oct. 17, 1952.
[87] "Thomas Challenges Ike's Statement on Socialism," *Buffalo Courier-Express*, June 12, 1952.
[88] "Thomas Hits Eisenhower Anti-Socialist Views; Asks SP Time to Reply," *Socialist Call*, June 13, 1952.

"I deny that there is a conflict between socialism and liberty," wrote Thomas in a telegram to Taft. "I should be willing to certify Governor Stevenson as a nonsocialist," he continued. "If he is a socialist, so in almost the same degree are Eisenhower and the Republican platform of 1952. Both accept 'social gains' of the last twenty years, all of which were regarded as socialistic in 1928 and 1932 when I was running for President."[89]

To nobody's surprise, Taft never responded.

Thomas, who spoke for his party's national ticket on several occasions that summer and autumn, later attended the party's final campaign rally in Reading, Pennsylvania, the Saturday before the election. In his Reading address, a rally in which he appeared side by side with Hoopes and Friedman, Thomas joined his party's nominees in declaring that neither major party was capable of ending the wave of corruption, waste and fear sweeping the country.[90]

Though no longer a candidate himself, Thomas took a keen interest in the 1952 presidential election and frequently commented on the campaigns waged by the two major-party nominees, Dwight Eisenhower and Adlai Stevenson.

Eisenhower, the Republican nominee, was something of a blank slate in Thomas's mind. There were simply too many unanswered questions, particularly when it came to foreign policy. "None of these questions can be properly answered simply by saying, 'I like Ike,'" Thomas remarked during an appearance at Rensselaer Polytechnic Institute in Troy, New York, earlier that year. "I also like Ike pretty well," he chortled, "but I am in the dark about what Ike likes."[91]

There's little question that Thomas, who had covered both major-party conventions that summer as a correspondent for more than a dozen daily newspapers, including the *Denver Post*, *St. Louis Post-Dispatch*, *Los Angeles Times* and the *New York Post*, personally preferred Stevenson to Eisenhower. Among other things, he thought the Illinois Democrat had given a spectacular acceptance speech.[92] "If as man, candidate, and President, he can live up to its extraordinary quality, our country will be greatly blessed," wrote

---

[89] "Thomas and Taft Debate Proposed," *Baltimore Sun*, Sept. 19, 1952.
[90] "Socialist Nominees End Party Campaign," *New York Times*, Nov. 3, 1952.
[91] "Norman Thomas Won't Run Again," *Pittsburgh Press*, Feb. 17, 1952.
[92] Swanberg, *Norman Thomas: The Last Idealist*, p. 356. Other major newspapers that carried his daily columns from the two major party conventions included the Cincinnati Enquirer, Des Moines Register and Tribune, Houston Post, Indianapolis Star, Milwaukee Sentinel, Minneapolis Star Tribune, Oakland Tribune, Portland Oregonian, San Francisco Chronicle, Seattle Times, Trenton Times, Washington Daily News and the Worcester Telegram.

Thomas.[93]

Thomas was also admittedly pleased by the Democratic platform, a document he described as "a consistent program for a democratic welfare state." The longtime Socialist was particularly impressed not only by the fact that the Democrats had courageously reiterated their support for the controversial civil rights plank of 1948 — an issue that had deeply divided the party four years earlier, resulting in Strom Thurmond's renegade Dixiecrat candidacy — but also urged immediate action "to improve congressional procedures so that majority rule prevails and decisions can be made after reasonable debate without being blocked by a minority in either house." Though he was somewhat disappointed that the party's platform didn't include a stronger plank on universal disarmament or make mention of civil liberties in the face of McCarthyism, Thomas thought — or at least hoped — that liberalism was finally reasserting itself within the Democratic Party.[94]

As in 1948 when the *Denver Post* hired him to report on the Democratic, Republican, and Progressive national conventions in Philadelphia, Thomas had a blast covering the two major-party conventions that summer. There were several memorable moments, not the least of which included being nearly trampled by a seemingly spontaneous parade for Ohio's Robert Taft outside Chicago's Conrad Hilton Hotel.

Barely getting out of the way, Thomas stood in the doorway laughing as Taft's supporters, led by a band playing "Onward Christian Soldiers," followed by a stream of supporters, chanting, "Taft for me, Taft for you, Taft will win in '52." Thomas was clearly amused. "It sounds so funny for Taft people to be singing "Onward Christian Soldiers," he cracked. "I was a Bull Mooser back in 1912 and that was Teddy Roosevelt's song. Anyway, it shows that the Republicans can heal a break after 40 years."[95]

Yet, true to his word, Thomas stuck with his rapidly-fading and increasingly irrelevant party until the bitter end, quietly pulling the lever on Row G for Darlington Hoopes on November 4th. Sadly, it was the last time the Socialist Party's presidential ticket would ever appear on the ballot in the state of New York.

Precisely as Thomas predicted, the 1952 presidential campaign proved to be an utter disaster for the Socialist Party. The relatively

---

[93] Norman Thomas: "Quality of Stevenson's Speech Proves Amazing," *Oakland Tribune*, July 27, 1952.
[94] Norman Thomas: "Platform is Socialistic, Welfare State Program," *Oakland Tribune*, July 24, 1952.
[95] "GOP Delegates Sing Ditties, Heckle Rivals at Chicago," *Pittsburgh Press*, July 7, 1952.

obscure Hoopes-Friedman ticket barely mustered 20,000 votes nationally — a far cry from the 139,570 votes garnered by Thomas four years earlier — while finishing far behind not only the Progressive Party's Vincent Hallinan, but also the Prohibition Party's "singing cowboy" Stuart Hamblen and the Socialist Labor Party's Eric Hass, a Nebraska-born De Leonist who was waging the first of four consecutive campaigns for the presidency. It was the first time in history that the Socialist Party's presidential ticket had been eclipsed by the latter party.

Thomas wasn't the least bit surprised by the party's relatively abysmal showing that year, but was delighted shortly after the election when the party's national executive committee, appearing to finally heed his advice, voted seven to three to stop running a presidential ticket — a recommendation supported by Hoopes himself.[96]

In January 1953, shortly after the election, Thomas urged the U.S. Senate to reject President Eisenhower's nomination of Charles E. Wilson as Secretary of Defense.[97] Citing concerns about Wilson's large holdings in General Motors — a major defense contractor — the venerable Socialist told the Senate's Armed Services Committee that it would be "immensely hurtful to public relations internationally" if the deep-pocketed GM executive was confirmed.

Famously remembered for saying "What's good for General Motors is good for the country" — a misquote he spent years trying to correct — Wilson owned nearly 40,000 shares of GM common stock at the time of his nomination. Wilson's nomination, warned Thomas in a telegram to the committee's chairman, would make everybody suspicious of U.S. foreign policy, believing that decisions were being made primarily to benefit the defense industry.[98] Despite spirited opposition from Oregon's Wayne Morse, Wilson was easily confirmed by the Senate.[99]

---

[96] "Socialists May Drop Presidential Tickets," *New York Times*, Dec. 15, 1952.
[97] "Thomas Opposes Wilson in Post," *New York Times*, Jan. 18, 1953.
[98] Norman Thomas, "Minks to General Motors," *Socialist Call*, Jan. 23, 1953.
[99] "Wilson Confirmed by Senate, 77 to 6, in 5-Hour Debate," *New York Times*, Jan. 27, 1953.

Chapter III

Keeping the Faith

Though his days as a political candidate were now behind him, Thomas managed to keep his name — and that of his beloved but dwindling party — in the news, regularly issuing press releases, holding press conferences, publishing pamphlets, and writing books, all while maintaining a grueling speaking schedule. Remaining fully engaged in the pressing issues of the day while occasionally pricking the nation's conscience, the gentle and amiable Socialist continued to travel the country for the next fifteen years, logging nearly as many miles in any given year as he had as a presidential candidate. He was tireless.

At the outset of the Korean War, the six-time presidential aspirant proposed that the United States should recognize Communist China on the condition that the Chinese government "will loyally cooperate in the United Nations and prove it by appropriate action in regard to Korea." In making his proposal — an idea strongly opposed by the powerful China Lobby — Thomas expressed a willingness to give Chairman Mao, the Communist revolutionary and founder of the People's Republic of China, an opportunity to prove that he wasn't another Joseph Stalin.

Thomas, however, abruptly withdrew his proposal in June of 1950 when an estimated 135,000 troops from the North Korean People's Army poured across the 38th parallel, the boundary dividing the China and Soviet-backed Democratic People's Republic of Korea in the north and the pro-Western Republic of Korea to the south, triggering the first major conflict of the Cold War.[1]

Though deeply pained by the outbreak of hostilities in Korea, Thomas — in keeping with his deeply-held anticommunist beliefs — wholeheartedly supported U.S. involvement in the troubling

---
[1] Swanberg, *Norman Thomas: The Last Idealist*, p. 336.

and potentially disastrous conflict, which quickly escalated into a full-scale war that eventually claimed the lives of several million soldiers and civilians, including more than 36,000 U.S. servicemen and women. "On the whole," wrote Thomas, "I think it is better to back the U.N. against this aggression than to have permitted it to go unchallenged. That would have certainly invited ultimate world war."[2]

As the war dragged on, however, Thomas grew increasingly critical of the U.S. role in Asia because he believed American strategy in that region had failed miserably, especially in the critical "war of ideas," largely due to continuing U.S. support for South Korean President Syngman Rhee, Chiang Kai-shek, head of the exiled Chinese nationalist government in Taiwan, and the French in Indo-China, each of whom he described as "almost universally disliked in Asia." Having recently returned from a seven-week tour of Japan, Thailand, Burma, Indo-China and the Philippines on behalf of the Congress for Cultural Freedom, an anticommunist advocacy group secretly established and funded by the CIA — a fact completely unknown to him at the time — Thomas was also sharply critical of the gross mishandling of prisoners by the U.S. military on Koje Island.[3] Like most Americans, Thomas applauded when President Eisenhower finally brought the Korean War to an end.

In early 1953, Thomas launched the Union for Democratic Socialism, a purely educational organization somewhat analogous to an American version of the Fabian Society in Great Britain. Though it never attracted a large following and lacked the kind of influence he might have hoped for, Thomas had taken great pains in quietly organizing his new group. Making it clear from the outset that his new organization wasn't a political party nor a substitute for either the Socialist Party or the Social Democratic Federation, Thomas was extremely careful in who he initially approached about joining his new organization. The last thing he wanted was to be seen as interfering or meddling in the delicate unity negotiations then taking place between those two groups.[4]

The decision to form the Union for Democratic Socialism was explained in the "Statement of Aims" adopted at the group's founding conference in New York City on March 21:

> The march of history in tumultuous years has created new

---

[2] Ibid.
[3] "U. S. Fails in Asia, Thomas Declares," *New York Times*, June 18, 1952.
[4] Norman Thomas, "Toward UDS," *Socialist Call*, Apr. 10, 1953.

problems for democratic socialism. These call for new answers. Communism and fascism have taught us that collectivism may be the collectivism of an intolerable slave state. The abolition or severe limitation of private ownership under the profit system has by no means brought with it guarantees of freedom, peace, and plenty for the peoples of the earth.

Calling on socialists to reexamine some of their basic principles and beliefs while adopting a new approach to addressing the great evils of the times — the persistence of poverty, widespread social and economic injustice, and the always present threat of war — Thomas and the other founders suggested that the historic Marxian insistence on public ownership of the means of production should be discarded in favor of a more enlightened "diversity of forms of ownership, including public, cooperative and private ownership" relevant to the economic realities of modern America.[5]

While it remained largely a paper organization for most of its short existence, Thomas, who served as the group's chairman, was nevertheless successful in recruiting a number of prominent members, many of whom believed in socialism but felt compelled to work within the Democratic Party. Novelist Upton Sinclair and his wife, who were among the earliest to join, the financially independent and generous Albert Sprague Coolidge and literary critic Van Wyck Brooks were active in the short-lived organization, while A. Philip Randolph, always personally loyal to Thomas, served as its vice-chairman. Despite a relatively successful founding conference, the Union for Democratic Socialism petered out after only three or four years.

Concurrent with the launching of the Union for Democratic Socialism, Thomas published a forty-page pamphlet reassessing some of the basic tenets of socialism and the socialist movement in the United States. "My own lack of success in building a strong Socialist or Socialist-inspired party as one of the major parties in our two-party system," he wrote almost apologetically, "deprives me of a right to dogmatize on what must be done. But as I read the lessons of the past, the first job of Socialists is today in the strictest sense one of education...education of themselves in the meaning of democratic socialism for our time, and then the education of their fellow Americans, especially in the great labor unions. We no longer educate by running pro forma political campaigns," he said. "This I acknowledge with sorrow."

---

[5] Rev. Benjamin L. Masse, "Socialism, New Style," *The Living Church*, Vol. CXXVII, No. 6 (August 9, 1953), p. 10.

The simple truth, wrote Thomas, "is that here in America more measures once praised or denounced as socialist have been adopted than once I should have thought possible, short of a Socialist victory at the polls." The "march of events," he continued, compelled "at the very least a considerable qualification of some of the most important doctrines of Marxism, including even the basic notion of the class conflict." Marx's prediction that the working class would rise up and overthrow their capitalist exploiters, Thomas said, could never happen in this country, precisely because an individual's "productive powers in the age of applied science have been greater than he could have dreamed."

The United States, he continued, has "a middle class in a true economic sense, while those who think of themselves as belonging to the middle class are even more numerous. Salaried and high wage employees regard themselves as members of the middle class, a notion that has been strengthened by the fairly wide distribution of stock ownership in this country." Pointing to Britain, Thomas maintained that the long-held socialist concept of nationalization or state ownership wasn't a cure all for society's ills:

> Britain's problems admit no solution on a purely national level. What British socialism had done for the workers — once the veritable wage slaves of Britain — is magnificent. But it must be admitted that the nationalization of industry in Great Britain and elsewhere has not been the simple solution of all problems which many socialists in their age of faith had assumed.

Declaring that a "completely non-competitive society would be dull and stagnant," Thomas said that "social ownership" of the means of production, would be far preferable to the nationalization of industry:

> Two things have happened since World War I to lessen somewhat insistence on state ownership, First, not only the dictatorial Fascist and Communist states have sharpened our fears of the state as the master of human society, but experience with the broadened activities of relatively democratic states like Britain and America has made us more aware than formerly of the dangers of statism — and the economic inadequacies of nationalism — against which we must always be on guard.
>
> At the same time that we have been learning to guard against statism as an expression of socialism, we have learned that it has been possible, to a degree not anticipated by most earlier

socialists, to impose desirable social controls on privately owned enterprises by the development of social planning, by proper taxation and labor legislation, by the growth of powerful labor organizations.

While seemingly championing a competitive economy, Thomas nevertheless insisted that socialism still had a very important role to play. "Socialism will put a floor under family incomes at a rate sufficient for decent living," he wrote, "but for years to come the problem of increasing production must take precedence in socialist planning, over the problem of achieving the noblest system of distribution from the standpoint of pure ethics. St. Francis of Asisi," he quipped, "is not our guide to an economy of abundance."

Asserting that socialism was "not a panacea against war," Thomas also firmly rejected Marx's thesis that capitalism was the root cause of war. "The explanation of the wars of our time cannot be derived from any economic theory which does not take into account nationalism; of the older imperialism that was born of Western capitalism and nationalism, and the newer Communist imperialism under Stalin, who has succeeded in imposing a Russian imperial pattern on what started out as an international working class movement."

Largely owing to the efforts of Katrina McCormick Barnes, secretary of the League for Industrial Democracy, Thomas's pamphlet was widely circulated and arguably received more coverage and editorial comment than any of his previous writings. Barnes, ironically, was the daughter of the late Republican Sen. Medill McCormick of Illinois and a niece of conservative *Chicago Tribune* publisher Robert R. McCormick.[6]

Though drastically moderating his own longstanding views about socialism, Thomas nevertheless emerged as one of Sen. Joseph R. McCarthy's harshest critics during this period, repeatedly lambasting the Wisconsin lawmaker's anticommunist crusade and warning almost anybody who would listen that the victory we want "can never be won by beginning to imitate communism in the denial of basic freedoms here at home."[7]

Throughout this bleak and dreary period, the lanky, fast-talking Socialist — arguably the country's most consistent civil liber-

---

[6] Raymond P. Brandt, "Norman Thomas Discards Marx's Interpretation of History — 'Socialism is Not a Panacea,'" *St. Louis Post-Dispatch*, Mar. 1, 1953.

[7] "Rabbis Hear Thomas Cite 'Evils' of McCarthyism," *Philadelphia Inquirer*, Mar. 15, 1953.

tarian — maintained that liberals were partly to blame for the anti-communist hysteria sweeping the country. "Liberals have a large share of the responsibility for the growth of McCarthyism," he told the commission on Justice and Peace of the Central Conference of American Rabbis meeting in Atlantic City in March 1953. "It is entirely inexcusable that liberal disunity and poor tactics permitted the passage of the two McCarran bills on internal security and immigration over President Truman's veto. It is completely inexcusable," he added, "that in so many American towns, decent people let relatively small groups of 'super patriots' censor public libraries, lists of speakers and so forth."[8]

Thomas was right, particularly when it came to the bungled, if not bizarre, tactics employed by Senate progressives in trying to derail the McCarran Act a few years earlier.

The McCarran Act, known more formally as the Internal Security Act of 1950, established a Subversive Activities Control Board to investigate persons suspected of engaging in subversive activities and required communist-affiliated organizations, including "front groups" and "infiltrated" organizations to register with the U.S. Attorney General. Groups designated as such were required to provide the names of their officers and members, financial records, and any printing equipment under their control. Individual members were barred from holding office in a labor union or working in a public office and were prohibited from obtaining a passport or seeking employment in a defense plant — the latter two of which were struck down by the U.S. Supreme Court in *Aptheker v. Secretary of State*, 378 U.S. 500 [1964] and *United States v. Robel*, 389 U.S. 258 [1967].

Trade unions deemed to have been infiltrated by Communists, moreover, were subject to the loss of all rights under national labor laws. The McCarran Act also provided for the deportation of Communist aliens. The legislation, sponsored by Pat McCarran, a Democratic senator from Nevada, had the overwhelming support of lawmakers in both parties.

The McCarran Act raised many serious constitutional questions, including a separate order requiring individual Communist Party leaders to register with the Attorney General, which was subsequently declared unconstitutional on the grounds that it violated one's right against self-incrimination (*Albertson v. Subversives Activities Control Board*, 382 U.S. 70 [1965]).

Thomas, who shared many of Truman's concerns about the

---

[8] "Thomas Urges Fight on McCarthyism," *Poughkeepsie Journal*, Mar. 15, 1953.

law, was deeply troubled that many lawmakers freely admitted that they had never read the President's courageous and powerful veto message, nor the lengthy bill itself. "Senators and Representatives voted for it in many cases simply because they feared the electorate," wrote Thomas.

Describing such cowardice as "an ominous commentary on the nature of our democracy," Thomas praised those who opposed the legislation — a small band led by Senators Hubert H. Humphrey of Minnesota, Paul H. Douglas of Illinois, William Langer of North Dakota, and Tennessee's Estes Kefauver — and expressed deep disappointment in Ohio Sen. Robert A. Taft, regarded by many as one of the country's leading civil libertarians. "Senator Taft," lamented Thomas, "lost his claim to respect, namely that he in the past supported civil liberty, by voting for the bill. Hence, the more honor to the little company who stood steadfast for the one thing which, more than any other, makes democracy worth fighting for."[9]

When President Truman, who had vigorously denounced the legislation as a "mockery of the Bill of Rights" and "a long step toward totalitarianism," as well as "the greatest danger to freedom of speech, press, and assembly since the Alien and Sedition Laws of 1798" — vetoed the bill, only 48 House members, including Montana's Jerry J. O'Connell and ex-Socialist Andrew Biemiller of Wisconsin, and a mere ten members of the U.S. Senate, voted to sustain Truman's veto.[10] Incredibly, the House of Representatives had voted overwhelming to override Truman's veto within an hour of receiving his veto message. Anxious to get out of Washington for the weekend, most House members didn't even bother to read it.[11]

North Dakota's "Big Bill" Langer, arguably the most independent-minded lawmaker in the Senate who had praised Truman as "a brave man and a great president" for courageously vetoing the anti-subversive legislation, was also expected to uphold the president's veto, but collapsed at the end of a marathon speech during a 19 ½-hour filibuster and had to be rushed to the hospital.[12]

---

[9] Norman Thomas: "McCarran Act Madness," *Socialist Call*, Sept. 29, 1950.
[10] "Truman's Veto Text: 'This Bill Would Help Communists,'" *St. Louis Post-Dispatch*, Sept. 23, 1950; "Vote of 286-48 Polled Within Hour After Truman Calls Measure 'Mistake,'" *Washington Post*, Sept. 23, 1950; "Senators Override Communist Controls Veto," *Baltimore Sun*, Sept. 24, 1950.
[11] "Stampede," *Washington Post*, Sept. 23, 1950.
[12] "Veto Filibuster Nears Windup; Vote Awaited; Langer Collapses on Floor," *Minneapolis Star*, Sept. 23, 1950.

In the end, congressional Democrats, who enjoyed a 12-seat majority in the Senate and outnumbered their GOP colleagues by a staggering 95 seats in the House, came up woefully short in sustaining their president's extraordinarily courageous veto.[13]

The same thing was true some eighteen months later when Congress successfully overrode Truman's veto of the McCarran-Walter Act, immigration and naturalization legislation that Truman had denounced in some of the strongest language of his presidency. The bill's co-author was Rep. Francis E. Walter, a Pennsylvania Democrat and prominent member of the infamous House Un-American Activities Committee — a committee he once assailed for "abuse of power" — who was closely affiliated with the controversial Pioneer Fund.

Like many of its critics, Truman viewed the immigration legislation as an archaic, racially-motivated and discriminatory continuation of the 1924 law establishing immigration quotas while doing little to assist refugees, the displaced, and immigrants forced to flee their countries of origin. According to Truman, the new law only served to intensify "the repressive and inhumane aspects" of the nation's existing immigration legislation.[14]

"In no other realm of our national life are we so hampered and stultified by the dead hand of the past as we are in this field of immigration," asserted Truman in angrily vetoing the legislation in late June.[15]

Joined by eight Republicans, only eighteen Democratic senators voted to sustain Truman's veto.[16] Two additional votes in the Senate would have upheld the president's veto. A day earlier, the House rejected the president's veto by a margin of 278-113, seventeen votes more than the necessary two-thirds majority needed.[17]

Among its many features — the bill had no fewer than 164 separate sections — the Immigration and Nationality Act of 1952 permitted the U.S. government to deport immigrants or naturalized citizens engaged in subversive activities and barred suspected subversives from entering the country. It was used widely to prevent ex-Communist Party members and "fellow travelers" from entering the United States, including those who hadn't associated with the party in decades.

---

[13] The 91st Congress was a fairly conservative body, dominated more often than not by a Republican-southern Democratic coalition.
[14] "President Vetoes Immigration Bill as Discriminatory," *New York Times*, June 26, 1952.
[15] "Text of Truman's Message to House on Veto of Immigration Bill," *New York Times*, June 26, 1952.
[16] "Congress Enacts Immigration Bill Over Truman Veto," *New York Times*, June 28, 1952.
[17] "Alien Bill Veto Is Overridden By House," *Washington Post*, June 27, 1952.

While the comprehensive legislation maintained the quota system for immigration, it did remove all racial barriers to immigration, but Asians, Africans, and eastern and southern Europeans were assigned relatively small quotas until Congress, responding to extensive lobbying from various ethnic groups, removed the discriminatory and restrictive national origins quota system — an idea long championed by Thomas — with the passage of the Immigration Act of 1965.

Thomas, who initially favored the alternative and far more progressive Lehman-Humphrey immigration and naturalization bill — failed substitute legislation that McCarran claimed would "flood" the country with Asian immigrants — sharply criticized the controversial McCarran-Walter Act, which, despite "a few decent provisions," essentially gave "outrageous powers" to the federal bureaucracy while "perpetuating and intensifying racist standards."[18]

Thomas was also deeply troubled by the country's growing reactionary trend and the failure of liberals to effectively counter that trajectory. "By and large," he wrote in the summer of 1952, "the so-called liberals of both parties have been fighting mostly a defensive battle and fighting it badly." It was almost as though they were merely trying "to ride out the storm," said Thomas, adding that "a bolder and abler liberal leadership might have written a different chapter in American history."[19]

Returning from a six-week tour of Europe the following summer, Thomas said that U.S. prestige on that continent was at "an all-time low" due to McCarthyism. "Who is running the show, the president or the McCarthys or McLeods?" he asked, referring to State Department security chief Scott McLeod, who had recently stated that no member of the Socialist Party should be employed by the department. "Between Senator McCarthy and Mr. McLeod," Thomas told reporters, "I think Secretary of State John Foster Dulles should carry heavy insurance on his political life."[20]

Nothing made Thomas's blood boil more than those who questioned the loyalty and patriotism of Socialist Party members or the tendency of those on the right to make little, if any, distinction between Socialists and Communists.[21] McLeod was guilty of

---

[18] "Senate Rejects Liberal Substitute For McCarran's Immigration Bill," *New York Times*, May 22, 1952; Norman Thomas, "No Wonder U.S. Politics Confuse Other Peoples," *Oakland Tribune*, June 26, 1952.

[19] "No Wonder U.S. Politics Confuse Other Peoples," *Oakland Tribune*, June 26, 1952.

[20] "Norman Thomas Scores M'Carthy," *Trenton Evening Times*, Aug. 18, 1953.

[21] Swanberg, Norman Thomas: *The Last Idealist*, p. 364.

both. A former Senate staffer who owed his position to Vice President Richard M. Nixon, McLeod was once described as "one of the most powerful and least known men in the Eisenhower administration." He was the principal U.S. government official responsible for the firing of career State Department employees charged with disloyalty or homosexuality during that shamefully dark period in American history. According to William V. Shannon, a Washington correspondent and columnist for the *New York Post*, nervous colleagues referred to him as "The Lord High Executioner," possessing virtually unlimited authority to fire any employee, including those whose politics he might have disagreed with, on national security grounds.

When questioned by Thomas, the ultraconservative 39-year-old security chief — taking five weeks to respond to Thomas's letter — frankly admitted that he "would never knowingly employ a Socialist to fill such a (policy-making) position within the department. I simply feel it would be impossible for a Socialist to make or influence policy in a manner which would carry out the intentions of President Eisenhower. Whenever I become aware that any person who occupies such a position is a Socialist," he continued, "I shall use my best efforts to see that he is removed from the position." Thomas, who was in Europe by the time McLeod responded, was furious.

Theodore Kaghan, one of those who had been removed by McLeod from his post as a public affairs officer in Germany, related how veteran State Department employees feared for their livelihoods. "McLeod has taken this place over for McCarthy," one of them told him. "Nothing happens, nothing is said, that McLeod doesn't get almost immediately. People don't even talk at staff meetings anymore," the employee told Kaghan, for fear that they might be viewed as dissenting or nonconformist and would be immediately reported to McLeod.[22]

Protesting the firing of several socialists in foreign posts — none of whom were in actual policy-making positions — and citing an overall decline in morale in the Foreign Service as a result of the endless investigations and purges pursued by the cocky, high-and-mighty McLeod, Thomas expressed his concerns to President Eisenhower, asking for a meeting where he could discuss the distressing situation. Ike forwarded his letter to Secretary of State John Foster Dulles, who promptly reassured Thomas that he did not question the loyalty of Socialists and had the highest respect for

---

[22] William V. Shannon, "Terror to Insecure Homburgs," *New York Post*, Aug. 9, 1953.

many of them, "including, of course, yourself." But, in his reply, Dulles also said that it was proper to employ individuals who reflected the administration's beliefs. "I believe that Mr. McLeod's position is a sound one," he wrote.

Thomas then took off the gloves, responding firmly to Dulles:

> I still think it necessary that I should seek to see the President himself because events show that the present policy is not confined to your Department....I hear of an increasing number of little "S" socialists who are discharged...One can, of course, interpret policy making positions to include almost any position in which the judgment and discretion of its occupant are important. I do not think you would tend thus to define the phrase. If you do, you will wreck the civil service.
>
> It is certainly true that many of those discharged by Mr. Stassen [the Mutual Security Administrator] are far more loyal to your program than some of your party brethren in the Senate, or than Messrs. [Roy] Cohn and [G. David] Schine. Finally, I do object very seriously to a situation in which announcements of administration policy in a matter so important as this should come from a security officer in your department or any other. It is along these lines that I want to make the case, and to make it to the President, before trying to make it a public issue.[23]

Thomas's terse reply to Dulles resulted in a White House meeting with President Eisenhower on October 27. During their half-hour meeting, the president told Thomas that Socialists shouldn't be excluded from government civil service jobs and that his administration would be issuing a "reasoned statement" on the matter defining what constitutes a "policy making" position in government.

Emerging from the meeting, Thomas told reporters that he believed the administration ought to have its own people in policy-making positions, but that McLeod seemed to think that such jobs extended down to lowly clerical positions. Thomas, who said that he wasn't personally aware of any socialists who had been fired because of their political beliefs, stated that it was nevertheless probably true based on past statements made by McLeod and Sen. Joseph R. McCarthy. He was aware, however, of "blundering attempts made to get rid of alleged Socialists" and sympathizers in the Foreign Operations Administration, which appeared to be act-

---

[23] Swanberg, Norman Thomas: *The Last Idealist*, pp. 366-367.

ing on McLeod's principle, but when questioned about those specific firings, department officials maintained that they were part of unavoidable budget cuts.[24]

Thomas found Eisenhower to be "an extremely decent man" who "listened patiently and without objection or criticism" to what his Socialist visitor had to say. "He assured me that he knew socialists were loyal and he did not dispute my assertion that at the very least there was among us no higher percentage of blabber mouths to threaten security than among Republicans," wrote Thomas shortly after their meeting. Thomas was also struck by Eisenhower's knowledge of socialism — a much better grasp and understanding than he had expected. Thomas, however, was a little surprised that Eisenhower's White House Chief of Staff Sherman Adams — the "Abominable No Man" — sat in on their meeting and was relieved when he later discovered that Adams was also in the room when FBI director J. Edgar Hoover met with Eisenhower at the White House earlier that year. "I was relieved," quipped Thomas. "It means I wasn't a peculiar character."[25]

On his seventieth birthday in 1954, Thomas was honored at a gala reception at the Town Hall Club in New York City commemorating his half century of labor on behalf of social justice — and socialism. For nearly two hours, Thomas stood and personally greeted what seemed like a never-ending line of well-wishers. Between handshakes, he sat briefly with two of his young granddaughters — one on each knee — sipping ginger ale and talking to a reporter. Thomas absolutely adored his grandchildren. All of the handshaking reminded him of his years on the campaign trail. "I never was very good at this," he chuckled, "and now age doesn't help."[26]

In addition to singing "Happy Birthday, Dear Norman," the thousand or so friends, admirers and former supporters in attendance that evening presented the startled grand old man of American Socialism with a check for $10,000. Thomas was visibly moved, but kept his wits about him. "As an old-time Socialist," he quipped, "I always thought people forged signatures on $10,000 checks." It was an unusually large gift for someone whose sundry causes and organizations — and there were many — usually operated on shoestring budgets and were often in the red, constantly

---

[24] "President OKs Hiring of Socialists," *Philadelphia Inquirer*, Oct. 28, 1953.
[25] Norman Thomas, "A Talk with Eisenhower," *Socialist Call*, Nov. 1, 1953; Swanberg, *Norman Thomas: The Last Idealist*, p. 367.
[26] "Norman Thomas, at 70, Gets Gala Party and a $10,000 Check from His Admirers," *New York Times*, Nov. 22, 1954.

strapped for cash and desperately waiting for the next donation. Thomas, who spent a good portion of his earlier years trying to keep the Socialist Party of America solvent and much of his later life desperately struggling to raise enough money to keep his various organizations afloat, promised to put the money to good use promoting disarmament and civil liberties.[27]

Thomas, incidentally, left a relatively modest estate valued at approximately $150,000, the bulk of which went to his children and other relatives, when he died fourteen years later.[28]

When the Socialists finally threw in the towel in 1960, four years after the party's disastrous showing during the second Eisenhower-Stevenson contest — a race in which Reading attorney Darlington Hoopes limped home with an abysmal 2,192 votes nationally — Thomas and his fellow comrades tried in vain to have a measure of influence within the Democratic Party.

Among other things, the six-time former Socialist candidate for the presidency drafted a lengthy letter to the Democratic platform committee strongly urging the adoption of planks dealing with civil rights and peace while various party members manned a trailer and passed out literature to the delegates at the Democratic national convention in Los Angeles that summer.[29]

Like former First Lady Eleanor Roosevelt and Minnesota's Eugene McCarthy, the latter of whom delivered one of the greatest nominating speeches in history that summer — a speech William F. Buckley later described as a "dazzling oratorical cadenza" — Thomas felt the Democrats should have nominated the cerebral and quick-witted Adlai Stevenson for a third time in 1960. Thomas, who initially preferred Hubert H. Humphrey before he was eliminated by JFK in the West Virginia primary, believed that a Stevenson presidency offered the best chance of preserving the peace.[30]

Though he personally voted for John F. Kennedy in the razor-thin presidential election later that autumn, Thomas wasn't really impressed with either major-party candidate, remarking that one could flip a coin — heads or tails — in choosing between Kennedy and Nixon and pretty much come up with the same kind of president. "Neither of them is a crusader for anything in particular," observed Thomas earlier that summer, "but both of them are inclined

---

[27] Ibid.
[28] "Norman Thomas Left $150,000," *Washington Post*, Jan. 15, 1969.
[29] "Socialist Standard Finally Furled," *Washington Post*, Aug. 14, 1960.
[30] Ibid.

to be liberal." Both candidates, he added, were "very shrewd opportunists, which I suppose you have to be in politics."[31]

Though Thomas didn't meet personally with the newly-elected president as he had done so often with Franklin D. Roosevelt, he nevertheless was invited to the White House in early February 1961, shortly after Kennedy took office. While there was no specific purpose for his White House visit, he did meet with Richard N. Goodwin, assistant special counsel to the president. "Look," a grinning Thomas told reporters as he left the White House, "this administration, to its credit, is willing to listen to a lot of people, even if they are not Harvard men. They wanted to see if a Princeton man could talk."[32]

Interestingly, Thomas was deeply concerned by the growing federal bureaucracy during this period. "One of the great challenges of our times is to see how we can diminish bureaucracy rather than increase it," he said during a trip to California in 1960.[33] But he wasn't only concerned about government bureaucracy. "Oh, we're still a democracy, an imperfect democracy," he told a British television audience that spring, "but I'm not decrying it altogether. But practically we're governed by four bureaucracies. The civil government bureaucracy, the military bureaucracy, the bureaucracy of big management in big business and big labor…"[34]

Thomas maintained a hectic speaking schedule during the early 1960s, frequently lecturing on college campuses across the country. He inevitably drew large crowds, as was the case when he spoke at Vanderbilt University in the winter of 1962 where university officials were forced to move Thomas's scheduled speech from the original lecture room to the school's Benton Chapel when an overflow crowd of more than 600 turned out to hear the former six-time presidential candidate lecture on the role of third parties in American politics. In his warmly received address — arguably the most enthusiastic welcome of any speaker on the Vanderbilt campus since novelist Robert Penn Warren's appearance in 1959 — Thomas told the overflow crowd that the cards were stacked against third parties. "Nearly all of the ideas that have mattered in politics in this country since the start of the 19th century," lamented Thomas, "have come from minority parties. Now there isn't one."[35]

---

[31] "Norman Thomas Finds Kennedy and Nixon Alike," *Washington Post*, Aug. 1, 1960.
[32] "Norman Thomas Pays Call at White House," *Washington Post*, Feb. 3, 1961.
[33] "California Speaks," *Petaluma Argus-Courier* (Petaluma, CA), May 13, 1960.
[34] George Sokolsky, "Telling the British," *Ames Daily Tribune*, May 10, 1960.
[35] "Thomas Argues for Third Party," *Nashville Tennessean*, Feb. 6, 1962.

A normally happy warrior, few people in public life ever made Norman Thomas genuinely angry. New York Gov. Nelson A. Rockefeller was an exception. Thomas never cared for the nationally ambitious four-term governor, a product of enormous wealth and privilege. "He's the only governor in my long experience who hasn't the courtesy to answer a letter," the usually genial Thomas told a reporter in 1962. Unlike almost any other politician Thomas had ever encountered, Rocky really got under his skin. In fact, the mild-mannered Socialist's voice nearly quivered with anger every time he mentioned Rockefeller's name. "I can restrain my enthusiasm for him on lots of counts," sighed Thomas.[36]

In an obituary written for the Associated Press shortly after Thomas's death, former Milwaukee Mayor Frank P. Zeidler said that Thomas's life should not be viewed through the prism of his many failed candidacies, but rather by the lasting influence he had on so much of American society.[37]

His legacy, wrote Zeidler, who served three terms as mayor of the Brew City from 1948 to 1960 and later headed the Socialist Party-USA's ticket in the 1976 presidential election, surpassed that of many of the lesser presidents in U.S. history and probably approximated that of several of the country's greatest chief executives.[38]

According to Zeidler, Thomas's influence extended well beyond his frequent bids for public office. Through a generation of young Socialist scholars, the great dissenter was largely responsible for bringing about the country's war on poverty in the 1960s. Michael Harrington's *The Other America: Poverty in the United States* — a seminal work which is believed to have profoundly inspired President John F. Kennedy to develop antipoverty legislation, most of which was later put into effect during LBJ's "Great Society" — was one of the many things personally inspired by Thomas, said Zeidler.[39]

"If Thomas had a weakness," concluded the former Socialist mayor, "it was that he did not engage in the political wire-pulling and scheming that produces a political machine and produces a boss system. He was above it, and his party therefore suffered from excessive factionalism. He was unable to be harsh and merciless with his political opponents and did not therefore develop into a

---

[36] "Rockefeller Prime Target of Angry Norman Thomas," *Knickerbocker News*, Mar. 21, 1962.
[37] Frank P. Zeidler, "Without Being Elected to Major Office, Thomas Had Big Impact on U.S. Society," *Danville Register*, Dec. 27, 1968.
[38] Ibid.
[39] Ibid.

boss himself. Yet in the long run," concluded Zeidler, "this may have also been his greatest strength…for his idealism has inspired people in the United States for six decades."[40]

As biographer Murray B. Seidler noted, Thomas in many ways was America's greatest "successful failure."[41] But his life's work had not been in vain, as Thomas himself modestly acknowledged. "I suppose it is an achievement to live to my age and feel that one has kept the faith, or tried to," he said not long before his death. "It is an accomplishment to be able to sleep at night with reasonable satisfaction." It was an achievement, he added, to have played a part, even if it was a minor one, in some of the things that have been accomplished in the areas of civil liberties and improved race relations.

But Thomas was also painfully aware that not all of his efforts had gained acceptance. "I still heartily yearn for the nationalization of the steel industry," he once remarked. "In fact, I'm for public ownership of all natural resources. They belong to all the people and should not be for the private enrichment of the few."[42]

In his final years Thomas continued to grow increasingly pessimistic about the state of American politics, asserting that "our politics are clearly the politics of the garrison state." In delivering a commencement address at Haverford College in suburban Philadelphia in 1963, Thomas lamented that many colleges and universities were "profoundly, if subtly, affected by the mentality of this garrison state," a troubling development in which huge government contracts and other forms of federal largesse to academia were becoming "virtually a substitute for intellectual curiosity."[43]

In August of that year, Thomas participated in the historic March on Washington. As one who advocated for civil rights as long as anybody could remember, the 79-year-old Socialist leader, beaming with pride, sat as honored guest at the memorial ceremonies as more than 200,000 people streamed into the capital and made their way to the steps of the Lincoln Memorial. "I'm glad I lived long enough to see this day," said Thomas.[44] His only regret was that he couldn't join the marchers. "I have reached the age when I can only sit. My legs got old faster than I did," he quipped.[45]

---

[40] Ibid.

[41] "He's a Successful Failure," *Milwaukee Journal*, Dec. 5, 1961.

[42] "Norman Thomas, Prophet," *Decatur Herald*, Dec. 20, 1968.

[43] "Norman Thomas Scores 'Garrison State Mentality,'" *New York Times*, June 8, 1963.

[44] "200,000 March for Civil Rights in Orderly Washington Rally; President Sees Gain for Negro," *New York Times*, Aug. 29, 1963.

[45] "For 200,000 Who Were There It Was a Date to Live Forever," *New York Times*, Aug. 29, 1963.

In the autumn of that year — about three weeks before John F. Kennedy's assassination in Dallas — Thomas traveled to Mississippi to campaign for Aaron Henry, a Clarksdale pharmacist and head of the Mississippi branch of the NAACP. Henry was waging a dual write-in campaign for governor, which included participating in a mock election designed to dramatize the legal exclusion of nearly 400,000 eligible African-American voters. A founder of the Mississippi Freedom Democratic Party in 1964, Henry chose a white Methodist chaplain from historically black Tougaloo College as his running mate for lieutenant governor.[46]

"You almost have to have a passport to get into Mississippi," complained Thomas upon arriving in Jackson in late October. Thomas obviously wasn't impressed with either of the 41-year-old Henry's segregationist opponents — Democratic Lt. Gov. Paul B. Johnson, Jr., and Republican Rubel Phillips, a former public service commissioner — saying that neither candidate was discussing anything other than "who hates the Kennedys the most."[47]

Thomas was right. At times, both of Henry's opponents "sounded as though they were running for Kleagle of the Ku Klux Klan instead of governor," as journalist Curtis Wilkie so aptly described it. Both major-party candidates went out of their way to appeal to the state's most violent segregationists. While the Democratic nominee effectively distanced himself from JFK and the national Democratic Party, the Republican candidate, a former Democrat hoping to appeal to his former party's racist majority, focused his entire campaign on opposing civil rights and the Kennedy administration, lining the state's highways with billboards that boldly proclaimed, "K.O. the Kennedys" — creating a situation which could have proved terribly embarrassing for the rabidly-segregationist Magnolia State in the days immediately following Kennedy's cold-blooded murder in Dallas on November 22nd, as workers scurried across the state to paper over the defeated Republican candidate's sickeningly repugnant billboards.[48]

Still battling the two-headed Goliath, the aging Socialist also found time that autumn to stump for Richard Parrish, the Socialist Party's candidate for councilman at-large in Manhattan. Thomas and his longtime friend and associate A. Philip Randolph, president of the Brotherhood of Sleeping Car Porters, had personally

---

[46] "Norman Thomas Mocks Mississippi," *New York Times*, Nov. 1, 1963; "Miss. Negro Campaigns for Governor," *Jet*, Oct. 31, 1963, pp. 14-18.
[47] Ibid.
[48] Curtis Wilkie, *Dixie: A Personal Odyssey Through Historic Events That Shaped the Modern South* (New York, 2001), pp. 130-131.

recruited Parrish, a black special education instructor and vice president of the American Federation of Teachers, to run for city council earlier that year and later filed nominating petitions bearing an impressive 8,073 signatures — 5,000 were needed — placing his name on the November ballot.[49]

It was a remarkable feat given the fact that only two years earlier the party — lacking a sufficient number of valid signatures — had failed to place its citywide ticket headed by labor lawyer Joseph G. Glass for mayor, Samuel H. Friedman for controller and celebrated writer Michael Harrington of Manhattan for council president, on the November ballot.[50] Collecting far fewer signatures than their rival Socialist Labor and Socialist Workers parties that year, each of which submitted more than 12,000 signatures, the Socialist Party filed nominating petitions bearing only 587 signatures more than the requisite 7,500 valid signatures necessary and was quickly tossed from the ballot.[51]

Parrish campaigned on a solid working-class platform, calling for a city income tax to replace the regressive sales tax and sharply criticized the New York City Board of Education for dragging its feet in integrating the city's public schools. He also warned of a potentially "revolutionary situation" in Manhattan as a result of widespread poverty.[52]

One of three African-Americans running for at-large council seats in Manhattan, Brooklyn and Queens, the 47-year-old Parrish — the first Socialist Party candidate to appear on the ballot in New York City since the forlorn candidacy for president waged by Darlington Hoopes in 1952 — garnered 8,317 votes, or 2.5 percent, while finishing behind Democrat Paul O'Dwyer, brother of former Mayor William O'Dwyer, Republican Richard S. Aldrich, a cousin of Gov. Nelson Rockefeller, and the Liberal Party's Amos S. Basel, a 52-year-old lawyer and political gadfly who was waging his third bid for public office.[53]

The following spring — some 38 years after he delivered a moving eulogy to Eugene V. Debs on the front porch of his home in Indiana — Thomas returned to Terre Haute to formally dedicate the long-deceased labor leader and five-time Socialist presidential candidate's former house as a museum. The house, which had

---

[49] "Socialists Designate Negro for Councilman at Large," *New York Times*, June 17, 1963; "Primary Re-canvass Is Completed Here," *New York Times*, Sep. 14, 1963.
[50] "City Ticket Offered by Socialist Party," *New York Times*, June 21, 1961.
[51] "9 Entries Listed in Mayoral Race as Filing is Ended," *New York Times*, Sep. 20, 1961.
[52] "Liberal Party Testing Governor in Council Race," *New York Times*, Oct. 25, 1963; "Candidates Stress Bias and Narcotics," *New York Times*, Oct. 30, 1963.
[53] "Nominees' Color Discounted Here," *New York Times*, Nov. 8, 1963.

been owned by a college professor and later used as a fraternity house, had been restored by the Debs Foundation, a group organized by Terre Haute residents in 1962.[54]

In his remarks, Thomas spoke briefly of his personal association with Debs, telling the gathering that the cooperative society envisioned by the great Socialist leader — "a brotherhood of races and nations, and with it an end of bitter poverty and war" — was never more important than at the present time. "His own life should ever remain an inspiration," said Thomas.[55]

As was the case almost every four years since waging his last campaign for the presidency fifteen years earlier, Thomas was asked by a reporter in the autumn of 1963 if he might make one final dignified run for the Oval Office again the following year. "I'm not going to run," he quipped during an impromptu press conference at the Broome County Airport while on his way to a speaking engagement at Hartwick College in Oneonta, New York. "I have trouble walking now."[56]

But if he were to hypothetically mount another campaign, he added with a twinkle, he would run on the Socialist Party's 1962 platform. "I would be very concerned for civil rights and peace and for the apparent built-in unemployment that we have in this country," he said. "In a country as affluent as ours," he continued, "I would want to see that affluence better distributed." He also said that he would push "for socialized medicine, along the lines of the programs in England and Scandinavia. And I wouldn't send any more aid to Vietnam just to keep the Diem family in power."[57]

Before being whisked off to Oneonta by biographer Bernard Johnpoll, a political science professor at Hartwick, the veteran Socialist was asked if the Democratic Party had taken over his party's old program. "No, I wish it had," said Thomas. "I wouldn't have to worry as much."[58]

Another presidential campaign was never in the cards. Thomas, who turned eighty later that year, had made that abundantly clear during his party's 1964 national convention in Chicago. "Six times are enough," he told reporters. "It gets to be a joke after that many times. Maybe it got to be a joke before that."[59]

Thomas, who ran against every president from Herbert Hoover to Harry Truman and offered constructive criticism of every

---

[54] "Debs's Residence Becomes Museum," *New York Times*, May 10, 1964.
[55] Ibid.
[56] "Rights, Peace, Jobs Old Crusader's Goals," *Binghamton Press*, Oct. 8, 1963.
[57] Ibid.
[58] Ibid.
[59] "Thomas Hails Johnson; Raps Goldwater," *Chicago Tribune*, May 30, 1964.

successor who followed in their footsteps — Eisenhower, Kennedy and Johnson — later observed that he had been willing to go "part of the way with LBJ" in 1964, mostly because he thought Republican Senator Barry Goldwater was so dangerous, but subsequently voiced sharp criticism of Johnson's "picayune" war on poverty and for reneging on a 1964 campaign promise not to send American boys to Vietnam by vastly escalating U.S. involvement in Southeast Asia.[60]

While attending the Socialist Party's three-day national convention in Chicago earlier that spring — the last convention he ever attended — Thomas offered some high praise for President Johnson, saying that JFK's successor was much better than he expected. "We all have reason to be grateful for him," said Thomas, particularly when it comes to his handling of civil rights and poverty. "I ought to rejoice, and I do. I rub my eyes in amazement and surprise." He also had some kind words for Minnesota Sen. Hubert H. Humphrey, whom he personally preferred for the presidency and who was later tapped as LBJ's vice-presidential running mate after the president had narrowed his short list of choices down to Humphrey, fellow Minnesotan Eugene McCarthy, who quickly realized he was being used by Johnson to artificially build suspense at the 1964 Democratic national convention in Atlantic City, and Connecticut's Thomas Dodd. Humphrey, said Thomas, was "the type of Democrat I like and who would be a socialist if he got to England."[61]

In his Chicago press conference, Thomas also suggested that President Johnson's war on poverty was "a socialistic approach" to the problem — a remark quickly condemned by the pesky Socialist Labor Party, which took their aging Socialist rival to task for spreading what it described as "confusion" about socialism. In a stinging attack on Thomas, the SLP's weekly newspaper asserted that President Johnson's "war on poverty" was certainly not socialistic and that the Democratic president — like FDR several decades earlier — merely wanted to reform the capitalist system in order to preserve it. In their eyes, LBJ's approach to dealing with widespread poverty was merely an attempt to prop up the dying free enterprise system. "He wants to reform *capitalism* to save *capitalism*," argued the nation's oldest Marxist party, which was again running Eric Hass, editor of the party's newspaper, for president

---

[60] "Norman Thomas Dies," *Daily Capital News* (Jefferson City, Missouri), Dec. 20, 1968.
[61] "Johnson is Lauded, Goldwater Scored By Norman Thomas," *New York Times*, May 30, 1964; George Rising, *Clean for Gene: Eugene McCarthy's 1968 Presidential Campaign* (Westport, CT, 1997), p. 17.

that year.[62]

The Socialist Labor Party — a party that never tired of pummeling Thomas — then got really nasty, contending that the six-time presidential candidate was right when he had offhandedly suggested during his press conference that his own frequent bids for the White House had become something of a joke. "His campaigns were a joke because they offered no real alternative to capitalism," declared the *Weekly People*, the SLP's official organ. "The people who might have voted for him were really practical in voting for the Democratic presidential candidates instead, for these supporters of capitalism had a better chance of implementing — on behalf of capitalism — Mr. Thomas's patchwork reforms."[63]

Having grown accustomed to such attacks from the periphery of the American Left — he was routinely subjected to similar assaults from the SLP and the Communists throughout the 1930s and 1940s — Thomas remained undeterred and conducted a short nationwide speaking tour later that autumn urging voters across the country to support President Johnson against Republican challenger Barry M. Goldwater, whose election he believed would be tantamount to a "prescription for war."[64] He also believed the Republican nominee was being supported by some of the "worst racists in America."[65]

In his role as honorary national chairman, Thomas was joined in supporting LBJ's candidacy by nearly half of the party's national committee, including former Socialist Party-Social Democratic Federation national secretary Irwin Suall of Brooklyn, who later served as the Anti-Defamation League's fact-finding director, and author Michael Harrington, a former editor of Dorothy Day's *Catholic Worker* and inarguably the country's best known Socialist in the years following Thomas's death a few years later.[66]

Thomas, who had voted for John F. Kennedy in 1960, campaigned strenuously for the Johnson-Humphrey ticket, attacking Goldwater in speeches from Massachusetts to Hawaii. If elected, declared Thomas, the Arizona Republican "would not merely turn the clock back, he would stop it."[67]

Asked earlier in the year if his support for the Democratic ticket

---

[62] "Thomas Continues to Spread Confusion," *Weekly People*, Vol. LXXIV, No. 13, June 27, 1964.
[63] Ibid.
[64] "Many Socialists Backing Johnson; Thomas Will Tour Nation to Support President," *New York Times*, Oct. 11, 1964.
[65] "Barry's Thinking Called Dangerous," *Tucson Daily Citizen*, Oct. 28, 1964.
[66] Ibid.
[67] "Johnson Gets Backing of Norman Thomas," *Wisconsin State Journal*, Oct. 1, 1964.

would make any difference in the race, Thomas chuckled that even in the many campaigns in which he had strongly supported himself, it "never seemed to do me much good."[68]

Yet Thomas's support for LBJ did get some media attention, especially from some of the nation's conservative newspapers, including the *Chicago Tribune*, which said that everything was "coming up roses for Norman" now that the Democrats were "making his dream of a socialized United States come true."[69] The apoplectic editorial writers of the *Jefferson City Post-Tribune*, who described Thomas's enthusiastic endorsement of President Johnson as "scary" and "ought to be sobering news for those Americans who today have tipped their caps toward the Johnson-Humphrey ticket," while warning that the very future of the American way of life was at stake.[70]

It also drew the attention of local GOP organizations across the country, many of which ran newspapers ads — reprints of the *Chicago Tribune* editorial mentioned above, accompanied by a quote Thomas never made — reminding voters that Lyndon Johnson had been endorsed by the country's most prominent Socialist.[71]

The presidential election turned out almost exactly as Thomas anticipated. LBJ won by more than 16 million votes. "I wanted Goldwater decisively defeated and that happened," he said shortly after the election. "A large part of this big majority was more anti-Goldwater than for Johnson."[72]

The battle-scarred Socialist might have included himself in that category because it wasn't long before he began regretting his support for LBJ. In a letter to the *New York Times* in late December, only seven weeks after the election, the six-time presidential candidate expressed serious reservations about the escalating conflict in Southeast Asia, calling for an immediate cease-fire and bombing halt, as well as a prompt U.S. withdrawal from what he described as essentially a civil war.[73]

"President Johnson should press with all his skill and power

---

[68] "Johnson is Lauded, Goldwater Scored By Norman Thomas," *New York Times*, May 30, 1964.
[69] "Norman Thomas Finds a New Home," *Chicago Tribune*, Oct. 2, 1964.
[70] "Socialist Likes LBJ Ticket," *Jefferson City Post-Tribune*, Oct. 15, 1964.
[71] The ads, which appeared in hundreds of newspapers across the country, included the following quote falsely attributed to Thomas: "The American people will never knowingly adopt socialism, but under the name of liberalism they will adopt every fragment of the socialist program until one day America will be a socialist nation without knowing how it happened."
[72] "Socialism's Failure in U.S. Disappointment to Thomas," *Reading Eagle*, Nov. 21, 1964.
[73] "For Vietnam Withdrawal; Norman Thomas Asks Cease-Fire, U.N., China Roles in Talks," *New York Times*, Jan 3, 1965.

for an immediate cease-fire," wrote Thomas. "This should be accompanied by an agreement that no military should cross the lines set out in the cease-fire agreement, and that no further military aid should be extended by any country to the contending parties engaged while negotiations are initiated for neutralization, preferably of the entire area that was once French Indonesia." Suggesting that the UN should play a role in the negotiations, Thomas also said that Communist China's participation in any peace talks was imperative. More than anything else, however, the aging dissenter wanted the United States out of Vietnam. "In a bad situation," he concluded, "the worst thing possible is American participation in Vietnam's civil war, and the time for extrication is now."[74]

Fearing that the conflict in Southeast Asia could escalate into a "grave war," the aging prince of peace stepped up his antiwar activities during this period, frequently speaking on college campuses throughout the country. "We are saving our face at the cost of our soul," Thomas told students and faculty members at the University of Missouri in February of 1965.[75]

Secretary of Defense Robert S. McNamara, while defending the right of dissent, took issue with Thomas's statement that he "would rather see America save her soul than her face" in Southeast Asia. "How do you save your soul?" asked McNamara, a longtime admirer of Thomas. "Do you save your soul by pulling out of a situation, or do you save it by fulfilling your commitments?"[76] Some thirty years later, McNamara apologized, admitting that he had been wrong about the war in Vietnam. "We were wrong, terribly wrong," he wrote in his 1995 memoir. "We owe it to future generations to explain why."[77]

Nearly 2,000 persons gathered at the Astor Hotel a month following the 1964 presidential election to celebrate Thomas's eightieth birthday. Chief Justice Earl Warren, Martin Luther King Jr., who was on his way to Norway to receive the Nobel Peace Prize, several members of Congress, an assortment of labor leaders and a few current and former heads of foreign governments were among those who sent congratulations to the longtime Socialist. So, too, was Vice President Hubert H. Humphrey, who sent a telegram praising Thomas for consistently challenging "the evil faces of fascism and communism" and for making America a better

---

[74] Ibid.
[75] "Lodge Says Action in Vietnam is Wise," *New York Times*, Feb. 12, 1965.
[76] Mary McGrory, "McNamara Defends Dissenters' Rights," *Salt Lake Tribune*, Dec. 6, 1965.
[77] Robert S. McNamara, *In Retrospect: The Tragedy and Lessons of Vietnam* (New York, 1995), xx.

country.⁷⁸

Despite his advancing age, Thomas continued to maintain a relatively hectic schedule during the final years of his life. He rarely turned down an invitation to speak, making one public appearance after another. He particularly enjoyed the opportunity to appear on television, a medium still in its infancy when he stopped running for president in 1948.

Even in his late seventies and early eighties, Thomas always felt there was more work to do. He never intended to slow down and was slightly startled when *Dissent* magazine, a socialist publication founded and edited by Irving Howe, dedicated its tenth anniversary issue to him in 1964. "It makes me feel as I had died which I have not done yet," joked Thomas.⁷⁹

In the spring of 1966, Thomas debated the *National Review's* William F. Buckley, Jr., in the debut of his much-celebrated "Firing Line" program — the longest-running public affairs television show with the same host in television history. Thomas, who debated the erudite and witty conservative on at least a dozen occasions, sat stoically, seemingly staring ahead expressionlessly as Buckley — relying heavily on cue cards — asked him why he had supported the Korean War but now opposed U.S. involvement in Vietnam. Buckley maintained that if the United States failed in Vietnam, all of the countries in Southeast Asia and the Far East would be lost. Thomas vigorously disagreed, arguing that the U.S. could only win "if we lay Vietnam, North and South, barren." A military victory in Vietnam, warned Thomas, would force the U.S. to support a colony half way across the globe on the very borders of China.⁸⁰

It was a pretty fierce exchange, but the aging Socialist — in failing health and nearly blind — matched Buckley's legendary tiger-like toughness throughout the hour-long program. "Mr. Buckley, you seem to believe in cruelty as a necessary adjunct to this kind of war," asserted Thomas. "Your main point is that somehow we're going to contain communism this way, and we aren't. We may delay certain events in communism. We're not going to contain it."⁸¹

As his debate with the conservative polemicist clearly illustrated, Thomas had foreseen the tragedy of Vietnam — a conflict that eventually claimed more than 58,000 American lives — long

---

⁷⁸ "2,000 Hail Thomas at 80ᵗʰ Birthday," *New York Times*, Dec. 7, 1964.
⁷⁹ Swanberg, *Norman Thomas: The Last Idealist*, p. 446.
⁸⁰ "Norman Thomas Berates LBJ Lack of Peace Tries," *Nashville Tennessean*, Apr. 10, 1966.
⁸¹ "Vietnam: Pull Out? Stay In? Escalate?" Firing Line with William F. Buckley, Jr., Apr. 8, 1966.

before almost anybody else.

As his health continued to decline, travel became increasingly difficult, if not perilous, for the man fondly described as the grand old man of the American Left. Later that spring, Thomas was knocked to the ground and dragged down Manhattan's 19th Street when he inadvertently closed the door on his raincoat when getting out of a taxi cab in front of his office, near Park Avenue South. It wasn't until alert passersby shouted at the driver that the vehicle finally stopped. Thomas, who miraculously suffered only minor bruising and a scalp laceration, was briefly hospitalized, but remained in good spirits. Fortunately, he was spared any broken bones or internal injuries. "I wanted to just dust myself off and forget it," said Thomas from his hospital bed, "but we saw blood and the driver said he'd have to take me to a hospital."[82] The aging Socialist wasn't just putting on a brave face; he was worried that his next speaking appearance would be canceled if people heard that he had been hospitalized.

Following the accident — an unfortunate mishap that could have easily ended his life — friends and family wanted Thomas to retire, to give up the lecture circuit, but the six-time presidential candidate had no intention of slowing down. As a compromise, he promised never to travel alone again.[83] In the meantime, he couldn't wait to get back on the road and only reluctantly postponed that week's speaking engagements, telling reporters that if people didn't mind looking at his bruised face, he was hoping to meet the following week's commitments.[84]

To nobody's surprise, a bruised and limping Thomas could be seen leading a large group of antiwar demonstrators peacefully picketing in front of the White House some ten days later.[85] A few weeks after that, he was in the Dominican Republic as one of seventy unofficial observers trying to guarantee free elections in that country.[86]

Shortly before his death in late 1968 — some twenty years after he stopped running for president — the frail octogenarian, suffering from an ailing heart, nearly blind, and crippled by painful arthritis, could still be found lecturing against the Vietnam War on college campuses throughout the country.

Ambling along with the aid of a cane, Thomas frequently had

---

[82] "Thomas Recovering from Car Accident," *New York Times*, May 5, 1966.
[83] Steward, *Mr. Socialism*, p. 216.
[84] "Thomas Recovering from Car Accident," *New York Times*, May 5, 1966.
[85] "8,000 in Capital Picket for Peace," *New York Times*, May 16, 1966.
[86] Steward, *Mr. Socialism*, p. 216; "Balaguer Defeats Bosch in Dominican Balloting," *New York Times*, June 3, 1966.

to be assisted on and off the stage or speaking platform. After being introduced at an event in Long Island, the balding and bony Socialist slowly lifted himself out of his seat and shuffled ever so slowly across the stage to the podium, his cane in one hand and his other hand bracing his back. He appeared to be in pain. The audience watched patiently, fearing that he might not make it. He seemed to take forever. Finally reaching the podium, the frail and fragile-looking Thomas paused to catch his breath and then leaned forward and said in a clear, loud voice, "Creeping Socialism." The crowd ate it up.[87]

Widely regarded as "the conscience of America," the venerable Socialist leader had led the first antiwar protest in New York City in 1964 — long before the peace movement gathered steam — and as the war progressed and casualties mounted, students crammed into lecture halls across the country to hear his indictment against the war in Indochina. "If you can convince enough American people that you have the right idea in wanting us out of the Vietnam War," he told them, "then you'll convince Johnson."[88]

In what was claimed to be his "last public speech," an address to 109 students from thirty countries on behalf of the United States National Student Association on October 29, 1967, Thomas criticized the Johnson administration's Vietnam policy and its lack of progress on the antipoverty front. It was almost as if the students were listening to an apparition. "He was leprously white — the result of heart trouble," wrote biographer Dwight Steward. He was also blind and had to be guided to the podium by two people. Moreover, wrote Steward, Thomas was nearly completely deaf and couldn't really tell when the applause ended and he could begin speaking again.[89]

But his stentorian voice had lost none of its magic. It was loud and clear and the message was still that of a prophet. In his closing remarks to the students, the aging and frail Socialist accused the United States of living by its own version of the Ten Commandments: "Thou shalt not kill — retail; thou shalt kill wholesale at my command."[90]

That address, which took place at New York's Sheraton Atlantic Hotel, actually turned out to be Thomas's next-to-last public

---

[87] Gregory, *Norman Thomas: The Great Dissenter*, p. 209.
[88] Darcy G. Richardson, *A Nation Divided: The 1968 Presidential Campaign* (Lincoln, NE, 2002), pp. 7-8, 30-31.
[89] Steward, *Mr. Socialism*, p. 217.
[90] "Norman Thomas Makes 'Last Speech,'" *Daily Princetonian*, Vol. 91, No. 109, Oct. 31, 1967.

speech. Thomas simply didn't want to call it quits. There was always one more speech, one more audience, yet one more chance to enlighten a few in the Socratic tradition, something he had been doing without interruption for more than fifty years.

As it turns out, Thomas delivered his final speech a couple of weeks later in Chicago when he spoke at a meeting of SANE's trade union division, the peace organization he had helped to found a decade earlier. On his return flight to New York he suffered a serious stroke. It was only then that he finally realized he would have to give up the ghost once and for all. He had done as much as any mortal could in a single lifetime.

Asked in one of his later public appearances how he would like to be remembered, Thomas paused momentarily before answering. "I'd like to be remembered as Norman Thomas, as a man who was among the fortunate of the earth, who had no personal grievances, who therefore felt he had a great responsibility to do something in a world where there was a tremendous need to do a great deal."[91]

Expressing support for the "Dump Johnson" drive, the veteran Socialist leader endorsed Minnesota Sen. Eugene McCarthy's insurgent antiwar candidacy for the Democratic presidential nomination in March 1968. "Starting from practically nothing in August, that movement, spurned by Democratic Senators, including Robert Kennedy, found an admirable candidate in Senator Eugene McCarthy," he wrote in a letter to the *New York Times*.[92] Thomas had been highly critical of Sen. Robert F. Kennedy, who opposed LBJ's Vietnam policy yet professed continuing support for the president, accusing the New York senator of "lacking the courage to go with his convictions."[93] Though a close personal friend of Vice President Hubert Humphrey — the party's eventual nominee — the ailing Thomas followed McCarthy's candidacy closely, occasionally reiterating his support by offering words of encouragement.[94]

Urging Humphrey's defeat on the eve of the Democratic national convention in Chicago, Thomas called for a coalition between McCarthy's supporters and those of South Dakota Sen.

---

[91] "Time Hasn't Mellowed Norman Thomas — the Master Dissenter," *Boston Globe*, Apr. 30, 1967.
[92] "Thomas Expresses Hope for 'Dump Johnson' Drive," *New York Times*, Mar. 26, 1968.
[93] Paul Harvey, "GOP Offers No Vietnam Alternative," *Jefferson City Post-Tribune*, Jan. 26, 1968.
[94] "Ailing Norman Thomas Gives McCarthy Boost," *Oregon Statesman* (Salem, OR), June 18, 1968.

George McGovern, who belatedly entered the race following Kennedy's assassination in June. "The Vice President continues to plead to liberals to honor his role in domestic politics while, in effect, they shut their eyes to his stanch advocacy of the Johnson-Humphrey administration's Vietnam policies," wrote Thomas. "No memory of personal friendship should make us endorse a politician who has been so opportunistic about the terrible war in Vietnam," he continued. "The Vice President's record is an extraordinarily poor recommendation for a future administration. A coalition to defeat such a possibility is an absolute necessity. The McCarthy and McGovern forces must work together."[95]

Thomas became critically ill and was hospitalized at Huntington Hospital in June of 1968 with an undisclosed stomach ailment.[96] Many believed this would be the end, but Thomas, who was always full of surprises, rallied and hung on for another six months.

Thomas was interviewed from his bed at the Hilaire Farm Nursing Home while celebrating his 84th birthday on November 19th. The reporter was none other than Alden Whitman, the famous obituary writer for the *New York Times*. Thomas was in a particularly good mood, but rather gloomy about the state of the nation, much of which he blamed on the escalating war in Vietnam. "The effect of the war has been totally bad, spiritually, morally and economically," he told Whitman. "Think what we could have done to improve the quality of life at home with the money that's been spent in Vietnam! It's an awful world when the lives of our young men have to be disposed of by this war.[97]

"The state of the country is not too good," continued Thomas. "It's partly because the country lacks the leadership it needs" — something that wasn't likely to change with Richard Nixon's election a few weeks earlier.[98] Thomas, who never thought very highly of Nixon, had reluctantly endorsed his old friend Hubert H. Humphrey as the "lesser of two evils" during the final week of the 1968 campaign, but wasn't particularly surprised or glum about his defeat. "He was so equivocal in the campaign," sighed Thomas. "He would contradict himself and then deny doing it."

The 1968 campaign, however, hadn't been a complete bust for Thomas. Proudly pointing to an "Elect Lowenstein" poster hanging in his room, the aging Socialist was obviously encouraged that

---

[95] Norman Thomas, "For McCarthy-McGovern Coalition," *New York Times*, Aug. 22, 1968.
[96] "Norman Thomas Critically Ill," *Rome News-Tribune* (Rome, GA), June 17, 1968.
[97] "Norman Thomas, at 84, Worried by State of Nation," *New York Times*, Nov. 21, 1968.
[98] Ibid.

his good friend Allard K. Lowenstein — a quintessential liberal activist and 39-year-old leader of the "Dump Johnson" movement — had been elected to Congress from the fifth congressional district in heavily-Republican Nassau County. Lowenstein, a lawyer who couldn't stop running for Congress after losing his seat two years later, narrowly defeated Mason L. Hampton, a member of New York's Conservative Party who was running with GOP support.[99]

Upon learning of the Socialist leader's death on December 19, 1968, President Johnson — the last of the U.S. Presidents to feel the sting of Thomas's wrath — observed that with Thomas's passing America had lost "one of its most eloquent speakers, finest writers, and most creative thinkers." Johnson, who was recuperating from the flu at Bethesda Naval Hospital when he received word of his death, said that Thomas had kept the faith. "He was a humane, courageous man who lived to see many of the causes he championed become the law of the land."[100]

Countless others also eulogized the fallen Socialist.

"The death of Norman Thomas, six times the Socialist candidate for President, leaves an intellectual void in the nation's political life which no one in view may be able (or have the courage) to fill for years to come," observed the *Boston Globe*.[101]

The Rev. Donald S. Harrington of the Community Church of New York echoed similar sentiments at a memorial service for Thomas on December 23, 1968. "For over a generation he was the conscience of his country," said Harrington, a Unitarian minister who had actively supported Thomas during his final bid for the presidency twenty years earlier and later campaigned for lieutenant governor of New York with Franklin D. Roosevelt, Jr., on the Liberal Party ticket in 1966. "He was a kind of unofficial ombudsman for all America, as he crossed and crisscrossed the continent, arousing the consciences of men. With his long first finger upraised in denunciation or scorn, his wit flashing like a rapier, his cracking powerful voice thundering to the farthest reaches of a hall or arena or public square, he was unforgettably magnificent. Justice, freedom, world brotherhood and peace, I fear, will not see his like again."[102]

In one of his final speeches before entering a nursing home shortly after suffering a stroke two days before his 83rd birthday in

---

[99] Hampton, who had garnered 322,693 votes as the Conservative Party's candidate for New York attorney general in 1966, was hoping to become the first Conservative Party member of Congress.
[100] "Norman Thomas Dies at 84," *Hagerstown Morning Herald*, Dec. 20, 1968.
[101] "Norman Thomas, a Good Man," *Boston Globe*, Dec. 20, 1968.
[102] Gorham, *Leader at Large*, pp. 202-203.

November 1967, Thomas offered some affection as well as some criticism for the United States, suggesting that antiwar activists and dissenters should wash the American flag instead of burning it. "I don't like the symbolism of burning the flag of the country I love," he sighed.[103]

Thomas indeed loved his country, as eloquently expressed in an editorial tribute by an upstate New York newspaper shortly after his death:

> Even those to whom Thomas' ideas were anathema are to some extent in his debt. For he, as much as any public figure of the past several decades, elevated the quality of political dialogue in this country. Because of what he said, others often were moved to deal more substantively with issues than might have been the case had he remained silent. All of us, whatever our views on political and social questions, profit whenever that happens.
>
> Norman Thomas had a way of crystallizing problems, of stating them with clarity and brevity. One such formulation strikes us as a fitting way to close this modest tribute to an extraordinary American: If I were to pick out one question on which above all others humanity's fate depends, it would be this: 'Can and will we Americans avert World War III and preserve our freedom?' There spoke a man who loved his country and understood its profound responsibility in the world.[104]

Nearly forgotten today, Norman Thomas was not only a prophet, but arguably America's most persistent patriot and unapologetic defender of the country's endangered civil liberties, an often lonely and noble voice in the wilderness echoing the spirit and values that made this a Great Republic while consistently speaking — and acting — on behalf of its better self.

---

[103] "Norman Thomas Dies," *Daily Capital News*, Dec. 20, 1968.
[104] "Norman Thomas," *Oswego Palladium-Times*, Nov. 27, 1968.

Chapter IV

♦

Long Distance Runner

While a handful of individuals have sought the presidency over a longer period of time — the one-time "boy wonder" of American politics Harold Stassen, a tragic figure who ran regularly for the nation's highest office for nearly half a century, Minnesota Senator Eugene J. McCarthy, the gentle poet-politician who stunningly dislodged a sitting president of his own party in 1968 and sought the Oval Office four more times over the next twenty-four years, and controversial fringe candidate Lyndon H. LaRouche, Jr., a longtime advocate of the Hamiltonian-inspired American System of Political Economy who ran repeatedly for the presidency from 1976 to 2004, among them — nobody worked harder as a presidential candidate than Norman M. Thomas. He never skimped on any of his six consecutive bids for the White House. He was truly one of a kind.

Having inherited the role of Eugene Debs' successor as the public face and leader of the Socialist Party for more than four decades until his death in 1968, the former Presbyterian minister freely admitted that he had been something of a "Hobson's choice" when he was first nominated for president in 1928.

The Socialist Party at the time still had a wealth of talent within its ranks. But the party's other outstanding leaders that year — Victor Berger, the Socialist congressman from Wisconsin, or New York's Jacob Panken and Morris Hillquit, the latter two of whom were both getting along in years — weren't born in the United States and therefore had been ruled out as possible presidential candidates in the immediate post-Debs era. Daniel W. Hoan, the Socialist mayor of Milwaukee from 1916-1940, might have been a logical choice to head the party's ticket, but he didn't want to risk everything he had worked so hard to achieve at the municipal level for what almost certainly would have been a doomed candidacy at the national level.

In addition to California's Cameron King, a Stanford-educated lawyer, and the colorfully quotable Joseph W. Sharts, the party's candidate for governor of Ohio, there was also some talk of possibly nominating Freda Hogan, the longtime companion and later wife of Oklahoma City satirist Oscar Ameringer, the "Mark Twain of American Socialism."[1]

And while there had also been some serious speculation that James H. Maurer, a former three-term Socialist legislator from Pennsylvania — the man Thomas personally preferred — might seek the party's presidential nomination in 1928, the longtime labor leader eventually demurred, telling his comrades that he "felt that a younger and better qualified Socialist should assume the task of carrying the party's message."[2]

The Pennsylvanian preferred Thomas, a man who had clearly demonstrated his courage of conviction by joining the party at a time when war hysteria was sweeping the country. "What I like about Norman is that he came to us," Maurer once said, "when everybody else was running away."[3]

Though declining to run for president, the 63-year-old Maurer, who had been elected to the Reading city council the previous year during the Socialist Party's sweep of that blue-collar city, nevertheless happily agreed to serve as Thomas's vice-presidential running mate that year — a role he fulfilled again in 1932.

A one-time machinists' apprentice, Maurer was the longtime president of the Pennsylvania Federation of Labor, ably serving in that capacity from 1912 to 1928. Like his presidential running mate, Maurer had been sharply criticized in the press for speaking out against American involvement during World War I.

In nominating the avuncular Thomas, New York's Louis Waldman told the delegates that the nominee must be a loyal member of the party, an excellent public speaker and — in a some-

---

[1] Vaughn Davis Bornet, *Labor Politics in a Democratic Republic: Moderation, Division, and Disruption in the Presidential Election of 1928* (Washington, D.C., 1964), p. 85.
[2] James Hudson Maurer, *It Can Be Done: The Autobiography of James Hudson Maurer* (New York, 1938), p. 293.
[3] "Thomas Long Active Fighter for Socialism," *Socialist Call*, Nov. 30, 1935.

what strained analogy — someone of the stature of Abraham Lincoln, the enlightened Wendell Phillips, abolitionist William Lloyd Garrison, and the late Eugene V. Debs.

The delegates believed they had found their man. "When we go riding out on the Great Adventure," wrote one delegate who could hardly contain his enthusiasm, "we will have as gallant a spirit as ever set lance against the three black horsemen, Cruelty, Greed, and Fear."[4]

The witty and urbane Thomas was much more modest, admitting later that he only ran for president in 1928 because there "wasn't anybody else" willing to do it.

The same thing was true — if not moreso — in 1944, the year he waged his loneliest battle of all.

Maintaining that "no good man as a political Messiah can save America," Thomas accepted his party's presidential nomination in 1928 with dignity and grace, qualities that marked each of his six tries for the White House.[5]

In his eloquent acceptance speech to the delegates gathered at the Manhattan Opera House, the ex-minister insisted that he wasn't a legitimate successor to the beloved labor leader Eugene V. Debs — nobody could be, he said with a tinge of sorrow — but that it was his intention to continue to battle for the cause Debs "so greatly loved, and for which he so greatly suffered." He also acknowledged the party's deteriorated and weakened condition. "We are not building for this election but for education and for the future," he calmly told the delegates that year.[6]

The Socialist standard-bearer also reminded the delegates that success in the presidential campaign couldn't be measured in terms of votes, but rather in "the steady education of men and women in the possibilities…of peace, of freedom, of justice, of brotherhood, for all men everywhere." He also prophetically cautioned those who were hoping for some sort of national catastrophe to usher in the establishment of a socialist society — a view shared by many Communists and Socialists at the time. "The sad part of it is that there is no promise that out of convulsion you will get salvation," he warned.[7]

The Socialist platform that year was virtually tailor-made for a candidate like Thomas, a man whose appeal was largely aimed at intellectuals and middle-class liberals. In addition to calling for the

---

[4] Bornet, *Labor Politics in a Democratic Republic*, pp. 85-86
[5] Seidler, *Norman Thomas: Respectable Rebel*, p. 75.
[6] Bornet, *Labor Politics in a Democratic Republic*, pp. 85-86.
[7] Seidler, *Norman Thomas: Respectable Rebel*, p. 75.

collective ownership and democratic management of the country's basic industries, it also included separate planks calling for public ownership of the utilities, railroads, transportation and communications systems and conservation of the nation's natural resources. Among other things, the Socialists also advocated a shorter workweek, a public works program, unemployment insurance and government pensions for the elderly.

Though not nearly as harsh or difficult as what he would encounter sixteen years later, the 1928 campaign was hardly a joyride for Thomas and his running mate. Coming at the tail end of the "Roaring Twenties," a period of resplendent opulence for the nation's wealthiest citizens, the United States was enjoying a wave of prosperity unlike anything it had experienced before. The once-relevant Socialist Party, so desperately needed during the final days of the Gilded Age at the turn of the century, almost seemed like a relic. In fact, the party's membership had dwindled to only 7,793 members nationally, and the party's machinery was virtually nonexistent.

Making matters worse, the party's national office, then based in Chicago, was being badly mismanaged by national secretary William H. Henry, a somewhat lazy, incompetent and semi-literate man who occasionally dabbled in nativist and anti-Semitic activities. A native of Terre Haute, Indiana, Henry had replaced the highly-competent Otto Branstetter following his resignation as national executive secretary in February 1924. Henry clearly had no idea what he was doing and Thomas and other leading Socialists wanted him removed as soon as possible. "I am never so discouraged about Socialism as when I am talking to Comrade Henry," lamented Thomas.[8]

To circumvent the Chicago office, Victor Berger established a Socialist Action Committee based in New York with Morris Hillquit as its chairman. Algernon Lee, a slender, stoop-shouldered intellectual whose biting sarcasm was lost on most people, served as treasurer. G. August Gerber, a young and dynamic son of a veteran Socialist, served as secretary and campaign manager.

Gerber had a particular knack for getting the party on the ballot in states where its membership was small or virtually nonexistent. At the start of the 1928 campaign, the Socialist Party enjoyed permanent ballot status in only four states, but largely through Gerber's efforts, the Thomas-Maurer ticket eventually appeared on the

---

[8] Johnpoll, *Pacifist's Progress*, p. 59; David A. Shannon, *The Socialist Party of America* (Chicago, 1967), pp. 184-185, 192.

ballot in more than three-quarters of the states that year.[9]

Lacking the same level of familiarity and name recognition enjoyed by his predecessor Gene Debs, newspaper coverage was also somewhat hard to come by. One sympathetic columnist joked that Thomas would have to ride a bicycle backwards on the steps of the U.S. Capitol to get the same kind of exposure Herbert Hoover and Al Smith routinely received.

Thomas and Maurer nevertheless campaigned strenuously across the country that autumn, rebuilding the once-proud Socialist Party in the process. Frequently accompanied by New York publicist McAlister Coleman and the jocular August Claessens — arguably one of the funniest politicians in the party — the road-weary Thomas spoke in all but three of the nation's forty-eight states during the 1928 campaign.

While relying on radio as a new medium to reach a larger audience, Thomas only used two or three basic speeches during the campaign. Making only slight alterations depending on the audience, he later lamented that he almost gagged at their repetition.[10]

Occasionally traveling by bus, automobile and airplane, but usually by train, the lanky Socialist candidate stressed that prosperity under Coolidge had not conquered poverty and that there were still more than four million unemployed people in the country.

To remedy this tragic situation — and this was before the 1929 stock market crash and the ensuing Great Depression — Thomas called for a federal public works program at prevailing union wages, a shorter workday and workweek, and the adoption of a constitutional amendment to prohibit child labor. He also called for unemployment insurance and federal old-age pensions — an issue championed by the Socialists dating back to the original Social Democratic platform of 1900 — to be financed by increased corporate taxation, inheritance taxes, and increased taxes on the wealthy.

"Had this program been in force when the stock market crash occurred," wrote Thomas biographer Harry Fleischman, "the nation might have been spared one of the most searing and painful crises in its history."[11]

On foreign policy, the Socialist candidates closely followed the party platform that Thomas himself was instrumental in writing, calling for U.S. initiative for world disarmament and sharp cuts in

---

[9] Shannon, *The Socialist Party of America*, p. 192.
[10] Steward, *Mr. Socialism*, p. 132.
[11] Fleischman, *Norman Thomas: A Biography*, pp. 114-115.

military spending. The party's platform also urged U.S. entry into the League of Nations and a cancellation of all World War I debts and reparations, provided that both the Allied and Central Powers agreed to drastically reduce military expenditures.

While sharply criticizing the Soviet Union's "despotic and brutal" totalitarianism, the Socialist Party also called for "the speedy recognition of Russia" to foster international stability and promote good will. The platform also called for the withdrawal of all U.S. troops from Nicaragua, home rule for Puerto Rico and the Virgin Islands, and independence for the Philippines.[12]

The Socialist nominee was quite impartial when it came to his criticism of his two major-party opponents during the 1928 campaign. He would have been more than happen to finish ahead of either of them, thereby enabling the Socialist Party to form the nucleus of a new opposition party. Noting that Democrat Al Smith was known as the "Happy Warrior," Thomas joked that he wouldn't mind being called the "Happy Mourner" at the funeral of either party.[13]

While regularly flaying the Democrats for exploiting racial prejudice, Thomas was particularly put off by the religious bigotry that surfaced shortly after New York governor, a Catholic, captured the Democratic presidential nomination. He was particularly appalled by the ugly whispering campaign against the Democratic nominee and the prospect of a "Pope in the White House," an appeal to the crudest kind of religious bigotry found in American politics since the days of the stridently anti-Catholic and anti-immigrant Know-Nothing Party.

Thousands of Protestant ministers throughout the country railed against the Democratic candidate that year. "If you vote for Al Smith," cried one Protestant preacher, "you're voting against Christ and you'll be damned."[14]

In an open letter to the nation's Protestant leaders, Thomas tried to appeal to their sense of decency by assailing his former colleagues in the ministry for introducing "religious prejudice" into the campaign and for using the issue of prohibition as a "mask for religious partisanship."[15]

Thomas was also deeply disturbed that so many members of the Protestant clergy had injected themselves into the campaign on

---

[12] Ibid., p. 115.
[13] Rodney Dutcher, "Thomas, Socialist Candidate, Works Hard, Has Fun and Doesn't Worry," *Wisconsin Rapids Daily Tribune*, Oct. 15, 1928.
[14] Paul F. Boller, Jr., *Presidential Campaigns* (New York, 1985), p. 225.
[15] Fleischman, *Norman Thomas: A Biography*, p. 115.

Hoover's behalf and questioned why they believed the issue of prohibition was such a crucial "moral" issue while ignoring the equally important moral issues such as disarmament and poverty.

"The Bible, if memory serves me, contains no explicit Volstead Act," wrote Thomas to his former colleagues, "but it is fairly explicit on matters of the exploitation of the poor."[16]

Prohibition, of course, turned out to be a major issue during the 1928 campaign, especially with the nomination of a "wet" Catholic New Yorker on the Democratic ticket.

Unlike Smith, who made it clear that he favored local option, giving states the right to pass legislation permitting the sale of light wines and beer, and Hoover, who insisted that prohibition was "a great social and economic experiment, noble in motive and far-reaching in purpose" — thereby winning him the support of a large segment of the Prohibition Party, including that of national chairman D. Leigh Colvin — Thomas seemed to straddle the issue, urging a national referendum to settle the question once and for all.

Speaking to a crowd of 1,700 in New Haven in mid-October, the Socialist standard-bearer said that President Hoover could not make the Republican Party sufficiently dry enough to satisfy most Prohibitionists any more than Al Smith could make the Democrats wet enough to satisfy most of those opposed to prohibition.[17]

Believing that prohibition wasn't a "political" issue, Thomas had urged the Socialists not to adopt an official position on the matter in the party's platform — a view shared by a majority on the platform committee.[18] His failure to come out forcefully in favor of repeal undoubtedly hurt him in the party's stronghold of Milwaukee, with its large German population and once-thriving breweries, many of which were forced to produce other items, such as soft drinks, during prohibition simply to stay afloat while others were forced to close their doors forever.

In the eyes of many Milwaukeeans, prohibition had not only robbed thousands of citizens of their livelihoods, but had also robbed their city of its happiness.

By straddling the liquor issue, Thomas clearly hurt himself, especially in beer-guzzling Milwaukee, where local Socialists had hung signs throughout the city urging citizens to "VOTE SOCIALIST AND WET." Thomas polled only 18,000 votes in the entire state,

---

[16] Shannon, *The Socialist Party of America*, p. 198.
[17] Darcy G. Richardson, *Others: "Fighting Bob" La Follette and the Progressive Movement — Third-Party Politics in the 1920s* (New York, 2008), pp. 320-321.
[18] Bornet, *Labor Politics in a Democratic Republic*, p. 82; "Thomas Nominated by Socialist Party," *New York Times*, April 17, 1928.

whereas avowedly "wet" Socialists like Victor Berger and Walter Polakowski, an upholsterer and longtime union activist, garnered 40,536 and 18,885 votes in their respective congressional races in Milwaukee.

Thomas, who had been invited to campaign in Milwaukee only once between May and October, claimed that he really wasn't welcome in the party's stronghold, but Daniel Hoan, the longtime Socialist mayor of Milwaukee, blamed the party's poor showing in that city on Thomas's failure to take a firm stand against prohibition.

"This is the home of the breweries," Hoan wrote in a letter to Thomas shortly after the election. "The brewery workers were originally more nearly 100 per cent Socialist than other unions...They have been thrown out of employment and naturally are deeply incensed at the Prohibition law." The Milwaukee mayor claimed that many of the ex-brewery workers had been so angered by remarks made against Democrat Al Smith by Victor Berger and the Milwaukee Daily Leader "that they deliberately and intentionally voted for Smith and many of them deliberately voted the straight Democratic ticket."[19]

As New York's Louis Waldman later recalled, Thomas, representing what he called the "new Socialism" — unlike his predecessor Eugene V. Debs, who had been largely shunned by such institutions — was welcomed into the nation's churches, colleges, and civic organizations during the 1928 campaign. "But above all," added Waldman, who later became one of Thomas's most vocal adversaries, "he had those qualities of mind and character which appealed to the intelligent and educated young people of the country and which drew them into the ranks of the party in unprecedented numbers."[20] Like other Socialists, the Ukrainian-born Waldman was extremely optimistic about the party's future.

Taking the high road throughout the campaign, Thomas's candidacy attracted the support of a number of leading intellectuals, including that of theologian Reinhold Niebuhr of the Union Theological Seminary, Paul H. Douglas of the University of Chicago, Rev. John Haynes Holmes, and historian and biographer W. E. Woodward. Woodward had sent a letter to 700 writers and artists in August urging them to support Thomas and Maurer to "help lay the foundation for a powerful party of progress and social justice."[21]

---

[19] Johnpoll, *Pacifist's Progress*, p. 58
[20] Louis Waldman, *Labor Lawyer* (New York, 1944), p. 189.
[21] Shannon, *The Socialist Party of America*, p. 197

The Socialist standard-bearer also received a boost later that month when a group of thirty-six educators publicly endorsed his candidacy as the first step in building such a party. Those supporting Gov. Smith and President Hoover "are the same sterile and corrupt groups which have ruled the country for the last half century," stated the group's appeal in the form of a letter, signed by Paul Douglas. Other signers included sociology professors Isaac E. Ash of Ohio University and Edwin L. Clarke of Oberlin College.[22]

Moreover, Thomas-for-President clubs were formed on college campuses throughout the country and Thomas was given a rousing welcome at Harvard's Liberal Club. A committee of 120 intellectuals headed by Bishop Paul Jones was also formed to support his candidacy. Its members included W.E.B. Du Bois, Fola La Follette, the eldest child of the late Wisconsin senator, and Freda Kirchwey, a Barnard-educated civil rights and peace activist who later replaced Oswald Garrison Villard as editor of the *Nation*.[23]

Though questioning his ability to appeal to the working class, the *Christian Century*, the liberal Protestant weekly based in Chicago, applauded the Socialist Party's wisdom in nominating Thomas, describing him as "one of the clearest minded and most attractive leaders of liberal thought in the country," adding that if the party's goal was "to appeal to the intellectuals," they couldn't have made a better choice.[24]

Throughout the campaign, the indefatigable Thomas — a better all-around speaker than either Hoover or Smith — acknowledged that he had no chance of winning and told reporters that he was using his candidacy as a way of educating the electorate.

"I am telling the people that it is within their power, by intelligence and cooperation, to abolish poverty, enlarge the borders of freedom, rid the world of the menace of war and to realize the fellowship of which prophets and poets have dreamed," he asserted.[25]

As was his nature, Thomas refrained from personal attacks and instead gently criticized the policies of the country's two major parties while presenting his own candidacy as an idealistic and "plausible" alternative. "Smith and Hoover are about the best men in their parties, but what this country needs is a political realist," he asserted, adding that the country "can't be saved by any Messiahs. There is no cure-all. One thing imperatively needed is a party held

---

[22] "Educators Back Thomas," *New York Times*, Aug. 25, 1928.
[23] Johnpoll, *Pacifist's Progress*, p. 56.
[24] Ibid.
[25] "Fight With No Chance to Win," *New Castle News*, July 17, 1928.

together by some other force than a mere desire for office and special privilege."[26]

Thomas knew all along that he and the other minor-party candidates didn't stand a chance in the 1928 presidential election. Acknowledging that prohibition and religious and racial intolerance would be factors in the election, the Socialist candidate also realized that things looked considerably bleak for his Democratic opponent.

"On both sides, openly and secretly, there is great and unhealthy bigotry," said Thomas in late September. "The three R's — religion, race and rum — in the order named will sway thousands upon thousands of voters. Nevertheless, organization is very important, and I look to see the Republicans win because of their superior organization, if for no other reason."[27] If only his own party enjoyed that kind of organization, Thomas must have thought to himself.

The Socialist candidate echoed the same sentiment in the campaign's waning days. "I have been in thirty-seven states since the campaign started and I believe I know whereof I speak," he told reporters while campaigning in Boston toward the end of the campaign. "Smith will have to carry every doubtful state to be elected," he said. The New York Democrat might have a fighting chance in each of those states, Thomas added, but it was highly unlikely that he would win all of them.[28]

The former Presbyterian minister had read the tea leaves correctly. On Election Day, Herbert Hoover, promising a "chicken in every pot and a car in every garage," swept to an easy victory, carrying all but eight states while polling 21,430,743 popular votes, or more than 58% nationally. Democrat Al Smith, done in by booze, bigotry and prosperity, mustered less than 41% of the popular vote, garnering 15,016,443 votes. Thomas, who garnered more than 107,000 votes in the state of New York, including 50,973 from the five boroughs of New York City, received 267,420 votes in forty states, or seven-tenths of one percent nationally.[29]

While the Socialist ticket's relatively unimpressive national total was a far cry from the more than 4.8 million votes garnered by Wisconsin's Robert M. La Follette only four years earlier, or the 913,000 votes amassed by the late Eugene V. Debs during his final

---

[26] Johnpoll, *Pacifist's Progress*, pp. 55-56.
[27] "Mr. Thomas," *TIME*, Oct. 8, 1928.
[28] "Norman Thomas Says Hoover is the Choice," *Oshkosh Daily Northwestern*, Oct. 30, 1928.
[29] "Smith Won City by 453,805 Margin," *New York Times*, Nov. 29, 1928.

campaign for the presidency in 1920, Thomas had miraculously revived a party that many believed had been buried along with Debs in the cold clay of Indiana.

Thomas's vote might have been even greater if thousands of others had simply voted their conscience. After the election, in fact, dozens of voters told the Socialist standard-bearer that they wished they had voted for him. "Thanks for the flowers," quipped Thomas, "but I wish you hadn't waited for the funeral."[30]

The following year, Thomas was back on the campaign trail — this time running for mayor of New York City. Thomas, who opened his campaign with a blistering attack on the Tammany machine in Brooklyn's Ulmer Park in late July, was pitted against flamboyant and dapper Mayor Jimmy Walker, donning a silk hat and gray swallowtail coat, and colorful congressman Fiorello H. La Guardia, who was more or less the GOP's sacrificial lamb, in the 1929 mayoral contest.[31] La Guardia, incidentally, had actively supported Thomas during the 1925 mayoral contest.[32]

Describing New York City as one of "great luxury and greater poverty, a little beauty and immense ugliness, this market place where everything, even justice, is bought and sold," Thomas laid out his municipal program in the pages of the *New York Times* in late September. In addition to cleansing the machinery of justice, Thomas proposed a constructive housing program designed to move those currently living in decrepit tenement dwellings into garden apartments; the establishment of a unified city-owned subway system; the creation of public markets; a fairer system of taxation; and an improved public school system unencumbered by "glorified mediocrity, tainted by ecclesiastical, racial and partisan politics, and apparently run for the purpose of turning out docile robots for political and industrial bosses." He also promised to fight for lower milk prices and cheaper electric rates — all of which he freely admitted would require state and federal cooperation.[33]

The race was so lopsided that the Tammany-backed Walker, a swaggering, brassy symbol of the jazz age who preferred to spend summer afternoons at Yankee Stadium and winter evenings attending the latest Broadway premieres rather than tending to the nuts and bolts of running the country's largest city, barely campaigned.

Striking a condescending tone, Walker dismissed both of his

---

[30] Fleischman, *Norman Thomas: A Biography*, p. 116.
[31] "Thomas Attacks Rule of Tammany," *New York Times*, July 28, 1929.
[32] "La Guardia Backs Thomas," *New York Times*, Oct. 19, 1925.
[33] Norman Thomas, "Where the Socialists Stand," *New York Times*, Sep. 29, 1929.

rivals from the outset of the campaign, describing Thomas as "a permanent Socialist" and La Guardia as "a transient Socialist." As far as he was concerned, the Republicans really didn't have a candidate. "There is no Republican candidate," he brashly stated at an old-fashioned Tammany rally launching his reelection campaign in October. "I have two opponents that I know of. Both of them are Socialists."[34]

The fact that Walker preferred to spend more time with his showgirl mistress than on the campaign trail that autumn didn't deter Thomas from launching one attack after another on the top-hatted playboy whose fall from grace was still three years in the offing.

Denouncing the Walker administration as a "rule of racketeers," the Socialist candidate charged that the mayor had failed to preserve the city's five-cent transit fee, lacked a decent housing program and had allowed political favoritism to influence property assessments, including the underassessment of a property in the heart of the city's financial district which had only been assessed at between a quarter and third of its actual value. "What the favored landowner does not pay, the rest of us have to make up," said Thomas, reminding ordinary, working-class New Yorkers that they were subsidizing the wealthy and well-connected.[35]

Calling it a "an alarming cancer in the body politic," Thomas also accused the mayor of making a mockery of the city's criminal justice system, a system where the guilty often went free while the innocent lived in fear. "The Walker Administration has reached new low levels in ability, character and honesty," declared Thomas. "No magistrate is appointed without political pull, and few if any without payment of large sums of money, ranging from $30,000 to $75,000. Political activities are carried on freely by magistrates, and the average magistrate does business on the side, sometime for very dubious clients." Justice was for sale. It wasn't uncommon, said Thomas, for slick Tammany district leaders and their aides, acting as fixers — arranging verdicts through bribery or influence — to hang around the city's courtrooms and talk to the judges before and after hearing a case. Many magistrates, he contended, had been "unfair to the point of brutality," especially in cases involving labor unless the defendants were represented by fixers.[36]

---

[34] "Walker, Opening Campaign, Stands on 4-Year Record; Smith Hails Business Rule," *New York Times*, Oct. 16, 1929.
[35] "Thomas Denounces 'Racketeer Rule,'" *New York Times*, Sep. 23, 1929.
[36] "Thomas Denounces City Magistrates," *New York Times*, Nov. 4, 1929.

Focusing much of his attention on Tammany corruption during the course of the campaign — it was a tailor-made issue, especially since there was so much of it — Thomas singled out several city magistrates whom he believed were corrupt, all of whom were later indicted, resigned, or weren't reappointed to office.[37]

When the mayor accused his three rivals — La Guardia, Thomas and former police commissioner Richard E. Enright, who was running on an independent "Square Deal" ticket — of slandering the city, Thomas quickly fired back. "It is the height of cowardice for the mayor to throw out general ill-tempered attacks on his opponents," Thomas said briskly. "He cannot disprove a single statement I have made. As for besmirching the city, Mr. Walker's administration alone is responsible. The city to him is one large factory for the production of Tammany spoils."[38]

When Walker refused to accept Thomas's challenge to participate in a three-way debate with La Guardia on WNYC, the city-owned radio station, Thomas, in a particularly shrewd maneuver, challenged former Gov. Alfred E. Smith — a creature of the Tammany Tiger if there ever was one — to discuss the campaign issues that Walker had refused to address.[39]

"If Mayor Walker will not answer these questions," Thomas told a radio audience in late October, "I must ask his spokesman, ex-Gov. Smith to do it." There was a certain "irony that comes very close to tragedy" in Smith's endorsement of the mayor and his Tammany administration, continued Thomas, for "every New Yorker knows that in his heart of hearts Mr. Smith loathes the tactics of the present city administration and that time and again Tammany has rejected that which is nearest and dearest to Mr. Smith."[40]

As expected, Smith never responded to Thomas's challenge to discuss the issues, but the Socialist mayoral candidate had skillfully zeroed in on a potentially embarrassing sore spot for the Democrats. After all, several reporters had noted a few weeks earlier that the former governor, in endorsing the current Tammany administration, had merely urged the city's voters "to elect a straight Democratic ticket," but never mentioned Mayor Walker by name. Similarly, as the *New York Evening Post* pointed out,

---

[37] Gregory, *Norman Thomas: The Great Dissenter*, p. 87.
[38] "Opponents Accept Walker Challenge," *New York Times*, Oct. 4, 1929.
[39] "Walker Declines Debate," *New York Times*, Aug. 30, 1929; "Thomas Asks Smith to Speak for Walker," *New York Times*, Oct. 30, 1929.
[40] "Thomas Asks Smith to Speak for Walker," *New York Times*, Oct. 30, 1929.

Smith declined to be photographed with the mayor after the meeting. "In principle, conduct and political idealism," wrote the paper's editors, "the two men are as far apart as the two poles."[41]

With Walker refusing to mix it up with his challengers, Thomas and La Guardia, who desperately pleaded with his Socialist rival to withdraw from the race, often used each other as sparring partners with Thomas prevailing time and again.

Characterizing La Guardia as a "political chameleon," Thomas needled his Republican opponent for asserting that he had never made a deal with Tammany Hall during his political career. "The politest thing we can say about Mr. La Guardia's boast that he never made a deal with Tammany is that he suffers from an exceedingly bad memory," quipped Thomas. "If he did not make a deal in 1918, somebody made it for him," said Thomas, referring to the congressman's successful Democratic and Republican fusion campaign against Socialist Scott Nearing, an economics lecturer at the Rand School of Social Science, eleven years earlier — a race La Guardia won by about 8,000 votes.[42]

By a sheer stroke of luck, Mayor Walker appointed Thomas and two other prominent New York Socialists to the welcoming committee for British Prime Minister Ramsay MacDonald when he visited the city in early October.[43]

While serving on the reception committee for MacDonald, who had become that country's first Labour Party prime minister in 1924 and had just returned to power a few months earlier, Thomas bumped into *New York Times* publisher Adolph Ochs, who was also serving on the welcoming committee. Making small talk while waiting for MacDonald's ship to dock, Ochs told Thomas that he heard he was running for mayor again and hoped he would wage an issues-oriented campaign. "Mr. Ochs," replied Thomas, "I've always discussed issues. Last year, when I ran for president, your paper merely reprinted some wisecracks of mine two or three times over but never carried the substance of my remarks." The powerful publisher was obviously taken aback by Thomas's frank response. "Well," said Ochs, "I'll speak to my people and see what we can do."[44]

Ochs kept his word and from that moment forward Thomas's mayoral candidacy received considerably more coverage, much of

---

[41] "Walker's Unimpressive Start," *New York Evening Post*, Oct. 16, 1929.
[42] "Thomas Questions La Guardia on Fascism," *New York Times*, Sep. 16, 1929.
[43] "Socialists Plan Welcome; Norman Thomas to Be on Mayor's Committee to Great MacDonald," *New York Times*, Oct. 3, 1929.
[44] Fleischman, *Norman Thomas: A Biography*, p. 118.

it favorable, than previously. In the final month of the campaign, the *New York Times* ran more than six-dozen articles on Thomas's candidacy and mentioned him in most of the articles written about Walker and La Guardia. Thanks to the publisher, Thomas was given the full-dress treatment, the same amount of coverage routinely provided to major-party candidates.

Like blackbirds on a telephone wire, the city's other newspapers quickly followed suit. In fact, Thomas received far more extensive — and sympathetic — newspaper coverage in that election than in any of his previous campaigns for public office, and several leading columnists endorsed his candidacy outright.

In late October, Thomas picked up the endorsement of the *New York Telegram* and the *New York World*, two papers implacably opposed to continued Tammany misrule, but not exactly sold on La Guardia's candidacy.[45] The *Telegram*, which supported Hoover for president the previous year, said that the local GOP was "ready for burial, and a not very honorable burial at that," and that in spite of his party label "Thomas, better than La Guardia, provides a rallying point about which liberals of the city can seek to proclaim the end of the local Republican party and open the way for a real and lasting liberal movement" in New York City.[46]

The Socialist candidate also enjoyed the backing of the widely-respected and influential Citizens Union, a good government group long opposed to Tammany. Founded in 1897, the Citizens Union helped elect Seth Low as the city's first reform mayor in 1901. In recommending Thomas, the Citizens Union described the Socialist candidate as "a man of learning, ability and high ideals." Regardless of how voters might have felt about his party's platform, the reform group maintained that his "sincerity and fearlessness" alone — qualities sorely lacking in the current administration — warranted serious consideration. "If personal merit alone were to decide the contest, Mr. Thomas would win easily."[47]

Thomas was also endorsed by longtime New York Supreme Court Justice John Ford, a veteran of William Randolph Hearst's Municipal Ownership League who had supported "Fighting Bob" La Follette's insurgent candidacy for president in 1924. In endorsing the Socialist nominee, the 67-year-old jurist ripped into both of Thomas's major-party opponents. Characterizing Jimmy Walker's administration as a "continuous violation of his official oath," the

---

[45] "The Real Happy Warrior," *New York Times*, Oct. 31, 1929.
[46] "The Telegram Backs Thomas for Mayor," *New York Times*, Oct. 23, 1929.
[47] "La Guardia Opposed by Citizens Union in Campaign Survey; Walker Scored as Organization Mayor — Thomas Termed Best Man for Office," *New York Times*, Sep. 9, 1929.

judge said that he didn't expect La Guardia to be much better than the notorious Beau Brummel and nightclub patron who currently occupied City Hall, asserting that while the irascible Republican candidate hadn't had a chance to break his mayoralty oath yet, "he brazenly declares he will do so if elected."[48]

The pace of the mayoralty campaign was no less frantic than the presidential race Thomas conducted the previous year. Debs biographer McAlister Coleman, a former *New York Sun* reporter and perennial candidate himself who had accompanied Thomas during much of the 1928 presidential campaign, described a typical night during the mayoral campaign as an unforgettably exhilarating experience:

> It is seven o'clock in the evening and already there are gathering in front of the old-fashioned Thomas house on East 18th Street just beyond the thunder of the Third Avenue Elevated, reporters, the police escort, the ubiquitous and ever-faithful Eddie Levinson, and Joe Viola, who drives a car as Kreisler plays a violin.
>
> By 7:30 we are off. Immediately there comes to rushing reality the dream of every small New Yorker, namely, to ride on a fire-engine. For with the motorcycle cop ahead, sounding his siren, all speed laws are off as you dodge in and out of elevated pillars, under the noses of suddenly halted trucks, and through red lights at a speed of forty to fifty miles per hour. Of course this is a courtesy extended to all candidates. Nevertheless it gives you a wonderful sense of superiority to be riding in a Socialist auto past indignant Rolls Royces and Packards, waved to one side by the majestic arm of the law ahead. In one night, you go at this headlong pace from a meeting at the tip-end of the Bronx clear down to where cold winds are blowing along Coney Island's boardwalk.[49]

In a typical evening, continued Coleman, Thomas made at least a half-dozen campaign appearances and usually didn't arrive home until sometime after midnight, when the exhausted candidate and crew would inevitably be greeted by a smiling and hospitable Violet Thomas waiting patiently for them with hot beverages and refreshments. After a few hours of sleep, Thomas would be up at the crack of dawn to do it all over again.[50]

Toward the end of the campaign, Thomas said that it had been

---

[48] "Political Briefs," *Brooklyn Daily Eagle*, Oct. 25, 1929.
[49] Quoted in Fleischman, *Norman Thomas: A Biography*, p. 118.
[50] Ibid. p. 119.

his goal to awaken hope and faith in the kind of city New York could become in the near future. "In awakening hope we shall have to conquer that pervasive fear which characterizes New York's political life," he said — a fear that perpetuated Tammany's stranglehold on the city. A political machine which derives its power from "honest graft" and the cohesive force of public plunder could only be conquered by a political party with a programmatic set of solutions for the city's woes, as outlined in his campaign, a party committed to making government at all levels — federal, state and city — "our servant in winning plenty, peace and freedom."[51]

Acknowledging that his program wasn't infallible and would require a great deal of intelligence and social engineering to make it a reality, Thomas said he believed his fellow New Yorkers were up to the challenge. "To try to voice that challenge and reawaken hope and confidence in man's capacity to deal with his destiny here in the mighty city has been my purpose" throughout the campaign, wrote Thomas. "Every vote for the Socialist ticket will give an enormous impetus to this task of social pioneering. Not one vote will be wasted. In this spirit," he concluded, "we have sought and still seek the support of our fellow citizens whose labor of hand and brain creates all the wealth which makes our city strong."[52]

With the threat of an economic collapse hanging over the country, Thomas's longshot candidacy continued to gain momentum as the campaign entered the homestretch. The *New York Times* conceded that Thomas was likely to garner at least 100,000 votes and possibly more, but the discernible drift toward the dignified Socialist candidate in the final two weeks of the campaign didn't seem to worry the all-powerful Tammany organization, whose leaders remained convinced that most of his support would come at La Guardia's expense from Republicans, independents and independent Democrats who usually supported the opposing fusion ticket.[53]

In wrapping up his sixth campaign in as many years, Thomas conducted a whirlwind tour of the city on election eve, appearing on two radio programs, speaking at the First Presbyterian Church on West Eleventh Street, and addressing late-night outdoor meetings in Harlem, the Brownsville section of Brooklyn, and the

---

[51] "Three Candidates Sum Up the Issues," *New York Times*, Nov. 3, 1929.
[52] Ibid.
[53] "Drift of Voters to Thomas Does Not Disturb Tammany; Sees It as Republican Loss," *New York Times*, Oct. 21, 1929.

Lower East Side. In attacking Mayor Walker for refusing to discuss the issues while dragging former Gov. Al Smith "by the chains of false party loyalty in his triumphant procession" and charging that a vote for La Guardia was a vote to continue the city's "bondage to a bipartisan machine," Thomas implored New Yorkers to support the Socialist ticket, not only for "one short and bloodless battle at the polls," but to build a "permanent army of peaceful progress."[54]

The city's normally jaded voters responded in record numbers. Running strongest in the Bronx and Brooklyn, the tireless champion for the city's dispossessed and downtrodden received a staggering 175,697 votes as nearly one in every eight New Yorkers pulled the Socialist lever in the mayoral race. While Mayor Walker swaggered to a second term, rolling up an eye-popping 500,000-vote margin against La Guardia, his closest competitor, the extraordinarily impressive 12.3 percent showing by Thomas was, until then, the largest vote ever recorded in the city for a Socialist candidate.[55] La Guardia, who polled 367,675 votes, complained shortly after the election that many of the city's Republicans had voted for Thomas — and he was probably right.[56]

Needless to say, Thomas was ecstatic at the large showing of support, telling his election-night supporters that that the results had far exceeded his expectations. When he first declared his candidacy, he told the cheering crowd, he never expected to receive more than 50,000 votes. "Let no one deceive himself," continued Thomas. "The size of our vote will be a warning to Tammany and an inspiration to those of us who dare to have great dreams for our city."[57]

Buoyed by the more than 175,000 votes cast for Thomas in the mayoral contest, the Rev. John Haynes Holmes, who worked feverishly for Thomas, was convinced that his good friend could be elected mayor of New York City if the party was willing to drop the word "Socialist" from its name and sacrifice part of its program.[58]

Speaking a few weeks later at a "jubilation meeting" celebrating the party's strong showing in the recent mayoral election, Holmes maintained that the reason Thomas ran as well as he did was precisely because he didn't talk much about "the shibboleths and doctrines of socialism" and instead focused on the day-to-day

---

[54] "Thomas Sums Up Attacks on Rivals," *New York Times*, Nov. 5, 1929.
[55] "Socialist Peak Set by Thomas's Vote," *New York Times*, Nov. 6, 1929.
[56] Waldman, *Labor Lawyer*, p. 193.
[57] Ibid.
[58] "Socialists Refuse to Form New Party," *New York Times*, Nov. 18, 1929.

problems and pocketbook issues of concern to ordinary New Yorkers. "I am not crazy," asserted Holmes, "and I am profoundly convinced that we can elect Norman Thomas as our mayor. All that we need is a little time and a few brains. If the party can measure up to its candidate, then it can win, but hitherto the Socialist Party has lacked the intellectual leadership worthy of its candidate." There were tens of thousands of non-Socialist New Yorkers who would be willing to join in "a great alliance for victory," said Holmes, a twenty-year member of the party.[59]

Though Holmes' message had been politely received, most of the party's leadership, including Morris Hillquit and Thomas himself, turned thumbs down to his proposal. "Not on a golden platter," exclaimed Hillquit "would Norman Thomas ever accept the mayoralty of New York on such conditions." "Not even on a silver platter," added Thomas.[60]

Thomas's attention was temporarily diverted from politics a few weeks after the 1929 mayoral campaign when his wife, Violet, suffered a heart attack at their home on East Eighteenth Street. Though she quickly recovered, it was the second serious ailment that Violet, who had undergone pelvic surgery during the waning days of the 1928 presidential campaign, experienced during this period.[61]

In the meantime, the campaigns were now coming in rapid succession for the former Presbyterian minister. Nine months after the mayoral race had concluded, Thomas enthusiastically mounted his seventh campaign for public office in as many years. Running for a seat in the U.S. House of Representatives, the respectable rebel polled an astonishing 21,938 votes, or 22.1 percent of the vote, against Democratic congressman Andrew L. Somers, a 35-year-old former naval pilot, and Republican challenger Joseph G. Myerson in New York's overwhelmingly Democratic sixth congressional district. The Communist Party's Earl Browder, never really a factor in the race, was also a contestant, netting a woeful 802 votes, or less than one percent of the total in that race.

Running with the vigorous support of John Dewey's fledgling League for Independent Political Action (LIPA), which had been founded a year earlier and included such diverse religious and social progressives as W.E.B. Du Bois, Reinhold Niebuhr, Paul Douglas, the *Nation*'s Oswald Garrison Villard and Devere Allen, editor

---

[59] Ibid.
[60] Ibid.
[61] "Norman Thomas at Wife's Bedside," *New York Times*, Oct. 29, 1928; "Mrs. Norman Thomas Stricken," *New York Times*, Nov. 19, 1929.

of *World Tomorrow*, Thomas waged a vigorous campaign against his major-party rivals, criticizing the Democratic incumbent as a colorless lackey of powerful political boss John H. McCooey — the rotund and white-mustached Democratic leader who controlled Brooklyn politics for a quarter of a century — and promising to make the issue of rising joblessness throughout the country the cornerstone of his candidacy.

"Unemployment is a national calamity and there must be a national remedy," declared Thomas in announcing his candidacy on August 10, only twelve weeks before the election.[62]

Given his national following, the country's best-known Socialist clearly scared the daylights out of his two major-party rivals that autumn.

Somers, who was seeking a fourth term in the House, nevertheless welcomed Thomas's candidacy and said that he was "flattered" by his Socialist opponent's opening attack. "If all Mr. Thomas can say about me after my six years in Congress is that my record is colorless then I feel flattered," remarked Somers.[63]

Republican Myerson was less welcoming, criticizing Thomas as an outsider who "knows nothing whatsoever about conditions in the district." He also accused his Socialist rival of using his congressional candidacy as "a public forum where he can urge his views upon the entire nation." A Manhattan lawyer living in Brooklyn, Myerson said he was confident that the district's voters wouldn't allow "the glamour of a name to blind them to their own best interests."[64]

Thomas didn't deny the charge. In fact, coming off of his relatively impressive 175,000-vote showing in the city's mayoral contest the previous autumn — a race in which he more than quadrupled his 1925 performance — he did precisely what Myerson alleged by using his widely-watched congressional candidacy that autumn to articulate his party's national agenda. As the party's leading national spokesman, it seemed like the appropriate thing to do.

In a half-hour radio address broadcast nationally in mid-October, the white-haired dean of American socialism outlined his party's program to alleviate joblessness, including a comprehensive public works program, a five-day workweek (the forty-hour week didn't become law until 1938), and unemployment insur-

---

[62] "Thomas Will Run for Congress Seat." *New York Times*, Aug. 11, 1930.
[63] "Somers 'Flattered' By Thomas Attack," *New York Times*, Aug. 12, 1930.
[64] Ibid.

ance — the latter of which, he said, would be shouldered by industry and affluent Americans.

In his national radio appearance, Thomas also called for hefty increases in income and inheritances taxes on the wealthy. "There is no justice in a system in which one child is born heir to untold wealth while another, perhaps scarcely a block away, has no assurance of food enough to grow to healthy manhood," he asserted.[65]

This is not to suggest that Thomas intentionally neglected or deemphasized local issues during his congressional campaign. In fact, the opposite was true. While virtually ignoring his Republican opponent, the well-known Socialist traded barbs with the Democratic incumbent on a variety of local and national issues throughout the three-month campaign, while constantly tying the three-term lawmaker to McCooey's corrupt Brooklyn machine.

From the outset, it was clear that Thomas had put Somers on the defensive. In one of the sharpest exchanges between the two men, the Democratic congressman angrily responded to one of Thomas's allegations by denying that he was McCooey's puppet and part of "a political machine which has prostituted justice and treated public office as private plunder." He also accused Thomas, who lived in Manhattan, of being an "opportunist."[66]

Contrary to the optimistic claims of August Gerber, the Socialist Party's state campaign manager, and other party leaders who exuberantly predicted the former presidential candidate would prevail in Brooklyn's sixth congressional district, Thomas never really expected to win.[67]

"I had hoped for a vote of 30,000, although candidly I did not expect to be elected," admitted Thomas on election night. He added, however, that he was "greatly encouraged" by the party's organization in the district and the "educational effect of the campaign."[68]

Somers, the son of an Irish nationalist who later sponsored legislation calling for the creation of a separate Jewish army during World War II — an idea championed by militant Zionists Hillel Kook (aka Peter Bergson) and Benzion Netanyahu, father of Israeli Prime Minister Benjamin Netanyahu — was reelected by nearly

---

[65] "Thomas Outlines Broad Aid for Idle," *New York Times*, Oct. 16, 1930.
[66] "Somers Hits Back at Thomas Attack," *New York Times*, Sept. 10, 1930.
[67] "Sees 250,000 Votes Cast by Socialists," *New York Times*, Nov. 2, 1930. A few days before the election, Gerber predicted that Louis Waldman, the party's gubernatorial candidate, would garner a quarter of a million votes and that the Socialists would elect Thomas and Judge Jacob Panken to Congress. He also expected the party to elect at least seven Socialists to the New York legislature, including three state senators.
[68] "Socialists Elated in Spite of Defeat," *New York Times*, Nov. 5, 1930.

17,000 votes.⁶⁹

As the party's best known public figure, Thomas had also lent his considerable support — and time and energy — to the party's other congressional candidates in New York City that fall. He stumped vigorously for the party's ticket in every borough.

It was an impressive array of candidates, to put it mildly.

One of the party's most widely-watched congressional races that fall occurred in the state's 17th district where Socialist Heywood Broun, a popular sportswriter and syndicated columnist for the *New York Tribune* and *New York World*, polled an impressive 6,841 votes, or nearly 15%, against his major-party rivals in a hard-fought contest decided by fewer than 700 votes.⁷⁰

A fierce champion of the underdog, strong supporter of labor unions and sharp critic of social injustice, the 42-year-old Broun, who later wrote for several other New York newspapers, including the *New York Post*, was one of the most quotable newsmen around.

He was also one of the most widely read newspaper columnists in the country, always armed with a memorable one-liner. "A liberal is a man who leaves the room when the fight starts," he once said. Another Broun gem: "The tragedy of life is not that man loses, but that he almost wins." Irreverent and amusing, his caustic observations always contained more than a grain of truth. "Poor people wouldn't be such a bother if they didn't starve so publicly," he commented while watching a New York City breadline in 1932.⁷¹

Broun, who converted to Catholicism shortly before his premature death in 1939, once remarked that whenever he was unsure about what position he should take on a public issue he would wait until Bishop William Thomas Manning of New York, a rigid Episcopal prelate, made a pronouncement on the subject and then adopt the opposite position.⁷²

The father of Heywood Hale Broun, the legendary and flamboyant rust-colored mustached CBS Sports commentator, the elder Broun founded the American Newspaper Guild with several other New York reporters and writers in 1933 and served as the organization's president from its inception.⁷³

---

⁶⁹ Rafael Medoff, *Militant Zionism in America: The Rise and Impact of the Jabotinsky Movement in the United States, 1926-1948* (Tuscaloosa, Alabama, 2002), pp. 73-74.
⁷⁰ "Heywood Broun Out for Congress," *New York Times*, Aug. 4, 1930.
⁷¹ "It Isn't True That Nobody Starves in America," *New York Times*, June 4, 1967.
⁷² John C. Cort, *Dreadful Conversions: The Making of a Catholic Socialist* (New York, 2003), pp. 47-48.
⁷³ "Newspaper Guilds Unite Nationally," *New York Times*, Dec. 16, 1933.

Frequently accused of being a Communist — a charge he vigorously denied — the one-time drama critic expected by be expelled from the Socialist Party and resigned his party membership in the spring of 1933, shortly after appearing with members of the Communist Party at a rally demanding the release of the martyred Tom Mooney and the Scottsboro Nine.

Announcing his resignation in his column in the *New York World Telegram*, Broun later explained to reporters that he was being expelled from the Socialist Party for defying the party's policy against a "united front" with the Communists by speaking on the Scottsboro case at two Communist-sponsored meetings.[74]

Hoping to unseat Republican congresswoman Ruth B. Pratt, a Wellesley-educated former member of the Board of Aldermen and the first woman ever elected to Congress from the Empire State, while leaving the Democratic nominee — City Magistrate City Louis B. Brodsky — in the dust, the genial, disheveled-looking Broun waged a vigorous campaign for Congress in 1930, not unlike the dogged congressional campaigns waged by Norman Thomas, Jacob Panken, B. Charney Vladeck, and several other New York Socialists that autumn. He wept when he lost.

On the campaign trail, the veteran newspaperman described the growing ranks of jobless Americans as a "tragic national crisis" and accused President Hoover of maintaining a politically partisan and highly unsympathetic attitude toward the unemployed. He also called for deep cuts in defense spending. Claiming that three-quarters of the federal budget was spent on the military, Broun, who had served as a foreign correspondent in France during World War I, urged Congress to direct those huge outlays to alleviate the growing unemployment crisis, arguing that "the nation's wealth should be spent for the benefit of those who create it."

Calling for steep tax increases on corporations and wealthy individuals, the legendary reporter also pointed to the socialist government in Vienna, Austria, as a model government that should be emulated in the United States. The socialist government in that Austrian municipality was investing heavily in apartments for workers, making it possible for working-class residents in that city "to live in comfort and decency" — equivalent, he said, to some of the nicer apartment buildings along Park Avenue in his own congressional district.[75]

Despite more than quadrupling the party's showing in the dis-

---

[74] "Heywood Broun Quits Socialists," *New York Times*, April 29, 1933.
[75] "Broun Sees Hoover Biased on Idleness," *New York Times*, Sept. 8, 1930.

trict in the previous congressional election — a race in which Socialist Bertha Mailley, executive secretary of the Rand School, polled only 1,600 votes — Broun was deeply disappointed by his setback. "I am sorry I lost," he said mournfully. "I got fewer votes than I expected. I expected at least 10,000...I am frankly disappointed. I expected to get more votes, but I did not expect to win." Looking forward to a rematch in 1932, Broun took solace in the fact that the party had "gained enough votes to make it seem reasonable to expect ultimate victory."[76]

Despite their relatively strong showings, Thomas and Broun weren't the party's most prolific congressional vote-getters in New York City that fall. The top honor belonged to veteran Socialist Judge Jacob Panken, a Ukrainian-born lawyer who finished ahead of his Republican opponent while polling a startling 25.9% in a four-cornered race in Manhattan's silk-stocking fourteenth congressional district.

While actively supporting Norman Thomas's candidacy, Panken made headlines in the closing days of the 1928 presidential campaign when he publicly ridiculed Herbert Hoover's widely-covered speech in Madison Square Garden, an address in which the Republican nominee blasted Democratic candidate Al Smith's program as bordering on state socialism. Nothing could have been further from the truth, declared Panken, reminding his audience that the Socialists favored government ownership and democratic management of the country's basic industries — an idea completely disavowed by the Democrats.[77]

The biographically-neglected East Side agitator, who served as a municipal judge in New York City for more than two decades and had come within 2,300 votes of capturing the same congressional seat eight years earlier, garnered an impressive 6,793 votes against eclectic Democrat William I. Sirovich, a physician, editor and playwright who served nearly seven terms in Congress until his untimely death in 1939.

Edward E. Spafford, a retired Navy lieutenant commander and former national commander of the American Legion, was the Republican nominee in that four-cornered race. An avid anti-Communist who reportedly once boasted that he had been personally decorated by Benito Mussolini with the Order of the Crown of Italy and later briefly organized a small right-wing party to oppose Mayor Fiorello La Guardia's re-election in 1937, Spafford finished

---

[76] "Socialists Elated in Spite of Defeat," *New York Times*, Nov. 5, 1930.
[77] "Panken Says Smith is not Socialistic," *New York Times*, Oct. 24, 1928.

135 votes behind the second-place Panken.[78]

Panken made Tammany corruption the leading issue in his congressional campaign.[79] It was a fight the former municipal judge had been waging for years.[80] But he ultimately paid a price for doing that when his campaign headquarters on Seventh Avenue was vandalized in late October. His office was trashed and his campaign signs were ripped down, all in an apparent effort to find a list of allegedly illegal voters that Panken had been compiling as evidence of potential Tammany fraud.[81]

Not the least bit intimidated by the break-in or by any other shenanigans the Tammany Tiger might be planning, Panken continued to focus on the real pocketbook issues of concern to voters in the fourteenth district. Late in the campaign, he urged President Hoover to call a special session of Congress to deal with the country's mounting unemployment crisis — a plea that was largely ignored.[82]

On Election Day, Panken's nephew — a deputy attorney general for the state of New York — was apparently beaten at his polling place by Tammany thugs while Panken's wife was personally responsible for the arrest of an illegal registrant who was attempting to vote in one of the district's precincts.[83]

Another particularly strong Socialist congressional campaign in New York City that year was waged by B. Charney Vladeck, the low-keyed general manager of the *Jewish Daily Forward* who sought to unseat a two-term Democrat in Brooklyn's eighth congressional district.

A former two-term Socialist member of the New York city council, Vladeck was later returned to city council on the American Labor ticket in 1937, representing Manhattan. One of six successful American Labor Party candidates elected to city council that year under the city's newly-enacted system of proportional representation, Vladeck served as minority leader in the council — with a brief stint as majority leader during a heated political-tug-of-war over Mayor La Guardia's proposed budget in early 1938 — until

---

[78] "Anti-Reds Formed to Oppose Mayor: E. E. Spafford, Ex-Head of Legion, Announces New Party Under Liberty Bell Emblem," *New York Times*, Oct. 4, 1937.
[79] "Panken Will Run as Tammany's Foe," *New York Times*, Aug. 18, 1930.
[80] "Panken Sees Need to Fight Tammany," *New York Times*, Sep. 5, 1927.
[81] "Panken Headquarters Raided and Wrecked; Socialist Candidate Charges It Was Done to Seize List of Alleged Illegal Voters," *New York Times*, Oct. 27, 1930.
[82] "Panken Urges Hoover to Summon Congress; Telegraphs Appeal for Special Session to Hasten Relief for Unemployed," *New York Times*, Oct. 22, 1930.
[83] "Irregularities in New York Election," *Lowell Sun*, Nov. 4, 1930.

his untimely death in October of that year at the age of 52.[84]

Gov. Herbert Lehman, Mayor Robert Wagner and Norman Thomas spoke at Vladeck's funeral service and more than a half million mourners crowded the streets of the East Side to pay their final respects.[85] Anticipating a huge turnout — a tribute to his immense popularity — loudspeakers carried the services to crowds that had gathered blocks from the Daily Forward Building where the services were held.[86]

As remarkable and accomplished as any of the other leading New York Socialists of that era, Baruch Charney Vladeck was a close friend and ally of Mayor Fiorello H. La Guardia.

Vladeck, whose 1930 candidacy was supported by John Dewey's League for Independent Political Action and was later enthusiastically endorsed by Rabbi Stephen S. Wise, the influential leader of Brooklyn's Free Synagogue, polled a spectacular 23,662 votes, or nearly seventeen percent, in his uphill battle against his major-party opponents.[87]

Though not quite comparable to the ingeniously witty August Claessens, a former Socialist state legislator whose droll speaking style delighted friend and foe alike, or Oklahoma's legendary Oscar Ameringer — the incredibly witty "Mark Twain of American Socialism" — the quick-witted Vladeck possessed a delightful and biting sense of humor.

When several foreign-born members of the city council were being attacked by a speaker who claimed that his grandfather had been a neighbor of Abraham Lincoln — "a native-born American" — Vladeck, who spoke with a heavy Yiddish accent, responded that his own ancestors "were neighbors of Moses, and everybody knows that Moses was secretary to God." While being attacked by an Irish speaker who accused him of fomenting a revolution in Russia and attempting to do the same thing in this country, Vladeck didn't miss a beat. "What were your ancestors doing in Ireland when that country was fighting for its freedom?" he asked the startled speaker. "Either they were in jail most of the time or they were not good Irishmen!"[88]

---

[84] "Session in Tumult: Coalition in Surprise Move Picks Vladeck Majority Leader," *New York Times*, Jan. 12, 1938; "B. C. Vladeck Dies; City Councilman," *New York Times*, Oct. 31, 1938.
[85] "Half Million See Vladeck Funeral," *New York Times*, Nov. 3, 1938.
[86] "Rites Tomorrow for B.C. Vladeck," *New York Times*, Nov. 1, 1938.
[87] "Dewey Supports Vladeck," *New York Times*, Sept. 15, 1930; "Wise Endorses Vladeck; Rabbi Urges Election of Brooklyn Socialist to Congress," *New York Times*, Oct. 21, 1930.
[88] Philip Henry Lotz, ed., *Distinguished American Jews* (Freeport, N.Y., 1970), p. 28.

At least in the party's strongholds in New York City, Milwaukee, and Reading, Pennsylvania, the Socialist Party was clearly the biggest beneficiary of the sharp economic downturn among the nation's minor parties that autumn.

In addition to the strong showings posted by Panken, Vladeck, Thomas and Broun, at least two other Socialist congressional candidates in New York City also put up impressive numbers, including Russian-born Abraham I. Shiplacoff, a former Socialist state assemblyman and alderman from the poverty-stricken Brownsville section of Brooklyn.

Shiplacoff, who was affectionately known as "the Jewish Eugene Debs," polled an impressive 12.4% in a bid for Congress from New York City's 10th district. Samuel Orr, famously remembered as one of the five Socialists expelled by the New York State Assembly during the Red Scare of 1919-1920, polled almost twelve percent of the vote in the nearby 23rd congressional district.

Fielding congressional candidates in seventy-seven districts nationally, the Socialist Party waged several other highly competitive U.S. House races in 1930.

In Wisconsin, the party's James P. Sheehan, a veteran labor leader, came within 1,176 votes of defeating Republican William H. Stafford in a bid to reclaim the late Victor Berger's seat in Congress, while Milwaukee lawyer and former Socialist state Senator William F. Quick, Sr., running 12,000 votes ahead of his Democratic opponent, finished a strong second in the state's 4th congressional district while amassing 20,789 votes.[89]

In Pennsylvania, retired cigar maker and longtime labor activist Andrew P. Bower, who had been active in the party since its founding, polled a relatively impressive 11,309 votes, or 13.3%, in the party's Berks County stronghold in the fourteenth congressional district,

Though expressing regret that the American electorate had continued "the habit of never rising above answering one old party's failure by voting for the other," Thomas was generally satisfied with his party's performance in the 1930 mid-term elections.

Reviewing returns from across the country, the once and future presidential hopeful said that the Democrats, having gained more than fifty seats in the U.S. House of Representatives — eventually taking control of that body for the first time since 1914 — now had enough power "to make trouble in Washington," but not

---

[89] Stafford garnered 27,533 votes to Sheehan's 26,357 and Democrat Thomas O'Malley's 10,947. An Independent Communist candidate finished a distant fourth with a negligible 469 votes.

enough to solve the deepening economic crisis or deal effectively with any of the country's other pressing problems "because Democrats cannot agree among themselves on any of these issues."[90] Some things never change.

The next twelve months were characteristically busy ones for the country's best-known Socialist. He not only formally gave up his Presbyterian ministry after twenty-five years, but also found himself spending several hours in a dingy jail cell after being arrested along with 45 others for taking part in an "illegal" picket line on behalf of striking silk workers in Paterson, New Jersey, in September.[91]

Earlier that year, Macmillan published his latest book, *America's Way Out: A Program for Democracy*. A 324-page prescription for what ailed the United States, Thomas's book was also something of a campaign book for the 1932 presidential election — a point driven home in a lengthy yet generally favorable review by William MacDonald in the *New York Times*.[92]

In setting out "what the country of Mr. Hoover and the Wall Street barons of finance would be like" in a Socialist administration, wrote MacDonald, an American history professor at Brown University, Thomas had little difficulty showing "that the existing political and economic order, grounded in capitalism and the fruit of capitalistic nurture, falls far short of even approximate perfection and that progress, if it exists at all, is dishearteningly slow" and that "incomes are grossly unequal, that the contrasts of wealth and poverty are distressingly sharp, that wage earners of all classes are haunted by fear born of insecurity, and that personal freedom and justice are often grievously denied."[93]

The whole system, wrote Thomas, was designed to further enrich the affluent — many of whom inherited their wealth — without any regard to their ability or effort while creating "a new type of misery" for the unemployed and impoverished. "No one can read it," concluded MacDonald, "without feeling convinced that Mr. Thomas greatly desires a better world and is ready to go a long way to attain it."[94]

Keeping his eye closely riveted on national developments,

---

[90] "Socialist Vote Gain Hailed by the Party," *New York Times*, Nov. 6, 1930.
[91] "Norman Thomas Seized as Silk Strike Picket; Jailed in Paterson With 45, Then Freed in Bail," *New York Times*, Sep. 4, 1931; "Thomas as Minister Quits Presbytery," *New York Times*, Oct. 6, 1931.
[92] "A New Program for Democracy," *New York Times*, Mar. 29, 1931.
[93] Ibid.
[94] Ibid.

Thomas was deeply worried about the country's rapidly expanding level of joblessness and the accompanying poverty that came with those who suddenly found themselves unemployed. It often kept him up at night.

Millions of Americans had been thrown out of work in the months following the frenzied, speculation-driven 1929 stock market crash and the United States didn't have any kind of social safety net to protect those who suddenly found themselves without any income or means by which to feed their families and keep a roof over their heads. Bread lines, begging, and soup kitchens became the order of the day, the only way countless poor and working-class, hungry Americans survived. That was life in the pre-Franklin Roosevelt laissez-faire Great Republic.

In the two dreary and increasingly desperate years following the stock market crash, the country's Gross Domestic Product (GDP) plunged from $103.6 billion (in current dollars) to $76.5 billion — eventually falling to $56.4 billion as Roosevelt took office in 1933 — while the nation's unemployment rate increased five-fold, soaring from a healthy 3.2 percent in 1929 to 16.3 percent in 1931 before eventually swelling to more than a quarter of the working population during the devastatingly bleak winter of 1932-33.

To alleviate the suffering of the millions who lost their livelihoods as a result of the dramatic economic downturn of the financial oligarchy's making, Thomas proposed a low-interest $5 billion loan from the Federal Reserve to provide unemployment relief for the jobless. The loan, he said, could be repaid relatively quickly through increased income and inheritance taxes on the wealthy. Thomas made his bold but largely ignored proposal during the closing session of the League for Industrial Democracy's 1931 annual summer retreat at Camp Tamiment in the Poconos.[95]

In his speech, Thomas lamented that the large number of business and bank failures and declining prices over the previous eighteen months were leading to an inevitable clash between creditors and debtors, similar to that experienced in the early 1890s. "The real wealth and power in this country still belong to the people who own the vital resources of the country, and any system of planning must take into account that of money, banking and credits as a vital part of the program, if the country is to recover from its present slump," asserted Thomas.[96]

Thomas rarely had anything positive to say about President Hoover, but a few days later found himself praising the embattled

---

[95] "Asks Five Billion for Relief of Idle," *New York Times*, June 29, 1931.
[96] Ibid.

President's proposal for a one-year debt moratorium to save Germany from economic collapse — something the Socialist Party had been advocating for more than a dozen years. "I think that Hoover's debt plan is one of the very few intelligent forward things he has done," Thomas told a conference of ministers at the Union Theological Seminary a few days after his speech in the Poconos. The collapse of Germany, he said, threatened all of Europe, if not all of Western Civilization. "Although Hoover's plan does not go far enough," he concluded, "it is good as far as it goes."[97]

When Gerard B. Swope, the dynamic, MIT-educated president of General Electric proposed a plan for stabilizing industry later that autumn — a proposal enthusiastically supported by the U.S. Chamber of Commerce but swiftly rejected by President Hoover — Thomas thought he sensed a whiff of fascism. While Swope's plan, an antecedent to the New Deal's National Industrial Recovery Act (NRA), was about as complete a repudiation of capitalism ever proposed by a captain of industry, Thomas said that the plan nevertheless showed an unmistakable "drift to an American version of fascism rather than to any worthwhile type of socialism."

Though far more original than the "sickening mixture of platitudes" offered by most industrialists at the time, Thomas didn't believe that the Swope Plan — a proposal that earned the GE executive a gold medal from the National Academy of Social Services in 1932 — was an adequate substitute for the prevailing system. One of its most troubling aspects, argued Thomas during a debate on New York's WOR radio, was that the GE executive was essentially proposing "a system of capitalist syndicates" which would undoubtedly "be strong enough to control the government which regulates them."[98]

Sandwiched between his 1930 congressional campaign and his second try for the presidency at the height of the Great Depression two years later, Thomas actively campaigned for President of Manhattan Borough in a special election held in November 1931. Running against Democrat Samuel Levy — Tammany's candidate — and Republican Edward C. Carrington, Thomas was again endorsed by the widely-respected Citizens Union, a good government watchdog group which described the former Presbyterian minister as "the best qualified of the three candidates," possessing "exceptional intellect, learning and courage, qualities badly needed at City Hall."[99]

---

[97] "Hoover's Debt Plan Praised by Thomas," *New York Times*, July 2, 1931.
[98] "Swope Plan Fascist, Says Norman Thomas," *New York Times*, Oct. 5, 1931.
[99] "Thomas Endorsed By Citizens Union," *New York Times*, Oct. 16, 1931.

Denouncing Tammany's "tin box" regime headed by Mayor Jimmy Walker, the colorful former Tin Pan Alley songwriter who presided over an orgy of corruption, while criticizing the city's ineffective and complacent Republican Party as "a kind of political kept woman by the Tammany Hall organization," Thomas made civic honesty the major issue in his campaign.[100] He also had some stern words for the widespread public indifference displayed by New Yorkers when it came to municipal corruption, saying that at the very moment when the breakdown of the old economic order was most apparent, "there is also the most justifiable cynicism about the honesty and capacity of all our governmental agencies, and especially of the bipartisan band of plunderers who rule New York."

Thomas simply couldn't understand why there was so much public apathy. "The great masses, deprived of Socialist hope and vision, with hearts filled with cynicism or despair," he wrote, "docilely vote for those who rob them in the hope that the robbers may throw them a few bones."[101]

Levy's election was never in doubt and the real contest was for runner-up honors between the wealthy Carrington, a steamship operator and chairman of the Great Lakes-Hudson Waterways Association who unsuccessfully sought the Republican nomination for governor in an attempt to unseat Franklin Roosevelt the previous year, and Thomas, running once again on the Socialist ticket. The Carrington-Thomas battle got quite nasty at times, with Thomas denouncing his Republican foe as a "political midget" and Carrington returning the favor by describing Thomas as a "political mosquito."

Claiming that voting for his Socialist opponent was akin to throwing one's vote away, Carrington, who had managed Teddy Roosevelt's Bull Moose campaign in Maryland nearly two decades earlier, urged the voters of Manhattan not to be distracted "by the buzz of a political mosquito or become involved in the dubious Don Quixotic adventure of charging a windmill."[102]

Carrington, whose candidacy had been irreparably damaged during five hours of grueling testimony a few weeks prior to the election as part of the widely-watched Seabury inquiry into Tammany corruption, nevertheless managed to limp in ahead of his

---

[100] "Thomas Denounces City Republicans," *New York Times*, Sep. 26, 1931; "Thomas Scores Tammany," *New York Times*, Oct. 14, 1931; "Thomas Denounces the 'Tin Box' Regime," *New York Times*, Nov. 1, 1931.
[101] "Thomas Deplores Apathy of Public," *New York Times*, Oct. 12, 1931.
[102] "Col. Carrington Retorts," *New York Times*, Sep. 27, 1931.

Socialist rival on Nov. 3rd, finishing about 17,000 votes ahead of Thomas, who polled more than 48,000 votes, or 13 percent of the total.[103]

Thomas, who had one of his tires slashed while visiting a precinct in Manhattan's twenty-third election district on the day of the election, charged that election officials in three districts had illegally intimidated voters, including physically manhandling Socialist poll workers in two districts, while officials in another district refused to count any Socialist votes — charges that eventually resulted in the removal of one of the election officers and the censure of seven others.[104]

---

[103] "Carrington Admits Hiring of Olvany for Deal With City," *New York Times*, Oct. 22, 1931; "Carrington Backing Dwindles, Rivals Say," *New York Times*, Oct. 26, 1931; "Carrington's Chances for Borough Presidency Seen as Slight Due to Inquiry Testimony," *New York Times*, Nov. 1, 1931; "Levy Plurality 181,219," *New York Times*, Nov. 4, 1931. Preliminary returns showed Levy garnering 247,110 votes to Carrington's 65,891 and 48,438 for Thomas. The Communist Party's Israel Amter, a former classical musician who directed the party's National Committee of Unemployed Councils, polled 1,789 votes in the four-cornered race.

[104] "Thomas Calls Vote a Tammany Theft," *New York Times*, Nov. 4, 1931; "Socialists Measure Gains in City Vote," *New York Times*, Nov. 5, 1931; "Thomas Files Complaint," *New York Times*, Nov. 6, 1931; "Oust Election Head on Thomas Charges," *New York Times*, Dec. 2, 1931.

Chapter V

"Such a Little Man, So Big a Depression"

Following his spirited but unsuccessful bid for President of the Borough of Manhattan — his eighth campaign in as many years — Norman Thomas returned to the national stage at the height of the Great Depression in 1932.

The presidential election that year was a turning point in American history, arguably producing the greatest president since Abraham Lincoln, an activist chief executive who wasn't afraid to use the power of the presidency and the vast resources of the federal government to improve the lives of ordinary citizens while laying the groundwork for economic growth and eventual prosperity, resulting in the creation of a vibrant and expanding middle class — a segment comprising only 15 to 20 percent of the U.S. population prior to the Great Depression. It was a period of tremendous despair, but also one of widespread hope for a better tomorrow. Things, after all, couldn't possibly get any worse.

As the election year approached, the Democrats were hoping to recapture the White House for the first time in a dozen years. The party's prospects looked promising, probably brighter than at any time since the antebellum period.

As might have been expected, there was no shortage of candidates seeking the party's presidential nomination that year. Leading the pack was New York governor Franklin D. Roosevelt, a fifty-year-old former assistant Secretary of the Navy in the Wilson administration. Scion of an affluent New York family, Roosevelt had served briefly as an anti-Tammany member of the New York legislature before falling victim to the powerful Tammany Tiger in an unsuccessful bid for his party's nomination to the U.S. Senate in 1914.

Though somewhat disappointed by his failed Senate campaign — losing to Tammany's James W. Gerard by more than a two-to-one margin in a primary he knew, deep down, he wouldn't win — the patrician New Yorker remained active in Democratic politics, serving as James Cox's vice-presidential running mate during the 1920 Harding landslide and stumping vigorously for Al Smith eight years later.

A distant relative of the late Theodore Roosevelt, FDR, who was unable to use his legs after being stricken with polio in 1921, proved to be a wildly popular vote-getter, narrowly winning the Empire State's hotly-contested gubernatorial contest against the GOP's Albert Ottinger during the 1928 Hoover landslide and winning re-election two years later by clobbering hapless Republican challenger Charles H. Tuttle, a former U.S. attorney, by more than 725,000 votes — nearly doubling Al Smith's record-breaking margin of 386,000 in 1922.[1]

Despite his immense popularity among New York voters and the widespread support he was receiving from party leaders in the South and West, Roosevelt's nomination was anything but certain. The Democratic field was overflowing with contenders, many of them seemingly viable candidates — and the powerful Tammany Tiger certainly wasn't in his corner.

Among others, FDR faced serious opposition from former New York governor Alfred E. Smith, the party's nominee four years earlier, and Speaker of the House John N. Garner of Texas, a thirty-year veteran of Congress. Garner, a staunch prohibitionist, had the solid backing of former Treasury Secretary William G. McAdoo, a California-transplant who had been a major contender for the Democratic presidential nomination in 1920 and 1924. He also enjoyed the support of the influential Hearst newspaper chain. Of the two, Smith proved to be Roosevelt's most formidable — and perplexing — rival. The "Happy Warrior," after all, had been instrumental in persuading FDR to run for governor in 1928.

Posing a serious threat to Roosevelt's chances, Smith's unexpected candidacy in 1932 came as something of a jolt to most political observers. The former New York governor, who withstood a seemingly endless barrage of anti-Catholic propaganda during his lopsided loss to Herbert Hoover in 1928, had vowed that he would

---

[1] Black, *Franklin Delano Roosevelt: Champion of Freedom*, p. 207.

never run for public office again. Nobody expected him to mount a fourth campaign for the presidency.

And certainly no one was more surprised by Smith's entry into the Democratic field than Roosevelt himself. After all, FDR had campaigned for the man he affectionately dubbed the "Happy Warrior" in 1920, 1924 and again in 1928. Roosevelt had stumped vigorously for Smith throughout New York in the latter campaign, speaking out forcefully against the "vile thing" of religious bigotry. Why Smith later turned on Roosevelt remains something of a mystery to historians, but the answer can probably be gleaned from his close ties to the tainted Tammany machine, an organization that feuded with FDR dating back to his days in the New York legislature.

But that might be an oversimplification. While it was true that Smith and other Tammany Democrats believed Roosevelt was something of a political lightweight — not the kind of leader the nation needed in a time of crisis — biographer Robert A. Slayton believes Smith was primarily motivated by a need for personal redemption, "the chance to redeem himself, to finally overcome the hate-mongers of 1928 who had hurt him so badly."[2]

As was the case four years earlier, Smith's candidacy was amply financed when he entered the Democratic sweepstakes, again enjoying the generous support of Delaware million John J. Raskob, a former Du Pont and General Motors executive who had managed his 1928 campaign.

In addition to Roosevelt, Smith and Garner, a number of other presidential hopefuls, mostly favorite-sons, also entered the crowded contest for the Democratic nomination in 1932, including four-term Gov. Albert C. Ritchie of Maryland, a reformer who had climbed his state's political ladder by battling the price-fixing policies of the state's privately-held utility companies. A single-issue candidate of sorts, the 55-year-old Ritchie, making his second bid for the Democratic presidential nomination, campaigned primarily for the repeal of prohibition.

There was also speculation that former Secretary of War Newton D. Baker, the 60-year-old ex-mayor of Cleveland who fought diligently for the League of Nations and against U.S. isolationism, or Owen D. Young, the dynamic chairman of the General Electric Company who drafted a much-heralded plan for German reparations following World War I, would enter the race, especially if there appeared to be a deadlocked convention.

---

[2] Robert A. Slayton, *Empire Statesman: The Rise and Redemption of Al Smith* (New York, 2001), pp. 365-366.

Among the many other favorite-sons candidates were former Virginia Gov. Harry Byrd, Ohio Gov. George White and Melvin A. Traylor, a wealthy banker from Chicago. Former Sen. James A. Reed, who led the movement to keep the United States out of the League of Nations following World War I, again enjoyed the backing of the Missouri delegation.

Last but certainly not least was Oklahoma's newly-elected governor, William H. Murray, a 62-year-old former two-term congressman who had spent five of the previous seven years in South America helping to colonize southeast Bolivia.

Considered a demagogue by some and hailed as a hero by others, the shaggy-haired and walrus-mustached Murray, a rip-snorting survivor of Oklahoma's pioneer days, had been the first candidate to throw his hat into the ring in 1932. In early 1931, "Alfalfa Bill," as he was dubbed, visited Lincoln's tomb in Springfield, Illinois, and asked God to "send us another Lincoln."

Apparently answering his own prayer, Murray formally launched his presidential candidacy in a speech in Okmulgee, Oklahoma, in August 1931, before 3,000 supporters who cheered him on as "a Moses to lead the American people out of depression."

Appealing to the prevailing prejudices and suspicions of Midwesterners toward the Eastern establishment — an animosity dating back to the Populist Era — the modern-day Moses, a power in the southwest with a considerable following in Oklahoma and Texas, immediately took to the campaign trail, warning a Labor Day crowd of 20,000 at Chicago's Soldiers' Field of the dangers of the "vicious gambling den" known as Wall Street. Murray's appearance, according to one observer, was the best show the Windy City had seen in months.

Coining the campaign alliterative, "Bread, Butter, Bacon, and Beans," the Oklahoma governor was as intensely hued as any presidential prospect who ever skipped lightly across the American landscape. While undoubtedly the most colorful candidate in the relatively crowded Democratic field, Murray — garnering only 23 votes on the first ballot — wasn't really a factor as the party's delegates gathered in Chicago that summer to nominate a challenger to President Hoover.

On the Republican side, Herbert Hoover's nomination to a second term was never really in doubt, especially after his party's insurgents refused to put up a serious challenger. Facing only token opposition from former Sen. Joseph I. France of Maryland, the hapless Hoover was easily nominated for a second term at the party's national convention in Chicago in June.[3]

The Socialists, meanwhile, had high hopes as the country prepared for the quadrennial ritual that would determine the leader of the free world.

"We are facing the greatest opportunity we ever had," exclaimed Emil Seidel, the former mayor of Milwaukee who ran for the U.S. Senate that year. "The world is dropping the barbarism of capitalism. Socialism is being born," he said excitedly.[4]

Though he didn't think it was likely, even a political pragmatist like Norman Thomas, who again headed the party's national ticket that year, refused to rule out the remote possibility of a Socialist Party victory at the ballot box in 1932. "I expect to get the largest Socialist vote in history this year," he stated while campaigning in Salt Lake City later that autumn. "I do not expect to be elected," he added, "but if the voters would wake up before Election Day my election would not be impossible."[5] The American people were hurting and they were hurting badly. Anything was possible.

Convening in Milwaukee's Municipal Auditorium on May 20, the Socialist Party again nominated Thomas for the presidency. His nomination had been a forgone conclusion once Daniel Hoan, then in his sixteenth year as the city's mayor, had taken his name out of consideration. James H. Maurer was again named for the party's second spot. The 68-year-old Maurer enjoyed smooth sailing once Meta S. Berger, the widow of Socialist congressman Victor Berger of Milwaukee, declined the party's vice-presidential nomination.[6]

The sentiment among delegates had clearly been for Berger to run as Thomas's co-star that year. Though largely ignored by historians, the 59-year-old Berger was the longest-serving elected official in the history of the Socialist Party, winning five consecutive terms on the Milwaukee school board between 1909 and 1939.

Consistently campaigning in Milwaukee's non-partisan school board races as a publicly-identified Socialist, Berger had served as president of the Board of Education after winning a second term in

---

[3] Roseboom, *A History of Presidential Elections*, pp. 433-434. Ex-Sen. France was forcibly removed from the platform when he tried to withdraw and place former President Calvin Coolidge's name in nomination at the Republican national convention.
[4] "State Socialists Select Metcalf to Head Ticket," *Wisconsin Rapids Daily Tribune*, June 20, 1932.
[5] "Socialist Candidate Advances Observations on Present Scene," *Salt Lake Tribune*, Oct. 12, 1932.
[6] Shannon, *The Socialist Party of America*, p. 216.

1915 — a remarkable feat considering that there were only five Socialists on the 15-member board at the time. During her long tenure as a school board member in one of the country's largest school districts, she was tremendously influential in improving both the quality of education in that city and the living standards of its teachers.

There wasn't much Maurer, who desperately wanted to run again, could do in the face of the seemingly spontaneous Berger boom. So he sat silently and waited. Socialist candidates, after all, could never appear too eager — a point made by Pennsylvania's national committeewoman Lilith M. Wilson. "Socialists have a way of turning down those who have a desire to stand out in front of the party," said Wilson, one of two Socialist members of the Pennsylvania legislature at the time. "Our candidates, like all our leaders, must be subservient to the party, otherwise, out they go."[7]

Berger's vice-presidential candidacy had been actively promoted by delegates from New Jersey who were planning to place her name in nomination. The idea quickly spread like wildfire among the delegates. The nomination, in fact, was hers for the taking, but she eventually decided against it. "I think it is the proper thing to do," she said in deferring to Maurer.[8]

Thomas, who was nominated unanimously, accepted his party's nomination in a short three-minute speech. His voice trembling with emotion, the former Presbyterian minister told the cheering delegates that "the world has to choose between catastrophe and socialism. The time for action is now, rather than after all the people are dead of starvation," he said.[9] That wasn't mere hyperbole; without a social safety net, millions of his fellow citizens were suffering — and suffering badly.

While Thomas's second nomination for the presidency was never in doubt — even New York's Old Guard recognized that he was the party's only viable national candidate — the Socialist Party's national convention in Milwaukee that year marked the beginning of a lengthy and extremely bitter split that would leave the party barely a shell of its former self by the time the next presidential election rolled around.

In what essentially amounted to the opening salvo in the acrimonious four-year struggle between the party's militants and the Old Guard, resulting in the irreparable split of 1936, Thomas was

---

[7] "Hillquit Asks Socialists to Disarm World," *Wisconsin State Journal*, May 21, 1932.
[8] "Norman Thomas Selected by Socialist Convention," *Nevada State Journal*, May 23, 1932.
[9] Ibid.

determined to remove Morris Hillquit as the party's national chairman. He desperately wanted to replace the New York labor lawyer with Milwaukee Mayor Daniel Hoan, who had amassed an impressive record by governing Wisconsin's largest city in an honest and efficient manner for the previous sixteen years. Having carefully avoided the growing Militant-Old Guard conflict, Hoan was an almost ideal person to lead the party's renaissance. Like a growing number of the party's rank and file, the Milwaukee mayor believed that Hillquit was "woefully weak on matters of organizational tactics," but had been reluctant to openly challenge him until persuaded by Thomas that he was the only one in the party who could possibly unseat the New Yorker.

Internal politics aside, Thomas was happy to be back on the national stage promoting his party's solutions to the country's deepening economic crisis. Having offered a remedy for the nation's staggering unemployment crisis in his latest book, *America's Way Out: A Program for Democracy*, published the previous spring, Thomas was more than eager to make his case directly to the American electorate.[10]

He had a much larger audience this time around. In fact, many prominent non-Socialists believed his candidacy at the height of the Great Depression could lead to a broader and more dynamic third-party movement — one that might actually compete for power in traditionally two-party America.

In his book *The Coming of a New Party*, the University of Chicago's Paul H. Douglas, wary of left-wing Socialists and deeply impressed by the Minnesota Farmer-Labor Party's ability to put Floyd B. Olson in the governor's chair while electing Magnus Johnson and Henrik Shipstead to the U.S. Senate and winning eight congressional races between 1922 and 1930 — a startling accomplishment that eventually caught the eye of many New Dealers, including Roosevelt himself — had proposed the creation of a new liberal party to be formed in early 1933, shortly after the 1932 presidential election.

The nucleus of that embryonic movement later merged with the Farmer-Labor Political Federation (FLPF), a semi-autonomous unit within the League for Independent Political Action (LIPA) under the intellectual leadership of Minnesota's Howard Y. Williams, Alfred Bingham, the aristocratic editor of *Common Sense*, writer

---

[10] "For Unemployment Cure; Norman Thomas in New Book Offers Five Measures as Solution," *New York Times*, Mar. 24, 1931.

Archibald MacLeish and philosophers John Dewey and Lewis Mumford.[11]

Actively campaigning for Thomas that year, Douglas believed that liberals had no other choice than to support the Socialist nominee. "For the purposes of this campaign, there is only one party that liberals can support, the Socialist Party, but after the election there is a great possibility of a new group, a Farmer-Labor Party, coming into being," he declared. The Socialists, he added, would probably be a strong faction in the new party, helping to galvanize others to action while keeping the party honest.[12]

Though not a Socialist himself, Douglas vigorously championed Thomas's candidacy throughout the 1932 campaign. "Roosevelt is about two percent better than Hoover," he said while pacing the floor of the Thomas-for-President headquarters in New York, "but Thomas is fifty percent better than either of them."[13] The Chicago economics professor, who later served three terms in the U.S. Senate from Illinois as a Democrat, believed that it would be a "great victory" if Thomas shattered the party's previous record by polling a million votes, but optimistically believed the Socialist candidate would garner "more than two million votes."[14]

In the meantime, John Dewey, the LIPA's founder and guiding light, had been imploring leading progressives, including Nebraska Sen. George W. Norris, a nominal Republican who broke with his party to support Democrat Al Smith in 1928, to join his movement for more than a year. Arguably one of the nation's most influential philosophers, the 73-year-old Columbia University professor wrote to Norris in December 1930 reminding him of the shabby treatment he had received at the hands of the Republicans during his bid for re-election earlier that year and urging him to sever ties with his lifelong party and help give birth to a new liberal movement. In his letter, which was made public on Christmas day, Dewey stressed that such a party could conceivably be in a position to win the White House as early as 1940.[15]

Dewey was optimistic that the aging Norris, who had clearly been targeted for defeat earlier that year by Robert H. Lucas, executive director of the Republican National Committee — presumably without Hoover's knowledge — would break from the GOP

---

[11] Roy V. Peel, *The 1932 Campaign: An Analysis* (New York, 1935), p. 207.
[12] "Educator Sees New Party, With Roosevelt, Pinchot as Members," *Salt Lake Tribune*, Sep. 24, 1932.
[13] Ibid.
[14] Ibid.
[15] Norman L. Zucker, *George W. Norris: Gentle Knight of American Democracy* (Urbana, Illinois, 1966), p. 16.

"and participate in the thrill and enthusiasm of a great movement."[16] But he was profoundly disappointed when the "Gentle Knight of American progressive ideals," as FDR once described him, flatly rejected the professor's sincere overture, essentially repeating many of the same arguments he used in declining the Farmer-Labor Party's presidential nomination in 1928.

"I think," replied Norris, "experience has shown that the people will not respond to a demand for a new party except in case of a great emergency where there is practically a political revolution."[17] Presumably, the Great Depression didn't fit the Nebraska lawmaker's description of a "great emergency."

Arguing that it would be futile to organize a new party with any hope of success as long as the Electoral College was still in existence, the longtime Nebraska lawmaker told reporters that he had no interest in joining a third-party movement and, instead, would lead a fight in Congress to abolish the Electoral College so that it would be possible for someone to run for the presidency as an independent, unencumbered by any party apparatus. "I'm not a candidate for president," he insisted. "I'll not be a candidate for president. I'll probably be dead before this reform can be brought about."[18]

Though deeply disappointed, Dewey and the LIPA nevertheless threw themselves into the 1932 presidential campaign with all the enthusiasm and might they could muster, making what can only be described as a yeoman's effort on behalf of the cash-strapped Thomas campaign — a candidacy virtually abandoned by New York's right-wing Old Guard.

At its third annual convention in Cleveland during the second week in July, the League adopted a comprehensive platform and, without a candidate of its own, endorsed Norman Thomas for the presidency, qualifying its endorsement of the Socialist standard-bearer by stating that it did "not necessarily support every feature in the ultimate program of the Socialist Party."[19]

The delegates attending the LIPA convention read like a "Who's Who" of the country's liberal intelligentsia. In addition to Dewey and economist Paul H. Douglas, the LIPA convention included William Mahoney, the Farmer-Labor mayor of St. Paul, Minnesota, Oswald Garrison Villard of *The Nation*, John Kvale, a

---

[16] "Proposes Norris Leave Ranks and Join Third Party," *Zanesville Signal*, Dec. 26, 1930.
[17] George W. Norris to John Dewey, December 1930, George W. Norris Papers. Manuscript Division, Library of Congress.
[18] "Norris to Stick With Republican Stamp on Lapel," *Zanesville Signal*, Dec. 27, 1930.
[19] "League Seeks Unified Plan; Supports Norman Thomas, But Not All of His Views," *Manitowoc Herald-Times*, July 13, 1932.

Farmer-Labor congressman from Minnesota, Quaker pacifist Devere Allen of Connecticut and B. Charney Vladeck, the longtime Socialist editor of the *Jewish Daily Forward*. The League's executive director Howard Y. Williams of St. Paul, who later embraced the Communist Party's call for a national Farmer-Labor Party, also played a major role at the convention.

In his address to the convention, Dewey predicted that the United States would plunge into fascism if the Hoover administration continued to pursue its current economic policies. Claiming there wasn't a snowball's chance in hell that the League would support FDR over Norman Thomas, the Columbia University professor saved most of his oratorical firepower for the Republicans, sharply denouncing the administration's economic theory that prosperity for the wealthy eventually trickles down to the working-class and the poor and that prosperity was just around the corner. "If the administration continues to act on that policy," he declared, "the outcome will be some form of economic dictatorship — or Fascism."[20]

Reaffirming its "solidarity with the American worker and farmer," the preamble to the League's platform urged the hastening of "the end of the present depression and substituting intelligent political leadership for misrule."

In addition to calling for the abolition of child labor and the enactment of unemployment insurance and old-age pensions, the League's 600-word platform included a six-hour workday for federal employees without any cut in pay; a 75% tax on incomes over $5 million and estates valued in excess of $100,000; a twenty-five percent reduction in the Hawley-Smoot tariff; transformation of the Department of Labor "from a bureau of propaganda and deportation into a public agency serving the interests of labor;" and federal appropriations of not less than $250 million for direct relief and three to five million dollars a year for "useful public works."[21]

In a plank dealing with civil rights and justice, the League dealt briefly with the thorny issue of prohibition. "While on democratic principles we recognize the right of the people to vote on the abolition or modification of the 18th amendment, we condemn the Re-

---

[20] "Pictures U.S. as Filled With Discontent," *Elyria Chronicle-Telegram*, July 9, 1932.
[21] "Liberal League Backs Thomas for President," *El Paso Herald-Post*, July 11, 1932; "7 'Third Party' Candidates Nominated for Presidency and Others Appear Likely," *Syracuse Herald*, July 24, 1932.

publican and Democratic parties for subordinating urgent economic issues to the liquor question" — a position generally shared by Norman Thomas.[22]

The LIPA convention came off smoothly, except for one particularly rancorous debate over a proposal to endorse William Browder of Chicago, the Communist Party's candidate for the U.S. Senate from Illinois and brother of Earl Browder, who later served as the party's general-secretary until both of them were expelled from the party as enemies of the working class. Dewey led the fight against the proposal to endorse Browder, arguing that the "Communists have as their aim the disruption of all parties and unless this fellow is an exception, he favors the same principle."[23]

The League's support for Thomas in the autumn campaign was far from inconsequential, as one of Thomas's biographers claimed, especially in New York where the party's stingy "Old Guard," which controlled the city and state machinery, put almost all of its resources into Morris Hillquit's campaign for mayor — a reasonable expenditure, to be sure — but squandered the rest on Louis Waldman's hopeless gubernatorial quest while virtually ignoring Thomas's presidential campaign.

The LIPA, which then boasted some 10,000 members nationally, opened a Thomas-for-President office in the same Nineteenth Street building that housed Harry W. Laidler's League for Industrial Democracy. The League, moreover, raised almost forty percent of Thomas's $43,000 campaign budget that year, while the party contributed a relatively meager $26,000 — or barely more than a quarter of its pre-depression 1928 fund.[24] One curious contributor to the Thomas campaign in 1932 was Henry A. Wallace, the future vice president. A registered Republican who voted for the Democratic ticket that year, Wallace discreetly chipped in $25 to the Socialist Party's presidential campaign fund.[25]

Though a few observers estimated that Thomas might receive as many as 5 million protest votes — a vastly exaggerated figure,

---

[22] Ibid.
[23] "Liberals Plan a Third Party for Next Year; Endorse Socialist Nominee for President — Refuse Approval to Communist," *Stevens Point Daily Journal*, July 12, 1932.
[24] Swanberg, *Norman Thomas: The Last Idealist*, p. 135; Fleischman, Norman Thomas: A Biography, p. 135. The Socialist Party raised $25,663.36 for the presidential campaign while the Independent Committee for Thomas reportedly received $17,302.31 in contributions.
[25] Cabell Phillips, "That Baffling Personality, Mr. Wallace," *New York Times Magazine*, Feb. 8, 1948, p. 172.

as it turned out — there was absolutely no chance the respected ex-Princeton valedictorian would win the White House in 1932.[26]

Yet, the dignified Socialist campaigned like he was running to win, giving more than 200 speeches in thirty-eight states. Strapped for cash and armed only with an arsenal of ideas, Thomas barnstormed the county as if he was on the verge of pulling off the biggest political upset in American history.

Among other things, the fast-talking Socialist relentlessly pushed the idea of a capital levy on wealth throughout the autumn campaign. An idea originally championed by the British Labour Party, Thomas claimed that a capital levy would "take care of the national debt, unemployment relief and a considerable part of the reduction of municipal and farm debts."[27]

Addressing a crowd of 4,000 at the Ohio State Fairgrounds in late October, the Socialist candidate asserted that such a tax was both "just and practicable."[28] He then explained precisely how a capital levy would work:

> According to the scale of capital levy formerly proposed by the British Labor Party for Great Britain, a man with $30,000 would pay $250 (5 per cent on excess over $25,000); then by a graduated scale up so that a man worth $50,000,000 would pay $29,574,000 or 59 per cent of the total.
>
> This would raise somewhere between 46 and 57 billion dollars in America. The exemption could be raised to $250,000 and still we could raise between 30 and 44 billion.
>
> Such a tax could be practicable, the exact rate, heavily graduated, could be determined by careful study of needs. The tax would be levied only once, on individual, not corporate bodies, and on total net wealth, not capitalized income. Exemptions could be put high enough to avoid the administrative difficulties of collecting on small fortunes.
>
> The procedure would be relatively simple. Assessments would follow the procedure of ordinary inheritance tax. Payments could be by cash, government bonds, or approved se-

---

[26] "Socialists' Candidate for President Favors 'Orderly Revolution' at Polls," *Sandusky Star-Journal*, Aug. 11, 1932.
[27] "Norman Thomas Proposes Capital Levy for Relief," *Portsmouth Times* (Portsmouth, Ohio), Oct. 21, 1932.
[28] Ibid.

curities. A board of referees might permit installment payments. Bonds paid in could be cancelled; cash would be used to purchase and retire bonds.[29]

Economic reconstruction, concluded Thomas, "requires the transfer of our national resources, our public utilities, our banking system, our monopolies and near-monopolies from private to public ownership and control."[30]

In defending his proposal, Thomas explained that a capital levy on wealth was profoundly fair and justified "because it would fall equitably on all members of the owning class as piecemeal confiscation or debt repudiation would not." He also said that his proposal wasn't intended to replace the nation's existing income and inheritance taxes — all three components were necessary if the United States, already sinking in a sea of red ink, was going to avoid an even greater debt crisis.[31]

Thomas also promised to nationalize the Federal Reserve and require all of the nation's commercial banks to join it, a proposal later promulgated by "Maury's Mavericks," a progressive congressional study group formed by Democratic Rep. Maury Maverick of Texas during the Great Depression — a bold proposal that eventually cost the colorful San Antonio lawmaker and other members of his group their seats in the U.S. House of Representatives.[32]

"We shall forbid banks to have affiliates with market securities by selling them to the banks," asserted the Socialist candidate during a campaign appearance in Hartford, Connecticut, in late October. The plan, he explained, was to "enlarge the postal savings bank into a general banking system" with segregated commercial and individual savings accounts. Thomas said that he expected this publicly-owned bank to rapidly surpass privately-owned

---

[29] Ibid.
[30] "Advocates Levy on Large Fortunes to Liquidate Debts," *Thomasville Times-Enterprise* (Thomasville, GA), Oct. 21, 1932.
[31] "Capital Tax on Wealth to Lift Nation's Debt is Proposed by Thomas," *Escanaba Daily Press*, Oct. 21, 1932.
[32] "Power Chiefs Now Gunning for Maverick," *St. Petersburg Independent*, July 18, 1936; "Maury Maverick, Texas New Dealer, Defeated in Democratic Primary," *Bend Bulletin*, July 25, 1938; Richard B. Henderson, *Maury Maverick: A Political Biography* (Austin, 1970), pp. 118, 122, 176-183. Wealthy utility executive Ralph W. Morrison of Texas, a member of the Federal Reserve Board, reportedly spent $150,000 — the equivalent of more than $2.5 million in today's currency — in an effort to defeat Maverick in the 1936 primary. Morrison had been a financial angel to Jack Garner's campaign for the Democratic presidential nomination in 1932. With Roosevelt's assistance, Maverick survived the 1936 campaign, but was unseated two years later, narrowly losing to fellow Democrat Paul J. Kilday, a Georgetown-educated lawyer from San Antonio.

banks in deposits "without catastrophic suddenness and without requiring the purchase or confiscation of private banks."[33]

Declaring repeatedly that the Socialist Party intended "to change the system that inevitably breeds unemployment," Thomas faulted both of his major-party opponents for failing to adequately address how they would deal with the country's massive joblessness. A capital levy, he asserted, had to be part of any economic recovery program, "if for no other reason than to lighten the load of government and foreign debts."[34]

Thomas flatly rejected the austerity mongers who argued that the nation's severe economic crisis required that everybody sacrifice something. Millions were already jobless and hungry, retorted Thomas. The simple fact, he said, was that they literally had nothing more to sacrifice. "In the storm of this great depression," he later wrote, "we may all be in the same boat, but there is still a vast difference between travelling in the first cabin and in the stokehole."[35]

In that same vein, Thomas ridiculed Roosevelt's plan to balance the federal budget by taxing beer. A tax on beer, designed to raise several hundred million dollars a year, was one of the Democratic nominee's more ludicrous proposals for reducing the ballooning federal deficit, asserted Thomas.

He was absolutely right. As hard to believe as it might be considering joblessness had reached a staggering 25 percent nationally, Roosevelt — sounding like a fiscal conservative — actually campaigned for a balanced budget that year, proposing a staggering 25 percent reduction in federal spending. During his famous "Bonus, Budget and Beer" address at Forbes Field in Pittsburgh, a speech reportedly drafted by Gen. Hugh "Iron Pants" Johnson and heavily influenced by financial oligarch Bernard Baruch — and one that Roosevelt long regretted ever making — the New York governor attacked President Hoover for failing to balance the budget and for being one of the biggest spenders in American history.[36]

---

[33] "Thomas Would Socialize All U.S. Industry," *Albuquerque Journal*, Oct. 31, 1932.
[34] "Thomas Talk Stirs 12,000 in New York," *Syracuse Herald*, Nov. 4, 1932.
[35] Norman M. Thomas, *Human Exploitation in the United States* (New York, 1934), p. 142.
[36] "Roosevelt Lays U.S. Deficit to Hoover," *Pittsburgh Press*, Oct. 20, 1932; "Roosevelt Says Hoover Theories Wrecked U.S. Finances," *Pittsburgh Press*, Oct. 20, 1932; "Roosevelt Opposes Cash Bonus Now; Urges Beer Tax to Balance Budget," *New York Times*, Oct. 20, 1932; Rosenman, *Working with Roosevelt*, p. 86; Michael Hiltzik, *The New Deal: A Modern History* (New York, 2011), p. 119.

In a speech in Newark, New Jersey, in late October the Socialist standard-bearer charged that FDR's proposal was unfair to workers. "His idea that beer can be taxed heavily enough to balance the budget is comical," asserted Thomas. Taxing beer, he argued, would never solve the problem of a ballooning federal deficit and, even if it could, what Roosevelt was really proposing was to balance the budget on the backs of working-class Americans, rather than the rich.[37]

While his proposal for a capital levy on wealth was sharply condemned by the *New York Times*, which wondered aloud how Thomas "could bring himself to make a proposal so unworthy of his intellectual quality," some of the sharpest criticism hurled in his direction during the campaign came from the rival Communists, offering their usual spicy condemnation of the Socialist Party, and the tiny Socialist Labor Party, the nation's oldest Marxist party.[38]

William Z. Foster, the Communist Party nominee who had suffered a serious heart attack in September and spent the remainder of the campaign recuperating at his home in the Bronx, called Thomas a "slick magician" running on "the third party of capitalism built up by Wall Street as a weapon against the revolutionary movement of the Communist Party."[39]

The Socialist Labor Party, whose lineage dated back to the Workingmen's Party of the United States of the late 1870s, had nominated Verne L. Reynolds, a former steamfitter who was living in New York and running a newspaper advertising agency at the time of his candidacy, for president that year. The 48-year-old Reynolds, who had been the party's vice-presidential candidate in 1928, was thrust into a leading role during the former campaign when the party's presidential nominee Frank T. Johns, a 39-year-old Portland carpenter, tragically lost his life while valiantly trying to save a young boy who had fallen into the Deschutes River a few days after being nominated for the presidency.[40]

While Reynolds ripped Thomas as a "typical bourgeois reformer," Eric Hass, a studious and soft-spoken Nebraskan who not only headed the party's ticket in four consecutive presidential elections between 1952 and 1964 and ran for mayor of New York City on a half-dozen occasions, but also edited the *Weekly People*,

---

[37] "Thomas Has Program for World Peace," *Olean Times Herald*, Oct. 29, 1932.
[38] "Open Season for Promises," *New York Times*, Oct. 22, 1932.
[39] "Foster Ill, Ends Campaign; Communist Candidate for President Suffers Hearts Attack," New York Times, Sep. 15, 1932; "20,000 Reds Demand a 'Soviet America,'" *New York Times*, Nov. 7, 1932.
[40] "Frank T. Johns Drowns," *New York Times*, May 22, 1928; "Drowns in Unsuccessful Attempt to Rescue Boy," *Chicago Tribune*, May 21, 1928.

the party's official organ, for thirty consecutive years — tapping away on his typewriter from 1938 to 1968 — spent much of his time that autumn denouncing the rival Socialist Party for leading American workers astray by promising reforms that would merely prop up the badly battered capitalist system. An advertising salesman prior to joining the SLP a few years earlier, the 27-year-old Hass maintained that the reform agenda offered by Norman Thomas and the Socialists would do little more than prolong the country's decaying economic system.[41]

Aaron M. Orange, the Socialist Labor Party's candidate for governor of New York, also criticized Thomas, suggesting that the former Presbyterian minister's candidacy was nothing more than an attempt to "patch up the collapsed capitalistic system." Speaking to an audience of seventy in Hartford, Connecticut, in late October, the Socialist Laborite argued that Thomas was no different than President Hoover, Franklin D. Roosevelt and the Communist Party's William Z. Foster, saying that all four men were nothing more than "a bunch of politicians whose promises are utterly incapable of fulfillment."[42]

Declaring that his party's four rivals were offering little more than a band aid to a system hemorrhaging out of control, the 27-year-old Orange asserted that the platforms of the four rival parties were almost identical when it came to solving the nation's unemployment problem and farm crisis. They're nothing but "efforts to patch up capitalism," he intoned.[43]

Orange, a Columbia University-educated public schoolteacher from the Bronx who later ran for vice president on his party's ticket in 1940, also ridiculed the Socialist Party nominee's proposal to appropriate $5 million for immediate unemployment relief, saying that Thomas's proposal was as politically impractical as his earlier proposal to impose a capital levy on the wealthy in an effort to raise an additional forty to fifty billion dollars for the federal treasury. "If Hoover and Roosevelt are willing to promise every part of the country a heaven on earth," he quipped, "Thomas is willing to promise two heavens, or to double any other promise."[44]

To the extent that he was even aware of it, Thomas took the SLP's criticism in stride, preferring instead to focus all of his attention on his major-party rivals.

---

[41] "Radical Spanks Radical Groups," *Wisconsin State Journal*, Sep. 29, 1932.
[42] "Says Thomas Would Patch Up Capitalism," *Hartford Courant*, Oct. 31, 1932.
[43] Ibid.
[44] Ibid.

In an attempt to counter Roosevelt's endorsement by the sons of the late "Fighting Bob" La Follette, the Wisconsin Socialist Party's executive committee sent out a last-minute appeal to the progressives in that state urging support for the Thomas-Maurer ticket. Pointing to a statement made by La Follette during his 1924 presidential campaign in which the late Senator envisioned "a militant political movement, independent of the two old party organizations," the Wisconsin Socialists urged the state's progressive and liberal-minded voters to ignore the appeals from those supporting one of the major-party candidates.[45]

Asserting that the Republicans had nominated a man who had "blundered through three years of the present depression," while the Democrats had turned to a man who was constantly "trimming his sails to catch every wind that blows," the Wisconsin Socialists — offering what they described as "a more cheerful choice" than either the hapless Hoover or the patrician Roosevelt, representing "the darkest reaction of the South" — reminded the state's progressives that the Socialist Party had been their dependable allies during the previous forty years, fighting alongside them for the state's progressive legislation now under attack and being destroyed by deep-pocketed, predatory interests.[46]

Thomas essentially repeated the same message in an election eve appearance in Milwaukee when he wondered aloud "what old Bob La Follette would say to his son, the governor of Wisconsin, if he knew of his apostasy?" He then accused the La Follette brothers — Sen. Robert M. La Follette, Jr., and Philip La Follette, the latter of whom had just been defeated for the Republican nomination in a bid for a second term as governor — of endorsing Roosevelt in attempt to exact revenge on the GOP.[47] "The La Follettes knew what Roosevelt was when they endorsed him for revenge," asserted Thomas. "Well, we Socialists are not interested in the revenge of the La Follette dynasty. We're interested in the welfare of the United States."[48]

Though saving some of his sharpest barbs for his Democratic rival, Thomas aimed much of his firepower on Herbert Hoover that autumn, blaming the Republican president for the deepening depression. Daniel W. Hoan, the popular Socialist mayor of Milwaukee, doubling as chairman of the Socialist Party's national

---

[45] "Socialists Ask Progressives for Support," *Stevens Point Daily Journal*, Oct. 31, 1932.
[46] Ibid.
[47] "Thomas Hits at Roosevelt in Wisconsin," *Syracuse Herald*, Nov. 8, 1932.
[48] Ibid.

campaign committee, echoed the same theme while stumping extensively for the party's national ticket that during the fall campaign. Speaking to a crowd of more 2,000 in Brooklyn in early October, the Milwaukee mayor said that he had traveled to New York "in search of Hoover prosperity, supposed to be somewhere round the corner. I thought it might have been round some corner in New York," he quipped, "but I can't find any signs of it."[49]

Like the party leaders themselves, most observers expected Thomas, at a minimum, to garner in excess of a million votes — the highest popular vote total in the party's history. Many believed Thomas would run even stronger. A *Literary Digest* poll, albeit far less scientific than today's modern polls, indicated that the Socialist candidate would garner as many as two million votes, shattering Eugene Debs' relatively strong showing a dozen years earlier.[50]

"The Socialist vote in this year's election is expected to exceed a million," wrote the editorial writers for the *Wichita Daily Times* in Wichita Falls, Texas. The expected increase in the party's vote totals, they said, was largely due to the candidate himself, "an anomaly as a Socialist nominee" whose differences with his predecessor Gene Debs in both style and substance were "wide and many."

Thomas, they wrote, had given the Socialist Party an air of respectability that had been lacking in the past.[51]

"There is nothing in the least incendiary about Thomas, as mild-mannered a gentleman as ever campaigned for office," the editorial continued. "He makes the sort of speech that educated people like to hear, even if they do not agree with it, and he is being heard in this campaign by thousands of folks, who, in earlier years, would not have thought for a moment of being seen in a Socialist meeting."[52]

"There is the possibility," the editorial concluded, "that the Socialists can develop enough strength to give them the balance of power in Congress. In next month's election their vote may be large enough in a few states, not to win, but to upset the calculations of one of the major parties. Whatever the party's future, the probability is that Thomas has brought it to a more important position than it has ever held before."[53]

While focusing most of his attention on his own national campaign that fall, Thomas also hoped to influence New York's 1932

---

[49] "2,000 Hear Mayor Hoan," *New York Times*, Oct. 7, 1932.
[50] Fleischman, *Norman Thomas: A Biography*, p. 135.
[51] "Thomas and the Socialists," *Wichita Daily Times*, Oct. 22, 1932.
[52] Ibid.
[53] Ibid.

mayoralty contest, a special election triggered by the resignation of Mayor Jimmy Walker, the colorful song-writing and wisecracking politician who left office under the threat of criminal indictment some sixteen months before the end of his term.

The Socialists had nominated ailing labor lawyer Morris Hillquit to run in the special election. An immensely popular figure at the ballot box who once came within 413 votes of winning a seat in Congress on the Socialist ticket, the 63-year-old Latvian-born lawyer had waged a spectacular bid for the mayor's office fifteen years earlier, garnering more than 145,000 votes, or nearly 22 percent, in a fiercely fought quadrangular struggle won by Tammany's John F. Hylan. Remarkably, Hillquit finished some 89,000 votes ahead of the hopeless Republican nominee in that race.

In an attempt to sway New Yorkers in the 1932 special election, Thomas, in collaboration with Paul Blanshard, a young minister-turned-apostate who served as field director for the League for Industrial Democracy, co-authored a book called *What's the Matter With New York?* Published by the Macmillan Company and coming on the heels of the famous Seabury investigation, Thomas's book was widely read that fall.[54]

In an address at New York's Madison Square Garden five days before the November election — his first campaign appearance in the city since September 21st — Thomas urged an enthusiastic crowd of more than 20,000 to rally behind Hillquit's surging candidacy in the city's special mayoral election:[55]

> The one ray of light in this municipal darkness will be the immense vote our Socialist candidate, Morris Hillquit, will receive not alone from Socialists, but from all who resent Tammany's brazen contempt of ordinary decency in putting up a respectable puppet for an office requiring what Mr. Hillquit, and only Mr. Hillquit among the candidates, conspicuously offers: Ability, honesty and conviction.[56]

Yet Hillquit, Thomas continued, would be the first to agree with him that the city's real problem wasn't necessarily the "effrontery of Tammany," but rather "the breakdown of a capitalist system which is little more than a legalized racket." The great opportunity for the Socialist Party on Tuesday, said Thomas, wasn't so

---

[54] "Norman Thomas' Book about New York City Politics Announced," *Galveston Daily News*, Sep. 11, 1932; "An Anatomy of Corruption in the City of New York; What's the Matter With New York: A National Problem," *New York Times*, Oct. 16, 1932.
[55] "20,000 Hail Thomas at Rally in Garden," *New York Times*, Nov. 4, 1932.
[56] "U.S. Hope Lies in Big Protest, Says Socialist," *Salt Lake Tribune*, Nov. 4, 1932.

much merely throwing out the Tammany rascals, but putting socialism into the lives and consciousness of the American people at the city, state and national levels. "Tammany," he said, was "more corrupt yet scarcely less futile for good than Wall Street's two old parties in the national field."[57] In closing, the Socialist standard-bearer urged the voters of New York City to cast a large protest vote on Tuesday. "Vote your hopes, not your fears," he exhorted the overflow crowd. "You owe no man the obligation to vote for less."[58]

The 1932 campaign came to an end with President Hoover rumbling across the vast wastelands of Wyoming, Utah and Nevada, where he made a final appeal for support. A supremely confident Roosevelt concluded his campaign with a speech in Poughkeepsie, New York, while Thomas, asserting that the balloting wasn't an end for his party "but the beginning of a new and greater crusade," raced to Wisconsin to give a closing address in the party's stronghold of Milwaukee.[59]

In his final appearance of the campaign, Thomas told some 12,000 cheering supporters in Milwaukee that the campaign, as conducted by the two old parties — "divided only by lust for office" — had been one of superficiality and invective. "It has been a campaign marred, as usual, by economic and political coercion," said Thomas.[60]

While saying it was almost wasting one's breath to talk about Hoover, a man whose candidacy had become so maudlin that he pathetically kept referring to himself and Lincoln in the same sentence — "Me and Lincoln" Hoover kept saying, as if there was any comparison between the two men — Thomas saved his sharpest criticism for his Democratic rival, savaging FDR for his associations with Tammany Hall, his less-than-impressive record on utilities, and his position on the issues, particularly widespread joblessness.[61]

In his election-eve address, the Socialist nominee also faulted Roosevelt for failing to utter so much as a single word of protest when Democratic election officials in Florida, Louisiana and Oklahoma, working on his behalf, arbitrarily kept the Socialist Party and other minor parties off the ballot.[62]

---

[57] Ibid.
[58] Ibid.
[59] "Heaviest Vote in History May Be Polled Today," *Lubbock Morning Avalanche*, Nov. 8, 1932.
[60] "Thomas Hits at Roosevelt in Wisconsin," *Syracuse Herald*, Nov. 8, 1932.
[61] Ibid.
[62] Ibid.

The Democrats and Republicans, he contended, didn't understand the breadth and depth of the current depression, the severity of which the country had never quite experienced before. "What both old parties hope is that we should drift out of this depression as we have done in former crises," said Thomas. That was "cold comfort," he continued, "for the record of the last century shows that we never have had true prosperity and security, but are always either going up in a gamblers' boom or coming down into cruel depression. If we ever come partially out of this depression it will be only as a man might recover from smallpox in time to get the cholera. None of the fundamental causes of depression has been or can be met by this capitalism which Hoover extolls and Roosevelt seeks to sugarcoat with promises impossible of fulfillment."[63]

As the votes trickled in on Nov. 8th, Thomas issued an election night "victory statement" from Chicago, saying that the campaign had been a huge success. "If we get 1,000,000 votes, we will be moderately encouraged," he said, adding that every vote over 1,500,000 would be "decidedly encouraging." Acknowledging that he didn't expect to win, the Socialist candidate said that every vote over two million — the figure indicated by the *Literary Digest* survey showing Thomas receiving almost 5% of the vote nationally — would be "cause for tremendous jubilation."[64]

At least that's what Thomas said publicly. Privately, he had braced himself — and his relatively small campaign staff — for a disappointing showing. "I want to tell all of you that I'm not going to get a big vote tomorrow," he told a couple of staffers over coffee the day before the election. "For instance, at my wonderful meeting in Milwaukee last Saturday, hundreds came up to shake my hand. One young man came up to me with tears in his eyes and said, 'I believe in everything you say and I agree entirely with your principles, but my wife and I can't vote for you. The country can't stand another four years of Hoover.' You can multiply that couple by thousands, if not millions," said the dejected candidate. "I can't help but sympathize with the feelings of that young man," he added, "but our vote will be small."[65]

Sadly, Thomas was right. Though tripling his 1928 showing, the Socialist standard-bearer fell short of the million-vote mark, officially polling 884,781 votes nationally, or 2.2 percent. Thomas's total was also far shy of the two to three million votes forecast by

---

[63] Ibid.
[64] "Norman Thomas Gives Statement," *Oil City Derrick*, Nov. 9, 1932.
[65] Fleischman, *Norman Thomas: A Biography*, pp. 135-136.

the party's managers only a few weeks earlier.⁶⁶ While there were numerous allegations that the Socialist Party's vote totals had been deliberately undercounted — veteran *St. Louis Post-Dispatch* reporter Paul Y. Anderson insisted that Thomas polled at least two million votes, but that election officials didn't bother to produce an accurate count in countless precincts across the country where the Socialists lacked poll watchers — Thomas's total, while impressive by minor-party standards, was nevertheless disappointing.⁶⁷

While the party's presidential showing came as a sharp blow to many of the party's leaders and activists, almost all of whom believed Thomas would easily shatter the million-vote threshold, particularly at a time when a quarter of the working population couldn't find employment, the Socialists still had plenty of reason to be optimistic about the party's future. Based on the returns in other contests across the country, there were plenty of bright spots to build upon.

The party's most spectacular showing occurred in New York City's special mayoral election where the ailing Morris Hillquit polled a staggering 251,656 votes, or 12.6 percent.

The Socialists also put up highly respectable fights in at least a half-dozen congressional races across the country that autumn, including a 27 percent showing by Raymond S. Hofses, the longtime editor of the *Reading Labor Advocate*, in Pennsylvania's fourteenth congressional district. Hofses, a member of the Reading school board and a perennial Socialist candidate for public office, garnered 19,319 votes in a hotly-contested race decided by fewer than 6,500 votes.

Hofses carried Reading in his losing battle — a city that gave Norman Thomas more than thirty percent of its vote — but lost badly in the district's rural areas. In addition to the strong showing by Hofses, Reading's veteran Socialist state lawmakers Darlington Hoopes and Lilith B. Wilson were both reelected to the Pennsylvania legislature that year with nearly forty percent of the vote, garnering an impressive 11,828 and 11,290 votes, respectively, in their bids for a second term. Moreover, city councilman William C. Hoverter, the Socialist Party candidate for state treasurer, won a plurality in Reading, as did the party's candidate for the State Senate.⁶⁸

---

⁶⁶ "Socialists Claim 2,000,000 Votes," *New York Times*, Oct. 16, 1932.
⁶⁷ Fleischman, *Norman Thomas: A Biography*, p. 136.
⁶⁸ Kenneth E. Hendrickson, "Triumph and Disaster: The Reading Socialists in Power and Decline, 1932-1939, Part II," *Pennsylvania History*, Volume 40, Number 4 (October 1973), p. 386.

"SUCH A LITTLE MAN, SO BIG A DEPRESSION"

In Milwaukee, upholsterer Walter Polakowski — the only Socialist in the Wisconsin Senate at the time and the author of an ambitious $12 million public relief bill — polled a respectable 20.3% of the vote in that city's fourth congressional district while Herman O. Kent, a former Socialist assemblyman, tallied 23.3% in the neighboring fifth district. In California, J. Stitt Wilson, the former mayor of Berkeley, garnered 22,767 votes, or 22.5%, in a three-cornered race while two Socialists in New York City — B. Charney Vladeck, business manager and editor of the *Jewish Daily Forward*, and former state assemblyman Samuel Orr — polled 31,930 and 21,349 votes, respectively, in four-cornered races against incumbent Democratic lawmakers.

One of the party's most celebrated congressional candidates that autumn was theologian Reinhold Niebuhr of the Union Theological Seminary, a close personal friend of Norman Thomas. An eloquent critic of unregulated capitalism and co-founder of the Fellowship of Socialist Christians, Niebuhr polled a relatively disappointing 3,582 votes, or less than five percent, against entrenched Democratic lawmaker Sol Bloom in New York's nineteenth congressional district.

Another well-known Socialist congressional candidate that year was John T. Scopes, the young, chain-smoking biology teacher at the center of the celebrated "Monkey Trial" seven years earlier. In one of the most widely-watched trials in American history, Scopes had voluntarily stepped forward to challenge a Tennessee law prohibiting the teaching of Charles Darwin's theory of evolution.

Scopes, who shunned the limelight, became an almost forgotten figure when the trial turned into an oratorical duel between aging special prosecutor William Jennings Bryan, a three-time presidential candidate, and 68-year-old attorney Clarence Darrow. Scopes was also represented by Arthur Garfield Hays, general counsel for the ACLU, and the debonair Dudley Field Malone, an internationally-famous divorce lawyer who had once served as an assistant Secretary of State for Bryan during the Wilson administration. Malone, whose riveting "duel to the death" speech received the largest ovation of any during the eleven-day trial, had been a serious contender for the Farmer-Labor Party's presidential nomination in 1920.

The sandy-haired Scopes, whose conviction was later overturned by the Tennessee Supreme Court, had disappeared from the limelight following the trial. He spent a couple of years studying at the University of Chicago and working as a geologist in Venezuela for three years before moving back to his father's farm in Paducah, Kentucky, where he tended to the family garden and read voraciously. He had been jobless for more than a year when the Socialist Party of Kentucky nominated him for Congress. During the campaign, he told curious reporters that he now considered himself "a private in the army of the unemployed."[69]

His fame had been fleeting. A somewhat shy and introverted man, Scopes had found it exceedingly difficult to deal with the publicity generated during his trial in 1925. "I could not get accustomed to interviews by the press and the resulting publicity," he told a reporter shortly after announcing his candidacy.[70]

Believing that capitalism was "headed for a collapse," the 31-year-old Scopes — a longtime admirer of the late Eugene V. Debs — publicly endorsed Norman Thomas for president that year.[71] A lifelong Socialist, Scopes limited his own campaign to a single speech in Louisville. Running for one of Kentucky's nine at-large seats in the U.S. House, the young man who had been at the center of the famous Monkey Trial nevertheless led the Socialist congressional ticket in that state with 3,273 votes.

Emil Seidel, the former Socialist mayor of Milwaukee, waged the party's strongest U.S. Senate race that autumn, polling 65,807 votes in Wisconsin. Journalist Devere Allen, an Oberlin-educated Quaker pacifist, polled over three percent of the vote in Connecticut; labor lawyer and longtime party war-horse Charles Solomon received 143,282 votes in New York's U.S. Senate race won by popular Democrat Robert F. Wagner.

In Pennsylvania, perennial Socialist candidate William J. Van Essen, a Pittsburgh optometrist waging the fifth of seven campaigns for the U.S. Senate over a period spanning thirty years, garnered a not-too-shabby 91,556 votes — his strongest showing ever. The "Grand Old Man of Optometry," as he was affectionately known, had polled fewer than 27,000 votes as the party's nominee for the U.S. Senate only two years earlier.

Remarkably, Van Essen polled 24.8 percent of the vote in Berks County, home of the Reading Socialists, and picked up quite a few votes in some of the party's old strongholds of East Pittsburgh, Pitcairn, Turtle Creek and Wilkinsburg in populous Allegheny

---

[69] "Evolution Case Dead Issue to Scopes; Jobless Now, He Seeks Post in Congress," *Portsmouth Times* (Portsmouth, OH), Sept. 22, 1932.
[70] Ibid.
[71] "Scopes Will Support Thomas for President," *Telegraph-Herald* (Dubuque, IA), Sept. 26, 1932.

County — struggling working-class communities in western Pennsylvania that had routinely elected Socialists to local office during the party's heyday twenty years earlier.

"Doc" Van Essen, a former member of the party's national executive committee who waged several campaigns for mayor of Pittsburgh and once arranged for Gene Debs to sit for a portrait by renowned local artist Martin B. Leisser, a close friend of Andrew Carnegie and founder of the Pittsburgh Art Society, probably ran for office on more occasions than any other Socialist in Pennsylvania history.[72] The biographically-neglected Van Essen was also a close personal friend of James H. Maurer, the Socialist Party's vice-presidential candidate, and had provided much of the inspiration and enthusiasm for the insurgent La Follette-Wheeler ticket in Allegheny County in 1924 — a populous county that gave the Wisconsin progressive an eye-opening 31.3 percent of the vote.[73]

Despite polling nearly 100,000 votes — the party's best showing ever in a U.S. Senate race in the Keystone State — Van Essen's impressive showing wasn't enough to land him in third place in that hard-fought contest. Those bragging rights belonged to Dr. Edwin J. Fithian, chairman of the board of the Cooper-Bessemer Company and president of the Grove City National Bank who was waging the first of two campaigns for the U.S. Senate on the Prohibition ticket. Fithian, whose banking and manufacturing concerns employed more than 1,700 people, garnered 106,597 votes, or 3.8 percent, in that contest, nearly costing embattled Republican Sen. James J. Davis his seat.[74]

In Wisconsin, Frank B. Metcalfe, who narrowly edged out Milwaukee alderman William Coleman to win the Socialist Party's nomination, waged the party's most competitive gubernatorial campaign that year, garnering 56,965 votes, or slightly more than five percent of all votes cast. Metcalfe, a Milwaukee county supervisor, had also been the party's gubernatorial nominee in 1930, a year when large numbers of Socialists broke ranks and supported insurgent Republican Philip F. La Follette, son of the late Robert M. La Follette.

In the party's New York stronghold, where the Old Guard had wasted precious resources on the party's ill-fated gubernatorial ticket, Louis Waldman, running far behind the party's statewide

---

[72] "Socialists Here Observe Passing of Eugene Debs," *Pittsburgh Press*, Oct. 20, 1930.

[73] "Van Essen Talks on La Follette Aims," *Pittsburgh Post-Gazette*, Oct. 20, 1924.

[74] "Local Prohibitionists Join State-Wide Drive to Elect Dr. Fithian," *Clearfield Progress*, Nov. 7, 1932

ticket, polled a relatively unimpressive 102,959 votes — considerably fewer than the more than 177,000 cast for Norman Thomas — while narrowly finishing ahead of Colgate Divinity School theology professor John F. Vichert, the Law Preservation Party's little-known nominee who reluctantly entered the race with only five weeks remaining in the campaign.[75]

---

[75] "Backing of Drys Promised Vichert," *Christian Science Monitor*, Oct. 7, 1932; "Dr. Vichert Decides to Run," *New York Times*, Oct. 7, 1932.

Chapter VI

Factionalism & Fascism

Thomas received a much-needed reprieve in 1933 — his first break from the campaign trail in nine years — but he stayed busy, perhaps busier than at any other time in his life. Unlike the late Eugene Debs, who steadfastly remained aloof from internal party squabbles, Thomas found himself deeply immersed in the bitter and bloody battle for the party's soul during this period, freely lending his imprimatur to the militants in their longstanding battle with the party's Old Guard.

The long-simmering feud between the Old Guard and party's left-wingers came to a head during the party's midterm convention in Detroit in the late spring of 1934 when the party committed itself to a revolutionary program advocating resistance to war by any means necessary, including use of a general strike, and to the belief that democracy itself shouldn't stand in the way of proletarian rule in the event of a complete economic collapse.

While it didn't directly mention a "dictatorship of the proletariat" — the party's right-wing forces managed to block a resolution containing that specific language a few days earlier — the party's "Declaration of Principles" overwhelmingly adopted in Detroit and subsequently ratified by a margin of 5,933 to 4,872 in a referendum of the national membership was the most profoundly militant stance taken by the party since the antiwar declaration adopted by the St. Louis convention of 1917.[1]

Siding with the party's left-wingers in the Detroit controversy after trying but failing to achieve a suitable compromise acceptable to both factions, Thomas found himself targeted by the Old Guard in the ensuing war between the two factions. Many of Thomas's longtime friendships were badly frayed and some were lost forever in the bitter factional fight following the Detroit convention. Needless to say, it also made for an extremely awkward, if not entirely uncomfortable, experience for Thomas later that autumn when he ran for the U.S. Senate on a slate chosen and dominated by the party's right-wingers.

Saddened by the recent deaths of Morris Hillquit and longtime editor Abraham I. Shiplacoff, the "Jewish Eugene V. Debs" who served as the party's floor leader in the state assembly during World War I when he and four other Socialist lawmakers were unceremoniously expelled from that body, and torn apart by the deep division in the party stemming from the "Declaration of Principles" adopted in Detroit earlier that spring, the badly-divided New York Socialists, pulling together one last time, waged a spirited campaign during the 1934 mid-term elections.

One of the most fascinating developments during that campaign, of course, was the tenuous relationship between Thomas, the party's nominee for the U.S. Senate, and gubernatorial candidate Charles Solomon, a key member of the party's Old Guard.

Solomon had been the party's candidate for mayor the previous autumn. Adding some color to a race that already had plenty, the Socialist lawyer, running a poor fourth in the mayoral race, polled a relatively paltry 59,846 votes — barely a quarter of the votes garnered by Morris Hillquit in the 1932 special election and only about a third of the 175,000 votes cast for Thomas in 1929 — against fusion candidate Fiorello H. La Guardia, Democratic incumbent and longtime Tammany foot soldier John P. O'Brien, and the Recovery Party's Joseph V. McKee while finishing ahead of the Communist Party's Robert "Fighting Bob" Minor, the brilliant radical cartoonist for the *Daily Worker*.[2]

---

[1] "Socialists Rout Right Wing Chiefs in Party," *Manitowoc Herald-Times*, June 4, 1934; "Soocialist Party More Radical," *Ithaca Journal*, Nov. 5, 1934; Daniel Bell, *Marxian Socialism in the United States* (Ithaca, 1996), pp. 166-168.

[2] Darcy G. Richardson, "Fusion's Greatest Triumph: Major Parties Play Minor Role in 1933 NYC Mayoralty Campaign," *Uncovered Politics*.

Thomas, returning from a nationwide tour, gave twenty speeches on Solomon's behalf and — putting aside his profound differences with the party's Old Guard — delivered the principal address at the party's mass rally at Madison Square Garden in the closing days of that campaign.[3]

Having previously turned down a cabinet-level position in the La Guardia administration, Thomas was deeply concerned about the party's poor showing that year and was particularly irked when Solomon eagerly accepted an appointment as a magistrate in the newly-elected mayor's administration — a position he held for twenty-three years until his forced retirement in 1959 — saying that it made the Socialist Party "look like a job bargaining party."[4]

A lawyer and labor leader, Solomon had been at odds with Thomas, the party's titular national leader, since the divisive Detroit convention in early June.[5] A delegate to that convention, Solomon had vigorously opposed the party's Declaration of Principles, "not because it is radical," he said, "but because it is reckless. The only mass resistance you will get as a result of this declaration will be the mass resistance of the people against you." He also warned that adoption of the declaration would drive many long-time members out of the party.[6]

A graduate of Brooklyn Law School, the 45-year-old Solomon easily defeated Coleman Cheney of Saratoga Springs, a Skidmore College economics professor who was backed by the party's militant faction, including Thomas, to win the party's gubernatorial nomination at its badly-divided and rancorous state convention at the Rand School of Social Science in New York City in early July. Solomon trounced Cheney by a margin of 79 to 33. He was joined on the statewide ticket by a slate that had been almost universally supported by the Old Guard.[7] Norman Thomas, the party's nominee for the U.S. Senate — the only left-winger to appear on the Socialist Party's statewide ticket that fall — was the lone exception.[8]

The state convention had been completely controlled by the party's Old Guard, a fact made clear with the re-election of Louis Waldman as state chairman and the adoption of a resolution

---

[3] "Thomas Returns to Aid Socialists; Will Make 20 Speeches in Next Three Days," *New York Sun*, Nov. 2, 1933.
[4] Johnpoll, *Pacifist's Progress: Norman Thomas and the Decline of American Socialism*, p. 107.
[5] "Charles Solomon, Unorthodox Magistrate, Dies," *New York Times*, Dec. 10, 1963.
[6] "Left Wing Seizes Socialist Party," *New York Times*, June 4, 1934.
[7] "Socialists Expected to Name Solomon; Nomination for Governor at the State Convention Predicted, With Thomas for Senator," *New York Times*, June 28, 1934.
[8] "Thomas Nominated in Harmony Move," *New York Times*, July 2, 1934.

sharply denouncing the party's Declaration of Principles adopted in Detroit.[9] Every candidate and resolution favored by Thomas was beaten back by the party's Old Guard.[10]

In a bitterly-contested session, Thomas was nominated only after journalist and historian James Oneal, candidate of the right-wing forces, graciously withdrew from the contest for the sake of party unity. As it was, Thomas narrowly escaped with a majority, receiving 58 votes to 38 against, with 16 others abstaining altogether.[11]

Hailed only a few weeks earlier for winning control of the national party at its tumultuous convention in Detroit, Thomas had barely survived an open rebellion in his home state. In fact, most observers believed that Oneal, a founding member of the party who had played a decisive role in the bitter party split of 1919 and the only "right-winger" elected to the party's national executive committee in Detroit a few weeks earlier, would have easily defeated Thomas if he had remained in the race.[12]

Like Thomas, who actively recruited and vigorously supported Cheney for governor, Solomon had voted against nominating Thomas for the U.S. Senate, but both men later professed a desire for harmony. Needless to say, neither man was completely happy that the other was on the ticket.[13]

"The conduct of the convention was outrageous," Thomas wrote Mayor Daniel Hoan of Milwaukee, "and the speeches against the Declaration were extreme." Thomas dreaded the idea of campaigning with members of New York's "Old Guard," the same folks he had been battling at the national level during the previous two years. For him, the 1934 campaign was nothing short of torture.[14]

Though it made for an uneasy pairing, Thomas temporarily put aside his differences with the Old Guard and campaigned vigorously for the entire Socialist ticket, including Solomon, that autumn, proving that he was a better man than many of his erstwhile critics among the party's right-wingers.

Nationally, the Socialist Party faced a particularly troubling dilemma that year when best-selling novelist Upton Sinclair, a lifelong Socialist who had been the party's gubernatorial nominee in

---

[9] "Socialists Expected to Name Solomon; Nomination for Governor at the State Convention Predicted, With Thomas for Senator," *New York Times*, June 28, 1934.
[10] "Socialists Fight Thomas Program," *New York Times*, July 1, 1934.
[11] Fleischman, *Norman Thomas: A Biography*, p. 166.
[12] Swanberg, *Norman Thomas: The Last Idealist*, pp. 171-172.
[13] "Thomas Nominated in Harmony Move," *New York Times*, July 2, 1934.
[14] Swanberg, *Norman Thomas: The Last Idealist*, pp. 171-172.

California in 1926 and 1930 — polling more than 50,000 votes in the latter contest and nearly as many in his earlier bid — announced that he had switched parties and was seeking the Democratic nomination for governor of California.[15]

Deeply influenced by economist Thorstein Veblen, the muckraking journalist had joined the Socialist Party of Eugene V. Debs a few years after its founding in 1901. He had long been considered one of the party's most influential propagandists and had also been the party's nominee for a congressional seat in Los Angeles in 1920 — the year Debs waged his final campaign for the presidency from a jail cell — and for the U.S. Senate two years later.

Initially bursting onto the national scene in 1906 with the publication of *The Jungle*, a graphic depiction of the horrific and unsanitary conditions in Chicago's meatpacking industry, Sinclair's book was an instant bestseller and helped secure passage of the Pure Food and Drug Act later that year. It was one of some ninety books and tracts authored by the Pulitzer-prize winning journalist over his lifetime.[16] As the late Howard Zinn noted, Sinclair's prolific literary output was "intended to bury capitalism under a barrage of facts, and to present socialism in a way that Americans could accept."[17]

Running on a socialist-leaning platform to "End Poverty in California," Sinclair's Democratic candidacy had a disastrous effect on the Socialist Party in California, attracting such leading lights in the party as future Democratic congressman Jerry Voorhis, Kate Richards O'Hare, and former Berkeley Mayor J. Stitt Wilson.[18] "The Sinclair movement is the nearest thing to a mass movement toward socialism that I have heard of in America," Voorhis wrote Thomas.[19]

Sinclair, who had been generally supportive of Roosevelt's New Deal but thought it didn't go far enough, had discussed his prospective candidacy on the Democratic ticket with Norman Thomas before entering the race. The two men had been friends for more than fifteen years. Worried that Sinclair's candidacy would virtually destroy the party in California, Thomas tried in vain to dissuade Sinclair from running as a Democrat.

---

[15] "Sinclair to Run on Democratic Ticket," *Berkeley Daily Gazette*, Sep. 14, 1933.
[16] Peter Dreier, *The 100 Greatest Americans of the 20th Century: A Social Justice Hall of Fame* (New York, 2012), p. 91.
[17] Howard Zinn, *The Zinn Reader: Writings on Disobedience and Democracy* (New York, 1997), p. 470.
[18] Johnpoll, *Pacifist's Progress*, p. 136.
[19] Seymour Martin Lipset and Gary Marks, *It Didn't Happen Here: Why Socialism Failed in the United States* (New York, 2001), pp. 209-210.

THE LOWEST EBB

In a last-ditch effort to convince his friend of the merits of his EPIC program, Sinclair even sent Thomas the proofs of his not-yet-published book, *I, Governor of California, and How I Ended Poverty*, but Thomas wasn't impressed and almost immediately began denouncing the EPIC program in the party's newspaper. He continued to repudiate Sinclair's plan for the next fourteen months. As an unfortunate result, their long friendship was temporarily strained.

Almost pathetically, the Socialist Party's Milen C. Dempster also got into the act, urging the world-renowned novelist to abandon his candidacy and throw his support to him. A former Unitarian clergyman from San Francisco, the little-known Dempster had the impossible task of carrying the left-wing party's tattered banner in the gubernatorial contest. "What you do now may swing the course of history," he wrote Sinclair in late October. "You have become a man of greater power than ever before. For the cause dearest to your heart, I am pleading with you to withdraw your candidacy and to throw your support to the Socialist Party."[20]

The good-natured Sinclair took his rival's preposterous suggestion in stride. "I have a million votes and Mr. Dempster has about 5,000," he laughed. "I think it would be easier for Mr. Dempster to throw his support to me."[21]

Sinclair was right. Though not quite polling a million votes, the muckraking journalist came pretty close to achieving that level of support in November when some 879,537 Californians voted for him against incumbent Republican Gov. Frank E. Merriam. Merriam was reelected, polling 1,138,620 votes, while another 302,519 — the difference in that widely-watched race — voted for Raymond L. Haight, a young Los Angeles attorney and former state corporation commissioner who ran as the nominee of the ballot-qualified Commonwealth and Progressive parties. The little-remembered Dempster, who brought up the rear — polling a negligible 2,947 votes — was even outdistanced by the Communist Party's Sam Darcy, the party's Ukrainian-born state chairman and organizer of a mass demonstration of the unemployed in New York City at the onset of the Great Depression.

As Thomas feared, Sinclair's candidacy on the Democratic ticket spelled the beginning of the end for the Socialist Party in California. While the party was able to exceed the 3 percent requirement and maintain its legal ballot status that year due to the more than 108,000 votes cast for George R. Kirkpatrick, Hiram Johnson's

---

[20] "Dempster Calls on Sinclair to Quit," *Oakland Tribune*, Oct. 29, 1934.
[21] "Sinclair Will Not Quit Race," *Galveston Daily News*, Oct. 30, 1934.

lone challenger in the state's U.S. Senate contest, party membership plunged by nearly ninety percent between 1933 and 1935.[22] The party lost its permanent ballot status in the Golden State following the 1938 mid-term elections, forcing Thomas to seek refuge with the ballot-qualified Progressive Party during the 1940 presidential campaign and to wage forlorn write-in efforts in the state in 1944 and 1948.[23]

In the meantime, Thomas had turned his attention to his own Senate race in New York. Running against Sen. Royal S. Copeland, a conservative Democrat who was seeking a third term, and Republican challenger E. Harold Cluett, a fiscally conservative Troy industrialist who urged New Yorkers to "go back to the shrewd common sense of Calvin Coolidge, the sound, simple sense that made the country for 150 years the most prosperous and happy that civilization has known," Thomas barnstormed the state with his usual energy and enthusiasm.[24]

Accompanied by his wife Violet, Thomas campaigned vigorously, concentrating most of his efforts in upstate New York and Long Island while leaving most of the city to Solomon. Driving from one small town to the next, Thomas would often speak to local townspeople while standing on the rumble seat of his Chevrolet.[25] Though curious, local residents — mostly denim-clad farmers — were somewhat suspicious about the stranger campaigning from his car seat and would keep their distance, usually standing several feet away as Thomas spoke. "Come in closer," Thomas would say. "I don't have smallpox and the worst thing you can catch is socialism."[26]

Socialism, he told his audiences, was the only way out of the Great Depression. The free market simply wasn't working. "Under Hoover we waited for prosperity and under Roosevelt we are chasing prosperity," said Thomas. "The New Deal tells us to produce less so we can have more. Why should we reduce the supply of cotton when the people who raise the cotton haven't sheets or underclothes? Nero fiddled and the old parties don't even play a good tune. We want to change that system, not tinker with it and

---

[22] Lipset and Marks, *It Didn't Happen Here*, p. 210.
[23] "Socialists Fail to Qualify Party on Official Ballot," *Los Angeles Times*, Nov. 16, 1938; "Count Shows Symes Polled 22,569 Votes," *Socialist Call*, Jan. 14, 1939. The Socialist Party lost its ballot status in California when writer and longtime party activist Lillian B. Symes failed to meet the three percent threshold, polling a relatively disappointing 22,569 votes, or less than one percent, in her bid for the U.S. Senate.
[24] "Cluett Urges Return to Coolidge 'Sense,'" *New York Times*, Oct. 24, 1934.
[25] Fleischman, *Norman Thomas: A Biography*, p. 166.
[26] Gorham, *Leader at Large*, p. 139.

patch it up." Socialism, he explained, wasn't simply government ownership. It was much more than that. It meant social ownership. "That is what we have been working for and that is the way out for America."[27]

In Thomas's view, the New Deal was falling woefully short in stimulating any kind of real economic recovery. The American people were still hurting — and they were hurting badly. Speaking at a Socialist Party rally in Yonkers, the perennial Socialist candidate declared that eleven million people were still unemployed while a staggering 22 percent of the population was living at or below the poverty level. Equally grim, lamented Thomas, was the fact that the per capita income of those lucky enough to be "gainfully" employed was less than $500 per year — hardly a living wage.[28]

"Our supposedly civilized government is trying to starve us into prosperity through a cut in production," asserted Thomas, who had been highly critical of the AAA's curtailment of crop production and livestock during the early years of the depression and long believed that scarcity was the only method known by capitalists to produce prosperity — prosperity for the wealthy, that is. "We need 41,000,000 more acres under cultivation to properly feed and clothe the American people," said Thomas. "We have had the wit to invent machinery, but not the brains to use it. We never have overproduction," he added, "just under-consumption."[29]

Thomas also ripped into Roosevelt's National Recovery Administration, charging that the NRA, symbolized by the Blue Eagle and later ruled unconstitutional, was doing little to alleviate scarcity while guaranteeing the profits of companies through price-fixing — in a sense, "subsidizing scarcity." He viewed it as a form of creeping fascism.[30] "There will be no recovery until the working class controls the tools," he maintained.[31] The pied piper of American socialism also criticized Gen. Hugh Johnson, the blustering and domineering head of the NRA, as a dishonest enemy of the workers, but said that the former army officer's removal as administrator of the NRA would make little difference. "But even if you did get rid of Johnson," he told a crowd in Schenectady, "the Blue

---

[27] "Norman Thomas Addresses 1,500 at Mass Meeting," *Olean Times-Herald*, Oct. 9, 1934.
[28] "World Facing New Conflict, Thomas Fears," *The Herald Statesman* (Yonkers, N.Y.), Nov. 1, 1934.
[29] Ibid.
[30] Swanberg, *Norman Thomas: The Last Idealist*, p. 158.
[31] "Socialists Taunt Foes; Norman Thomas, Solomon, Claessens Speak Before 200 Here," *Daily Argus* (Mount Vernon, N.Y.), Oct. 22, 1934.

Eagle would be just as blue as before because the system would still be there."[32]

Thomas had been highly critical of the NRA almost since its inception — and of the irascible Johnson, in particular, telling a Harvard audience earlier that year that the colorful NRA administrator reminded him of "a barker outside a lion tent." Predicting that the National Recovery Administration would become "as useless as the Prohibition Amendment or as a straitjacket more appropriate to a Fascist State than a socialistic one," Thomas said that under Johnson's leadership there was a "growing tendency in the NRA to use it as means for forbidding strikes and pickets." He also charged that it had done little for the nation's consumers.[33]

Though mainly focusing on economic issues, Thomas also occasionally attacked his Democratic opponent, ridiculing the two-term incumbent for failing to take a position on the crucial issues facing the country. "Senator Copeland stands for everything," quipped Thomas, "consequently he stands for nothing. He seems to have an automatic calculator which always places him on the popular side of the question. When he isn't sure on what side the people of New York would want him to be, he develops a cold and doesn't vote in Congress."[34]

A few weeks before the election, Thomas told reporters that he had found no great enthusiasm for the New Deal on the campaign trail — and even less for a return to the days of Hoover — resulting in what he described as an "amazing apathy," a sense of hopelessness among the electorate, particularly among farmers in rural, upstate New York, many of whom were forced to slaughter their cattle because they couldn't afford the high price of western grain to get them through the winter. "As long as relief is kept up there will continue to be a sort of discontented acquiescence to the New Deal on the part of the worst off," sighed Thomas, who nevertheless predicted a sizable increase in the Socialist Party's support at the ballot box on Nov. 6th.[35]

His prediction proved uncannily accurate. While Marvin B. Baxter, the Socialist mayor of West Allis, posted one of the party's most impressive performances nationally by polling more than 20 percent of the vote in a five-way free-for-all in Wisconsin's fourth

---

[32] "Thomas Asks Socialization of Industries," *Schenectady Gazette*, Sep. 25, 1934.
[33] "Norman Thomas Lauds Roosevelt," *Boston Globe*, Mar. 16, 1934.
[34] "Socialists Taunt Foes; Norman Thomas, Solomon, Claessens Speak Before 200 Here," *Daily Argus* (Mount Vernon, N.Y.), Oct. 22, 1934.
[35] "Thomas Sees Wide Gains," *New York Times*, Oct. 14, 1934.

congressional district, the New York Socialists didn't fare too badly themselves that autumn.

B. Charney Vladeck, a member of the Municipal Housing Authority, received more than 22,000 votes, or nearly 12.2 percent, in Brooklyn's eighth congressional district and Rachel Panken, the wife of municipal judge Jacob Panken, posted a respectable showing in the fourteenth congressional district in Manhattan while Harry W. Laidler, the longtime executive director of the League for Industrial Democracy and a close friend of Thomas, made a relatively strong showing in his race for New York City controller. Thomas himself garnered an eye-opening 194,952 votes, or 5.27 percent — his strongest statewide showing ever — in the U.S. Senate contest. Thomas received 128,824 votes in New York City alone, an impressive figure that narrowly eclipsed Solomon's statewide total of 126,580.[36]

Sadly, it was the last reasonably significant showing Thomas would ever make as a candidate for public office. For all intents and purposes, the 1934 mid-term elections also marked the end of what he later described as the Socialist Party's "Indian Summer," the period marking the early years of the Great Depression when the party briefly experienced a resurgence of sorts.[37]

Thomas, to nobody's surprise, remained characteristically busy in the months following his unsuccessful Senate campaign. As mentioned in a previous chapter, in March of 1935 the intrepid Socialist conducted a whirlwind speaking tour of the South, drawing much-needed public attention to the plight of the nation's 1.4 million sharecroppers — black and white alike — who were barely eking out a living or had been displaced altogether as a result of the New Deal's Agricultural Adjustment Act (AAA), which incentivized landowners to reduce production acreage in order to drive up agricultural prices.

A monumental failure on the part of Henry Wallace's Department of Agriculture, the policy of encouraging production restrictions — paying farmers to reduce acreage, plow under their surplus crops and slaughter their excess livestock to achieve income "parity" — didn't provide for any substantive safeguards for the powerless tenant farmers. As Thomas so stridently pointed out in speeches and newspaper articles across the country, tens of thousands of sharecroppers had been displaced by the department's implementation of the cotton acreage reduction program

---

[36] "Hylan Vote 15,489 in City's Canvass," *New York Times*, Nov. 28, 1934.
[37] Shannon, *The Socialist Party of America*, p. 235.

alone. The lowly tenant farmer, he astutely observed, was the true "Forgotten Man" of the Great Depression.

Appalled by the deplorable living conditions he witnessed first-hand during his tour of the South — worse than anything he had ever seen in the most destitute slums of New York City — Thomas tried as he might to convince the Secretary of Agriculture to change his policies.

Despite a Democratic wave the previous autumn, nothing was happening in the nation's capital.

"Once more," wrote columnist Walter Lippmann, "we have come to a period of discouragement after a few months of buoyant hope. Pollyanna is silenced and Cassandra is doing all the talking." Lippmann's much-quoted column appeared in March 1935, several months after the Democrats had swept the 1934 mid-term elections. Despite enjoying overwhelming majorities in both houses of Congress, not a single important piece of the president's legislative agenda had reached his desk.[38] Roosevelt was growing impatient, but more importantly so were the American people, a nation still stuck in the throes of the Great Depression.

Irritated and restless voices of discontent began rising across the country, leading to considerable speculation that a formidable third-party challenge — or perhaps several of them — could be in the offing in 1936.

From the airwaves came the mellow-rich and mesmerizing voice of Father Charles E. Coughlin, the outspoken and controversial radio priest from Royal Oak promising economic and social justice while stepping up his vituperative and personally abusive attacks on the president; from the Deep South rose the noisy populism of Huey Long, the incendiary Winn Parish wave maker and his Every-Man-a-King "Share Our Wealth" program; and from the Midwest emerged the dynamic Floyd Olson, the radical Farmer-Laborite governor of Minnesota who famously warned Roosevelt in early 1935 that the New Deal would have to move much faster if he was going to avoid a serious third-party challenge and who was now believed to be seriously entertaining the possibility of building a national Farmer-Labor Party. All three men had actively supported Roosevelt against Hoover in 1932. To a country in despair, none of them could be taken lightly.

Roosevelt was worried — and for good reason. A poll commissioned by the Democratic National Committee in the spring of

---

[38] Alan Brinkley, *Voices of Protest: Huey Long, Father Coughlin and the Great Depression* (New York, 1982) p. 3; Arthur M. Schlesinger, Jr., *The Age of Roosevelt: The Politics of Upheaval* (New York, 1960, 2003), p. 8.

1935 showed Louisiana's Huey Long polling in double-digits with a relatively impressive 10.9 percent of the vote nationally, including grabbing a worrisome 14.5 percent in the Solid South. By comparison, Coughlin — the self-appointed spokesman for the country's dispossessed — was only garnering about one percent of the vote nationally in the DNC survey.[39]

The most striking feature of the poll, as Alan Brinkley pointed out, was the fact that Huey Long's support appeared to be evenly distributed across the country and he seemed to poll as strongly in urban areas as he did in rural communities. "In short," wrote Brinkley, the poll "strongly suggested that Long was neither a regional nor a rural figure," but a candidate with a truly national following.[40]

While the poll, which didn't include Gov. Olson's name, showed Roosevelt prevailing easily over a generic Republican opponent, it nevertheless exposed some of the president's potential vulnerabilities, particularly among voters on relief — an unusually large category given that the country's jobless rate was still hovering at a staggering 17 percent, down from a high of 25 percent at the height of the Great Depression. In that category, the insatiably ambitious Kingfish was polling at an impressive 16.7 percent nationally with nearly six percent favoring Coughlin and other prospective third-party candidates.[41]

Though keeping a close eye on Coughlin and Olson, the latter of whom had bluntly predicted an agrarian revolt at the ballot box unless farmers were paid a fair price for their products, the Roosevelt administration — believing they could ultimately prevent the Minnesotans from rebelling — was particularly concerned about Long's potential as a third-party candidate in 1936.[42] Unlike the pragmatic Farmer-Laborites, the fiery and unpredictable Louisianan — a "Messiah of the Masses" challenging concentrated wealth and power perhaps more effectively than any other political figure during the Great Depression, as historian Glen Jeansonne so brilliantly described him — clearly marched to the beat of his own drummer.[43]

Thomas, too, kept tabs on all three men during this period. Strongly supportive of the idea of organizing a national farmer-labor party, he and other Socialists were particularly interested in

---

[39] Brinkley, *Voices of Protest*, pp. 207-209, 284-286.
[40] Ibid., p. 208.
[41] Ibid., p. 286.
[42] George H. Mayer, *The Political Career of Floyd B. Olson* (Minneapolis, 1951), pp. 295-296.
[43] Glen Jeansonne, *Messiah of the Masses: Huey P. Long and the Great Depression* (New York, 1993), p. 189.

Gov. Olson's activities. Hoping to draw the immensely popular governor out on the prospects of a third-party coalition involving the Socialist Party and other like-minded groups, Thomas had sent Olson a congratulatory letter a year earlier, shortly after Minnesota's flourishing Farmer-Labor Party adopted a largely socialistic program, but had been somewhat disappointed by the governor's short and noncommittal response.[44]

A year later things appeared a bit more promising and Thomas, though not in attendance, watched with anxious anticipation as the Minnesota Farmer-Laborites, led by congressman Ernest Lundeen and Howard Y. Williams, national organizer for the Farmer-Labor Political Federation, agreed to take part in a planned a national third-party conference in Chicago over the 4th of July holiday in 1935 — a two-day gathering chaired by University of Chicago economist Paul. H. Douglas. Williams' FLPF collaborator Alfred M. Bingham, a New York publisher and son of former Republican Senator Hiram Bingham of Connecticut, was named secretary.

In addition to the Minnesota FLP and the Wisconsin Progressives, representatives from more than a half dozen organizations, including the National Farm Holiday Association, Howard Scott's Technocracy movement and the left-wing Commonwealth Builders, a precursor to the Seattle-based Washington Commonwealth Federation, attended the conference. The Socialists sent three observers.

The third-party conference, moreover, drew a wide array of leading progressives from across the country, including Tom Cheek, longtime president of the Oklahoma Farmers' Union, Mayor C. Henry Bloome of Rockford, Illinois, a former alderman who had been elected to the city's top office two years earlier on a Progressive ticket — a party backed by that blue-collar city's powerful Labor Legion — left-wing congressman Vito Marcantonio of New York who was one of two delegates that later bolted the convention, and Wisconsin's Thomas R. Amlie, a Progressive Party congressman sympathetic to Huey Long's Share Our Wealth program and Dr. Francis E. Townsend's Old Age Revolving Pension Plan who had consistently agitated for a far more radical New Deal.

One of the leaders who issued the call for the third-party conference, the 38-year-old Amlie was named permanent chairman of

---

[44] Swanberg, *Norman Thomas: The Last Idealist*, p. 157.

the organization, which dubbed itself the American Commonwealth Political Federation after delegates to the convention couldn't agree on a name for the yet-to-be organized party. Midwesterners naturally wanted "Farmer-Labor Party" as its name while participants from the East generally preferred the "Commonwealth Party."

Olson, whose name was prominently mentioned at the conference as a possible candidate for the presidency on the party's ticket in 1936 — went out of his way to avoid the meeting, but did send a somewhat encouraging note stating that he was "completely committed to a production-for-use program" and was ready to follow any movement that advocated such a policy. Wisconsin's Robert M. La Follette, Jr., who had also been mentioned as a presidential possibility, was also noticeably absent.

Denouncing it as a poor rehash of Upton Sinclair's EPIC movement, "which is nothing more than a gigantic public works program," and Huey Long's "share-the-wealth panaceas" with a few vague phrases about production-for-use, the Socialists immediately dismissed the Chicago conference as "much ado about nothing."[45]

Noting Olson's inexplicable absence from the meeting, Thomas also realized the fledgling movement inaugurated in Chicago wasn't going anywhere. The Socialist Party, he insisted, had to be an integral part of any realistically viable national Farmer-Labor Party, but there was little chance of that happening. By joining in the kind of coalition launched in Chicago, wrote Thomas, Socialists would be forced to tone down their message to "a kind of native American radicalism" — not socialism. He also didn't believe there was enough evidence of substantial organized labor and farmer support in Chicago to warrant a serious discussion of the matter.[46]

In the meantime, Thomas turned his attention to Huey Long and Father Coughlin — two potential rivals in 1936, both of whom he strongly believed represented a rising spectrum of fascism.

To the merriment of a New York audience, the Kingfish had once debated Thomas at Mecca Temple on the question of Long's seven-point scheme to "soak the rich" — a debate evoking hearty laughter, but clearly won by the lanky, quick-witted Socialist.[47]

During their spirited exchange, Thomas accused the Louisiana

---

[45] "Much Ado About Nothing," *Socialist Call*, July 13, 1935.
[46] "At the Front by Norman Thomas," *Socialist Call*, July 13, 1935.
[47] "Long and Thomas Argue Capitalism," *New York Times*, Mar. 3, 1934.

senator of aspiring to become a dictator. "It was just that sort of talk, Senator Long," asserted Thomas, "that Hitler fed the Germans."[48]

Some Socialists, of course, derisively referred to Long's "Share the Wealth" motto as "Spare the Wealth."[49] The vast majority of party members believed that Long's proposal was nothing more than a panacea, a half-baked idea that couldn't possibly deal effectively with the nation's growing income inequality. Thomas shared that view.[50]

"What we want — what we need," declared Thomas in responding to the Louisianan's proposal to redistribute the wealth by limiting an individual's fortune to $50 million, "is not a system which grotesquely keeps up its fat, a system such as this of Senator Long, which requires a surgical operation every so often to keep it in balance, to keep the capitalist below his $50,000,000 and the family unit above its $5,000, but a normal, wholesome functioning system" — a fair and equitable system of planning, production and distribution as proposed by the Socialist Party of America.[51]

In the summer of 1935, the Socialist Party's national executive committee authorized Thomas's long-anticipated tour of Louisiana, a trip that he had been planning since completing his campaign in Arkansas' share-cropping country on behalf of the Southern Tenant Farmers' Union. "We want it distinctly understood that the campaign is not merely anti-Long," said Thomas in announcing that he would be leading a sound-truck caravan through Louisiana in October. "It is directed against the whole demagoguery of Long's share-the-wealth program."[52]

Hoping that Thomas would have an opportunity to personally confront the profane prophet of prosperity for millions left behind during darkest days of the Great Depression who naively believed that Long's utopian proposals would indeed "make every man a king," party members were understandably excited to learn of the planned excursion into Huey Long's bailiwick. "Norman Thomas's invasion of Louisiana for the Socialist Party," wrote Richard Babb Whitten, executive secretary of the party's New Orleans local, "will be the first realistic work in America to defeat the political forces making for fascism."[53]

---

[48] Jeansonne, *Messiah of the Masses*, p. 120.
[49] "Turning the Tables: Norman Thomas Invades Huey's Home Territory," *Socialist Call*, June 1, 1935.
[50] "Long and Thomas Argue Capitalism," *New York Times*, Mar. 3, 1934.
[51] Ibid.
[52] "Norman Thomas to Campaign Against Share-the-Wealth," *Alexandria Daily Town Talk* (Alexandria, LA), July 13, 1935.
[53] "Norman Thomas Invades Huey's Home Territory," *Socialist Call*, June 1, 1935.

Meanwhile, the Louisiana senator was visibly irritated by Thomas's planned tour and went so far as to accuse President Roosevelt, with whom he had broken politically, of furtively sending the Socialist leader into his home state. "Anyway," cracked the supremely confident Kingfish, "Thomas won't get three people in Louisiana to listen to him."[54]

In the meantime, the Socialists vigorously denied Long's assertion that the party's speaking tour had been prompted by FDR. "Huey Long is justly nervous about Norman Thomas' forthcoming speaking tour in Louisiana," the party's national committee said in a statement in mid-July. While stating that they fully expected Thomas to deflate the Louisiana senator as a potential candidate for the presidency, the party took strong exception to the charge that President Roosevelt was sending Norman Thomas to Louisiana, calling Long's bald-faced assertion "utterly false." The Socialists then reminded the senator's constituents that they had been highly critical of the New Deal program of artificial scarcity — calling FDR's policy "wholly unsound" — but were equally critical of "Long's quackery."[55]

In the weeks leading up to Thomas's planned tour of the Pelican State, the Socialists accused the Louisiana "dictator" of deliberately undermining their caravan, charging that the flamboyant and demagogic Long had pressured local sound truck operators to refuse to rent vehicles and equipment to them. Long was clearly worried about the Thomas tour and his plans to warn Louisianans about their senator's "dangerous tendencies."[56]

Thomas never got the chance. The Socialist Party cancelled their planned caravan within days of Huey Long's assassination in September.

Returning from a speaking tour of the Midwest in late October, Thomas threw himself wholeheartedly into New York City's municipal election, campaigning tirelessly for the party's aldermanic and state assembly candidates — Old Guard and Militants alike — in the closing days of the 1935 off-year elections.[57]

In addition to dozens of candidates running for various municipal and judicial offices, the Socialist Party fielded nominees in each of the city's 65 aldermanic districts and placed no fewer than 62 candidates for the state assembly on the ballot — one in each of the

---

[54] "Socialist Threatens Drive Against Long," *Palm Beach Post*, July 14, 1935.
[55] "Socialist Party Brands Story by Long as 'False,'" *Monroe News-Star* (Monroe, LA), July 15, 1935.
[56] "Worried," *Socialist Call*, June 22, 1935; "The Life and Death of Huey Long," *Socialist Call*, Sep. 14, 1935.
[57] "Thomas in Whirl Wind N.Y. Campaign Windup," *Socialist Call*, Nov. 2, 1935.

assembly districts within the city.[58] Though the 1935 campaign marked the last time many of the Old Guard, including the colorful August Claessens who was running for alderman in Manhattan's sixth district, would appear on the ballot under the Socialist Party emblem, the sheer number of candidates running on the party's ticket was a remarkable feat for an organization so badly divided.

The party's left-wing faction did much of the heavy lifting that autumn. The *Socialist Call*, which had been launched in February, even offered to print 100,000 free copies of a special election supplement in an effort to spur and intensify interest in the campaign.[59]

Thomas, who always did more than his fair share on the stump, spoke at dozens of meetings and campaign events, including making nine separate appearances during the final weekend of the campaign.[60] He also found time to address a huge rally sponsored by the Westchester County Socialists in nearby Yonkers on the eve of the election.[61] For the first time in its history, the Socialist Party in Yonkers had a full slate of candidates in the field, headed by mayoral candidate Otto A. Reigelman.[62]

In appearance after appearance in the city that never sleeps, Thomas hammered away at an increasingly unpopular issue: the city's new sales tax. Speaking in the Flatbush section of Brooklyn, the lanky former presidential candidate denounced the sales tax — a regressive tax championed and signed into law by Mayor La Guardia, who had vigorously opposed a national sales tax as a congressman only a few years earlier — as akin to "soaking the poor to help the poor."

Thomas also sharply criticized the fact that $15 million of an estimated $66 million to be collected in its first year would be used to repay outstanding loans to the banks. Then as now, the financiers on Wall Street — anticipating a new income stream — predictably had their collective snouts buried deep in the public trough, making sure they slurped up more than their fair share of the city's revenues. Based on a funding formula in which the state of New York agreed to match the revenues from the city's sales tax dollar for dollar with a federal match of $2 for every dollar raised by the tax,

---

[58] "Complete List of the Candidates in the City," *New York Times*, Nov. 3, 1935.
[59] "100,000 Copies of CALL Election Supplement Offered Free to New York," *Socialist Call*, Oct. 19, 1935.
[60] "Thomas in Whirl Wind N.Y. Campaign Windup," *Socialist Call*, Nov. 2, 1935.
[61] "Norman Thomas Will Speak in Yonkers Monday Night; Socialist Leader at Giant Westchester County Rally," *Socialist Call*, Nov. 2, 1935.
[62] "Reigelman for Yonkers Mayor," *Socialist Call*, Nov. 2, 1935.

Thomas contended that the exorbitant payment to the bankers would ultimately deprive unemployed New Yorkers of some $60 million they desperately needed.[63]

Latvian-born Jacob Hillquit, brother and law partner of the late Morris Hillquit, and Samuel A. De Witt, a former Socialist member of the New York Assembly, were the party's marquee candidates that autumn. The 66-year-old Hillquit was a candidate for the Court of General Sessions in Manhattan while De Witt ran for a seat in Congress in a special election to fill a vacancy created by the resignation of four-term Democratic Rep. William F. Brunner, who gave up his congressional seat in September of 1935 shortly after winning the Democratic nomination for sheriff.

A poet, playwright and longtime friend of novelist Upton Sinclair, the 44-year-old De Witt was waging the second of three campaigns in a span of two years for the state's second congressional district seat in Queens. In a long-shot bid for the same seat a year earlier, De Witt polled a disappointing 3.2 percent of the vote yet somehow managed to finish ahead of the City Fusion Party's nominee — the "good government." reform-minded party that had played such a decisive role in La Guardia's remarkably stunning victory against the Tammany machine a year earlier. In finishing third in that race, the biographically-neglected Socialist also outpolled the Communist Party's Paul P. Crosbie, a World War I veteran and former Harvard classmate of Franklin D. Roosevelt who once served as a district captain in the powerful Queens Democratic organization, by more than 4,500 votes.[64] The left-wing De Witt ran again in 1936, but fared even worse than he had in his two previous attempts to win that seat.

A frequent candidate on the Socialist ticket, De Witt had been one of the five fabled Socialists expelled from the New York Assembly in 1920 on the grounds of disloyalty to the United States and for their membership in a "disloyal organization composed exclusively of perpetual traitors" intent on overthrowing the government by force and violence.[65]

Working closely with some of those who later assumed leadership roles in the party's Clarity Caucus, including civil rights attorneys Max and Robert Delson, De Witt was also a key ally of

---

[63] "Socialists to End Campaign Tonight," *New York Times*, Nov. 3, 1935; Mason B. Williams, *City of Ambition: FDR, La Guardia, and the Making of Modern New York* (New York, 2013), p. 103.

[64] "Paul P. Crosbie, 68, Communist Leader," *New York Times*, Aug. 2, 1949.

[65] "Expel the Five Socialist Assemblymen, Urges Majority Report, Charging Treason; Roosevelt to Oppose Ouster Move," *New York Times*, Mar. 31, 1920; "Oust 5 Socialists; Will Compel Party to Purge Itself," *New York Times*, Apr. 2, 1920.

Thomas and the Militants in their bitter struggle with the Old Guard during this period.[66] Concerned more with their own preservation than the party's historic revolutionary mission due to their increasingly close ties to some of the unions, he strongly believed that the party's right-wing forces had grown both complacent and corrupt and had virtually turned the Socialist Party of New York into a self-serving business of sorts. In his eyes, the Old Guard was beyond redemption and had to be replaced with fresh, new leadership.[67] "We must bury the old set-up and start a new Socialist Party right here, using whatever good timber there is left of the old house, but building mainly on the youth for foundation," he wrote Thomas earlier that year.[68]

Despite a gallant, last-minute flurry of activity by the party's titular leader, the Socialists took a drubbing at the polls on November 5th. Unable to capitalize on his late brother's extraordinary popularity, Hillquit was trounced in his bid for a judgeship while De Witt mustered only 4,901 votes, a decline of nearly a full percentage point from his showing the previous November.[69]

The 1935 off-year elections marked only the second time in a dozen years that Thomas himself wasn't a candidate for public office. Thomas, who voted early that morning at a cigar store on Third Avenue in New York's twelfth assembly district, spent most of Election Day tending to his regular activities, which included a fair amount of reading and writing. Earlier that morning, somebody had mischievously splashed the sidewalk of Thomas's polling station with red paint, but most of it had been mopped up before he and his wife arrived to cast their ballots.[70]

The election was barely over when the party's Old Guard launched yet another offensive in its long simmering feud with the party's left-wingers, setting off a series of fireworks that would eventually lead to the party's virtual disintegration.

Calling for the ouster of those allegedly engaged in "disruptive" activities, the New York City central committee, led by Louis Waldman, the party's state chairman, voted 69 to 47 to reorganize the local party by eliminating the party's militant faction, triggering what was arguably the most damaging split in the party's history.

---

[66] Johnpoll, *Pacifist's Progress*, p. 80.
[67] Swanberg, Norman Thomas: *The Last Idealist*, p. 189.
[68] Samuel A. De Witt letter to Norman Thomas, Thomas Papers, Mar. 31, 1935.
[69] "Socialists Poll 'Gratifying' Vote," *New York Times*, Nov. 6, 1935.
[70] "Farley Casts Early Vote," *New York Sun*, Nov. 5, 1935.

The purge had been a long time in the making and was clearly aimed at those who adhered to the party's revolutionary Declaration of Principles adopted in Detroit by a lopsided vote of 99-47 and later ratified by the party's entire membership in the spring of 1934. That declaration, while generally adhering to social democratic principles, called for proletarian rule in the event the capitalist system collapsed in general chaos and confusion — a doctrine strongly opposed by the Old Guard, which viewed it as an open declaration in favor of armed insurrection and a "dictatorship of the proletariat."

While Thomas himself wasn't subjected to immediate expulsion, the Old Guard made it clear that they were gunning for him, charging the two-time presidential candidate with willfully ignoring the party's rules forbidding cooperation with Communists in agreeing to publicly debate Earl Browder on the respective merits of socialism and communism.

Thomas, of course, scoffed at the idea that communism would begin to take hold in the United States. "We will have fascism in this country long before we have communism," he said. Acknowledging that he was a lifelong pacifist, Thomas nevertheless believed that the forces of fascism must be countered as vigorously as possible. "Let's do all we can now peacefully to minimize the need for violence," he said. "Let's make it plain we will do all in our power, and that if a fascist dictator comes with blood and iron we will not lie down as Germany did."[71]

That was more or less the same point he made during his highly controversial debate with Earl Browder at New York's Madison Square Garden the following week when he declared that both Communists and Socialists "recognize that they are in common danger from fascism in America and, if it is by any means possible, intelligent Socialists and Communists do not want to have to learn to get along together only in a concentration camp here in America."[72]

In refuting the specific charge that he had violated party policy in agreeing to debate Browder, Thomas said that his forthcoming November 27th debate with the Communist Party leader was being sponsored by the *Socialist Call*, a newspaper founded earlier that year which served as the official organ of the Socialist Party in Arkansas, Illinois, Missouri, Ohio and West Virginia. The paper had also been endorsed by recognized state party organizations in

---

[71] "Socialist Head Predicts Path Ahead for U.S.," *Decatur Daily Review*, Nov. 21, 1935.
[72] "Left Wingers Unite Fronts," *Des Moines Register*, Nov. 28, 1935.

five other states, including California and Massachusetts, and by the Young People's Socialist League of America.

Thomas maintained that the party's local organization had no right to interfere with a debate being sponsored under the paper's auspices. If the Old Guard-dominated local organization insisted on taking unfavorable action against him, he vowed to appeal their decision to the party's higher councils, including the national executive committee. "In the name of democracy," fumed Thomas, "our friends do some tyrannical things. This is not a bona fide attempt to maintain party discipline."[73]

There was obviously no love lost between Thomas and the Old Guard at this point, as evidenced in a separate interview earlier that week when the battle-scarred veteran of ten political campaigns in less than a dozen years wryly observed that the Old Guard, desperately clinging to power, was "like a mother who can't believe their child (the Socialist Party) has grown up. Some of them had even rather see the child dead than anyone else in control."[74]

A few days later the breach had clearly widened with both sides promising to carry the factional fight all the way to the party's national convention in Cleveland the following spring. Thomas was clearly in a fighting mood, describing the central committee's decision to oust the party's left wingers as "exactly the kind of thing that Hitler did in Germany — first he took the power and then he had a referendum."[75]

An all-out war ensued. In early December, Waldman called for Leo Krzycki's resignation as the party's national chair on the grounds that the Milwaukee Socialist had presided at the debate between Browder and Thomas at Madison Square Garden a few days earlier, a debate that he had once facetiously described as a "love feast," a celebration of sorts marking the beginning of a united front between the Socialist and Communist parties.

Describing it as a conspiracy engineered by the Communists, Waldman insisted that a united front between the two parties could have but one effect — precisely as the Communists intended all along — and that was the "destruction" of the Socialist Party nationally. "That Mr. Thomas, whom the Socialists have twice honored by naming him as their standard bearer, and Mr. Krzycki, the party's national chairman, should take part in this conspiracy

---

[73] "Socialists to Oust Party Left Wing," *New York Times*, Nov. 18, 1935.
[74] "Norman Thomas Sees Bogey of Fascism in U.S. by 1940," *Rochester Democrat and Chronicle*, Nov. 20, 1935.
[75] "Socialist Breach in State Widens," *New York Times*, Nov. 18, 1935.

in clear defiance of the decisions of the national executive committee, of which both of them are members, reveals the utter lack of responsibility which characterizes the present leadership of the Socialist Party nationally," said Waldman.[76]

A few nights later some 44 members, reportedly representing no fewer than thirty-six branches of the party, walked out of a meeting at the Rand School when the Old Guard refused to reconsider the expulsion of the party's militant faction. The secessionists immediately held their own meeting on East Seventeenth Street and formed their own organization — a move that was heartily endorsed by Thomas, who told the bolters that the way was now clear for the genuine Socialists in New York City to organize a strong and powerful party of the working class.[77]

The Old Guard wasted little time in responding, sharply criticizing Thomas for aligning himself with a group that believed in violence, force and armed insurrection. "It is regrettable that Norman Thomas, against his own better judgment, allowed himself to become the window dressing for a minority group which for six months has been persistently working to split the party. Instead of leading, he is being led," the party said in a joint statement issued by city chairman Algernon Lee and party secretary Julius Gerber.[78]

By then, both sides had dug in their heels. Rapprochement wasn't possible. In the meantime, the party's state committee, which was headed by Waldman, a man insanely jealous of Thomas's tremendous popularity among the party's rank and file, proclaimed that the left-wing bolters were an "outlaw organization" without standing in the party.

Meanwhile, both factions — the city's regular organization, headed by the scholarly Algernon Lee, the educational director of the Rand School of Social Science, and the secessionist militant group — held heavily-attended meetings to discuss how they should proceed. The always busy Thomas, who was in Detroit at the time helping to settle a dispute between rival automobile unions, stated in a letter addressed to the left wingers meeting at Irving Plaza that "we are not splitting the party," but "saving it from those who would destroy it."[79]

The rift quickly widened beyond the city and state limits. It was now a national battle, especially since it was widely assumed that

---

[76] "Waldman Insists that Krzycki Quit," *New York Times*, Dec. 2, 1935.
[77] "Socialist Meeting Split," *New York Times*, Dec. 5, 1935.
[78] "Socialists Weigh Thomas Expulsion," *New York Times*, Dec. 6, 1935.
[79] "State Socialists Outlaw Left Wing," *New York Times*, Dec. 9, 1935.

the party's NEC, controlled by the Thomas faction, would eventually revoke the New York party's state charter and organization and recognize the bolting left-wing group, which was then being led by temporary chairman Charles B. Garfinkel, a Russian-born former state assemblyman from the Bronx, as the official state party.

But the Old Guard wasn't about to go down without a fight, declaring that they were confident they would have the support of an "overwhelming majority" of party members in the city, state and nation in their fight against "any effort to foist upon us members who openly admit that they favor dictatorship and armed insurrection."[80] At the time, there were approximately 17,000 dues-paying members in the party nationally and as many as 100,000 registered voters across the country who were enrolled as Socialists, including slightly more than 15,000 in the state of New York.

Despite such bravado, the party's right-wingers were deeply worried. In fact, Waldman himself had long anticipated the schism brewing in the party and had already thoroughly prepared for the inevitability of a leftwing takeover.

Returning from the Detroit convention that famously approved the controversial Declaration of Principles, Waldman began quietly securing the party's most valuable assets in New York. Fearing that the militant-controlled NEC would eventually revoke the party's New York State charter and expel members of the Old Guard, the former Socialist assemblyman had spent the better part of 1935 and 1936 carefully rewriting the charters, bylaws and constitutions of the various assets controlled by the party's subsidiaries and devising legal techniques to protect their most valuable property, which included, among others, the *Jewish Daily Forward*, the world's leading Jewish newspaper which at the time had millions of dollars in reserve funds, the *New Leader*, a robust weekly newspaper with a fairly large circulation, radio station WEVD, and the Rand School of Social Science, which, coupled with the school's 2,100-acre Camp Tamiment in the Pocono Mountains, was worth a small fortune, from falling into the hands of the left-wingers.[81]

Waldman had good reason to worry. In the weeks immediately following the decision to expel the militants, the Old Guard suffered one embarrassing setback after another. Among other things, attorney Louis P. Goldberg, the author of the expulsion motion and a longtime law partner of the Old Guard's Charles Solomon, was soundly repudiated by his own Knickerbocker Village

---

[80] "Socialists Press Fight for Control," *New York Times*, Dec. 10, 1935.
[81] Waldman, *Labor Lawyer*, pp. 272-273.

branch, which sided with the seceding group.[82] Worse yet, Waldman's own assembly branch in downtown Brooklyn voted to support the Thomas faction while Algernon Lee's branch in Greenwich Village also went on record in favor of the left-wing bolters.[83]

The left-wing secessionists were elated. "New York's Socialists are speaking plainly," crowed Jack Altman, temporary secretary of the newly-constituted city central committee and business manager of the *Socialist Call*. "They have begun to make it plain that they want the wholesome leadership of Norman Thomas and the group he represents. The desire for a clean, healthy party is sweeping the branches. Waldman and Lee," he continued, "have been defeated by the Socialists who know them best, the members of their own district organizations. The membership is with us. It rejects the undemocratic policies of Waldman and Lee. Socialism is making itself heard in New York. The fine traditions of our past will soon be revived and wipe out the ignominy which the Old Guard has created."[84]

In its struggle for control of the local party, Thomas's left-wing faction was supported by a number of party luminaries, including Professor Reinhold Niebuhr, Protestant missionary Sherwood Eddy, writer Harry W. Laidler, African-American trade union organizer Frank R. Crosswaith, Elsie Gluck of the International Ladies' Garment Workers Union (ILGWU) and labor leader Murray Gross, many of whom believed the Old Guard's real objective was to deny Thomas the party's presidential nomination in 1936.[85]

Jack Altman was one of many others who shared that view, but went even further. "It is quite true that Old Guard leaders oppose Mr. Thomas for the presidential nomination," he said in a press statement on December 13, "but their opposition to Mr. Thomas as a candidate seems to be part of a general opposition to the running of any candidate against Roosevelt." Altman maintained that it was therefore "reasonable to assume that the Old Guard does not desire to carry on a fight against Roosevelt and the policies he represents. Apparently, they want to leave the field to Roosevelt and are now seeking to eliminate Norman Thomas. They will not succeed," he concluded. "The Socialists of this city and of the nation are opposed to the Roosevelt regime."[86]

---

[82] "Sees Old Guard Rejected," *New York Times*, Dec. 15, 1935.
[83] "Socialist Camps Fight for Control," *New York Times*, Dec. 11, 1935.
[84] "Waldman Loses in Home District," *New York Evening Post*, Dec. 10, 1935.
[85] "61 Socialist Leaders Back Thomas Group," *New York Evening Post*, Dec. 27, 1935.
[86] "'New Leader' or 'New Dealer'?" *Socialist Call*, Feb. 22, 1936.

The battle between the warring factions became even more heated when Thomas, returning from a speaking tour in the Midwest, personally declared war on the Old Guard. This was a fight to the finish, asserted Thomas in accusing the Old Guard of "sabotage and tyranny" in the administration of party affairs. It was clear that he no longer wanted any of them in a position of leadership. "The Old Guard have read themselves out of the party," he elaborated, adding that "if they want to be officers of any organization in the future, they will have to set up their own organization. And that organization will be a rival organization of the Socialist Party."

Pulling no punches during a somewhat lengthy interview with a *New York Times* reporter at his home on East Eighteenth Street in Gramercy Park, Thomas predicted that the Socialist Party would be completely reorganized, not only in New York City but also at the statewide level with control of the party shifting from Waldman and other members of the Old Guard to the left wing insurgents. Thomas also strenuously denied that he and the militants were trying to push the party in a Communist direction or that they were fighting the Old Guard in order to bring about a united front with the Communist Party. "It is utterly false and ridiculous that we advocate armed insurrection," he said. "What we want is a clean, inclusive, aggressive Socialist Party. What we reject is the rule or ruin policy of the handful of Old Guard leaders."

Thomas's remarks were quickly criticized by James H. Maurer, his vice-presidential running mate in 1928 and 1932. The 71-year-old Maurer, who was reportedly in declining health, accused Thomas of using "Tammany tactics" in an effort to seize control of the party while denouncing the left-wing bolters as "betrayers of the cause."[87] Waldman also weighed in, accusing Thomas of deliberately orchestrating the party split "because he knows that the New York state delegation will be unanimously opposed to his nomination for president at the national convention in May." It was the only way Thomas could possibly rid himself of potentially strong and dangerous opposition in Cleveland and capture a third consecutive presidential nomination, explained Waldman.[88]

Claiming to represent a majority of the party's statewide membership, the Thomas faction held an emergency convention in Utica in late December to lay the groundwork for a new state committee to supplant the existing Old Guard-dominated committee led by Waldman. In formally repudiating the Old Guard and setting up the machinery for a complete reorganization of the Socialist

---

[87] "Thomas Declares War on Old Guard," *New York Times*, Dec. 12, 1935.
[88] "Old Guard Replies to Thomas Threat," *New York Times*, Dec. 13, 1935.

Party in New York state, it was Thomas's hope that the newly established state committee would be recognized by the party's national executive committee, which planned to meet in Philadelphia the following week.[89] During the two-day convention, the leftists elected a new state committee and named attorney Max Delson as the party's new state chairman.[90]

As expected, the Old Guard responded with appropriate fury, denouncing Thomas as "a traitor working for the destruction of the party." One right winger called him "a lost leader," while others referred to him as "an open enemy of the party" and "an ally of the Communists." Citing a recent statement issued by the Pennsylvania state committee in support of the Old Guard, Waldman himself issued a stern warning to the party's national executive committee, cautioning that any action on the part of the NEC in recognizing the seceding New York insurgents would result in an irreconcilable split in the party nationally.[91]

Most observers expected the NEC, meeting in Philadelphia on January 4th, to revoke the charter of the existing state organization and officially recognize the secessionist left wing group headed by Thomas as the party's regular state organization. Though maintaining that its attempts to free the party of factionalism, dual organizations and members who openly advocated communism and armed insurrection, New York's Old Guard didn't even bother to send a delegation to Philadelphia, but the militants were well represented.

In addition to Delson, the group's chairman, Jack Altman and David P. Berenberg also appeared in person to press the left-wing case, reminding committee members that the Old Guard was deliberately sabotaging the party and unconstitutionally excluding younger members from actively participating in party work. Dr. Louis Sadoff, a militant dental surgeon and veteran of the late Morris Hillquit's 1932 mayoralty campaign who once proposed that the party be divided into separate Old Guard and left-wing units, each with its own bureaucracy, but agreeing to field joint electoral tickets — an idea that briefly intrigued Thomas — also spoke in favor of the left-wing faction.[92]

In a compromise of sorts, the party's national executive committee — by a vote of 8 to 2 — deposed the existing state committee

---

[89] "Move to Supplant Socialist Regime," *New York Times*, Dec. 29, 1935.
[90] "'Left' Socialists Set Up State Body," *New York Times*, Dec. 30, 1935.
[91] "Thomas Called 'Traitor,'" *New York Times*, Dec. 30, 1935.
[92] "Leftists Favored in Socialist Feud," *New York Times*, Jan. 5, 1936; Johnpoll, *Pacifist's Progress*, p. 164.

headed by Waldman, and in its place named a fifteen-member committee to run the state organization until a new state convention could be held, but no later than June 30. The NEC also suspended the charter of the New York state organization and placed the party in receivership.

The Thomas faction, which initially backed a proposal by Connecticut's Devere Allen, recognizing the left-wing group as the party's bona fide state organization, agreed to the compromise in the face of spirited opposition from NEC members Albert Sprague Coolidge of Massachusetts and Pennsylvania's Darlington Hoopes, both of whom passionately argued that giving the charter to the secessionist group would be setting a terrible precedent.

James Oneal of New York, an Old Guard member of the national executive committee who stormed out of the Philadelphia meeting, bitterly objected to the compromise, arguing that it was both "arbitrary" and "illegal" and essentially gave control of the party to Thomas's left-wing group.[93]

Back in New York, the Old Guard defied the NEC's ruling and vowed to ignore the suspension. They appeared to be on pretty solid ground. Barring a legal challenge, the existing state committee headed by Waldman remained the legally constituted state committee in New York.

In a statement released a day after the NEC meeting in Philadelphia, the Waldman-led organization maintained that it would "continue to function as the duly constituted state party" in New York and squarely placed the blame for the split at Thomas's feet, saying that "to Norman Thomas, who led the fight, who started out several years ago to fashion a party in his own image, and who finally realized that the Socialist Party is bigger than any individuals whom it may temporarily assign to a position of leadership, goes what credit he can derive for having split the national organization."[94]

In the meantime, James Maurer again attacked his former running mate, accusing Thomas of violating a trust and helping to destroy the party. Maurer, who had refused to meet with Thomas when he traveled to Reading immediately following the NEC meeting in Philadelphia, said that he was astounded by the news of the New York suspension and "the part played by Norman Thomas in this dirty deal." The former president of the Pennsylvania State Federation of Labor also exhorted party members throughout the country to raise their voices in protest against the

---

[93] "Socialists Depose New York Chiefs; Feud Spread Seen," *New York Times*, Jan. 6, 1936.
[94] "'Old Guard' Defies Socialist Ouster," *New York Times*, Jan. 7, 1936.

NEC's actions. "If it is tolerated," he concluded, "then democracy in the Socialist Party is dead."[95]

Connecticut's Jasper McLevy joined Maurer in lining up with the Old Guard a few days later. In a tersely-worded telegram to the NEC, the Bridgeport mayor sharply criticized the committee for suspending the New York charter, calling it a "disservice to the party and its principles" while making "a mockery out of the democracy that is fundamental in our organization." He also accused the committee members of willfully violating every tradition and ideal of the Socialist movement.[96]

Buoyed by the support of party members throughout the country, the Old Guard overwhelmingly repudiated the NEC's suspension of the New York state organization's charter during a crowded meeting at historic Beethoven Hall in Manhattan in mid-January. More than a thousand party members cheered as Waldman challenged the legality of the NEC's action. This was obviously going to be a bloody battle. "The national executive committee has declared war on the Socialists of New York State and we accept the declaration," thundered the recently deposed party chair. "So far as we are concerned and so far as all loyal Socialists in the country are concerned, the national executive committee no longer exists, for it has misused its power and acted in flagrant violation of the party constitution and democratic procedure."[97]

Waldman's faction received a substantial boost a few days later when a conference of a half-dozen eastern states, including the Maryland, Massachusetts and Pennsylvania state committees, met in a two-day session at the Hotel Pennsylvania and adopted a resolution declaring that the recent suspension by the NEC, consisting of a majority of Thomas supporters, was a violation of the party constitution and an attempt to establish a dictatorship over the party in New York and elsewhere. The resolution, which also enjoyed the support of the Finnish and Jewish Federations, also demanded that the party's charter be restored within thirty days.[98] Before adjourning, the delegates elected a seven-member committee to carry the fight for restoration of the New York state organization's charter into other states throughout the country.[99]

What initially began as a bitter internal schism seemingly limited to New York City had suddenly mushroomed into a battle for

---

[95] "Maurer Aids Fight on Thomas Faction," *New York Times*, Jan. 8, 1936.
[96] "Socialist Mayor Assails Thomas," *New York Times*, Jan. 10, 1936.
[97] "Socialists Here Defy Thomas Wing," *New York Times*, Jan. 17, 1936.
[98] "Socialist Breach Here Is Widened," *New York Times*, Jan. 19, 1935.
[99] "Socialists Press Factional Battle," *New York Times*, Jan. 20, 1935.

the party's soul involving virtually every Socialist Party member in the country, including a few thousand dues-paying members who never really belonged to either warring faction. The same thing was true for an even larger number of registered Socialists throughout the country. Dating back to the glory years of Eugene V. Debs when the party still held significant promise for the country's working class, most of them were loyal party supporters who regularly voted for the party's ticket, regardless of which faction happened to be in control of the party nationally.

Ignoring the NEC's suspension of its charter, the Waldman-led state committee continued to function as the legally recognized Socialist Party in the state and were fully prepared to defend their control of the party in the state's April 2 primary, a hotly-contested election that would not only determine which faction controlled the party's city and state organizations, but also the selection of delegates and alternates to the party's national convention in Cleveland later that spring.

Contending that fewer than a quarter of the party's statewide membership supported the left-wing organization, Waldman more than welcomed a showdown with the militants in the upcoming spring primary, saying that he was confident that the party's rank-and-file membership "can distinguish between communism, even if it is of the milk-and-water variety which the Socialist left wing advocates, and social democracy."[100] The militants immediately accepted the challenge.[101]

The Old Guard, however, had seriously underestimated the depth of Thomas's appeal, particularly among party centrists who didn't belong to either faction, many of whom rallied to his side during this bitterly divisive factional struggle. Jessie Wallace Hughan of the War Resisters League was one of them. Hughan, who had been highly critical of the party's militants in the past, famously told Thomas that as a rank and file member of the party she wasn't siding with either faction, but did "stand unequivocally for Norman Thomas."[102]

A number of other notable centrists — those who never identified with the Old Guard or the party's left-wing faction — also supported Thomas and the militants. Among the more influential moderates who backed Thomas during this duel to the death were Julius Hochman, general manager of the joint board of the International Ladies Garment Workers Union (ILGWU), former state

---

[100] "Waldman Seeks Test in Primaries," *New York Times*, Feb. 10, 1936.
[101] "Welcome Primary Test," *New York Times*, Feb. 12, 1936.
[102] Swanberg, *Norman Thomas: The Last Idealist*, p. 191.

party chairman S. John Block, a Manhattan attorney who had been one of the lawyers who defended the expelled Socialist state assemblymen in 1920, and writer Kirby Page, a longtime peace advocate and former editor of *The World Tomorrow*.[103]

As one might have expected, there was no shortage of sniping between the two camps as both sides prepared for what promised to be a bitter and bruising primary. One of the most damning incidents occurred during the final week of February when the Thomas-led militant faction accused the Old Guard of supporting FDR's reelection — a charge emphatically denied by the Waldman faction.[104]

Responding to an article written by Harry Rogoff, a longtime managing editor at the *Jewish Daily Forward*, in the February 15 issue of the *New Leader*, a newspaper controlled by the Old Guard, the militants accused the *New Leader* of tossing its hat in the air for the Roosevelt administration.

Rogoff, who later became the *Forward's* editor-in chief and an early critic of the war in Vietnam, was replying to a radio address by Thomas in which the former Presbyterian minister sharply criticized Franklin Roosevelt. Rogoff had vigorously defended the Democratic president and the New Deal in his article, maintaining that the American people were "in a much sounder condition, from a general economic point of view, than they were a year or two ago" and that "the New Deal has diminished the numbers of the hungry and the homeless, of the desperate and the impoverished, of the ruined and the embittered" — all of which was true.

But that's not how the left wingers viewed it. Rogoff's piece, wrote the editors of the pro-Thomas *Socialist Call*, was proof that the Waldman-led right wingers had "broken from the tradition of the Socialist movement." The Old Guard had betrayed the cause and was now "ready to support and even now defends the starvation relief program of a capitalist politician, Franklin D. Roosevelt." Urging readers to "brush aside the debris of the Old Guard," the paper continued:

> Socialists throughout the country may have been incredulous when it was charged that the Old Guard is disloyal to the basic concepts with which the Socialist Party has been identified. They now have surrendered the last element of Socialist character.

---

[103] "Socialist Party Split Leads to Primary Fight," *Binghamton Press*, Mar. 31, 1936.
[104] "Old Guard Socialists Disavow Roosevelt," *New York Times*, Feb. 24, 1936.

FACTIONALISM & FASCISM
> Much in the fight that has been going on within the party now becomes clear. The fight against Norman Thomas and the national executive committee of the party now becomes more understandable. It is a fight to prevent the Socialist Party from putting up a campaign against Roosevelt.[105]

As a result, Waldman and the Old Guard were clearly put on the defensive. "The *New Leader* never carried the editorial attributed to it by the supporters of Norman Thomas," Waldman clumsily tried to explain. "What did appear was a signed article by a contributor taking issue with Norman Thomas that Roosevelt was making for fascism, but pointing out that the President was far removed from socialism and characterizing his policies as inadequate."[106]

The militants, meanwhile, made Rogoff's article a major theme in the April primary. "Socialist sympathizers can now understand the situation, the issue having been so clearly drawn by the very words of the Old Guard," observed the *Socialist Call*. "This puts an end to the internal party fight...there is no doubt that the Old Guard is not merely out of the Socialist Party; it is out of the Socialist movement as well."[107]

With legal control of the city and state organizations at stake, both factions in New York City filed complete slates for state committee and for 24 delegates and alternate delegates to the party's May 23 national convention in Cleveland. Both sides also designated partial slates in upstate New York, where at least sixty-six of the eighty-eight assembly districts in that region were expected to be contested. It was the party's first major primary fight in the Empire State since the party's historic left-wing split in 1919.[108]

Charging that the insurgents were trying to commit the party to communist doctrines, the Old Guard immediately announced the formation of a Committee of One Thousand in support of its campaign and were later bolstered by the support of state committee members and representatives of other party-affiliated groups in Connecticut, Maryland, Massachusetts, Montana, New Jersey, Pennsylvania and Rhode Island, as well as the party's Finnish and Jewish Federations. Those groups and individuals, claiming to represent more than half of the party's dues-paying membership nationally, included Mayor McLevy's Bridgeport organization

---

[105] "'New Leader' or 'New Dealer'?" *Socialist Call*, Feb. 22, 1936.
[106] "Old Guard Socialists Disavow Roosevelt," *New York Times*, Feb. 24, 1936.
[107] "'New Leader' or 'New Dealer'?" *Socialist Call*, Feb. 22, 1936.
[108] "Socialist Slates Widen Party Split," *New York Times*, Mar. 4, 1936.

and Pittsburgh optometrist and perennial candidate William J. Van Essen, a longtime leader of the Socialist Party in western Pennsylvania.[109]

Accusing the Old Guard of essentially functioning as the left wing of the New Deal, Norman Thomas consistently denied that he and the militant faction intended to from an alliance with the Communist Party, asserting that what Socialists really needed was a "party strong enough in its fight against capitalism that it will make communism superfluous." There were better ways, he added, "for me to prove that I am a Socialist than cursing the Communists."[110]

Both factions made last-minute pleas for support on the eve of the election. Speaking on behalf of the Old Guard, Mayor McLevy of Bridgeport said that the party's increasingly left-wing philosophy had brought "chaos and confusion" into the ranks of the party. "The Detroit Declaration of Principles," he said in a radio address, had "divided the party on fundamentals" and that no reasonably informed member could afford to straddle the issue. "The Right Wing," he continued, "stands for repeal of the declaration and the restoration of democratic doctrines and principles upon which the Socialist Party was founded. We are opposed to dictatorship, either in the government or in the party."

Appearing jointly with McLevy on New York's WEVD, Waldman reminded listeners that Thomas, as a member of the national executive committee, had voted in favor of a united front with the Communists. Like McLevy, he also pointed out that the Declaration of Principles adopted in Detroit favored the use of violence, minority rule and dictatorship. "No amount of denials from the Left Wing," he concluded, "can conceal the facts. The declaration is there for everybody to read."

Thomas, in a statement released later that evening, described their joint appearance as a "desperate plea of men afraid of the truth." The real issue in the campaign, declared Thomas, was about rescuing the Socialist Party in New York from "an Old Guard oligarchy which tried a little fascist purge of its own to expel illegally those of us within the party who stood for aggressive socialism."[111]

From the moment the polls closed on April 2, it was clear that the Old Guard had suffered a staggering defeat. "It is now clear

---

[109] "Appeals to Socialists," *New York Times*, Mar. 9, 1936; "Old Guard Plans Socialist Battle," *New York Times*, Mar. 29, 1936.
[110] "Thomas Ridicules Charge He is a Red," *New York Times*, Mar. 30, 1936.
[111] "Socialists Issue Final Vote Pleas," *New York Times*, Apr. 2, 1936.

that we have won a very large majority on all the party committees," an elated Thomas said in a statement issued from his headquarters on election night. "We have also won a large majority of the total votes. For this victory we have to thank the rank and file, young and old, who put in a magnificent campaign not merely for victory in the primaries, but for constructive socialism.

"I am sure that the great majority of those who have supported the Old Guard are glad that a campaign of misrepresentation against us and for a socialism scarcely as radical as the New Deal has lost," continued Thomas. "This victory closes the chapter of intra-party controversy and opens a new chapter of victory for the workers. There is room and welcome in our ranks for all who know that socialism is our only hope of freedom, peace and plenty."[112]

As the votes slowly trickled in on primary night, the Old Guard nevertheless remained confident that it would ultimately prevail against the Thomas-led Militants. "The Left Wing has played its last card," asserted Waldman earlier in the evening. "There is no longer any basis for its existence in New York. The result is complete repudiation of Norman Thomas in his home state. He has been snowed under and will never be heard from again."[113]

It turned out that Waldman had been a little too quick in declaring victory. Within a few hours, it was clear that a majority of party members, particularly in New York City, had emphatically rejected the Old Guard, which prevailed in only a dozen of the state's 42 congressional districts in the battle for delegates to the party's national convention while failing to gain a majority on the all-important state committee. The results were utterly devastating for Waldman and the party's right-wingers.

Waldman himself was beaten badly in his bid to become a delegate to the national convention, losing to Isadore Fried, a young attorney who was later actively involved with the Liberal Party in Queens, by a decisive margin of 115 to 79.[114] In addition to Waldman, the Old Guard's casualties included such seasoned veterans as James Oneal, editor of the *New Leader*, August Claessens, party veteran Julius Gerber, and his son, G. August Gerber, and former state assemblyman William Karlin. Though narrowly managing to become a delegate to the party's national convention, Algernon Lee of the Rand School also went down to defeat when he was

---

[112] "Left Wing Leading in Socialist Fight," *New York Times*, Apr. 3, 1936.
[113] "Primary Sidelights," *Socialist Call*, Apr. 11, 1936.
[114] "Thomas Wing Wins Primaries in City," *New York Times*, Apr. 4, 1936; "New York Primary Results," *Socialist Call*, Apr. 18, 1936.

trounced in his bid for a seat on the party's state committee, losing to Joseph P. Lash, a CCNY student and leader in the Student League for Industrial Democracy, by two dozen votes.[115]

While losing control of the party in Buffalo, long an Old Guard bastion, the biggest blow to the party's right-wingers occurred in their stronghold in New York City. Polling a combined 3,552 votes to the Old Guard's 2,730 votes, the Thomas faction elected twenty of the city's twenty-four delegates to the party's national convention while winning an astonishing 48 of the city's 62 state committee seats.[116]

Interestingly, one of the victorious left-wingers was Margaret Lamont, daughter-in-law of Thomas W. Lamont, a longtime senior partner in J.P. Morgan & Company who recently took over as chairman of the investment firm following the death of J.P. Morgan, Jr., several months earlier. Married to philanthropist and prolific author Corliss Lamont, she defeated Simon Berlin, chairman of the Old Guard-dominated city committee, by a nearly five-to-one margin in a bid for the party's nineteenth congressional district delegate slot.[117] Thomas's wife, Violet, was also a big winner in the primary, drubbing the Old Guard's Louis P. Goldberg by a better than two-to-one margin in the race for delegate in the 16th congressional district.[118]

While the militants, whose campaign had been ably managed by Dr. Louis Sadoff, were ecstatic at the outcome, the Old Guard, claiming that it still controlled a majority of the party's dues-paying membership in the state — and the nation, for that matter — steadfastly refused to concede defeat and promised to carry their fight all the way to the party's national convention in Cleveland in late May.[119]

It was a vow they were determined to keep, even as the left-wingers solidified their hold on the statewide organization by trouncing the Old Guard at the party's state committee meeting at Buffalo's Hotel Statler a few weeks later, a two-day meeting in which Harry Laidler was elected as the party's new state chairman by defeating Waldman by a margin of 60 to 42. Knowing the odds were heavily stacked against him, Waldman didn't even bother to

---

[115] "Thomas Credits Young Aids With Defeat of Old Guard," *New York Evening Post*, Apr. 3, 1936; "New York Primary Results," *Socialist Call*, Apr. 18, 1936.
[116] "Thomas Wing Wins Primaries in City," *New York Times*, Apr. 4, 1936; "New York Primary Results," *Socialist Call*, Apr. 18, 1936.
[117] "Wife of Lamont's Son Wins in Socialist Vote," *New York Evening Post*, Apr. 3, 1936.
[118] "New York Primary Results," *Socialist Call*, Apr. 18, 1936.
[119] "Socialist Fight Foreseen," *New York Times*, May 11, 1936.

attend the meeting.[120] A few weeks later, the Socialist Party's NEC restored the party's state charter, vesting power in the left-wing committee chosen in Buffalo.[121]

Despite the double drubbing at the hands of the militants, who walloped them in both the primary and the subsequent reorganizational state committee meeting in Buffalo, the Old Guard still wasn't about to throw in the towel and promised a floor fight in Cleveland. August Claessens, who had briefly chaired the Buffalo meeting before being replaced by leftist Max Delson, who acted as temporary chairman, declared that "the fight is not yet over. We'll go to the national convention in Cleveland, where we believe we will control half or more of the votes."[122]

If unsuccessful in wresting control of the party from Thomas and the militants at the national convention, the party's right-wingers also threatened to launch a new party. "The Old Guard will not stand at the gates of a disintegrating Socialist Party which has by its policies abandoned a Socialist position and has become anything but socialistic," thundered Waldman shortly before the Cleveland convention. "It will organize a party independent of the present Socialist Party and will seek to draw to itself the elements of organized labor whose political awakening in the real sense has been indicated by interest shown in federal and state labor legislation."[123]

As expected, both factions sent full delegations to the party's national convention, where the final battle was expected to be waged.[124]

---

[120] "Left Wing of Socialists Achieves Sweeping Victory," *Buffalo Courier-Express*, Apr. 18, 1936.
[121] "State Socialists Get Back Charter," *New York Times*, May 13, 1936.
[122] "Left Wing Socialists Win First Victory in State in Forty Years," *Kingston Daily Freeman* (Kingston, N.Y.), Apr. 18, 1936.
[123] "State Socialists Get Back Charter," *New York Times*, May 13, 1936.
[124] "Seating Fights Face Socialist Convention," *New York Times*, May 17, 1936.

Chapter VII

Battling a Radio Priest

Party infighting aside, 1934 and 1935 were two of the busiest years in Thomas's extraordinarily hectic life. The ubiquitous Socialist was seemingly everywhere at once, involved in every kind of social and economic justice struggle imaginable.

In addition to all of his other activities, Thomas somehow also found time to write four more books between his 1932 and 1936 presidential campaigns — his fourth, fifth, sixth and seventh books.

The first of those four volumes, *The Choice Before Us*, was published by Macmillan in 1934 and was followed six months later with the publication of *Human Exploitation in the United States*. In 1935, Thomas wrote *War: No Glory, No Profit, No Need*, in which he expounded on his own pacifist beliefs while arguing that shared abundance and interdependence were the only ways to guarantee a secure and lasting peace. His fourth book during this period — the somewhat awkwardly titled *After the New Deal, What?* — was something of a campaign book, written as Thomas prepared to mount his third bid for the presidency in 1936.[1]

With his party badly fractured and forced to compete with radio priest Charles E. Coughlin's Union Party — a movement that appealed to thousands of disaffected voters on both ends of the political spectrum — Thomas's 1936 presidential campaign proved that the third time isn't always a charm and, indeed, can sometimes be downright disastrous.

Convening at the Municipal Auditorium in Cleveland, Ohio, in late May, Thomas was nominated for the presidency for a third

---

[1] Gregory, *Norman Thomas: The Great Dissenter*, pp. 147-149.

consecutive time, but his nomination wasn't unanimous as several right-wingers, including Bridgeport's Jasper McLevy, voiced their opposition when his name was placed in nomination by New York's Harry Laidler.[2]

Emerging from a field that included Mary Donovan Hapgood of Indiana, a member of the party's national executive committee and wife of Powers Hapgood, national organizer Roy Burt of Illinois and national party chairman Leo Krzycki of Milwaukee, George A. Nelson, president of the National Farmers' Union, was named as the party's vice-presidential candidate. A one-time Republican, the 62-year-old Nelson was a former state legislator and Speaker of the Wisconsin assembly. A former member of the University of Wisconsin board of regents, Nelson had carried the Socialist Party's banner in Wisconsin's 1934 gubernatorial contest.

Proclaiming that FDR's "Old Deal" had failed miserably, the Socialist platform called for the social ownership of the nation's mines, railroads, utilities and other key industries, as well as a thirty-hour workweek. It also called for a $6 billion federal relief package for the country's unemployed. Among other things, the Socialist platform also advocated an old-age pension program for persons over sixty to be financed by levying taxes on incomes and inheritances, and called for adequate medical care for the sick and disabled. The party of Debs and Thomas also proposed immediate relief for the nation's debt-ridden farmers, including the adoption of a crop insurance program and easier government credit. The party also promised a drastic reduction in the nation's military arsenal and pledged its "unconditional opposition to any war."

Ironically, the convention also radically modified the controversial "Declaration of Principles," removing the language that had so incensed the party's conservative members two years earlier, but it was too late to heal the breach between the Old Guard and the party's younger militants. There was simply too much bad blood between the warring factions to prevent what was now viewed as an inevitably damaging split from which the party would never fully recover.

Any hope of reconciliation between the warring factions ended when the convention refused to seat the Old Guard's New York delegation. Despite last-ditch attempts by Pennsylvania's Darlington Hoopes and Milwaukee Mayor Daniel Hoan to work out some sort of sort of compromise in the seating of New York's 44-member delegation — Hoopes had proposed seating half of each

---

[2] "Thomas Nominated Again by Socialists," *New York Times*, May 26, 1936.

delegation while Hoan suggested seating only a dozen Old Guard delegates, precisely the number the right-wingers were clearly entitled to based on the results of the state's April 2 primary — both proposals were swiftly rejected by the convention and the entire left-wing delegation was seated.[3]

The party's right-wingers were furious and made it clear they weren't going to hand over control of their state organizations to the militants. "We built up the Socialist Party in our states and we do not intend to surrender these organizations to an oligarchy," fumed Pennsylvania's William Van Essen.[4] Joining right-wing delegates and a handful of contested delegates from other states, New York's "Old Guard," led by Waldman, quickly established a competing organization — the Social Democratic Federation (SDF) — an organization that Thomas predicted would be "peculiarly unsuccessful."[5] Speaking to reporters at the convention shortly after the Old Guard announced their intentions, Thomas said that he could almost find it in his heart to feel sorry for them.[6]

Waldman's newly-christened organization briefly launched a "People's Party" in early July, but quickly joined New York's newly-created American Labor Party shortly thereafter.[7] Waldman, who was promptly named to the American Labor Party's executive committee while retaining his role as chairman of the short-lived People's Party, publicly endorsed President Roosevelt in late August. In announcing his support for FDR in a radio address over New York's WEVD, the labor lawyer couldn't resist taking a potshot at Thomas, faulting his one-time friend for pretending not to recognize any real differences between Roosevelt and Republican challenger Alf Landon.[8]

Unlike Waldman, Thomas wasn't too worried about Landon's candidacy. There was little danger of a Republican victory that year. Barring some sort of unexpected crisis or catastrophic event, the Socialist candidate was firmly convinced that FDR would be reelected — and probably by a relatively large margin.[9]

Having virtually conceded Roosevelt's reelection long before jumping into the fray, Thomas realized that his third bid for the White House would be much more difficult than the campaign he

---

[3] "'Old Guard' Forms New Party after Socialist Ouster," *New York Times*, May 25, 1936.
[4] "'Left' Socialists Win Round Here," *Cleveland Plain Dealer*, May 23, 1936.
[5] "Thomas Nominated Again by Socialists," *New York Times*, May 26, 1936.
[6] "'Old Guard' Forms New Party after Socialist Ouster," *New York Times*, May 25, 1936.
[7] "Old Line Socialists Form Own Party," *New York Times*, July 6, 1936; "Former Socialists Join Labor Party," *New York Times*, Aug. 2, 1936.
[8] "Waldman for Roosevelt," *New York Times*, Aug. 28, 1936.
[9] "Sees Roosevelt's Return," *New York Times*, May 6, 1935.

waged four years earlier, but he had no idea just how lonely a quest it would turn out to be, particularly since many of his previous supporters were now clearly in Roosevelt's corner.

Thomas, who would have preferred to run for Congress that year, had serious doubts about mounting another campaign for the presidency in 1936. According to biographer Harry Fleischman, he only consented to run again because "he did not feel that the New Deal was enough of an answer to America's problems as to make a Socialist campaign unnecessary."[10]

The former Presbyterian minister was also motivated to run, in part, by the misleading suggestion of economist James P. Warburg and others that Roosevelt was carrying out much of the Socialist Party's agenda through his New Deal programs. "Roosevelt did not carry out the Socialist platform," quipped Thomas, "unless he carried it out on a stretcher."[11]

According to Thomas, Roosevelt was anything but a Socialist. Citing the banking crisis as an example, the tall, increasingly white-haired Socialist faulted the president for putting the banks in order only to "turn them back to the same groups to wreck them." Speaking in Boston the previous October, he had also criticized FDR's housing administration for "making promises but failing to produce houses." Likening the Roosevelt administration to the Mussolini and Hitler regimes in Europe, Thomas famously asserted that the Roosevelt administration was all show and little substance, providing "little bread but much circus."[12]

That's not to say that Thomas didn't have some good things to say about some of FDR's New Deal policies, especially the creation of the Tennessee Valley Authority (TVA), which he called the only genuinely socialistic project of the New Deal — describing it as "a beautiful flower in a garden of weeds."[13] During his 1944 campaign eight years later, Thomas said the TVA exemplified "what socialism might do" and some of the techniques it would use in the process. "We've learned much that can be done under TVA and rural electrification," he told a group in Nashville that year. While his party advocated the nationalization of the country's natural resources, Thomas explained that a Socialist administration would favor a variety of social controls, including municipal ownership

---

[10] Fleischman, *Norman Thomas: A Biography*, p. 171.
[11] Ibid.
[12] "Roosevelt 'No Socialist'; Norman Thomas Likens President to Hitler and Mussolini," *New York Times*, Oct. 7, 1935.
[13] Philip Abbott, *The Exemplary Presidency: Franklin D. Roosevelt and the American Political Tradition* (Amherst, MA, 1990), p. 91.

of local water and power systems and more fully involving the cooperative movement in a democratic socialist economy. It wasn't as though the president and bureaucrats in Washington would be running everything, he said.[14]

Yet it was precisely because of Roosevelt's policies during the Great Depression that enthusiasm for the Socialist message dampened considerably, proving to be as damaging to the country's leading third party as any of its deep and irreconcilable internal schisms.

Roosevelt had impressed many Socialists long before he ran for president. Belle Waldman, wife of labor lawyer Louis Waldman, recalled a chance encounter with FDR in Rochester during the 1928 New York gubernatorial campaign. Her husband was running for governor on the Socialist ticket against Roosevelt at the time. After their brief meeting, Belle looked at her husband and said, "I think Roosevelt is the most formidable opponent that the Socialist Party will ever have in the United States. He will charm your working class away from you."[15] No truer words were ever spoken.

This was something Thomas freely acknowledged, but not until many years later. "What cut the ground out pretty completely from under us…was Roosevelt in a word," wrote Thomas. "You don't need anything more."[16]

With the positive effects of the New Deal beginning to be felt, life on the campaign trail was a difficult one for Thomas in 1936. Not only did he have to compete with Father Coughlin's Union Party on his right, but he also had to contend with the Communist Party's Earl Browder on his left.

As mentioned previously, the Socialist Party's Old Guard had been particularly upset when Thomas agreed to debate Browder in Madison Square Garden in late 1935, denouncing the event as a "united front" and potentially damaging to the party. "We regard unity with the Communists, either on specific or general issues, as suicidal from a tactical standpoint and as thoroughly dishonest as a matter of principle," charged the explosive Waldman, who also demanded that Krzycki resign as the party's national chairman for presiding in the debate between Thomas and Browder. "The Socialist Party has traditionally and constantly adhered to the principles of democracy and freedom," continued Waldman, while the

---

[14] "Thomas Lauds TVA Ideas," *New York Times*, Oct. 9, 1944.
[15] Waldman, *Labor Lawyer*, pp. 183-184.
[16] Schlesinger, *The Politics of Upheaval*, p. 180.

Communist Party "believes in dictatorship and the suppression of civil rights. Between the two there is an unbridgeable gulf."[17]

Although the Thomas-Browder debate was certainly no "love feast," as Thomas's critics asserted, the Communist leader had cleverly succeeded in driving yet another wedge between the Socialist Party's warring factions. Browder, who clearly enjoyed the discord he was provoking in the rival Socialist Party, widened the gulf between the two factions even further when he proposed — once again — a joint Thomas-Browder ticket on the eve of the Socialist convention in Cleveland. As was the case earlier in the year, Thomas adamantly rejected the offer.[18]

The Communist leader, campaigning that year under the slogan "Defeat Landon at all costs; vote for Earl Browder" — the first part of that bewildering slogan reflecting the party's true goal in 1936 — had initially suggested such a ticket earlier in the year when he approached Thomas and other Socialists about working together in forming a broad-based Farmer-Labor Party, an idea abandoned shortly thereafter on orders from Moscow, which feared that a mass Farmer-Labor Party that year would split the country's progressive vote resulting in a Republican-Liberty League fascist victory. Browder, who was still interested in providing some sort of "united front," then suggested a less threatening joint Socialist-Communist ticket headed by Thomas for president with Browder as his vice-presidential running mate — another proposal swiftly rejected by Thomas.[19]

Algernon Lee, president of the Rand School of Social Science and a protégé of the late Morris Hillquit, and Mayor Jasper McLevy of Bridgeport, Connecticut, were among the high profile Socialists who initially joined the fledgling Social Democratic Federation. Though they stuck it out for the duration of the 1936 presidential campaign, Darlington Hoopes, a three-term Socialist member of the Pennsylvania legislature, and other members of the party's stronghold in Reading, Pennsylvania, also eventually aligned with the SDF. Hoopes, who later headed the Socialist Party's presidential ticket in 1952 and 1956, only did so reluctantly.[20]

Thomas certainly didn't view the SDF's departure as a crushing setback to the party, nor was he particularly heartbroken to see

---

[17] "Waldman Insists that Krzycki Quit," *New York Times*, Dec. 2, 1935.
[18] "Reds Ask to Share Socialist Ticket," *New York Times*, May 20, 1936.
[19] Harvey Klehr, *The Heyday of American Communism: The Depression Decade* (New York, 1984), pp. 186-191; Fleischman, *Norman Thomas: A Biography*, p. 169; James G. Ryan, *Earl Browder: The Failure of American Communism* (Tuscaloosa, AL, 1997), pp. 109-110.
[20] Henderson, *Darlington Hoopes*, p. 76.

them leave. After all, their departure allowed him to consolidate his leadership of the party. The Social-Democratic Federation, he said caustically, wasn't "Socialist, Democratic or a Federation, but merely a half-way port to Tammany Hall."[21]

On August 2, the SDF, comprised largely of anti-Trotskyist members of the party's Old Guard, voted to formally affiliate with the newly-formed American Labor Party, thereby directly aiding Franklin D. Roosevelt's re-election campaign that year.
Coupled with the loss of Jasper McLevy's organization in Connecticut and the Finnish Socialist Federation — the party's largest foreign-language bloc — the departure of the Old Guard had a devastating effect on Thomas's party and on his 1936 candidacy.

In losing its right-wing elements — a loss comprising nearly 40 percent of the party's total national membership — the Socialist Party lost some of its most valuable financial and structural resources, including the powerful Workmen's Circle, one of the party's most reliable sources of revenue. In leaving their former comrades, the Old Guard took with them the *Jewish Daily Forward* and the *New Leader* — two of the party's most important print organs — as well as radio station WEVD, a New York City station launched nine years earlier in memory of the late Eugene V. Debs. Gone, too, was the Rand School. The Socialists also lost the support of the International Ladies' Garment Workers and the Amalgamated Clothing Workers unions, both of which subsequently followed the Old Guard into the American Labor Party.[22]

If things weren't already bad enough for Thomas, the party suffered yet another blow in July of that year when Reading's James H. Maurer, Thomas's running mate in 1928 and 1932 and a leading member of the party for forty years, abruptly announced his resignation from the party.

Denouncing the party's "trend toward communism," the 67-year-old "war horse" accused his one-time friend and ally Norman Thomas and the "sinister forces" on the party's national executive committee of "wrecking the Socialist Party" and betraying the confidence of the party's rank and file membership "by wrenching the party from its idealistic moorings of democracy."[23]

In announcing that he was leaving the party, Maurer was particularly critical of what he described as the autocratic nature of the party's national executive committee, then comprised of four law-

---

[21] Seidler, *Norman Thomas: Respectable Rebel*, pp. 163-164.
[22] Bell, *Marxian Socialism in the United States*, p. 169.
[23] "Maurer Quits Socialist Party on Communism," *Chicago Tribune*, July 8, 1936.

yers, three clergymen, three college professors and only one working-class individual — George M. Rhodes, president of Reading's Federated Trades Council, whose inclusion on the party's national executive committee was almost an afterthought. Saying that his resignation was the "most regrettable one in my entire political career," Maurer nevertheless said that he would continue to vote for the Socialist ticket.[24]

"The primary trouble is not old deal or new, more money or less," said Thomas in officially launching his candidacy in July at the National Education Association's national convention in Portland, Oregon. "You cannot have abundance in this machine age without planning for abundance. You cannot plan to produce or share abundance as long as profit for owners — increasingly absentee owners — is your god," he told the delegates.[25]

The New Deal, continued Thomas, had failed miserably. Again pushing the idea of a capital levy on wealth — an issue he strongly championed in 1932 — Thomas bemoaned the fact that ten to twelve million Americans were still unemployed while corporate profits were on the rise and wages — for those lucky enough to have a job — remained stagnant. While big business and the wealthy were recovering nicely, said Thomas, few others were sharing in the nation's so-called recovery. FDR's policies, he charged, were shamelessly "subsidizing scarcity — at great expense — and calling it prosperity." While it was true that the United States, like many other countries, was better off than in 1932, nobody in his right mind would say that the nation had achieved true prosperity, asserted Thomas, whose address to the NEA was aired nationally a few days later on NBC's Blue Network.[26]

Shortly after accepting his party's nomination, Thomas had been invited to address Francis Townsend's mass convention in Cleveland's huge Municipal Auditorium. Townsend, a 69-year-old physician who had launched a national movement for federal monthly pensions for those over sixty years of age — endearing him to millions of impoverished and dependent seniors — was, along with Father Coughlin and controversial evangelist Gerald L. K. Smith, one of the three principals behind the fleeting Union

---

[24] Ibid.
[25] "America Hears Thomas; Socialization is Solution, Parley Told," *Socialist Call*, July 11, 1936.
[26] "Norman Thomas: Socialists Give the Answer to the Problems of Today," *Socialist Call*, July 11, 1936.

Party insurgency that year — a short-lived movement that sapped much of the Socialist Party's strength.

Townsend, incidentally, had invited Roosevelt, Landon and Thomas to speak at his convention, but only Thomas and William Lemke — a Nonpartisan League Republican congressman from North Dakota and the Union Party's handpicked presidential candidate — accepted his invitation.

Amid a chorus of boos and catcalls, the dignified Socialist candidate proceeded to tell the 11,000 or so aging delegates why their founder's plan wouldn't work, likening Townsend's old-age plan to "treating tuberculosis with cough drops." His comment wasn't appreciated. The response from the Townsendites, wrote Fleischman, "sounded like a Greek chorus — with Thomas giving the solo and the audience responding antiphonally with boos."[27]

Playing "the role of one who shatters the faith of children in Santa Claus," as the *New York Times* described his appearance, Thomas also said it would be next to impossible to provide a lifestyle of abundance and security for the nation's elderly population under the present capitalist system in which profits were based on worker exploitation and "relative scarcity." It really didn't make any economic sense, he said, to expect people over sixty, those who were no longer working, to receive twice as much in income as they had received during their working years. "You can't keep capitalism and do this trick," he told them.[28]

While Thomas was speaking, Dr. Townsend and Francis Arbuckle, permanent chairman of the convention, had to step to the microphone repeatedly to remind the jeering delegates that Thomas was their guest and deserved to be heard. Smiling throughout his speech and dressed in a gray suit while looking as presidential as ever, the Socialist nominee displayed few signs of being unnerved or rattled by the hostile demonstrations that his words seemed to evoke.[29]

While addressing the issue of ballot access, Thomas took a swipe at the Rev. Gerald L. K. Smith, taking the rabble-rousing preacher to task for canonizing the late Huey P. Long of Louisiana, and questioning how he expected to get his candidate on the ballot in the state that his beloved "hero" had dominated until his assassination the previous year.

Reminding Townsend's followers that the late Robert M. La Follette found it impossible to get his name before the voters of

---

[27] Fleischman, *Norman Thomas: A Biography*, p. 171.
[28] "Thomas Tells Convention of Townsend Plan Flaws," *New York Times*, June 19, 1936.
[29] Ibid.

Louisiana a dozen years earlier, Thomas declared that it was virtually impossible for a minority party to get on the ballot in that state or to mount a write-in campaign for its candidate. Thomas said things were just as bad in Ohio, where a minor-party candidate needed 320,000 signatures to get on the ballot, and that Florida and North Carolina weren't much better.[30]

"If you really believe in democracy," Thomas thundered in a parting shot at Smith, "why don't you give it to us in the states where you live? Whatever you think about candidates and parties, isn't it fair in America that minority parties should be given a place on the ballot?"[31]

Thomas then turned his attention to Father Coughlin, reminding the Townsend throng that the radio priest still hadn't retracted his recent denunciation of the Townsend Plan as "economic insanity," and telling them that he didn't the think the nation would benefit from the kind of personal vilification and abuse Coughlin was heaping on FDR. If Coughlin was truly serious about rescuing the nation from the depths of depression, Thomas wondered why he hadn't proposed any constructive solutions, such as a capital levy on wealth.[32]

Two nights later and more than 500 miles from the boos and hissing of the hostile crowd that greeted him in Cleveland, Thomas continued his critique of the Union Party — a flash-in-the-pan that borrowed its name from Abraham Lincoln's 1864 reelection campaign — saying that he was skeptical that Father Coughlin's party would prove to be a serious threat to the two major parties that year.

"At this late date," he told the annual conference of the League for Industrial Democracy, meeting in Lake Mahopac, New York, "it will not be easy to get on the ballot. The only chance of success is a kind of triumvirate of Coughlin, Townsend and Smith, and historically triumvirates have usually fought among themselves." Rival messiahs, coupled with an ambitious politician and a platform reminiscent of the Nazi Party's platform in Germany during Hitler's rise to power a few years earlier, "do not make a very strong party," asserted Thomas. Conceding that it expressed "some noble aspirations" for the discontented, the Socialist standard-bearer ridiculed the Union Party's platform as one that "vaguely promises the impossible."[33]

---

[30] Ibid.
[31] Ibid.
[32] Ibid.
[33] "Thomas Ridicules New Lemke Party," *New York Times*, June 21, 1936.

The party's planks for farmers, stated Thomas, were entirely "for the benefit of land-owning farmers who will get the government to take their mortgages while they still grind the tenants down or exploit them as unmercifully as the planters exploit the sharecroppers in the cotton country, especially now in Arkansas." The Union Party's platform, he continued, promises plenty of profit for small businesses and farmers with a minimum of government interference, guaranteeing "in some miraculous way a nice living wage for workers in farms and factories" in small enterprises rather than conglomerates. "That's a good deal the way the Fascists began to talk in Italy and Germany," he said.[34]

Given the growing animosity between the Union Party's "three messiahs," Thomas joked that Lemke was "worse off than a man with three wives in the same house." Referring to Townsend as "Santa Claus" and describing Coughlin as "almost as good a showman as Hitler," Thomas said that Smith was "the worst demagogue of them all" and probably the most fascist. But he was also the least dangerous of the three, said Thomas, because he had no real following.[35]

Overshadowed throughout the campaign by the Union Party's William Lemke and virtually ignored by his major-party rivals, Thomas found himself subjected to attacks from those on his left throughout the 1936 campaign, particularly from the Communist Party's Earl Browder, who accused Thomas of "leading the Socialist Party into a blind alley" — a rather curious criticism since Browder's own candidacy that year was something of a charade, aiming all of its ammunition at Landon and the Republicans while openly rooting for Roosevelt's reelection.[36]

Thomas responded by accusing the Communists of colluding with the Democrats, charging that Moscow had instructed the CPUSA to provide "indirect support" to Roosevelt — a charge that infuriated Browder. "If correctly quoted," replied Browder, Thomas's speech "sounds as if it were borrowed from the Hearst editorial pages."[37]

Thomas also took his lumps from the Socialist Labor Party's Arnold Petersen, who said that when listening to Thomas, "one scarcely knows whether to weep or to laugh." The Socialist nominee, decried Petersen, was "a pathetic figure, walking around in

---

[34] Ibid.
[35] Norman Thomas, "Santa Claus with Three Wives: Lemke and His Three Messiahs," *Socialist Call*, Aug. 21, 1936.
[36] "Mild-Mannered Kansas Red Carries Communist Banner," *The Evening Leader* (Corning, N. Y.), July 16, 1936.
[37] Klehr, *The Heyday of American Communism*, p. 195.

circles in a hall of mirrors wherein all the reflections are of a posturing, gesticulating, but utterly futile Norman Thomas — self-acknowledged savior of capitalism."[38]

Undeterred, Thomas kicked off his seven-week autumn campaign on September 9th with a blistering attack on organized labor, declaring that neither Labor's Non-Partisan League, created in April by United Mine Workers of America president John L. Lewis and Sidney Hillman of the Amalgamated Clothing Workers of America to assist Roosevelt's re-election, nor the newly-established American Labor Party of New York "fill the requirements" of a genuine labor party. Maintaining that neither organization was independent of the capitalist parties, Thomas said that each was a "creature of powerful labor bureaucrats."[39]

Curiously, Thomas twice referred to Roosevelt's second term during his opening speech, as if the President's reelection was a forgone conclusion. "The course Roosevelt himself will take in his next term," he said in one reference, "depends far more upon what we make him fear than upon the blank check that Labor's Non-Partisan League would give him."[40]

Thomas, moreover, spent much of the 1936 campaign warning of the danger of creeping fascism in the United States — a danger he didn't detect in either of his major-party opponents, but rather from the Union Party's motley crew of Charles E. Coughlin, Gerald L. K. Smith, Francis Townsend and U.S. Rep. William Lemke. On the campaign trail, Thomas repeatedly referred to the little-known North Dakota congressman as "the puppet candidate of Father Coughlin." Going for the jugular, he also charged that the Union Party was the closest "parallel we have to American Fascism," adding that the party's platform resembled "the platform of the Nazi Party of Germany."[41] At one point in the autumn campaign, Thomas even went so far as to accuse Republican candidate Alf Landon of "using Lemke as a stooge to beat Roosevelt."[42]

In fairness to Lemke, however, the North Dakota congressman had never been particularly close to Coughlin and wasn't one of the large handful of senators and congressmen who regularly traveled to Royal Oak to consult with the influential priest. His relationship with Coughlin really didn't begin to blossom until early in 1936 when he co-sponsored the Frazier-Lemke Act, legislation

---

[38] Arnold Petersen, "Political Potpourri," *Weekly People*, Vol. XLVI, No. 29, Oct. 17, 1936.
[39] "Thomas Starts 7-Week Tour," *Reading Eagle*, Sep. 9, 1936; "Thomas Assails Labor's Politics; Sees Danger in Lemke," *New York Times*, Sep. 9, 1936.
[40] Ibid.
[41] "Thomas Flays Coughlin Group," *Pittsburgh Press*, Aug. 10, 1936.
[42] "Thomas Sees Party Periled," *Milwaukee Journal*, Oct. 13, 1936.

designed to guarantee government refinancing of all farm mortgages. Coughlin immediately took to the airwaves in support of Lemke's proposal.

Nor was Lemke some sort of country bumpkin, as he was so often portrayed in the press. The son of a prosperous farmer, Lemke was a Yale-educated attorney and had carefully built a political reputation as a spokesman for his state's agricultural interests.

On the other hand, he certainly didn't look like a typical presidential candidate. "Lemke is not a human being at all, but a werewolf," quipped H. L. Mencken. "I had several long gabbles with him in Cleveland. Get him on his favorite project — to dig 250,000 lakes out in cow country — and you will howl. With his glass eye, his bald head, and his large yellow freckles, he is the most astonishing looking candidate that I have ever seen."[43]

As a leader in Arthur C. Townley's Non-Partisan League, Lemke succeeded in making the League the dominant influence in North Dakota politics during his tenure as state chairman of the Republican Party from 1916 to 1920. He served as the state attorney general for the next year and a half, but was recalled in the same special election that forced Gov. Lynn Frazier from office. Though he and Frazier had framed some of the most progressive legislation in North Dakota history — laws that delighted the farmers yet infuriated the business community — the freckled-faced politician had made some powerful enemies. "If you had shot me on the streets of Fargo in 1919," he quipped a few decades later, "you wouldn't even have been prosecuted."[44]

Cast into the political wilderness for nearly a decade, "Liberty Bill" — as he was dubbed by Coughlin — ran unsuccessfully for governor as the Non-Partisan League's candidate in 1922, finishing some 29,000 votes behind the man who had replaced Frazier, and was trounced in mounting another comeback as the Farmer-Labor Party's candidate for the U.S. Senate four years later, garnering a dismal 4,977 votes while finishing last in a five-way race easily won by Republican Gerald P. Nye. Lemke's popularity was at an all-time low and his political career appeared to be over.

Lemke's political fortunes, however, improved dramatically in 1932 when he was elected to Congress as a Republican. He was re-elected overwhelmingly two years later. He eventually served nine terms in the U.S. House until his death in the spring of 1950.

---

[43] William E. Leuchtenburg, *The FDR Years: On Roosevelt and His Legacy* (New York, 1995), p. 119.
[44] "Washington Daybook," *Chillicothe Constitution-Tribune*, Feb. 11, 1939.

Though nominally a Republican, the North Dakota lawmaker had actively campaigned for Roosevelt in 1932, believing that the patrician Democrat would look kindly on his farm relief program.

The populist lawmaker later soured on FDR when the president, eyeing a chance to humiliate his outspoken critic from Royal Oak, helped to defeat the most recent version of the Frazier-Lemke Act. Lemke, who had managed earlier to maneuver the Bankruptcy Act through Congress — legislation enabling farmers to scale down their debts — despite Roosevelt's opposition, took the defeat personally. "I look upon Roosevelt as a bewildered Kerensky of a provisional government," he stated caustically. "He doesn't know from or where he's going."[45]

While Lemke's third-party candidacy soaked up much of the protest vote that ordinarily would have gone to Thomas, Roosevelt's unmistakable leftward lurch during the 1936 campaign proved far more costly to the Socialist nominee. The president's recent legislative accomplishments — the Social Security Act, the Public Utilities Holding Company Act and the establishment of the Works Progress Administration (WPA), all of which became law in 1935, as well as the Revenue Act of 1936, which taxed undistributed corporate profits — had tremendous appeal to many of those on the American Left, potentially costing Thomas the support of hundreds of thousands of voters who otherwise might have seriously considered voting for the Socialist ticket, as they had four years earlier.

If his legislative agenda wasn't damaging enough to the Socialists, Roosevelt — embracing a much more muscular position against Wall Street and the world's financial oligarchy — concluded his 1936 campaign that autumn with a blistering attack on wealth and privilege in a speech at Madison Square Garden on October 31, telling a cheering throng of 20,000 that he had "just begun to fight" for his New Deal program.[46]

"We had to struggle with the old enemies of peace — business and financial monopoly, speculation, reckless banking, class antagonism, sectionalism, war profiteering," FDR told the enthusiastic crowd. Wall Street and big business, he said in a particularly rousing speech, "had begun to consider the government of the United States as a mere appendage to their own affairs. We know now that government by organized money is just as dangerous as

---

[45] Jean Edward Smith, *FDR* (New York, 2008), p. 365.
[46] "Roosevelt Defies 'Organized Money' Foes, Pledges Continued Fight for New Deal Aims; Landon, Closing, Promises Happier America," *New York Times*, Nov. 1, 1936.

government by organized mob." Acknowledging that he was despised by the Lords of Finance and the leaders of industry, the president then said he welcomed their hatred. "I should like to have it said of my first administration that in it the forces of selfishness and of lust for power met their match," he continued with a dramatic cadence. "I should like to have it said of my second administration that in it these forces met their master."[47]

Even with as splendid and articulate a candidate as Norman Thomas, the Socialist Party couldn't possibly match Roosevelt's rhetorical brilliance — or his remarkable record of legislative achievement during his first term. Nobody could.

Thomas himself acknowledged that he would have been hard pressed to exceed Roosevelt's breathtaking accomplishments during his first one hundred days in office. Though he was initially concerned that the New Deal might lead to fascism and believed that Roosevelt's sweeping legislative program was being used to preserve the capitalist system, Thomas freely acknowledged that if he had been elected in 1932 his first hundred days wouldn't have been substantially different from Roosevelt's. At one point in the autumn of 1933, Thomas — in a speech at Madison Square Garden — even went so far as to say that he would gladly welcome FDR into the Socialist Party.[48]

Aware that the New Deal had sapped much of their strength, the Socialists nevertheless realized that Roosevelt's economic recovery still had a long way to go. There were still millions of forgotten men and women throughout the country, long-suffering souls whose lives hadn't yet improved in any significant way nearly four years after Herbert Hoover left office. It was "a sad commentary," lamented Reading's Raymond Hofses, when the Roosevelt administration talks about prosperity while eleven million Americans remained unemployed and countless others were "in dire need and on the border of starvation."[49]

Hofses, who was again running for Congress from Pennsylvania's fourteenth congressional district — his third straight try for that seat and his fifth of eleven campaigns for the U.S. House in a

---

[47] "The Text of President Roosevelt's Address as He Closed His Drive for Re-election," *New York Times*, Nov. 1, 1936.
[48] Johnpoll, *Pacifist's Progress*, pp. 103-105. Responding to a suggestion made by Abraham Cahan, the longtime editor of the *Jewish Daily Forward*, that the president was entitled to membership in the Socialist Party, Thomas said the he was willing to second the nomination if Roosevelt was willing to nationalize the coal and banking industries — something that wasn't totally out of the question in October 1933.
[49] "No Prosperity Signs Seen by Socialist," *Reading Eagle*, Oct. 22, 1936.

period spanning from 1924 to 1948 — blamed the captains of industry for the country's continuing depression, those who "weep crocodile tears just prior to the election for the unemployed and the aged, but refuse to appropriate sufficient funds to take care of them decently." Big business, he said, had done little to pull the country out of its economic quagmire.[50]

The defections of several leading Democrats, including two of the party's former presidential nominees — J.P. Morgan-affiliated lawyer John W. Davis and the increasingly bitter Al Smith, as well as former Secretary of State Bainbridge Colby, a close associate of Roosevelt-hating publisher William Randolph Hearst — had little impact on the election's outcome.[51]

On Tuesday, November 3, Franklin D. Roosevelt rolled to an unprecedented landslide victory, smashing the GOP's colorless Alfred M. Landon by a margin of 27,751,841 votes to 16,679,491. Carrying every state in the union except Maine and Vermont, FDR picked up 523 electoral votes to Landon's eight. The Union Party's William Lemke polled 892,390 popular votes, or just a shade below two percent nationally.

Lemke's relatively impressive showing aside, the Roosevelt landslide had a decisive and highly detrimental impact on the rest of the nationally-organized minor parties that year, especially the Socialist Party. As the results began trickling in, it immediately became clear that the Democratic strategy of appealing to working-class voters through Labor's Non-Partisan League had paid huge dividends.[52]

Perhaps because of the intra-party split between the party's Old Guard and the party's younger militants, possibly because of Lemke's protest candidacy, or maybe due to FDR's immense popularity, Thomas — waging his third straight campaign for the presidency — garnered only 188,497 votes in thirty-six states. His national total barely exceeded the 177,000 votes he had received in the state of New York four years earlier.

Despite a significant drop in support, New York was again Thomas's strongest state. Though losing more than half the support he enjoyed from New Yorkers four years earlier, Thomas polled 86,897 votes in the state, only slightly fewer than the 96,233 cast for Harry W. Laidler, the party's nominee for governor. Dar-

---

[50] Ibid.
[51] John B. Townley, "Bolters Do Little Damage to Roosevelt Candidacy; Lemke Strength is Steadily Declining in State," *Pittsburgh Press*, Oct. 25, 1936.
[52] "Radical Vote Hit in FDR Landslide," *Socialist Call*, Nov. 7, 1936.

win J. Meserole, the longtime president of the National Unemployment League who was running for Associate Judge of the Court of Appeals, was the party's leading statewide vote-getter in the Empire State, garnering 103,284 votes.[53] Vastly outdistanced by the newly-formed American Labor Party in the gubernatorial contest, the Socialists consequently lost their coveted third line on the New York ballot.[54]

On a positive note, the Socialist Party — along with the country's two other proletarian parties — taught the two major parties a lesson in fiscal responsibility that year by finishing the presidential campaign with a modest surplus. Running their campaigns as though money grew on trees, the Democrats and Republican parties both finished in the red.

Based on receipts and expenditure reports filed by national, state and related party organizations, the Socialist Party, which raised $27,258 for its national effort, ended up with a surplus of $2,296.[55] Moreover, toward the end of the 1936 campaign Thomas said that he had personally spent $5,614 on his campaign while vice-presidential running mate George Nelson of the Wisconsin Farmers' Union reported expenditures of $323.47.[56]

Similarly, the older Socialist Labor Party, which spent $31,659 during the 1936 campaign, ended up banking nearly $7,000 while the Communist Party, which reportedly spent $3.27 for every vote cast for the Browder-Ford ticket, raised and spent the most of any minor party that year, shelling out an impressive $270,489.40, or more than four times as much as Father Coughlin's Union Party and nearly ten times the amount expended by the rival Socialist and Socialist Labor parties. Unlike their left-wing counterparts, both of which finished the campaign with surpluses, the Communists ended the campaign with a small but manageable debt.[57]

Like the Communists, Father Coughlin's Union Party also finished the campaign in the red, reportedly spending $65,696 on behalf of William Lemke's candidacy while raising $62,884. The debt became Lemke's personal burden as he tried in vain to keep the party afloat beyond the November election.

By contrast, the spendthrift major parties finished the 1936 presidential campaign with huge deficits. Receiving overwhelming support from the financial oligarchs on Wall Street who

---

[53] "Party Vote 96,233 in New York State; 86,897 for Thomas," *Socialist Call*, Dec, 12, 1936.
[54] "Socialists Suffer Heavy Vote Loss," *New York Times*, Nov. 4, 1936.
[55] "1936 Campaign Cost Parties $23,973,329," *New York Times*, Mar. 5, 1937.
[56] Swanberg, *Norman Thomas: The Last Idealist*, p. 205.
[57] "1936 Campaign Cost Parties $23,973,329," *New York Times*, Mar. 5, 1937.

wanted to get rid of Roosevelt, the Republicans amassed a debt exceeding $1.1 million while the Democrats, again retaining control of the White House and both houses of Congress, piled up a deficit of more than $445,000.[58]

Though disappointed, Thomas accepted the election results philosophically, chalking up FDR's huge majority to an "exaggerated belief that a Landon victory would mean the end of relief, a virtual outlawry of labor unions, and perhaps an erection of concentration camps." Such was the magnitude of the anti-Republican propaganda that year.[59]

Acknowledging that the outpouring of support for Roosevelt contained "elements of conscious working class solidarity," Thomas nevertheless believed that the 1936 presidential election "almost wiped out numerically minor parties for the time being," largely because of the overwhelming desire to defeat Landon.[60]

Though he tried to hide his pessimism — at least in public — Thomas, who made more than 160 speeches and several radio addresses during the course of the campaign, was deeply discouraged.

In a letter to Maynard Krueger, a University of Chicago economics professor who would later join him as his vice-presidential running mate in the 1940 campaign, Thomas sounded like he was close to despair, admitting that he was "much more depressed" about the party's future than he had been at the beginning of the campaign. He also maintained that he was finished trying to lead the party, but would "rather passively" continue to support it through his writing and speaking engagements.[61]

"The Socialist Party lay in ruins," wrote W. A. Swanberg in his beautifully written and meticulously detailed 1976 biography of Thomas. "Politics was Thomas's life, and now his nineteen years of arduous building lay in rubble around him."[62]

---

[58] Ibid; G. William Domhoff, *The Power Elite and the State: How Policy is Made in America* (New York, 1990), pp. 233-234.
[59] Fleischman, *Norman Thomas: A Biography*, p. 173.
[60] Ibid.
[61] Swanberg, *Norman Thomas: The Last Idealist*, p. 205.
[62] Ibid., p. 206.

Chapter VIII

♦

Keep America Out of War

The Spanish Civil War — "a singularly cruel and dangerous military revolt engineered by the economic royalists of Spain," as Thomas personally described the conflict to President Roosevelt — caused a dilemma for many Socialist Party members, including Thomas himself.[1]

Unlike Thomas, many pacifists in the party were appalled when Jack Altman, secretary of the party in New York City, suggested in December 1936 that the party should form a "Eugene V. Debs Column" to provide manpower and financial assistance to the Spanish Loyalists in their struggle to repel the fascist uprising led by Generalissimo Francisco Franco and aided by Hitler and Mussolini.

Altman, who had specifically proposed the creation of a Debs Column consisting of 500 volunteers which would provide technical support to the Loyalists while fighting alongside the other International Brigades, was joined in this effort by Thomas, who briefly shed his pacifist principles and persuaded the party's NEC to establish a "Friends of the Debs Column" to raise money to transport the volunteers to Spain.

Despite Altman's claims that the group's goal of recruiting 500 volunteers had been "oversubscribed by many hundreds" — an exaggerated claim echoed by his militant allies at the *Socialist Call* — the Debs Column never came close to raising their initial goal of $50,000 and, in the end, recruited only a few dozen volunteers,

---

[1] Fleischman, *Norman Thomas: A Biography*, p. 174.

many of whom were left stranded in Paris lacking the means and resourcefulness to find their way to Spain.[2]

The Debs Column was a complete flop, contributing only a small handful of the more than 36,000 foreign volunteers who eventually fought for the Loyalist cause between 1936 and 1939. Earl Browder, general-secretary of the Communist Party USA, boasted in 1937 that sixty percent of the estimated 2,800 to 3,300 Americans serving on the side of the Spanish Republicans — the famous Lincoln Brigade, a third of whom perished in the conflict — were members of the Communist Party or the Young Communist League, while a majority of the remainder were believed to be fellow travelers. By the same token, the relatively inconsequential funds raised by Thomas for the Debs Column paled in comparison to the large sums of money raised for humanitarian aid and technical assistance by Browder's organization.

Moreover, it's more than likely that the few Socialists who actually participated in the much-heralded Debs Column — a small group that included Sam Romer, the former managing editor of the *Socialist Call* — probably found their way into the Lincoln Battalion by way of the Communist Party.[3]

Despite its relatively insignificant impact, Thomas nevertheless took quite a bit of heat for briefly abandoning his deeply-held pacifist beliefs and advocating in favor of armed intervention during the Spanish Civil War. The Fellowship of Reconciliation, headed by Thomas's longtime friend and ally John Nevin Sayre, issued a statement in early January condemning the formation of a Debs Column as "a grave mistake," creating a potential opening for American reactionaries to "pour a flood of money, munitions and recruits to General Franco's aid."[4]

The War Resisters League, founded in 1923 by Socialist and pacifist Jessie Wallace Hughan as part of the London-based War Resisters' International, also weighed in, sharply criticizing the party's sanctioning of the Debs Column in a series of blistering letters published in the *Socialist Call* and the *New Leader*.[5] The Rev. John Haynes Holmes, one of Thomas's closest and dearest friends who chaired or served as honorary chair of the War Resisters League from 1929 to 1943, personally expressed his dismay in a

---

[2] "Socialists Here Would Aid Spain," *New York Times*, Dec. 24, 1936; "$50,000 for 500 Men to Spain; First Contingent of Debs Column to Leave Jan. 19," *Socialist Call*, Jan. 2, 1937.
[3] Robert A. Rosenstone, *Crusade of the Left: The Lincoln Battalion in the Spanish Civil War* (New York, 1969), p. 112.
[4] "Socialist Move Deplored," *New York Times*, Jan. 11, 1937.
[5] Scott H. Bennett, *Radical Pacifism: The War Resisters League and Gandhian Nonviolence in America, 1915-1963* (Syracuse, 2003), pp. 54-55.

dramatic letter to Thomas, accusing him of betraying his pacifist principles and reminding his old friend that they had "stood fast when Belgians lifted cries as pitiful as those lifted by Spaniards today, and when Paris was beset no less terribly than Madrid" during World War I. "By what right," he asked, "does any Socialist today profane the sacred name of Debs by using it to designate a regiment of soldiers enlisted for the work of human slaughter?"[6]

Thomas, who had led the League for Industrial Democracy into a brief affiliation with the Communist-dominated American League Against War and Fascism — a group headed by Methodist minister Henry F. Ward, an ethics professor at the Union Theological Seminary in New York City, which initially attracted the support of an assortment of intellectuals, pacifists, anarchists, and members of the labor movement, including the CIO's John L. Lewis — shortly after its founding in 1933, was deeply conflicted

With ominous signs of a world in turmoil and on the brink of all-out war, Thomas helped to create the Keep America Out of War Committee in early 1938, soon renamed the Keep America Out of War Congress (KAOWC). This important yet largely-forgotten antiwar group — one of several such organizations that sprang up on the American Left during this period — was comprised largely of pacifists and socialists who were critical of Roosevelt's foreign policy.

The loosely-organized Congress, which remained active until the attack on Pearl Harbor when it was almost instantly transformed into the Thomas-led Post War World Council — a peace group that lived on for another quarter century — initially included an array of similar antiwar organizations, including the Quaker-based National Council for the Prevention of War, the Women's International League for Peace and Freedom, the American Friends Service Committee, the Fellowship of Reconciliation, the Commission for World Peace of the Methodist General Conference, and the Peace Committee of the General Conference of American Rabbis.

Curiously, one of the original groups operating under KAOWC's umbrella was something called World Peaceways, a fairly well-funded organization headed by advertising genius and popular writer Bruce Barton, the son of a Congregationalist minister who was convinced that only free enterprise — not socialism

---

[6] Gregory, *Norman Thomas: The Great Dissenter*, p. 173.

— could prevent another war.⁷ Described by the brilliant muckraking journalist George Seldes as a "native fascist," Barton had once praised Benito Mussolini *after* the Duce had already murdered thousands of his own citizens, curtailed civil liberties in Italy, and destroyed his country's labor unions.⁸

Having served briefly in the U.S. House as a Republican during this period, the controversial advertising executive was the GOP's candidate for the U.S. Senate in New York in 1940, losing by more than 400,000 votes in a race in which he preposterously claimed that Hitler favored Roosevelt's re-election and that he himself had been the victim of a whispering campaign portraying him as an intolerant isolationist harboring fascist views based on an article written ten years earlier.⁹

Originally incorporated in 1931 as World Peace Posters, Inc., Barton's World Peaceways organization actively promoted the establishment of a cabinet-level Secretary of Peace — an idea first championed by celebrated Philadelphia physician Benjamin Rush in 1793 and later echoed by such luminaries as women's rights activist Carrie Chapman Catt and Indiana Sen. Vance Hartke, and more recently, by country music pioneer Willie Nelson and former U.S. Rep. Dennis J. Kucinich of Ohio.

Sen. Robert M. La Follette, Jr., of Wisconsin was the featured speaker at KAOWC's first major public event, an antiwar rally attended by an estimated 4,500 at New York City's Hippodrome in March 1938. Thomas also addressed the rally. Other speakers included Oswald Garrison Villard, United Auto Workers president Homer Martin, retired Major-General William C. Rivers and writer Bertram D. Wolfe.¹⁰

In his remarks, the son of the late "Fighting Bob" strongly endorsed the Ludlow Amendment calling for a national referendum on any declaration of war by Congress as part of an eight-point program to keep the United States out of war.¹¹ "Our past experience should make us realize that we cannot preserve democracy either abroad or at home by trying to police the world," La Follette boldly declared to prolonged applause. "Nor can we salvage peace and democracy by organizing a holy crusade, nor by forging an

---

⁷ Patricia Faith Appelbaum, *Kingdom to Commune: Protestant Pacifist Culture Between World War I and the Vietnam Era* (Chapel Hill, N.C., 2009), p. 91.
⁸ George Seldes, *Facts and Fascism* (New York, 1943), p. 77.
⁹ "Barton Agrees to Enter Race," *Poughkeepsie Eagle-News*, Sep. 27, 1940; "Hitler, Roosevelt Linked by Barton," *New York Times*, Oct. 11, 1940; "'Whispering' Drive Charged by Barton," *New York Times*, Oct. 28, 1940.
¹⁰ "La Follette Maps Plan to Avoid War," *New York Times*, Mar. 7, 1938.
¹¹ Ibid.

iron ring around Germany, Italy and Japan…" Nor could it be accomplished, he added, "by simply out-bluffing the dictators." Martin, the UAW's first president and a man closely aligned with left-wing factions of the labor movement, told the crowd that, unlike 1917, organized labor would not be "goose-stepped into another war."[12]

In addition to organizing KAOWC, Thomas maintained a hectic political schedule during this period, briefly running for mayor in 1937 and waging his second campaign for governor of New York the following year. Much of his time, however, was consumed dealing with internal party strife and bickering — much of it his own making.

In the months following the 1936 campaign, Thomas again found himself smack in the middle of another bitter factional fight within the Socialist Party — this time a four-sided struggle. Thomas had always wanted to lead an "all-inclusive party," but he could have hardly imagined the quadrangular tug of war that ensued in the aftermath of the Old Guard's departure the previous year.

With their right-wing adversaries now ensconced in either the SDF or New York's rapidly-expanding American Labor Party, usually both, and no longer posing a threat, the party's militants and their assorted allies — all of whom had cooperated in battling the Old Guard — quickly broke into competing factions, each hoping to guide the Socialist Party of America's destiny now that the Old Guard had been routed from its ranks.

Thomas himself was part of the party's informal centrist faction, essentially those who might best be described as Social Democrats. This group also included an assortment of pacifists and a myriad of independent-minded progressives of varying stripes who never clearly aligned themselves with one of the party's other factions.

The Socialist Party's more left-wing elements formed what became known as the Clarity Caucus, headed by Herbert Zam, a former secretary of the Young Communist League, the mercurial Gus Tyler and the Delson brothers, two extremely intense and serious-minded young men who were out to change the world, while the original Militant group — "the balding young Turks of yesteryear," as historian Daniel Bell described them — under the direction of New York's Jack Altman, a seasoned veteran when it came

---

[12] "War Promotes Only Death," *Livingston County Leader* (Geneseo, New York), Mar. 18, 1938.

to party infighting, represented what was probably the largest of the four groupings.

Led by James P. Cannon and Minneapolis Teamster Vincent R. Dunne, the Trotskyists, who had entered the party *en masse* in 1936 — at Thomas's invitation, no less — comprised the fourth faction until their expulsion from the party fourteen months later.

The Trotskyists, who had eagerly accepted the invitation to join in building a more robust and radical Socialist Party — an invitation issued to all "who believe that the times require another American Revolution" — posed the biggest headache for the party's leaders and it wasn't long before Thomas began regretting the olive branch that he had personally extended to the anti-Stalinist Left a few years earlier.

Described by one historian as the "Pharisees of the revolution," wandering aimlessly across the landscape of the American Left in the eight years following their expulsion from the Communist Party, Trotsky's followers — led by Cannon, the foremost leader of American Trotskyism, and his then-colleague Max Shachtman, both of whom had been expelled for supporting Trotsky's position at the Sixth World Congress of the Comintern in 1928, had formed the Communist League of America (CLA) the following spring. The CLA later merged with pacifist A. J. Muste's American Workers Party in early 1935 to form the short-lived Workers Party of the United States.[13]

In joining the Socialist Party, the Trotskyists wasted little time making their presence felt. Having virtually captured the party's organization in California and Minnesota almost immediately upon their arrival, the Trotskyists, known as the Appeal group, enjoyed a large following in New York City, especially among the Young People's Socialist League (YPSL). Like the Clarity faction, they also produced their own publication, *The Socialist Appeal*, a mimeographed newsletter published by Albert Goldman of Chicago and YPSL leader Ernest Erber.

The 37-year-old Goldman had been one of the first Trotskyists to accept Thomas's offer to join the party. A civil rights lawyer who

---

[13] Founded in 1933, Muste's American Workers Party (AWP) attracted a number of leading lights on the U.S. Left, including intellectuals such as James Burnham, Sidney Hook, J. B. S. Hardman and Louis Budenz, the latter of whom edited *Labor Action*, the party's weekly newspaper. Growing out of the Conference for Progressive Labor Action (CPLA), an insurgent labor group centered around Brookwood Labor College in Katonah, New York, where the Dutch-born Muste, a former minister and leader in the famous Lawrence textile strike of 1919, served as dean of the faculty — a post he held for a dozen years — the AWP played a critical role in the Toledo Auto-Lite strike in the spring of 1934, a key labor victory in the pre-CIO period.

later was not only a defendant, but also the lead defense attorney for the Socialist Workers Party during the famous Minneapolis trial of 1941 when nearly two dozen party leaders, including James P. Cannon, Grace Carlson and Farrell Dobbs, were prosecuted under the notorious Smith Act, Goldman had given up his rabbinical studies to become a tailor before eventually turning to law. The exiled Leon Trotsky was one of his clients. Acting as a scout of sorts for Cannon and other Trotskyists to follow, Goldman was enthusiastically welcomed into the Socialist Party after breaking with the American Workers Party in November 1934.

Thomas and other party leaders were fine with Goldman's membership and that of other Trotskyists, so long as they joined as individuals and not as a group or faction.

With the Trotskyists clearly on their way out, Thomas turned his attention to New York City's 1937 mayoral election — another issue that had deeply divided the various factions. Though he personally had some genuine affection for Mayor Fiorello H. La Guardia — the "pragmatic radical," as the late Howard Zinn described him — who had made considerable progress in taming the Tammany Tiger, Thomas tentatively agreed to run for mayor in 1937 on a ticket that included Frank R. Crosswaith, a prominent African-American trade union activist and close friend and ally of A. Philip Randolph, for city controller and longtime labor lawyer Murray Baron for city council president. In conditionally accepting his party's nomination — the shortest candidacy in his long career — Thomas reserved the right to withdraw from the race if negotiations with the larger American Labor Party, which was enthusiastically supporting La Guardia's reelection, proved fruitful.[14]

Thomas recognized, moreover, that the immensely popular La Guardia would be impossible to defeat. Regardless of how vigorously he campaigned, he realized that he didn't have a prayer of generating anything remotely resembling the kind of support he received in the city's 1929 mayoral contest when he garnered a staggering 175,000 votes. "It would be hard to match La Guardia," Thomas freely acknowledged in conditionally entering the race that summer. "It would be harder to beat him. It would be tough to elect a Socialist mayor."[15]

Hoping that an alliance with the American Labor Party would help strengthen the city's growing labor movement, possibly leading to the development of a national labor party, the Socialists were

---

[14] "Socialists Name Thomas for Mayor," *New York Times*, July 14, 1937.
[15] "Socialist Support Dangled Before La Guardia in Race," *Brooklyn Daily Eagle*, July 13, 1937.

disappointed that La Guardia was again actively seeking the Republican nomination. Recognizing the value of making identical nominations, it was the Socialist Party's stated intention to only support candidates who weren't also running on one of the major-party tickets.[16]

Though disappointed that the ALP was willing to support a candidate running on one of the old party tickets, Thomas nevertheless withdrew from the race in late September, thereby leaving party members free to support La Guardia as labor's choice in the mayoral contest. Thomas, meanwhile, had been endorsed by the party's state convention for delegate-at-large to the state constitutional convention.[17]

In dropping out of the mayoral race, Thomas stopped short of endorsing La Guardia and, in fact, bitterly assailed the mayor for accepting the Republican nomination.[18] Thomas, of course, had long considered the local GOP "the kept woman of Tammany" and — dating back to his second bid for the mayor's office in 1929 — had long criticized the city's Republican leaders for routinely collaborating with the Tammany Tiger for their share of the spoils.[19]

Declaring that his decision to withdraw from the race was made only after "lengthy deliberation," Thomas — speaking for the party — explained that his decision to withdraw was motivated in large part by a desire to help forge a better working relationship with the rival ALP. "We are persuaded that the ALP, or great sections of it, may play an enormously important role in the imperative task of building on a nationwide scale a genuine Farmer-Labor Party," he said, adding that the creation of a national Farmer-Labor Party was an idea the Socialists had long advocated and pursued. "We are determined to preserve our own identity and keep our own flag flying for the great purpose of achieving the cooperative commonwealth," he continued. "But equally are we determined to keep in friendly relations with the forward movements of the workers and to cooperate with them so far as our principles permit."[20]

---

[16] "Socialists Name Thomas for Mayor," *New York Times*, July 14, 1937.
[17] "Thomas Quits Race for Mayor Today," *New York Times*, Sep. 26, 1937.
[18] "Thomas Withdraws as Mayoralty Candidate; La Guardia Not Backed," *Socialist Call*, Oct. 9, 1937.
[19] Swanberg, *Norman Thomas: The Last Idealist*, p. 118.
[20] "Thomas Withdraws as Mayoralty Candidate; La Guardia Not Backed," *Socialist Call*, Oct. 9, 1937.

With the modest goal of polling a minimum of 50,000 votes to maintain the party's statewide ballot status in New York, Thomas ran for governor the following year.[21]

Slated against three-term Democratic incumbent Herbert Lehman, a wealthy banker who had succeeded Roosevelt as governor, and young New York City prosecutor Thomas E. Dewey, the Republican nominee, Thomas opened his campaign with a number of outdoor speeches in Queens in early October.[22] Having tried unsuccessfully to engage his major-party opponents in a series of three-cornered debates in all four corners of the state, Thomas used his longshot candidacy to criticize the enactment and enforcement of election laws designed to protect the country's two old parties while virtually legislating the nation's smaller parties out of existence.[23]

Pointing to the example of a newly-organized labor party which had been recently barred from the ballot in Illinois on a myriad of technicalities, Thomas declared that if the trend continued "it will be difficult, almost to the point of impossibility," for any minor party to wage anything resembling a national campaign in 1940. "It would take something close to political revolution for any party, new or minor, to get on the ballot in as many as three-fourth of our states," he warned.[24]

As a result of losing its coveted ballot line in the state when Thomas polled only 24,890 votes in that fall's gubernatorial contest — the party needed a minimum of 50,000 to maintain its recognized status — the Socialist Party of New York decided in a referendum shortly after the election to allow individual party members to join and actively participate in the American Labor Party.[25]

In announcing the decision, state chairman Harry W. Laidler, who had long advocated the creation of a national Farmer-Labor Party, said that he was confident that Socialist Party members could make a positive contribution to the ALP while still maintaining their Socialist activities. "We are convinced that Socialists can make a genuine contribution to labor party development in this state," he said. "We consider the American Labor Party as the electoral expression of the working class in New York. It is imperative that the strength of this party be increased. Socialists will dedicate

---

[21] "Thomas to Head Socialist Ticket," *New York Times*, Aug. 28, 1938.
[22] "Thomas Opens Campaign," *New York Times*, Oct. 6, 1938.
[23] "Thomas Invites Rivals to Debate," *New York Times*, Oct. 11, 1938.
[24] "Thomas Deplores 'Old Party' Power; Socialist Nominee Warns Ticket May Be Barred From the Ballot in 1940," *New York Times*, Nov. 6, 1938.
[25] "State Socialists to Join Laborites," *New York Times*, Dec. 25, 1938.

themselves to that end, seeking to contribute to the labor party's vitality as a political force."[26]

As difficult as the 1936 presidential campaign had been for Thomas, a year when he played second fiddle to Father Coughlin's Union Party, the 1940 presidential campaign was even worse — much worse.

Mounting his fourth consecutive campaign for the nation's highest office, Thomas once again emerged as Roosevelt's most significant minor-party challenger, similar to the role he had played in 1932 at the height of the depression. But things were different now.

Viewed as "largely a wastebasket for disgruntled liberals to throw away their votes," as Henry Luce's *TIME* magazine so caustically described it, hardly anyone noticed when the Socialist Party, convening at the National Press Club Auditorium in Washington, D.C., in early April, just as Hitler was preparing to invade Denmark and Norway, unanimously nominated Thomas for the presidency for a fourth consecutive time. Keynote speaker Maynard C. Krueger was tapped for the vice presidency.[27]

With his wire-rimmed glasses, the pipe-smoking Krueger looked every bit the intellectual that he was. Having studied history and international politics before specializing in economics, the scholarly-looking professor had emerged as a leading spokesman for campus opposition to the war during this period, frequently assailing the nation's fixation with Adolf Hitler. He was a popular and witty lecturer and regular guest on the University of Chicago's widely-respected "Round Table" radio program.[28]

Some 210 credentialed delegates representing twenty-eight states attended the three-day convention, the first national convention ever held by a political party in the nation's capital. Approximately two-thirds of the delegates were union members. One of them was Leonard Woodcock, a 29-year-old machine assembler from Detroit who later served as president of the United Auto Workers (UAW) and as Jimmy Carter's ambassador to the People's Republic of China.

A number of well-known Socialists attended the 1940 convention, including Joseph H. Coldwell of Providence, Rhode Island, who had been Eugene V. Debs' cellmate at the Atlanta Penitentiary during World War I. Coldwell, who was given a rousing welcome,

---

[26] Ibid.
[27] "Socialists Convene," *TIME*, April 15, 1940.
[28] James C. Schneider, *Should America Go to War? The Debate over Foreign Policy in Chicago*, 1939-1941 (Chapel Hill, 1991), p. 179.

urged the Socialists to exchange their customary clenched fists for "the outstretched hand of comradeship," but tradition prevailed.[29]

In his keynote address, Krueger flailed away at the private profit system, arguing that capitalism had developed a serious case of "hardening of the arteries" and was in dire need of an overhaul. "We will get the kind of expansion which private enterprise fails to give us," he declared, "only by resorting to public enterprise, which is the only possible alternative to the private profit system. A public enterprise can expand as far as usefulness of its product justifies expansion, because it represents production for use, not production for profit." Under the two old parties, asserted Krueger, the country's economic system was gradually being transformed into one of state capitalism, "heavy on the armament side, light on the standard-of-living side."[30]

A rising star in the party who turned thirty-five on January 16, 1941 — four days before he and Thomas would have been inaugurated — the University of Chicago economist argued that public enterprise was the only realistic alternative to the capitalist system. "Public ownership and operation of a business does not mean that it has to be completely centralized," he asserted. "It can be very much decentralized and it is even desirable that a substantial amount of competition be maintained among the various decentralized units of any industry organized by public enterprise."[31]

The highly-articulate Krueger explained that the Socialists were committed to making the economic system work by expanding opportunities for employment, markets and investment. The Socialist Party, he said, would pursue two major policy objectives, one to increase consumption and the other to increase investment.

Attacking the two major parties, the professorial Chicagoan said that the American people were "waking up" to the fact that the Democrats, beholden to the entrenched power of the southern Bourbons, were not "a fit instrument for sustained social progress," and that there was "no sleight of hand by which the Republican Party can be taken away from big business."[32]

Although Mary Donovan Hapgood of Indianapolis and A. Philip Randolph, president of the International Brotherhood of Sleeping Car Porters, were prominently mentioned as possible

---

[29] "Socialists Reject Soviets; Stand with Thomas for No War," *Christian Science Monitor*, April 9, 1940; "Thomas Again Head of Socialist Ticket," *New York Times*, April 8, 1940.
[30] "Socialists Hear Greater Public Ownership Plea," *Capital Times* (Madison, WI), April 6, 1940; "Socialists Adopt Isolation Stand to Bar War Entry," *New York Times*, April 7, 1940.
[31] Ibid.
[32] "Public Ownership Declared Need at Socialist Session," *Reno Evening Gazette*, April 6, 1940.

vice-presidential candidates that year, Krueger faced no opposition at the convention. Like Thomas, his nomination was unanimous.

While there was little suspense regarding the outcome of the party's presidential and vice-presidential nominations, the convention wasn't completely void of drama. The most heated battle took place over adoption of the party's antiwar plank, which pitted the isolationist supporters of Norman Thomas against a faction supporting economic assistance to Great Britain and other nations committed to defeating the Nazis and Fascists.

Though also opposed to direct U.S. entry into the war, the minority supporting aid to the counties opposed to Nazi Germany were led by Jack Altman of New York City and the persistent Alfred Baker Lewis of Cambridge, the wealthy secretary of the Socialist Party of Massachusetts who emerged as the leader of the party's internationalist wing.

The minority resolution, which had been offered to the convention by New York's Lazar Becker, a former Communist who made his way to the Socialist Party via the Revolutionary Workers Party organizing committee — a short-lived group he co-founded with Benjamin Gitlow — favored extending non-military economic aid to the Allies while expressing deep sympathy for those determined to overthrow Hitler's menacing Nazi regime. It also sharply criticized those who were advocating an armistice or negotiated peace in the European war.[33]

Thomas, who was among a half-dozen party members who spoke for the majority, declared that "our best service to socialism is not to join the collective suicide pact," a dramatic step that he believed would eventually lead to U.S. military involvement in the conflict. While opposing economic aid to the Allies, Thomas said the United States could nevertheless play an important role in the war by helping to mediate a negotiated peace between the warring countries, one that could eventually lead to disarmament.[34]

Lewis, who was personally opposed to direct U.S. military involvement in the war, spoke for the minority, arguing that eight times as many Americans would support entering the conflict if Hitler appeared on the verge of victory. Therefore, he contended, it was imperative to provide economic assistance to those countries fighting the Nazi menace as a way of keeping the United

---

[33] Swanberg, *Norman Thomas: The Last Idealist*, p. 241; "Socialists Adopt Isolation Stand to Bar War Entry," *New York Times*, April 7, 1940; "Thomas Again Head of Socialist Ticket," *New York Times*, April 8, 1940.

[34] "Thomas Again Head of Socialist Ticket," *New York Times*, April 8, 1940.

States out of the conflict. Following a vigorous debate, the minority report was overwhelmingly defeated by a margin of 159 to 28, with nearly two-dozen delegates apparently abstaining.[35]

Thomas, who had been extremely reluctant to run that year — and that's something of an understatement — made it clear that he wouldn't possibly entertain the idea of mounting a fourth consecutive campaign for the presidency if the party failed to adopt an uncompromisingly isolationist position on the war. Any measures even remotely resembling "steps short of war" would be entirely unacceptable to him. With the adoption of a satisfactory platform, however, Thomas willingly agreed to once again serve as the nation's moral catalyst.

Shortly after being nominated Thomas and Krueger appeared on the platform as Elizabeth Morgan, daughter-in-law of Arthur E. Morgan, the brilliant and visionary former director of the Tennessee Valley Authority, played an accordion strapped around her neck and led the delegates in singing "Solidarity Forever" and "The Internationale," while members of the Young Socialist League paraded around the hall chanting, "The Workers are Eager for Thomas and Krueger." (Krueger, as mentioned previously, was pronounced to rhyme with eager.)[36]

Graciously accepting his party's nomination, Thomas — a little older, but looking as presidential as ever — reminded the delegates that he had resolved not to run for president that year and that it was his deepest desire to see the Socialist Party cooperate with some larger group, possibly an independent Farmer-Labor Party, "representing the awakening interest and intelligence of the producing and consuming masses of Americans in the conquest of our wholly unnecessary poverty."

Unfortunately, he said, no such farmer-labor movement had emerged. He agreed to run, he carefully explained, because not running a ticket that year would clearly have been an "abdication in the face of the enemy." If the Socialists didn't address the crucial issues facing the country in that "year of crisis and confusion," he said, elaborating on his point, then "no party will proclaim what our platform says about the things necessary for plenty, peace and freedom as the rightful possession of 130,000,000 Americans."[37]

It was up to the Socialist Party, Thomas eloquently continued, to fight for peace and democracy and the elimination of poverty in the United States:

---

[35] Ibid.
[36] Ibid.
[37] Ibid.

> I make no prophesy of the size of our vote. But this I affirm: If we can make our fellow citizens stop and listen to our program for keeping America out of war, and abolishing poverty, if we can make our words like a burr to stick on their minds and consciences in this hour of darkness, doubt and confusion, we shall not have failed.
>
> We shall instead have played our part here in this late great land where democratic progress is possible, in delivering the people from the apathy and despair from which war and fascism are born.
>
> America and American democracy need not fail. And the success of our democracy shall be as a great light whose rays may pierce open the clouds of war and totalitarianism under which our brethren grope in the motherlands of civilization in Europe and Asia.
>
> The magnitude and adequacy of our success lie not wholly in our hands. But if we carry on as this convention has begun, we shall have proved ourselves worthy of our great name and our great tradition. We shall be the bearer of hope to mankind.

Resigned to the fact that he would once again be just a minor footnote in the presidential election while acknowledging that he was once more "a voice crying in the wilderness," Thomas nevertheless campaigned vigorously that year, far outpacing each of his minor-party rivals. As in his three previous presidential campaigns, the former Presbyterian minister roamed the country from coast to coast while attacking Roosevelt and Willkie on domestic and foreign policy, suggesting on more than one occasion that both of his major-party rivals had some sort of "Messianic complex."[38]

Thomas's fourth campaign for the presidency was greeted with a kind of grudging respect, even from some of the nation's more conservative quarters. His candidacy, said one newspaper, provided a healthy influence in the land. "Like Voltaire," wrote the *Bradford Era*, a small daily in rural Pennsylvania, most "Americans do not agree with a word he may say (although that may be qualified in this instance) but they will give their lives for his right to say it. Thomas is a thinker, a brilliant speaker, a challenging mind and a continual reminder of certain pitfalls, which America must sidestep to escape disaster."[39]

---

[38] "Five Minor U.S. Parties Seek to Elect President," *Fresno Bee*, Oct. 14, 1940.
[39] "Thomas Is Candidate," *Bradford Era*, Apr. 16, 1940.

THE LOWEST EBB

For a brief moment that spring it appeared as though Thomas, enjoying some breathing room over Prohibitionist Roger Babson and the Communist Party's Earl Browder, might suddenly be destined for another fourth-place finish when CIO chieftain John L. Lewis, a lifelong Republican who had supported Roosevelt in 1932 and 1936, threatened to put a third-party ticket in the field. Boasting more than four million members nationally, Lewis's powerful CIO had reportedly loaned or contributed $500,000 to FDR's 1936 reelection campaign.[40]

Lewis, who had hinted at the possibility of building a nationally-organized third party to unite the country's dispossessed laborers and farmers as early as the summer of 1937 following Roosevelt's failure to support the steelworkers during the ill-fated "Little Steel" strike, had grown increasingly critical of the administration in the intervening years.[41] He had also voiced strong opposition to a third term, predicting that Roosevelt would suffer an "ignominious defeat" in he ran again.[42]

In 1938, Lewis and the CIO seriously considered breaking with Roosevelt by putting a third-party ticket in the field in Pennsylvania, running Lt. Gov. Thomas Kennedy for governor and former Attorney General Charles J. Margiotti for the U.S. Senate against the party's regular nominees, both of whom enjoyed FDR's support. The combative and fast-talking Margiotti, one of the most famous trial lawyers in Pennsylvania, and the blue-collar Kennedy, who later succeeded Lewis as president of the UMW, had both been defeated in the bruising Democratic gubernatorial primary earlier that spring. As was the case two years later, Lewis' third-party threat in 1938 proved idle.[43]

Since nobody had called his bluff, Lewis continued to persist in his agitation for a CIO-led third party movement. Speaking at an annual miners' meeting in West Virginia in early April of 1940 — only seven months before the election — the paradoxical labor leader, a man revered by millions yet scorned by millions more, declared that he was "serving notice upon the political parties in this country — and I don't expect anything from the Republicans — that America cannot be permitted to drift, drift, while politicians merely hope, hope."[44]

---

[40] "Lewis Seeks Nucleus for Third Party," *Pittsburgh Press*, Apr. 2, 1940.
[41] Melvyn Dubofsky and Warren Van Tine, *John L. Lewis: A Biography* (Urbana, 1986), pp. 240-241.
[42] "Sidney Hillman Disagrees With Lewis on Third Term," *Pittsburgh Press*, Jan. 28, 1940.
[43] "CIO to Run Kennedy as Independent Say Rumors," *Deseret News*, May 23, 1938.
[44] "Lewis Threatens Third Party Move," *New York Times*, Apr. 2, 1940.

In threatening to create a new party, the United Mine Workers president charged that Roosevelt hadn't done nearly enough for organized labor. He was also deeply disturbed by the country's staggering jobless numbers, a figure the CIO's research department placed at 11,934,000. "Not a single, solitary suggestion is being made in America on how to provide Americans with work," barked Lewis, adding that involving the United States in the escalating conflict in Europe wasn't a solution to the nation's economic woes. "Those in this country who may secretly hope that America may be drawn eventually into the European war and that this will be an answer to the economic and political questions that beset the land are in for a fool's awakening," he warned.[45]

Thomas wasn't the least bit worried about Lewis' latest threat, describing it on the eve of the Socialist Party convention in Washington as "political romanticism." While making it clear that the Socialists wanted nothing to do with the CIO leader's plans, Thomas questioned the wisdom of launching a third-party movement that late in the year, saying it would be almost impossible for Lewis to get his new party on the ballot in more than a few states.[46]

Moreover, the former coal miner's threat of fielding a third-party ticket in the 1940 presidential election appeared to have fallen flat when Montana's Burton K. Wheeler — Lewis's choice to head such a ticket — initially disavowed any interest in running on a third-party ticket.[47]

Wheeler later had a change of heart, suggesting during a dramatic and unexpected appearance at a Townsend Club convention in St. Louis in early July that unless the Democratic Party adopted an ironclad pledge to keep the United States out of war, there would be a great uprising of the masses and the creation of a strong peace party. "If we get into another war," the Montanan told the wildly cheering delegates, "we might as well forget about old age pensions and everything else." Wheeler and Lewis were both cheered enthusiastically in St. Louis, but nothing ever came of their third-party threat.[48]

With the threat of a Lewis or Wheeler-led party removed, Norman Thomas was again the leading minor-party candidate for the presidency, a familiar role he assumed in both the 1928 and 1932 campaigns.

---

[45] Ibid.
[46] "Thomas Assails Lewis Threat," *St. Petersburg Times*, Apr. 6, 1940.
[47] "Wheeler Will Refuse to Lead Third Party," *Pittsburgh Press*, Apr. 2, 1940.
[48] "Wheeler Gives Ultimatum: Anti-War Pledge or 3rd Party," *Toledo Blade*, July 3, 1940.

Thomas took a break from the campaign trail in late July to testify against the draft. Describing military conscription as "the basic principle of totalitarianism," Thomas told the House Armed Services Committee — then called the Committee on Military Affairs — that compulsory military training was "a measure far better calculated to establish the principle of universal regimentation than to provide efficient defense."[49]

Any form of military conscription, said Thomas, would provide an enormous impetus for American militarism and imperialism. "Armament makers, investment bankers and oil prospectors will be provided by this measure with an army so powerful that it will be a standing temptation to them and to their government to impose their will by force on our neighbors," he told the committee.[50]

In late August, the Thomas-Krueger ticket picked up the endorsement of an independent committee comprised of actors, authors and educators. Contending that there was "no essential difference in the foreign and domestic policies of the two major candidates," members of the new committee, which included such luminaries as philosopher John Dewey, artist John French Sloan and literary critic Van Wyck Brooks, announced that they were supporting the Socialist ticket because Norman Thomas was "the only candidate with a record of unwavering opposition to reaction and militarism at home and abroad."[51]

Life on the road during the 1940 campaign presented more than its share of problems for Thomas, the most heart-wrenching of which occurred in Illinois when Ruth Adams, a young Socialist who was scheduled to drive him to Carbondale, was killed in an automobile accident while on her way to Springfield to pick up the candidate.[52] Another dramatic incident occurred while campaigning in Billings, Montana, when a hotel where Thomas was staying caught on fire, shooting flames some fifty feet above the dome of the $600,000 Northern Hotel and completely destroying the four-story structure. It was a close call, but fortunately Thomas and the other 75 guests escaped unharmed.[53]

Access to the ballot proved to be a particularly troublesome obstacle for the undermanned Socialists that year. The party even struggled mightily to obtain 23,000 signatures to place the

---

[49] "Draft Defended by La Guardia; Thomas Opposed," *Knickerbocker News*, July 26, 1940.
[50] Ibid.
[51] "New Group Backs Thomas; Finds 'No Essential Difference' in the Two Major Candidates," *New York Times*, Aug. 25, 1940.
[52] Fleischman, *Norman Thomas: A Biography*, p. 197.
[53] "Thomas Flees Hotel Fire," *Daily Sentinel* (Rome, N.Y.), Sep. 13, 1940.

Thomas-Krueger on the ballot in the party's stronghold of New York. It encountered even more difficulty elsewhere.

In Indiana, for example, the party needed 8,000 valid signatures and each of those signatures had to be notarized — an onerous task, to put it mildly.[54] In California, where the party lost its qualified status two years earlier, Thomas was forced to turn to the ballot-qualified Progressive Party for a place on the ballot.[55]

Despite the myriad of obstacles facing third-party candidates in 1940, Thomas nevertheless managed to have a little fun on the campaign trail. As in his previous campaigns, the Socialist candidate's spontaneous and marvelous sense of humor — equaled only by the witty and urbane Eugene McCarthy and the dry humor of Arizona's Morris K. Udall a few decades later — set him apart from his rivals.

Nobody could possibly forget the Thomas one-liner about Herbert Hoover in 1932, when he asked his audiences not to hold the President responsible for the country's economic plight because "such a little man could not have made so big a depression," or when he described Tom Dewey in 1948 as "clad each day in a pair of platitudes." Harry Truman, he quipped during the same campaign, "proves the old adage that any man can become president of the United States." Everybody chuckled, too, when the perennial Socialist candidate occasionally joked that while he'd "rather be right than President, at any time I am ready to be both."[56]

It had long been rumored that Thomas was related to Tom Dewey, his opponent in the 1944 and 1948 campaigns. When leaving the White House after a short visit with President Truman in 1951 in preparation for a trip to India to attend an international conference on cultural affairs, Thomas was asked by a reporter if it was true that he and Dewey were distant relatives. "He has never advertised it and neither have I," laughed Thomas. "There are times when the less you know about your family, the better."[57]

Dry humor had long been one of Thomas's trademarks. The 1940 presidential campaign was no exception. Thomas had plenty

---

[54] "Willkie Called 'Political Enigma' By Perennial Socialist Candidate," *Indianapolis Star*, June 29, 1940.
[55] "Progressives Put Thomas on Ballot," *Bakersfield Californian*, Sep. 21, 1940. Thomas defeated Wisconsin Sen. Robert M. La Follette, Jr., who wasn't actively seeking the nomination, by a vote of 40-8 on the first and only ballot at the party's state convention in Sacramento. One delegate voted for Republican nominee Wendell L. Willkie. Shortly after the Thomas-Krueger ticket was nominated, several California Progressives complained that the Socialists had "stacked" the convention.
[56] "He's a Successful Failure," *Milwaukee Journal*, Dec. 5, 1961.
[57] "Norman Thomas, Dewey Related?" *Pittsburgh Press*, Mar. 1, 1951.

of fun at his rivals' expense, but nothing was probably quite as humorous as his delightful reaction to Wendell Willkie's acceptance speech in Elwood, which he described as "a synthesis of Guffey's First Reader, the Genealogy of Indiana, [and] the collected speeches of Tom Girdler and the New Republic." The Republican candidate, he quipped, "agreed with Mr. Roosevelt's entire program of social reform and said it was leading to disaster."[58]

While his keen wit enlivened the otherwise dull race — at least to the extent that his voice was even heard that autumn — most of the 1940 campaign was pure drudgery for the battle-scarred Socialist. As hard as he tried, he couldn't seem to catch a break.

When Willkie, for example, challenged FDR to a series of debates — a proposal swiftly rejected by the White House — Thomas quickly weighed in, saying that he applauded Willkie's desire to revive the Lincoln-Douglas debate tradition and then challenged his Republican opponent to a face-to-face debate on a wide-range of issues facing the country.

Thomas might have reasonably expected a positive response from Willkie. The two men, after all, were on friendly terms — they were both trustees of the New York Town Hall — and had debated a year and a half earlier in New York City on the issue of government ownership of utilities.

Describing him as something of a "political enigma," Thomas also had some fairly positive things to say about his Republican rival that year. "I don't know what kind of president he would make," he told a reporter for the *Indianapolis Star*, but "he may surprise his own party by being the most liberal leader the Republicans have ever had." Thomas also believed that Willkie was "a sincere advocate of civil liberties."[59]

Needless to say, Thomas would have loved to go toe-to-toe with Willkie that autumn. "In principle your position and the President's on vital issues is the same," Thomas wrote in a telegram to the Republican nominee on August 19. Arguing that his own position on "peacetime conscription and economic policy is very different and emphatically worth public discussion," Thomas said the national interest would be served with or without President Roosevelt's participation.[60]

When Willkie ducked his Socialist rival's challenge to a debate, Thomas's supporters began picketing outside the GOP nominee's

---

[58] Seidler, *Norman Thomas: Respectable Rebel*, p. 92.
[59] "Willkie Called 'Political Enigma' By Perennial Socialist Candidate," *Indianapolis Star*, June 29, 1940.
[60] "Asks Willkie to Debate," *New York Times*, Aug. 20, 1940.

hotel in New York, carrying banners demanding that Willkie accept the challenge to debate. When informed of the protesters, Willkie laughed and said that he wouldn't participate in a one-on-one debate with Thomas. "I'm very fond of Norman," he told reporters, "and if he can get Mr. Roosevelt to join us, I'll be glad to participate in a tri-partite debate."[61] Refusing to take no for an answer, an exasperated Thomas challenged Willkie to another face-to-face debate in Elmira, New York, in late October, but was again rebuffed.[62]

In the meantime, Willkie had stunned most of his party's conservative and isolationist elements that year by essentially accepting almost all of the major objectives of Roosevelt's foreign and domestic policies.

While mildly criticizing the Democrats for failing to adequately stimulate business activity, Willkie's refusal to issue a wholesale indictment of the New Deal's economic policies helped to mollify independents and moderates and liberals in both parties, but it also opened him to criticism from conservatives that he was little more than a "me too" candidate, a mere echo of Roosevelt — a charge that was reinforced by the fact that he also embraced the administration's policy toward Great Britain, which now stood virtually alone in its struggle against brutal Nazi aggression.

By early October, Willkie's handlers realized that their candidate's opposition to a third term — the GOP's only consistent rallying cry that year — was failing to gain traction. They were worried, too, that Willkie's thoughtful criticism of Roosevelt for failing to bring about a full and lasting economic recovery, was falling on deaf ears. As the summer turned to fall, Willkie's candidacy was going nowhere — and fast. Biographer Ellsworth Barnard called it the "Willkie Slump."[63]

Losing steam, the Republican standard-bearer dramatically changed tactics and began campaigning as an out-and-out "peace candidate" — a dramatic shift in his public position that caught Thomas and his left-wing Socialist Party almost completely by surprise.

Ironically, that was precisely what Thomas had advised Willkie and the GOP to do earlier that summer while campaigning

---

[61] "Willkie is Picketed; But He Says He Is Willing to Debate With Thomas,"*New York Times*, Aug. 27, 1940; "Willkie Blasts Roosevelt for Defense Delay," *Chicago Tribune*, Aug. 27, 1940.

[62] "Thomas Challenges Willkie to Debate; Socialist Asks Opponent to Face Him at Elmira," *New York Times*, Oct. 25, 1940.

[63] Ellsworth Barnard, *Wendell Willkie: Fighter for Freedom* (Marquette, Michigan, 1966), p. 209.

in Indianapolis. "If I were a Republican," said Thomas, grinning at the very prospect, "I would charge that Franklin Roosevelt has played fast and loose with the American people on this war talk. First, he would have us believe that the United States could dominate world trade without war, and now he says we can't even defend Omaha from an invader." Suggesting that FDR's foreign policy had given the Germans "as much reason to declare war against the United States as Hitler needs," Thomas said that he believed "the American people will refute Mr. Roosevelt because he has come so perilously close to bringing us into war."[64]

Up to this point in the campaign, the 55-year-old Thomas had been campaigning as the only genuine isolationist or peace candidate in the race. For months, he had been saying that the two major parties weren't offering the voters a choice on the issue of war or peace, but Willkie's sudden change of strategy altered all of that.

Though Willkie privately saw eye to eye with FDR on aid to Great Britain, then sustaining nightly aerial attacks from the German *Luftwaffe*, he was keenly aware of the strong desire of most Americans to stay out of the conflict and in early October began warning that Roosevelt's reelection would mean "wooden crosses for sons and brothers and sweethearts."[65]

Whether Willkie was entirely sincere in his rhetoric or not, his antiwar stance was music to the ears of his party's isolationists — and there were many of them at the time. Though he privately supported the so-called "Destroyer Deal," FDR's executive order agreeing to the exchange of fifty aging U.S. destroyers in return for 99-year leases for American bases on British territory in the Atlantic and the Caribbean, Willkie — under enormous pressure from his party's isolationists, including Michigan's Arthur Vandenberg — publicly charged that the destroyers deal was "the most arbitrary and dictatorial action ever taken by any President in the history of the United States."[66]

In his new role as the savior who would keep America out of war, Willkie began telling voters that Roosevelt's pledge to stay out of the European conflict was just another empty promise, not unlike his vow to balance the federal budget in 1932. Pushing the envelope even further, the Republican candidate went so far as to

---

[64] "Willkie Called 'Political Enigma" By Perennial Socialist Candidate," *Indianapolis Star*, June 29, 1940.
[65] Scott John Hammond, Robert North Roberts and Valerie A. Sulfaro, *Campaigning for President in America, 1788-2016* (Santa Barbara, 2016), p. 673.
[66] Ibid.

suggest that if Roosevelt won a third term the United States would be at war by the spring of 1941.

Willkie's promise to keep America out of the war momentarily breathed new life into his floundering campaign, one that had been lagging in the polls since early September when Gallup, in a poll released on September 20, reported that Roosevelt was winning 55 percent of the popular vote and leading in all but ten of the forty-eight states.[67] But it came at a heavy price, subjecting the Republican nominee to some of the most intense and mean-spirited attacks imaginable during the closing weeks of the campaign.

From the Left, Thomas sharply disputed Willkie's claim that he would keep the country out of war, declaring in a speech in Rochester, New York, that the Republican nominee had been "captured by the same interventionists school" as Roosevelt — words that while certainly not his intention surely comforted the British, who were deeply worried that the U.S. would put an isolationist in the White House that year.[68]

Thomas also believed that Willkie was as likely to plunge the country into war "about as fast and on about the same terms" as Roosevelt.[69] If anything, asserted Thomas, Willkie was more of a spokesman for a dying capitalist system, which, "having failed to conquer poverty at home, seeks expansion through armament economics, imperialism and war" than the Democratic incumbent had been.[70]

Though Thomas personally conceded that a relatively strong case could be made for U.S. involvement in the growing European conflict, the Socialist standard-bearer believed that an even stronger case could be made to stay out of it. He seriously doubted the sincerity of both Roosevelt and Willkie when they pledged to keep the United States out of the war, especially since both men favored peacetime conscription and massive military preparedness.

What really angered him, however, was his belief that both major-party candidates were deliberately deceiving the American people into a war they obviously didn't want.[71] "Both were convinced, I think, that we were going to have to go to war," reflected Thomas a few years later, "but did not have the courage to tell the people. Either that or they were incomprehensibly stupid, which I

---

[67] Barnard, *Wendell Willkie: Fighter for Freedom*, p. 209.
[68] "Peace Proponents Said to Have One Choice," *Los Angeles Times*, Oct. 26, 1940.
[69] "Republicans and Democrats Hurl Speeches and Statements in Heat of Vote Campaign," *Racine Journal-Times*, Oct. 31, 1940.
[70] "Peace Proponents Said to Have One Choice," *Los Angeles Times*, Oct. 26, 1940.
[71] Fleischman, *Norman Thomas: A Biography*, p. 198.

am not inclined to believe they were. As a result of such policy, we were prepared for neither peace nor war."[72]

Thomas had made this point throughout the campaign. Wrapping up a two-day visit to California, where his name appeared on the ballot as the nominee of the ballot-qualified Progressive Party, he told a national radio audience on September 21 that it would be "exceedingly ill advised" if the American people allowed the recent statements by Willkie and Roosevelt promising to keep the country out of the war in Europe to "lull them into false security."

Pointing to the country's massive military buildup and peacetime conscription — policies favored by both major-party candidates — Thomas claimed that both of his opponents were so deeply committed to a program stopping just short of full-scale U.S. military involvement that it might be impossible to avoid going over the threshold for which they originally intended to stop short. They were playing a very dangerous game, he said.[73]

Thomas was particularly disturbed by the enactment of a peacetime draft. It was evidence that the country was unmistakably headed toward war. "They put it over beautifully and painlessly," he observed in an interview with the Harvard student newspaper on the eve of the election, "but now the novacane is wearing off and opposition is developing. It is probable," he gloomily prophesied, "that after the election the government will crack down on this and all other opposition or criticism."[74]

Thomas's rebuke of Willkie, assailing his rival as a tool of interventionists clamoring for war, was fairly mild compared to the blistering salvos launched by the Democrats against the Republican candidate that fall.

Speaking in Philadelphia in late October, Democratic vice-presidential candidate Henry A. Wallace, getting down and dirty, charged that Nazi agents had been ordered to spend significant sums of money to help Willkie defeat President Roosevelt. It was a breathtaking allegation and one that would be repeated throughout the remainder of the campaign.

In his particularly vicious attack, Wallace claimed that Willkie's mind was in a constant "state of confusion" and that he made up in bluster for what he lacked in knowledge. "This fact explains, I

---

[72] "Norman Thomas Thinks Browder Conservative," *Los Angeles Times*, Sep. 29, 1944.
[73] "Fight for Keeping Out of War Extolled by Norman Thomas," *Los Angeles Times*, Sept. 22, 1940.
[74] "Thomas Pledges Party Will Fight On; Predicts FDR Win," *Harvard Crimson*, Nov. 5, 1940.

believe, why the Nazi agents in this country have been ordered to work for his election," said Wallace.[75]

"The friends of the totalitarian powers have decided that the ignorance and lack of leadership of the Republican candidate qualify him as their candidate," continued the vice-presidential candidate, adding that Adolf Hitler "would rejoice to see in control of our government a party whose leaders cannot see what is before their eyes. He would rejoice," concluded Wallace, "to have in office a well-meaning but inexperienced man who cannot understand the Nazi plots, and who is unable to lead his own party except into confusion."[76]

In an address at New York's Madison Square Garden a few days later, Wallace again asserted that Hitler and the Nazis wanted Willkie to defeat Roosevelt. Speaking at rally sponsored by the American Labor Party on October 31, Wallace declared that "millions of Americans know from personal observations that there is Nazi propaganda and Nazi pressure for the election of the Republican candidate" and that various Nazi organizations were "marching in the Republican parade." Hitler, he said, "has decided that if Roosevelt can be defeated, England would be discouraged, South America would turn away from the United States, and he would have an easier time with his somewhat delayed plans for world conquest."[77]

Willkie immediately denounced the vice-presidential candidate, calling his politically-charged remarks "reckless and irresponsible."[78]

While carefully skirting the candidate's German ancestry, the vicious Democratic attacks that autumn, echoed by one administration spokesman after another, hurt Willkie not only politically, but also on a deeply personal level. They were excruciatingly painful since Willkie, an internationalist all his life, had strongly repudiated isolationism and had promised to "outdistance Hitler in any contest he chooses."[79]

Though he contended throughout the 1940 campaign that Roosevelt had "courted a war for which this country is totally unprepared and which it emphatically does not want" and had personally promised not "to send one American boy into the shambles of a European war," Willkie nevertheless supported the major

---

[75] "Wallace Charges Nazis are Ordered to Assist Willkie," *New York Times*, Oct. 26, 1940.
[76] Ibid.
[77] "Willkie Warns U.S. of One-Man Rule, Citing President's 'My Envoy' Remark; Wallace Charges Nazi Pressure Here," *New York Times*, Nov. 1, 1940.
[78] Ibid.
[79] Roseboom, *A History of Presidential Elections*, p. 469

objectives of FDR's foreign policy, including aid to beleaguered Britain, which was being pounded almost nightly by Nazi air raids.

Recognizing the additional menacing threat to that country posed by German U-Boats, the Republican nominee, as mentioned previously, refused to criticize Roosevelt when he originally proposed an agreement giving Great Britain fifty World War I vintage naval destroyers in exchange for 99-year leases for naval and air bases on British territory in the western hemisphere. It was only after considerable pressure from his party's sizable isolationist wing that he finally spoke out against it.[80] He also courageously supported legislation calling for a peacetime draft — the first in American history — deeply angering a majority of Republicans in Congress.[81]

Moreover, Willkie had taken an unequivocal stand against "race hatred, bigotry and Hitlerism" long before he ever decided to run for president. There was never any doubt about his feelings toward Hitler and those who sympathized with him. "I consider anti-Semitism in America as a possible criminal movement and every anti-Semite as a possible traitor to America," he said in early July.[82]

The Republican nominee had also repudiated the support of any group or individual supporting him on the basis of racial or religious prejudice and had bluntly rejected the support of Father Coughlin's organization when an editorial praising Willkie's candidacy appeared in the pages of *Social Justice*, the weekly magazine of the Coughlinites, in late August.[83]

Wallace, of course, wasn't alone in trying to link Willkie's candidacy to the Nazis and their appeasers in the United States. When Willkie repudiated Coughlin and other potential supporters who were promoting religious and racial intolerance, Edward J. Flynn, the Bronx political boss who had replaced James A. Farley as chairman of the Democratic National Committee, was quick with a rebuttal. "Mr. Willkie can repudiate their support — as he has in one case, at least — from now until doomsday. The fact still remains that these fellow travelers still support him, by disseminating the vilest sort of anti-Roosevelt propaganda."[84]

---

[80] Barnard, *Wendell Willkie: Fighter for Freedom*, pp. 205, 227-229; "Willkie is Cheered in Chicago Loop," *New York Times*, Sept. 14, 1940.
[81] Roseboom, *A History of Presidential Elections*, p. 469.
[82] Barnard, *Wendell Willkie: Fighter for Freedom*, p. 222.
[83] "Willkie Rejects Coughlin Backing," *New York Times*, Aug. 28, 1940.
[84] "Flynn Supports Wallace Charge," *New York Times*, Sept. 1, 1940.

New York Gov. Herbert Lehman, Roosevelt's successor then halfway through his fourth and final term, also attacked the Republican nominee, saying that nothing "could give Hitler, Mussolini, Stalin, and Japan more satisfaction than the defeat of...Franklin D. Roosevelt." Journalist Dorothy Thompson — regarded as one of the two most influential women in America — also chimed in, hysterically suggesting in a radio broadcast that "a vote for Wendell Willkie is a vote for fascism." Thompson made the same charge in a column that was so inflammatory that the *New York Herald Tribune* flatly refused to publish it.[85]

Willkie's vigorous protestations notwithstanding, there was, unfortunately, more than a measure of truth in the highly-sensational charges made by Wallace and other supporters of the administration, a fact unbeknownst to the Republican standard-bearer at the time and something that would have been completely beyond his control even if he was aware of it.

It's absolutely true that Hitler would have liked nothing more than to see Roosevelt go down to defeat in 1940. Just as British intelligence had tried to influence the Republican nominating process earlier that year, the German government, in fact, had spent lavishly in a largely unsuccessful attempt to influence both the Republican nomination and the outcome of the general election.

Working through Hans Thomsen, an attaché in the German embassy who later boasted that he had personally inserted a plank in the GOP's platform stressing "Americanism, preparedness and peace," the Nazis placed a number of full-page advertisements in the *New York Times* that autumn supporting isolationist candidates in both major parties.[86]

Additional evidence of direct Nazi involvement in the 1940 presidential campaign surfaced six years later when O. John Rogge, a special assistant to the U.S. Attorney General who won convictions that helped break up Huey Long's political machine in Louisiana and actively sought the Progressive Party's vice-presidential nomination in 1948, said in a speech in Swarthmore, Pennsylvania, that Nazi leaders in Germany, working through a special committee in the German Foreign Office established by Nazi Foreign Minister Joachim von Ribbentrop — one of a dozen Nazi leaders sentenced to death at Nuremberg — spent a great deal of time and effort on proposed schemes to defeat Roosevelt in each of his three campaigns for reelection.[87]

---

[85] Barnard, *Wendell Willkie: Fighter for Freedom*, p. 259.
[86] Manchester, *The Glory and the Dream*, p. 225.
[87] "Nazis' Plan to Defeat Roosevelt Described," *Los Angeles Times*, Oct. 23, 1946.

Rogge, the chief prosecutor in the government's mass sedition conspiracy case against thirty suspected Nazi sympathizers, including controversial Wichita evangelist Gerald B. Winrod and self-styled fascist Joseph E. McWilliams, the former pinup boy of the Christian Front, was fired by Attorney General Tom C. Clark — Ramsey Clark's father — for violating the Justice Department's longstanding rules and regulations regarding secrecy a few days after his Swarthmore speech.[88]

While Nazi involvement in the 1940 presidential election was never disputed, there was also quite a bit of evidence of British intrigue in the campaign. The Rev. John Haynes Holmes, who feared the nation had "gone dangerously mad" in the face of the European situation, was one of those who strongly suspected that Great Britain had influenced the outcome of the presidential contest, asserting shortly after the election that "under the influence of the cleverest kind of British propaganda," the Roosevelt administration had deliberately conspired to break down overwhelming resistance to the war. "Britain," he said, was "fighting her own battle for the protection and perpetuation of her far-flung empire."[89]

While fending off the vicious attacks from Wallace and other Democratic partisans, Willkie appeared to receive a badly-needed boost when John L. Lewis, the powerful and unpredictable leader of the four million-member CIO, dropped a political bombshell in the campaign's closing days, strongly urging organized labor to abandon Roosevelt and support the Republican nominee.[90] A third term, said Lewis, "would be a national evil of the first magnitude."[91]

In a nationally-broadcast radio address on October 25 — at a cost of $60,000, it was the most extensive radio hook-up ever marshaled by a labor leader up to that point in American history — the CIO chieftain charged that FDR had betrayed labor and was planning to involve the United States in the world war during his third term. Lewis, who had encouraged Montana's Burton K. Wheeler to mount a third-party candidacy earlier that summer and even

---

[88] "Clark Ousts Rogge for Speech Linking Americans With Nazis," *New York Times*, Oct. 26, 1946.
[89] "Civil Liberties Head Fears Conscription; John Haynes Holmes Sees Nation 'Gone Dangerously Mad,'" *New York Times*, June 12, 1940; "America Urged by Dr. Holmes to Oppose War," *Buffalo Courier-Express*, Mar. 10, 1941.
[90] "Lewis Declares for Willkie; Says Roosevelt Means War and Dictatorship in Nation," *New York Times*, Oct. 26, 1940.
[91] Robert H. Zieger, *John L. Lewis: Labor Leader* (Boston, 1988), p. 110.

briefly considered heading such a ticket himself, said that Willkie's election was imperative for the country's welfare.[92]

Denouncing Roosevelt as "a Caesar" who wanted to impose a dictatorship in the United States and whose sole motivation and purpose in seeking an unprecedented third term in the White House was to lead the nation into war, Lewis asserted that Willkie would not "send the sons of American mothers and American fathers to fight in foreign wars" and would use the power and influence of the presidency to prevent war and maintain peace between nations. He also promised to resign as head of the CIO if Roosevelt was elected to a third term. "Sustain me now, or repudiate me," he told his listeners.[93]

Several left-wing leaders in the CIO heeded Lewis's plea, including Harry Bridges of the militantly left-wing west coast longshoremen's union who was already under attack as a Communist, but most of the country's larger unions, especially those affiliated with the AFL, remained loyal to Roosevelt.[94]

It was against this intriguing cloak-and-dagger backdrop that Thomas heroically campaigned in 1940, quietly canvassing the country in search of votes for America's better self.

As the only militantly antiwar candidate in the race, support came from some pretty unusual and rather strange quarters that year. In a column thirty years later, John P. Roche, a veteran of that campaign, recalled receiving a $5,000 check from a woman in Los Angeles who urged Thomas to protect the nation from the "international Zionist conspiracy." Though Roche believed Thomas would've personally returned the check in a heartbeat, he rather suspected that the woman's note was conveniently misplaced by the back office and that the funds eventually found their way into the campaign's coffers. That was a lot of money in those days.[95]

As in 1936, Thomas once again found himself competing with the Communist Party's Earl Browder and the tiny Socialist Labor Party's John W. Aiken on his left.

The 40-year-old Aiken, an expert furniture polisher, joined the SLP at an unusually early age and quite by accident, discovering the party as a sixteen-year-old in 1912 when a copy of *The People*, then edited by Daniel De Leon, blew into his front yard in Chelsea,

---

[92] "Lewis, C.I.O. Chief, Urges Willkie Vote," *Los Angeles Times*, Oct. 26, 1940.
[93] Ibid.
[94] "Bridges Hails Lewis Talk," *New York Times*, Nov. 2, 1940.
[95] John P. Roche, ""Weird Coalition Defeats AID," *Daytona Beach News-Journal*, Nov. 14, 1971.

Massachusetts. Hoping to find comics in the newspaper, the inquisitive teenager picked it up and read it closely. He liked what he read and wrote to the party's headquarters asking for literature, becoming a lifelong party member shortly thereafter.

Within a decade, the bushy-haired Aiken was running for statewide office on the party's ticket. He kept running for the next quarter of a century, his high-water mark occurring during the hotly-contested and razor-thin 1930 Massachusetts gubernatorial contest when he nearly polled the difference between Republican incumbent Frank G. Allen and Democrat Joseph B. Ely, an Al Smith acolyte who later opposed the New Deal and backed Alf Landon against Roosevelt in 1936. Impressively, Aiken outdistanced Alfred Baker Lewis, the Socialist Party's wealthy and widely-recognized nominee, by nearly 6,400 votes in that campaign.

A self-educated man who voraciously consumed the works of Karl Marx for nearly a quarter century while studying anthropology, economics, history, law and sociology at night, Aiken was one of the party's brightest members. An artist and something of a romantic, he was as comfortable chatting in his thick Boston accent about the merits of Thomas Chippendale, the famous English cabinetmaker, or the simple style of U.S. furniture maker Duncan Phyfe, as he was in discussing the works of Karl Marx and Friedrich Engels.

He was also an extremely modest individual, a quiet man who kept largely to himself. In fact, when he died in virtual obscurity in December 1968 — five days before Socialist Norman M. Thomas passed away — his longtime neighbors in the East Hartford, Connecticut, mobile home park where he had lived for nearly a decade, had no idea that Aiken had ever been involved in politics and had twice sought the presidency.

"You're kidding," said the surprised manager of the trailer park who had known Aiken for more than nine years when informed of his late tenant's political past. Even Aiken's wife from whom he had been separated for a number of years wasn't quite sure where he lived in the years preceding his death. But that's the way the retired furniture finisher wanted it, requesting that no obituaries be published upon his death.[96]

The low-key radical, who was then waging his second campaign for the White House — he crisscrossed the country in a used 1934 Chevrolet four years earlier, polling a hugely disappointing

---

[96] "He Died Obscure But TIME Magazine Covered John Aiken," *Hartford Courant*, Dec. 25, 1968.

12,790 votes — was never really a factor in the 1940 presidential election.

The Communist Party's Earl Browder, who denounced Norman Thomas as "a social fascist" during the 1932 presidential election, was of much greater concern to Thomas and the Socialists.

A man riddled with contradictions and complexities and possessing a feisty independent streak that couldn't be tamed, ultimately leading to his fall from grace within the Communist hierarchy, Browder was arguably the preeminent leader of the Communist Party in the United States during the Great Depression and World War II, a heady period when the party boasted a membership of 100,000 and arguably exerted its greatest influence.

The son of a disabled homesteader and elementary schoolteacher whose ancestors settled in Virginia in the 1650's, more than 100 years before the American Revolution, Browder was born in Wichita, Kansas, in 1891, and was raised with his seven siblings in a poor farming family that had been heavily influenced by Populism, the great agrarian movement that had swept Kansas and other farming states of the Great Plains shortly after his birth.

Like his predecessor and adversarial successor William Z. Foster, Browder was forced to leave school at an early age to help support his family, working as an errand boy in a department store and later as a messenger for Western Union. Despite his lack of formal education, Browder — again like Foster — was intellectually inquisitive, possessing an almost insatiable appetite for knowledge. He also harbored Foster's deep hostility toward economic injustice, a lifelong resentment undoubtedly shaped by the fact that he had to quit school at the age of nine, before completing the third grade, shortly after his father — a schoolteacher and avowed socialist who freely inculcated his children with a strong sense of class-consciousness — became an invalid, possibly the result of a nervous breakdown.[97]

The younger Browder joined the Socialist Party in 1906, when he was barely fifteen years old and actively campaigned for Eugene V. Debs in the 1908 and 1912 presidential campaigns.

"While other boys scanned the sports pages and talked about baseball heroes such as Honus Wagner and John McGraw," wrote James G. Ryan in his magnificent and meticulously researched biography of the Kansan, "Browder peddled party periodicals and urged adults to elect Debs." For a small monthly fee, the budding Marxist also purchased fifty "Socialist classics" and devoured the

---

[97] Ryan, *Earl Browder*, p. 8.

works of Friedrich Engels, Karl Marx and Karl Kautsky, the intellectual and political conscience of German socialism and arguably the most influential Marxist theorist in the years following Engels' death in 1895. Browder was particularly impressed by Kautsky's *Road to Power*.

Like thousands of other left-wing party members, however, Browder left the Socialist Party in disgust seven years later, shortly after the IWW's William D. "Big Bill" Haywood, the fiercely radical leader of the miners' union and a man that the young Browder admired immensely, was unceremoniously expelled from the party's national executive committee for allegedly endorsing the use of sabotage and violence in labor disputes.

Relocating to Kansas City in 1912, Browder drifted politically during this period and at one point even turned down an offer to join the powerful Pendergast machine before eventually joining the Workers' Educational League, a local affiliate of William Z. Foster's Syndicalist League of North America, founded in 1912. A forerunner of the far more influential and significant Trade Union Educational League (TUEL), Foster's Syndicalist League sought to radicalize existing American Federation of Labor trade unions. Kansas City was one of eleven U.S. cities with an autonomous league.

Browder, who headed the local Bookkeepers, Stenographers, and Accountants Union, an AFL union, and represented it on the Kansas City (Missouri) Central Labor Council, worked as an accountant for a subsidiary of Standard Oil during this period. In his spare time, he edited the *Toiler*, the League's monthly publication. He later managed a farm cooperative and served on the Cooperative League of North America's national council.

Browder, who briefly rejoined the Socialist Party in 1917 after being arrested for conspiring to obstruct the country's draft laws during World War I — spending a year in prison for failing to register for the draft — was subsequently sentenced to 16 months in Leavenworth in mid-1919 on the conspiracy charge. During his prison stay at Leavenworth, he was named as an honorary charter member of the Communist Party.

Browder subsequently immersed himself in the party and later emerged as the faction-ridden organization's leader following a protracted battle between William Z. Foster and Lithuanian-born Jay Lovestone — a quarrel ultimately settled by Moscow in which Foster was severely admonished, Lovestone was unceremoniously removed as the party's national secretary, and Browder, whose role in the factional fight was minimal, was named as the party's new chief.

Campaigning far more strenuously against Alf Landon than for himself during the 1936 presidential campaign, Browder received 80,160 votes in thirty-five states — a slight drop from the 103,000 votes cast for William Z. Foster four years earlier.

While Norman Thomas was deeply disappointed by his own showing in that election, Browder was tickled pink by the results, not necessarily by the number of votes cast for the Communist ticket, but by the sheer size of Roosevelt's victory.

"The balloting on Nov. 3 could be called 'the great repudiation,'" gloated the tart-tongued Communist in a post-election statement. "The large majority of people were first of all voting against Hearst, against the Liberty League, against Wall Street, against Landon, against reaction, fascism and jingoism."[98]

Breaking with Roosevelt's foreign policy upon the signing of the Soviet-German pact in 1939, Browder was singing a completely different tune in 1940. Roosevelt was now the enemy.

In what was otherwise one of the most heady and exciting periods in its history, the 1940 presidential election proved to be the most difficult campaign ever conducted by the Communist Party.

Facing obstacles of almost unfathomable proportions — burdensome and oppressively onerous hurdles deliberately placed in its path by the two major parties, the Justice Department and state election officials, as well as members of the fascist-leaning American Legion — it was easily the most arduously painful and punishing campaign ever experienced by a minor party in U.S. history. In magnitude, it even surpassed the churlish, heavily-funded and carefully orchestrated campaign by state and national Democrats to thwart democracy more than sixty years later by attempting to keep longtime consumer advocate Ralph Nader's 2004 independent presidential candidacy off the ballot in as many states as possible.

Though initially hoping that John L. Lewis and the CIO would provide the spark for a new "Farmer-Labor Party," one that would unite opponents of the war with other left-leaning New Dealers, the Communist Party went ahead with its own national convention at New York's Royal Windsor Hotel. As fully expected, Browder was again chosen for the nation's top spot.[99]

James W. Ford, the son of a coal miner whose grandfather had been lynched by the Ku Klux Klan, once again came along for the

---

[98] Klehr, *The Heyday of American Communism*, p. 197
[99] "Earl Browder to Seek Presidency," *Appleton Post-Crescent*, June 3, 1940.

ride. A former Alabama steelworker, Ford was one of the party's most prominent African-American members. Appearing on the party's national ticket for the third and final time, the 47-year-old Ford had been William Z. Foster's running mate in 1932 and campaigned with Browder four years later.[100]

"The masses of the United States cry out for a new party, for a modern Abraham Lincoln," thundered Browder in his acceptance speech, "as the only road toward the solution of the crisis of today, the crisis of the breakdown of capitalism, the crisis of imperialist war that threatens destruction to the world. Accepting your nomination, I pledge our party to cooperate with labor and the people toward this great goal."[101]

Outlining his party's program, Browder said that the Communist Party "gives voice to the deepest convictions of the great majority of the American people when it calls for a halt to the deliberative drive into the war. We speak for the people," he declared, "when we demand a stop to the blood-soaked trade in munitions and instruments of war. We speak for the millions when we resolve, 'The Yanks are not coming.'"[102]

The Communists quickly got an inkling of how extraordinarily difficult things were going to be that year when a number of radio stations across the country, including WCKY in Cincinnati and WCAU in Philadelphia, refused to air Earl Browder's acceptance speech from Madison Square Garden during the closing session of the party's national convention.

Moreover, officials of the Columbia Broadcasting System, one of three national networks that carried Browder's speech, albeit an abbreviated version, said that they would ask for a revision of the nation's broadcast communications laws so that individual radio stations wouldn't be compelled to provide time to "any political party if it is proven to be subservient to a foreign power."[103]

The most devastating blow of all, however, occurred in its New York stronghold when Browder and Ford and the party's entire statewide ticket — Israel Amter for the U.S. Senate and Frank Herron and feminist Elizabeth Gurley Flynn for representatives-at-large — were knocked off the ballot on a technicality, one that involved some heavy-handed tactics by the fervently anti-communist American Legion.

---

[100] Fraser M. Ottanelli, *The Communist Party of the United States: From the Depression to World War II* (New Brunswick, 1991), p. 203; William Z. Foster, *History of the Communist Party of the United States* (New York, 1952), pp. 290-291.
[101] "Browder Proposes Creating 3d Party," *New York Times*, June 3, 1940.
[102] Ibid.
[103] "Storm Raised by Communists," *Los Angeles Times*, June 1, 1940.

The Communist Party's petitions, filed shortly before midnight on October 8 and bearing 43,760 signatures — 20,000 more than submitted by the Socialist Party and 25,000 more than the Prohibitionists turned in — were immediately challenged by Edward A. Vosseler, state commander of the American Legion, who instructed legion posts throughout the state to investigate the authenticity of the signatures on the Communist petitions.[104]

As in West Virginia and elsewhere, the American Legion had been determined to keep the Communists off the ballot in as many states as possible that year. In January, national commander Raymond J. Kelly declared that the Communist Party was "a criminal conspiracy and a revolutionary movement and not a bona fide political party" and should be barred from the ballot throughout the country.[105]

"We ought to quit coddling these radical groups," Kelly told a reporter prior to attending a luncheon hosted by officials of the New York Stock Exchange. "We have gone too far in allowing people who would destroy our government to enjoy the same rights as people who are willing to abide by the fundamental precepts of democracy." Arguing that there was a point where freedom ends and treason begins, the American Legion national commander questioned why state election officials would allow the Communist Party to appear on the ballot as a legitimate political party. "The Communists are using the Bill of Rights as a cloak to destroy those rights in the nation," he asserted.[106]

Cognizant of the fact that the Communists had garnered more than 106,000 votes in the state's at-large U.S. House race two years earlier and worried that its presidential ticket would improve upon the 35,609 votes polled in New York in 1936, Browder firmly believed that the Democrats had conspired to keep the Communist Party off the ballot in the Empire State to enhance Roosevelt's chances of carrying the state against its adopted son, Wendell Willkie.

Testifying before the U.S. Senate Committee on Campaign Expenditures in late October, Browder accused the Democrats of working in tandem with the American Legion and deliberately using "fraud" and "intimidation" to convince 160 of the 200 regis-

---

[104] "Three New Slates in Field in State: Communists, Socialists and Prohibitionists File Petitions," *New York Times*, Oct. 9, 1940.
[105] "Kelly Proposes Reds be Taken Off Ballot," *New York Times*, Jan. 29, 1940.
[106] Ibid.

tered voters in Greene County who had signed the party's nominating petitions to testify under oath that they had not been aware of what they were signing.[107]

According to Browder's testimony, many of the signers had been threatened with the loss of their jobs — especially those employed by the WPA — or, in the case of older voters, possibly the forfeiture of their old-age pensions. The American Legion stopped at nothing to convince the signers to retract their signatures. This was clearly an act of brazen intimidation, since the authenticity of the signatures was never in question.[108]

In a radio appearance a few days earlier, Browder alleged that the Democrats were attempting to "steal" as many as 200,000 Communist votes in New York to make the state and its forty-seven electoral votes safe for Roosevelt. "If Mr. Roosevelt cannot win this election without Communist votes," he declared, "he has no right to win at all." In his radio broadcast, the Communist Party leader also lambasted the state's newspapers for publishing the names of those who had signed the party's nominating petitions.[109]

The Democrats vigorously denied Browder's accusations. "The Democrats want no part of Mr. Browder or anything he stands for — and that goes for New York state, West Virginia, and the rest of the country," retorted Sol A. Rosenblatt, counsel for the Democratic National Committee."[110]

Another particularly wrenching experience took place in Illinois where the state election board barred the party from the ballot on the grounds that the party's petitions lacked a minimum of 200 signatures in each of at least fifty counties, thereby sustaining an objection lodged by Leonard W. Esper, an American Legion commander in Springfield.[111]

Party activists had faced one unforeseen obstacle after another when trying to get the party on the ballot in the Land of Lincoln, including an assault on ten party members from Chicago and Evanston while petitioning in the town of Pekin. The ten party activists, including two women, were physically attacked by a menacing crowd and had to seek shelter in the nearby courthouse. Their automobiles were also set on fire by angry townspeople. After spending the night in jail for their own safety, the ten Communists

---

[107] "Browder Charges Democratic Plot," *New York Times*, Oct. 26, 1940.
[108] Ibid.
[109] "Browder Charges Democratic 'Steal'" *New York Times*, Oct. 23, 1940.
[110] "Browder Charges Democratic Plot," *New York Times*, Oct. 26, 1940.
[111] "Illinois Electoral Board Bars Reds from Ballot," *Chicago Tribune*, Sept. 24, 1940.

were taken to Peoria the following morning under the protection of sheriff's deputies and state patrolmen where they boarded a train back to Chicago.¹¹²

Party workers faced similar hostilities in Rockford about a month later when a crowd of about 150 people, organized and instigated by the local American Legion, pummeled a group of petitioner circulators, slapping and punching several of them. The unruly mob also tried to overturn their cars. As in Pekin, the Communists were again rescued by police and deputy sheriffs, but not before the crowd seized the party's nominating petitions and other literature and burned them on the courthouse steps.¹¹³

Convinced of a conspiracy by state and local authorities to thwart the party's ballot access efforts, the Communists filed a lawsuit in federal court in August seeking to restrain Attorney General John E. Cassidy, a Democrat, and 33 other law enforcement officials from interfering with efforts to place the Communist Party on the ballot.

Alleging a general conspiracy to deprive the plaintiffs of their constitutional rights, the lawsuit cited numerous incidents of party members and sympathizers being arrested, beaten or chased out of town for circulating nominating petitions and distributing literature. At least thirty party activists had been arrested during the party's petition drive.

Filed on behalf of nine party members, including Ira Silbar, who was being held in a Lewistown jail for nearly a month on charges of criminal syndicalism for distributing party literature, the party also sought $90,000 in damages.¹¹⁴ The party's plea for injunctive relief was later dismissed by a federal judge.¹¹⁵

Indiana also proved to be a nightmare when the state election board — without so much as even a cursory review of the party's nominating papers — rejected the party's petitions bearing more than 11,000 signatures on the grounds that some of the signatures may have been invalid and that the Communist Party advocated overthrowing the U.S. government by force. Dating back to William Z. Foster's initial campaign on the Workers' Party ticket sixteen years earlier, the Communist ticket had appeared on the ballot in the Hoosier State in every presidential election since 1924.

---

112 "10 Communists Released After a Night in Jail," *Chicago Tribune*, May 27, 1940.
113 "Seize Reds in Rockford," *Chicago Tribune*, June 23, 1940; "Deny Communist Plea for Ballot 'Plot' Injunction," *Chicago Tribune*, Sept. 7, 1940.
114 "Illinois Reds Sue for Damages in Battle to Thwart Ballot Ban," *Chicago Tribune*, Aug. 18, 1940
115 "Deny Communist Plea for Ballot 'Plot' Injunction," *Chicago Tribune*, Sept. 7, 1940.

Adding insult to injury, Indiana's Secretary of State later forwarded copies of the 239 sheets of signatures on the party's nominating petitions to the Dies congressional investigating committee in Washington to determine if any of the signers were illegal aliens or had criminal records.[116]

One of those arrested for circulating Communist Party petitions that year was a young Max Weiner, a fiery consumer activist who later founded the Philadelphia-based Consumers Education & Protective Association (CEPA) and the Consumer Party, a left-leaning party that regularly fielded candidates in Pennsylvania between 1967 and 1995. The 28-year-old Weiner, who joined the party in late 1933 after he was unable to land a teaching job, had been convicted on charges of fraudulently obtaining signatures on the party's petitions, conspiracy to violate state election laws, and making false affidavits.[117] He was fined $500 and given an eight-month jail sentence.[118]

And so it went in state after state that year.

The Communists, of course, did have some success against the mean-spirited, if not outright fascist, attempt by the American Legion to subvert democracy by keeping the party off the ballot in 1940.

One example occurred in Rhode Island, where various American Legion chapters had lobbied hard to deny them a spot on the general election ballot. In that state, Secretary of State J. Hector Paquin, a Republican, ruled that there was nothing in the state election statutes to bar them from the ballot. Unfortunately, the Socialist Party, which had filed nominating petitions containing 800 signatures, wasn't as fortunate in the Ocean State, losing a place on the ballot for the second consecutive election cycle when more than 300 signatures were tossed out by election officials.[119]

While nothing compared to the inexcusably abysmal treatment afforded Earl Browder and the Communist Party that year, the 1940 presidential election was one of the most difficult campaigns for the country's nationally-organized minor parties in American history, with ballot access barriers clearly proving to be the largest impediment.

---

[116] "Communist Ticket Barred from Ballot in Indiana," *Chicago Tribune*, Oct. 9, 1940; "Open Probe of Communist Party Members in Indiana," *Hammond Times*, Oct. 17, 1940.
[117] "Red Vote Jury Convicts Two," *Pittsburgh Press*, Nov. 8, 1940.
[118] "Weiner and Zvon Get Jail Terms; File Appeals," *Harrisburg Evening News*, Mar. 31, 1941.
[119] "Move to Bar Communists Hits Snag in Rhode Island," *Christian Science Monitor*, Oct. 4, 1940.

According to University of Wisconsin professor Edward A. Ross and pacifist John Haynes Holmes, the Harvard-educated founder of the American Civil Liberties Union and close ally and friend of Norman Thomas, the Communist Party was barred from the ballot in fifteen states that year while petitions for the Socialist and Socialist Labor parties had been rejected in eleven and five states, respectively — the result, observed Holmes and Ross, of a "studied campaign of obstruction and intimidation."[120]

Despite the legal obstacles and ballot access difficulties facing both of their parties that year, Thomas and Browder mixed it up quite a bit during the autumn campaign, frequently trading barbs as each tried to establish supremacy on the left.

Thomas found the entire tenor of the 1940 presidential campaign, particularly the lack of substance on the crucial issues facing the country, absolutely appalling. He believed that both major-party candidates were deliberately waging "phony" campaigns while ignoring the real issue of war and peace. "There are no differences of importance between Roosevelt and Willkie," he scoffed while campaigning in Pittsburgh in early November. "Both of them are agreed on all steps short of war in order not only to aid England but the British Empire."[121]

The Socialist candidate's criticism of his major-party rivals also extended to domestic policy. "It is not merely in the all-important issues of war or peace that this is a phony campaign," he asserted, but also on domestic issues where the differences between the Democrats and the Republican parties were so "inconsiderable" as to be almost non-existent. In his mind, the same capitalist influences had captured both major parties. Having failed to conquer unemployment, he asserted, both parties were now looking toward economic expansion through imperialism and war. "That is the way of disaster," said Thomas. Moreover, he concluded, both major parties had colluded in creating a "monopolization of the ballot by the Republican and Democratic parties."[122]

Thomas and Krueger ended their longshot campaign with a joint appearance at New York's Mecca Temple on the eve of the election. Speaking to a crowd estimated at 2,000 — a far cry from the sellout crowd that gathered to hear Thomas's sensational

---

[120] "Minority Parties Curbed," *New York Times*, Nov. 3, 1940.
[121] "Thomas Denounces 'Phony' Campaign," *New York Times*, Nov. 2, 1940.
[122] Ibid.

windup to the 1932 campaign, or the 12,000 who gathered at Madison Square Garden four years earlier — the Socialist duo urged the nation's voters to give peace a chance.[123]

Claiming that the country was evenly divided "between those who think we must be saved from Willkie and those who think we must be saved from Roosevelt," Thomas asserted that the millions of "tortured souls" searching for the lesser of two evils should support the Socialist ticket rather than canceling each other out by voting for one of the two major-party candidates. "Those who have refused to support our Socialist cause lest they permit the greater evil to overtake them cannot even agree which is the greater evil," he said, reading from a prepared six-page manuscript.[124]

Thomas also reminded his audience that he was the only bonafide peace candidate in the race. Questioning Roosevelt's "zeal for peace," Thomas told the pint-sized crowd that a vote for the Socialist Party would put pressure on FDR to keep the country out of war, asserting that the larger the vote, the harder it would be for Roosevelt to ignore.[125]

In addition to criticizing the recent deportation proceedings initiated against Raissa Browder, the Russian-born wife of Communist Party leader Earl Browder who had furtively entered the country through Canada nearly six years earlier, the lean Socialist standard-bearer charged the Roosevelt administration with "slavishly" supporting British foreign policy toward Spain and the Far East.[126]

He also said that he was growing "sick and tired" of William Allen White's efforts to plunge the country into war, accusing the iconic journalist's Committee to Defend America by Aiding the Allies of committing acts that "the United States would consider acts of war if directed against her."[127]

In his address, Krueger bemoaned the fact that while millions of Americans recognized that Norman Thomas was an honest man and that the Socialist Party platform made a lot of sense, they nevertheless maintained that it wasn't "practical politics" to vote for the party.

"The point isn't that Norman Thomas is an honest man," he told the delegates, or that the Socialist program makes sense. "The point is that you can take the good sense they talk and make it

---

[123] "Thomas Appeals for Protest Vote; Socialist Ends Campaign with Plea to All 'Unwillingly for Roosevelt or Willkie,'" *New York Times*, Nov. 4, 1940.
[124] Ibid.
[125] Ibid.
[126] Ibid.
[127] Ibid.

'practical politics' by delivering to Norman Thomas the support that his honesty and his sincerity and his program deserve."[128]

In addition to attacking Wendell Willkie, whose experience as an executive of the Commonwealth and Southern Corporation — a "holding company whose business is pushing pieces of paper around" — was sharply belittled, the University of Chicago economist saved his most vicious attack for labor leader Sidney Hillman, the bespectacled founder and president of the Amalgamated Clothing Workers of America and co-architect of the American Labor Party, as a vehicle for Socialists and other left-wing voters to support Franklin Roosevelt's re-election without formally aligning with the Democrats.[129]

A left-wing fixture in that state's politics for nearly two decades, the ALP — launched in 1936 with FDR's implicit blessing — was an outgrowth of Labor's Non-Partisan League, a group founded by the CIO's John L. Lewis and initially chaired by George L. Berry of the AFL's International Printing Pressmen's Union to explicitly marshal organized labor's support for Roosevelt's re-election that year.

The party was the brainchild of David Dubinsky, president of the International Ladies Garment Workers Union (ILGWU), and Alex Rose of the hatters' union. In addition to Louis Waldman and his recently-created SDF, Sidney Hillman of the Amalgamated Clothing Workers union, a leading figure in Labor's Non-Partisan League who had served on the labor advisory board of Roosevelt's National Recovery Administration, was also one of the party's founders.

While Labor's Non-Partisan League, working exclusively inside the Democratic Party, contributed immeasurably to FDR's success in 1936 — raising and spending approximately a million dollars on Roosevelt's behalf, including a $500,000 lump sum contribution from Lewis and the United Mine Workers — the American Labor Party's role in that campaign had a far more lasting impact on the body politic, not only adding 274,925 votes to Roosevelt's total, largely from New York City's working-class Jewish neighborhoods where the Socialist Party once held such great appeal, but also in establishing a permanent independent political force in city and state politics for years to come.

Professor Krueger wasn't impressed. In his view, the ALP, always a sore spot for the Socialist Party, was no friend to working-class New Yorkers. "If you follow the example of Sidney Hillman,"

---

[128] Ibid.
[129] Ibid.

Krueger asserted, "you can help sell the whole working class down the road to war — because that's what Sidney Hillman is doing — he's reselling the whole war program back to an unwilling rank and file." Hillman's American Labor Party, he concluded, was "a disgrace to the very name of an independent labor organization."[130]

As Thomas and his wife Violet quietly cast their ballots on Tuesday, Nov. 5th, the Socialist candidate told reporters that the 1940 presidential election had been "the worst campaign in all my political memory."[131]

Recognizing that it wouldn't be him, the evangelical reformer also said the next president would face a gargantuan task in keeping the country out of war while preventing incipient fascism from taking hold in the United States.[132]

In the closing days of the 1940 campaign, it looked like Willkie was making a race of it, but the polls — still somewhat in their infancy — were all over the place.

While Democratic national chairman Edward J. Flynn claimed 427 electoral votes for Roosevelt and Republican national chairman Joseph W. Martin predicted that Willkie would win with 324 electoral votes, the nation's pollsters differed sharply on the election's outcome.[133]

In an election eve statement, Dr. George Gallup's American Institute of Public Opinion gave Roosevelt 198 electoral votes to 59 for Willkie, but left 274 electoral votes in doubt. The American Opinion Forecasts poll, conducted by Edward J. Wall, reported 52% for Roosevelt, but conceded that Willkie might win in the Electoral College while *Fortune* magazine's Elmer Roper, the modest, curly-haired pollster whose scientific sampling method proved to be the most accurate in 1936, gave Roosevelt 55.2 percent of the popular vote against Willkie.

Two other national surveys predicted a decisive Willkie victory. One of those was publisher Emil Hurja, the "wizard of Washington" who predicted that Willkie would win by nearly a million votes. In 1936, Hurja had been deadly accurate, telling James A. Farley that FDR would carry 46 of 48 states. Political analyst Rogers C. Dunn, who later received national acclaim for predicting Harry Truman's come-from-behind victory over Tom Dewey in 1948,

---

[130] Ibid.
[131] "50,000,000 Americans Vote Today," *Lowell Sun*, Nov. 5, 1940.
[132] "Thomas," *Hattiesburg American*, Nov. 5, 1940.
[133] "Party Heads See Victory On Tuesday," *Hartford Courant*, Nov. 3, 1940.

also got it wrong, giving Willkie 364 electoral votes to 124 for Roosevelt in his survey of forty states.[134]

Most pundits, moreover, believed that support for minor-party candidates for president in 1940 would likely be the least significant since the turn of the century, a prognostication that was seemingly reinforced by a national survey conducted earlier that autumn by George Gallup's American Institute of Public Opinion.

Despite the presence of two nationally-recognized third-party candidates — Socialist Norman M. Thomas and Prohibitionist Roger W. Babson, the white-haired "Yankee Genius" who had accurately predicted the stock market crash of 1929 — the Gallup survey indicated that the nation's third parties weren't expected to have much of an impact on the outcome of the FDR-Willkie contest, a race believed to be tightening considerably in the final weeks of the campaign. "Whereas all third parties combined polled 2.6 percent of the total vote four years ago, the indicated vote for all third parties at present does not exceed one percent," Gallup reported in early October.[135]

Attributing the lion's share of support for third-party candidates in 1936 to Rep. William Lemke's relatively large showing on Father Coughlin's Union Party ticket, Gallup gloomily predicted that Thomas, the leading third-party candidate in 1940, would garner roughly the same number of votes he received four years earlier when he polled 188,000 votes nationally.

Based on his findings, Gallup predicted that the well-known Socialist nominee would receive approximately 200,000 votes, but even that figure proved overly optimistic. "Communist candidate Earl Browder is even weaker than he was in 1936, when he polled 80,000 votes," Gallup noted, concluding that none of the minor-party candidates for president could expect to receive much more than a token "protest" vote.[136]

Norman Thomas, meanwhile, was convinced that FDR was headed toward a third straight victory, saying that he would be "a vastly surprised man" if Roosevelt didn't win the election — and by a relatively comfortable margin. "There has been nothing I've seen in this campaign that indicates that Willkie has a chance to win," said Thomas while campaigning in Pittsburgh on November 2. He was right.[137]

---

[134] Roseboom, *A History of Presidential Elections*, p. 474; "The Press: Polls on Trial," *TIME*, Nov. 18, 1940.
[135] "Third Party Vote; It May Be the Smallest Since the Turn of the Century, Gallup Survey Finds," *New York Times*, Oct. 5, 1940.
[136] "Third Party Vote," *New York Times*, Oct. 5, 1940.
[137] "Thomas Sees Roosevelt Victory," *New York Times*, Nov. 3, 1940.

THE LOWEST EBB

As in 1936, Elmer Roper again proved to be the country's most accurate pollster as Franklin D. Roosevelt, carrying thirty-eight states, rolled to an unprecedented third term, defeating Republican challenger Wendell Willkie by a margin of 27,243,466 to 22,334,413 while posting a lopsided Electoral College majority of 449-82.

Norman Thomas, who would return for a fifth straight bid for the White House in 1944, limped into third place, garnering a less-than-spectacular 116,514 votes, or slightly more than two-tenths of one percent of the total — a decline of nearly 72,000 votes from his relatively meager showing four years earlier.

The Socialist Party was no longer simply lying in ruins, as was the case following the devastating 1936 campaign. Its remnants, the rubble of its long and storied history, could barely be seen by even the most astute political observers. For all intents and purposes, the Socialist Party was dead.

Chapter IX

Flirting with America First

Norman Thomas characteristically took his 1940 defeat in stride, reiterating that the campaign between Roosevelt and Willkie had been the "most disgraceful and disappointing" in his long career — and one that he hoped would soon be forgotten. "I have just one hope for America and that is that we get down to principles and cut out the bitterness and the mudslinging," he said on election night as the results slowly trickled in. "There are issues before us, issues that transcend personality, issues that need not merely a President but the intelligent interest of the people, issues of peace and war, life and death," he said. "An aroused and awakened people can help to keep America out of war and use our machinery, the kind of machinery that is so marvelously working here now, for the conquest of poverty." He also congratulated President Roosevelt on his overwhelming victory and wished him all the success in the world in leading the American people in that endeavor.[1]

Needless to say, Thomas remained focused on the imminent threat of war in the weeks and months following the 1940 campaign. He was generally satisfied with the president's State of the Union address in January — FDR's famous "Four Freedoms" speech — but was deeply concerned by Roosevelt's lack of specifics in clarifying what types of demands he would make on Congress for aid to Great Britain and other nations resisting attacks by fascist aggressors. He was also worried that the country's domestic

---

[1] "Thomas Bids America Forget Campaign," *New York Times*, Nov. 6, 1940.

agenda would suffer immensely if Roosevelt had been accurate in telling Congress that "our actions and our policy should be devoted primarily — almost exclusively — to meeting this foreign peril."[2]

The best way to fight Hitler and fascism, Thomas responded, was "by keeping America out of war and making our own democracy work. With our vast resources and our noble heritage, we can, if we will, do that very thing, even if darkness should fall upon Europe. And the light we shall kindle by our success will, in time, rekindle the light of a purer democracy in Europe itself."[3]

Growing increasingly concerned that the United States was plunging headlong into war, Thomas stepped up his antiwar activities during this period. He understood that half measures were doomed to fail and he knew instinctively that an undeclared or limited war, one in which the U.S. supplied arms but not troops — a position articulated by both of his major-party opponents in the recent presidential campaign — would have disastrous consequences.

"We have no right to go halfway into war unless we are ready for total war, war with Japan as well as the Axis, war on two oceans and on five continents, war which require us to send or try to send our boys by the hundreds of thousands, eventually the millions, to Singapore and Shanghai, Java, Cambodia and the Philippines, as well as to Europe," Thomas told his readers in the *Socialist Call*. What Hitler had not yet been able to accomplish across thirty miles of the English Channel, he explained, the United States would have to do across 3,000 miles of the Atlantic and 5,000 miles of the Pacific. It would be a nearly impossible task.[4]

"If the war lasts long enough the kind and degree of victory both the President and Mr. Churchill demand for the British Empire," said Thomas, "will go beyond the defense of Britain to a military re-conquest of the European continent, virtually unthinkable without American troops." America's best intentions, he added, couldn't "alter the grim fact that in such a war the most probable victor is exhaustion and stark ruin, perhaps such a breakup of the whole western civilization that Stalin, another cruel but patient dictator, by his armies and devoted Communist followers will pick up the pieces and shape his own totalitarian world."[5]

---

[2] Norman Thomas, "The President's Incomplete Message," *Socialist Call*, Jan. 18, 1941.
[3] Ibid.
[4] Norman Thomas, "On the State of the Nation," *Socialist Call*, Jan. 25, 1941.
[5] Ibid.

While debating the lend-lease issue with Frank Kingdon, chairman of the New York chapter of William Allen White's interventionist Committee to Defend America by Aiding the Allies, on WJZ's "Town Meeting of the Air" in January, about ten weeks after the election, Wendell Willkie suddenly popped up from the audience with an impassioned plea for the nation to grant President Roosevelt the necessary authority to lend military aid to Great Britain. The debate quickly turned into a heated exchange between the two recently defeated presidential candidates.[6]

Up to that point, Thomas seemed to have the upper hand in the debate, winning sustained applause from the crowd for his eloquent noninterventionist stance. Refuting the argument that it was possible for the United States to wage a partial or limited war without eventually committing U.S. troops — a position echoed by many in favor of lend-lease — Thomas said that those who believed such nonsense were living "in a fool's paradise" and were in for a rude awakening.[7]

"The odds against limited undeclared war as the terrible months drag on are overwhelming," said Thomas. "Almost certainly, sooner or later we shall have to fight on two oceans and three continents; against Japan as well as the Axis. We shall have to furnish troops for a military re-conquest of Europe and Africa and probably parts of Asia and the islands of the sea…"

Thomas also said it would be virtually impossible for one of the belligerent nations to successfully invade the United States. "I have never seen contradicted the oft-quoted statement that a successful invasion of the U.S.A. would require at least 1,000,000 troops who in turn would need the services of eight million tons of shipping, plus a navy big enough to defeat ours in our waters and pulverize our coastal defenses…No man or superman could unite sullen slavery in a half-starved Europe successfully to support such a venture against us."[8]

When Willkie argued during the question and answer period that a Nazi victory would destroy civilization as we know it, Thomas responded by saying sarcastically that neither Roosevelt or Willkie had made any hint of the kind of extraordinary authority and power FDR was now seeking during the recent presidential campaign.[9]

---

[6] "Willkie Lifts a Radio Debate Out of the Fire," *New York PM*, Jan. 17, 1941.
[7] Ibid.
[8] Ibid.
[9] Ibid.

Willkie quickly struck back, telling the audience that "the American people also had the privilege of voting for Mr. Thomas. If I recall the results of the mandate of the American people," he said, "Mr. Roosevelt got some 27,000,000 votes; I got 23,000,000 votes and I have never seen a public record of how many Mr. Thomas got." It was a pretty cheap shot, one almost unbecoming of the former Republican nominee. Thomas, who had too much class to dignify Willkie's remark, didn't respond and let his former opponent prattle away. "We will keep America out of war if we supply to the fighting men of Britain sufficient resources so they may crush and defeat the ruthless dictatorship of Hitler," concluded Willkie.[10]

A few days later, Thomas testified against the Lend-Lease Bill before the House Foreign Affairs Committee, telling the congressional committee that some aid to Great Britain might be justified to resist a German invasion of that country, but cautioned that any assistance provided by the United States would potentially run the risk of being used by Winston Churchill, whom he described as "an imperialist to the core," to reconquer the continent of Europe. "I would trust him even less than Lloyd George to remake the world," Thomas said bluntly.[11]

Invited to testify by the Republican minority led by isolationist congressman Hamilton Fish of New York, the four-time Socialist candidate for the presidency astutely observed that adoption of Lend-Lease would inevitably lead to direct U.S. involvement in the European conflict. Testifying a day before Charles Lindbergh appeared before the same committee, Thomas essentially agreed with Senate Minority Leader Charles L. McNary of Oregon, the GOP's vice-presidential candidate in 1940, who had stated in earlier House testimony that he was opposed to the bill because it "grants extraordinary and total power to one person — President Roosevelt."[12]

In concurring with the Oregon lawmaker, Thomas said that he had both praised and criticized Roosevelt's use of executive emergency powers in the past, but that Lend-Lease was going entirely too far. "In no sense, then, do I make a personal or partisan attack on Mr. Roosevelt when I say that no man, not even an angel from heaven, who asks such breathtaking powers of war or peace with such vague limitations, should be trusted with them," he said. "If democracy in this crisis gives sole control of peace or war to one

---

[10] Ibid.
[11] "Thomas Pictures Democracy Upset in Lend-Lease Bill," *New York Times*, Jan. 23, 1941.
[12] Ibid.

man it has already surrendered the front line trenches to the principle of totalitarian dictatorship."[13]

Testifying before the Senate Foreign Relations Committee a few weeks later, Thomas acknowledged that the Axis powers were a menace, but scoffed at the notion that Adolf Hitler posed any direct threat to the United States. "It is a dangerous world, but I am more afraid of our rushing faster and faster into our own brand of Hitlerism than I am of anything Hitler can do to us," Thomas told the committee. "Even if we allow him many years," he continued, "I do not think it will be easy for Hitler in the unhappy event of victory over Great Britain, to organize a sullen, half-starved Europe, with a jealous Stalin at his rear, to conquer the Western Hemisphere."[14]

The bottom line, continued Thomas, was that passage of Lend-Lease virtually guaranteed direct U.S. military involvement in the war. "It is wholly improbable that we will avoid the necessity of sending men. Indeed, this bill which you now are considering is backed almost equally by those who believe that it is the way to slide America gradually into war and by those who still believe somehow that it is the way to stop short of war," he stated in his testimony. "The greatest danger which this bill increases, not diminishes, is that we shall find ourselves in total war," a conflict requiring thousands of U.S. troops in Europe, Asia and "perhaps in Africa."[15]

Non-interventionists on both the left and right agreed with Thomas. The Rev. John Haynes Holmes asserted that the bill — patriotically labeled HR 1776 — would give President Roosevelt unprecedented dictatorial powers while American Labor Party congressman Vito Marcantonio worried that U.S. planes and other military equipment could potentially be used "in massacring the Indian tribes who are seeking independence and freedom from British exploitation." If Great Britain was really fighting America's war, facetiously remarked Republican congressman Paul W. Shafer of Michigan, "we had best accept a dominion status and be done with it."[16]

Later that month, Thomas appeared with Senators Burton K. Wheeler of Montana and North Dakota's Gerald P. Nye at a rally

---

[13] Ibid.
[14] "Senators Warned of War in Aid Bill," *New York Times*, Feb. 4, 1941.
[15] "Thomas Claims Aid to Britain Will Bring War," *Amsterdam Evening Recorder* (Amsterdam, N.Y.), Feb. 3, 1941.
[16] Justus D. Doenecke, *Storm on the Horizon: The Challenge to American Intervention, 1939-1941* (Lanham, MD, 2003), p. 167.

co-sponsored by the New York chapter of the America First Committee and the Keep America Out of War Congress at the Mecca Temple on West Fifty-fifth Street.[17]

In his address, which was broadcast over the Mutual Broadcasting System network, Wheeler — one of the leading noninterventionists in the U.S. Senate — told the cheering crowd of 3,500 that the United States was already providing Great Britain every conceivable form of aid short of war and that the real purpose of Lend-Lease was to grant the President "the right to intervene in the present bloody European conflict — and that power of intervention is the power to wage war." Sen. Nye concurred, adding that the Lend-Lease bill would give Roosevelt powers "in excess of powers ever granted to a President even when our country was at war."[18]

In his remarks to the overflow crowd, Thomas vigorously denounced fascism and Nazism, but warned that Lend-Lease would take the issue of war and peace "out of the hands of the American people or Congress." Those promoting the legislation, he said, were leading the United States "into an armed imperialism" of a dangerous and "necessarily fascist" nature, "however much they may protest to the contrary."[19]

During this period, Thomas also participated in a lively debate with the America First Committee's John T. Flynn, a frequent critic of the Roosevelt administration, and banker James P. Warburg, the son of the late Paul Warburg, the driving force behind the creation of the Federal Reserve and later a founding member of the Council on Foreign Relations, at Long Island's Woodmere High School.[20]

The younger Warburg, an economic advisor to President Roosevelt and believed by many to be part of the president's original "Brain Trust," argued in favor of Lend-Lease, saying that the more aid the United States provided now the less it will have to do later. He also conceded that effective aid to Britain might require "the eventual use of our Navy" or the "sending abroad of pilots and ground crews" — and possibly an all-out military commitment. Aiming to enslave the entire world, the totalitarian Axis Powers, he said, can and will be defeated "if we shake off our lethargy and

---

[17] "Wheeler and Nye Carry Fight Here," *New York Times*, Feb. 21, 1941.
[18] Ibid.
[19] Ibid.; "Isolationist Rally Here Cold-Shoulders McWilliams; Followers Applaud Wheeler, Nye and Thomas, But Are Repudiated," *New York Evening Post*, Feb. 21, 1941. Several hundred followers of Joe McWilliams' anti-Semitic American Destiny Party attended the rally, but were rebuffed by event organizers.
[20] "J. P. Warburg Asks Passage of Bill," *New York Times*, Jan. 29, 1941.

stop listening to the voices of defeatism and of those who cannot or will not face reality."[21]

While Flynn vehemently opposed the legislation, asserting that "no dictator ever had a power greater or more exclusive" than that proposed in the Lend-Lease bill, Thomas told the crowd of several hundred that he "wouldn't trust an angel from heaven with the power Mr. Roosevelt asks for himself."[22] While professing a belief in helping the democratic nations of Europe "within limits," Thomas said that the United States had "neither the power nor the wisdom to play God to the world."[23]

In the meantime, a handful of former and current party members tried to portray a serious "split" in the Socialist Party over the party's official position regarding Lend-Lease and the question of aid to Great Britain. Several newspapers covered the imaginary split. The seven dissenters — Jack Altman, Gus Tyler, Reinhold Niebuhr, Frank R. Crosswaith, Alfred Baker Lewis, Murray Lewis and Lazar Becker — had strongly repudiated Thomas's testimony before the House Foreign Affairs Committee. The seven had also signed a petition supporting H.R. 1776.[24]

In a statement signed by Thomas, national secretary Travers Clement and Robert Parker, the party's administrative secretary, the Socialist Party responded immediately, reiterating that the party was unified on the question of opposition to Lend-Lease. "The seven signers of this petition — with the exception of two (Lazar Becker and Murray Gross) who were brought up on charges some time ago and whose cases are pending — are former Socialists who resigned or were dropped from the party when they found themselves in disagreement with the party position. These individuals do not speak for any section of the party nor was their withdrawal to support President Roosevelt in any way equivalent to a split."[25]

Thomas's vigorous opposition to U.S. involvement in the war also drew the ire of his critics in the Social Democratic Federation, those who represented the party's "Old Guard" prior to the 1936 split. Labor lawyer Louis Waldman was foremost among those critics, sharply repudiating Thomas and the Socialist Party's opposition to Lend-Lease. Asserting that the position expressed by Thomas and other members of his party did not reflect the views

---

[21] Ibid.
[22] "Famous Trio Hold Debate," *Poughkeepsie Eagle-News,* Jan. 29, 1941.
[23] "J. P. Warburg Asks Passage of Bill," *New York Times,* Jan. 29, 1941.
[24] "Attempt to Discredit Socialist Party Fails," *Socialist Call,* Feb. 8, 1941.
[25] Ibid.

of "genuine Socialists devoted to the preservation of democracy," Waldman — pointing to the Detroit declaration calling for mass resistance to war — argued that his former comrades were deliberately sabotaging the country's national defense.[26]

"Socialists who go up and down this land denouncing the lease-lend bill, President Roosevelt and effective aid to Britain undoubtedly do not speak for the million Socialist voters in the United States," said Waldman. "The spokesmen of the Socialist Party who loudly assert that they are opposed to the bill because it may lead us into war with Hitler know perfectly well that by their propaganda they are powerless to protect the United States against war, but are undoubtedly of great help to Hitler. Under the guise of being opposed to effective aid to Britain these Socialists are really sabotaging our national defense."[27]

Waldman also took exception to those who argued that Lend-Lease would give Roosevelt dictatorial powers, maintaining that the discretion delegated to the president under Lend-Lease was completely constitutional and consistent with his authority to conduct the nation's foreign affairs as commander-in-chief. "The issue really is whether we have faith in the capacity and leadership of President Roosevelt to defend the United States by more effective aid to Britain," said Waldman. "On that the American people have already spoken."[28]

August Claessens, a former Socialist assemblyman who later chaired the SDF, also emerged as one of Thomas's most vociferous critics during this period. Like Waldman, the 56-year-old New Yorker had been quick to condemn the four-time presidential candidate's congressional testimony opposing Lend-Lease in 1941, believing that in the face of the Hitler menace the kind of isolationism advocated by Thomas was based on "purely provincial selfishness."[29]

Claessens, the SDF's national secretary at the time, argued that Thomas represented only a small fraction of the country's Socialists. "There are some 900,000 Socialist voters in the nation," said Claessens. "Only 100,000 voted for Thomas and for the views he expresses. Eight hundred thousand campaigned and voted for Roosevelt because of his foreign policy. Democratic Socialists are

---

[26] "Waldman Assails Aid Bill Opponents; Repudiates Stand of Thomas and Socialist Party as 'Sabotage of Defense,'" *New York Times*, Feb. 20, 1941.
[27] Ibid.
[28] Ibid.
[29] "Socialist Group Hits Thomas View," *New York Times*, Jan. 23, 1941.

wholeheartedly in favor of the lease-lend bill and for all aid to Britain as the best means of national defense today."[30]

Claessens, who had traveled extensively with Thomas during the 1928 and 1932 presidential campaigns, also criticized those in the press who continued to describe Thomas as the country's "Socialist leader" and successor to Eugene V. Debs, vigorously asserting that Thomas's views had been overwhelmingly repudiated by a majority of the nation's Socialists, as well as by Socialists in other countries. "Mr. Thomas has a right to speak for himself but he cannot speak for American Socialists," Claessens wrote in a letter-to-the-editor in the *New York Times* about seven months before Pearl Harbor. A majority of Socialists, he maintained, had long since parted company with Thomas.[31]

Despite strenuous opposition from isolationist lawmakers — Rep. Hamilton Fish of New York denounced it as a "fascist bill" and a "confession that representative government has failed in America," Missouri's Champ Clark called it "the King's royal tax for the support of the British Empire" while colleague Gerald P. Nye of North Dakota railed against it for twelve straight hours on the floor of the Senate — the lend-lease legislation, giving the president powers that no other chief executive in American history had ever requested, passed the House by a vote of 260-165 in early February and was approved a month later by a lopsided 60-31 margin in the Senate.[32]

President Roosevelt, using six different pens — one for every three letters in his signature — signed the bill into law ten minutes after it reached his desk on March 11, and immediately asked Congress for nine billion dollars in lend-lease funding.[33]

In addition to his KAOWC activities and his seemingly never-ending party responsibilities, both of which kept him fairly busy, Thomas also spoke several times under the auspices of the newly-formed America First Committee (AFC) during this period, believing that it was an effective way to strengthen the nation's democratic, antiwar forces while influencing the masses against war and fascism.[34]

---

[30] Ibid.
[31] August Claessens, "Comment on Norman Thomas," *New York Times*, June 5, 1941.
[32] Barnard, *Wendell Willkie: Fighter for Freedom*, p. 274; Manchester, *The Glory and the Dream*, pp. 230-231; "May Loses Motion," *New York Times*, Jan. 13, 1941; "House Passes British Aid Bill," *Berkeley Daily Gazette*, Feb. 8, 1941; "Oratory-Wearied Senate Passes Lend-Lease Measure," *Eugene Register-Guard*, Mar. 9, 1941.
[33] "Roosevelt Signs Aid Measure With Six Pens Ten Minutes After It Reaches White House," *New York Times*, Mar. 12, 1941.
[34] "Thomas, On America First," *Socialist Call*, May 31, 1941.

Thomas initially declined the America First invitation, which included an offer to pay his expenses, but no speaking fees. Realizing that his own antiwar organization, which was perpetually operating in the red and rarely had two nickels to rub together, couldn't provide the same sort of large speaking venues offered by the relatively well-funded America First organization, Thomas eventually relented and agreed to speak at several of their events, beginning with a speech in the city's Mecca Temple in February where he joined Senators Burton K. Wheeler and Gerald P. Nye, as well as KAOWC's own John T. Flynn, in vigorously denouncing Lend-Lease.[35]

A noninterventionist organization founded in September 1940 by second-year Yale law student R. Stuart Douglas, Jr., and headed by retired Gen. Robert E. Wood of Chicago, chairman of Sears, Roebuck and the group's leading financial angel, the short-lived America First Committee initially attracted a wide array of prominent members, including ultraconservative *Chicago Tribune* publisher Robert McCormick, World War I flying ace Eddie Rickenbacker, Avery Brundage, a one-time track star and longtime president of the U.S. Olympic Association, and John C. Cudahy, a former U.S. ambassador to Poland and Belgium and minister to Ireland who — prior to Pearl Harbor — had advocated a negotiated peace with Hitler. Automaker Henry Ford was also a member of America First.[36]

Future President Gerald R. Ford and future Supreme Court Justice Potter Stewart, both of whom graduated from Yale Law School in 1941, also joined the noninterventionist group and a young John F. Kennedy, a recent Harvard graduate, made a $100 contribution.[37]

The America First Committee also enjoyed the support of several well-known activists on the American Left, including writer Sinclair Lewis and journalist and publisher Oswald Garrison Villard, the pacifist grandson of the famous abolitionist William Lloyd Garrison. New York lawyer and publicist Amos Pinchot, a veteran of Teddy Roosevelt's insurgent Bull Moose campaign of 1912 and younger brother of former Pennsylvania governor Gifford Pinchot, was also actively involved with the America First Committee, the largest antiwar organization in American history.

---

[35] Swanberg, *Norman Thomas: The Last Idealist*, pp. 245-246.
[36] "Ford in America First," *New York Times*, Sep. 25, 1940.
[37] Ruth Sarles, *A Story of America First: The Men and Women Who Opposed U.S. Intervention in World War II* (Westport, CT, 2003), pp. xxii, 12.

Like journalist John T. Flynn, Amos Pinchot — once a leading light of the Progressive Era — was drifting from the political left to what is now called the "Old Right" during this period and rather curiously had supported reactionary newspaper publisher Frank Gannett, the darkest of dark-horse candidates, for the Republican presidential nomination earlier that year.[38] Pinchot, who had actively supported FDR in 1932, came to believe that the New Deal was prolonging the depression and broke with the administration three years later.[39] By the autumn of 1940, the 67-year-old Pinchot believed that Harold Ickes and other Roosevelt enthusiasts were laying the groundwork for a virtual dictatorship by clamoring for war. "When a nation's judgment has been systematically sapped by fear, hysteria and war fever, passed around by politicians impressed with their holy duty to hang on to their jobs," he said, "there are few things that cannot be put over in the name of public safety." The speeches by Roosevelt and his aides, particularly Harold Ickes, he added assuredly, were "war statesmanship, pure and simple."[40]

Pinchot, who had been a member of Skull and Bones while a Yale undergraduate, emerged as one of Charles Lindbergh's most outspoken defenders following the aviator's fateful speech in Des Moines in September 1941. While Flynn and other America First leaders were deeply distressed by the Iowa speech, Pinchot vigorously defended the Lone Eagle, insisting that the group's most prominent spokesman wasn't anti-Semitic and was being unfairly condemned for speaking the truth. "As a group," said Pinchot, "the Jews of America are for intervention."[41]

Coupled with the suicide of his oldest daughter four years earlier, the distraught Pinchot grew increasingly despondent by world events and tried to take his own life shortly after the U.S. entered World War II. He was institutionalized for the remainder of his life.[42]

---

[38] Doenecke, *Storm on the Horizon*, p. 159.
[39] "Amos Pinchot Foe of New Deal Now; Assails Monetary Policy," *New York Times*, July 24, 1935.
[40] "Amos Pinchot Sees Dictatorship Peril," *New York Times*, Sep. 4, 1940.
[41] Kathryn S. Olmsted, *Real Enemies: Conspiracy Theories and American Democracy, World War I to 9/11* (New York, 2009), p. 53.
[42] "Rosamond Pinchot Ends Life in Garage," *New York Times*, Jan. 25, 1938; "Amos Pinchot Tries to Commit Suicide," *New York Times*, Aug. 7, 1942. Pinchot's daughter Rosamond, a well-known stage actress, took her own life in January 1938. Mary Pinchot Meyer, a daughter from his second marriage, was alleged to have been John F. Kennedy's mistress. The ex-wife of Cord Meyer, a high-ranking CIA official recruited by Allen Dulles in 1951, Mary was mysteriously murdered in the autumn of 1964, about eleven months after President Kennedy was assassinated in Dallas. For fascinating accounts of Mary's life and the

Though he later denied it, high-powered Wall Street lawyer John Foster Dulles, a managing partner at Sullivan & Cromwell who later served as Secretary of State during the Eisenhower administration, was also an avid supporter of the America First Committee. His law firm, in fact, had drafted the organization's articles of incorporation at no charge.[43] A staunch Roosevelt critic and key figure in cementing Wall Street's control over the country's foreign policy apparatus in the immediate aftermath of FDR's death in the spring of 1945, Dulles also reportedly contributed $500 per month to the fledgling AFC prior to the Japanese attack on Pearl Harbor — briefly putting him at odds with his brother Allen Dulles, later the first civilian director of the CIA, who at the time was towing the Council on Foreign Relations' stridently interventionist line.[44]

Impressed by Hitler's humble origins, Dulles reportedly wept when his law firm decided to drop its German clients a few years earlier and, even as the hostilities escalated, didn't believe the Axis Powers posed a threat to the United States. "Only hysteria entertains the idea that Germany, Italy, or Japan contemplates war upon us," he told the Economic Club of New York in March 1939, barely a week after the Nazi conquest of Czechoslovakia. Even after the Nazi invasion of Poland later that year, Dulles — lamenting Great Britain's declaration of war against Germany in early September — continued to maintain that Hitler's forces weren't a threat to the United States and that the country shouldn't become embroiled in the European conflict.[45]

Organized in response to famous Kansas editor William Allen White's Committee to Defend America by Aiding the Allies and launched shortly after the destroyers-for-bases deal was made public during the 1940 presidential campaign, at its peak the America First Committee boasted between 800,000 and 850,000 dues-paying members in approximately 450 chapters across the country, with its greatest strength in the Middle West, mostly within a 200-mile radius of Chicago.[46]

---

lingering mystery surrounding her death, see Nina Burleigh, *A Very Private Woman: The Life and Unsolved Murder of Presidential Mistress Mary Meyer* (New York, 1998) and Peter Janney, *Mary's Mosaic: The CIA Conspiracy to Murder John F. Kennedy, Mary Pinchot Meyer, and Their Vision for World Peace* (New York, 2013).

[43] Stephen Kinzer, *The Brothers: John Foster Dulles, Allen Dulles, and Their Secret World War* (New York, 2013), pp. 53-54.

[44] Glen Yeadon and John Hawkins, *The Nazi Hydra in America: Suppressed History of a Century; Wall Street and the Rise of the Fourth Reich* (Joshua Tree, CA, 2008), p. 86.

[45] Kinzer, *The Brothers*, p. 54.

[46] Wayne S. Cole, *Charles A. Lindbergh and the Battle Against American Intervention in World War II* (New York, 1974), p. 117.

Representing a broad cross-section of American isolationism, its membership also included such notables as Gen. Hugh S. Johnson, former head of the National Recovery Administration, George N. Peek, the original administrator of the New Deal's Agricultural Adjustment Administration (AAA), University of Chicago president Robert M. Hutchins, Washington socialite Alice Roosevelt Longworth, the outspoken daughter of the late Theodore Roosevelt, New York investment banker Edwin S. Webster, Jr., Chicago industrialist Sterling Morton, labor activist Kathryn Lewis, the daughter of longtime United Mine Workers of America (UMWA) president and powerful CIO boss John L. Lewis, deep-pocketed window shade manufacturer William H. Regnery, actress Lillian Gish — "the First Lady of American Cinema" — and diplomat and future Connecticut governor Chester Bowles, a Democrat, to mention but a few. Automaker Henry Ford also served on the organization's national committee, but wasn't an active participant and didn't contribute financially.

Despite Henry Ford's involvement in the organization and that of many other known anti-Semites, the America First movement nevertheless attracted several prominent Jewish members, including Lessing J. Rosenwald, a retired director of Sears, Roebuck and Company who became a national committee member in September 1940. A longtime opponent of Zionism, Rosenwald later served as president of the American Council for Judaism. Former Republican congresswoman Florence P. Kahn of California — the first Jewish woman to serve in the U.S. House of Representatives — was also a member of the group's national committee.[47]

Dr. Charles Fleischer, a former rabbi of Boston's Temple Israel and one-time editor of the *New York American*, also played an important role in the noninterventionist organization. The German-born Fleisher, a member of the New York chapter, resigned from the committee shortly after Lindbergh's controversial Des Moines speech.[48] Dr. Hyman Lischner, a highly-respected physician from Los Angeles and former president of B'nai B'rith in San Diego, was also supportive of America First.[49]

Moreover, a number of prominent politicians, ranging from Montana's Burton K. Wheeler and North Dakota's Gerald P. Nye to former Wisconsin Gov. Philip La Follette and New York's con-

---

[47] Sarles, *A Story of America First*, p. 49.
[48] "Quits America First; Dr. Charles Fleischer Assails the 'Hostile Speech' of Group," *New York Times*, Oct. 20, 1941.
[49] Sarles, *A Story of America First*, pp. 49-50.

troversial isolationist congressman Hamilton Fish lent their support, serving as speakers or advisors for the America First Committee.

Though he died a few days before it was officially launched, Minnesota's Ernest Lundeen, a staunch isolationist and one of two Farmer-Laborites representing that state in the U.S. Senate before Henrik Shipstead bolted to the GOP, was also strongly supportive of the America First Committee's objectives.[50]

In fact, thirty days before his death in a violent plane crash, the Minnesota lawmaker had urged the formation of a nationally-organized third party committed to the principles of "strict neutrality and America First" to challenge the interventionist policies of the two major parties in the 1940 elections. He was convinced that both Roosevelt and Willkie, acting on behalf of Great Britain, were leading the nation into an unnecessary war. Both major parties, said Lundeen in calling for a hastily-organized national convention in Chicago, were intent on "aiding Great Britain to the limit of our capacity, and placing at that nation's disposal all American resources to the end that the British Empire may win the war."[51]

Recognizing that "Wall Street bankers" and like-minded pundits in the "plutocratic" press were the ones clamoring loudest for U.S. intervention in the European conflict, Ohio Sen. Robert A. Taft — a serious contender for the Republican presidential nomination in 1940 — was also closely identified with the committee.[52] Along with Wheeler, the principled Ohioan had been one of the first politicians of national stature to encourage its creation.[53] Even former President Herbert Hoover, while refusing to align himself directly with the America First Committee, sympathized with the movement and reportedly helped raise funds for the organization.[54]

Sen. Wheeler, who had been the late "Fighting Bob" La Follette's vice-presidential running mate in 1924, emerged as one of FDR's sharpest critics within the America First movement, telling

---

[50] Jennifer A. Delton, *Making Minnesota Liberal: Civil Rights and the Transformation of the Democratic Party* (Minneapolis, 2002), p. 13.

[51] "Lundeen Issues Call for Anti-War Party To Be Formed in Chicago by Farmers, Labor," *New York Times*, Aug. 2, 1940.

[52] Bill Kauffman, *America First! It's History, Culture, and Politics* (Amherst, N.Y., 1995), pp. 19-20.

[53] Cole, *America First*, p. 167.

[54] Justus D. Doenecke, Editor, *In Danger Undaunted: The Anti-Interventionist Movement of 1940-1941 as Revealed in the Papers of the America First Committee* (Stanford, CA, 1990), p. 15. As honorary chairman of the National Committee on Food for the Small Democracies, the former president didn't want to detract from his efforts to rally public support to feed 27 million Europeans, mostly women and children who had been left destitute during World War II, by publicly associating with the America First Committee.

a radio audience in January 1941 that Lend-Lease was Roosevelt's new triple-A and would "plow under every fourth American boy" — a particularly harsh reference to the Agricultural Adjustment Administration's controversial program of burying crops and killing livestock in order to increase prices on those products during the early days of the New Deal. It was an incendiary comment the Montana lawmaker later regretted.[55]

The group's biggest draw — and indeed its most popular speaker — was famed aviator Charles A. Lindbergh, arguably the second most popular figure in the country. Lucky Lindy had been speaking out against U.S. involvement in the European conflict long before the launching of the America First Committee. He was convinced that the nation's interventionists were seizing every opportunity to push the United States "closer to the edge" of war. "We are in danger of war today not because European people have attempted to interfere in America," he said earlier that spring, "but because we American people have attempted to interfere with the internal affairs of Europe."[56]

Thomas never formally joined the America First Committee, but he welcomed every opportunity to address their rallies, the largest of which occurred at New York's Madison Square Garden on May 23. Receiving a rousing reception from a capacity crowd of 22,000 when he made his entrance on the platform with Lindbergh, Wheeler and novelist Kathleen Norris, the movement's chief propagandist, Thomas — speaking under the auspices of the Keep America Out of War Committee — literally had the audience repeating every line of his speech when he recited Roosevelt's pledge that American boys wouldn't be sent into harm's way to fight in any foreign wars.[57] His inclusion of journalist Dorothy Thompson on a short list of the nation's leading "warmongers" drew the loudest reaction of the evening with the sound of boos and hisses filling the sold-out Garden.[58]

The following week, Thomas again urged Congress to pass legislation requiring a national referendum on whether the country should enter the war, something he had initially proposed earlier. Speaking at the second annual Keep America Out of War Congress in Washington, D.C., Thomas said that U.S. foreign trade, accounting for only six percent of the nation's annual output, wasn't

---

[55] Lynne Olson, *Those Angry Days: Roosevelt, Lindbergh, and America's Fight Over World War II, 1939-1941* (New York, 2013), p. 276.
[56] Manchester, *The Glory and the Dream*, p. 220.
[57] "Lindbergh Joins in Wheeler Plea to U.S. to Shun War; 22,000 at Madison Sq. Garden Peace Rally Cheer Leaders' Attacks on Intervention," *New York Times*, May 24, 1941.
[58] "But No Boos for Hitler," *New York Post*, May 24, 1941.

worth "the cost in blood and treasure of one week of modern war." The United States, he declared, was "doomed to become a fascist state" if it entered the war, regardless of which side ultimately prevailed.[59]

In his remarks to the group, which included representatives from the Fellowship of Reconciliation, the National Council for the Prevention of War, the War Resisters League and the Women's International League for Peace and Freedom, the four-time presidential candidate ridiculed those who were suggesting that the United States might be vulnerable to a military or economic attack, calling those assertions an "hysterical falsehood."[60]

In the unlikely scenario that Adolf Hitler somehow seized the British fleet, said Thomas, "it would be years before the master of a sullen and hungry Europe could even dream of turning that navy and his other military resources to so difficult a task as the invasion of America by way of Boston or Brooklyn." U.S. entry in the war, he concluded, would "prolong it indefinitely" and drain a "hungry, neurotic Europe" of its human and material resources while subjecting the American people to a systematic campaign of "propaganda censorship which would grow heavier with every month and would eventually destroy democracy."[61]

The previous evening, KAOWC sponsored an antiwar rally in Washington's Turner Arena, drawing a crowd of 2,500. In addition to Thomas and John T. Flynn, the crowd heard from a wide range of speakers, including Montana's Burt Wheeler and Martha Taft, the gregarious and outspoken wife of Ohio Sen. Robert A. Taft. The inimitable Alice Roosevelt Longworth, daughter of the late Teddy Roosevelt, was one of the dignitaries who shared the platform with Thomas. In a particularly hard-hitting speech, Wheeler brought the house down by saying that members of the House and Senate "might as well go home, for Congress is now just a sounding board for President Roosevelt, almost the same as the Reichstag is for Hitler. The president," declared Wheeler, "is now playing the game of the Morgans and the Rockefellers and of others whom until recent days he denounced."[62]

Hitler's invasion of Russia on June 22, the beginning of "Operation-Barbarossa" in which three million German troops opened a second front by launching three parallel offensives against the disorganized Red Army, didn't seem to weaken Thomas's isolationist

---

[59] "Thomas Urges Vote on War in Referendum," *Buffalo Courier-Express*, June 1, 1941.
[60] Ibid.
[61] Ibid.
[62] "Anti-War Group Assails President," *New York Times*, May 31, 1941.

stance. If anything, it strengthened his resolve to keep the United States out of the escalating conflict. In a statement issued the following day, Thomas said:

> As always, Socialist sympathy will go to the people, in this case the Russian people, who are the victims of aggression at Hitler's hands. Hitler cannot rehabilitate himself by becoming a crusader against the crimes of Stalin. But for Stalin we have no sympathy. In every way his cruelty and duplicity have equaled Hitler's own. It was his agreement with Hitler which unleashed the military force of which he is now a prospective victim. The lion has now turned on the jackal and marches Finnish troops against the dictator who assayed the conquest of Finland.
>
> We shall watch with interest to see how fast American Communists and the organizations which they control or influence will become propagandists for American entry into the war on the side of the 'great democracies,' Stalin's dictatorship and the British Empire.
>
> We, whose concern has been to keep America out of war in order to make our own democracy work and whose interest is in peace and not in Stalin, see in the tangled course of events new reason for maintaining the fight to keep America out of war.[63]

Needless to say, Thomas was subjected to plenty of abuse for his willingness to associate with the America First Committee. According to columnist William F. Buckley, Jr., students at CCNY shouted "Heil Hitler!" when Thomas spoke on their campus in 1941.[64] In declaring that "Hitler's unconscious tools" in the United States "serve him to better purpose than those in his own pay," Secretary of the Interior Harold Ickes branded Lindbergh as the country's leading Nazi dupe while expressing dismay that America First — an organization he denounced as fascist and anti-Semitic — had been given a certain level of legitimacy and respect by a wide range of individuals, including "decent Socialists, such as Norman Thomas."[65]

As criticism mounted, the *Socialist Call*, then edited by national secretary Travers Clement, naturally came to Thomas's defense,

---

[63] "Isolationist Stand in U.S. is Unshaken," *New York Times*, June 23, 1941.
[64] William F. Buckley, Jr., "The Father of McCarthyism," *Herald Statesman* (Yonkers, N.Y.), Dec. 4, 1979.
[65] "Ickes Brands Lindbergh No.1 Nazi Dupe," *Washington Post*, April 14, 1941.

reminding readers that Eugene Debs had faced similar criticism during World War I. "For many months now much the same kind of smear campaign has been waged against the Socialist Party and its national chairman, Norman Thomas, as was directed against the Party and Eugene V. Debs in the first World War," wrote Clement, who had managed the party's presidential campaign in 1940. An intrinsic part of the smear campaign, continued Clement, was the technique of singling out an unsavory group or individual who also opposed U.S. entry into World War II and then holding all of the antiwar forces responsible for the utterances of that group or individual.

Then citing the examples of Gerald P. Nye, who foolishly spoke at a rally of Gerald L. K. Smith's Committee of One Million in Detroit, and Sen. Burton K. Wheeler of Montana, who had been accused of anti-Semitism as a result of a radio address in which he mentioned the role of international bankers — specifically, the Rothschilds and Warburgs — in the drive for U.S. intervention in the European conflict, Clement concluded:

> The Socialist Party is not the keeper of Nye, Wheeler or anyone else outside the Socialist Party. We do not accept responsibility for their actions any more than we charge the responsibility for the J. P. Morgans, the Nicholas Murray Butlers and Ellery Sedgwicks to liberal interventionists.
>
> Nor are we the keepers of the America First Committee with which we have no affiliation whatever. Nationally, that has pursued a decent anti-war policy, though isolationist, not socialist, in tone. If any of its local units have permitted themselves to get involved in any way with questionable or pro-fascist elements, we condemn them vigorously and urge Socialists to have nothing whatever to do with them.[66]

Like so many others, Thomas and other Socialist Party members were appalled by Charles Lindbergh's shocking speech in Des Moines, Iowa, on September 11, 1941, an address in which the famous aviator accused the British, FDR and Jews for pushing the United States to the brink of war.

"We are on the verge of war," Lindbergh told the crowd of more than 8,000 in Des Moines that evening, "because of war agitators in this country. The three most important groups who have been pressing this country toward war," he asserted, "are the British, the Jewish, and the Roosevelt administration. Behind these

---

[66] "Debs Faced It Too," *Socialist Call*, Mar. 22, 1941.

groups, but of lesser importance," he continued, "are a number of capitalists, anglophiles and intellectuals who believe that their future and the future of mankind depend upon the domination of the British Empire."

These groups, declared the country's leading isolationist, "planned, first to prepare the United States for foreign war under the guise of American defense" and "to involve us in the war, step by step, without our realization" by creating "a series of incidents which would force us into the actual conflict. These plans were of course, to be covered and assisted by the full power of their propaganda."

In his speech, Lindbergh took all three groups to task, accusing the British of devoting every effort imaginable to draw the U.S. into the war so that they could "shift to our shoulders a large portion of the responsibility for waging it and for paying its cost" and condemning the Roosevelt administration for engaging in "subterfuge" by promising the American people peace while deliberately leading the country into war.

Though acknowledging their desire to defeat the Nazis — "the persecution they suffered in Germany would be sufficient to make bitter enemies of any race" — Lindbergh nevertheless went on to sharply criticize Jewish groups in the United States for "agitating for war," breathtakingly adding that "their greatest danger to this country lies in their large ownership and influence in our motion pictures, our press, our radio and our government.

"We are on the verge of war for which we are unprepared," Lindbergh concluded, "and for which no one has offered a feasible plan for victory — a war which cannot be won without sending our soldiers across the ocean to force a landing on a hostile coast against armies stronger than our own."[67]

Thomas, who long believed that the committee's isolationist program was entirely inadequate in advancing the cause of noninterventionism, was stunned by Lindbergh's public remarks and quickly disassociated himself from the America First Committee.

In his capacity as national chairman of the Socialist Party, Thomas issued a statement on behalf of the party vigorously denouncing Lindbergh's speech in Des Moines. "Many groups and elements in this country are attempting to drive us into war," declared Thomas. "This issue cuts across all racial lines. No one race is responsible. The Socialist Party has many Jews in its ranks and

---

[67] "Lindbergh Blames British, Roosevelt and Jews," *Des Moines Register*, Sep. 12, 1941.

these take their stand with the Party against American involvement. No race or people can be made the scapegoat for this crime.

"We are glad that Lindbergh puts himself so definitely on record against the Nazis as he did when he said that 'no person with a sense of dignity of mankind can condone the persecution of the Jewish race in Germany,'" continued Thomas. "We share his fears that a wave of anti-Semitism such as this country has never known may follow this war. But when Lindbergh singles out the Jews as a race for major responsibility and speaks of their power and influence as apart from others in American life, he helps to create the conditions which give rise to the very wave of persecution he warns against. It is a plain matter of fact that most of the financial interests and great newspaper publishers are not Jewish," concluded Thomas. "Their influence in the aggregate is far greater than that of those who are Jewish."[68]

The Keep America Out of War Congress also sharply condemned Lindbergh's Des Moines speech, asserting in a September 18th statement that it deeply regretted and disagreed with "Lindbergh's implication that the American citizens of Jewish extraction or religion are a separate group, apart from the rest of the American people, or that they are unanimously for our entrance into the European war." As much as it welcomed the aviator's denunciation of Hitler's treatment of Jews in Germany, the group stated that it strongly deplored "that aspect of his speech which, whatever his intentions, may help to arouse the same intolerant and un-American treatment of racial and religious minorities here."[69]

Even before Lindbergh's infamous De Moines speech, Thomas had returned to the political hustings earlier that year, actively campaigning for George W. Hartmann, the Socialist Party's candidate for mayor of New York City. A lifelong educator and former chairman of the Society for the Psychological Study of Social Issues who had studied with the leading Gestalt psychologists in Berlin and Leipzig during the early years of the Great Depression, Hartmann had been Thomas's running mate for lieutenant governor in 1938.

In explaining why his party wasn't throwing its support to Mayor La Guardia, as had been the case in 1937, Thomas explained that the mayor's failure to create an independent organization to carry on his work made it impossible for the Socialist Party to support him again. He also cited the mayor's fiscal policies — balancing the budget largely at the expense of education while

---

[68] "Roosevelt and Lindbergh," *Socialist Call*, Sep. 27, 1941.
[69] "Lindbergh Talk Scored," *New York Times*, Sep. 21, 1941.

refusing to establish a more equitable system of taxation — as two of the main reasons why the Socialists felt it was necessary to field their own candidate. He also criticized the mayor for refusing to bargain with the city's rapid transit workers.[70]

Thomas, who may have privately regretted withdrawing from the mayoral contest four years earlier, had long since grown critical of La Guardia, accusing the short and stout Napoleon of New York of using his office "as a lever to put America into war."[71]

It was a view shared by the party's mayoral candidate. Hartmann, a professor of psychology at Columbia University's Teachers' College who later founded the controversial "Peace Now" movement, essentially campaigned as a single-issue, antiwar candidate. Throughout the campaign, the colorful antiwar activist accused La Guardia of beating the drums of war and told his audiences that the only reason President Roosevelt was backing the incumbent fusion mayor instead of his own party's nominee was because he believed it would help "plunge the United States into war."[72]

"Overshadowing every other issue at the moment is the great question of war or peace for this country," declared Hartmann. "This issue is too sweeping in its implications to be sidestepped or soft-pedalled on the spurious ground that being Mayor of New York City has little or nothing to do with it.[73]

"A sufficient retort to this childish reasoning," continued Hartmann, "is to ask where is the present mayor and what is he doing? If he is not helping in the deadly business of getting us ready for war, just what is he doing? La Guardia is a federal appointee and an open political ally of President Roosevelt. Together both of them are doing everything in their power, by fair means or foul, to thrust a doubting and unwilling people into this stupid war." Calling for La Guardia's defeat on the issue of the war alone — "a fatal defect which justifies the defeat of any candidate for any position at any time in any place" — was completely warranted, said Hartmann.[74]

Accusing La Guardia of "pulling a Roosevelt," Hartmann said that New York City "needed a full-time mayor, not one who

---

[70] "Won't Back Mayor," *New York Sun*, June 6, 1941.
[71] "Socialists Assail Mayor, Pick Slate," *New York Times*, June 6, 1941. Samuel H. Friedman, who was then serving as publicity director for the Workers' Defense League, was the Socialist Party's candidate for city comptroller and Brooklyn lawyer Joseph G. Glass was nominated for president of the city council.
[72] "Socialist Makes Plea; Hartmann Asks Support for Mayoralty as 'Peace Candidate,'" *New York Times*, Oct. 25, 1941.
[73] "Socialist Asks O'Dwyer Define Attitude on War," *Brooklyn Eagle*, Aug. 25, 1941.
[74] Ibid.

would harness the people of our city to a war they are overwhelmingly against."⁷⁵

The Socialist candidate also strongly urged Democratic challenger William O'Dwyer to issue an unequivocal statement on the issue of war and peace. "Don't pull a Willkie on us," he implored the Democratic candidate in late August. "Stop being so silent and mysterious, Mr. O'Dwyer, and share your thoughts with your constituency."⁷⁶

Hartmann was convinced that O'Dwyer, in refusing to address possible U.S. involvement in the growing international conflict, was merely acting on the advice of cynical Tammany strategists who believed that "what people don't know won't hurt them" — and the less said the better. It seemed like déjà vu to many older New York Socialists who fondly remembered the late Morris Hillquit's heroic antiwar candidacy for mayor nearly a quarter of a century earlier, a year when the Socialist Party nearly carried the Bronx while winning the support of more than one in every five New Yorkers and nearly tripling the Republican Party's meager showing in the mayoral race. "Tammany played this trick in 1917, the last time we went to war under circumstances suspiciously similar to the present," charged Hartmann.⁷⁷

Accusing La Guardia of having "out-Tammanied Tammany" during his eight years in office, the 38-year-old psychology professor, moreover, believed the enormously popular mayor had everybody fooled and was anything but a progressive. "If what Mr. La Guardia has done justifies the name of liberal and progressive, then Hitler is a Zionist and Mussolini is a Quaker," asserted Hartmann.⁷⁸

Thomas must have cringed in late October when he read Hartmann's interview in the city's *PM* newspaper, a left-leaning tabloid with a circulation of about 165,000 readers. The interview, which took place in Hartmann's cramped, book-lined office at Teachers' College, started out smoothly enough with Hartmann criticizing both La Guardia and O'Dwyer for endorsing Roosevelt's foreign policy while asserting his own antiwar beliefs. "I am the candidate who is opposed to all kinds of war," he said.⁷⁹

Things got really hairy a few moments later when the little-known Socialist candidate said that he wouldn't have advocated

---

⁷⁵ "La Guardia Tried 'A Roosevelt,' Socialist Candidate Charges," *Socialist Call*, Aug. 2, 1941.
⁷⁶ "Socialist Asks O'Dwyer Define Attitude on War," *Brooklyn Eagle*, Aug. 25, 1941.
⁷⁷ Ibid.
⁷⁸ "Mayor Pays Only Lip Service to Reform, Socialist Leader Holds — Hartmann Says Rival 'Out-Tammanies Tammany,'" *New York Times*, Nov. 3, 1941.
⁷⁹ "Interview With a Candidate Who Doesn't Expect to Win," *New York PM*, Oct. 30, 1941.

armed resistance in any of the countries invaded by the Nazis. "I think in that respect, the Danes were the smartest of all," said Hartmann. "They didn't resist. They saved their men and money." Hitler's invasions, he said flatly, were "a lot of sprouts."[80]

Eager to discuss issues most candidates would shy away from — he seemed to relish controversy — Hartmann then told the somewhat startled and incredulous reporter that Charles A. Lindbergh had been right to make the kind of anti-Semitic remarks that he delivered in his notorious Des Moines speech some six weeks earlier — a speech met with considerable outrage in many quarters.[81]

"This will probably all turn up in the paper as anti-Semitism on my part," he conceded, "but we ought to face the facts." The Jewish people, he elaborated, had "a deep interest in the outcome of the war" — and that was precisely what Lindbergh was trying to say in his Des Moines speech. Incredibly, Hartmann's only criticism of the famed aviator was that he lacked "a constructive policy" and tended to come across as something of a hayseed.[82]

Asked what had happened to the Socialist Party in Germany after Hitler's rise to power, Hartmann hesitated for a moment and then sheepishly responded in a half-whisper. "Well," he said, "I believe it has disappeared."[83]

The *Jewish Daily Forward*, an organ of the rival Social Democratic Federation, and the Communist Party's *Daily Worker* quickly pounced on the *PM* interview and strongly denounced Hartmann — and Thomas — as Nazi sympathizers. The *Forward* went further, calling them outright Nazis. "Scratch a pacifist," wrote the *Forward*, "and you find a Nazi, a Fascist and an anti-Semite."[84]

In the meantime, Hartmann vehemently denied some of the quotes attributed to him, particularly the comments regarding Lindbergh's views on Jewish "responsibility" for the country's current war drive, and demanded a retraction. "The absurdity of this charge must be apparent from the fact that my campaign manager, Irving Barshop, and my running mates, Samuel Friedman, Joseph Glass and Leonard Lazarus are all prominent Jewish Socialists who are working with me to keep America out of war," declared Hartmann in demanding a retraction. After repeated demands, a

---

[80] Ibid.
[81] Ibid.
[82] Ibid.
[83] Ibid.
[84] "N.Y. Election Smear," *Socialist Call*, Nov. 15, 1941.

carefully-worded retraction finally appeared in the paper's afternoon edition on Election Day, several hours after many New Yorkers had already cast their ballots.[85] Threatened with a libel suit, the *Forward*, too, later issued a retraction of sorts, but it came long after the election.[86]

Whether he had been accurately quoted or not, Thomas and other party members were undoubtedly embarrassed by some of Hartmann's off-the-cuff remarks during the interview. Coming so soon after Lindbergh's controversial speech in Des Moines, where Lucky Lindy blamed the British, Roosevelt and the Jews for pushing the United States to the brink of war, the last thing Thomas wanted to see was his name again linked with the famous aviator. By then, Lindbergh was toxic. Thomas, who had placed the activist-scholar's name in nomination at the party's convention in June, nevertheless stood by his party's mayoral nominee until the bitter end — undoubtedly motivated, in large part, by his growing dissatisfaction with Mayor LaGuardia's administration.

Anxious to show the party's flag after the Socialists had failed to field a mayoral candidate of their own in 1937, Thomas had been unusually effusive in his praise of Hartmann when placing his name in nomination at the party's citywide convention in early June, describing the little-known psychology professor as "my friend and comrade in a score of struggles" and commending him for "his courage in accepting a very difficult task."[87]

Having reluctantly supported La Guardia four years earlier, Thomas didn't want to make the same mistake again. Among other things, he was deeply disappointed that La Guardia, while cozying up to organized labor, was unwilling to do battle with Wall Street and merely paid "lip service" to the ideals of progressivism and meaningful reform. "He is one of the best equilibrists in the business," quipped Thomas, adding that the mayor's famous tantrums and outbursts were all for show. "There isn't a better or more calculating showman in America," said Thomas.[88]

A deeply troubled soul who later committed suicide, Hartmann was never really a factor in the 1941 mayoral contest, polling a relatively inconsequential 24,145 votes, or approximately one

---

[85] Ibid.
[86] "Better Late Than Never," *Socialist Call*, Dec. 20, 1941.
[87] Benjamin Harris, "The Perils of a Public Intellectual," *Journal of Social Issues*, Vol. 54, No. 1, 1998, p. 83.
[88] "Socialists Assail Mayor, Pick Slate," *New York Times*, June 6, 1941; "Mayor Pays Only Lip Service to Reform, Socialist Leader Holds," *New York Times*, Nov. 3, 1941.

percent of the total votes cast, to La Guardia's 1,186,518 and Democratic challenger William O'Dwyer's 1,054,235.[89] It was the closest of La Guardia's three successful mayoral campaigns. Despite a relatively paltry showing, Hartmann described his own performance at the polls as "a moral victory for the peace forces of this great city."[90]

Due to a geographical quirk, Hartmann actually carried one of the city's precincts in that election when Rabbi Nathan Wolf, the lone registered voter in the 46th election district of the 10th Assembly District, cast his ballot for the Socialist candidate "for the reason that he is against war." Wolf was a registered Democrat who frequently split his ballot. By 1941 — the ninth consecutive year in which the rabbi found himself as the only registered voter in his precinct — Wolf, a widower with a 19-year-old son who attended Yeshiva College, had become something of a celebrity and was accompanied at the polls by a policeman, four election inspectors and at least two reporters.[91]

Incidentally, it was estimated that the rabbi's single vote cost New York City taxpayers as much as $500 in every election.[92] Wolf, who was affiliated with the Times Square Temple — he lived at the synagogue — routinely voted for Norman Thomas for president. According to several newspaper accounts, Wolf was singlehandedly responsible for "the mighty landslide for Norman Thomas" at his polling place in 1940. The rabbi's precinct, moreover, was the only precinct in the country carried by Thomas in the 1940 presidential election.[93]

The war raging in Europe and elsewhere hit closer to home for Thomas and his wife, Violet, shortly before Thanksgiving of 1941 when their twenty-one-year-old son Evan, the youngest of the Thomas children, informed them that he wanted to do his part in defeating fascism. He told his startled parents that he would be sailing to Egypt with a friend as part of the American Field Service, a World War I organization that had been reactivated and eventually provided nearly 2,200 U.S. volunteer ambulance drivers in war-torn France, North Africa, the Middle East, Italy, Germany, India and Burma.[94]

---

[89] "Mayor Candidate in '41 Found Dead," *New York Times*, June 12, 1955.
[90] "Sees a 'Moral Victory,'" *New York Times*, Nov. 6, 1941.
[91] "Lone Voter Picks Socialist," *New York Evening Post*, Nov. 4, 1941; "Rabbi is the Lone Voter in One Election District," *New York Times*, Nov. 5, 1941.
[92] "Rabbi Casts His $500 Vote With the Usual Fanfare," *New York Evening Post*, Nov. 3, 1936.
[93] "Supply vs. Demand Problem," *Brooklyn Eagle*, Dec. 22, 1940.
[94] Fleischman, *Norman Thomas: A Biography*, p. 201.

Needless to say, Norman and Violet were shocked and deeply saddened, yet reluctantly accepted their son's decision. Evan, who abhorred violence and warfare and fully shared his father's opposition to U.S involvement in the escalating conflict, was a senior at Princeton at the time.[95]

On the fateful morning of December 7, Thomas and his wife drove to Princeton University to pick up the rest of Evan's personal belongings. Earlier that day, it was announced that Thomas had agreed to debate Clark M. Eichelberger, the national chairman of the Committee to Defend America by the Allies, in Pittsburgh later that week on the question of whether the United States should enter the war against Germany. It was a debate Thomas was looking forward to with great anticipation.[96]

Later that afternoon, Thomas learned of the surprise attack on Pearl Harbor while speaking with one of Evan's professors. Needless to say, Thomas was stunned by the news. His life's work appeared to have been in vain. "I feel as if my world has pretty much come to an end, that what I have stood for has been defeated, and my own usefulness made small," he wrote despondently to Maynard Krueger.[97]

The assault on Pearl Harbor and America's immediate entry into the escalating world conflict signaled the death knell for the America First Committee, which quickly disbanded. Thomas's Keep America Out of War Congress wasn't far behind.

In what had been billed as a gala dinner at New York's Town Hall on December 11th, only four days after the surprise attack in the Pacific, turned out to be the organization's swan song as one featured speaker after another refused to attend. Among those who cancelled was longtime Vassar College President Henry Noble MacCracken, who was scheduled to deliver a speech opposing the use of any American expeditionary forces in the war. John T. Flynn, chairman of the New York chapter of the America First Committee, and poet Michael Strange also declined to attend the dinner.

Nevertheless, more than a hundred KAOWC members and supporters showed up on that Thursday evening to hear Thomas speak on "The Bill of Rights in War Time," a speech he largely put aside to denounce the "treachery" of the Japanese attack while la-

---
[95] Ibid.
[96] "Debate on Intervention Scheduled for Thursday," *Pittsburgh Press*, Dec. 7, 1941.
[97] Swanberg, *Norman Thomas: The Last Idealist*, pp. 257-258.

menting that if the course of action advocated by the Keep America Out of War Congress had been followed, the war could have been averted.

In his speech, Thomas told the dinner guests that Japan's envy had been aroused by British, Dutch, and U.S. imperialism in the Far East during the previous half-century. The United States, he said, "should stop the business of trying to play Lord God Almighty around the world" — a remark that drew loud applause.[98] He also asked for a thorough probe of "the amazing disaster in the Pacific, which cannot be explained altogether in terms of the treachery of Japan's surprise attack." Reminding his audience that the 150th anniversary of the Bill of Rights was only a few days away, Thomas said that its essential principles were never more applicable than at the present time. "Even in the midst of war we are faced with the problems of democratic control of economic processes for the common good," he asserted. "If we are to make this war any sort of road to a lasting peace, we must keep and apply the great American tradition of civil liberty."[99]

KAOWC was formally dissolved a few days after the dinner, at which time the group's governing committee, refusing to completely throw in the towel, launched the Provisional Committee Toward a Democratic Peace, an organization whose vastly repurposed goals included the "enforcement of the Bill of Rights, with particular vigilance for the protection of freedom of speech, press and assembly, and the maintenance of religious tolerance and elimination of racial discrimination; equal distribution of the economic burden of the war, and the earliest possible attainment of a just and lasting peace."

In addition to Thomas, the new organization's governing committee included Oswald Garrison Villard, the Rev. John Haynes Holmes, dramatist and KAOWC vice chairman Morrie Ryskind, Dorothy Detzer of the Women's International League for Peace and Freedom, Albert W. Palmer, president of the Chicago Theological Seminary, and economist W. Jett Lauck, peace activist Charles F. Boss, Jr., historian Harry Elmer Barnes and journalist Devere Allen. Layle Lane, a longtime labor activist and vice president of the American Federation of Teachers who had ran for office on the Socialist ticket on no fewer than three occasions, was also a member of the provisional committee.[100] Topeka-born Mary W. Hillyer, a veteran of the League for Industrial Democracy and

---

[98] "Peace Group Dines, Still is Critical," *New York Times*, Dec. 12, 1941.
[99] "Thomas Asks U.S. Liberties Be Kept," *Baltimore Sun*, Dec. 12, 1941.
[100] "Anti-War Group Changed," *New York Times*, Jan. 2, 1942.

longtime Thomas supporter, stayed on as the group's executive secretary.[101]

Rechristened as the Post War World Council shortly thereafter, Thomas's new organization, which eventually included peace activist A. J. Muste on its board, sought to lay the groundwork for a democratic and anti-imperialist conclusion to the war. Advocating universal disarmament, a strengthening of the United Nations, an end to racial discrimination and global poverty, Thomas — cranking out bi-monthly newsletters and occasional pamphlets even as his eyesight was failing — kept the Post War World Council afloat until late 1967 when his failing health led to the organization's dissolution.

Worried about potential British brutality in dealing with the campaign of nonviolent disobedience by the nationalist supporters of Mahatma Gandhi — the "Great Soul" — in British-ruled India, Thomas met with Secretary of State Cordell Hull in Washington in August of 1942 to urge the Roosevelt administration to use all of its power and influence to avert any unnecessary bloodshed in India and to help "establish a satisfactory provisional government, and to work out terms of cooperation between India and the United Nations."[102]

Possibly fearing a repeat of the infamous 1919 Jallianwala Bagh Massacre, also known as the Amritsar Massacre, an act of stunning brutality in which British soldiers fired indiscriminately into a large crowd of unarmed, nonviolent protestors in Punjab, killing nearly 1,500 people and wounding more than 1,100 others, Thomas compared the volatile situation in India to the Sinn Fein uprisings in Ireland during Easter Week of 1916, when the barbaric and repressive measures employed by the British turned public opinion in support of Irish independence.[103]

After receiving assurances from Secretary Hull that the United States, while not formally offering to act as a mediator in the situation, had made its views known to both sides involved in the struggle, Thomas provided reporters with a copy of a letter in which he urged President Roosevelt to issue a public statement emphasizing that neither U.S. troops or arms — including lend-lease equipment provided to Great Britain — would be used, either directly or indirectly, against the citizens of India. To do anything less, the letter continued, would "make a mockery of those great ideals in whose

---

[101] Swanberg, *Norman Thomas: The Last Idealist*, pp. 264-265.
[102] "U.S. Said to Offer Aid on India Issues," *New York Times*, Aug. 18, 1942.
[103] Ibid.

behalf you have so eloquently assured us that this war is being fought."[104]

Later that autumn, Thomas returned to the campaign trail, this time to "pinch hit" for Coleman Cheney, the Socialist Party's nominee for governor of New York.[105] The 42-year-old Cheney, a professor of economics at Skidmore College in Saratoga Springs, had been drafted and inducted into the U.S. Army in July of 1942, making an active campaign that autumn virtually impossible. Cheney had been Norman Thomas's running mate for lieutenant governor in 1938, the year the party lost its automatic ballot status in the Empire State.

The Socialist Party joined Cheney, who had also served in World War I, in asking for a deferment or furlough until after the election, but their request was denied. Cheney consequently spent the entire campaign in Colorado where he was stationed.[106]

Despite Army regulations prohibiting active service members from seeking public office, his name remained on the November ballot.[107]

Thomas, who campaigned vigorously for Cheney — giving speeches in Rochester, Geneva, Buffalo, Syracuse, Auburn and Schenectady — sharply criticized the Army's refusal to grant Cheney a deferment in a radio address in early October. "Suppose Cheney, the only gubernatorial candidate in uniform, had been nominated by the Republican or Democratic parties or even the American Labor Party, would he not have been granted a deferment to campaign?" It was a fair question.[108]

The Socialist Party and Thomas, in particular, had grown increasingly critical of the American Labor Party during this period, viewing their left-wing rival as little more than an appendage of the Democratic Party — a perception that was further reinforced when the larger ALP ignored the Socialist Party's suggestion that it should follow their lead and offer their gubernatorial nomination to Cheney in absentia.

---

[104] Ibid. The letter to President Roosevelt was signed by Thomas, the Rev. John Haynes Holmes, John T. Flynn of the America First Committee, ACLU executive director Roger Baldwin and a dozen others.
[105] "Thomas to Tour State," *New York Times*, Oct. 17, 1942; "Thomas Takes Stump," *New York Sun*, Oct. 17, 1942.
[106] "Socialists Nominate Cheney for Governor," *New York Times*, June 22, 1942; "Cheney Deferment Asked," *New York Times*, July 4, 1942; "Cheney is Inducted Despite Party Plea," *New York Times*, July 11, 1942.
[107] "Cheney Stays On Ticket," *Knickerbocker News*, Oct. 17, 1942. By the time the Army informed the Socialist Party of the War Department regulation in mid-October, it was too late for the party to make a substitution.
[108] "Draft Ruling Assailed," *New York Times*, Oct. 5, 1942.

When the ALP refused to seriously consider the Skidmore professor's candidacy and nominated Dean Alfange by acclamation, the Socialists, in a blistering statement issued by party executive secretary Irving Barshop, lashed out at their left-wing rival, asserting that the American Labor Party "had given up its one chance to be really independent and free of old party ties." Pointing out that Alfange, a longtime Tammany Democrat, wasn't even a member of the ALP, the Socialists declared that the American Labor Party, with whom it had eagerly cooperated two years earlier in the vain hope that it would prove to be an independent force in New York politics, wasn't deserving of the support of progressive and working-class voters.[109]

Maynard Krueger, the party's newly-elected national chairman, echoed the concerns of the New York Socialists in a speech at the Church of All Nations on Second Avenue in late September. "The American Labor Party seems to have muddied the waters of independent political action so that in some places it is accepted as the symbol of independent political action by labor," he argued, adding that it was "the responsibility of the New York Socialists to make it clear that what is being represented today by the American Labor Party is not the principle of independent political action."[110]

Thomas, meanwhile, campaigned vigorously for the party's statewide ticket. Often appearing with Samuel H. Friedman, the party's candidate for lieutenant governor, Thomas told a crowd of 400 in Schenectady that there was "very little difference" between the major-party candidates and "the only issue seems to be who supported the President more before Pearl Harbor."

Thomas and Friedman, editor of the *Socialist Call*, the party's national weekly, told the Schenectady audience that while the other parties talked about winning the war, the Socialist Party's candidate for governor was actually doing something about it — he was serving his country in the armed forces.[111]

---

[109] Ibid; "Connolly Chosen for Congress," *New York Times*, Feb. 15, 1941. Alfange had been Tammany's candidate in a special election in Manhattan's "Silk Stocking" 17th congressional district in the spring of 1941, placing second in a three-way contest that included the American Labor Party's Eugene P. Connolly. A founder of the National Maritime Union who had worked closely with John L. Lewis in organizing the Congress of Industrial Organizations and later served on the New York City Council, Connolly — campaigning on a platform promising to keep the United States out of World War II — enjoyed the backing of left-wing congressman Vito Marcantonio in his 1941 congressional campaign.

[110] "A.L.P. is Criticized; Socialist Party Head Says It Does Not Represent Labor," *New York Times*, Sep. 27, 1942.

[111] "Thomas in Plea for Cheney at Boro Socialist Rally," *Brooklyn Eagle*, Oct. 24, 1942.

Speaking in Buffalo in late October, the four-time presidential candidate declared that the nation was heading toward a dictatorship. "We are moving toward a dictator who tries to be more or less popular," he said at rally at the Salem Evangelical and Reformed Church. "It has not happened yet," he added, "but we are on the road in that direction." While acknowledging that Roosevelt had "done some good things in peace time and war," Thomas said that his administration was "far from being infallible." He also said that continuing criticism of the administration's ineffective handling of the war was completely warranted.[112]

In marked contrast to some of the enthusiastic rallies witnessed at the close of previous Socialist campaigns, the 1942 afternoon finale in a ballroom at the Hotel Diplomat in New York City was a quiet and sparsely-attended affair, drawing fewer than 300 supporters. Cheney, who was still in an Army training camp in Colorado, addressed the group in a previously recorded message.[113]

Deploring the lack of any substantive difference in the choices offered by the two major parties, Thomas told the party faithful that New Yorkers could have saved themselves the time and trouble of holding an election if a little girl in a "white dress with a red, white and blue sash" had been permitted to pick the winner by drawing a slip of paper from a fishbowl in Albany. It really didn't matter which major-party candidate prevailed, he said. "It cannot be said that either the American Labor Party or the Communist Party has helped the situation much," he added.[114]

Sounding a more positive note, Thomas offered a few kind words for Wendell Willkie in his remarks to the pint-sized crowd. "I am glad to bear testimony," said Thomas, "to the surprising excellence of Mr. Willkie's latest speech — he either got converted or changed his ghost writer — in so far as it dealt with the substitution of racial cooperation for imperialism." The comment was a reference to Willkie's speeches in China earlier that month in which the former Republican presidential nominee raised some eyebrows, particularly in Britain, by saying that World War II "must mean an end to the empire of nations over other nations" and that the days of colonial rule were numbered.[115]

Despite Thomas's strenuous efforts on behalf of the party's ticket, the Socialist Party once again took it on the chin. Cheney ran

---

[112] "Nation Seen Heading Into Dictatorship," *Buffalo Courier-Express*, Oct. 28, 1942.
[113] "Socialists Have 'Record' Rally," *Knickerbocker News*, Nov. 2, 1942.
[114] "Few Attend Final Socialist Rally," *New York Sun*, Nov. 2, 1942.
[115] "Global Offensive Urged By Willkie," *New York Times*, Oct. 7, 1942; "Cheney Talk Heard at Socialist Rally," *New York Times*, Nov. 2, 1942.

a distant fifth in the governor's race, garnering a meager 21,911 votes — a shade below the 24,890 votes garnered by Thomas four years earlier — while finishing behind Republican winner Thomas E. Dewey, Democrat John J. Bennett, Jr., the ALP's Dean Alfange and the Communist Party's Israel Amter, the latter of whom more than doubled Cheney's showing.[116] Cheney's relatively disappointing showing, moreover, was far short of the 50,000 votes needed to requalify the Socialist Party for a permanent place on the New York ballot.

The rest of the Socialist Party's statewide ticket — Samuel H. Friedman for lieutenant governor, labor lawyer Joseph G. Glass for attorney general, and the Rev. Herman J. Hahn of Buffalo for controller — didn't fare much better, nor did New Rochelle engineer Amicus Most and African-American teacher and writer Layle Lane, the party's candidates for the state's two at-large seats in Congress. In New York, the party was as dead as a doornail.

Nationally, the situation looked even worse. The 1942 midterm elections had been another all-around disaster for the Socialist Party. Even Milwaukee's beloved and picturesque Robert Buech, an aging former alderman, sheriff, supervisor and member of the city election commission whose political career spanned the Socialist Party's rise and decline in that city, failed to break the modest three percent mark in his bid for the U.S. House in the party's stronghold in Wisconsin's fourth congressional district.

---

[116] Michael J. Dubin, *United States Gubernatorial Elections, 1932-1952: The Official Results by State and County* (Jefferson, N.C., 2014), pp. 9, 165. Dewey won in a landslide, garnering 2,148,546 votes to Bennett's 1,501,039 and 403,626 for the ALP's Alfange. The Communist Party's Israel Amter polled 45,220 votes while the Socialist Labor Party's Aaron Orange brought up the rear, tallying a scant 3,496 votes.

Chapter X

♦

The Loneliest Quest

Moments after being nominated in 1944, Norman Thomas and his vice-presidential running mate delivered their acceptance speeches over the Blue Network, a quasi-public affairs radio network covering media markets in about three-quarters of the country.

The fact that Thomas neither anticipated — nor desired — another nomination for the presidency was obvious in his remarks accepting his party's highest honor. "This convention knows that I did not come to it with an acceptance speech in my pocket," he told the delegates in Reading. "Ever since 1940 I had believed and said that personal, and I thought party, considerations should preclude my undertaking for the fifth time the burdens and responsibilities of an extraordinarily difficult campaign. But I was firmly convinced," he continued, "that our party owed it to its own integrity and to its own concept of democracy to raise, in the face of all odds, a banner around which men could rally in the cause of plenty, peace and freedom. I was scarcely in a position to urge my party and its devoted workers, the Jimmy Higginses, who are our real heroes, into an arduous undertaking in which I should decline."[1]

Thomas knew the campaign ahead was going to be the most

---

[1] "Norman Thomas, 'Why Socialist Vote This Year is So Essential,'" *Socialist Call*, June 16, 1944.

difficult of all. "Year by year, in state after state," he told the delegates, "Democrats and Republicans tighten their monopoly on the ballot. Even the Communists, recognizing that fact, have decided to bore from within. We shall offer about the only articulate and organized opposition to this old-party monopoly."[2]

In accepting his party's fifth straight nomination for the presidency, Thomas foresaw a particularly bitter campaign ahead, one in which emotions would be aroused and the American people more or less divided along class lines. Predicting a minimum of difference in the vague generalities offered by the two major parties, the Socialist standard-bearer quipped that "the choice between Tweedledum and Tweedledee will scarcely be worth the cost."[3]

Roosevelt, he said in his afternoon radio address, "will be praised and attacked as the patron of labor, a disguised Socialist or worse. Yet the President, by his own statement, backed by his own deeds, is no longer 'Dr. New Deal' but "Dr. Win the War.' He has backed no important progressive legislation since 1937; and he has supported conscription of labor and given indications of supporting permanent post-war conscription."[4]

Joking that the New Dealers were now "a government in exile," Thomas ridiculed the "strange chorus" of Communists, Wall Street bankers, farmers, small businessmen and labor leaders who were singing the praises of free enterprise as the solution for the nation's prolonged unemployment crisis — widespread joblessness "that the original free enterprise system did so much to breed" in the first place.[5]

"The commanding heights of the modern economic order — natural resources, money, banking and credit, monopolies and semi-monopolies, including, of course, public utilities — must be socially owned and controlled," he declared. He also defended the Socialist Party's call for the nationalization of industry, assuring the American people that the Socialist Party's proposals would include safeguards against the establishment of an omnipotent bureaucratic state.[6]

In his radio address, Thomas also elaborated on his party's call for "an immediate political peace offensive based on the offer of an armistice to the peoples of the Axis nations."[7]

---

[2] Bertram Benedict, "The Socialist Vote," *Pittsburgh Press*, Oct. 4, 1944.
[3] "Socialist Ticket Headed by Thomas," *New York Times*, June 5, 1944.
[4] Ibid.
[5] Ibid.
[6] Ibid.
[7] Ibid.

Defeating a minority proposal relying entirely on "popular pressure" to bring an end to the war, the party's peace offensive, written by Thomas, had been overwhelming adopted by a vote of 83-42.[8] Needless to say, Thomas was more than a little pleased that the delegates approved his plank calling for the United Nations to begin "an immediate political peace offensive based on the offer of an armistice to the peoples of the Axis nations," a peace initiative that mandated the Axis powers to immediately disarm and withdraw from conquered territories. It also required the Axis countries to form new governments and to return all of the gold, artwork, archaeological treasures and other property stolen by the Nazis.[9]

Under such a peace initiative, the Socialist nominee told his radio audience, the Allied forces would assist in settling boundary disputes and aid in the creation of regional federations consisting of smaller nations as part of a world federation. The party's peace plan would also offer the opportunity of self-government to occupied colonial lands. A fundamental ingredient of the party's proposal, explained Thomas, was the recognition that people on every continent deserved freedom and the right to determine their own form of government in a world in which "political and economic arrangement for removing the causes of war, settling disputes, guaranteeing security and conquering poverty" had been established.[10]

Thomas expanded on several of the points made in his radio address in a book published earlier that spring, one of dozens of blueprints for peace that hit bookstores during that period. In his book *What Is Our Destiny?* — Thomas's first book since the attack on Pearl Harbor — the Socialist standard-bearer sharply condemned the internment of Japanese-Americans on the west coast, racial segregation in the army, and the saturation bombing of Germany. He also laid out a provocative eight-point plan for peace, one that not only sought to expand the socialist economic doctrine of government ownership to international public ownership, but also to raise the standard of living in the poorest countries and regions of the world through "an inclusive world confederation, with powers limited to this sort of cooperation for peace and plenty."[11]

Clearly written for posterity, Thomas spent several chapters attempting to justify his own opposition to U.S. involvement in the

---

[8] "Socialist Convention Backs Peace Offensive," *Los Angeles Times*, June 4, 1944.
[9] "Socialists Demand a Peace Offensive," *New York Times*, June 4, 1944.
[10] "Socialist Ticket Headed By Thomas," *New York Times*, June 5, 1944.
[11] "Norman Thomas Blueprints the Future," *New York Times*, April 9, 1944.

war, and wondered how so many Americans could have confidence in the administration's ability to work miracles in faraway lands when most people regarded "most of its domestic policies as a monument to folly."[12]

Maintaining that there were "no forces which can make our country act effectively to police the earth or play God to it," Thomas specifically called for an end to imperialism and colonialism; a reduction in arbitrary interference in trade; an equitable distribution of the world's raw materials; parity between the world's monetary systems; a healthy flow of capital into developing and underdeveloped nations; an end to immigration restrictions; minimum international standards for working conditions; and freedom of the air and seas. "We may neither perfectly predict nor completely control our collectively destiny," he eloquently concluded, but it was still within the power of the American people to shape that destiny "in terms of such plenty, peace and freedom as in our haunted sleep we have not dared to dream."[13]

Unlike the strong antiwar stance adopted by the party during World War I, the Socialist Party had adopted a resolution lending its "critical support" to the Allied cause at its 1942 national convention in Milwaukee — a position reluctantly championed by Thomas himself.

"Mr. Socialist," as he was known to millions of Americans, ran on a platform that autumn urging the United States and its Allies to seek a democratic peace rather than insisting upon an "unconditional surrender" by the Axis powers. Though the patrician rebel believed that a Nazi victory would be "the lowest circle of hell," he nevertheless strongly felt that a statement of democratic peace terms would be the most reasonable approach to ending the deadly conflict.

After Japan's sneak attack on Pearl Harbor on December 7, 1941, rabid anti-Japanese feelings spread throughout the country, fanned by unsubstantiated rumors of a fifth column in the United States allegedly communicating with enemy submarines off America's shores while planning massive sabotage. One particularly xenophobic congressman proposed rounding up every Japanese-American in the United States, Alaska and Hawaii and "putting them in concentration camps."

Though Roosevelt didn't necessarily share the congressman's hysterical view, he nevertheless signed Executive Order 9066 in February 1942, giving the U.S. Army's Lt. Gen. John DeWitt, head

---

[12] Ibid.
[13] Ibid.

of the Western Defense Command, authority to arrest every Japanese-American on the West Coast. Denied due process, some 110,000 Japanese-American men, women and children — 70,000 of whom were born in the United States — were subsequently uprooted from their homes, schools and workplaces and shipped to American-style concentration camps on the West Coast where most of them remained for three years. It was one of the most shameful episodes in American history. Fascism, it seemed, was alive and well on both sides of the Atlantic.

Given the anti-Japanese frenzy sweeping the country, only a handful of courageous Americans spoke out against what historian Eugene V. Rostow described as "our worst wartime mistake."

Speaking for America's conscience, Norman Thomas was one of those few intrepid yet lonely voices. Imprisoning American citizens of Japanese descent, he said, "is a good deal like burning down Chicago to get rid of gangsters…The worst feature of the whole bad business is the small volume of protest and the considerable volume of applause from the West Coast for this establishment of military despotism." No less a pamphleteer than Thomas Paine, the eternal Socialist candidate published a brochure called *Democracy and Japanese Americans*, describing in vivid detail the shameful internment of Japanese-American citizens. Few of his fellow countrymen, however, bothered to read it.

As sure as the sun rises, Thomas addressed this issue head-on during the 1944 campaign, condemning the shameful wartime internment of Japanese-Americans and arguing that they should be welcomed back to the Pacific Coast following the war. "You cannot indulge in racial prejudice and hope very honestly for a lasting peace," he said during a campaign appearance in Seattle. "And that applies to Japanese-Americans on the West Coast."[14]

Having developed an almost personal animosity toward Roosevelt during the 1940 campaign — something that clearly wasn't evident in the 1932 or 1936 elections — Thomas focused most of his fire during the 1944 presidential election on FDR's failed domestic and foreign policies, accusing the President of acting without congressional or popular approval while desperately scheming to involve the United States in the war in Europe by deceptive and nefarious means.

Though aiming much of his fire at Roosevelt that year, Thomas was also highly critical of Thomas Dewey, whom he had person-

---

[14] "Thomas Would Let Japanese on Coast," *Christian Science Monitor*, Sep. 2, 1944.

ally campaigned against in New York's 1938 gubernatorial election. "It is a pity that the Republicans couldn't pull out of their hats anything better than Dewey," Thomas told a rally at Reading's Socialist Park in the summer of 1944. "He will be nominated largely on the fact that he said nothing about vital issues."[15] The Socialist nominee also accused the New York governor of sidestepping every important issue in his Chicago acceptance speech, an address in which the Republican governor railed against the New Deal while accusing the Roosevelt administration of being "consistently hostile to and abusive of American business and American industry."[16]

In a radio address a few days later, Thomas posed several domestic and foreign policy questions to the Republican nominee — none of which were ever satisfactorily answered. "We know what we are fighting against, but what are we fighting for?" queried Thomas. "Are you satisfied with any official statement of our war and peace aims, and if not, what do you propose?" He also wanted to know how Dewey planned to reduce the size of the country's peacetime federal bureaucracy and, more specifically, which of Roosevelt's New Deal agencies he planned to abolish.

Among other things, the five-time presidential candidate then asked Dewey how he planned to provide full employment in the postwar period. He also asked the Republican candidate what his prospective administration planned to do with the "new public domain," the thousands of wartime factories and plants built with taxpayer dollars, following the war.[17]

Much tougher on Roosevelt than he had been during the 1932, 1936 and 1940 campaigns, the Socialist standard-bearer came out swinging against the man in the White House, accusing FDR of failing to pursue any major progressive legislation since 1937 and lacking any sort of program to conquer poverty in the United States.[18] Prior to the war, asserted Thomas, Roosevelt had failed to alleviate joblessness and instead merely subsidized the unemployed, which made up about 23 percent of the American workforce.[19]

Though FDR had proposed a "Second Bill of Rights" in his 1944 State of the Union address, a bold vision of the government's

---

[15] "Socialist Chief Talks Politics," *Wilkes-Barre Times Leader*, June 26, 1944.
[16] "Text of Governor Dewey's Formal Acceptance of the Presidential Nomination," *New York Times*, June 29, 1944.
[17] "Norman Thomas Asks Dewey's Postwar Views," *Washington Evening Star*, July 1, 1944.
[18] "Thomas Charges Roosevelt Paves Way to New War," *Los Angeles Times*, July 31, 1944.
[19] "Norman Thomas Hits Roosevelt War Plan," *Palm Beach Post*, July 31, 1944.

role in providing economic security for the American people, Thomas and his running mate didn't believe the president's sweeping set of demands went far enough in eliminating poverty.

Roosevelt's "Economic Bill of Rights," based in part on a memo from Chester Bowles, the lanky, long-jawed advertising executive who served as the director of the Office of Price Administration (OPA), included the right to a meaningful and remunerative job; the right to earn enough to provide adequate food and clothing and recreation; the right of every farmer to raise and sell his products at a reasonable price guaranteeing a decent living; the right of every business, large and small, to trade in an atmosphere of freedom from unfair competition and domination by monopolies at home or abroad; the right of every family to a decent home; the right to adequate medical care; the right to adequate protection from the economic fears of old age, illness, accident, and unemployment; and the right to a quality education.[20]

Thomas was also deeply worried that Roosevelt, if re-elected, would continue a peacetime draft, saying in July that the President had "advocated total conscription of human beings in war and gives signs of supporting permanent military conscription of our youth in peace."[21]

According to the Socialist standard-bearer, Roosevelt's foreign policy — or lack of foreign policy, to be more precise — was unfairly aiding big business while "unnecessarily prolonging this war and inviting the next." Bemoaning the death of the New Deal, the Socialist standard-bearer also slammed the President for failing, by his own admission, to vigorously support any progressive legislation during the previous seven years.[22]

Thomas had been growing increasingly critical of FDR's foreign policy, suggesting in February 1944 that the Roosevelt administration was "paving the way for World War III by Balkanizing Europe on instructions from Moscow and London" while essentially underwriting the British and Dutch empires in Asia.[23]

"I think this blind marriage to Churchill and Stalin is hurting the situation," he said during a speech in Chicago. Russia, he predicted, would have more power, both in Europe and Asia, at the end of the war than Hitler could ever possibly dreamed of having. "The greatest danger of the next war comes from Asia," he noted, "and we will have no reason to believe that Stalin, or his successor

---

[20] Jordan, *FDR, Dewey, and the Election of 1944*, p.66.
[21] "Norman Thomas Hits Roosevelt War Plan," *Palm Beach Post*, July 31, 1944.
[22] Johnpoll, *Pacifist's Progress*, pp. 217, 245.
[23] "Thomas Sees F.D.R. Breeding Another War," *Chicago Tribune*, Feb. 26, 1944.

in Russia, will feel disposed to help us defend England's empire there."[24]

In addition to charging that the Allies were "stupidly wrong" in insisting on an unconditional surrender, Thomas belittled the President's foreign policy as "the most irresponsible, personal, even dictatorial in the world, except Russia's." The British, he said, could at least question Churchill's policy. Thomas, moreover, charged that Roosevelt hadn't even consulted with the State Department during the conferences at Cairo and Teheran, meetings that he believed had unnecessarily prolonged the war.

Thomas had long been a critic of secret diplomatic meetings on the issues of war and peace, believing that excessive secrecy at Dumbarton Oaks and other global parleys was unnecessary in a free and open democratic society. The participants at Dumbarton Oaks, he said, had been so tight-lipped that there was almost "something ominous" about it. "If this is a democracy, we are entitled to at least some general information about that policy for which our sons are dying," Thomas concluded, adding that he blamed Congress and the American people "for not making the President speak out."[25] Ironically, it was a view shared by some conservatives, the most vocal of whom was U.S. Rep. Clare Boothe Luce of Connecticut, arguably FDR's most severe critic.

Thomas, of course, strongly believed that the participants at Dumbarton Oaks — the conference at which the United Nations was formulated — had surreptitiously produced a sinister and nefarious plan "by which three countries can rule the world, a phony internationalism which is a mere façade for a triple alliance."[26] He believed it was a recipe for disaster. "No alliance in history," Thomas told an audience of Bucknell University alumni that year, "has lasted beyond the purposes of the individual allies."[27]

It was a theme that Thomas had been hammering away at for weeks, if not months. "Wars will arise out of a punitive peace and out of an organization of the world in which a cartel of potentially rival imperial powers, Russia, Britain, and America, will try to exploit, economically and politically, the rest of the world," he said while campaigning in Boise, Idaho, in late August.[28]

Nobody could have convinced the highly-principled Socialist candidate that Roosevelt, Churchill and Stalin hadn't "deliberately

---

[24] Ibid.
[25] Ibid; "Norman Thomas Sees Peril of New World War," *Chicago Tribune*, Sept. 13, 1944; "Norman Thomas Assails Secret Global Parley," *Chicago Tribune*, Sept. 18, 1944.
[26] "Thomas Slaps at Peace Plan," *Milwaukee Journal*, Nov. 1, 1944.
[27] "Thomas Discusses Issues," *New York Times*, Sep. 16, 1944.
[28] "New War Forecast," *Christian Science Monitor*, Aug. 29, 1944.

turned their backs" on any and all paths that might have led to peace. Thomas firmly believed that the "Big Three" were playing "the old imperial game of power politics in which the pawns are men, and victory means death."[29]

Thomas was particularly critical of the media's tendency to glorify the personalities of the three main architects of the postwar world — Stalin, Churchill and Roosevelt — and in that order. "Roosevelt has the most potential power," he said while campaigning in Louisville, "but less knowledge of what to do with it."[30] Roosevelt, he elaborated in a speech, was "at a loss in dealing with such masters of power politics as Stalin and Churchill," both of whom knew exactly what they wanted.

> Of the Big Three, only Stalin and Churchill know exactly what they want. Probably that includes peace and for the sake of that peace, concessions might have been won from both of them which Mr. Roosevelt has either not sought or has sought ineffectively. Today both Stalin and Churchill are definitely committed to the aggrandizement of their own countries and can think of no way to win peace other than the old way of power politics which has always failed. There are Americans who will accept this statement regarding Churchill and the British Empire, but hotly deny it of Stalin. Other Americans will do the exact opposite with equal vehemence. On the record both Stalin and Churchill are playing the same sort of power politics game.[31]

In an October 17th radio address, Thomas charged that Stalin had diverted his war effort "to make sure of his supremacy in the Baltic areas and the Balkans, where at last Russia has found access to warm water. Churchill," Thomas told his listeners, "lets Americans supply reinforcements for the for the attack on the German fortress while he hastens to free Greece before Stalin includes it along with the rest of the Balkans in his sphere of influence. It is a preposterous joke to tell us that this sort of maneuvering is in line with any honest internationalism or that an America which would refuse to underwrite it would perforce be guilty of the sin called 'isolationism.'"[32]

The greatest difficulty in obtaining a lasting peace, said

---

[29] "Thomas Accuses 'Big 3,'" *New York Times*, Oct. 18, 1944.
[30] "Norman Thomas Misses Train, But Not Chance to Lash Opponents," *Louisville Courier-Journal*, Sep. 21, 1944.
[31] "The 'Phony Internationalism' of Dumbarton Oaks," *Socialist Call*, Oct. 20, 1944.
[32] "Thomas Accuses 'Big 3,'" *New York Times*, Oct. 18, 1944.

Thomas, wouldn't be in developing a postwar structure for international cooperation — the United Nations — but rather in the "struggle for spheres of influence" by Soviet Premier Joseph Stalin and British Prime Minister Winston Churchill. "So many are the causes of conflict in the world," he asserted in yet another radio address, "so keen are the latent rivalries among the victors and so provocative of war is imperialism, that if by a miracle all the Germans and Japanese could be destroyed, Stalin and Churchill would go on demanding strategic frontiers and maneuvering for spheres of influence." As for Roosevelt, asserted Thomas, he would probably continue "the futile task of trying to appease them both by underwriting their empires with the lives of our sons."[33]

This was a point Thomas drove home repeatedly throughout the campaign. Campaigning in Buffalo earlier that summer, Thomas said that he considered it a crime "for one American boy to die to restore Dutch rule in Java or British rule in Burma or Malaysia." He also decried the "monstrous hypocrisy of calling this a war of true liberation" when in reality the war was threatening to place most of postwar Europe under Stalin's rule while virtually guaranteeing restoration of white supremacy in the Far East.[34]

The Socialist standard-bearer was unrelenting in his criticism of Roosevelt's foreign policy. He even brought up the issue of Pearl Harbor, asking some pointed questions of Secretary of State Cordell Hull earlier that summer.[35]

Reacting to British Cabinet Minister Oliver Lyttelton's startling contention that the United States had deliberately provoked the attack on Pearl Harbor — "a diplomatic blunder" for which the minister of production later apologized — Thomas asked the Secretary of State if the administration had been planning a military offensive against Japan at the time of the attack and, if so, was it intended to forestall future Japanese designs on the United States, uphold white imperialism in Asia, or simply to defend China against Japanese aggression? "Is the administration now committed to opposition to all imperialism in Asia or only Japanese imperialism?" asked Thomas. "Is it now appeasing Mr. Churchill — and powerful American interests — by silence on this question, even as it has appeased him by refusing to press for the feeding of children of Hitler's victims for which both Houses of Congress unanimously asked?"[36]

---

[33] "Thomas Warns of Perils," *New York Times*, Oct. 24, 1944.
[34] "Thomas Assails Major Party's War Programs," *Buffalo Courier-Express*, Aug. 8, 1944.
[35] "Thomas Puts Foreign Policy Queries to Hull," *Washington Post*, June 26, 1944.
[36] Norman Thomas: "Some Questions to Secretary Hull, As Yet Unanswered, On How We

Thomas's questions to Hull were prompted not by Lyttelton, but by Churchill himself in an address to the House of Commons on January 28, 1942, when the British Prime Minister intimated that it was his policy to stay out of the war in the Far East until the United States entered the conflict. "It would appear that the British Prime Minister knew far more about the administration's intentions, and that at an early date, than did Congress or the American people," asserted Thomas.[37]

While waiting for Hull's response — a reply that would never come — Thomas was harshly scolded by the *Washington Post* for having the audacity to ask such prickly questions. It was obvious, intoned the *Post* in a particularly nasty editorial, that the Roosevelt administration had not been planning a military offensive against Japan at the time of the sneak attack on Pearl Harbor. "Had it been planning such an offensive and had it embarked upon it prior to Pearl Harbor, a great many million human lives might have been spared....But the administration was so beset by men like Norman Thomas, who wrote books and made speeches to prove that the events in Asia and Europe were none of our concern, that it was slow in planning even an adequate defense. When it advocated even the most elementary measures of security, Mr. Thomas accused it of warmongering."[38]

Thomas took such criticism in stride and continued to hammer away at the man in the White House, forcefully expressing his criticism of Roosevelt's foreign policy later that summer in an open letter to Reinhold Niebuhr, chairman of the Union for Democratic Action. Declaring that the president's "underwriting of white supremacy in the Far East and the Balkanization of Europe between Moscow and London is an invitation to a new war," Thomas questioned how the proposed "triple alliance" of Great Britain, the Soviet Union and the United States — with China thrown in for good measure — could possibly prevent the outbreak of future wars when all previous alliances had failed. "That fallacy," he said in his July 25th letter, "lies at the heart of the President's great design."[39]

Thomas, of course, was desperately trying to shame his old friend into abandoning Roosevelt and supporting his candidacy, as Niebuhr had enthusiastically done in 1932 and 1936. It didn't work. As was the case four years earlier, the famous theologian

---

Got Into War — And Where We Go From Here...," *Socialist Call*, July 7, 1944.
[37] Ibid.
[38] "$64 Question," *Washington Post*, June 30, 1944.
[39] "Norman Thomas Assails F.D.R. Foreign Policy," *Chicago Tribune*, July 31, 1944; "Norman Thomas Hits Roosevelt War Plan," *Palm Beach Post*, July 31, 1944.

stuck with FDR, but not before issuing a stinging rebuke of Thomas's candidacy:

> One of the more interesting ironies of this time has been the spectacle of American Socialists talking of "winning the peace"; if America and the democratic world had listened to those Socialists who before Pearl Harbor were telling us that our capitalist society was not pure enough in heart to take up arms against fascist aggression, Hitler would be making [his] peace today.
>
> [Your political] irresponsibility, which led to the folly of your pre-Pearl Harbor isolationism, stems from your inability to conceive of politics as the art of choosing among possible alternatives. This blindness makes it impossible for you to correctly gauge the political climate of the country.
>
> America, in the years immediately ahead, may be the scene of basic political realignments. But America will not in the foreseeable future be called on to make a choice between socialism and reaction. A sizeable Socialist vote in November will prove nothing and influence no one. The realistic actual choice before Americans is that of reverting to the period of Hoover-Coolidge normalcy...or of moving militantly forward in the determination to make the last four years of the Roosevelt era a period of social reconstruction and reform...
>
> I remind you once again that the battles ahead will not be simple contests between unmitigated evil and absolute good, and that a true perspective cannot be had from the Olympian heights of Socialist dogma.[40]

Niebuhr's response was one of the harshest criticisms ever hurled at Thomas. Coming from somebody Thomas had long considered a close personal friend, it was also one of the most hurtful.

Elaborating on his criticism of Roosevelt in remarks recorded for a broadcast to U.S. troops overseas in September, Thomas said that he had serious doubts about the President's ability to assure a continuing peace following the war.

Accusing the administration of not planning effectively for either war or peace, the Socialist candidate said that based on the President's record of handling the prewar issues, "there is no reason to accept the indispensability of the Roosevelt administration for handling of the peace. The record of Cairo and Teheran, the

---

[40] Johnpoll, *Pacifist's Progress*, pp. 247-248.

terms of the President's so-called 'great design' for peace and the proceedings at Dumbarton Oaks so far as we know them," asserted Thomas, "show an intention to base our peace upon a cartel of empires which in the light of all we know of history and observation is far more likely to lead to new war — a view also expressed by the Socialist Labor Party's Edward Teichert.[41]

Suggesting that Roosevelt's record in the months leading up to U.S. involvement in World War II didn't support the omniscience which the President's supporters glowingly attributed to him, Thomas said:

> In 1940 when the Nazi power was at its height, Roosevelt did not say we must prepare rapidly and very soon enter the war to save ourselves and the world. He said that we must take the sort of steps to aid one belligerent which always in history has led to war — that latter fact he forgot to mention — but by these steps short of war we shall remain at peace. After the election the President proceeded to extend help to the Allies, which included actual convoying of their soldiers.[42]

In his shortwave radio address to the troops, the former Presbyterian minister and social worker, who had accurately predicted during the 1940 campaign that the U.S. would enter World War II by declaring war on Japan, also accused the Roosevelt administration of helping to arm the Japanese by purchasing $702 million of gold from them during that country's war with China, "which was completely useless to us," and that the President and Congress did little "to prevent the sale of scrap to Japan." By pursuing such policies, argued Thomas, the U.S. government, in effect, "helped to arm our enemies."[43]

Turning to domestic policy, Thomas acknowledged that the New Deal had contributed to the nation's recovery, but that there was still far too many jobless Americans and it wasn't until the war that the administration was able to change the horrible fact that as many as 40 percent of the U.S. population "lived barely on or below the level of proper subsistence in respect to food."[44]

Though he focused most of his remarks on Roosevelt, Thomas also took a shot at Republican nominee Tom Dewey toward the

---

[41] "Thomas Doubts F.D.R.'s Ability to Handle Peace," *Los Angeles Times*, Sep. 25, 1944; "Presidential Nominee Sees New War Peril," *Los Angeles Times*, Sep. 5, 1944.
[42] Ibid.
[43] Ibid; "Norman Thomas Thinks Browder Conservative," *Los Angeles Times*, Sep. 29, 1944.
[44] Ibid.

end of his taped remarks. "Again, let no Republican argue that I am presenting a case for Gov. Dewey," he concluded. Dewey, he said, "favors the system which led to the Great Depression and wants nothing better than a slightly more sophisticated and I hope more honest version of Harding's return to normalcy."[45]

Each of Roosevelt's opponents, including the Republican nominee, owed the Socialist Party — and more specifically, campaign manager Harry Fleischman — a huge debt of gratitude for forcing the War Department to issue a ruling calling for equal time for all political parties to address U.S. soldiers overseas in a series of weekly shortwave radio broadcasts.[46]

Aware that the 1942 Soldier Vote Act, which included provisions authored by North Dakota's independent-minded "Wild Bill" Langer provided for equal radio time for the nation's minor parties to address U.S. troops overseas, Fleischman had written to Major Gen. F. H. Osborn requesting equal time for Thomas. Osborn responded that while the law provided for equal time for every presidential candidate who was on the ballot in at least a half-dozen states, no time had yet been granted to any candidate. In responding, Osborn — almost as an afterthought — asked Fleischman if he thought President Roosevelt's speech in Bremerton, Washington, on August 12 was of a "political" nature. Fleischman responded affirmatively.[47]

On August 25, Osborn wrote to Fleischman again, this time granting equal time to the Socialist Party, but six hours later, Assistant Secretary of War John J. McCloy — a Wall Street lawyer, banker, and Henry Stimson protégé who later headed the World Bank, chaired the Council on Foreign Relations and served as chairman of the Rockefeller family's Chase Manhattan Bank — reversed the War Department's decision and denied the Socialist candidate equal time.[48] In announcing his decision, which he claimed was made without Roosevelt's input, McCloy said that the president's Bremerton "report," delivered on the deck of a destroyer in the Puget Sound Navy Yard, was "not political, and, accordingly, no time will be granted to the Socialist Party on such basis."[49]

Thomas, who was campaigning in Denver, wasn't the least bit

---

[45] Ibid.
[46] "Army Yields Radio Time to All Parties; Socialists Win Battle to Make Broadcasts to Troops Overseas," *Socialist Call*, Sep. 8, 1944.
[47] Fleischman, *Norman Thomas: A Biography*, p. 212.
[48] Ibid., p. 213.
[49] "Army Rules Roosevelt Address Was Political, Then Denies It," *New York Times*, Aug. 26, 1944.

surprised by McCloy's decision. In fact, he wasn't surprised by anything when it came to the duopoly. "I had feared something of the sort," he told reporters.[50] The War Department's decision, he added, meant that "the troops abroad will get very little chance to hear anything else than their master's voice."[51] He also believed Roosevelt had "directly or indirectly" determined that his own speech was "not a political talk."[52]

McCloy, a leading Establishment figure who later served on the widely-discredited Warren Commission investigation into John F. Kennedy's assassination, insisted that his decision to reverse the War Department's original ruling had been made free of any White House influence.[53] Nobody believed him, of course, and it was only a matter of hours before several leading Republicans, including RNC chairman Herbert Brownell, Jr., and Nebraska Sen. Kenneth S. Wherry, joined with Thomas and the Socialists in criticizing the reversal of the Army's initial ruling and demanding equal time for Dewey. "It would be interesting to know where the order for reversal came from," said Brownell.[54]

In a particularly playful mood, Roosevelt himself whimsically suggested that his Bremerton speech, a rambling and admittedly poorly-delivered address about his recent trip to Hawaii and the Aleutian Islands, had been "non-political." In a delicious dig at Republicans who were suggesting that McCloy had succumbed to White House pressure, the president stated during a press conference that his Bremerton speech was equivalent to giving a dissertation on the growing, planting and selling of Christmas trees. (Roosevelt, incidentally, grew Christmas trees commercially at his Hyde Park estate.)[55]

In the meantime, Fleischman was furious, telling reporters that McCloy's "highly partisan and political" reversal of the War Department's earlier ruling was a clear violation of the Soldier Voting Law. "It is significant that time was granted for the Socialist broadcast by regular Army officers and should now be reversed by a political appointee of President Roosevelt," asserted Fleischman, adding confidently that a reconsideration of the issues involved would lead to a reversal of McCloy's "arbitrary, unfair and unjust decision" preventing soldiers serving abroad from hearing all

---

[50] "Army Yields Radio Time to All Parties," *Socialist Call*, Sep. 8, 1944.
[51] "Thomas Criticizes Ban," *New York Times*, Aug. 26, 1944.
[52] "Socialist Radio Curb Attacked," *Milwaukee Journal*, Aug. 26, 1944.
[53] "M'Cloy Says He Acted Free of White House," *New York Times*, Aug. 29, 1944.
[54] "Republicans Insist on Radio Equality," *New York Times*, Aug. 27, 1944.
[55] "F.D.R. Will Make First Campaign Speech Sept. 23," *St. Petersburg Times*, Aug. 30, 1944; Rosenman, *Working with Roosevelt*, pp. 461-462.

sides of the issues.[56]

He was right. Wasting little time, the Socialist Party's campaign manager fired off another letter to the War Department reiterating his party's belief that Roosevelt's speech in Bremerton was indeed of a political nature.

"In his Bremerton talk," wrote Fleischman, "Roosevelt stated that the common people of Japan are equally guilty with their warlords of imperialist grabbing and promoting warlike policies, and that the people, as well as their rulers, cannot be trusted. We Socialists emphatically disagree with this political position. We urge a political peace offensive based on the offer of an armistice to the peoples of the Axis nations, on condition that they overthrow their fascist and imperialist rulers, withdraw their military forces from all occupied territory and rapidly disarm. Such a policy, we believe, would shorten the war by inviting revolt in Germany and Japan, would save American lives and would lead to a lasting peace.[57]

"But whether or not the War Department prefers Roosevelt's policies to those of the Socialist Party," concluded the young Socialist, "certainly the soldiers should have a chance to hear both sides of this political discussion."[58]

While making no mention of Roosevelt's Bremerton speech, the War Department announced two days later that it would grant equal time to all five parties on the ballot in at least six states — the Democratic, Republican, Socialist, Prohibition and the Socialist Labor parties — to deliver a series of weekly political broadcasts on the Army's short-wave radio facilities overseas.[59]

The Socialists were naturally ecstatic. "We have won a splendid victory for free speech," wrote Fleischman, who continued to press for additional equal time for Thomas based on Roosevelt's speech in Bremerton.[60]

Under the agreement, the five parties were each allocated two half-hour broadcasts and three fifteen-minute programs which would be aired over the Army's thirteen shortwave stations, reaching every theatre of the war. In addition, the two thirty-minute broadcasts were to be sent to nearly 120 Army radio stations across the globe. Under the terms of the agreement, each of the speeches

---

[56] "Fleischman Calls It 'Politics,'" *New York Times*, Aug. 26, 1944.
[57] "Army Yields Radio Time to All Parties," *Socialist Call*, Sep. 8, 1944.
[58] Ibid.
[59] "Army Radio Time Offered 5 Parties to Talk to Troops," *New York Times*, Aug. 28, 1944.
[60] "Socialist Victory for Free Speech," *Socialist Call*, Sep. 8, 1944.

had to be rebroadcasts of programs previously aired on commercial stations in the United States — the costs of which had to be borne by the political parties.[61] Moreover, each of the broadcasts were subjected to the same code of wartime practices as every U.S. broadcaster and had to be cleared with the Office of Censorship before being transmitted to the Army.[62]

The agreement, of course, didn't guarantee that the Socialist, Prohibition and Socialist Labor parties would be heard by soldiers serving abroad as often as the major-party candidates since the arrangement didn't place any restrictions on the Army's regular broadcast news coverage of the presidential campaign, most of which was gleaned from commercial news services focused almost entirely on the Roosevelt and Dewey candidacies.[63]

Already running on fumes, the cash-strapped Socialists, whose half-hour broadcasts were scheduled for Sept. 20 and Sept. 28, with the fifteen-minute broadcasts scheduled for three separate days in late October, scurried to raise an estimated $15,000 to pay for the broadcasts, including the original commercial broadcasts and the transcriptions, as well as enough recordings to reach the nearly 120 Army radio stations abroad.[64] Thomas made the first thirty-minute broadcast on September 20th and retired Brigadier General Herbert C. Holdridge, who had publicly endorsed the Socialist ticket a few weeks earlier, spoke to the U.S. troops overseas during the party's second half-hour program eight days later.[65]

During the ensuing fight for equal time, a drama that made front-page headlines across the country, Thomas continued to attack both of his major-party opponents. "Whether you vote for Roosevelt or Dewey, you vote for the same principles and toward the same results, capitalism, imperialism, and unemployment at home, from which ultimately comes fascism," he said in a speech in Buffalo a few weeks earlier.[66]

Throughout the autumn campaign, Thomas maintained that there weren't any substantive differences in the Democratic and Republican platforms of 1944. "Roosevelt and Dewey are running

---

[61] "Overseas Talks Begin Sept. 20; $15,000 Needed," *Socialist Call*, Sep. 15, 1944; "Whirlwind Campaign to Raise $15,000 Radio Fund in 10 Days," *Socialist Call*, Sep. 15, 1944.
[62] "5 Parties Share Radio to Soldiers," *New York Times*, Sep. 15, 1944.
[63] Ibid.
[64] "Overseas Talks Begin Sept. 20; $15,000 Needed," *Socialist Call*, Sep. 15, 1944.
[65] "Thomas Warns on Losing Peace," *New York Times*, Sep. 21, 1944; "Assails Major Parties; Holdridge, Thomas Backer, See War Plants 'Plowed Under,'" *New York Times*, Sep. 29, 1944.
[66] "Thomas Assails Major Party's War Programs," *Buffalo Courier-Express*, Aug. 8, 1944.

on virtually interchangeable platforms," he asserted during a campaign appearance in Connecticut. "If I read you their respective planks without labels, you couldn't tell which was which, and what is worse, you couldn't tell with any definiteness what either of them means," said Thomas. "It is only the Socialist Party which offers you a clear-cut program definitely related to winning plenty, peace and freedom."[67]

Not that it really mattered. After all, the Democratic and Republican platforms were essentially meaningless. "It is one of the wonders of American politics that neither the congressional nor the presidential candidates of the two major parties are bound by party platforms or their own promises," observed Thomas while participating in a symposium at Wellesley's Summer Institute for Social Progress.[68]

He also attacked the country's major banks, proposing once again that the nation's money, banking and credit system should be collectively owned and managed — in short, calling for the nationalization of the Federal Reserve. "In war and peace," he declared, "there must be an end of this business of permitting private banks to create interest-bearing money to their profit but to our great cost. We must collectively own the natural resources like oil and coal and iron which were certainly not God's gift to the Rockefellers. These resources have been shockingly wasted under private ownership," he said, adding that absentee ownership of land should also be eliminated.[69]

Though he once again found himself subjected to occasional sniping from the Communists, the 1944 presidential campaign was the first in which Thomas didn't have to worry about a Communist Party opponent. In 1928, when he first sought the nation's highest office, Thomas and the Socialists were severely lambasted by William Z. Foster and the Communists, then known as the Workers' Party, for having supported "Fighting Bob" La Follette's insurgent bid for the presidency four years earlier. By supporting the aging Wisconsin lawmaker's candidacy, argued the Communists, the Socialist Party had exposed its own "capitalist" nature. Needless to say, Thomas was mildly amused that sixteen years later, the same Communists who leveled those charges were now criticizing him for refusing to join Earl Browder in supporting

---

[67] "Peace Terms Criticized By Thomas," *Hartford Courant*, Oct. 16, 1944.
[68] "Sen. Burton Advocates GOP 'Square Deal,'" *Boston Globe*, July 6, 1944.
[69] Ibid.

the CIO's Political Action Committee in its drive to aid the Democrats.[70]

Convening at New York's Riverside Plaza Hotel, the Communist Party had formally dissolved itself as a political party earlier that spring and was immediately reconstituted as the Communist Political Association, an organization whose stated mission called for "a more democratic and progressive America" and the establishment of a lasting peace. Working within the traditional two-party system, the short-lived association was committed to supporting progressive candidates who would work for peaceful cooperation between the United States and Russia in the postwar period.

Promising to fight for "the continuance of Roosevelt's leadership, and the election of a victory Congress," the newly-formed organization, headed by Browder, claimed some 80,000 dues-paying members, including some 22,000 who had been enlisted during the previous three months, shortly after the Communist Party initially announced its intention to disband as a political party.[71]

There were some in the party who vehemently disagreed with the decision to convert the party into a "nonpartisan" left-wing pressure group, the most vocal of whom included William Z. Foster, the party's former general secretary and three-time presidential candidate, and longtime party organizer Sam Darcy, but their dissent was stifled by Earl Browder, the party's soft-spoken and occasionally aloof general secretary and former Roosevelt foe who managed to convince the party's rank-and-file membership that organizational adaptation was necessary and that the party could have a much greater impact by working within the existing two-party system.

Later disapprovingly interpreted by the party's international leadership — meaning, of course, that it was a view shared by Moscow — as liquidating the only truly independent working-class party in the United States, Browder's decision to disband the party and form the Communist Political Association eventually led to his unceremonious expulsion from the party fifteen months after the 1944 presidential election.

In the interim, the publicity-seeking Browder, who was prominently featured in Republican attacks on the administration dur-

---

[70] "Pacific States: Thomas Reports Coast Unions Beset by Internal Tensions," *New York Times*, Oct. 1, 1944.
[71] "Communists Disband Party in U.S.; Back Roosevelt for Fourth Term," *New York Times*, May 21, 1944; Klehr, *The Heyday of American Communism*, pp. 410-411.

ing the autumn campaign — and apparently enjoyed every minute of it — spent much of that year rallying support for the Democratic ticket, vigorously defending the president's new vice-presidential running mate to disappointed Henry Wallace supporters on the left while dismissing rumors of Roosevelt's failing health as pro-Nazi propaganda.

Browder, who had waged a thinly disguised effort to reelect Roosevelt in 1936, but actively campaigned against him as the Communist Party's nominee again in 1940 — a year when his party, having abandoned its Popular Front strategy, faced widespread public distrust and resentment stemming from the notorious Nazi-Soviet Pact — also sharply attacked the Republican candidate, asserting that Dewey's election would signal an end to the prospects of post-war cooperation between the United States and the Soviet Union.

A Dewey victory, he told an enthusiastic and nearly sold-out crowd at New York's Madison Square Garden in late September, would also mean that the U.S. was abandoning the idea of a permanent international peace organization while inviting the nations of Europe to drive Communists and those who sought to cooperate with them out of public life, thereby risking the possibility of plunging those European countries into a "devastating civil war" once the threat of Nazi domination was removed.

Dewey and his supporters, declared the Communist leader, were waging a campaign as though it was "more important for Dewey to win the election, by whatever means, than it is for America to win the war."

In the meantime, Thomas, who was once wonderfully described as the country's only mobile national monument besides San Francisco's world-famous cable cars, again mounted a whirlwind campaign, logging more than 15,000 miles while visiting thirty-six states.[72] Again and again, he urged his fellow citizens to support the ideals of democratic socialism as the best way to avoid an inevitable drift toward fascism in the wake of what he described as a dying capitalist system.[73]

As in past campaigns, the good-natured, perpetual candidate frequently used humor to make his point, telling a radio audience that he had to speak quickly because he only had few minutes of air time to discuss what Roosevelt and Dewey would normally take hours to evade.[74]

---

[72] "Thomas to Carry Socialist Message Across the Nation," *Socialist Call*, Aug. 11, 1944.

[73] "Large Socialist Vote Is Urged By Thomas," *New York Times*, Oct. 10, 1944.

[74] Gregory, *Norman Thomas: The Great Dissenter*, p. 209.

Thomas also sharply criticized Sidney Hillman's powerful Political Action Committee, characterizing the group's activities as "company unionism in politics." In an open letter to the 57-year-old founder and president of the Amalgamated Clothing Workers Union in late September, the Socialist candidate scolded the CIO leader for squandering an excellent opportunity for independent political action on behalf of the nation's workers and for aligning his organization with "that extraordinary conglomeration of Northern city political machines and Southern Bourbons, known as the Democratic Party."[75]

Ironically, Thomas almost seemed like he was echoing Tom Dewey and the Republicans by stating that the CIO's Political Action Committee was "run by a man who is temporarily the boss of America — Sidney Hillman." The PAC, he said, didn't practice democracy and was "run from the top down. Hillman is the boss."[76]

Thomas stepped up his criticism of Hillman a few weeks later, mocking the New York labor leader's support of FDR. "Look how little Roosevelt has really given labor," the Socialist candidate said in late October. "About the only thing labor obtained from him was a job for Hillman in the House of Bosses."[77]

Thomas, of course, had long been a critic of the powerful labor leader. Hillman, he remarked in an interview with the *Harvard Crimson* a few days before the 1940 election, would wield disproportionate influence if the United States entered the world war and that "would be a major catastrophe, for Hillman is as complete a Machiavelli as ever walked the earth."[78]

In the meantime, Thomas and his comrades in the Socialist Party were completely powerless to take advantage of the serious rupture in Hillman's American Labor Party and could only watch from the sidelines as yet another ballot-qualified party dwarfing their own — the Liberal Party — sprung into existence in New York earlier that year.

In his July 25 letter to Reinhold Niebuhr, mentioned earlier, Thomas proclaimed that the Liberal Party wasn't a genuine alternative in 1944, gently reminding the theologian that the leaders of the Liberal Party broke with the Communist-dominated American Labor Party only to support the same presidential candidate as the ALP and the Democrats.[79]

---

[75] "PAC Tactics Scored by Norman Thomas," *New York Times*, Sept. 27, 1944.
[76] "Norman Thomas Thinks Browder Conservative," *Los Angeles Times*, Sept. 29, 1944.
[77] "Thomas Won't Choose Between His Rivals," *New York Times*, Oct. 23, 1944.
[78] "Thomas Pledges Party Will Fight On; Predicts FDR Win," *Harvard Crimson*, Nov. 5, 1940.
[79] Seidler, *Norman Thomas: Respectable Rebel*, p. 219.

As was customary in each of his half dozen campaigns for the presidency, Thomas spoke at his alma mater in September. Not that there was much competition, but he was far and away Princeton's favorite radical. Addressing a crowd of 450 students and faculty in Alexander Hall, Thomas said that "America is afraid of the peace. War brings security that we lack in time of peace," he said, "and there is an underlying defeatism about our ability to cope with the problem of joblessness after the war."[80]

Sponsored by the Princeton Roundtable organization, Thomas spoke on the subject "What Will Peace Bring?" It wasn't logical to be pessimistic about the postwar period, asserted Thomas, adding that the war had demonstrated the country's enormous capacity for production. Coupled with the knowledge that there was "plenty to go around," he said, no more wars ever needed to be fought for the sake of economic security.[81]

"We can have peace, and security, and freedom — all three," he concluded, "if we believe in fellowship and cooperation rather than race prejudice, if we take a more intense interest in democracy, and if maximum disarmament is established."[82]

Despite the incredibly long odds facing his candidacy, Thomas worked as hard during his 1944 campaign as he had in each of his previous bids for the presidency. Crisscrossing the country twice that year, he even went out of his way to meet with supporters in states where his name wasn't on the ballot and where he had little hope of registering any kind of significant protest against Roosevelt and Dewey.

Arizona was one of those states. In a brief stop in Tucson in early October — the return leg of his second trip to the West Coast — Thomas held an impromptu press conference at the railroad station, telling reporters that he was the only candidate running for the president who was willing to discuss the issues.[83]

One of those issues, Thomas explained, was the demand by the Allies for an "unconditional surrender," a doctrine that he believed was unnecessarily prolonging the war. "The peace is being lost as fast as the war is being won," he declared. He also criticized the tentative plans for an international organization following the war, declaring there was a strong danger that it would result in a triple

---

[80] "No Need for Pessimism Concerning the Peace, Says Norman Thomas," *Daily Princetonian*, Vol. 2, No. 93, Sep. 13, 1944.
[81] Ibid.
[82] Ibid.
[83] "Thomas 'Shocked' By Party Tactics," *Tucson Daily Citizen*, Oct. 2, 1944.

alliance between the three major powers, particularly if it was carried out in the same fashion as the Dumbarton Oaks Conference. A system that depends on competitive armaments wouldn't be capable of keeping the peace, he said.[84]

On a lighter note, Thomas told the reporters that he hadn't hired any moving vans to help him move into the White House. His campaign would be a success, he said, if he was able to "smoke out" his major-party rivals on a few key issues.[85] Thomas, who was greeted at the station by a small group of party members and several students from the University of Arizona, encouraged his supporters to cast a write-in vote before departing on the next train.[86]

Rose Schuyler of Tucson, a former party member in New York City, quickly organized the Arizona write-in effort, instructing Thomas's supporters to write-in the names of the party's four electors: Ruth Greenbert, Polly E. Dougherty, Mildred R. Craig, and Elizabeth B. Pendleton.[87] Unfortunately, Arizona election officials never tallied any write-in votes for the Socialist ticket.

During that west coast trip, Thomas had sharply criticized Roosevelt's handling of foreign policy as not only prolonging the current war but inviting the next one, telling an audience in Los Angeles that the "administration's present policies, which Dewey apparently accepts, both prolong this war and invite the next. It is possible that ruling groups in Britain and Russia, although not the people, may have something to gain by the Balkanization not only of Germany, but of all Europe, under the rival power politics of Moscow and London," declared Thomas. "We Americans have everything to lose by underwriting it with the lives of this and the next generation of our sons."[88]

Though generally opposed to Roosevelt's foreign policy, Thomas nevertheless occasionally offered a few words of praise for the wartime president. After listening to Roosevelt's prayer to the U.S. troops on the evening of the Normandy invasion in early June — a daring amphibious assault led by Gen. Dwight Eisenhower involving an estimated 156,000 U.S., British and Canadian forces along a fifty-mile stretch of France's heavily fortified northern coast marking the beginning of the end of the war in Europe — the Socialist candidate sent the president a telegram praising the

---

[84] Ibid.
[85] Ibid.
[86] Ibid.
[87] "Third Party Votes May be Cast Nov. 7," *Tucson Daily Citizen*, Oct. 25, 1944.
[88] "Thomas Says Allies are Inviting Next War," *Miami News*, Sep. 30, 1944.

"ideals of liberation and lasting peace" expressed in his prayer and encouraging him to outline a "political invasion of Europe" to parallel the military invasion that had been so carefully planned and executed.[89]

While praising the president, Thomas expressed some disappointment that the Office of War Information's radio broadcasts at the time had made no direct appeal to the people of Europe, failed to refer to the invading Allied forces as "Armies of Liberation," and made no mention of any humanitarian relief.[90]

Thomas also remained strongly opposed to the idea of postwar military conscription. On September 12th, he debated the issue with Representative James W. Wadsworth (R-N.Y.), sponsor of the Gurney-Wadsworth Bill — one of two bills in Congress calling for universal postwar conscription — and the American Legion's Warren H. Atherton, who was widely recognized as one of the fathers of the G.I. Bill. Footage of the debate, which was aired live on WOR radio in New York, was later used in newsreels and seen in movie theaters across the country.[91]

---

[89] "Broadcasts Criticized," *New York Times*, June 8, 1944.
[90] Ibid.
[91] "Start Fighting Conscription!," *Socialist Call*, Dec. 22, 1944.

Chapter XI

"A Grim Experience"

Thomas traveled light that year, accompanied only by his wife Violet, a suitcase full of clothes, a flat iron and a typewriter. Crisscrossing the country at least twice, Thomas logged nearly as many miles as he had in 1932 when he gave 214 speeches in thirty-eight states.[1]

The grueling campaign clearly took a toll on Thomas and his wife. In early October, the five-time presidential aspirant indicated that this would be his final campaign, telling a gathering of Socialists in California that he planned to retire from politics at the conclusion of the 1944 election. "This is my last campaign," he said almost matter-of-factly. "At a meeting of the party in Chicago in January I shall formally retire from active politics."[2]

Not in the best of health to begin with, Violet was also showing signs of strain. She had accompanied her husband on four of his five presidential campaigns, but stayed home with their five small children during his initial bid for the presidency in 1928. The stress and rigor of the 1944 campaign was almost too much for her.

In a letter to her daughter, Frances, Violet complained about life on the road. There didn't seem to be nearly as much interest or enthusiasm in her husband's campaign this time around, she lamented. Party meetings and campaign events had been poorly at-

---

[1] Fleischman, *Norman Thomas: A Biography*, p. 132.
[2] "Norman Thomas is Expected to Retire," *Joplin News Herald*, Oct. 2, 1944.

tended. Thomas often found himself speaking to a handful of supporters and was lucky if a reporter showed up. "At Albuquerque there were only two Socialists to plan our meeting," she wrote her daughter, and one of the organizers was elderly and deaf and the other had died just before they arrived. She also complained that their hotel room was "disreputable dirty" with no food accommodations whatsoever. Worse yet, she concluded, it was almost impossible to attract any newspaper coverage.[3]

Violet nevertheless persevered, telling a reporter for the *Pittsburgh Post-Gazette* that her faith in her husband had never wavered, regardless of the increasingly long odds that he faced in wartime America. "It takes the country a long time to recognize a great man," she said somewhat wistfully, "but each year Norman is more and more welcome in the cities where he speaks." She also strongly hinted that the 1944 campaign would probably be her husband's final bid for the presidency and knew that she would never reside in the White House. "I don't know about the wives of other candidates, but I personally never expect to be First Lady," she said candidly.[4]

Thomas's sister, Emma, also hoped that the 1944 effort would be her brother's final campaign for the presidency. Emma Thomas, a Baltimore social worker with little interest in politics yet who shared her famous brother's intelligence and wit, said shortly after the election that she had voted for her older brother so often that she had lost count. Like Violet, she bravely stuck by him through thick and thin, admitting that she had "created quite a commotion at the polls and was a little embarrassed" when she tried to write in her brother's name that year because he wasn't on the ballot in Maryland. "It's too bad he keeps on running," she sighed, "because the Socialist Party ought to get some new blood. But as long as he does I'll stick by him."[5]

With a large portion of its most active members serving in the armed forces or in Civilian Public Service camps for conscientious objectors, the Socialist Party experienced a severe manpower shortage during the 1944 campaign.[6] Campaign manager Harry Fleischman later estimated that more than a quarter of the party's membership — including many of its youngest and most active volunteers — were unavailable for those reasons. Consequently,

---

[3] Swanberg, *Norman Thomas: The Last Idealist*, p. 288.
[4] "Wife of Socialist Norman Thomas Expects Never to Be First Lady," *Pittsburgh Post-Gazette*, Sep. 8, 1944.
[5] "Thomas' Sister Would Retire Him," *Baltimore Sun*, Nov. 16, 1944.
[6] "We've Got a Manpower Shortage of Our Own — And Help is Wanted!," *Socialist Call*, July 28, 1944.

given the party's increasingly weakened state, access to the ballot proved particularly difficult for the country's leading third party.[7]

Though Thomas managed to qualify for the ballot in Connecticut and Iowa — two states where he failed to appear on the ballot in 1940 — the Socialist Party was unable to qualify in a half-dozen other states, including vote-rich California, Illinois, Maryland and Massachusetts, where Thomas's name had appeared on the ballot four years earlier. Even qualifying in New York proved to be something of a struggle.

With the Progressive Party no longer on the ballot, Thomas had little chance of securing a spot on the ballot in California, where 220,000 valid signatures were due in early March. Pointing out that no minor party was able to clear that difficult hurdle, the Socialist candidate blasted the law's provisions as "now the most reactionary in the country" and appealed directly to Gov. Earl Warren to include a measure easing the state's ballot access requirements for independent nominations during a special legislative session in June, but to no avail.[8] He was then forced to wage a forlorn write-in effort.

While the party eventually succeeded in obtaining more than 12,000 valid signatures to earn a spot the ballot in populous New York, it might not have been possible without the truly inspiring efforts of a man who was totally blind, but nevertheless helped the party overcome the state's burdensome county distribution requirement — an onerous ballot access requirement that wasn't invalidated until 1970 — by single-handedly collecting more than the fifty valid signatures required in each of at least three rural upstate counties.

Accompanied by his wife, E. Marshall Bush personally collected all of the signatures needed in Cayuga, Chemung and Steuben counties. Bush, who lived in Elmira, had been a delegate to the party's national convention in Reading. His amazing example was widely publicized in the party's newspaper in an effort to motivate other party members to do their part in what was clearly shaping up to be one of the most difficult presidential campaigns in the party's long and storied history.[9]

Thanks to the heroic efforts of Rose Parker, a young party activist from Philadelphia, and Elwood Keppley, an organizer for Local Berks, the party also qualified for the ballot in Pennsylvania

---

[7] "Socialist Vote Kept Low by Restrictive Laws," *Socialist Call*, Nov. 17, 1944.
[8] "Socialists Ask Change in Qualification Law," *Sacramento Bee*, May 15, 1944.
[9] "We've Got a Manpower Shortage of Our Own — and Help is Wanted!" *Socialist Call*, July 28, 1944.

by obtaining more than 10,000 signatures — a minimum of 8,500 were needed — earlier that year. Assisted by other volunteers in the Keystone State, Parker and Keppley, the latter of whom later chaired the party in Reading and became editor of the *Reading Labor Advocate*, were able to obtain all of the signatures in a remarkably short ten-day period.[10]

But successes were few and far between. In Maryland, for example, the Socialists filed nominating petitions containing 125 signatures for three presidential electors — Baltimoreans Elisabeth Gilman, director of the Baltimore Open Forum, Zelma C. Smith, a housewife, and Jerome Tucker, a clerk — and naming Norman Price, a machinist from Baltimore, as the party's nominee for the U.S. Senate. The Socialist Party petition, filed on April 17, was rejected by the attorney general's office a few days later on the grounds that it contained an insufficient number of signatures. In his ruling, Attorney General William C. Walsh, a Democrat, cited the state's election code requiring that the number of signatures "shall not be less than 2,000 when the nomination is for an office to be filled by an election participated in by voters of the entire State…"[11]

During its struggle to qualify for the ballot in Indiana, the Socialist Party experienced a kind of Jim Crow in reverse when Eleanor Guttman of Bowling Green, Kentucky, and Ann Rodgers of Chicago were arrested in July after a waitress refused to serve them at a restaurant in a Greyhound bus terminal in Evansville.

The two young women, both of whom were white, had been part of a four-member petitioning team canvassing in Indiana and Illinois that summer. When they arrived at the bus station, they deliberately sat in an area marked "This Section For Colored Patrons Only" — a section that was completely unoccupied at the time — and were arrested and jailed when they calmly but firmly refused to move to the bus depot's "white section." Though prodded by the police, the two Socialists stood their ground. "In a democratic society," they told the arresting officer, "people should not be segregated by color." As they were waiting to be taken to jail where they were briefly held incommunicado, the two women told a crowd, largely comprised of soldiers and sailors, that they were being arrested for non-violently protesting Hitler's ideology of racial supremacy, as practiced in the United States.[12] Though initially

---

[10] "Getting Signatures for Socialist Ballot Petitions," *Socialist Call*, Apr. 7, 1944.
[11] "Socialists Seek to Enter Ticket in Md. Election," *Washington Post*, Apr. 18, 1944; "Md. Socialist Nominations Ruled Invalid," *Washington Post*, Apr. 20, 1944.
[12] "It Happens in Evansville!" *Socialist Call*, Dec. 1, 1944; "Socialists Tried for Defying Jim

convicted and fined, the case against the two young women was later dismissed on appeal.[13]

The party also heroically attempted to gain a place on the ballot in Louisiana for the first time since 1912.[14] Led by Marjorie Geier of New Orleans, a civil rights activist and secretary of the party in Louisiana, the Socialist Party held a state central committee for the purpose of nominating presidential electors on September 10, shortly after volunteers obtained approximately 1,100 signatures on nominating petitions — a minimum of 1,000 valid signatures were needed, according to the state's general election statute — and submitted them to the Secretary of State in a timely manner.[15]

The Secretary of State immediately sought an opinion from the Attorney General, who ruled that the secretary wasn't authorized to print the names of the Socialist Party's electors on the November ballot for two reasons: not all of the names on the party's nominating petitions had been certified by parish registrars as being party members; and, secondly, the Socialist Party wasn't a legally recognized party in Louisiana. The last point referred to the state's draconian primary law declaring that a political party couldn't be officially recognized unless it had received five percent of the entire vote cast in the last gubernatorial election or the last presidential election.[16]

Geier, a white southerner who later served on the board of the Urban League in New Orleans, and fellow party member Alice M. Labouisse, a faculty member at Newcomb College and the daughter of a late Louisiana Supreme Court justice, remained undeterred by the Attorney General's ruling and later qualified as official write-in candidates for presidential elector. According to newspaper reports, the pair received a scattering of write-in votes, including at least seven in New Orleans.[17]

In addition to the party's ballot access woes, the cash-strapped Socialists were forced to stretch every dollar raised, spending most

---

Crow," *Socialist Call*, Jan. 8, 1945.
[13] "Continue Fight Against Jim Crow," *Socialist Call*, Apr. 9, 1945.
[14] "We've got a Manpower Shortage of Our Own — and Help is Wanted!" *Socialist Call*, July 28, 1944.
[15] "Socialist Party's Petition is Signed," *Times-Picayune*, Sept. 2, 1944.
[16] "Socialist, Prohibition Parties May Have Names on La. Ballots," *State Times Advocate* (Baton Rouge, LA), Sept. 30, 1944.
[17] "Socialist Elector Candidacies Filed," *Times-Picayune*, Oct. 27, 1944; "Overton High," *State Times Advocate*, Nov. 10, 1944. There were 69 write-in votes for presidential electors included in the state's official canvass that year, 55 of which were cast for the Prohibition Party's electors in Caddo and La Salle parishes (See, "Final State Vote Tabulation Made," *Shreveport Times*, Nov. 16, 1944.)

of its limited resources on radio spots and the printing and distribution of more than 700,000 campaign leaflets. With barely three and a half weeks remaining in the 1944 presidential campaign, the party had not yet reached the half-way mark toward its modest goal of raising $100,000. Unlike its pesky SLP rival — a party that vastly outspent both the Prohibitionists and the Socialists that year — the Socialist Party didn't come close to meeting its fundraising goals.[18]

Despite the party's ballot access and financial woes and realizing that it was probably his final campaign for the presidency, Thomas nevertheless kept on plugging until the bitter end. He wasn't about to go down without a fight.

In a late October campaign appearance in Lake County, Indiana — a state where the relatively well-organized Prohibitionists had slated candidates in each of the state's eleven congressional districts compared to only one for the Socialists, and where Claude Watson outpolled his Socialist rival by a lopsided margin of 12,574 to 2,223 — Thomas cast a suspicious eye on both of his major-party rivals, saying that the campaign conducted by Democratic and Republican parties had been "on the lowest level in all my long experience."[19]

"The noise of controversy over the selective use of history enables Dewey and Roosevelt and their supporters to evade the issues that matter and discuss even secondary issues superficially," he said while speaking at the La Salle Hotel in Hammond.[20]

In his address, Thomas accused his chief rivals of supporting imperialism, almost guaranteeing another war in the future — not peace, as they claimed — regardless of what kind of postwar international structure was put in place. "It is preposterous to believe that rival empires with competitive armaments will permanently and effectively set aside parts of those armaments to be used against an aggressor who is likely to be one of themselves," he wryly observed.[21]

Rushing to Bridgeport in the campaign's final hours where he was accompanied by Darlington Hoopes, Gen. Holdridge and Mayor Jasper McLevy, Thomas fired salvos at both of his major-party opponents, saying that the Republicans had been right about the "extraordinary contradictions in Roosevelt's promises and performances," but that the Democrats had been equally correct about

---

[18] "Full Steam Ahead in Last Month of Socialist Campaign," *Socialist Call*, Oct. 13, 1944.
[19] "Thomas Casts Fishy Eye on Both Major Parties," *Hammond Times*, Oct. 29, 1944.
[20] Ibid.
[21] Ibid.

"Dewey's somersaults on foreign policy."[22]

Asserting that the scourge of widespread unemployment was a "curse second only to war," the Socialist standard-bearer maintained that the postwar policies of both major parties would result in widespread joblessness.[23] Speaking at Bridgeport's Central High School, Thomas aimed most of his criticism at FDR that night, reminding his audience that the President had "assured us in 1932 that he would balance the budget, reduce taxes and cut down the number of federal agencies. He repeated his assurance that he would balance the budget in 1936," continued Thomas, "and in 1940 he assured us again and again and again that he would not put our sons into foreign wars, and that steps which in all human experience have led to war would lead to peace."[24]

Thomas also questioned the conventional wisdom that the United States had been attacked by Japan on Dec. 7, 1941, without cause or warning. "This ignores Secretary Hull's ultimatum (to Japan) on November 26," he said, and "overlooks the fact that the President told Mr. Churchill but not the Congress or the American people, that he would enter the eastern war even if not attacked. The Prime Minister's statement to this effect on January 29, 1942," added Thomas, "has never been denied."[25]

Receiving word of Wendell Willkie's unexpected death on October 8th, Thomas briefly suspended his campaign to join dozens of other prominent politicians and world leaders in paying tribute to his globe-trotting rival from the 1940 campaign. "America," mourned Thomas, "has lost a distinguished and useful citizen."[26]

Toward the end of the campaign, Thomas complained that he had never witnessed a more disappointing national election, especially considering the gravity of the issues facing the country. "Most of the discussion has been on personalities," he lamented in a speech in the nation's capital in late October. "One would think we were electing a dictator who is under no compulsion to outline policies except in the vaguest terms," he said.[27]

That caustic comment wasn't necessarily meant as a knock on FDR for seeking an unprecedented fourth term — Thomas didn't believe in term limits — but rather a criticism of both Roosevelt and Dewey for failing to adequately address the U.S. economy in the post-war period.

---

[22] "Both Parties Draw Fire of Thomas," *Hartford Courant*, Nov. 5, 1944.
[23] "Thomas Assails Rivals' Programs," *New York Times*, Nov. 5, 1944.
[24] "Both Parties Draw Fire of Thomas," *Hartford Courant*, Nov. 5, 1944.
[25] Ibid.
[26] "Tributes to Willkie," *Boston Globe*, Oct. 9, 1944.
[27] "Thomas Criticizes Tone of Campaign," *New York Times*, Oct. 25, 1944.

THE LOWEST EBB

It was almost impossible to find a Republican who could recall anything that happened between 1929 and 1933, continued Thomas, deliciously adding that "no Democrat remembers that, until the war brought us such temporary prosperity that literally millions of Americans fear the peace, the best that Roosevelt could do with the capitalist system was to subsidize unemployment for some 10,000,000 workers."[28] It was harsh language, but true.

Both parties, he said in another speech, were suffering from "selective amnesia" that year, with the Republicans completely forgetting that the stock market crash of 1929 and the seemingly never-ending Great Depression began under their watch while the Democrats couldn't seem to remember that the only way they partially pulled the country out of that deep depression during peacetime was by borrowing heavily from the Socialist platform.[29]

Thomas was right. Then again, he was almost always right. Prior to World War II, neither major party really had any earthly clue about how they might end the decade-long economic crisis that featured a relatively devastating recession within a depression. "It is the worst possible commentary on our civilization that it has required a war to dispose of the unemployment problem," opined Thomas in a speech earlier that summer in Oberlin, Ohio.[30]

Under Roosevelt or Dewey, Thomas predicted that the United States would likely squander the opportunity to build a fairer society based on social and economic justice, as well as creating a lasting peace, in the postwar period. "I really feel badly about it," he told the *Louisville Courier-Journal's* Marion Porter. "This is our golden chance to win the peace and then conquer poverty," he said. "The defeat of Nazism is clearing the way for something better. But both parties have the same reconversion ideas. They will hand the economic system back to business, which is unable, through the profit system, to get results," thereby resulting in another economic downturn and new foreign conflicts. "Militarism and imperialism," he added, almost matter-of-factly, "are the ancient and respectable forms of boondoggling for depression."[31]

Pressed by a reporter in late October to identify which of his major-party rivals he would prefer to see elected, Thomas insisted that he had no preference between President Roosevelt and Republican challenger Tom Dewey. "I'm equally gloomy about both

---
[28] Ibid..
[29] "Thomas Slaps at Peace Plan," *Milwaukee Journal*, Nov. 1, 1944.
[30] "Thomas Assails Post War Programs of Both Parties," *Oberlin News-Tribune*, Aug. 3, 1944.
[31] "Norman Thomas Misses Train, But Not Chance to Lash Opponents," *Louisville Courier-Journal*, Sep. 21, 1944.

candidates," he candidly admitted moments after arriving at La Guardia Field following a campaign swing through Michigan. "Both are taking us into a new depression and both are taking us into a new war. For the magnitude of the issues involved," he said with a faint hint of disgust in his voice, "this campaign is on the lowest level I have ever seen."[32]

Most voters, Thomas elaborated, were voting against one of the major candidates rather than for one of them. "They either want to 'lick' Roosevelt or they want to 'lick' Dewey," he said, adding that he wasn't blaming either candidate, but rather the country as a whole, which "doesn't think beyond tomorrow morning."[33]

Thomas had clearly soured on the electorate and, unlike in his previous campaigns for the nation's highest office, freely shared that criticism with any journalist willing to listen. "I am the only presidential candidate in the United States talking issues, but I don't think the people care too much about issues," he told a *Louisville Courier-Journal* reporter while waiting for a train in September. "The average American likes not to know — then he can hope. Otherwise we never could have the kind of campaigns we've had in this country." Apathy, he added, was "the greatest threat to the American political situation."[34]

During the course of the campaign, the Socialist candidate also expressed serious qualms about Missouri Sen. Harry S. Truman, Roosevelt's vice-presidential running mate. Truman, said Thomas during an appearance in St. Louis in late October, would probably be "the worst president we've ever had" if he were to succeed FDR as the nation's 33rd chief executive. Describing the Missouri lawmaker as "a creature of one of the worst bosses in American history," Thomas charged that Truman had never written a speech on his own regarding any public issue of importance.[35]

Described by one reporter as "a little fellow who can talk like a house afire," vice-presidential hopeful Darlington Hoopes also waged a vigorous campaign that fall, urging his audiences around the country to support the Socialist ticket as the only alternative to a one-way trip to hell.[36]

Blaming the free enterprise system for the prospects of widespread unemployment, poverty, fascism, and future world wars, the former state legislator said that World War II had proven that

---

[32] "Thomas Won't Choose Between His Rivals," *New York Times*, Oct. 23, 1944.
[33] Ibid.
[34] "Norman Thomas Misses Train, But Not Chance to Lash Opponents," *Louisville Courier-Journal*, Sep. 21, 1944.
[35] "Thomas Appraises Truman as President," *Christian Science Monitor*, Oct. 28, 1944.
[36] "Candidate of Socialists Sees Bleak Future," *Los Angeles Times*, Oct. 18, 1944.

the United States, in a time of crisis, could produce for use and not for profit. If the federal government continued to plan for use rather than for profit in the postwar period, the fast-talking Hoopes argued that the United States could provide decent housing for every American family in an atmosphere of "plenty, peace and freedom" for all.[37]

As in 1952 and 1956 when he headed the party's ticket, Hoopes put the issue of race at the forefront, deploring the fact that both major parties had cowardly evaded the issue in their respective platforms.

Reminding his audiences that the Socialist platform had strongly condemned "Jim Crowism, and every form of race discrimination and segregation," Hoopes strongly condemned the Democrats for ignoring the controversial issues of the poll tax and anti-lynching legislation and criticized the Republicans for sanctimoniously parading its legacy as the party of Lincoln and emancipation while generally siding with conservative southern Democrats in defeating legislative measures beneficial to African-Americans.

The little-known Reading attorney also tore into both parties for the hypocrisy of drafting blacks to fight in "armies of liberation" against the Nazis when those same soldiers were being subjected to discriminatory practices in virtually every facet of life in their own country. In his speeches around the country, the vice-presidential candidate said there was little moral difference between Hitler's "damnable dogma of a superior race" and persecution of Jews than the kind of "white supremacy" openly practiced by southerners and generally accepted and adapted in modified form in the North.[38]

While campaigning on the west coast, Hoopes told reporters that he was pessimistic about the country's future, especially the prospect of massive joblessness after the war. "The major party candidates talk glibly about unemployment, but have no concrete program," said Hoopes. "The so-called free enterprise system can't possibly do the job," he continued, asserting that, according to the American Federation of Labor's carefully-researched estimates, unemployment was still *a staggering ten million before the attack on Pearl Harbor.* Add in seven or eight million more due to technological advances during the war, he lamented, coupled with an additional three million or so young people just entering the workforce,

---
[37] Henderson, *Darlington Hoopes*, pp. 118-119.
[38] Ibid., pp. 119-120.

and you have nearly twenty million Americans without jobs.[39] That was the stark and gloomy postwar economy envisioned by the Socialists in 1944.

As a solution, the former Pennsylvania legislator said that the Socialist Party would remove the profit motive from industry and create jobs based on need, in much the same way the government had done successfully in the interests of the war.[40]

The Reading attorney clearly didn't share his running mate's unmistakable pessimism about the party's prospects that year, telling reporters in late October that "there is increasing support and enthusiasm for the Socialist campaign in all sections of the nation where I have travelled. Workers groups, farmers groups, cooperative members, and others are planning to roll up a large Socialist vote so that pressure 'from the left' can be put on the winning candidate for President."[41] Hoopes wasn't delusional, but he was certainly going to be sorely disappointed on November 7th.

On a positive note, the Thomas-Hoopes ticket received a major boost that summer when Bridgeport Mayor Jasper McLevy and the Connecticut Socialists — estranged from the national party since 1936 — voted overwhelmingly to endorse the Socialist Party's presidential ticket.[42] After three hours of debate at the party's state convention in Bridgeport, the Socialists in the Constitution State voted 36-5 to nominate eight presidential electors pledged to the Thomas-Hoopes ticket.[43] This was wonderful news for Thomas since the Socialists in that state had adamantly refused to name presidential electors and place his name on the ballot in 1940, forcing his dispirited supporters to wage a half-hearted write-in effort on his behalf.[44]

Bridgeport City Clerk Fred Schwartzkopf, who along with McLevy had been instrumental in securing an endorsement for Thomas and Hoopes, headed the party's petition drive that summer — and did a spectacular job. With a goal of collecting 15,000 raw signatures, Schwartzkopf's crew easily surpassed the minimum number of valid signatures required to place the party's

---

[39] "Candidate of Socialists Sees Bleak Future," *Los Angeles Times*, Oct. 18, 1944.
[40] Ibid.
[41] "Socialist Candidate to Speak Here Today," *Wilmington Morning Star*, Oct. 22, 1944.
[42] "Connecticut Socialists Back in National Fold," *Hartford Courant*, July 2, 1944; "Socialists Vote Support of Thomas," *Hartford Courant*, Aug. 14, 1944; "Thomas-Hoopes Ticket is Endorsed in Connecticut," *Socialist Call*, Aug. 25, 1944.
[43] "Connecticut Socialists Meet," *New York Times*, Aug. 14, 1944.
[44] "No Electors on Socialist State Slate," *Hartford Courant*, Sep. 16, 1940; "Write-In Votes Are Possible For Norman Thomas," *Hartford Courant*, Nov. 4, 1940.

presidential ticket on the ballot.⁴⁵

Renewing a friendship that had been sorely strained for nearly a decade, McLevy personally campaigned with Thomas during a rally in Hartford in October and made several other appearances with him in Bridgeport.⁴⁶ For a brief shining moment it seemed like old times as Thomas and McLevy — once again comrades-in-arms — applauded one another and shook their heads in approval as they addressed the voters of Connecticut that autumn.

The Bridgeport mayor, who — like clockwork — was again running for governor on the Socialist ticket, was one of those who had initially encouraged the reluctant Thomas to mount a fifth consecutive campaign for the presidency in 1944. "Any little disagreements should be forgotten in these crucial times, when the choice between democratic socialism and totalitarianism is at stake," McLevy told the Connecticut Socialists that summer. "We owe it to our boys and girls in the armed forces to work for a peace which will make future wars impossible." The only way such a peace would be possible, he implored, was by putting a Socialist in the White House — and that undoubtedly meant another Thomas candidacy.⁴⁷

Thomas also received the support of an independent organization headed by Unitarian minister and antiwar activist John Haynes Holmes, a Harvard-educated pacifist who helped found the American Civil Liberties Union and the NAACP. Holmes, who had recently given up his role as honorary chair of the War Resisters League — he served as the WRL's chair or honorary chair continuously from 1929 to 1943 — had long considered Thomas one of his closest friends and most important allies and unfailingly stood by the Socialist nominee in both balmy times, as well as in darker days. The 1944 presidential campaign was obviously one of the latter.⁴⁸

"In no campaign in recent years have the differences between the major parties been so slight," the group said in an August statement announcing its support for the Socialist ticket. "A vote for either Roosevelt or Dewey means a vote for more of the same — of a war economy, of imperialism, of post-war depression. We urge Americans to vote for a future of hope and not of fear."⁴⁹

---

⁴⁵ "In the Final Stretch to Get On the Ballot in Some States: Help Give That Needed Push!," *Socialist Call*, July 21, 1944.
⁴⁶ "Norman Thomas, McLevy Will Speak Here Today," *Hartford Courant*, Oct. 15, 1944.
⁴⁷ "Thomas-Hoopes Ticket is Endorsed in Connecticut," *Socialist Call*, Aug. 25, 1944.
⁴⁸ "Group to Back Thomas," *New York Times*, Aug. 21, 1944; Bennett, *Radical Pacifism: The War Resisters League and Gandhian Nonviolence in America, 1915-1963*, p. 27.
⁴⁹ Ibid.

"A GRIM EXPERIENCE"

The Socialist standard-bearer also received a ringing endorsement from African-American author and newspaper columnist George S. Schuyler — the "Black Mencken." Arguably the first black journalist to gain national prominence, the 49-year-old Schuyler was a longtime columnist for the *Pittsburgh Courier*, one of the leading African-American newspapers in the country, and an occasional contributor to H. L. Mencken's *American Mercury*. An acerbic critic of the status quo, Schuyler previously had been a regular columnist for *The Messenger*, a Harlem-based magazine founded in 1917 by A. Philip Randolph and Chandler Owen, the latter of whom studied economics at Columbia University, once ran for the New York Assembly on the Socialist ticket, and later wrote speeches for GOP presidential candidates Wendell Willkie and Thomas E. Dewey.[50] During this period, Randolph and Owen were known as the "Lenin and Trotsky" of Harlem.[51]

As a one-time member of the Socialist Party before drifting increasingly to the right during the McCarthy Era and eventually clashing with almost every major civil rights leader during the 1960s, Schuyler had been one of the first to publicly call for compensation for the 112,000 citizens of Japanese heritage who had been forced into internment camps during World War II.[52]

Schuyler, who had the uncanny ability to see around corners yet died in virtual obscurity in 1977 — some nine years after Thomas — predicted that the U.S. government would round up and imprison members of the Japanese-American community shortly after Pearl Harbor, writing in his *Pittsburgh Courier* column that "the Japanese Americans are overwhelmingly loyal, but they have always borne the burden of white American suspicion, and that burden will increase. Thousands may be penned in camps."[53]

Like Raymond C. Hoiles, the libertarian-leaning publisher of the *Santa Ana Register* whose criticism of one of the most shameful episodes in American history has long since become legendary, the little-remembered Schuyler also had been right on the mark.[54]

An intrepid duo acting on behalf of the country's better self,

---

[50] Johnpoll, *Pacifist's Progress*, p. p. 246; "George S. Schuyler, Black Author," *New York Times*, Sep. 7, 1977; "Civil Rights Gadfly George Schuyler Dies," *Virgin Islands Daily News*, Sep. 15, 1977.

[51] Manning Marable, *Race, Reform, and Rebellion: The Second Reconstruction and Beyond in Black America, 1945-2006* (Jackson, MS, 2007), p. 20.

[52] Greg Robinson, *A Tragedy of Democracy: Japanese Confinement in North America* (New York, 2009), p. 276.

[53] Oscar Renal Williams, *George S. Schuyler, Portrait of a Black Conservative* (Knoxville, TN, 2007), p. 105.

[54] Steven Greenhut, "Standing Against the Tide," *The Tribune* (Seymour, Indiana), Nov. 23, 2005.

during the 1944 campaign Schuyler and Thomas joined with Roy Wilkins, editor of the NAACP's *The Crisis*, and Fred Hoshiyama of the Japanese American Citizens League who had been forcibly removed from his home in northern California and sent to a dreary internment camp in Utah after Japan bombed Pearl Harbor, in addressing a mass rally in New York City protesting Mayor LaGuardia's feverish objection to the placement of relocated Japanese-American citizens in that city.[55]

Schuyler couldn't understand how so many black leaders from historian W.E.B. DuBois to singer and actor Paul Robeson and the Rev. Adam Clayton Powell — each of whom actively campaigned for FDR's re-election — could support "a party guilty of a thousand crimes" against the African-American community. "If Roosevelt were an angel from Heaven on high, his criminal surrender of the Negro soldier and sailor to the Jim-Crow system of the unreconstructed and Democratic South was enough to damn him in the eyes of every red-blooded Negro with any feelings of pride," he wrote shortly after the election. If the self-appointed "leaders" of the black community had to support a capitalist party, he continued, Dewey and the Republicans were probably a better choice, "but if they were really intelligent, informed and interested in racial welfare, they should have urged their people to vote for Norman Thomas and the Socialist Party, to which the only alternative is ultimate slavery."[56]

As in his previous campaigns, Thomas had made the issue of racial prejudice a central feature of his 1944 candidacy, even venturing into the Deep South to make his case. "Americans have been fed a lot of falsehoods and we've paid a terrible price for race prejudice," he said while campaigning at Dillard University in New Orleans that autumn. The two major problems facing mankind, he said, were war and poverty, both of which were exacerbated by race supremacy. Neither issue, he declared, could be solved in terms of racial superiority because "there is no historical or scientific authority that one race is greater than another."[57] In addition to supporting an anti-lynching law and federal legislation outlawing the poll tax, Thomas called for the vigorous enforcement of the Fourteenth Amendment, thereby drastically reducing the number of representatives in Congress from those southern

---

[55] George Lipsitz, *The Possessive Investment in Whiteness: How White People Profit from Identity Politics* (Philadelphia, 2006), p. 200; "Mayor Protests Japanese in East," *New York Times*, Apr. 27, 1944.

[56] George S. Schuyler, "Views and Reviews," *Pittsburgh Courier*, Nov. 11, 1944.

[57] "Americans Paid for Prejudice, Says Thomas," *New York Age*, Oct. 21, 1944.

states which continued to deny the right to vote to racial minorities.[58]

In addition to Schuyler's influential support, Thomas also received an unexpected endorsement in September from retired Brigadier General Herbert C. Holdridge, one of the most colorful and eccentric characters to appear on the American political landscape in decades. Declaring that there weren't any substantive differences between the two major parties and that the Socialist Party was the only political party in the country that hadn't surrendered to "economic oligarchy," Holdridge, while reserving his right to disagree with certain aspects of the party's platform, said that the Socialists were "on the right track."[59]

A graduate of West Point and the only general to retire from active duty during World War II, Holdridge took an active part in the Socialist campaign that autumn, barnstorming the country for Norman Thomas and addressing various party meetings.

"In electing Dewey, instead of Roosevelt," Holdridge thundered at a dinner in New York commemorating the eighteenth anniversary of Eugene Debs' death, "you don't change horses in the middle of the stream, you merely change jockeys of the same old capitalistic horse, both competing for the privilege of leading the country into fascism."[60]

When the War Department offered equal time to the five nationally-organized parties to address U.S. soldiers abroad, the 52-year-old Holdridge was asked to give an address on behalf of the Socialist Party. In his remarks, the retired general charged that the Democrats and Republicans were woefully unprepared to deal with the problems of postwar reconstruction and that both parties were committed to a policy of "plowing under abundance in order to create a world of artificial scarcity."[61]

The retired military officer also said that hundreds of plants and factories built with taxpayer money during the war would soon be considered surplus and that government officials would eventually do exactly what industry leaders proposed, namely sell them to big business for a few cents on the dollar, entice municipalities to purchase some of them, or demolish them altogether — as long as they were never used to compete with the plants and factories owned by the industrialists. By pursuing such a policy, he concluded, the two major parties were essentially ripping off

---

[58] "'Terrible Price Paid for Race Bias' – Thomas," *Pittsburgh Courier*, Oct. 14, 1944.
[59] "Holdridge for Thomas," *New York Times*, Sept. 17, 1944.
[60] "Socialist Assails Both," *New York Times*, Oct. 21, 1944.
[61] "Assails Major Parties," *New York Times*, Sept. 29, 1944

American taxpayers while guaranteeing "a gigantic monopoly to the profits system of free enterprise."[62]

Holdridge, who continued to dabble in politics long after the 1944 campaign — becoming something of a laughingstock by frequently seeking the Democratic nomination for president, waging an aborted campaign as the virtually non-existent American Vegetarian Party's candidate for the Oval Office in 1952 and briefly running for vice president on the Prohibition ticket in 1956 — reiterated his support for the Socialist Party's national ticket in an election-eve statement released by the Independent Committee for Norman Thomas and Darlington Hoopes.

"Both President Roosevelt and Governor Dewey," declared Holdridge, "have underwritten the misnamed system of free enterprise, which has meant unemployment, wars, racial and religious discrimination." A vote for either of them wasn't only a wasted vote, he argued, but also a confession of failure. Imploring others to join him, the retired general declared that he was voting for Thomas and Hoopes "because they insist on the democratic control of the resources of the country by the people in their own interest, an end to discrimination against any group and real freedom under democracy."[63]

Other notable endorsements of the Thomas-Hoopes ticket in that relatively dreary and lonely year included artist and author Cyrus Leroy Baldridge, Dr. Henry Neumann of the Brooklyn Society for Ethical Culture, and Rabbi Isidor B. Hoffman, a former executive director of the Jewish Peace Fellowship and a longtime counselor to Jewish students at Columbia University. A large Socialist vote, said Hoffman, "would hearten the labor and socialist forces in other countries whose courageous stand against totalitarianism of both the right and the dictatorship of the left are the inspiration and hope for a truly democratic world — a world in which imperialism and the supreme curse of war will be banished."[64]

Aging labor editor Justus Ebert and Elsie Elfenbein, executive director of the Post War World Council, also endorsed Thomas and Hoopes, as did the Rev. Paul F. Boller of the Far Rockaway Presbyterian Church in Queens. In endorsing the Socialist ticket, Rev. Boller said that he didn't consider it a wasted vote to cast his ballot for the things he truly believed in, namely, the rights of conscientious objectors, the fair treatment of Japanese-Americans,

---

[62] Ibid.
[63] "Backs Norman Thomas," *New York Times*, Nov. 6, 1944.
[64] "Why We're Supporting Thomas-Hoopes," *Socialist Call*, Nov. 3, 1944.

equality for African-Americans and a blanket indictment of racial discrimination.[65]

The famously-named Rev. John Paul Jones, a Jesuit master of novice brothers at the Novitiate of St. Andrew-on-Hudson in Poughkeepsie, New York, also publicly supported Thomas, saying that while he didn't necessarily agree with everything the Socialist nominee had to say, Thomas was the only candidate demanding honesty, intelligence and "fearless leadership."[66]

Thomas also gained the endorsement of Sam Marino, president of a CIO Barber and Beauty Culturists Union local. Marino, who endorsed the Socialist candidate during a radio broadcast on New York's WBNX, said that voting for Thomas was only way "to prevent an American brand of fascism."[67]

With virtually all of the major unions and liberal newspapers supporting Roosevelt, votes for Norman Thomas and the other minor-party candidates were particularly hard to find that year. Yet, support for the five-time presidential candidate, as infrequent and miniscule as it was, often came from some of the most unexpected quarters. Thomas might have been surprised to learn that Russell Kirk, the gifted prophet of American conservatism, was among the lonely few who cast a ballot for the Socialist Party's presidential ticket in 1944. Kirk, who famously debated Thomas seventeen years later, supported him that year largely out of gratitude for his steadfast and principled refusal to join America's rush to war in the years and months preceding Pearl Harbor.[68]

Jeannette Rankin also voted for Thomas that year. In fact, Rankin, a lifelong Republican who had been the first woman elected to Congress and the only member of the House and Senate to vote against U.S. entry in both world wars, voted for Thomas in each of his six presidential campaigns.[69]

The Rev. Ernest Fremont Tittle, a noted pacifist and longtime pastor of the First United Church in Evanston, Illinois — one of the country's most prominent Protestant churches — also supported the Socialist standard-bearer. Tittle, who voted for Thomas several times beginning in 1928, had been strongly opposed to U.S. entry in World War II, even after Hitler's Wehrmacht ravaged much of Europe and threatened Britai "I can see only ruin ahead if the United States becomes a belligerent in Europe or in Asia — ruin for

---

[65] Ibid.
[66] Ibid.
[67] "Marino Asserts Socialist Vote is Blow at American Fascism," *Socialist Call*, Nov. 3, 1944.
[68] David Frum, *Dead Right* (New York, 1995), p. 154.
[69] "Dignitaries Honor Memory of First Woman in Congress," *Nashua Telegraph*, May 2, 1985.

us and for all mankind," he said while insisting on American isolation in the growing global conflict.[70]

Thomas might have been pleasantly surprised to learn that literary critic and man of letters Edmund Wilson, the former editor of *Vanity Fair* and longtime book reviewer for the *New Yorker* and the *New York Review of Books*, had also cast a ballot for him, just as he had done in 1936, 1940 and did again in 1948.[71] Noted sculptor Louis Mayer — not to be confused with the MGM movie mogul of the same name — also supported the Socialist ticket that year. Mayer, who long admired Thomas and was fully cognizant of the difficulties in waging a presidential campaign in wartime America, personally contributed $500 to the party's meager campaign fund.[72]

While not a single major union in the country backed his forlorn candidacy, Thomas was gratified to receive the sporadic support of individual union members across the country, including a group in Milwaukee which formed a rank and file labor committee and urged fellow trade unionists to support Thomas and Hoopes as the only candidates who "have suggested how the productive capacity of the nation could be used for full employment in peace as well as war."[73]

Reflecting a minor revolt of sorts against the "political dictatorship" of the CIO's Sidney Hillman and the AFL's Philip Murray, Thomas also received the support of a hastily-formed independent labor committee in Reading, Pennsylvania.[74]

Declaring that the Roosevelt administration had "become increasingly reactionary" and that supporting the Republican nominee was "entirely out of the question," three CIO officials in New Hampshire also endorsed Thomas late in the campaign. Speaking as individuals and not for their organizations, the three officials, all members of the United Steelworkers of America and led by Earl M. Bourden, vice president of the New Hampshire State CIO Council, accused Roosevelt of abandoning the New Deal and appointing too many Wall Street-types, corporate executives and conservatives to his administration. The fact that southern senators and northern big city bosses were able to pressure the president into dumping Vice President Henry Wallace, they said in a joint

---

[70] Joseph Loconte, "The Prince of Peace Was a Warrior, Too," *New York Times*, Jan. 28, 2003; Robert Moats Miller, *How Shall They Hear Without a Preacher? The Life of Ernest Fremont Tittle* (Chapel Hill, 1971), p. 395.

[71] Lewis M. Dabney, ed., *Edmund Wilson: Centennial Reflections* (Princeton, 1997), p. 181.

[72] "How Famous Sculptor Helps Keep Alive Social Conscience," *Socialist Call*, Aug. 4, 1944.

[73] "Milwaukee Unionists Support Norman Thomas," *Socialist Call*," Nov. 3, 1944.

[74] "Reading Unionists Hit Old Parties, Support Thomas," *Socialist Call*, Sep. 8, 1944.

statement endorsing Thomas, made it clear that the Democratic Party was still controlled by the party's reactionaries.[75]

Thomas also picked up a number of other endorsements from individual union officials, including that of Louis Nelson, manager-secretary of the Knit Goods Workers, Local 155 of the International Ladies Garment Workers Union (ILGWU). "I voted against supporting Roosevelt for the fourth term at the recent ILGWU convention, not because I'm against the fourth term, nor because I'm for Dewey," said Nelson in endorsing Thomas in late August.[76]

Nelson's lone dissent at the ILGWU's national convention in Boston in early June prompted a loud chorus of boos from the other garment workers and was only silenced when union president David Dubinsky intervened, telling the angry delegates that their behavior was "contrary to the practice of the ILGWU in matters of opinion."[77]

In explaining his support for Thomas a few months later, Nelson said that his decision was based on "the actual record of the Roosevelt administration during the last five years and the prospect for jobs and a lasting peace after the war. The programs of the Democrats and Republicans," he said, "assure us of neither jobs nor security."[78]

Despite these occasional expressions of support, the 1944 presidential campaign was an extraordinarily arduous and painful experience for Thomas, both politically and personally. Never before had he been subjected to such disdain and venom. Despite his tireless efforts to establish asylum for Jewish and other displaced refugees in the United States, the Socialist candidate was vehemently attacked by several leading Jewish newspapers for calling for an early negotiated peace, one designed to avoid the vengeful and unreasonably punitive terms contained in the Treaty of Versailles at the end of World War I. Abe Cahan's *Jewish Daily Forward* denounced Thomas and the Socialist platform for offering peace to Hitler on a silver platter, while a cartoon in the *Jewish Morning Journal* portrayed Thomas as a quisling.[79]

How quickly some of them had forgotten, or possibly never

---

[75] "New Hampshire Union Officials Declare Support of Thomas," *Socialist Call*, Oct. 20, 1944.
[76] "Roosevelt 'Increasingly Anti-Labor,' Two Union Leaders Back Thomas," *Socialist Call*, Sep. 1, 1944.
[77] "Garment Workers Union Backs a Fourth Term for the President," *New York Times*, June 8, 1944.
[78] "Roosevelt 'Increasingly Anti-Labor,' Two Union Leaders Back Thomas," *Socialist Call*, Sep. 1, 1944.
[79] Swanberg, *Norman Thomas: The Last Idealist*, p. 291.

knew, that it was Thomas who had personally pleaded with Roosevelt to open America's doors to Jewish refugees when it became clear that Hitler planned to exterminate all the Jews in Europe — men, women and children alike. "We are willing to fight Hitler," Thomas observed at the time, "partly because of his anti-Semitic cruelty, but we have not been willing to take any bold and aggressive action to rescue Jewish refugees or even temporarily to modify our immigration laws in this historic land of asylum."[80]

The worst attack, however, was leveled by *The International Teamster*, official organ of the Teamsters, which accused the Socialist nominee of "fawning on the Germans and Japs while they were killing Thomas's fellow countrymen." Likening Thomas to Hitler, the Teamster publication said that the two men were "just a couple of Socialist boys looking at the world through blood-smeared glasses."[81]

Thomas was enraged by the sheer ugliness of the Teamster attack. Charging "malicious libel," he filed a $500,000 libel suit against Daniel Tobin, president of the Teamsters and chair of the Democratic Party's national labor committee, and Lester M. Hunt, the author of the article.[82]

It took a couple of years, but Thomas, who was represented by attorney Joseph Glass, the party's mayoral candidate in 1945 and 1949, eventually won a settlement shortly before the case went to trial. The full terms of the settlement were never disclosed, but the Teamsters had to pay all court costs and issued a public retraction in December 1946, acknowledging that Thomas's opposition to peace-time conscription was "not a reflection upon his patriotism or loyalty as a citizen of the United States." The retraction also stated that the five-time Socialist candidate for the presidency was "one of the earliest critics of Fascism and Nazism and at no time in any way condoned any of Hitler's crimes..."[83]

There was no shortage of criticism for Thomas in 1944. An Illinois newspaper reminded its readers that the Socialist candidate had personally taken an attitude reminiscent of the antiwar position adopted by the Socialist Party during World War I, stating in an editorial that Thomas had been closely identified with the America First movement prior to Pearl Harbor. "In some of his addresses, he had preached a doctrine of isolation greatly at variance with the presumed internationalism of Socialists," the paper noted.

---

[80] Fleischman, *Norman Thomas: A Biography*, p. 209.
[81] Ibid., pp. 211-212.
[82] "Thomas Sues Tobin for $500,000 in Libel Charge," *Socialist Call*, Nov. 10, 1944.
[83] Fleischman, *Norman Thomas: A Biography*, p. 212.

"Although Mr. Thomas carefully qualified his statements, and could not be directly chargeable with the appeasement of Germany advocated by Col. Lindbergh, he was always lukewarm on resistance to the Axis peril..."[84]

Thomas even found himself subjected to abuse and blistering criticism from abroad when economist and political theorist Harold J. Laski, in article published a few days before the Labour Party's December conference in Great Britain, took a few potshots at America's best-known Socialist. "I know that Thomas is a warmhearted, sincere Socialist who hates the forces of fascism, whether in Europe or Asia, no less bitterly than we," wrote Laski in an arrogant British tone. "But it is difficult for us not to feel that he has led his party into a cul-de-sac (blind alley) and made it not only insignificant in numbers but utterly unrealistic in outlook."[85]

Unlike their counterparts in the United Kingdom, the Socialist Party in this country never adopted the pragmatic and bare-knuckled realism of the British Socialists who set out to capture a political party more than fifty years earlier — taking over the Independent Labour Party, which wasn't their first choice — and eventually gaining control of the government.

Stating that the Socialist Party in the United States was as "muddle minded" as the Independent Labour Party in his own country, Laski said that if the attitude in Great Britain had been the same as the one advocated by Thomas, "we should now be a province in a Nazified Europe instead of a free nation which sees victory near at hand."[86]

The English writer was brutal. "To see the American Socialist party, at one of the great turning points in modern history, thus reduced to an influence which is as insignificant intellectually as numerically, is a tragedy of the first order," continued Laski. "For just when we have supreme need of American Socialists to help in the common task, they are not in a position to give help. They seem to have no conception of what is happening in the world.[87]

"Thomas seems to us to wash his hands of the problems of the real world," wrote Laski. "He speaks, no doubt with all his old eloquence, of a perfectionist paradise, of whose coming occurrence none of us in Europe sees an atom of evidence."[88]

Laski also faulted Thomas and the Socialist Party for failing to

---

[84] "Yes, There's a Third Party," *Freeport Journal-Standard*, Oct. 5, 1944.
[85] "Our Socialists Called Feeble," *Milwaukee Journal*, Dec. 7, 1944.
[86] Ibid.
[87] Ibid.
[88] Ibid.

make any serious inroads with organized labor. "We do not see any evidence that Thomas and his followers exert any influence in the AFL; it is clear from the activities of the PAC that the CIO has no interest in the American Socialist Party. Socialism means virtually nothing in the America of 1944 and there is no evidence that it is likely to mean anything more in the America of 1948."[89]

Calling the Socialist Party in the United States "a small circle of high-minded idealists" totally out of touch with reality, the British economist said there had never been a greater need for a Socialist Party on the other side of the pond than at the close of the war. "When we need, as never before, a strong American Socialist Party with which to discuss the grave issues of the day, it refuses to recognize those issues; it even turns against us with indignation because we urge the obligation to act."[90]

The once-proud party headed by Thomas, concluded Laski, was "guilty in this hour of terrible responsibility of a crime for which they will not be acquitted at the bar of history. For at the very moment when they should be pressing toward power," he concluded, "they are turning their backs on it. They risk peace for us as well as for themselves. It is not easy to pardon that attitude."[91]

The 1944 campaign was also a pretty lonely quest for the man considered the "dean" of American presidential politics. Many of his past supporters and former Socialist colleagues were now Democrats actively campaigning against him — or, more precisely, totally ignoring his presence altogether.

The list of defectors was pretty long, including former Milwaukee Mayor Dan Hoan, who was running for governor of Wisconsin as a Democrat, and Andrew J. Biemiller, a former Socialist assemblyman who was campaigning for Congress as a Democrat in the state's fifth congressional district. Unable to resist, Thomas good-naturedly needled both of the ex-Socialists during the 1944 campaign, suggesting that the two men were now far more interested in furthering their own political careers than in the principles that initially inspired their political involvement. Biemiller, who had been one of the party's most influential militants, had managed Thomas's presidential campaign in the Midwest in 1932. "I can remember when Andy was a left-wing Socialist and I was too conservative for him," quipped Thomas.[92]

In addition to the loneliness and biting criticism hurled in his

---

[89] Ibid.
[90] Ibid.
[91] Ibid.
[92] "Thomas Slaps at Peace Plan," *Milwaukee Journal*, Nov. 1, 1944.

direction, Thomas also had to endure the occasional indignities of trying to run for president on a minor-party ticket — something to which he had grown quite accustomed. Despite the tremendous personal abuse, occasional indignities and arduous nature of the campaign, there were a few bright spots here and there for the weathered and weary Socialist. The highlight of the campaign may have occurred when Thomas defeated his major-party rivals in a poll at Yale Divinity School, garnering 59 votes to FDR's 58 and 46 for Dewey.[93]

In a sweeping victory, Thomas also won a mock election held at the Civilian Public Service camp in Big Flats, New York, garnering 59 votes to 29 for Dewey. Roosevelt only received two votes in that mock election, tying the Prohibition Party's Claude Watson while beating the Socialist Labor Party's Edward Teichert by a single vote.[94] The Socialist Party nominee also stomped Roosevelt and Dewey in a straw poll conducted by the Elmira Area Purchasing Agents Association in late October.[95]

But the bright spots were few and far between. It wasn't as though voters were overtly hostile, it was just that nobody really wanted to hear what he or any of the other minor-party candidates for the presidency had to say that year. "The paradox of the situation," wrote Thomas in an article for *Commonweal* magazine shortly after the election, "is that during my long political experience the general tendency has been to a steadily diminishing respect or affection for the old parties coupled with an increasing reluctance to give any consideration to a third party, especially in a presidential election. That tendency," he added, "was peculiarly strong in the last election."[96]

Elaborating further, Thomas said the problem facing a Socialist candidate wasn't hostility or the threat of physical violence. Open hostility had rarely been a problem. "More eggs and vegetables were thrown at Wendell Willkie in 1940 than I ever saw in five presidential campaigns," wrote Thomas. The real problem facing a Socialist candidate for president was the party's lack of organization and adequate funding to wage a truly credible national campaign, a difficulty made worse by a woeful lack of newspaper and

---

[93] Johnpoll, *Pacifist's Progress*, p. 246; "Thomas Wins Poll at Yale Divinity School," *Socialist Call*, Oct. 27, 1944.

[94] "Thomas Wins," *Socialist Call*, Nov. 10, 1944.

[95] "Norman Thomas Wins Poll on Merits of Speeches by Purchasing Agents," *Corning Leader*, Oct. 28, 1944. Thomas also garnered 11.5 percent of the vote in a straw poll conducted at the Farmers Union state convention in Chippewa Falls, Wisconsin, in late October. See, "Gets Farmer Votes," *Socialist Call*, Nov. 10, 1944.

[96] Thomas, "Reflections of an Old Campaigner," *Commonweal*, Dec. 22, 1944, p. 246.

radio coverage. "It has been the general rule of the press that candidates are entitled to space in proportion to the strength of their parties — a rule which tends to doom the weak to permanent weakness," he lamented.[97]

While it was unquestionably the most difficult of his six campaigns for the presidency — he once described it as a "grim experience" — Thomas was nevertheless immensely proud of the campaign that he and his running-mate had waged that year.[98]

Reflecting on it almost twenty years later, Thomas wrote that he was "perhaps prouder of our 1944 campaign and its platform than any of my six presidential campaigns." He was particularly pleased by the party's foreign policy platform, which called for an early and lasting peace settlement and the establishment of an international organization to keep the peace and promote economic and social justice following the war.[99]

In addition to its presidential ticket, the Socialist Party fielded ballot-qualified gubernatorial candidates in seven states, ran eleven candidates for the U.S. Senate, and nominated thirty-three candidates for the U.S. House of Representatives. It was a far cry from 1932, at the height of the Great Depression, when the Socialists offered the American electorate ballot-qualified choices in no fewer than nineteen Senate races, including special elections in Colorado and New Jersey, while fielding candidates for the House in nearly 200 congressional districts in thirty-three states.[100]

Maynard Krueger, who failed to get on the ballot as the nominee of the short-lived American Commonwealth Party in his Chicago congressional district, had agreed to stay on as the Socialist Party's national chairman at the party's convention in Reading and actively campaigned for the Thomas-Hoopes ticket.

Krueger had been unusually optimistic about the Socialist Party's prospects that year. While visiting Los Angeles in June, the left-wing economist said that he expected the party's presidential ticket to receive "a bigger vote" than any election since 1932 — the year Roosevelt stole the party's thunder. Most liberals, he said, now recognized that the New Deal was dead and that any real economic reforms would have to come from the Socialists.

Asserting that "Roosevelt never went very far to the left," Krueger asserted that the President's New Deal administration really hadn't accomplished much more than Hoover probably

---

[97] Ibid, p. 247.
[98] Gregory, *Norman Thomas: The Great Dissenter*, p. 200.
[99] Norman M. Thomas, *Socialism Re-Examined* (New York, 1963), p. 127.
[100] "Drys Top Minor Parties in List of Candidates," *Chicago Tribune*, Nov. 2, 1944.

would have done during a major depression. In fact, he argued, FDR didn't even go as far to the left as the Tories in Great Britain during the height of the Great Depression — a remark that contained more than a grain of truth.[101]

Like other party activists, Krueger was deeply concerned about the postwar economy. During a speech at the Whittier Institute of International Relations in California in late June, the University of Chicago economist said the United States faced two profound questions in the immediate aftermath of World War II.

"First, will the United States build a 'welfare-centered economy,' forsaking the state-power centered economy under which it now functions? And, second," he asked, "what kind and degree of public enterprise will America encourage in the reconstruction period?" The United States, he asserted, had not yet answered those perplexing questions.

Predicting that the European countries wouldn't return their industry, newspapers and systems of communications to private enterprise following the war, Krueger also said that if Great Britain and the United States continued their policy of trying to restore an outmoded system of free enterprise in the postwar period, it was likely that the people of Europe would "resort to the totalitarian-collectivism of Russia."[102]

In the meantime, Norman Thomas continued to barnstorm the country in search of support for his eight-point peace plan. Nothing annoyed the Socialist candidate more than the demand by the Allies of an "unconditional surrender" — "a term President Roosevelt threw out in a gay moment at Casablanca," chided Thomas.[103]

Thomas absolutely deplored the term "unconditional surrender," calling it "something meant to divert us from thinking and make us drunk with emotional wine" while offering nothing to the German people except more unnecessary Allied and German deaths.[104]

Realizing that their fate had already been sealed, asserted Thomas in a speech at the Hartford High School auditorium in mid-October, the German people were not fighting in the hope of victory, but in the increasingly remote hope of salvaging something of their country. Comparing the determination of the German people to the way the Russians valiantly fought during the

---

[101] "Socialist Sees Heavy Gains for His Party," *Los Angeles Times*, June 28, 1944.
[102] "Free Enterprise Draws Blast at Whittier Parley," *Los Angeles Times*, July 1, 1944.
[103] "Thomas Slaps at Peace Plan," *Milwaukee Journal*, Nov. 1, 1944.
[104] "Peace Terms Criticized By Thomas," *Hartford Courant*, Oct. 16, 1944.

Battle of Stalingrad, a close quarters and bloody conflict waged with little to no regard for military and civilian casualties, Thomas said that by imposing the unreasonable demand of "unconditional surrender" instead of peace terms that offered some hope to the masses, the Allies had virtually eliminated the possibility that as many as a half a million German people might revolt against Hitler and the Nazi regime, thereby bringing the war to a quicker end.[105]

This was a theme Thomas repeated throughout the campaign. Failure on the part of the Allies to offer terms more definite than a simple unconditional surrender tended to unite a desperate people who might otherwise be ready to concede if it were not for fear of harsh retribution, he said. Consequently, the use of such a "grandiose phrase" as "unconditional surrender" instead of more fundamental considerations was merely serving to prolong the war, argued Thomas.[106]

"How can the masses rise with no slogan but unconditional surrender?" asked Thomas, who added emphatically that he wasn't suggesting a soft peace with Hitler and the Third Reich. "The terms could be hard, but they should offer the people something to look forward to," he said.[107] Those were the words of a true statesman.

The Socialist Party, said Thomas while stumping in California in late September, was merely advocating reasonable terms of surrender. "We Socialists propose no peace with Hitler at all. We believe that specific war criminals should be tried and punished." Any peace terms, he told a crowd of 2,000 at the Embassy Auditorium in Los Angeles, should be based on "disarmament of enemy countries" and their "complete renunciation of conquest," as well as restitution of property and compensation to refugees.[108]

The Socialist candidate repeated his criticism of FDR's demand for an unconditional surrender throughout the campaign. In a speech at Yale University earlier that summer, Thomas explained that his opposition to an unconditional surrender was based, in part, on the fact that "there is no nation good enough to enforce a punitive peace against Japan or Germany and no nation bad enough to deserve it." Germany, he argued, should be subjected to an international war crimes tribunal and should also be required to make any necessary retribution, but the peace terms must be

---

[105] Ibid.
[106] "Thomas Assails Post War Programs of Both Parties," *Oberlin News-Tribune*, Aug. 3, 1944.
[107] "Peace Terms Criticized By Thomas," *Hartford Courant*, Oct. 16, 1944.
[108] "Norman Thomas Fights Partitioning of Reich," *Los Angeles Times*, Sep. 30, 1944.

reasonable.[109]

Any excessively punitive policies after the war would lead to resentment not unlike that experienced in the South during the period of reconstruction following the Civil War, noted Thomas. "If such a punitive peace is enforced, one of the present allies, probably the United States, will be drawn to help Germany within the next ten years," he said.[110] As it turned out, it happened much quicker than that.

"Unconditional surrender," declared Thomas while addressing a crowd of 750 at Milwaukee's historic Solomon Juneau Auditorium on the final day of October, might mean "a sentence of death to the boy you love. That's what you'll get for voting for Roosevelt or Dewey. Under such terms the German people would be cowardly not to fight on. It would have lessened German resistance," continued the stentorian-voiced Socialist, "and brought the boys home sooner for Roosevelt to have said to Germany that if she consented to disarmament and agreed to renounce conquest she also would be included in the benefits of any cooperative world organization."[111]

Unless the world was prepared to accept perpetual war in Europe, Thomas said on another occasion, "there must be no partition of Germany, no assignment of German territories, no slavery of Germans in Russian work camps and no attempted reduction of the German economy to a peasant level."[112]

An ideal peace, Thomas articulated during an annual Town Hall event in Oberlin, Ohio, would involve the demand of an awakened people from all nations that "the power of the few over the many be ended" and that the nations of the world renounce "the fool's gold profits of imperialism and racial prejudices." As a practical first step, he suggested, the United States should immediately make it absolutely clear that it will "refuse to underwrite any program of imperialism or Balkanization."[113]

Thomas envisioned "a fellowship of free men who harness machinery for the good of all, with the state as a useful, powerful servant but never as an instrument for dominance by the few. Planning democratically for the common good, as we now plan

---

[109] "Norman Thomas Asks for 'Peace of Reconciliation,'" *Yale News Digest*, Vol. II, No. 8, Aug. 18, 1944.
[110] Ibid.
[111] "Thomas Slaps at Peace Plan," *Milwaukee Journal*, Nov. 1, 1944.
[112] "Norman Thomas Fights Partitioning of Reich," *Los Angeles Times*, Sep. 30, 1944.
[113] "Thomas Assails Post War Programs of Both Parties," *Oberlin News-Tribune*, Aug. 3, 1944.

autocratically for victory in the war, is a slow job," he sighed. "Democracy and freedom are not a normal way of life for man," he concluded, "and it takes time and thought and labor to achieve them and maintain them."[114]

While the Roosevelt and Dewey campaigns each made a concerted bid for black support, Thomas was at his best when appealing to African-American voters. Speaking in Pittsburgh in early September, the Socialist standard-bearer declared that a lasting peace was incompatible with racial inequality. "It is completely illogical," he said, "to believe that the United States can settle the tangled racial problems of the world, although it cannot, or will not, prevent discrimination against Negro soldiers in a war for freedom."[115]

In a plea for anti-discriminatory legislation to outlaw lynching and the poll tax while denouncing all forms of racial and religious bigotry as vicious and illogical in every aspect, Thomas declared that the days of white supremacy were numbered. If the United States was going to oppose white supremacy in Burma, India, and other colonial possessions of the British Empire, then it was imperative that the country should practice what it preaches here at home, asserted Thomas.[116]

Thomas also came out strongly in favor of lowering the voting age to eighteen — a measure supported by Georgia Gov. Ellis G. Arnall, South Carolina Gov. Olin D. Johnston, ex-Democratic National Committee chairman Frank C. Walker, and Michigan Sen. Arthur Vandenberg. While acknowledging that there certainly wasn't anything magical about giving twenty-one-year-olds the wisdom to actively participate in the electoral process, Thomas said that he wished "we could find magic to give them wisdom at any age, but boys and girls compelled to face war so realistically at 18 should be given a vote."[117] Thomas, of course, had raised some serious objections to drafting 18 and 19-year-olds when Congress, responding to Henry Stimson's request to increase the army's strength from 4,250,000 to 7,500,000 men, vigorously debated the issue in the autumn of 1942.[118]

---

[114] Ibid.
[115] "Race Hate Peril to Nation," *Pittsburgh Courier*, Sep. 16, 1944.
[116] Ibid.
[117] "F. M. Brewer, "The Voting Age," *Pittsburgh Press*, Sep. 14, 1944. The state of Georgia, which had adopted a constitutional amendment lowering the voting age in 1943, allowed those who had turned eighteen by the day of the election to participate in the 1944 presidential election — the first time in American history that voters under the age of 21 were allowed to cast ballots.
[118] "Committee Votes for Draft of 18-19 Youths," *St. Petersburg Times*, Oct. 15, 1942.

"A GRIM EXPERIENCE"

For a brief moment in late September it appeared that Thomas might be afforded an opportunity to mix it up with his major party rivals when George Denny, Jr., executive director of the League for Political Education and the host of "America's Town Meeting of the Air" invited Roosevelt, Dewey and Thomas to participate in a forum on his October 26th program.[119]

Denny's proposal would have been the closest thing to a debate between the leading presidential candidates that year, but the idea was nixed when the two major-party candidates refused to participate. Turning to surrogates, Denny then scheduled a debate between Secretary of the Interior Harold Ickes and Sen. Homer Ferguson (R-Mich.), but neglected to invite a representative from the Socialist Party.

With about three weeks remaining in the campaign, the Rev. John Haynes Holmes, whose independent committee had officially endorsed Thomas and Hoopes a few weeks earlier, reiterated his support for the Socialist ticket in a statement contending that Thomas was "presenting the only program of constructive statesmanship that will bring America security and world peace."[120]

In his October 14th statement, Holmes maintained that a vote for Roosevelt or Dewey was clearly a wasted vote, "for it makes little difference to the fate of mankind which candidate is elected. The results will be the same. But a vote for Norman Thomas," he declared, "will count as impressive support of sound policy and true ideals in the present crisis. A million votes for Norman Thomas," Holmes concluded, "would do more to stabilize this nation and help in the cause of peace than any other result in this campaign."[121]

Other prominent members of the Independent Committee for Thomas and Hoopes included former party activist Devere Allen, who was then working as a foreign correspondent and editor of *Worldover Press*, George S. Schuyler of the *Pittsburgh Courier*, A. J. Muste of the Fellowship of Reconciliation, and poet Lenore G. Marshall, one of the founders of SANE (the National Committee for a Sane Nuclear Policy) in 1957.[122]

In early November, Thomas participated in a New York City Town Hall-sponsored debate on the merits of the profit system.

---

[119] "Forum of 3 Candidates Invited to 'Town Meeting,'" *Washington Post*, Sep. 24, 1944.
[120] "Holmes Backs Thomas; Praises Socialist for 'Sound Policy and True Ideals,'" *New York Times*, Oct. 15, 1944.
[121] Ibid.
[122] "Independent Committee for Thomas and Hoopes Formed," *Socialist Call*, Aug. 11, 1944.

His sparring partner was wealthy industrialist Henning W. Prentis, Jr., president of the Armstrong Cork Company. A former director of the U.S. Chamber of Commerce and past president of the powerful National Association of Manufacturers, Prentis had been a vociferous critic of FDR's New Deal during the Great Depression.

During their lively exchange, Prentis argued that the dangers inherent in government planning and control of the economy could lead to a loss of freedom in the United States. Without a profit motive, he stated, the free enterprise system couldn't survive, and without private competition, each of the liberties the American people cherished — personal, political and economic — would be jeopardized and eventually disappear. There simply was no satisfactory substitute for the profit motive, he argued.[123]

"The profit motive provides the only system under which the consumer has virtually unlimited freedom of choice in satisfying needs," asserted Prentis. "It provides the lifeblood of our private hospitals, colleges, museums and libraries. It helps support the church. It is the only system that can build up an economically competent mass of independent citizens, without which political freedom cannot survive."[124]

Not only could a satisfactory substitute for the profit motive be found, countered Thomas, but it was imperative that one be established immediately if democracy was to be saved, poverty abolished, and wars prevented. Moreover, said Thomas, it was deeply insulting to all of the young men risking their lives in World War II to suggest that human beings were only motivated by personal profit or gain.[125]

State intervention in the economy had become a necessity, continued Thomas, noting that the private profit or capitalist system had failed to provide adequate employment or abundance in any country in the world prior to World War II. "Nowhere will a system recognizable as private capitalism by the laissez faire economists be reestablished after this war," he concluded. "We must plan in the service of a nobler God than private profit or see civilization perish under dictatorship in chronic depressions and recurring wars."[126]

---

[123] "Merits of Profit System Debated By Socialist Leader, Industrialist," *New York Times*, Nov. 3, 1944.
[124] Ibid.
[125] Ibid.
[126] Ibid.

Chapter XII

The "Great Jasper" Returns

Though the Socialist Party had been further decimated in the 1942 congressional mid-term elections — only one of their candidates for the U.S. Senate polled as much as one percent of the vote that autumn, and that's primarily because he was running in a race featuring only one major-party candidate — the party nevertheless put up a brave front in 1944.

Fielding candidates for the U.S. Senate in Colorado, Connecticut, Indiana, Iowa, Kansas, Missouri, Pennsylvania, Washington and Wisconsin, as well as in a special election in New Jersey to replace Republican Sen. W. Warren Barbour, a former amateur heavyweight boxing champion who died the previous November, many of the party's candidates that autumn had been cajoled into running by the man they deeply admired — Norman Thomas.

If Thomas was willing to subject himself to the trials and tribulations of another exceedingly difficult campaign in what was clearly shaping up to be one of the leanest years in the party's storied history, then they, in good conscience, should do no less. A number of the party's old warhorses — those who stuck with the Socialist Party through thick and thin — entered the fray that year, but so did an even larger number of political newcomers.

One of those old veterans was Pennsylvania's J. Henry Stump, then serving in his third non-consecutive term as mayor of the blue-collar city of Reading. Like Bridgeport's Jasper McLevy, the 64-year-old Stump was arguably one of the party's better known candidates for the U.S. Senate that year. Another was Mario B. Tomsich, a prominent labor lawyer and economist from Gary, the party's U.S. Senate nominee in Indiana. Long active in the American Civil Liberties Union, the largely-forgotten Tomsich frequently lectured on the economic aspects of a just and durable peace during World War II. He had been the Socialist Party's nominee for governor of the Hoosier State in 1936.

The party's best showing in a Senate race, however, occurred in Wisconsin, where 31-year-old labor historian Walter H. Uphoff — a relative political newcomer who was the working as a field representative for the party — posted a somewhat respectable 9,964 votes, or roughly eight-tenths of one percent, in a race where the Progressive Party's Harry Sauthoff, a four-term congressman, attracted the bulk of the state's left-wing support that autumn.

During the course of his uphill campaign, Uphoff received some high praise from legendary *Capital Times* columnist Aldric Revell. "For our money," wrote Revell, commenting on one of the candidate's recent radio appearances, "this was the most intelligent and the most honest and decent address of the campaign."[1]

"We need statesmen today who have convictions and who stand for principles of freedom and justice whether they win or lose at the polls," asserted Uphoff in his radio address.[2] That was fine, but what really caught Revell's attention was the young Socialist's ability to speak straight from the shoulder:

> Full utilization of our manpower and productive capacity is not only possible, but absolutely necessary, if we are to avert the chaos that Germany experienced during the twenties and which provided the soil on which the seeds of fascism grew. Full employment for every willing and able-bodied person, including all returning service men, must be given an A-1 priority rating by our legislatures and by Congress.
>
> Since capitalism has shown itself incapable of doing the job, our system of money, banking and credit, our natural resources, our public utilities and monopolies, must be controlled by society. Social control, to be effective, requires social ownership, but not autocratic administration by agents of a bureaucratic state. Socialized enterprise should be administered by public corporations operated for the people's benefit."[3]

Uphoff, whose wife Mary Jo had been deeply involved with

---

[1] "Hokum and Hogwash vs. Honest Realities: That's How Wisconsin Campaign Looks to Columnist," *Socialist Call*, Sep. 1, 1944.
[2] Ibid.
[3] "Times Columnist Praises Socialist," *Socialist Call*, Oct. 20, 1944.

KAOWC's Youth Committee Against War, was very active in the Wisconsin Committee Against Peacetime Conscription during this period and was later involved in peace movements in Minnesota and Colorado. Uphoff is probably best remembered as the author of *Kohler on Strike*, a widely-read account of one of the longest labor disputes in American history. He was also one of the first individuals to challenge Wisconsin's notorious Joe McCarthy in a political debate.[4] A fascinating couple, the Uphoffs, who named their son after Norman Thomas, later turned their interests to parapsychology, writing and lecturing extensively on that subject.[5]

Carle Whitehead of Denver, a 66-year-old Columbia University-educated attorney who had been involved in every major campaign in Colorado since 1932, carried the party's banner against Republican Eugene Millkin, a member of the Senate Finance Committee, and Democrat Barney Whatley in that state's U.S. Senate race. Briefly intrigued by Howard Scott's short-lived technocracy movement, Whitehead was a close personal friend of Norman Thomas and served on the ACLU's local executive committee. A long-distance runner in the Thomas tradition, Whitehead waged four campaigns for the U.S. Senate and an equal number for the House on the Socialist ticket before his death in 1955.[6]

In Kansas, the party's U.S. Senate nominee was 33-year-old Arthur G. Billings, a former University of Texas economics instructor and conscientious objector who had recently been released from Fort Leavenworth where he was being held for refusing to take the U.S. Army's oath of induction after being drafted. A lower federal court had initially ruled that Billings couldn't use the conscientious objection defense since he was an agnostic, but he was eventually set free in a ruling by the U.S. Supreme Court after being held since August of 1942.[7]

The party's senatorial aspirants also included Connecticut's Spencer Anderson, who had been one of dozens of Socialists elected to the Bridgeport city council between the early 1930s and the late 1950s. Ray C. Roberts, a member of the party's executive committee in Seattle, carried the party's banner in Washington's U.S. Senate race, a contest won comfortably by the modest and low-key Democrat Warren G. Magnuson. In addition to fielding little-known candidates in Iowa and Missouri, the Socialist Party's

---

[4] John Nichols, *The "S" Word: A Short History of an American Tradition...Socialism* (Brooklyn, 2011), p. 107.
[5] "World of Physics; Mind Over Matter," *Madison Capitol Times*, July 22, 1982.
[6] "Carle Whitehead, 77, Perennial Candidate, Dies in Denver Sun," *Greeley Daily Tribune*, Jan 3, 1955; Swanberg, *Norman Thomas: The Last Idealist*, p. 145.
[7] "Arthur Billings Enters Senate Race in Kansas," *Joplin Globe*, June 18, 1944.

list of U.S. Senate aspirants that year even included a member of the armed services — labor organizer Morris Riger of Newark, the party's nominee to fill the remainder of the late William W. Barbour's U.S. Senate seat in New Jersey. Riger, who received 1,593 votes, or one-tenth of one percent of the vote, was serving in the army and was stationed in France during the autumn campaign.

Though none of the party's down-ballot candidates polled particularly well, the 33 Socialist candidates for the U.S. House of Representatives in 1944 included a bevy of party heavyweights — both literally and figuratively — not the least of whom was biographically-neglected Raymond S. Hofses, the longtime editor of the *Reading Labor Advocate*, in Pennsylvania's fourteenth congressional district.

A former member of the Reading school board and a perennial Socialist candidate for public office, Hofses — a whale of a man — was an immensely popular figure in that blue-collar city dating back to his gridiron days when he played center for the Reading High School football team. The longtime secretary-treasurer of the Reading Cooperative Publishing Association was also one of the party's leading all-time vote getters and had garnered an eye-opening 19,319 votes, or 27 percent, against his Democratic and Republican opponents in a previous bid for Congress a dozen years earlier.

In terms of percentage of the votes received that autumn, the little-remembered Reading Socialist was by far the party's most successful congressional candidate in 1944. Moreover, Hofses, who polled 3,501 votes, or nearly 4.4 percent of the vote, in his uphill battle against freshman Democratic congressman Daniel K. Hoch and Republican challenger Randolph Stauffer, was one of only eight Socialist candidates for the U.S. House who broke the relatively modest one percent threshold in that extraordinarily lean year for the nation's minor parties.

Half of those eight contests occurred in the party's one-time stronghold of Wisconsin — the only state in the nation in which Norman Thomas polled as much as one percent of the vote that year — and included a spirited effort by Edwin W. Knappe, a former Socialist assemblyman and assistant city attorney, who had the misfortune of campaigning against ex-Socialist-turned-Progressive Andrew Biemiller who was running for Congress as a Democrat in Milwaukee's fifth congressional district once represented by the late Victor Berger. By 1944, the fifth district, which included the city's North Shore suburbs and other Republican territory, was considered something of a swing district.[8]

A Marquette-educated lawyer who had joined the Socialist Party 39 years earlier when he was first eligible to vote, Knappe firmly believed that the Roosevelt administration hadn't done nearly enough to stimulate the economy in the years prior to World War II — a view generally shared by his comrades. "The wasted, idle years of the depression were entirely unnecessary," asserted Knappe while running for Congress two years earlier, "because the powers of government could have been used to initiate and direct the production that private interests could not bring into being."[9] He was right. The so-called "job creators" weren't creating too many of them before Pearl Harbor.

Given Frank Zeidler's spirited campaign for mayor earlier that spring, a race in which the 31-year-old younger brother of the late "Singing Mayor" Carl Zeidler was barely nosed out in the primary, the Milwaukee Socialists had high hopes for Knappe's candidacy.

Waging the second of three campaigns for the fifth district seat, the 60-year-old Knappe, however, was never really a factor in the four-cornered race, garnering fewer than 4,800 votes in a race the Biemiller won by nearly 10,000 votes. Knappe probably would have run stronger had it not been for the presence of the Progressive Party's Irvin I. Aaron, a mover-and-shaker in the Milwaukee Cooperative League, who was listed on the ballot as an independent because he failed to poll the requisite number of votes in the Progressive primary. Aaron, who later urged the Wisconsin Progressives to rejoin the Republican Party when that party collapsed in the spring of 1946, garnered 2,103 votes in the congressional contest.

The Wisconsin Socialists posted similar numbers in the neighboring fourth congressional district where 42-year-old Stanley Budny, a painter and decorator by trade, campaigned against a two-term Democratic incumbent and half-hearted Republican opposition that autumn. A Socialist member of the City Election Commission, the German-born Budny, who later served as executive secretary to Milwaukee's Socialist Mayor Frank P. Zeidler in the 1950s, was once described by the longtime Socialist mayor as

---

[8] "Ex-Union Official Biemiller Says Progressives Face a Tough Road," *Milwaukee Journal*, Jan. 28, 1979. The 38-year-old Biemiller, who had campaigned for "Fighting Bob" La Follette in his home town of Sandusky, Ohio, when he was eighteen, was a staunch advocate of national health insurance and later drew significant opposition from the American Medical Association, causing his defeat in 1950.

[9] "Election Laws Revise Urged," *Milwaukee Journal*, Aug. 23, 1942.

"an exemplary public servant and a wonderful diplomat."[10] Like Knappe, Budny unfortunately wasn't really a factor in his 1944 congressional campaign, polling a disappointing 4,170 votes in a lopsided race decided by nearly 50,000 votes.

John C. Boll of Sheboygan Falls, a member of the party's state executive committee, also managed to barely break the one percent threshold in his hopeless battle in Wisconsin's sixth congressional district — a race easily won by Republican Frank B. Keefe, a three-term lawmaker who served on the congressional committee that investigated the attack on Pearl Harbor — as did little-known Alma farmer Adolph Maassen, the lone opponent to the Progressive Party's Merlin Hull in the state's 9th congressional district, which included the cities of Eau Claire and Chippewa Falls.

In addition to Hofses and the four candidates in Wisconsin, only three of the party's other congressional candidates polled as much as one percent of the vote that autumn, including Norwalk bus driver Stanley W. Mayhew, the party's nominee in Connecticut's widely-watched fourth congressional district, and Leverne Hamilton, a quick-witted rancher from Roundup, who campaigned for one of Montana's two U.S. House seats. Hamilton, who got along marvelously with Norman Thomas, garnered 841 votes — precisely one percent of the total — in the state's first congressional district while losing to freshman Democratic Rep. Mike Mansfield, a young former history and political science professor who later became the longest-serving Senate Majority Leader in U.S. history. Hamilton, who had briefly served in the Montana legislature as a Democrat in 1931, was a frequent candidate for Congress, waging unsuccessful bids on the Socialist ticket in 1940, 1942, 1944, 1950 and 1952.

In Virginia, perennial candidate Clarke T. Robb, who had been stricken by polio and confined to a wheelchair, polled 925 votes, or 1.8 percent, against seven-term congressman Howard W. Smith, a rabid segregationist and outspoken critic of the Congress of Industrial Organizations (CIO). A product of the powerful Byrd organization and sponsor of the draconian Smith Act of 1940 — the first federal peacetime sedition statute enacted in the United States since 1798 — the Virginia lawmaker had to fend off three pesky challengers to win an eighth consecutive term in 1944, including a spirited campaign waged by Elizabeth C. Murray, a staunch Roosevelt supporter and daughter of the late U.S. Sen. William E. Chilton of West Virginia, one of Woodrow Wilson's closest allies in the

---

[10] "Obituaries: Stanley Budny," *Milwaukee Sentinel*, June 28, 1994.

U.S. Senate. Murray, who had three sons serving in the armed forces and campaigned on the spectacular slogan, "Vote for a three-star mother against a triple-plated heel," finished second in the four-cornered race, polling nearly 21 percent of the vote against Smith while running as an Independent Democrat.[11]

Beyond its relatively limited roster of House and Senate candidates that fall, the Socialists also fielded a number of gubernatorial candidates, including the write-in candidacy of the Rev. George Lyman Paine of Cambridge, an Episcopal minister and frequent Socialist candidate, in Massachusetts.[12] A noted pacifist, Paine had been the party's candidate for the U.S. Senate in 1942.

The picturesquely-named Jasper McLevy, the Socialist mayor of Bridgeport who was mounting the tenth of his fifteen tries for the governor's chair in Connecticut, and Wisconsin's George A. Nelson, Thomas's vice-presidential running mate in 1936, were the party's leading candidates for state chief executive.

The 70-year-old Nelson, who owned a small dairy farm near Milltown, spent most of the campaign attacking former Milwaukee Mayor Daniel Hoan for abandoning the Socialists for the greener pastures of the Democratic Party.[13] Nelson, who had been the Farmer-Labor Progressive Federation's nominee for lieutenant governor in 1938, was immensely proud to once again be running on the Socialist Party ticket.

"Humanity First," the slogan adopted at the party's national convention in Reading, must become the basis for the country's domestic and foreign policies, said Nelson. "The Socialist Party stands, not for America First, Britain First, or Russia First, but for the welfare of all peoples." Deploring what he perceived as widespread voter apathy, the one-time Alaska gold miner said that he was convinced that if his friend Norman Thomas was given equal radio time and newspaper coverage "the Socialist vote polled in this country and in Wisconsin, would scare the daylights out of the old parties."[14]

Unfortunately, like Thomas nationally, Nelson was never a factor in the Wisconsin race, polling a relatively disappointing 9,183 votes, or only a small fraction of the nearly 45,000 votes he received in a previous bid for governor a decade earlier.

While many of the party's nominees that autumn were either

---

[11] Drew Pearson, "Washington-Merry-Go-Round," *Free Lance-Star* (Fredericksburg, MD), Oct. 30, 1944.
[12] "Write in Vote," *Socialist Call*, Oct. 13, 1944.
[13] "State Socialist Replies to Hoan Charge," *Racine Journal-Times*, Sep. 25, 1944.
[14] "Socialists Put Humanity First," *Socialist Call*, Oct. 20, 1944.

political novices or completely unknown, that certainly wasn't the case with 66-year-old Jasper McLevy of Bridgeport, a veteran campaigner who was once again running for governor of Connecticut.[15]

A perennial Socialist office seeker, McLevy had finally been elected mayor of Bridgeport, Connecticut, in 1933 after nearly a dozen failed attempts. A roofing contractor who ran for mayor of Bridgeport in every mayoral contest dating back to 1911, McLevy eventually held the office for twenty-four years before losing a bid for an unprecedented thirteenth term by a mere 161 votes in 1957.[16] A previous mayor, of course, had already put the working-class city of Bridgeport on the map. His name was Phineas T. Barnum, owner of the world-famous Barnum & Bailey circus. One of the world's greatest showmen, Barnum served as a Republican mayor in the mid-1870s and helped transform Bridgeport from a quiet port city to a bustling manufacturing center.

As in Milwaukee, one of the few other American cities with a long Socialist tradition, McLevy's brand of "sewer socialism" was hardly mired in doctrinaire Marxism, focusing instead on a series of progressive reforms, honest government and the efficient delivery of basic municipal services.

Born in 1878, McLevy drifted toward socialism after reading Edward Bellamy's utopian novel, *Looking Backward*. He went to work at an early age and eventually started his own roofing business. A leader in the Bridgeport Building Trades Council, McLevy organized the city's Central Labor Union and also served for a time as vice president of the Connecticut Federation of Labor. McLevy's tenacity and persistence were richly rewarded when he captured the mayoralty in 1933. McLevy's stunning victory — he garnered 49% of the vote against his major party rivals — came at a time when Bridgeport's unemployment rate had swelled to 25%, the city was a million dollars in debt, and the incumbent Democratic mayor had asked city workers to take a drastic twenty percent pay cut in order to meet the city's payroll.

McLevy was re-elected two years later with 56% of the vote, carrying with him the entire Socialist city council slate. During his 24-year tenure as mayor, McLevy proved to be as fiscally conservative as any budget-cutting Republican, sharply reducing the city's debt while consistently holding the line on taxes, improving the

---

[15] "McLevy Again Expected to Run for Governor," *Hartford Courant*, June 12, 1944; "McLevy Nominated Again," *New York Times*, Aug. 13, 1944.
[16] "Tedesco Elected by 161 Votes Ending M'Levy's 24-Year Reign," *Bridgeport Telegram*, Nov. 6, 1967.

city's credit rating, eliminating wasteful government spending and attracting new businesses to the city. In addition to streamlining city services, the long-serving Socialist mayor pulled Bridgeport from virtual bankruptcy while earning a Triple-A credit rating for his blue-collar city. McLevy also pioneered one of the earliest civil service systems in the country while vastly improving the city's crumbling infrastructure, including a modernized and expanded sewage system.

A stickler for a balanced budget, the frugal working-class mayor, who had been sharply criticized for suspending the city's snow removal services during the winter, famously blew off his critics, saying, "The good Lord brought the snow, the good Lord will take it away." He was right — by early spring not a single snowflake could be found in Bridgeport.

Ironically, the business community was generally pleased with its Socialist mayor. "He is a good, honest, Scotsman, who has handled our money carefully," said the president of one local company. Tax crusader Vivien Kellems, a stormy petrel of Connecticut politics in the 1950s, once made a similar observation, describing the Bridgeport mayor as "the best damned Republican of them all."[17] That was pretty high praise and explains, in a nutshell, why more than a few registered Republicans in Connecticut routinely voted for the down-to-earth slate roofer in state and local elections.

Running for governor like clockwork, the Socialist mayor received a staggering 166,253 votes in Connecticut's 1938 gubernatorial election — causing the defeat of two-term Democratic Gov. Wilbur L. Cross, a well-known literary critic and former Yale University English professor. McLevy ran for governor on fifteen occasions, waging his last campaign for the state's highest office as an octogenarian in 1958. Incredibly, McLevy's name graced the ballot on no fewer than 54 occasions — always as a Socialist candidate — during a span of nearly sixty years.

Largely owing to McLevy's immense popularity in Bridgeport, the Socialists captured five seats in the Connecticut legislature in 1934, including three seats in the state Senate where the party held the balance of power between seventeen Democrats and fifteen Republicans.

All five Socialists hailed from Bridgeport. "Neither party has a majority," observed the *Christian Science Monitor*, "and neither can carry through legislation without the help of the Socialists."

The Socialists now held the "whip-hand" in the state's general

---

[17] "McLevy, Soapbox Champ, Took Formality Out of City Hall," *Bridgeport Post*, Nov. 19, 1962.

assembly. "While Democrats were electing their entire state ticket for the first time since 1912 and picking up 12 seats in the lower house of the Legislature," the paper noted, "Bridgeport's new enthusiasm for Socialism was too strong."[18]

An utterly novel experience for Connecticut Socialists, it was the first time in twenty years that a third-party candidate had been elected to the state legislature and the first time ever that the Socialist Party had been represented in that body. John M. Taft, a foreman for the Bridgeport Brass Company who doubled as a member of the city's common council, a post he was first elected to in 1933, was the party's floor leader in the Senate.

Under Taft's leadership, the Socialist bloc in the legislature avoided any strikingly radical proposals and to the utter dismay and anger of the party's left-wing activists frequently sided with the Republicans on several crucial issues, including support for a controversial state sales tax — a proposal initially opposed by the party — in exchange for GOP support for unemployment relief. Later serving as president of Bridgeport's common council, the 38-year-old Taft died tragically of a massive heart attack in 1937 while attending the Socialist Party's annual banquet in Bridgeport.[19]

Along with Taft, the mellifluously-named Audubon J. Secor, a 48-year-old engineer, and 52-year-old Albert E. Eccles, an immensely talented engraver and close ally of Mayor McLevy, also served in the upper chamber. Jack C. Bergen, a 28-year-old architect, and Harry G. Bender, a 43-year-old factory inspector, were the victorious Socialist representatives. Believing that it unfairly shifted the burden of taxation to the working class, Bergen had vigorously opposed his party's support for a state sales tax in 1935 — a proposal supported by McLevy — and later joined Devere Allen and the party's militant faction in forming Connecticut's short-lived Labor Party in 1938.[20]

Buoyed by the party's success in the 1934 legislative contests, the Socialists made a concerted effort to expand the party's influence beyond Bridgeport and its surrounding communities in 1935, a year in which nearly all of Connecticut's 169 towns and cities held

---

[18] "Socialists Attain Power Over Rivals in Connecticut," *Christian Science Monitor*, Nov. 9, 1934.
[19] "Socialists Press Connecticut Gains," *New York Times*, Sept. 8, 1935; "John M. Taft Succumbs to Heart Attack," *Hartford Courant*, April 26, 1937.
[20] Cecelia Bucki, *Bridgeport's Socialist New Deal, 1915-1936* (Urbana, 2001), p. 239; "The Socialists in the Legislature," *Hartford Courant*, Nov. 8, 1934; "Connecticut Goes a Little to the Left: Five Socialists Elected to the Legislature for the First Time," *New York Times*, Nov. 11, 1934; "Bergen Hits Sales Levy as Unjust," *Hartford Courant*, Mar. 9, 1935; "Bergen Sees Passing Sales Tax Possible," *Hartford Courant*, Apr. 14, 1935.

municipal elections.

While hoping to displace the Democrats as the ranking minority party in Republican-dominated communities, the Socialists held out hope of carrying several towns and cities, including Plainfield, a traditionally Democratic town, and the city of Norwalk, the state's eighth largest city and a place where Socialist support at the ballot box had increased twenty-fold between 1930 and 1934.[21] Waging their strongest campaign ever for local offices in Connecticut, the Socialists fell short in Plainfield and Norwalk, but in several communities surpassed McLevy's relatively strong showing the previous year.[22]

It would be another twelve years, however, before the Socialists finally elected a mayor in Norwalk when Irving C. Freese was swept into office.

Overwhelmed in the Roosevelt landslide of 1936 — FDR claimed nearly 64 percent of the vote in Bridgeport — the Connecticut Socialists were wiped out at the ballot box that year, losing all five seats in the legislature while McLevy, waging yet another campaign for governor, limped into third place with 20,993 votes, a significant decline from his remarkable seven percent showing two years earlier. The results were absolutely devastating.

Despite competing in 24 of the state's 35 state senatorial districts, not a single Socialist came close to winning and all three Senate incumbents — Eccles, Secor and Taft — were soundly beaten in their bids for a second term, as was Harry Bender in his bid for reelection as a state representative. Bender and his running mate William S. Neil, a member of the Bridgeport Common Council who had replaced Jack Bergen as the party's nominee in that district, took a real shellacking in their contest, finishing fifth and sixth in a 6-candidate field while losing to their Democratic opponents by more than 21,000 votes.

Coming on the heels of the national party's devastating split in 1936, Connecticut's Old Guard had barely lifted a finger for the party's presidential ticket that year; Norman Thomas garnered only 5,683 votes — far fewer than the more than 20,000 votes that he received four years earlier and only a fraction of the totals received by the party's other statewide candidates in 1936. Moreover, only 2,783 votes were cast for Thomas in the party's stronghold in Fairfax County compared to 13,887 votes for Mayor McLevy in the governor's race, including 9,048 in the city of Bridgeport alone.

---

[21] "Socialists Press Connecticut Gains," *New York Times*, Sep. 8, 1935.
[22] "Connecticut G.O.P. Sees Gain," *New York Times*, Oct. 13, 1935.

McLevy, who had been elected chairman of the Social Democratic Federation at the its founding national confab in Pittsburgh in the spring of 1937, bounced back with a vengeance in 1938, waging one of the strongest statewide campaigns in the party's history while providing a much-needed glimmer of hope for the nation's alternative parties.[23]

The Nutmeg Socialists put up a real battle against the two major parties that autumn, virtually turning each of the state's eight statewide races into genuine three-way affairs while winning four state legislative contests and coming remarkably close to snatching a seat in Congress.

It was truly an incredible feat, all the more remarkable given the fact that the party's left-wing militants loyal to Norman Thomas and led by Devere Allen, the internationally-recognized peace activist and member of the party's national executive committee, contested that election by fielding their own Labor Party ticket against the larger and much more powerful McLevy faction.

The rift between the party's right-wing and left-wing factions, which led to an irreconcilable split at the party's 1936 state convention in Hartford, had its roots in the party's turbulent national convention in Detroit two years earlier when the party adopted its controversial Declaration of Principles.

Weighing in on the side of New York's Old Guard, McLevy had angered his party's militants earlier that year when he scolded Norman Thomas shortly after the party's national executive committee suspended the charter of the New York organization. In a blistering telegram to the NEC, the Bridgeport mayor accused the faction headed by Thomas of performing "a disservice to the party and its principles" while making a "mockery" of the party's democratic process. With more than a touch of hyperbole, McLevy also said that their actions smacked of fascism — the very thing the Socialist Party bitterly opposed. "You have violated every tradition and ideal of the Socialist movement," he wrote angrily.[24]

There was also some speculation that McLevy, representing the party's right-wing faction, was likely to challenge Thomas for the party's presidential nomination at the party's national convention in Cleveland later that spring.

"Communism has crept into the Socialist Party and we may have this situation — Jasper McLevy might be the right-wing's candidate for the presidency in 1936," said George Mara, a special assistant to U.S. Attorney General Homer S. Cummings. "That is

---

[23] "Mayor McLevy Will Head Right Wing Socialists," *Hartford Courant*, May 31, 1937.
[24] "Socialist Mayor Assails Thomas," *New York Times*, Jan. 10, 1936.

possible and very close to being probable."[25] McLevy's presidential candidacy, of course, never materialized.

In the meantime, everything came to a head during the party's September state convention in Hartford, an acrimonious meeting that nearly ended in fisticuffs before the party's left-wingers stalked out and — with written authorization from the party's National Executive Committee — held their own convention nearby in which they organized their own Socialist Party of Connecticut, drafted a platform, and nominated their own slate of candidates headed by journalist Devere Allen for governor.[26]

"We shall wage an energetic campaign to elect our state ticket, which is composed of candidates with experience in presenting the Socialist view of Connecticut affairs, and we shall push our national candidates, Norman Thomas for president and George A. Nelson for vice-president," said Allen in a prepared statement.[27]

"As for the disaffiliated former Socialist Party of Connecticut, which has now been disowned by the national organization," continued Allen, "we can cheerfully give credit to the McLevy administration in Bridgeport for honesty in government, but it has never followed a Socialist program and has repeatedly caused embarrassment by giving mere lip service to Socialist principles."[28]

Believing that his faction represented the national party, Allen, who had been the Socialist Party's nominee for the U.S. Senate in 1932 and 1934, wasted little time in trying to keep Mayor McLevy and the rest of the right-wing ticket, which included three incumbent Socialist state senators from Bridgeport, off the November ballot. While confident that his side would ultimately prevail, he promised to fight all the way to the Supreme Court, if necessary.[29]

"We shall not indulge in personalities," Allen declared, "but we are justified in pointing out that for the last three years, ever since their eyes became dazzled with political prestige, the leaders of the Old Guard in Connecticut have sabotaged the Socialist Party in the nation."[30]

Among other things, Allen accused McLevy of trying to convert the Socialist Party of Connecticut into his personal political machine, one that no longer advocated socialism, but merely

---

[25] "Socialist Mayor Viewed as Candidate for the Presidency," *Christian Science Monitor*, Mar. 4, 1936.
[26] "Socialist Party Split is Forced by McLevy at State Convention," *Hartford Courant*, Sep. 14, 1936.
[27] Ibid.
[28] Ibid.
[29] "Fight Opens for Socialist Ballot Place," *Hartford Courant*, Sep. 15, 1936.
[30] Ibid.

pushed "measures which have long been advocated and accomplished in other states by Republicans and Democrats." The final straw, said Allen, had been McLevy's support for a state sales tax, "a form of taxation universally recognized as bearing down most heavily upon the poorest section of the population."[31]

Declaring that the Socialist cause had survived greater rifts in the past and would survive the current "desertion and betrayal of those who have been suddenly elevated to public office and whose success has gone to their heads," Allen and the other left-wingers in Connecticut promised an energetic campaign that fall, one that included close cooperation with organized labor and the development of a Young People's Socialist League. They also promised a vigorous campaign on behalf of the party's national ticket of Norman Thomas and George A Nelson — a ticket the McLevy faction was unlikely go out of its way to promote.[32]

A bitter legal wrangle ensued as both sides vigorously argued that they should be recognized as the official Socialist Party in Connecticut and therefore entitled to the party's line on the November ballot. McLevy and Allen both met separately with the state attorney general and deputy secretary of state on September 16 to press their respective cases.

Allen argued that the old Socialist Party no longer existed because it had divorced itself from the national party at its Hartford convention a few days earlier and that his group should now be recognized as the official party in Connecticut. McLevy, on the other hand, was more than confident that the courts would rule in his favor. "I am waiting for a Connecticut court to say that a group of Connecticut citizens, whether they are Socialists, Republicans or Democrats, can't run their own affairs," he said.[33]

McLevy's faction was eventually awarded a place on the ballot by the Connecticut Superior Court on October 21 — nineteen days before the election — thereby leaving the left-wingers out in the cold. Hartford lawyer Harold Strauch, counsel for the Allen group, said it was too late to file an appeal, but left open the possibility that injunctive relief could be sought after the election to prevent the McLevy faction from using the Socialist Party name, which he claimed was the property of the Socialist Party of America, in future elections.[34] Needless to say, Allen's faction was disheartened

---

[31] Ibid.
[32] "Socialist Party Split is Forced by McLevy at State Convention," *Hartford Courant*, Sep. 14, 1936; "2 Socialist Tickets Filed in Connecticut," *New York Times*, Sep. 15, 1936.
[33] "McLevy, Allen Talk Separately With Officials," *Hartford Courant*, Sep. 17, 1936.
[34] "McLevy Side Wins Ballot Recognition," *Hartford Courant*, Oct. 21, 1936.

by the ruling.

Norman Thomas was also deeply disappointed by the ruling, believing that it was "harmful to a sound democracy" and a particularly perilous development for the Socialist Party.[35] Acknowledging that it was too late for further legal action, the former Presbyterian minister said that a sound democracy "requires that party names should mean something and that there should be party responsibility. If each state is a law to itself conceivably," he continued, "under peculiar circumstances, a state convention of any party might be captured by enemies of its generally accepted principles, who would then be entitled to its name. There would be no national standards and no national principles that could be enforced." The result, he said, would be confusion for the voters and further injury to the democratic process.[36]

In his statement, which reached Hartford on October 23 — two days after the court ruling — Thomas also took a swipe at McLevy, criticizing the Bridgeport mayor and his handful of Socialist allies in the legislature for supporting a state sales tax — a proposal that had been roundly condemned not only by the national party, but also by the Connecticut organization. "The true Socialist Party of Connecticut will carry on," he concluded.[37]

The two factions were naturally still at odds when McLevy launched his 1938 gubernatorial campaign — his seventh bid for the office. Adopting the slogan "Everybody wins with Jasper," the Socialist Party conducted one of the most vigorous campaigns in memory, scaring the living daylights out of leaders of both major parties.[38]

In addition to McLevy, the Socialists nominated a rather impressive statewide ticket, which included Wallingford's Martin F. Plunkett, president of the Jewelry Workers' Union, for lieutenant governor. A perennial Socialist candidate who had been indicted for violating the Espionage Act during World War I and later demanded Eugene Debs' release from federal prison, Plunkett was a longtime state chairman of the Socialist Party.[39]

Harry Schwartz, Bridgeport's city attorney who had long been active in the American Civil Liberties Union, was chosen for state attorney general. A key figure in McLevy's administration, the 38-

---

[35] "Conn. Ruling Seen Danger by Thomas," *Hartford Courant*, Oct. 23, 1936.
[36] Ibid.
[37] Ibid.
[38] "Party Slogan Adopted by Socialists of State," *Hartford Courant*, Oct. 20, 1938.
[39] "M'Levy is Nominated to Head State Ticket," *New York Times*, Aug. 28, 1938.

year-old Schwartz was responsible for drafting the city's merit system and its civil service laws. He also authored Connecticut's first housing law. David Mansell, an architect from Old Greenwich who later waged a spirited congressional campaign against Clare Boothe Luce — garnering 15,573 votes on the Socialist ticket against the wealthy socialite and a freshman Democratic lawmaker in 1942 — was nominated for state controller.[40]

McLevy's candidacy had deeply worried both major parties that fall, so much so that a "Stop McLevy" campaign had been launched by supporters of the Democratic and Republican candidates; the thought of Connecticut electing the first Socialist governor in American history was unthinkable — or worse — in their minds.

Receiving rousing receptions throughout the state, the mayor himself predicted an upset victory eight days before the election. Receiving rousing receptions throughout the state, the mayor himself predicted an upset victory eight days before the election.[41]

There was something noticeably different about the 1938 campaign, McLevy told a reporter during a meeting at the party's headquarters in Hartford in late October. He believed that a stunning victory at the polls, once thought impossible, was within his grasp. "In this campaign people are really taking their votes seriously, he said with only a touch of bravado. "It is for that reason I am confident of what the result will be. In the past few weeks," he continued, "I have made a tour of all parts of Connecticut. The surprisingly large attendance at all my rallies and the enthusiasm of people everywhere are greatly encouraging signs."[42]

Al Kamm, a Hartford Socialist who was managing the party's statewide campaign, concurred, saying that he had personally given out 23,000 McLevy campaign buttons in the city of Hartford alone. Acknowledging that some voters in McLevy's hometown would be sorry to lose him as mayor, Kamm said that most Bridgeport citizens viewed McLevy's candidacy for governor as a very positive development. "Bridgeport's loss," he said, "will be the whole state's gain."[43]

While McLevy barnstormed the state, Devere Allen and his left-wing allies conducted a vigorous petition drive to qualify their recently-formed Labor Party on the November ballot, obtaining

---

[40] Ibid.
[41] "The Jasper McLevy Factor," *Hartford Courant*, Oct. 29, 1938; "McLevy Sees Socialist Win Next Tuesday,"*Hartford Courant*, Nov. 1, 1938.
[42] Ibid.
[43] Ibid.

far more signatures than required — a development that heartened Norman Thomas and the party's NEC. "Connecticut and especially Connecticut labor needs one really independent party not flirting with old party machine politicians and dedicated alike to keeping America out of war and to work for the triumph of genuine democracy, political and economic," Thomas wired Allen.[44]

In addition to running Allen for governor, the Labor Party had slated, among others, Harold Strauch of Hartford for attorney general, Philip C. Brainard of Waterbury for the U.S. Senate, and Jack Bergen of Bridgeport — one of the five Socialists elected to the state legislature in 1934 — for the state's at-large seat in the U.S. House of Representatives.[45] Connecticut voters now had a smorgasbord of candidates from which to choose.

Though Allen was never a factor, the highly competitive gubernatorial campaign that autumn was further complicated when a week before the election Albert Levitt, an eccentric law professor from Redding, demanded a spot on the ballot for the Union Party. The Harvard-educated Levitt had some experience in third-party politics. Running under the aegis of an Independent Republican ticket, also known as the "dry Republicans," Levitt had teamed up with lawyer and Yale University professor Milton Conover in 1932 to prevent the election of "wet" Republicans in Connecticut. Conover ran for the U.S. Senate that year while Levitt campaigned for governor.[46]

A political mischief maker extraordinaire, Levitt convinced a Superior Court judge in the final days of the 1938 campaign that the Union Party was entitled to a place on the ballot based on its showing in 1936, thereby allowing the group which he now controlled and which no longer had any connection to Father Coughlin's original organization, to name Raymond E. Baldwin, the Republican candidate, as its own nominee for governor. It was a brilliant move. The 3,046 votes cast for Baldwin on the Union Party ticket made the difference in the race between Baldwin and Democratic incumbent Wilbur Cross — a race decided by a mere 2,688 votes.[47]

Levitt's shrewd legal maneuvering notwithstanding, the real story in that race was the spectacular 166,000-vote showing by McLevy against his two major-party rivals, a 26.3 percent share of

---

[44] "Devere Allen Says Labor Party Sure of Place on Ballot," *Hartford Courant*, Sep. 11, 1938.
[45] Ibid.
[46] Allen B. Lincoln, "The Independents," *Hartford Courant*, Oct. 28, 1932.
[47] "Union Party Victorious In Court Battle," *Hartford Courant*, Nov. 2, 1938; Curtiss S. Johnson, *Raymond E. Baldwin: Connecticut Statesman* (Chester, Connecticut, 1972), pp. 67-71; Wilbur L. Cross, *Connecticut Yankee: An Autobiography* (New Haven, 1943), p. 417.

the vote in which the Bridgeport mayor placed second in two of the state's eight counties, finishing slightly ahead of his Republican rival in Hartford County and defeating the incumbent Democratic governor in Fairfield County, which included McLevy's stronghold in Bridgeport.

Incredibly, McLevy also ran extremely well in a number of traditional Republican strongholds, including the town of Glastonbury, where the Republicans swept every other office while giving the Bridgeport Socialist a plurality.[48]

While McLevy led the entire ticket, each of the party's candidates for the state constitutional offices also exceeded six figures in the 1938 election, ranging from a high of 109,434 votes for Martin Plunkett for lieutenant governor (the governor and lt. governor were elected separately) to 102,785 votes cast for David Mansell in the state comptroller's race.

Moreover, the unusually-named Bellani Trombley, a political neophyte who later waged a somewhat disappointing campaign for mayor of Hartford, garnered an impressive 99,282 votes, or nearly 16%, as the party's candidate for the U.S. Senate and labor leader Arthur F. King of Norwich, a member of the Textile Workers' Union, polled an equally sensational 99,717 votes for Connecticut's at-large seat in the U.S. House of Representatives.

Charles H. McLevy, brother of Mayor McLevy and business agent for the carpenters' union, also put up quite a fight in the state's fourth congressional district — one of the most competitive House districts in the country. Many believed that McLevy's 35,328 votes, or 24.9 percent, enabled Clare Boothe Luce's stepfather Albert E. Austin, a physician and wealthy banker from Old Greenwich, to unseat freshman Democratic lawmaker Alfred N. Phillips, a former mayor of Stamford.

The party's most surprising result that year, however, occurred in Connecticut's first congressional district where Hartford's Edward C. Roffler polled an astounding 24,718 votes, or 15.7 percent, enabling Republican challenger William J. Miller, a legless World War I veteran, to narrowly unseat a three-term Democratic lawmaker.

Roffler's unexpected performance in that hotly-contested race was all the more stunning given the fact that he hadn't done a lick of campaigning and wasn't even aware that his name and those of several other local Socialist candidates had been added to the ballot until late on the Thursday before the election — literally less than

---

[48] "Town Goes To McLevy, Republicans," *Hartford Courant*, Nov. 9, 1938; "McLevy Gets 1228 Votes In Election," *Hartford Courant*, Nov. 9, 1938.

five days before voters went to the polls — when a Superior Court judge, deciding a case brought by the Union Party, ruled that the Socialist Party's initial filing should have been accepted without nominating petitions. "We forgot all about them," exclaimed a startled Al Kamm, the Hartford chairman who was managing McLevy's gubernatorial campaign. "We nominated them, filed their names with the secretary and the town clerk, and then when we were told they were ineligible because there were no petitions we just forgot about them."[49]

As expected, McLevy carried Bridgeport by a plurality of nearly 6,000 votes and finished ahead of the Democratic incumbent in Fairfield, Stratford and Trumbull, but lost badly in most of the fourth district's other communities.

Impressively, the Socialists captured four seats in the Connecticut legislature that year. Ex-Sen. Audubon Secor avenged his 1936 defeat by unseating the Democratic lawmaker who beat him in Bridgeport's 21st district and was joined in the State Senate by James Tait, who later served as Bridgeport police commissioner. Tait slaughtered his major-party opponents, piling up a 3,495-vote plurality against his closest rival in the 22nd state Senate district.

The Socialists also came close to winning a third Senate seat in Bridgeport's 23rd district where Louis Hafele, who later served several terms as president of the Bridgeport common council and as city clerk, lost a tightly contested three-cornered race to a Democrat by a heartbreakingly narrow margin of 116 votes.

While Sadie K. Griffin, Bridgeport's only female member of the Board of Aldermen — a post she held for fourteen consecutive years from 1935 to 1949 — and William S. Neil, both of whom won comfortably, were the only two Socialists elected to the assembly in 1938, the party nevertheless waged several highly competitive assembly races throughout the state.

Impressively, the four Socialist candidates for the legislature in Fairfield and Stratford outpolled their Democratic rivals while waging competitive campaigns. In Hartford, where a Socialist local had just been formed only a few months earlier, self-styled taxpayers' champion Elias Starquist of the city's Citizens, Taxpayers and Property Owners League and running mate Leon W. Parker polled 11,170 and 11,090 votes, respectively, on the Socialist ticket against their major-party rivals, one of whom included future Democratic governor and three-term U.S. Senator Abraham A. Ribicoff.[50]

---

[49] "Socialists Finally Get Ballot Places," *Hartford Courant*, Nov. 4, 1938.
[50] "Local to be Formed by Socialists," *Hartford Courant*, Aug. 20, 1938.

THE LOWEST EBB

In Waterbury, the two Socialist candidates for state representative garnered more than thirty percent of the vote and in Danbury, where policemen, firemen, teachers and other municipal workers went weeks without pay during the Great Depression, the party's assembly candidates grabbed a quarter of the vote against their Democratic and Republican rivals. It was a remarkable feat for Connecticut's third party.

Meanwhile, Devere Allen's short-lived Labor Party performed disastrously at the polls that autumn, with Allen finishing dead last with a pathetically miniscule 773 votes in the governor's race — some 6,500 votes behind the Socialist Labor Party's little-known Joseph Borden. The rest of the Labor Party ticket was demolished in similar fashion; one almost needed a magnifying glass to read their vote totals.

McLevy, who began quietly drifting away from the Social Democratic Federation in late 1938, ran for governor again in 1940 and 1942, polling 18,090 votes in the former contest and 34,537 in the latter. The Connecticut Socialists really took it on the chin in the former election, losing all four of their legislative seats — and losing them badly.

Waging his eighth consecutive gubernatorial campaign and his tenth bid for that office dating back to 1924, McLevy was pitted against Republican Gov. Raymond E. Baldwin, who was seeking a third nonconsecutive term, and Democrat Robert A. Hurley in the 1944 campaign. Hurley, the state's first Catholic governor, had unseated Baldwin in 1940 before losing a rematch in 1942 — a contest in which the Bridgeport mayor had polled the difference.

McLevy, who had been easily reelected to a sixth term as mayor the previous autumn, was joined on the Socialist ticket by running mate Harry L. Bowman, a frequent candidate for mayor of Norwich and the party's most prolific vote-getter in that city.

Waterbury's John W. Ring ran for Congressman At-Large, his fifth bid for a seat in the U.S. House. A machinist and toolmaker and longtime member of the International Association of Machinists, Ring had polled 15,369 votes, or 16.2 percent, as the party's candidate in the state's fifth congressional district in 1938 and was the party's nominee for mayor of Waterbury the following year.

Stanley W. Mayhew of Norwalk, vice president of the Connecticut Federation of Labor, was the party's nominee in the fourth congressional district. A bus driver and former resident of Bridgeport, Mayhew had been McLevy's running mate for lieutenant governor in 1942. Another of the party's many perennial candidates, Mayhew's 1944 candidacy was the first of six consecutive congressional campaigns waged by the longtime union activist.

The Socialists had always fiercely contested the fourth district seat in Fairfield County, which included the party's stronghold in Bridgeport. It was a predominantly blue-collar district thickly peppered with factories, manufacturing everything from military armaments to clothing, small tools, aluminum goods and electrical equipment. The Socialists had mounted several competitive campaigns in the district during the previous decade. In addition to Charles McLevy's impressive showing in 1938, Arnold E. Freese of Norwalk, state secretary of the party and brother of that city's future Socialist mayor, Irving Freese, polled an astounding 21,021 votes, or 17.1 percent, while running for the seat in 1934.

The battle for the district's seat in 1942 had been one of the most widely-watched congressional races in the country that autumn, featuring wealthy playwright Clare Boothe Luce, wife of *TIME*, *Life* and *Fortune* magazine founder and publisher Henry R. Luce, one of the leading establishment figures in the country. Considered one of the most powerful women of the twentieth century, Luce was hoping to unseat the district's Democratic incumbent that autumn.

Incredibly, Luce didn't declare her candidacy until August 31, barely ten days before her party's state convention in Bridgeport — a convention, coincidentally, in which she was slated as the keynote speaker. The 39-year-old foreign correspondent had been extremely coy about her intentions until it was absolutely certain that the Republican nomination was hers for the taking. In fact, at one point she actually dropped out of the contest, citing unfamiliarity with the district and its citizens.[51] Republican leaders nevertheless persuaded her to run and she officially received the party's blessing when five of her six opponents, including Westport industrialist Vivien Kellems, the celebrated critic of the federal income tax, withdrew from the race during the party's nominating convention.[52]

Kellems had become something of a lightning rod on the American Right a few years later when she boldly denounced the federal income tax as "a monstrous invasion of the rights of free people" and declared that she would no longer deduct the federal withholding tax from her employees' paychecks on the grounds that federal withholding was unconstitutional and had been sold

---

[51] "Mrs. Luce Decides She Will Seek Nomination as Congress Candidate," *New York Times*, Sept. 1, 1942; "Mrs. Clare Luce Named Keynoter for Republicans," *Hartford Courant*, Sept. 6, 1942.
[52] "Mrs. Luce Winner Over 6 Opponents," *New York Times*, Sept. 15, 1942.

to the American public as a wartime measure.⁵³

Kellems, who later became only the second woman to ever appear as a guest on NBC's "Meet the Press," had defiantly dared federal authorities to indict her as a way of testing the constitutionality of the federal tax collecting system. Refusing to indict her, the government seized the amount due from her bank account. Kellems then sued in federal court, demanding the funds be returned. When her case finally came to trial in 1951, the jury ordered the federal government to return the funds. The constitutionality of the withholding issue was never resolved.⁵⁴

In announcing her own candidacy for the fourth congressional district seat in August, the vivacious Kellems, who was one of the five candidates to eventually withdraw from the race, took a delicious dig at her wealthy socialite rival, saying that she didn't consider Luce a resident of the state. "It would be very difficult to conduct a political campaign in Connecticut from the ivory tower of the Waldorf-Astoria," she quipped.⁵⁵ Kellems later assailed her opponent as lacking any new or original thought and one whose nomination "would be a victory for those who wish to nullify our Constitution and substitute an evil internationalism for our true democracy."⁵⁶

The daughter of a small town Oregon minister, Kellems said that the United States was losing the war and that she was running for Congress "to help stem the tide and turn defeat to victory."

Kellems, whose manufacturing firm made cable grips invented by her brother and used in mounting guns on battleships and in supporting cables leading to gun turrets, said that she was tired of dealing with "the stone wall of bureaucracy, inefficiency, incompetence, and plain lunacy in Washington" in her efforts to help the nation's war effort. "Hundreds of our ships are torpedoed and sunk off our coast while for months I have been pleading in vain for material to make the tools for operating minesweeping equipment that would prevent many of these sinkings," she contended.⁵⁷

Kellems was regarded as Luce's strongest Republican opponent. In pulling out of the race a month later, shortly after the district's Republican leaders rallied behind her rival's candidacy, the

---

⁵³ Bill Kauffman, *Ain't My America: The Long, Noble History of Antiwar Conservatism and Middle-American Anti-Imperialism* (New York, 2008), pp. 185-186.
⁵⁴ Murray N. Rothbard, *For a New Liberty: The Libertarian Manifesto* (Auburn, AL, 2006), p. 105.
⁵⁵ "Opens Congress Race with Slap at Clare Boothe," *Chicago Tribune*, Aug. 18, 1942.
⁵⁶ "Miss Kellems Assails Opponent," *New York Times*, Sept. 13, 1942.
⁵⁷ "Opens Congress Race with Slap at Clare Boothe," *Chicago Tribune*, Aug. 18, 1942.

45-year-old Kellems could hardly contain her disappointment, saying that she realized the cards had been stacked against her from the outset. It also provided a glimpse into her feisty nature, a trait that would last a lifetime. "But the very weight and power of the forces opposing me presented a challenge which I could not resist," she admitted. "It is my first real experience in politics, and I have enjoyed it thoroughly and have learned a lot," she said, adding that she didn't intend to retire from politics.[58]

True to her word, the prominent Connecticut businesswoman and fiercely combative tax protestor waged several campaigns for the U.S. Senate during the following decade, twice seeking the Republican nomination and running as an independent or write-in candidate on three occasions, including polling 6,219 write-in votes against Prescott Bush in 1956.

The irrepressible industrialist also ambitiously set out to change Connecticut's election laws, hoping to get rid of the straight party lever, establishing a direct primary and reducing the number of petition signatures required of independent and third-party candidates. Kellems, who held a graduate degree in economics from the University of Oregon and started but never completed work toward a doctorate from Columbia University in 1921, also ran for governor of Connecticut and was nominated for the vice presidency against her wishes on the right-wing Constitution Party ticket headed by an equally reluctant Gen. Douglas MacArthur in 1952. In 1964, she co-chaired the Connecticut's Citizens Committee for Goldwater-Miller.[59]

Connecticut's fourth district was one of the most competitive congressional districts in the country. Over the previous twenty years the district had swung back and forth between the two major parties like a constantly swinging pendulum. Le Roy D. Downs, the Democratic incumbent in 1942, had narrowly defeated Luce's stepfather, the late Albert E. Austin, a physician and banker from Old Greenwich, to capture the seat two years earlier after Austin himself — polling less than 44 percent in a race in which the Socialist candidate garnered nearly a quarter of the vote — had unseated a freshman Democratic lawmaker in 1938.

In 1942, Luce was determined to reclaim her stepfather's seat in Congress for the GOP. It was clear from her keynote address to the Republican state convention in early September that the

---

[58] "Mrs. Luce Winner Over 6 Opponents," *New York Times*, Sept. 15, 1942.
[59] "Vivien Kellems Loses Suit to Gain Place on Ballot," *Hartford Courant*, Oct. 24, 1956; "Vivien Kellems Continues Fight on Election Laws," *Hartford Courant*, Nov. 9, 1956; "She'd Rather Fight Than Switch," *Hartford Courant*, Sept. 28, 1964.

wealthy socialite was going to make Roosevelt's yearlong "bungling and muddling" of the war, as she famously described it, the centerpiece of her congressional campaign.

Acknowledging that this was "the toughest war in history" — a phrase FDR himself had used — Luce lambasted the Democratic administration for talking tough, but acting far less aggressively. "The fact remains that while the administration and many of its appointees have talked a tough war, so far, unhappily, they have fought a soft one," she declared. "A soft war is an improperly conducted one. A soft war is a war in which the greatest shortage always turns out to be a shortage of victory." As such, the wealthy New Yorker promised the cheering delegates a "hard war but a happy peace."[60]

This, of course, was an old theme with the woman who once aspired to be an actress. During the 1940 presidential campaign, she had sharply criticized the President for not being tougher on Hitler, accusing Roosevelt even then of waging a "soft war." Every powerful leader in the world had a symbolic gesture, she said. Churchill had the "V" for victory sign, Hitler had his Nazi salute and Mussolini had his pompous strut. When asked about Roosevelt, Luce cleverly licked her finger and held it in the wind.[61]

Clare Boothe Luce's celebrity status made that year's congressional campaign one of the most widely-watched races in the country, creating an opportunity that the Socialist Party wasn't about to pass up. David Mansell, an architect and longtime Socialist from Old Greenwich, eagerly carried the party's banner against Congressman Downs and Clare Boothe Luce that autumn.

The 62-year-old Mansell received a boost late in the campaign when Ely Culbertson, one of the world's best known bridge players, publicly endorsed his candidacy. Culbertson, a prominent Democrat who had unsuccessfully sought his party's nomination for Connecticut's At-Large seat the U.S. House in 1940, urged voters in the fourth district to support Mansell's candidacy. Describing himself as a strong supporter of Roosevelt's policies, the famous and highly extravagant card player said that he was unable to support his own party's nominee because the freshman congressman "simply hasn't got what it takes to sit in the next Congress, which may decide the destiny of our country and of the world."[62]

---

[60] "Mrs. Luce, in Keynote Speech, Attacks Administration for Fighting 'Soft War,'" *Hartford Courant*, Sept. 11, 1942.
[61] Manchester, *The Glory and the Dream*, p. 227.
[62] "Culbertson Urges Votes for Socialist," *Hartford Courant*, Oct. 30, 1942.

Mansell wasn't the only outsider running against Congressman Downs and his celebrity challenger that fall. Lester P. Barlow, a world-renowned explosives inventor who had briefly sought the Republican nomination, qualified as an independent after submitting petitions bearing more than the 2,200 signatures.[63]

The longtime resident of Stamford had invented some of the first aerial bombs and torpedoes used in World War I, but the patents on his weapons were kept secret by the U.S. government and Barlow received no payment for his inventions until 1940 when Congress, after a lengthy court battle, finally awarded a payment of $529,719 for use of his destructively deadly inventions. It was estimated that the U.S. had dropped about 500,000 bombs designed by Barlow during the First World War.

Not without controversy, the ill-tempered inventor reportedly tried to interest American military officials in a secret superweapon he claimed could destroy cities 1,000 miles from its launching point, but when the U.S. expressed little interest in the weapon he reportedly traveled to Moscow and turned it over to Soviet officials in 1932 in return, he said, for a pledge that it would never be used except to force total disarmament of the world's military powers.[64] A man of ideas, in 1925 Barlow proposed the construction of a billion-dollar interstate highway system, similar to the one eventually developed in the 1950s.[65]

Politically, Barlow had been a strong supporter of Robert M. La Follette and briefly served as a lieutenant in Huey P. Long's Share-the-Wealth movement. A political gadfly of sorts, he frequently clashed with members of Congress and other government officials and once called for FDR's impeachment.[66] As president of the World War Veterans, Barlow tried desperately to stampede the Farmer-Labor Party's 1920 national convention in Chicago into nominating "Fighting Bob" for the presidency against his wishes, triggering a noisy, 45-minute demonstration on behalf of the Wisconsin progressive.[67] Barlow, who was then living in Minneapolis, received ten votes for the party's vice-presidential nomination at that convention.[68]

---

[63] "To Oppose Mrs. Luce," *New York Times*, Sept. 18, 1942.
[64] "Lester P. Barlow is Dead at 80; Built World War I Aerial Bomb," *New York Times*, Oct. 6, 1967.
[65] "Federal Highway Engineer's Dream," *Evening Independent* (St. Petersburg, Florida), Oct. 20, 1925.
[66] "Lester Barlow, Inventor of Aerial Bombs, Is Dead," *Cedar Rapids Gazette*, Sept. 6, 1967.
[67] "Salt Lake City Man Wins," *New York Times*, July 15, 1920.
[68] "Christensen and Hayes Head New Farmer-Labor Fusion Party Slate," *Fitchburg Daily Sentinel*, July 15, 1920.

Running on a "win-the-war" platform, the 55-year-old inventor — unlike the Socialist Party's Mansell — was never really a factor in the 1942 campaign, but made headlines across the country when he refused to shake hands with his witty and outspoken Republican rival during a candidates' forum in Stamford.[69]

In one of the most intensely-scrutinized congressional races in Connecticut history, Clare Boothe Luce, who had repeatedly accused President Roosevelt and the United States of waging a "soft war" — a charge she had been making long before Pearl Harbor — prevailed on Election Day, garnering 63,719 votes to 57,861 for Democrat Downs and Mansell's 15,573. Barlow, the controversial bomb-maker, finished last with a disappointingly skimpy 914 votes, or less than one percent of the total.

Mansell's 11.3 percent share of the vote in 1942 was the Socialist Party's strongest congressional showing in the country that autumn and marked the third time in the previous eight years that the Socialist nominee in that district had received a double-digit percentage against Democratic and Republican opposition.

Downs, the Democratic incumbent, attributed his defeat to the relatively large vote received by his Socialist opponent, including an astonishing 11,029 votes in the party's Bridgeport stronghold, on which Downs had heavily counted.[70]

Not surprisingly, the district's hotly-contested battle in 1944 was again one of the most widely-watched congressional races in the country. Even President Roosevelt was paying close attention.

Coupled with a bitterly-contested U.S. Senate race between Republican Sen. John A. Danaher and Democratic challenger Brien McMahon, a former federal prosecutor who accused the incumbent of being an isolationist and an obstructionist, Connecticut was braced for the largest voter turnout in the state's history.[71]

Hoping to reclaim the fourth congressional district seat, the Democrats enthusiastically nominated Margaret E. Connors, a young Bridgeport attorney, as Luce's challenger, thereby setting up one of the country's first U.S. House races where both major parties nominated female candidates. Luce, of course, had been one of only eight women to serve in the U.S. House of Representatives during the 78th Congress, so the Connors candidacy was something of a stroke of brilliance by the Democrats.

---

[69] "Barlow Declines to Shake Hands With Mrs. Luce, Crowd Walks Out," *Hartford Courant*, Oct. 27, 1942.

[70] "Mrs. Luce Wins Race for House; Pledges Work for 'Fighting War,'" *New York Times*, Nov. 4, 1942.

[71] "Record Vote May be Cast in Connecticut," *Naugatuck Daily News*, Nov. 7, 1944.

The 29-year-old Connors was an impressive candidate. Graduating cum laude from Wellesley College where she majored in history and government before earning a law degree from Yale, Connors specialized in workmen's compensation and civil liberties cases and had already won four cases before the State Supreme Court.

Connors was hardly a political novice, having run for a seat in the Connecticut general assembly in 1940 when she was still in law school. She lost that race narrowly, but was later appointed Deputy Secretary of State, becoming the first woman and, at age 25, the youngest person to hold that position. She was later elected chair of the Fairfield County Federation of Democratic Women's clubs.[72] While at Yale, Connors also worked briefly in the New Haven office of the Department of Justice, earning her a brief newspaper mention as "Connecticut's first G-woman."[73]

The dark-haired, blue-eyed Connors, a low-key and disarming woman who measured her words carefully, focused primarily on the issues of peace and postwar unemployment during her congressional campaign. "I'm particularly interested in the problem of employment. Everything else depends on it," she said shortly after winning the Democratic nomination by acclamation after the only other candidate, magazine writer Charles E. Calkins, withdrew from the race.

A self-described New Deal Democrat, Connors hammered away at joblessness throughout the campaign, promising a postwar economy that would provide abundance for all. "It's time we stopped talking of full employment as meaning 10,000,000 unemployed as in 1940. By full employment we should mean work for everybody who wants it."[74]

Rep. Luce, meanwhile, thought long and hard about seeking a second term in 1944. Coupled with a rift in the state's GOP leadership, Connors' endorsement by the powerful CIO — support that Luce had actively sought — was seen as a blow to the glamorous congresswoman's reelection hopes. Observers put her chances of winning a second term at no better than fifty-fifty. With organized labor lining up behind her Democratic rival, Luce briefly thought

---

[72] "Margaret Connors is Basing Fight With Clare Boothe Luce on Citizenship and Her Brains," *Southwest Times* (Pulaski, VA), Sep. 5, 1944.
[73] "Margaret Connors Will Oppose Mrs. Luce for Congress Seat," *Charleston Gazette*, Aug. 10, 1944.
[74] "Margaret Connors is Basing Fight With Clare Boothe Luce on Citizenship and Her Brains," *Southwest Times* (Pulaski, VA), Sep. 5, 1944; "Monroe Writer Would Run Against Mrs. Luce," *Hartford Courant*, July 7, 1944.

seriously about not running for a second term that fall, but eventually decided to give it a whirl.[75]

In accepting her party's nomination, Luce again lashed out at the Roosevelt administration. Coining a colorful new phrase — the "ramsquaddled do-gooding" New Deal bureaucrats — while assailing FDR as "a sort of super-duper highly cultured political boss," the freshman congresswoman accused Roosevelt of allowing 50,000 American Communists to infiltrate the Democratic Party.[76]

"Mr. Roosevelt knows this as well as you and I do," the celebrity lawmaker told the GOP's nominating convention in Greenwich, adding that the three-term Democratic president "seems content to accept their services whether they manifest themselves secretly in the CIO Political Action Committee, in branches of his government or at the polls." While refusing to mention her Democratic opponent by name, the sharp-tongued playwright and bitter Roosevelt critic also faulted the "weak and vacillating" Democratic Party for failing to plan for a postwar economy, saying it was "just as incapable of preventing a new depression as it was of curing the last one."[77]

The race between Luce and her Democratic challenger was a particularly nasty and bitterly-contested campaign with Connors mocking the Republican congresswoman for describing the GOP's Tom Dewey as "the inevitable man" to lead an ailing nation and cleverly lumping Luce in with such repugnant Republican figures as New York's Hamilton Fish, the *Chicago Tribune's* Robert McCormick, anti-Semitic writer Elizabeth Dilling, author of *The Red Network*, and the self-aggrandizing minister of hate Gerald L. K. Smith. She also faulted the freshman Republican lawmaker for a number of inconsistencies, contending that Luce's congressional voting record didn't match her rhetoric. She also sharply criticized the incumbent for suggesting that only in a Republican administration would U.S. soldiers "find the kind of world he has been fighting for," when Luce herself inexplicably failed to show up in March when the U.S. House was voting on legislation providing a federal soldiers' ballot for American troops overseas.[78]

---

[75] "Connecticut G.O.P. Row Hits Mrs. Luce's Election Chances," *Dunkirk Evening Observer*, July 31, 1944; "Clare Boothe Luce Seeks Reelection Expressing Confidence in Victory," *Hartford Courant*, Aug. 1, 1944.
[76] "Clare Boothe Hits New Deal's 'Ramsquaddled Do-Gooding,'" *El Paso Herald-Post*, Aug. 10, 1944.
[77] Ibid.
[78] "Democratic Rival Scores Clare Luce," *Hartford Courant*, Sep. 24, 1944; "Opponent Lashes at Clare Luce," *Hartford Courant*, Oct. 2, 1944.

The campaign had been contentious from the outset, with Connors accusing Luce of having accomplished little in Congress other than to oppose Roosevelt in an almost knee-jerk fashion. "Mrs. Luce is perfectly charming, lovely to look at, puts on a wonderful show — you can see the actress in every gesture — but I have long considered her a menace," said Connors upon winning the Democratic nomination in August.[79]

Connors also attacked her Republican rival for suggesting in a speech in Philadelphia — one of eight speeches Luce made on behalf of the Dewey campaign that fall — that there was "something sinister and harmful to the American people in the secrecy with which the Dumbarton Oaks conference has been conducted." Quoting widely-respected columnist Walter Lippmann, Connors compared the secrecy of Dumbarton Oaks to that which surrounded the Philadelphia convention which drafted the U.S. Constitution in 1787.[80]

Luce — a flippant, female Joe McCarthy in the making — responded in kind, accusing her Democratic opponent of speaking under the auspices of the Communist Party when she spoke at an event in Bridgeport sponsored by Sidney Hillman's Political Action Committee. Never at a loss for words, the freshman congresswoman also suggested that President Roosevelt "was a lame duck playing ringmaster as my opponent rode into the ring on a tired, decrepit Democratic donkey with a tin can marked 'Earl Browder' tied to its tail."[81]

Luce, whose name had been mentioned as a possible keynote speaker at the Republican national convention earlier that summer, hammered away at the Communist theme throughout the autumn campaign. "Communism, through Sidney Hillman," she asserted during a speech in Boston, "has bought, paid for and acquired the biggest single interest in a great American institution, the Democratic Party."[82]

The eyes of the nation, including those in the White House, were riveted on the fascinating and widely-watched race between Luce and Connors in Connecticut's fourth congressional district. Consequently, the Socialist Party's Stanley Mayhew barely received any attention at all. In an October 30th radio address — his only one of the campaign — Mayhew criticized both of his major-

---

[79] Sylvia Jukes Morris, *Price of Fame: The Honorable Clare Boothe Luce* (New York, 2014), p. 91.
[80] "Eight Talks for Dewey Planned by Mrs. Luce," *Hartford Courant*, Sep. 26, 1944; "Democratic Rival Raps Speech by Clare Luce," *Hartford Courant*, Oct. 1, 1944.
[81] "Feminine Candidates Trade Digs," *Hartford Courant*, Oct. 10, 1944.
[82] "Democratic Party Bought by Reds, Clare Luce Avers," *Hartford Courant*, Oct. 22, 1944.

party opponents, saying that both women seemed to be conducting a personal feud rather than a political campaign.[83]

"I have been watching the very elaborate and very expensive campaigns of my two lady opponents, and they leave me, as they probably leave you, amused and somewhat bewildered," lamented Mayhew. Insisting that he had no personal animosity toward either of his opponents, the little-known and underfunded Norwalk bus driver nevertheless voiced some strong feelings about the political parties they represented. Declaring there wasn't the slightest difference between either major party, Mayhew said that both old parties "support a decaying system that will always create poverty and depressions, and more and more unemployment and distress."[84]

In his radio broadcast, the longshot Socialist candidate also took a swipe at both of his rivals, suggesting that Clare Boothe Luce wasn't really a resident of the state and that "both she and Connecticut would be happier if she returned to Broadway, and went back to writing shows." His Democratic opponent, he continued, wasn't much better. According to Mayhew, Connors was a product of the notoriously corrupt Hague, Flynn and Kelly machines. "I have no use for that kind of setup," he asserted.[85]

"I think we have had enough of playwrights, and lawyers and professional politicians in Congress," concluded Mayhew. "Most Connecticut voters are either workers or families of workers or small business and professional people who depend on the prosperity of the workers." Stressing his involvement in organized labor, particularly his role as vice president of the Connecticut Federation of Labor, Mayhew said that it was "high time that a worker who knows and sympathizes with the problems of the working people should represent this district in Congress."[86]

In the meantime, Connors predicted that she would defeat Luce "by around 5,000 votes." Speaking at a press conference at the Democratic national headquarters in New York, Connors based her prediction, in part, on last-minute appearances in the district by Vice President Henry A. Wallace, who was scheduled to speak in Bridgeport on Nov. 2nd, and a planned whistle-stop visit by FDR on the final weekend of the campaign. She also based her prognostication on the belief that Luce was woefully out of

---

[83] "Rival Women 'Bewildering' to Socialist," *Hartford Courant*, Oct. 31, 1944.
[84] Ibid.
[85] Ibid.
[86] Ibid.

touch with voters in the district, particularly female voters.[87]

"The principal issue in the industrial section of Fairfield County is that of jobs," said Connors. "Mrs. Luce had advocated that when the war is ended women should leave their jobs and go back to their homes. This, I believe, is a great mistake. The government, by subsidies and other means, should make available jobs to everyone who desires to work." During her press conference, she also sharply criticized the incumbent for refusing to debate the issues.[88]

As expected, Connors received a huge boost in the final days of the campaign when President Roosevelt's train briefly stopped in Bridgeport, the first stop on a four-city tour of New England on Saturday, November 4th. Accompanied by John G. Winant, the U.S. Ambassador to Great Britain, and movie and radio producer Orson Welles, FDR told a cheering crowd at the Bridgeport train station that he looked forward to a White House visit from Margaret Connors as a newly-elected member of Congress.[89]

Roosevelt, of course, would have liked nothing better than to see Luce, one of his most outspoken congressional critics, defeated by her young Democratic challenger. In fact, he expected it to happen. "My friend (Margaret Connors) seems to be winning," an elated Roosevelt told supporters in Hyde Park early in the evening on election night. Nothing would have given him greater pleasure than to see the Republican congresswoman go down to defeat, he told the jubilant crowd. "That would prove a mighty good thing for the country," he said, adding almost apologetically that his comment was a pretty "rough thing to say about a lady."[90]

Though the race had been neck-and-neck for several hours, Luce eventually overtook her Democratic challenger, escaping with a razor-thin victory, polling 102,043 votes to 100,035 for Connors. Socialist Stanley Mahew, polling slightly more than the difference between his major-party rivals, garnered a somewhat paltry 2,448 votes, or 1.2 percent of the total votes cast.

In the meantime, Jasper McLevy waged a vigorous campaign in the governor's race. Perhaps proudest of the fact that his scandal-free Socialist administration in Bridgeport had implemented a civil service and merit system for municipal employees during his first term as mayor, McLevy sought to expand civil service reform

---

[87] "Margaret Connors Predicts Victory By 5000 Margin," *Hartford Courant*, Nov. 1, 1944.
[88] Ibid.
[89] "Fourth Term Bid to New England States," *Atchison Daily Globe*, Nov. 4, 1944.
[90] "Looks Like Another Four Years, FDR Tells Friends," *Benton Harbor News-Palladium*, Nov. 8, 1944.

to the state level. Instead of relying on a patronage system influenced by "the rise and fall of political tides," the Bridgeport mayor, as in his previous bids for the governor's office, told voters that a successful civil service system was the only scientific way to guarantee efficiency, integrity and good government since every public employee, regardless of their position, would be "relieved of the concern of party obligation and can devote themselves wholly to doing a good job."[91]

In early October, McLevy found himself attacked in the pages of the widely-read *In Fact* newsletter, a weekly publication edited by longtime investigative journalist and press critic George Seldes, a crusty left-winger whose self-published *Facts and Fascism*, a 286-page classic exposing corporate media fascism in the United States in the period prior to and during the early months of World War II, had been released in 1943.[92]

The October 2 issue of Seldes' newsletter accused the Bridgeport mayor of being "a splitting and disruptive candidate" who was acting in collusion with Republican Rep. Clare Boothe Luce and ex-GOP national committeeman Samuel F. Pryor, Jr., in an effort to help swing Connecticut into the GOP column.[93]

It was a charge echoed by many of Luce's opponents that autumn, including the CIO's powerful Hillman-led Political Action Committee, which was conducting a massive voter registration drive in Connecticut in an attempt to oust Rep. Luce from Congress while bolstering FDR's prospects in that important battleground state, a state that Roosevelt failed to carry in 1932 and in which he defeated Willkie by only 56,000 votes in 1940. Luce's critics — the widely-read Seldes being the principal prevaricator — charged that McLevy had entered into some sort of backroom deal with the Republican congresswoman by nominating Stanley Mayhew for Congress specifically to siphon votes away from Democratic challenger Margaret Connors in what was expected to be a nip-and-tuck contest.[94] Given the fact that the Socialists always fielded a candidate in that district, it was ludicrous charge on its face.

According to McLevy, huge quantities of Seldes' *In Fact* newsletter had been placed in factories and office buildings throughout

---

[91] Bucki, *Bridgeport's Socialist New Deal, 1915-1936*, pp. 169, 184-185; "McLevy Asks Spread of Civil Service," *Hartford Courant*, Sep. 28, 1944.
[92] "McLevy Hits at Criticism in Pamphlet," *Hartford Courant*, Oct. 8, 1944.
[93] Ibid.
[94] "Labor Vote Holds Key in Connecticut," *New York Times*, Oct. 10, 1944.

the state in an attempt to discredit his candidacy. He was understandably furious, saying the article was filled with "filthy, deliberate lies."[95]

In response to the article's allegation that he had met privately with Rep. Luce at a State Street tavern, McLevy responded scornfully, asserting that the newsletter's smear was "so nasty and foul as to be ridiculous." and for a thousand reasons. "Can anyone in his right mind picture the swanky Mrs. Luce and Jasper McLevy, the tea drinking roofer, strolling arm in arm into a tavern?

The fact is that I have only spoken to Mrs. Luce once or twice in my whole life," continued McLevy, "and then only to exchange greetings on a public platform when we happened to be guests at the same public occasion." He also strenuously denied ever having a political conversation, directly or indirectly, with either Luce or Republican national committeeman Pryor.[96]

"This sheet attacks me and abuses me and lies about me simply because an increasing number of Connecticut voters have dared to vote for me for public office and because the Socialist Party has dared, under our American system, to nominate candidates to oppose Republican candidates and, what seems to annoy them most, to oppose Democratic candidates," said the indignant mayor. "No Fascist wolf masquerading in sheep's clothing as a 'Liberal' is going to kick that soap box out from under my feet without one hell of a fight."[97]

While fending off the false and nasty attacks of those who charged that he was involved in some sort of deal with Rep. Luce, McLevy also had to contend with a challenge on his left flank from the Socialist Labor Party's Joseph C. Borden of Darien. Usually just a minor nuisance, the SLP — arguably waging the most determined national campaign in the party's history — made a particularly spirited effort in Connecticut that fall, nominating a nearly full statewide ticket on a platform calling on the working-class to reject legislation promoting mandatory national service and permanent militarism in the United States and "to organize politically and industrially to put an end to capitalism and to establish the socialistic commonwealth of labor."[98]

Borden campaigned vigorously that fall, asserting throughout the campaign that the real issue in 1944 was socialism vs. capitalism. Lumping McLevy in with his major-party rivals, the Darien

---

[95] "McLevy Hits at Criticism in Pamphlet," *Hartford Courant*, Oct. 8, 1944..
[96] Ibid.
[97] Ibid.
[98] "Socialist Labor Party Chooses State Ticket," *Hartford Courant*, May 8, 1944.

resident charged that all three of his opponents were supporting a system that breeds poverty and war in the midst of plenty. "In this campaign, as in all campaigns since 1892, it is the Socialist Labor Party against the field," declared Borden.[99]

Like his hardy band of comrades, the little-known Socialist Labor candidate had long argued that the Socialist Party — "left wing, right wing and drumsticks" — was not a genuine party of socialism and that McLevy himself had "remained ominously silent on Marxism and social revolution since taking office in Bridgeport" eleven years earlier. The Socialist Party, he contended, never understood that socialism couldn't be established without the working class seizing control of industry — something that Thomas and McLevy never advocated.[100]

Augmenting Borden's efforts there, Edward A. Teichert and Arla Albaugh both campaigned vigorously in Connecticut. Teichert, the party's presidential candidate, spent four full days in the state — two of them in McLevy's Bridgeport stronghold — in late October. He also made a passionate and informative 15-minute statewide radio broadcast on Saturday, October 28, at the conclusion of his four-day campaign swing.[101]

McLevy, who barnstormed the state almost to the point of exhaustion, speaking throughout the state while shaking every hand in sight, wrapped up his tenth campaign for governor by calling for a postwar plan of international cooperation that would raise the living standards of other nations and prevent another major depression. The Socialist Party, he said in a speech in Waterbury in early November, was the only party offering a plan for peace designed to raise the standard of living in other countries. "Only in that way," he explained, "can the danger of competition which caused the last depression, and is likely to cause the next, be removed. Only in that way can danger of future wars be prevented."[102]

International cooperation with poorer nations, said McLevy, was also vital in preventing another economic downturn. Only by assisting those countries in establishing democratic governments and fostering the development and growth of labor unions to assure that their workers received wages comparable to those in the United States, could the United States guarantee that citizens in

---
[99] "'Build Better World Now,' Borden Tells Conn. Voters," *Weekly People*, Vol. LIV, No. 32, Nov. 4, 1944.
[100] Joseph Borden, "Only One Party of Socialism," *Weekly People*, Vol. XLVI, No. 28, Oct. 10, 1936.
[101] "Socialist Labor Heads to Tour Connecticut," *Hartford Courant*, Oct. 23, 1944.
[102] "McLevy Asks for Peace to Prevent Depression," *Hartford Courant*, Nov. 3, 1944.

those nations would have the purchasing power to buy American products, he said. If the U.S. was not able to sell its manufactured goods to them, he concluded, the U.S. and global economy would experience a depression similar to the one that it had painfully endured during the thirties — if not worse.[103]

The Bridgeport mayor waged a valiant campaign that autumn, but failed to poll the difference between his major-party rivals — something he had spectacularly managed to do in five of his previous nine gubernatorial campaigns, including both of the fiercely competitive contests between Baldwin and Hurley in 1940 and 1942.

Amassing nearly half of his support in his native Fairfield County, McLevy polled 16,475 votes to Gov. Baldwin's 418,289 and former governor Hurley's 392,417. Despite making a vigorous effort, the Socialist Labor Party's Borden garnered a relatively insignificant 1,398 votes. In retaining the governorship, Baldwin ran about 28,000 votes ahead of his party's presidential ticket while McLevy, who always ran well ahead of his party's ticket, more than tripled Norman Thomas's showing in the state.

---

[103] Ibid.

Chapter XIII

A New Party with Big Dreams

Not only did Norman Thomas and the Socialists have to compete with Sidney Hillman's left-wing American Labor Party in the party's one-time stronghold in New York, long the center of the Socialist Party's universe, but they now also had to contend with the newly-formed Liberal Party, a hastily-created entity organized in the spring of 1944 in opposition to Hillman and the ALP's increasingly leftward drift.

A brilliant and inventive political tactician who once studied to be a rabbi and later worked his way up as an immigrant clothing worker in New York's garment district to become one of organized labor's most powerful — and pilloried — leaders, Hillman had led thousands of rank-and-file Socialist Party members into the Roosevelt camp in 1936 through the newly-formed ALP, a halfway house of sorts between the Democratic and Socialist parties.

Largely viewed as a refuge for those New Yorkers who couldn't bring themselves to support a Tammany ticket, it came as little surprise when the Hillman-led American Labor Party, which had delivered nearly 275,000 votes to Roosevelt in 1936 and more than 417,000 votes in 1940, including 317,000 in New York City alone — assuring the Democratic president the state's forty-seven electoral votes against Wendell Willkie in the latter campaign — enthusiastically endorsed FDR for a fourth term earlier that spring, more than ten weeks before he was formally re-nominated at the Democratic national convention in Chicago.[1]

---

[1] "Roosevelt Draft Advocated by ALP," *New York Times*, May 7, 1944.

At that very moment, however, a deeply bitter struggle for control of the ALP was taking place, pitting the influential Hillman, a former Socialist, and the party's left-wing elements against a moderate or right-wing faction led by another former Socialist, David Dubinsky, the anti-Communist president of the International Ladies' Garment Workers Union (ILGWU), eventually leading to the formation of the Liberal Party of New York — and yet another third-party presidential nomination for Roosevelt in the country's most populous state.

Like Hillman, Dubinsky had also been instrumental in furnishing FDR with a massive base of support on the American Labor ticket in 1936 and 1940, especially among the city's robust needle trades. Like his adversary, Dubinsky — an idealist with his feet planted firmly on the ground — had also enthusiastically come out in favor of a fourth term for Roosevelt, calling for his reelection and a post-war reconstruction program which would provide full employment during a convention of the ILGWU in Boston earlier that spring.[2]

Although the American Labor Party had been founded eight years earlier by anti-Communists and pro-New Dealers, Dubinsky and other party moderates had grown deeply alarmed by the fact that thousands of Communists in New York City began enrolling in the party shortly after the Communist Party lost its official recognition as a ballot-qualified party when political cartoonist and radical journalist Robert Minor, the Communist Party's candidate for governor, failed to garner 50,000 votes in the state's 1936 gubernatorial election.[3]

Prior to then, members of the Communist Party had been officially excluded from the ALP, but according to critics had quietly infiltrated the left-wing party under Hillman's sympathetic watch. By 1938, the Communists controlled the ALP in Manhattan and within five years gained control of the party's machinery in most of the city's other county organizations while threatening the moderates' increasingly fragile hold on the Bronx.[4]

In an effort to unify the American Labor Party for the crucial 1944 presidential campaign, Hillman had proposed as early as August 1943 that every trade union — primarily the left-wing unions affiliated with the powerful CIO — be entitled to representation in

---

[2] "Keep Roosevelt In, Dubinsky Pleads," *New York Times*, May 30, 1944.
[3] "Communists Lose Status as Party," *New York Times*, Nov. 5, 1936. Finishing a distant fourth in that race behind the Socialist Party's Harry W. Laidler, Minor garnered 35,609 votes in the 1936 gubernatorial campaign.
[4] Joseph F. Zimmerman, *The Government and Politics of New York State* (Albany, N.Y., 2008), p. 60.

the party's leadership, based on their dues-paying membership. Hillman's proposal also provided adequate provisions for representation on the party's controlling body by progressives who supported the party, but weren't specifically affiliated with any trade unions.[5]

Dubinsky, who had risen to power in the ILGWU following an intensely bitter battle with Communists in the late 1920's, was in no mood to now cooperate with them in the American Labor Party. He was convinced, rightly or wrongly, that Hillman's plan for the ALP could have no other effect than to deliver the entire party over to the Communists.[6]

Interestingly, as many as thirty unions affiliated with the CIO, whose increasingly influential Political Action Committee was headed nationally by Hillman himself, agreed with the party's right-wingers and urged the founder of the Amalgamated Clothing Workers to abandon "the campaign he is waging for the election of Communist candidates" to the American Labor Party's state committee. Declaring that they would fight every attempt by the Communists or any other totalitarian elements to capture the party, the CIO officials warned that turning over any aspect of the party's administration to the Communists was wrong in principle and politically dangerous.[7]

Hillman responded in kind, arguing that his "unity" plan safeguarded the party against control "by Communists, Socialists, or any other group" and firmly maintained that he would continue to strengthen and unify the party with or without their help. It was his intention, he said, "to build the broadest, strongest and most democratic possible ALP, a party which will register its maximum effectiveness on the side of peace and progress in the elections of 1944."[8]

Hillman's proposal, which was soundly rejected by the party's leadership twice in a span of eight days, set the stage for a hostile confrontation between the party's increasingly potent left-wing and Dubinsky's moderate forces.

In formally rejecting Hillman's plan on January 12, the party's moderate or right-wing forces, who still maintained a tenuous hold on the party's state executive committee, denounced it as "illegal, undemocratic and immoral," arguing that its adoption

---

[5] "ALP Heads Reject Hillman Proposal," *New York Times*, Jan. 21, 1944.
[6] David Dubinsky and A. H. Raskin, *David Dubinsky: A Life with Labor* (New York, 1977), p. 272.
[7] "30 CIO Officials Criticize Hillman," *New York Times*, Feb. 10, 1944.
[8] Ibid.

would transform the ALP into a narrow trade union party under the exclusive control of the state CIO with the Communist-controlled CIO in New York City playing a disproportionate role in the party's leadership. Such an outcome, said worried party leaders, would destroy the ALP's effectiveness in the 1944 presidential election while generally harming the labor movement.[9]

Holding out hope that his proposal would eventually gain acceptance, Hillman dismissed the allegation that he was entering into a united front with the Communists as utter "nonsense" and "silly." If anything, he said during an interview at the Amalgamated headquarters shortly after being rebuffed by the executive committee, his proposal would lessen the likelihood of Communist control by broadening the party's base.[10]

If his plan failed to win the approval of the party's executive committee, Hillman made it clear that the CIO and other unions aligned with it were prepared to duke it out in the primary, adding that a committee headed by Harry Chapman of the Brotherhood of Railway Clerks, an AFL affiliate, had already been formed to direct the CIO's primary campaign.[11]

Hillman continued to press his unity proposal during a second meeting of the party's executive committee on January 20, only to be rebuffed again. The second conference, held at the invitation of CIO leaders, was a virtual replay of the earlier meeting, with the party's right-wing leadership refusing to budge on an issue they viewed as vital not only to the party's credibility, but also its long-term viability as a liberal and progressive force in New York politics.[12]

A minority on the committee, however, sided with Hillman. These included New York CIO chairman Louis Hollander, R. J. Thomas, president of the United Auto Workers, then an affiliate of the CIO, Emil Rieve, president of the Textile Workers Union, and Harry Chapman of the Railway Clerks, who was heading the CIO's campaign to dislodge the right-wingers in the March 28 primary.[13]

Though it appeared to the public as an abrupt schism in the party's ranks, the bitterly-contested primary that followed was actually the culmination of four years of factional disputes within the party — a contest in which the moderates, led by Dubinsky and

---

[9] "Right Wing of ALP Rebuffs Hillman," *New York Times*, Jan. 13, 1944.
[10] Ibid.
[11] Ibid.
[12] "ALP Heads Reject Hillman Proposal," *New York Times*, Jan. 21, 1944.
[13] Ibid.

ALP co-founder Alex Rose of the Millinery Workers, were clearly the underdogs and in immediate danger of losing control of the party.

The acrimonious and irreconcilable showdown that ensued even caused alarm in the White House. Deeply concerned that the internecine warfare in the party whose founding he had strongly encouraged eight years earlier might become a source of considerable embarrassment, President Roosevelt, hoping to prevent an all-out war among his supporters, conferred privately with Hillman and Dubinsky in separate meetings at the White House. If FDR had hoped to be a peacemaker he sure had an unusual way of showing it as both men emerged from their secret meetings with the President convinced that he was on their side.[14]

Meanwhile, the rival Socialist and Socialist Labor parties watched the ALP slugfest with keen interest. In a front-page article in the *Weekly People*, the SLP explained that the slugfest taking place in the American Labor Party had nothing to do with opposition to Roosevelt's intention to seek a fourth term or the president's stated determination to save capitalism through reforms. That had long been conceded by everyone involved — Hillman and his Stalinist allies, Dubinsky and his trade union allies, as well as the party's so-called "Socialist" politicians — argued the De Leonists. "The struggle is a power struggle for the control of the bargaining machine known as the American Labor party." In the end, it made little different which faction prevailed, declared the SLP, since "the workers corralled would be strongly influenced (in many cases, decisively influenced) to support capitalist politicians and capitalism itself."[15]

The Socialists echoed a similar view, saying that the American Labor Party had long since failed as a viable vehicle for independent labor action. "The experiment in independent labor political action," wrote Samuel H. Friedman, chairman of the party in New York City, "failed from the start — from the moment that ALP leaders adopted the policy of supporting Republican and Democratic candidates, and later admitting Communists and fellow travelers to their ranks." It was a recipe for disaster.[16]

"The joker in the whole deal," concluded Friedman, was that, except for the charges of alleged Communist control and a personal feud between Dubinsky and Hillman, the issues involved in

---

[14] Dubinsky and Raskin, *David Dubinsky*, pp. 274-275.
[15] "Which Faction Will Run Rulers' ALP?" *Weekly People*, Vol. LIII, No. 49, Mar. 4, 1944.
[16] "It's Time for Genuine Experiment in Independent Labor Political Action!," *Socialist Call*, Apr. 7, 1944.

the ALP split weren't really about anything of substance. "Both sides," he wrote, had "vowed eternal loyalty to President Roosevelt, despite his increasingly anti-labor record, his appeasement of the 'economic royalists' he had formerly flayed (at least verbally), and his proposal for a national slave act for the conscription and crucifixion of labor."[17]

Rejecting Mayor La Guardia's last-minute attempt to play the role of peacemaker, the party's right-wing forces refused to go down without a fight. On the eve of the primary election, Dubinsky's forces took out full-page advertisements in the city's leading newspapers denouncing Hillman as a "collaborator" of the Communists — a charge that had little effect in a wartime environment in which world leaders such as Roosevelt and Churchill were seen actively "collaborating" with Communists in the Soviet Union to defeat Hitler's armies. In retrospect, as Hillman biographer Matthew Josephson observed, it seemed politically foolish "to 'wave the bloody shirt' of old left-right quarrels."[18]

Determined to maintain his hold on the party, Hillman, speaking from his heart, told a crowd of 5,000 at the Manhattan Center how deeply disappointed he was that his opponents had resorted to using "Red smear" tactics to gain control of the party.[19]

In the end, the party's right-wing forces were no match for Hillman's superior organizing skills. With Mayor La Guardia more or less remaining neutral and ALP congressman Vito Marcantonio, "chief spear carrier for the pro-Communist faction in Manhattan" lining up behind the Hillman faction's "fake facade of labor unity," as Dubinsky bitterly described it, the left-wingers prevailed in the primary, running much stronger than expected in upstate New York while capturing between 550 to 600 of the party's 750 state committee seats. Approximately 87,000 ALP members participated in the hotly-contested primary.

The overwhelming victory by the radicals paved the way for Hillman, head of the CIO's powerful Political Action Committee — the nation's first political action committee — to replace sociologist George S. Counts, a Columbia University professor aligned with Dubinsky's faction, as the party's new state chairman. The overwhelming victory by the leftists was so complete that the right-wingers even failed to carry their traditional stronghold in

---

[17] Ibid.
[18] Matthew Josephson, *Sidney Hillman: Statesman of American Labor* (Garden City, N.Y., 1952), p. 606.
[19] Ibid.

the Bronx, losing in each of its eight assembly districts.[20]

Viewing the primary as a last-ditch effort to prevent the American Labor Party from falling under Communist domination, the party's moderates were proud of the battle they waged in the March 28 primary — and were braced for the eventual outcome.

"We have no regrets," asserted Rose and Counts in a joint election-night statement. "We fought a good fight for great principles. The Browder-Hillman coalition won the primaries. The Communists who controlled Manhattan, Brooklyn and Queens have now extended their control to the whole party." From that moment on, they said despairingly, the ALP would be controlled by Communist Party leader Earl Browder, regardless of whom the party decided to put up as its fronts.[21]

While spurning offers of conciliation, Dubinsky also took the defeat in stride. "We were not heartbroken," he recalled in his 1977 autobiography co-authored by longtime *New York Times* labor correspondent A. H. Raskin, "because the important thing in our view was to be rid of them. We didn't want to stay in the same party with them and provide a front." Dubinsky actually sounded relieved by the way things turned out. "Even if we had prevailed in the primary," he elaborated, "that would not have been the end of it. They would have used their power in the county organizations to disrupt the party until they succeeded in either dominating or destroying it."[22]

The longtime labor leader was nevertheless disappointed by Mayor La Guardia's failure to come out in opposition to the Hillman forces. "The mayor helped," he said sarcastically. "He cost us at least 5,000 votes."[23]

From the beginning of the crisis that eventually split the party in two, the party's moderates had been worried that Hillman's attempt to force them into an alliance with the Communists would isolate the party, demoralize the party's non-Communist membership and render the ALP completely ineffective as a political force in New York politics.

Alex Rose, believed by many to be one of the nation's shrewdest political strategists, had been particularly critical of Hillman, ar-

---

[20] Dubinsky and Raskin, *David Dubinsky*, pp. 275-276; "Leftists Win ALP Control in State Vote," *New York Times*, March 29, 1944; "Hillman is Elected State Head of ALP," *New York Times*, April 9, 1944.
[21] "Leftists Win ALP Control in State Vote," *New York Times*, March 29, 1944; "Concede Reds Take Control of NY's ALP," *Chicago Tribune*, March 29, 1944.
[22] Dubinsky and Raskin, *David Dubinsky*, p. 276.
[23] "Concede Reds Take Control of NY's ALP," *Chicago Tribune*, March 29, 1944.

guing that his proposal to develop a party superstructure comprised of trade union leaders, including Communists and other left-wingers, with full control of party policy, was nothing short of advocating a merger with the Communist Party.

"For five years," Rose said in a joint statement with Counts earlier that year, "Communists fought to make the American Labor Party their political home. They made no bones about." By joining a united front with them, they charged, Hillman was now actively "assisting them in their efforts to achieve their objective."[24]

"The American people will never have confidence in the American Communists, who betrayed the interests of American democracy during the tragic days of 1940 and 1941," asserted Rose, "nor in anyone who associates with them in any political enterprise." Manhattan lawyer Dean Alfange, the ALP's candidate for governor in 1942 who favored a fourth term for the President, echoed Rose's sentiments, ominously warning that the Hillman-Communist alliance would be "the kiss of death for President Roosevelt."[25]

Hillman, who calmly reproached the party's right-wingers for using what he described as "Red smear" tactics during the bitter primary campaign, officially took over the reins of the American Labor Party on April 8 during a meeting of the party's new state committee — a meeting, incidentally, that was boycotted by most of the party's right-wing faction.[26]

Having already sent up several trial balloons in favor of a fourth term while declaring that the CIO would enthusiastically support the wartime president if he ran again, Hillman made it clear upon assuming the chairmanship that Roosevelt's re-election was the party's highest priority, telling the party's new state committee that uniting the country's labor and progressive forces was essential to making that happen.[27]

In the meantime, Rose, Counts and Alfange took the lead in establishing the Liberal Party, an influential fixture in New York politics from 1944 until it lost its permanent ballot status fifty-eight years later.

The 46-year-old Alfange served as the group's spokesman. Born in Istanbul to Greek parents and raised in Utica, New York, Alfange was a great admirer of Roosevelt and had chaired the

---

[24] "ALP Heads Renew Fight on Hillman," *New York Times*, Feb. 3, 1944.
[25] "Labor Right Wing Plans State Fight," *New York Times*, Jan. 15, 1944.
[26] "Hillman is Elected State Head of ALP," *New York Times*, April 9, 1944.
[27] Ibid,; Melvyn Dubofsky and Warren R. Van Tine, eds., *Labor Leaders in America* (Champaign, IL, 1987), p. 228; Josephson, *Sidney Hillman*, pp. 598, 606.

Democratic Party's foreign-language speakers' bureau during FDR's bid for a third term in 1940. Deeply committed to Roosevelt's fourth term, Alfange also served as vice-chairman of the Emergency Committee to Save the Jewish People of Europe during World War II, testifying before the House Foreign Affairs Committee and frequently calling for aid to the Jews against the Nazis. He was also one of the first to voice opposition to U.S. military involvement in Vietnam, criticizing American military aid to the French government in Indochina as early as 1954.

Within a week of the March 28 primary, the three men met behind closed doors with approximately 400 liberal and labor leaders at New York's Park Central Hotel to discuss the formation of a new party.[28]

A few weeks later, Alfange, who chaired the nascent party's Labor and Liberal Committee, announced the formation of a platform and program committee headed by Columbia University professor John L. Childs and laid plans for a statewide convention to be held in New York City later that spring.

Interestingly, half of the party's three dozen-member organizing committee, which included such well-known figures as George S. Counts, former state chair of the American Labor Party, A. Philip Randolph, president of the Brotherhood of Sleeping Car Porters, Grace H. Gosselin, a former WPA official and director of the East Side Settlement House, novelist George Tichenor III, editor of the *Co-operator*, a publication of the cooperative movement, and the League for Industrial Democracy's Harry W. Laidler, a longtime proponent of a national Farmer-Labor Party, were individuals not previously affiliated with the ALP.[29]

As expected, members of the Social Democratic Federation — those who comprised the Socialist Party's Old Guard prior to the devastatingly bitter split of 1936 — immediately flocked to the newly-organized Liberal Party. While Norman Thomas and the Socialists were generally amused by the SDF's latest transformation, the older Socialist Labor Party pulled no punches in denouncing the Liberal Party as capitalism's latest effort to confuse working-class New Yorkers.

The Liberal Party's platform, wrote the SLP's Max Hoffman, was a "foot-in-mouth affair," as much an indictment of the capitalist system and a warning of its impending collapse as an attempt to save it through a series of reforms. The party's demands for

---

[28] "Labor Right Wing Maps State Drive," *New York Times*, April 6, 1944.
[29] "Machinery Set Up for New Party By Group Seceding From the ALP," *New York Times*, April 24, 1944.

curbing the growing concentration of wealth in the United States and its call for a substantial reduction in income inequality, wrote Hoffman, were in direct conflict with the party's stated support of capitalism, which preserves and extends those very conditions.[30]

In criticizing the Liberal Party's lone socialist plank calling for "public ownership of utilities, of natural resources and of monopolistic enterprises, wherever this is necessary to maintain production or to serve other desirable social ends," the Socialist Labor Party was quick to point out that the Liberal platform explicitly stated that it was not opposed to private enterprise and, indeed, believed that it had "a large role in the economy of the future."[31]

The SLP concluded:

> At present, the activities of the Social Democrats and other elements of the Liberal party are centered in New York State. The forecast is made, however, that the movement will spread. Whether it does or not, it typifies a move in the interest of capitalism that is against the interests of all American workers.
>
> The American workers are in need of a fundamental change in social relations. The cause of their problems is private-property and class-ruled society. No reforms within capitalism can benefit them. The one change that can benefit them is the transformation of society from its capitalist basis to a Socialist basis. Organized on class lines in Socialist Industrial Unions and supporting the political aims of the Socialist Labor Party, the workers can bring into being a society in which all the means of wealth-production would be commonly owned and democratically managed for the good of all. The forces that prevent this organization and that deter the adoption of this aim are necessarily reactionary and pro-capitalist. The Liberal party is but the latest of such forces.[32]

Casting a jaundiced eye toward New York's latest political party — one billing itself as a "party of destiny" — the *Socialist Call*, the official organ of the Socialist Party, was also quick to criticize the new party, reminding its readers that the founders of the Liberal Party were virtually the same men who had organized the American Labor Party eight years earlier. "Having repudiated their child when the Communist-Hillman junta kidnapped it,"

---

[30] "Liberal Party's Platform is Foot-in-Mouth Affair," *Weekly People*, Vol. LIV, No. 13, June 24, 1944.
[31] "Capitalism's Latest Party Formed to Confuse Workers," *Weekly People*, Vol. LIV, No. 10, June 3, 1944.
[32] Ibid.

wrote the paper in a blistering editorial in early June, the party's leaders had now given birth to yet another unsavory party not only dedicated to the same lack of principles as in 1936, but destined once again to commit "adultery with the old capitalist parties."[33]

Writing in the same edition, Thomas himself expressed similar skepticism. Mildly criticizing the Liberal Party's platform — "it is sound rather than rousing in its rejection of imperialism, and timid rather than convincing" in its support of public ownership of the nation's utilities, natural resources and monopolistic enterprises — Thomas wondered how the Liberal Party, comprised of many ex-Socialists, could expect to achieve any measure of success when they were essentially adopting the "same tactics and program" of their now despised ex-colleagues in the American Labor Party in supporting Roosevelt, "an old party leader whose progressive quality today, whatever may have been true in the past, is deduced simply from fear of his Republican opponent."[34]

"The Roosevelt whom these sworn enemies now vie with one another to endorse" wrote Thomas, "is today the champion of no progressive legislation, has been silent on the poll tax issue, advocates labor conscription, strongly inclines towards postwar military conscription, and has a foreign policy which heads straight to new wars by underwriting white imperialism in the Far East and Stalin's sphere-of-influence politics in Europe."[35]

While stating that he could fully understand why the Communists, now firmly ensconced in the ALP and "whose sole principle is loyalty to Stalin," could endorse FDR's bid for a fourth term, Thomas said that he was baffled by the Liberal Party's apparent willingness to embrace the same electoral strategy as the Communists. "This is more bewildering," he added, "when one remembers the scurrilous Communist abuse of Roosevelt when he was a genuine New Dealer, and the liberal and labor suspicion of some of his acts in his present role of Dr. Win-the-War."[36]

Despite such criticism, the Liberals enthusiastically forged ahead, organizing what they hoped would be a party of significant state and national consequence. Approximately 1,100 delegates attended the opening session of the party's founding convention, a two-day event held at the Hotel Roosevelt on May 19-20.

---

[33] "That 'Liberal Party,'" *Socialist Call*, June 2, 1944.
[34] "FDR's Triple Indorsement and the Three Great Issues that are Really Important," *Socialist Call*, June 2, 1944.
[35] Ibid.
[36] Ibid.

A NEW PARTY WITH BIG DREAMS

One of nine speakers during the opening session, Alfange gave the keynote address, describing the Liberal Party of New York as "a party of destiny," possibly the nucleus of a nationally-organized third-party movement.[37]

Senator Robert F. Wagner and David Dubinsky also addressed the convention, the former explaining that while he remained a Democrat, he nevertheless recognized that the cause of "progress and humanism" in the United States was not bound by party lines. The country's reactionary forces, he warned, were again on the march and it was the duty of the Liberals and their allies in the Democratic Party to prevent their ascendancy to power. "We must win the peace at home," he declared, "through political and economic democracy, resulting in more social security, better housing, full employment and a high national income, fairly distributed among all the people."[38]

Described as "the shining symbol of genuine American liberalism," Franklin D. Roosevelt was nominated for a fourth term by acclamation. In addition to nominating Henry A. Wallace for vice president, the Liberal delegates also gave their stamp of approval to Sen. Wagner, who was facing a spirited challenge from Republican Thomas J. Curran, a former alderman from Greenwich Village who had been appointed New York Secretary of State by Gov. Dewey in 1943, in his bid for a fourth term to the U.S. Senate.[39]

A buoyant Alex Rose, a mover-and-shaker in the party until his death in 1976, predicted that the fledgling Liberal Party, bolstered by the 310,000-member ILGWU, would provide at least 400,000 votes for Roosevelt in the presidential election — a figure not too far off the mark.[40]

In addition to selecting 25 vice chairs and 109 members of the party's state executive committee, Professor John L. Childs was named as the party's first state chairman, a post he held until the spring of 1947 when he was replaced by Adolf A. Berle, Jr., a former diplomat and member of Roosevelt's original "brain trust." Ex-state controller Joseph V. Leary was chosen as state secretary of the party and Manhattan's Harry Uviller of the International Ladies Garment Workers Union was named party treasurer. Alex Rose became chairman of the Liberal Party's administrative committee.[41]

---

[37] "New Liberal Party Formed Officially," *New York Times*, May 20, 1944.
[38] Ibid.
[39] "New Party Fixes 400,000-Vote Goal for Roosevelt," *New York Times*, May 21, 1944.
[40] Ibid.
[41] Ibid.

Reinhold Niebuhr of the Union Theological Seminary, an ex-Socialist and member of the NC-PAC, an offshoot of Sidney Hillman's powerful CIO Political Action Committee, was named vice chairman of the party in late July. At the time, the 52-year-old Niebuhr was serving as president of the Union for Democratic Action, a World War II interventionist group and forerunner of Americans for Democratic Action.[42]

Before adjourning, the delegates, whose numbers swelled to more than 1,500 by the convention's closing session, also ratified a platform condemning isolationism and imperialism and calling for the creation of a permanent international organization — the United Nations — with the authority and power to prevent and check aggression, by whatever military and economic measures necessary, and to "eliminate the political, social and economic causes of war."[43]

Recognizing that the United States could no longer rely on laissez-faire economics when dealing with depression and unemployment, as well as the very real danger of runaway inflation in the post-war period, the Liberals also called for the establishment of a permanent National Economic Council, accountable to the Congress and the President, to guarantee full employment and the highest level of production possible while maintaining a high standard of living for the American people.[44]

"Only a political party which thoroughly believes in and is prepared to fight for the basic and elementary right of all people to work, live and play on the basis of their merit and need and without discrimination or segregation," concluded the party's platform, "can cultivate in the American people those moral and spiritual impulses and attitudes upon which our commonwealth depends and without which we cannot keep our free institutions."[45]

The Liberal Party, which adopted the Liberty Bell as its emblem, immediately set out to gain a place on New York's general election ballot, collecting more than 175,000 signatures for its congressional, state and national candidates prior to the state's August 16 deadline.

The party's petitions, filed an hour before the midnight deadline, included the name of Vice President Henry A. Wallace, but Truman's name was later substituted in his place. Though an ob-

---

[42] "Dr. Niebuhr Takes Liberal Party Post," *New York Times*, July 28, 1944.
[43] "Digest of Platform Adopted by New Liberal Party," *New York Times*, May 21, 1944.
[44] Ibid.
[45] Ibid.

jection to the party's petitions had been lodged by former congressman John J. O'Connor, the conservative Democrat purged by FDR in 1938 and then aligned with the American Democratic National Committee, the anti-fourth term organization mentioned in a later chapter, Secretary of State Thomas J. Curran — Wagner's Republican opponent in the U.S. Senate race — overruled O'Connor's objections and placed the Liberal Party on the ballot.[46]

Contending that neither party held a national nominating convention that year and therefore were not eligible to nominate presidential electors, O'Connor later sued in a desperate attempt to prevent the American Labor and Liberal parties from naming presidential tickets.

O'Connor's lawsuit, however, was dismissed by state Supreme Court Justice Francis Bergan, a former court reporter and nine-year veteran of the state's highest court, in a 1,200-word opinion issued on September 6. Bergan had ruled a week earlier that the names of Roosevelt and Truman would appear as the American Labor and Liberal Party candidates for president and vice president, respectively, on the state's absentee ballots being mailed to military personnel overseas, thereby giving the Democratic incumbent three lines on the New York ballot. Determined to hamper FDR's re-election prospects, O'Connor refused to back down, but was forced to give up the ghost when New York's Court of Appeals refused to consider his appeal a month later.[47]

While the Liberals initially applauded Secretary of State Curran's decision to dismiss O'Connor's objections and place the party on the ballot, they weren't at all happy when he decided, shortly thereafter, to list the party last on the statewide ballot, placing Roosevelt's name on the Liberal ticket in the last column after Socialist Norman M. Thomas and the Socialist Labor Party's Edward A. Teichert.[48]

In a letter to Curran threatening legal action, the Liberal Party's executive committee protested the party's ballot position as "prejudicial and discriminatory" and requested that the Secretary of State change the order of the ballot so that all three parties that had

---

[46] "Liberal Party Names Wallace for V. President," *Salamanca Republican-Press*, Aug. 17, 1944; "Truman is Listed by Liberal Party," *New York Times*, Aug. 20, 1944; "Liberal Party Wins," *New York Times*, Aug. 26, 1944.

[47] "State War Ballot Ruling," *New York Times*, Aug. 29, 1944; "Court Denies Plea to Bar ALP Electors," *New York Times*, Sept. 7, 1944; "Lets ALP Pick Roosevelt," *New York Times*, Oct. 6, 1944.

[48] "Ballot Bias Seen by Liberal Party," *New York Times*, Sep. 25, 1944.

nominated Roosevelt would appear on successive lines, preventing the potential for massive voter confusion on Election Day.[49]

The letter, signed by state chairman John L. Childs, state secretary Joseph V. Leary and Alex Rose, chairman of the party's administrative committee, pointed out that the Liberal Party's statewide nominating petitions had contained 52,000 signatures — more than quadrupling the 12,000 required — compared to 19,352 for the SLP (listed on the New York ballot as the Industrial Government Party) and only 18,335 for the Socialist Party.[50]

In their letter, the Liberal Party leaders also seriously challenged a statement made by a deputy Secretary of State, who maintained that the positioning of the three independent parties on the ballot was determined by the order in which their petitions had been received. This was "obviously not the true reason for depriving the Liberal Party candidates of their proper place on the ballot," claimed the party's outraged leaders, because the Socialist Labor Party had filed its nominating petitions before those of the Socialists, yet, according to the Secretary of State, would be listed on the ballot after the Socialist Party.[51]

The Liberal Party's hopes for gaining a coveted fourth spot on the general election ballot, however, were dashed when a state Supreme Court justice, in a ruling in early October, dismissed the party's lawsuit demanding that the party be listed ahead of the Socialist and Industrial Government (SLP) parties.[52]

The Liberals, who hoped to be listed on the ballot right next to or immediately below the American Labor Party, had argued that they should take precedence over the two socialist parties because they had nominated a full statewide ticket and their nominating petitions contained far more signatures than either of the two older socialist parties. In their lawsuit, they also contended that the Liberal Party's nominees were, for the most part, identical to those of the Democratic and American Labor parties, and that the present order of parties, placing the party in the sixth column on the ballot, was both "prejudicial and confusing to the independent voters."[53]

---

[49] Ibid.

[50] Ibid. The Socialist Labor Party, of course, was just happy to be back on the ballot in the nation's most populous state after having been arbitrarily denied a place on the New York ballot during the 1936 and 1940 presidential campaigns.

[51] Ibid.

[52] "Liberals Lose Ballot Suit," *New York Times*, Oct. 7, 1944; See also, *Matter of Childs v. Curran*, 183 Misc. 195 (1944); "S.L.P. Gives Liberals Drubbing in Court," *Weekly People*, Vol. LIV, No. 30, Oct. 21, 1944.

[53] Ibid.

The pragmatic nature of the Liberal Party's endorsement policy — a longstanding practice enabling the party to gain concessions and patronage from New York's two major parties — was evident almost from the party's founding.

During its initial foray into the murky and often convoluted world of New York politics, the Liberals not only nominated Roosevelt, Truman and Wagner, but all of the Democratic candidates for statewide office with the exception of two judicial candidates. In addition to cross-endorsing nine Democratic congressional candidates — all of whom were victorious in November — the Liberal Party backed ex-city councilman Louis P. Goldberg against "isolationist" Democratic lawmaker Andrew L. Somers in Brooklyn's 10th congressional district.[54]

While still a member of the ALP, Goldberg had been among the earliest to urge a fourth term for Roosevelt, arguing that FDR should seek another term — not as a Democrat — but as the nominee of a nationally-organized labor party. "If America is still at war in 1944," he said in March of 1943, "President Roosevelt should be the candidate of a youthful, vigorous, progressive national labor party."[55]

The former Brooklyn councilman, who had been elected on the American Labor ticket in 1942 and was twice returned to the New York City council on the Liberal ticket, serving from 1946-49, was a former Socialist and had run for the New York Supreme Court on the party's ticket on no fewer than seven occasions between 1919 and 1939. He had also co-authored a somewhat sensational book with Eleanore Levenson titled *Lawless Judges*, published by the Rand School Press in 1935.

A longtime veteran of Harry W. Laidler's League for Industrial Democracy, the NYU-educated lawyer later served as national chairman of the Social Democratic Federation, an organization whose growth had grown stagnant since its founding by the Socialist Party's "Old Guard" in 1936. Under the leadership of Alex Kahn, Gus Claessens, Jacob Panken, Charles Solomon, Goldberg and several other veteran Socialists, the SDF voted to align itself with the Liberal Party in the spring of 1944, shortly before the party's founding.

Working closely with Milwaukee Mayor Frank P. Zeidler, Goldberg was later instrumental in bringing about the SDF's merger with the Socialist Party in January 1957, shortly before his death

---

[54] "Slates are Filed by Minor Parties," *New York Times*, Aug. 17, 1944.
[55] "Fourth Term Urged Here," *New York Times*, March 20, 1943.

later that year. Goldberg's detractors in the SDF complained bitterly that Goldberg had "'stolen' the SDF and unified it illegally with the SP" and proceeded to organize the Democratic Socialist Federation (DSF).[56]

First Lady Eleanor Roosevelt helped the Liberals launch their 1944 campaign as the featured speaker at a dinner at New York's Hotel Commodore on August 2, telling the overflow crowd of more than 1,800 that they were "the most hopeful group in the country and perhaps the whole world." Admitting that she was by no means a fan of political machines, especially notoriously corrupt organizations like Tammany, Mrs. Roosevelt strongly encouraged the Liberal Party to take a lesson from them by organizing from the precinct level up and by electing representatives capable of responding to the will of the people.[57]

While the First Lady was obviously the biggest draw that evening, the most interesting speech may have been delivered by former Wendell Willkie adviser Russell W. Davenport, a novelist and magazine publisher whose appearance that night seems to lend considerable credence to the notion that the Liberal Party was actively planning to run Willkie for mayor of New York City in 1945, possibly as a springboard to a national third-party effort in 1948.

Despite losing to Roosevelt in 1940 and being drubbed in the Wisconsin GOP primary earlier that spring, many believed the 52-year-old Willkie still had his eye on the presidency. This was probably what David Dubinsky was alluding to in his remarks earlier that night when he strongly hinted at a future coalition of labor and liberal forces in a third-party movement of national scope.[58]

A former classmate of *TIME* magazine's Henry Luce and a member of the secretive Skull & Bones Society while a student at Yale, Davenport sharply denounced the platforms of both major parties in his dinner speech, accusing the Democrats of "chiseling on principles" and asserting that the Republicans — the party that had callously rejected Willkie's visionary candidacy earlier that spring — was even worse. The Republican platform, he said, was derelict on both domestic and foreign policy.[59]

Suggesting that millions of Republicans around the country felt the same way he did, Davenport, who later emerged as the de-facto leader of the GOP's internationalist wing following Willkie's

---

[56] "Votes to Join New Party," *New York Times*, May 4, 1944; "Louis P. Goldberg;, Lawyer, 68, Dead," *New York Times*, Dec. 12, 1957; Henderson, *Darlington Hoopes*, p. 152.
[57] "New Liberal Party to Open Drive Here," *New York Times*," July 26, 1944; "Davenport Balks at Dewey Support," *New York Times*, Aug. 3, 1944.
[58] "Davenport Balks at Dewey Support," *New York Times*, Aug. 3, 1944.
[59] Ibid.

untimely death on October 8 — a role he shared with Minnesota's Harold E. Stassen — charged that Thomas Dewey failed to grasp the basic concepts of international cooperation and world freedom and that he could not, in good conscience, support his candidacy.[60]

A former managing editor of *Fortune* magazine, the 45-year-old Davenport was considered one of Willkie's closest personal and political friends. He was also Willkie's principal speechwriter during the 1940 presidential campaign and again during his short-lived bid for the Republican nomination earlier that year. Despite his assertion that he was speaking only for himself that evening, it's more than likely that the Yale-educated publisher was really acting as an emissary for Willkie, especially since it has been widely established that the former Republican nominee for president, who lived on Fifth Avenue and had an office on Broad Street, had personally reached out to Dubinsky and other Liberal Party leaders earlier that spring to discuss such a strategy.[61]

Realizing that the Republicans would never again nominate a liberal for the presidency, the genial, tousled-haired Willkie had become something of a political orphan by the spring of 1944. Despite the fact that his brief public career had taken him from a virtual unknown at the age of forty-eight to a statesman of international stature, respected by millions, in a span of only four years, he was for all intents and purposes a man without a party. Overwhelmingly rebuked in the Wisconsin Republican primary earlier that spring, Willkie had all but given up on the GOP, a party that had never completely come to terms with the fact that it had nominated a genuine liberal for the presidency in 1940 — and wasn't about to try it again. Given the hostility he encountered in trying to win the Republican nomination for a second time, Willkie was obviously in search of a new political home and appeared to have found it in New York's Liberal Party, a nestling creation with boundless possibilities.

In May of that year, at almost the precise moment the Liberal Party was being launched, Willkie had called Dubinsky completely out of the blue and arranged to meet with him and several other Liberal leaders to discuss his future plans and those of the party.

---

[60] Ibid.
[61] "Willkie Man May Key New Liberal Party," *Boston Herald*, Aug. 1. 1944. Before accepting the Liberal Party's invitation, Davenport had asked Willkie if he would have any objection. "Certainly not," Willkie reportedly responded. "All my other friends are expressing opinions, why shouldn't you?"

Intrigued by Willkie's unexpected phone call, Dubinsky immediately contacted Alex Rose and the two men arranged a dinner meeting with Willkie at Dubinsky's apartment on West Sixteenth Street. They also invited the party's three intellectual leaders — State Supreme Court Justice Samuel Null and Columbia University professors John L. Childs and George S. Counts, the former chair of the ALP — to join in the discussion.[62]

What transpired following the dinner was one of the most extraordinary third-party strategy sessions of all time. According to Dubinsky, Willkie wasted little time explaining the need to get started on building a national third-party, a liberal coalition that he would be more than happy to lead. The two major parties, he said, were moribund and he was deeply worried that the Democrats would fall victim to the same reactionary forces as the Republicans once FDR, whose health was continuing to deteriorate, passed from the scene.[63]

Rose and Dubinsky cautioned that it would be a mistake to announce his intentions too soon and urged him to consider running for mayor in 1945 on a Liberal-Republican fusion ticket — an idea that Willkie welcomed enthusiastically. Willkie, who had already been toying with the idea of possibly running as a third-party candidate before declaring for the Republican presidential nomination in February of that year, grew visibly excited by the prospect as the men drank coffee and brandy, admitting that the New York mayoralty would be a perfect springboard for launching a third-party presidential candidacy in 1948.[64]

Ostensibly created as an alternative to the American Labor Party and to assist in Roosevelt's bid for a fourth term, the Liberals now had a long-range plan. "Once Willkie won the mayoralty in New York and had won the ear of the media and the interest of the people," wrote labor guru-turned-syndicated columnist Gus Tyler, "he could then have a public rostrum from which to declare for the presidency in 1948. The Liberal Party had a future not just in New York City but across America."[65]

Like Dubinsky and other Liberal Party leaders, Willkie kept his long-range plans closely guarded, but sought the counsel of William L. Shirer, the noted historian and foreign correspondent who believed that Willkie would be a formidable candidate for mayor

---

[62] Dubinsky and Raskin, *Dubinsky*, p. 286.
[63] Ibid.
[64] Ibid., pp. 286-287.
[65] Gus Tyler, *Look for the Union Label: A History of the International Ladies' Garment Workers' Union* (Armonk, N.Y., 1995), p. 223.

and the presidency.[66]

Growing increasingly excited about the idea, Willkie then discussed the plan with his old friend Gifford Pinchot, the former Republican governor of Pennsylvania who was actively supporting Roosevelt's bid for a fourth term. Now in his late seventies, Pinchot was serving on the executive committee of Sidney Hillman's National Citizens' Political Action Committee (NC-PAC) and was later named national chairman of the Independent Voters for Roosevelt, an organization actively supporting a fourth term.[67]

The 79-year-old Pinchot, a founding member of Teddy Roosevelt's Bull Moose Party in 1912 who had briefly toyed with the idea of mounting his own third-party candidacy for the White House in 1932, liked the idea and encouraged Willkie to pursue "a new setup in American politics." Shortly after their meeting, the aging conservationist visited FDR in the White House to discuss Willkie's idea of organizing a national Liberal Party.

Roosevelt, who had long been intrigued by the idea of uniting the liberals in both parties under a single banner, was visibly excited by the prospect of a new party and sent White House counsel Sam Rosenman, an amiable former judge who doubled as FDR's speechwriter, to meet privately with Willkie at the St. Regis Hotel in New York City on July 5.

Imagining the kind of field day the press would have if the former GOP presidential nominee was seen meeting with the President's envoy in the middle of a presidential campaign, Willkie took extra precautions not to be seen publicly with Rosenman, at one point ducking into a bedroom when room service delivered lunch to the two men.

During their clandestine meeting, Willkie told Rosenman that they should wait until after the election to pursue the idea.

An unusually impatient Roosevelt couldn't wait until after the election to explore the idea and shot off a letter to Willkie on July 13 — the first of three such letters FDR excitedly sent to the former utility executive that summer — inviting his one-time Republican rival to meet with him at either the White House or Hyde Park shortly after the election.

Roosevelt was so intrigued by the idea that presidential advisor Rexford G. Tugwell, a member of FDR's original brain-trust who learned economics at the feet of radical Scott Nearing and Si-

---

[66] Neal, *Dark Horse*, p. 316.
[67] Josephson, *Sidney Hillman*, p. 626; "Pinchot Heads Group Backing Fourth Term," *Pittsburgh Press*, Sept. 24, 1944.

mon N. Patten, the innovative and brilliant founder of the American Economic Association, at the University of Pennsylvania's Wharton School of Business back in the days when that institution still taught the American School of Political Economy, later asserted that had the two men lived, Roosevelt might have sought a fifth term as a Liberal Party candidate in 1948, possibly with Willkie as his vice-presidential running mate.[68]

America could have done a lot worse. A political comeback, a seemingly implausible leap from the mayor's office to the Oval Office in a span of three short years, might have been in the offing had Willkie lived — and with it an opportunity to expand the Liberal Party nationally in 1948.

Was it really such a far-fetched idea? After all, Willkie had already given the idea plenty of thought. Keenly aware of the possibility that he would be repudiated in a second attempt at the GOP's nomination, Willkie had carefully considered the possibility of running as a third-party candidate in 1944 — an intriguing fact missed by most of his biographers.

In a story published by the *St. Louis Post-Dispatch* in early December 1943 — long before he declared his candidacy for the Republican nomination — it was reported that Willkie, intrigued by the idea of being a wildcard in that year's presidential sweepstakes, had "thoroughly explored the possibility of forming a third political party," including researching the technicalities of getting a third-party presidential candidate on the ballot in each of the forty-eight states, but eventually decided against the feasibility of such a candidacy because the obstacles would have been virtually insurmountable.[69]

The article, written by Marquis W. Childs, a respected Pulitzer-prize winning Washington reporter for the *Post-Dispatch*, quoted an authoritative source close to Willkie who maintained that the former utility executive had seriously considered leading an independent movement out of the GOP if the party rejected his views on internationalism and named a compromise candidate unacceptable to him and other liberal Republicans at the party's national convention in Chicago. When asked about the story, Willkie remained characteristically coy, declining to comment on its veracity.[70]

---

[68] "F.D.R.'s Plans for Own Party Told by Tugwell," *Los Angeles Times*, Sept. 19, 1957
[69] "Third Party Declared Studied," *New York Times*, Dec. 12, 1943; "Willkie Surveying Outlook for Third Party, Paper Says," *Chicago Tribune*, Dec. 12, 1943; "Willkie to Try New Role: Free Lance Political Critic," *Wisconsin State Journal*, April 6, 1944.
[70] Ibid.

A NEW PARTY WITH BIG DREAMS

After being thoroughly rejected in the Wisconsin primary, Willkie spent the next several months in political seclusion, only occasionally sallying forth to comment on politics and world events.

Those who believed that the tattered and rain-soaked "Willkie for President" posters still dotting the Wisconsin landscape symbolized the political grave of the Wall Street lawyer who blitzed the state a few months earlier might have been in for a rude awakening had fate not intervened. Willkie certainly didn't sound like a gloomy and beaten man. In fact, it was quite the opposite. Within weeks of his Wisconsin drubbing, Willkie was already plotting his political resurrection. The White House, he believed, might still be in his future. "It was a good fight," he wrote a friend shortly after the Wisconsin primary, "but there are many battles yet ahead."[71]

One thing was certain. Willkie was determined that Wisconsin wouldn't be the end of the road. He was equally resolute in his belief that he wasn't going to be just another one-hit wonder in American politics and that bigger and better things lie ahead, balmier days that might have included life at 1600 Pennsylvania Avenue. He realized, too, that his future wouldn't involve the GOP, an increasingly reactionary party that had never completely welcomed him into its fold. This was never more painfully obvious than during his disastrous attempt at a second presidential nomination earlier that year.

The fact that Willkie had given Roosevelt by far his toughest race for the presidency in three elections and even ran stronger in heavily-populated New York state than Gov. Dewey, the popular racket-busting prosecutor who was then serving the first of three consecutive terms as the state's chief executive, managed to do against the ailing president four years later, meant nothing to the Republican leadership. Nor were they moved by the 22.3 million votes cast for Willkie in 1940 — until then, the largest popular vote ever received by a losing candidate for the presidency.

Willkie, who had once served on Tammany Hall's New York County Democratic Committee — an issue Roosevelt's supporters exploited during the 1940 presidential campaign — and had been a delegate to the Democratic national convention in 1924 and a contributor to Roosevelt's presidential campaign in 1932, was never fully trusted or embraced by the GOP establishment. "Well, Wendell," quipped a Republican official from his home state, "you know back home in Indiana it's all right if the town whore joins the

---

[71] Bill Severn, *Toward One World: The Life of Wendell Willkie* (New York, 1967), p. 211.

church, but they don't let her lead the choir the first night."[72]

The utility tycoon had more than his share of Republican critics during his few short years in the party. One particularly influential detractor was Ernest T. Weir, a wealthy steel executive and former chairman of the party's national finance committee, who remarked that Willkie "never was a good Republican." Willkie's inflated sense of his own importance and his propensity to publicly criticize those in his own party who disagreed with him did more harm than good, said Weir, a self-made man possessing only an eighth-grade education who had climbed his way to the top of the steel industry.[73]

As the party's finance director, Weir had worked closely with Willkie during the 1940 presidential campaign. The founder of Weirton Steel and chairman of the National Steel Corporation — one of the nation's largest steel producers at the time — also faulted the former utility executive for failing to accept his role as the titular head of the party following the 1940 election, leaving the GOP without any real leadership at the national level.[74]

Edgar Monsanto Queeny, heir to the Monsanto chemical fortune, echoed similar sentiments. Queeny, who introduced Willkie at a luncheon for 150 Republican and business leaders as "America's leading ingrate," was still reeling from the fact that he had raised $200,000 for Willkie's 1940 presidential campaign without receiving so much as a word of thanks from the candidate. Queeny, who led the Missouri delegation at the 1940 Republican national convention — delivering twenty-six of his state's thirty votes to Willkie on the sixth ballot — had clearly soured on the former GOP nominee.[75]

In the fall of 1943, the president of the Monsanto Chemical Company sent a questionnaire to Willkie demanding written answers within ten days. The nine questions, as TIME magazine noted, were of the "have-you-stopped-beating-your-wife" variety. Willkie, who was vacationing in Maine when the questions arrived and didn't see the Monsanto executive's ultimatum until the ten-day deadline had passed, said that it would be impossible to answer the questions in their entirety without writing another book. He then offered to travel to St. Louis to address Queeny's concerns in person, an overture that did little to mollify the wealthy

---

[72] Mark H. Leff, "Strange Bedfellows: The Utility Magnate as Politician," James H. Madison, ed., *Wendell Willkie: Hoosier Internationalist* (Bloomington, IN, 1992), p. 24.
[73] "Willkie Never was any Good to GOP: Weir," *Chicago Tribune*, April 8, 1944.
[74] Ibid.
[75] Donald Bruce Johnson, *The Republican Party and Wendell Willkie* (Urbana, IL, 1960), pp. 250-251.

chemical manufacturer and other Missouri Republicans.[76]

Even Rep. Joseph W. Martin, Jr. of Massachusetts, the conservative lawmaker tapped by Willkie to head the Republican National Committee in 1940, was actively working to block his nomination — a particularly dastardly act considering that Willkie had repeatedly asked Martin to manage his 1944 campaign.[77]

Martin, whose chairmanship was largely viewed as a compromise between the party's emerging internationalist wing and the isolationists, had resigned as RNC chair in late 1942, shortly after that year's mid-term elections. By the following autumn, the veteran Massachusetts congressman was conspiring with Alf Landon in an effort to frustrate Willkie's candidacy. Landon's goals that year, according to biographer Donald R. McCoy, were to deny Willkie a second chance at the Republican nomination and to prevent Roosevelt from winning a fourth term.[78]

Willkie's biggest critic within the GOP, however, was none other than John D. M. Hamilton, the Kansas Republican Willkie had unceremoniously sacked as the party's national chairman shortly after capturing the Republican presidential nomination four years earlier. Hamilton, who had been Alf Landon's choice to head the party in 1936, long contended that Willkie had personally promised him another term as national chairman in 1940, but instead was relegated to executive director of the party — a humiliating demotion in his eyes — when Willkie named Massachusetts Republican Joseph W. Martin, minority leader in the U.S. House of Representatives, as the party's new national chairman in July of that year.[79]

Still seething at having been replaced as the party's national chair and amply financed by Monsanto's Queeny and Sun Oil's Joseph N. Pew, Jr. — a wealthy reactionary who despised both Willkie and Roosevelt — Hamilton, who was then practicing law in Philadelphia, took on the role of a one-man truth squad, canvassing the country in the months leading up to the 1944 Republican primaries and recruiting various favorite-son candidates in an

---

[76] "U.S. At War: No, Thanks," *TIME*, Sep. 27, 1943.
[77] James J. Kenneally, *A Compassionate Conservative: A Political Biography of Joseph W. Martin, Speaker of the U.S. House of Representatives* (New York, 2003), p. 109.
[78] Donald R. McCoy, *Landon of Kansas* (Lincoln, NE, 1966), p. 503.
[79] "G.O.P. Leaders Hail Willkie's Choice of Martin," *Chicago Tribune*, July 10, 1940; Johnson, *The Republican Party and Wendell Willkie*, p. 111; Neal, *Dark Horse*, p. 123. According to the *Chicago Tribune*, Willkie initially wanted to name a three-member committee to direct the party, comprised of Martin, Hamilton and Russell W. Davenport, his pre-convention campaign manager, but party leaders convinced him to use the party's existing structure.

effort to derail Willkie's impending candidacy.[80]

Hamilton, who once served as Speaker of the Kansas House of Representatives, campaigned in twenty states during the autumn of 1943, irreparably damaging Willkie's prospects for a second consecutive nomination in the process.[81] In state after state, the former Kansas politician-turned-Philadelphia attorney repeatedly alleged that Willkie was in cahoots with Roosevelt and wasn't a good fit for the GOP — a charge that resonated with millions of rank-and-file Republican voters.[82]

In January 1944 — two months before the first-in-the-nation New Hampshire primary and only eleven weeks before the April 5th Wisconsin primary, Willkie's first crucial test in America's heartland — Hamilton, who was clearly still in a state of discomfiture, accused Willkie's handlers of trying to stampede Republicans into nominating him for a second time.[83]

The "Willkie blitz," as he called it, was "a deliberate attempt to foreclose the Republican presidential nomination many months before the Republican national convention even assembles, to the exclusion of every other possible choice." By falsely claiming that they already had 300 to 500 delegates "in the bag," Willkie's managers, he asserted in a nationally broadcast radio address, were putting undue pressure on party leaders throughout the country to commit themselves to his candidacy before any other candidate "had a chance to be heard." At the conclusion of his twenty-state tour, Hamilton said that most party leaders refused to "subscribe to the theory that the Republican Party, like the Democratic Party, has only one indispensable man."[84]

A large number of Republican leaders shared Hamilton's reservations about Willkie. To them, he was still an interloper — a Democrat at heart — despite having honorably carried the Republican banner against FDR four years earlier.

Realizing that most of the party's powers-that-be weren't in his corner, and likely never would be, Willkie nevertheless plunged ahead, believing that he could circumvent the party's establishment and make his case directly with the American people.

Arguably, he wasn't the darkest horse in the stable — that dubious honor probably belonged to Illinois congressman Everett M.

---

[80] "Hamilton on Tour Opposing Willkie," *New York Times*, Nov. 5, 1943; "U.S. At War: Mr. Pew's Ambassador," *TIME*, Nov. 15, 1943.
[81] Neal, *Dark Horse*, pp. 285-286.
[82] Thomas Fleming: *The New Dealers' War: F.D.R. and the War Within World War II* (New York, 2001), p. 349.
[83] "Hamilton Assails 'Willkie Blitz,'" *Chicago Tribune*, January 16, 1944.
[84] Ibid.

A NEW PARTY WITH BIG DREAMS

Dirksen — but the spokesman for internationalism still faced an awfully steep climb if he was going to wrest the nomination from New York's Thomas E. Dewey, the party's prohibitive favorite.

In gearing up for the 1944 contest, Willkie was fully aware that 63 percent of likely Republican voters surveyed in the late summer of 1943 believed that he would be the party's weakest potential candidate in the general election.[85] He also knew he couldn't count on the support of most of the party's elected officials, particularly congressional Republicans.

In early June 1943, longtime Republican Rep. Leo Allen of Illinois released the results of a poll in which 180 of the 207 Republicans in the House had participated. Allen's poll found that 51 of his colleagues preferred Dewey, 33 were for MacArthur, 32 for Bricker, and only 13 for Willkie.[86] Even more worrisome was the fact that only six of the 168 Republican members of Congress surveyed in November 1943 favored Willkie's candidacy, compared to 89 who were predisposed to Thomas E. Dewey, thirty for Gen. Douglas MacArthur, a dozen for Ohio Gov. John W. Bricker and ten for Ohio's Robert A. Taft — none of whom had yet tossed their hats into the ring.[87] Unfortunately, Willkie could never figure out how to crack congressional resistance to his candidacy.

Making matters worse, C. Nelson Sparks, a former mayor of Akron, Ohio, published a highly-critical and controversial book about Willkie in the autumn of 1943, in which he alleged that the young utility executive was nothing more than a "New Deal 'fellow traveler'" whose candidacy was part of an elaborate "conspiracy of the New Dealers and the Willkie internationalists to force the United States into an acceptance of a permanent union of world government with Europe and Asia."[88]

Sparks, who had managed the favorite-son candidacy of New York's Frank E. Gannett, an outspoken and wealthy newspaper publisher who had more or less tossed his "crumpled and weather-beaten hat" into the ring for the Republican presidential nomination in 1940, alleged that the real story behind Willkie's nomination that year "makes the Teapot Dome scandal look like a Sunday school affair."[89]

In his mockingly titled *One Man — Wendell Willkie*, an obvious

---

[85] "Willkie G.O.P.'s Weakest Hope, 63% Say in Poll," *Chicago Tribune*, Aug. 30, 1943.
[86] Barnard, *Wendell Willkie: Fighter for Freedom*, p. 427.
[87] "Willkie Gets 6 of 168 Votes in Congress Poll," *Chicago Tribune*, Nov. 5, 1943.
[88] James H. Madison, *Wendell Willkie: Hoosier Internationalist* (Bloomington, IN, 1992), xviii; Thomas E. Mahl, *Desperate Deception: British Covert Operations in the United States, 1939-44* (Washington, D.C., 1999), pp. 156, 175, 180.
[89] "Book on Willkie Stirs Up Debate," *Milwaukee Journal*, Nov. 27, 1943.

play on Willkie's best-selling *One World* published earlier that spring, the former mayor of Akron claimed that the amiable and urbane Thomas W. Lamont of J. P. Morgan and other high-powered Wall Street titans spent lavishly at the party's national convention in Philadelphia in an attempt to persuade delegates to switch to the dark-horse Hoosier.

According to Sparks, the so-called "Miracle in Philadelphia" wasn't so miraculous, after all. Involving more than a little British intrigue, it was a carefully planned and orchestrated effort on the part of some of Wall Street's most powerful financiers. Relying on a notorious forged letter, Sparks contended that the entire episode had been engineered by Harry Hopkins, one of Roosevelt's closest advisors and a man many believed was being groomed by the president as a possible successor. Among other things, Sparks alleged that the deep-pocketed Lamont offered an attractive loan to *Minneapolis Star Journal and Tribune* publisher John Cowles, acting as a go-between, in exchange for arranging Minnesota Gov. Harold Stassen's dramatic eleventh-hour switch from Dewey to Willkie — a charge categorically denied by Cowles.[90]

Sadly, support for a second Willkie candidacy had seemingly all but vanished long before the industrialist-turned-foreign emissary entered the fray in 1944. Even among the delegates who had dramatically nominated him in Philadelphia four years earlier, there appeared to be little enthusiasm for a repeat performance. In a survey of those delegates in September 1943, only 17.6% indicated a preference for Willkie.[91]

Despite his relatively late start — by the time he officially announced his candidacy in mid-February, Dewey had virtually sewn up the nomination — Willkie believed that he could once again defy the odds and magically throw the Republican convention into an uproar, resulting in a last-minute stampede and perhaps a second miraculous nomination for the presidency.

Coming after more than a year of speculation, Willkie's candidacy hardly came as a surprise. "Everybody knows it anyway," he said while officially declaring his candidacy in Portland, Oregon, on February 14.[92]

If Willkie was hoping for a repeat of the 1940 pre-convention campaign, a year when he didn't actively compete in the primaries, he was in for a rude awakening, beginning and ending with the Wisconsin primary — his first real test of strength — in early

---

[90] "Cowles Denies Willkie Deal, Flays Sparks," *Pittsburgh Press*, Dec. 10, 1943;
[91] "Dewey Leads in Poll Among '40 Delegates," *New York Times*, Sept. 6, 1943.
[92] "Willkie Declares Candidacy for '44," *New York Times*, Feb. 15, 1944.

April.

Why Willkie chose Wisconsin as his make-or-break state in 1944 remains something of a mystery. The state had been drifting rightward for more than a dozen years and even its most popular progressive figure, Sen. Robert La Follette, Jr., son of the late "Fighting Bob," had become an outspoken critic of FDR's interventionist policies.

Coupled with the fact that an ultraconservative such as John B. Chapple, a fiery small-town newspaper editor who had long feuded with his party's moderates, could twice win the party's U.S. Senate nomination in the previous decade and in which the rising political star of a former Marine by the name of Joseph R. McCarthy, whose fabricated war record would send him to the U.S. Senate two years later under the slogan "Wisconsin Needs a Tail Gunner in the Senate," should have been enough to give Willkie serious second thoughts about his Wisconsin strategy.

The state also had a large German-American population, especially in Milwaukee, and more than its share of prewar isolationists. Moreover, Robert McCormick's hostile *Chicago Tribune* — a newspaper that absolutely loathed everything Willkie stood for — enjoyed a large circulation in the state, particularly in southern Wisconsin.[93] In short, the Badger State was a calamity waiting to happen.

Despite a spirited effort that left him emotionally drained and physically exhausted while reducing his booming voice to a bare whisper, it came as no surprise that the Wisconsin primary turned out to be an utter disaster for the one-world Willkie, who had nearly carried the state against FDR only four years earlier.

Barnstorming the state during a fourteen-day, 1,500-mile speaking tour which often found him plowing through snowdrifts in the weeks leading up to the primary, Willkie was unable to win a single delegate while polling a pitifully disappointing 6,439 votes, or 4.6%, in the state's non-binding preferential primary.

Dewey, long considered the party's frontrunner, won the lion's share of the state's 24 delegates, while Harold E. Stassen, the youthful ex-governor of Minnesota, and Gen. Douglas H. MacArthur — both of whom were undeclared candidates and serving on active duty in the South Pacific during the primary — picked up seven delegates between them.[94]

Willkie was particularly irked by Stassen's candidacy, the first of a breathtaking ten tries by the ex-Minnesota governor for his

---

[93] Fleming, *The New Dealers' War*, p. 351.
[94] "Willkie Withdraws," *New York Times*, April 9, 1944.

party's presidential nomination between 1944 and 1992. Their friendship had already been strained by Stassen's unflattering review of Willkie's best-selling *One World* the previous spring, a book review that caused Willkie a great deal of personal pain. In his *New York Times* review, Stassen wrote that Willkie had "a tendency to be dogmatic and belligerent" in stating the principles which he had been courageously fighting for in international affairs and faulted his friend for overemphasizing the wrongs of British colonialism while understating the evils of communism.[95]

The 37-year-old Stassen had delivered the keynote address at the party's national convention in Philadelphia four years earlier. As the face of the party's future, the youthful Stassen's enthusiastic endorsement of Willkie on the eve of the presidential balloting as the person "best fitted for leadership…in preparing to make this country safe for any eventuality" was seen as a major turning point in the convention.[96]

Stassen, who served as Willkie's floor manager during the "Miracle at Philadelphia," had personally informed Willkie that he had no plans to run for president in 1944. "I'm young enough to try later," he told Willkie before leaving for active duty in the Pacific. "I'm saying this because I really feel this way. Your thinking and mine are very much alike. I think the hope of the party in 1944 lies with you."[97]

Stricken by the presidential bug shortly thereafter — an intoxicating addiction that would last a lifetime — Stassen, who was too smart not to realize that whatever success he managed that year would come at Willkie's expense, later inexplicably consented to allow his name to be placed on the Wisconsin, Nebraska and Oregon primary ballots, a decision that Willkie found deeply troubling, especially since both men agreed on the issue of internationalism and Stassen had personally promised him that he wouldn't run that year, even going so far as instructing his supporters to rally behind his friend from Indiana. Willkie never really forgave Stassen for reneging on his promise.[98]

Wisconsin was the end of the road for the 1944 Willkie-for-President campaign. A bigger flop was hard to imagine.

Though he had won a majority of the delegates in the New Hampshire primary three weeks earlier, Willkie deliberately made

---

[95] Harold E. Stassen, "Report on a Wakening World," *New York Times*, April 11, 1943.
[96] Johnson, *The Republican Party and Wendell Willkie*, p. 82; "Stassen Backs Willkie Drive," *Los Angeles Times*, June 27, 1940.
[97] Barnard, *Wendell Willkie: Fighter for Freedom*, pp. 453-454.
[98] Barbara Stuhler, *Ten Men of Minnesota and American Foreign Policy* (St. Paul, MN, 1973), pp. 150-151.

Wisconsin the testing-ground of his strength with the party's rank-and-file voters. It was a gamble from the beginning — and one that cost him dearly.

Given the enormity of his defeat, Willkie promptly dropped out of the race the following day, barely six weeks after formally announcing his candidacy. His staggering setback was widely viewed as a sharp repudiation of the GOP's internationalist wing by the party's prewar isolationists — a drubbing that looked even worse given the fact that he was the only presidential aspirant who actively campaigned in the state.

"I deliberately entered the Wisconsin primary," Willkie told supporters in Omaha where he had been campaigning in the expectation of a strong showing in Nebraska's April 11 primary, "to test whether the Republican voters of the state would support me personally and in the advocacy of every sacrifice and cost necessary to winning and shortening the war and in the advocacy of tangible, effective economic and political cooperation among the nations of the world for the preservation of peace and the rebuilding of humanity." He then conceded. "As I have said many times, this country needs new leadership. It is obvious now that I cannot be nominated."[99]

Willkie's strategy had been predicated on a strong showing in Wisconsin followed by a successful showing in neighboring Nebraska, at the foot of the Oregon Trail, and culminating with a lopsided victory in the Oregon primary on May 19th. Without the Badger State, his path to a second nomination in 1944 was essentially closed.

A deeply disappointed Willkie then got in a parting shot. "The result of the primary is naturally disappointing and doubly so," he concluded, "since the candidate who led the poll for delegates is known as one active in organizations such as America First, opposed to the beliefs which I entertain." Willkie's reference was a dig at Secretary of State Fred R. Zimmerman, a one-time America First adherent and suspected ex-Ku Klux Klan member who organized the Dewey-for-President movement in Wisconsin. Zimmerman, who had served as governor of Wisconsin in the late twenties, had threatened to hound Willkie throughout the state, refuting his arguments at every campaign stop, but couldn't raise the money for such an undertaking.[100]

A popular politician and the top vote-getter in the state's

---

[99] "Willkie Flop in Wisconsin Stirs Capital," *Chicago Tribune*, April 6, 1944; "'Can't Win: I Quit' — Willkie," *Chicago Tribune*, April 6, 1944.
[100] Johnson, *The Republican Party and Wendell Willkie*, p. 280.

crowded delegate-at-large race — Zimmerman garnered 143,031 votes while the leading Willkie candidate polled only 49,535 votes — the 63-year-old Secretary of State took delight in the state's stunning repudiation of Willkie. "This proves the contention of Abraham Lincoln that you can't fool all the people all of the time," he declared, adding that Wisconsin Republicans recognized that there was little difference between Willkie and Roosevelt.[101]

Reaction to Willkie's withdrawal — a dramatic climax to a spirited and lightning-quick battle for the party's soul — was decidedly mixed. Finding little to cheer about in the Wisconsin results, the mood in the White House was reportedly gloomy. Sen. Warren R. Austin of Vermont, who later gave up his Senate seat to serve as the first U.S. Ambassador to the United Nations — a post tailor-made for Willkie had he lived — refused to comment on Willkie's withdrawal. The 66-year-old Austin was considered Willkie's strongest internationalist proponent in the U.S. Senate. "The primary results in Wisconsin," asserted Montana's Burton K. Wheeler, "ought to convince the internationalists that the people are opposed to their visionary schemes for making the world over in one fell swoop and destroying America in the process."[102]

Wheeler, who had been Robert La Follette's vice-presidential running mate in 1924, said that he wasn't the least bit surprised by the results in Wisconsin. "Nationalism is as strong today as it ever was, and is getting stronger," he said. Sen. Robert A. Taft of Ohio said that Willkie had "recognized the inevitable," but expressed disappointment that he had chosen to attack his fellow Republicans in bowing out of the race, while New York Rep. Hamilton Fish — certainly no fan of the homespun Hoosier — described Willkie's withdrawal as "an unselfish and patriotic act."[103]

On the political fringe, longtime critic Gerald L. K. Smith of the right-wing America First Party delighted in Willkie's misfortune, claiming that his repudiation by the voters in Wisconsin was "a victory for the America First crusade." Smith's supporters had picketed Willkie the previous spring when he addressed the general assembly of the Presbyterian Church in Detroit, many of them carryings signs and handing out leaflets denouncing Willkie as a "New Deal stooge" and "Communist bootlicker" — protests that

---

[101] "Wendell Willkie Withdraws from GOP Presidential Race," *Wisconsin State Journal*, April 6, 1944; "Dewey's Vote is About 41 Pct. of G.O.P. Total," *Chicago Tribune*, April 6, 1944; "Willkie Bows Out," *LIFE*, April 17, 1944, p. 38.
[102] Ibid.
[103] Ibid.

A NEW PARTY WITH BIG DREAMS

absolutely amused Willkie. "I doubt if anyone was ever so fortunate in the nature of his opposition," he cracked. Willkie had also sharply denounced the rabble-rousing Smith and his indigenous America First movement during the Wisconsin primary, suggesting that any candidate who did not reject "America First and Gerald L. K. Smith cannot possibly be elected president."[104]

Rep. Joseph W. Martin of Massachusetts, the Republican leader of the House who had betrayed the chain-smoking utility executive by lending his support to Alf Landon's anti-Willkie movement in the months leading up to the 1944 primaries, was certain that the former presidential candidate "would continue to help arouse the public to the need of a new administration in Washington."[105]

Senate Minority Whip Kenneth S. Wherry of Nebraska echoed Martin's remarks. "I think it's a courageous statement by a man who has shown the courage of a real leader," said Wherry. "If that's his final conclusion, I sincerely hope he will continue to fight for those principles with the Republican Party, for it will take a united Republican Party to win this most important election in the 160 years of the nation's existence."[106]

While most newspapers agreed that Willkie had little choice other than to withdraw in light of the shellacking he took in Wisconsin, a few expressed regrets that he dropped out of the race so early. "They Have Defeated Wendell Willkie...and the Hope for a GOP President," screamed a front-page headline of an editorial in the *Wisconsin State Journal*. "The defeat of Wendell Willkie was more than a personal tragedy for one man, more than the defeat of one man. It can also mean the defeat of a party at a time when America needs its victory," wrote the newspaper.[107]

"Millions of Americans will deeply regret his departure," observed the *Boston Herald*, "for they have regarded and still regard him as the most stimulating and vigorous Republican who has come forward in a generation." Similarly, a Buffalo newspaper lamented his withdrawal from the race while urging him to remain in public life, "where his figure looms larger than ever before."

The *Baltimore Sun* insisted that Willkie's candidacy had been a "powerful stimulant" in forcing Republican and Democratic lead-

---

[104] "'America First' Victory Says Gerald L. K. Smith," *Racine Journal-Times*, April 6, 1944; Barnard, *Wendell Willkie: Fighter for Freedom*, p. 426.
[105] "Willkie Withdraws," *New York Times*, April 9, 1944.
[106] "'Step Toward Unity' or 'Back to Old Guard' — Willkie Move Stirs Up a Froth of Comment," *Racine Journal-Times*, Apr. 6, 1944.
[107] "— Disaster," *Wisconsin State Journal*, April 6, 1944.

ers alike to reassess the issues facing the country, while the *Cleveland Plain Dealer* praised him for rejuvenating the GOP and "fighting unceasingly to rid the Republican Party of isolationist and obstructionist elements."[108]

The *Hartford Courant* echoed similar sentiments, commending Willkie for making "an important contribution in arousing the nation, and particularly some elements within the Republican Party, to an appreciation of the role America appears destined to play in world affairs."[109]

On the other hand, Robert R. McCormick's arch-conservative and nationalistic *Chicago Tribune*, which dismissed Willkie as a "minor nuisance" and no longer a threat to the Republic, and a few of the other usual suspects were delighted to see him leave the race.[110] "The New Dealers will now have to look around for another straw-man to sell to the Republicans if they can," sarcastically intoned the *New York Daily News*, "and then concentrate all of their efforts on re-electing Roosevelt."[111]

North Dakota's Gerald P. Nye, the leading isolationist in the U.S. Senate, said that he was surprised that Willkie had mentioned the America First movement in his statement of withdrawal. By alluding to it, said Nye, Willkie was acknowledging that non-interventionism was still a prominent force in American politics.[112]

Stopping in Chicago on his way back to New York, Willkie — smiling broadly and saying that he felt "wonderful" — refused to elaborate on his withdrawal. When asked if he thought Dewey would be the party's nominee, the former presidential candidate grinned, saying, "You know as much about that as I do." As he climbed the steps of Chicago's crowded Union Station, reporters could hear a smattering of cheers and a few boos from the crowd that had gathered below.[113]

Willkie spent the next several months in political seclusion, only occasionally commenting publicly on politics and world events. Except for a few close friends and advisors, nobody was aware of his surprise phone call to the Liberal Party's David Dubinsky later that spring.

Like Louisiana's Huey Long whose plans to shake and rattle

---

[108] "Newspapers Discuss Willkie's Withdrawal from Race," *New York Times*, April 6, 1944.
[109] Ibid.
[110] "The End of Mr. Willkie," *Chicago Tribune*, Apr. 6, 1944.
[111] "Newspapers Discuss Willkie's Withdrawal from Race," *New York Times*, April 6, 1944.
[112] "'Step Toward Unity' or 'Back to Old Guard' — Willkie Move Stirs Up a Froth of Comment," *Racine Journal-Times*, Apr. 6, 1944.
[113] "Willkie is Silent on His Next Steps," *New York Times*, April 7, 1944.

A NEW PARTY WITH BIG DREAMS

the depression-era two-party system in 1936 were ended by an assassin's bullet a year earlier, Willkie's closely-guarded plans for a national comeback in 1948 tragically came to a screeching halt when he succumbed to heart failure on October 8, 1944, following a short illness.

Willkie's death marked the passing of a third major U.S. political figure in the span of less than six weeks. New York's Al Smith, the "Happy Warrior" who rose from newsboy and fishmonger on the sidewalks of New York to win four terms as governor and head the Democratic ticket against Hoover in 1928, died four days earlier.[114] Nebraska's George W. Norris, the majestically honest and independent-minded former five-term senator and "Father of the TVA" — winning his fifth and final term in the U.S. Senate in 1936 as a bona-fide independent — lost his life in early September, shortly after suffering a cerebral hemorrhage at his rural home.[115]

Believing that it would be a "tragedy" if Roosevelt was denied a fourth term, the 83-year-old Norris was serving as honorary chairman of the National Citizens Political Action Committee at the time of his death.[116]

One can only speculate as to what might have happened if Willkie had lived and followed through with his carefully-laid plans for a political comeback. With Mayor La Guardia refusing to seek a fourth term in 1945, the New York mayoralty, according to Dubinsky and other Liberal Party founders, was certainly within his grasp and who knows what might have happened in 1948.

Given the Liberal Party's remarkably auspicious beginnings — delivering more than 329,000 votes to Roosevelt, exceeding his margin of victory over Dewey in the state in 1944 — gaining permanent ballot status two years later when more than 177,000 New Yorkers voted for Democrat James M. Mead for governor on the Liberal line, and electing the president's oldest son, Franklin D. Roosevelt, Jr., to Congress in a special election in Manhattan's twentieth congressional district against Democratic and Republican competition in the spring of 1949, the sky appeared to be the limit for America's newest party.[117] Maybe it was a party of destiny, as its leaders claimed.

---

[114] "Alfred E. Smith Dies Here at 70," *New York Times*, Oct. 4, 1944.
[115] "Norris Dies, Ill Five Days after Stroke," *Omaha World-Herald*, Sep. 3, 1944.
[116] "Norris Accepts Post for Political Action," *New York Times*, Aug. 6, 1944; "Ex-Senator Norris Dies in Nebraska," *New York Times*, Sep. 3, 1944.
[117] "Roosevelt Wins House Seat By Majority Over 3 Rivals; Tammany Candidate Second" *New York Times*, May 18, 1949. In addition to running on the Liberal Party line, Roosevelt qualified for a second line on the ballot by obtaining 25,630 signatures on independent nominating petitions to run under the label of the Four Freedoms Party. Garnering three-

Moreover, almost anything would have been possible in a genuine three-way race for the White House between Truman, Dewey and Willkie in 1948, a contest that would have been further complicated by the significant fourth and fifth-party candidacies of former Vice President Henry A. Wallace and Dixiecrat J. Strom Thurmond with venerable Socialist Norman M. Thomas, as usual, playing the role of a political Jeremiah.

By 1948, the American people were slowly growing tired of the Democrats — sixteen years in the White House had been enough — yet they weren't at all happy with the "do-nothing" Republican-controlled 80th Congress. They were looking for something different — something bold and imaginative. Anything was possible in post-war America. After all, the American people had courageously defeated fascism, miraculously pulling themselves out of a decade-long depression in the process. It was a brand new world and the future looked increasingly bright for the country and its citizens who had made the world safe for democracy.

The only thing missing, the Liberal leaders believed, was a White Knight on a horse to lead them into that promising future, an idealistic leader of great integrity, brilliance and persistence who could show them the way. We'll never know, but the hopeful Hoosier — a man some would say was far ahead of his time — might have been the gallant leader they were looking for.

Unfortunately, that dream — the elusive aspiration of expanding the Liberal Party nationally — died with Willkie in early October of 1944. The country had not only lost "the only man in America who has proven that he would rather be right than President" and whose independence and greatness of character placed him above partisan politics at the cost of losing the leadership of his own party, as Harry Bridges of the longshoremen's union so eloquently put it, it also lost the one political figure capable of putting New York's young Liberal Party on the national map.

Describing him as a "bold human leader to whom all liberal-minded Americans looked for guidance," Alex Rose and John L. Childs mourned Willkie's passing in a joint statement. His death was clearly a blow to the Liberal Party. "The Liberal Party, its members and supporters, share with millions throughout the world a keen feeling of loss at the untimely death of this great American."[118]

---

quarters of his 40,882 votes on the Liberal ticket, Roosevelt swamped Democrat Benjamin Shalleck, a municipal judge, by more than 16,000 votes while his Republican and American Labor Party opponents ran far behind.
[118] "Messages Extol Willkie as a Powerful Influence in Crusade to Form Better World

President Roosevelt also paid tribute to Willkie, whom he considered a close friend, saying the country had lost a great citizen, a man of tremendous courage whose fortitude and intrepid spirit prompted him "more than once to stand alone and to challenge the wisdom of counsels taken by powerful interests within his own party." FDR's sentiment was echoed by Socialist Norman Thomas, who mourned that "America has lost a distinguished and useful citizen."[119]

In a tribute to Willkie a few weeks later, Childs described the former presidential candidate as a "trusted friend and adviser of the leaders of the Liberal Party" and one who was deeply interested in the party's formation and success.[120] "It was a crushing moment," recalled Dubinsky. "The national third-party project died with him. So far as I was concerned, it died for all time." Nobody else of similar stature ever came along, he lamented.[121]

While mourning Willkie's sudden passing that cold, gray autumn, Dubinsky and other Liberal Party leaders tried to refocus their attention on the campaign at hand.

In keeping with their goal of providing 400,000 votes for Roosevelt, the Liberals conducted a vigorous campaign for the president's re-election. Impressively, the party printed and distributed a million pamphlets urging New Yorkers to be "front line citizens" and support the Liberal ticket.[122] Party leaders also made a concerted effort to peel off support from the rival American Labor Party, mailing letters to the 186,000 enrolled ALP voters in New York City and urging them to switch their party affiliation to the Liberal Party.[123]

Beginning on October 17, the party also aired a series of five radio broadcasts in New York City on "Dewey and His Record," the last of which featured Sen. Robert Wagner discussing Dewey's record on social legislation.[124] Appearing in a separate radio broadcast on the eve of the election, the Liberal Party's Dean Alfange accused Dewey of being on both sides of every important issue, asserting that the New York governor had once preached nationalism and isolationism and was now touting international cooperation. Faulting Dewey for flip-flopping on Lend-Lease and

---

Relations," *New York Times*, Oct. 9, 1944
[119] "FDR, Dewey Pay Tribute to Willkie," *Hartford Courant*, Oct. 9, 1944; "Willkie Funeral to be Tomorrow," *New York Times*, Oct. 9, 1944.
[120] "Wallace, Truman Cheered by 20,000 at Liberal Rally," *New York Times*, Nov. 1, 1944.
[121] Dubinsky and Raskin, *David Dubinsky*, p. 287.
[122] "Liberal Party Pamphlets Ready," *New York Times*, Oct. 2, 1944.
[123] "ALP Members Urged to Quit the Party," *New York Times*, Oct. 7, 1944.
[124] "Liberal Party on Air," *New York Times*, Oct. 17, 1944.

for once proposing a two-nation alliance with Great Britain in an attack on the Dumbarton Oaks conference, Alfange ridiculed the double-talking Republican nominee for denouncing the New Deal in Pennsylvania while praising it in California.[125]

The Liberal Party's 1944 campaign drew to a close with a rousing rally of 20,000 supporters at New York's Madison Square Garden on October 31, an event featuring Vice President Henry A. Wallace and Harry S. Truman, the dapper ex-haberdasher who replaced him on the Democratic ticket three months earlier. The event — the only joint appearance by the two men that autumn — captured headlines across the country, making millions of Americans aware of the existence of New York's Liberal Party for the first time ever.[126]

Though the two men walked down the center aisle arm-in-arm in a display of unity, and while Truman heaped lavish praise on the Vice President — calling him "the greatest Secretary of Agriculture this country ever had" — Wallace didn't return the favor when it came his turn to speak. The best Wallace could do was to assert that Truman wasn't a "reactionary Democrat" and, in a backhanded endorsement of his successor, told the packed audience that he was personally content in supporting "all brands of Democrats who are in favor of Roosevelt."[127]

Administration officials and others who were hoping that any remaining traces of resentment on the part of the Vice President and his supporters over the almost cavalier manner in which he had been discarded by Roosevelt in favor of Truman — a second-rate politician by any objective standard — at the Democratic national convention in Chicago would be lost in a flurry of enthusiasm for his replacement were sorely disappointed.

They also must have been worried by the wildly enthusiastic reception the Liberal Party had given to Wallace, especially compared to the polite but somewhat subdued applause that greeted the Missourian. Unlike Truman, Wallace struggled to quiet the crowd amid shouts and cries of "Wallace in 1948."[128]

In his speech, the Vice President warmly praised FDR and hinted at his own political future. "This has been and is a people's war," he declared. "The peace must be a people's peace. The way

---

[125] "Dewey Inconsistent, Alfange Declares," *New York Times*, Nov. 4, 1944.
[126] "Wallace, Truman Cheered by 20,000 at Liberal Rally," *New York Times*, Nov. 1, 1944.
[127] Ibid.
[128] Ibid.

to get it is to reelect Roosevelt and then make the Democratic Party into a truly liberal party."[129]

In addition to Truman and Wallace, a number of Broadway celebrities also took part in the rally at Madison Square Garden, including Frank Sinatra, the immensely popular 28-year-old crooner who later performed at fundraising events for Henry Wallace and the Progressive Party. Sinatra, who sang and danced for the crowd, said that he had been warned that his political activities could hurt his career. "Well, the hell with that," he told the cheering audience. "I'm more interested in good government than in my own future." Singer Ethel Merman, Danish humorist Victor Borge, tap dancer Bill "Bojangles" Robinson, actress Benay Venuta and Polish singer and actor Jan Kiepura were among the other entertainers who made appearances that night.[130]

The Liberals put up quite a fight in their inaugural campaign, enabling Roosevelt to garner 329,325 votes on the party's line on Nov. 7, about 12,000 more than his margin of victory in the state over Dewey. Though not quite as spectacular as the 496,405 votes cast for FDR on the older American Labor ticket, it was an auspicious beginning for New York's Liberal Party.

In addition to making a similar contribution to Sen. Wagner's re-election and supporting seven Democratic candidates for the U.S. House — all of whom were victorious — the Liberals also backed Louis P. Goldberg, a former American Labor councilman from Brooklyn, against ten-term Democratic incumbent Andrew L. Somers and his Republican rival in New York City's tenth congressional district. Running exclusively on the Liberal Party ticket, the 55-year-old Goldberg garnered 20,719 votes, or 15.2 %, in a race easily won by Somers. Moreover, votes cast on the Liberal and American Labor lines, either separately or collectively, provided the margin of victory for three Democratic congressional candidates in New York City alone. The two parties also provided the winning margin for three major-party candidates for the State Senate and five for the Assembly.[131]

Needless to say, the Liberals were ecstatic about the role they had played in the 1944 campaign and immediately began making plans to establish their party on a permanent basis. Having polled more than 300,000 votes in New York City, the party immediately announced plans to participate in the city's 1945 municipal campaign with an eye on the state's 1946 gubernatorial election, where

---

[129] Ibid.
[130] Ibid.
[131] "ALP, Liberal Vote Elected 11 Here," *New York Times*, Nov. 29, 1944.

party leaders were confident that the Liberal Party would garner more than the 50,000 votes needed to give the new party full political status with the Democratic, Republican and American Labor parties.[132]

"The Liberal Party emerges from this campaign as it entered it — free from strings, commitments or obligations to any other party," asserted party leaders in a statement issued shortly after the election. The Liberal Party, they continued, would retain its independence for the political battles — municipal, state and national — that loomed ahead.[133]

Expressing hope that they would be able to attract the support of progressives in both major parties, party leaders said that liberalism will "never become a dynamic force in American politics by riding the coattails of either of the two old parties. It can and will become the arsenal of social progress and political reconstruction in America by taking the lead in the inevitable realignment of political forces in our country into two clear-cut parties."[134]

---

[132] "New Party's Rise to Power Seen; Liberals May Swing City Election," *New York Times*, Nov. 10, 1944.
[133] "City Role Planned By Liberal Party," *New York Times*, Nov. 16, 1944.
[134] Ibid.

Chapter XIV

A Colorful Dry Crusader

Struggling for political relevancy more than a decade after the repeal of national prohibition, the Prohibition Party — America's aging yet dauntless dry alternative — also entered the fray in 1944. It was the nineteenth consecutive time since 1872 that the tireless teetotalers had entered a national ticket in the country's quadrennial ritual.

More than anything else that year, the Prohibitionists were hoping to rebound from what had been one of the most disappointing presidential campaigns in the party's history when white-haired economist and statistician Roger W. Babson — puritanical to the core, but arguably the best known candidate in the party's history — polled a staggeringly small one-eighth of one percent of the vote in the 1940 presidential election, a tiny fraction of the million votes that he expected to receive.

In the two presidential campaigns following repeal of national prohibition in late 1933, the Prohibition Party, which twice played the role of spoiler at the national level — costing the Republicans the presidency in 1884 and again in 1916 — had become an increasingly distant also-ran in the nation's presidential elections, a relic of sorts in American politics.

Cheered by the news that three party members had been recently swept into office in Cherrytree Township in the party's long-time stronghold of Venango County — a western Pennsylvania county that once elected 205 Prohibitionists to public office — the Prohibition Party nominated Claude A. Watson of Highland Park, California, for the presidency and selected Floyd C. Carrier of

Takoma Park, Maryland, as his vice-presidential running mate at the party's national convention in Indianapolis in November 1943.[1]

Carrier, a minister and physician who attended Yale University, was general secretary of the American Temperance Society. Citing a serious lung disease, he later withdrew from the ticket and was replaced by Andrew N. Johnson, a 67-year-old Methodist minister and widely-known lecturer from Wilmore, Kentucky.[2] Johnson, who had been the Prohibition Party's candidate for governor of Kentucky the previous year, hit the campaign trail that autumn, telling his audiences that a vote for the Prohibition ticket wasn't a wasted vote. "You don't throw your vote away," he declared, "you throw it up — to Heaven."[3]

Johnson's candidacy — coming exactly eighty years after another vice-presidential candidate of the same name appeared on Lincoln's Union Party ticket in 1864 — was not only a curiosity of sorts, but also a pleasant reminder in war-time America of that earlier Johnson. Coincidentally, Hollywood, in one of its rare historical moods, produced a movie about the original Andrew Johnson called "Tennessee's Johnson," which had hit the big screen only a few months before the little-known Kentuckian, a namesake of the seventeenth president, replaced Floyd Carrier on the Prohibition ticket that year.[4]

Unlike the original Andrew Johnson of Tennessee who succeeded Honest Abe in the White House following the assassination of America's sixteenth president in 1865, the dry Johnson from Kentucky, a graduate of Asbury College, had been a pretty avid student and had learned to read and write long before he reached the age of twenty-one.[5]

Though his active campaigning was somewhat limited, Johnson's candidacy nevertheless galvanized Prohibitionists in the whiskey-drinking Bluegrass State, which impressively fielded a complete slate of congressional candidates for the first time since 1902.[6]

Despite wartime travel restrictions, some 226 delegates from

---

[1] Roger C. Storms, *Partisan Prophets: A History of the Prohibition Party* (Denver, Colorado, 1972), p. 51.
[2] "Prohibition Party Names Wilmore, Ky., Man," *Middlesboro Daily News*, Feb. 2, 1944.
[3] "Support for Drys' Candidates Urged," *Wilmington Morning News* (Wilmington, Delaware), Oct. 21, 1944.
[4] "Viewpoints," *Valparaiso Vidette Messenger*, Nov. 2, 1944.
[5] Ibid.
[6] "The Prohibition Party Solicits the Christian Vote," (Political Advertisement), *Middlesboro Daily News*, Nov. 4, 1944.

twenty-seven states and the District of Columbia traveled to Indianapolis to celebrate the party's diamond jubilee, marking the party's 75th anniversary, and to nominate a presidential ticket. Another 233 representatives of the National Youth Prohibition Committee also took part in the historic proceedings in Indianapolis.[7]

The Prohibition Party's nineteenth national nominating convention — the earliest of any party fielding candidates in the 1944 presidential election — heard a keynote address from former national chairman D. Leigh Colvin of New York, the party's presidential nominee eight years earlier, who told them that the country had not yet recovered from two devastating setbacks: the attack on Pearl Harbor and repeal of national prohibition, the latter of which he described as "the worst moral defeat of modern times."[8]

"On Dec. 7, 1941," said Colvin, "the United States suffered its worst military defeat since the burning of Washington in 1814, and on Dec. 5, 1933, the two major parties in a joint attack rushed repeal through so quickly the moral forces scarcely knew what had happened."[9]

Colvin was one of at least eleven individuals who had been mentioned as possible candidates to carry the party's banner in the 1944 presidential campaign. It was an impressive list, including several other past standard-bearers such as William F. Varney of New York, former Georgia congressman William D. Upshaw and economist Roger W. Babson, the party's nominee in 1940 — none of whom actively sought the party's nomination in Indianapolis. Several state delegations were pledged to Babson when they arrived in Indianapolis, but the snowy-haired economist, undoubtedly disappointed by his showing four years earlier, eventually decided against mounting a second campaign for the presidency.[10]

As in previous Prohibition conventions, aging former congressman Charles Hiram Randall of California, one of only two Prohibitionists to ever serve in Congress, was also mentioned as a possible presidential candidate, but the race eventually boiled down to a two-way contest between Watson and Sam Morris of Texas.[11]

Enjoying the support of Michigan Prohibitionists and the unusually large Indiana delegation, the 58-year-old Watson — a longtime host of the "Weekly Open Forum," a popular Los Angeles-

---

[7] Storms, *Partisan Prophets*, p. 51.
[8] "Prohibition Party Opens Convention," *Schenectady Gazette*, Nov. 11, 1943.
[9] Ibid.
[10] "Prohibitionists in Convention to Name Candidates," *Dunkirk Evening Observer*, Nov. 10. 1943.
[11] Ibid.

based radio series — arrived in Indianapolis as a prohibitive favorite for the party's nomination. Watson had been the keynote speaker at the party's 1940 national convention, delivering a rousing appeal for a coalition of the nation's Christian and patriotic forces and a stinging denunciation of the New Deal as an expression of defeatism and moral bankruptcy — instantly winning over the hearts and minds of a large number of party activists.[12]

Claiming to be a "conscientious objector" to the federal government's policy of allowing the sale of liquor in and around army bases, Watson had also received the pre-convention endorsement of the relatively large, 52-member California delegation at the party's state convention in Los Angeles earlier that spring. The California Prohibitionists had endorsed Morris as their favorite son's vice-presidential running mate.[13]

Watson's favorite-son candidacy was being boomed by J. W. Farr of Oakland, chairman of the party's state central committee. Farr had toured the state earlier that year in an effort to drum up support for Watson's candidacy while simultaneously increasing the party's voter registration figures, which in the autumn of 1943 stood at a meager 5,389. While the Prohibitionists weren't in any immediate danger of slipping below the state's new and relatively stringent requirement of maintaining at least one-tenth of one percent of the total registration figure to remain on the California ballot, Farr had ambitiously hoped to register 100,000 Prohibitionists by the 1944 general election.[14]

Despite Watson's apparent lead among the party's rank-and-file, Morris, who enjoyed a huge radio following, was arguably the better known of the two candidates, but Watson — an overwhelmingly favorite among party activists, defeated Morris by a margin of 131-31 to easily capture the nomination on the first ballot. Morris was then offered the party's vice-presidential nomination by acclamation, but declined. The Los Angeles lawyer, one of the party's most popular vote-getters, then magnanimously offered to withdraw from the ticket if Morris would agree to run for president, but the Texan declined that, too.

In addition to tabling a proposal by New York's William F. Varney to change the party's name, the Prohibitionists re-elected Edward E. Blake as the party's national chairman and named F.

---

[12] "Drys' Keynoter Rips New Deal for Defeatism," *Chicago Daily Tribune*, May 9, 1940.
[13] "Lawyer Put Up as 1944 Dry Candidate," *Los Angeles Times*, May 23, 1943.
[14] "Prohibitionists Boom L.A. Man for President," *Modesto Bee and News-Herald*, Sept. 9, 1943.

W. Lough of Winona Lake, Indiana — the summer home of evangelist Billy Sunday — as vice chair. Charles L. Hill of Rosendale, Wisconsin, was elected party treasurer and James A. W. Killip of Philadelphia, a Yale and University of Pennsylvania-educated physical education instructor who later ran for governor of Pennsylvania, was re-elected as the party's national secretary.[15]

In an address to the delegates earlier in the convention, the 36-year-old Killip, a lifelong professional magician who toured with the USO during World War II, predicted that the Prohibition Party would eventually become the nucleus for a successful third party, one powerful enough to capture the White House.[16]

Highly critical of the "rapidly growing tendency toward totalitarian government" in the United States, the Prohibitionists adopted a platform promising to "decentralize the national administration and restore to the several states their constitutional place in government." The party also pledged to "do away with all bureaucratic devices with overlapping functions which are causing enormous waste of public funds and manpower" and to "conduct government by constitutional methods."[17]

The party's platform also urged "constructive cooperation and collaboration with all nations in some form of world organization" — the United Nations, as it turned out — in the postwar period, "but military alliance with none."

In addition to the party's usual demand for national prohibition, the dry delegates called for tougher laws to enforce "higher standards of decency" in literature, motion pictures, radio and the stage — all of which were blamed for the increased wave of juvenile delinquency sweeping the nation.

Calling for lower taxes, the fiscally conservative Prohibitionists also adopted planks setting a one percent limit on property taxes and vigorously condemning the Roosevelt administration's "extravagance and maladministration of government funds." As in 1916, the Prohibitionists also came out in favor of a constitutional amendment for a single, six-year presidential term, an idea first advocated by President Rutherford B. Hayes in 1876.[18]

Throughout the first half or so of the twentieth century, the Prohibition Party, which once nominated presidential candidates of

---

[15] "Prohibition Party Picks State Man," *Wisconsin State Journal*, Nov. 13, 1943.
[16] "Prohibition Party Urges End to Totalitarian Trend," *Christian Science Monitor*, Nov. 18, 1943; "James A. W. Killip, 77, Teacher and Magician," *Philadelphia Inquirer*, May 16, 1984.
[17] Ibid.
[18] Ibid.

some national stature, tried repeatedly — and in vain — to nominate a "big name" candidate for the presidency, not only during the period when the eighteenth amendment was the law of the land, but in the years immediately thereafter. They tried to recruit silver-tongued William Jennings Bryan in 1920 and Idaho's William Borah, who kept the party on pins and needles waiting for a definitive response in 1932, when fervor for repeal of national prohibition was sweeping the country.

Some twenty years later, the Prohibitionists tried to regain their relevancy by attempting to entice pipe-smoking General Douglas MacArthur to accept their presidential nomination, but the insubordinate protean and paradoxical "American Caesar" — a man admired by millions who was then hanging out in the Waldorf-Astoria on New York's Park Avenue, sipping an occasional cognac while busily puffing away his last shot at glory in the GOP, a party pining for a completely different five-star general that year — wouldn't hear of it.[19]

Ironically, and clearly without his consent, the reluctant former Supreme Allied Commander responsible for overseeing Japan's postwar transition to democratic self-rule was later offered up as a symbolic protest candidate by the relatively inconsequential, ultra-right Christian Nationalist and Constitution parties — the former founded by the hate-preaching racist and anti-Semitic gadfly Gerald L. K. Smith — and both seemingly determined to prove the general's famous line that "old soldiers never die; they just fade away."[20]

Possessing considerable political acumen, the Prohibitionists — though waning in both relevance and influence — consistently reached out to some of the most consequential figures of their time.

Bryan, who still boasted a large following, was a three-time Democratic nominee for president and had been Secretary of State during the Wilson administration; Borah, the legendary "Lion of Idaho," was the longtime chairman of the powerful Senate Foreign Relations Committee; and the aging MacArthur had been one of

---

[19] "'Mac' Rejects Prohibition Nomination," *Kokomo Tribune*, Nov. 13, 1951; "Singer-Evangelist Prohibition Nominee," *Council Bluff Nonpareil*, Nov. 16, 1951. In declining the Prohibition Party's offer, MacArthur reportedly said that he had "always understood and respected the high moral and spiritual tone" of the party's activities. The Prohibitionists ended up nominating "Singing Cowboy" Stuart Hamblen, an evangelist and recovering alcoholic, for president that year.

[20] George E. Sokolsky, "Christian Nationalist Party Backing Douglas MacArthur," *Syracuse Post-Standard*, Oct. 30, 1952; Marquis Childs, "MacArthur May Beat Eisenhower," *Freeport Journal-Standard* (Freeport, Illinois), Nov. 1, 1952; "Eight Minor Parties Seek 'Protest' Votes," *Charleston Daily Mail*, Nov. 3, 1952.

the nation's greatest and most beloved military leaders known to virtually everybody in the country — and beyond.

While it never quite worked out for the third-party teetotalers, they nevertheless always made the most of what they had.

Watson, for instance, wasn't particularly well known and certainly didn't have the cachet or wide name recognition of a Bryan, Borah or MacArthur — nor was he nearly as well-known as Roger Babson four years earlier — but the dry party couldn't have found a more capable, dynamic and energetic spokesman than the little-remembered Los Angeles lawyer, a true believer who campaigned doggedly — and valiantly — for the White House in 1944 and again in 1948.

At the time of his nomination, Watson, an ordained minister who held two doctorates, was serving as general counsel to the Free Methodist Church of North America. He was also the national treasurer of the World's Christian Fundamentals Association, an interdenominational organization founded twenty-five years earlier by Baptist minister William Bell Riley — "The Grand Old Man of Fundamentalism" — to oppose the teaching of evolution in the nation's public schools. Riley had personally urged William Jennings Bryan to act as counsel in the famous Scopes Trial in 1925. Watson had previously served as a vice president of the organization.

Married and the father of three children — two of whom were in the military — Watson had twice run for attorney general of California on the Prohibition ticket, polling 93,085 votes in 1938 and 81,988 votes in 1942, or nearly four percent of the vote both times. His strongest showing ever occurred a decade later when he garnered a remarkable 332,173 votes, or 30.5 percent, in a race for Los Angeles district attorney.

Watson was hoping to have even better luck in 1944. After all, he was the first candidate to enter the fray. "If the old adage is true that the early bird catches the worm," he joked in early February, "then I will be the next president."[21]

The son of a Free Methodist minister, Watson was literally born in a log cabin in rural Manton, Michigan, on June 26, 1885.[22] After briefly attending Michigan's Alma College, he played minor league baseball for a brief period and later worked as an accountant and auditor for a subsidiary of the U.S. Steel Corporation. He later became general manager of the Four Drive Tractor Company,

---

[21] "Prohibition Party Leader Heard," *Bellingham Herald*, Feb. 6, 1944.
[22] Gordon G. Beld and David C. McMacken, *A History of Alma College: Where Plaid and Pride Prevail* (Charleston, S.C.), p. 123.

Inc., headquartered in Big Rapids, Michigan.

Ordained as a minister in the Free Methodist Church in 1911, Watson was admitted to practice law in California seventeen years later, eventually establishing his own law firm in Highland Park, a suburb of Los Angeles, where he continued to practice law into the late 1970s.

Watson, who agreed to run for vice president in 1936 after legendary World War I hero Alvin C. York declined the party's nomination, was a frequent Prohibition candidate for public office, waging at least nine campaigns on the party's ticket.

Believing that the third time might be the charm, Watson had been prominently mentioned as a possible nominee for the White House again in 1952 — a year when the Prohibitionists publicly flirted with General Douglas MacArthur before nominating country musician and songwriter Stuart Hamblen, the "singing cowboy" — and waged his last campaign at the age of seventy-eight when he again briefly sought the Prohibition Party's presidential nomination at the party's national convention in St. Louis in the late summer of 1963.[23]

In addition to waging a nominal campaign for Los Angeles district attorney in 1952, Watson also ran for California attorney general on five occasions, mounting the last three candidacies for that office following his 1944 bid for the White House. Running on the Prohibition ticket, he garnered a mildly respectable 85,688 votes, or 3.3 percent, in 1946 and 96,732 votes, or 2.7 percent, four years later.

Hoping to unseat Democrat Edmund G. (Pat) Brown, the Los Angeles lawyer surprised Prohibition activists in 1954 when he suddenly switched parties and ran for state attorney general in the Republican primary. Believing he had a realistic chance of defeating corruption-tarnished former attorney general Fred N. Howser for the Republican nomination, Watson didn't bother to cross-file in the Prohibition primary — leaving Montebello lawyer Edwin M. Cooper unopposed for the dry party's nomination. Watson's candidacy, unfortunately, was never taken seriously by the press and he was trounced in the June GOP primary, garnering 154,609 votes while finishing a distant third to Brown and Howser, both of whom had cross-filed. Brown, a rising star in Democratic politics, captured both major-party nominations that year.[24]

As his son Robert explained not too long after his father's death

---

[23] "'Mac' Rejects Prohibition Nomination," *Kokomo Tribune*, Nov. 13, 1951; "Prohibition Party to Pick Candidate," *Chillicothe Constitution-Tribune*, Aug. 30, 1963.

[24] "Brown, Repudiate Foe are in Attorney General Race," *Modesto Bee and News-Herald*, May 6, 1954; "Knight Primary Vote Sets Record," *Oakland Tribune*, Aug. 5, 1954.

in 1978, Watson never really believed that he had "lost" any of the elections in which he competed. "My father was a great influence on my life," said the younger Watson. "He said you never lose an election if you espouse your convictions. You may not get elected, but you haven't lost the election." The younger Watson, who briefly dabbled in politics himself, felt the same way.[25]

A nationally-recognized speaker, the 1944 and 1948 Prohibition standard-bearer also wrote a number of books during his lifetime, including *Traitors to America*, *God's Plan for Civil Government*, *Fifth Columnists in America*, *Bloody Hands* and *Repeal Has Succeeded*, all of which stressed the need for Christianity in government.

Though not quite as puritanical as Roger Babson, the party's 1940 nominee, Watson was still very much a socially conservative Prohibitionist. He was concerned with many of the same cultural issues as his predecessor, including juvenile delinquency and what he viewed as the declining morals and values of the nation's youth. Juvenile delinquency was on the rise in the United States, he said, because the country had "more adult delinquents than juvenile delinquents," a condition he blamed on the fact that more and more women had taken full-time jobs in industry during the war and were neglecting their children and their homes as a result.[26]

Watson was particularly troubled by the seemingly rampant increase in teenage pregnancy across the country, another wartime phenomenon. "I know of one high school on the Pacific Coast that in the last school year, 1942-1943, had over 600 expectant mothers," he said during his 1944 presidential campaign. "This is only a sample case of what prevails throughout the nation."[27]

The former Free Methodist preacher was also deeply concerned about the steep decline in church attendance in the United States — a seemingly irreversible trend experienced by almost every major denomination during this period. During the 1944 campaign, Watson frequently lamented the fact that no more than eight percent of the U.S. population regularly attended Sunday morning worship and that only two percent were motivated to go to a second service.[28] He was also critical of the church's role in combating the evils of alcohol. "The church has a grave responsibility regarding alcoholic beverages," he said while campaigning in Missouri, "but in recent years it has largely failed to meet it with

---

[25] "Roybal Sure Bet to Return to Congress," *Los Angeles Times*, Nov. 5, 1978.
[26] "Dry Candidate Sees Need of Third Party," *Joplin Globe*, March 31, 1944.
[27] Ray B. White, *The False Christ of Communism and the Social Gospel* (1946, republished, Whitefish, Montana, 2007), pp. 213-214.
[28] Clarence H. Benson, *Techniques of a Working Church*, (1946, republished, Whitefish, Montana, 2005), p. 32.

intelligence and enthusiasm."[29]

Watson also believed that the church had an important role to play in American politics. "The liquor business is in politics, the profit-makers are in politics, every predatory interest in in politics," he told a crowd of 400 in Portland. "If the church is to accomplish anything it, too, must enter the political field because if religion is not in politics we have a debauched nation."[30]

Though advocating the establishment of a Christian government — one in which the nation's political leaders "believe in the Bible and follow its commands" — Watson nevertheless insisted that he favored the separation of church and state. "But I do with all my soul believe in a union of righteousness and state," he said. It was a minister's duty, he added, to discuss politics and offer guidance to his parishioners.[31]

Believing that American democracy was being "kidnapped by those who on the one hand pay it lip service and on the other hand pilfer from us the liberties we hold so dear," the Prohibition candidate maintained that the moral quality of a political party was no higher than the most degenerate and anti-social condition that it permitted to exist, and by supporting parties — Democratic or Republican — that catered to such immorality and wickedness was to be an accessory to their evil deeds.[32]

Promising to eliminate the "crushing curse" of bureaucracy while winning World War II as quickly as possible, the pink-cheeked Prohibitionist enthusiastically accepted his party's presidential nomination at a ceremonial rally attended by 750 cheering supporters at the Philharmonic Auditorium in Los Angeles on January 9, some two months after the Prohibition Party national convention in Indianapolis.

"Today we find the liquor power again strongly entrenched, in legal and quasi-legal partnership with government everywhere, its corrupting and demoralizing hand reaching into the far corners of the country we all so dearly love," asserted Watson. "It is the same old liquor power, the same liquor traffic," he said, "but in even more insidious form than when the righteous wrath of an aroused nation sounded its death knell."[33]

---

[29] "Dry Candidate Sees Need of Third Party," *Joplin Globe*, March 31, 1944.

[30] "Prohibitionist Heard by 400," *The Oregonian*, Jan. 31, 1944.

[31] "'Christian Political Party' Proposed by Dry Speaker," *San Diego Union*, June 20, 1944.

[32] "Righteous Government Needed to Save America," *News-Herald* (Franklin, Pa.), May 5, 1944.

[33] "Bureaucracy Elimination Aim of Prohibition Party," *Christian Science Monitor*, Jan. 10, 1944; "Dry Candidate for President Opens Drive," *Los Angeles Times*, Jan. 10, 1944; "Watson Urges Drive on Entrenched Liquor," *New York Times*, Jan. 10, 1944.

According to the dry standard-bearer, the American people never lost faith in national prohibition. "Primarily," he elaborated, "repeal came because of the utter and disgraceful and scandalous failure of enforcement on many fronts. The country was in the throes of a great economic depression. The people in general were disturbed and harassed. The liquor interest, as a matter of course, took advantage of the situation...They did their utmost to discredit prohibition through promoting the bootleg racket and by any and every means at their command. And they did their utmost to discourage the weak-kneed public officials charged with the responsibility for enforcing the laws voted into the statutes by the vast majority of our people under the machinery of our American democracy. They flouted the express will of our people, our constitution and our laws.[34]

"Overlapping, liberty-destroying bureaucracy is strongly enthroned in this fair land of ours," he declared, and with each passing day was "extending its tyrannical rule by leaps and bounds." Turning his sights on the two major parties and the discriminatory election laws that protected them from any meaningful political competition, the Prohibition candidate charged that the election laws in many states were designed to keep the Democrats and Republicans in power, providing them with a monopoly on the ballot while denying minority parties the right of free expression. It was an old refrain, echoed by many minor-party hopefuls before and since Watson.

Watson had little faith in the two major parties to correct any of the nation's ills. "I submit in all earnestness and candor that neither of the old major parties is capable of correcting the evils and abuses that stalk the land."[35]

While believing in minimal government interference in the free market, the longshot aspirant firmly believed that government had an important role to play in society. "We believe in the right of the citizen to establish the enterprise of his choice, and that government should not compete with the citizen in business," he said. "But we are utterly opposed to the establishment of monopolies of trade or wealth, which, under the guise of free enterprise, would stifle competition and make a mockery of liberty. Our party is pledged to the strengthening and enforcement of the laws against gambling, the narcotics traffic and commercialized vice, which every wide-awake citizen knows are openly violated and nullified

---

[34] Ibid.
[35] Ibid.

by the inaction of the parties in power."[36]

Taking time from his private law practice to wage war on the liquor traffic — almost always paying his own expenses along the way — the dry crusader blamed almost all of the country's woes on repeal of national prohibition.

According to Watson, the nation's liquor bill exceeded $7 billion in 1944. That was the equivalent of six dollars a minute for every minute since the birth of Christ, said Watson. "All of this money," he quipped, "has been spent for something which makes a man see double and think half" — a line he used throughout the campaign.[37]

According to Watson, repeal had actually prolonged World War II. "America today faces three major enemies — Germany on one side, Japan on the other, and King Alcohol in our own country," he wrote in 1945. "While patriotic citizens saved tin cans, shaving-cream and toothpaste tubes, and even tinfoil chewing-gum wrappers to provide steel for the weapons of war, thousands of beer haulers were collecting the big No. 10 gallon-size heavy cans at cafes, restaurants, and hotels. Half of all they collected went to make caps for beer bottles. What patriotic mockery," he grumbled.[38]

After observing what he described as the negative impact of alcohol on U.S. military training camps during his tour of the South earlier that spring, Watson even went so far as to declare that "the liquor traffic remains the most perilous, pro-Hitler activity in the United States today."[39] He also said that he was concerned by reports that drinking water wasn't available to U.S. troops at Guadalcanal, site of the first major Allied offensive against Japan and a major turning point in the long and vicious "island-hopping" battle in the Pacific. "It's been reported there was no cold water for the men at Guadalcanal, but there was plenty of iced beer," Watson told a reporter for the *Brooklyn Eagle* during a campaign stop in New York later that spring. "Now, of course, I'm a lawyer and I don't know that to be a fact, but it's what has been reported and stated by some of the boys who claim to have been there," he said.[40]

Watson was also highly critical of the fact that Roosevelt occasionally served cocktails in the White House and reportedly had

---

[36] Ibid.
[37] "Watson Urges United Action for Dry Cause," *Macon Telegraph*, Mar. 24, 1944.
[38] Claude A. Watson, *Repeal Has Succeeded* (Winona Lake, IN, 1945), pp. 7-8, 11, 13, 15.
[39] "Liquor Issue Topic," *Cincinnati Enquirer*, Apr. 28, 1944.
[40] "Dry Era Returning, Says Prohibition Chief," *Brooklyn Eagle*, May 16, 1944.

enjoyed a couple of drinks with Prime Minister Churchill — well, the hard-drinking Brit actually consumed quite a few more than that — during the Teheran conference in late 1943.

"Unless God Almighty moves America," the Prohibition nominee told a student audience at Seattle Pacific College, "there will be only one Christian voice at the world peace table, and that will not be Winston Churchill, who came over here in 1931 to campaign against the 18th Amendment and represent the liquor interests of England, or the man we have now with his bar in the White House and his cocktail drinking at peace conferences. The only voice that will represent God Almighty and Christ," said Watson, was "a man converted from heathendom — Chiang Kai-shek, the Chinese general."[41]

Believing that national prohibition would again be the law of the land, Watson cautioned that a new prohibition law — or constitutional amendment — would be meaningless without an administration committed to its enforcement. "A law is not self-executing," he said. "Too often prohibition is put on the books and then John Barleycorn is elected to administer it."[42] National enforcement, he said during a campaign stop in San Francisco a few weeks later, could only be accomplished by electing a party committed to prohibition.[43]

On the campaign trail, Watson repeatedly encountered those who argued that prohibition couldn't be legislated. "Tell that to the OPA with its restrictions against sugar and tires," he typically responded, adding that the brewers and distillers themselves didn't believe such nonsense. "If the government can restrain the sale of food and tires it can restrain the sale of liquor — tires or toddies, which shall it be?"[44]

Between campaign appearances, Watson managed to devote some time that summer to assist a dry organization determined to close saloons throughout the state of California. Armed with a court order stemming from a test case involving a Glendale bar, California Drys, Inc., an organization founded five years earlier with the goal of seeking a restoration of national prohibition, aimed to close as many of the state's estimated 10,000 saloons as possible. "The court held that an establishment selling more than 50 percent liquor is a saloon and section 22 of the California liquor

---

[41] "Watson Raps Cocktails in White House," *Seattle Daily Times*, Feb. 5, 1944.

[42] "Prohi Party's Candidate Expresses Election Views," *The Oregonian*, Jan. 30, 1944.

[43] "Presidential Campaign Comes to Town; Prohibition Candidate Gives Answers," *San Francisco Chronicle*, Feb. 15, 1944.

[44] "'Christian Political Party' Proposed by Dry Speaker," *San Diego Union*, June 20, 1944.

control law prohibits saloons," declared the plump candidate in throwing his support behind the movement.[45]

Despite his strong opinions regarding the liquor industry and the evils of alcohol, Watson didn't want to be portrayed as some sort of dour, narrow-minded and priggish person when it came to an individual's right to consume alcoholic beverages. "The Prohibition Party during all its 75 years of history has never had a plank prohibiting drinking," he asserted while campaigning in Atlanta earlier that year. "It opposes the manufacture, sale and distribution of whiskey. A person does not get protamine poisoning by cooking his own food. If every drinker was left to manufacture his own whiskey, liquor would not be the menace it is today."[46]

Like almost every minor-party candidate in American history, the former Methodist minister was also continuously confronted with the "wasted vote" syndrome, the fear of throwing one's vote away. "No man loses his vote who votes his honest Christian convictions," he told a large gathering at San Diego's First Presbyterian Church in June. "I'd rather chase a rabbit for six months and not catch it than a skunk for six minutes and catch it," he added to a round of applause and laughter.[47]

While the obstacles placed in Watson's path weren't nearly as coercively restrictive as those encountered by the Communist Party's Earl Browder four years earlier, getting around the country proved unusually difficult for the Prohibition standard-bearer during the 1944 presidential campaign due to wartime travel restrictions.

Shortly after winning his party's nomination, Watson was informed by the chief of staff for traffic and priorities in Washington that his air travel would be severely restricted and that such travel privileges were being strictly reserved for missions directly related to the war effort. Watson was naturally skeptical. "I am wondering if this is to be a general policy for all presidential candidates when they are nominated," he sighed.[48]

Watson, who owned two automobiles, including one with more than 78,000 miles that he hoped to trade in for a newer

---

[45] "New Organization Seeks Prohibition," *San Luis Obispo Telegram-Tribune*, Aug. 12, 1939; "Drys Launch Drive to Close California Saloons," *Riverside Daily Press*, June 22, 1944.
[46] "Prohibition Party Candidate Believes Man Ought to Make Own Whiskey," *Atlanta Constitution*, Mar. 26, 1944.
[47] "'Christian Political Party' Proposed by Dry Speaker," *San Diego Union*, June 20, 1944.
[48] "Prohibition Party Nominee Can't Get Air-Travel Room," *Christian Science Monitor*, Dec. 15, 1943.

model, received more bad news in January 1944, when he was forbidden by federal authorities from purchasing a new car to canvass the country. The Office of Price Administration (OPA), a federal agency created in 1941 to prevent wartime inflation, advised the Prohibition Party standard-bearer that he didn't need a new car for his campaign. "There is nothing in the regulations to prevent Mr. Watson from acquiring another second-hand car," said the district OPA automobile ration chief, "but the rules are quite clear as to his right to buy a new one. He doesn't need it."[49]

Things got even worse the following month when the Prohibition candidate was denied gasoline for a planned tour of the South. Watson, who had earlier gained approval for a 10,000-mile allotment from his local rationing board, was notified that his request had been denied by the OPA's headquarters in Los Angeles and that his application was being forwarded to the regional office in San Francisco for further review.

Watson was furious. "If Willkie can tie a special car on a train and Vice President Wallace can burn up gasoline in an Army bomber campaigning for a fourth term then I think I'm entitled to a little gasoline," he declared. "I guess those bureaucrats don't want to give me the gasoline for fear I might swing some of the southern Democrats to the Republican Party," he said.[50] Given the widespread coverage of his outrage, the OPA's regional office approved Watson's request for a 10,000-mile gasoline ration a few days later.[51]

Every campaign has its share of ups and downs — and God knows the plump and prosperous Prohibitionist had his more than his share of the latter — but two of Watson's most disappointing experiences that year involved groups that he might have reasonably assumed would at least be sympathetic, if not entirely supportive, of his candidacy.

The first occurred in early March when a Dallas church refused to let Watson use its facilities for a public address after initially granting him permission. "We didn't want to mix politics and the church," explained the minister. "The elders granted permission to use the church when told it would not be a political meeting. Newspaper and radio advertising later indicated it was to be a political meeting."

A disappointed Watson, who had already given more than

---

[49] "Prohibition Party Candidate Loses His Plea for a New Car," *Los Angeles Times*, Jan. 5, 1944.
[50] "Prohibition Candidate Denied 'Gas' for Tour," *Los Angeles Times*, Feb. 25, 1944.
[51] "Prohibition Candidate Gets 10,000 Miles Extra 'Gas,'" *Los Angeles Times*, Feb. 29, 1944.

thirty-five speeches since winning the Prohibition nomination — many of them in houses of worship — said that was the first time one of his talks had been cancelled with so little notice.[52]

The second incident took place later that month when the Woman's Christian Temperance Union — long sympathetic to the aims of the Prohibition Party — abruptly withdrew its sponsorship of a Watson speech in Memphis, forcing the dry candidate to cancel his appearance. Describing Watson as "a fine man and a worthy candidate," a spokeswoman for the group explained that they were pulling out "because prohibition is an unpopular subject and we do not like to stir up too much publicity" — an explanation that obviously left a bewildered Watson, who had frequently addressed WCTU gatherings in the past, scratching his head.[53]

It appeared that Queens College professor Hugh A. Bone had been right when he wrote in the *National Municipal Review* the previous autumn that minor political parties were fast becoming one of the domestic casualties of World War II.

In any event, it hadn't been a particularly promising start for Watson's long-shot campaign. In addition to being denied air travel and the right to purchase a new car, the candidate's younger brother pleaded guilty in early 1944 to driving under the influence. Apparently not everyone in the Watson family agreed on sobriety. C. Arthur Watson, who was later sentenced to two years on probation, admitted in court that he had consumed three alcoholic beverages after taking some codeine for a throat infection. Needless to say, newspapers had a field day with Watson's arrest and conviction on charges of driving while intoxicated.[54]

While that embarrassing saga was soon forgotten, government restrictions on Watson's air travel remained a sore spot for the candidate throughout much of the campaign — so much so, in fact, that he later obtained a pilot's license and flew across the country in his own Stinson Voyager during the 1948 presidential campaign, becoming the first candidate for the Oval Office to pilot his own plane during a presidential election.

Commenting on newspaper reports that First Lady Eleanor Roosevelt had flown a total of 58,467 miles — including a flight to Miami Beach for a relaxing weekend getaway and a 23,000-mile journey to the South Pacific and Australia — since the imposition

---

[52] "Prohibition Candidate Refused Use of Church, Speaks at School," *Dallas Morning News*, Mar. 4, 1944.
[53] "Unpopular," *San Francisco Chronicle*, Apr. 2, 1944.
[54] "Brother of Dry Party's Chief is Tipsy Driver," *Chicago Tribune*, Jan. 28, 1944; "Prohi Official's Brother Guilty on Drunk Charge," *Nevada State Journal*, Feb. 12, 1944.

of gas rationing in the spring of 1942, Watson questioned Mrs. Roosevelt's right to "fly in Army bombers from Timbuctoo to the tropics" while a bona-fide candidate for the presidency such as himself was being denied the right to travel by air at all. Watson made his remarks on April 3, shortly after his own flight reservations from Kansas City to Los Angeles had been canceled due to military priorities.[55]

Furious that Secretary of War Henry L. Stimson had refused to grant him a permit for air travel, Watson accused President Roosevelt of being fearful of the Prohibition Party, suggesting that the President was afraid to duke it out with the nation's leading dry party in a fair and open campaign.

When reporters questioned FDR about Watson's statement during a presidential news conference shortly thereafter, the bewildered President turned to one of his assistants and asked who "this damn character" Watson was. When informed that he was the Prohibition Party candidate for president, Roosevelt immediately ordered his assistant to grant Watson the requested permit in front of the amused reporters.[56]

Despite Roosevelt's apparent intervention on his behalf, Watson continued to experience difficulties in traveling by air, as was the case in late June when his reservation for a flight to San Jose was cancelled at the last-minute by government order, preventing the Prohibition candidate to address a Free Methodist conference in that city.[57]

One of the major highlights of Watson's 1944 candidacy occurred in the spring of that year when he was a featured speaker at the second annual conference of the National Association of Evangelicals (NAE) in Columbus, Ohio.

Tentatively organized in St. Louis two years earlier for the purpose of fostering and promoting evangelical Christianity, the NAE claimed about 800,000 members when Watson addressed their national conference in April. By the time Watson waged his second campaign for the presidency in 1948, the NAE boasted a membership of approximately 3,000,000 representing more than two-dozen different denominations, including several relatively small denominations.

Interestingly, Dr. Rutherford L. Decker — a longtime Baptist missionary and the Prohibition Party's presidential nominee in

---

[55] "Wife of F.D.R. Piles Up Miles on Air Travel," *Chicago Tribune*, April 2, 1944; "First Lady's Air Travel Challenged," *Los Angeles Times*, April 4, 1944.
[56] Storms, *Partisan Prophets*, p. 52.
[57] "Appearance Prevented," *Petaluma-Argus Courier* (Petaluma, CA), June 23, 1944.

1960 — was vice president of the NAE and headed the national organization's Rocky Mountain region when Watson was invited to speak in 1944. The mustached-Decker, who was preaching in Colorado during this period, later served as president of the NAE, a group whose membership at the time included pioneer religious broadcaster Bob Jones, Sr., the fundamentalist founder of Bob Jones University, and well-known Baptist minister David O. Fuller, the latter of whom had been educated at the Princeton Theological Seminary.

In his fiery speech, Watson admonished the Protestant clergy to become more politically involved. According to scripture, asserted Watson during his address to the NAE conference, God wanted the righteous people of the Earth to "organize for political action to establish the ethics of the Christian religion in our administration of government." By taking the reins of power in all three branches of government, he declared, the nation's moral forces could destroy "every immoral and anti-social and debauching force" in American society. If the United States could send millions of young men "to lick Japan and lick Germany and put Italy down," there was no reason why it couldn't muster the strength to crush the liquor industry and the other evil forces throughout the land.

Reminding his audience that prayer was insufficient and that a "Christian citizen's most powerful weapon is his vote," Watson pleaded with the evangelicals to put aside their party loyalties and unite "under a great Christian philosophy for political action," a movement that had the potential to "elect the next President of these United States."[58]

The cure to virtually all of the nation's moral and social ills, he told a work study group during the conference, could be found in five words: evangelize, educate, agitate, legislate and administrate. "Laws are not self-executing," said Watson. "We must organize and administer according to Christian ethics. Separation of the church and state doesn't mean separation of righteousness and the state."[59]

Largely due to his own diligence, Watson received a decent amount of coverage on the campaign trail, much of it positive. He was especially proud of an article that appeared in the *Brewers Journal*, the liquor industry's leading publication, which described the Prohibitionist as an intelligent and capable candidate and said that

---

[58] Axel R. Schafer, *Countercultural Conservatives: American Evangelicalism from the Postwar Revival to the New Christian Right* (Madison, WI, 2011), pp. 46-47.
[59] "United Effort in Fight for Prohibition Urged," *Columbus Dispatch*, April 16, 1944.

if by some miracle Watson should be elected, "we wouldn't have a wild man in the White House." That was high praise. Needless to say, Watson carried that article with him throughout the campaign.[60]

On the other hand, there were a few journalists who had some fun at Watson's expense — but, as the old adage put it, any publicity was better than none. One of those was *Atlanta Constitution* columnist Jack Tarver who found plenty of humor in the fact that the Prohibition candidate had opened his five-city swing through Georgia with a stop in Savannah. "Mr. Watson is wasting his time, of course," wrote the witty Tarver, "but one cannot but admire the man's audacity: Inaugurating a dry campaign in Chatham County is like beginning a pugilistic career by hitting Joe Louis in the eye." During the entire "noble experiment," he added, "not a single Savannahan, so far as I can ascertain, ever passed on for lack of lubricant." If Watson managed to defeat Roosevelt and Dewey, Tarver concluded, it will have less to do with his own popularity and appeal than "the fact that many citizens who wouldn't ordinarily vote a dry ticket remember so well that, during prohibition, whiskey was easier to get."[61]

Returning to Los Angeles in the middle of June after conducting a campaign tour that took him to half the states in the country, Watson said that he had encountered widespread opposition to the concept of socialized medicine during his travels. "What right has the state to say that pills, dope, or surgeons' knives are more efficacious than prayer?" he asked. In his travels, the Prohibition standard-bearer said he also found growing sentiment against government regimentation and bureaucracy — disturbing trends that he claimed were leading to a totalitarian society. Declaring that alcoholism was the most dangerous "ism" facing the United States, Watson called upon all church-going people to join "in a great Christian party to speed the way to victory."[62]

Addressing party members at the headquarters of the reform-minded Twentieth Century Association in Boston earlier that spring, the bone-dry White House aspirant called on the nation's moral and patriotic forces — the country's largest unorganized group, as he described it — to organize politically to combat the forces of evil and selfishness.

---

[60] "Prohibition Party Candidate Believes Man Ought to Make Own Whiskey," *Atlanta Constitution*, Mar. 26, 1944.
[61] Jack Tarver, "Prohibition Party Can't Lose This Year," *Atlanta Constitution*, Mar. 24, 1944.
[62] "Dry Party Nominee Reports Opposition to State Medicine," *Christian Science Monitor*, June 17, 1944.

"We are sending 5,000,000 men across the seas to hold political parties responsible for the international banditry they have committed in administering governments in Europe," he declared. "We hold the National Socialist Party responsible in Germany, the Fascist Party responsible in Italy, and the military party responsible in Japan. Should it then be unreasonable," he asked, "for us to apply the same doctrine to political parties in our own land and hold them to strict accountability for the administration of government in which they permit social evils to exist which they could destroy?"[63]

Outlining a five-point program entitled "God's Program for Civil Government," the self-assured Prohibition nominee stated that Christians would be willing to pay higher taxes if the government was administered by righteous men and women who acknowledge God as the author of civil government and who were spiritually committed to eliminating evil and selfishness. "Democracy was, after all, built on spiritual ideals, not material ones," he said.[64]

Watson, who had lunched with Roger W. Babson earlier in the day, then turned his attention to national prohibition, arguing that if the six billion dollars spent on liquor in 1943 had been given to the nation's colleges and churches, "we could reeducate the United States in the direction of temperance." Instead of destroying lives and exploiting "human weakness and appetites," that money could also have been used to build 25 strategically-placed radio stations throughout the world to teach the spiritual ideals of government and good will, he said, an investment that would go farther in saving the planet from another catastrophic world war than any treaties signed at a liquor-induced conference of world leaders. "If I were elected President," he concluded, "I would set up such a group of radio stations."[65]

Like Babson who wanted to change the party's name to the Commonwealth Party, Watson also favored changing the party's name to reflect a broader set of issues, but cautioned that such a change should wait until after the November election since full or partial Prohibition tickets had already been placed in the field in nearly thirty states. While campaigning in Dallas, the former clergyman suggested the "American Party" or the "National Party" as

---

[63] "Watson Rallies Pro-Social Units to Start Action," *Christian Science Monitor*, May 13, 1944.
[64] Ibid.
[65] Ibid.

an appropriate future moniker for the party.[66]

Unlike Babson, however, the fast-talking Watson focused almost exclusively on the evils of alcohol. While Babson spoke about a wide-range of moral issues during his campaign four years earlier, Watson couldn't stop talking about how repeal had failed and how the liquor industry was destroying the country. In fact, he was convinced that sooner or later national prohibition — the country's "noble experiment" — would again be the law of the land.

"Prohibition," he said during a 24-hour campaign stop in Brooklyn, "is on its way back and the forces bringing it back faster than anyone else are the liquor people. They're doing more to bring it back than anyone else by their failure to police their industry and by their lack of supervision. If they didn't give us so much to holler about," he said, "the sentiment for prohibition's return wouldn't be as great as it is." By its very nature, continued Watson, it was impossible to police the liquor industry. "Today the liquor traffic is worse than the old saloon. They've taken a polecat, put a ribbon around its neck and put it in the parlor, but it's still the same old kitty," he quipped.[67]

When pressed, Watson gladly spoke about other issues, reminding his audiences that the Prohibition Party wasn't some sort of Johnny one-note, single-issue entity. Among other things, he said during a campaign appearance in Oregon, the party was also advocating a single six-year term for the presidency and had a detailed plank dealing with returning servicemen after the war, providing both proper care and jobs to those who had put their lives on the line for the country. "We want postwar planning to expand industry along creative lines," he stated, adding that if the United States could provide jobs for everybody during wartime, it could certainly do the same in peacetime.[68]

While running for the presidency again in 1948, the former Free Methodist minister boldly predicted that he would receive 24,000,000 votes — enough to put him in the White House.[69] Though stopping short of making any such outlandish claim in

---

[66] "Candidate Favors Change in Name of Prohibition Party," *Galveston Daily News*, Mar. 4, 1944; "S.F. Judgeship Race," *San Francisco Chronicle*, Mar. 4, 1944. Watson, of course, later soured on the idea of changing the party's name once he was informed by California's Secretary of State — his home state — that the state's election statutes didn't include a provision for a qualified party to change its name except by circulating a new petition bearing a minimum of 226,429 signatures or obtaining 22,543 new registrations or changes in existing registrations.

[67] "Dry Era Returning, Says Prohibition Chief," *Brooklyn Eagle*, May 16, 1944.

[68] "Prohi Party's Candidate Expresses Election Views," *The Oregonian*, Jan. 30, 1944.

[69] "Their Hats Also Are in the Ring," *St. Petersburg Times*, Oct. 24, 1948.

1944, Watson strongly hinted that a union of the nation's dry voters in wartime America still wielded enough power to elect a Prohibitionist to the presidency.

"Thirty-seven percent of the voting population favors national prohibition," Watson told a workshop at the second annual meeting of the National Association of Evangelicals in Columbus, Ohio. "If they would unite into a great third party, they could control the legislative and administrative branches of the United States government."[70]

Unlike his latter campaign for the presidency when he predicted that he would be elected "if the church people vote like they pray," and had dispatched his wife to the White House to measure the drapes in anticipation of his victory, Watson refused to make any wild predictions about winning the presidency that autumn. He nevertheless believed that his candidacy would determine the outcome of the 1944 presidential election based on his belief that "the Prohibition Party holds the balance of power" in the nation.[71]

Watson also believed that he would poll the largest popular vote for president in the party's 75-year history, surpassing the 271,000 votes polled by California's populist-leaning John Bidwell in 1892. Voters in the so-called Bible Belt, he said during an appearance in Portland, were so angry at Roosevelt "that they could chew nails."[72] At a minimum, he believed the Prohibition Party could play the role of spoiler in the 1944 presidential election, in much the same way the party had determined the outcome in 1884 and again in 1916. "Our party may determine the winner this fall," he said with an air of confidence while campaigning in Dallas in early March.[73]

The Prohibition standard-bearer based his prediction on growing dissatisfaction with Roosevelt and the New Deal in the Solid South. "There are a horde of southern Democrats who are disgusted with the present administration," he said during a campaign appearance in Houston, "but who will not vote a Republican ticket, and because of this situation the votes cast for the Prohibition Party may very probably turn the election."[74]

Speaking at the county courthouse in Joplin, Missouri, in late

---

[70] "Drys Could Control U.S. Says Watson," *Hartford Courant*, April 16, 1944.
[71] "The Minor Party Candidates," *Mason City Globe-Gazette*, Nov. 4, 1944; "No Meat, No Drink," *TIME Magazine*, Aug. 11, 1947; Storms, *Partisan Prophets*, pp. 54-55.
[72] "Prohi Party's Candidate Expresses Election Views," *The Oregonian*, Jan. 30, 1944.
[73] "Prohibition Candidate Refused Used of Church, Speaks at School," *Dallas Morning News*, Mar. 4, 1944.
[74] "Prohibition Vote May Turn Election," *Brownsville Herald* (Brownsville, TX), Mar. 6, 1944.

March — some three months before the Republican Party convened in Chicago — the Los Angeles attorney said that he hoped his candidacy would help "to speed the day of victory and return America to the principles of Jefferson and Lincoln" by crystallizing opposition to the failed policies of the Democrats and Republicans in the formation of a Christian-oriented, national third-party movement.[75]

Watson's optimism was shared by Edward E. Blake, the party's energetic and industrious national chairman who predicted a few weeks before the election that his party's presidential standard-bearer "will poll the largest vote ever cast for a Prohibition Party presidential candidate."

Believing that "sentiment against prohibition was greatly overrated and sentiment for it correspondingly underrated," Blake based his prediction on the fact that Watson, who began actively campaigning on January 9, had been given a much-needed "head start" on his major-party rivals and had already visited thirty states by the time FDR and Dewey were nominated.

According to Blake, the dry party was centering most of its fire on the toss-up states of Michigan, where the party boasted fourteen candidates for Congress, and the whiskey-producing state of Kentucky — Andrew Johnson's home state — where the party was running evangelist preacher Robert H. Garrison for the U.S. Senate and had fielded candidates in each of the state's nine congressional districts.[76]

Returning to Los Angeles in early April, Watson predicted that thousands of southern Democrats were going to defy tradition and vote against Roosevelt's New Deal in November. "Everywhere in the Deep South," he told reporters following his whirlwind tour of ten southern states, "I found a rising tide of anger against bureaucracy, invasion of states' rights and governmental waste. Many southern voters are going to vote the Republican and Prohibition tickets for the first time," he said. "They are no longer slaves of tradition."[77]

In early September, Blake announced that Watson would take part in a series of five broadcasts to be heard by servicemen in war zones around the world as part of a public service offered by the War Department, beginning with a speech broadcast from Los

---

[75] "Dry Candidate Sees Need of Third Party," *Joplin Globe*, March 31, 1944.
[76] "Prohibition Candidate Tells Program," *Oakland Tribune*, Jan. 16, 1944; "Prohibition Party Making 'Supreme Bid,'" *Lowell Sun*, Oct. 11, 1944; "Drys Making Bid for Record Minority Vote," *Daily Journal-Gazette* (Mattoon, Illinois), Oct. 12, 1944.
[77] "Prohibition Candidate Tells Democrat Revolt," *Los Angeles Times*, Apr. 7, 1944.

Angeles on Sept. 21. A second radio address by Watson was scheduled for Sept. 29th. Andrew Johnson, the party's vice-presidential candidate, and Sam Morris, radio's "Voice of Temperance," were also slated to take part in the broadcasts as spokesmen for the party.[78]

Thanks to North Dakota's "Wild Bill" Langer, the Nonpartisan League veteran who had a soft spot for the nation's minority parties and insisted on eliminating every form of political bias and partisanship from any and all government-sponsored information or materials sent to U.S. troops abroad, joked one nationally-syndicated columnist, American soldiers now had an opportunity to hear the Prohibition Party's standard-bearer as they downed cans of beer in the foxholes of the South Pacific or toasted the liberation of Paris with glasses of free-flowing champagne in French nightclubs.[79]

Despite the seriousness of his cause, the rotund and good-natured Prohibitionist nevertheless enjoyed a few lighter moments on the campaign trail in 1944, the most humorous of which might have been an appearance at the Bonehead Club in Dallas, Texas, where Harry McDaniel, a club member and magician, pulled a half-empty bottle of whiskey from Watson's coat pocket when he entered the club. Watson had been the club's guest of honor that day and thoroughly enjoyed the prank, particularly the widespread publicity it generated. The Bonehead Club, of course, was widely known for its friendly insults and practical jokes on national figures.[80]

The Dallas pranksters weren't the only ones who had some fun at Watson's expense that year. A few journalists did, too. Expressing its delight in discovering a trade paper's headline that read, "Equal Radio Time Accorded FDR, Dewey and Dr. Watson," one newspaper syndicate couldn't resist poking a little fun at the Prohibitionist.

"Splendid, we thought, splendid and wise. It was comforting to know that after confusing charges and countercharges, we may spin our dial for an equal dose of Sherlock Holmes' delightful companion and stooge," wrote an editorial writer for the Copley newspaper chain. "We hope we may be forgiven a slight feeling of letdown when we found that the headline referred to Dr. Claude A.

---

[78] "Prohibition Party to Address Soldiers," *San Mateo Times*, Sept. 8, 1944.
[79] Walter Fitzmaurice, "Getting News of the Campaign Before the GIs Overseas," *Brooklyn Eagle*, Aug. 31, 1944.
[80] "Magician 'Finds' Bottle in Dry Leader's Pocket," *Wisconsin State Journal*, March 5, 1944.

A COLORFUL DRY CRUSADER

Watson, the Prohibition Party's candidate for president."[81]

Though limiting his campaign activities to a handful of appearances in the South and a few states in the mid-Atlantic, Andrew Johnson, Watson's little-remembered running mate, also added some additional color, if not levity, to the Prohibition cause that year.

Asserting that the country needed a "little less horsepower and a little more horse sense," Johnson longed for a return to national prohibition — a noble experiment, as he described it, that had been abandoned by both major parties. Under the eighteenth amendment, he told his audiences that fall, high school enrollment quadrupled and college enrollment had tripled. "The Democrats didn't want it, the Republicans didn't want it," he quipped, "so it was an orphan raised on a bottle by that great distiller, Andrew Mellon."[82]

Johnson, who claimed he never drank a bottle of beer or smoked a cigarette in his entire life and was "so dry that I rattle when I turn over," said that whiskey — "that nauseating bilge water," as he put it — not only subsidized the press through advertising revenue, but had also corrupted the nation's legislature, "rendering unfit great statesmen, cursing unborn generations" and "impoverishing industry."

The little-known Methodist pastor also zealously attacked the liquor industry, describing it as a "Trojan horse running loose over the highway." Those "avaricious distillers," he told a small gathering of Methodists in Richmond, "would rather see the United States bow to Germany and Japan than lose any of their trade." Prohibition, he insisted, didn't interfere with individual rights, "but abolishes a public wrong."[83]

An aging William D. Upshaw, the fiery former congressman from Georgia who headed the Prohibition ticket in 1932, also stumped for the party's candidates that autumn, telling voters that their "only hope for doing anything or getting anywhere against liquor is to unite and vote with the Prohibition Party." Upshaw, who strongly urged Republican Tom Dewey to "smash the liquorized [sic] political gangsters" in his acceptance speech in late June — a plea that fell on deaf ears — argued repeatedly during the campaign that the American people were fed up with "gov-

---

[81] "Well, We Can Hope," *San Luis Obispo Daily Telegram*, Oct. 6, 1944.
[82] "Prohibition Party Candidate Addresses Church Audience," *Richmond Times-Dispatch*, Oct. 19, 1944.
[83] Ibid.

ernmental connivance in the debauchery of our soldier-defenders."[84]

While Roger Babson, the party's nominee in 1940, didn't take an active role in Watson's campaign, D. Leigh Colvin, the party's former chairman and its candidate for president eight years earlier, could be found once again stumping for national prohibition that autumn. So, too, was his wife, Mamie, who was elected national president of the Women's Christian Temperance Union in September.[85] Both of them were predicting a return of national prohibition, but with better enforcement than the last time.[86]

Having dedicated his life to fighting the evils of alcohol, the 64-year-old Colvin, who was serving as treasurer of the World Prohibition Federation — a post he held from 1934 to 1948 — toured the country that fall, asserting that booze might have played a critical part in the Japanese sneak attack on Pearl Harbor on that fateful Sunday morning of December 7, 1941. "That Saturday night the highways around Pearl Harbor were congested with taxicabs carrying drunken sailors and naval officers, and every taxi driven by a Jap," said Colvin, sounding like some sort of half-crazed conspiracy theorist. "It was so bad," he added, "some thought perhaps fifth columnists were responsible."[87]

Despite the obstacles facing America's minor parties during the war, the Prohibition Party's presidential ticket qualified for a place on the ballot in twenty-seven states that autumn. That was a couple states fewer than economist Roger Babson had managed in 1940, but still more than any other nationally-organized minor party that year, including the better-known Socialist Party ticket headed by Norman Thomas, which appeared on the ballot in only twenty-six states. The Socialist Labor Party, waging one of the most impressive campaigns in its history, qualified in just fifteen states.

Ballot access requirements in some states were simply too difficult for the tiny dry party. In Georgia, for example, where Watson had actively campaigned earlier that spring — making appearances in Savannah, Macon, Gainesville, Athens and Atlanta — the Prohibitionists were determined to place the party's ticket on the ballot, but were thwarted by draconian ballot-access legislation approved by the Georgia legislature a year earlier. That legislation, primarily designed to keep Communist Party candidates off the Georgia ballot, required minor-party and independent candidates

---

[84] "William Upshaw Speaks Here on Prohibition," *Bellingham Herald*, July 4, 1944.
[85] "WCTU Head Retires After Eleven Years," *San Francisco Chronicle*, Sep. 19, 1944.
[86] "Sees Return of U.S. Prohibition," *Cleveland Plain Dealer*, Sep. 16, 1944.
[87] "Liquor Pearl Harbor Cause?" *Hutchinson News Herald*, Oct. 24, 1944.

to obtain signatures equal to a staggering five percent of the electorate, due thirty days before the election. The Prohibitionists, whose presidential ticket appeared on the ballot in the Peach State in 1932, 1936 and 1940 and in eleven of the previous fifteen presidential elections, eventually despaired of collecting the more than 15,000 valid signatures necessary and were forced to wage a futile write-in effort in the state.[88]

One of the dry party's most impressive ballot access drives that year took place in Illinois, where party activists obtained more than 25,000 signatures in 94 counties, including 5,000 in Cook County, and managed to beat the state's August 29 midnight deadline — with three hours to spare.[89]

Claude Watson, who traveled more than 55,000 miles while visiting no fewer than thirty-two states during his uphill quest for the nation's highest office, personally helped in several of the party's ballot access efforts.[90] In September, he traveled to Oregon to address the party's nominating convention at Portland's Norse Hall — a convention that drew 400 attendees, 150 more than the 250 qualified electors necessary to place Watson and his running mate on the ballot as independents.

Criticizing President Roosevelt in his address to the Portland gathering, Watson declared that neither major party was addressing the moral issues facing the country and that America's salvation lies in a religious revival. "It makes no difference if a man has one term or five terms, but what does make a difference is whether or not he is a righteous man." The Roosevelt administration, "which puts the bottle to people's lips," wasn't a righteous presidency, he told the delegates.[91]

With each passing quadrennial election it became exceedingly more difficult for the country's oldest minor party to qualify for a place the ballot, but nowhere was the situation more nerve-rackingly tense than in Pennsylvania, where the Prohibitionists must have momentarily thought they were experiencing a nightmarish case of *déjà vu*.

As in 1940, when statistician Roger W. Babson was barred from the ballot because the party had neglected to include the names of any presidential and vice-presidential candidates on its nominating petitions, it appeared for a while as though Watson's name

---

[88] "Watson Opens Georgia's Presidential Campaign," *Atlanta Constitution*, Mar. 23, 1944; "Write-In Votes Asked in Georgia by Prohibitionists," *Atlanta Constitution*, Oct. 29, 1944.
[89] "Prohibition Party Candidates File," *Illinois State Journal* (Springfield, Illinois), Aug. 30. 1944.
[90] Storms, *Partisan Prophets*, p. 52.
[91] "'Dry' Choices to Seek Votes," *The Oregonian*, Sep. 21, 1944.

would also be kept off the ballot there.[92]

This would have been only the second time in the party's history that its presidential ticket didn't appear on the ballot in the Keystone State — a state that had recently elected several Prohibitionists to local office and where the party had provided critical support to former governor Gifford Pinchot's successful comeback bid fourteen years earlier. Worse yet, it looked as though the party's entire statewide ticket might be knocked off the ballot on a technicality, a circumstance much different than the one encountered four years earlier when the party's statewide ticket remained on the ballot after Babson and his vice-presidential running mate were excluded.

In any case, the State Election Bureau had accepted the party's nominating petitions containing more than the minimum of 6,515 signatures, or one-half of one percent of the highest vote cast in the last election, prior to the state's filing deadline for minor parties in early April, but claimed at the time that the party had neglected to include candidates' affidavits from its presidential and vice-presidential candidates. Since party officials maintained that the candidates' affidavits had been filed with the bureau prior to the filing deadline, the initial decision by the election officials sparked a firestorm of protest from Prohibitionists across the country.[93]

"Keen resentment was expressed by Prohibitionists, not only in Pennsylvania, but throughout the nation, by the news stories accompanying this decision, which inferred that the entire state ticket was ruled off the November ballot," said James A. W. Killip, the party's state chairman. While fully prepared to file a lawsuit, Killip and other party officials appealed to the Secretary of State, whose predecessor kept Babson off the ballot four years earlier, arguing that officers of the party's national convention in Indianapolis the previous autumn had already certified the names of its presidential ticket to the Secretary of State prior to filing the party's nomination papers on April 5.[94]

---

[92] "Drys Lose Fight on Ticket Place," *Chester Times*, Oct. 25, 1940; "2 Prohibition Candidates Denied Place on Ballot," *Gettysburg Times*, Oct. 25, 1940; "Dry Standard Bearer Ruled Off Pa. Ballot," *Warren Times-Mirror*, Oct. 25, 1940; "Babson Off Pennsylvania Ballot," *New York Times*, Oct. 26, 1940. Given the state's early filing deadline, Pennsylvania had long recognized the right of substitution, but the Prohibition Party's nominating petitions for its statewide candidates in 1940, filed shortly before the state's April 3 deadline for independent and minor party candidates and before the party's national convention in Chicago, inexplicably left the presidential and vice-presidential slots blank, preventing the Prohibitionists from later making substitutions.

[93] "Prohibition Party Ruled Off Ballots," *Gettysburg Times*, Apr. 11, 1944.

[94] "Prohibitionist Will be on Ballot," *Indiana Evening Gazette*, June 2, 1944.

Party leaders were ecstatic when the Secretary of State, reversing himself, ruled in the party's favor in early June. Describing it as a victory not only for the Prohibition Party, but for democracy itself, Killip commended the Secretary of State for "reviewing the decision and justly interpreting the law, which provides minorities for the opportunity of expression at the ballot box, rather than attempting to invoke a hardship or disfranchise minorities."[95]

---

[95] Ibid.

Chapter XV

Slim Pickings

Although it was relatively slim pickings compared to other periods in American history, the Prohibition Party fielded more gubernatorial and congressional candidates in 1944 than any other nationally-organized minor party, including the once-vibrant Socialists.[1] They actually won a couple of local races that year, too, when four Prohibitionists were swept into minor offices in Jewell County, a dry hot-spot in north central Kansas.

In addition to slating gubernatorial candidates in ten states, the Prohibition Party ran eleven candidates for the U.S. Senate and fifty-one for the U.S. House of Representatives. They also fielded hundreds of candidates for state and local offices that year.

The Socialist Party, which appeared on the ballot in only twenty-five states that year — down from thirty in 1940 — fielded candidates for governor in eight states, placed nominees for the U.S. Senate on the ballot in ten states, and ran candidates for the House in thirty-three congressional districts.

With their ranks severely depleted first by the American Labor Party and then by the recently-formed Liberal Party, the Socialists didn't bother to field any congressional candidates in New York that year. In declining to nominate a candidate for the U.S. Senate — leaving the SLP's Eric Hass as the only minor-party aspirant for that office — the Socialist Party urged voters in the Empire State to

---

[1] "Drys, 73 In Field, Top 6 Minor Parties; Socialists Are Second With 53 Candidates and Socialist Labor Third With 20," *New York Times*, Nov. 2, 1944; "Drys Top Minor Parties in List of Candidates," *Chicago Tribune*, Nov. 2, 1944.

ignore the Democratic and Republican parties and their "minor satellites" altogether and to exclusively support the party's presidential ticket as the only effective means of ending the economic system that "perpetuates depressions, war and fascism."[2]

In addition to its presidential slate, which appeared on the ballot in fifteen states, the Socialist Labor Party fielded candidates for 79 federal, state, and local offices, including a candidate for mayor of St. Louis. Including write-in candidates, the SLP had gubernatorial nominees in ten states while fielding a dozen candidates for the U.S. Senate and nine for the U.S. House of Representatives.[3]

With millions of American soldiers stationed around the world and women expected to make up more than sixty percent of the electorate that year, pundits and party leaders alike had declared 1944 as a "woman's year," yet curiously women weren't expected to make any significant gains in Congress because, as U.S. Rep. Mary T. Norton of New Jersey, a 19-year veteran of the House and dean of the women members of Congress, bluntly put it earlier that year, "women won't vote for women."[4]

But that didn't stop the dry party from trying. Of the Prohibition Party's more than five dozen candidates for Congress, eight of them were women. In addition to Josephine B. Sulston of Tacoma who ran for the U.S. Senate from Washington, the Prohibitionists nominated three women for the U.S. House from Kentucky; Elizabeth Stephens Carr for representative-at-large in Illinois; Margaret Cameron Lowe and Savilla K. Dormida in New Jersey's sixth and eighth congressional districts, respectively; and Cora C. Schott in the fifth district of Oklahoma, encompassing Oklahoma City.[5]

Remarkably, the party's eight female congressional candidates represented the second highest number fielded by any party that year. The Democrats, who claimed only one female member of the House at the time — New Jersey's Norton — fielded a dozen women for the U.S. House while the Republicans nominated only seven candidates for Congress, five of whom were incumbents seeking reelection.[6]

Unlike the Prohibitionists, neither major party nominated a woman for the U.S. Senate in 1944. Democrat Hattie W. Caraway

---

[2] "No Socialist Choice Picked for Senate," *New York Times*, June 11, 1944. By a vote of 17-16, the Socialists narrowly rejected the idea of fielding a candidate for the U.S. Senate during the party's state convention at the Hotel Pennsylvania on June 10.
[3] "Socialist Labor Party Tickets," *Weekly People*, Vol. LIV, No. 31, Oct. 28, 1944.
[4] "This is a Woman's Year at the Polls, But Men Candidates Crowd the Ballots," *Evening Independent* (St. Petersburg, Florida), Oct. 31, 1944.
[5] Ibid.
[6] Ibid.

of Arkansas, a reliable Roosevelt administration supporter who had been badly beaten in her state's August primary — finishing a distant fourth in a contest eventually won by former University of Arkansas president J. William Fulbright — was the only female member of the U.S. Senate at the time.[7]

Washington's Josephine B. Sulston, a longtime activist in the Prohibition Party who had previously served as the party's Pierce County chairperson, was an ordained minister. A resident of Tacoma, she and her husband had jointly shared a pulpit as pastor and associate pastor of the city's Nazarene Church for more than twenty years. It was the first husband and wife ministry in the city's history. Prior to her marriage, Sulston had held several pastorates of her own in Maine, Rhode Island and Vermont.[8] As the only female candidate for the U.S. Senate in the autumn of 1944, the little-remembered Sulston was pitted against Democrat Warren G. Magnuson, Republican Harry P. Cain, and the Socialist Party's Ray C. Roberts. Sulston polled 1,598 votes in the race which was nearly won by the Republican candidate, who had taken a leave of absence as mayor of Tacoma to serve as an Army paratrooper in Europe and hadn't actively campaigned.[9]

Other notable Prohibition nominees that fall included Indiana's Carl W. Thompson, a former county prosecuting attorney and mayor of Winchester who ran for the remaining two months in the late Frederick Van Nuys term in the U.S. Senate. The Rev. George G. Holston of Linn Grove ran for the full six-year seat in a race won narrowly by Republican Homer Capehart, an outspoken critic of the New Deal who had made a personal fortune in the jukebox industry. Holston and Thompson, a perennial Prohibition office-seeker who was waging the third of five campaigns for the U.S. Senate over a sixteen-year period, were joined on the Prohibition Party's ticket that autumn by gubernatorial hopeful Waldo E. Yeater, editor and founder of *The Farmer's Exchange*, a weekly agricultural publication serving northern Indiana and southern Michigan.[10]

Impressively, the highly-organized Prohibitionists in the Hoosier State fielded more than eighty candidates for state, congressional and county offices that year, many of whom waged active campaigns. One of their candidates was South Bend farmer and poet Granville B. Leeke, who ran for the U.S. House in the state's

---

[7] "Cotton Ed, Caraway Lose Races," *Dallas Morning News*, July 26, 1944.
[8] "Married, They Share Pulpit," *Kansas City Star*, Mar. 6, 1921.
[9] "Prohibition Party Candidates Filed," *Bellingham Herald*, July 26, 1944.
[10] Storms, *Partisan Prophets*, p. 51.

third congressional district. The little-remembered Leeke, who was born in Philadelphia, later ran for vice president on Indianapolis realtor John Zahnd's National Greenback Party ticket in 1948.[11]

The party's best known and most successful congressional candidate in Indiana was the Rev. Jasper A. Huffman, a kind of "pied piper" theologian who taught at various Christian colleges and also served as the longtime president and dean of the Winona Lake School of Theology, a respected summer seminary program. Huffman also helped to found Bethel College in 1947. A devoted proponent of evangelical scholarship, Huffman also wrote numerous books and frequently lectured at Bible conferences across the country.[12] In his 1944 campaign for Congress — one of several campaigns he waged on the Prohibition ticket — Huffman garnered 3,206 votes, or nearly two percent of the vote.

In Illinois, the party slated Willis R. Wilson, a minister and president of the Chicago Evangelistic Institute's board of trustees, for governor and nominated longtime Prohibitionist Enoch A. Holtwick for the U.S. Senate.[13] A professor of history and government at Greenville College, Holtwick later headed the party's ticket against Dwight Eisenhower and Adlai Stevenson in the 1956 presidential election.

Temperance activist Elizabeth Stephens Carr of Harvey — a small, Chicago-area town founded in 1891 as a model for Christianity and temperance — was the party's nominee for the state's lone congressional at-large seat, a race won by Emily T. Douglas, wife of University of Chicago economist Paul H. Douglas, a onetime advisor to Pennsylvania's Gifford Pinchot and a leading voice of liberalism in the U.S. Senate for eighteen years.[14]

Charles Palmer, an 81-year-old Swarthmore-educated Quaker who had cast his first vote in a presidential election in 1884 when he proudly marked his ballot for the Prohibition Party's John P. St. John, was the party's nominee for the U.S. Senate in Pennsylvania. A perennial Prohibition candidate, Palmer could still be found running for office in his nineties — waging a campaign for a seat on the Pennsylvania Superior Court in 1954 at the age of ninety-one — and was still practicing law in his Ridley Park office a decade later, at the age of 101. "You get better health by keeping busy," he famously said.[15]

---

[11] "2 Candidates Named by Greenback Party," *Omaha World-Herald*, Jan. 16, 1948.
[12] Dr. Paul Erdel, "Great Preachers of the Missionary Church," *Reflections*, Vol. 9 (Spring and Fall 2007), pp. 9-10.
[13] Storms, *Partisan Prophets*, p. 51.
[14] "Illinois Drys Choose Slate for Fall Race," *Chicago Tribune*, April 23, 1944.
[15] "Mr. Palmer is 101; Works as Usual," *Delaware County Daily Times*, July 9, 1964.

The Reverend E. Tallmadge Root, the party's state chairman and a former longtime executive secretary of the Massachusetts Federation of Churches (later known as the Massachusetts Council of Churches), waged a vigorous campaign for the U.S. Senate against Republican Leverett Saltonstall, then governor of Massachusetts, and Democrat John Corcoran, the mayor of Cambridge, in a special election for the seat previously occupied by Henry Cabot Lodge, Jr., who earlier that year became the first U.S. Senator since the Civil War to resign his Senate seat to serve in the armed forces.

Root was confident that the Prohibitionists would post an exceptionally strong showing in Massachusetts that autumn. "I have never seen so much interest in the prohibition cause in Massachusetts and am confident that tomorrow's election will bring an increase in our vote," he said on the eve of the election. Referring to a Gallup Poll showing that 34 percent of the nation's voters favored a return to national prohibition, Root said that he had "never been more certain of ultimate victory than today, no matter how many years it may take."[16]

The minister's optimism, however, proved to be wishful thinking. Claude Watson garnered only 973 votes in the Bay State while Root himself polled a negligible 3,269 votes, or only a quarter of the 12,296 votes cast for the Socialist Labor Party's Bernard G. Kelly, the only other minor-party candidate in the race.

The Rev. Robert H. Garrison of Louisville, pastor of that city's Calvary Methodist Church, had a little better luck in Kentucky's U.S. Senate contest when he finished ahead of his little-known Socialist Labor Party rival in a race won somewhat handily by longtime Democratic incumbent Alben W. Barkley, the future vice president. In addition to the Rev. Harold H. Vigneulle, a former music director and soloist who waged a lonely campaign for Delaware's only House seat, and Indiana, which ran candidates in each of the state's eleven congressional districts, Kentucky was one of three states where the Prohibitionists had managed to field a complete slate of congressional candidates that year.

The 64-year-old Garrison, who had been battling the liquor traffic for more than thirty years and claimed to have been personally responsible for closing more roadhouses in Kentucky than anybody else in the state's history, was a graduate of Emory and Vanderbilt universities and had studied law for a year at the University of Chicago. Garrison, who once came within 26 votes of winning a

---

[16] "Prohibition Leader Sees Prospect of Increased Vote," *Christian Science Monitor*, Nov. 6, 1944.

seat in the Kentucky legislature while running as a Republican, later served as the Prohibition Party's longtime state chairman in Kentucky and ran for governor on the party's ticket in 1955, polling a somewhat disappointing 2,687 votes against former governor and ex-U.S. Senator A. B. "Happy" Chandler, a one-time commissioner of major league baseball, and Republican candidate Edwin R. Denney, a Lexington lawyer, former circuit court judge and ex-federal prosecutor who had served a single term in the state legislature a decade earlier.[17]

Garrison's luck wasn't much better in 1944. Waging an active campaign for the U.S. Senate that autumn, the Louisville minister dutifully supported his party's presidential nominee, but had some rather nice things to say about Watson's major-party opponents. "Governor Dewey comes closer to my personal platform," he said candidly, "but I am a great admirer of President Roosevelt also."[18] Never a factor in the race, Garrison garnered only 1,808 votes, or two-tenths of one percent, in his longshot bid for the U.S. Senate.

While longtime Methodist minister George Holston emerged as the party's leading Senate vote-getter by amassing 12,213 votes in Indiana's hotly-contested battle between Republican Homer E. Capehart and the state's Democratic governor — a race decided by fewer than 22,000 votes — Hollis B. Parrish, a 67-year-old Birmingham attorney, recorded the party's strongest performance in a U.S. Senate election that autumn, polling 3,162 votes, or nearly 1.3 percent, in Democratic Majority Whip J. Lister Hill's lopsided victory in heavily-Democratic Alabama.

The Rev. Seth A. Davey, a graduate of Northern Michigan University, carried the party's torch in Michigan's gubernatorial election that autumn. The 41-year-old Hastings minister and former school teacher came from a long line of Episcopalian and Methodist pastors, a lineage that began five generations earlier in England where three of his ancestors became Episcopalian ministers after graduating from Oxford. Davey, who eventually had ten children — eight sons and two daughters — had been a pre-med student before accepting his calling to the ministry. His unexpected change of vocation surprised and puzzled some of his classmates, several of whom later became prominent in the medical field, but Davey had the perfect response. "Those you serve eventually die," he told

---

[17] "8 Ran With No Victory Thought," *Louisville Courier-Journal*, Nov. 9, 1955.
[18] "Garrison Predicts Victory for Drys," *Louisville Courier-Journal*, Oct. 2, 1944.

them. "Mine live forever."[19]

One of more than five dozen Prohibition candidates to grace the Michigan ballot in 1944, the dynamic Methodist minister had led the unsuccessful dry cause in rural Barry County's local option election the previous fall — the first such election in Michigan in nearly a decade.[20] Barry County, of course, was the only county in the state to vote against repeal when Michigan, swarming with bootleggers who smuggled liquor into Detroit from Canada, became the first state in the nation to ratify the 21st Amendment, repealing national prohibition, more than a decade earlier.[21]

Claude Watson, the party's presidential nominee, made a concerted effort in Michigan that year, inaugurating the Prohibition Party's statewide campaign with an address at Alma College, his alma mater, in late May.[22] In addition to Rev. Davey, other notable Prohibitionists running for office in the Wolverine State that autumn included George Bennard, composer of "The Old Rugged Cross," often referred to as one of America's favorite hymns. Written in 1913, it was one of more than 300 hymns that he authored during his lifetime. The renowned evangelist, who was never too sure that he actually wrote the hymn — he thought God might have written it — was the party's candidate for state treasurer.[23]

The Rev. George A. Emerich of Hillsdale, a retired pastor and publisher of the *Human Relations Digest*, waged the first of three bids for attorney general that autumn while E. Harold Munn, a young member of the Hillsdale College faculty who was put in charge of the party's statewide radio communications during the campaign, ran for the State Senate from Michigan's 10th senatorial district.

Though unable to match the more than 6,500 votes cast for presidential nominee Claude Watson, Dr. John Mason Wells, a professor of religion and philosophy at Hillsdale College, was the party's next highest statewide vote-getter in Michigan that autumn, garnering 5,883 votes while running for Secretary of State —

---

[19] "Family Has Seven Generations of Ministers," *Ludington Daily News* (Ludington, Michigan), Nov. 20, 1968.
[20] "Voters to Settle Wet-Dry Question," *Lansing State Journal*, Nov. 1, 1943; "Prohibition Loses in Barry County's Local Option Poll," *Battle Creek Enquirer*, Nov. 3, 1943.
[21] "Wet Landslide Sweeps Michigan; Barry County Leading Drys," *Lansing State Journal*, Apr. 4, 1933; "State Wets Get 99 Out of 100 Votes," *Ironwood Daily Globe*, Apr. 5, 1933; "State Casts Die for Repeal, Blazing Trail for Nation," *Detroit Free Press*, Apr. 11, 1933. Barry County's Eugene Davenport, a former dean of the College of Agriculture at the University of Illinois, cast the lone vote against repeal at the Michigan repeal convention.
[22] "Watson Opens Vote Drive in State Friday," *Detroit Free Press*, May 25, 1944.
[23] "Dry Forces Name Hastings Pastor," *Lansing State Journal*, July 19, 1944; "Author of Famed Hymn in Hospital," *Los Angeles Times*, Feb. 1, 1958.

a somewhat modest showing that he would nearly double two years later in a second bid for the same office.

Charles R. Miller, a longtime Presbyterian clergyman, carried the party's banner in Montana's gubernatorial election.[24] The Hamilton minister — one of only two Prohibitionists to appear on the ballot alongside the party's presidential ticket that fall — had been the party's U.S. Senate candidate two years earlier, polling a modestly respectable 2,711 votes, or 1.6 percent, while finishing third in that race, more than a thousand votes ahead of the Socialist Party's E. H. Helterbran, a union official from Billings. Miller was less fortunate in his 1944 gubernatorial campaign, receiving only 960 votes, despite being the only minor-party candidate in the race.[25]

In Arizona, longtime dry activist Charles R. Osburn waged his fourth campaign for governor on the Prohibition ticket. His first try was as a write-in candidate in 1938 when the party made a gallant, but unsuccessful last-minute attempt to qualify for the ballot.[26] He had better luck in 1940 and 1942, qualifying for the ballot in both races. A former president of the Temperance Federation of Arizona and one-time member of the state's board of control, a three-member board that included the governor and state auditor which was responsible for the supervision of the state's penal, charitable and educational institutions, the 64-year-old Osburn was one of five statewide Prohibition candidates in Arizona who qualified for the general election ballot in 1944 when the party submitted nominating petitions signed by 777 voters from seven counties earlier that spring.[27]

Though his candidacy didn't generate much coverage that year, Osburn nevertheless had the pleasure of accompanying his party's presidential nominee when the colorful Los Angeles attorney dropped in unexpectedly on the state's Democratic governor during a two-day swing through the state in late February.[28]

The Rev. Albin Walter Gehres, a 75-year-old retired pastor who had been instrumental in reviving the Prohibition Party in Arizona a decade earlier, was slated as the party's nominee for one of the

---

[24] "Prohibition Party Puts Candidate Into Montana Race," *Helena Independent-Record*, July 21, 1944.
[25] Sumner M. Crane, a 50-year-old World War I veteran from Casade County who ran for a state legislative seat, was the only other Prohibitionist to appear on the Montana ballot in 1944.
[26] "Drys Attempt to Revive Party," *Arizona Republic*, Sept. 20, 1938.
[27] "Prohibition Party Gets Place on State Ballot," *Tucson Daily Citizen*, Apr. 18, 1944.
[28] "Dry Candidate Campaigns Here," *Arizona Republic*, Feb. 29, 1944.

state's two at-large seats in the U.S. House.[29] Gehres, who was originally from Indiana, had carried the party's banner in Arizona's 1940 U.S. Senate campaign, polling an extremely modest 579 votes in a lopsided race won handily by Democrat Ernest W. McFarland, one of the catalysts behind the adoption of the G.I. Bill during World War II.

Only seven of the party's more than four dozen candidates for the U.S. House of Representatives that autumn garnered more than one percent of the vote in their uphill races. One of them was Robert G. Burnham, a perennial Prohibition office seeker from Pennsylvania who was waging his fourth congressional campaign since 1934. Burnham, who had been the party's nominee for governor in 1938, was a lifelong educator and had served on the school board — an elected position — in the Clarion and Clarion-Limestone school districts in north-central Pennsylvania for more than 33 years during his long and remarkable career.

A man of varied interests, Burnham owned a chicken hatchery and a relatively lucrative business producing and selling gas to two of the area's largest gas suppliers. His firm had interests in more than eighty gas wells in the region. Burnham, who could still be found tutoring local third graders to read and write well into his eighties — "In my early days," he quipped, "even the village idiot could read" — had quite a few hobbies, including genealogy, photography and collecting Indian arrowheads. He was also an avid birdwatcher and reportedly had as many as 35 nesting boxes on his vast farmland near Corsica. The lifelong Prohibitionist was also a prolific letter writer and his letters-to-the-editor frequently appeared in newspapers in Clarion, Jefferson and Venango counties — the latter a one-time Prohibition Party stronghold.[30]

In his 1944 congressional campaign, Burnham polled 1,152 votes, or 1.5 percent, against his major-party rivals, a noticeably modest decline from his relatively impressive showing a decade earlier when the well-known Clarion Township dry crusader and poultry man garnered 2,550 votes, or nearly three percent, while running for the same seat.

Despite a severe dearth of candidates, the Prohibition Party of California also waged an active campaign in 1944, but it was a far cry from the party's spirited effort only two years earlier — a campaign electrified by the unexpected congressional candidacy of Robert P. Shuler, the fiery pastor of the Trinity Methodist Church in downtown Los Angeles.

---

[29] "Prohibition Party Planned," *Arizona Republic*, May 4, 1934.
[30] "Keeping Busy is No Problem," *Oil City Derrick*, Jan. 27, 1973.

Shuler, who captured the Republican and Prohibition nominations in the state's August 25 primary — winning the crowded GOP primary by more than 3,000 votes — faced three-term Rep. Jerry Voorhis, a left-leaning Democrat and one-time Socialist, in the 1942 campaign. The Prohibitionists couldn't have been more thrilled. They fondly remembered "Fighting Bob" Shuler's spectacular campaign for the U.S. Senate on the Prohibition ticket a decade earlier, a year when the crusading firebrand of the airwaves garnered a staggering 560,088 votes, or nearly 26% of the total, while spectacularly carrying Orange and Riverside counties.

Pitted against former Secretary of the Treasury William G. McAdoo, the Democratic nominee, and Republican Tallant Tubbs, an affluent state senator from San Francisco who happened to be married to the daughter of the enormously wealthy Pillsbury family, which then controlled the telephone monopoly on the Pacific Coast, Shuler's widely-watched 1932 candidacy delighted partisan Prohibitionists across the country.

Born in a log cabin in Virginia's Blue Ridge Mountains in the waning days of Rutherford B. Hayes' administration, the lanky, 52-year-old evangelist waged one of the most impressive third-party campaigns in U.S. history. As the first U.S. Senate candidate in California history to cross-file and actively seek the nominations of the Democratic, Republican and Prohibition parties, Shuler, a registered Prohibitionist who was unopposed for that party's nomination, outpolled his Democratic and Republican rivals in the August primary, garnering a whopping 291,279 votes while scaring the daylights out of politicians in both major parties. His totals included nearly 199,000 votes in the Republican primary and more than 86,000 in the Democratic primary, finishing a respectable third in both contests. Running unopposed, Shuler also received 4,940 votes in the relatively quiet Prohibition primary.

Shuler's support cut across the political spectrum as evidenced by the fact that he also received a scattering of write-in votes in the Socialist and Liberty Party primaries, polling 677 write-in votes in the Socialist primary while 367 members of William H. "Coin" Harvey's fledgling Liberty Party also took the time and trouble to scribble in his name in their primary.

By comparison, McAdoo, who was the late Woodrow Wilson's son-in-law and twice a serious candidate for the Democratic presidential nomination, polled 269,746 votes in his party's primary while the "wet" Tubbs, who narrowly captured the Republican nomination when Shuler split the party's dry vote with a three-term congressman from Los Angeles, received 217,047 in the

GOP primary.[31]

Many believed that Shuler could win the three-way general election. Promising a "real hot-blooded campaign," the 51-year-old father of seven formally entered the race for the U.S. Senate in December 1931, about a month after the Federal Radio Commission, in a unanimous ruling, revoked his radio license, permanently removing his radio station, KGEF, from the air.

"I am not interested in partisan politics," Shuler said in a prepared statement announcing his candidacy, "and will go into the campaign on the Republican, Democratic and Prohibition ballots." Denouncing political partisanship, the fiery evangelist said that the sooner the people take their government out of the hands of the politicians, the more likely they will be in "salvaging something from the wreckage which is now apparent."[32]

While pledging to "keep America dry," the ruddy, blue-eyed minister maintained that the issue of "free speech" would be the centerpiece of his campaign. "This decision has been forced upon me," he stated in announcing his candidacy. "I find myself denied the privilege of free speech and by that denial a precedent established that may oppress and afflict my fellow-men, thus depriving American citizens of their constitutional rights and establishing a menacing and dangerous censorship, contrary to all accepted standards." The airwaves, he stated empathically, must be as free as the press.[33]

"With greed, graft and sordid selfishness gradually bringing the great middle class in America to a state of dependence," Shuler argued that this was no time for a special interest-dominated and self-serving bureaucracy "to muzzle men's lips and stifle the voices of those who protest at conditions." Promising to fight for a new law governing the airwaves — one that guaranteed the constitutionally-protected right of free speech — the pioneering evangelist declared that he would carry this issue directly to the American people, contending that they were not ready "for the slavery that manacled Europe in the Dark Ages."[34]

In addition to entering the Republican primary, Shuler also sought the Democratic nomination against five other candidates, but wasn't given much of a chance of winning that primary.

The battle for the Republican nomination, however, was a completely different story. Given his enormous following among

---

[31] "Figures Reveal Shuler Menace in Senate Fight," *Modesto News-Herald*, Oct. 2, 1932.
[32] "Shuler Bid for Senate Announced," *Los Angeles Times*, Dec. 15, 1931.
[33] Ibid.
[34] Ibid.

traditionally dry voters in Los Angeles — one of the few remaining prohibition strongholds in the country — Shuler's candidacy wasn't to be taken lightly.

With hundreds of precincts in Los Angeles reporting earlier than the rest of the state, the controversial minister actually led the entire Republican field in the early balloting on primary night and victory fleetingly appeared within his grasp.[35] He was eventually overtaken later in the evening, but not before throwing a genuine scare into the state's Republican establishment.

One can only speculate as to what the outcome might have been had Shuler not inexplicably sent a memo to Protestant ministers in southern California on the Saturday before the primary urging them, in the spirit of unity, to support his opponent Joe Crail, a three-term Los Angeles congressman supported by old Hiram Johnson Progressives and the Anti-Saloon League, so as to avoid splitting the party's moral and dry vote. As it turned out, the two men were old acquaintances; the congressman, in fact, had appointed William Reeves Shuler, the pastor's son, to West Point where he later became captain of the football team. Shuler's magnanimous gesture came too late and the party's dry vote was badly splintered, enabling the soaking wet Tubbs to eke out a narrow victory against his dry rivals.[36]

Though virtually every major newspaper in the country hailed the victories by Tubbs and the flip-flopping McAdoo, who was personally dry but promised to support his party's national platform calling for repeal of the eighteenth amendment, as "one for the wets," it was clear that the state still possessed a particularly large dry constituency, especially in southern California. As such, it would be an understatement to suggest that leaders in both major parties were deeply worried about Shuler's presence in the November election.[37]

Appealing to California's struggling, Depression-era middle-income and working-class populations, Shuler's populist-tinged platform demanded that control of the U.S. government should be removed from the hands of the wealthy and the privileged. Not unlike Louisiana's Huey P. Long, the famous Methodist preacher whose radio audience had swelled to more than 50,000 regular listeners before his radio station was yanked from the airwaves in

---

[35] "McAdoo Takes Long Lead in California Senatorial Contest," *Salt Lake Tribune*, Aug. 31, 1932.
[36] Royce D. Delmatier, Clarence F. McIntosh and Earl G. Waters, *The Rumble of California Politics 1848-1970* (New York, 1970), pp. 232-233.
[37] Ibid., p. 233; "Shuler Key Figure in California Vote," *New York Times*, Oct. 14, 1932.

late 1931, also sought to limit personal fortunes to no more than a million dollars and advocated tariffs to protect American workers — an issue also supported by both McAdoo and Tubbs. He was also as unrelenting in his opposition to repeal of the national and state dry laws as any temperance leader in the country, frequently excoriating the evils of liquor from his pulpit and radio microphone.[38]

Though he was frequently introduced as "the dryest man in the United States" at campaign events, Shuler desperately tried to avoid being labeled as a single-issue candidate and, while publicly praising the benefits of the eighteenth amendment, believed that the issue of prohibition was something of a distraction. The most vital issue was bread, not liquor, he asserted, adding modestly that his only purpose in running for the Senate was to serve humanity.[39]

Shuler's overriding message was a populist one. "All the candidates on the ticket with me are millionaires," he said of his opponents while campaigning in Bakersfield in early September. "They live up there in a class by themselves. They have a different look on life than we do. We, the great common class, are down here and those fellows up there do not know a thing about us."[40]

Shuler boasted several important endorsements during the fall campaign, perhaps the most important being that of the influential Anti-Saloon League, an organization that he had once publicly denounced in his magazine as "an adjunct of the Republican machine engaged in the whitewashing of the city administration and taking care of certain judges whose reputation for law-enforcement is shady."[41] The League had actively supported Congressman Crail in the Republican primary.

The fighting preacher also enjoyed the support of Los Angeles Mayor John C. Porter, a Republican and longtime ally who had sharply criticized his own party's nominee for advocating the repeal of the eighteenth amendment on campaign billboards throughout the state.[42] A used auto parts dealer who promised to maintain Los Angeles as a bastion of native-born Protestantism, Porter owed his own election three years earlier to the fearless radio preacher's merciless vilification of his opponents.

---

[38] "Preacher Turns Senate Race to a Battle Royal," *Chicago Tribune*, Nov. 3, 1932.
[39] "Triangular Battle for Senate Rages Over California," *Alton Evening Telegraph*, Oct. 21, 1932.
[40] Robert Shuler, *Fighting Bob Shuler of Los Angeles* (Indianapolis, 2011), p. 329.
[41] "Champion 'Ag'inner' of Universe in Shuler," *Los Angeles Times*, June 1, 1930; "Both Parties Claim Vote in California," *New York Times*, Oct. 9, 1932.
[42] "Shuler Backing Laid by Porter to Coincidence," *Los Angeles Times*, Oct. 1, 1932.

Several national pundits gave the politically-potent Shuler a fighting chance of pulling off a major upset in the campaign's closing days. Given the fact that Los Angeles, representing 43 percent of the state's voting population, normally supported dry candidates and that voters in the county had cast a combined 179,366 votes for the crusading preacher in the Republican, Democratic and Prohibition primaries, nobody was willing to dismiss Shuler's insurgent candidacy that fall.[43]

Newspapers across the country were caught up in the fascinating three-way Senate struggle, a contest that drew more attention in California than the presidential race between Roosevelt and Hoover. The *New York Times*, for example, suggested there was a "good chance" that Shuler could slip in between McAdoo and Tubbs, particularly if the voters who had supported his dry rivals in the primary rallied to his side.[44] Under the headline, "Crusading Pastor May Sit in U.S. Senate," another New York newspaper declared in late October that Shuler had an "even chance" of winning against McAdoo and Tubbs.[45]

The colorful pastor, moreover, was consistently drawing large crowds throughout the state and people were listening. "That the old party politicians fear that perhaps too many believe him," wrote a reporter for the *Chicago Tribune*, "is evidenced as the campaign nears a galloping close with Shuler just as close to that Toga as either McAdoo or Tubbs."[46]

Shuler, who reportedly spent only $6,662 in his uphill battle against his amply-financed opponents — the equivalent of a relatively modest $110,000 by today's standards — received a last-minute boost when the *Los Angeles Record*, a liberal Scripps-Howard newspaper that had been vigorously supporting McAdoo, suddenly and inexplicably endorsed the Prohibition pastor's candidacy in its afternoon edition the day before the election — literally only an hour after the same paper glowingly endorsed the Democratic candidate in an earlier edition.

Long hostile to the hometown preacher, the Los Angeles newspaper had denounced Shuler as a "self-appointed Apostle of Hate," a "bigot and blatherskite" who lacked the intelligence and decency to represent California in the U.S. Senate in its earlier edition, but completely reversed itself in the later edition, praising

---

[43] "Triangular Battle for Senate Rages Over California," *Alton Evening Telegraph*, Oct. 21, 1932.
[44] "Both Parties Claim Vote in California," *New York Times*, Oct. 9, 1932.
[45] "Crusading Pastor May Sit in U.S. Senate," *Olean Times Herald* (Olean, N.Y.), Oct. 29, 1932.
[46] "Preacher Turns Senate Race to a Battle Royal," *Chicago Tribune*, Nov. 3, 1932.

Shuler's long list of achievements and enthusiastically urging voters to support his candidacy. While the sudden switch of allegiance remains something of a mystery, it was believed at the time that the newspaper's new owner personally favored Shuler and that two out-of-town newspaper executives had intervened on his behalf, urging the *Record's* editorial board to do something dramatic, simply to stir things up and sell more papers. The newspaper's editor, a staunch McAdoo supporter, resigned in protest.[47]

While the fiery evangelist obviously benefited from dry Republicans who couldn't, as a matter of principle, support a "wet" Republican or bring themselves to vote for a Democrat, Shuler's jaw-dropping 560,000-vote showing nevertheless gave penurious Prohibition partisans throughout the country a glimmer of hope that their venerable organization — a party that punished the GOP by throwing the 1884 and 1916 presidential elections to the Democrats — could again be a factor in national politics. To many Prohibitionists, the colorful and fiery evangelist appeared to be the ideal person to lead that resurgence.[48]

They briefly experienced that same sensation again in 1942 when the nationally-recognized Methodist minister unexpectedly threw his hat into the ring in California's twelfth congressional district. As was the case a decade earlier, Shuler announced his congressional candidacy shortly after again being forced off the air, at least temporarily.[49] He said running for office was the only way he could guarantee his own free speech.[50]

Reminiscent of his 1932 Senate candidacy, the controversial radio minister, this time focusing almost exclusively on sin and sanctity, again waged a particularly aggressive campaign, trading barbs with his Democratic opponent every step of the way.

Once again sounding the siren for freedom of speech while lambasting his Democratic opponent as a former member of the Socialist Party and extreme leftist supporter of the New Deal, Shuler aimed his candidacy at small businessmen, farmers and manufacturers — none of whom, he claimed, had been given a fair shake during the Roosevelt presidency.

As in 1932, he again focused on the middle-class. "The middle-class people made America. They have preserved America. They

---

[47] "Campaign Cost Reports Filed by Contenders," *Los Angeles Times*, Dec. 1, 1932; "Two Million Will Vote in California Today," *Los Angeles Times*, Nov. 8, 1932; Delmatier, McIntosh and Waters, *The Rumble of California Politics 1848-1970*, pp. 261-262.
[48] "Drys Prepare for Comeback; New Leaders Already Seeking Candidate for 1936," *Salt Lake Tribune*, Dec. 19, 1932.
[49] "Station in L.A. Bars Rev. Shuler," *Sacramento Bee*, Apr. 3, 1942.
[50] "Shuler Ponders Congress Bid," *Los Angeles Times*, Apr. 15, 1942.

are winning this war and will win it, if it is won. The nation will perish without them," declared the Republican-Prohibition candidate, whose two youngest sons had joined the Navy shortly after the sneak attack on Pearl Harbor. The middle class, continued Shuler, wouldn't survive after the war if small and medium-sized businesses were to give way to technological advances, monopoly, political opportunism and greed. The New Deal, he said, had "produced theorists in droves," but had "produced no sane, sound thinker who is successfully dealing with this important matter."

Portraying Rep. Voorhis, who later emerged as one of Richard Nixon's fiercest critics, as "a rich man's son" who briefly worked in a factory and as a ranch hand to better understand the difficulties facing working-class Americans, Shuler mockingly compared the wealthy, pipe-smoking and Yale-educated congressman's blue-collar sojourn to what "rich society women do when they go slumming." He also said that type of experience was pretty common among "these 'lefty' young statesmen, whose radicalism now threatens constitutional government and many of whom were born with silver spoons clinking against their baby teeth."[51]

Shuler's spirited efforts forced the heavily-favored Voorhis, who intended to remain in Washington for the duration of the election, to return the district in late October and wage a vigorous campaign.[52] It was a hard-fought and fascinating race, but the spellbinding radio minister, who had been endorsed by the *Los Angeles Times* — a newspaper that had poked fun at his Senate candidacy a decade earlier — nevertheless fell short on Election Day, losing to Nixon's future nemesis by approximately 13,000 votes.

Things were quite different in 1944. Lacking a candidate of Shuler's charisma and celebrity, the Prohibition Party's most promising prospects in California appeared to be limited to a couple of relatively low-key state assembly contests where Prohibition candidates had quietly emerged as the only challengers to incumbent Republican lawmakers in the general election.

One of those was the Rev. Wesley G. Edwards of Santa Ana, a crusading pastor determined to close every saloon in California. "The old-time saloon has returned, only it is worse," declared Edwards, the party's state treasurer, in announcing earlier that summer that the Prohibition Party hoped to force the closure of every

---

[51] "Shuler Urges Postwar Plan for Servicemen," *Los Angeles Times*, Sept. 23, 1942.

[52] "Spirited Race for Congress from 12th District Concluded," *Los Angeles Times*, Nov. 3, 1942.

bar in the state whose receipts from the sale of food did not constitute at least 51 percent of the establishment's receipts.[53] The colorful Methodist minister had also led an unauthorized raid on slot machine operators in an unincorporated area of Orange County that same summer — seizing sixteen slot machines in the impromptu raid, but unceremoniously losing his special deputy's badge in the aftermath. Despite reportedly dropping out of the race shortly before the election, the fighting preacher nevertheless polled a respectable 4,221 votes, or 13.7 percent, on Election Day.[54]

The party's most familiar candidate that year, of course, was former Prohibition congressman Charles H. Randall, a former editor of the *Highland Park Herald* who was mounting yet another comeback for a seat in the U.S. House of Representatives, a position he held for three terms during World War I.

Randall was the party's grand old man — not only in California, but nationally. He was also one of only two congressional candidates running on the party's ticket in California that year. (The other was little-known Johannes Nielson-Lange, who was waging an uphill battle against Los Angeles supervisor Gordon L. McDonough, a Republican, and Democrat Hal Styles, a well-known radio producer, in the nearby fifteenth congressional district.)

Though getting up there in years, the 79-year-old former congressman took his campaign fairly seriously that fall while running against Republican incumbent Carl Hinshaw and Democratic challenger Archibald B. Young in California's twentieth congressional district. Though caustically dismissed by the *Los Angeles Times*, as "a political chameleon and perennial contender," Randall still had quite a few supporters in the district and the party had always fared reasonably well there.[55] Former Prohibition Party national chairman Virgil P. Hinshaw, a transplanted Oregonian, had polled a mildly impressive 6,864 votes, or more than five percent, in the same district two years earlier.

A leader in the Lincoln-Roosevelt League of Highland Park — the first local Progressive Republican organization established in southern California — Randall had been elected to the state legislature as a Republican in 1910, but was narrowly defeated in his bid for re-election as an independent two years later, losing to his

---

[53] "Violations Claimed in Bar Food Sales," *Bakersfield Californian*, July 21, 1944.
[54] "Fighting Preacher Loses His Badge," *Fresno Bee*, July 29, 1944; "Retirement Plan Up in Orange County," *Los Angeles Times*, Nov. 5, 1944.
[55] "'Times' Recommends Candidates for House," *Los Angeles Times*, May 14, 1944.

Republican challenger by 900 votes. The Democratic nominee finished third in that five-way contest. Ironically, Prohibitionist Enoch A. Holtwick, a young high school teacher from Englewood who later headed the Prohibition Party's national ticket in the 1956 presidential election, nearly polled the difference in that race, garnering 696 votes, or 6.2 percent of the total.

Running on the Democratic and Prohibition tickets, Randall narrowly defeated the Progressive Party's Charles W. Bell, Republican Frank C. Roberts and Socialist Henry A. Hart to win a seat in Congress from California's newly-created ninth congressional district in 1914. Following in the footsteps of Minnesota's Kittel Halvorson, a 43-year-old Scandinavian farmer who was elected to Congress with strong Farmer Alliance support in 1890, Randall became only the second Prohibitionist ever elected to Congress.[56] Since the Minnesotan was closely identified with Farmers' Alliance, Randall is generally recognized as the first and only Prohibitionist to ever serve in the U.S. House of Representatives.

Competing against strong wet and dry opposition, including a candidate backed by the powerful Anti-Saloon League, Randall ran as an out-and-out Prohibitionist in the razor-thin 1914 contest, declaring that every "moral or civic reform which now holds a conspicuous place in the Progressive, Republican or Democratic platforms was demanded in Prohibition platforms long before they were taken by other political parties."[57]

Aided immensely by Earl H. Haydock, a young University of Southern California student who recruited forty other students from the Intercollegiate Prohibition Association on southern California campuses and spent the entire summer of 1914 canvassing door-to-door in the district — registering more than 20,000 voters in the process — Randall, an ex-state legislator and former member of the Los Angeles Municipal Park Commission, was able to squeak by his Progressive and Republican rivals in the general election, garnering 28,097 votes to Bell's 27,560 and 25,176 for the GOP's Frank Roberts to capture the state's ninth congressional district seat.[58]

Socialist Henry Hart, a former member of the Los Angeles Aqueduct Investigating Board which investigated the Owens Valley-Los Angeles water controversy a few years earlier, brought up the

---

[56] Storms, *Partisan Prophets*, p. 19.
[57] Gilman M. Ostrander, *The Prohibition Movement in California, 1848-1933* (Berkeley, 1957), p. 125.
[58] D. Leigh Colvin, *Prohibition in the United States: A History of the Prohibition Party and the Prohibition Movement* (New York, 1926), pp. 409-410.

rear with 10,084 votes, or more than eleven percent of the vote in that highly-competitive, four-cornered contest.

Understandably, there was a tremendous amount of speculation as to whether Randall would take his seat in Congress as a Democrat or as a Prohibitionist. He chose the latter, saying in a statement that while he supported most of President Woodrow Wilson's policies, one of his first acts in the U.S. House would be to introduce a prohibition measure making it illegal to manufacture, transport or sell liquor anywhere in the United States.[59]

The Los Angeles newspaperman wasted little time making his mark in the 64th Congress. As soon as he took his seat on December 6, 1915, Randall introduced three pieces of prohibition legislation, including a bill to prohibit interstate liquor traffic.[60] As a lawmaker, the Nebraska-born Randall exerted tremendous energy and influence in the wartime drive for national prohibition and later co-authored the eighteenth amendment to the Constitution.

Somewhat self-righteous and single-minded, the Los Angeles lawmaker sharply criticized General John J. Pershing during the First World War for allowing American troops in France to drink wine and later introduced legislation that would have prevented U.S. citizens from drinking alcoholic beverages anywhere in the world, regardless of what country they were residing in at the time.[61] He also sponsored legislation making it a federal crime to send liquor advertisements through the mail to dry areas where state and local laws specifically prohibited such advertising.[62]

Prior to passage of the prohibition amendment, the California congressman had demonstrated his considerable legislative ability by pushing the so-called "Reed-Randall Bone Dry Act" through both houses of Congress in 1917. The legislation barred the interstate shipment of all alcoholic beverages — except for scientific, sacramental or medicinal purposes — into any state that prohibited "the manufacture or sale therein of intoxicating liquors" and was initially sponsored as an amendment in the U.S. Senate by Missouri's James A. Reed in a clever attempt to embarrass the Anti-Saloon League, which was on record as opposing any "bone-dry" legislation in communities where public opinion didn't demand such harsh measures.[63]

---

[59] "Randall Announces He Is a Prohibitionist," *San Jose Mercury* News, Jan. 1, 1915.
[60] "Prohibitionist Files Anti-Liquor Bills," *Christian Science Monitor*, Dec. 17, 1915.
[61] Norman H. Clark, *Deliver Us from Evil: An Interpretation of American Prohibition* (New York, 1976), p. 127.
[62] Richard F. Hamm, *Shaping the Eighteenth Amendment: Temperance, Reform, Legal Culture, and the Polity, 1880-1920* (Chapel Hill, 1995), p. 238.
[63] Clark, *Deliver Us from Evil*, p. 127.

Although he was focused almost exclusively on the issue of prohibition, Randall joined Montana's unshakable and courageous Jeannette Rankin and forty-eight other lawmakers in voting against U.S. entry in World War I. He later authored the War Prohibition Act, prohibiting the manufacture and sale of all intoxicating beverages containing more than 2.75 percent alcohol, and was instrumental in obtaining its passage.

Garnering 2,500 votes more than all of his primary opponents combined, Randall captured the nominations of the Democratic, Republican, Progressive and Prohibition parties in sailing to an easy re-election victory in 1916 against former congressman Charles W. Bell, who was running as an independent, and Socialist Ralph L. Criswell. Running on his familiar arid platform, he won a third term in 1918 when he defeated the mellifluously-named Montaville Flowers by more than 7,000 votes.

Again running on the Prohibition and Democratic tickets in a predominantly Republican district, the ardently dry congressman was trounced in his bid for a fourth term in 1920, losing to the GOP's Charles F. Van de Water by a margin of 62,952 to 36,675.

The conservative-leaning *Los Angeles Times*, a newspaper never particularly fond of Randall, provided his Republican opponent, a wealthy Long Beach banker, with all the ammunition he needed, criticizing Randall's willingness to run on any ticket, including, on past occasions, the Socialist and Progressive tickets.

"Randall is that strange creature of the primary law," intoned the *Times* in a pre-election editorial, "which seeks for political purposes to be all things to all men and who in consequence serves but one — himself." In its glowing endorsement of Randall's rival, the city's largest newspaper also severely condemned the three-term congressman for his free trade beliefs and for voting against U.S. involvement in World War I.

The newspaper also sharply rebuked the Prohibitionist congressman for voting against the draft and four other wartime measures. "He played the part of a pacifist until the thunder of indignation from his district warned him to be still," observed the *Times*.[64] Needless to say, the newspaper's editors were delighted when Van de Water sent Randall to an early retirement. Tragically, however, the 48-year-old Van de Water died in an automobile accident a few weeks later, moments after attending a victory celebration in his honor in nearby Pomona.[65]

---

[64] "Van de Water vs. Randall," *Los Angeles Times*, Aug. 30, 1920.
[65] "Van de Water is Killed," *Los Angeles Times*, Nov. 20, 1920; "Celebrated His Election; Slain in Auto Wreck," *Chicago Tribune*, Nov. 21, 1920.

Following Van de Water's untimely death, Randall again competed for his seat in a special election the following February, but again came up woefully short, this time losing to Republican Walter F. Lineberger, a mortgage banker from Long Beach.

As in the preceding general election, the man long regarded as the father of national prohibition never stood a chance in the special election. Among other things, he was sharply criticized for impugning his opponent's military service and was severely rebuked for abusing his franking privilege while vastly exaggerating his legislative accomplishments in the official *Congressional Record*.

Refuting Randall's claim that he had sponsored twenty-nine bills that eventually became law, Galen H. Welch, the GOP chairman in the ninth congressional district, accused the beleaguered ex-congressman of deliberately misleading his constituents by falsifying his congressional record and called for an official investigation by the U.S. House of Representatives. "Not a single bill or resolution introduced by Randall...was acted upon by the House in any way whatsoever," asserted Welch. "Not the slightest attention was paid to his bills."[66]

Making matters worse, Republican women's groups also viciously assailed Randall during the second campaign, accusing the embattled Prohibitionist lawmaker of missing important votes on a wide range of issues of paramount concern to them, including legislation calling for uniform divorce and marriage laws and an eight-hour workday for women. According to his female critics, he also failed to vote on critical child welfare and maternity legislation. Randall, who had been conspicuously absent when Congress voted on each of those measures, apparently also missed a couple of votes on bills related to prohibition — the issue nearest and dearest to him.[67]

Despite waging a desperate, last-minute campaign to hang onto his seat, Randall went down to an overwhelming defeat for the second time in three months, losing to his Republican opponent by a margin of 32,442 to 21,056. Again running as a Democratic-Prohibition fusion candidate, Randall polled 41 percent of the vote in a rematch with Lineberger two years later. Subsequent attempts at a comeback were also stymied by the district's voters in 1924 and 1926.

During his 1924 congressional campaign, Randall was unexpectedly nominated for the vice presidency by the newly-created

---

[66] "Official Record Gives Lie to Randall Boast," *Los Angeles Times*, Jan. 30, 1921; "Randall Slurs Anger Veteran," *Los Angeles Times*, Feb. 7, 1921.

[67] "Women Deride Lazy Record," *Los Angeles Times*, Jan. 20, 1921.

American Party, a pro-Ku Klux Klan, anti-Catholic organization that was hoping to merge with the Prohibition Party on a dry ticket headed by Pennsylvania's Gifford Pinchot. Like Pinchot, who told party leaders that under no circumstances would he accept their nomination, Randall also declined the dubious honor, saying that he wanted to focus on his congressional candidacy. Leander L. Pickett, a little-known evangelist from Wilmore, Kentucky, replaced Randall on the American Party's ticket.[68]

Despite receiving a last-minute endorsement from Sen. Burton K. Wheeler, Bob La Follette's vice-presidential running mate, and appearing on the ballot as the Democratic, Prohibition and Socialist nominee, the former three-term congressman fared poorly at the polls that autumn, losing again to Lineberger by more than 52,000 votes.[69]

Earlier that spring, Randall threw his support to insurgent Republican Sen. Hiram W. Johnson, the former governor of California who was waging an uphill battle against President Calvin Coolidge for the Republican presidential nomination. Johnson, of course, had been the late Teddy Roosevelt's co-star on the Bull Moose ticket a dozen years earlier.

Randall had been highly critical of Coolidge during this period, accusing the Republican chief executive of deliberately resisting every attempt to improve the enforcement of the nation's prohibition laws. "The wets," he bitterly charged, "have more influence than the drys in President Coolidge's enforcement bureau." Randall was particularly furious over the removal of what he described as three of the most effective prohibition enforcement officers in southern California, chief among them being Harold H. Dolley — a man characterized by several judges as the single most powerful enforcement agent in California.

In announcing his support for the state's senior senator — ironically, a man he would challenge four years from then — Randall said that while Johnson's record wasn't everything he could hope for, the longtime progressive nevertheless deserved a great deal of credit for supporting the Eighteenth Amendment and the Volstead Act, the latter over a presidential veto.[70]

Licking his wounds after own congressional drubbing that

---

[68] "American Party Names Candidates; It Will Seek Klan and Dry Support for Nations and Randall," *New York Times*, June 4, 1924; "Angeleno Quits Race for Vice-President," *Los Angeles Times*, Aug. 22, 1924.

[69] "Coolidge Lead in California Passes the Quarter-Million Mark," *Los Angeles Times*, Nov. 6, 1924.

[70] "Dry Chief to Give Support for Johnson," *San Bernardino County Sun*, May 5, 1924.

year, Randall was elected to the Los Angeles city council the following year.[71] He was also named president of the State Law Enforcement League.[72]

But Randall longed to return to Washington. Though facing a recall election in an attempt to remove him from the Los Angeles city council at the time — a recall initiated by San Fernando Valley property owners that he easily survived — he ran for his old congressional seat again in 1926.

As in the past, the *Los Angeles Times* — a newspaper long hostile to the Prohibitionist lawmaker — did everything in its power to thwart Randall's comeback that year, denouncing him as "a typical politician and officeholder, more interested in advancing his personal interests and perpetuating himself in office than in rendering efficient and disinterested service to those who placed him there." Long critical of his opposition to high tariffs, the then-solidly Republican newspaper seemed to be particularly bothered by the fact that Randall — a political free spirit — routinely sought multiple party nominations, including frequently seeking the GOP's nomination. "By tradition and inclination, lamented the paper, "Randall is anything but a Republican."[73]

The voters apparently agreed as Randall, running on the Democratic and Prohibition tickets, was buried once again in the general election, losing to his Republican opponent by a margin of 102,270 to 61,719.

More than willing to cross party lines in the furtherance of national prohibition, Randall joined the Prohibition Party's national chairman D. Leigh Colvin and several other party leaders in strongly supporting Herbert Hoover's candidacy for president in 1928. Randall, whose name appeared on the Prohibition Party's presidential primary ballot in Wisconsin earlier that spring, had been a longtime admirer of the Secretary of Commerce and had actively supported Hoover's bid for the Republican presidential nomination in 1920, publicly endorsing his fledgling candidacy a few weeks before the important California primary, a widely-watched race that pitted the former director of the Belgian relief effort against California's popular progressive Hiram W. Johnson.

In a message to the Prohibition Party's national convention in Chicago that summer, the former Prohibition congressman implored the delegates to support Hoover's candidacy against Democrat Al Smith. Asserting that the Republican standard-bearer was

---

[71] "Randall is Winner in Council Race," *Van Nuys News*, June 5, 1925.
[72] "Former Solon New Law League Head," *Santa Ana Register*, Dec. 7, 1925.
[73] "In the Ninth District," *Los Angeles Times*, Aug. 30, 1926.

personally and politically dry and that the GOP had "committed itself to the greatest forward movement since the adoption of the Eighteenth Amendment," Randall urged the Prohibition Party to nominate Hoover and his vice-presidential running mate Charles Curtis of Kansas as its standard bearers.

"If the Republicans had shown any evidence of collusion or evasion in naming candidates to run upon such a platform," said Randall, "then I would be the last man to recommend that our party join the Republican Party in the election of its candidates."[74]

Randall, who had drafted the dry party's planks favoring national prohibition and condemning the nation's "power trust," nearly convinced the Prohibition delegates to nominate Hoover, but a narrow majority preferred their own ticket that fall and eventually named New York's little-known William F. Varney for president on the second ballot. A switch of only eleven votes on the second ballot would have given Hoover the Prohibition Party's nomination. Randall was later instrumental in convincing California Prohibitionists to name Hoover's Republican presidential electors at the party's state convention in Sacramento. Despite some initial opposition from the convention floor, Randall's resolution was eventually adopted by unanimous vote.[75]

Though still a loyal Prohibitionist, both in name and spirit, Randall also challenged the immensely popular Senator Hiram W. Johnson — Hoover's old nemesis — in the Republican primary that summer.

The contest was a classic David vs. Goliath struggle. Announcing his insurgent candidacy on July 29, a few weeks after the Prohibition Party's national convention in Chicago, Randall attacked the 61-year-old Johnson — arguably the most dominant political figure in California history — as a "destructive" force in Washington, one that had heaped "vindictive abuse" on every president from Taft to Coolidge.

According to Randall, those presidents included Woodrow Wilson, whom Johnson had hounded "from one end of the land to the other." Johnson, he said scathingly, had also been "a member of that small, willful band in the Senate which sent the President to his grave — as surely a casualty of the war as any soldier who died on the battlefield."[76]

The former Prohibition congressman also questioned his ri-

---

[74] "Back Hoover, Prohibition Party Urged," *Christian Science Monitor*, July 11, 1928.
[75] "Drys Name Republican Electors," *Los Angeles Times*, Sept. 19, 1928.
[76] "Randall's Hat Goes into Ring," *Los Angeles Times*, July 20, 1928.

val's loyalty to Hoover, criticizing the incumbent Senator for failing to attend the Republican national convention in Kansas City and reminding the press that while seeking the GOP presidential nomination eight years earlier, Johnson had accused Hoover of waging "the filthiest, nastiest, most disreputable campaign ever waged" in California, suggesting that Hoover would stop at nothing to win the presidency. Randall, who had endorsed Hoover during the 1920 Republican presidential primaries, said that Californians would be committing "an unpardonable sin" while perpetrating "a monumental blunder" if they re-elected Johnson to a third term in 1928. The former governor would be nothing but a thorn in the side to Hoover's "humanitarian and constructive" administration, he argued.[77]

As expected, Randall also took the incumbent to task on the issue of national prohibition, suggesting that Johnson's re-election to the U.S. Senate could endanger the eighteenth amendment. "Hiram Johnson's votes in favor of wine and beer and weakening proposals are not reassuring to friends of the dry law, no matter what he may promise today," he said. "Loyalty, loyalty! Loyalty to the President of our choice and loyalty to the Constitution — including the Eighteenth Amendment! This is my platform," he declared.[78]

Despite a spirited effort on his part, Randall, who was virtually unknown outside the Los Angeles area, was no match for the immensely popular Johnson, losing the Republican primary by a more than four to one margin.[79] Having narrowly defeated Wiley J. Phillips, a Methodist Episcopal minister and the longtime editor of the *California Voice*, the state's largest prohibition newspaper, in the party's primary, Randall nevertheless remained in the race as the Prohibition Party's nominee. He polled 92,106 votes in November, or about a third of the total garnered by his equally hapless Democratic rival in a race Johnson won by a smashing margin.

Following his involuntary retirement from Congress, the impeccably dressed and distinguished-looking Randall served on the Los Angeles city council from 1925-1933 before suffering a crushing defeat at the hands of political newcomer Jim Wilson, a North Hollywood realtor, in the city's 1933 municipal election. The longtime Prohibitionist, who had survived a recall petition earlier in his council career, was one of seven incumbent councilmen who went

---

[77] Ibid.
[78] Ibid.
[79] "Johnson Still Piles Up Votes," *Los Angeles Times*, Aug. 30, 1928; "State Primary Vote Lighest for Years," *San Bernardino Daily Sun*, Sept. 25, 1928. Johnson received 420,219 votes in the Republican primary to Randall's 92,710.

SLIM PICKINGS

down to defeat that year.[80] Randall's eight years on the council included a stint as council president, a post he held at the time of his ouster and from which he had declared war on Mayor John Clinton Porter while excoriating the city's "power and paving trusts."[81]

When the *Los Angeles Times* asked Randall, in a feature story titled "What's the Matter with Los Angeles?" — an article obviously inspired by William Allen White's powerful editorial aimed at the Populists in 1896 — what he would do to improve the city if he had the power of Mussolini in Italy, the former Prohibition lawmaker said that he would "establish a semi-military law-enforcement brigade" to "strike terror in the hearts of the reckless and drunken drivers" in the city. He also stated that he "would hold up to contempt and then fire every judge on the bench who yields to politics and influence in relaxing rigid and inexorable punishment for the law violator."

Given that Los Angeles, like every other major American city, was then in the throes of the Great Depression, Randall's hardline, law-and-order response seemed a bit curious, even during a period of rampant crime. He spoke little about improving economic conditions in the city. Then again, in responding to the same question the mayor of Los Angeles said that he would line up all of the city's gangsters and racketeers "before a firing squad in front of a brick wall," so that the metropolis could be made safe for human habitation.[82] Organized crime, it appears, was on everybody's mind.

Using his council seat as a springboard in yet another bid for Congress, Randall edged past fellow councilman Carl Jacobson — the man he narrowly defeated for the council presidency the previous year — and several other candidates in the 1932 GOP primary in California's thirteenth congressional district, encompassing a portion of Los Angeles and South Pasadena.[83]

Running as a Republican while actively supporting President Hoover's bid for re-election that year, the Highland Park resident spent most of the campaign denying reports that he had consistently voted with the Democrats during his three terms in the U.S. House of Representatives, particularly on the thorny issue of low tariffs, which — as in past campaigns — his opponents maintained had adversely affected citrus growers in the district. Randall tried

---

[80] "Recall Petition Filed Against Councilman Charles H. Randall," *Los Angeles Times*, July 20, 1926; "Shaw Winner in Race for Mayor: Seven Out of Ten of Present Council Lose," *Los Angeles Times*, June 7, 1933.
[81] "Council Makes Randall Chief," *Los Angeles Times*, July 2, 1931.
[82] "What's the Matter with Los Angeles?" *Los Angeles Times*, Feb. 28, 1932.
[83] "Randall Casts His Sombrero," *Van Nuys News*, June 9, 1932.

to counter his critics by reminding them that as a member of Congress he had supported the Emergency Tariff Act in 1920 — a tariff that took effect the following year — which placed duties on California farm products, including 1¼ cents per pound on lemons.[84]

Gaining the support of numerous Republican organizations, including the East Hollywood Republican Club, Randall was supported by the "big four" railroad brotherhoods, the Los Angeles Unemployed Voters Association, the Southern California Board of Strategy and numerous other temperance and church groups in his latest bid to return to Washington. He also enjoyed the support of several veterans' organizations.

Though receiving substantial majorities in Atwater Park, Griffith Park and Silver Lake — areas that he represented in city council for the previous seven years — Randall put up a valiant fight against his Democratic opponent in November, but came up short, losing by fewer than 12,000 votes. Considering that FDR and the entire Democratic ticket carried virtually every part of Los Angeles county by a wide margin, Randall's 1932 candidacy — one of a dozen bids for a seat in the U.S. House of Representatives — was his strongest congressional campaign in more than a decade. It's fair to say that were it not for the overwhelming Democratic landslide that autumn, Randall's fifth attempt to regain a seat in the House following his overwhelming defeat in 1920 might have proven successful.

While deeply disappointed in the outcome, Randall was nevertheless pleased by the support of his own constituents, a large number of whom split their tickets to support his Republican candidacy, enabling the indefatigable dry activist and city council president to carry some neighborhoods in his council district by as much as a three-to-one margin. "After seven years in the city council serving the first council-manic district, it was indeed gratifying to have such support from the people of my own section," he said shortly after the election.[85]

Like most dry adherents, Randall was troubled and saddened by the growing clamor for repeal during this period. Nothing bothered the former congressman more than the notion that national prohibition had somehow been "put over" on the American people while the country was distracted by World War I. Randall, who was still a member of the U.S. House when the eighteenth amendment was ratified in 1919, tried to set the record straight:

---

[84] "The Watchman," *Los Angeles Times*, Nov. 8, 1932.
[85] "Randall Thanks Valley Friends," *Van Nuys News*, Nov. 10, 1932.

Strange stories exist about how national prohibition came into being. One of the most popular is that it was "put over" on the American people while the boys were in France during World War I. The plain truth is that prohibition was "put over" by the action of more than two-thirds of the members of each House of Congress, all of whom had been elected in November, 1916, while all the boys were still here in the United States.

Furthermore, Congressmen had very little to do with the actual enactment of the law, for it required that both houses of the legislatures of 36 states should first ratify it. Thirty-six state legislatures completed the job in 13 months, the shortest time within which any amendment was ever ratified. But prohibition was so popular that states continued to ratify as their legislatures met even after its passage was assured, until all but two — Connecticut and Rhode Island — had done so.

How little sense there is in this oft-repeated slogan of the wets — "put over" — is also proven by the simple fact that 33 states had already gone dry by their own state laws. These 33 states comprised 80 percent of the area of the United States and 50 percent of the population. If we include the dry areas in wet states (made through local option) then when prohibition was "put over," it was put over after 95 percent of the area and 68 percent of the population of our country was already living in dry territory, made so by independent action before any national prohibition amendment was passed by Congress.[86]

Mounting yet another bid for Congress in 1934 — this time as a third-party aspirant — the indefatigable dry champion polled 18,760 votes on the Progressive and Prohibition tickets in a crowded, five-way race easily won by Democratic incumbent Charles Kramer, the man who defeated him two years earlier. Randall tried again six years later, but with a similar outcome, this time polling 36,406 votes, or 21.7 percent, on the Prohibition ticket as one of two minor-party candidates running against the same four-term Democratic incumbent.

The results were even worse in 1944 when the aging ex-congressman garnered a negligible 3,615 votes — by far his worst showing ever in a congressional campaign.

In 1947, seven years after the death of his second wife, Randall married longtime WCTU leader Eva C. Wheeler. He was 82 at the time and she was 74. Randall remained active in the temperance

---

[86] Margaret A. Gee, "The Voice of the People," *San Luis Obispo Telegram-Tribune*, Mar. 28, 1944.

movement and the Prohibition Party for the remainder of his life.[87] Following a brief illness that he carefully concealed from most of his close friends and supporters, Randall died in February 1951 at the age of eighty-five, only three months after waging his "last hurrah" as the Prohibition Party's nominee in California's 45th assembly district.[88]

---

[87] "Charles Randall and Eva Wheeler of W.C.T.U. Wed," *Los Angeles Times*, May 14, 1947.
[88] "Services Planned Today for Charles H. Randall," *Los Angeles Times*, Feb. 21, 1951.

Chapter XVI

"The Noblest Spartan Band in the Land"

"I was originally a member of the old revolutionary, up-on-its-hind-legs fighting Socialist Labor Party...I believe that the working class, by fighting, by never fusing, by never making terms with the enemy, could emancipate itself." – Jack London

Those words spoken several decades earlier by a young Jack London still inspired the devoted members of the tiny Socialist Labor Party (SLP) as they gathered at the Cornish Arms Hotel in New York City on April 29, 1944, to nominate a presidential ticket.

Thirty-four credentialed delegates representing sixteen states and three foreign language federations, as well as a fraternal delegate from the Socialist Labor Party of Canada, attended the party's national convention, which took place in a festively-decorated room adorned with large, full-color portraits of twenty leading socialist theoreticians and writers, including Marx, Engels, Daniel De Leon and Lewis Henry Morgan, the pioneering nineteenth-century anthropologist whose theories of social evolution — particularly his groundbreaking book *Ancient Society* — had so profoundly influenced De Leon.

The enormous portraits, framed in red and gold, and the other decorations adorning the hall were the work of German-born artist and famous animal sculptor Paul Herzel, a longtime party member who was once awarded the coveted Barnett Prize from the National Academy of Design for a sculpture of a boa constrictor strangling a tiger. It was called "The Struggle." Herzel, whose works were once displayed at the Bronx and Central Park zoos in New York, served as the party's treasurer for twenty years. Several of his paintings were acquired by the Moscow Museum of Modern Western Art. He was also one of the party's most prolific signature gatherers and spent countless hours distributing party literature on New York street corners.[1]

The Socialist Labor Party, which had competed in every presidential election since 1892, nominated Edward A. Teichert, a little-known steelworker from Greensburg, Pennsylvania, for the presidency and named the equally obscure Arla A. Albaugh, a professional photoengraver from Massillon, Ohio, as his vice-presidential running mate. The little-known Teichert was the younger brother of Emil F. Teichert, the party's vice-presidential nominee in 1936.

Echoing previous SLP nominees, the 40-year-old Teichert called for the "unconditional surrender of capital and the inauguration of an industrial republic of labor" in his brief remarks following his nomination:[2]

> It is up to us to bring to birth this new and happy world. No one will do it for us. No political Moses will lead us out of this wilderness and into the Promised Land. We must do it ourselves. We must unite politically under the banner of the Socialist Labor Party, not to demand reforms such as old-age pensions, but to demand the abolition of capitalism....In asserting your independence from capitalist opinion, you also pledge yourself to continue the struggle beyond election and until freedom is won. For this fight *will* go on.
>
> Make no mistake about that. It will go on until the American workers unite, as a class, politically and industrially, to consummate their historic mission — politically under the banner of the Socialist Labor Party, and industrially into one big Socialist Industrial Union.[3]

---

[1] "Historic 21st National Convention Outstanding for Solid Achievement," *Weekly People*, Vol. LIV, No. 7, May 13, 1944; "Paul Herzel, 79, Animal Sculptor," *New York Times*, May 12, 1956; "In Memoriam," *Weekly People*, June 2, 1956.
[2] "National Slate Named," *New York Times*, May 1, 1944.
[3] "National Executive Committee of the Socialist Labor Party," *Twenty-first National Convention Socialist Labor Party, April 29-May 2, 1944: Minutes, Reports, Platorm, Resolutions, Etc.* (New York, 1946), p. 3.

Albaugh, the youngest candidate to appear on a national ticket that fall, made a similar plea in his acceptance speech, telling the delegates that he and his running mate weren't coming to them with "flypaper promises," but with a sound program that could turn the United States into "a veritable paradise."[4]

In his brief remarks, Teichert's co-star said the only thing preventing that from becoming a reality was the transformation of the instruments of wealth-production into collective property to be managed for the benefit of the people by the workers who operate them. Once the Socialist Industrial Union is established, he told the cheering delegates, it "becomes both the power to enforce the fiat of the ballot, and the framework for the glorious Industrial Republic of Labor."[5]

Claiming 3,000 members nationally, the SLP adopted a platform calling for a socialist reconstruction of American society — "a world of social ownership, democratic management of the industries, jobs and plenty for all, human brotherhood, and enduring peace." It stated:

> The present global war — the greatest crisis ever to face civilized man — grew out of the prewar struggle among the capitalist powers for the markets and resources of the world. The chaos it has wrought is evidence of the breakdown of the capitalist system, of its inability to manage for the benefit of society the immensely productive machinery created under it.
>
> Capitalism could not solve the problems besetting society before the war began; it cannot solve the immensely greater problems which will arise when the war ends.
>
> For more than a decade prior to the outbreak of World War II the factories stood idle or operated part-time, while the army of unemployed workers numbered millions. The reason is self-evident. The capitalists, owning the instruments of production and using them to exploit the propertiless [sic] workers, could not find markets for labor's product. Only one "market" could absorb the abundant output of our fields and factories. That market is war.[6]

Denouncing FDR's New Deal as a doomed attempt to bolster the dying capitalist system while failing to adequately provide for a viable postwar economy, the Socialist Labor Party's platform

---

[4] Ibid.
[5] Ibid.
[6] Ibid.

called on working-class Americans to "repudiate the barbarous social system that exploits the mass of useful producers for the benefit of the few" and put an to "this insane social system of capitalism."[7]

Impressively, the party raised $50,000 toward its fundraising goal of $100,000 for the campaign at a dinner given for the delegates on the first night of the four-day convention.[8] That lofty figure, incidentally, was shattered four years later when the party raised nearly $65,000 at its "May Day-Communist Manifesto" Centennial Celebration dinner attended by 500 members and supporters during its 1948 national convention.[9]

Nevertheless, the $50,000 war chest represented an auspicious beginning and compared favorably to the paltry $8,000 raised by Norman Thomas and the Socialists at their convention in Reading. Among the party's many contributions received that evening were checks from U.S. soldiers serving as far away as England and from combat zones in the South Pacific.[10]

With a campaign budget of $100,000, promised Eric Hass, editor of the party's newspaper, the SLP would "carry on a million dollar campaign" — and for all intents and purposes, they did precisely that.[11] A campaign budget of $100,000 in 1944, incidentally, was the equivalent of raising about $1.4 million in 2019 — a pretty daunting task for a party as small as the Socialist Labor Party. One of the most disciplined minor parties in American history, the SLP never squandered any of its precious resources. It knew how to stretch every dollar.

In addition to adopting a platform and nominating a presidential ticket, the 47 delegates representing 21 states attending the party's twenty-first national convention unanimously re-elected Arnold Petersen as national secretary — a post the iron-willed Petersen held from Daniel De Leon's death in 1914 until his resignation in 1969 — and retained Eric Hass as editor of the *Weekly People*, the party's official organ.[12]

Predicting the demise of capitalism and its replacement by an

---

[7] Ibid.
[8] "Candidates: Teichert, Albaugh; $50,000 Start for Campaign," *Weekly People*, Vol. LIV, No. 6, May 6, 1944.
[9] "Party's Celebration in New York Raises $65,000 for the Campaign," *Weekly People*, Vol. LVIII, No. 7, May 15, 1948.
[10] "Candidates: Teichert, Albaugh; $50,000 Start for Campaign," *Weekly People*, Vol. LIV, No. 6, May 6, 1944.
[11] "Teichert and Albaugh Address May Day Rally," *Weekly People*, Vol. LIV, No. 7, May 13, 1944.
[12] "National Slate Named," *New York Times*, May 1, 1944.

"industrial republic of labor," Petersen asserted that the capitalist system was dying in the most brutal form that force could assume and had inadvertently released forces during the war that were shaping themselves into the very forms and structures that would "replace the tottering and collapsing edifice of capitalism."[13]

"Capitalism," declared Petersen in his rousing address to the delegates, had been born and raised and eventually reached maturity "through ruthless force and bloody violence." It was little wonder, he continued, that it was now expiring "in the most brutal form that force can assume, and amidst a violence hitherto thought impossible in any society claiming to be civilized, its victims — and even many of its beneficiaries — drowning in rivers of blood."[14]

The new and higher civilization that will emerge in its wake, said Petersen, could only be socialism, or — more precisely — the Socialist Industrial Republic of Labor. "For socialism is but another name for ordered progress," he elaborated, "with equality for all and special privileges for none, in harmony with the laws of nature and an intelligent and conscious direction of social forces for the benefit of all in mutual fellowship and fraternal relations.[15]

"In the conscious and deliberate furtherance of this great goal, the Socialist Labor Party stands alone," continued Petersen. "In the principles and program of our party alone are found the answers to the problems besetting the world. Only through the program of the Socialist Industrial Unionism will it be possible to realize the promise with which our technological age is instinct — only through the organizing of the workers on the Socialist Industrial Union plan, enabling them to take control of their affairs, and the the further progress of society, can the challenge of the future be adequately met. All else," he said, "spells stagnation or retrogression."[16]

The longtime national secretary then reminded the delegates that it was up to each and every one of them to organize the working class "until every hall in the country shall echo and re-echo with the voice of the S.L.P., and every street corner in the land is turned into a public forum where the order of business will be the one and only demand — or two in one, if you will — 'Capitalism must be destroyed — The Socialist Industrial Republic of Labor must be established.'[17]

---

[13] "Capitalism's End Seen," *New York Times*, April 30, 1944.
[14] "Fighting Socialist Labor Party Girds for Great 1944 Campaign; Heroic Task Lies Ahead," *Weekly People*, Vol. LIV, No. 7, May 13, 1944.
[15] Ibid.
[16] Ibid.
[17] Ibid.

"It is in this spirit, and with this high purpose, we face the future," concluded Petersen. "And in this spirit we enter this great historic campaign, knowing that we alone are right, our cause alone just, and that social progress can follow no other path than the one indicated in the principles and program of the Socialist Labor Party."[18]

According to his critics, Petersen was every bit as autocratic and authoritarian as Daniel De Leon, the dogmatic, Curacao-born socialist theoretician and polemicist who guided the party from the early 1890s until his death in 1914. Like De Leon, Petersen had completely dominated the Socialist Labor Party during his thirty years as national secretary and would continue to do so for another quarter century. Nobody else in American history ever served at the helm of a political party longer than Petersen.

Trained as an accountant, the Danish-born Petersen joined the Socialist Labor Party in 1908, but had to argue for six to eight months before finally being admitted to the party's Section Bronx. "We don't want anybody who doesn't fully understand our program," he was told by William A. Walters, a factory worker and member of the party who urged Petersen to continue studying the works of Karl Marx and party apostle Daniel De Leon before applying for admission.[19]

Petersen, whose fascination with Mark Twain brought him to America's shores in 1905, was finally accepted as a member of the party in 1908 and quickly moved into a position of leadership. At De Leon's urging, he eventually replaced the beleaguered and weary Paul Augustine as the party's national secretary in February 1914, only three months before the ailing De Leon's death on May 11.

Petersen never had second thoughts about accepting the post. "To be told by De Leon that a certain course was one's duty and then not follow it was unthinkable," he recalled. Petersen, who initially earned $22 a week as the party's national secretary, inherited a party on the brink of bankruptcy. The party had only $79 in its coffers, a deplorable condition that Petersen quickly remedied by eliminating commercial printing and relying more heavily on the party's own publishing arm, which included the New York Labor News Company, for the printing of party pamphlets and literature.[20] Remarkably, he kept the party afloat through two world

---

[18] Ibid.
[19] "A Political Rebel Looks Back to '08," *New York Times*, March 8, 1964.
[20] Ibid.

wars and a Great Depression in an environment of almost unrelenting persecution.

Petersen was a quintessential true believer, an unshakable sectarian whose allegiance to the Socialist Labor Party was surpassed only by his belief that the party's moment of glory would eventually come to pass, a day when De Leon's SLP would usher in a socialist government, deriving its strength and working-class representation from industrial unions, to replace the decaying capitalist system. "There are a thousand hacking at the branches of evil to one who is striking at the root," he said, quoting Henry David Thoreau, in a 1964 interview with the *New York Times*.[21]

During World War II, Petersen was instrumental in saving the life of Henry P. Weber, an army private and party member who had been sentenced to death by hanging for refusing to take part in drills with his unit stationed at Camp Roberts in central California. A conscientious objector who had been denied an opportunity to apply for that status by his local draft board, the 27-year-old Weber, a logger and foreman in a Portland shipyard, had twice refused to shoulder a weapon and take part in training exercises with his unit, leading to his court martial and conviction.[22]

At least five servicemen who were members of the Socialist Labor Party had refused to bear arms in what they perceived as a "capitalistic war." Two of them were given non-combat duties, another was discharged from the army, and a fourth was sent to a conscientious objector camp.[23]

The most famous of the five, Weber's case was obviously the most disturbing, involving serious ramifications for future military draftees who might otherwise qualify for conscientious objector status. When Weber's father-in-law, a party organizer in Vancouver, Washington, appealed for help against his son-in-law's "barbaric sentence," Petersen and the Socialist Labor Party immediately intervened, organizing a massive public outcry against the soldier's conviction. Petersen told reporters that several other party members had been granted conscientious objector status during the war because of their involvement with the Socialist Labor Party, but that Weber had been "ill-advised" by his draft board.

Weber's life was spared a few days later when his sentence was commuted to life in prison. That sentence, too, was later commuted. Applauding Weber's principled and courageous stand against the war, Petersen said that the soldier's belief in "peaceful

---

[21] Ibid.
[22] "Soldier is Saved from Execution," *New York Times*, Feb. 8, 1945.
[23] "Justice, Not Martyrdom," *Wisconsin Rapids Daily Tribune*, Feb. 13, 1945.

revolution" was in keeping with the SLP's basic tenets. "The whole philosophy of our party is based on the belief that the war is the social outgrowth of capitalist conditions," said Petersen. "We believe that such conditions should be changed through the ballot box."[24]

Under Petersen's leadership, the party also experienced a number of expulsions in the years leading up to the Great Depression, the most damaging of which was the so-called "Bronx Disruption" of 1927 when the entire Bronx section — the largest section in the party — was unceremoniously expelled by the NEC.[25]

This bitter episode began when Joseph Brandon and other members of Section Bronx wrote letters critical of Olive M. Johnson, editor of the *Weekly People*, questioning some of the things that she had written in the party's newspaper. A former head of the Scandinavian Socialist Labor Federation who later succeeded the deposed Edmund Seidel as editor of the party's newspaper — potentially the most influential position within the SLP — Johnson responded that her critics were essentially making a flank attack on Daniel De Leon's "Socialist Reconstruction of Society."[26]

Petersen resolved the issue by expelling Brandon and another member of Section Bronx. The strong-willed and energetic Brandon, a linotype operator who nearly faced a firing squad for refusing to carry a rifle during World War I, had been the party's nominee for mayor of New York City in 1925 when he was barely twenty-eight — the same year, incidentally, that Olive Johnson ran for president of the board of alderman. He had also been the party's candidate for New York attorney general in 1924 and for the U.S. Senate in 1926.

When a majority of the section's members later sided with Brandon, the NEC expelled the entire section and placed former longtime national secretary Henry Kuhn, whose loyalty and almost slavish devotion to the late Daniel De Leon bordered on religious fanaticism, in charge of reorganizing what had long been the party's most effective unit.[27]

Under Petersen's leadership, expulsions and suspensions became commonplace in the SLP. In fact, in 1944 the entire Seattle branch of the party, which experienced quite a bit of internal dissent of its own, was censured and eventually expelled from the

---

[24] "Socialist Labor Party Promises Aid to Pvt. Henry Weber," *Mason City Globe-Gazette*, Feb. 7, 1945.
[25] Frank Girard and Ben Perry, *The Socialist Labor Party 1876-1991: A Short History* (Philadelphia, PA, 1991), p. 52.
[26] Ibid.
[27] Ibid., pp. 52-53.

party and had to be reorganized.

As a result, Petersen's detractors grew in numbers during this period. Nathan Dershowitz, a longtime party member who was expelled from Section New York in March of 1947, emerged as one of his most vociferous critics.[28] In a blistering article published later that summer, Dershowitz alleged that the Socialist Labor Party, under Petersen's authoritarian control, had become something of a money-making venture, one that provided Petersen and other employees of the national office with a pretty decent lifestyle.[29]

According to Dershowitz, the party's 1,600 members were being "systematically milked to the tune of about $200,000 annually," much of it used to finance the party's national office, including meeting a payroll of close to $1,000 a week (or about $13,000 per week in today's currency). As of January 1946, moreover, the party had $150,000 in the bank — a significant sum for a tiny proletarian party in those days and a far cry from the $79 in the party's treasury when Petersen, at the ailing De Leon's personal request, succeeded Paul Augustine as national secretary thirty-two years earlier. "Whatever its insolvency otherwise," wrote Dershowitz, "the SLP is quite solvent financially."[30]

Dershowitz further maintained that anyone who inquired about the salaries of those employed by the national office or otherwise questioned the party's expenditures was treated like a "party criminal" and was automatically guilty of committing *Lèse-majesté*, as had been the case with a recent party member in New York. That unfortunate individual, he said, was immediately charged with "conspiracy" and expelled for trying to discredit the national office.[31]

"The ruling bureaucracy of the party, like any other vested interest, concentrates its attention on preserving its control, maintaining its cash balance and ensuring a steady source of income," continued Dershowitz. "The one party activity which it pursues with any enthusiasm and method, aside from the periodic purges, is the scientific appropriation of funds. Everything else is either irrelevant or merely contributory."[32]

In his bitter departure from the party, Dershowitz argued that it was "absurd to think that those who surrender to SLP totalitarianism can seriously attack class society." Maintaining that those

---

[28] "Expulsion," *Weekly People*, Vol. LVI, No. 51, Mar. 22, 1947.
[29] Nathan Dershowitz, "The Socialist Labor Party," *Politics* [New York], Vol. 5, No. 3, (Summer 1948), pp. 155–158.
[30] Ibid., p. 155.
[31] Ibid.
[32] Ibid., pp. 155-156.

who readily accept and slavishly submit to the kind of authoritarian rule exhibited by Petersen cannot possibly work for freedom, the ex-Socialist Laborite said that the party of Daniel De Leon died a long time ago. "What now passes for it is a grotesque caricature, an imposition on the American working class."[33]

During his long tenure at the party's helm, Petersen also consistently opposed any attempts at unity with the Socialist Party — an idea advocated by Eugene Debs as early as 1914. An internal power struggle ensued within the SLP when the Socialist Party proposed a unity conference in early 1917, eventually resulting in the removal of unity advocate Edmund Seidel as the party's national editor and the suspension and expulsions of several prominent New York members, including Julius Hammer, father of oil baron Armand Hammer, who was also briefly a member of the Socialist Labor Party.[34]

Throughout this period and thereafter, Petersen consistently balked at the idea of working with other groups, believing that, unlike the SLP, most of them were reformist and non-revolutionary in nature.[35] Petersen, moreover, routinely dismissed those critical of his authoritarian handling of internal party matters, claiming that the party had never experienced any splits during his watch, saying that "...no one, no group, ever 'split off' from the Socialist Labor Party. The expulsion of individuals from the party constitutes removal of unfit material," he explained in his own defense, adding that "excrescences removed from a party are 'expulsions' — that and nothing more...the SLP has no interest whatever in refuse deposited in the 'garbage can.'"[36]

As a result, under Petersen's leadership the SLP grew stagnant, remaining rooted in the past, unyielding and unwilling to change with the times — "the most consistent Marxist organization in America," as Daniel Bell guilelessly observed, yet "a bleak cenotaph to the cold genius of Daniel De Leon."[37]

On the other hand, the recession and depression-riddled "free enterprise" system never had a more passionate foe. "Any moron, by virtue of ownership, can be a capitalist," Petersen liked to say.[38]

---

[33] Ibid., p. 157.
[34] Girard and Perry, *The Socialist Labor Party 1876-1991*. pp. 40-43.
[35] Ben Perry, "Petersen, Arnold (1885-1976)," *Encyclopedia of the American Left* (Urbana, Illinois, 1992), p. 575.
[36] Lewis A. Coser, *Greedy Institutions: Patterns of Undivided Commitment* (New York, 1974), p. 111.
[37] Bell, *Marxian Socialism in the United States*, p. 36.
[38] Arnold Petersen, *Daniel De Leon: Social Scientist* (New York, 1945), p. 33.

"The pleas and whining of the 'free enterprisers' are particularly nauseating, because they are so hypocritical," wrote Petersen. "They know that there is no such thing as 'free enterprise' except for the small minority owning the instruments of production and all that goes with such ownership. They are obviously talking about capitalism. There can be no free enterprise where the vast majority are totally divorced from the tools of production, to which they can secure access only by selling themselves into wage slavery. To the vast majority there is not, there cannot be, either freedom or individual enterprise in such a situation. When the plutocracy and their allies talk about private property rights being sacred, when they say that where there is no 'private property' (as they understand it) there can be no freedom, they lie, or they babble like fools."[39]

No free or decent society could possibly exist when it relies on the "robbery of one class by another," argued Petersen.[40]

A prolific writer, the silver-haired Petersen authored numerous books during his lifetime, including a highly laudatory two-volume biography of De Leon. He also published more than sixty pamphlets, including numerous essays on De Leon and De Leonism. Petersen, whose undying devotion to De Leon bordered on outright hero worship, believed the late socialist theoretician was not only the country's greatest social scientist, but once argued that compared to De Leon, Daniel Webster was a "second-rank" orator while the spell-binding Robert Ingersoll and William Jennings Bryan were mere "run-of-the-mill" rhetoricians.[41]

An indefatigable and unapologetic defender of De Leon and his legacy, Petersen frequently took issue with what others had said or written about his mentor. De Leon's faithful disciple was particularly upset by Irving Stone's unflattering depiction of De Leon in *Adversary in the House*, a biographical novel about Eugene V. Debs, published in 1947, bitterly condemning the famous writer for years following publication of that book.

It wasn't by coincidence that the third day of the convention coincided with May Day, the annual celebration of international proletarian solidarity. The Socialist Labor Party celebrated that special day with a spirited rally at the Cornish Arms Hotel featuring the party's newly-minted candidates for president and vice president, both of whom promised to do everything within their

---

[39] Arnold Petersen, "The 'Free Enterprise' Fantasy," *Daniel De Leon: Internationalist* (New York, 1944), p. 43.
[40] Ibid., p. 44.
[41] Arnold Petersen, *Daniel De Leon: Social Architect* (New York, 1953), p. 19.

power to reach millions of workers before Election Day. "Only through the adoption of our program can we have peace and plenty for all," Teichert told the capacity crowd. "Capitalism befuddles the minds of the workers. It is up to the SLP to disperse that fog, to put our program before the workers."[42]

Teichert concluded his warmly received address by asking the party faithful to imagine a socialist future. "Could there be anything more worthwhile than to establish a society where our class will enjoy all the fruits of our labor and where for the first time in the history of the human race we will be able to live like human beings?"[43]

Eric Hass, who chaired the event, urged the party's tiny band of supporters to help the spread the word. "We must have the help of all workers who already know that capitalism must be destroyed," he asserted. "We have two allies — that mighty ally — historic forces, and a slow awakening by the workers of this country."[44]

Veteran national field organizers John P. Quinn and Joseph A. Pirincin, either of whom would have been a logical choice to head the party's ticket in the 1940s were it not for their foreign birth, were quickly pressed into action.

Quinn, who was born in Great Britain and later ran for governor of New York and mayor of New York City on the party's ticket in the early 1920s, traveled with Teichert that summer and fall while the Yugoslavian-born Pirincin, who doubled as the party's candidate for governor of Ohio, was placed in charge of the party's national ballot access efforts. Then based in Cleveland, Pirincin had spent four or five weeks in Pennsylvania earlier that year gathering signatures before heading to Michigan.[45] A former resident of Pittsburgh whose interest in the party dated back to 1919, the 40-year-old Pirincin had been the Socialist Labor Party's candidate for governor of Pennsylvania in 1942.

Unlike the more widely-recognized Socialist Party, whose leadership and candidates during the previous four decades included an occasional millionaire such as J. G. Phelps Stokes, California businessman Henry Gaylord Wilshire or Robert Hunter, a social worker who married the daughter of one of the richest men in America, the Socialist Labor Party was solidly anchored to a

---

[42] "Teichert and Albaugh Address May Day Rally," *Weekly People*, Vol. LIV, No. 7, May 13, 1944.
[43] Ibid.
[44] Ibid.
[45] "J. Pirincin, National Organizer," *Weekly People*, Vol. LIV, No. 7, May 13, 1944.

working-class base, a foundation consistently reflected in the party's choice of candidates for public office. This was generally true throughout the party's long and fruitless history, and it was certainly the case in 1944.

Little-remembered Frank J. Knotek, whose name graced the Pennsylvania ballot for nearly a quarter century, was a retired toolmaker from Erie. He was one of eight ballot-qualified candidates for the U.S. Senate on the Socialist Labor ticket that year, two of whom were running in special elections in Massachusetts and New Jersey.

Like many other seasoned veterans who spent a lifetime promoting the party's aim of a "stateless, classless society of free producers," Knotek devoted virtually every spare moment to promoting socialism and the Socialist Labor Party. A prolific letter writer and tireless party organizer, Knotek ran for the U.S. Senate on at least a half-dozen occasions, including a write-in effort when the SLP was barred from the ballot in 1938. In his 1944 campaign — the third of his six bids for the Senate — the 77-year-old Knotek garnered a relatively disappointing 1,989 votes, finishing behind Reading Mayor J. Henry Stump, the Socialist candidate, and the Prohibition Party's Charles Palmer.

Knotek virtually dedicated his entire life to the Socialist Labor Party and the cause of socialism. Like many other party activists, he spent a lifetime running for a battery of public offices — losing them all. Hardly a week passed when he wasn't seen passing out party leaflets at the gates of Erie factories or along the city's busy State Street. "The workers," he often asserted, "must be educated to realize their own strength. The workingman is a sleeping giant. He must be made to realize that the means of production belong to those who produce — the workers."[46]

Knotek's frequent candidacies and steady stream of letters-to-the-editor prompted the *Erie Dispatch* to run a full-page story about him in 1950. Headlined "Frank Knotek: Erie's No. One Socialist," the article included several photographs, including a picture of Knotek as an eight-year-old orphan in class-conscious Vienna.[47]

Another photo, a close-up, carried the caption, "Frank Knotek of McKean has been crusading for Socialism for the past 61 years." Of course, the *Dispatch* couldn't resist also using a photo of him furiously pecking away on his typewriter — producing yet another

---

[46] "In Memoriam: Frank Knotek," *Weekly People*, Vol. LXVIII, No. 35, Nov. 29, 1958.
[47] Ibid.

one of his thousands of letters-to-the-editor. He regularly sent letters not only to the Erie newspapers, but to papers in Buffalo, Miami, Pittsburgh and elsewhere.[48]

Extolling his boundless energy and relentless determination, National Secretary Arnold Petersen frequently used Knotek's example as an inspiration to motivate other party members. "May you long continue to harass the enemy, and inspire your comrades," Petersen wrote his Erie comrade following a lengthy illness in the early 1950s.[49]

A deeply committed party activist, Knotek was precisely the kind of person the late Daniel De Leon had in mind when he described the Socialist Labor Party as "the noblest Spartan band in the land."[50]

Following his 1944 candidacy, Knotek waged three more campaigns for the U.S. Senate, making his final appearance as an octogenarian in 1952 when he polled a meager 1,897 votes. John P. Quinn, the party's longtime national organizer, recalled an evening he spent in Erie during that campaign. It was the year of the first presidential campaign between Gen. Dwight Eisenhower and Adlai Stevenson of Illinois. Eric Hass, waging the first of four campaigns for the Oval Office, was the Socialist Labor Party's nominee. A young Richard M. Nixon, whose dogged pursuit of Alger Hiss catapulted him into the national limelight, was Eisenhower's vice-presidential running mate.

When Quinn arrived in Erie earlier that day, he found the 85-year-old Knotek passing out leaflets on the street. He spent the entire day and evening distributing literature in downtown Erie. "In the evening, while I was broadcasting, he went over to the Nixon meeting and passed out the remainder of his leaflets," recalled Quinn, who was obviously moved by the elderly Pennsylvanian's determination and loyalty to the cause. "Then he was going to sit at the bus station until 10:30 at night to get the only bus that would take him home." Knotek lived about 15 or 20 miles outside of Erie. Quinn then told Knotek that he would give him a lift home, but the aging Senate candidate politely refused, telling his comrade that he would be fine taking the bus and that he — the road-weary Quinn — needed to get some rest.[51]

Quinn persisted, but had a heck of a time convincing Knotek to eventually accept a ride. Knotek made every excuse he could

---

[48] "A Tribute to Frank Knotek," *Weekly People*, Vol. LX, No. 19, Aug. 5, 1950.
[49] "Follow Knotek's Example," *Weekly People*, Vol. LXI, No. 47, Feb. 23, 1952.
[50] "Our Spartan Role," *Weekly People*, Vol. LIV, No. 14, July 1, 1944.
[51] "Field Reports and Headquarters Notes," *Weekly People*, Vol. LXII, No. 31, Nov. 1, 1952.

think of, telling Quinn that the rural roads where he lived were in pretty bad shape and he would ruin his automobile if he gave him a ride home. "I finally convinced him that it was best for my sake that I drive him home," continued Quinn. "I did that, and got him to his home at least an hour before his bus would have done so. He insisted on paying for my room in Erie and for my dinner. Then he handed me $25, five from his son Frank and twenty from himself, and told me told me to credit the contribution to Section Erie. He is a wonderful old man," said Quinn admiringly. "It is remarkable how active he is and how well he looks."[52]

Retiring to his 36-acre farm in rural McKean County a few years earlier, Knotek remained active in the SLP until "paralyzed, dizzy and half blind" — to use his own words — he was eventually forced to give up the ghost. With great sadness and regret, the selflessly devoted SLP activist resigned as organizer of Section Erie shortly before his death at the age of ninety-one in the fall of 1958.[53]

Like his indefatigable counterpart in Pennsylvania and indicative of the working-class nature of the party's candidates, John C. Butterworth, a perennial SLP office seeker and the party's nominee for the U.S. Senate in New Jersey, was a retired silk worker from Paterson. Butterworth, who was born in England, joined the SLP in 1893 and remained an active party member until his death in 1952. There was also Adolf Wiggert of Milwaukee, another frequent candidate who was running for the U.S. Senate from Wisconsin. Born in Berlin, Germany, the 38-year-old Wiggert was an electrician in the construction industry and had been the party's nominee for attorney general of Wisconsin in 1938 and for lieutenant governor in 1942. Wiggert could still be found running for office on the party's ticket a couple of decades later.

In addition to Knotek, Butterworth and Wiggert and the party's other usual suspects — Eric Hass, the longtime editor of the *Weekly People* who was running in New York, and eighty-year-old retired coal miner and part-time minister William W. Cox of Missouri, who had been the party's presidential nominee in 1920 and was then waging the last of his numerous campaigns on the Socialist Labor ticket — the party's senatorial aspirants that year also included Dundee-born Bernard G. Kelly in Massachusetts, little-known Yona M. Marret of Kentucky, and feisty Frank Schnur in Illinois.

Eric Hass was clearly the party's star candidate for the U.S. Senate that year. The young Nebraskan had been the party's golden

---

[52] Ibid.
[53] "In Memoriam: Frank Knotek," *Weekly People*, Vol. LXVIII, No. 35, Nov. 29, 1958.

boy since joining the party in 1927, shortly after listening to one of Verne Reynolds' many street corner talks on socialism.[54]

Described as a "proletarian fighter of heroic proportions," William Wesley Cox had been a candidate on the Socialist Labor ticket on more than two dozen occasions, including five tries for the U.S. Senate, four for governor of Missouri, and at least two campaigns for mayor of St. Louis. In addition to running frequently for various municipal and township offices, he was also the party's vice-presidential nominee in 1904.

A longtime party organizer from Springfield, Kelly had garnered 16,347 votes as the party's nominee for Massachusetts Secretary of State in 1942, impressively tripling the totals amassed by his Socialist and Prohibition rivals in that race. One of the party's few female candidates in 1944, the 43-year-old Marret had joined the party a decade earlier and worked in the meatpacking industry in Louisville until her retirement in 1963.

A custom tailor from Chicago who had served as secretary of the Illinois Socialist Labor Party and as a member of the party's NEC, the 56-year-old Schnur was waging the second of three campaigns for the U.S. Senate on the party's ticket that year. Born in Austria-Hungary in 1888, Schnur joined the party in 1908, shortly after arriving in the United States. Like Pennsylvania's Knotek and other "lifers," Schnur committed almost his entire life to the SLP.

Possessing a keen intellect and rapier wit that could figuratively shred his opponents to pieces, Schnur — regarded as something of a disciplinarian in the Petersen tradition — was also considered one of the party's most beloved and respected figures and party members were profoundly saddened by his death in 1959.

"To know Frank Schnur, to converse and discuss the social question with him," eulogized Georgia Cozzini, "was an experience which always left one richer in knowledge, for he was the best kind of teacher — never pedantic, nor officious, nor attempting to impress others with how much he knew. He had the rare gift of being able to draw out the thoughts and expressions of others. In a few words he could sum up a discussion's logic or fallacies."[55]

Though garnering less than two-tenths of one percent of the vote in a race won by incumbent Democrat Scott W. Lucas, an early critic of Wisconsin's red-baiting Joe McCarthy, the little-known Schnur nevertheless outpolled Prohibitionist Enoch A. Holtwick by more than 1,500 votes in his 1944 U.S. Senate race.

---

[54] Brooks Atkinson, "Critic at Large: Socialist Labor Party Candidate Awaits People's Call to 'Save Civilization,'" *New York Times*, Sept. 26, 1961.
[55] "In Memoriam: Frank Schnur," *Weekly People*, Vol. LXVIII, No. 44, Jan. 31, 1959.

Holtwick, who had written his master's thesis on the "Role of the Third Party in American Politics," was a future Prohibition Party candidate for president who taught history and political science at Greenville College, a four-year Christian college founded by the Free Methodist Church in 1892.

In Oregon, the unusually-named Upton A. Upton ran for the U.S. Senate as a write-in candidate. The 66-year-old Upton, a former postal worker who had served briefly on the party's national executive committee, had waged four previous campaigns for the U.S. House, polling a high of 3,973 votes, or slightly more than three percent, in 1928. He had also served as publicity director for the late Frank T. Johns, the Socialist Labor Party's candidate for president in 1924.[56] Upton's write-in candidacy was never a factor in the 1944 Senate contest, a race easily won by Republican Wayne Morse, dean of the University of Oregon Law School.

In addition to Upton's candidacy for a full six-year term, the Oregon SLP also fielded a write-in candidate in a special election for the four years remaining in the late Charles L. McNary's Senate term. McNary, who had served as Willkie's vice-presidential running mate in 1940, had been overwhelmingly reelected to a fifth term in 1942 — garnering more than 77% of the vote against his hapless Democratic opponent — but succumbed to cancer in February 1944.

The Socialist Labor Party also fielded write-in candidates for the U.S. Senate in California and Ohio. Herbert Steiner, a 35-year-old party organizer and lecturer from San Francisco who campaigned vigorously for the party's national ticket that autumn — making several radio appearances and giving numerous lectures on the West Coast — was the party's nominee in California while Louis P. Wettstein, a 61-year-old cabinetmaker from Cleveland who had joined the party when he was nineteen, carried the party's banner in Ohio.[57] A member of the party's NEC, Steiner's 1944 U.S. Senate candidacy was the first of many write-in campaigns that he waged for governor and the U.S. Senate in California over the next three decades.

The SLP also boasted nine candidates for the U.S. House of Representatives in 1944, including at least one woman — little-known Magdalena Schmidt, who ran in Missouri's eleventh congressional district. In addition to a half dozen candidates for Congress in Missouri — all of whom performed poorly at the ballot

---

[56] "Johns Opens Campaign," *Oregonian*, May 28, 1924.
[57] "Socialist Labor Party Tickets," *Weekly People*, Vol. LIV, No. 28, Oct. 7, 1944.

box — the Socialist Labor Party also fielded an ardent Arnold Petersen loyalist in New Jersey's 8th congressional district and ran Carl V. Soderback of Portland in Oregon's third district.

While the party typically posted poor showings in congressional elections that autumn, Walter J. Klobuchar, an ex-coal miner and longtime party activist originally from Hammond, Indiana, surprised a few political observers by finishing ahead of the Prohibition Party's better-known Elizabeth Stephens Carr, a realtor and field organizer for the WCTU, while garnering 6,588 votes for the lone At-Large congressional seat in Illinois. The 39-year-old Klobuchar, who worked as an electrical foreman in a Chicago war plant, was never a factor in that race, a contest easily won by Democrat Emily Taft Douglas, a former actress and wife of future U.S. Senator Paul H. Douglas who was then serving with the Marines in the South Pacific.[58] The daughter of famous sculptor Lorado Taft, Douglas won by nearly 200,000 votes, but was unseated two years later.

The party's gubernatorial candidates in 1944 also included a number of blue-collar workers, chief among them being 33-year-old Henning A. Blomen of Massachusetts, a machine assembler from Cambridge who later served as the party's vice-presidential candidate in 1964 and as its presidential nominee in the tumultuous year of 1968.[59]

Describing himself as "just an ordinary working man," the low-key Blomen, whose parents migrated to the United States from Sweden before he was born, was an eloquent spokesman for socialism, arguably one of the most effective public speakers in the party's long history. "Capitalism," he said while running for president in 1968, "is like a top...as long as it keeps spinning, it's okay." But its inherent contradictions will be its downfall, he said, adding that the so-called free enterprise system was only being kept alive by massive deficit spending.[60]

Waging the fourth of thirteen campaigns for governor of Massachusetts (several of them as a write-in candidate) over a period spanning nearly four decades, the tousle-haired Blomen — one of only two minor-party candidates for governor on the ballot in the Bay State — posted his strongest gubernatorial showing to date, polling 5,176 votes in his 1944 effort while finishing nearly 2,200 votes ahead of the Prohibition Party's nominee.

---

[58] "Representative in Congress," *The Pantagraph* (Bloomington, IL), Oct. 19, 1944.
[59] "Blomen, Taylor Head SLP National Ticket for '68," *Weekly People*, Vol. LXXVIII, No. 7, May 18, 1968.
[60] "Spotlight Avoids Henning Blomen," *Asbury Park Press*, Oct. 24, 1968.

Philadelphia's George S. Taylor, who later teamed up with Blomen as the party's vice-presidential candidate in 1968, was another working-class candidate who ran on the Socialist Labor Party ticket in 1944. The 29-year-old Taylor, who worked as an electronics engineer, was the party's nominee for Pennsylvania auditor general — an office he also sought in 1936 and 1940.[61] Having joined the SLP in 1936 when he was barely 21 years of age, Taylor was a frequent SLP candidate for public office, waging at least a half-dozen campaigns for governor of Pennsylvania and three for the U.S. Senate, as well as campaigning for mayor of Philadelphia on a couple of occasions.

One of Taylor's most impressive campaigns occurred in Pennsylvania's 1962 gubernatorial election, a year he garnered 14,340 votes against wealthy Republican William W. Scranton and Democrat Richardson Dilworth, the former mayor of Philadelphia. During that campaign, the little-known electronics engineer demanded equal time under the Fairness Doctrine, resulting in no fewer than 21 television appearances and 51 radio broadcasts — almost all of which were a half-hour in length.[62]

Despite waging numerous campaigns on the party's ticket over a period of more than thirty years, it wasn't until 1971 — a year he commanded a modest 948 votes while running for mayor of Philadelphia against the legendary and polarizing Frank L. Rizzo, "America's toughest cop," and silk-stocking Republican W. Thacher Longstreth — that the native born Pennsylvanian finally sensed a breakthrough of sorts. It was the first time in his long career as a Socialist Labor Party candidate and organizer that he had concluded a campaign "without once being told to go back to Russia" — a country, of course, that he had never visited. "At least they're beginning to distinguish between us and that ill-fated experiment in Russia," he grumbled.[63]

Louis Fisher, the party's nominee for Illinois Secretary of State that year, was another blue-collar worker who frequently ran for public office on the Socialist Labor Party ticket. Fisher, who joined the party when he was 22, was deeply angered by the Roosevelt administration's policy of creating artificial scarcity by destroying livestock and burying thousands of acres of crops in the midst of hunger and starvation during the Great Depression. Fisher, whose

---

[61] "Sample Ballot," *Bristol Courier* (Bristol, Pa.), Nov. 4, 1936; "Industrial Government Party Lists Candidates," *Harrisburg Evening News*, Apr. 2, 1940.
[62] "Field Notes," *Weekly People*, Dec. 22, 1962.
[63] "Mayoral Non-Hopefuls Glad They Ran," *Philadelphia Daily News*, Nov. 2, 1971.

outrage — like that of many others at the time — led him to socialism and directly into the ranks of the world's second-oldest socialist party.

A lifelong party activist who made his living as a silk spotter in the dry cleaning industry, Fisher previously ran for governor of Wisconsin and later campaigned for governor and the U.S. Senate in Illinois before heading his party's ticket in the 1972 presidential election, garnering the largest popular vote in the party's history.[64] Frequently using humility and humor, the trim, neatly-bearded Chicagoan panned Democratic nominee George S. McGovern as a tool of the capitalist system throughout the 1972 campaign, accusing the Democratic candidate of "just fooling the populists" while maintaining that the evils of capitalism and the SLP's prescription for replacing it with socialism was "the only hope for the future of mankind." McGovern's reform program was simply inadequate. "When you've got a mosquito problem in a swamp, you don't go after them with a flit gun," the spry, 59-year-old quipped, "you drain the swamp."[65]

Charles Ginsberg of Indianapolis, the party's nominee for Indiana Secretary of State, was another blue-collar worker. A lifelong boilermaker, the 54-year-old Ginsberg joined the party 27 years earlier and served in various capacities, including stints as the party's state secretary and party organizer, as well as an instructor and lecturer on Marxian science. He spent 36 years in service to the party and waged several campaigns for governor of Indiana, mounting his last effort in 1952, eleven months before his death at the age of 63.[66]

While most of the party's candidates that year had what could be described as traditional blue-collar occupations — men like Akron rubber worker William Farkas, who ran for lieutenant governor of Ohio, Charles E. Storm, a Chicago electrician who ran for governor of Illinois, 37-year-old machinist James Sim, the party's nominee for Secretary of State in Michigan, or Joseph Mackay, a painting contractor from Norwalk who ran for state comptroller in Connecticut — there were several notable exceptions.

For instance, Dr. O. Alfred Olson, a practicing physician from Rockford, was the party's nominee for state auditor in Illinois. Ol-

---

[64] "Socialist Labor Party Plans Presidential Campaign," *New York Times*, April 11, 1972.
[65] "Socialist Labor Party Choice Undeterred By Empty Chairs," Minneapolis Star, Sep. 27, 1972; "Socialist Candidate Tells Goals of Party Movement," *Minneapolis Tribune*, Sep. 27, 1972.
[66] "Charles Ginsberg," *Indianapolis News*, Oct. 15, 1953.

son's daughter, Helen, was slated as one of the party's three candidates for trustee of the University of Illinois that year. Long active in the party's local and state organization, the Rockford doctor had been the party's candidate for governor in 1936.[67]

Another exception was Joseph C. Borden, the party's candidate for governor of Connecticut that year. Borden was a Harvard-educated New York City librarian. One of a half-dozen gubernatorial candidates fielded by the party that year, Borden probably did as much, if not more, to publicize the Socialist Labor Party and its beliefs than any other party activist in the country during this period. A frequent candidate for public office and a prolific writer whose letters-to-the-editor were regularly published in the *Hartford Courant* and other Connecticut newspapers, Borden understood the importance of running candidates in elections with little chance of success.

Walter Steinhilber, a frequent Socialist Labor candidate between 1944 and 1970, was an extremely talented and fairly renowned graphic artist who regularly produced editorial cartoons for the *Weekly People* and other SLP publications. Steinhilber, whose works included hundreds of water colors, some of which still appear in New York art galleries, was a candidate for the New York Court of Appeals in 1944.

Like so many of the party's candidates, Steinhilber was a long-distance runner, a perennial aspirant willing to use any soapbox to further the party's cause. A quarter century after his 1944 campaign for the Court of Appeals, Steinhilber was still running for office. In 1969, he waged a campaign for president of the New York City Council and a year later was the Socialist Labor Party's candidate for State Controller — a race in which the 73-year-old commercial artist polled 6,908 votes.

Similarly, Michigan's Theos A. Grove was also a perpetual Socialist Labor Party candidate for public office, frequently running for governor and other offices. The 40-year-old Grove, who joined the party in 1932, was a practicing chiropractor. In both his 1944 gubernatorial campaign and in a bid for the U.S. Senate four years later, Grove focused much of his firepower on the "spurious socialism" of Norman Thomas and his party, charging that the rival Socialist Party was advocating "nothing but a patched-up capitalism with its own politicians in place of Democrats or Republicans."[68]

---

[67] "Doctor, Daughter on S-L State Ticket," *Rockford Morning Star*, Mar. 28, 1944.
[68] "Marxian Socialism Program Advocated," *Battle Creek Enquirer*, Oct. 22, 1948.

Grove's running mate for lieutenant governor in 1944 was 32-year-old James C. Horvath, a General Motors employee and another constant candidate on the party's ticket. In addition to waging a couple of campaigns for the state's second spot, the didactic and doctrinaire Horvath, who once famously debated a member of the New Left during the war in Vietnam in a forum hosted by the *Detroit Free Press*, waged no fewer than four campaigns for governor between 1964 and 1974. Horvath posted his strongest showing in 1966 when he garnered 8,017 votes as the only minor-party candidate running against Gov. George W. Romney and Democratic challenger Zolton Ferency, a Michigan State University criminal justice professor and three-time Democratic state chairman who was later instrumental in the founding of the left-wing Human Rights Party.[69]

Mary K. Gesensway of Philadelphia, the party's nominee for Pennsylvania state treasurer in 1944 — her second try for that statewide post — was the wife of Latvian-born composer and violinist Louis Gesensway, a longtime member of the Philadelphia Orchestra who once performed a concert for First Lady Eleanor Roosevelt.[70]

Louis Gesensway, the son of a rabbi who became a professional musician at the remarkably young age of twelve and whose chamber works have been performed worldwide, studied violin at the Toronto Conservatory, now the Royal Conservatory of Music, where he famously helped organize the new Toronto Symphony Orchestra with flutist Abe Fenboque in 1923, following a five-year hiatus. Described as "America's foremost young composer," Gesensway, playing first violin, was part of a string quartet that performed at the Socialist Labor Party's annual Thanksgiving Affair at New York's City Center Casino shortly after the 1944 presidential campaign.[71]

This writer had an opportunity to speak with Mary Gesensway on a couple of occasions in the mid-eighties, about a decade after her husband had passed away. The Gesensways were a remarkable couple. Dignified, urbane and cultured, they were lifelong members of the Socialist Labor Party and frequently held picnics and other party gatherings at their cottage along the banks of the Rancocas Creek in Mt. Holly, New Jersey.

---

[69] "Old Leftist Scorns the New Protest," *Detroit Free Press*, Mar. 29, 1966.
[70] "Socialist-Laborites Name '44 Candidates," *Pittsburgh Press*, Mar. 1, 1944.
[71] "Medley of Fun and Beauty Lined Up for N.Y. Affair," *Weekly People*, Vol. LIV, No. 31, Oct. 28, 1944.

It was in those very waters that Mary Gesensway single-handedly saved the lives of two women following a canoe mishap in 1941. Gesensway, who had been canoeing nearby, dove in the water when she saw the two women clinging to their overturned canoe. Overcome by fatigue, one of the women slipped under the surface at which point Gesensway dove in and dragged the drowning woman ashore. She then returned and pulled the second victim to safety.[72]

Firm believers in the SLP's long-anticipated Socialist Industrial Union, the Gesensways had been arrested for distributing party literature during World War II — a difficult and dangerous period for all of the country's dissenters. As it turned out, Louis Gesensway, who died in 1976, had been arrested twice, charged both times with littering the streets of Philadelphia while handing out party leaflets. The Gesensways frequently made their spacious home in the city's Mount Airy section available for party activities and Mary, the party's local chairwoman at the time, presided over a rally for vice-presidential candidate Arla Albaugh at Philadelphia's Sylvania Hotel when he visited the city during the summer of the 1944 presidential campaign.[73]

Originally from Indiana, Mary Gesensway was a frequent candidate for public office in Philadelphia, running for city council and the city commission on the Socialist Labor Party ticket in the 1950s and 1960s. A candidate for an at-large seat on the city council in 1971 — the last year the SLP appeared on the ballot in a Philadelphia mayoral race — she remained active in the party until shortly before her death at the age of eighty-seven in 1993.[74] Gesensway garnered 2,216 votes, including 227 military absentee ballots, in her bid for state treasurer in 1944.[75]

Similarly, Herman A. Johansen of Monroeville, another frequent Socialist Labor candidate from Pennsylvania, had a Ph.D. in chemistry from the University of Oregon and worked as a research chemist for the Westinghouse Electric Corporation.

The party even had an occasional entrepreneur within its ranks, as was the case with Milton Herder of White Plains, New York, another longtime member. Herder, who attended the University of Pennsylvania as an undergraduate and later studied at the Pennsylvania Museum School of Art, owned an advertising

---

[72] "Mary K. Gesensway; Socialist Labor Hopeful," *Philadelphia Daily News*, June 29, 1993.
[73] "Socialist Rally Hears Candidate," *Philadelphia Inquirer*, Aug. 11, 1944.
[74] "Four Minority Parties Put Up Candidates for Mayor and Councilman-at-Large Seats," *Philadelphia Inquirer*, Oct. 24, 1971.
[75] "FDR's Official Pa. Majority Reached 105,431 Votes," *Gazette and Daily* (York, Pa.), Dec. 13, 1944.

agency in Manhattan. "Socialism is necessary," he asserted while running for governor of New York in 1966, "to salvage the human race."[76] Herder, who was born and raised in Philadelphia, was perhaps best remembered for famously stating that he looked forward to a "world in which man can live by cooperation, not competition."[77]

While the party usually fielded working-class candidates, a surprising number of the Socialist Labor Party's rank-and-file members also didn't hold what one would describe as typical blue-collar jobs.

One of those was cultural evolutionist Leslie A. White, a leading scholar on the life and career of American anthropologist Lewis Henry Morgan and whose own views had been deeply influenced not only by Morgan but also by Charles Darwin and Herbert Spencer. White was widely believed to have been a member of the Socialist Labor Party during the Great Depression.

"It was White's political commitment to the Socialist Labor Party," wrote biographer William J. Peace, "that shaped the corpus of the evolutionary work for which he is so well known." While the neo-evolutionist never ran for office on the party's ticket and went to great lengths to conceal his decades-long involvement in the party, the University of Michigan professor embraced Marxism long before it was fashionable in anthropology and frequently contributed articles to the *Weekly People* during this period under the pseudonym of John Steel. According to Peace, it was in those anonymous articles in the party's newspaper that the world famous anthropologist originally honed his arguments on the theory of cultural evolution, arguing that it could function as both a science and a "principle of action."[78]

Having been introduced to the SLP by his friend and former colleague Marvin Farber, an internationally-recognized philosopher and second generation member of the SLP, White believed that anthropology and particularly the concept of cultural evolution could provide a rational and humane way of understanding the transition from a capitalist society to a socialist society.[79]

White, who served as president of the American Anthropological Society in the 1960s, eventually had a bitter parting of the ways with the SLP when Eric Hass, editor of the *Weekly People*, retracted

---

[76] "Socialist Candidate Visits in Ellenville," *Kingston Daily Freeman* (Kingston, N.Y.), Nov. 3, 1966.
[77] "Timely Quotes," *Fond du Lac (Wisconsin) Commonwealth Reporter*, May 3, 1966.
[78] William J. Peace, *Leslie A. White: Evolution and Revolution in Anthropology* (Lincoln, NE, 2004), pp. 69-70.
[79] Ibid.

a glowing review of White's *The Science of Culture: A Study of Man & Civilization*, and later published a devastatingly critical review written by three members of the party's NEC.[80]

Popular 1960s science fiction writer Dallas McCord "Mack" Reynolds, the son of Verne L. Reynolds, a steamfitter-turned-advertising salesman who headed the Socialist Labor Party's ticket in the 1928 and 1932 presidential campaigns, was also a devoted party member. Like his father, the younger Reynolds, whose radical perspective on politics was often reflected in his prolific writings, was an activist in the Socialist Labor Party for twenty-five years and had accompanied John W. Aiken, the party's little-remembered presidential candidate, on his national tour in 1940.[81]

---

[80] Ibid.
[81] "Hard-Hitting '44 Campaign Planned by Calif. S.L.P.," *Weekly People*, Vol. LIV, No. 6, May 6, 1944.

Chapter XVII

A Steelworker for President

The son of a German coal miner and farmer who escaped Prussian militarism and immigrated to the United States, Edward A. Teichert — the youngest of the half-dozen men seeking the presidency that autumn — was born in Greensburg, Pennsylvania, in 1904.[1] A steelworker for twenty years, he was married and had three children: Edward, Gail and Shirley. Eighteen-year-old Edward was serving in the armed forces during his father's 1944 presidential campaign as a member of Gen. George Patton's Third Army in Europe.[2]

The Socialist Labor Party ran deep in the Teichert family's blood. Ernest Teichert, the candidate's father, had been a faithful party member for years, as were the candidate's five brothers and two sisters. The Teicherts lived and breathed the SLP and the family farm in Greensburg had been the scene of many fundraising events and other SLP-related activities.[3]

Emil Teichert, the candidate's older brother, was a former office worker in the statistical department of the Pennsylvania Railroad in Pittsburgh and had been the party's candidate for vice president in 1936. Unfortunately, he was injured in an automobile accident after making only four campaign appearances that year and was laid up for most of the campaign.[4] The older Teichert had been a

---

[1] "Socialist Labor Candidate Only 40," *Washington Post*, Oct. 29, 1944.
[2] "Edward A. Teichert Jr., 73, educator, theater founder," *Daily Record* (Morristown, N.J.), Sep. 23, 1999.
[3] "Candidates: Teichert, Albaugh; $50,000 Start for Campaign," *Weekly People*, Vol. LIV, No. 6, May 6, 1944.
[4] "Chevrolet Campaign," *TIME*, Nov. 2, 1936.

frequent SLP candidate for state and municipal office, twice running for lieutenant governor of New York and waging a spirited campaign for mayor of New York City in 1937. He also worked briefly as the acting editor of the *Weekly People*, the party's official organ.[5]

A member of the Socialist Labor Party since 1930, Edward A. Teichert worked as an assistant foreman at the Railway Industrial Engineering Company, a structural steel plant, in Greensburg — an industry in which he had toiled for some twenty years. He also had been a delegate to the party's national conventions in 1936, 1940 and 1944 and served as state secretary of the SLP in Pennsylvania for a dozen years. He was also a popular party lecturer, often traveling to New York City to lecture in Aaron Orange's weekly classes on socialism.[6]

Teichert, who later quit the Socialist Labor Party along with the entire Greensburg section in 1977, only a few months after the party's final presidential campaign in the year of America's Bicentennial, was also the party's presidential nominee in 1948 — a year the press accurately dubbed him the "forgotten man" in the crowded contest between President Truman, Republican Thomas E. Dewey, former Vice President Henry A. Wallace, Dixiecrat J. Strom Thurmond and the Socialist Party's Norman M. Thomas.[7]

Teichert was employed as a steelworker for more than thirty years and later worked as a Good Humor ice cream salesman for another fourteen years, retiring from his second occupation in his mid-seventies, only a year or two before his death in 1981.

Like Teichert, the 38-year-old Albaugh was also a member of the party's lecture staff and spoke frequently at party gatherings in Ohio and Pennsylvania. During the 1944 campaign, he was a resident of Massillon, Ohio — a city that had once elected the colorful "General" Jacob Coxey as mayor. Struggling financially, Albaugh had joined the Socialist Labor Party in 1934. "Poverty or the threat of poverty had never affected me so greatly as it did that year," he said.[8]

Albaugh, who attended the Cleveland School of Art and the

---

[5] "Aiken Nominated by Socialist-Labor Party; Seeks Presidency on Revolutionary Program," *New York Times*, April 27, 1936; Girard and Perry, *The Socialist Labor Party 1876-1991*, p. 58; "Emil Teichert, 74, Leader in Socialist Labor Party," *New York Times*, Jan. 11, 1972.

[6] "The Minor Party Candidates," *Times Recorder* (Zanesville, Ohio), Oct. 27, 1944

[7] "Socialist Labor Candidate Forgotten Man of Politics," *Free-Lance Star* (Fredericksburg, Va.), July 31, 1948.

[8] "Socialist Party Names Candidate," *Altoona Tribune*, Aug. 18, 1944.

Ohio School of Commercial Art, was also a perennial SLP candidate for public office, mounting no fewer than a half-dozen campaigns for governor of Ohio, all but one of which were write-in efforts, and also running for numerous offices on the party's ticket in neighboring Pennsylvania.[9] In fact, Albaugh was the party's nominee for governor of Ohio at the time of his vice-presidential nomination later spring, having been nominated for the state's top office at the party's state convention in Cleveland in early February.[10] In 1948, when Teichert was paired with New York subway dispatcher Stephen Emery, Albaugh served as their national campaign manager.

Albaugh's most impressive campaign arguably occurred in Ohio's 1946 gubernatorial contest — a year the SLP fought tooth-and-nail to obtain a place on the ballot after miraculously collecting 44,796 signatures — when he garnered 11,203 votes in a close race between incumbent Democrat Frank J. Lausche and Republican challenger Thomas J. Herbert.[11] Relocating to Pennsylvania, he later polled 10,387 votes as the Socialist Labor Party's nominee for the U.S. Senate from that state in 1962.

The mustached Massillon Marxist was a true believer and one of the party's most tireless advocates. "Capitalism should be abolished because it cannot function unless it denies to the wage workers — the actual producers — the enjoyment of the abundance they produce," he said during the 1944 campaign. "Along with a great increase in wealth, capitalism also produces great poverty, general insecurity and war. Economic laws inherent in the capitalist system rule out a capitalist solution of the problem of distributing labor's tremendous output."[12]

A lithographic artist, photograph engraver and musician who had his own big band — "Albaugh's Hi-Seven Band" — and once owned a flower shop in Cleveland, Albaugh later retired to Hollywood, Florida, where he remained active in the Socialist Labor Party until his death in 2003 at the age of 96.

Like the Prohibition Party's Claude Watson, Albaugh had been subjected to gasoline rationing during the 1944 campaign by his local rationing board, severely curtailing his ability to roam freely across the country. The rationing board reasoned that he could travel by bus or rail. Albaugh complained to the Office of Price Administration (OPA) in Cleveland, but it wasn't until the

---

[9] "Social Labor Candidates," *Mansfield News-Journal*, Nov. 3, 1946.
[10] "One Nominee Chosen," *Lancaster Eagle-Gazette* (Lancaster, Ohio), Feb. 8, 1944.
[11] "Party Asks Ballot Spot," *Evening Independent* (Massillon, Ohio), Aug. 23, 1946.
[12] "Socialist Labor Candidate Asks End of Capitalism," *Cleveland Plain Dealer*, Oct. 14, 1944.

Akron Beacon Journal sympathized with his plight in an editorial on June 25, 1944, that the board relented and provided enough gasoline ration stamps to allow the vice-presidential candidate to travel 18,000 miles during the course of the autumn campaign.[13]

While national publicity was always extraordinarily difficult for Socialist Labor Party candidates to obtain, Teichert's nomination in 1944 somehow attracted the attention of the popular "The Talk of the Town" column in *The New Yorker* magazine. "Our favorite radical party, by a long shot, is the Socialist Labor Party," wrote literary critic and *bon vivant* Stanley Edgar Hyman a few months after the party's national convention in New York City.[14]

"We feel a certain admiration for the Socialist Labor Party, its program, and its candidate," continued the witty and urbane Hyman, who was married to well-known novelist and suspense writer Shirley Jackson. "We don't suppose he will be elected this fall, but if, someday, while the three thousand enrolled Socialist Laborites are marching around the citadel of Wall Street, blowing on their ram's-horns, the walls come tumbling down, we will take it in our stride. We think we'd rather have them overthrow capitalism than anyone else we know."[15] That was pretty high praise for the tiny Marxist party, particularly coming from such a discerning and influential man of letters.

That was an exception, of course, rather than the rule. The few mainstream publications that bothered to take notice of the SLP's presidential ticket that year usually did so dismissively. The *Washington Post*, for instance, was quick to point out that, as far as they could tell, the Socialist Labor Party had never carried as much a single precinct in an election, let alone occasionally elect somebody to Congress, a state legislature or a municipal office as the rival Socialists had done repeatedly. "The Socialist Labor vote is also dwindling," observed the *Post*, noting that the party's support at the presidential level had shrunk to an abysmal 14,861 votes in 1940. "Evidently it has not been able to offset the death rate among the older generation by more than a negligible number of recruits."[16]

Most newspapers and magazines simply ignored Teichert's candidacy altogether, while those that did briefly mention him often got things wrong, including his name. One Minnesota news-

---

[13] A. A. Albaugh, "Ohio Days Revisited," Letter-to-the-Editor, *Miami News*, Aug. 2, 1986.
[14] "The Talk of the Town," *The New Yorker*, July 22, 1944
[15] Ibid.
[16] "Long Shots," *Washington Post*, Nov. 6, 1944.

paper, for instance, referred to him as "Egbert," instead of Edward.[17]

The relatively obscure Socialist Labor candidate eventually became accustomed to such slights. While waging his second campaign for the presidency in 1948, Teichert was inadvertently handed an application for an entertainer's role when he visited the CBS radio network in New York to record a radio spot. "I'm not an entertainer," he told the surprised receptionist. "I'm not looking for a radio job. I'm running for president on the Socialist-Labor ticket. I'm here to do a broadcast."[18]

Of course, it wasn't always easy for the Socialist Labor Party to find a candidate who was willing and able to take a leave of absence from his job to campaign on a full-time basis, but they found such a candidate in Teichert, who energetically campaigned from coast-to-coast that year.[19]

While Wall Street, corporate and big labor money flowed to the Roosevelt and Dewey campaigns like water rushing through a collapsed dam, Teichert took an unpaid, five-month leave from his job in 1944 and again in 1948 to wage a poor man's campaign for the presidency. It was a tremendous personal sacrifice, one that went largely unnoticed by the "Greatest Generation," yet was deeply appreciated by the party's tiny membership.

Embarking on what party leaders had described as "the greatest campaign in the history of the Socialist Labor Party," Teichert kicked off his herculean effort in 1944 with several campaign events in nearby Pittsburgh, about forty miles from his home in Greensburg, on June 24th and June 25th.

Accompanied by longtime national organizer John P. Quinn — a veteran of every SLP presidential campaign between 1920 and 1972 — Teichert's initial itinerary showed him traveling to no fewer than forty-eight cities in eighteen states. They traveled by automobile throughout the campaign, including a six-week tour of the West Coast and Rocky Mountain states. As the campaign progressed, additional campaign appearances were added to Teichert's hectic schedule.[20] Quinn, a machine pattern-maker, served as the party's national campaign manager that year.

Drawing modest crowds throughout most of the campaign,

---

[17] "Gubernatorial Candidate Files," *Moorhead Daily News*, Aug.1, 1944.
[18] "Get on the New Quiz Show if You Want to Be Named President," *Pittsburgh Press*, May 16, 1948.
[19] Girard and Perry, *The Socialist Labor Party 1876-1991*, p. 65.
[20] "Historic 21ˢᵗ National Convention Outstanding for Solid Achievement," *Weekly People*, Vol. LIV, No. 7, May 13, 1944; "Itinerary of E. A. Teichert," *Weekly People*, Vol. LIV, No. 13, June 24, 1944; "Candidates Are on Tour," *Weekly People*, Vol. LIV, No. 14, July 1, 1944.

Teichert occasionally found himself addressing fairly large audiences, as was the case when he spoke to a Labor Day audience of approximately 500 at the Embassy Auditorium in Los Angeles.[21]

Invariably, campaign manager Quinn would conclude Teichert's public appearances with a fundraising appeal. "And now," Quinn would say over and over again that summer and autumn, "since this movement is for our benefit when it is installed, we ask you to contribute generously to its progress" — usually raising enough money to help the pair get to their next campaign stop.[22]

Arla Albaugh, Teichert's vice-presidential running mate, embarked on a similarly grueling tour of the country, commencing with an appearance in Alliance, Ohio, in early July. Like Teichert, Albaugh was also on the road for the entirety of the campaign, visiting nearly five dozen cities in at least seventeen states. Usually traveling alone, Albaugh's campaign itinerary included a two-day swing through Louisville, Kentucky — the southernmost point on his schedule. He, too, traveled exclusively by automobile.[23]

An unassuming and friendly man, the self-taught Teichert — a man who studied economics, history and sociology, devouring almost everything he could get his hands on — proved to be one of the Socialist Labor Party's most articulate spokesmen.

In formally accepting the party's nomination in late August, the little-remembered De Leon adherent ridiculed the platforms of both major parties, asserting that they were filled with platitudes and vague promises that neither major-party nominee was likely to observe, let alone fulfill. "Socialism and socialism alone is the hope of humanity," he declared. "If the vast potentialities of this technological age are to be realized, capitalism must be abolished." Then and only then, he concluded, could "unemployment, poverty, the scourge of racism and anti-Semitism and the barbarity of war" be ended.[24]

According to Teichert, only the Socialist Labor Party's program of socialist industrial unionism was capable of ushering in a truly peaceful world. "The present global war, the greatest crisis ever to face civilized man," he explained, "grew out of the prewar struggle among the capitalist powers for the markets and resources of the world. The chaos it has wrought is evidence of the breakdown of

---

[21] "Presidential Nominee Sees New War Peril," *Los Angeles Times*, Sep. 5, 1944.
[22] "Teichert Asks a 4-Hour Day," *Des Moines Register*, Sep. 16, 1944.
[23] "Itinerary of A. A. Albaugh," *Weekly People*, Vol. LIV, No. 13, June 24, 1944.
[24] "Teichert Enters Race," *New York Times*, Aug. 28, 1944.

the capitalist system, of its inability to manage for the benefit of society, the immensely productive machinery created under it."[25]

Teichert hammered away at this theme throughout the autumn campaign, maintaining that capitalism had failed and that socialism offered the only hope for lasting peace and economic security. "The war," the little-known Pennsylvanian told a Detroit radio audience in late September, "is conceded by most students to be economic rather than ideological and it represents a capitalistic struggle for markets and spheres of influence. When the fighting ceases the same basic causes will constitute a continuing future threat."[26]

A slim, dark and intense yet personable man who had no illusions about his chances of occupying the White House, Teichert left school when he was fourteen to help support his large family. A voracious reader, he nevertheless had a solid grasp of history and a command of the English language that might have shamed some Ivy League graduates. He was also an engaging speaker, often using his hands for emphasis.

He could, on rare occasion, also be quite a fiery speaker. In one of his first campaign speeches, Teichert exhorted his audience at Cleveland's Public Hall to rise up against the established political order. "Workers of America," the normally mild-mannered Marxist shouted, "repudiate the barbarous social system that exploits the mass of useful producers for the benefit of the few who merely own! Repudiate the political representatives of capitalism, be they Republicans, Democrats, 'so-called Socialist' or Communist or 'Labor,' who preach the criminal falsity that capitalism can be reformed and that it is worth reforming."[27]

On the campaign trail, the little-known SLP hopeful told his audiences that the presidency should be abolished by constitutional amendment and replaced with democratically-managed industrial unions. He also said repeatedly that he was opposed to most of the country's existing unions — AFL and CIO alike — as spineless "servile minions to capitalism." The Socialist Labor Party, he said, would like to see those unions replaced by industrial unions that truly had the workers' interests at heart.[28]

Teichert also said that he would like to see the industrial unions replace the states. "Instead of states," he told a radio audience in

---

[25] "Capitalism and Socialism," *Vidette-Messenger* (Valparaiso, IN), July 5, 1944.
[26] "Capitalism Hit by Socialist Party's Choice," *Detroit Free Press*, Sep. 29, 1944.
[27] "Socialist Labor Nominee Asks: Insecurity or Plenty — Which?" *Cleveland Plain Dealer*, June 28, 1944.
[28] "Socialist Labor Candidate Sees Unions Instead of States," *Milwaukee Journal*, July 10, 1944.

Milwaukee in early July, "we shall have industrial constituencies, such as a steel workers' industrial union, a textile workers' industrial union" and so forth.[29]

During a speech in Milwaukee, the Greensburg native said that industrialization and capitalism had gloriously solved the problem of production, but had failed miserably when it came to distribution. The problem of distribution, he asserted, was something that the billions spent on the New Deal hadn't been able to solve.[30]

The little-known Socialist Laborite also advocated a four-hour workday, telling an audience in Des Moines that the country's unemployment crisis could be solved through a shorter workweek, and that American workers were entitled to "the full social value" of whatever they produced. U.S. workers, he said, must either organize politically and industrially to overthrow the capitalist system, or "figure out a way to live without eating."[31]

Like other party adherents, Teichert was no fan of the American Federation of Labor and the CIO, describing both organizations as "reformist." Neither union, he said while campaigning in Oregon, could be counted on for establishing socialism in the United States.[32]

"Although advocating the formation of Socialist Industrials unions to take over and operate the country's industries and business," Teichert elaborated during a stop in Kansas City a month later, "the Socialist Labor Party is strongly opposed to the CIO as well as the AFL. These are reformistic unions which cannot be used for the purpose of establishing socialism. Our party claims these and similar unions are actually organized and maintained in the interests of the capitalistic system."[33]

Teichert's comments were echoed by several other SLP candidates that year. Arla Albaugh, Teichert's vice-presidential running mate, equated the American Federation of Labor and the CIO as stepping stones to fascism, every bit as dangerous as Nazism. In some ways, declared Teichert's co-star, the organized labor movement was worse because it "advocates the proposition that capital and labor are brother."[34]

"There is no real union in existence," wrote Adolf Wiggert, a perennial Socialist Labor candidate running for the U.S. Senate in

---

[29] Ibid.
[30] "Socialist Presidential Candidate Full of Hope," *Milwaukee Sentinel*, July 10, 1944.
[31] "4-Hour Work Day Urged by Socialist," *Omaha World-Herald*, Sep. 17, 1944.
[32] "Socialist Labor Candidate Picks Faults of Capitalism," *The Oregonian*, Aug. 16, 1944.
[33] "Says the Unions Fail," *Kansas City Star*, Sep. 14, 1944.
[34] "Unions Terms Fascist Step," *Rockford Morning Star*, Sep. 5, 1944.

Wisconsin. "There can be no real union until the workers of America organize on class lines into socialist industrial unions as advocated by the Socialist Labor Party of America." Then and only then, argued the little-remembered Milwaukeean, would labor "be in a position to demand and get everything they produce."[35]

Like his party's previous presidential nominees, Teichert vigorously contended that the Socialist Labor Party's program could be put into effect through a constitutional amendment, providing for a peaceful transition from capitalism to socialism.

Predicting that the country was headed toward totalitarianism, the Socialist Labor aspirant also told the *Kansas City Star* that the United States had been "moving toward ownership and control by a few" — in other words, a financial oligarchy. "Economically," he said, "democracy has failed. It will no longer suffice in this country." Claiming that World War II was a capitalist struggle for markets and spheres of influence, Teichert argued that only socialism — ending the private ownership of income-producing property — could end the scourge of war.[36]

The Pennsylvania steelworker also took a few swipes at the rival Communist and Socialist parties during the campaign, suggesting that neither party offered anything other than mild reforms that the capitalist system had to grant to workers anyway to keep them from revolting.[37]

Like his party's previous nominees, Teichert was particularly critical of Norman Thomas and the Socialists, suggesting that the rival Socialist Party wasn't a genuine socialist organization. It was a point also driven home by Georgia Cozzini, the party's candidate for governor of Wisconsin, and other SLP activists. Teichert, in fact, had challenged Thomas to debate that very question during the 1944 and 1948 presidential campaigns.[38]

Cozzini, a 29-year-old Milwaukee housewife and mother of a young son who was waging her second campaign for governor of Wisconsin and later emerged as the party's nominee for the vice presidency in 1956 and 1960, accused the Socialist Party of "economic double-talk" that did little more than confuse the American

---

[35] Adolf Wiggert, "From Socialist Labor Party," *Milwaukee Journal-Sentinel*, May 25, 1944.
[36] "Says the Unions Fail," *Kansas City Star*, Sep. 14, 1944.
[37] "Socialist Presidential Candidate Full of Hope," *Milwaukee Sentinel*, July 10, 1944.
[38] "Who's the Socialist?" *Wisconsin State Journal*, Oct. 15, 1944; "Thomas, Dobbs Debate," *New York Times*, Oct. 18, 1948. Teichert had been highly critical of Thomas for refusing to respond to his debate challenges, but when Thomas finally agreed to debate his socialist rivals in 1948, the Socialist Labor Party nominee inexplicably refused to share a platform with Thomas and Farrell Dobbs, the Socialist Workers Party candidate.

electorate as to the true meaning of socialism. Socialism, she argued, was much more than government ownership of industries and utilities.

"Does it not stand to reason," she asked, "that being exploited through a bunch of politicians differs little from being exploited by privately owned corporations? In capitalist Canada, for example, one railroad system is privately owned, the other government owned," she contended, yet the workers in both systems were equally exploited. Cozzini elaborated:[39]

> There is only one scientific party of Socialism in America — the Socialist Labor Party — which has consistently declared that Socialism will come when the working class organizes in every industry into Socialist Industrial unions so that industries, designed, built, and operated from top to bottom by labor, shall become the collective property of labor. The industries will take the place of states as units of government, and the industrial vote will replace the political vote. Production will be carried on for use, and the abundant wealth created will be made available to all. This is *true* Socialism.[40]

While the postwar economy was the major issue in Teichert's low-key quest for the presidency that autumn, he was also deeply worried about his son's safety and the issue of war and peace in general. It was a concerned shared by Norman Thomas, whose son, Evan, had joined the American Field Service and was volunteering in a combat zone.

Teichert strongly believed that without socialism as a precondition, any postwar world organization, such as the United Nations, was doomed to fail. "Wars cannot be prevented without the removal of the basic sources of conflict," he asserted while campaigning in Wisconsin. "Those sources are the capitalist struggle for markets and spheres of influence, and the inability of capitalism to solve the domestic problems of unemployment and poverty, which are the breeding grounds for hatred and strife."[41]

Speaking in Tacoma, Washington, later that summer, the articulate yet little-known steelworker from western Pennsylvania predicted widespread unemployment following the war, asserting that the country's prosperity, the result of a war-expanded economy, would not last and that American industry would have an

---

[39] Georgia Cozzini, Letter-to-the-Editor, *Wisconsin Rapids Daily Tribune*, June 10, 1944.
[40] Ibid.
[41] "Socialist Labor Candidate Sees Unions Instead of States," *Milwaukee Journal*, July 10, 1944.

extremely difficult time finding adequate peacetime markets. "Capitalism never has been able to solve unemployment," he maintained, "despite the honest efforts of the New Deal."[42]

The Socialist Labor Party, which had budgeted $100,000 for the national campaign — not a penny of which was wasted on political consultants — made excellent use of the airwaves in 1944. In addition to availing itself of the free time granted to its presidential and vice-presidential candidates for their acceptance speeches on each of the four major networks — 15-minute slots on CBS, NBC, the Mutual Broadcasting System and the Blue Network, the immediate predecessor of the American Broadcasting Company — the SLP purchased airtime on WABY in Albany, New York, KYA in San Francisco and WQXR in New York City for regular weekly 15-minute broadcasts between September 29 and November 3.[43]

Among other stations, the party also bought additional airtime for Teichert and Albaugh on KSTP in Minneapolis-St. Paul on Sept. 14; WHO in Des Moines, Iowa, on Sept. 15; WGN in Chicago on Sept. 23; WSBT in South Bend, Indiana on the 24th of September; WOWO in Indianapolis on the following day; and WLEU in Erie, Pennsylvania, on October 4th. The party also purchased a half-hour slot for an address by Eric Hass on "Socialism Means Jobs for All" on New York's WXQR.[44]

In addition, Section Los Angeles — one of the party's most active groups — sponsored "The Voice of the Socialist Labor Party," a fifteen-minute radio broadcast that was aired over station KFAC in Los Angeles every Sunday evening throughout the presidential campaign.[45]

On Saturday, Nov. 4 — three days before the election — the Socialist Labor Party preempted the immensely popular "Mysterious Traveler" radio program on New York's WOR with coverage of the party's Town Hall rally featuring Teichert and Albaugh.

Some radio stations, however, initially refused to air the party's broadcasts. In Cleveland, for example, radio station WJW — the city's popular ABC affiliate — turned down one of Teichert's speeches in late June on the grounds that it was "not acceptable." This occurred after the station's management had agreed to sell the SLP fifteen minutes of airtime for $102 and had signed a contract

---

[42] "Socialist Labor Leader Predicts Lack of Jobs," *Christian Science Monitor*, Aug. 9, 1944.
[43] "Free Time Granted Socialist-Laborites; Buy Quarter-Hours on WQXR, KYA, WABY; $100,000 Fund," *Broadcasting: The Weekly Newsmagazine of Radio*, Sep. 18, 1944.
[44] Ibid.
[45] "Radio Broadcasts," *Weekly People*, Vol. LIV, No. 33, Nov. 11, 1944.

to that effect several days earlier.[46] A spokesman for WJW, moreover, later told the *Cleveland Plain Dealer* that the script was rejected because of its "vitriolic nature" — a rather outlandish claim considering that Teichert's speech contained no personal attacks and merely critiqued the capitalist system.[47]

In rejecting Teichert's prepared script, the radio station, which was owned by the Akron-based General Tire & Rubber Company, initially contended that Teichert's speech was "definitely subversive, un-American and certainly not in the public interest." WJW executives also slyly intimated that the FBI was interested in the script, which had been provided to the radio station beforehand. A second, revised script was also rejected.[48]

Arnold Petersen, the party's national secretary, immediately filed a complaint with the Federal Communications Commission, telling the FCC in early July that the very same script had been approved the following day by WCAE in Pittsburgh. Vigorously maintaining that the principles of the party were consistent with the interests of the American people, Petersen also accused the radio station of practicing unwarranted censorship and discrimination against the Socialist Labor Party, charging that WJW had "violated the laws and regulations under which it holds its license" and was in clear violation of the rules and provisions of the Federal Communications Act of 1934.[49]

Cognizant of the fact that the party's script had been approved and accepted by several other radio stations, WJW's attorneys then contended that the station's owners were justified in denying the party's presidential candidate access to the airwaves by the mere fact that the SLP wasn't on the ballot in Ohio — a specious argument, to be sure, and something they had no way of knowing when they originally rejected the party's radio script on June 25th. The station's management must have been clairvoyant because the Socialist Labor Party didn't even file its Ohio nominating petitions until five days later, and it wasn't until July 26 — long after the party filed its formal complaint with the FCC — that the Secretary of State ruled that the party had failed to qualify for the ballot due to an insufficient number of valid signatures.

Despite such obstacles, hundreds of thousands of voters across the country eventually heard the SLP's candidates on the airwaves

---

[46] "S.L.P. Protests Radio Gag on Presidential Candidate Teichert," *Weekly People*, Vol. LIV, No. 16, July 15, 1944.
[47] "Teichert and WJW in Time Dispute," *Cleveland Plain Dealer*, June 26, 1944.
[48] Ibid.
[49] "A Presidential Candidate Denied Freedom of Speech," *Weekly People*, Vol. LIV, No. 16, July 15, 1944.

that summer and fall.

Some of Teichert's national radio addresses that autumn weren't particularly well received. An Iowa editor, it seems, was so alarmed that a candidate of the Socialist Labor Party had been given air time that he felt compelled to attack the obscure left-wing candidate and his party in a blistering editorial.

Acknowledging that Teichert "sounded sincere" and that his "arguments were smooth and convincing," the editor of the *Sioux County Capital* went on to hysterically editorialize that if the SLP's seemingly benign solutions didn't work, the party would almost certainly resort to violence, consisting of "rubber hoses across the throat, gas pipes on the head and firing squads in the alley" as a way of educating the American people.[50]

Confusing the Socialist Labor Party with Soviet totalitarianism, this particularly reactionary editor was apparently stunned that a socialist candidate for president of the United States had been afforded an opportunity to present his views on the airwaves, suggesting that "if he were an advocate of 'capitalism,' he couldn't get on the air in Russia."[51]

The editorial writer also claimed that the ideas advocated by the Socialist Labor Party were as old as the Dark Ages, a throwback to medievalism when "every citizen was a pawn of the state, when nobody was allowed to own anything, and when the government settled all the details of life."[52]

Earlier in the campaign, a newspaper in upstate New York took issue with Teichert's contention that "the barbarous social system that exploits the mass of useful producers for the benefit of the few" needed to be repudiated. "Well, from a casual look around," observed the *The News of the Tonawandas*, "most of us would say that American labor, using the machinery and methods that capitalism has developed, is doing pretty well. Never has the manual worker made so much money and enjoyed such short hours and congenial working environment. On the other hand, never has capital had so much of its profit taken by the government — which is all of us — leaving so little, comparatively, for the capitalist owner to use for himself."[53]

Teichert and the SLP took such criticism in stride. Such right-wing ranting — typical dog-whistle politics, as the Australians

---

[50] "The First Time," *Sioux County Capital*, Sep. 21, 1944.
[51] Ibid.
[52] Ibid.
[53] "Capitalism and Socialism," *The News of the Tonawandas*, July 5, 1944.

would say — were to be expected from those who were completely unfamiliar with socialism and the party's long history of non-violence and peaceful participation at the ballot box.

While recognizing the tremendously long odds facing his candidacy, Teichert refused to concede defeat, contending that if a majority of Americans became aware of the Socialist Labor program anything was possible.

Visiting as many newspaper offices and radio stations as time permitted during his cross-country campaign tour, the Socialist Labor nominee told reporters in Seattle that it would be ridiculous to admit defeat while actively seeking support. "I know where I stand, and the issue will be decided on Election Day," he sighed when pressed to admit that his candidacy would be overwhelmingly rejected at the polls. Refusing to concede that his party would once again be a minor footnote in a presidential campaign, the amiably quiet Teichert always put on a brave face, insisting that lightning could strike, that the awakening working-class, ravaged by the deepest depression in U.S. history only to be followed by a world war of even greater and devastatingly horrific consequences, might finally elect one of its own to the presidency.[54]

As such, he wanted voters to know that he was the only bonafide socialist in the race. Responding to a gratuitous slander made by the Socialist Party of Iowa, which scurrilously referred to the Socialist Labor Party's "totalitarian program" while issuing its call for a statewide convention in Des Moines earlier that summer, Teichert challenged the Socialist Party's Norman Thomas to a public debate in late August.

In his August 31 letter to the Socialist Party's standard-bearer, Teichert accused Thomas and his party of "sailing under false colors," asserting that his better-known rival was more interested in reforming the capitalist system than in dismantling and replacing it:

> Workers throughout the nation, deeply perturbed by the portents of social and economic crisis, are groping for a solution to the problems confronting them. They have suffered a series of stunning blows at the hand of the employing class, its political State and their own leaders. Their confidence in the ability of capitalism to solve its own inner contradictions is deeply shaken. And there is much evidence that, notwithstanding the desperate efforts of the trade union leaders to herd them into the capitalist political fold, tens of thousands are prepared to

---

[54] "Socialist Confident," *Nevada State Journal*, Aug. 4, 1944.

repudiate the major parties. It is natural and it is right, therefore, that they should express their desire for a new social system by supporting Socialism.

You and I are candidates for the office of President of the United States on tickets designated as Socialist. The awakening members of the working class are confused by this anomaly. For, obviously, unless Socialism means all things to all men, there should be but one Socialist candidate for President. The fact that there are two can only signify that one is sailing under false colors, that he has usurped the name of Socialism for a program at war with the lofty aims and scientific principles of Karl Marx, the founder of Socialism.

I charge that it is you who have misappropriated this honored name. I charge that your party is interested in reforming capitalism, not with overthrowing it. I recall your own repeated plaint (or boast) that the major parties have 'stolen' Socialist Party planks. I need hardly remind you that the planks thus appropriated, or the reforms they demanded, were used to prop up the system of class rule, as, indeed, you yourself have admitted. The record speaks for itself. You and your party have shamelessly played the role of political gadfly to the major parties.

I hold that in preaching reforms, and in inculcating reliance on the State for a redress of grievances, you have palsied the workers' striking arm. The State is an instrument of class rule. Socialism teaches that it must go with class rule. I charge that you and your party, in repudiating this essential Socialist principle, prepare the workers, not for Socialism, but for State capitalism (Fascism), or Industrial Feudalism.[55]

Such a debate would serve many purposes, concluded Teichert. "Not only would it offer an opportunity to prove that the program of the Socialist Labor Party is the antithesis of totalitarianism — that it aims for the most complete democracy the world has ever known — but it would do much to clarify the minds of bewildered workers as to which of the parties representing themselves as Socialist has a moral claim to that honored name."[56]

Thomas, who declined a similar debate challenge from the Socialist Labor Party's Verne L. Reynolds during the 1932 presidential campaign, obviously wasn't interested in sparring with his

---

[55] "Teichert Challenges Thomas to Debate," *Weekly People*, Vol. LIV, No. 24, Sep. 9, 1944.
[56] Ibid.

lesser-known rival. "If the workers were indeed turning away from Roosevelt to some sort of socialism and were puzzled to choose between us," responded Thomas, "I might agree that a debate was the best use to make of our limited time and energy."[57] But there was no chance of that happening, said Thomas.

Worried that mixing it up with his left-wing rival would further marginalize his own candidacy, Thomas replied that he would be happy to recommend some sort of post-election debate with the Socialist Labor Party to his party's NEC. He also maintained that he had always been careful to distinguish the SLP from communism and to applaud its sincerity. "I know that it does not endorse violent revolution or dictatorship," he wrote. "I am inclined, however, to agree with the Iowa Socialists that despite your intention, your tactics, if they could be successful at all, would result in a totalitarian reorganization of society by the true believers."[58]

Thomas's reply, dated September 8th, prompted an immediate and uncharacteristically angry response from Teichert, who scolded his Socialist opponent for cowardly ducking a debate before the election. In his lengthy reply, Teichert made it clear that he wasn't particularly interested in any post-election round-table discussions between the Socialist Party and the SLP, nor was he looking forward to participating in any nice pink-tea "academic" conferences. "I think you are fully aware of the implications of a debate now," Teichert wrote bitterly, "and I am justified in concluding that you are deliberately and disingenuously evading the real issue."[59]

While there was no mention of Teichert's debate challenge in the *Socialist Call*, the Socialist Party's newspaper, the *Weekly People* — the official organ of the Socialist Labor Party — quickly weighed in, sharply criticizing Thomas for refusing to debate his SLP rival and reminding its readers that the silver-haired Socialist, who was "much too busy peddling his reform nostrums to discuss the question of Socialism," had turned down a similar debate request from the SLP's Verne Reynolds at the height of the Great Depression in 1932. Thomas and his party, thundered the *Weekly People*, realized that the Socialist Labor Party's program and logic would "cut Thomas's 'socialist' pretensions to bits. He knows this, and his party knows this," adding that it was childish for Thomas and his

---

[57] "Thomas Ducks Campaign Debate with Socialist Labor Party Nominee," *Weekly People*, Vol. LIV, No. 28, Oct. 7, 1944.
[58] Ibid.
[59] Ibid.

party to pretend the S.L.P. doesn't exist.⁶⁰

While the mainstream media ignored Teichert's debate challenge, Socialist Labor Party members tried to publicize it through letters-to-the-editor in newspapers across the country.

Accusing Thomas of "sailing under false colors" throughout his political career, William Farkas, the SLP's candidate for governor of Ohio, sharply criticized the better-known Socialist Party candidate for declining the debate invitation until the campaign was over.

Reminding the readers of the *Akron Beacon Journal* of a split in the socialist movement forty-five years earlier, Farkas wrote that in the intervening years "the two organizations have been distinguished by the difference between reform and revolution — the Socialist Party believing that capitalism could and should be reformed, the Socialist Labor Party insisting that capitalism should and must be abolished and that in its place must be erected the Industrial Republic of Labor."⁶¹

In the meantime, Teichert continued to hammer away at Thomas for the remainder of the campaign, asserting that the Socialist nominee and his party were more interested in reforming capitalism than bringing about a socialist society. It was a theme he repeated during the 1948 campaign, when the two men were once again rivals for the presidency.

Proclaiming in a radio address during the latter campaign that the Socialist Labor Party was standing alone in fighting the nation's reactionary forces, Teichert charged that all of the other parties, including the Socialist Party of Norman Thomas, were trying to reform a system that couldn't be reformed and to patch up a system that was well beyond repair. By perpetuating capitalism, he asserted, the whole world would eventually become "one vast, prostrate Hiroshima."⁶²

Arla Albaugh, Teichert's vice-presidential running mate, also waged a vigorous campaign in the autumn of 1944, grabbing headlines throughout the country by denouncing Sidney Hillman's powerful Political Action Committee. In a national radio address in September, Albaugh accused the Communists — the most vicious and reactionary of labor's foes, as he described them — of actively supporting Hillman's political action committee, but told his listening audience that they were sadly mistaken if they believed that the Communists were out to destroy capitalism. The

---

⁶⁰ Ibid.
⁶¹ William Farkas, "Organizations Differ," *Akron Beacon Journal*, Oct. 9, 1944.
⁶² "Candidate Fights Reaction Alone," *Washington Post*, Oct. 30, 1948.

Hillman committee, he charged, was headed and controlled by labor leaders who were not only servants of the capitalist system which exploited labor but whose personal incomes exceeded $20,000-$30,000 per year — a pretty lucrative salary in those days.[63]

"Capitalism has been very kind to them, and they, in turn, affirm emphatically their devotion to capitalism, which, in the modern manner of double-talk, they call free enterprise." He also said that the country's labor leaders, including the Communists, feared the uncertainty of the post-war era, a period when the United States was likely to experience rampant joblessness. "They fear unrest and upheaval as much as any millionaire nabob from Wall Street," said Albaugh. "They fear any change which would disrupt the pleasant and profitable relationship they now enjoy with employers and government officials."[64]

Campaigning in Rockford, Illinois, earlier that month, Albaugh asserted that the American Federation of Labor and the Congress of Industrial Organizations, the latter founded by John L Lewis in 1935, were helping to pave the way for fascism in America by advocating the proposition that labor and capital were brothers in a common struggle. In perpetuating that belief, claimed Albaugh, the two giant unions were creating a situation similar to the one that existed in Germany when the Nazis came to power. Even the celebration of Labor Day, he said, was something of a misnomer since laborers were merely celebrating what the capitalists gave them.[65]

"Revolution by ballot" was the only solution to an inevitable surplus of labor and goods in the post-war period when as many as ten million returning veterans were expected to join the workforce, declared Albaugh while campaigning in his home state of Ohio, where the SLP had been forced to wage a write-in campaign after narrowly failing to qualify for the ballot. The abolition of private ownership of production and distribution, he told an audience in Akron, would bring about a much-needed system of production for use "wherein goods produced by labor will be retained for those who perform useful labor." Under a new government ushered in by the Socialist Labor Party, he continued, "the Socialist Industrial Republic of Labor will elect representatives from where

---

[63] "Communists Worst Foes of Labor, Says Socialist Candidate," *Chicago Tribune*, Sept. 23, 1944; "Socialist Labor Party Assails Hillman Group," *Christian Science Monitor*, Sept. 25, 1944.
[64] Ibid.
[65] "Unions Terms Fascist Step," *Rockford Morning Star*, Sep. 5, 1944.

we work instead of from where we live, and we will have an Industrial Congress instead of a political one." Unlike the present U.S. workplace, the workers in various industries would democratically elect their own foremen and management committees, he explained.[66]

"Capitalism should be abolished," Albaugh told anybody willing to listen that autumn, "because it cannot function unless it denies to the wage workers — the actual producers — the enjoyment of the abundance they produce. Along with a great increase in wealth," he told a crowd in Cleveland, "capitalism also produces great poverty, general insecurity and war. Economic laws inherit in the capitalist system rule out a capitalist solution to the problem of distributing labor's tremendous output."[67]

While campaigning in Pittsburgh a few months earlier, the Socialist Labor candidate for vice president stated that if all the goods produced in the United States went to the workers who produced them, every gainfully employed citizen in the country would be earning the equivalent of $10,000 per year — a significant increase over the national median income at the time — and that if the waste inherent in capitalism was eliminated, that income might be as high as $20,000 annually, enabling the nation to adopt a four-hour workday.[68]

Meanwhile, Eric Hass, the party's candidate for the U.S. Senate in New York, delivered the party's radio address to American troops overseas. Largely due to the prodding and persistence of Harry Fleishman, the Socialist Party's young campaign manager, the War Department had authorized a series of weekly talks to soldiers stationed around the world that autumn by representatives of all five parties — Democratic, Republican, Prohibition, Socialist and Socialist Labor.

In his address, the 39-year-old Hass told the members of the armed forces that capitalism could not provide full employment and that the Socialist Labor Party was "the party of the future, the party of the working class." Hass also urged all members of the working class, in and out of uniform, to exercise their constitutional rights and "demand the abolition of private ownership of the industries and the establishment of a socialist commonwealth of labor."[69]

---

[66] "Vote Revolution is Albaugh Plea," *Massillon Evening Independent*, Oct. 12, 1944.
[67] "Socialist Labor Candidate Asks End of Capitalism," *Cleveland Plain Dealer*, Oct. 14, 1944.
[68] "Socialist Wants Labor in Power," *Pittsburgh Press*, Aug. 16, 1944.
[69] Fleischman, *Norman Thomas: A Biography*, pp. 212-213; "Army Promises 5 Parties Equal Broadcast Time," *Chicago Tribune*, Aug. 28, 1944; "Capitalism Held Failure," *New York Times*, Sept. 19, 1944.

Continuing to operate in the shadow of the larger Socialist Party, the Socialist Labor Party waged a particularly aggressive campaign that year, proving, in the words of the late Eugene V. Debs, that it was still "that little band of valiant comrades — frenzied fanatics if you please, but still of the stuff of which revolutions are made." Throughout most of the party's history, Debs noted, "they were a mere handful, and yet they fought as if they had legions behind them.[70] That was certainly true in 1944.

Despite a promising development in Ohio — Albaugh's home state — ballot access was once again a major problem for the Socialist Labor Party. The party's presidential ticket ultimately appeared on the ballot in fifteen states that autumn, a slight improvement over the fourteen states in which its presidential ticket appeared in 1940.

In addition to regaining a spot on the ballot in Illinois — a state where John W. Aiken failed to qualify four years earlier — by obtaining 29,825 signatures from 52 counties, the SLP, successfully petitioning under the Industrial Government label, also qualified for a place on the ballot in the party's stronghold of New York.[71]

The Socialist Labor Party had failed to appear on the ballot in New York during the 1936 and 1940 presidential campaigns. In 1936, the party was arbitrarily knocked off the ballot in New York on a flimsy technicality that enabled the newly-formed American Labor Party — specifically created to support Roosevelt's re-election that year — to appear on the ballot in the country's most populous state.

Since New York's election law prohibited any two parties from using the same word in their names, the appearance of the "Social Labor Party" — the party's actual designation in the Empire State during this period — would have prevented the ALP from qualifying for the ballot that autumn. The technicality, which allegedly involved duplicate signatures on the SLP and American Labor Party nominating petitions, resulted in the lower courts tossing out twenty-three signatures from Putnam County, thereby leaving the SLP nine signatures short of the required minimum of fifty signatures in each county. In what can only be described as a remarkable coincidence, nearly two dozen voters in that small scenic county had apparently signed the nominating petitions for both parties.[72]

---

[70] Stephen Coleman, *Daniel De Leon* (Manchester, U.K., 1990), p. 153.
[71] "Socialist Labor Party Candidates File Nominations," *Freeport Journal-Standard* (Freeport, Illinois), Aug. 29, 1944; "Slates are Filed by Minor Parties," *New York Times*, Aug. 17, 1944.
[72] "Bars Two Tickets Off State Ballot; Court of Appeals Rejects Pleas of Union and Social Labor Parties," *New York Times*, Oct. 24, 1936.

In upholding the lower court ruling, the New York Appellate Court ignored the SLP's contention that its petitions had been circulated in June, two months before the American Labor Party even began collecting signatures in that county. Dishearteningly, it was the first presidential election since 1888 that the SLP and its familiar arm and hammer emblem had failed to appear on the New York ballot in a presidential election. New York, moreover, had traditionally been the party's strongest state, twice giving the Socialist Labor Party nominee for president more than one percent of the total and providing Verne L. Reynolds with 10,339 popular votes — nearly a third of his national total — in the 1932 presidential election.[73]

The Socialist Labor Party suffered another heartbreaking setback in New York in 1940 when the party's nominating petitions, bearing 14,000 signatures — 2,000 more than necessary — apparently lacked any signatures from Chenango County, thereby failing to comply with the state's onerous requirement of at least fifty signatures from each county.[74]

In addition to the populous states of New York and Illinois, the Socialist Labor Party's presidential ticket also qualified for the ballot in Maine, a state where it had also failed to appear on the ballot in 1940.[75] Teichert, who garnered 335 votes in the state, was the only minor-party candidate for president to qualify in Maine that year, but — sadly — it was the next-to-last time the Socialist Labor Party's presidential ticket would ever appear on the ballot in the sparsely-populated Pine Tree State.[76]

The party also qualified for the ballot in a dozen other states, including Connecticut where — along with the Socialist Party — the Socialist Labor Party was one of only four parties to appear on the November ballot.[77] Party activists also collected an impressive 9,610 signatures on nominating petitions by early May to qualify in Michigan.[78] The party also managed to get on the ballot in Kentucky, where party activists submitted nominating petitions bearing 1,336 signatures — 336 more than required. Almost all of those signatures were from the Louisville vicinity.[79]

In all, the Teichert-Albaugh ticket appeared on the ballot in

---

[73] Ibid.
[74] "Three New Slates in Field in State," *New York Times*, Oct. 9, 1940.
[75] "Maine Presidential Ballots to List Socialist Laborites," *Christian Science Monitor*, Sep. 6, 1944.
[76] "Dewey Maine Margin Set at 14,803 Votes," *Boston Herald*, Nov. 26, 1944.
[77] "Four Parties Have Places on Ballots," *Hartford Courant*, Oct. 19, 1944.
[78] "Fourth Party Files Petitions," *Detroit Free Press*, May 5, 1944.
[79] "Socialists Likely to Get On Ballots," *Louisville Courier-Journal*, June 24, 1944.

Connecticut, Illinois, Iowa, Kentucky, Maine, Massachusetts, Michigan, Minnesota, Missouri, New Jersey, New York, Pennsylvania, Virginia, Washington and Wisconsin, representing a total of 252 electoral votes — 14 shy of the 266 needed to win an Electoral College majority.

Despite spending a couple of days in Portland earlier that summer, Teichert's tiny De Leonist party was hoping again to petition its way onto the ballot, but was unable to qualify in Oregon, a state where the party's national ticket had appeared on the ballot in every presidential election since 1920.[80] The party had managed to qualify in Oregon using the more difficult petition method four years earlier — a year when their rival Socialist Party was disqualified on a technicality — by obtaining 18,918 signatures on nominating petitions, some 620 signatures more than required.[81]

Despite herculean efforts, the party also fell short in Ohio, home of some of the party's most reliable and dedicated members. Party activists were initially encouraged earlier that year when Ohio Secretary of State Edward J. Hummel, a Republican, reversed a 1942 ruling made by his predecessor, allowing the Socialist Labor Party to petition for a place on the ballot. Hummel's predecessor, Democrat John E. Sweeney, had issued a ruling denying the Communist and Socialist Labor parties access to the ballot.

"No political party, or group, which advocates, either directly or indirectly, the overthrow by force or violence, of our local, state or national government or which carries on a program of sedition or treason by radio, speech or press or which has in any manner any connection with any foreign government or power or which in any manner has any connection with any group or organization so connected or so advocating the overthrow...shall be recognized or be given a place on the ballot in any primary or general election held in the state of Ohio or in any political subdivision thereof," asserted Sweeney in announcing his June 1942 ruling. "As long as I am Secretary of State," he added, "the ballot of Ohio will not be used as a transmission belt to import foreign ideals and subversive movements." The SLP had condemned Sweeney's statement as slanderous.[82]

In reversing Sweeney's 1942 ruling in April, Hummel maintained that the Socialist Labor Party was entitled to a spot on the

---

[80] "Socialist Labor Party Seeks Place on Ballot," *Eugene Guard*, Aug. 16, 1944.
[81] "Socialists Seek Spot on Ballot," *The Oregonian*, Sep. 14, 1940; "Socialists Off Oregon Ballot," *The Oregonian*, Oct. 4, 1940.
[82] "S.L.P. Entitled to Place on Ballot; Ohio State Sec'y Reverses Sweeney," *Weekly People*, Vol. LIV, No. 6, May 6, 1944.

ballot provided the party met all of the state's ballot access requirements.[83]

Hummel's decision came after months of correspondence and intensive personal lobbying on the part of Louis P. Wettstein, the SLP's state secretary. His dogged determination and persistence made all of the difference. Wettstein, who was running for the U.S. Senate that year, diligently furnished the Secretary of State with an affidavit and sample nominating petition, copies of the party's 1936 and 1940 national platforms, a certified statement setting forth the method of selecting the party's state executive officers, their names and addresses, a copy of the party's Ohio bylaws, and sixteen SLP publications supporting the party's affidavit that the party, historically resorting to the "peaceful and civilized means" of the ballot box to place its program before the American electorate, had never advocated the overthrow of the government by force or violence.[84]

At first blush, it appeared that the SLP had indeed qualified for the ballot in Ohio when the party, which needed a minimum of approximately 17,000 valid signatures, submitted 20,496 signatures from 35 counties — two more than the 33 counties required — in late June, but election officials later tossed out several thousand signatures for various reasons, leaving the party short of the minimum necessary.[85]

Refusing to unfurl the white flag of surrender after such a devastating setback, the Ohioans then pursued a vigorous write-in effort for their ticket, including placing a number of paid political ads in the *Cleveland Plain Dealer* and other Ohio newspapers. Joseph Pirincin, the party's candidate for governor, gallantly promoted the write-in drive in a number of last-minute radio broadcasts resulting from the SLP's complaint to the Federal Communications Commission in June demanding equal time for its candidates. Pirincin's first address, a fifteen-minute speech on Cleveland's WJW (now WRMR 1420 AM), was aired on October 29th — nine days before the election.[86]

Teichert, who picked up the support of four of the country's foreign-language newspapers — more than 160 endorsed Roosevelt — campaigned vigorously until the bitter end, telling audiences in upstate New York that the country would face massive joblessness after the war. He also predicted that as many as 25 to

---

[83] Ibid.
[84] Ibid.
[85] "Socialist Labor Petitions Filed," *Cleveland Plain Dealer*, July 1, 1944.
[86] "Write-In Vote is Urged," *Cleveland Plain Dealer*, Oct. 30, 1944.

30 million Americans would be unemployed. "If we don't establish socialism in post-war America," he asserted, "we'll have totalitarianism."[87]

Spending nearly a week in Massachusetts — a state where the Socialist Party's Norman Thomas wasn't on the ballot — Teichert made a number of radio appearances and gave several public speeches, including talks at Melha Temple in Springfield and Boston's famous New England Mutual Hall.[88] During a four-day swing through neighboring Connecticut in late October, the little-known Socialist Labor candidate gave speeches in New Haven and South Norwalk and spent two days in the Socialist Party's stronghold in Bridgeport before delivering a 15-minute radio address over a combined statewide radio network from the studios of WSRR in Stamford.[89]

Following his tour of Connecticut, Teichert made a couple of quick campaign stops in New Jersey and nearby Philadelphia before returning to his home in western Pennsylvania, where he gave a radio address over Pittsburgh's WCAE, an affiliate of the Mutual Broadcasting System, and was the featured speaker at the Socialist Labor Party's rally on the roof garden of the city's Mayfair Hotel. In his speech, Teichert told the party faithful that the war was evidence of a "breakdown of the capitalist system" and that socialism was the only "hope of humanity."[90] Barely able to catch his breath, the little-known steelworker then made two radio addresses over local Washington, D.C., stations on Saturday, November 4th, before racing to New York City to take part in the party's grand finale later that evening.[91]

On Tuesday, October 31, Eric Hass delivered a national radio address over the nationwide Blue Network. His half-hour talk, titled "No Lasting Peace Without Socialism," was broadcast live on nearly 120 stations in thirty-six states and the District of Columbia.[92]

Hass, who devoted as much time and energy to the party's national campaign as he did actively campaigning for the U.S. Senate — all while maintaining his demanding editorial responsibilities at

---

[87] "Foreign Language Press for Roosevelt," *Boston Herald*, Nov. 6, 1944; "Socialism After War Urged by Candidate," *Rochester Democrat and Chronicle*, Oct. 13, 1944.
[88] "Teichert Will Speak at Meeting Thursday," *Springfield Republican*, Oct. 15, 1944.
[89] "Socialist Labor Heads to Tour Connecticut," *Hartford Courant*, Oct. 22, 1944.
[90] "Names in the News," *Pittsburgh Press*, Nov. 4, 1944.
[91] "Dewey, Roosevelt Will Climax Drives Tonight," *Ogden Standard Examiner*, Nov. 4, 1944.
[92] "Hass Blue Network Talk Oct. 31 on Permanent Peace Through Socialism," *Weekly People*, Vol. LIV, No. 31, Oct. 28, 1944.

the *Weekly People* — told his national radio audience that the Socialist Labor Party abhorred isolationism and favored the idea of a world organization to maintain the peace, but that such an organization, as formulated in the recent Dumbarton Oaks Conference laying the groundwork for the postwar United Nations, was doomed to failure if it wasn't built on the proper foundation:

> The Socialist Labor Party abhors isolationism. We believe devoutly in world organization. But we also know that, if world organization is not to be a mockery, it must rest on the bedrock of common interests. Socialism alone supplies this sound and solid foundation for concord and for the free cultural and material intercourse between the peoples of the world. Socialism does this by destroying the parent evil — the exploitation of wage labor. Socialism does this by making it possible for workers to achieve living standards in keeping with our capacity to produce. By producing for use, instead of for sale and profit, Socialism abolishes the problem of surpluses that have to be disposed of in foreign markets. Surpluses under Socialism will be planned surpluses. And they won't be the curse they are today; they will be a blessing, for the larger they are, the less we shall need to work, and the more time we shall have for leisurely pursuits. Socialism means peace, not for ten years or twenty, or for "our time," but forever, because it effectively and permanently removes the cause of war.[93]

The feisty Socialist Labor Party concluded its 1944 presidential campaign with a huge rally at New York's Town Hall on Saturday, Nov. 4th. Except for a few empty seats in the upper balcony, the auditorium was packed. Billed as "the greatest political campaign in the history of the Socialist Labor Party," the Town Hall rally was a fitting climax to what was arguably the most intensive presidential campaign ever conducted by the tiny SLP.

The highlight of the evening was Teichert's national radio address over the Mutual Broadcasting System (see Appendix E), a half-hour speech carried by 131 radio stations in thirty states and the District of Columbia in which the Socialist Labor candidate exhorted the working-class to "repudiate the barbarous social system that exploits the mass of useful producers for the benefit of the few." [94]

---

[93] "Socialism for Lasting Peace," *Weekly People*, Vol. LIV, No. 33, Nov. 11, 1944.
[94] "Teichert Town Hall Speech, Nov. 4, To Be Carried Over Mutual Network," *Weekly People*, Vol. LIV, No. 29, Oct. 14, 1944; "Candidate's Nationwide Broadcast Climaxes SLP's Greatest Campaign," *Weekly People*, Vol. LIV, No. 34, Nov. 18, 1944.

Chapter XVIII

Rumbling on the Right

In addition to the Thomas, Watson and Teichert candidacies, Gerald L. K. Smith, the vitriolic, rabble-rousing racist and anti-Semite who fancied himself as the voice of isolationism in the United States and a power in national politics, also entered the fray as the nominee of his own hastily-created America First Party.

Smith's right-wing party was a joke. Though he claimed otherwise, Smith's miniscule and short-lived party, of course, had no genuine connection to the America First Committee, the popular and well-financed prewar isolationist movement that disbanded shortly after Pearl Harbor.

Arguably the most controversial figure in the Union Party triumvirate of 1936, Smith had endorsed Wendell Willkie's candidacy during the 1940 presidential campaign, before vehemently turning on him four years later.

Marching to the beat of his own drummer in 1940, the anti-Semitic Detroit crusader, who was then heading something called the Committee of One Million — another of his many creations — spent most of his time that autumn vigorously attacking FDR and the New Deal. "If all the reds and pinks were deported from America," he thundered during a speech in Lima, Ohio, "about half the New Deal office holders would have to leave the country." Declaring that Willkie would "help us proclaim America for Americans," Smith told an outdoor crowd of 3,000 who braved the cool winds that October afternoon that the Republican nominee would emerge victorious on Nov. 5.[1] As usual, he was wrong.

Determined to remain in the limelight, the fundamentalist preacher and one-time Huey Long lieutenant ran unsuccessfully for the U.S. Senate from Michigan in 1942. Promising to imbue the U.S. Senate with "guts," the former director of Long's "Save Our Wealth" crusade and veteran of Father Coughlin's Union Party of 1936 had waged a spirited campaign for the Republican nomination in the state's September primary, achieving a reasonably strong showing of more than 120,000 votes while losing to Judge Homer E. Ferguson, the party's endorsed candidate.[2]

The controversial preacher had made the prospect of gasoline rationing the central focus of his campaign for the Republican nomination, asserting that the nation's rubber supply had been badly bungled during the war effort and suggesting that Henry Ford, the famous automaker who financed a series of Smith radio broadcasts during this period and once impulsively told the rabble-rousing preacher that he would make a great president, should be put in charge of managing the nation's rubber production. A synthetic substitute for rubber could be made, Smith told his audiences, from "practically anything" grown on farms.

Moreover, he argued that gasoline rationing would severely harm Michigan autoworkers, reduce farmers to "hitch hiking bondage," strand suburbanites and virtually destroy the nation's rural churches. His slogan, "tires for everybody," proved to be a novel and relatively effective campaign gimmick, but not quite enough to propel him to victory in the GOP primary.[3]

Smith, who had outspent Ferguson by $4,500 in the primary, was nevertheless pleased by his "sensationally large" showing and promised to support the Republican nominee in November. However, when Judge Ferguson refused to confer with him shortly after the primary and the Republican state chairman informed him that he wouldn't be allowed to address the party's state convention, Smith stayed in the race as a write-in or sticker candidate, dramatizing his "tires for everybody" theme by crisscrossing the state, frequently driving over the speed limit to make his point. On Election Day, Smith polled the difference between his two major-party rivals, garnering 32,173 write-in or sticker votes to Ferguson's 589,652 votes and Democratic Sen. Prentiss Brown's

---

[1] "Smith Charges Many 'Reds' in Federal Posts," *Lima News*, Oct. 18, 1940.
[2] Leo P. Ribuffo, *The Old Christian Right: The Protestant Far Right from the Great Depression to the Cold War* (Philadelphia, 1983), pp. 160-162.
[3] Ibid., p. 160; Glen Jeansonne, "Gerald L. K. Smith: From Wisconsin Roots to National Notoriety," *The Wisconsin Magazine of History*, Vol. 86, Issue 2 (Winter 2002-2003), p. 26.

561,595.[4]

When Wendell Willkie stumbled in the Wisconsin primary two years later while trying to capture the GOP's presidential nomination for a second time, nobody was happier than Smith, who immediately claimed that Willkie's repudiation by the Republican voters in Wisconsin was "a victory for the America First crusade."[5]

Willkie, who recognized a demagogue when he saw one, had sharply denounced the rabble-rousing Smith and his indigenous America First movement during the Wisconsin primary, suggesting that any candidate who did not reject "America First and Gerald L. K. Smith cannot possibly be elected president."[6]

The delusional Smith, who maintained an office in Detroit's Industrial Bank Building staffed by an office manager and four or five young women, believed that he was a real mover-and-shaker in American politics and threatened to field a third-party ticket if neither major party nominated a nationalist for president.

As such, the flamboyant demagogue floated the names of several presidential possibilities, including famed aviator Charles A. Lindbergh and World War I fighting ace and Medal of Honor recipient Eddie Rickenbacker — at one point even suggesting a Lindbergh-Rickenbacker ticket — but neither of the famous high-flying duo wanted anything to do with Smith and his rag-tag army of political misfits.

The former Huey Long lieutenant also approached Sen. Gerald P. Nye that year, but the North Dakotan was more concerned with his own re-election to the U.S. Senate — and for good reason. Smith also organized a short-lived Republican Nationalist Revival Committee, proposing longtime *Chicago Tribune* publisher Robert McCormick — a leading pre-WWII isolationist — as a possible Republican standard-bearer. Along with several others, he also asked General Douglas MacArthur to consider running.

Smith also suggested that Montana's Burton K. Wheeler — the only Democratic officeholder on his not-so-short list of presidential possibilities — would make a fine candidate on the America First ticket. He also proposed the possibility of retiring isolationist Sen. Robert R. Reynolds of North Carolina, who ignominiously tried to launch his own Nationalist Party during this period. While "flattered and honored" by Smith's suggestion, Reynolds — citing his four previous marriages — eventually ruled out a possible White

---

[4] Ibid., pp. 161-162.
[5] "'America First' Victory Says Gerald L. K. Smith," *Racine Journal-Times*, April 6, 1944
[6] Glen Jeansonne, *Gerald L. K. Smith: Minister of Hate* (Baton Rouge, 1997), p. 153.

House candidacy.⁷

Given his deep disdain for President Roosevelt, Smith wanted more than anything to be able to support the Republican nominee that year, hinting strongly that he might be able to support Thomas Dewey or Ohio Gov. John W. Bricker.

While Bricker apparently wasn't aware of Smith, Dewey wanted nothing to do with him, stating on the eve of the Wisconsin primary that "the Gerald L. K. Smiths and their ilk must not for one moment be permitted to pollute the stream of American life."⁸

Speaking in Chicago on July 10 — less than two weeks after the Republican national convention had adjourned in that city — Smith told reporters that he would ask his America First organization to approve a resolution demanding that Gov. Dewey withdraw in favor of Bricker as the Republican nominee. He also urged the Democrats, who would be meeting in the same city the following week, to nominate Wheeler for president.⁹

If the Democrats nominated FDR and Dewey refused to step aside in favor of Bricker, asserted Smith, the America First Party would hold its own national convention and nominate its own candidate for president. "If we call our own convention," he said, "I am convinced that our people will attempt to draft Charles A. Lindbergh for President."

In the meantime, Bricker's unfamiliarity with Smith proved to be quite embarrassing for Dewey — and for the entire GOP, for that matter — when a reporter asked the Ohio governor about Smith's support during a joint press conference in Albany, New York, in late July. "If he votes the Republican ticket, his vote would count the same as anyone's," said Bricker, almost nonchalantly, completely unaware that Smith was viewed as a political pariah by almost everybody in the country — and most certainly by the press. An obviously embarrassed Dewey winced noticeably as his running mate spoke those words.¹⁰

Bricker's unexpected response to the reporter's question stunned most observers, including several sympathetic newspapers that immediately threatened to withhold their support from the Republican ticket. "It's 'Curtains' for Dewey if Bricker Is Writing the Ticket," headlined an Iowa newspaper while the widely-read *Wisconsin State Journal*, in a telegraph to Dewey, demanded

---

⁷ Julian M. Pleasants, *Buncombe Bob: The Life and Times of Robert Rice Reynolds* (Chapel Hill, 2000), pp. 243, 250-255
⁸ "Liberty Must Be Secured, Says Dewey," *San Francisco Chronicle*, Apr. 5, 1944.
⁹ "America Firster Demands Bricker," *Pittsburgh Press*, July 10, 1944.
¹⁰ "Candidates, Bad Eggs, Rodents," *Wisconsin State Journal*, Aug. 2, 1944.

that he repudiate Smith's support in no uncertain terms.[11]

In the meantime, Smith's phantom America First Party, meeting in Detroit, nominated Bricker for vice president on a ticket headed by the controversial Smith — an action immediately denounced by Dewey and his running mate.[12] The America First convention took place shortly after Smith had denounced Dewey in a series of vitriolic attacks, including one in which the rabble-rousing preacher suggested that the New Yorker should step aside and permit the governor of Ohio to stand as the GOP's presidential candidate against Roosevelt.[13]

Describing it as "ridiculous," Bricker, who had clearly learned his lesson by not denouncing Smith earlier, wasn't the least bit amused by his nomination and immediately denounced Smith's effort to link his name with the America First Party as "the cheapest sort of demagoguery." Thomas Dewey also lambasted Smith, comparing the right-wing evangelist to Adolf Hitler and denouncing his contemptible attempts to associate himself and his party with Gov. Bricker as a "sinister effort to smear the Republican candidate for Vice President."[14]

Except for a few sensational headlines, Smith's third-party candidacy never really got off the ground and he and his vice-presidential running mate, Henry A. Romer, a little-known funeral director from St. Henry, Ohio, eventually withdrew from the race and reluctantly endorsed Dewey and Bricker — a development that was almost certainly met with displeasure by both of the Republican nominees.[15]

In terms of sheer frivolity, Smith's candidacy was exceeded by two other minor candidacies that year, including the nominee of retired Indianapolis real estate broker John Zahnd's National Greenback Party, a largely paper organization which nominated the Rev. Leo Charles Donnelly, a physician-turned-pastor of Detroit's Westminster Community Church, for the nation's highest office. Like most of the party's previous presidential nominees, the little-known Donnelly — a former orthopedic surgeon who once had his medical license revoked and was later arrested for peddling a soluble mixture of distilled water and vitamins as a phony

---

[11] "It's 'Curtains' for Dewey if Bricker is Writing the Ticket," *Mason City Globe Gazette*, July 31, 1944; "Dewey Lashes Gerald Smith as Hitler-Like Race Baiter," *Wisconsin State Journal*, Aug. 1, 1944.
[12] "Gerald L. K. Smith Nominated for President," *Joplin Globe*, Aug. 1, 1944.
[13] "Dewey Claims Gerald Smith 'Race Baiter,'" *Mason City Globe-Gazette*, Aug. 1, 1944.
[14] "Dewey Lashes Gerald Smith as Hitler-Like Race Baiter," *Wisconsin State Journal*, Aug. 1, 1944; "Bricker Rips Gerald L. Smith and His Party," *Chicago Tribune*, Aug. 2, 1944.
[15] "America Firsters Endorse Dewey," *Pittsburgh Press*, Sep. 25, 1944.

cure for cancer — actively campaigned on a platform calling for monetary reform, but didn't appear on the ballot anywhere in the country.[16]

The other, of course, was the frivolous write-in candidacy of the volatile Agnes Waters, one of the most vile and hateful anti-Semitic and racist figures in the increasingly marginalized isolationist movement during World War II. One of the more sickening leaflets distributed by one of the so-called mothers' groups Waters claimed to represent during this period demanded that Major Gen. Lewis B. Hershey, director of the U.S. Selective Service, "shoot all Jews and Communists in government service and civilian jobs."[17]

A successful realtor who once served as secretary to feminist Alice Paul of the National Woman's Party, the 51-year-old self-described "pistol-packing mama" had long claimed to be the legislative representative for the Philadelphia-based National Blue Star Mothers of America — not to be confused with the better-known and far more reputable Blue Star Mother organizations throughout the country — and two or three similar right-wing groups associated with the so-called "Mothers' Movement" led by anticommunist author and right-wing fanatic Elizabeth Dilling, both of which were loosely affiliated with Gerald L. K. Smith's America First Party.[18]

A familiar figure on Capitol Hill who could still be found running for president as a write-in candidate against John F. Kennedy and Richard M. Nixon some sixteen years later, the shrill and high-strung Waters — a woman who never uttered a single criticism of Hitler during the entire course of the war — had unsuccessfully sought the presidential nominations of both major parties earlier that year.

A relatively attractive woman with graying hair who once publicly asserted that President Roosevelt should be charged with treason and shot for allowing the Japanese sneak attack on Pearl Harbor — an inflammatory statement that prompted an immediate FBI investigation — the placard-carrying crackpot announced her little-noticed candidacy in the spring of 1942, declaring that the time had come for "a good old, old-fashioned American revolution of mothers." Comparing herself to the French heroine Joan of

---

[16] "Greenback Party Names Pastor for President," *Indianapolis Star*, Mar. 22, 1944.
[17] "When is a Mother?" *The News of the Tonawandas* (North Tonawanda, N.Y.), Mar. 29, 1944.
[18] Glen Jeansonne, *Women of the Far Right: The Mothers' Movement and World War II* (Chicago, 1996), p. 212. An irrational Roosevelt hater and widely-known critic of Judaism, Dilling actively campaigned for Thomas Dewey that year, but nevertheless accused the Republican nominee of "fawning at the feet of international Jewry."

Arc, Waters said that it was "high time the women of America took over the driver's seat since the men have made a hell of a mess of things everywhere."[19]

Though her quixotic bid for the White House received little attention, Waters managed to keep herself in the news for much of the next two years. In the winter of 1943, for example, the widow of a World War I veteran and one-time Roosevelt supporter made newspaper headlines across the country when she was forcibly removed from a U.S. House Foreign Affairs Committee meeting after heckling U.S. Rep. Clare Boothe Luce shortly after the freshman Connecticut lawmaker had been thoroughly upbraided by J. William Fulbright, a young Democratic congressman and former president of the University of Arkansas.[20]

Gossip columnist Walter Winchell also gave Waters plenty of ink during this period, none of which was favorable. Deeply concerned about the remnants of the numerous fascist organizations "that crawled into the walls after Pearl Harbor and now are crawling out again," Winchell wanted to know why Waters hadn't been charged with sedition. Reminding his readers that he had repeatedly "exposed her swastika activities," the famous newspaper and radio commentator wondered aloud why the controversial Waters was able, time and again, to deliver pro-Nazi testimony on Capitol Hill.[21]

While she personally preferred New York's embattled Hamilton Fish for the presidency that year, Waters appeared to have given up the ghost regarding her own candidacy when — to the surprise of many — she inexplicably began urging Roosevelt's reelection during the summer of 1944.

"Dewey is a Communist and the Republicans are Communist controlled," she told a somewhat startled audience in Milwaukee in late July, adding that FDR and the Democrats were, too, but to a lesser degree. "The world is ablaze tonight," continued the militant noninterventionist, an outspoken proponent for a negotiated end to the war as advocated by the fringe Peace Now movement. "We must put out the fire with immediate peace," she said. "War doesn't pay. Both sides lose."

---

[19] "Crusading 'Mother' Faces FBI Inquiry," *San Luis Obispo Telegram-Tribune*, Apr. 17, 1942; Jeansonne, *Women of the Far Right*, p. 148.

[20] "Scholarly Arkansan Rips Into 'Globaloney' Speech," *Omaha World-Herald*, Feb. 17, 1943. The 37-year-old Fulbright, who later served as chairman of the U.S. Senate Relations Committee during the war in Vietnam, had sharply criticized Luce for advocating a "narrow, imperialistic policy of grab" for postwar America — a dangerous policy, argued Fulbright, that would almost certainly guarantee a third world war.

[21] Walter Winchell, "A Reporter's Report to the Nation," *Cincinnati Enquirer*, June 8, 1943.

Apparently exonerating Roosevelt of any responsibility for Pearl Harbor — a complete reversal of her earlier position — Waters, a lifelong Democrat who had supported FDR in 1932 and 1936 but later accused the three-term president of plotting with the British monarchy to drag the United States into the war as a pretext to create a world government, told the sparse crowd assembled in Milwaukee's Fine Arts Building that she still had a number of unanswered questions about the greatest military disaster in U.S. history and seriously doubted the Japanese could have spanned the Pacific without the knowledge of U.S. intelligence agencies. "If we can't get the traitors out of offices by peaceful means," she added with her usual flair, "we can shoot them out."[22]

As was the case four years earlier when the threat of a serious third-party movement led by CIO chieftain John L. Lewis or Montana's Burton K. Wheeler evaporated shortly after the Democratic national convention in Chicago, the Democrats and Republicans didn't face any significant challenge from outside the two-party system in 1944.

As in 1940, there had been some sporadic discussion of organizing a serious third-party movement in the months leading up to the 1944 presidential election, perhaps the most tantalizing of which was former Secretary of War and ex-Kansas governor Harry H. Woodring's proposal to organize a Commonwealth Party of America as a viable alternative to the country's two major parties.

Woodring, who had been the first governor west of the Mississippi to endorse Roosevelt's candidacy in 1932 and proudly seconded his nomination at the Democratic national convention in Chicago later that summer, was determined to deny FDR — a man he deeply admired and whose political ambitions he once actively promoted — a fourth term in the White House.[23]

Woodring was convinced — mistakenly, as it turned out — that millions of Democrats throughout the country were as disillusioned with their own party as he was.[24]

A former Democratic governor in an overwhelmingly Republican state who owed his razor-thin 1930 victory in Kansas to controversial radio quack John R. Brinkley's spectacular write-in can-

---

[22] "'Peace' Parley Is Held Here," *Milwaukee Journal-Sentinel*, July 26, 1944.
[23] "Harry H. Woodring Dies at 77; War Secretary Under Roosevelt," *New York Times*, Sept. 10, 1967.
[24] Keith D. McFarland, *Harry H. Woodring: A Political Biography of FDR's Controversial Secretary of War* (Lawrence, KS, 1975), p. 242.

didacy, Woodring had been named as Roosevelt's second Secretary of War following the death of George H. Dern, a wealthy mining executive with reputed pacifist leanings and no previous military experience, in the summer of 1936.

As Secretary of War, Woodring insisted on the appointment of General George C. Marshall as Army Chief of Staff in 1939 over the objections of several prominent congressmen. Before turning on him a dozen years later — "he would sell out his grandmother for personal advantage" — Woodring considered his recommendation of Marshall as his greatest service to the nation.[25]

Widely viewed as an isolationist, the conservative Kansan was later ousted from the Cabinet after a bitter falling out with FDR in June 1940 and was replaced by Henry L. Stimson, the aging Wall Street lawyer who served in the same post during the Taft administration nearly three decades earlier and who later became Herbert Hoover's Secretary of State.

A member of Skull & Bones while an undergraduate at Yale, Stimson was a leading figure in the Eastern Establishment, educated at Phillips Academy in Andover, Yale University and Harvard Law, traveling in the same elite circles as W. Averell Harriman, the patrician heir to a railroad fortune who twice sought the Democratic presidential nomination, and other members of that privileged and insular Wall Street-dominated class.

Stimson's law firm represented Kuhn, Loeb & Company, the powerful New York banking house with labyrinthine connections to the City of London and other international finance quarters. Stimson was also a close friend of George Harrison of the New York Fed — a protégé of influential banker Benjamin Strong, the J.P. Morgan representative at Jekyll Island and longtime head of the Federal Reserve Bank of New York blamed by many for the speculative bubble leading to the stock market crash of 1929. Harrison, who advised Stimson on issues of international finance, was a firm believer in the idea that a nation's central bank should be kept in private hands, separate from the national government.[26]

Described by historian Charles Beard as an "old Republican hand of the imperialist school — war for glory and trade and to divert attention from domestic troubles" — the 72-year-old Stimson, was indeed a highly partisan Republican.[27] Despite the fact

---

[25] Ibid.
[26] Liaquat Ahamed, *Lords of Finance: The Bankers Who Broke the World* (New York, 2009), pp. 55-56, 408, 454; David Wessel, *In Fed We Trust: Ben Bernanke's War on the Great Panic* (New York, 2009), p. 37.
[27] Sean Langdon Malloy, *Atomic Tragedy: Henry L. Stimson and the Decision to Use the Bomb Against Japan* (Ithaca, N.Y., 2008), p. 5.

that he later made a point of serving under presidents of both parties, Stimson had actively opposed FDR when he sought a second term as governor of New York in 1930, accusing Roosevelt in a radio address of being unfit to deal with New York's scandal-plagued judiciary.[28]

According to Woodring, whose forced resignation briefly threatened to develop into a cause célèbre, he had been forced out of the administration for refusing to strip the nation's defenses to aid the Allies, prompting a firestorm of protest and indignation from a number of non-interventionist lawmakers in both parties, including North Dakota's fiercely isolationist Gerald P. Nye, who demanded Roosevelt's immediate resignation from office.[29]

Woodring, who personally blamed "a small clique of international financiers who wanted the United States to declare war" for his ouster as Secretary of War, proposed the formation of the Commonwealth Party of America shortly after the 1942 mid-term elections, the results of which he and many others viewed as a complete repudiation of the New Deal.[30]

The Republicans, winning 209 seats, had significantly trimmed the 100-plus seat majority enjoyed by the Democrats in the U.S. House of Representatives and gained ten seats in the U.S. Senate that November, cutting the overwhelming Democratic margin in the upper chamber from 66-28 in the previous session to a much narrower 57-38 majority in the 78th Congress, with the remaining seat held by Wisconsin Progressive Robert M. La Follette, Jr.

Having spent most of his time at his home in Topeka tending to his agricultural and timber interests since leaving Washington in 1940, Woodring was about to embark on a political odyssey that would totally consume his life for the next sixteen months.

Reaching out to what he called the "lost souls" of both major parties, the 52-year-old former governor of Kansas proposed the formation of a new Commonwealth Party in a speech to the Kansas Grange in Topeka on December 11, 1942. Describing the New Deal as "a philosophy of government gone mad," the ex-Kansas governor said his new party would appeal to dissident elements in both old parties, specifically those voters who were fed up with the New Deal and those unable to find effective leadership in what he described as "an impotent Republican Party."[31]

---

[28] "Stimson Raps Gov. Roosevelt for 'Unfitness,'" *Binghamton Press*, Oct. 29, 1930.
[29] "Woodring Blast Starts Battle," *Los Angeles Times*, June 22, 1940
[30] "Call for a New Party Sounded by Woodring," *Chicago Tribune*, Dec. 12, 1942.
[31] "Woodring Urges New Party to Fight on Bureaucracy," *Los Angeles Times*, Dec. 12, 1942.

Indicating that he would personally head the new party, if necessary, Woodring fully expected the Commonwealth Party to field a presidential ticket in 1944, but claimed that the party's real strength would be demonstrated in 1948, "the year America's course will be determined."[32]

He also predicted that FDR would not seek a fourth term in 1944. "Roosevelt will be too smart and too cagy to run again as he senses the trend," he said confidently. Nevertheless, Woodring refused to rule out the possibility of Roosevelt's continuing political involvement, suggesting the possibility of a major political realignment in the future in which the three-term ex-President might join forces with one-time rival Wendell Willkie in the founding of a Liberal Party.[33]

In announcing the party's formation — a bold proposal that made headlines across the country — Woodring forcefully rejected the notion that wholesale Republican gains in 1942 reflected some sort of trend toward the GOP.

"The voters of America cried out for a change in the recent election," he declared. "Republicans were voted into office everywhere and New Deal Democrats were kicked out of public places in wholesale manner." The Republicans weren't successful the previous November because they were Republicans, he asserted, or because their party offered substantive change or took exception to the New Deal. They won, he argued, because they were the only party competing against the Democrats.[34] In other words, the GOP picked up seats in the House and Senate by default.

In Woodring's view, the Republican Party wasn't a viable alternative. As the nation's minority party, he charged, the Republicans had utterly failed to meet their responsibilities. "The party as such," said Woodring, "has done nothing, said nothing, and the recent meeting of the [party's] national committee in St. Louis indicated it doesn't intend to do anything."[35] The New Deal Democrats were thrown out, continued the former governor, because the American people can no longer "stomach their philosophies" and refuse to "submit to bureaucratic regulation and Washington paternalism."[36]

Woodring, who was still obviously bitter about his ouster from FDR's cabinet, then twisted the knife. "Everywhere in these United

---

[32] "Call for a New Party Sounded by Woodring," *Chicago Tribune*, Dec. 12, 1942.
[33] "Woodring Proposes a New Party," *Daily Capital News* (Jefferson City, Missouri), Dec. 12, 1942.
[34] "Woodring Urges New Party to Fight on Bureaucracy," *Los Angeles Times*, Dec. 12, 1942.
[35] "Call for a New Party Sounded by Woodring," *Chicago Tribune*, Dec. 12, 1942.
[36] "Woodring Urges New Party to Fight on Bureaucracy," *Los Angeles Times*, Dec. 12, 1942.

States there is an increasing demand for constitutional guarantees of state and personal rights and a return of the government to the people," he said, adding that there was a growing resentment against government agencies and bureaucrats usurping the power of the courts. "If Congress ever intended to give one individual or these agencies the power to by-pass our courts, it was done without the consent of the people," he declared. "Now regulation, domination, restriction, supervision and squandering of public moneys has become a philosophy of government gone mad. It is repulsive alike to honest, conscientious, liberty-loving Democrats and Republicans."[37]

With the exception of a few lonely voices, Woodring's proposal for a new constitutionally-based party was more or less greeted with a collective yawn. His Commonwealth Party of America had been stillborn.

Interestingly, former Republican presidential candidate Alf Landon, who unseated Woodring as governor of Kansas nearly a decade earlier, was among the few who offered encouragement. "Don't jump on Woodring," he advised one Kansas editor. "He represents a great [flock] of Democrats that are coming our way. Let's woo them."[38]

Roosevelt apparently wasn't too upset by Woodring's attempt to launch a new party; he even sent him a Christmas present later that year.[39]

Failing to get the Commonwealth Party off the ground and fearing FDR would seek another term in the White House, the former Secretary of War later organized and briefly chaired the American Democratic National Committee (ADNC), a right-wing organization whose name — cleverly mirroring that of the official DNC — was most likely intended to deliberately mislead and cause confusion among the party's rank-and-file, leaving some poorly-informed Democratic voters with the false impression that the party's national officers were actively working against Roosevelt's nomination.

The organization's name must have been even more confusing to some unsuspecting voters later that summer when the ADNC, while continuing to support Democratic electors opposed to Roosevelt in the southern states, publicly endorsed the Republican ticket of Dewey and Bricker in the North, giving the illusion that the national Democratic Party was badly divided in its support of

---

[37] Ibid.
[38] McCoy, *Landon of Kansas*, p. 488
[39] McFarland, *Harry H. Woodring*, p. 242.

FDR.[40]

While consistently maintaining that it was his intention to "restore the party to Jeffersonian principles," Woodring himself had stated in the spring of 1944 that he wouldn't lose any sleep if the Republicans captured the presidency that year. At one point, he publicly declared that if the ADNC was unsuccessful in blocking Roosevelt's nomination to a fourth term at the Democratic national convention in July, "we might adopt the 1860 formula" by holding a national convention below the Mason-Dixon Line and nominating a southern Democrat for the presidency. A split of that magnitude, even if it meant putting a Republican in the White House, he said, would be "preferable to the destruction of our democracy."[41]

In 1860, southern Democrats dissatisfied with Stephen A. Douglas' candidacy held a separate convention in Charleston and nominated Kentucky's John C. Breckinridge for president, thereby dividing the party and enabling Lincoln to win the presidency with only 39 percent of the popular vote.

Woodring even offered the names of some potentially suitable candidates to head such a ticket, a list that included Virginia's Harry F. Byrd, Joseph B. Ely, a former governor of Massachusetts, ex-Postmaster General James A. Farley, Sen. Walter F. George of Georgia and Iowa's Guy Gillette, the latter of whom had been targeted for defeat in 1938 by the Roosevelt administration for opposing the president's court-packing plan the previous year.[42] Among others, he also mentioned Kentucky's Alben W. Barkley and former New Jersey Gov. Charles Edison, a wealthy industrialist and son of famous inventor Thomas Edison, as possibilities for the nation's highest office.[43] Woodring seemed to be offering the ADNC's support to almost anyone and everyone and at one point had even suggested 72-year-old Cordell Hull — the longtime Secretary of State — as a possible candidate to succeed Roosevelt.[44] Hull's name elicited little excitement among the party's rank-and-file.

Suggesting one name after another, Woodring's growing list of potential candidates — a seemingly nonstop cavalcade of some of the biggest names in American politics — kept growing in the months leading up to the 1944 presidential campaign. Several of

---

[40] Ralph M. Goldman, *The Future Catches Up: Selected Writings of Ralph M. Goldman*, Vol. II (Lincoln, 2002), p. 136; "Anti-New Dealers Adopt Dewey Link: Will Back Republican Ticket in Northern States, Support Elector Bolt in South," *New York Times*, July 25, 1944.
[41] "Break of Southern Democrats is Seen," *Augusta Chronicle*, Mar. 10. 1944.
[42] Ibid.
[43] "Third Party Sighted if Roosevelt Runs," *Canton Repository*, Mar. 5, 1944.
[44] "A Call for Hull," *Kansas City Star*, Feb. 4, 1944.

them expressed an interest, but with the exception of former Gov. Ely of Massachusetts — a man of exceptional courage, candor and independence who firmly believed in the doctrines expressed in Walter Lippmann's *The Good Society* — nobody was willing to risk his political future in a quixotic campaign to unseat a popular wartime president, particularly one who had pulled the country out of the worst depression in American history.

Almost every prominent Democrat who ever feuded with FDR during the previous twelve years seemed, at one time or another, to be included in Woodring's ever-expanding list of potential Roosevelt challengers for the Democratic nomination. The former Kansas governor, whose unceremonious ouster from FDR's Cabinet had been instigated, in part, by Secretary of the Interior Harold Ickes, appeared to be looking for somebody with a grudge against Roosevelt — ideally someone like himself, a Democrat who had been wronged or scorned by the administration and who possessed a bull-sized taste for revenge.[45]

While visiting Texas in March, the final stop in a southern tour that had taken the former Secretary of War through Georgia, Florida, Louisiana and elsewhere, Woodring added the colorful W. Lee "Pappy" O'Daniel of Texas, a successful flour salesman-turned-politician who once compared his colleagues in Washington to "stinkweed" and bitterly complained that Roosevelt had surrounded himself with a "a group of pussyfooting, pusillanimous politicians who were not fit to run a peanut stand," to his lengthy list of potential giant slayers.[46] Believing that the country would be doomed if the "Washington Dynasty" wasn't stopped, the Texas lawmaker clearly wasn't happy in the nation's capital. "Every time I turn around up here," he told a reporter, "I bump into a building or a bureaucrat."[47] During an interview in Houston, Woodring described the state's junior senator, a persistent critic of the Roosevelt administration, as "an outstanding example of the type of man who would be acceptable to us" as a presidential nominee.[48]

According to longtime nationally-syndicated labor columnist Victor Riesel, Woodring actually ordered staffers at the ADNC headquarters in Chicago's Palmer House that winter to circulate

---

[45] Doris Kearns Goodwin, *No Ordinary Time: Franklin & Eleanor Roosevelt: The Home Front in World War II* (New York, 1944) p. 24.
[46] Bill Crawford, *Please Pass the Biscuits, Pappy: Pictures of Governor W. Lee 'Pappy' O'Daniel* (Austin, Texas, 2004), p. 45.
[47] "O'Daniel Speaks Here Tonight," *Amarillo Daily News*, Oct. 25, 1944.
[48] "O'Daniel, Byrd Outstanding Men, Says Woodring," *Richmond Times-Dispatch*, Mar. 18, 1944.

nominating petitions to place the colorful Texan on the April 11 Illinois Democratic presidential primary ballot. Despite obtaining the requisite number of signatures, Woodring's underlings, delayed by a snowstorm, arrived at the state capitol in Springfield fifteen minutes after the filing deadline. Though it remains unclear whether O'Daniel had personally authorized such an effort, the mad dash through the snow-covered roads in the Land of Lincoln on that cold winter night was as close as old Pappy would ever come to running for president.[49]

Despite spending nearly a year and half trying to recruit a challenger for the Democratic nomination or possibly a candidate to run against Roosevelt in the general election, Woodring curiously maintained that he still considered the president a good friend — and a great humanitarian. "Franklin D. Roosevelt will go down in history as the father of the renaissance of the common man," he declared in February while floating the names of several potential rivals. "I am proud to call him my friend." His objection to a fourth term, explained Woodring, was primarily due to the kind of men Roosevelt had surrounded himself with — a "palace guard" aided by an unidentified "wire-pulling Rasputin" on the U.S. Supreme Court which had nefariously usurped leadership in his administration.[50]

During a packed press conference from his suite at New York's Waldorf-Astoria later that month, Woodring vowed to raise a $1.5 million war chest for a 48-state fight to prevent a fourth term. Accompanied by New York's John O'Connor, the former conservative Democratic congressman who had been famously targeted for defeat by FDR six years earlier, the former Kansas governor said that his group's initial goal was to deny Roosevelt the Democratic nomination. "The real objective of our organization is not to support any Republican," he asserted, "but to organize the Democrats against a fourth term and recapture control of the party." As such, he said the ADNC hoped to field a presidential candidate in as many Democratic primaries where there was still sufficient time to do so.

Admitting that he didn't yet have a candidate who was willing to openly challenge Roosevelt for the Democratic nomination, Woodring said that he had recently spoken to former Massachusetts Gov. Joseph B. Ely, an outspoken critic of federal expansion

---

[49] Victor Riesel, "Queens Coughlin Chief Leads Stop-FDR Party Here," *New York Post*, Feb. 25, 1944.
[50] "Woodring 'Nominates' Hull for President, Raps 'Palace Guard,'" *Seattle Daily Times*, Feb. 4, 1944.

under the New Deal, by telephone and believed that a slate of district delegates pledged to the 63-year-old ex-governor would appear on that state's Democratic primary ballot on April 25. He also hoped to encourage other favorite-son candidates to follow Ely's example in trying to block Roosevelt's reelection. "Our purpose is to organize all Democrats in the party against a fourth term," said Woodring.

Keeping the idea of a national third-party movement afloat, the former Secretary of War also told reporters during his New York press conference that he could foresee a scenario in which an ADNC-backed candidate running outside the duopoly might garner enough electoral votes to throw the election into the House of Representatives.[51]

Woodring shared the view that opposition to Roosevelt and the New Deal, particularly among Democrats, was far more extensive than commonly believed — and it wasn't simply limited to the South. He privately agreed with New Orleans industrialist John U. Barr, national chairman of the Draft-Byrd-for-President organization, who argued that dissatisfaction with Roosevelt's New Deal wasn't based exclusively on racial factors and it certainly wasn't limited to those in southern states. According to Barr, it was far more widespread and extended across party lines. "Southern Democrats — along with millions of good Americans of both parties in other sections — are deeply alarmed at the totalitarian trend of the New Deal and are determined to get rid of it before it is too late," he said.[52]

This opposition was clearly reflected in the ADNC's executive committee assembled by Woodring during his short tenure with the group. They weren't all southerners by any stretch of the imagination. It was a relatively substantial group that included former Sen. James A. Reed of Missouri, an aging Kansas City lawyer who fought vigorously to keep the United States out of the League of Nations in 1919 and later unsuccessfully sought the Democratic presidential nomination in 1924, 1928 and 1932.

In addition to Reed, at one time or another during its brief 10-month existence, the American Democratic National Committee counted five former governors, three former U.S. House members, an ex-state attorney general, an elected statewide officeholder in Texas, two former state party chairmen, and at least two university

---

[51] "Anti-Roosevelt Democrats Vow 48 State Fight," *Chicago Tribune*, Feb. 25, 1944; "Nation-Wide Fight on Fourth Term Planned Here by Woodring Group," *New York Times*, Feb. 25, 1944.

[52] "Politics Center of Dixie Revolt," *Palm Beach Post*, June 23, 1944.

presidents among its members — each warning of an apocalyptic future if FDR succeeding in winning a fourth term.

Gleason L. Archer of Boston, president and founder of Suffolk University, ex-Rep. John J. O'Connor of New York, former Iowa congressman-turned-western fiction writer Otha D. Wearin, ex-Michigan governor William A. Comstock, who was then serving on the Detroit city council, Dr. Robert E. O'Brian, a former Iowa secretary of state, and New York financier Robert M. Harriss, a prominent patron of conservative causes, were among those personally recruited by Woodring. Edward F. Judge, vice president of the Scullin Steel Company in St. Louis, was named treasurer in late February.[53]

O'Brian, a former Methodist minister who served as Iowa's secretary of state from 1937-39, was a prime mover in the founding of the organization. O'Brian was quick to point out that the ADNC wasn't a third party movement, nor was it supporting a specific candidate for the Democratic presidential nomination. "But we are all agreed that the New Dealers shall not usurp the name and power of the Democratic Party." According to O'Brian, the anti-administration group originated during informal talks with party leaders across the country who were concerned about the direction of the party and what they perceived as a trend toward totalitarianism.[54] "We aren't happy about the situation," sighed O'Brian. "But we think the future of our country is more important than that of our party. We can see no other way to protect our form of government."[55]

A wealthy cotton broker, the 54-year-old Harriss was a longtime financial advisor to Father Coughlin and had managed Joseph V. McKee's spectacular 1933 mayoral campaign on the Recovery Party ticket in Queens when the former acting mayor was running against incumbent Mayor John P. O'Brien, a Tammany Democrat, and Republican-Fusion challenger Fiorello H. La Guardia. The Dallas-born investor later headed a Queens "Democrats for Willkie" organization in 1940.[56] Harriss told a congressional investigating committee that he contributed $3,500 to the American Democratic National Committee.[57] In addition to contributing generously to the ADNC cause, Harriss also funded Texas Sen. W. Lee "Pappy" O'Daniel's political activities to the tune of $1,000 that

---

[53] "E. F. Judge is Treasurer of Anti-New Deal Group," *St. Louis Star-Times*, Feb. 28, 1944.
[54] "Anti-New Deal Democrats Plot Control," *Los Angeles Times*, Feb. 3, 1944.
[55] "Democratic Bolt," *San Bernardino Sun*, Mar. 23, 1944.
[56] "Robert Harriss, Cotton Broker," *New York Times*, Sep. 27, 1971.
[57] "Dewey Backers Odd Bedfellows," *Gazette and Daily*, Oct. 21, 1944.

year while also reportedly giving money to "Cotton Ed" Smith's National Farm Committee and publisher Frank Gannett's arch-conservative Committee for Constitutional Government.[58]

Publisher Henry Regnery of Chicago, a former member of the isolationist America First Committee who had personally financed the initial publication of the conservative *Human Events* magazine that same year, also served on the ADNC's executive committee. Some of the lesser-known individuals who served on the group's executive committee included H. W. Kramer, publisher of the little-remembered *National Free Press*, wealthy St. Louis realtor William Warren, attorney Harry Weiss of St. Paul, Minnesota, and Lee Merriweather of St. Louis, a former assistant ambassador to France during the Wilson administration who was then serving as president of the Jeffersonian Democrats of America.

Mankato attorney John E. Regan, a former state representative who had twice been the Democratic candidate for governor of Minnesota and later stumped the state with Henry Wallace, who was then running for vice president, as the party's nominee for the U.S. Senate in 1940, was also later appointed to the ADNC's executive committee.

Regan deeply disliked Roosevelt for defeating Al Smith for the Democratic presidential nomination in 1932 and for cooperating with Gov. Floyd Olson and Minnesota's Farmer-Labor Party later that autumn while the conservative Mankato lawyer was bravely holding aloft the Democratic banner in the state's three-cornered gubernatorial campaign easily won by his Farmer-Labor opponent. The scrappy Minnesotan, who was appointed to the committee in June, was tasked with organizing a convention of delegates from all of the country's anti-New Deal Democratic organizations in the event of Roosevelt's nomination for a fourth term.[59]

Ted R. Ewart, a Dallas publicity man who was then working for newspaper publisher Frank Gannett's Committee for Constitutional Government, also became a member of the ADNC executive committee after meeting with Woodring during the latter's swing through Texas in March. The 49-year-old Ewart, who once played an active role in defeating the famous "Ham and Eggs" $30-a-week pension plan in California, was initially offered the role of campaign manager in Texas, but eventually served as head of the national organization's finance committee.[60]

---

[58] Stetson Kennedy, *Southern Exposure: Making the South Safe for Democracy* (Tuscaloosa, AL, 1991), p. 140.
[59] "Today's Digest of Nation's News," *Minneapolis Star-Tribune*, June 22, 1944.
[60] "Post Offered Dallasite to Oppose F.R.," *Dallas Morning News*, Mar. 1, 1944.

M. C. Roberts, founder of New Mexico's Club for Constitutional Government, a coalition of anti-New Deal Democrats and likeminded Republicans, was also a member of the committee. A wealthy feed and seed dealer originally from Texas, Roberts — a lifelong Democrat — believed that Roosevelt's New Deal was destroying the party. "We're not fighting the Democratic Party," declared Roberts, "we're out to lick the New Deal — and to return the party to the Democrats." Roberts, who had been organizing opposition to FDR in New Mexico for several months, was deeply concerned that the New Deal was undermining private enterprise and crushing individual initiative while maintaining that any "progress must come through production and industry and not from social gains or planned economy." Soldiers returning from the war, he argued, should be offered good-paying jobs in the private sector, not government handouts.[61]

As one might have expected, a number of politically prominent southerners also served on the ADNC's executive committee, including at least one elected official — James E. McDonald, the longtime Texas Secretary of Agriculture. Other southerners on the committee included pastor and historian Marshall Wingfield of Memphis, national commander of the Sons of Confederate Veterans, and former State Senator E. Wales Brown of Shreveport, Louisiana. Junius M. Futrell, an austerity-minded former governor of Arkansas, and former Oklahoma attorney general George F. Short also briefly served on the ADNC's national committee.

The most controversial member of the committee, however, might have been New York's William J. Goodwin, a somewhat pompous Roosevelt hater, isolationist and avowed anticommunist who once tried to run for mayor of New York City on his own newly-created "American Rock Party." A former Democratic district leader in Queens, Goodwin — a man who later admitted under oath that he had never voted for Roosevelt — served as the ADNC's national treasurer.[62]

One of the group's most quotable members, the Fordham-educated public relations specialist — a longtime foe of the New Deal — claimed that the United States was "writhing in the grip of theorist monsters with cat-like grins on their faces and false promises on their tongues."[63]

---

[61] "Coalition Club Opens Campaign Here Tomorrow," *Las Cruces Sun-News*, Sep. 10, 1943; "State Constitutional Government Club Official to Speak," *Albuquerque Journal*, Sep. 28, 1943.
[62] "These Men Contributed to the Hate-Roosevelt Campaign; GOP Industrialists, Fronters Joined to Finance Drive," *New York PM*, Oct. 19, 1944.
[63] "Two Democrats Speak," *Pampa News* (Pampa, TX), July 21, 1944.

The dapper-looking Goodwin was also one of the organization's most influential and popular committee members as evidenced by the fact that the ADNC wholeheartedly recommended that he would be their choice for vice-president on a third-party ticket headed by Sen. W. Lee "Pappy" O'Daniel of Texas — a candidacy the colorful Texan eventually decided against.[64] Retiring Sen. Robert R. Rice of North Carolina — the "Tar Heel Fuhrer" — told his supporters that Goodwin was to the ADNC "what Jim Farley was to the National Democratic Executive Committee in 1932 and 1936."[65]

The 47-year-old Goodwin, who was then living on a small estate on Long Island and later worked as a lobbyist for Chiang Kai-shek's Chinese Nationalist government (Taiwan) in Washington, D.C. — earning approximately $415,000 a year from that client alone by today's standards — ran for Congress in 1936 with the backing of Father Coughlin's National Union for Social Justice, but lost in the Democratic primary.[66] Four years later, he managed Vice President John Nance Garner's nascent presidential campaign in New York when FDR was seeking a third term.[67] Later that autumn, he endorsed Republican Wendell Willkie, earning him the wrath of other Democratic leaders in Queens.[68]

Goodwin always managed to keep his name in the news. In 1941, for example, he testified before the Senate Foreign Relations Committee in opposition to the administration's Lend-Lease legislation. During his widely-covered testimony, he warned that given its large foreign-born population there would likely be a civil uprising in New York City if the legislation was approved. "New York City is a veritable powder keg," he testified, "and our entry into this war might touch it off." In his testimony, which made the front page of the *New York Times*, the New York publicist also claimed that the La Guardia administration was "permeated with Communists."[69] Goodwin's testimony immediately drew the ire of some of the city's most prominent civic leaders, many of whom denounced his testimony as a "shameful misrepresentation" and "utterly unfounded and untruthful."[70]

---

[64] "Third Party Dems to Run O'Daniel," *Whitewright Sun* (Whitewright, TX), July 13, 1944.
[65] Victor Riesel, "Coughlin Back in Politics, Directs War on Roosevelt," *New York Post*, June 30, 1944.
[66] "Insurgents Routed Here," *New York Times*, Sep. 16, 1936.
[67] "Garner Will Raise Third-Term Issue," *New York Times*, Mar. 7, 1940.
[68] "Bill Goodwin Repudiated By His Lieutenants," *Long Island Daily Press*, Nov. 1, 1940.
[69] "New Yorkers Say Civil Uprising Will Come Here if We Enter War," *New York Times*, Feb. 8, 1941.
[70] "'Civil War' Augury Draws Fire Here," *New York Times*, Feb. 9, 1941.

In a letter to the committee's chairman in October, Goodwin again criticized the administration's policies. "By a series of steps, of which this revision of the Neutrality Act is one, you are being committed to the full program of your Executive, which program pretends to be the destruction of Hitler," he wrote Sen. Tom Connally of Texas. "Why should America destroy Hitler?" If anybody was violating international law, it was the United States — not Germany, he said. "We are not champions of freedom of the seas, but hypocritical starvation blockaders of non-belligerent women and children."[71]

Goodwin was also mentioned in journalist Avedis Derounian's explosive book, *Under Cover*, a blistering exposé of native fascism published by E. P. Dutton in 1943. Eventually selling over a million copies, Derounian's sensational book was the best-selling work of nonfiction in the country in 1944. Using the pseudonym John Roy Carlson, Derounian, an Armenian journalist who came to the United States when he was twelve, quoted Goodwin as saying that there was "nothing wrong with fascism. Hitler has done a good job for Germany" — a remark Goodwin strenuously denied ever making. "I haven't read the damn book," he told a reporter for the left-leaning *PM* newspaper shortly after it was published. "But from all I've heard about it, I am proud to be in it."[72]

If it was any consolation to Goodwin, Derounian's fascinating but deeply-flawed book — an exaggeratedly frightening page-turner — relying on a shockingly heavy use of guilt-by-association and filled with false and unsubstantiated claims, had unfairly smeared many decent and reputable pre-war isolationists and noninterventionists. Even such honorable men as Ohio's Robert A. Taft and Montana Sen. Burton K. Wheeler, two of no fewer than fourteen U.S. senators cast in a provocatively negative light, as well as Socialist Norman Thomas, the latter of whom was depicted as a "zealot" who had actively cooperated with both Communists and fascists in an effort to deliberately sabotage the nation's defense, were savagely skewered by the author.[73]

Sen. Gerald P. Nye of North Dakota, who was running for reelection in 1944, was also maligned in the 544-page narrative and believed that he had been the victim of "clever editing," telling the *St. Louis Post-Dispatch* that he thought Derounian's book was little more than "unadulterated propaganda, intended alone to smear

---

[71] "Let's Look at the Record of Dewey Rally Backers," *PM*, Oct. 25, 1941.
[72] "WJZ Drops McNutt for Coughlinite Cash," *PM*, Sep. 24, 1943.
[73] Ribuffo, *The Old Christian Right*, p.192.

certain individuals." Anybody who read the book, said Nye, would be left with "the impression that I was part of a great undercover movement in the United States to undermine our own government and to show favor to the enemy countries."[74]

Wheeler's friend, John T. Flynn, a tenacious muckraking journalist who had chaired the America First Committee in New York, believed Derounian's book was part of a larger "conspiracy" to discredit virtually every prominent American who had been opposed to U.S. entry in World War II prior to the attack on Pearl Harbor. Flynn, who was inclined toward conspiracy theories since his earliest days as a reporter, denounced *Under Cover* and Derounian's follow-up volume, *The Plotters*, as "a long, dull catalogue of repetitious drivel aimed at discrediting Roosevelt's foreign policy critics.[75]

In the autumn of 1941, Goodwin, stymied in his attempt to seek the Democratic nomination for president of the New York city council, abruptly decided to run for mayor as a third-party candidate shortly before the city's filing deadline. The fence-jumping political adventurer from Queens wasted little time in attacking his two major-party opponents. "Since Mayor La Guardia and his stooge, William O'Dwyer, are both behind this drive to push the country into a foreign war, I am running for mayor so that the people against war will have a chance to show it with their votes," he declared. "Our campaign will be against convoys, communism and Quislings."[76]

Running on his own American Rock Party, a name he incorporated the previous year, Goodwin launched his mayoral candidacy in a radio address in which he identified himself as a follower of Charles Lindbergh, Senators Gerald Nye and Burton K. Wheeler and other members of the American First Committee.[77] A former member of the Coughlinite Christian Front, Goodwin was asked about support from members of that group. "I am not against the Christian Front," he responded, "but I am against anything anti-Semitic. The Christian Front is not anti-Semitic."[78]

Goodwin's mayoral candidacy, however, proved to be short-lived. Despite obtaining nearly 10,000 signatures on his nominating petitions in a relatively short two-week period, the city's Board

---

[74] "How Carlson's 'Under Cover' Became a Political Sensation, Passionately Denounced and Lavishly Praised," *St. Louis Post-Dispatch*, May 7, 1944.
[75] John E. Moser, *Right Turn: John T. Flynn and the Transformation of American Liberalism* (New York, 2005), p. 172.
[76] "Isolationist Gets in Race for Mayor," *New York Times*, Sep. 24, 1941.
[77] "Expect O'Dwyer to 'Tell Off' Tiger," *Brooklyn Eagle*, Oct. 16, 1941.
[78] "Let's Look at the Record of Dewey Rally Backers," *PM*, Oct. 25, 1944.

of Elections subsequently determined that he didn't have enough valid signatures.[79] Goodwin sued, but a Supreme Court justice in Queens, in an eleventh-hour ruling, upheld the board's decision to exclude him from the ballot a week before the election on the grounds that only 5,366 of the 9,655 signatures on his nominating petitions were valid. He needed a minimum of 7,500.[80]

Goodwin nevertheless kept his American Rock Party alive for the next few years and even ran several candidates for public office under its banner, but with increasingly disappointing results. In 1943, Goodwin's tiny party blanketed Queens with leaflets quoting an archbishop from Dubuque, Iowa, who was a close friend and ally of Father Coughlin, proclaiming that "the forces of Christ...are about to come to close grips with the anti-Christs — those saboteurs of God and Country — who have penetrated our bastions, infected large groups of our people with their clever program of demoralization and de-Christianization, and in consequence prepared this republic for evil days.[81] In March 1944, the New York publicist reportedly told other members of the ADNC during a highly secretive meeting at the Canadian Pacific Building on Madison Avenue that his Coughlinite party would, in effect, become the Queens section of the national organization.[82]

Switching parties several years later, the talkative New Yorker — he was a loose cannon, to put it mildly — actively supported Ohio's Robert A. Taft for the Republican presidential nomination in 1948 and again in 1952, serving as chairman of the Volunteers for Taft in metropolitan New York in the latter campaign. Goodwin, who wasn't the least bit circumspect, couldn't stop talking about the Ohio senator.

According to nationally-syndicated columnist Drew Pearson, the well-dressed publicist once boarded a plane to Cincinnati during the 1948 campaign, quickly took his seat and immediately began talking incessantly to the passenger seated next to him. A devout Catholic, Goodwin told his fellow passenger everything he could about the Ohio senator's campaign, including little-known details about his recent trip to Nebraska to help round up delegates, and how he was now on his way to Cincinnati to convince the archbishop to support Taft's candidacy. The only thing he didn't convey to his fellow passenger was the fact that he was a paid lobbyist for Chiang Kai-shek. As the plane was preparing to

---

[79] "Goodwin Petitions Voided by Board," *New York Times*, Oct. 22, 1941.
[80] "Goodwin Loses in Court," *New York Times*, Oct. 28, 1941.
[81] "Coughlinites Get Fraction of Queens Vote," *New York Post*, Nov. 3, 1943.
[82] "Brooklyn Coughlinites," *New York Post*, Mar. 24, 1944.

land, Goodwin leaned over and asked his traveling companion for his name. "My name is Kroll," the passenger replied. "Jack Kroll." Goodwin was stunned. He had just divulged a tremendous amount of valuable insider knowledge to the director of the CIO's political action committee, which was doing everything in its power to thwart Taft's candidacy that year.[83]

Goodwin, who had briefly belonged to the short-lived Christian Front — an anti-Semitic organization with pro-Nazi sympathies — later claimed that he had personally "laid the groundwork" for Sen. Joseph R. McCarthy's infamous investigation into alleged Communist infiltration in the State Department, but vehemently denied that he had been feeding information to the Wisconsin lawmaker.[84]

With the New York chatterbox now firmly ensconced in the national organization, the fledgling American Democratic National Committee, which was still headed by Woodring, struggled to make meaningful strides in its efforts to derail Roosevelt's bid for a fourth term. In early March, Woodring announced that he would be conducting a nationwide tour, beginning with a quick stop in New England followed by a more extensive tour of the South.[85]

In Boston, where he met with Democrats from several nearby states, Woodring — a son-in-law of former Massachusetts Sen. Marcus A. Coolidge — told reporters that the ADNC's goal was to "take the Democratic Party out of the hands of 'Hopkins and Company' and return it to the Jeffersonian Democrats" at the party's national convention in July. "Our real fight," he said, "is against the men of the 'palace guard' — the men around the throne who are advising Roosevelt and are a sinister influence in our government."[86] Based on samplings, Woodring claimed that 35 to 40 percent of the country's Democrats were opposed to a fourth term. He also said that he found anti-Roosevelt sentiment in New England to be "very encouraging."[87]

Accompanied by New York's Robert Harriss, the deep-pocketed Texas native who had strongly recommended that Goodwin be given a major role in the organization, the irreconcilable insurgent then ventured into the Solid South, a region brimming with anti-Roosevelt sentiment.

---

[83] Drew Pearson, "Washington Merry-Go-Round," *Greensboro Daily News*, Apr. 23, 1950.
[84] "Goodwin Admits Role in Charges," *New York Times*, Apr. 11, 1950; "Goodwin Clarifies Place in Red Inquiry," *New York Times*, Apr. 12, 1950.
[85] "Woodring Plans Wide Anti-New Deal Fight," *Nashville Tennessean*, Mar. 3, 1944.
[86] "Woodring Scores 'Palace Guard' Around FDR," *Elmira Star-Gazette*, Mar. 6, 1944.
[87] "35 Pct. of FDR's Party Reported Anti-4th Term," *Chicago Tribune*, Mar. 7, 1944.

As mentioned previously, Woodring had suggested that the ADNC "might adopt the 1860 formula" and hold a separate convention below the Mason-Dixon Line where it would nominate a southern Democrat for president. The chain-smoking ex-governor candidly admitted that such a strategy could result in a Republican victory, but added that such an outcome would be "preferable to the destruction of our democracy."[88] When he made those remarks in Atlanta, Woodring — a man who usually chose his words carefully — had no idea that some southerners would be deeply offended by his suggestion.

"Woodring Foresees Southern Secession" screamed the sensational headline of a South Florida newspaper.[89] The term "southern secession," of course, had a very clear and distinct meaning in American history, particularly in the South, and that's obviously not what the retired Kansas banker said or implied during his appearance in Atlanta.

The sharpest rebuke to Woodring's proposal, however, came from the *Asheville Citizens-Times* in North Carolina, which described his comment as "an unfortunate historical allusion," while viciously calling the ADNC chairman a "malcontent" who was "trying to foster a revolt against President Roosevelt within the Democratic Party." The editorial writer pulled no punches in lambasting the former cabinet member:

> Mr. Woodring was no great shakes as Secretary of War. Among our grievances against President Roosevelt is the fact that he kept this incompetent so long in his cabinet. That Mr. Woodring will be able to inspire any genuine rebellion within the Democratic fold is most unlikely. He is hardly a big enough man to serve as a rallying figure for discontented Democrats.
>
> But Mr. Woodring was certainly not felicitous in his historical allusion when he suggested the other day that in the event of Mr. Roosevelt's nomination the South "might adopt the 1860 formula" and hold a separate Democratic convention. No Southern Democrat can contemplate the grievous blunder of 1860 with any emotion save that of shivery remorse.
>
> The only effect of the "1860 formula" was to condemn the Democratic Party to defeat, to insure Lincoln's election and to lay the train of the War Between the States. Perhaps the nation gained from the end result, but the South is still paying the

---

[88] "Woodring Asserts South's Democrats May Put Up Ticket," *Jackson Sun* (Jackson, TN), Mar. 10, 1944.
[89] "Woodring Foresees Southern Secession," *Palm Beach Post*, Mar. 10, 1944.

heavy price of that tragic mistake...

> If any Southern Democrat is unable to vote for Mr. Roosevelt, then he should adopt the honorable course of bolting the party and of embracing the opposition. There is no dishonor in an honest change of party allegiance. But he should not advocate "the formula of 1860." Leaving a party is one thing, but a conspiracy to wreck it is another and quite different matter.[90]

Woodring appeared unshaken by the harsh criticism and continued on his whirlwind tour of the South. Along the way, he kept adding names to his ever-expanding list of potential candidates to challenge Roosevelt.

Stopping in Jacksonville, Florida, a day after his Atlanta appearance, Woodring told the *Jacksonville Journal* that Sen. Alben W. Barkley was one of nine men "available" to head the committee's ticket if Roosevelt ultimately decided to seek a fourth term.[91] The president, of course, had been silent about his intentions up to that point.

In New Orleans a few days later, Woodring suggested yet another name, that of Gov. Sam Houston Jones — a man on virtually nobody's list of prospective presidential hopefuls that year. According to Woodring, Jones was certainly "presidential timber." The 46-year-old Jones, who was barred by law from succeeding himself that year, had defeated Earl Long, the late Huey Long's brother, in 1940. "Jones is a great patriot and a great southerner," said the Kansan while declining to discuss the Louisiana governor's specific qualifications for the presidency.[92]

Woodring was obviously aware that Jones, working closely with Gov. Frank Dixon of Alabama, an avowed racist, had called for an independent "Southern Democratic Party" based on white supremacy a year earlier during the 1943 Conference of Southern Governors — a proposal that was wisely rejected by most of the region's governors who clearly realized that such an endeavor would be suicidal, resulting in diminished congressional power and federal patronage for the South.

In stating that it might be time for the "Solid South" to abandon its blind allegiance to the Democratic Party, the Louisiana gover-

---

[90] "An Unfortunate Historical Allusion," *Asheville Citizens-Times*, Mar. 12, 1944.
[91] "Woodring Asserts Barkley 'Available' if Roosevelt Runs," *Louisville Courier-Journal*, Mar. 11, 1944.
[92] "Gov. Jones Called 'Presidential Timber' for '44," *Alexandria Daily Town Talk*, Mar. 15, 1944.

nor, in a widely-publicized article published in the *Saturday Evening Post* in March 1943, accused the Roosevelt administration of denying the South its share of public investments while charging that the administration's economic policies "continued to kick an already prostrate South in the face." Jones was clearly in a fighting mood, as the following excerpts demonstrate:

> It is abundantly and increasingly clear that the New Deal high command hopes to use the war as an instrument for forcing the "social equality" of the Negro upon the South. White southern boys in the armed services, who, perhaps, have an understanding of and affection for the Negro race not shared by their comrades from other sections, do not improve in morale when they are told that one of the things they are fighting for is social equality of the Negro. They would renounce any such war aim, rightly or wrongly.
>
> The New Deal Democrats have their method of solving the race problem, and we have ours. Ergo, let's affiliate with a group which supports our own view. Or create a group, if necessary...There is a possibility of an independent Southern Democratic Party...consider the result when a bloc of 115 electoral votes takes effect in a college of 531 in all. Subtract those votes from the already-shaky New Deal Democratic column and very little dependable comfort remains for current officeholders. We may support a Democrat, a South Democrat, a Republican, or a Mr. No-Party-At-All, but you can be sure that he is going to be a man prepared to speak and act our language. One thing can save the New Deal Democratic Party — that is, a complete reversal of attitude toward the South.[93]

Jones, in effect, had laid down the gauntlet, putting FDR on notice. By then, of course, Woodring's list of potential candidates also included Gov. Dixon, so one can only assume that the former Kansas governor knew exactly what he was doing in throwing the Louisiana governor's name into the increasingly volatile mix.[94]

In Texas the following week, the former Kansas governor suggested a couple of more names — one that made a splash in newspapers across the country. Woodring and Harriss spent several days in the Lone Star State. While there Woodring urged Texas Democrats to take control of the Democratic state convention in May and select delegates opposed to a fourth term.

---

[93] Sam H. Jones, "Will Dixie Bolt the New Deal?" *Saturday Evening Post*, Mar. 6, 1943, pp. 20-21, 42, 45.
[94] "Woodring Lists Byrd Candidacy," *Fort Lauderdale News*, Mar. 15, 1944.

"Get in the front seats, fill the precinct conventions and crowd out the New Dealers," exhorted Woodring at a luncheon hosted by wealthy industrialist and ex-state party chairman Eugene B. Germany, an implacable Roosevelt foe, at the Hotel Adolphus in Dallas. "Name delegates to the national convention who are real states' rights, Jeffersonian, constitutional Democrats, who will be uninstructed or for a real Democrat like Gov. Coke Stevenson." Stevenson was well-liked by the party's regulars, particularly the rebellious right-wingers who later organized the Texas Regulars.

Woodring then told the twenty or so businessmen in attendance that the New Dealers were able to nominate Roosevelt every four years by controlling the party's machinery nationally through federal employees and by directing the flow of federal funds. "This has gone on until we no longer have representative government, but a bureaucratic control of government," he bemoaned.

Delving into policy, the former Kansas governor outlined what he perceived to be a dangerous scheme concocted by the New Dealers to bring about state capitalism. "The program," he explained, "is for industry and business to have no reserves when peace comes with which to convert from a war to a peace economy. The result will be unemployment and hunger, because industry can't furnish jobs due to the government policy. The President will then ask Congress for fifty billion dollars to take care of the unemployed and to save business, and he will then dole out the money." It will 1933 all over again, said Woodring. "And the final result of such a situation will be state capitalism, according to plan."[95]

Stevenson, who was running for reelection, wasn't the only Texan whose name had been floated by the ADNC chairman as a potential challenger to Roosevelt during his March visit to the state. As mentioned earlier in this chapter, Woodring had remarked a few days earlier in Houston that Sen. W. Lee "Pappy" O'Daniel, one of the state's most popular political figures, would be "an outstanding example of the type of person who would be acceptable to his group" as a presidential candidate.[96] Woodring's overture made headlines across the country.

O'Daniel, who rose to fame and political glory by playing hillbilly music and "passing the biscuits," responded in his charmingly folksy way that he was flattered by the offer and in hearty

---

[95] "Fight to Stop F.R. Asked By Woodring," *Dallas Morning News*, Mar. 22, 1944.
[96] "Dissident Demo Wants O'Daniel Type as President," *El Paso Herald-Post*, Mar. 17, 1944.

agreement with the aims of Woodring's organization, but remained noncommittal.[97] The genial, strapping ex-governor and former radio personality — the greatest showman in Texas politics who would later do everything in his power to try to swing the state's 23 electoral votes away from Roosevelt in November — would be approached by the increasingly desperate American Democratic National Committee again in August, several weeks after the Democratic national convention in Chicago, urging him to run for president as a third-party candidate.[98]

Stopping in Oklahoma City on his return trip to Chicago, an exhausted Woodring boasted that the ADNC had established organizations in a dozen states. "Our investigation reveals that we can enter a ticket of real Democrat[ic] candidates, if that becomes necessary, in every state south of the Mason-Dixon line, as well as many of those north of the line." Speaking at a private luncheon, Woodring advised those in the audience to organize a delegation to the party's national convention in Chicago instructed to oppose FDR's bid for a fourth term.[99]

In the meantime, the Republicans, who had been following the ADNC developments with more than glancing interest, were naturally delighted by what appeared to be a growing schism in the Democratic Party. Buoyed by their own off-year successes when they captured five out of six U.S. House seats in special elections while picking up a couple of more congressional seats earlier that year, Republican officials were increasingly confident that 1944 would be their year.

But they may have been celebrating too soon, as former Democratic congressman John J. O'Connor sternly warned them in late March. O'Connor was the ADNC's general counsel.

In a letter to the GOP's House minority leader Joseph W. Martin, Jr., of Massachusetts, O'Connor — still very much a Democrat at heart — cautioned Martin's Republican colleagues to "sober up from their cockiness" and stop celebrating. "When a fourth term finishes its job of destroying our traditional form of government," Connor informed Martin, "it will also bury what is left of the two 'great' parties. And if ever we do get out of the pit, there will be a new party alignment, bearing little resemblance to what we had…"[100]

---

[97] "O'Daniel Declares Few Favor FDR," *Dallas Morning News*, Mar. 20, 1944.
[98] "American Democrats Ask O'Daniel to Run," *Washington Evening Star*, Aug. 15, 1944.
[99] "12 States Move to Block Fourth Term for FDR," *Miami Daily News-Record* (Miami, OK), Mar. 23, 1944.
[100] "GOP Warned to Stop Celebrations," *Ithaca Journal*, Mar. 31, 1944.

THE LOWEST EBB

Things changed dramatically for the anti-Roosevelt group a few days later when Woodring, catching nearly everybody by surprise, unexpectedly announced that he was stepping down as national chairman of the ADNC, effective immediately. Woodring's sudden resignation, coming shortly after his lengthy tour of the South, received widespread newspaper coverage.

In a statement issued from the ADNC headquarters in Chicago, Woodring declared that many Democratic leaders opposed to the Roosevelt administration "appear too timid, politically and economically, to stand up and be counted." The frustrated chairman, who had been the public face of the organization since its inception, lamented that while several hundred thousand dollars had been faithfully pledged to the fledgling stop-Roosevelt effort, "only a small part of this has been received." In his view, there simply wasn't enough time nor were there sufficient funds to organize the party's rank and file in the manner that he had initially contemplated. Though he promised to "unflinchingly" support the efforts of his successor, Woodring remained aloof from the organization for the remainder of the presidential campaign.[101]

There was plenty of speculation about the former Secretary of War's abrupt resignation. Keith McFarland, Woodring's biographer, believed that Woodring's longtime friendship with FDR and his insistence that the organization refrain from attacking the president directly — preferring instead that any criticism should be directed exclusively at the New Dealers and the so-called "Palace Guard" surrounding Roosevelt — was a key factor in his decision to step down.[102]

While McFarland's explanation is certainly plausible, it differed sharply from the testimony given by Iowa's Robert O'Brian, the group's secretary, before a House investigating committee later that year. "Mr. Woodring was determined to employ methods of collecting donations which I was confident were in violation of the Corrupt Practices Act," testified O'Brian. "I opposed his ideas strongly and consistently. It is my impression that he resigned in anger over my position in the matter."[103]

While Woodring's personal friendship with Roosevelt and O'Brian's sharp criticism of his handling of the ADNC's fundraising activities might have been factors in his sudden resignation, a St. Louis newspaper might have been closer to the truth when it

---

[101] "Woodring Quits New Party for Lack of Support," *Louisville Courier-Journal*, Apr. 3, 1944.
[102] McFarland, *Harry H. Woodring*, p. 245.
[103] Kennedy, *Southern Exposure*, p. 145.

took issue with Woodring's assertion that administration critics within the Democratic Party were too timid to stand up to the president. According to the *St. Louis Star-Times*, there were plenty of anti-Roosevelt Democrats willing to be labeled as such. A quick glance of almost an issue of the *Congressional Record* made that abundantly clear. The problem, according to the paper, was that few, if any, of them were willing to join Woodring's curious mixture of pique, extreme conservatism and unabashed isolationism. "That was an unacceptable concoction even for the intransigent Tories whose support he sought."[104]

Woodring, moreover, had been subjected to quite a bit of abuse from the press, some of which undoubtedly got under his skin. Shortly before announcing that he was stepping down, *Atlanta Constitution* columnist Gladstone Williams claimed that the former Secretary of War was "still sore because he was ousted from the cabinet as an incompetent after the outbreak of the European war." According to the Atlanta writer, there was "no bigger rat-hole" ever conceived than Woodring's American Democratic National Committee, an organization seemingly "made up of all the soreheads in the Democratic Party."

Describing Woodring as a "cat's paw" for Big Jim Farley, the former postmaster general, Williams argued that the Kansan's true motivation in forming the ADNC was to exact revenge on Roosevelt while positioning himself for a high-level position in a Republican administration. "Obviously the backers of the Farley-Woodring program are not so dumb as to think they have a ghost of a chance of defeating Mr. Roosevelt," wrote Williams. "What they are shooting at is something entirely different. They hope to develop a schism with the Democratic Party that will be an important contributing factor in the defeat of the Democratic ticket in the November election, and thus feather their nests with the new Republican administration."[105]

---

[104] "Exit Mr. Woodring," *St. Louis Star-Times*, Apr. 3, 1944.
[105] Gladstone Williams, "Woodring Party Another Grass Roots," *Atlanta Constitution*, Mar. 22, 1944.

Chapter XIX

"The Great Flop of 1944"

Promising to intensify the group's national organizing efforts, Boston's Gleason Archer assumed the ADNC chairmanship upon Woodring's unanticipated departure. Former congressman John J. O'Connor of New York was elected vice-chairman, a role in which he quickly became one of the organization's leading spokesmen. The American Democratic National Committee, he told reporters shortly after Woodring's resignation, was one of the few political movements with the potential to save the country from the New Dealers. "Despite customary half apologies and punch pulling by other movements, including the Republicans, we guarantee to pull no punches," he declared.

With Woodring no longer in the picture, O'Connor made it clear that the ADNC wouldn't hesitate to criticize Roosevelt directly — and to do so vehemently. "No one has ever exposed this man for what he is," asserted the bitter New Yorker. "He is the first multimillionaire President — born a Bourbon with all thoughts plutocratic while he pretends to get down in the sewer with the man with the pick and shovel. We must try to convince that fellow in the sewer that he has been deluded." O'Connor, who had been an early Roosevelt supporter in 1932, maintained that none of FDR's supporters from that campaign remained with him beyond 1937 "when he started his rampage...to satisfy the starry-eyed radicals."[1]

---

[1] "We'll Put Real Tag on FDR, Says O'Connor," *Chicago Tribune*, Apr. 4, 1944.

Nobody had a bigger ax to grind against Roosevelt than O'Connor, whose brother happened to be the president's former law partner. Representing New York's "Silk Stocking" district, the former chairman of the powerful House Rules Committee — a post he occasionally used to block New Deal legislation when angered — was considered to be a major contender for majority leader in the next session of Congress when he was targeted for defeat by FDR in 1938.

Roosevelt, who favored Sam Rayburn of Texas as the next majority leader, recruited attorney James H. Fay, a member of Ed Flynn's powerful Democratic organization in the Bronx, to challenge O'Connor in the Democratic primary that year. Most political observers expected O'Connor to survive the challenge, but Fay narrowly defeated the outspoken New Deal critic by a little more than 500 votes in the primary. Fay had to face O'Connor again in November after the nine-term congressman unexpectedly captured the Republican nomination by defeating former diplomat and future CIA director Allen W. Dulles, the party's endorsed candidate. The embattled congressman also appeared on the November ballot on an independent Andrew Jackson Party line. That, too, was a tight race with Roosevelt's candidate edging out O'Connor by a margin of 24,500 to 22,037.[2]

Nursing a bull-sized taste for revenge, O'Connor, who failed in a bid to regain his House seat in 1940, had briefly threatened to enter a third-party candidate in the 1940 presidential election on the "Andrew Jackson Party" — a party that he had personally organized after losing the Democratic primary in 1938 — but later ended up supporting Republican Wendell Willkie.[3]

Thrust into a leadership position, the 63-year-old Archer was a prolific writer — most of the courses taught at the Suffolk Law School used his textbooks — and later authored the ADNC's so-called "Declaration of Chicago." He was also an advisory member of newspaper publisher Frank Gannett's Committee for Constitutional Government. An unapologetic Roosevelt critic, Archer had recently published a book excoriating the Democratic president. Along with Morris A. Bealle's explosive *Washington Squirrel Cage*, it was one of two books sponsored by the ADNC that year.

---

[2] Thomas P. Wolf, William D. Pederson, and Byron W. Daynes, *Franklin D. Roosevelt and Congress: The New Deal and Its Aftermath* (Armonk, N.Y., 2001), pp. 64, 112; "Dulles Put in Race Against O'Connor," New York Times, Aug. 20, 1938; "O'Connor is Loser; Fay Margin is 2,590," *New York Times*, Nov. 9, 1938.

[3] "Jackson Party Formed," *New York Times*, Sep. 26, 1938; "O'Connor Proposes Third-Party Move," *New York Times*, Jan. 8, 1940; "Plans Democratic Split," *New York Times*, July 12, 1940; "O'Connor Aids Willkie," *New York Times*, July 26, 1940.

THE LOWEST EBB

In *On the Cuff*, a book filled with charts and tables showing the level of increased taxation and rising government debt during Roosevelt's three terms, Archer maintained that FDR's administration had placed the nation "on the road to regimentation and bankruptcy" and argued that private enterprise was the only system that could effectively restore economic prosperity. "Under the cover of war necessity," he wrote, "the administration has created conditions, with bureaucratic restrictions and taxation, under which nearly all the smaller industries of the nation are endangered, and similar peril is confronting the larger industries as well. Can anyone believe that the inevitable inching up of 'social gains' is not a deliberate process of destruction of private industry?"[4]

In assuming the ADNC chairmanship, Archer promised a renewed effort, vowing a "fight to the finish" against the New Deal Democrats while telling reporters that the ADNC planned to organize in all 48 states. "Woodring has been doing the inspirational work of getting things going," he said of his predecessor, "and now the time has come when we have to organize."[5]

The first test of Archer's leadership — and that of the entire anti-Roosevelt movement within the Democratic Party, for that matter — occurred a few days later when the Suffolk University president thrust himself smack dab in the middle of the Massachusetts primary where former Gov. Joseph B. Ely was boldly challenging FDR's bid for a fourth term.

An outspoken critic of the New Deal, the Harvard-educated Ely announced his candidacy in late February, telling reporters that "everyone knows my position. I don't believe in a fourth term; I didn't believe in a third term. I'm a Jeffersonian Democrat, and I can't change," he said. "This will simply give the voters a chance to express themselves one way or another."[6]

In declaring his candidacy, Ely said that he didn't plan to enter any other Democratic primaries. The former governor's announcement was accompanied by a suggestion that conservative Democrats should start a Bull Moose movement and nominate their own ticket if they were unsuccessful in forestalling Roosevelt's nomination in Chicago later that summer. "It is entirely possible," said former Democratic state chairman Charles H. McGlue, who headed Ely's campaign committee, "that if Mr. Roosevelt is

---

[4] "Anti-New Deal Book Edition is Curbed by WPB," *Chicago Tribune*, Apr. 22, 1944.
[5] "Woodring Quits Leadership of Anti-New Deal Democrats; Succeeded by College Head," *Cincinnati Enquirer*, Apr. 3, 1944; "Stop Roosevelt Group Plans Campaign Against Fourth Term," *Palladium-Item and Sun-Telegram* (Richmond, IN), Apr. 4, 1944.
[6] "Joseph B. Ely is Candidate for President," *Berkshire Eagle*, Feb. 21, 1944.

nominated, the Ely forces would join with other 'Jeffersonian Democratic' groups in the country to nominate a separate slate for president and vice-president."[7]

A close personal friend of former New York Gov. Al Smith, Ely had been the first Democrat elected governor of Massachusetts in sixteen years when he narrowly defeated Republican Gov. Frank G. Allen in 1930 by fewer than 16,000 votes. He had an easier time two years later when he thrashed his Republican opponent by more than 120,000 votes. Ely decided not to seek a third term in 1934.

Ely's impassioned 1932 nominating speech for the "Happy Warrior" was arguably one of the greatest convention speeches in history, comparable to Eugene McCarthy's nominating speech for Adlai Stevenson in 1960. Herbert Bayard Swope, the Pulitzer prize-winning former reporter and editor of the widely-read *New York World* — one of the country's most liberal newspapers during its day — compared it to Robert G. Ingersoll's spellbinding speech for James A. Garfield in 1880 while others equated it to William Jennings Bryan's famous "Cross of Gold" speech in 1896.

The Massachusetts governor, who had briefly threatened not to seek a second term that year if Roosevelt emerged as the party's presidential nominee, reminded the delegates in Chicago that Al Smith, clobbered by Hoover in 1928, had done much of the party's heavy lifting following that disastrous defeat. "After his defeat, who reorganized the party?" Ely asked. "Who carried on the battle? Who has set the course?" The progressive New Yorker, he said, was the man who held the Democratic Party together during some of its leanest years in the period immediately preceding the Great Depression, positioning the party to come to the aid of the American people when they needed it the most. Unlike the patrician Roosevelt, Smith dropped out of school when he was fourteen and worked in a fish market to support his family. He knew what it meant to struggle financially. From the rural South to the sidewalks of New York, he was one of our own, declared Ely.

Pricking at his party's conscience, the Yankee Protestant told the delegates — many of whom still refused to support a Catholic — that "the prejudices of our Protestant ancestors against entrusting government to those of a different religious faith have long since been wiped away by many a successful experience through which we have found that a man imbued with faith in God, what-

---

[7] "Fourth Term Foes Bring Campaign into Open," *Pittsburgh Press*, Feb. 21, 1944.

ever the creed, may be entrusted safely with the reins of government...As I stand here," concluded Ely, "I devoutly believe that a Divine Providence has given us this man and preserved him so that you might make him the instrument for the preservation of popular government and democratic freedom. Let us end government by doubt, let us establish a government of decision, of action, and of progress. For the Democratic Party, for the United States of America, for the needs of humanity, I give to this convention the name of Alfred E. Smith."

Ely's heartfelt speech evoked a 52-minute demonstration and visibly moved Smith to the point of tears, but couldn't prevent Roosevelt's fourth-ballot nomination.[8] As one of the last of the Smith irreconcilables, Ely took weeks to publicly support his party's nominee — and did so only reluctantly after meeting with Roosevelt in Albany in late July.[9]

The Massachusetts governor soured on Roosevelt's presidency fairly quickly, fearing the New Deal would lead to socialism.[10] Like his political idol, Ely eventually joined the Liberty League, an organization founded for the purpose of upholding and protecting the constitution and later played a prominent role in the founding of the National Jeffersonian Democrats in the summer of 1936, an organization led by ex-Missouri Sen. James A. Reed, former Secretary of State Bainbridge Colby, former congressman Joseph W. Bailey, Jr., of Texas, and New York's Henry Breckinridge, which tried to purge President Roosevelt and the New Dealers out of the Democratic Party.[11] Calling for Roosevelt's defeat in November, the Jeffersonian Democrats were deeply worried that the administration was exerting itself in every conceivable way to strike down the structure of democratic government while replacing it with a collectivist state.[12]

Ely vigorously defended the former group against attacks from Roosevelt's supporters, asserting that FDR couldn't have been elected in 1932 without the help of some of the League's most prominent members, most notably Al Smith and John J. Raskob, former chairman of the Democratic National Committee. "Finding no other weakness in the armor of the American Liberty League

---

[8] David Pietrusza, *1932: The Rise of Hitler and FDR — Two Tales of Politics, Betrayal, and Unlikely Destiny* (Guilford, CT, 2016), p. 160.
[9] "Ely to Run, Backs Roosevelt," *Boston Globe*, Aug. 1, 1932.
[10] "Ely Fears New Deal as State Socialism," *Boston Globe*, Sep. 22, 1933; "Gov. Ely Fears Socialist State," *Boston Globe*, July 28, 1934.
[11] Seth Shepard McKay, *Texas Politics, 1906-1944* (Lubbock, TX, 1952), pp. 404, 406-409.
[12] "Roosevelt Defeat Urged by Bolters; Wide Drive Mapped," *New York Times*, Aug. 9, 1936; "Text of 'Jeffersonian Democrats' Statement," *New York Times*, Aug. 9, 1936.

because its principles cannot be assailed," he asserted, "all the propaganda of the government bureaus is directed to the fact that the DuPonts, very wealthy men, I assume, have made substantial contributions in order that these principles may be brought to the public attention. The principles of the league are those espoused by Washington, Jefferson and Lincoln and the Democratic Party itself. They cannot be made bad because they now have the approval of DuPont."[13]

Neither group made much headway; the Liberty League failed precisely because it was viewed as an organization made up primarily of men of wealth while the short-lived National Jeffersonian Democrats, as Ely himself later described it, "was still-born because it was a meeting of men without the means to bring it to life."[14]

Ely's outspoken criticism of the New Deal during this period nevertheless led to a brief presidential boom on his behalf in early 1936.[15] But Ely had another candidate in mind that year. Declaring that he would "back him to the sky," Ely once again preferred Smith, assuming, of course, that the party's 1928 nominee was willing to seek the Democratic nomination for a fifth consecutive time. Ely was particularly irked that Roosevelt had never consulted the man he once described as the "Happy Warrior" during his first three years in office. It wasn't until Smith was scheduled to give the Liberty League's keynote address at a widely-publicized dinner at the Mayflower Hotel in Washington in January 1936 that he finally received an invitation to the White House, which he promptly declined. "They've had three years to consult with him about state and national affairs and they never once asked his opinion about a thing," snarled Ely. "Why should they start now?"[16]

The former Massachusetts governor also charged that the New Deal brain trust "would destroy Smith's influence with the American people and besmirch his reputation to achieve their own wild purposes." The president, he said in a speech in Boston, "forgot the pledges of the Democratic party, and the fundamental principles of the constitution, as well as the names of the leaders of his party, under the beguiling influence of the fanciful theories and impractical schemes of inexperienced men."[17] Like Smith, Ely "took a walk" that year, refusing to support his party's nominee while

---

[13] "Ely in Defense of Liberty League," *Boston Herald*, Apr. 2, 1936.
[14] Joseph B. Ely, *The American Dream* (Boston, 1944), p. 190.
[15] "Ely Stops Presidential Boom," *Boston Globe*, Feb. 8, 1936.
[16] "Ely Would Back Al Smith Should He Be Candidate," *Springfield Republican*, Dec. 31, 1935.
[17] "'Ely Upholds Smith, Assails Robinson," *New York Times*, Feb. 6, 1936.

backing Republican Alf Landon during the autumn campaign.[18]

Strongly opposed to a third term, Ely actively supported New York's James A. Farley for the Democratic presidential nomination in 1940, but abruptly left the Democratic national convention in Chicago that summer when confronted with Farley's unexpected motion to make Roosevelt's nomination unanimous.[19] He continued to speak out against a third term during the autumn campaign and later conspicuously appeared with Al Smith at the Boston Symphony Hall where the former New York governor was speaking under the auspices of "Democrats for Willkie."[20]

Gleason L. Archer, who had just taken over the reins of the ADNC following Woodring's resignation a few days earlier, attended a meeting at the Ely-for-President headquarters in Boston in early April to give his organization's support to the former governor's candidacy. "Eleven years ago, a group of social reformers got possession of the Democratic Party and have since continued to operate under its framework," he said in a prepared statement given to reporters. "Needless to say, none of the palace guard are or have been Democrats," he continued. "We believe that it is high time that the Democratic Party took away from this alien group the party which they kidnapped in 1933."

Declaring that his organization was "in no sense a third party movement," Archer said that the ADNC hoped to organize throughout the country and would hold a national convention or caucus in advance of the Democratic national convention in Chicago. The ADNC, he concluded, planned to formulate a national platform and would decide at that time which one of our numerous Democratic leaders, including Ely, would be the strongest challenger to Roosevelt at the Democratic national convention.

Ely also addressed the meeting, telling the relatively small crowd that he was against "regimented democracy," which he described as "bureaucracy, government by rule and regulation, and an economy that is lurching toward inflation, to the point where government must put a ceiling on what a man can earn."[21]

With twenty-six candidates for delegate in seven of the state's fourteen congressional districts pledged to his candidacy, Ely

---

[18] "Smith and Ely Demand Party Drop Roosevelt," *Boston Globe*, June 22, 1936; "Ely to Stump for Gov. Landon," *Boston Herald*, June 23, 1936; "Ely Urges Democrats to Vote for Landon," *Springfield Republican*, Oct. 8, 1936.
[19] "Ely Quits Chicago, Undecided on 'Walk,'" *Boston Globe*, July 19, 1940.
[20] "Ely Blasts Third Term," *Boston Herald*, Oct. 7, 1940; "1928 Democratic Standard Bearer Scores Roosevelt," *Springfield Republican*, Nov. 1, 1940.
[21] "Ely and Archer Ask Defeat of Roosevelt as Nominee," *Boston Globe*, Apr. 6, 1944.

waged an active campaign in the April primary. Formally launching his campaign in Boston three weeks earlier, the Westfield attorney — one of the state's most prominent trial lawyers — said that his favorite-son candidacy would focus principally on Roosevelt's domestic policy. Assailing bureaucracy — "government by rule and regulation," as he described it — the former governor maintained that the president's domestic agenda pursued in the nine years prior to World War II had "hampered our war program and will hamper rehabilitation. We've got to renew our faith in the government the founders planned and we must be united in that faith if we are to preserve the American way of life and have any influence in the establishment of a just peace," asserted the would be giant slayer.[22]

Stepping up his attack the following week in an address at Boston's Copley Plaza Hotel celebrating Thomas Jefferson's birthday, the fiscally conservative ex-governor declared that failures on the part of the Roosevelt administration had prolonged the war and would result in the unnecessary loss of additional American lives.

In one of the most passionate speeches of his career, Ely — almost sounding like the Socialist Party's Norman Thomas — lambasted the administration's failure to adequately explain to the German people what they might reasonably expect in the event that their leaders yielded to our demand for an "unconditional surrender." Our intentions toward Germany, he added, should be better defined and the principle of self-determination — the one thing that might lead to a quicker end to hostilities — should be restated and amplified:

> The argument will be made that serious objections to a fourth term will sustain the morale of the German people, therefore jeopardizing the lives of American youth.
>
> It is my firm conviction that the morale of the German people is sustained by the faults and inadequate policy of this administration in dealing with that very subject, and that these failures have prolonged the war, and will be the cause of sacrificing our sons, brothers, husbands and sweethearts.
>
> In plain terms, the words 'unconditional surrender' do not mean anything when the white flag is lifted and the German people, under proper leadership, ask for an armistice. The terms should now be plainly stated and understood. This is the

---

[22] "Joseph B. Ely Opens Campaign," *Boston Herald*, Apr. 6, 1944.

way to break the morale of Germany and to shorten the war.[23]

Like the Socialist Party's Thomas, the former Massachusetts governor told the Jefferson Day celebrants that he had some serious concerns about role the Soviet Union might play in postwar Europe and warned that the United States shouldn't surrender "one whit of our sovereign power" to an ideology whose purpose and future direction wasn't clearly defined:

> We must favor the maintenance of military and naval establishments sufficient to back up whatever position we may take in international affairs, and retain the full determination of how that force shall be used.
>
> When we are satisfied that the Russian aim is not revolutionary in a world sense, but is ready to recognize the principle of self-determination and to give assurance she will refrain from interfering in the governments of other peoples, it will be time enough for us to talk about the surrender of sovereignty for the purpose of policing the world.

Ely also warned that there was an inherent danger in breaking the two-term precedent for any American president, suggesting that it could not only lead to conflicts among the three branches of government, but might also create a situation where a demagogue, appealing to certain elements of the population, could potentially destroy representative government while establishing a virtual dictatorship in the United States.[24]

During his address to the Jefferson Day banquet, Ely said that he had received a copy of the *Daily Worker*, the Communist Party's newspaper, featuring an article with the sensational headline, "Conspiracy in the Bay State." The article, written by Otis A. Hood of Boston, a former Communist Party candidate for governor, described Ely and several other prominent Massachusetts Democrats, including Sen. David I. Walsh and Boston District Attorney William J. Foley, as "defeatist conspirators." Needless to say, he found it mildly amusing.

Quoting from the article, Ely reminded the gathering that the CIO's Political Action Committee (PAC) was funding the drive for a fourth term. "The political action committee of the CIO," he said, "is controlled by men who do not believe in the basic faith of this

---

[23] "Ely Attacks War 'Errors,'" *Boston Herald*, Apr. 14, 1944.
[24] "'Ely Condemns Russia's Plans to Rule Europe' Blasts FD's Supporters," *Boston Globe*, Apr. 14, 1944.

nation and would overthrow the fundamental balance of our government, take over the power in the presidency and make us children of the state." They were the real conspirators, he added.[25]

Despite carrying Brockton, Hyde Park, Quincy and a number of surrounding communities — the only places where the anti-Roosevelt forces did a mailing to every Democratic household — Ely's delegates generally ran poorly in the April 25 primary, losing statewide by a roughly four-to-one margin while prevailing in only one of the state's fourteen congressional districts. Ely himself, however, was elected as one of the party's twelve at-large delegates and undoubtedly took more than a little satisfaction in the fact that he had outpolled eight-term congressman and future Speaker of the House John W. McCormack by nearly 1,000 votes in the congressman's Boston bailiwick. McCormack, who eventually spent 42 years in Congress, was one of the Roosevelt administration's closest allies on Capitol Hill and an outspoken advocate of a fourth term.[26]

With only a dozen candidates in the field, each of the twelve candidates for delegate at-large was virtually assured of a spot in the Massachusetts delegation in Chicago. Ely finished fourth overall, polling 29,938 votes statewide, approximately 5,000 votes behind top vote-getter U.S. Sen. David I. Walsh, another prominent Democrat with serious reservations regarding a fourth term.[27] Measured simply in terms of the statewide vote for delegates at-large, those who shared Ely's belief that Roosevelt had betrayed the country's two-term tradition and had already overstayed his welcome didn't do badly at all.

Claiming only three delegates, including himself, the former Massachusetts governor decided not to attend the Democratic national convention in Chicago later that summer. Except for perhaps a smidgeon of symbolic value, it would have been a complete and utter waste of time for the dignified ex-governor who had been briefly poised to be the white knight of the party's leaderless right to attend what was shaping up to be yet another coronation for the "Indispensable Man."

Accusing the New Deal of centralizing "the power to control, regiment and license business, agriculture and labor" in Washington while making the American people "subservient to bureau-

---

[25] "Ely Attacks War 'Errors,'" *Boston Herald*, Apr. 14, 1944.
[26] "Ely's Vote Tops McCormack's," *Boston Herald*, Apr, 29, 1944.
[27] "Walsh Led Democrats in Primary Contest; Ely Finished Fourth," *Boston Globe*, May 5, 1944.

cratic bosses, political bosses and labor bosses," Ely endorsed Republican Tom Dewey in an October 31 radio address over the Yankee Network. The presidency during the previous twelve years, he charged, had grown too powerful and had reduced Congress to a "position of comparative impotence." Through this unprecedented concentration of power, charged Ely, Roosevelt had "acquired a vast army of satellites who must work for his continuance in office to keep their positions. The machine is too big and too powerful for Congress to overcome," he said. "Only the people can save us."[28]

Declaring that "there will be war" if Roosevelt, who was still being deliberately coy about his intentions, decided to seek a fourth term, Archer announced on April 13 — twelve days before the Massachusetts primary — that the ADNC planned to hold a caucus in early June, probably in St. Louis, to select a presidential ticket and adopt an anti-New Deal platform in advance of the Democratic national convention in Chicago. Though he didn't have a specific presidential candidate in mind — he mentioned Sen. Byrd of Virginia, ex-Gov. Ely of Massachusetts and Georgia Sen. Walter George, one of many who survived Roosevelt's 1938 purge, as possibilities — Archer said that the candidates chosen by the caucus "must be true followers of Thomas Jefferson who, by their deeds as well as by their promises, have demonstrated their loyalty to American ideals." As far as a platform was concerned, the Bostonian joked that one had already been prepared. "We may take some planks from the Democratic platform of 1932, which promised to balance the budget and reduce national expenditures 25 per cent. That platform is as good as new," he said grinningly. "It never has been used."[29]

By late April, the ADNC claimed to have established state committees in seven states in the South, as well as in eight western and four eastern states. There was clearly momentum, stated an upbeat Archer, who reiterated that the group's call for a pre-convention caucus in St. Louis was going according to plan and that they hoped to be organized nationally by the beginning of May. "If the New Deal and the 'Palace Guard' surrounding President Roosevelt were given four more years of political life, the shackles of regimentation would be affixed to American business and American life for generations," he said in a statement from the group's head-

---

[28] "Ely Goes on Air for Dewey Tuesday," *Boston Globe*, Oct. 29, 1944; "Ex-Gov. Ely to Vote for Dewey; Sen. Walsh Attacks Truman," *Boston Globe*, Nov. 1, 1944.
[29] "Anti-4th Term Democrats to Offer Nominee," *Chicago Tribune*, Apr. 14, 1944.

quarters in Chicago. "President Roosevelt," he continued, "is personally responsible for the machinations of this group and with them, he must be eliminated."[30]

Stepping up his attack on the three-term president, Archer said that for the first time in American history "we are being ruled by men who are not of our choosing" — and that Roosevelt was to blame:

> Twelve years ago our party was taken from us by a group of alien minded conspirators who needed a cloak of respectability to establish themselves in power. Their scheme succeeded. They got possession of the United States Treasury, which they have shamelessly used to overawe the legislative branch of government...
>
> They have used dollars instead of the machine guns which were found necessary in Russia and Germany. Under a pretense of social gains they have endeavored to set up a regimented society in American with themselves as perpetual overlords.

These men — the bureaucratic New Dealers and internationalists, as he called them — could only be removed by defeating Roosevelt, "their indulgent patron and protector who now occupies the White House," concluded Archer.[31]

With Archer serving as ringmaster, the ADNC quickly evolved into a political circus. It might not have been the greatest show on earth, but it featured a new performance almost daily.

In early May, Archer proposed that the GOP should nominate Virginia Sen. Harry F. Byrd as a fusion candidate for the presidency. Describing the ultraconservative Virginian as a "virile southern Democrat," the ADNC chairman asserted that Byrd was the only candidate capable of cutting heavily into Roosevelt's support in the traditionally Democratic South, and that without heavy support from that region any Republican candidate was doomed to defeat.[32] Not surprisingly, there was little reaction from the GOP hierarchy to Archer's proposal.

Barely a week later, Archer announced that the ADNC was prepared to back Gov. John W. Bricker if the Ohioan captured the Republican presidential nomination. Declaring that the "only

---

[30] "Opposition to New Deal Will be Established," *Rushville Republican* (Rushville, IN), Apr. 26, 1944.
[31] "4th Term Foes to Wage Battle on 'Globalism,'" *Chicago Tribune*, Apr. 26, 1944.
[32] "Anti-Fourth Term Democrats Proffer Sen. Byrd to GOP," *Chicago Tribune*, May 4, 1944.

practical method of preventing the reelection of President Roosevelt and purging New Deal influence from the Democratic Party may be to support a Republican for president," Archer expressed the hope that the Ohio governor would be willing to serve a single term. "Everyone knows there is a mess to clean up," he said in a statement from Washington, D.C. "It will take a one-term President with no ambition to succeed himself to do a thorough job."[33] Archer's statement, which apparently caught some committee members by surprise, was reportedly issued by Ralph W. Moore, a gregarious, back-slapping and fast-talking Washington-based lobbyist from Texas who once boasted that he probably had "more friends on Capitol Hill than anyone else in town." Moore served as the ADNC's assistant treasurer.[34]

Bricker, who supported a constitutional amendment for a single six-year term or two four-year terms, was naturally flattered by the suggestion. "I have felt throughout the country this rising sentiment on the part of old line Democrats to support a Republican candidate," he said while campaigning in Nebraska."[35]

Though Archer maintained that the decision to support Bricker had been reached during a series of regional conferences with ADNC leaders, some committee members vigorously denied that they intended to support the Ohioan — or any Republican presidential candidate, for that matter. John O'Connor, the group's combative vice chair, immediately fired off a letter to Thomas E. Dewey, the presumptive Republican nominee, asserting that the committee was working for the nomination of a "real Democrat" and wouldn't decide until after the Democratic national convention whether or not to support the Republican candidate against Roosevelt. In his letter to Dewey, the former New York congressman said the statement attributed to Archer was made "without consultation with the committee."[36]

A few weeks later, Archer told the press that the ADNC was "seeking a coalition with the Republican Party" in the 1944 presidential election as party of a longer term strategy of "putting the historic [Democratic] party back on its feet." In making the announcement, the ADNC chairman stressed that this was not a third-party movement, adding that Democratic Party "must be

---

[33] "Anti-4th Term Group Favors Bricker," *Chicago Tribune*, May 13, 1944.
[34] "Dem Group Denies Bricker Support," *Fort Lauderdale News*, May 16, 1944; Drew Pearson, "Lobbyist from Texas," *Syracuse Post-Standard*, Oct. 24, 1947.
[35] "Fourth Term Opposers to Back Bricker," *Lincoln Star*, May 12, 1944.
[36] "Democratic Help for GOP is 'Undecided,'" *Battle Creek Enquirer*, May 16, 1944.

purged of New Dealers."[37] If it wasn't already obvious to everybody, it was now clear precisely where the organization was headed. "The name, the declared purpose nor any other pretense could cover or camouflage its shape as a simon-pure Republican aid society," observed a Tennessee newspaper.[38]

In the meantime, Archer and the ADNC were ecstatic when the party's reactionary forces overwhelmed Roosevelt's supporters at the regular Texas Democratic state convention in Austin later that month (see chapter 16). "We are delighted with the news from Texas," crowed Archer, who immediately tried to take credit for the stunning repudiation of Roosevelt in the Lone Star State. "Since Texas was the first state to organize a branch of our committee, with Commissioner of Agriculture J. E. McDonald as our vice chairman for the Southwest, we are gratified at this significant response to our efforts," said Archer. Claiming that Texas was now lost to Roosevelt, Archer predicted similar results in other southern states. "From our knowledge of what is actually going on below the Mason and Dixon Line," he said with his usual bravado, "we confidently predict future developments that will electrify the nation."[39]

In a fundraising letter in early June, Archer contended that the 1944 presidential campaign was the last opportunity to "save America from foreign-minded wolves." Reminding potential donors of the evils of Roosevelt's domestic policies, the Boston attorney alleged that the New Deal had been ignited by "alien-minded internationalists, striving to submerge us as a people in a world state — headed by some alien group — and to blot out forever our sovereignty as a nation. A fourth term for Mr. Roosevelt," wrote Archer, "means four more years for his New Deal to communize the business and industry of the United States; poison American education; destroy every ideal bequeathed to us by the founders of the republic; wipe out human liberty; [and] make robots of American citizens in some dreamy international setup, controlled by aliens." In short, freedom itself was at stake.[40]

The organization's pre-convention caucus, which had originally been slated for St. Louis on June 1, took place at Chicago's Hamilton Hotel on June 19. The highlight of the poorly attended two-day meeting was the fiery keynote address by Missouri's

---

[37] "'American Democrats' Seek G.O.P. Coalition," *Los Angeles Times*, June 5, 1944.
[38] "Birds of a Feather," *Nashville Tennessean*, June 17, 1944.
[39] "Texas Revolt Called Blow at New Deal," *Rochester Democrat and Chronicle*, May 25, 1944.
[40] "Says U.S. Faces Last Chance to Keep Free," *Chicago Tribune*, June 13, 1944.

James Reed, who accused FDR of flouting his oath to uphold the constitution. "The man who has taken that oath," Reed told a radio audience, "and thereafter seeks to destroy or undermine the constitution has laid the crime of treasonable perjury upon his soul and has forfeited the right to the respect and confidence of all decent men."

Denouncing the 1933 National Recovery Act as a first step toward creating a dictatorship and lashing out at FDR for attempting to pack the Supreme Court in 1937, the 82-year-old Missourian sharply criticized the Democratic president for characterizing the constitution as a document belonging to the horse and buggy era. Reed, who died of pneumonia less than three months later, was also highly critical of Roosevelt's bid for a fourth term, describing it as "one of egotism run mad and of ambition that has consumed the conscience."

His considerable oratorical skills undiminished by his advancing years, the white-haired former three-term senator also used his address to launch a not-so-subtle attack on Thomas E. Dewey, Roosevelt's likely Republican challenger, for failing to be more forthcoming about the issues facing the country. "Aspirants for the presidency ought frankly and clearly to present their views and policies to the American electorate," he thundered, adding that the American public had the right to know where somebody who eagerly aspired to the presidency stood on the issues. "No man living is so great that he can demand that this, the highest office in the world, must be forced upon him."[41]

The anti-fourth termers also heard from Sen. W. Lee "Pappy" O'Daniel, who told them that the New Deal had "set up machinery for the biggest racket the world has ever seen for the purpose of perpetuating itself in power." The Roosevelt administration, he asserted, had transferred part of the federal government's taxing power "to a gang of labor leader racketeers by supporting the check-off collection of union dues. From this swag taken by the labor leader racketeers campaigns are paid for to help re-elect the members of Congress and the President, who set up the legal authority for the racket."[42] The New Dealers, continued O'Daniel, had "stolen everything the Democratic Party has except our principles, and they tried to make up for not stealing our principles by stealing the Communist Party platform."[43]

"If any of you folks have any doubts about the fact that the

---

[41] "Jim Reed Flays Blows by FDR at Constitution," *Chicago Tribune*, June 21, 1944.
[42] "'Election Racket' Laid to New Deal," *Philadelphia Inquirer*, June 20, 1944.
[43] "End New Deal and 'Racket,' O'Daniel Asks," *Chicago Tribune*, June 20, 1944.

New Deal is a communistic organization," the fiery Texan told the assembled delegates, "then I think these doubts should have been removed a few days ago when the Communist Party in the United States dissolved and announced that they would support the New Deal party."[44]

O'Daniel, who once called Roosevelt a greater menace than Hitler, also called for a thorough cleansing of Washington, beginning with a six-year term limit for president, vice president and members of Congress. "I think after six years in Washington we should permit these men to go back home and make an honest living under the laws they themselves have passed," he chided. The Texas senator also predicted that the upcoming Democratic national convention would fail to meet southern demands for a white supremacy plank in the party's national platform and restoration of the party's two-thirds rule. "That means the revolt must continue beyond the convention," he asserted.[45]

Former Georgia Gov. Eugene Talmadge, dressed in his customary red suspenders, also addressed the gathering, but appeared uninspired by the relatively disappointing turnout — fewer than 75 delegates attended the Chicago meeting — and sat down after a relatively short speech in which he maintained that "the New Deal no more represents the Democratic Party than a kidnapper represents his victim when he writes a ransom note."[46]

During the two-day meeting, Talmadge made it clear that he favored an all-southern Democratic ticket and was opposed to the idea of any sort of coalition with the Republicans, as advocated by Archer and other ADNC leaders. The former Georgia governor also strongly hinted that if the Democratic national convention in Chicago adopted a platform unsatisfactory to his state's anti-Roosevelt Democrats — namely, a platform containing a racial equality plank — they might put an independent slate of presidential electors on the November ballot.[47]

In his address to the caucus, former New York congressman John J. O'Connor of New York — the only Democratic member of Congress unseated during Roosevelt's famous "purge" of the party in 1938 — stated that the country was about to experience "the greatest onslaught ever yet made on free speech" in the coming presidential campaign.

---

[44] "O'Daniel Scores New Deal Policy," *Illinois State Journal* (Springfield, IL), June 20, 1944.
[45] William E. Leuchtenburg, *The White House Looks South: Franklin D. Roosevelt, Harry S. Truman, Lyndon B. Johnson* (Baton Rouge, 2005), p. 137; "Dissident Group Continues Its 4th Term Caucus," *Charleston Evening Post*, June 20, 1944.
[46] "End New Deal and 'Racket,' O'Daniel Asks," *Chicago Tribune*, June 20, 1944.
[47] "Anti-4th Termers Continue Caucus," *Akron Beacon Journal*, June 20, 1944.

"Under the New Deal," said O'Connor, "the freedom of the press has had a better chance of surviving than free speech via radio. That somewhat peculiar contrast has arisen because the federal government has a more direct control over the operation of the radio through the legislative power to license and regulate the use of the air for the purposes of broadcasting." Consequently, he continued, the American people were about to be subjected to the greatest assault on free speech in U.S. history, "rivaling, if not equaling similar suppressions of free speech in other parts of the world, especially the Russian brand of 'control,' which, like every other idea originating in Moscow, has been made so 'popular' here by reason of presidential favoritism and executive decree."[48]

Though a resolution to support a coalition ticket comprised of Ohio Gov. John Bricker and Sen. Harry F. Byrd of Virginia — an idea pushed by New York's William J. Goodwin and Ralph W. Moore of Texas — was tabled after a lengthy debate, the conferees in Chicago managed to approve several other resolutions, including one calling for a constitutional amendment limiting presidential tenure to a maximum of eight years, before adjourning. They also approved a resolution prohibiting the United States from participating in "entangling alliances or international commitments such as setting up a world police force capable of involving us in future wars without the consent of Congress."[49]

Incidentally, the brief Byrd for vice president boom on the Republican ticket — an idea initially championed by O'Connor — gained some currency that summer. O'Connor talked it up at the Republican national convention in Chicago in late June and convinced a number of leading Republicans, including former RNC chairman Harrison E. Spangler and Minnesota congressman Harold Knutson, that the idea had some merit. A Dewey-Byrd ticket, O'Connor told them, could help the GOP crack the so-called "Solid South." House Minority Leader Joseph Martin of Massachusetts was also intrigued by the possibility, but the idea was eventually rejected by Dewey advisor Edwin Jaeckle, a wealthy Buffalo lawyer who helped engineer the New York governor's presidential nomination. "If the Republican Party, with 26 fine Republican governors and a host of members in the Senate and House, has to go into the opposition camp for its vice-presidential candidate," scoffed Jaeckle, "then we'd better throw in the sponge right

---

[48] "Campaign Will Bring Assault on Free Speech," *Tucson Daily Citizen*, June 23, 1944.
[49] "New Deal Critics Decide to Act if F.D.R. is Nominee," *St. Louis Post-Dispatch*, June 21, 1944.

now."[50]

In addition to approving several other resolutions, the ADNC also sharply condemned the Roosevelt administration for "bypassing the courts and substituting bayonet rule for the orderly processes of law" and for substituting executive orders in place of laws passed by Congress. They also denounced "usurpation of judicial powers by various bureaus and executive agencies."

Most importantly, the New Deal critics approved a resolution recommending that their executive committee call a national convention of all of the anti-New Deal organizations in the country "as soon as practicable after the major party conventions" in the event that Roosevelt was re-nominated in Chicago the following month.[51]

Former congressman John J. O'Connor, Charles H. McGlue, a former state chairman of the Massachusetts Democratic Party, Minnesota's John Regan, former state Rep. E. Wayles Browne of Louisiana and former Oklahoma attorney general George F. Short, were tasked with calling the convention.[52] Interestingly, McGlue, who once served in the Massachusetts House and chaired the Massachusetts Democratic state committee on five occasions, later managed George C. Wallace's 1968 presidential campaign in the Bay State and served as legal advisor during the successful petition drive that garnered 61,238 signatures to place the former Alabama governor on the Massachusetts ballot that autumn.[53]

Even before the Democrats convened in Chicago on July 19, however, Robert E. O'Brian, the committee's secretary, revealed that the ADNC planned to hold a nominating convention to choose a Democrat to run against Roosevelt on a third-party ticket. "We are under strong pressure to put a presidential and a vice-presidential candidate in the field," said O'Brian in early July. "Our candidates will be offered as the true Democratic Party ticket whom members of the party may support without a feeling of desertion. Our committee has held all along that it is the New Dealers who have abandoned the party of Jefferson."

In divulging the committee's plans, the former Iowa Secretary of State said he expected the ADNC-backed candidates would be designated as the official Democratic ticket in several southern states, including Alabama, Louisiana, Mississippi, South Carolina

---

[50] Drew Pearson, "Dewey Campaign Plans Set," *Detroit Free Press*, June 29, 1944.
[51] "New Deal Critics Decide to Act if F.D.R. is Nominee," *St. Louis Post-Dispatch*, June 21, 1944.
[52] "New Deal Foes Plan Conclave," *Rochester Democrat and Chronicle*, June 22, 1944.
[53] "The Campaign Trail: Yankee Area for Wallace," *Austin American-Statesman*, Sep. 29, 1968.

and Texas — state's where the party's state central committees had already taken a stand against a fourth term. O'Brian also indicated that the convention call would be issued by the five members of the ADNC's newly-formed executive committee, which was scheduled to meet in Chicago on July 20, the second day of the Democratic national convention held in that same city. Their convention, he added, would likely be held in New Orleans since the anti-Roosevelt forces were likely to find their greatest source of strength in the South.[54]

The convention, of course, never materialized, but it wasn't for lack of trying. Gleason Archer and other ADNC committee members spent most of the remaining summer courting "Pappy" O'Daniel of Texas, but made little headway.

Recognizing O'Daniel's tremendous vote-getting ability, the ADNC hoped that the junior senator might be able to carry Texas outright or — at the very least — swing the state's 23 electoral votes into the Republican column. A national third-party candidacy, moreover, didn't seem beyond the realm of possibility. After all, the Texas senator had recently revived his newspaper, the immodestly titled *W. Lee O'Daniel News* — a publication devoted to lambasting the New Deal — which quickly attracted 100,000 subscribers nationally. He also had been fueling speculation that a presidential candidacy could be on the horizon by purchasing time on forty smaller radio stations — his speeches were eventually aired on 124 stations in 44 states — while availing himself of speaking opportunities across the country to rail against the "Roosevelt dynasty and the bureaucrats."[55]

Yet O'Daniel remained noncommittal. Finally, in mid-August Archer made one final appeal, desperately pleading with the folksy Texan to heed their call. "It is important in the best interest of our beloved country that you lead the fight to secure electoral votes of Democratic states and prevent them from going to the Browder-Hillman candidate," Archer wrote in an August 14 telegram to the colorful Texas senator and longtime critic of the New Deal.

O'Daniel's immediate reaction to Archer's telegram was surprisingly positive, telling reporters that the ADNC was composed of Democrats unhappy with the way left-wingers, including an assortment of Communists and Socialists, had taken over the party

---

[54] "Anti-New Deal Democrats Eye Third Ticket," *Chicago Tribune*, July 6, 1944.
[55] "Third Party Dems to Run Lee O'Daniel," *Dallas Morning News*, July 9, 1944; Kennedy, *Southern Exposure*, p. 137. In initially approaching O'Daniel in early July, the ADNC had suggested New York's William Goodwin as a possible vice-presidential running mate.

machinery. "What they are trying to do is defeat the New Deal and save the country, as well as restore the old Democratic Party," he said.[56] Archer's hopes and those of other ADNC leaders were understandably high after hearing O'Daniel's initial response, but after thinking it over for a little more than a day the folksy Texan ultimately decided against a presidential candidacy.[57]

Deeply disappointed by O'Daniel's refusal to run, the ADNC changed its focus a few days later. While continuing its southern strategy of putting up independent electoral slates instructed to support a conservative Democrat in opposition to Roosevelt — a strategy they hoped to employ in Alabama, Arkansas, Florida, Georgia, Louisiana, Mississippi, South Carolina and Texas — John J. O'Connor, who was now chairman of the ADNC's executive committee, announced that the ADNC would form "Democrats for Dewey" organizations in at least a dozen northern states, including populous states such as New York, Illinois, Michigan and Ohio.

In announcing their plan in late August, spokesmen for the ADNC claimed that similar groups had already been established or were in the process of being organized in California, Colorado, Iowa, Kansas, Maryland, Massachusetts, Minnesota, Missouri, Oregon, South Dakota and West Virginia.[58] By the middle of September, the ADNC claimed organizations in thirty-six states with functioning headquarters in sixteen cities, including three in New York City alone. In addition to the group's national headquarters in Chicago, the anti-fourth termers had also opened offices in Baltimore, Boston, Cleveland, Detroit, Fort Worth, Johnstown, Pennsylvania, Los Angeles, Memphis, Milwaukee, Minneapolis, Nashville, Oklahoma City, San Francisco and Washington, D.C.[59]

While there was plenty of criticism levelled at the ADNC for aligning with the GOP, particularly in crucial northern battleground states, there were others who were cheering them on, including wealthy newspaper publisher Robert H. Gore, a former Chicagoan who served as Roosevelt's campaign finance chairman in 1932. The American Democratic National Committee, observed Gore's *Fort Lauderdale News*, was "the story of a group of outstanding American citizens who have dedicated their 'all' to returning the Democratic Party to its former status — free of isms and bureaucracies. These men are so interested in the future of America

---

[56] "O'Daniel Weighs Presidential Bid," *Amarillo Daily News*, Aug. 15, 1944.
[57] "O'Daniel Turns Down Presidential Effort," *Lubbock Morning Avalanche*, Aug. 17, 1944.
[58] "Democrats Link North in Revolt Over 4th Term," *Chicago Tribune*, Aug. 31, 1944.
[59] "Anti-New Deal Democrats' Aim: To Get Out Vote," *Chicago Tribune*, Sep. 16, 1944.

they are prepared to join former political opponents to rid the country of 'enemies' that have taken over their own party. That's patriotism with a capital 'P.'"[60]

In the meantime, Archer tapped former congressman Martin L. Sweeney of Cleveland to head the ADNC's "Democrats for Dewey" organization in the crucial battleground state of Ohio, a state narrowly carried by Roosevelt in 1940 and one that Dewey desperately needed if he was going to have any chance to unseat Roosevelt. A switch of fewer than 73,000 votes from Roosevelt to Willkie four years earlier would have given the Republican standard-bearer the state's 26 electoral votes — the fourth-largest electoral prize in the country.

"Don't get the idea that we're Republicans," Archer told newsmen in announcing in early September that Sweeney would head the effort in Ohio. "We're trying to reconstruct the Democratic Party as it existed prior to 1933. We're trying to destroy this unholy New Deal-Communist alliance." Sweeney, who had finished a surprising second in the state's six-way Democratic gubernatorial primary a few months earlier, concurred, telling reporters that he and other Ohio Democrats resented the prominent roles played by Earl Browder, Sidney Hillman and other leftists in Roosevelt's reelection campaign. "We won't permit the country to be Hillmanized," asserted the former six-term congressman.[61]

O'Connor, who incorporated the "Democrats for Dewey" organization in New York earlier that summer, played an active role in trying to rally disaffected Democrats in the state to Dewey's banner during the autumn campaign, but apparently not many Democrats were interested. In fact, fewer than two hundred turned out to hear former Queens borough president George U. Harvey, who was then living in Connecticut, and longtime isolationist John T. Flynn, a founder of the then-defunct American First Committee, viciously assail Roosevelt and his "useless federal agencies" at a widely-publicized rally organized by the Queens branch of the American Democratic National Committee in late October.[62] The rally, incidentally, was held at Lost Battalion Hall on Queens Boulevard, a facility built in the late 1930s with funds and labor provided by the New Deal's WPA.[63]

Despite the small turnout in Queens and similar meager

---

[60] "Editor's Corner," *Fort Lauderdale News*, Sep. 2, 1944.
[61] "Sweeney Heading Ohio 'Bolt' Group," *Cleveland Plain Dealer*, Sep. 8, 1944.
[62] "Harvey to Speak for Dewey," *New York Times*, Oct. 21, 1944; "Dewey Rally in Queens," *New York Times*, Oct. 27, 1944; "176 Turn Out to Hear Harvey," *Long Island Daily Press*, Oct. 27, 1944.
[63] "Queens Dewey Rally Has Familiar Look," *New York Post*, Oct. 27, 1944.

crowds at other ADNC-sponsored events around the state, O'Connor remained reasonably optimistic about Dewey's chances in New York and predicted in the final week of the campaign that the Republican standard-bearer would win the presidency. Reportedly basing his forecast on reports from the 40 states where there was organized Democratic opposition to the Roosevelt-Truman ticket, O'Connor believed there was a hidden or "concealed opposition" of at least five percent among alienated Democratic rank-and-file voters in both rural and urban areas throughout the country — none of whom were likely to admit that they planned to vote for Dewey.[64]

Julius F. Smietanka, a well-known Chicago lawyer, headed the ADNC's efforts in heavily-populated Illinois, a state Roosevelt carried by 102,000 votes out of more than 4.2 million votes cast four years earlier. The 71-year-old Smietanka, who twice served on the Chicago Board of Education and as collector of internal revenue during the Wilson administration, had been strongly opposed to FDR's bid for a third term in 1940 and actively supported "Cactus Jack" Garner's bid for the Democratic presidential nomination that year. He believed there was even more reason to oppose the president's fourth term candidacy.

"We are at the crossroads of an epoch where party loyalty to the national ticket must be disregarded to save the country," said Smietanka, adding that genuine Democrats "steeped in the political philosophies of Jefferson, Cleveland, and Wilson, cannot sit by and allow the country to go to pot without raising our voices in an effort to put a stop to this tragedy."[65] In the campaign's closing days, the Chicago attorney also questioned Roosevelt's fitness and ability to represent U.S. interests in peace negotiations.[66]

Former Gov. William Comstock, who had been widely credited with swinging his state into Willkie's column in 1940, led the effort in Michigan. Willkie had carried the state by a razor-thin margin of 8,200 votes.[67] In a letter to the state's Republican leaders, Comstock, who was then a member of the Detroit city council, summed up his feelings on the topic of a fourth term. "You know me as a Democratic governor in the true sense — not a New Dealer, conspiring with Communists and fellow travelers to dim

---

[64] "O'Connor Says Dewey Will Win Presidency," *Buffalo Courier-Express*, Nov. 3, 1944; "Alienated Democrats Expected to Beat FDR," *Knickerbocker News*, Nov. 3, 1944.
[65] "Democrat Foes of F.D.R. Find Revolt Spreads," *Chicago Tribune*, Sep. 8, 1944.
[66] "F.D.R.'s Acts Belie Fitness to Decide Peace — Smietanka," *Chicago Tribune*, Nov. 2, 1944.
[67] "State Democratic Faction Promises Help in Drive Against Fourth Term," *Detroit Free Press*, Apr. 5, 1944; "Democrat Bolt Seen by Comstock if FDR Runs," *Battle Creek Enquirer*, Apr. 5, 1944.

our sovereignty and destroy our liberties," wrote Comstock. "The time has come when we must forget labels, Republican or Democrat, and join forces against a common political foe. We must wipe out the New Deal in November and elect the Dewey-Bricker ticket, to preserve our American system of government."[68] As in 1940, the GOP again enthusiastically welcomed the former Democratic governor's help.

Establishing a headquarters in Milwaukee, the ADNC's "Democrats for Dewey" organization in Wisconsin was headed by Kenosha attorney Edward A. Quinn, a veteran of the Rev. Charles E. Coughlin's National Union for Social Justice who later became an outspoken supporter of Sen. Joseph R. McCarthy. "We are all real Democrats," said John N. Zimmerman of Milwaukee, the group's vice chairman, "and our main interest is the eventual reorganization of the Democratic Party as it was before the New Deal wrecked it. We believe the first thing to do is to defeat President Roosevelt in his bid for a fourth term, and we regard the 'Democrats for Dewey' club as the vehicle we must ride to reach that end."[69] Running on a "Stop Politics, Win the War" slate, Zimmerman had polled approximately 75,000 votes while running for delegate to the Democratic national convention earlier that spring.[70]

Charles H. McGlue of Massachusetts was in charge of ADNC activities in New England. A former Democratic state chairman, McGlue established a Dewey-Bricker headquarters on Beacon Street in Boston and served as regional director for the six states in that region.[71] Along with ADNC chairman Archer, McGlue had actively supported former Gov. Joseph B. Ely's favorite-son candidacy in the Massachusetts Democratic primary earlier that year.[72]

Recognizing that many Democrats in the region would refuse to support a Republican ticket, McGlue tried unsuccessfully to launch a massive write-in or sticker campaign in his home state of Massachusetts on behalf of "Jeffersonian Democrats" later that autumn. McGlue's proposed slate of anti-Roosevelt presidential electors, announced in early October, included such prominent Bay State Democrats as former Ambassador to England Joseph P. Ken-

---

[68] "Save America," *Escanaba Daily Press* (Escanaba, MI), Sep. 28, 1944.
[69] "Dewey Democrats in Wisconsin Draw State-Wide Backing," *Chicago Tribune*, Oct. 13, 1944.
[70] "Democratic Group to Campaign for Dewey in State: Callahan," *Green Bay Press-Gazette*, Oct. 7, 1944.
[71] "Jefferson Democrats to Fight Roosevelt," *Springfield Republican*, July 23, 1944.
[72] "McGlue Heads Anti-Roosevelt State Group," *Boston Globe*, Mar. 7, 1944; "Ely-Pledged Slate Assures Fight to Control State Delegation," *Boston Herald*, Mar. 8, 1944.

nedy, ex-Gov. Joseph B. Ely, former Sen. Marcus A. Coolidge, Boston district attorney William J. Foley, former Boston Mayor John F. Fitzgerald and State Treasurer Francis X. Hurley.

However, there was one major hurdle. Massachusetts didn't provide a method for writing in presidential electors. "When you have a ballot with no electors on it and no opportunity to write in your own choice, it becomes nothing but political legerdemain, or a pig-in-a-poke," asserted McGlue.[73]

Seeking a writ of mandamus compelling the Secretary of State to print an entirely new set of ballots that included write-in spaces for the state's sixteen presidential electors, McGlue declared that Massachusetts voters had been denied an opportunity to cast such write-in votes since 1932. In 1935, he argued in his petition to the state's highest court, the legislature amended the state's election statute so that it required blank spaces after the names of all candidates for federal and state offices, "except for presidential electors." In 1941 and again in 1943, the legislature amended the law and in each case deleted the clause "except for presidential electors." It was obvious, contended McGlue, that the state legislature intended that ballots should contain blank spaces for presidential electors, as was required for every other federal and state office.

The state's highest court disagreed, thwarting McGlue's last-ditch attempt to give Massachusetts Democrats an alternative to what he described as the "choice of electors selected by the New Deal-Communist clique."[74]

Led by James R. Thompson of Oakland, a former head of the state National Guard, the anti-Roosevelt Democrats in California, establishing headquarters in Los Angeles, San Francisco and Oakland, formed a statewide "Democrats for Dewey" organization as early as June and later campaigned all-out for the Republican nominee.[75]

Adopting the slogan "No Fourth Term or Fifth Term, Either," the Californians were buttressed in their efforts by Los Angeles attorney James W. Mellen, a one-time Roosevelt enthusiast who broke with the New Deal over the National Recovery Act (NRA). A self-described "Jeffersonian Democrat" who ran unsuccessfully for the Democratic U.S. Senate nomination in 1938, Mellen gave dozens of ADNC-sponsored radio addresses throughout the state

---

[73] "'Jeffersonian Democrats' Seeking Place on Ballot," *Berkshire Eagle*, Oct. 3, 1944.
[74] "Charges Ballots Lack Write-In Elector Space," *Fitchburg Sentinel*, Oct. 3, 1944; "McGlue Asks New Ballot," *Boston Herald*, Oct. 4, 1944; "McGlue Group Plans Stickers for Electors," *Boston Herald*, Oct. 5, 1944.
[75] "Democrats for Dewey Organize," *Oakland Tribune*, Aug. 3, 1944.

that autumn. He had also been one of the first prominent California Democrats to publicly endorse Dewey, doing so in a widely-publicized telegram to the New York governor as he was preparing his acceptance speech in late June:

> The opportunity to restore to the American people the constitutional freedom which is now being destroyed lies in your hands. Ten million Jeffersonian Democrats of this nation await your call. Why not issue this call in your acceptance speech tonight? We Jeffersonian Democrats of California are pledged to your candidacy and to the restoration of our constitutional freedom.[76]

Louisville insurance broker George Keene Gray headed the "Democrats for Dewey" campaign in Kentucky — a state Roosevelt carried by 147,000 votes four years earlier. Hoping to influence the state's undecided Democrats, Gray believed that the ADNC effort might make the difference in a tight contest between FDR and Dewey. "With as close an election as is in prospect it is entirely possible that our organization could help decide it," said Gray, the ADNC chairman in the Bluegrass State. "Outside of winning the war, the most important thing facing us is to defeat the New Deal," he added.[77]

In late August, the American Democratic National Committee demanded equal time from the War Department to present its case to soldiers serving overseas in the same short wave radio broadcasts offered to the country's five nationally-organized political parties actively competing in the 1944 presidential election, but their request was ultimately denied."[78]

Archer continued to push the ADNC's anti-Roosevelt message throughout the fall campaign. Standing in front of the Jefferson Memorial in the nation's capital on October 11, the Suffolk University president unveiled what he described as the country's "second Declaration of Independence," a document that accused the president of placing himself "in a stratosphere of his own creation as commander in chief." Listing a litany of grievances against the three-term chief executive, Archer asserted that the second declaration should be a warning to future presidents "who seek to perpetuate themselves in power." Among other things, the document stated:

---

[76] "Jeffersonian Democrat Will Support Dewey," *Los Angeles Times*, June 29, 1944.
[77] "'Democrats for Dewey' Movement Being Organized By Louisville Man," *Louisville Courier-Journal*, Sep. 20, 1944.
[78] "Anti-New Deal Group Applies for Radio Time," *Chicago Tribune*, Sep. 1, 1944.

> When, in the course of human events, a free people find tyranny growing apace in their land, it becomes necessary to act immediately to save their freedom. To delay invites disaster. To wait may be too late. For tyranny feeds upon its own power.
>
> We hold that tyranny from within the United States of American in 1944 is just as destructive to the rights of man as tyranny from without was destructive to the rights of our ancestors in 1776.[79]

Summing up the case against Roosevelt in much the same way that the Founding Father presented the case against King George in the original Declaration of Independence, the declaration's list of grievances was quite extensive:

> He has set class against class and race against race. He has divided the nation into large minority groups, each fighting for its own selfish interests by catering to him for special governmental favors.
>
> Through the vast power of the federal government and by the acts of his servants, he has seriously attacked the freedom of the press and the freedom of radio. He has seriously impaired freedom of speech in America. He has used the Internal Revenue Department to attack the integrity of American citizens of high standing. These attacks have made many Americans afraid to speak their convictions freely…
>
> He has endeavored to destroy the equal power of the three separate branches of government…He has sought to make the courts of the United States subservient to his will…He has superimposed a government of men over and above the government of laws as established by our Constitution…
>
> He has endeavored to destroy the rights of the various states which were banded together under the Constitution of the United States. He has tried to center all power in the hands of the federal government at Washington and to assume all this vast power for himself.
>
> Holding all these things to be true as a matter of public record throughout the years, we do hereby declares ourselves independent of Franklin Delano Roosevelt, the man. Let this be a

---

[79] "Offers U.S.A. a 2d Declaration of Independence," *Chicago Tribune*, Oct. 12, 1944.

warning also to future presidents who seek to perpetuate themselves in power.[80]

Nobody, however, campaigned harder for the ADNC that year than New York's revenge-minded John O'Connor, who attacked Roosevelt and the New Deal in a number of crucial battleground states. O'Connor, who was initially elected to Congress in a special election in 1923 and was quickly appointed to the powerful Rules Committee — highly unusual for a freshman member of the House — and became chairman of the committee nine years later, arguably campaigned more aggressively than the Republican nominee during the 1944 presidential campaign. He certainly logged more miles than the dapper New York governor.

O'Connor had been in attack mode the entire year, reminding longtime Democrats around the country that their party was now in the hands of Earl Browder, Sidney Hillman and the Liberal Party's David Dubinsky, the latter of whom he described as a "leftist, pinkish radical." Dubinsky's new party, he asserted earlier that spring, was an "illegitimate off-cast" of Hillman's left-wing American Labor Party. "What a triumvirate to be running, not only the affairs of our Party of Jefferson, but actually directing the destinies of a nation of 130 million people, with whom they have nothing in common," he lamented.[81]

Determined to unseat Roosevelt, O'Connor took it upon himself to personally organize "Democrats for Dewey" organizations in several dozen states that autumn. The Harvard-educated attorney, who still retained considerable clout in New York's Tammany organization, also had a lot on his mind that autumn. His son had been reported missing in action in August, but it was later revealed that he was being held as a prisoner-of-war by the Germans — something the former New York congressman wasn't aware of until a day or two before the election.[82]

O'Connor rarely passed up an opportunity to remind his audiences that Communist leader Earl Browder was actively supporting Roosevelt, but saved some of his sharpest rhetoric for the CIO's Sidney Hillman, reminding his audiences that Roosevelt had allegedly instructed Democratic national chairman Robert Hannegan to "clear everything with Sidney" — a charge Hannegan vigorously denied.

---

[80] "4th Term Foe Reads Second 'Declaration,'" *Rochester Democrat and Chronicle*, Oct. 12, 1944.
[81] "Pass in Review," *Fort Lauderdale News*, May 30, 1944.
[82] "Ex-Solon's Son a Prisoner," *Minneapolis Star-Tribune*, Nov. 7, 1944.

Describing the labor leader as the "gargoyle-looking Hillman," O'Connor claimed that the Lithuanian-born head of the Amalgamated Clothing Workers of America had never actually held a blue-collar job. His parents were wealthy, O'Connor told a Rhode Island newspaper editor during the heat of the campaign. "He was a revolutionist in Russia, for which diversion he was out of circulation for a while. On his release, he sought new pastures in our country — but not to toil," continued O'Connor. "His wife has worked as a pants maker operator, but Sidney has always been wealthy and has lived by exploiting the working man, like his patron, Franklin D., who never worked a day in his life. Our first multimillionaire president! Friend of the man with the pick!"[83]

O'Connor's fiery speech in Mankato, Minnesota, in early October, in which the former New York congressman mercilessly lambasted Roosevelt, Hillman and Browder — accusing the latter two of openly operating as a "Fifth Column" in the United States with Hillman, "or whatever his real name is, standing behind the throne as Rasputin," and both men "alternating in making trips to the Great White Father in Moscow" — made headlines in anti-Roosevelt newspapers across the country. O'Connor's Minnesota address, laced with vitriolic anti-Semitic rants, was arguably the most controversial speech of the entire 1944 presidential campaign.

Despite giving it everything he had, the campaign ended on a somewhat sour note for O'Connor, who was forced to abruptly cancel an election-eve radio address because he claimed his prepared speech had been "censored beyond recognition" by the radio station. The station — New York's WMCA — confirmed that his remarks had been censored, saying that without proof certain charges made by the ex-congressman "might be deemed libelous."[84] The former congressman charged that the station's owner Nathan Strauss, a former director of the National Recovery Administration (NRA) in New York, was a member of Hillman's PAC. "I believe the entire speech was submitted to Hillman for approval," said O'Connor.

Excerpts from O'Connor's never-delivered speech were published by the *Chicago Tribune* on Election Day, and, in addition to remarks highly critical of Hillman which had been deleted by the station's management, included the following explosive passage that also had been censored:

---

[83] "Pull No Punches!" *Newark Daily Advocate* (Newark, OH), Oct. 11, 1944.
[84] "Anti-Fourth Term Radio Address Censored Out," *Los Angeles Times*, Nov. 7, 1944.

The other great issue is Pearl Harbor and the disgraceful debacle that was permitted by our President to happen there has not been answered by those charged with offenses that are only paralleled by what happened at West Point during the Revolutionary War, while they have continued to muzzle General Short and Admiral Kimmel, whose disclosures would rock the world.[85]

Like many other Roosevelt detractors, O'Connor believed that Admiral Husband E. Kimmel and General Walter C. Scott, shouldering the entire blame for the attack on Pearl Harbor, had been unfairly scapegoated by the Roosevelt administration to divert blame from themselves.

The ADNC, moreover, had sponsored and widely distributed former *Washington Times* reporter and one-time *Plain Talk* magazine editor Morris A. Bealle's controversial *Washington Squirrel Cage*, a 65-page book dismissing the official Pearl Harbor commission inquiry headed by Supreme Court Justice Owen J. Roberts as a "whitewash" and accusing the "incredibly naïve" Roosevelt of inexplicably ignoring the warnings of Secretary of State Cordell Hull and Joseph C. Grew, the U.S. ambassador to Japan, while tragically taking the army and navy off high alert ten days before the treacherous attack on Dec. 7, 1941.

Described as "the literary gem of 1944" by the *Fort Lauderdale News*, a newspaper highly sympathetic to both the ADNC and John U. Barr's Draft Bryd movement, Bealle's short and breezy narrative, liberally sprinkled with satire, described how the president had been clearly outwitted by Japanese ambassador Kichisaburō Nomura:

> The army and navy had been heeding the warnings of Ambassador Grew for weeks and maintaining a close watch on all avenues of attack by the Japanese. Baron Nomura and his partner came to Washington in November and the first thing they did was to tell our gullible President that this alertness was irritating Japanese people and making difficult the task of Tojo's plenipotentiaries.
>
> Nomura told Mr. Roosevelt that this close watch was embarrassing them, it indicated suspicion and ill feeling toward Japan, and that if the 'watch were lowered' and an attitude of confidence in Japan displayed, their task of averting the war would be much easier.

---

[85] "Radio Gag Bans Attack on Reds and New Deal," *Chicago Tribune*, Nov. 7, 1944.

History's biggest sucker swallowed the bait and lowered our watch, after telling Mr. Churchill that he was 'babying Japan along' and the American people that 'every man is at his battle station from Singapore to Honolulu.'[86]

On the whole, things ended rather badly for the entire American Democratic National Committee, which found itself subjected to intense scrutiny by a congressional investigating committee looking into the organization's finances during the final weeks of the 1944 campaign. According to Truman Felt, Washington correspondent for the *St. Louis Star-Times*, it was the first time in U.S. history that campaign expenditures were the subject of extensive open hearings by the both the House and Senate.[87]

While claiming to be looking into the funding of some 168 groups, including the CIO's Hillman-led Political Action Committee (PAC) and Frank Gannett's Committee on Constitutional Government — the latter of which refused to voluntarily release its financial records to the House Campaign Expenditures Committee, a committee comprised of four Democrats and three Republicans — it was clear from the outset that the ADNC and Texas Sen. W. Lee "Pappy" O'Daniel's activities, which Democratic committee members believed were interrelated, were the real targets of the probe by Roosevelt's allies on Capitol Hill.

Accused of violating the Corrupt Practices Act by Rep. Clinton P. Anderson, a New Mexico Democrat who chaired the House committee, the ADNC hearings began in Washington on October 6 with testimony from national chairman Gleason Archer.

"You said you are organized to uphold the constitution, yet when Congress, created by the constitution, passes a law such as the Corrupt Practices Act, you avoid it," averred Anderson. Testifying under oath, Archer admitted that some of the organization's activities were indeed "political," and not exclusively "educational," as he had initially maintained. He also told the committee that the group's financial records were available at the ADNC's headquarters in Chicago, where the congressional committee would be resuming its investigation the following day. The evasion charged by the House committee chairman was based on the ADNC's failure to file a report of the organization's contributions

---

[86] "Book Puts Full Pearl Harbor Blame on F.D.R.," *Chicago Tribune*, Aug. 12, 1944; "Pass in Review," *Fort Lauderdale News*, Sep. 14, 1944.
[87] "The Capital's Spectacular Political Expense Probe," *St. Louis Star-Times*, Oct. 6, 1944.

and expenditures with Congress as required under the act.[88]

In Chicago, several ADNC officers were subpoenaed to appear before Anderson's congressional committee, including James C. Crummey, the group's accountant, who told the committee that he had been "tremendously overloaded with work" and that it was the responsibility of William J. Goodwin, the organization's treasurer, to file the required reports.[89] Before leaving Chicago, however, Crummey provided the congressional committee with a partial list of the group's contributors.

Crummey's list of receipts and expenditures showed contributions totaling $89,342 received through the ADNC's Chicago headquarters and an additional $8,500 that had been sent directly to the organization's national treasurer in New York. At least seventeen individuals had contributed $1,000 or more with the largest contributions coming from Houston oil tycoon Hugh R. Cullen and philanthropist William L. Volker of Kansas City, both of whom contributed $5,000. Cullen had also reportedly contributed $25,000 to O'Daniel's political activities that year. A self-made millionaire, Volker had given generously to several free market and libertarian organizations, including the Foundation for Economic Education, and had personally paid Friedrich von Hayek's salary at the University of Chicago while also providing the funds which enabled Austrian economist Ludwig von Mises to teach at New York University, enabling both men to promulgate their austerity-driven nonsense about the free market.[90]

In table-thumping testimony before the Senate Campaign Expenditures Committee the following week, William J. Goodwin, the ADNC's national treasurer, testified that the organization had deliberately tried to protect the identities of some of their contributors from "busybodies and newspapers," particularly such "miserable papers" as the *New York Post* and the city's left-leaning *PM* newspaper — both of which provided some of the most hostile press coverage of the anti-Roosevelt group that year. During his testimony, Goodwin admitted that the ADNC had not filed a report of contributions and expenditures with the Clerk of the

---

[88] "Anti-Fourth Term Group is Charged with Evading Law," *St. Louis Star-Times*, Oct. 6, 1944; "Anti-Roosevelt Group Fail to Comply with Corrupt Practices Act," *Sacramento Bee*, Oct. 7, 1944.
[89] "House Probers Open Election Hearings Today," *Chicago Tribune*, Oct. 7, 1944; "Chairman Withdraws Charge Against 13 GOP Legislators from Committee's Record," *Cincinnati Enquirer*, Oct. 8, 1944.
[90] "Democrats Fighting Fourth Term List Names of Backers," *Chicago Tribune*, Oct. 10, 1944.

House, as required by law, and had accepted money from corporations — a clear violation of the Corrupt Practices Act.

Insisting the organization was "patriotic" and not "political," Goodwin, in a prepared statement, lashed out at Clinton P. Anderson, chairman of the House committee investigating the ADNC, for linking him with Joe McWilliams, the notorious communist-baiter and anti-Semitic defendant in one of the most widely-watched sedition trials during World War II, telling the Senate investigators that McWilliams was a paid provocateur for the Communists whose sole purpose was to discredit "authentic Christian Americans." He also told the committee that the ADNC had helped to purchase radio time for Sen. O'Daniel of Texas. "We were trying to do all we could to stimulate anti-New Deal activities," he said.[91]

The widely-watched Senate hearings, which focused as much on the funding of the Texas senator's political activities as on the American Democratic National Committee itself, provided more details about the ADNC's sources of funding, including financial assistance the group received from major industrialists, as well as an assortment of isolationists actively working against a fourth term. It was estimated that $90,000 of the $128,465 received by the ADNC came from approximately forty Republican donors.

Among the group's major donors — some of whose identities hadn't been previously disclosed during the House committee hearing in Chicago a week earlier — were members of the du Pont family, owners of the famous Delaware-based chemical company, who had given a total of $3,500 to the ADNC. The du Pont's reportedly gave more than $106,000 to various Republican committees during that election cycle.

Charles E. Merrill, co-founder of the Merrill Lynch investment banking firm, and Marjorie N. Morawetz of New York, the wealthy widow of Victor Morawetz — a leading corporate and railroad attorney and longtime counsel for J. P. Morgan & Co. — gave $5,000 apiece while Philadelphia banker Samuel F. Houston contributed $4,000. Robert K. Harriss, the commodities broker who had been deeply involved with the ADNC from its founding in February, chipped in $3,500, a sum that was matched by Houston oilman Harry Weiss, president of the Humble Oil Company. Edward F. Hutton, a Long Island fundraiser for one of Frank Gannett's committees, contributed $3,000.[92]

---

[91] "Say Anti-Roosevelt Organization Violates Corrupt Practices Act," *Gazette and Daily*, Oct. 19, 1944; "Dewey Backers Odd Bedfellows," *Gazette and Daily*, Oct. 21, 1944.

[92] Kennedy, *Southern Exposure*, p. 152.

THE LOWEST EBB

Wealthy businessman Max C. Fleischmann, who famously refused to turn over his private Lockheed airplane to the government in 1941 — telling the Roosevelt administration that his aircraft was "not essential for England's defense" — contributed $2,500.[93] The widow of New York investment banker Van Santvoord Merle-Smith also gave $2,500. Gen. Robert E. Wood, former head of the America First Committee and president and chairman of retail giant Sears, Roebuck & Company, gave $1,462.73 directly to the ADNC while personally underwriting Gleason Archer's anti-Roosevelt book published earlier that year by Suffolk University and distributed by the ADNC.

Automobile entrepreneur Charles W. Nash, chairman of the Nash-Kelvinator Corporation, the 27th largest recipient of U.S. military contracts during World War II, Texas oilman and rancher Marrs McLean, the longtime finance chairman for the Republican Party of Texas, and publisher Henry Regnery of Chicago, a 32-year-old heir to a textile manufacturing fortune, were among a dozen contributors who gave $1,000 to the ADNC.[94] Senate probers also discovered that McLean, who later became a key figure in Robert A. Taft's unsuccessful bid for the Republican presidential nomination in 1952, had also written a check for $2,500 to O'Daniel's newspaper.[95]

---

[93] "Identify Plane Operator Whom F.D.R. Assailed," *Chicago Tribune*, June 24, 1941.
[94] Kennedy, *Southern Exposure*, pp. 152-153. Wood provided $3,500 for the publication of Archer's anti-Roosevelt screed.
[95] "Mrs. O'Daniel Takes Stand," *Baltimore Sun*, Oct. 20, 1944.

Chapter XX

The Draft Byrd Movement

There were, of course, many other prominent Democrats throughout the country who shared the ADNC's hostility to FDR and the New Deal, but never formally joined the Chicago-based anti-Roosevelt organization. Most of them, of course, were southerners sired on Jim Crow desperately clinging to the notion of white supremacy.

Gov. Frank M. Dixon of Alabama was one of them. An unapologetic segregationist and longtime states' rights champion, Dixon had also fired a salvo at the Roosevelt-led Democratic Party during this period, accusing it of "dynamiting" the social structure of the South while strongly hinting at the possibility of an independent Democratic southern movement in the 1944 presidential election.

Coincidentally, Dixon, who later emerged as a leader in the 1948 Dixiecrat bolt and refused to vote for John F. Kennedy as an unpledged Democratic elector from Alabama in 1960 — defiantly casting a protest vote for Virginia's Harry F. Byrd — issued his not-so-thinly-veiled threat during remarks at the annual dinner of the Southern Society at New York's Waldorf-Astoria Hotel on the same day that Woodring made his announcement about the formation of the Commonwealth Party in Topeka in December 1942.[1]

Denouncing the bloated bureaucracy in Washington and the rapid extension of federal authority in virtually every aspect of American life, Dixon claimed that white southerners had about as much as they could take and were prepared to draw a line in the

---

[1] "Gov. Dixon Scores U.S. Bureaucracy," *New York Times*, Dec. 12, 1942.

sand. "The retention of democracy," he declared, "requires the exercise of its functions." A few more years of what he caustically described as "the mess-of-pottage form of government" under FDR, and the United States would be fair game for a "two-penny American Hitler whom the future will surely bring" — a bureaucratic administrator who will plan "our democratic privileges into oblivion." It was time, he said, for those who love democracy to do a little planning, too.[2]

Dixon was particularly critical of the Works Project Administration (WPA), identifying it as the principal instrument of an increasing concentration of power in the nation's capital. Like other Democratic politicians in the Deep South, the Alabama governor was especially annoyed by the administration's support for anti-poll tax legislation and by the adoption of the Fair Labor Practices Act, signed into law as an executive order by FDR on June 25, 1941, which prohibited racial discrimination in the national defense industry, thereby preventing defense contractors in the South from discriminating against African-Americans in their hiring practices.[3]

Coming in response to a planned march on Washington by civil rights activists A. J. Muste, leader of the Fellowship for Reconciliation, Bayard Rustin and A. Philip Randolph to protest racial discrimination in the military, Executive Order 8802 was the first federal law promoting equal opportunity and prohibiting discrimination in federal hiring based on race.

A nephew of writer Thomas Dixon, Jr., whose controversial novel *The Clansman* was the basis for the explicitly racist movie "Birth of A Nation," Dixon was outraged by these developments, firmly believing that the South's survival was entirely dependent on the principle of segregation — "separation of the races, not mistreatment of any one," as he put it. Dating back to the Civil War and subsequent Republican rule during Reconstruction, Dixon lamented that southerners had always been placed in a difficult position. "Today their position is anomalous in the extreme," he decried. In "dynamiting" Dixie, he elaborated, their own party's national leaders had aroused "bitterness and recrimination" in the South, an anger that would likely be registered at the ballot box, possibly resulting "in the defeat of the next Democratic candidate for President."[4]

---

[2] Ibid.
[3] Ibid.
[4] "South to Break Its Party Chains, Says Gov. Dixon," *Chicago Tribune*, Dec. 12, 1942; "Frank Dixon, 73, Rebel Democrat," *New York Times*, Oct. 12, 1965.

THE DRAFT BYRD MOVEMENT

According to Dixon, the South was rife with talk of forming a southern Democratic Party and "the election of unpledged representatives to the electoral college." He and his fellow southerners were determined to "break our chains," he asserted. "We will find some way," he concluded, "and find it regardless of the effect on national elections if this senseless attack keeps up."[5]

Coupled with Woodring's threat of organizing a third-party in 1944, Dixon's opening salvo — a loosely-coordinated precursor to the much stronger sectional Dixiecrat movement that supported South Carolina's Strom Thurmond in 1948 — deeply worried some national Democratic leaders, who quickly huddled in an emergency session in Omaha to diagnose the situation. The emergency meeting, attended by a special assistant to FDR, the vice chairman of the Democratic National Committee, and party leaders from nine Midwestern states, hoped to stifle the rumblings of discontent within the party.[6]

Hoping to take advantage of that growing discontent was the nearly year-long effort to draft Virginia's Harry F. Byrd for the presidency, a movement headed by New Orleans industrialist John U. Barr, a little-remembered rope and twine manufacturer who had been championing the reluctant senator's candidacy more than a year before voters finally headed to the polls on November 7, 1944.

Later derisively described as a "retired New Orleans businessman with a passion for any cause to the right of slavery," the 55-year-old Barr launched the Byrd-for-President Committee in late October 1943, ostensibly to encourage the Virginia lawmaker to consider seeking the Democratic presidential nomination in 1944.[7] Barr, who pumped a lot of his own money into his seemingly quixotic Draft Byrd crusade, was the proprietor of Federal Fibre Mills — the largest mill of its kind in the world when he sold it in 1947.[8] Barr and a handful of his New Orleans business associates reportedly put up the first $25,000 for the fledgling campaign to draft the fiscally prudent Virginian.[9]

In addition to serving as a director of the National Association of Manufacturers and the Louisiana Manufacturers Association, Barr was also a vice-president of the virulently anti-labor Southern

---

[5] Ibid.
[6] "Third Party Threats Worrying Democrats," *Gastonia Daily Gazette*, Dec. 12, 1942.
[7] "White Citizens Council Started in 'Black Belt,'" *Pittsburgh Courier*, Sep. 4, 1965; "Southerners Launch Drive to Draft Byrd for President," *Louisville Courier-Journal*, Oct. 29, 1943.
[8] "Rightist Deep-South Federation Gets Under Way — But What is It?" *Louisville Courier-Journal*, Mar. 18, 1956.
[9] "Drafting a Real Democrat," *Macon Telegraph*, Oct. 31, 1943.

States Industrial Council, an ultraconservative Nashville-based organization founded in 1933 in response to New Deal policies that threatened to reshape the South's economic, political, social, and cultural landscape.[10]

The only son of a Presbyterian minister, Barr was a newcomer to politics that year, but quickly emerged as an important yet largely forgotten figure in the region's defiant political resistance to the early civil rights movement. With a mind for detail and a flair for organizing, the pleasant, deep-voiced southerner was a key behind-the-scenes player in the Strom Thurmond-led Dixiecrat movement of 1948, a year when the New Orleans manufacturer — painfully aware of what had transpired four years earlier — quietly placed an independent slate of presidential electors under a "States' Righters" label on the Louisiana ballot and only removed them once he was absolutely sure there wouldn't be any last-minute shenanigans by national Democratic officials looking to replace the state Democratic Party's official list of electors, all of whom were pledged to the segregationist's candidacy.[11] Thurmond easily carried the state in November, defeating President Harry S. Truman, who ran without a party label in the Cajun State, by nearly 70,000 votes.

Barr had fond memories of Thurmond's candidacy, a campaign energized by rebellious southern Democrats, enabling the South Carolinian to carry four states in the Deep South while nearly throwing the election into the House of Representatives. "Just 12,486 votes in Ohio and California would have thrown the election into the House where the South could have won," he said years later. "That's how close we came."[12] He was right — Truman carried Ohio by a razor-thin 7,107 votes and narrowly took California by 17,865 votes — and a switch of 12,486 votes in those two states would have denied the Democratic president an Electoral College majority.

Barr, who wore his politics on his sleeve, also resisted Democratic nominee Adlai Stevenson's candidacy four years later, profusely praising Louisiana Gov. Robert F. Kennon, a Democrat, for displaying "rugged integrity" in endorsing Republican Dwight Eisenhower while strongly repudiating "the shabby Truman mess" and its continuation under a handpicked successor who was

---

[10] Kari Frederickson, *The Dixiecrat Revolt and the End of the Solid South, 1932-1968* (Chapel Hill, 2001), p. 158; Kennedy, *Southern Exposure*, p. 200.
[11] "States' Righters to Be on Ballot," *Times-Picayune*, Aug. 27, 1948; "Original States' Rights Electors to Be Withdrawn," *Alexandria Daily Town Talk*, Oct. 9, 1948.
[12] "Biggest States Rights Backer Works Behind the Scenes," *News Journal* (Wilmington, DE), Sep. 17, 1956.

closely surrounded by "traitors who have grown politically fat by their hatred of southern Democrats."[13]

Along with Clarence E. Manion, the former dean of the University of Notre Dame Law School and longtime conservative radio and television host, Barr co-chaired the late-starting States' Rights presidential campaign waged by former IRS Commissioner T. Coleman Andrews in 1956 — a campaign in which Barr enthusiastically claimed that the Richmond accountant had "an excellent chance" of carrying several southern states.[14]

Again promoting the possibility of a deadlocked Electoral College strategy, Barr had personally organized the National States Rights Conference in Memphis in mid-September of that year, a carefully controlled gathering that drew 317 delegates from a dozen splinter parties and organizations in 25 states. The Memphis conference officially endorsed the Andrews candidacy, but thwarted the efforts of an ambitious minority to simultaneously launch a nationally-organized third party — a proposal made by Clarence Manion, who called for the founding of a new party on the "political and moral right" in his keynote speech. It was a thorny issue that briefly threatened to drive a wedge between the Memphis participants.

Declaring that the creation of a third-party would "sabotage" their efforts, Barr personally played a decisive role in defeating the motion. "This is a federation of independent state parties," he asserted during the heated floor debate. "If we form a third party, the Republicans and Democrats will kill us," he continued. "We'd be dead. We couldn't win. If you believe in states' rights, practice states' rights."[15] The clincher, however, came when Barr quoted a recent telephone conversation with Andrews in which the former IRS commissioner said that he wasn't "interested in trying to create a new third party." He also quoted Andrews, who was unable to attend the conference, as saying that the objectives of the states' rights groups "had been, as I understood it, to restore the two-party system, and I would be content and happy if we succeeded in accomplishing it."[16]

Limiting his active campaigning to evening and weekends, Andrews appeared on the ballot in fourteen states that autumn.

---

[13] "Barr Commends Action by Kennon," *Shreveport Times*, Sep. 8, 1952.
[14] "States'-Rights Leader Hopes to Carry 'Most of 10 States,'" *Louisville Courier-Journal*, Oct. 15, 1956.
[15] "States' Righters Veto Third Party," *Los Angeles Times*, Sep. 16, 1956.
[16] "States' Righters Split on Issue of '3rd Party,'" *Palm Beach Post*, Sep. 15, 1956.

Thomas H. Werdel, a former Republican congressman from California, was his vice-presidential designee. Despite Barr's optimism, the Andrews-Werdel ticket — running strongest in Louisiana, where they polled 44,520 votes, or 7.2 percent, on the States' Rights ticket, and in Harry F. Byrd's Virginia stronghold where they garnered more than six percent of the vote while carrying rural Prince Edward County — was never a factor in the rematch between President Eisenhower and Democratic challenger Adlai Stevenson.

Barr played a much more important role during this latter period as chairman of the Federation for Constitutional Government (FCG), an organization initiated by Sen. James O. Eastland of Mississippi in early 1955. It was the pinnacle of Barr's public career. Committed to defending the South while promoting laissez-faire capitalism and limited government interference in the private sector, the retired New Orleans industrialist initially envisioned the FCG as a national organization. In fact, he made no mention of segregation when incorporating the group earlier that year, but Senator Eastland's remarks to the group's founding members at the Peabody Hotel in Memphis in December 1955 left little doubt as to the organization's true purpose. "Generations of southerners yet unborn will cherish our memory," declared the Mississippi lawmaker, "because they will realize that the fight we now wage, will have preserved for them their untainted racial heritage, their culture, and the institutions of the Anglo-Saxon race."

From its inception, moreover, the federation included a number of leading southern-based segregationist and states' rights groups, most notably the States' Rights Council of Georgia, the Committee for Individual Rights in Virginia, and the various White Citizens Councils flourishing throughout the region during the relatively tumultuous mid-to late-fifties — a period in which the South increasingly found itself politically alienated from the rest of the country. Barr himself was a member of the Citizens Council of New Orleans. In addition to Eastland, the powerful chairman of the Senate Judiciary Committee and bellicose voice of the segregationist Citizens' Councils, the group's original advisory committee included Louisiana's ruthless segregationist Leander Perez, who worked closely with Barr in launching the FCG. Gov. Marvin Griffin of Georgia and Sen. Strom Thurmond of South Carolina, as well as a sprinkling of congressmen and former governors, were also prominent committee members.[17]

---

[17] "Dixie Mix Foes Form New States Rights Group," *Orlando Sentinel*, Oct. 24, 1955.

THE DRAFT BYRD MOVEMENT

Thrust into the limelight in his role as chairman, Barr defended the organization's association with the White Citizens' Councils, telling *Minneapolis Tribune* reporter Richard P. Kleeman and Pulitzer Prize-winning journalist Carl Rowan that the Federation for Constitutional Government was willing to "cooperate with any organization that has as its purpose the preservation of constitutional government — and as long as the White Citizens councils have that purpose, we will collaborate with them."[18]

Though widely depicted as a political novice during the 1944 presidential campaign, the mild-mannered, graying businessman wasn't quite the neophyte described by most reporters and, in fact, impressed many of the journalists that he encountered on the campaign trail that year, including J. Oliver Emmerich, Jr., the longtime publisher of Mississippi's *McComb Enterprise*.

Emmerich, who spent considerable time with Barr during a conference in Memphis that spring, said that chairman of the Byrd committee was "no mental sloth. He is not a political will-o'-the wisp," wrote Emmerich. "He's the kind of a man who knows what he is doing and who has political perception. He knows the obstacles ahead; the danger of failure; the chances of victory. One thing is certain," continued the Mississippi editor, "he knows that the effort of the Byrd-for-President movement is certain to benefit Dixie and the nation."[19]

Recognizing the preeminent role the South would be required to play if there was any chance of stopping or reversing the country's "drift toward bureaucratic collectivism and national bankruptcy," Barr's initial objective in 1944 was to assure that all fifteen southern delegations to the Democratic national convention in Chicago the following summer were pledged to the Virginian. Byrd apparently hadn't been informed about Barr's fledgling organization prior to its founding — something the New Orleans businessman freely acknowledged. "Senator Byrd has not been consulted about this undertaking," said Barr, "and will not be until a sufficient number of southerners have subscribed to the movement to demonstrate to him that he has a large and growing body of support."[20]

Informed of Barr's activities, Byrd declared that he had no in-

---

[18] Richard P. Kleeman and Carl T. Rowan, "Dixie Divided: Segregationists Seek Conservatives' Aid," *Minneapolis Tribune*, Feb. 6, 1956.
[19] "That Byrd-for-President Rally," *McComb Daily Enterprise*, Apr. 22, 1944.
[20] "White Citizens Council Started in 'Black Belt,'" *Pittsburgh Courier*, Sep. 4, 1965; "Southerners Launch Drive to Draft Byrd for President," *Louisville Courier-Journal*, Oct. 29, 1943.

tention of becoming a candidate for the presidency. He also confirmed that he hadn't spoken with Barr and, in fact, didn't even know him, prompting one Washington columnist to quip, "Byrd and Barr, and Barr and Byrd. About each other they ain't heard."[21]

In the meantime, Barr acted quickly, hiring a small staff and opening a temporary Byrd-for-President headquarters in the St. Charles Hotel in New Orleans. From the outset, Barr insisted that the effort to draft the Virginian wasn't part of any potential third-party movement, as had been recently advocated by South Carolina Sen. Ellison D. "Cotton Ed" Smith. It was strictly designed to prevent a fourth term for President Roosevelt. "It is not a third party movement," asserted Barr during a stop in the nation's capital in mid-December, but rather an effort to pressure the Democratic Party to "purge itself of bureaucracy and wastefulness. It is a movement to revitalize the Democratic Party and to preserve the two-party system in this country."[22]

During his visit to the nation's capital, Barr told reporters that Byrd-for-President clubs had already been formed in a half-dozen southern states — Alabama, Florida, Louisiana, Mississippi, North Carolina and South Carolina — and that similar groups were in the process of being formed in Arkansas, Georgia, Tennessee, Texas and West Virginia. "It is our present purpose to organize the South first and then expand into other sections of the country," he explained.[23]

The New Orleans manufacturer, who corresponded regularly with the Virginia senator once the movement picked up steam — a dialogue that continued for several years — acknowledged that his hastily-organized group faced a particularly daunting task. The same thing would have been true, observed Barr, for anybody opposing Roosevelt's bid for a fourth term. "The main difficulty we have encountered so far has been defeatism and the hesitancy of some people — particularly business and political leaders — to 'stick their necks out,'" he said while in Washington. "We in Louisiana — where this movement for Senator Byrd had its inception — understand this and are not surprised by it because we have personally known dictatorship. Huey Long," he continued, "had thousands of people scared to move and this partial paralysis of

---

[21] George Dixon, "One-Time Press Agent Recalls When Byrd Became Blood Brother of the Sioux," *Shreveport Times*, Dec. 20, 1943.
[22] "Byrd Presidential Boom Aimed to Nip Fourth Term for FDR," *Long Beach Independent* (Long Beach, CA), Dec. 15, 1943.
[23] "Byrd-for-President Clubs Organized in Six Southern States, Planned in Others," *St. Louis Post-Dispatch*, Dec. 15, 1943.

the opposition was one of the sources of his power. A similar condition of intimidation and fear now exists throughout the country and it will not be finally overcome until the New Deal is decisively repudiated at the polls and we return to the processes of a constitutional democracy."[24]

By late February, Barr claimed to have organized Byrd-for-President groups in no fewer than fourteen states, mostly southern and border states, but also such unlikely places as Pennsylvania and Ohio.[25] Barr, who personally conferred with the intensely private Virginia lawmaker in late February, wasn't the least bit discouraged by Byrd's latest protestation that he wasn't a candidate for the presidency and no intention of becoming one.[26] In fact, the exact opposite was true. Barr was now more convinced than ever that the reluctant Virginian would indeed heed the call of a genuine presidential draft and immediately announced that his organization would "intensify" its efforts to make it happen.

"Senator Byrd has stated that he is not a candidate and does not expect to become one," admitted Barr at a hastily-scheduled press conference following his meeting with the Virginia senator. "But if someone is not a candidate, does not want to be a candidate, but can be drafted as a candidate, it is my feeling that it is the right of the rest of us to take counsel as to our country's interests and to discuss his qualifications. If enough of us agree — and we have ample evidence that, politics and personalities aside, Senator Byrd would be the practically unanimous choice of the Democratic National Convention — then we may accomplish something. Few men in history have refused presidential nominations," he continued. He also predicted that with an adequate campaign "well over 50 percent" of the southern delegates to the Democratic national convention later that summer could be lined up for the hesitant Virginian. (Eleven southern states, including Texas, had a total of 276 delegates.)

Barr, who denied that the Byrd-for-President Committee had any official connection to Harry Woodring's widely-publicized American Democratic National Committee, also told skeptical newsmen in Washington that he didn't believe Roosevelt would be a candidate for reelection, largely because he didn't think the three-term president would want to risk the "probability of defeat

---

[24] "Byrd Backers in Presidency Race Gaining," *Baltimore Sun*, Dec. 15, 1943.
[25] "Move to Draft Byrd for President Making Progress," *Greenwood Commonwealth* (Greenwood, MS), Mar. 1, 1944.
[26] "Byrd Talks With Principal Backer," *Monroe News-Star* (Monroe, LA), Feb. 29, 1944.

if he runs." Faced with almost certain defeat and the strong likelihood of an even more hostile Congress if he won, Barr — readily admitting that he had never voted for FDR — said that it was difficult to imagine why the war-weary and increasingly exhausted president would even want a fourth term in the first place.[27]

Barr, who consistently emphasized that his criticism of Roosevelt was based entirely on the president's domestic policies and not on his handling of the war, also told reporters that his organization would be opening Byrd-for-President headquarters in Washington and New York shortly. He clearly envisioned a national effort.[28]

Despite the fact that preliminary delegate counts in early March showed that Roosevelt already had the pledged support of 476 delegates — four-fifths of the 589 required — to three for ex-Massachusetts Gov. Ely and that it would take something short of a miracle to deny Roosevelt another nomination, Barr remained undeterred and continued his one-man crusade to put Harry F. Byrd in the White House.[29]

The graying and bespectacled Louisiana businessman found plenty of encouragement in editorials during this relatively heady period, several of which appeared in newspapers outside the Deep South. Commenting on Barr's efforts to draft the Virginia legislator, Iowa's *Sioux City Journal* noted that "if the entire Solid South and the border states mentioned got behind Senator Byrd, they could build him into a formidable candidate by the time the convention was held in July."

The Virginian, the paper concluded, was probably "the foremost Democratic opponent of New Dealism in our government. He has been outspoken in his criticism of bureaucracy, debt, extravagance and waste, and in recent years he has led all others of like mind in the South and in the nation at large. An exponent of economy in government, a man who proved as governor of Virginia the fact of his understanding of administrative problems, and one of the recognized leaders of his party in the Senate, Senator Byrd at 56 makes a powerful appeal to Democrats not only in the South but throughout the country."[30]

Sensing some momentum, Barr announced in late March that

---

[27] "Byrd to Stay as Senator," *Baltimore Sun*, Mar. 1, 1944.
[28] "Draft-Byrd Group Plans Convention," *New York Times*, Mar. 1, 1944.
[29] "Moves Started to Halt Roosevelt; Woodring and Others Seek New Nominee," *Cincinnati Enquirer*, Mar. 2, 1944; "Big Delegate Vote Assured President," *New York Times*, Mar. 2, 1944.
[30] "Drafting Senator Byrd," *Sioux City Journal*, reprinted in the *Argus-Leader* (Sioux Falls, S.D.), Mar. 5, 1944.

his fledgling Draft-Byrd-for-President organization would hold four regional meetings in the South during the month of April, beginning with an April 10 meeting of Byrd's supporters from North Carolina, South Carolina, Virginia and West Virginia in Greensboro, North Carolina. Four days later, a second meeting was scheduled for Atlanta, which would include representatives from Alabama, Florida and Georgia. A third meeting, to be held in Memphis on April 17, was expected to include delegates from Arkansas, Kentucky, Mississippi, Missouri and Tennessee, with a final meeting planned for Dallas on April 20 with representatives attending from Texas, Louisiana and Oklahoma.[31] The movement appeared to be taking flight.

In the meantime, Barr traveled to Richmond, Virginia, to meet with some of the senator's supporters.[32] During the two-hour meeting, which was boycotted by most of the senator's closest friends and allies at Byrd's request, Barr told the approximately 35 attendees that he had met with the senator in late February and that he fully understood how deeply the Virginian felt about the seriousness of the issues facing the country. "We know, you know and all America knows that, regardless of his personal desires or inclinations, Harry Byrd will never refuse the clear call of duty. He is a patriot, worthy of Virginia," he said. Despite the relatively small turnout, Barr described the Richmond meeting as "a decisive step in final preparations to bring to the service of the nation, as Chief Executive, one more of Virginia's great statesmen."[33]

Remmie L. Arnold, a wealthy pen manufacturer who later sought the Democratic nomination for governor — a candidacy in which the one-time Byrd supporter actively sought black support and was endorsed by Arthur W. Mitchell, the New Deal's first African-American congressman — was named as the group's state chairman. Arnold, a two-term Petersburg city councilman, was the second largest pen manufacturer in the world.[34]

Given the small turnout in Richmond — some observers claimed only twenty-six showed up for the meeting — the Norfolk *Virginian-Pilot* couldn't resist ridiculing the rope manufacturer, claiming that the only thing Barr had offered Sen. Byrd was "enough rope to hang himself with."[35]

Stopping in Washington just prior to the Richmond meeting, a

---

[31] "Byrd-for-President Bloc Calls Parleys in the South," *Philadelphia Inquirer*, Apr. 10, 1944.
[32] "Byrd Presidential Backers to Confer," *Newport News Daily Press*, Mar. 30, 1944.
[33] "'Draft Byrd' Move Opens in Virginia," *Baltimore Sun*, Apr. 1, 1944.
[34] Ibid.; Dennis S. Nordin, *The New Deal's Black Congressman: A Life of Arthur Wergs Mitchell* (Columbia, Missouri, 1997), p. 286.
[35] "The Upper South," *New York Times*, Apr. 9, 1944.

visibly elated Barr told reporters that the movement to draft the ultraconservative senator was quickly growing into a "genuine crusade." Though refusing to estimate the Virginian's overall potential strength at the Democratic national convention later that summer, the New Orleans industrialist said that Byrd was the "outstanding choice" of most Democrats in the South, the vast majority of whom were tired of the New Deal. "I do not know how to correctly label the New Deal," he sneered. "It is a little bit of fascism, a little bit of Nazism, some communism, and a lot of state socialism, mixed together like a pot of Mulligan's stew. But whatever it is, the masses want no more of it, and millions of these masses are seeking an outlet for their determination in a Draft-Byrd-for-President movement."[36]

"I am not a politician," Barr elaborated. "I know little or nothing of the mechanics of political machinery, yet I do have some knowledge of human nature and am convinced that the Democratic Party faces catastrophe if New Deal politicians attempt to force the New Deal program down the throats of the American people for another four years."[37]

Barr was absolutely delighted a few days letter when he received a letter from North Carolina Sen. Josiah W. Bailey, a longtime critic of the New Deal, endorsing Byrd for president. In his letter, Bailey expressed "unreserved confidence" in Byrd, describing him as "one of the finest men in this whole country." The author of the controversial 1937 Conservative Manifesto — a bipartisan document sharply criticizing Roosevelt's New Deal policies — laid it on pretty thick in his letter to Barr:

> [Byrd] understands government. He knows the details of the task of president. His views are sound. His standards are the highest. His integrity is beyond question, and I do not think under any circumstances, anywhere, his integrity would be questioned. He has great ability.
>
> I am always glad to have evidence that our party can produce men of presidential caliber, and as long as Harry Byrd is living we can be sure that he would not fail the American people.
>
> I know his views and I know his character. I know his spirit. He is a fine, strong, noble, high-minded man and as thorough

---

[36] "Declares Byrd for President Drive Growing," *Chicago Tribune*, Mar. 31, 1944.
[37] "Byrd Backers Growing Happy," *Columbus Daily Enquirer* (Columbus, GA), Mar. 31, 1944.

THE DRAFT BYRD MOVEMENT

an American as ever breathed the air of this country.[38]

Bailey, who had threatened the Roosevelt administration on the floor of the Senate several months earlier by suggesting the possibility of a newly-created Southern Democratic Party to oppose the New Deal, even went so far as to predict that FDR wouldn't seek another term — a view expressed earlier by Barr. "I seriously question whether President Roosevelt will seek a fourth term," Bailey told newsmen. "I think most of the delegates probably will be for him, but I question whether he will run."

The three-term North Carolina senator also proposed a Democratic ticket headed by Byrd with former DNC chairman James A. Farley, who was adamantly opposed to a fourth term, as his vice-presidential running mate, but made it clear that he intended to support his party's nominee — even if it was Roosevelt — in November.[39] Party loyalty was important to the 71-year Bailey, especially given the fact that he owed his stunning 1930 Democratic primary victory over longtime Sen. Furnifold M. Simmons, in large part, to the incumbent's refusal to support his party's nominee, Al Smith, in the 1928 presidential election.

In the meantime, Barr focused his attention on recruiting "big name" speakers for the upcoming southern conferences in Greensboro, Atlanta, Memphis and Dallas. He didn't do too badly for a political novice. The April 10th Greensboro meeting, which attracted nearly five-dozen participants from Virginia and the two Carolinas, was keynoted by former Sen. Edward R. Burke, an anti-New Deal Democrat from Nebraska. Burke, who lost his Senate seat in 1940, had been a severe critic of Roosevelt's court-packing plan in 1937 and, along with New York's Royal S. Copeland, joined a coalition of southern and border-state Democrats later that summer in opposing much of Roosevelt's New Deal agenda.

In addressing Byrd's supporters in the King Cotton Hotel ballroom, Burke heaped praise on the Virginia lawmaker and said that a fourth term was a greater threat to the Republic than any foreign dictator. "The United States needs a president who believes in our constitutional system of limited powers — limitations that will be effective only so long as we maintain a careful observance of the

---

[38] "Sen. Bailey Backs Byrd as President With High Praise," *Alexandria Town Talk*, Apr. 6, 1944.

[39] "Byrd and Farley Ticket Proposed," *Indianapolis Star*, Apr. 6, 1944. Farley, who had unsuccessfully challenged Roosevelt for the Democratic presidential nomination four years earlier, had seriously considered allowing his own name to be placed in nomination for the presidency at the Democratic national convention later that summer, but eventually supported Byrd.

division of those powers between three coordinate branches of government," he told the participants. Charging that "a continuation of the policies of the present national administration through a fourth term for President Roosevelt would place in real peril the foundation principles upon which a free people have built the most splendid republic the world has known." Refuting Roosevelt's diehard supporters, the Nebraskan also said that successful prosecution of the war wasn't enough and "ought not to be a factor in the coming campaign."[40]

Stark S. Dillard, president of the Dillard Paper Company, assisted Barr in handling publicity for the Greensboro conference and was subsequently appointed state chairman of the Draft-Byrd-for-President movement in North Carolina.[41]

State Rep. Joseph C. Jenkins of Gainesville, Florida, a vociferous critic of the New Deal, was the keynote speaker at the Atlanta conference, a two-day event that drew a disappointingly small crowd of 51 men and five women from Georgia, Alabama and Florida.[42] Jenkins had chaired the insurgent Byrd campaign in the Sunshine State and polled 74,097 votes as an at-large delegate pledged to the Virginia senator in the May 2 Florida Democratic primary a few weeks later — a contest in which Byrd's supporters captured a sizzling 45 percent of the statewide vote while electing four of the state's 18 delegates to the party's national convention in Chicago.[43]

Campaigning aggressively throughout the state that spring, the Gainesville lawyer accused the Roosevelt administration of allowing itself to be "surrounded and hogtied by a radical, theoretical, extravagant, power mad, bureaucratic New Deal clique" while asserting that the conservative Virginian was "probably the only Democrat who can win the 1944 presidential election."[44] Singing Byrd's praises — he "successfully ran his father's newspaper at 15 years of age," cut wasteful spending while leaving a large surplus as governor of Virginia, and had consistently opposed FDR's "alphabetical asininities" as a member of the U.S. Senate — Jenkins warned that the country's future "lies in the hands of militant

---

[40] "Burke Tells Byrd Supporters Fourth Term for Roosevelt Would Ruin Nation," *Greensboro Daily News*, Apr. 11, 1944.

[41] "Dillard Made State Chairman of Byrd-for-President Move," *Greensboro Daily News*, Apr. 13, 1944.

[42] "Byrd Backers Meeting Here," *Atlanta Constitution*, Apr. 14, 1944.

[43] "Floridians Name Jenkins Head of Byrd-for-President Drive," *Fort Lauderdale News*, Mar. 3, 1944; "Complete Official Vote Tabulations From Primary Contain No Surprises," *Palm Beach Post*, May 12, 1944.

[44] "As One Democrat to Another," *Fort Lauderdale News*, Mar. 29, 1944.

Americans."[45]

Jenkins, who eventually spent ten years in the Florida legislature, wasn't particularly bothered by the relatively sparse crowd that attended a midday luncheon on the Rainbow Roof of Atlanta's famous Hotel Ansley. "Defeatists and those scared of the New Deal bureaucrats stayed away," he stated almost matter-of-factly.[46] Obviously embarrassed by the scarcity of participants — organizers were expecting at least 250 people — a red-faced Barr tried to put a positive spin on the disappointing turnout, explaining to reporters that very little advance work had been done in Atlanta. "I consider the gathering entirely satisfactory," he said.[47]

The five-state conference in Memphis a few days later attracted a much larger crowd to hear former Mississippi Gov. Martin S. "Mike" Conner viciously attack the New Deal while vigorously defending white supremacy. In his keynote speech, Conner called upon southern Democrats to regain control of the party or "walk out" if it remained under the control of the New Dealers. "We have nothing left to lose and our right as free men to regain," he thundered.[48] Addressing the only session open to the press during the two-day meeting, the ex-governor further charged that FDR's New Deal had indulged in "wild extravagances and wanton waste" and predicted that Roosevelt's domestic policies would result in the "destruction of the American economic system of individual enterprise."

Conner, who was then serving as commissioner of the Southeastern Conference (SEC) — a conference that didn't have a single African-American scholarship athlete until 1967 when Kentucky's Nate Northington made his brief debut on the gridiron and hoopster Perry Wallace of Nashville played for Vanderbilt University's basketball team — told the attendees from Tennessee, Arkansas, Kentucky, Mississippi and Missouri that southerners had been the Democratic party's most loyal supporters, sustaining it "in the lean and somber years of defeat, which have been many, just as loyally as the flush and joyous years of victory, which have been few."

Invoking the names of Presidents Jefferson, Jackson, Cleveland and Wilson, Conner asserted that the party's foundational principles of constitutional government, state sovereignty and individ-

---

[45] "Jeffersonian Democrats Hear Jenkins Flail FDR During 'Byrd' Rally," *Fort Lauderdale News*, Apr. 20, 1944.
[46] "Absence Makes the Heart," *TIME*, Vol. XLIII, No. 17, Apr. 24, 1944.
[47] "Senator Byrd Supporters Hold Meeting," *Macon Telegraph*, Apr. 15, 1944.
[48] "Southern Democrats Promise 'Walkout' if FDR Nominated," *Fort Lauderdale News*, Apr. 21, 1944.

ual freedom were under assault by the New Dealers, whom he described as "revolutionists" foisting an un-American philosophy of government on the unsuspecting citizens of the United States. "Our party," he continued, "has a long and glorious record of service to the people of America in defense of individual and states' rights, and against the encroachments of special privilege and centralized power."

Conner, who succeeded populist race-baiter Theodore G. Bilbo as governor of the Magnolia State at the height of the Great Depression in 1932, then tossed some red meat to the wildly enthusiastic crowd, declaring that the issue of white supremacy trumped every other issue in the campaign. "This issue," said Conner, who was enthusiastically cheered and applauded throughout his speech, "is being forced upon us, not by the people of any section, but by foolish New Deal politicians. We must let the political reformers and communistic equalizers of the New Deal know that the South is white and we are going to keep it white, regardless of costs or political affiliations."

In defending white supremacy, the former Mississippi governor reminded the Memphis audience of Abraham Lincoln's speech during the fourth Lincoln-Douglas debate in September 1858, in which the Great Emancipator declared that he wasn't — and never had been — "in favor of bringing about in any way the social and political equality of the white and black races." Lincoln, he said, also stated in that speech that there was "a physical difference between the white and black races which I believe will forever forbid the two races living together on terms of social and political equality. And inasmuch as they cannot so live, while they do remain together there must be the position of superior and inferior, and I as much as any other man am in favor of having the superior position assigned to the white race."[49]

Traveling with fellow New Orleans businessman James J. Kramer, the Draft-Byrd organization's executive secretary, Barr arrived in Dallas a few nights later. Encouraged by the success of the Memphis meeting, which drew as many as 200 participants from five states, Barr announced that the group's efforts would be expanded to the Northeast and Midwest following the Texas meeting. "Hundreds of thousands of Democrats of the North will desert the Democratic Party and tip the scales in favor of the Republican Party unless we unify our ranks by purging the New Deal," he told the *Dallas Morning News*.

---

[49] "Conner Calls Upon Democrats to Condemn New Deal Policies," *Clarion-Ledger* (Jackson, MS), Apr. 18, 1944.

The travel-weary New Orleans businessman further maintained that a switch of only a million votes in the North would doom the Democrats to certain defeat. "That is how precarious our position is," he said. "A Jeffersonian Democrat like Senator Byrd would not only reunite our party, but would bring into the fold many Democrats who started their exodus from the party in 1940." Byrd's candidacy, he concluded, would also have tremendous appeal to large numbers of independents and Republicans looking for "a statesman rather than a politician for president."[50]

The tri-state Dallas meeting on April 20 drew about sixty people, most of them from the host city, but also included several Byrd supporters from other parts of Texas, as well as from Louisiana and Oklahoma. Dallas assistant district attorney Allen Melton and John Bickett, Jr., chairman of the University of Texas Board of Regents, were among those in attendance, as was Connie C. Renfro, a prominent Dallas attorney who had been active in several anti-New Deal groups and had publicly supported Wendell Willkie in 1940.

Convening at the Hotel Adolphus, the draft Byrd supporters heard from three principal speakers, including Barr, Zach Lamar Cobb, a native Texan who was then living in California, and magazine publisher Peter Molyneaux, the latter of whom presided over the meeting.[51] Barr told the gathering that it was time for southern Democrats to refute the claim of Roosevelt supporters that they "talk a good game, but fold up in a crisis."[52]

Cobb, a former campaign manager for "Cactus Jack" Garner in 1932 who later actively supported the vice-president's long-shot quest for the Democratic presidential nomination in 1940 — a breathtakingly audacious gamble doomed from the outset — declared that it was time for the South to stop supporting national Democratic leaders they no longer believed in. "The South cannot follow the American Labor Party of Sidney Hillman," asserted Cobb to a round of enthusiastic applause. "As the North saved the union in the War Between the States," he continued, "the South now has the opportunity to save the nation. If the issue is forced this fall between the bureaucracy of revolutionary regimentation and the return of the American system of free enterprise and liberty under the constitution there will be no doubt as to the outcome."

Tyler attorney L. L. James, who gained national attention later

---

[50] "Byrd Backer Urges Purge of New Deal," *Dallas Morning News*, Apr. 20, 1944.
[51] "Tyler Attorney Heads Draft-Byrd Democrats," *Dallas Morning News*, Apr. 21, 1944.
[52] "Byrd Backers Unite in Texas; Lash New Deal," *Chicago Tribune*, Apr. 21, 1944.

that summer when he joined fourteen other Texas delegates in walking out of the Democratic national convention in Chicago when it refused to seat the entire regular delegation, was named state chairman of the draft Byrd movement. A longtime critic of the New Deal who described himself as an American first and a Democrat second, the Tyler lawyer had led a delegation from Texas to Washington to fight FDR's court-packing scheme in 1937.[53]

Arriving in New York the following week, Barr hinted for the first time that the "Draft Byrd" movement could potentially lead to a third-party movement in the general election. In an interview at the Belmont-Plaza Hotel, the Louisianan stopped just short of predicting such an effort, telling George Van Slyke, a reporter for the *New York Sun*, that in the event Byrd wasn't nominated there was a strong possibility that anti-New Deal Democrats would rally behind another candidate in November. "Should the national convention be able to force a fourth-term nomination or the selection of another candidate indorsing the New Deal philosophy," asserted Barr, "there would be an avalanche of anti-New Deal votes cast, but few Republican votes. The Democrats," he predicted, "will have tough sledding in many of the southern states." He continued:

> Patriotism is strong in the South, as loyal to the nation and in support of the war as anywhere in the country. But the people are growing war weary and are rebellious because they now are convinced that the federal administration is taking advantage of the war to perpetuate unnecessary regimentation which they are fearful may be carried on after the war is ended to fasten the New Deal permanently on the nation.

The South would certainly play a deciding role in the 1944 presidential election, Barr elaborated, noting that many Democrats in that region were finally finding the courage to speak out against both the New Deal and a fourth term. "Citizens who have hesitated about taking part in an organized revolt against bureaucracy until safely screened by the curtains of polling places are now becoming outspoken," he said. The strength of southern resistance to the New Deal would become crystal clear to the rest of the nation shortly, continued Barr. "Within the next few days several primaries in the South will shed light on the actual proportions of this revolt. In Florida and Alabama, two New Dealers are fighting for

---

[53] "Tyler Attorney Heads Draft-Byrd Democrats," *Dallas Morning News*, Apr. 21, 1944; "15 Texas Regulars Walk Out as Dems Seat Rump Group," *Dallas Morning News*, July 21, 1944.

their lives," he said, referring to the spirited primary challenges being waged against Senators Claude Pepper of Florida and Alabama's Lister Hill, both of whom were ardent supporters of the New Deal. Clues as to what Democrats might reasonably expect to see in the North and Midwest in November, he added, might be found in the results of those southern primaries.[54]

Needless to say, Barr was more than a little pleased by the results of the Florida primary in early May, asserting that the results in both the presidential and U.S. Senate contests indicated that Democrats in the Sunshine State were almost evenly divided between those who supported the New Deal and those who were opposed.[55] Running much stronger than expected, Byrd's delegates captured four of the state's eighteen delegates to the national convention, including one of the state's three at-large delegates, while garnering approximately 45 percent of the popular vote. (Florida, incidentally, abandoned its unit rule at the national convention, enabling the state's four Byrd delegates to vote for the Virginian on the convention's first and only ballot.) In the state's widely-watched U.S. Senate primary, liberal incumbent Sen. Claude Pepper, an outspoken Roosevelt supporter who was given a tremendous amount of outside help in the primary, prevailed by a relatively unimpressive margin of 9,604 votes against the combined totals of four lesser-known candidates.[56]

In a press release issued shortly after the Florida primary, Barr's committee pointed out that Roosevelt's machine, aided by 65,000 federal employees in the state and "scads and scads of money, with the gift of a toll-free bridge two days before the election and with big newspaper advertisements" was only able to defeat Byrd's fledgling campaign by approximately 21,000 votes — a somewhat startling outcome given the limited resources and lack of organized campaigning on the part of those opposed to the New Deal. Coupled with Pepper's narrow majority in the Senate primary, the Louisianan said it was hardly an impressive display of strength.[57]

In surveying the results, Barr daringly predicted that if Roosevelt, who was still being coy about his intentions, decided to run again, Florida "will go Republican in the November election," as was the case sixteen years earlier when Floridians rejected Al

---

[54] "Byrd Backer Assails New Deal," *New York Sun*, Apr. 26, 1944.
[55] "Byrd-for-President Chairman Predicts Florida to Go to GOP," *Jackson Sun*, May 7, 1944.
[56] "Report of Canvass Board Confirms Unofficial Return," *Fort Lauderdale News*, Apr. 12, 1944.
[57] "Fourth Term Opponents Still May Offer Nominees," *Philadelphia Inquirer*, May 22, 1944.

Smith's candidacy and overwhelmingly supported Republican nominee Herbert Hoover. "Our people are set, and with the normally Republican vote added, the vote in Florida will be at least 60 to 65 percent anti-New Deal," he said.

On the other hand, Barr was almost completely dismissive of Sen. Lister Hill's primary victory in Alabama's closely-watched Senate primary where the majority whip, a strong proponent of the New Deal, had racked up a 25,000-vote margin over challenger James A. Simpson, a prominent Birmingham attorney and state senator who was loathed by organized labor. Hill's victory, inferred Barr, was bought and paid for by the New Deal. "Government purchases in the Birmingham steel and iron districts and government operations in Mobile and other sections of Alabama are enormous," he asserted. When coupled with some 64,000 people in Alabama who were on the federal payroll, accounting for "a goodly portion of the votes Mr. Hill secured," his primary victory wasn't at all surprising, said Barr.[58]

Barr was even more delighted a few weeks later when the Democratic state convention in South Carolina — one of only nine state delegations to cast at least a few ballots against FDR at the Democratic national convention in Chicago — supported a constitutional amendment limiting presidential tenure to two four-year terms while sharply condemning "the tendency of some of the leaders of the national party to unduly favor regimentation, collectivism, bureaucratic control and other methods and means characteristic of totalitarian government." It was language tailor-made for a Byrd candidacy. In addition to choosing an uninstructed delegation and adopting a resolution insisting on continued segregation, the South Carolinians also reserved the right to review the actions of the Democratic national convention at a special state convention in early August.[59] "The New Deal steamroller," quipped Barr, "ran out of steam."[60]

The graying-haired chairman of the insurgent Byrd movement was also strongly encouraged by recent developments in Texas, where the May 23 Democratic state convention in Austin chose an uninstructed delegation to the party's national convention and named fifteen presidential electors adamantly opposed to FDR and the New Deal, a raucous affair which led to a dramatic and widely-publicized bolt by the president's supporters who held a

---

[58] "Byrd-for-President Chairman Predicts Florida to Go to GOP," *Jackson Sun*, May 7, 1944.
[59] "S.C. Democrats Would Limit Presidents to Two Terms," *Greenville News*, May 18, 1944; "Barr is Pleased," *Greenville News*, May 18, 1944.
[60] "97,000 in Florida Voted for Byrd," *Miami News*, May 21, 1944.

rump convention of their own which left them temporarily scurrying for a way to place a full slate of 23 Roosevelt electors on the November ballot. "The results of the Texas convention prove conclusively that the Democratic Party is resolved to keep its traditions," exclaimed an obviously elated Barr.[61]

Expanding the Byrd movement to the Midwest, Barr announced in late May that his organization would be opening an office in Chicago to promote the Virginian's candidacy. During a brief stop in the Windy City, he said that Byrd's chances of winning the nomination were improving rapidly. Once again, he also predicted that FDR wouldn't be a candidate for reelection, suggesting that Roosevelt's decision would be based exclusively on political circumstances and not — as many had suggested — health considerations.[62]

Still hoping to persuade the Virginia senator to become an avowed candidate, Barr met with Byrd in Washington a few days later — it was their second meeting that year — but failed to make any headway in convincing the austerity-minded lawmaker to enter the fray. Undeterred, Barr reminded reporters shortly after their meeting that Byrd was still the leading choice of Texas and South Carolina Democrats, and that the electoral votes of those states and elsewhere could be in serious doubt in November if certain conditions weren't met at the Democratic convention in Chicago.[63]

Though admittedly flattered by the attention, the frugal Virginian remained focused on cutting the bloated federal bureaucracy. Keenly aware of the nation's severe labor shortage — a situation exacerbated by the fact that more than 11 million Americans were in uniform and another 288,563 civilian federal employees were working abroad — Byrd was deeply concerned that the number of civil service employees had been growing by leaps and bounds and had reached a staggering 3,305,460 in April, including 47,619 who had been hired during the previous four months. Charging that the federal government was the "chief hoarder of manpower" and that there wasn't a single agency in the federal government that wasn't "grossly overmanned," Byrd called for an immediate reduction of at least 300,000 non-essential civilian federal employees, saving U.S. taxpayers an estimated $700 million annually.

"We have been at war now for a little more than two and a half

---

[61] "Texas Voter Most Puzzled Individual in Party Split," *Lubbock Morning Avalanche*, May 26, 1944.
[62] "Byrd Backers Optimistic on Vote Chances," *Circleville Herald* (Circleville, Ohio), May 29, 1944.
[63] "Uninstructed Delegation is Advocated," *Wilkes-Barre Evening News*, June 2, 1944.

years," Byrd declared in a widely-publicized Senate speech on June 23. "We have mobilized our resources, both in material and manpower, in private employment, but the facts stand out that no real or sincere effort has been made to eliminate useless federal employees so that every unnecessary employee can be transferred to some essential activity and those within the draft age inducted into the armed services." Describing the federal workforce as "the greatest single reservoir of manpower existing," Byrd sharply criticized the Roosevelt's administration's failure to make the necessary reductions. "Why should not the federal government," he asked, "make the same sacrifices in the supervision of its own personnel that our government is requiring of every citizen?"[64]

In the meantime, Barr stepped up his one-man crusade later that weekend. Pointing to recent Democratic developments in Florida, Louisiana, South Carolina and Texas, Barr declared that the New Deal had finally reached "the day of political reckoning with the long-suffering Southland." In a widely-published statement issued from New York, the well-traveled New Orleans manufacturer maintained that Sen. Byrd, as the Democratic nominee, was virtually guaranteed every one of the 124 electoral votes from the Solid South and another 56 in Delaware, Kentucky, Maryland, Missouri, Oklahoma and West Virginia.[65] That same level of support from southern and border states, he said, couldn't be assured if a New Deal proponent — including Roosevelt himself — was nominated in Chicago.[66] Nominating Byrd, he added enthusiastically, would be "the best thing that has happened to our party in twelve years."[67]

Speaking the following day at the Sherman Hotel in Chicago where he quickly established a Byrd-for-President headquarters, Barr reiterated his support for the Virginia senator, saying that several million independents in crucial battleground states outside the South would likely back the Virginian if he was the Democratic nominee. "The day the country at large learns that the Democratic Party is no longer the temporary home of commies, and wild-eyed experimenting pinks, millions of independents will flock to our party," he asserted. Barr, who recently completed a tour of New York, New Jersey and Ohio, told reporters that he was surprised to find that opposition to the New Deal was as prevalent in those

---

[64] "Byrd on Economy," *Poughkeepsie Journal*, June 28, 1944.
[65] "180 Byrd Electoral Votes Sure, Says Barr," *Baltimore Sun*, June 5, 1944.
[66] "124 Votes of South in Doubt, Barr Says," *New York Times*, June 5, 1944.
[67] "South is Balking," *Greenville News*, June 6, 1944.

states as it was in the South.⁶⁸

Following his brief stop in Chicago, Barr raced to Mississippi for that state's Democratic convention a few days later. Accompanied by Kramer, the group's executive secretary, Barr was delighted by the both the outcome and speed of the convention, the party's shortest Democratic state convention in memory. In addition to naming an uninstructed slate of delegates to the national convention and choosing a footloose and free slate of presidential electors, the Mississippians approved four measures instructing the state's 20 delegates to insist on the restoration of the national party's two-thirds rule and to oppose any attempt to place racial equality or abolition of the poll tax in the party's national platform, and to fight any encroachment on states' rights.⁶⁹

Barr, a native of the Magnolia State, had nothing but praise for the rebel Democrats, characterizing their convention as "merely the result of deliberate planning," adding that "the Democrats of Mississippi knew what they wanted and set out to get it the quickest way." Praising the convention's actions as a powerful political expression filled "with courage and hope for an anxious nation," Barr said the smoothly-run and streamlined convention was evidence that Mississippi — one of only three states to cast all of its votes for Byrd at the national convention — was "acutely aware of her responsibilities as a dominant Democratic stronghold, as already indicated in Texas and South Carolina." Barr had also attended both of those state conventions.⁷⁰

A couple of days later Barr huddled with approximately forty other Democratic leaders from six states at a highly secretive conclave in Shreveport, Louisiana, to discuss what steps might be taken to prevent Roosevelt's reelection. While the closed-door meeting was off limits to the press, one participant, speaking on the condition of anonymity, said that representatives from at least a half-dozen states — Louisiana, Florida, Mississippi, South Carolina, Arkansas and Texas — participated in the day-long session.

According to the anonymous source, all of the participants were in agreement that the two-thirds rule on presidential and vice-presidential nominations should be restored at the Democratic national convention in Chicago, and that planks supporting states' rights and opposing social equality should be included in

---

⁶⁸ "Sees New Deal Label Party's Tag of Defeat," *Chicago Tribune*, June 5, 1944.
⁶⁹ "Delegates to National Convention Directed to Vote as Unit, Fight for Restoration of Two-Thirds," *Clarion-Ledger*, June 8, 1944.
⁷⁰ "Byrd Supporter Says Convention 'Planned,'" *Clarion-Ledger*, June 8, 1944.

the party's national platform — none of which was likely to happen. Much of the discussion, said the unidentified spokesman, focused on "the principles of restoring the Democratic Party to its former position and driving out the Communists and New Dealers."

While the group decided against creating a formal organization, the various states represented had been working chiefly toward nominating presidential electors opposed to a fourth term, with the goal of cobbling together a block of approximately 100 southern electors who wouldn't, under any circumstances, support FDR or any other New Deal nominee in the Electoral College. In addition to Barr and Kramer, other prominent participants included ex-Gov. Martin Conner of Mississippi; Eugene B. Germany, a former Texas state party chairman; Mississippi newspaper publisher J. Oliver Emerich, Homer Casteel, a Mississippi public service commissioner; and E. Wayles Browne, a member of the ADNC and vice-chairman of the Louisiana Democratic Party. Given its conspiratorial nature, many of those attending the Shreveport meeting were never publicly identified.[71]

In the meantime, a number of influential southerners found the idea of deliberately fielding Democratic electors who intended to vote against their party's nominee highly troublesome, a misguided strategy that could seriously backfire on the South. To most of them, it was a deeply-flawed way of expressing the region's growing opposition to the New Deal and a fourth term.

Virginius Dabney, the longtime editor of the *Richmond Times-Dispatch*, was one of its most thoughtful critics. In a commencement address at the College of William & Mary that spring, Dabney declared that such a strategy could result in the abolition of the Electoral College. Dabney, an authority on political and economic issues involving the South and a courageous and outspoken leader in southern racial collaboration, told the William & Mary graduates that while it was a generally positive development to see southern states exhibiting their political independence in the days leading up to the Democratic national convention in Chicago, the idea of fielding faithless presidential electors in the general election carried a certain risk that could potentially further weaken the South's once-powerful influence in national politics.

If carried to fruition, asserted the award-winning editor, the threat of a bolt by the Texas and South Carolina electors might be

---

[71] "Southern Anti-4th Term Demos Discuss Plan for Action Here," *Shreveport Times*, June 10, 1944.

the worst thing that could happen to the South. "Suppose, for example, that the election in November is extremely close, and that even though Mr. Roosevelt should carry these two states by substantial margins, the electors from those states were to vote for some other Democrat, and thereby throw the presidency to Mr. Dewey," said Dabney. In that scenario, he continued, "the Electoral College might not survive, and we might come quickly to choosing our president by popular vote." That would be an utter disaster for the southern states, he concluded, particularly since most of those states currently "enjoy far greater influence under the existing electoral arrangement than they would in competition with the heavily populated states under a system of direct elections."

In his address, Dabney also asserted that those advocating a separate electoral strategy clearly weren't acting in "the best southern tradition." Some of their language, he boldly stated, had been "inflammatory and harmful to cordial race relations" and often bordered on demagoguery. "The emphasis in these declarations," he added, "has not been in the right place, irrespective of whether one is for Mr. Roosevelt or against him."[72]

Echoing Dabney's concerns, Dr. Howard P. Johnson, an associate professor of history at Tulane University, also denounced the so-called "rebel bloc." Asserting that such a strategy was typical of the "hate-Roosevelt campaign," Johnson said that the faithless elector proposal championed by southerners adamantly opposed to a fourth term would establish a dangerous precedent, essentially depriving the American people of their right to choose the president of the United States. "By attempting to take advantage of a long dead portion of our written constitution," he said, "the sponsors of such action would now suddenly make members of the Electoral College independent voters, despite the fact that by common agreement since 1796 they have been merely party agents. It is appalling that a proposal so subversive of American democratic practices should ever have been seriously entertained by responsible people."[73]

As the Democratic national convention in Chicago neared, Barr continued to believe in the impossible, insisting that the reluctant Virginian — defying the odds — still had a fighting chance to capture the party's presidential nomination, despite what he described as the "steamrolling" tactics of the president's managers.

---

[72] "Dabney Fears Texas and S.C. Bolt Would Kill Electoral Plan and Hurt Influence of South," *Newport News Daily Press*, June 5, 1944.
[73] "Johnson Scores 'Electoral Revolt,'" *Times-Picayune*, Sep. 6, 1944.

"The events of the past six weeks," he declared with more than a touch bravado in early July, "and the news from Texas, Louisiana, Florida, Mississippi, South Carolina and other southern states, should convince even the most profound skeptics of six months ago that the New Deal has been defeated in the very places where it expected its greatest strength." Hinting that Byrd's supporters had some sort of "secret weapon" they would unveil in Chicago, Barr intimated that if Roosevelt, who still hadn't officially announced his intentions, was to seek a fourth term, "we shall not be caught napping there, and in this regard we must again refrain from writing more with the admonition that "a word to the wise should be sufficient.'"[74]

Ignoring the fact that Roosevelt had already accumulated more than 800 pledged delegates — only 589 were needed — to only three for former Massachusetts Gov. Joseph B. Ely, the president's only declared challenger, and dismissing public opinion polls, including a recent survey by *Fortune* magazine showing the wartime president defeating any likely Republican challenger by more than 17 percentage points, Barr still believed there was a chance Roosevelt wouldn't run, especially if his advisers "ever summon sufficient courage to inform him of the strength and determination of the opposition."[75]

Sounding increasingly shrill as the Democratic convention approached, the New Orleans manufacturer declared that any attempt to nominate Roosevelt for a fourth term would "wreck the Democratic Party west of the Mississippi River." Basing his observation on "concrete evidence" provided by James J. Kramer in his recently-completed tour of the western states, Barr — desperately hoping to worry Roosevelt's self-assured managers — claimed that the wildfire spread by the Draft-Byrd movement in the west proved that the "dissatisfaction of the Democrats does not spring from the South, and makes crystal-clear that the race question is only one of the issues" in the 1944 campaign.

"There is no connection between the New Deal hatreds of the cattle and sheep ranches of the west and cotton planters of the south other than that they both are, and have long been, the victims of constant New Deal bureaucracy, regimentation and stupidity," argued Barr. Democrats in that region, he continued, "admit that

---

[74] John M. Cummings, "Heavy Pressure is on to Renominate Wallace," *Philadelphia Inquirer*, July 7, 1944.
[75] "Administration Opponents May Set Off Convention Fireworks," *Palladium-Item*, July 7, 1944; "Don't Tell Mr. Barr," *Nashville Tennessean*, June 24, 1944.

only a Democrat of Senator Byrd's caliber can save the party in California, Washington, Oregon, Montana, Idaho and Utah" — six states Roosevelt carried against Willkie four years earlier. "Bitter strife among the Democrats of New Mexico" — another western state that went for Roosevelt in 1940 — made that state "even more doubtful," he added. He also hinted that there would be a post-convention caucus of southern and western Democrats to "protect the future interests of these geographic minorities."[76]

Barr's scare tactic, of course, was later rendered moot when FDR swept all seven states that autumn, albeit winning each of them by smaller margins than in 1940.

Huddling with the Mississippi delegation as delegates were still arriving in Chicago by the trainload, Barr applauded vigorously when former Gov. Conner, in a particularly fiery speech, urged his state's delegates "to stand up and fight" for their principles. Barr couldn't have been happier when the delegation voted moments later to enforce the unit rule, assuring Byrd of all twenty of the state's votes on the first ballot.

"The action of the Mississippi delegation is a clear indication of what the genuine Democrats of our country want," Barr said excitedly, adding that, "if all of the delegates to the convention were as free as the Mississippi delegation to follow the dictates of their conscience — their desire for the best interests of the party and the nation — Senator Byrd would be the Democratic nominee on the first ballot." The action of the Mississippi delegation, he continued, "should put the captors of our convention on notice to the effect that the 180 electoral votes of the southern and border states no longer intend to be bossed and kicked around by some 400,000 New York Communists."[77]

While all eyes were riveted on the seething suspense surrounding the party's vice-presidential nomination, Barr — focused almost exclusively on the presidential balloting, but more than willing to exploit the looming vice-presidential contest to further Byrd's nascent candidacy — spent most of his time during the closely-watched convention visiting as many southern delegations as possible while buttonholing individual delegates from other parts of the country in hotel corridors and on the convention floor.

Hoping to foment a last-minute southern revolt, the New Orleans businessman reminded virtually everyone he spoke with that there was a rumor circulating that the CIO and northern big city bosses would veto any southern vice-presidential possibility

---

[76] "Sees End for Demos if FDR is Nominated," *Shreveport Times*, July 10, 1944.
[77] "State Delegates to Vote for Byrd," *Clarion-Ledger*, July 18, 1944.

— a rumor given more than a little credibility by news reports that Roosevelt had convinced former senator and ex-Supreme Court Justice James F. Byrnes of South Carolina, director of the Office of War Mobilization who had been eagerly seeking the nomination, to withdraw from the crowded race for the party's second spot. At the time of his withdrawal, the party's bitterly contested vice-presidential free-for-all featured not only Vice President Henry A. Wallace — the lanky, tousle-haired incumbent abandoned by FDR yet determined to fight to the finish — and Missouri Sen. Harry S. Truman, but also at least eight favorite-son candidates, five of whom hailed from southern and border states.[78] Roosevelt believed that Byrnes was probably the most qualified person for the job, but was deeply concerned about his outspoken racial views.[79]

It was a rumor Barr was more than happy to spread. "I have heard it said that orders were issued that no one south of the Mason and Dixon line should be considered for the vice-presidency," he told anybody within earshot. Byrnes's abrupt withdrawal from the vice-presidential race had irked countless southern Democrats already troubled by the growing influence of CIO leaders Sidney Hillman and Philip Murray in the party's national councils. Now some of them were furious — and Barr exploited that anger for all it was worth. Cheered by reports that the "Dixie revolt" had spread to five more southern delegations, Barr was now telling reporters that Sen. Byrd would receive more than 125 votes on the first ballot — an increase from the somewhat more modest 100 votes that he had predicted a day earlier.[80]

Buoyed by the news that former DNC chairman James A. Farley intended to cast his half-vote in the New York delegation for the Virginia senator and that at least one prominent West Virginia delegate intended to break from his state's solidly pro-Roosevelt delegation to support his longtime friend from the Old Dominion, Barr was thrilled when Ruth Nooney of Jacksonville, Florida, agreed to place Byrd's name in nomination, describing the 53-year-old mother of three — two of whom were serving in the armed forces — as "one of the earliest workers in the state of Florida who

---

[78] "F.D.R. is Willing to Take Truman; Byrnes Gives Up," *St. Louis Post-Dispatch*, July 19, 1944; "Sharp Race Looms for Second Place," *New York Times*, July 20, 1944. Favorite-son candidates from the southern and border states included J. Melville Broughton, the governor of North Carolina, Tennessee Gov. Prentice Cooper, Sen. John H. Bankhead of Alabama, Senate Majority Leader Alben W. Barkley of Kentucky, and House Speaker Sam Rayburn of Texas.
[79] Leuchtenburg, *The White House Looks South*, p. 136.
[80] "Spread of Southern Revolt into Five More States is Threatened," *Circleville Herald*, July 20, 1944.

dedicated their efforts toward freeing the state and the nation from the shackles of the alien-controlled New Deal bureaucracy."[81]

One of the four Floridians pledged to the reluctant Virginian, the little-known Nooney had polished off her rivals in Florida's May 3 Democratic primary, polling an eye-opening 19,149 votes in the state's second congressional district — some 1,477 votes more than the top Roosevelt delegate in that district.[82] Though portrayed as a political novice in newspaper accounts describing her nominating speech, Nooney actually had a long record of civic and political involvement. Among other things, she founded the parent-teacher association in Duval County and served as its first president. A close political ally of state Sen. Edgar W. Waybright, a prominent Jacksonville attorney, she had also been a delegate to the 1928 Democratic national convention in Houston, where she opposed New York Gov. Al Smith's nomination, largely over the issues of prohibition and immigration. Stressing Tammany Hall's "contempt for the South," Nooney actively campaigned for Republican Herbert Hoover later that autumn.[83]

The soft-spoken southerner remained active in Democratic politics for years following her 1944 moment in the limelight, attending the 1948 Democratic national convention at Philadelphia's Convention Hall as a delegate initially pledged to Mississippi Gov. Fielding L. Wright, Dixiecrat Strom Thurmond's vice-presidential running mate later that fall — a ticket Nooney actively supported.[84] She was a delegate again in 1952, supporting Sen. Richard B. Russell of Georgia in his uphill quest for the party's presidential nomination against eventual nominee Adlai Stevenson, the sagacious and witty governor of Illinois, and liberal populist Sen. Estes Kefauver of Tennessee.[85] In late 1955, Nooney was named to the advisory committee of the recently-formed Federation for Constitutional Government, which was chaired by Barr. She was the only Floridian who served on the confederation's original advisory committee.[86]

In any case, Nooney, who was born and raised in Alexandria, Virginia, was startled when Barr asked her in the wee morning hours prior to the presidential balloting to make Byrd's nominating speech. "I turned white as a sheet, they tell me," said Nooney.

---

[81] "Will Nominate Byrd," *Sandusky Register*, July 20, 1944.
[82] "Official Vote Tables Uphold Early Count," *Miami News*, Apr. 12, 1944.
[83] "Women Delegates Seek Party Vote for Hoover," *Orlando Evening Reporter-Star*, Oct. 30, 1928.
[84] "Wright Entries Leading in State Delegate Races," *Fort Myers News-Press*, May 9, 1948.
[85] "Florida Split on Candidates," *Miami News*, July 21, 1952.
[86] "Dixie Mix Foes Form New States Rights Group," *Orlando Sentinel*, Oct. 24, 1955.

"It was such a surprise," she added, "I didn't have time to get my breath." While many women had given seconding speeches in previous conventions, in presenting Byrd's name to the convention Nooney became the first woman in history to place a presidential candidate in nomination at a major-party convention, according to news reports at the time. "I am first against Roosevelt, and then I am for Senator Byrd," she said later. In fact, Nooney had never met the Virginia senator until a few moments after placing his name in nomination.[87]

In placing Byrd's name in nomination, Nooney was lustily jeered by Roosevelt's supporters, prompting the convention chairman to bang his gavel repeatedly while shouting that there wasn't a Democrat alive entitled to that sort of unwelcoming and hostile response. "We will have no more of that," he authoritatively thundered. Continuing in her soft southern accent while cheered by the placard-waving Louisiana, Mississippi, Texas and Virginia delegations, the low-key Jacksonville native — making it clear that she was speaking without Byrd's consent or knowledge — described the Virginian as "a great lawmaker, farmer and businessman," "an outstanding governor," and a man with the "courage of his convictions" who was fully capable of handling the difficult issues of the presidency. Former Gov. Dan Moody of Texas seconded Byrd's nomination.[88]

The anti-fourth term resistance was short-lived. Moments later Roosevelt was nominated, garnering 1,086 votes to Byrd's 89. The southern rebellion had failed — and failed miserably.

Though deeply disappointed, Barr quickly made it clear that he had just begun to fight. He was still determined to deny FDR a fourth term and remove the New Dealers from Washington. While refusing to comment on Byrd's relatively meager showing in Chicago, Barr told reporters that he intended to keep his organization intact to assist in the formation of a third-party ticket.

Barr, who liked to describe the draft Byrd movement as having "started from scratch by a group of amateurs riding from Baton Rouge to New Orleans," also renewed his threat of fielding anti-administration electors in as many southern states as possible with the hope that dissident Democratic electors might wield the balance of power in the Electoral College. Barr, moreover, believed there was a distinct possibility that such a strategy could throw the election into the House of Representatives in the event of a closer-

---

[87] "Pepper Continues Fight for Wallace," *Miami News*, July 21, 1944; "Floridian Nominates Senator Byrd," *Richmond Times-Dispatch*, July 21, 1944.
[88] "Roosevelt Nominated for Fourth Term by Democrats," *Baltimore Sun*, July 21, 1944.

than-expected contest between Roosevelt and Dewey.

"The events of the next thirty days may develop the fighting names and slogans under which we will wage our battle," Barr said in a statement issued from Washington in late July, about a week after the Chicago convention. Noting that Mississippi and Texas had already freed their electors to vote for a Democrat other than the party's nominee and that similar steps were reportedly being taken in several other southern states, including Alabama and Louisiana, the New Orleans industrialist declared that "there will be a genuine Democratic ticket for the Electoral College." In his statement, Barr didn't indicate whether Byrd would be the movement's standard-bearer.[89]

In the meantime, Barr and his cohorts spent the next several weeks studying various ballot access laws throughout the South while seriously entertaining the idea of mounting write-in campaigns for electors where feasible. They also collaborated with likeminded anti-Roosevelt leaders throughout the region during this period, including former Texas Gov. Dan Moody, ex-governor Mike Conner of Mississippi, and John K. Breedin, founder of the Southern Democratic Party in South Carolina. Barr was also in close consultation with Sam Jones, the former governor of Louisiana.[90]

While keeping its headquarters in the same suite of the St. Charles Hotel in New Orleans, Barr renamed the Draft-Byrd-for-President organization in mid-August.[91] "There is much that still must be done in our effort to restore and perpetuate constitutional government," he said in announcing the organizational change.[92]

Rechristened as the Constitutional Democracy Crusaders, a kind of clearinghouse for like-minded individuals and organizations, Barr told a luncheon testimonial given in his honor by New Orleans business leaders that the group's work for the restoration and preservation of constitutional government would continue with renewed vigor. "One of our main objectives," he asserted, "will be to do everything within our power and means to destroy the political dictatorship of Messrs. Hillman, Browder and Dubinsky, and restore to the Democratic Party its traditional complete independence." One of the organization's first tasks, he said, was to guarantee "that the will of the people is fully and freely expressed

---

[89] "Byrd Backers Plan to Assist 3d-Party Birth," *Louisville Courier-Journal*, July 28, 1944.
[90] "Expect 'Solid South' to 'Go Down Line' in November," *Charleston News and Courier*, Aug. 6, 1944.
[91] "Constitutional Democracy," *Times-Picayune*, Aug. 20, 1944.
[92] "Workers for Byrd Plan to Continue Organization," *Morning Advocate* (Baton Rouge, LA), Aug. 16, 1944.

in the forthcoming November elections."[93]

Things didn't go quite as swimmingly that autumn as Barr and other dissident southern Democrats had originally anticipated. Many of the region's most fiercely anti-administration Democrats simply threw in the towel following the Democratic national convention in Chicago. That was clearly the case with Mobile attorney Sam M. Johnston, who angrily resigned as an Alabama Democratic elector in early September rather than support the party's nominees. In resigning, Johnston scornfully denounced the national party as some sort of mythical beast "devouring with a carnivorous appetite its own flesh and blood, its mother whose body gave it birth and at whose breasts it was nurtured for more than a century — the Southland."[94]

Several other Democratic electors in the South, some of whom were almost anxious to assume the role of "faithless elector" by voting against the Roosevelt-Truman ticket in the Electoral College, simply never got the chance.

In Louisiana, a hotbed of New Deal resentment, five of the state's ten Democratic electors resigned in late September rather than sign a pledge, demanded by the party's state committee, that they would support the Roosevelt-Truman ticket.[95] Three other electors opposed to Roosevelt refused to sign the pledge, but were removed and replaced by the state committee on October 7.[96] The three dissident electors, which included the widely-respected and influential E. Wayles Browne, an at-large elector from Shreveport, Bronier Thibaut of Donaldsonville, and George L. Billeaud of Broussard — subsequently appealed to the courts contending that the Democratic state committee had no right to make any changes to the ballot after the state's statutory October 3 filing deadline, but were denied relief.[97]

A member of the American Democratic National Committee and vice chairman of the Louisiana State Democratic Committee, the 64-year-old Browne had proposed in early September that Louisiana's ten electors should be allowed to act as "free agents," guided by their own conscience — a proposal reportedly favored by at least five of the Democratic electors. There was plenty of dis-

---

[93] "Byrd Backers to Continue Campaigns," *Shreveport Times*, Aug. 16, 1944.
[94] "Mobile Attorney Quits as Elector," *Anniston Star* (Anniston, AL), Sep. 3, 1944. Leuchtenburg, *The White House Looks South*, p. 136.
[95] "5 Electors in Louisiana Quit," *Monroe News-Star* (Monroe, LA), Sep. 28, 1944.
[96] "Seven New Electors on Revised List," *Shreveport Times*, Oct. 8, 1944.
[97] "Court Turns Down Appeal on Electors," *Shreveport Times*, Oct. 15, 1944; "Court of Appeals Upholds Ouster of Rebel Electors," *Weekly Town Talk* (Alexandria, LA), Oct. 21, 1944.

cussion surrounding the Shreveport attorney's controversial proposal and, at one point, there was even talk of a potential Byrd-Truman compromise ticket. Complicating matters even further, there was also some speculation that the Republicans might include some of the state's ten Democratic electors who agreed to bolt on their own electoral slate. Browne's proposal naturally alarmed nervous administration supporters, who acted quickly to quell the incipient rebellion before it spread to other southern states.[98]

Needless to say, Barr was outraged by the unexpected developments in Louisiana, arguably the most serious blow to his fantasy of thwarting Roosevelt's bid for a fourth term in the Electoral College. Denouncing the actions of the state committee in demanding a loyalty pledge from the party's duly nominated electors, Barr charged that state committee members had been intimidated by "a combination of the old Long machine with the newly-elected state administration, pressured by the New Deal."

Describing it as "the third Louisiana Purchase," Barr angrily contended that the state committee's actions was the "equivalent to an open letter to Mr. Sidney Hillman and his fellow travelers, notifying these enemies of the South that that they can insult us, cure and vilify us — but that we like it, and that we will take it, and continue to bend our knees, bare our backs, and ask for more."[99]

There were thousands of Louisianans who had never wavered in their faith and loyalty to the Democratic Party, asserted Barr, who maintained that his organization would do everything in its power to give Louisiana Democrats an opportunity to vote for free and independent Democratic electors in November. "They want to vote for a Democrat — they devoutly want a Democratic administration — but if they are forced to vote the Republican ticket to voice their protest, the combination of pressure politics that caused free and independent electors to resign can thank themselves for the defection."[100]

The unforeseen setback in his home state of Louisiana, where eight of the Democratic Party's ten original electors might reasonably have been expected to vote for Senator Byrd or possibly another anti-New Deal Democrat, had a sobering effect on the man who did everything in his power that year to prevent FDR's fourth term. Barr grew noticeably quieter as the election neared. Though

---

[98] "Fourth Term Bolt by La. Electors Being Talked," *Shreveport Times*, Sep. 10, 1944.
[99] "New Deal, Long Machine Dominate Central Committee, Asserts Barr," *Alexandria Daily Town Talk*, Sep. 29, 1944.
[100] "Sees New Deal Pressure in La. Committee Action," *Shreveport Times*, Sep. 29, 1944.

he continued to issue anti-Roosevelt missives from his headquarters in New Orleans during the final weeks of the campaign, some more scurrilous than others, Barr realized that his efforts that year had largely been in vain and, more importantly, that the battle had been lost.

Chapter XXI

♦

A Minor Southern Revolt

With John U. Barr's unwavering support and encouragement, Gov. Dixon's warning of a southern revolt in 1944 eventually came to fruition, albeit in a much, much more limited way than the saber-rattling Alabama governor and other southern Democratic leaders originally envisioned.

The movement's most significant activity took place in the Lone Star State where the heavily-bankrolled Texas Regulars, a group of conservative Democrats opposed to FDR and the New Deal, nearly kept the Roosevelt-Truman ticket out of the Democratic column while later placing a slate of anti-Roosevelt electors on the state's November ballot.

Hoping to prevent Roosevelt's fourth term, similar schemes took place in a couple of other states in the Solid South that autumn, most notably in Georgia and South Carolina, where the bolters enjoyed the tacit support of former Georgia Gov. Eugene Talmadge and colorful lame-duck Senator Ellison D. "Cotton Ed" Smith of South Carolina, respectively.

Talmadge, who hated Roosevelt with a passion and had seriously entertained the idea of challenging him on a "Grassroots" third-party ticket in 1936, was still an immensely popular figure in Peach State politics while Smith, the 80-year-old chairman of the Senate Agricultural Committee who blamed his recent primary defeat on his longstanding opposition to the New Deal, still had a relatively large following in South Carolina, especially among the state's struggling farmers.

A bitter critic of the New Deal who spent his entire congressional career trying to "keep the Niggers down and the price of cotton up," Smith had been pummeled in his bid for a seventh term a few months earlier, losing by more than 50,000 votes to a pro-Roosevelt New Dealer in the state's July 25th Democratic primary — a loss he blamed directly on FDR, who had openly supported his challenger, Olin D. Johnston, in 1938 and again in 1944.

An unapologetic champion of states' rights and white supremacy who routinely railed against the country's anti-lynching laws, Smith was one of the Roosevelt administration's harshest critics. "I served under five Presidents," he snarled, "before I had to run into an outfit like this, challenging the sovereignty of the states and violating the constitution at every step."[1]

Smith, who had been targeted in FDR's largely unsuccessful purge in 1938 before finally being unseated six years later, was looking to exact revenge on the man he held responsible for his defeat and in late September — two months after losing his bid for re-nomination — organized a National Agricultural Committee to rally the nation's farmers against Roosevelt. Smith, who helped organize the Farmer's Protective Association in 1901 and later emerged as one of the leading figures in the Southern Cotton Association, had long considered himself the voice of America's agricultural interests. Adopting the slogan "Farmers for Freedom," Smith's hastily-organized group planned to hold mass meetings in rural communities across the country, urging farmers to turn out in large numbers to defeat Roosevelt on Nov. 7th.[2]

Insisting that he was trying to resuscitate the old Democratic Party rather than organize a new party — the kind of anti-New Deal third-party that ex-Gov. Woodring spoke about in his 1942 speech in Topeka — the octogenarian told a two-day founding session in Washington that the American farmer had been held in bondage to the New Deal for a dozen years. "It is time to break the shackles," he thundered. The nation's farmers, he continued, had been needlessly subjected to price controls by the Office of Price Administration (OPA), an agency established through executive order just prior to U.S. entry in World War II, "and other forms of bureaucratic red tape." Those who worked the land, said Smith, weren't really free. "This committee proposes to gain economic

---

[1] "Cotton Ed Smith, Dean of Senate, Hates New Deal so Much it Hurts," *The Gallup Independent*, Feb. 16, 1940.
[2] "Cotton Ed Smith Forms Farm Fight Against Roosevelt," *Dallas Morning News*, Sep. 23, 1944.

freedom for the farmer."³

Though fewer than a dozen Roosevelt foes attended the opening session, participants who sat in on at least part of the two-day meeting included Washington lobbyist Ralph Moore, a former longtime leader of the Texas Grange who served as the group's secretary, Robert E. O'Brian of Des Moines, a former Iowa Secretary of State and a key member of Woodring's American Democratic National Committee (ADNC), and South Carolina's John K. Breedin, chairman of the Southern Democratic Party who was later instrumental in placing a slate of eight presidential electors favoring Harry F. Byrd on the ballot in the Palmetto State — a rogue electoral slate that actually outpolled the Dewey-Bricker ticket in that solidly-Democratic state.[4]

An avowed critic of the president for nearly a decade, the aging South Carolina senator — a quintessential product of the Old South — told newsmen that the people of the Palmetto State had actually done him the "greatest favor" imaginable by rejecting him in the state's July primary, "because I'm free now to do as I damn please. I'm going to do everything I can to redeem the people of my state."[5]

Believing that the South had been "ignored and insulted" at the Democratic national convention in Chicago, Smith announced in August that he intended to support the eight anti-Roosevelt presidential electors nominated by the state's newly-organized Southern Democratic Party. Praising the renegade electoral ticket for having "the guts and brains and courage" to oppose FDR's fourth term, Smith criticized those in the Democratic Party who were afraid to oppose the president. "What in the name of God Almighty is the matter with people that they are afraid of themselves, afraid to take a stand for what they know is right?" he asked. "I have stood for constitutional government, the original movement, all my life and I am not going to quit now," continued Smith, who died shortly after the election. "I will vote my convictions for what I think is best for my country and for my state."[6]

While Smith, the state's senior senator, publicly supported the Southern Democratic Party's pro-Byrd presidential electors that autumn, John Breedin was the real mover and shaker in the incipient anti-Roosevelt third-party rebellion in South Carolina.

---

[3] Ibid.
[4] Ibid.
[5] "Less Than One Dozen Antis Answer Cotton Ed's Call," *Charleston Evening Post*, Sep. 22, 1944.
[6] "Cotton Ed to Support Southern Democratic Party's Electors," *Charleston News and Courier*, Aug. 22, 1944.

A Manning attorney, economist, newspaper columnist and founder of Anderson College, the little-remembered South Carolinian had been a leader in the state's austerity-minded Farmers and Taxpayers League, an organization comprised largely of white farmers and Low Country planters which had been particularly influential during the Great Depression. The state's politicians ignored the league during that period only at their own peril.[7] Not surprisingly, the 58-year-old Breedin was also a member of the stridently anti-Roosevelt American Democratic National Committee.

A lifelong Baptist who once taught military history at The Citadel and somewhat incongruously spent ten years in South America serving as the educational director for the Pontifical Catholic University in Lima, Peru, Breedin founded the Southern Democratic Party in late March 1944, specifically to oppose Roosevelt's fourth term. The idea of a Southern Democratic Party, not unlike the Southern Democratic movement that supported John C. Breckinridge in the four-cornered 1860 presidential election, had been circulating throughout the South since the previous autumn when North Carolina Sen. Josiah Bailey, admonishing the administration during the debate over the soldier vote legislation, threatened such a movement. "We can form a Southern Democratic Party and vote as we please in the Electoral College," he boldly stated, "and we will hold the balance of power in this country."[8] The South Carolinian was trying to make Bailey's threat a reality.

Charging that FDR was "willing to inflame the white people of the South" in exchange for the support of African-Americans in the North, Breedin wasn't the least bit subtle about his new party and the constituency it hoped to represent. "Our party is a white man's party," he told reporters shortly after the party's founding. "We do not mean to deceive the Negroes and we shall not betray the white people."[9] As such, the Manning lawyer was thrilled to have Smith's support in his anti-Roosevelt crusade, describing the virulently racist six-term senator as the "last apostle of the old line democracy in the South."[10]

Like John U. Barr of the fledgling draft Byrd movement and the ADNC's Harry Woodring, Breedin announced that he would be making his own tour of the South later that summer to gauge the strength of opposition to Roosevelt among anti-New Dealers in

---

[7] Bryant Simon, *A Fabric of Defeat: The Politics of South Carolina Millhands, 1910-1948* (Chapel Hill, 1998), pp. 75-76.
[8] Kennedy, *Southern Exposure*, p. 131.
[9] "Breedin is Head New S.C. Party," *Greenville News* (Greenville, S.C.), Apr. 4, 1944.
[10] "Smith's Call Brings Less Than Dozen," *Gaffney Ledger* (Gaffney, S.C.), Sep. 28, 1944.

that region. "The spoon-fed, office holding New Dealers are a numerous clan, fighting desperately for their jobs, favors and the little, brief authority of public position, but the unofficial masses are disgusted with a government buying power with public money," he said in a brief statement announcing his southern tour.[11]

Breedin also attended the Democratic national convention in Chicago and was one of four South Carolinians who took part in an anti-fourth term caucus on the eve of the convention, telling delegates from Louisiana, Mississippi, Texas and elsewhere that his group planned to place a slate of electors on the ballot in South Carolina favoring another Democrat in the event of Roosevelt's nomination. Acknowledging that it might be difficult in getting the names of anti-Roosevelt electors on the ballot in some states, Breedin encouraged the assembled delegates to explore the possibility of doing the same thing in their respective states. "Under South Carolina law," he said, "any party or group may propose a ticket for the general election. This may not be the case in some states."[12]

True to his word, Breedin's insurgent, race-tinged party named its eight presidential electors a few months later. It was a fairly impressive slate consisting of at least one highly successful industrialist, a couple of newspaper editors, a Baptist minister, a founder of the National Cotton Council of America, a former state representative, a physician, and the wife of a small cotton farmer who had four sons in the military. They were all lifelong Democrats.[13]

South Carolina voters were fascinated to learn that T. Yancey Williams, a former state legislator, and retired Greenville farmer Jesse S. Plowden — two of the party's electors — rode with the infamous Red Shirts, a white supremacist paramilitary group that often resorted to violence while trying to intimidate black and white voters alike into supporting Democratic candidates and restoring white Democrats to power during the final years of Reconstruction. Plowden was only fourteen years old when he participated in an 1876 Red Shirts ride on behalf of Democratic gubernatorial candidate Wade Hampton, a fierce foe of radical Reconstruction and the first southern governor to be inaugurated in opposition to its policies. During the 1944 campaign, the 82-year old Plowden said that he still kept his red shirt hanging in a closet,

---

[11] "Breedin Plans Tour of Southern States," *Charleston Evening Post*, July 11, 1944.
[12] "4 South Carolinians Attend Anti-fourth Term Caucus," *Charleston Evening Post*, July 19, 1944.
[13] "Anti-New Deal Party Selects Eight Electors," *The State* (Columbia, S.C.), Sep. 14, 1944.

ready for an emergency.¹⁴

Arguing that the nomination of anti-Roosevelt electors in South Carolina wasn't "merely a formal and useless gesture," Breedin maintained that his party's eight electors, coupled with similar Democratic defections in Texas, Louisiana, Mississippi and Virginia, could result in a southern bloc of anti-fourth term electors holding the balance of power in the Electoral College, thereby throwing the election into the House of Representatives. "With each state having one vote in the House," he told a Kiwanis club meeting in Charleston that summer, "the New Deal Democrats might come with us to save their chairmanships, and the Republicans might side with us to keep the New Dealers out of power." Anything was possible in that scenario, he said.

For all intents and purposes, continued the articulate South Carolinian, the Democratic national convention in Chicago "had no legal effect on the election" for the men and women who will cast the truly important ballots for president — the presidential electors — were yet to be determined. "As a matter of law, all the double-dealing, hocus-pocus and flimflamming of the Chicago convention may amount to nothing at all, for the men who will cast the ballot for the president are yet to be elected," he asserted, adding that while Democratic electors might have a certain moral obligation to support their party's presidential and vice-presidential nominees, there was no legal or constitutional framework compelling them to do so.¹⁵

Returning to that theme frequently during the autumn campaign, the former history professor insisted that the election of either Roosevelt or Dewey was far from a foregone conclusion. "Read your history and refresh your memory," he told a radio audience in Columbia in late October, reminding his listeners that five men vied for the presidency in 1824 — John C. Calhoun, Andrew Jackson, John Quincy Adams, William H. Crawford and Henry Clay — but the U.S. House of Representatives chose Adams for president despite the fact that Jackson had received a plurality of the popular vote.¹⁶ It was entirely possible, he said on another occasion, that neither Roosevelt nor Dewey would have the necessary 266 electoral votes to win the election. "If we Americans are willing to sacrifice the principles, in order to be on the winning

---

¹⁴ "Southern Democratic Elector," *Charleston News and Courier*, Oct. 3, 1944.
¹⁵ "Breedin Asserts South May Gain Balance of Power," *Charleston News and Courier*, Aug. 11, 1944;
¹⁶ "Breedin Urges Vote for His Electors," *Charleston Evening Post*, Oct. 24, 1944.

side, we are really sacrificing our nation itself."[17]

Arguing that it took "more courage, more real manhood, more vision and statesmanship to stand alone in a righteous cause than to swallow one's pride and conscience" while standing in a line for a political handout, Breedin went on the offensive against those in the Democratic Party who desperately clung to party loyalty while denouncing the Southern Democrats. "There are still great Roosevelt projects for those who bow the knee to Baal," he said sardonically, "but the history of America, the history of England, the history of human freedom rebuke the time-servers, the pottage-eaters, the favor-seekers — and tell in glowing terms of those who dared to defy the king and all his favors and power."[18]

Though deeply disappointed that he wasn't able to persuade Sen. Pappy O'Daniel of Texas to actively stump in South Carolina, Breedin did most of his party's heavy lifting that autumn, actively campaigning for his party's electoral ticket while railing repeatedly against the "easy money men" supporting the president's fourth-term candidacy. Those who had profited handsomely from the war, he declared, were strongly supporting Roosevelt. "What I have observed," he stated in a radio address, "is that people who have accumulated anything through years of hard work, through thrift, are not for Mr. Roosevelt. They have learned the value of a dollar, they have learned self-discipline; they are not wildcat speculators nor overnight capitalists making great fortunes out of the use of government money and government plants."[19]

The only thing holding the regular Democrats in line for the Roosevelt-Truman ticket, he asserted in another radio appearance, was "the Roosevelt policy of spending, of favors, of contracts." Describing the national Democratic Party as the "spiritual descendant" of the children of Israel crying for the fleshpots of Egypt, the fiscally conservative lawyer said that FDR's New Deal had "neither principle nor tradition, nor anything, but the free-spending of the people's tax money; the riding high and wide and handsome of those nearest the public treasury."[20]

Criticizing the president for failing to adequately prepare the nation for war, it wasn't surprising that Breedin also personally

---

[17] "Breedin Says Stalin Takes Land, Lets Roosevelt Talk," *Charleston News and Courier*, Nov. 3, 1944.
[18] "Breedin Lauds Byrd Followers," *Greenville News*, Nov. 3, 1944.
[19] "Anti-New Dealer Will Be Invited to Speak in S.C.," *The State*, Sept. 22, 1944; "'Easy Money Men' Want Fourth Term, Breedin Asserts," *Index-Journal* (Greenwood, S.C.), Oct. 17, 1944.
[20] "Breedin's Party Supporting Byrd for President," *Charleston Evening Post*, Oct. 10, 1944.

blamed Roosevelt for the devastating sneak attack on Pearl Harbor. "It is a matter of established record that Mr. Churchill urged Mr. Roosevelt to take the Japanese in hand, but Mr. Roosevelt told Mr. Churchill that he could baby the Japanese along for a while," he asserted in a radio address on WCSC in Charleston. "That was his expression: he could baby the Japanese along. Well, he babied them along and that baby hurled the foulest indignity against us ever suffered by the United States."

The rebellious Democrat also promoted the reluctant Byrd at every opportunity, telling his audiences that the frugal Virginian, as a former governor and current member of the U.S. Senate, was uniquely qualified for the presidency:

> Senator Byrd is a native of Virginia, a Southerner to the marrow; a man who has risen in the world through his hard work and ability. He is said to be the most extensive apple grower in the world. As governor of Virginia, he established a record for administrative efficiency which still compels the admiration of the nation. He brought to the office of the governor those qualities which made him a success in his business and enabled him to reorganize the government of Virginia from the kind of slap-dash and haphazard sort of government that we have in South Carolina into an organization that was compact, efficient, and economical. If there is anything in the world needed by America at this day, it is exactly the sort of thing Mr. Byrd did in Virginia to be applied to our national government.[21]

While hoping for a stronger showing that autumn, Breedin was nevertheless pleased that his upstart party, polling 7,799 votes in the presidential race, had finished ahead of the state's dormant Republican Party, which polled a combined 4,610 votes for Dewey, including a miniscule 63 votes cast for the GOP nominee by the tiny "Tieless Joe" Tolbert faction.[22] Claiming that South Carolina needed "a vigilant political organization" that was both "alert and aggressive," Breedin announced immediately after the election that the Southern Democratic Party would remain a permanent organization in the state for the foreseeable future.[23]

---

[21] "Breedin Says Stalin Takes Land, Lets Roosevelt Talk," *Charleston News and Courier*, Nov. 3, 1944.

[22] Until displaced in 1938, Tolbert had been a prominent leader of the Republican Party in South Carolina dating back to William Howard Taft's presidency. The white leader of the party's Black & Tan faction, the longtime national committeeman — a rather disheveled-looking guy who never wore a necktie — was once regarded as one of the most powerful Republican patronage brokers in the South.

[23] "Breedin Claims His 'Party' Will Continue Active," *Gaffney Ledger* (Gaffney, S.C.), Sep. 11,

While the anti-Roosevelt Democrats in South Carolina ran a slate of presidential electors pledged to Virginia's Harry F. Byrd, the Independent Democrats of Georgia, a group that had vigorously opposed FDR's bid for a third term in 1940, also placed a slate of unpledged presidential electors opposed to Roosevelt's reelection on the November ballot.

Vowing to spend a considerable amount of money, the independent Democratic slate in Georgia was identical to the state's Republican list of electors headed by Clint Hager, a former GOP state chairman, and Wadley Mayor R. G. Foster — both representing an all-white faction of the Republican Party that had been denied recognition by the GOP national convention and the RNC. Certified by the Secretary of State, the twin electoral slates consisted of the same six Democrats and six Republicans. "We divided our ticket between Republicans and Democrats because there are a lot of good Democrats who have told us they would join us if they could, and this will give them a chance," explained Foster, who said that he was personally supporting Dewey. "If we win," he added, "each elector will decide for himself who he wants for president."[24]

Strongly opposed to FDR's bid for a third time, Georgia's Independent Democrats had been involved in the same sort of mischief in 1940 when they placed an electoral ticket consisting of six anti-Roosevelt Democrats and six Republicans pledged to Wendell L. Willkie on the state's November ballot — a slate of electors subsequently approved and duplicated by the state's miniscule Republican organization.[25]

Declaring that "we have not left the old Democratic Party — it left us," the Independent Democrats of Georgia held a convention at Macon's Dempsey Hotel in early October of that year to adopt a platform and ratify a list of presidential electors.[26] In addition to naming their own electors and adopting a platform castigating the New Deal, the Independent Democrats — while praising Willkie — sharply criticized the state's regular Democratic organization for "surrendering to the control of one man." They also pledged their support to the entire regular Democratic statewide ticket — 77 candidates in all, including all ten of the party's congressional

---
1944.
[24] "Anti-Roosevelt Slate in Georgia; Foes Form Coalition Ticket for Dissatisfied Democrats," *Trenton Evening Times*, Aug. 11, 1944.
[25] "Independent Democrats Convene in Georgia," *Washington Evening Star*, Oct. 6, 1940; "Georgia Backers of Willkie Weld Election Front," *State-Times Advocate*, Oct. 9, 1940.
[26] "Willkie Men Will Confer Here Today; Independents Plan Additional Assault Against Third Term," *Macon Telegraph*, Oct. 3, 1940.

nominees.[27] Many of those nominated by the independents later withdrew, preferring to be listed on the ballot only as the regular Democratic nominees.[28]

Interestingly, the 1940 Macon convention, which attracted 274 delegates, was chaired by Perry attorney Sam A. Nunn, the father and namesake of former Sen. Sam Nunn, a cerebral yet hawkish centrist lawmaker who later represented the state in the U.S. Senate from 1972-96. Like other leaders of the nascent party, the elder Nunn believed that many of the state's citizens simply couldn't bring themselves to vote for a Republican ticket — something they obviously have no problem doing three-quarters of a century later — but were more likely to support Willkie and his running-mate if their names appeared on an independent Democratic line.[29]

Though all but seven of the 77 Democrats nominated in Macon eventually removed their names as Independent Democratic nominees, the new party was nevertheless given its own column on the general election ballot along with the Democratic, Republican and Prohibition parties.[30]

Unlike the vast majority of those running on the state's regular Democratic ticket, Talmadge — a colorful politician prone to histrionics yet arguably the most dynamic force in Georgia politics since the late Populist Thomas E. Watson — proudly kept his name on the ballot as the party's nominee that fall, a fact that delighted the self-styled Independent Democrats. The Wild Man of Sugar Creek refused to budge. Though he had publicly declared that he intended to support the national Democratic ticket, his heart was clearly with the anti-Roosevelt forces. The Independent Democrats — dubbed "Willkiecrats" by their detractors — were naturally buoyed when the 56-year-old former governor, declaring that he wouldn't reject the support of any "conscientious Georgian," publicly defended his decision to remain on the independent ticket late in the campaign.[31]

After two unsuccessful bids for the U.S. Senate, the suspender-snapping Talmadge, a man who once seriously harbored presidential ambitions of his own, had launched a political comeback the previous year and was hoping — after a four-year absence —

---

[27] "Fourth Georgia Political Group to Back Willkie," *Times-Picayune* (New Orleans, LA), Oct. 4, 1940.
[28] "Many Georgia Democrats Shun Independent Ticket," *Washington Evening Star*, Oct. 13, 1940.
[29] "Fourth Georgia Political Group to Back Willkie," *Times-Picayune*, Oct. 4, 1940; "Independent Democrats Convene in Georgia," *Washington Evening Star*, Oct. 6, 1940.
[30] "State Ballot Gets Approval from Rivers," *Macon Telegraph*, Oct. 16, 1940.
[31] "Leaders of Three Georgia Parties Voice Final Appeals," *Macon Telegraph*, Nov. 5, 1940.

to win yet another term as the state's chief executive. Along with Commissioner of Agriculture Tom Linder and five others, including an incumbent Democratic congressman, all of whom accepted the dual Independent Democratic designation, Talmadge's name consequently appeared on the ballot twice in 1940 — once under the traditional Democratic emblem and again as the nominee of the fledgling Independent Democratic Party.[32]

It's not that Georgia's demagogue for all seasons really needed their help, but it was highly symbolic nonetheless. Talmadge's comeback had already been virtually guaranteed when he easily defeated Commissioner of Agriculture Columbus Roberts, a wealthy dairy farmer, in the state's all-important Democratic primary two months earlier — a race in which the former governor carried 136 of the state's 159 counties.[33] Facing only minor opposition in November, the virulent racist who had frequently feuded with President Roosevelt and once longed to occupy the office he held was returned to the governor's mansion with a staggering 99.6 percent of the vote.

Georgia's Independent Democratic movement, moreover, proved to be a nightmare for the national GOP. Unlike the situation four years earlier when the state's regular Republican organization, acting with the national party's blessing, merely rubber-stamped the electors chosen by the Independent Democrats, the unusual coalition that developed in 1944, comprised of a small band of anti-Roosevelt Democrats still loyal to the segregationist Talmadge and a lily-white faction of Republicans on the outs with their own party, left the national GOP without its own slate of presidential electors in Georgia.

Though never realistically expecting to carry any states in the Deep South, Dewey's managers, including Herbert Brownell, chairman of the Republican National Committee, were nevertheless furious and subsequently took legal action, but eventually lost their fight to have the party's officially sanctioned electors pledged to Dewey and Bricker placed on the November ballot when the Georgia Supreme Court sustained a lower court's earlier dismissal of its lawsuit against the Secretary of State.[34]

---

[32] "Gene Heads State Slate of Bolters; Independents Certify Talmadge Candidate with Willkie Ticket," *Macon Telegraph*, Oct. 9, 1940.

[33] "Talmadge of Georgia Wins Governorship," *Washington Evening Star*, Sep. 12, 1940.

[34] "GOP Asks Court Rule on Georgia Electors," *Augusta Chronicle*, Aug. 20, 1944; "Georgia Court Refuses to List GOP Electors," *Richmond Times-Dispatch*, Oct. 7, 1944; "Brownell Sees No Recourse in Georgia Ballot Denial," *Washington Evening Star*, Oct. 8, 1944. The RNC maintained that a biracial faction headed by national committeeman Wilson Williams of Columbus, the son of a Confederate soldier, and Ben Davis, an African-American

Though technically unpledged — some electors preferred Dewey while others favored Virginia's Harry F. Byrd — the *Savannah Morning News* strongly encouraged the Independent Democratic electoral slate to openly support Byrd rather than possibly be seen as offering nominal support to the Republican nominee. "The Morning News has for many months expressed the opinion that the type of man needed in the White House today is Senator Harry F. Byrd of Virginia, and once more we unhesitatingly recommend him to the electors under the Independent Democratic ballot as their choice for the presidency, as a sheer matter of political honesty and principle," the paper editorialized in early September. The anti-New Deal Democratic electors, the newspaper concluded, were providing an "excellent opportunity to do what Georgia and the South should have done long ago" — namely, breaking from the national Democratic Party and making the Solid South politically competitive for the first time since the Civil War.[35]

In neighboring Alabama, a group of anti-fourth termers aligned with the ADNC tried to launch an American Democratic Party with a slate of electors steadfastly opposed to the Roosevelt-Truman ticket. With the colorful Sen. W. Lee "Pappy" O'Daniel of Texas — a longtime Roosevelt critic — as their keynote speaker, this group of renegade Democrats held a rather poorly-attended convention in Birmingham in August and, in addition to naming a U.S. House candidate in the state's ninth congressional district, nominated eleven presidential electors.[36] The poorly-organized Alabama faction favored O'Daniel for president.[37] The party, however, failed to appear on the November ballot when a circuit court judge later sustained the state attorney general's ruling that the nominations were made after the legal deadline.[38]

A similar anti-Roosevelt, anti-New Deal effort was attempted in Florida, where the newly-organized "Independent Party" — the brainchild of Jacksonville attorney Edgar W. Waybright, Jr. — cobbled together an impressive list of presidential electors that included St. Petersburg Mayor George S. Patterson, Will M. Traer, publisher of the *Winter Park Herald*, prominent Orlando attorney Harry M. Voorhis, and Carl Hanton, the longtime editor of the *Fort*

---

journalist and longtime activist from Atlanta, had been recognized by the party's national committee and seated at the Republican national convention, represented the state's legitimate Republican Party.

[35] "Georgia's Independent Electors," *Savannah Morning News*, reprinted in *Williamsport Sun-Gazette* (Williamsport, PA), Sep. 6, 1944.

[36] "Birmingham Anti-FDR Group Chooses Electors," *Anniston Star*, Aug. 13, 1944.

[37] "Anti-Fourth Term Group Backs O'Daniel," *Pittsburgh Press*, July 12, 1944.

[38] "Anti-Roosevelt Ticket Ruled Out," *Dothan Eagle*, Oct. 1, 1944.

Myers News-Press.[39]

Holding their state organizing convention at an all-day session in Jacksonville in late August, the anti-Roosevelt Democrats elected I. Beverly Nalle, a Jacksonville realtor, as the party's chairman, approved a states' rights platform, and adopted the slogan, "Rule by Roosevelt to end in 1944."[40] Claiming the party was "composed of real Democrats pledged to save their country and party from a fourth term and the New Dealers," Nalle described the new party as the "white Democratic Party of Florida."[41]

Ruth Nooney of Jacksonville, the shaky-voiced woman who had placed Byrd's name in nomination amid a smattering of boos at the Democratic national convention a month earlier, was one of the convention speakers, telling the restive Floridians that the New Dealers in Chicago, dominated by the "communistic" CIO, northern big city bosses and racial troublemakers, had run "roughshod over the fundamentals principles of the Democratic Party and constitutional government."[42]

Brushing aside the notion that "only one man has qualifications to be president," the Floridians condemned "the efforts of any group stirring up racial questions for a political purpose" and demanded that any racial questions involving the South should be left to the southern states — and not the federal government — to resolve. The party also pledged to carry out the plank adopted in the 1932 Democratic national platform, but quickly discarded by Roosevelt, calling for "the "immediate and drastic reduction of unnecessary government expenditures by abolishing useless commissions and offices." They also added some platform language of their own by calling for the immediate elimination of "the multitude of unnecessary and oppressive bureaus which have since been created."

Condemning government favoritism involving corporations, labor or any other group or groups as "un-American," the anti-New Dealers, hoping to appeal to working-class Floridians, declared that "labors gains shall not be lost either through racketeering or communistic leadership of labor on the one hand, or by a return of the exploitation of labor by capital on the other, and we declare that it is the inalienable right of every citizen... to engage in useful work without interference from any governmental bureau or bureaus."

---

[39] Leuchtenburg, *The White House Looks South*, pp. 135-136.
[40] "Florida Dems Name Electors to Oust FDR," *Fort Lauderdale News*, Aug. 29, 1944.
[41] "Florida Organizes Independent Party," *Charleston News and Courier*, Aug. 29, 1944.
[42] "New Democrat Party is Formed by Florida Bloc," *Chicago Tribune*, Aug. 30, 1944.

In demanding a "vigorous and effective prosecution of the war" and the "speedy return" of those fighting abroad, the Independent Party of Florida also favored a "broad program of vocational and educational training for disabled veterans," as well as guaranteed medical care. In addition to calling for adequate assistance for surviving spouses and their dependents, the party also supported federal aid for other returning veterans until they could reestablish themselves in the private sector.[43]

Though the party's founding convention had been attended by more than fifty delegates from virtually every section of the state, the Independent Party was rebuffed by Secretary of State R. A. Gray in its attempt to place its eight presidential electors on the November ballot a few days later. Relying on an opinion by the state attorney general, Gray cited the state's five percent registration requirement for minor party ballot access — a draconian requirement by any stretch of the imagination — in keeping the independent, anti-Roosevelt electors off the ballot. It was the same statute that denied the older Prohibition and Socialist parties, as well as Gerald L. K. Smith's far-right America First Party, a spot on the ballot in the Sunshine State.[44]

Attorneys for the Independent Party had argued that a 1943 statute gave them the right to place their electors on the November ballot — an argument made earlier that year by the Prohibition Party — but the Secretary of State maintained that the new law had been enacted primarily to enable the Republicans to name their candidates by convention rather than in a primary election. According to Gray, the new law defined a minority political party as one which failed to elect a majority of its electors in two consecutive presidential elections — a provision that clearly discriminated against any new or recently-formed party.[45]

In the meantime, several Florida newspapers urged the Secretary of State to place the party's electors on the ballot. "We sincerely hope that Mr. Gray will give this matter considerable thought before he makes his final decision," wrote the *Fort Lauderdale News*. "Every American has been promised the right to vote as he sees fit and the omission of these electors' names on the November ballot would be a step away from democracy — the one thing that Americans are fighting and dying for these days."[46] But the Secretary of

---

[43] Russell Kay, "Too Late to Classify," *Fort Myers News-Press*, Sep. 1, 1944.
[44] "Gray Declines to Put Party on Ballot," *St. Petersburg Times*, Sep. 3, 1944.
[45] "Gray Rules Out New Party Names on State Ballot," *Fort Myers News-Press*, Sep. 3, 1944.
[46] "Editor's Corner," *Fort Lauderdale News*, Sep. 6, 1944.

State refused to reconsider his position, maintaining that a recognized political party was one that had at least five percent of the state's registered voters, thereby forcing the Independents to take legal action.

During the ensuing legal battle, Gray argued that there would be nothing to protect the general election ballot from being flooded with dozens of parties and hundreds, if not thousands, of candidates, resulting in a "chaotic condition on the possible length of the ballot" if the court ruled in the party's favor. Gray's claim was quickly rebutted by Edgar Waybright, the party's attorney, who told the court that "at least from 1895 to 1931 what is called a 'chaotic condition' existed in this state, and there was no chaos." He also stated that prior to 1931 the state didn't have a five percent registration requirement for political parties and that Florida's ballot had never been overcrowded.[47]

In its late September ruling, the state's highest court maintained that the 1943 statute would have been sufficient to place the party's electors on the ballot if it had been shown that the Independent Party had been "bound together in some kind of an organization" and that in "at least two consecutive presidential elections they attempted but failed to elect a majority of the electors for president and vice president."[48]

Refusing to go down without a fight, the Independents briefly considered waging a write-in campaign for their eight presidential electors.[49] The *Fort Myers News-Press*, which had been highly supportive of the party during its brief existence, even suggested the idea of a "sticker" campaign, suggesting that such a method would be far preferable to making Florida voters "carry along a bottle of smelling salts for use while voting either the national Democratic or Republican tickets."[50]

The party, however, abruptly abandoned that strategy a few days later when its executive committee decided to support Republican Tom Dewey. Though supporting all of the other Democratic nominees for state and local office, the Independents also endorsed Miles H. Draper, the Republican candidate running against Democratic Sen. Claude Pepper, an outspoken champion of the New Deal.

In deciding to throw its support to the Republican nominee, the

---

[47] "Anti-Roosevelt Party Calls for Place on Ballot," *Fort Myers News-Press*, Sep. 12, 1944.
[48] "White Democrat Party is Denied Place on Ballot," *Fort Myers News-Press*, Sep. 30, 1944.
[49] "Supreme Court Rules Against Anti-FDR Party," *Fort Lauderdale News*, Sep. 29, 1944.
[50] "White Democrats Barred," *Fort Myers News-Press*, Oct. 1, 1944.

party's executive committee also adopted a fiery resolution asserting that Roosevelt and Truman weren't "legitimate Democratic nominees," but were instead "the nominees of a convention stacked and packed by the South-hating New Deal bureaucrats who have stolen the name and machinery of the Democratic Party for the purpose of undermining and destroying the American system of government." With similar fury, the resolution continued:

> These modern day carpetbaggers are controlled and directed by the Sidney Hillman-controlled and operated Political Action Committee of the Communistic-dominated element of the CIO and are subtly and savagely using the race issue in the South for the purpose of creating and perpetuating hatred of the South and against southerners among the foreign-born population of the big cities of the North.[51]

Despite their relatively limited resources, the Independents ran newspaper ads throughout the state and distributed more than 100,000 campaign brochures supporting the Dewey and Draper candidacies. The response was overwhelming. "We are absolutely swamped with mail and telephone calls," said Nalle. "In fact, with our small staff and shoestring campaign fund, it is impossible for us to answer all of the mail and telephone messages we have received."[52]

The spirited campaign waged by the anti-Roosevelt Democrats that autumn contributed significantly to Dewey's nearly thirty percent showing in the Sunshine State — the strongest GOP performance in the state in a presidential election since 1928 when Floridians, rejecting Al Smith's Catholicism, overwhelmingly supported Herbert Hoover. The 143,205 votes cast for Dewey in Florida that fall was more than twice the number of votes received by President Hoover in 1932, and 17,000 more than the 126,158 votes garnered by Willkie in 1940. The same thing was true in the U.S. Senate race where Draper, a Tampa attorney, garnered nearly 29 percent of the vote in his uphill battle to unseat Pepper.

Equally troubling for the White House was the seemingly considerable anti-Roosevelt sentiment among rebellious Democratic electors in several other southern states, including Louisiana, where five of the state's ten Democratic electors resigned in late September rather than conform to an edict issued by the party's

---

[51] "New Independent Party to Support Dewey, Bricker," *Fort Myers News-Press*, Oct. 5, 1944.
[52] "Independent Party Pleased in Florida," *Palm Beach Post*, Nov. 5, 1944.

state central committee requiring each elector to individually pledge his or her support to the party's nominees. "I am not enough of a good politician to think one way and vote another," remarked one of those who had resigned.[53]

One of the most intriguing developments, however, occurred in Mississippi, another steamy cauldron of anti-Roosevelt sentiment. In late October, three of the state's nine Democratic electors chosen at the party's state convention in June announced that they planned to vote for Sen. Byrd in the Electoral College, even as the Virginia senator continued to stress that he wasn't a candidate for the presidency. Interestingly, all three of the bolting electors were attorneys.

In a statement announcing their defection, the three Democratic electors contended that Roosevelt's reelection would be "inimical to the best interests of Mississippi and the South." They also maintained that the June Democratic state convention in Jackson freed them from any obligation to support the party's presidential and vice-presidential nominees if the national convention failed to restore the two-thirds rule and adopted a racial plank "obnoxious to the South."[54] It was widely rumored that a fourth Democratic elector would also refuse to support Roosevelt in the Electoral College and that another Democratic elector had expressed opposition to the president's bid for a fourth term on several occasions.[55] As such, Roosevelt was only guaranteed the support of four of his party's nine electors in that traditionally Democratic state.

Meanwhile, Sen. Byrd maintained that he hadn't received any communication whatsoever from the three bolting electors and quickly reiterated his previous statements that he wasn't a candidate for the presidency. "I have not encouraged support from any source and I have no intention of doing so," he said in a statement from Winchester, Virginia.[56]

While the three renegade electors acknowledged that they had conditionally agreed to support the party's national ticket shortly after the Democratic national convention in Chicago, they insisted that a number of recent developments prompted their last-minute defection:

---

[53] "Five Louisiana Electors Resign," *Augusta Chronicle*, Sep. 28, 1944.
[54] "3 Mississippi Electors Bolt To Harry Byrd," *Clarion-Ledger*, Oct. 29, 1944; "Senator Byrd Repeats He Is Not Candidate," *McComb Daily Journal* (McComb, MS), Nov. 1, 1944.
[55] "Legislature Will Purge Electors," *Hattiesburg American* (Hattiesburg, MS), Oct. 31, 1944.
[56] "Legislature Meets Thursday; Will Revise Party Elector Laws," *Hattiesburg American*, Nov. 1, 1944.

Since that time many things have transpired proving beyond doubt that the election of Roosevelt and Truman would be inimical to the best interests of Mississippi and the South. Their appeal to the negro vote in the North, promising to do away with race segregation in the South, their open acceptance of support from Communists and from Sidney Hillman of the Political Action Committee of the CIO, and other derelictions, convinces us that these two men no longer represent the Democratic Party as we know it, or as Mississippians have known it for more than fifty years.[57]

When the three obstinate electors — Clarence Morgan, Frank E. Everett and W. G. McLain, the latter a grandson of a Confederate soldier — subsequently refused to resign, Gov. Thomas L. Bailey called a special legislative session, resulting in a new last-minute set of Democratic presidential electors chosen by the legislature. The new slate included four of the electors named earlier that year at the state Democratic convention in Jackson.[58]

Since it was too late to print and distribute a revised official statewide ballot the Democratic-dominated legislature took the extraordinary step of authorizing the printing and distribution of a short supplementary ballot, a pink-colored ballot containing the names of the newly-named nine electors pledged to Roosevelt and Truman. The famous pink ballots were rushed to the polling places in the state's 84 counties by siren-blaring state highway patrolmen on Saturday, November 4, less than 72 hours before Mississippians would head to the polls.[59]

Desperately clinging to the goal of denying FDR a fourth term, former congressman James J. O'Connor, representing the stridently anti-Roosevelt ADNC — a group firmly behind Dewey's candidacy at that late stage of the campaign — was highly critical of the actions taken by the Mississippi legislature, predicting that the extraordinary measure of providing a supplemental presidential ballot could potentially result in the unseating of the state's entire Democratic congressional delegation. According to O'Connor, those wishing to cast a straight Democratic ticket would have to mark two separate ballots; the supplementary pink ballot for the Roosevelt-Truman electors and the official statewide ballot for the party's congressional candidates, thereby creating the possibility of

---

[57] "3 Mississippi Electors Bolt To Harry Byrd," *Clarion-Ledger*, Oct. 29, 1944.
[58] "Three Electors Refuse to 'Quit Under Fire'; Governor Calls Special Session of Legislature," *McComb Enterprise*, Nov. 1, 1944; "House Passes Supplementary Ballot Bill," *Clarion-Ledger*, Nov. 3, 1944.
[59] "New Roosevelt-Truman Ballots are Distributed," *Biloxi Daily Herald*, Nov. 4, 1944.

a tremendous amount of confusion and chaos at the ballot box and seriously jeopardizing the prospects of several of the party's candidates for the U.S. House.

It was a charge quickly refuted by Bailey, a Roosevelt loyalist. "Mr. O'Connor, like most Republican propagandists, is talking through his hat," the governor firmly responded. "His fear about the unseating of Mississippi congressmen does not disturb me or any other Mississippi Democrat in the least. In short, it's Republican twaddle." In signing the bill, Bailey denied that he had been in consultation with the Roosevelt administration. "I feel there is no danger to the Roosevelt-Truman ticket, either in the state or nation," he said confidently. "This legislation," he added, "was predicated on the theory that every voter qualified to vote is entitled to express his conviction in the selection of the president."[60]

In addition to the dual Democratic electoral tickets, the Republicans also placed two separate lists of presidential electors on the Mississippi ballot, one sponsored by Perry W. Howard's black and tan faction which had been seated at the Republican national convention and the other representing the state's "lily white" Independent Republican Party headed by George L. Sheldon, a former governor of Nebraska. Though largely inconsequential in one-party Mississippi, both sets of electors were pledged to Dewey, the national party's nominee.

Consequently, Mississippians were confronted with four separate sets of presidential electors — 36 names in all, including four who appeared on both the regular Democratic ticket and the supplementary Roosevelt-Truman ballot — when they went to the polls on Nov. 7th.

---

[60] "Roosevelt Voters to Get Pink Slip," *Hattiesburg American*, Nov. 4, 1944.

Chapter XXII

The Texas Regulars

While the fledgling anti-Roosevelt movements in Georgia, South Carolina and elsewhere barely caused a stir, the story was quite different in the Lone Star State, where the amply-financed Texas Regulars, organized by dissident conservative Democrats as an anti-New Deal third-party movement, posed a potentially greater threat to Roosevelt's re-election prospects than any other renegade Democratic organization in the South.

Some of the Texas Regulars, of course, had never forgiven FDR for dumping Vice President John Nance Garner, a fellow Texan, from the Democratic ticket in 1940.[1] Primarily concerned with their own pocketbooks, many of the wealthier Regulars were angry about increased federal regulations under Roosevelt's New Deal, particularly wartime rationing and price controls, both of which they believed impeded the free market. The word "sacrifice" apparently wasn't in their vocabulary.[2]

Dedicated exclusively to denying FDR a fourth term, the short-lived Texas Regulars, whose autumn campaign was augmented by a speaking tour conducted by colorful Sen. W. Lee "Pappy" O'Daniel — the former host of an immensely popular hillbilly music radio show — were officially founded in late September 1944,

---

[1] Sean P. Cunningham, *Cowboy Conservatism: Texas and the Rise of the Modern Right* (Lexington, KY, 2010), p. 25.
[2] Judith N. McArthur and Harold L. Smith, *Minnie Fisher Cunningham: A Suffragist's Life in Politics* (New York, 2003), p. 169.

shortly after a pro-Roosevelt faction narrowly regained control of the party at a second state convention that year.[3]

Denouncing the recent *Smith v. Allwright* Supreme Court decision outlawing the party's all-white primary while demanding restoration of the party's two-thirds rule for nominating a presidential ticket — a rule that had been abolished in 1936, severely diminishing the ability of southern delegations to dictate to the national convention — the Regulars had dominated an earlier state convention in May to determine the party's 23 presidential electors and select a delegation to the party's national convention later that summer.

Outmaneuvering the party's liberal and moderate elements at the precinct and county levels, the regulars — financed by wealthy Texas oilmen determined to repudiate the New Deal and deny Roosevelt another term — had legally packed the convention and completely controlled the proceedings. Incredibly, only a couple of Roosevelt's most prominent backers in the state were named as Democratic presidential electors and even fewer were selected as delegates to the party's national convention in July.

Held in the State Senate chamber in Austin, the convention's atmosphere was so hostile to FDR's New Deal and the idea of a fourth term that most of Roosevelt's supporters, including Rep. Lyndon B. Johnson, an energetic and capable young congressman representing the city of Austin and the surrounding hill country, decided to bolt the convention and hold a pro-Roosevelt "rump" convention of their own in the adjoining House chamber.

Johnson, who happened to be a close personal friend and confidant of the president, tried in vain to heal the rift. "Before we go off half-cocked," he cautioned the bolters, "it's extremely important that we give every Democrat and every so-called Democrat another opportunity to say whether they expect to vote for the party nominee in November." The future president wanted the party's delegates and, more importantly, its electors to pledge support for the party's presidential nominee in November. He already knew the answer, but just wanted to make sure. "When I bolt a convention it's going to be a Hoovercrat Republican convention," he told those assembled in the Senate chamber. Viewed by some of the Regulars as "Roosevelt's pinup boy," LBJ received the confirmation he was looking for when the party's reactionaries overwhelmingly rejected his proposal, making it clear that they were opposed to a fourth term.[4]

---

[3] "Texas Regulars, New Political Party, Born," *Dallas Morning News*, Sep. 26, 1944.

[4] Robert Dalleck, *Lone Star Rising: Lyndon Johnson and His Times 1908-1960* (New York,

In addition to selecting delegates and alternates to the party's national convention in Chicago, both conventions nominated presidential electors — the Regulars choosing an uninstructed slate of electors generally hostile to Roosevelt while the bolting faction chose an electoral slate firmly pledged to FDR's fourth-term candidacy. A lengthy and bitterly-contested legal battle, involving two separate court cases, ensued to determine which of the two warring factions was entitled to place their twenty-three electors in the Democratic column on the general election ballot. The Roosevelt faction lost the first round in June when the state Supreme Court, upholding the party's 100-year practice of naming presidential electors by convention, refused to compel the state Democratic Executive Committee to certify twenty-three Roosevelt electors nominated at their rump convention to appear on the July 22 primary ballot along with the 23 uninstructed electors named by the regular convention in Austin.[5]

In the meantime, both factions of the strife-ridden party sent a full 48-person delegation to the Democratic national convention, which convened at Chicago Stadium, the Windy City's historic all-purpose indoor arena, on July 19.

The Regulars, led by former Gov. Dan Moody and Eugene B. Germany, a wealthy Dallas industrialist and former state party chairman who had openly supported Republican Wendell Willkie four years earlier, were initially recognized as the state's official delegation in Chicago. The convention's credentials committee, however, recommended seating both delegations with each faction entitled to 24 seats, or one-half vote per delegate — a recommendation that was overwhelmingly supported by the convention, leading to a walkout by 33 delegates and alternates from the right-wing regular faction. The adopted recommendation effectively diluted the regulars' strength by half.

Frustrated by their failure to influence the party's national platform, particularly on the thorny issue of states' rights, the regulars returned to their hotel shortly after Roosevelt was easily nominated for a fourth term — a lopsided first-ballot victory in which the regulars split their two-dozen votes evenly between FDR and Virginia's Harry F. Byrd — and named a committee to confer with other disgruntled southern leaders. They also quickly organized themselves, naming former State Senator Clint C. Small of Austin, a lawyer for the Humble Oil and Refining Company, as their chair-

---

1991), pp. 261-262.
[5] "Pro-Roosevelt Group Loses in High Court," *Dallas Morning News*, June 23, 1944.

man. Eugene Germany and a few other prominent regulars remained in Chicago for the next few extra days to explore the possibility of launching a third-party movement in support of Harry Byrd's candidacy in November. "We are going back to Texas and see that our votes are cast for a real Democrat," fumed the deep-pocketed Germany.[6]

Despite their drubbing in Chicago, the regulars still clung to the belief that the 23 uninstructed presidential electors nominated earlier that spring would appear in the state's Democratic column in November and made it clear that they intended to fight to the finish to make that happen.

During this period, Texas had two state conventions in presidential election years. By tradition and law, the May convention named delegates to the party's national convention and nominated a slate of presidential electors whose names would appear on the November ballot. Held in September, the second convention — known informally as the "governor's convention" — was tasked with electing state party officers and drafting a platform for the party's nominees.

Unlike previous years, a full-scale legal controversy erupted when Roosevelt's supporters served notice that they intended to take over the September convention in Dallas and appoint an entirely new slate of presidential electors pledged to Roosevelt and Truman. The Roosevelt loyalists were supported in this effort by Democratic national committeeman Myron G. Blalock, who argued that the later convention had the legal authority to remove electors who would not remain loyal to the party's presidential nominee.

A former state representative and ex-state party chairman who had vigorously opposed repeal of the party's two-thirds rule in 1936 and actively championed Vice President Garner's doomed candidacy for the Democratic presidential nomination in 1940, the 53-year-old Blalock controlled virtually all of the state's federal patronage during this period and was arguably the most powerful Democrat in the Lone Star State. He was also widely respected by Roosevelt's allies and the Texas Regulars alike, and was largely viewed as a peacemaker during the raging dispute between the two factions.

"I am hoping that when the smoke of battle clears away, we will find both crowds working and voting for the election of the party's nominee," he said during a press conference shortly after

---

[6] "Southerners Plan Party to Aid Byrd," *Dallas Morning News*, July 21, 1944.

the divisive Austin convention. "If there is going to be a contest before the convention in Chicago, and if it can be avoided, I hope to be instrumental in seeing that both sides get a fair hearing." From the outset, Blalock insisted that he wasn't favoring either side in the struggle. "I am proceeding," he asserted, "by conferring with men who might have influence on both sides."[7]

Prior to the Democratic convention in Chicago, Blalock had tried to hammer out a compromise in the seating of the Texas delegation, proposing that the regular delegation should be seated, except for those who explicitly didn't intend to support the party's presidential nominee in November, the latter of whom would be replaced by alternate delegates who had been selected at the regular convention earlier that spring. In the spirit of harmony, he also promised that he would personally support the resolutions adopted by the regulars at the party's Austin convention and, if those demands were rejected by the national convention, the Texas electors would be free to support another Democratic candidate who favored the resolutions adopted earlier that spring.[8]

With the exception of wealthy Dallas businessman Eugene Germany and a few others, Blalock's compromise was welcomed by most of the regulars and by the vast majority of those in the Roosevelt camp. Germany, who was quick to criticize Blalock's proposal, wanted the entire regular delegation seated, arguing that it was impossible for delegates to pledge support to the party's nominee before knowing if the planks approved by the Austin convention — specifically, a denunciation of the *Smith v. Allwright* Supreme Court decision abolishing the state's all-white primary and restoration of the party's "two-thirds rule," which had been eliminated in 1936 — were acceptable to the national convention.[9]

Blalock, whose attempt to lessen the bitter party strife in Texas was eventually rendered moot when the party's national convention in Chicago decided overwhelmingly to seat both delegations, with each delegate entitled to one-half vote, later embraced a last-minute plan put forward by Gov. Coke Stevenson calling for two separate sets of Democratic electors. "The people will vote overwhelmingly for the nominees of the Democratic Party if given the chance to do it, no matter how the ticket is arranged," said Blalock, whose brother Horace later became one of the 23 electors for the

---

[7] "Blalock is Seeking to Bring Texas Demo Factions Together," *Corsicana Daily Sun* (Corsicana, TX), May 25, 1944.
[8] "Blalock Offers Harmony Program, Urges Support of Party's Nominees," *Dallas Morning News*, July 15, 1944.
[9] Ibid.

renegade Texas Regulars. "But it will be very unfair to force a Democrat to scratch the Democratic ticket in order to vote for the nominees."[10]

Stevenson had offered his compromise solution shortly before the Dallas convention, suggesting that both factions should be permitted to place their presidential electors in the Democratic column in November and allow voters to choose between the two competing slates, but it was immediately rejected by leaders of both factions.

Believing they would have a majority at the Dallas convention, the pro-Roosevelt Texans were determined to supplant all of the anti-Roosevelt electors and had no desire to see any of them listed as Democratic electors on the November ballot, while the anti-Roosevelt Democrats were confident that the law was on their side and that they would ultimately prevail in court, regardless of what transpired in Dallas. Roy Sanderford, one of the anti-Roosevelt leaders with whom Stevenson had conferred, stated publicly that he had no objection to the names of pro-Roosevelt electors appearing on the general election ballot, but didn't want them to appear in the Democratic column.[11]

Previously shunning the idea of trying to play peacemaker in the increasingly bitter dispute, Stevenson was obviously disappointed that his proposal — one that he described as "eminently fair" to both sides — had been rejected by leaders in both camps. "It strikes me that the rank and file of Democrats would say this is a fair way out, but the leaders disagree," sighed Stevenson.[12] Deeply discouraged, Stevenson later hinted that he wouldn't attend the Dallas convention.[13]

Stevenson, who initially proposed that both sets of presidential electors should be placed in a parallel position under the Democratic column and clearly labeled as "Pro-Roosevelt" and "Anti-Roosevelt" or by some similar headings, quickly had a change of heart and renewed his efforts to bring about a satisfactory solution to the elector dilemma. On September 6th, six days before the Dallas convention, the governor met with President Roosevelt at the White House to discuss the Texas situation and immediately upon his return began contacting leaders of both factions. Roosevelt,

---

[10] "Governor Will Insist Convention Act on His Dual Elector Plan," *Dallas Morning News*, Sep. 11, 1944.
[11] "Texas Factions Each Confident," *Times-Picayune*, Sep. 5, 1944.
[12] "Stevenson Shuns Role of Umpire," *Dallas Morning News*, May 17, 1944; "Both Democratic Groups Reject Governor's Party Peace Plan," *Dallas Morning News*, Sep. 3, 1944.
[13] "Stevenson's Hope for Party Peace Wanes, May Not Attend Meet," *Dallas Morning News*, Sep. 10, 1944.

who had been deeply worried about the recent political developments in Texas, reportedly gave a thumbs up to Stevenson's proposal calling for a double-barreled set of Democratic presidential electors during their hour-long meeting.[14]

Roosevelt was clearly concerned about the drama unfolding in Texas, telling Houston's Jesse Jones, the former head of the Reconstruction Finance Corporation who was then serving as Secretary of Commerce, that the situation in the Lone Star State reminded him of the dramatically bitter Democratic split of 1860, which enabled Abraham Lincoln and the Republicans to capture the presidency.[15]

On the eve of the Dallas convention, Stevenson reiterated his plea for a dual set of presidential electors under the Democratic column, asserting that he would insist that the convention act on his proposal. Describing his plan as "the fairest to all concerned," the governor maintained that it was the only way Texas Democrats could express themselves — one way or another — on the party's presidential and vice-presidential nominees while still casting a Democratic ballot.[16]

Stevenson's proposal differed slightly from the one offered by former Gov. Dan Moody, who had aligned himself with the regulars at the Democratic national convention in Chicago. The former two-term governor had proposed that both sets of electors should be listed perpendicularly in the Democratic column with one list of electors under the other to make a single, uniform column where voters could choose one set or the other, or if voters preferred, they could scratch names from both lists to vote for a total of no more than twenty-three electors — the number of electors Texas was entitled to in the Electoral College.

Insisting that the Dallas convention could not legally remove or substitute the 23 electors nominated in May, Moody cautioned Roosevelt's supporters that time was running out and that they should seriously consider a compromise, such as the ones offered by Gov. Stevenson and himself. "The rights of thousands of people in the important proceedings of electing a President and Vice-President being involved, those who assume to act for them should not adopt uncertain methods of protecting such important rights, where certain methods are available," warned Moody, adding

---

[14] "If Anybody Asks F.R., He'll Favor Stevenson General Election Plan," *Dallas Morning News*, Sep. 9, 1944.
[15] Leuchtenburg, *The White House Looks South*, p. 138.
[16] "Governor Will Insist Convention Act on His Dual Elector Plan," *Dallas Morning News*, Sep. 11, 1944.

that it was almost too late for the president's supporters to come up with an alternative plan without jeopardizing the Roosevelt-Truman ticket's chances of appearing in the Democratic column in the Lone Star State. "The time for taking the necessary steps is short — too short to speculate on the results of litigation or on uncertain methods," said Moody.[17]

Meanwhile, George A. Butler, the party's state chairman, welcomed Stevenson's proposed comprise, calling it "a step in the right direction." Stopping short of making a full-throated endorsement of Stevenson's plan, Butler said that it was important that Texas Democrats be given two sets of electors in November. "I'm not saying how it should be done," he demurred, "but the people are the best court." Butler, who was closely aligned with the regulars yet promised to preside in a fair and impartial manner, remained hopeful that an amicable solution could be worked out at the Dallas convention on September 12th. "There will be no steamroller tactics, and on questions of importance, we are going to give a roll call," he stated shortly before the Dallas convention.[18]

Though cautiously optimistic that they would ultimately emerge victorious, Butler and the other regulars had no idea what was in store for them as the delegates began arriving at the Fair Park Auditorium in Dallas on that dry and humid day in September. They came in droves, accompanied by dozens of reporters and hundreds and hundreds of spectators anxious to see which side would prevail in what was expected to be an historic fight to the finish.

Most observers were anticipating the most contentious Democratic state convention since 1928, a year when the party was badly split over Al Smith's candidacy and many of the state's leading Democrats, troubled not only by the New Yorker's views on prohibition, but also by his Catholicism, ended up supporting Herbert Hoover. Their support that autumn enabled the former Secretary of Commerce to edge out the "Happy Warrior" by nearly 26,000 votes, thereby becoming the first Republican presidential nominee in history to carry Texas.[19]

The tumultuous 1944 state convention, which was covered live by radio station KGKO, began with a protracted fight over the seating of the disputed Dallas delegation where a pro-Roosevelt slate

---

[17] "Governor Renews Effort To Heal Intraparty Split," *Dallas Morning News*, Sep. 8, 1944.
[18] "Voters Deserve Right to Pass on Electors They Want, Butler Says," *Dallas Morning News*, Sep. 5, 1944.
[19] "Texas Political History Repeated: Party Split Wide Open as in 1928," *Dallas Morning News*, Aug. 21, 1944; "Dems Setting Stage to Fiery Convention," *Dallas Morning News*, Aug. 28, 1944.

had been chosen after the regulars bolted the raucous county convention in late July — a disorderly session in which police officers had briefly stepped in to keep the peace — and held a rump convention of their own.[20]

The convention's credentials committee in Dallas recommended seating the regulars, but the pro-Roosevelt forces, led by Robert W. Calvert, a former Speaker of the Texas legislature and floor leader for the Roosevelt faction, vociferously objected, demanding a roll call vote on the question. Despite strong support from the big city delegations of Dallas, Fort Worth, Houston and San Antonio, a motion to table Calvert's proposed amendment was narrowly defeated by a razor-thin vote of 803-774. A second roll call vote on Calvert's original amendment also passed by a similar margin of 799-769.[21] A switch of only fifteen votes on the first roll call vote or a mere sixteen votes on the second would have left the chagrined Roosevelt forces on the outside looking in. That's how close it was.

More importantly, the president's supporters then would have been forced to place an independent slate of Roosevelt-Truman electors on the November ballot if they had any hope of winning the state's 23 electoral votes, a potentially nightmarish situation where Roosevelt's electors would have been listed separately from the party's other candidates from governor all the way down the ballot — a situation made even more dicey by the fact that the names of a party's presidential and vice-presidential candidates weren't listed on the ballot. Voters only saw the names of a party's presidential electors. Coupled with the fact that hundreds of thousands of Texans were accustomed to voting a straight Democratic ticket and had never previously split their tickets, that scenario could have proven disastrous for the president.

In any case, the Roosevelt delegation from Dallas was immediately seated and from that moment on the fourth termers were in full control of the convention — and the party. With most of the regulars deserting the convention after the second roll call vote, the Roosevelt faction quickly appointed a committee headed by populist eight-term congressman Wright Patman, a vocal critic of the nation's banking system who once tried to impeach Treasury Sec-

---

[20] "KGKO Has Democratic Convention," *Dallas Morning News*, Sep. 12, 1944; "Pro-Roosevelt Forces Control Most Conventions; Rump Meetings Held," *Abilene Reporter-News*, July 30, 1944.
[21] "Fourth Termers Take Over State Convention," *Dallas Morning News*, Sep. 13, 1944.

retary Andrew Mellon, to choose a new slate of presidential electors to replace those selected in Austin four months earlier.[22] As a consequence, Gov. Stevenson never had an opportunity to present his dual elector proposal to the delegates. The Roosevelt loyalists also elected a new state executive committee. Harry L. Seay, a former insurance executive and prominent Dallas civic leader, became the party's new state chairman, replacing George Butler.[23]

Tradition had been shattered. "This was the first time in Texas political history that the so-called 'governor's convention' in September of presidential years has dealt with the question of electors," observed the *Amarillo Daily News*. "By custom, Texas has always chosen its electors at the May convention."[24]

Though keenly disappointed, the regulars remained confident that there was no legal or moral authority to set aside the electors who had been chosen at the party's May convention, fifteen of whom were committed to voting for a Democrat other than Roosevelt.[25] "All we have to do is sit tight and defend our position if it is attacked," said Connie Renfro, one of the anti-Roosevelt leaders, shortly after the fourth termers narrowly prevailed on the critical roll call votes.[26] "Under the plain provisions of our law, the action taken by the September convention is of no binding or legal effect whatever," the anti-New Dealers maintained in a formal statement issued the following day.[27]

Despite the fact that Roosevelt's supporters, fighting stubbornly every inch of the way, had prevailed in Dallas, it was clear that the party's months-long drama was far from over. The stop-Roosevelt movement was as determined as ever to deny the Democratic president a fourth term. "We have been astounded at the amount of interest and support our movement has brought," said Eugene B. Germany shortly after the regulars had been narrowly defeated in Dallas. "I had calls Wednesday from California, Tennessee and Washington about the movement. We now believe strongly that one half of the Democrats and all of the Republicans in Texas are against Roosevelt."

The regulars also took some satisfaction in the fact that the New

---

[22] "F.R. Opposition Purged; New Electors Named," *Dallas Morning News*, Sep. 14, 1944.
[23] "Strong Fourth Termers Take Control of Party Affairs after Upheaval," *Dallas Morning News*, Sep. 14, 1944; "Democrats Replace Butler, Simons with Seay, Kittrell," *Dallas Morning News*, Sep. 14, 1944.
[24] "Pro-Roosevelt in Control at Dallas," *Amarillo Daily News*, Sep. 13, 1944.
[25] "15 Electors Favor Byrd as Roosevelt Foes Launch Fight," *Dallas Morning News*, Aug. 21, 1944.
[26] "Anti-F.R. Dems Keenly Disappointed," *Dallas Morning News*, Sep. 13, 1944.
[27] "Stop-Roosevelt Move Explodes in New Fury," *Dallas Morning News*, Sep. 14, 1944.

Dealers — enjoying the advantages of the heavily-funded CIO Political Action Committee and an administration more than willing to use government contracts, judicial appointments and bureaucratic parity payments for its own political benefit — had barely managed a majority in Dallas, garnering less than 51 percent of the vote on the only two roll call votes taken during the convention. "This movement," they asserted in a statement issued on the second day of the Dallas convention, "will continue to grow in stature and in strength and there is no doubt but by Nov. 7 the regular Democrats of Texas will win a decisive victory for the party at the polls."[28]

Even before the Dallas convention adjourned, the Roosevelt faction began feverishly mapping out its legal strategy for removing the party's original electors and placing its 23 new electors on the Democratic ticket. Anticipating one of the shortest but most contentious court battles in Texas history, former Gov. James V. Allred, Robert W. Calvert and 39-year-old Corsicana attorney Tom L. Tyson were prepared to argue before the Texas Supreme Court on behalf of the pro-Roosevelt electors named in Dallas while Frank J. Knapp of Houston and Connie C. Renfro were tasked with representing the electors originally chosen at the Austin convention in May. Knapp and Allred had already faced off earlier that year when the pro-Roosevelt faction tried to compel the state Democratic executive committee to place their electors on the July primary ballot — a plea rejected by the state's highest court when it upheld the party's right to name its electors at the May convention.[29]

Knapp had argued brilliantly on behalf of the regulars in the earlier lawsuit when the pro-Roosevelt faction, looking for a second bite of the apple, demanded that the party's presidential electors should be chosen in the July 22 primary instead of at the earlier May convention, asserting that the petitioners sought to have the Supreme Court pass judgment on a political matter in which the Democratic Party was supposed to have exclusive control. In his reply to the court, Knapp argued that the petitioners had willingly acquiesced to party proceedings in both precinct and county conventions earlier that spring, and that sixteen of the relators had been duly elected as delegates to the state convention in Austin. "In accordance with democratic principles and accepted rules and regulations of the Democratic Party of which they were members," he

---

[28] Ibid.
[29] "Opposing Democrats Map Elector Strategy," *Dallas Morning News*, Sep. 17, 1944.

argued, "they were bound to accept the will of the majority of delegates to the state convention. It is apparent that relators do not enter this court in good faith and good conscience, but to the contrary, their hands are sullied by acts of participation and acquiescence in the accepted and established party proceedings, the results of which they now seek to overthrow."[30] The court agreed.

In the meantime, Roosevelt's surrogates, led by Rep. Wright Patman and Harry Seay, the party's new state chair, demanded that Secretary of State Sidney Latham immediately certify the newly-chosen electors from the Dallas convention. Latham, however, held his ground, saying that he wasn't going to be stampeded or pressured into accepting the revised list of Democratic electors and that he needed more time to study the unprecedented legal issues involved before deciding on the matter.

With the pro-Roosevelt faction threatening to seek a mandamus if he failed to rule in their favor and the regulars indicating that they would seek an injunction if he did, Latham — facing a looming September 25 midnight filing deadline that was only nine days away — realized the issue would eventually be decided by the state Supreme Court, regardless of which way he ruled.[31] After carefully reviewing the legal questions, Latham, insisting that he had put all political considerations aside in coming to a decision, rejected the substitute filing of the Dallas convention the following day, thereby setting the stage for the Roosevelt group's petition for mandamus.[32]

Roosevelt's supporters were naturally outraged by Latham's decision. "We are bitterly disappointed that any official would not follow the latest expression of the Democratic Party," asserted Patman in angrily denouncing the Secretary of State.[33] Along with several other Roosevelt leaders, Patman had spent the better part of two days trying to convince Latham to accept the Dallas electors. The only thing the quintessential agrarian populist didn't do was get down on his knees and beg, but he came close.[34] Then again, as the *Dallas Morning News* editorialized, it was difficult to see how Latham could have ruled any differently, especially since both law and tradition appeared to be on his side, while the prospect of certifying both slates of electors in the Democratic column — the novel idea pushed earlier by Gov. Stevenson and ex-Gov. Moody

---

[30] "State Court to Hear F. R. Electors' Pleas," *Dallas Morning News*, June 15, 1944.
[31] "Ruling on Electors Will Be Made Today," *Dallas Morning News*, Sep. 15, 1944.
[32] "May Electors Held Legal Dem Choices," *Dallas Morning News*, Sep. 16, 1944.
[33] Ibid.
[34] "Ruling on Electors Will Be Made Today," *Dallas Morning News*, Sep. 15, 1944.

and strongly favored by the Dallas newspaper — didn't appear to be an option available to him without the consent of both factions in the controversy.[35]

Both sides quickly prepared for the legal showdown triggered by Latham's decision. Having already prevailed in the first round back in June, the regulars were confident that the state's highest court would uphold the Secretary of State's ruling. They also had a three-pronged legal strategy they believed would virtually assure a positive outcome for the May electors.

The first thing they would argue, Renfro told the *Dallas Morning News*, was that the Democratic Party of Texas was not a legal branch of the national Democratic Party and that its electors weren't under any legal obligation to support the nominees of the national party. "If that is denied," said Renfro, one of the lead attorneys for the regulars, "I will demand a jury trial to prove it." If, on the other hand, the Supreme Court agreed with his argument and sent the case to the lower courts to decide, it would be too late to replace the May electors before the state's September 25 filing deadline.

Without revealing his strongest argument, Renfro also told the Dallas newspaper that he planned to rely heavily on an earlier ruling in *Pulliam v. Trawalter*, 120 S.W.2d 108 (Tex. App. 1938), where the Texas Court of Appeals held that an individual who participated in a nomination of a candidate was prohibited from becoming a candidate against that nominee. "Since the electors are chosen by conventions every person who participated in the precinct, county and state conventions were eligible potential candidates for elector and cannot move to displace those selected in the first or May convention," argued the Dallas attorney.[36]

With both sides accusing the other of engaging in dirty politics, the Texas Supreme Court heard two hours and fifteen minutes of heated oral argument during the mandamus proceeding on September 20.

During the hearing, Robert W. Calvert of Hillsboro, one of the lead attorneys for the Roosevelt faction, claimed that the anti-Roosevelt electors chosen in May were attempting to sabotage the party while subverting the will of the people. Former Gov. Allred, also pleading the case of the Dallas convention, echoed Calvert's remarks and told the court that the regulars were "asking the court to approve of something that will operate as a fraud on the voters of Texas. These gentlemen," he said, "in effect have vacated and

---

[35] "Latham's Ruling," *Dallas Morning News*, Sep. 17, 1944.
[36] "Dem Elector Fight Set in High Court," *Dallas Morning News*, Sep. 19, 1944.

organized a new party, and they are attempting to embezzle the name of the Democratic Party and the vote of the party."

Woodville Rogers of San Antonio, another attorney representing the September convention, chimed in that the Democratic Party had every right to toss out its enemies. "No man has an inherent right to enter a party he has fought for years, nor the right to come into court unless he has clean hands," shouted the highstrung Rogers. "They are boring from within to sabotage the party." Quoting at length from court decisions supposedly buttressing his claim, Rogers maintained that the September convention had more power than the May convention to select presidential electors — a claim quickly disputed by Frank Knapp, one of the attorneys for the regulars representing the fifteen May electors removed by the Dallas convention.

"It is an undisputed fact that the Democratic Party has always chosen the elector nominees at the May convention in accordance with party usage and custom since 1905," countered Knapp, adding that the opposing attorneys had failed to cite even a single authority supporting their argument that the September convention had the power to remove and replace the electors chosen in May. "The September convention lacked authority, regardless of reason or cause, to substitute the electors," he argued. "Under the statutes of Texas the power does not exist to withdraw a nominee and the nominee has a vested right which cannot be taken away." Tradition and custom, continued the Houston lawyer, gave the May convention the exclusive authority to choose the party's electors and, in the absence of a statutory regulation, "ripens into a rule of law which is binding upon the party."

During his pleading, Knapp refuted the opposition's argument that the regulars were trying disenfranchise Roosevelt's supporters in the Lone Star State. If anything, he said, it was the national Democratic Party that had already disenfranchised a large portion of Texas Democrats when it refused to seat the state's full delegation at the party's national convention in Chicago earlier that summer. It was a valid point.

In response to a question regarding absentee ballots for soldiers and how those serving overseas might be disenfranchised if the May electors were allowed to remain on the ballot — another issue raised by the Roosevelt lawyers — Renfro told the court that the regulars had no desire to deprive any citizen, civilian or military, of his or her right to vote and were more than willing to have "the nominees of the rump convention (the pro-Roosevelt bolters in May) placed on the ballot in a column plainly marked Roosevelt-

Truman."

The justices promised a speedy decision.[37] While both sides were anxiously awaiting on pins and needles as the state's highest court deliberated the issue, the pro-Roosevelt electors from the regular May convention in Austin were reduced from eight to seven when state Rep. Henry W. Rampy of Winters resigned due to his ineligibility to serve as an elector while also running for the state legislature. Depending on the court's ruling, there was now the possibility that the regulars could have sixteen anti-Roosevelt electors instead of fifteen in the Democratic column in November. Texas law specified that if a presidential elector died or resigned prior to the election, the other electors were empowered to name a successor.[38]

That potentially troubling development, however, turned out to be a moot concern for Roosevelt's leaders when the Texas Supreme Court, in a unanimous ruling issued on Saturday, September 23, directed Secretary of State Latham to certify the names of the pro-Roosevelt Democratic electors on the November ballot.

In its decision, announced by Chief Justice James P. Alexander, the state's highest court ruled that the Democratic Party of Texas was "free to handle the matter as it saw fit, so long as there was no fraud or oppression and the members of the party were given a reasonable opportunity to express their views" — all of which the court maintained had been satisfied by virtue of the Dallas convention. "To hold otherwise would force the party to retain as its representatives those who are no longer agreeable to it." Alexander, the first person in Texas history to serve as chief justice without having previously served on the court by appointment or as an associate justice, continued:

> This was clearly a matter within the inherent power of the party. The sufficiency of the cause for the withdrawal of the nominations is not a matter for this court to determine. That was a matter that rested entirely with the party. The party has thus spoken its will, and in the absence of a valid law to the contrary, it is entitled to have that will carried into execution.
>
> It is urged that it has long been the custom of the party to select its nominees for presidential electors at the May convention. This may be true, but it does not appear that there is any prevailing custom or established usage by which the party may

---

[37] 'Dirty Politics!' is Cry," *Amarillo Globe-Times*, Sep. 20, 1944.
[38] "Pro Dems Face Setback," *Amarillo Globe-Times*, Sep. 21, 1944; "Anti-Roosevelt Electors on State Ticket May Be Increased to 16," *Lubbock Morning Avalanche*, Sep. 22, 1944.

not subsequently withdraw its nominations when it is found that the nominees previously selected by it are not in accord with the will of the majority of the party. Compliance with the usage and custom speak through a properly constituted authority and at the same time when the members of the party will have an opportunity to be heard. Both of these requirements have been met in this instance.[39]

The Roosevelt forces applauded the decision. "In the Texas situation, the overwhelming evidence was that a majority of the Democrats of Texas wanted the right to vote the straight Democratic ticket, including the nominees for president and vice-president," said Secretary of Commerce Jesse Jones, a Texan who had kept Roosevelt closely informed of developments in the Lone Star State. "The decision of the Texas Supreme Court gives them that right, a right that should never have been in doubt."[40] Harry Seay, chairman of the party's new executive committee, echoed the Commerce Secretary's sentiment. "This is a great victory," he said. "It ends all questions as to where the electoral vote will go."[41]

The *Dallas Morning News* — a paper that had enthusiastically embraced Gov. Stevenson's compromise proposal prior to the Dallas convention and later endorsed Republican Tom Dewey — was somewhat critical of the court ruling, asserting that the justices had overlooked "the fact that the majority in the September convention, came possibly, if not probably, from arbitrary rulings in county conventions, as in Dallas County, that a Democrat is not a Democrat unless he is a Roosevelt Democrat." By putting its "stamp of approval on bolting in the early convention by any faction that may think that it has an opportunity to win in a second race," the paper continued, the court was setting a precedent for future cat-and-dog fights between the May and September presidential conventions. The Supreme Court ruling, it concluded, "reunites the party but less solidly than would have been done if the whole controversy had been referred to the one really supreme tribunal of democracy — the people of the state."[42]

The regulars, meanwhile, refused to throw in the towel. Denied the right to file a motion for a rehearing due to the state's

---

[39] "Pro-FD Electors On, Antis Off Presidential Ballot," *Abilene Reporter-News*, Sep. 23, 1944.
[40] "Fourth Term Electors Recognized," *Longview Daily News* (Longview, TX), Sep. 24, 1944.
[41] "Antis, Ruled Out By Court, Form New Party for Fight," *Lubbock Avalanche-Journal*, Sep. 24, 1944.
[42] "Decision on Electors," *Dallas Morning News*, Sep. 24, 1944.

looming September 25 filing deadline, several prominent members of that faction, including Renfro, Dallas millionaire Eugene B. Germany and J. Hart Willis, among others, had gathered in Austin awaiting the Supreme Court's decision. Meeting in a closed-session convention moments after the court's adverse ruling, the regulars quickly consulted with other anti-Roosevelt leaders around the state by telephone in coming to a consensus.

The hastily-organized convention, which was chaired by lawyer and oil executive Edgar E. Townes of Houston with Renfro serving as secretary, resolved to place its own set of electors on the November ballot, possibly under the label "Constitutional Democrats." In a formal statement issued immediately after the convention, the regulars declared that the purpose of their new party was "to certify persons for presidential electors and give the voters of Texas an opportunity to register their votes in the November election for electors who will stand for the true Jeffersonian principles of democracy and for the restoration of constitutional government, freedom of the press and freedom of private enterprise."

Claiming that "a large majority of the Texas people resent and condemn the usurping of the Democratic Party name by Communists, big-city machine politicians, Bronx Negro politicians and the CIO political action committee, headed by the foreign-born Sidney Hillman," the belligerent regulars asserted that "the fight has just started and will be waged increasingly upon the high planes of principles until victory is ours in November." The decision to field its own slate of electors was a blow to the Texas GOP leadership, which had already extended a cordial invitation to the dissidents to support the Republican electors.[43]

Under threat of possible legal action by the state Democratic executive committee, the regulars, who had considered "Jeffersonian Democrats," "Constitutional Democrats" or "Regular Democrats" as possible names for their new party, opted against using the word "Democratic" in the party's name when it filed its slate of electors on Monday, September 25.[44]

Adopting "Texas Regulars" as the party's name, the party filed its slate of 23 presidential electors before the midnight deadline. Except for two electors who had asked that their names be replaced, thirteen of the fifteen original electors nominated at the regular convention in May agreed to serve as electors. In making its filing,

---

[43] "Court Upholds Fourth Termers; Antis Organize, Set New Electors," *Dallas Morning News*, Sep. 24, 1944.

[44] "New Party Name to be Revealed Late Today by Anti-New Dealers," *Big Spring Daily Herald* (Big Spring, TX), Sep. 25, 1944.

the Texas Regulars chose Roy Sanderford of Belton as chairman of the party's nominating convention. Hamilton Rogers of Fort Worth was listed as secretary.[45] A former military flight instructor and ex-state senator who years earlier had famously flown his own plane nearly 300 miles from rural Belton — an old Ma and Pa Ferguson stronghold in central Texas — to his corporate office in Dallas and back every weekday, Sanderford had served as permanent chairman of the party's state convention in Austin earlier that spring.[46]

"The cardinal purpose of this party is to restore constitutional government to the United States and elect a Democrat as the next president," declared Sanderford at a press conference shortly after filing the party's paperwork with the Secretary of State. "We do not propose to be deterred by a flimsy Supreme Court decision that would either destroy the Democratic Party or surrender it to the satellites of Hillman and Browder, et al."[47]

Latham placed the Texas Regulars in the third column on the ballot, next to the Republican column, largely on the theory that the breakaway Democratic faction was likely to receive far greater support than the Prohibition, Socialist and America First parties, although each of those parties had nominated presidential and vice-presidential candidates and qualified for the ballot earlier than the state's newest party. In addition to the Democrats, Republicans and Texas Regulars, the Prohibitionists were the only other party on the general election ballot with a full slate of 23 electors, a list that included Sam Morris, the famous "Voice of Temperance" who usually concluded his radio program by saying that "all the beer and whiskey should be taken down and poured in the river." The Socialists filed thirteen electors while Gerald L. K. Smith's America First Party named only three.[48]

Having secured a place on the ballot, the Texas Regulars wasted little time renewing their appeals to anti-Roosevelt Democrats throughout the state. Merritt H. Gibson of Longview, a county judge who was later named campaign manager for the new party, issued an appeal "to every Democratic citizen of Texas, as a matter of patriotism and love of state and country, to vote for

---

[45] "Anti-FDR Democratic Electors on State Ballot as 'Texas Regulars,'" *Abilene Reporter-News*, Sep. 26, 1944.
[46] "Texas' First Aerial Commuter," *Dallas Morning News*, Aug. 18, 1929.
[47] "Texas Regulars File Slate; Demos Active," *Lubbock Morning Avalanche*, Sep. 26, 1944.
[48] "Regulars Placed Third on Ballots," *Longview Daily News*, Sep. 27, 1944; "Gets Third Place," *Lubbock Morning Avalanche*, Oct. 11, 1944; Gene Fowler and Bill Crawford, *Border Radio: Quacks, Yodelers, Pitchmen, Psychics, and Other Amazing Broadcasters of the American Airwaves* (Austin, 2002), p. 119.

presidential electors under the heading Texas Regulars. You owe this to yourself and Democratic principles," he continued, "for we have always stood and fought together for these very things — states' rights, freedom of enterprise, white supremacy — which have made Texas and this country the best on earth, but which are now endangered by a group...who in fact are enemies of democracy as you, your fathers and grandfathers knew it."[49]

A few days later, Martin Dies, the seven-term congressman and former New Dealer who led the infamous House Un-American Activities Committee (HUAC), a committee co-founded by New York's Samuel Dickstein — the only known member of Congress who had been actively engaged in espionage for the Soviet Union while serving in the U.S. House of Representatives — which made sensational headlines across the country while squandering a small fortune in supposedly tracking down alleged "subversives" on the federal payroll in the late thirties and early forties, publicly threw his support to the Texas Regulars.

Blasting Roosevelt and the New Deal during a speech in Dallas, Dies asserted that "the simple truth is that the New Dealers themselves do not believe in our form of government. They have been doing all within their power," he told a dinner in his honor hosted by the city's Southern Democratic Club, "to subvert and undermine it by intrigue, deception, and un-American propaganda."[50]

The 44-year-old Dies, who once tried to impeach Secretary of Labor Frances Perkins — the first woman to ever serve in a U.S. Cabinet — for failing to deport fiery West Coast labor leader Harry Bridges, the Australian-born head of the International Longshoremen's and Warehousemen's Union, for his alleged affiliation with the Communist Party, told the dinner gathering that Roosevelt, in a heated exchange at the White House, had personally insisted that the House investigative committee should "confine its work to the Nazis and Fascists and lay off the CIO. This I refused to do," said Dies, "knowing at the time that my decision would bring down upon my head the wrath of the president and those who blindly follow his leadership."[51] From that moment on, he continued, "the New Deal coalition of Socialists, Communists, officeholders, crack-

---

[49] "Creager Bares Move to Unite Texas Regulars, Republicans," *Abilene Reporter-News*, Sep. 28, 1944; "Merritt H. Gibson to Lead Campaign Texas Regulars," *Longview Daily News*, Oct. 5, 1944.
[50] "Dies Charges New Deal With Intrigue, Deceptive Tactics," *Lubbock Avalanche-Journal*, Oct. 1, 1944.
[51] "Dies Fires Blast at New Dealers," *Abilene Reporter-News*, Oct. 1, 1944.

pots and labor politicians launched a furious assault upon our investigation."

The Texas congressman then told the large and enthusiastic crowd at the Hotel Adolphus that he and his family had been subjected to years of threats and intimidation by supporters of the administration, eventually undermining his health and eventually leading to his decision not to seek another term that year. "While we were working days and nights to discover the agents and activities of the Axis powers, the New Deal agencies spent their time and the public's money investigating and obstructing the work of our committee," said Dies. They sent their stooges into my district to investigate my record as a lawyer, my private life, and my income for a period of years, in hopes that they could find something to smear me with."[52]

Charging that the "New Deal has opposed, harassed, and obstructed" his committee's investigations throughout his tenure as chairman, the lame-duck Texas congressman, a bitter Roosevelt critic, concluded his fiery speech by saying that he felt it was his duty "to join those fearless and unterrified Democrats of Texas who dare to fight for the restoration of our party to democratic principles and the American concept of government."[53]

Dies, who had been bitterly opposed by the CIO when he unsuccessfully ran for the U.S. Senate in special election to replace the late Morris Sheppard in 1941 — a race narrowly won by Pappy O'Daniel — addressed a statewide rally in Fort Worth on October 11, asserting that the "un-American character of the New Deal is shown by its policy in promoting class and racial consciousness in America," which he claimed was deliberately designed "to stir up hatred against southern people." Taking an active part in the campaign, the lame-duck congressman also scheduled appearances on behalf of the Texas Regulars in Houston, San Antonio, San Angelo, and in various parts of the Rio Grande Valley and west Texas.[54]

Meeting in Austin in early October, the Texas Regulars laid out their plans for an extensive statewide campaign, featuring heavy newspaper and radio advertising. Roy Sanderford was named as the party's publicity director.[55] Houston's Lamar Fleming, Jr., a di-

---

[52] "Dies Charges F. R. Sought to Block Communist Probe," *Dallas Morning News*, Oct. 1, 1944.
[53] "New Dealers Rapped by Chairman Dies," *Brownsville Herald*, Oct. 1, 1944.
[54] "Dies Says He'll Stump State in Effort to Beat New Deal," *Abilene Reporter-News*, Oct. 11, 1944.
[55] "Roy Sanderford is Named Chairman of Regulars Committee," *Corsicana Semi-Weekly Light* (Corsicana, TX), Oct. 6, 1944.

rector of the National Cotton Council, a trade group that had recently persuaded the Senate Banking and Currency Committee to include a provision in pending legislation to boost the price of cotton textiles — a measure expected to cost consumers between $225 million to $335 million a year — was named finance chairman. Fleming, who was then running Anderson, Clayton & Company, the world's largest cotton firm, and later served on the board of directors of the Federal Reserve Bank of Dallas, contributed $1,000 to Pappy O'Daniel's political activities that year.[56]

The party simultaneously announced the opening of a campaign headquarters in the Littlefield Building in Austin. The Austin conference, attended by approximately 35 party leaders, also adopted an eight-point statement of principles. During the meeting, Eugene B. Germany of Dallas announced that the group's electoral votes would be cast for Virginia's Harry F. Byrd and that a vice-presidential candidate would most likely be named later.[57]

Declaring that the party's main objective was to "consolidate the anti-New Deal vote in Texas and elect our electors who will cast their votes for Harry Byrd of Virginia," Germany told the Austin gathering that "a vote for Dewey and Bricker is a vote for the New Deal and Roosevelt. Republicans, being a minority party in this state, can best help their national ticket by aiding the Texas Regulars and preventing the 23 Texas votes from being cast for Roosevelt."[58]

The naming of Byrd as the party's presidential standard-bearer — obviously without his consent — was done, in part, to facilitate military votes being cast overseas. Unlike the official Texas ballot, federal absentee ballots didn't list a party's presidential electors and provided only one space to indicate an individual's presidential preference. Byrd's refusal to allow his name to be printed on the soldier ballot put the Texas Regulars at a great disadvantage, particularly since as many as 80,000 military absentee ballots were expected to be cast by Texans serving in the Armed Forces. "The instructions to Texas Regular electors pledged them to vote for some Democrat other than Roosevelt, but no definite person was named," wrote historian Seth McKay, "a fact which may have cost the party thousands of votes."[59]

---

[56] "Regulars Seek to Restore Integrity," *Longview Daily News*, Oct. 6, 1944; "A Study of the Cotton Lobby; Its Part in the Current Fight," *Baltimore Sun*, June 4, 1944; "O'Daniel Activities Paid for Mostly by Big Donors," *Abilene Reporter-News*, Nov. 13, 1944.
[57] "Regulars Set Principles in Asking for Support," *Odessa American*, Oct. 5, 1944; "Texas Regulars to Choose V-P," *Abilene Reporter-News*, Oct. 7, 1944.
[58] "Texas Regulars Specify Goals," *Amarillo Daily News*, Oct. 5, 1944.
[59] McKay, *Texas Politics, 1906-1944*, p. 453.

A few days later, the Texas Regulars published their platform, a relatively short document calling for a constitutional amendment limiting presidential tenure to no more than two four-year terms. While promising to restore and protect constitutional government in the United States, the party's platform, which was drafted by Merritt Gibson, Clint C. Small of Austin and former state Sen. Temple H. McGregor — the latter of whom once ran for governor of Texas on ex-Gov. James Ferguson's short-lived American Party ticket in 1920 — also pledged to work for the restoration of the national Democratic Party's two-thirds rule for nominating candidates for president and vice-president.

The platform, which had been adopted in principle at the party's hastily-organized founding convention on September 23, also reaffirmed its allegiance to the Democratic national platform of 1932 and sharply deplored the fact that the Roosevelt administration had "flagrantly disregarded the cardinal principles of that solemn compact with the American people." It also strongly condemned what it described as the persistent efforts to destroy the right of Texas to segregate its public schools and public transportation systems while criticizing attempts by the Roosevelt administration "to deny the right of states to require payment of a poll tax or of a registration fee as a prerequisite for the right to vote."

> Our action has been impelled by numerous governmental abuses during the past decade, including but not limited to, the gradual encroachment by the federal government upon states' rights, the ever increasing tendency to disregard constitutional limitations, the insidious infiltration of corrupt, sinister and radical elements into positions of honor and trust in our national government, and, more recently, by the fact that the control of the great Democratic Party has passed into the hands of the coalition of political bosses, greedy war profiteers, and Communist groups, whose avowed purposes will necessarily destroy our constitutional form of government.[60]

Dismissing the Texas Regulars as an inconsequential factor, state Democratic leaders asserted that Roosevelt would sweep the state with at least 750,000 votes while claiming the rebel breakaway faction wouldn't receive more than 50,000.[61] Speaker of the House Sam Rayburn, who served in Congress from Woodrow Wilson's

---

[60] "Texas Regular Party Announces Platform," *Paris News* (Paris, TX), Oct. 8, 1944. For McGregor's 1920 gubernatorial candidacy, see Richardson, *Others: "Fighting Bob" La Follette and the Progressive Movement — Third-Party Politics in the 1920s*, pp. 81, 109.
[61] "Texans Predict Roosevelt Win," *Indianapolis Star*, Oct. 14, 1944.

administration to the beginning of John F. Kennedy's presidency, predicted that their showing would be "so small that even the Republicans will be able to laugh at them. It will be the costliest campaign," he added, "and they will get the smallest number of votes of any election in the history of Texas."[62]

Believing that rank-and-file Democrats were more or less evenly split between Roosevelt and their own slate of unpledged electors, the Texas Regulars were undeterred by such projections and enthusiastically announced on October 21 that Texas Sen. W. Lee "Pappy" O'Daniel and his famous hillbilly band would be barnstorming the state on their behalf during the final two weeks of the campaign.

"We can't lose now," crowed Gibson in announcing O'Daniel's support for the anti-Roosevelt ticket. "The Texas Regulars consider victory in the bag," he proclaimed. "Everyone is familiar with Senator O'Daniel's valiant fight against the New Deal bureaucrats. He has been fighting for four years and it is only natural for him to align himself with our cause in Texas where the balance of power in the final outcome of the national election will lie. Senator O'Daniel," he concluded, "is a real Democrat who believes in the Jeffersonian principles of the party."[63]

Other than his strong opposition to Roosevelt and the New Deal, O'Daniel didn't have a lot in common with the leaders of the Texas Regulars and had never been dependent on support from men like Dallas businessman Eugene Germany and former Gov. Dan Moody. He had his own unique network of friends and supporters throughout the state, especially among older folks in the state's rural areas and small towns. O'Daniel, moreover, didn't even bother to attend the party's state convention in Austin earlier that spring and was a conspicuous no-show at the party's national convention in Chicago later that summer. He sort of knew the fix was in and was half right when he predicted a month earlier that the regulars wouldn't be seated in Chicago. "In line with the New Deal's policy to do most everything wrong," he said during a press conference in June, "I expect they will seat the 'pout' delegation" — a reference to the pro-Roosevelt rump convention. The colorful senator was also noticeably aloof when Texas Democrats gathered in Dallas for the all-important second convention in September.[64]

---

[62] "Rayburn Blames GOP for Much of U.S. Lack of War Preparation," *Lubbock Morning Avalanche*, Oct. 18, 1944.
[63] "Pappy and Band to Tour Texas," *Lubbock Avalanche-Journal*, Oct. 22, 1944.
[64] McKay, *Texas Politics, 1906-1944*, p. 463; "New Deal Setup Called Racket," *Lubbock Morning Avalanche*, June 20, 1944.

But O'Daniel nevertheless considered himself a Democrat and wasn't about to be pushed out of his own party. "I do not propose to let any gang of Communists run me out of the Democratic Party," he declared in announcing his support for the Texas Regulars.⁶⁵ Accompanied by wealthy oilman Arch H. Rowan of Fort Worth, one of the party's 23 electors, O'Daniel and his motorized caravan of country entertainers began their two-week musical tour across Texas with appearances in Fort Worth and Wichita Falls on October 24, followed by stops in Childress, Amarillo, Lubbock, Big Spring, San Angelo and Abilene over the next three days. In all, O'Daniel gave more than two dozen speeches for the Texas Regulars, all but one of which were broadcast over a statewide radio network.

Before hitting the campaign trail, O'Daniel had been temporarily distracted by a congressional investigation into the financing of his political activities, particularly the revival of his newspaper, which he began publishing again in July following a hiatus of several years. Notified that the Senate Campaign Expenditures Committee planned to send investigators to Texas, the former flour salesman didn't appear the least bit worried about the congressional probe. "It's the same old New Deal smear squad in action," scoffed O'Daniel. "They're just interested as stooges of the administration in smearing American citizens who believe in defending and upholding the constitution."⁶⁶

On October 12 — twelve days before the genial, strapping senator and his hillbilly band were to begin their whirlwind tour of the Lone Star state — the Senate committee subpoenaed Garfield Crawford, O'Daniel's treasurer, to appear in Washington the following week.⁶⁷ Crawford testified that "subscriptions" to the senator's weekly newspaper and contributions to the O'Daniel-sponsored Common Citizens Radio Committee came to $127,000 — a figure far less than what had actually been contributed. Included in that amount, he said, were $25,000 donations from Republican Sen. Edward H. Moore of Oklahoma and Houston oil magnate Hugh R. Cullen.

O'Daniel's teary-eyed wife, who managed the *W. Lee O'Daniel News* along with the couple's two sons, both of whom were serv-

---

⁶⁵ "O'Daniel to Fight F.R. in Texas, But Says He'll be Nonpolitical," *Dallas Morning News*, Oct. 22, 1944.
⁶⁶ "Senate to Probe O'Daniel's Part in Campaign," *Dallas Morning News*, Sep. 23, 1944.
⁶⁷ "O'Daniel's Treasurer Subpoenaed in Senate Expense Investigation," *Dallas Morning News*, Oct. 13, 1944.

ing in the military at the time, also testified before the Senate committee, scolding committee chairman Theodore Green (D-R.I.) for his "vicious and unwarranted attack" on her family and for publicly "insinuating that the *W. Lee O'Daniel News* is some sort of crooked, or unlawful or unworthy publication."[68]

O'Daniel later divulged that Green's Senate investigating committee had barely scratched the surface when it came to his fundraising prowess, boasting in his newspaper that Senator Green's "gumshoe snoopers failed to find a record of even one half of the money the *News* had taken in because most of it was sent to its head office in Washington and deposited in its Washington bank." O'Daniel's wife later submitted documentation to the Senate committee showing a reported income for the *W. Lee O'Daniel News* totaling $313,338.24 as of October 31, 1944.[69]

Although O'Daniel had never lost a statewide contest, the state's leading Democrats didn't appear to be too worried about his sudden high-profile involvement with the Texas Regulars. "O'Daniel is too well known now in Texas to mislead the voters," said Robert F. Peden, chairman of the state's Roosevelt-Truman organization.[70] Other Democrats heaped opprobrium on the reactionary senator while at least one leading party member firmly believed that O'Daniel and his hillbilly band would be widely ignored by the vast majority of the state's rank-and-file Democrats. "No act of the state organization will lend popular interest to the dying campaign of the Texas Regulars," said Corsicana attorney Tom Tyson, head of the Roosevelt-Truman speaker's bureau. "We had anticipated all along they would use Pappy. Some have called him their secret weapon...but it is a dud."[71] O'Daniel, he said confidently, wouldn't be able to puncture Roosevelt's immense popularity among Texans. "News that the junior senator is to tour this state to personally attack the president will be very disappointing to many of his former followers who are wholeheartedly supporting our great president." It was quite fitting, Tyson bluntly added, "that Senator O'Daniel should be the chief mourner at the political funeral of the Texas Regulars."[72]

Yet some Democrats were clearly worried about O'Daniel's

---

[68] "$127,000 for O'Daniel Activities Collected, Office Manager Says," *Dallas Morning News*, Oct. 20, 1944.
[69] Kennedy, *Southern Exposure*, p. 142.
[70] "Texas Regulars Elector Will Be on O'Daniel Tour," *Longview Daily News*, Oct. 23, 1944; "Pappy's Show Hits the Road Today," *Abilene Reporter-News*, Oct. 24, 1944.
[71] "Demos Ignore Pappy's Tour," *Abilene Reporter-News*, Oct. 23, 1944.
[72] "O'Daniel to Fight F.R. in Texas, But Says He'll be Nonpolitical," *Dallas Morning News*, Oct. 22, 1944.

role in promoting the Texas Regulars. Herman Jones, an Austin attorney and a Roosevelt leader in the state, questioned the fact the anti-fourth term party hadn't complied with Texas law in certifying the names of its presidential and vice-presidential candidates at least twenty days prior to the election. "The time for compliance with this law lapsed about a week ago," said Jones. "This morning I called the Secretary of State's office and was advised that the Texas Regulars had ignored the statue." Citing article 3079c of the Texas Statutes, Jones maintained that the Texas Regulars were required by law to inform the voters who their candidates were. "They should prompt Pappy to tell the people whether their choice is Gerald L. K. Smith, Gerald Nye, Hamilton Fish, or some other person," cracked Jones, knowing full well that Virginia's Harry Byrd was the preferred choice of the group's 23 unpledged electors.[73]

The concern raised by the Austin attorney turned out be a moot issue when Secretary of State Latham informed him that the statute in question was a 1931 law that, ironically, had been held invalidated years earlier by former Attorney General James V. Allred — a staunch Roosevelt supporter — and the courts.[74]

Given the strict gasoline rationing at the time, other leading Texas Democrats questioned how O'Daniel was able to acquire enough gasoline to make a 3,000-mile speaking tour of Texas, especially since no application for such a purpose had been filed with the Office of Price Administration (OPA). The Regulars responded, saying that O'Daniel was relying on friends throughout the state for transportation, using legally-issued gasoline coupons, during his statewide tour and, as such, permission from the OPA wasn't necessary.[75]

The Regulars, of course, weren't the least bit amused that Roosevelt's supporters were trying to thwart O'Daniel's planned speaking tour by turning to a federal agency. "It is plain to see that they (the Roosevelt Democrats) will not hesitate to use all the alphabetic agencies of the sour and sorry alphabet soup to suppress free speech and free action," asserted campaign manager Gibson somewhat hyperbolically. "Has the time at last arrived when Americans cannot be trusted to handle the issues of the day? Is this to be the last election in which free choice is to be allowed? When

---

[73] "Regulars Flay Pro Action over Gasoline for O'Daniel's Tour," *Lubbock Morning Avalanche*, Oct. 25, 1944.
[74] "Pappy, Connally and Bricker Woo Voters," *Abilene Reporter-News*, Oct. 25, 1944.
[75] "Regulars Flay Pro Action over Gasoline for O'Daniel's Tour," *Lubbock Morning Avalanche*, Oct. 25, 1944.

American town hall and fork of the creek debate is silenced, then goodbye free press, free speech; goodbye America!"[76]

The Republicans, likewise, weren't entirely pleased by O'Daniel's speaking tour. Some even suggested this his actions were unwittingly aiding Roosevelt's chances of carrying the state. "We agree with the Senator that the country is headed for ruin if Roosevelt is elected," said Walter Rogers, state director of the Dewey-Bricker campaign, "but we cannot understand why, if this be true, they do not come out and support the only man running against President Roosevelt — Gov. Thomas E. Dewey." Republican leaders were particularly miffed that O'Daniel had personally blocked several last-ditch attempts at forging a coalition between the Texas Regulars and the GOP, reportedly telling the former that he couldn't possibly support a ticket bearing the Republican label, even if the Regulars controlled a majority of the electors on a united ticket.[77]

Almost from the moment the Texas Regulars qualified for the ballot rumors and speculation abounded that there would likely be a coalition between the anti-fourth termers and the Republicans, the state's perennial minority party.

In late September, longtime Republican national committeeman Renfro B. "Rennie" Creager of Brownsville confirmed that an effort was underway to bring about some sort of coalition between the Texas Regulars and the Republicans — an undertaking that initially caught several of the former group's leaders by surprise. "It would be too bad if a common ground could not be found for a united front," said Creager, a lily-white Republican who had managed to keep his party's black and tan faction at bay while controlling the state's federal patronage during the Harding, Coolidge and Hoover administrations. A close personal friend of the late Warren G. Harding, Creager's iron-fisted reign as the undisputed leader of the Texas GOP from 1923 until his death in 1950 amounted to a virtual fiefdom.

Informed of Creager's comments, Sanderford, state chairman of the Texas Regulars, said that he wasn't aware of any such proposal. Eugene Germany, likewise, told reporters in Dallas that he hadn't heard anything about the possibility of combining forces with the Texas Republicans. "Last Saturday there was some talk," he said, referring to the party's September 23 founding convention

---

[76] "O'Daniel Speaks Here Tonight," *Amarillo Daily News*, Oct. 25, 1944.
[77] "O'Daniel Act Called Aid to Victory of F.R.," *Dallas Morning News*, Nov. 2, 1944; "O'Daniel to Conclude Campaign Here Nov. 6," *Dallas Morning News*, Oct. 31, 1944.

in Austin, "but we've formed a political party since then."[78]

A steady stream of proposals and counter proposals appeared in Texas newspapers over the course of the next several weeks and, on at least a couple of occasions, a joint effort appeared to be imminent.[79] There were even reports in several Texas newspapers that Germany, director of the Regulars' campaign in northeast Texas, had met privately with Republican national chairman Herbert Brownell, Jr., in New York on October 9 to discuss the possibility of a merger or coalition between the two groups.[80]

Since Texas law allowed electors to withdraw up to twenty days prior to the election, time was quickly slipping away.[81] Hoping to forge a last-minute united front against Roosevelt, leaders from both camps met at a hastily-called conference at the Rice Hotel in Houston on Sunday, October 16. Along with a few others who briefly attended the all-day meeting, the Republicans were represented by national committeeman Creager, Walter Rogers, director of the Dewey-Bricker campaign in Texas, and John F. Lucey of Dallas, one of the state's most widely-respected Republican leaders. Lucey had reportedly declined the Republican nomination for governor earlier that year. In addition to Germany, Edgar E. Townes, chairman of the party's executive committee, and John H. Crooker of Houston, one of its 23 electors, represented the Texas Regulars. Little headway was made as the Regulars rejected two proposals offered by the GOP, which, in turn, rebuffed two proposals made by the Regulars.[82]

The Republicans initially suggested that the Texas Regulars should form a "Democrats for Dewey" organization, similar to what was taking place in neighboring Oklahoma. When that proposition was rejected, GOP leaders then suggested that they would be willing to replace twelve of their own twenty-three electors with members named by the Regulars. In that scenario, the remaining eleven Republican electors would be instructed to support Dewey for president, but the twelve electors representing the Texas Regulars would be free to vote for any candidate of their choice. That, too, was turned down.

The Regulars countered with two proposals of their own. The first was a demand that the Republicans remove their 23 electors from the ballot — a proposal quickly rejected by Creager and the

---

[78] "Creager Bares Move to Unite Texas Regulars, Republicans," *Abilene Reporter-News*, Sep. 28, 1944.
[79] McKay, *Texas Politics, 1906-1944*, pp. 458-459.
[80] "Texas Coalition Talk is Revived," *Lubbock Morning Avalanche*, Oct. 11, 1944.
[81] "Regular Democrats Ignore GOP Bait," *Longview Daily News*, Sep. 28, 1944.
[82] "Regular-Republican Leaders Disagree," *Big Spring Herald*, Oct. 16, 1944.

other Republicans in the room. Recognizing that the Republicans would never agree to the removal of their electors, the Regulars then proposed that the Republican electors should be allowed to remain on the ballot, but as Election Day neared GOP state leaders would agree to endorse the Regulars' electors by calling on their party's rank and file to disregard the Republican electors. That proposal was also rejected.

Though failing to reach an agreement, Rogers and Germany, the latter of whom was far more amenable to working with the Republicans than most of the Texas Regular leadership, insisted that some progress had been made during the Houston conference. "We talked it over in a friendly attitude and some progress was made," said Rogers. "It is hoped that something may result from the meeting."[83] Germany, who later attended a Dallas rally for Gov. Bricker, Dewey's vice-presidential running mate, concurred, expressing confidence that the Texas Regulars and the GOP would be "fighting side by side soon for our common purpose — the smashing of the New Deal bureaucracy."[84]

Despite such optimism, it was growing increasingly clear that a coalition simply wasn't in the cards. If there was any doubt, those concerns were quickly laid to rest by Gibson, campaign manager for the Texas Regulars. "The Texas Regulars will not withdraw in favor of Republicans," Gibson declared in a formal statement issued in Austin shortly after the Houston conference, "but will continue the fight until the Democratic Party in Texas is freed of Communistic and alien influence." The party's 23 electors, he added, were furnishing a "common meeting ground for all persons opposed to the New Deal to vote against Roosevelt without having to go Republican."[85]

Whatever flickering hope remained for a united campaign against FDR was extinguished a few days later when Creager withdrew the GOP's earlier proposal for a joint ticket made up of electors from both groups. "It is now too late for a mixed ticket," said the longtime national committeeman in slamming the door on any and all coalition proposals made during the climactic negotiations in Houston a few days earlier.

Creager cited several reasons for opposing the proposals made by the Texas Regulars. Coupled with the fact a number of Dewey-Bricker electors would have refused to withdraw, Creager said that it would have been virtually impossible to convince a majority

---

[83] "Regulars Carry Plea for Unity to Lucey," *Dallas Morning News*, Oct. 16, 1944.
[84] "GOP Woos Regulars for Bricker Rally," *Dallas Morning News*, Oct. 17, 1944.
[85] "GOP, Regulars Unable to Reach Agreement," *Amarillo Daily News*, Oct. 17, 1944.

of Dewey's supporters to back the Texas Regulars. He also questioned the legality of the Texas Regulars' nominating method, suggesting that they were "treading on thin ice" from a legal standpoint and could be subject to a court challenge. "In the event suits were brought and adverse decisions rendered or even delayed by the courts," he said, "there is grave danger that both the anti-Roosevelt people and the Republican Party in Texas would be without a ticket or candidate, and, therefore, Roosevelt would win in Texas by default."

Expressing dismay at the resistance to a mixed ticket — the GOP offered the anti-Roosevelt Democrats 12 or 13 electors of their choosing — Creager sharply refuted the argument made repeatedly by the Texas Regulars that hundreds of thousands of Texans would simply refuse to cast a Republican ballot, regardless of the composition of the party's electoral slate. "There is no such ignorant and widespread prejudice against voting for the electors under a Republican heading, as was argued," he stated. "During the last twenty years, 75 percent of the Democrats of Texas have on one or more occasions voted a Republican ticket," he continued. "A vote for the Texas Regulars is a half-vote for Dewey. Why not a whole vote?"[86]

In the meantime, O'Daniel — in a prelude to his widely-publicized statewide speaking tour — told a radio audience in Fort Worth that the "New Deal dynasty," as he often called it, had virtually abandoned the constitution and warned that the United States faced "greater danger at home of losing our democracy than we do on the fighting fronts." Describing the constitution as the nation's only safeguard against the growing federal bureaucracy — "a document second in sacredness only to the Bible" — the colorful Texan cautioned that the U.S. couldn't remain free and continue enjoying individual rights and liberties by discarding the constitution. "No man can be trusted as president," he said in a not so thinly-veiled attack on FDR, "if he does not believe in the constitution of the United States."[87]

Occasionally heckled and booed while risking defeat for the first time in his meteoric political career by aligning so publicly with the Texas Regulars, O'Daniel denied that his speaking tour was of a political nature. Nobody, of course, believed him. "We haven't any candidate this year — the Democrats, that is," he told an incredulous reporter in Wichita Falls. "These talks of mine, for that

---

[86] "Texas GOP Closes Door on Coalition," *Dallas Morning News*, Oct. 19, 1944.
[87] "O'Daniel Voices New Deal Fears," *Amarillo Daily News*, Oct. 25, 1944.

reason, won't be political," he said, "but will be based on my crusade for a constitutional amendment to limit the tenure of the president and members of Congress." (O'Daniel wanted to limit the president and members of the U.S. Senate to a single six-year term while limiting members of the House to a maximum of three two-year terms.)[88] The state's junior senator also said that he hadn't returned to Texas "to tell the people of this state how to vote, but merely to report faithfully as their hired hand just what is going on in the nation."[89]

Though much of the old magic — the fire and good-natured wisecracking and ridicule that marked his four previous statewide campaigns — seemed to be missing, the once-popular former flour salesman and radio personality nevertheless campaigned vigorously against Roosevelt's reelection that autumn, reminding his Texas audiences that the only difference between a democracy and a monarchy was the length of tenure in office.

Frequently referring to the president as "Franklin the Fourth," O'Daniel charged that the Democratic Party was no longer recognizable and had "degenerated into nothing more than a political machine to pass out patronage and perpetuate the New Deal in power." The New Deal, he said repeatedly, had been a disaster, a period in which business and industry had been virtually destroyed, race problems had been exacerbated, morality was at an all-time low, and agriculture had been placed on a subsidy basis from which it could never free itself without disastrous consequences. Moreover, he asserted, the country no longer had a bona-fide opposition party.

According to O'Daniel, the GOP's Tom Dewey — the "me-too" candidate — simply wasn't an option. "The professional politicians in the Republican Party," he said during an appearance in Abilene, "are just as bad as those in the New Deal dynasty and they look alike to me. The Republican National Committee is either dumb or deceitful, and I don't think it's dumb. Anybody with any sense knows Dewey and Bricker haven't got a 10 to 1 chance of carrying Texas. Why, then, are they putting up posters all over Texas asking you to vote the Republican ticket? It looks to me like the Republicans want Roosevelt and Truman to get Texas' 23 electoral votes."

Maintaining that he was making the fight as a matter of princi-

---

[88] "O'Daniel Hits Campaign Trail for Regulars," *Fredericksburg Standard* (Fredericksburg, TX), Oct. 25, 1944.
[89] "O'Daniel Schedules Talk at Childress," *Brownsville Herald*, Oct. 25, 1944.

ple and not for any selfish or personal reasons, the former songwriter-turned-senator also said that it was his fervent hope that southern presidential electors would "vote for some outstanding southern Democrat" who really believes in the principles of the Democratic Party. "In the name of God, wake up," implored O'Daniel. "The pillars of democracy fall while the voice of the New Deal Jacob mesmerizes the people every four years again, and again and again."[90]

Drawing much smaller crowds than in previous campaigns, O'Daniel's strenuous two-week campaign on behalf of the Texas Regulars fell far short of expectations. In Wichita Falls, where he kicked off his statewide tour, the crowd size was estimated at only about a quarter of his previous campaign appearances. Similarly, in Amarillo, O'Daniel drew the smallest crowd to ever attend one of his performances in that city — and it wasn't a particularly enthusiastic crowd, at that. "It may have been the sad reality of war," wrote a reporter for the *Amarillo News*, "or it may have been the attitude of the people toward a man no longer highly popular, but the reception seemed certainly cold." Things weren't much better for the senator in San Angelo, where a crowd of only 600 to 700 people showed up — approximately one-tenth the number of folks who had turned out during his first race for governor six years earlier. Worse yet, O'Daniel drew only 615 people in Waco.[91]

Though failing to have the kind of impact the Texas Regulars were desperately counting on, O'Daniel's statewide tour wasn't without some tense and dramatic moments. While speaking to a crowd of 2,500 in Houston on November 2, O'Daniel could barely be heard over the deafening chants of "We want Roosevelt" and the shouting that accompanied a non-stop melee that erupted between his supporters and those of the president's backers. More than a dozen bloody fistfights ensued — one woman jumped on the back of a policeman during the slugfest and another smashed an umbrella over the head of a member of the audience — as the Texas senator tried to complete his thirty-minute radio address. "As O'Daniel began speaking," wrote a reporter for the *Houston Post*, "the jeers became louder and more determined, and never did let up."[92]

Toward the end of his speech, John H. Crooker, a spokesman

---

[90] "O'Daniel Attacks 'Communistic Control' of Democratic Party," *Lubbock Morning Avalanche*, Oct. 27, 1944; "O'Daniel Asks Defeat of All 'New Deal Gang,'" *Abilene Reporter-News*, Oct. 28, 1944.
[91] "O'Daniel Heckled, Booed at Rally; Blames Washington," *Paris News*, Nov. 3, 1944.
[92] McKay, *Texas Politics, 1906-1944*, p. 462.

for the Texas Regulars, grabbed O'Daniel's microphone and began addressing the audience. "I am ashamed of the people of Harris County for this disgraceful conduct," he shouted. "This is the most disgraceful scene I've ever seen. This gang of ruffians came here to break up this meeting. You can guess for yourself who sent them, but the right of free speech shall prevail."[93]

As many as 500 men and women, young and old, joined in the rumpus. At one point an egg was tossed, barely missing O'Daniel while splattering a supporter standing next to him and splashing into the hair of a photographer from the *Houston Chronicle* and several others. "What we wanted to do was keep the fellow, O'Daniel, from speaking because he's trying to break up this nation," yelled the egg thrower as he was being arrested for disorderly conduct. According to at least one witness, one of the rioters tried to get on the stage, shouting, "I'll cut O'Daniel's heart out." It was unclear whether he was brandishing a knife or not, although O'Daniel himself said that he saw several knives drawn during the tumultuous half-hour scuffle. Forty or fifty quick-thinking supporters immediately flanked the senator on the platform when the fighting broke out.

Fifteen uniformed police officers and twenty plain-clothed detectives in the audience couldn't quell the riotous atmosphere. O'Daniel, who somehow managed to finish his radio address amid the noisy bedlam and confusion, later issued a scathing statement blaming the outbreak of violence on "the communists, labor leader racketeers, New Deal fellow travelers and lawless element, which constitute the principal backing of the New Deal party." Describing it as "another disgraceful Gestapo performance for the White House," O'Daniel also said that he been reliably informed prior to his Houston speech to expect such chaos since it had been prearranged, "presumably on orders from Washington."[94] The editor of the *Houston Post* — a newspaper that supported Dewey — described the shameful episode as "the most disgraceful thing that ever occurred in the history of this city."[95]

O'Daniel had plenty to say about the Houston incident the following day. "If anybody would have said just a few short years ago that such an un-American demonstration as took place here in

---

[93] "O'Daniel Booed Off Air for Anti-Roosevelt Speech," *St. Louis Star-Times*, Nov. 3, 1944.
[94] "Boos, Catcalls Meet Sen. O'Daniel at Houston Talk," *Pampa News*, Nov. 3, 1944; "Riot Flares as O'Daniel Uses Radio," *Dallas Morning News*, Nov. 3, 1944; "O'Daniel Lays Heckling on White House," *Del Rio News-Herald* (Del Rio, TX), Nov. 3, 1944; "Senator O'Daniel Blames Washington for 'Rioting' During Houston Meeting," *El Paso Herald-Post*, Nov. 3, 1944.
[95] McKay, *Texas Politics, 1906-1944*, p. 462.

Houston could have taken place in Texas, where people believe in law and order and freedom of speech, nobody would have believed it," he remarked wistfully. "But it did happen in America. And it did happen in Texas."

O'Daniel, who gave no signs of being rattled during the ruckus, said that he wasn't the least bit surprised by the outbreak of violence "because I know it is the regular order of the day from here on out under the sign of Franklin the Fourth. It was his stooges," he added, "who continually shouted praises to his name in exactly the same manner as the Gestapo and the goose-steppers in Germany shout 'Heil Hitler.'" He also stated that he didn't consider it a personal assault, but rather an attack on American democracy. "I cannot believe the people of Texas will go to the polls and re-elect a president who has protected and encouraged this kind of lawlessness in our nation," he scoffed.[96]

As it turned out, the Houston skirmish was the second major disruption the Texas senator had been subjected to that day. In a situation remarkably similar to that experienced by the American Democratic National Committee's John O'Connor on the eve of the election, radio station WOAI — the control station for the Texas Quality Network — abruptly cancelled O'Daniel's statewide radio address in Victoria for "technical reasons" earlier that afternoon, prompting the enraged senator to accuse the radio station's owners of buckling under pressure from Washington. Unlike O'Connor's radio address, O'Daniel's speech had already been approved by the station's management. "The radio station operators won't cross the communistic New Deal dynasty because the New Deal would ruin them," O'Daniel angrily thundered. "The radio stations know they will be penalized if they carry my speeches."[97]

With calls for calm and civility from the state's Democratic leadership — state chairman Harry Seay asked FDR's supporters to politely refrain from booing — and surrounded by 85 police officers determined to prevent a repeat of the Houston incident, O'Daniel's final speech at the Fair Park Auditorium in Dallas was a fairly tranquil affair. Standing on stage next to a large Texas Regulars emblem bearing the words "Keep the White in Old Glory," O'Daniel — urging the packed crowd to ignore the pleadings of Republican leaders calling on anti-Roosevelt Democrats to support Dewey — told the audience that the only way to defeat Roosevelt

---

[96] "Senator O'Daniel Blames Washington for 'Rioting' During Houston Meeting," *El Paso Herald-Post*, Nov. 3, 1944.

[97] "Pappy Booed Off Air at Houston Regular Rally," *Abilene Reporter-News*, Nov. 3, 1944.

in Texas was by supporting the new party's electors.[98]

As O'Daniel was concluding his two-week effort on behalf of the Texas Regulars, James E. McDonald, the state's immensely popular agriculture commissioner, announced his support for the party's 23 presidential electors. McDonald's support wasn't completely surprising since he had abandoned Roosevelt in 1936 and 1940, supporting the Republican ticket in both presidential elections.

Running unopposed while seeking an unprecedented eighth term that fall, McDonald — the longest-serving agriculture commissioner in Texas history up 'til that time — was a frequent critic of the New Deal's agricultural policies.[99] While serving as one of several vice-chairmen of Harry Woodring's American Democratic National Committee earlier that year, the 63-year-old farm commissioner, determined to do everything in his power to prevent FDR's fourth term, proposed the possibility of a coalition ticket headed by Republican John W. Bricker of Ohio for president and Virginia's Harry F. Byrd for vice president — a ticket that was briefly championed by the ADNC.[100]

The Regulars also received an unexpected boost a few days later when John F. Lucey, one of the state's most prominent Republicans, endorsed the renegade Democratic electors. A wealthy oilman and close personal friend of former President Hoover — the Texan had worked closely with Hoover in feeding the Belgians after World War I and later served on the president's emergency unemployment committee at the outset of the Great Depression — the 69-year-old Lucey was considered one of the most widely respected Republicans not only in Texas, but in the entire South. His endorsement was expected to influence a large number of rank-and-file Republican voters in the Lone Star State.

Lucey, who had tried in vain to bring about a coalition between the Regulars' electors and the GOP electors pledged to Dewey and Bricker — holding last-minute meetings between leaders of the two groups in Houston and Dallas in the campaign's closing weeks — maintained that he was acting independently and hadn't even informed his own party's leadership of his decision when publicly announcing his support for the Regulars. "Divided we

---

[98] "Seay Urges No Booing of O'Daniel," *Dallas Morning News*, Nov. 5, 1944; "85 Police Guard Rally for O'Daniel," *Dallas Morning News*, Nov, 7, 1944.
[99] "McDonald May Repeat 1940 Bolt," *Dallas Morning News*, Sep. 9, 1944; "M'Donald Joins Regulars, Hits Partisan Votes," *Dallas Morning News*, Oct. 27, 1944.
[100] "Bricker-Byrd Ticket Asked By McDonald," *Dallas Morning News*, June 12, 1944.

certainly lose," he said, "united we may win." His unexpected announcement caught the state's Republican leaders by complete surprise, particularly since Lucey had spent years — and much of his own money — trying to make the Republican Party a viable entity in one-party Texas.[101]

Declaring that they would be in a "supreme trading position with both the Democratic and Republican parties" if their electors prevailed, the Texas Regulars unveiled their plans for defeating Roosevelt. Assuming that neither major-party candidate had an Electoral College majority, their multifaceted plan, as outlined by campaign director Merritt Gibson, called for different strategies, depending on which party controlled the House of Representatives in the new Congress.

If the Democrats controlled the House, the Texas Regulars planned to tell the GOP that they should "join with us in defeating Roosevelt or we will throw the election into the House." In that scenario, Gibson said the Regulars would seriously consider aligning with the Republicans — even if they insisted on a Dewey presidency — on the condition that the GOP electors would agree to unite behind a Democratic vice-presidential candidate in the Electoral College, possibly "someone like Sen. Byrd of Virginia, Coke Stevenson of Texas, or some other good Democrat who believes in constitutional government." There would be nothing wrong with such a coalition ticket, asserted Gibson, who later served as national campaign chairman for Strom Thurmond's Dixiecrat candidacy in 1948. In fact, he thought it would be a really healthy thing. "We aren't supposed to be concerned about this war as Democrats or Republicans, but as Americans," he said, "and since everything else is run on a coalition basis, why not our government?"

In the unlikely event that the House had a Republican majority, the Regulars said that they would initially work with other dissident Democratic electors in the South and try to swing their support to a Democrat other than Roosevelt. If a majority of Democratic electors refused to work with the rebellious Texans on a compromise candidate — someone acceptable to both sides — Gibson said that the Regulars were willing to say, "All right, we will throw our votes away (i.e., give them to someone who obviously cannot win the election), and send the election into the House, which being Republican, will make Dewey president."

But even in the latter scenario, Gibson maintained that the Texas Regulars would continue to jockey for control of the vice-

---

[101] "Lucey Says He'll Vote for Regulars Electors," *Dallas Morning News*, Nov. 3, 1944.

presidency by considering a trade of their electoral votes for Dewey provided the GOP was willing to support their choice of a Democratic vice-presidential candidate. "We prefer to beat Roosevelt with a good Democrat," he added, "but since our primary purpose is to defeat him, we would rather see Dewey elected…"[102]

Like Texans themselves, the state's daily newspapers were sharply divided between the three competing parties. Three of the state's largest papers were evenly split with the *Houston Chronicle* endorsing Roosevelt, the *Dallas Morning News* backing Dewey, and the *Houston Press*, a Scripps Howard afternoon newspaper that once employed a young Walter Cronkite, throwing its support to the Texas Regulars.

The *Houston Chronicle*, which came out in favor of Roosevelt's reelection shortly after the split in the Democratic Party earlier that spring, issued a strong endorsement on the final weekend of the campaign, declaring that "the best interests of the nation and world alike in the period ahead call for the reelection of President Roosevelt and election of Sen. Harry S. Truman as Vice President."[103] In an editorial that attracted an enormous amount of attention and an unusually large number of letters-to-the-editor, both pro and con, the *Dallas Morning News* faulted the president for failing to bring about a full economic recovery prior to World War II despite his extraordinary "pump-priming activities" while asserting that Dewey would be a welcome change from an administration that had become "stagnant with the odor of autocracy."[104]

In a front-page editorial appealing to its predominantly Democratic readership, the *Houston Press* maintained that the only way to defeat Roosevelt and "insure the election of Mr. Dewey" was to support the Texas Regulars. "We believe it is imperative that the people regain control of the government of the United States and compel it once again to become responsive to their needs," the editorial stated. "This they cannot do with the yoke of autocratic rule of Franklin D. Roosevelt around their necks, and advocates of foreign ideologies, star-gazing faddists and bosses of corrupt political machines hamstringing their effort. They can do it, we believe, through the election of Thomas E. Dewey as President. And to the attainment of that end, we believe the people of Texas can contribute most by voting for the Texas Regulars' ticket of electors," the paper concluded, apparently ignoring the fact that a majority of the electors on the third party ticket had already indicated that they

---

[102] "Regulars Detail Plans for Roosevelt Defeat," *Abilene Reporter-News*, Nov. 2, 1944.
[103] "Texas Press is Split 3 Ways over Politics," *Amarillo Daily News*, Nov. 7, 1944.
[104] "We Choose Mr. Dewey," *Dallas Morning News*, Oct. 15, 1944.

would support Virginia's Harry F. Byrd or another Democrat if given an opportunity to throw the election into the House of Representatives.[105]

Many of the state's big city newspapers were opposed to a fourth term, but Roosevelt scored plenty of endorsements from newspapers in medium-sized cities and smaller communities throughout Texas. Among others, the president enjoyed support from the *Corpus Christi Caller-Times*, the *Austin American-Statesman*, the *Waco News-Tribune*, the *Big Spring Herald*, and the *Port Arthur News*.[106]

"If we could not see Mr. Willkie in 1940, certainly we cannot see Thomas E. Dewey in 1944," wrote the *Abilene Reporter-News*. Similar sentiments were expressed by the *Wichita Falls Times and Record News* and the *El Paso Times*. The *Tyler Courier-Times and Telegraph* was typical of the medium-sized newspapers that stood unflinchingly by the wartime president. "Nothing would please Hitler and Hirohito more than for the Allied leader who is directly responsible for their defeats and impending overthrow to be repudiated at the hands of the American people," it declared in endorsing FDR. "This desire of the enemy will not be realized because President Roosevelt will be re-elected."[107]

With virtually no chance of carrying the state, Dewey nevertheless received a remarkably large number of newspaper endorsements, including those of the *Beaumont Enterprise* and the *Houston Post*, a newspaper owned by former Gov. William P. Hobby's family. It was the first time in the history of the Beaumont newspaper that it had backed a Republican candidate for the presidency.[108] Other notable endorsements were issued by the *Galveston News* — the state's oldest newspaper and the first one to endorse the Dewey-Bricker ticket — the *Amarillo Globe-News*, the *Pampa News* and the *Lufkin News*, the latter paper claiming that a vote for the Texas Regulars would do little good other than possibly enabling Roosevelt's electors to win with a minority of the popular vote.

Like Dewey, a surprising number of newspapers also endorsed the Texas Regulars, including the *San Antonio Express*, which editorially urged support for the party's unpledged electors in order to "break up New Deal domination" of the Democratic

---

[105] "Houston Paper for Texas Regulars," *El Paso Herald-Post*, Nov. 3, 1944; "Texas Regulars Present Hopes," *Amarillo Daily News*, Nov. 4, 1944.
[106] "Many Newspapers Have Taken Sides," *Pampa News*, Nov. 7, 1944.
[107] "Texas Press is Split 3 Ways over Politics," *Amarillo Daily News*, Nov. 7, 1944.
[108] Leuchtenburg, *The White House Looks South*, p. 138.

Party.[109] The San Antonio newspaper had been highly sympathetic to the Regulars throughout the internecine warfare waged by the party's two factions that year. "The Texas Regulars are fighting a battle of principle, for every person who calls himself a citizen," it editorialized earlier. "By the same token, they are fighting for free electoral choice — undominated [sic] by corrupt political machines — by citizens everywhere in the United States. That fight is a call to free men everywhere, but especially in Texas."[110]

The *Canyon News*, a relatively smaller publication in north Texas, had been one of the first newspapers to endorse the Texas Regulars, doing so in an editorial dated October 12. Asserting that Dewey didn't have prayer of carrying the state and that a vote cast for the Republican nominee meant "a vote thrown away," the Randall County newspaper urged its readers to break from tradition and support the Texas Regulars electors as "the only chance to help defeat Roosevelt in November."[111]

In addition to editorial endorsements from the *Lubbock Avalanche and Journal*, the *Temple Herald*, and the *Midland Reporter-Telegram* and several other newspapers, the Texas Regulars also received the blessing of the widely-read *El Paso Herald-Post*, which caustically dismissed the state's GOP as an "emasculated group" that was "no more effective in Texas than the Spit and Whittle Club of Possum Hollow in the Big Thicket." In urging its readers to "strike a blow for the Republic" by supporting the dissident Democratic electors, the paper's Nov. 3 editorial stated that "the Texas Regulars will get two or three times as many votes as the Republicans," while arguing that a vote for the Republican ticket was "just thrown away."[112]

All three parties forecast victory as more than a million Texans headed to the polls on November 7th. Merritt Gibson, campaign director for the Texas Regulars, predicted his party's unpledged electors would narrowly defeat Roosevelt's Democratic electors by a margin of 40 to 38 percent with Dewey and the Republicans claiming the remaining 22 percent.[113] Gibson's prediction was partly based on the claims of Judge Edgar E. Townes, chairman of the party's executive committee, who asserted that the Texas Regulars

---

[109] "State's Oldest Paper Backs GOP," *Pampa News*, Sep. 28, 1944; "Texas Press is Split 3 Ways over Politics," *Amarillo Daily News*, Nov. 7, 1944.
[110] "Texas Regulars Fight a Battle of Principle," *San Antonio Express*, Oct. 9, 1944.
[111] "Vote for Texas Regulars," *Canyon News*, Oct. 12, 1944.
[112] "Many Newspapers Have Taken Sides," *Pampa News*, Nov. 7, 1944; "Why We're Voting for the Texas Regulars," *El Paso Herald-Post*, Nov. 3, 1944.
[113] "Voting Heavy Over Nation; FDR Leads in 1st Returns," *Brownsville Herald*, Nov. 7, 1944.

— polling exceptionally well in the party's Houston stronghold — would safely carry populous Harris County, the most densely-populated area of the state. "I believe Harris County is from 65 to 70 percent anti-New Deal," said Townes, who based his prediction on a last-minute switch by many of Houston's Republican-leaning voters to the Regulars.[114] With the possible exception of Tulsa, Oklahoma, Houston was considered the most reactionary community in the United States at the time.[115]

Without a presidential candidate of their own, the severely disadvantaged Democratic-turned-third party faction faced an impossibly difficult uphill climb in their spirited quest to capture the state's twenty-three electoral votes. Texas was expected to remain safely in the Democratic column. Few, if any, expected the Texas Regulars to alter the outcome in the Lone Star State, with most prognosticators pegging their maximum strength in the neighborhood of 50,000-65,000 votes.[116]

The Regulars more than doubled those predictions on Election Day, but fell far short of denying Roosevelt the state's twenty-three electoral votes.

Sweeping 245 of the state's 254 counties, the president won overwhelmingly, polling a lopsided 821,605 votes to Dewey's 191,425. Running remarkably strong in heavily-populated Harris County, where the issue of white supremacy had clearly resonated with Houston's substantial reactionary and racist electorate, while finishing ahead of the Republican ticket in more than a third of the state's counties, the Texas Regulars garnered 135,439 votes, or nearly 11.8 percent of the statewide total.

The Regulars, moreover, carried rural Washington County, an area that traditionally gave Pappy O'Daniel huge majorities, and came within 68 votes of winning tiny Austin County, a predominantly German-American county in southeastern Texas, approximately thirty-five miles west of Houston. In Washington County — the party's lone bright spot — the anti-Roosevelt electors polled more than 52 percent of the vote, garnering 2,101 votes to 1,387 for Roosevelt and 534 for Dewey.[117]

---

[114] "Texas Citizens Expected to Roll Up New Poll Record," *Pampa News*, Nov. 7, 1944.
[115] Gunther, *Inside U.S.A.*, p. 827.
[116] "Third Party Threat Discounted in Estimates of Results," *New York Times*, Nov. 5, 1944.
[117] McKay, *Texas Politics, 1906-1944*, p. 464; *Texas Almanac, 1945-46*, p. 531; "Washington County Gives Texas Regulars Election Majority," *Taylor Daily Press*, Nov. 9, 1944.

Chapter XXIII

A Couple of Last Hurrahs

As trying as it was for the country's nationally-organized minor parties, the year nineteen hundred and forty-four also marked the end of the line for two of the most successful statewide third parties in U.S. history.

The Minnesota Farmer-Labor Party — which was never less than the second largest party in the state during its extraordinary existence between 1918 and 1944 — was one of the most vibrant and successful statewide third parties in American history. At its peak in the mid-thirties, the Farmer-Labor Party virtually dominated politics in the Gopher State, controlling not only the governor's office, both U.S. Senate seats and five of the state's nine U.S. House seats, but also seven of the nine other statewide elective offices. The party also controlled the officially "non-partisan" lower chamber of the Minnesota legislature.

Minnesota's Farmer-Labor Party, which had won four consecutive gubernatorial elections and five U.S. Senate races while winning no fewer than twenty-five campaigns for the U.S. House of Representatives during its spectacular 26-year-history, waged its last statewide campaign during the 1942 mid-term elections before quietly merging with Hubert H. Humphrey's Democratic Party in 1944.

The party's "last hurrah" in Minnesota politics not only exposed the deep rifts within the party — a seemingly never-ending schism between the party's left-wingers, led by mercurial former Gov. Elmer A. Benson, and its more moderate or conservative faction, led by rural newspaper publisher Hjalmar Petersen — but also made the party particularly vulnerable to a long-avoided merger with the state's weaker Democratic Party.

In what was probably one of the most bewildering elections in American history, Minnesota's political landscape in 1942 had a little something for everybody: the tragic death of a U.S. Senator; the third-party candidacy of a grieving widow hoping to reclaim her husband's seat in the Senate; a sitting senator who had to briefly give up his seat for two months because of a quirk in a state statute; the announced resignation of a governor in the midst of a campaign for reelection to a third term; a perennial candidate and maverick who ran for both governor and the U.S. Senate in the same election cycle; and more political comebacks than one could shake a stick at.

Historian Millard L. Gieske perhaps put it best when he suggested that politics in the Gopher State that year had taken on the qualities "of a Gilbert and Sullivan opera as alliances shifted back and forth to accommodate expediency, ambition, and, occasionally, ideology and/or principle."[1]

Sadly, the 1942 campaign also marked the Farmer-Labor Party's "last hurrah" in Minnesota politics.

Let's begin with the state's gubernatorial election, a race that had been nearly turned upside-down when 35-year-old Harold E. Stassen, who was seeking a third term as governor but with his eye clearly on the biggest prize of all — the presidency — announced early in the campaign that he planned to resign and enlist as a naval reserve officer immediately after the state's 1943 legislative session.

The young, silo-shaped Stassen, who was only expected to serve three months of his third term, made no secret of the fact that he wanted Northfield farmer Edward J. Thye, a former state dairy and food commissioner, to succeed him as governor the following year and — to prove his point — had thrown his full support behind Thye's candidacy in the lieutenant governor's race, a bold and audacious maneuver that quickly drew the ire of Stassen challenger Martin A. Nelson. Nelson, an Austin attorney seeking his party's gubernatorial nomination for a third time, accused the young Republican governor of essentially appointing a "crown

---

[1] Millard L. Gieske, *Minnesota Farmer-Laborism: The Third-Party Alternative* (Minneapolis, 1979), pp. 309-310.

prince" as his successor.²

A conservative isolationist, Nelson was resentful that he had been squeezed out by the younger Stassen as a possible Republican candidate for governor in 1938. A former aviation instructor and attorney who had been the GOP's nominee for governor against the Farmer-Labor Party's Floyd B. Olson and Elmer A. Benson in 1934 and 1936, respectively, the 53-year-old Nelson, supported by the party's old guard, proved to be no match for the dynamic Stassen, losing to the youngest governor in American history by 76,000 votes — or by an approximately three-to-two margin — in the September primary.

Thye, Stassen's choice for lieutenant governor, also emerged victorious in the GOP primary, defeating incumbent C. Elmer Anderson by a comfortable 50,000-vote margin.

Anderson, a native of Brainerd where he later served as mayor (1976-86), had been Stassen's lieutenant governor for two terms, beginning in 1938 at the remarkably young age of twenty-six. Miffed at the cavalier and ungracious treatment accorded him by Stassen, Anderson had remained in the Republican primary as one of six challengers to Thye, Stassen's handpicked successor.³

After several failed attempts at unity, the badly-divided Farmer-Labor Party's last foray in state and national politics proved to be yet another classic battle between the party's left-wing forces, led by Benson and the party's Popular Front, and the party's anti-communist faction, led by William Mahoney of St. Paul.

On the surface, it appeared that the left-wing's hatred of Stassen and Hjalmar Petersen's personal animosity toward the governor might have been enough to bring about a truce between the party's warring factions in an effort to block Stassen's political advancement. It was no secret that Minnesota's insatiably ambitious "Boy Wonder" was itching to run for president — a desire, as it turned out, that would last a lifetime.

Despite several failed attempts at unity, the party again faced a bitterly divisive primary with Petersen, the former lieutenant governor and a leader of the party's rural moderate wing, defeating Paul A. Rasmussen, a former state budget director, to gain the party's gubernatorial nomination for the second time in two years.

Petersen, who published a weekly newspaper in Askov, was then serving a six-year term as a state railroad and warehouse commissioner — the last Farmer-Laborite to hold statewide office

---

² "Postwar Policy of U.S. Big Issue for Minnesota," *Chicago Tribune*, Sep. 6, 1942.
³ Gieske, *Minnesota Farmer-Laborism*, pp. 312-313.

— a post he had been elected to in 1936 after serving briefly as Minnesota's chief executive for 4½ months following Floyd Olson's death. Hoping to avoid a bloodbath with his party's left-wingers, Petersen refrained from heavy campaigning during the primary and survived handsomely without the backing of the powerful Farmer-Labor Association, defeating Rasmussen by a margin of 66,405 votes to 39,362.[4]

Petersen welcomed a general election rematch with Minnesota's young governor, the same "Boy Wonder" who thrashed him by 205,000 votes only two years earlier.

Aware that there had been considerable speculation that the conservative, anti-Stassen wing of the Republican Party might throw its support to him if Martin A. Nelson was defeated in the primary — a possibility that later took on new life when the defeated Austin attorney unexpectedly filed as an independent candidate for the U.S. Senate in what many perceived as an attempt to siphon votes from Stassen's handpicked candidate in that race — the 52-year-old Petersen waged a vigorous campaign in the autumn of 1942, attacking the Stassen administration's excessive spending and alleged sympathy for Wall Street. As the author of Minnesota's first income tax legislation, Petersen was also highly critical of Stassen's record on taxation, especially his iron-ore tax policies.[5]

Turning up the heat, Petersen accused the governor of running the most fiscally irresponsible administration in Minnesota history and charged that Stassen's plans to join the navy during his third term was nothing more than a cheap "political trick."[6]

Recognizing that nearly half of the Republicans who had turned out in the September primary refused to support Stassen — including the more than a third who had voted for Nelson — Petersen, who had briefly flirted with the GOP in 1938, believed he could pull an upset against the young and rising national Republican star.

Petersen, who had briefly succeeded the magnetic Floyd Olson as governor in 1936 after having already lost his party's nomination for governor to Elmer A. Benson earlier that spring, was even willing to put aside his longstanding feud with his bitter Farmer-

---

[4] Ibid., p. 314; John Earl Haynes, *Dubious Alliance: The Making of Minnesota's DFL Party* (Minneapolis, 1984), p. 96; "Stassen, Ball and Thye Nominated by Minnesotans," *Evening Huronite*, Sept. 10, 1942.

[5] Ibid., pp. 314-315; "Anti-Administration Set-Up Seen with Candidate Filings," *Brainerd Daily Dispatch*, July 31, 1942; "Former Governor of Minnesota, Petersen, Dead," *Winona Daily News*, March 29, 1968.

[6] "Minnesota Voters to Polls Tuesday," *Brainerd Daily Dispatch*, Nov. 2, 1942.

Labor arch-rival in his quest for an upset victory against the Navy-bound Stassen. Remarkably, the two men called a truce during the final six weeks of what turned out to be the Farmer-Labor Party's final statewide campaign, making several joint appearances at party rallies throughout the state.[7]

Putting their differences aside wasn't a particularly easy thing for either man to do given the intense animosity that had been simmering between them since their unbelievably bitter primary in 1938, a blood-soaked and carnage-strewn campaign in which one of Benson's supporters angrily decried that Petersen would "go down in history side by side with Judas Iscariot and Benedict Arnold." Many historians believe that Petersen's attempt to unseat a sitting governor of his own party that year was the beginning of the Farmer-Labor Party's eventual decline as a viable force in Minnesota politics.[8]

Petersen's daughter, Evelyn, who had recently graduated from the University of Minnesota, worked fulltime on her father's campaign, organizing his schedule, handling most of his correspondence and traveling around the state for him. It was an almost impossible task since most voters were focused on the war rather than politics. Wartime rationing of gasoline, delays in printing due to manpower shortages and scheduling difficulties related to the war took their toll on the campaign — and on Petersen's daughter. "If it isn't a scrap drive," she complained, "it's a blackout that interferes with the speaking schedule."[9]

Despite a spirited effort on his part, Petersen again fell short in trying to unseat Harold E. Stassen, losing to the Republican "Boy Wonder" by a margin of 409,800 to 299,917 in a race where the Democratic nominee, polling an inconsequential 75,151 votes, was never a factor.

Stassen, who ran behind five of his party's nine statewide candidates, was held to 51.6 percent of the vote, a significant drop from the nearly sixty percent he amassed four years earlier while dramatically wresting control of Minnesota's state government from Elmer Benson and the Farmer-Laborites.

Petersen, who faced minor Socialist Labor and Communist opposition on his Left — a situation not encountered by the party's other statewide candidates that year — far outpaced the rest of the

---

[7] Gieske, *Minnesota Farmer-Laborism*, p. 314.
[8] Steven J. Keilor, "A Country Editor in Politics: Hjalmar Petersen, Minnesota Governor," *Minnesota History*, Vol. 48, No. 7 (Fall 1983), p. 283
[9] Steven J. Keillor, *Hjalmar Petersen of Minnesota: The Politics of Provincial Independence* (St. Paul, 1987), p. 193.

Farmer-Labor Party's statewide ticket, running more than 86,000 votes ahead of Benson in the hotly-contested U.S. Senate race and more than 49,000 votes in front of St. Paul labor leader Juls J. Anderson, the party's nominee for lieutenant governor.[10]

Petersen, who later ran against young congressman Eugene McCarthy of St. Paul for the DFL's U.S. Senate nomination in 1958, some fourteen years after the merger of the state's Democratic and Farmer-Labor parties, carried a number of strongly Farmer-Labor counties in the upper Minnesota River Valley in his 1942 campaign. He also won a plurality in several counties in northwestern and north-central Minnesota, as well as the state's rural counties with large Scandinavian populations. Largely owing to his non-interventionist views, he also won several predominantly German-American counties in the lower Minnesota River Valley.[11]

The 1942 Senate race in Minnesota — actually there were two contests for the same seat on November 3, 1942 — was truly a wild and wooly affair, a four-cornered battle for the seat once held by the Farmer-Labor Party's Ernest Lundeen, a 62-year-old isolationist lawmaker who had been tragically killed along with 24 others in a plane crash in Virginia, near the foothills of the Blue Ridge Mountains, in late August 1940 while returning to Minnesota to attend a Townsend rally.[12] According to historian Albert Eisele, the cause of that crash, which occurred during a violent thunderstorm, remains shrouded in mystery more than three-quarters of a century later. Given the possibility that sabotage might have been involved based on Lundeen's alleged association with a German-American poet and Nazi propagandist, the FBI never officially closed its investigation into what at the time had been the worst aviation accident in American history.[13]

In any case, Gov. Stassen appointed Republican Joseph H. Ball, a 34-year-old newspaper reporter and staunch ally who shared the governor's pre-Pearl Harbor support for FDR's foreign policy, to the U.S. Senate seat about six weeks after Lundeen's death.[14] Stassen apparently never considered naming Lundeen's grieving widow to the seat, despite the fact that she had been her husband's legislative aide for his entire 23-year career. Their ideological and party differences were simply too great.

---

[10] Gieske, *Minnesota Farmer-Laborism*, pp. 316-317.
[11] Keilor, *Hjalmar Petersen of Minnesota*, p. 194.
[12] "Sen. Lundeen, 24 Others Die in Plane Crash," *Wilmington Morning Star*, Sep. 1, 1940.
[13] Albert Eisele, "Death of Senator from Minnesota Still Shrouded in Mystery," http://www.minnpost.com/politics-policy/2009/09/death-senator-minnesota-still-shrouded-mystery (Retrieved 05/28/2014).
[14] "Joseph H. Ball Named Senator for Minnesota," *Chicago Tribune*, Oct. 15, 1940.

THE LOWEST EBB

Ball was still wet behind the ears. In fact, in taking office on October 14, 1940, the tall and lanky journalist with thick black hair became one of the youngest members to ever serve in the U.S. Senate, rivaled only by the brilliant "American System" architect and advocate Henry Clay of Kentucky in the early nineteenth century and later during the Great Depression by West Virginia's Rush D. Holt, the son of a small-town Socialist mayor and the youngest person ever popularly elected to the Senate.

Due to a quirk in Minnesota's election law, Ball's appointment to the U.S. Senate in 1940 was only effective until the next regularly-scheduled election on November 3, and not for the remainder of Lundeen's term, which would have ended in January 1943. As a consequence, Minnesota voters cast ballots in two U.S. Senate races for the same seat on the same day — a "short term" election for the remaining two months in Lundeen's original term and one for the new six-year term, beginning on January 3, 1943.[15]

While Republican placeholder Arthur E. Nelson, a former mayor of St. Paul and apparently no relation to Martin Nelson, won the race for the "short term" seat by defeating the Farmer-Labor Party's Al Hansen, the party's unsuccessful candidate for mayor of Minneapolis in 1941, and Democrat John E. O'Rourke, the race for the full six-year term was a real donnybrook.

On the Republican side, Ball, the young newspaperman appointed by Stassen twenty-five months earlier, drew a slew of challengers, including three in his own party, the most problematic of which was the candidacy of Walter K. Mickelson, a former secretary to isolationist Senator Henrik Shipstead and publisher of the New Ulm Journal.

Shipstead, who served in the U.S. Senate for 24 years before involuntarily giving up his seat in 1946 when he lost a hotly-contested primary to Stassen's successor Edward J. Thye, had bolted from the Farmer-Labor Party and became a Republican in 1940. Shipstead's sudden conversion to the GOP was a difficult transition and was hardly welcomed by Stassen and other leaders of the party's internationalist wing in Minnesota.

Promising to vote with Shipstead in virtually all matters facing the U.S. Senate, Mickelson's bruising primary challenge to Ball quickly developed into a fight to the finish between the party's internationalists and its pre-war isolationist faction.[16]

Defending the isolationist cause, Minnesota's normally mellow senior senator involved himself extensively in what otherwise

---
[15] "Stassen, Thye Nominated," *Brainerd Daily Dispatch*, Sept. 9, 1942.
[16] "Who Owns the House?" *TIME*, Sept. 7, 1942.

-678-

had been a somewhat somnolent primary campaign, actively stumping for Mickelson while railing against FDR and the forces determined to purge Congress of its prewar noninterventionists. Those seeking to punish the prewar isolationists, argued Shipstead while defending his own record, were "more interested in winning elections than in winning the war."[17] Despite Shipstead's active involvement in the hotly-contested primary, Stassen's candidate survived, defeating Mickelson and his other challengers by a relatively comfortable margin.[18]

In the meantime, leaders of the Farmer-Labor Party expected state Supreme Court Justice Harry H. Peterson, who had been endorsed by the Farmer-Labor Association's state convention in June, to seek the U.S. Senate seat once held by Farmer-Laborite Lundeen.

Peterson, 51, had served as attorney general during Olson's administration where he had helped author the Minnesota Mortgage Moratorium Law, creating a moratorium on farm foreclosures during the Great Depression, and successfully argued it before the U.S. Supreme Court, establishing the right of states to adopt moratoria on bank foreclosures.[19]

Having never firmly committed to the race, the highly-respected Peterson stunned FLP leaders when he inexplicably took his name out of consideration two days before the filing deadline and, in a scathing denunciation of the powerful Farmer-Labor Association, accused association leaders, including Paul A. Rasmussen, of double-crossing Hjalmar Petersen in the governor's race and charging that the association was dominated and controlled by left-wing troublemakers.[20]

Peterson's allegation of "double-crossing" was believed to have severely damaged the Farmer-Labor Association's slate of endorsed candidates and brought considerable pleasure to Minnesota Republicans who believed that a divisive Farmer-Labor primary, pitting the party's moderates against the left-wingers, would virtually assure a Republican victory in November.[21]

With Peterson unexpectedly out of the picture, the Farmer-Labor primary quickly turned into a real free-for-all with former governor Elmer A. Benson, a vehement left-winger, forced to fend off challenges from three other last-minute aspirants, including two

---

[17] "Smearers Put Votes Ahead of War; Shipstead," *Chicago Tribune*, Aug. 20, 1942.
[18] "Stassen, Thye and Ball Leading in Minnesota Primary," *Bismarck Tribune*, Sept. 9, 1942.
[19] Richard M. Valelly, *Radicalism in the States: The Minnesota Farmer-Labor Party and the American Political Economy* (Chicago, 1989), p. 93.
[20] Gieske, *Minnesota Farmer-Laborism*, p. 311.
[21] "Late Filings Set State Political Pot Boiling," *Brainerd Daily Dispatch*, July 30, 1942.

unabashed nationalists: ex-Farmer-Labor congressman Henry M. Arens and Norma Ward Lundeen, widow of the late senator.

Benson's candidacy had set off a divisive factional brawl within the party, prompting William Mahoney of St. Paul to stitch together an anti-Communist slate headed by Hjalmar Petersen for governor and Arens for the U.S. Senate. Mahoney had resigned from the Farmer-Labor Association shortly after the state convention, denouncing it as thoroughly dominated by communists.

Having served as lieutenant governor during Olson's first term, the 70-year-old Arens had been elected to the U.S. House of Representatives in 1932 as an at-large Farmer-Labor congressman before being unseated by a Democrat in a three-cornered race two years later. A respected leader in the farm cooperative movement whose candidacy provided the Mahoney faction's anti-communist slate with an air of respectability, Arens campaigned vigorously against Benson, accusing him of having a mediocre administration as governor, cooperating with the Communist Party, and enriching himself as banking commissioner during Olson's administration — a highly-inflammatory charge for which Arens was unable to provide any specific evidence that Benson had engaged in any illegal activities.[22]

While the 46-year-old Benson, whose left-wing faction had narrowly taken control of the Farmer-Labor Association in January 1941, was clearly the favorite in this triangular contest, all eyes were briefly focused on Norma Lundeen.

An unabashed isolationist yet extremely progressive on domestic issues, Lundeen's husband — as a Republican congressman — had voted against U.S. entry in World War I and, until the sneak attack on Pearl Harbor, had vociferously opposed American involvement in the Second World War.

Though the country was now at war, there were some who believed that the Lundeen name still possessed a hint of magic in Minnesota Farmer-Labor circles. The late senator, after all, had garnered a staggering 62% of the vote only six years earlier while trouncing his Republican opponent to win the U.S. Senate seat once held by the Farmer-Labor Party's Magnus Johnson, the foghorn-voiced champion of the state's dirt farmers and working-class voters. Moreover, Lundeen's widow boasted more than a few powerful allies in her own right, especially among Minnesota's relatively large ethnic German population.

---

[22] Haynes, *Dubious Alliance*, pp. 94-96.

Nobody had expected Norma Lundeen to seek her late husband's seat. In fact, the mother of two grown children, had unexpectedly entered the race on July 25, shortly before the filing deadline, saying at the time that she strongly desired to carry on her late husband's work in Washington while promising an all-out prosecution of the war.[23]

The charming 46-year-old widow waged a relatively low-key campaign, quietly yet passionately defending her late husband's record and presciently warning the voters of Minnesota that the internationalists — including the Farmer-Labor Party's Benson — would keep U.S. troops in Europe, Africa and Asia following the war, making them the policemen of the world.[24]

"When this war is over," asserted Lundeen, "we must insist that our sons be returned to America." Otherwise, she cautioned, the United States would find itself enmeshed in "continuous intrigue" around the globe, one in which the American people would eventually lose control of their own country and find their own children "pushed out of their cradle of liberty."[25]

Asserting that "internationally-minded political connivers" had stacked the deck in the state's U.S. Senate contest, Lundeen charged that if Republican Joseph H. Ball and the Farmer-Labor Party's Benson were nominated in the primary, Minnesota voters would have no choice in the general election because both men saw eye-to-eye on foreign policy and it would make no difference to the internationalists in Washington which of them was elected.[26]

Lundeen, however, was never a serious factor in the primary. By then, the Lundeen name had been too badly damaged by revelations, following her husband's death in 1940, that he had associated with known some fairly seedy characters on the far right, the most damaging of which was his longtime association with George Viereck, the controversial German-American poet and novelist who was then serving a two-to-six year prison sentence for having worked as a publicist and propagandist for the Nazis following Hitler's rise to power in Germany.[27]

Viereck, who had actively supported Robert M. La Follette's insurgent candidacy for the presidency in 1924, had cultivated friendships with several leading isolationist lawmakers during this

---

[23] Gieske, *Minnesota Farmer-Laborism*, p. 308; "Mrs. Lundeen is Candidate," *Mason-City Globe Gazette*, July 25, 1942.
[24] "Postwar Policy of U.S. Big Issue for Minnesota," *Chicago Tribune*, Sept. 6, 1942.
[25] Ibid.
[26] Ibid.
[27] "Viereck is Sentenced to 2 to 6 Years; Reads 1,000-Word Statement to Court," *New York Times*, March 14, 1942.

period, including New York's Hamilton Fish, Jr., but Senator Lundeen was arguably his closest ally in Congress.

A paid propagandist for Germany during World War I, Viereck, a reputed nephew of the Kaiser, convinced the isolationist Senator from Minnesota to head the Make Europe Pay War Debts Committee, a pre-Pearl Harbor group organized by Viereck in 1939 and funded, at least in part, by the German government and whose chief purpose was to discredit the interventionists.[28]

Later called the Islands for War Debts Defense Committee, the militantly anti-interventionist organization argued that European nations still owed the United States $14 billion in war debts and demanded that those countries should give up their island possessions in the Western Hemisphere as repayment — a proposal that found sympathy and encouragement from newspaper publisher Frank Knox and former Secretary of the Treasury William G. McAdoo, who had long supported such a proposal.[29]

The thick-lipped Viereck, who reportedly earned more than $100,000 singing the praises of Adolf Hitler while excoriating the British, was later indicted by a grand jury shortly after the devastating sneak attack on Pearl Harbor and was subsequently convicted on charges that he had deliberately concealed information when he registered as an agent of a foreign government. It turned out that he had also helped write speeches for several isolationist congressmen, including ghostwriting at least six speeches for Lundeen — all of which came out during his closely-watched trial in early 1942, seven months before the Minnesota primary.[30]

Testifying as a witness for the defense in Viereck's trial, Norma Lundeen said that she had never heard Viereck utter a single un-American remark and that if she had he certainly wouldn't have been welcome in their home.[31] She later made a dramatic plea for justice for her late husband's memory, but was denied an opportunity to speak directly to the jury. "People are thinking my husband is on trial," she pleaded in an anguished voice. "I'm entitled to a little justice."[32]

During and after the trial, the mainstream media — playing to the war hysteria that swept the country after Pearl Harbor — delighted in dragging the Lundeen name through the mud at every

---

[28] Jeansonne, *Women of the Far Right*, p. 31.
[29] Doenecke, *Storm on the Horizon*, p. 123.
[30] "Axis Agents: Safeguard for Viereck," *TIME*, Mar. 16, 1942.
[31] "Lundeen Widow Testifies for Suspected Spy," *Chicago Tribune*, Feb. 26, 1942; "Viereck All Right, Mrs. Lundeen Says," *New York Times*, Feb. 26, 1942
[32] "Viereck's Letter Barred at Trial," *New York Times*, Mar. 3, 1942.

opportunity. It wasn't surprising, therefore, that Henry Luce's always colorfully-descriptive *TIME* magazine, in a particularly vicious swipe at the late lawmaker, referred to Norma Lundeen shortly before the primary as "the 46-year-old widow of British-hating, German-loving Senator Ernest Lundeen."[33]

Just as she failed to find justice in the courtroom, the soft-spoken and attractive Lundeen found little fondness and impartiality for her husband's memory at the ballot box as Benson, still enormously popular among Farmer-Laborites in the Twin Cities and with miners on the northern iron ranges, easily captured the party's U.S. Senate nomination, garnering 66,051 votes to Lundeen's 24,163 and 17,163 for Arens.[34]

Like Petersen in the state's gubernatorial race, Benson campaigned vigorously during the ensuing four-cornered campaign that autumn, a contest both complicated and enlivened by the insurgent independent candidacy of Martin A. Nelson, who filed independent nominating papers to run for the U.S. Senate after losing to Harold E. Stassen in the Republican gubernatorial primary in September. Nelson unexpectedly filed nominating petitions containing 2,897 signatures — 2,000 were needed — an hour before the filing deadline in early October.

The unexpected entry of the conservative Republican as an independent candidate led many Farmer-Labor leaders, including Benson himself, to believe that Nelson's candidacy would split the Republican vote just enough to allow the former governor to pull off one of the most dramatic political comebacks in recent U.S. history.[35] The former Farmer-Labor governor, who had already been campaigning tirelessly, redoubled his efforts when the Austin attorney joined the race.

Benson, who had been elected governor by the widest margin in Minnesota history six years earlier and later campaigned for Henry A. Wallace's Progressive Party candidacy in 1948, believed he had an outside chance in the three-cornered race and savored the prospect of rejoining and perhaps leading the nation's progressive forces in the U.S. Senate.

Benson, of course, had served briefly in the Senate when he was appointed to fill the unexpired term of that late Thomas D. Schall after the Republican lawmaker was tragically struck and killed by a hit-and-run motorist in suburban Washington in December 1935.

---

[33] "Who Owns the House?" *TIME*, Sep. 7, 1942
[34] Gieske, *Minnesota Farmer-Laborism*, p. 314; Haynes, *Dubious Alliance*, p. 96.
[35] "Minnesota's Perennial Candidate," *Mason City Globe-Gazette*, Oct. 21, 1942.

But Benson and the other Farmer-Labor candidates again found themselves vastly outspent by their Republican opponents and — in addition to begging and borrowing from almost any source they could find — had to rely on the sometimes mysterious fundraising operation of Clarence Fisher, an advertising representative for the *Farmer-Labor Leader*, formerly the *Union Advocate* and later called the *Minnesota Leader*, who used various aliases and generally charged the party an exorbitant 40 percent commission on every dollar he raised.[36] Having earned his spurs in the third-party movement, Fisher later served as the assistant finance director for Minnesota's Democratic-Farmer Labor Party (DFL) in the 1950s.

Putting his considerable ideological differences with Franklin D. Roosevelt aside, Benson embraced the Communist Party's Popular Front wartime position of uniting the nation's progressive forces behind the president's war effort, describing the war as "a fight to the bitter end between the tyrant's way of life and the democratic way of life." The war, he elaborated, was about democratic principles and the right to vote. In Benson's view, there was no room for compromise between fascism and democracy.[37]

Like Petersen's uphill struggle against Stassen in the state's gubernatorial contest, Benson was unable to buck the national Republican trend that year, a trend fueled by growing anguish and frustration with the reversals suffered by the United States in the war, beginning with the sneak attack on Pearl Harbor and culminating in the recent setbacks by U.S. troops in the Solomon Islands.

The American electorate was also growing restless and angry on the home front, blaming the Democrats for gasoline rationing and shortages in rubber production and farm labor, coupled with the Roosevelt administration's inability to check inflation. An anti-inflation measure, providing stabilization of farm prices and industrial wages, signed into law by FDR on October 2, 1942, was considered too little, too late by a majority of Americans.

Consequently, the widely-read *Chicago Tribune* was predicting that the GOP would gain as many as forty seats in the U.S. House and five to ten seats in the U.S. Senate while picking up between four to six governorships.[38] Like today's electorate, the so-called "Greatest Generation" didn't seem to know exactly what kind of future it wanted.

---

[36] Gieske, *Minnesota Farmer-Laborism*, p. 315.
[37] Haynes, *Dubious Alliance*, p. 97.
[38] "Predict Smashing Gains for Republicans," *Chicago Tribune*, Nov. 1, 1942.

The *Tribune's* prognosticators were nevertheless pretty accurate. It wasn't quite a tsunami, but the 1942 mid-term elections turned out to be a destructively brutal wave for Democrats and third-party aspirants across the country. The Republicans gained 47 seats in the House, trimming the Democratic majority in that body to 222-209, with four seats held by third-party congressmen. The GOP also picked up ten seats in the Senate, where the Democrats clung to a 57-38 majority with the Wisconsin Progressive Party's Robert M. La Follette, Jr., holding the other seat.

As expected, the Republicans also won 18 of the 33 gubernatorial elections that autumn — a net pickup of two from the Democrats — and gained another governorship following the untimely death of the Progressive Party's Orland S. Loomis in Wisconsin a month before he was to be sworn in as the state's 31st chief executive, for a net gain of three governors.

Despite a spirited campaign, Benson's hopes for a political comeback were dashed when he, too, fell victim to the onslaught of voter discontent sweeping the nation, losing to his Republican opponent by a margin of 356,297 to 213,995. Even the 109,226 conservative votes cast for independent Martin A. Nelson, largely siphoned from the GOP's Joseph Ball, weren't enough to put the former Farmer-Labor governor within striking distance of his Republican rival. Democrat Edward Murphy, a former St. Paul assistant attorney, brought up the rear in the governor's race, polling 78,959 votes.

Benson, who received 86,000 fewer votes than Petersen, angrily blamed President Roosevelt for his overwhelming defeat, accusing FDR of refusing to help his campaign while privately confiding to a friend that the Roosevelt administration had no idea how to win the war. He also accused Roosevelt of allowing "a group of political and economic racketeers" to run the country. Intellectually bankrupt and Fascist-minded people had been placed in charge of the government from top to bottom, he lamented to the Farmer-Labor Association's Viena Johnson, a hardcore Popular Front activist.[39]

The rest of the Farmer-Labor Party's statewide slate also went down to defeat that year, led by labor leader and ex-socialist Juls Anderson, the party's candidate for lieutenant governor who polled more than a quarter of a million votes while losing to Stassen's handpicked successor, Ed Thye.

In addition to sweeping every statewide office and winning

---

[39] Haynes, *Dubious Alliance*, p. 98.

overwhelming control of both houses of Minnesota's non-partisan legislature, the Republicans also won eight of the state's nine congressional seats.

Harold C. Hagen, a former newspaper publisher and legislative aide to retiring Farmer-Labor congressman Richard T. Buckler, was the party's only successful candidate for Congress in 1942, narrowly defeating his Republican opponent by a scant 604 votes. The 40-year-old Hagen joined the GOP two years later, just as the FLP was merging with the Democrats, and was reelected five times as Republican before losing his seat a decade later when 42-year-old schoolteacher Cornelia Knutson pulled one of the biggest political upsets in the country.[40]

Railroad and Warehouse commissioner Charles Munn, a one-time progressive Republican and ex-Speaker of the Minnesota House who had bolted from the GOP to support the Farmer-Labor Party's Floyd B. Olson's bid for reelection in 1932, waged a hard-fought campaign on the party's ticket in the state's third congressional district, but fell approximately 15,000 votes short in his bid to unseat Republican lawmaker Richard P. Gale. William Mahoney, one of the party's original architects and the former mayor of St. Paul, and Francis H. Shoemaker, the colorfully combative ex-congressman who was mounting his fifth comeback attempt for a seat in Congress, were also among the Farmer-Labor Party's congressional casualties on Nov. 3.

Mahoney, who lost overwhelmingly in St. Paul's fourth district, only managed a quarter of the vote in his race, while the wildly rambunctious Shoemaker, who had been elected to Congress in 1932 as a recent Leavenworth prison parolee, finished a distant third in the state's seventh congressional district, nearly 4,000 votes behind his Democratic rival. Shoemaker, who had briefly dabbled in the Townsend movement, continued to run for Congress long after the Farmer-Labor Party had vanished from the scene, seeking a Republican nomination in 1946 and entering the seventh district's DFL primary in 1950. He lost badly in both attempts.[41]

In neighboring Wisconsin, a state with a strong tradition of political insurgency, the Progressive Party was also showing signs that it wouldn't be around much longer. Sadly, the 1944 campaign would be its swan song and the Wall Street-controlled duopoly —

---

[40] Gieske, *Minnesota Farmer-Laborism*, p. 316; "National Affairs: The Midwest," *TIME*, Nov. 15, 1954.
[41] Frederick L. Johnson, "From Leavenworth to Congress: The Improbable Journey of Francis H. Shoemaker," *Minnesota History*, Vol. 51, No. 5 (Spring 1989), p. 177.

in Wisconsin and nationally — has lived happily ever since then.

No party in the twentieth century had ever threatened the two major parties quite like the Minnesota Farmer-Labor and Wisconsin Progressive parties during the Great Depression. As hard to believe as it might be today, for most of their existence both parties enjoyed major-party status, neither ever being less than the second-most powerful political party in their respective states and for much of that time they were actually the dominant parties.

At the urging of their supporters, the sons of the late "Fighting Bob" La Follette tried to create a new, nationally-organized Progressive Party in the spring of 1934. Despite initial resistance from "Young Bob" La Follette, the older of La Follette's two sons, and several others — mostly officeholders aligned with the La Follette wing of the GOP, both nationally and in Wisconsin — the party was officially launched on May 19 during a conference of progressive leaders in Fond du Luc.

That autumn, Philip La Follette, who had lost his bid for renomination for a second term as governor two years earlier when Republican primary voters — "angry bees," as he had described them — overwhelmingly rejected his candidacy in favor of former Gov. Walter J. Kohler, was swept back into office on the newly-formed Progressive ticket.[42]

Trailing throughout much of the campaign, the 37-year-old La Follette narrowly defeated incumbent Democrat Albert G. Schmedeman by a margin of fewer than 14,000 votes to regain the governor's chair. La Follette, who didn't formally enter the 1934 gubernatorial race until late that summer and only after it became clear that his comeback attempt wouldn't hurt his brother's chances for re-election to the U.S. Senate, benefited immensely by the fact that a large number of Socialists, particularly in the party's Milwaukee stronghold, abandoned their own party's nominee to aid his third-party candidacy.[43]

Robert M. La Follette, Jr., Phil's older brother and a reliable supporter of FDR's New Deal, easily retained his Senate seat that autumn, trouncing both of his major-party rivals while rolling up a 217,000-vote plurality on the Progressive line.[44]

Secretary of State and longtime ally Theodore Dammann of Milwaukee, a four-term Republican incumbent who left the GOP

---

[42] Philip La Follette and Donald Young, ed., *Adventures in Politics: The Memoirs of Philip La Follette* (New York, 1970), pp. 181, 209-216.
[43] Ibid., pp. 212, 216.
[44] Ibid., p. 216.

and ran with the La Follette brothers on the newly-formed Progressive slate, was also swept into office on the party's ticket.

Impressively, the Wisconsin Progressives — enjoying the enthusiastic support of numerous farm and labor organizations while promising a bold extension of the New Deal — also captured seven of the state's ten congressional seats that year while winning a comfortable plurality in the Assembly and winning 14 of the 33 seats in the State Senate.[45] It was an auspicious beginning for the new party, arguably the closest thing to a statewide third-party sweep since 1854, when the Know-Nothing Party overwhelmed the two major parties in Massachusetts, winning virtually every office in the Bay State.

Thomas R. Amlie a 37-year-old former Republican congressman deeply influenced by economist Thorstein Veblen and whose views had been radicalized by the Great Depression, eventually leading to his outright rejection of both capitalism and the New Deal, was among the seven Wisconsin Progressives elected to the U.S. House that autumn.[46]

Nobody had agitated longer or more convincingly for a new party in Wisconsin than the agrarian-born Amlie, who had suffered the same fate as Phil La Follette in 1932 and had taken the early lead the following year in convincing other progressives around the state, including numerous labor unions and farm organizations, of the necessity of such a party.

Needless to say, Amlie was tickled pink when the Progressive Party began looking like it would become a reality earlier that year. "I am satisfied," he said shortly after a February meeting arranged by La Follette, "that the convention in Madison last Saturday is going to result in the formation of a new party in Wisconsin. Under the leadership of Phil La Follette," he added, "I am sure this party will go completely to the left" — precisely the direction the former congressman preferred.[47]

Amlie, of course, believed that capitalism was doomed, but didn't necessarily believe that it should be replaced with socialism

---

[45] Michael J. Dubin, *Party Affiliations in the State Legislatures: A Year by Year Summary, 1796-2006* (Jefferson, N.C., 2007), p. 202. The Progressives held 45 seats of the 100 in the Wisconsin Assembly during the 1934-36 sessions, compared to 35 seats controlled by the Democrats and only 17 by the Republicans. The Socialist Party held three seats. The Progressives also outnumbered the Democrats by one seat in the State Senate — 14 to 13 — while the once-dominant GOP claimed a mere six seats.

[46] Theodore Rosenof, "The Political Education of an American Radical: Thomas R. Amlie in the 1930's," *Wisconsin Magazine of History*, Vol. 58, Number 1 (Autumn 1974), pp. 19-30.

[47] John Kasparek, *Fighting Son: A Biography of Philip F. La Follette* (Madison, WI, 2006), pp. 148-150.

or any other "ism." The Wisconsin Progressive Party would show the way.

The left-wing lawmaker, who had attended the national Farmer-Labor Party convention in 1920 and vigorously supported "Battling Bob" La Follette's insurgent candidacy for the White House in 1924, had long encouraged the creation of a progressive third-party movement — not only in Wisconsin, but nationally — was one of the most radical members of the House during this period, an honor he briefly shared with Montana's young Jerry O'Connell, New York's "rebel in the House" Vito Marcantonio, and Minnesota Farmer-Laborite John T. Bernard, a suspected Communist.[48]

Gerald J. Boileau, a diminutive yet fiery young World War I veteran who escaped poverty in northern Wisconsin by working his way through Marquette University Law School and becoming district attorney for Marathon County six years after the war, was among the six other Progressives elected to the U.S. House in 1934. Initially elected to the U.S. House as a Republican four years earlier, Boileau — a close friend and ally of New York's colorful Fiorello H. La Guardia — served as whip for the Progressive coalition in the Seventy-second Congress.[49]

Representing the state's sprawling seventh congressional district, the 34-year-old Boileau was a leading spokesman for the state's agriculture and dairy interests who frequently clashed with Secretary of Agriculture Henry A. Wallace and spent much of the Great Depression pushing for legislation enabling farmers to refinance their mortgages at 1 ½ percent with a ½ percent annual payment on the principal — a wildly popular idea proposed in the original Lemke-Frazier Refinance Bill and vigorously promoted by the powerful Farmers' Union.[50]

Thwarted in an attempt to win the Progressive Party's U.S. Senate nomination in 1938, Boileau lost his congressional seat (and his important position on the House Agriculture Committee) later that autumn in what was an all-around disastrous year for the Wisconsin Progressives. A comeback attempt in 1940 also proved futile.

Returning to the governor's office in early January 1935, Phil La Follette wasted little time putting together a recovery program for

---

[48] Ibid.
[49] James L. Lorence, "Gerald J. Boileau and the Politics of Sectionalism: Dairy Interests and the New Deal, 1933-1938," *Wisconsin Magazine of History*, Vol. 71, Number 4 (Summer 1988), pp/ 277-278.
[50] Ibid., pp. 278, 281-282.

his depression-ravaged state, the centerpiece of which involved the creation of the Wisconsin Finance Corporation, a state bank that was to be initially capitalized with $100 million from the state's relief grant from the federal government. Communities throughout the state, at their own discretion, would then issue bonds to finance public works in their localities, financed by the state bank.

The Wisconsin Progressives scored an even more impressive statewide victory in 1936. Like the Farmer-Labor Party's dynamic but ailing Floyd B. Olson in neighboring Minnesota, the Wisconsinites virtually ignored William Lemke's third-party candidacy in that year's presidential race — veteran Progressive congressman Thomas R. Amlie dismissed the Union Party as "just another cheap money third party" — and wholeheartedly supported FDR's bid for reelection.

Though Phil and Robert La Follette both had some serious reservations about the President's claim that he had ended the depression, the Progressives — working in harmony with the Roosevelt administration — performed beyond their wildest dreams at the ballot box that year, winning all five of the state's constitutional offices and holding on to their seven seats in Congress. They also increased their pluralities in both the State Senate and Assembly, capturing 16 of the 33 seats in former and 46 of the 100 seats in the latter, while Phil La Follette glided to an easy third-term victory.[51]

La Follette absolutely demolished his major-party challengers that fall, garnering 573,724 votes, or 46.4 percent, to Republican Alexander Wiley's 363,973, or 29.4 percent, and Democrat Arthur W. Lueck's 268,530, or 21.7 percent. Roosevelt, meanwhile, carried Wisconsin by a greater than two-to-one margin, thrashing Alf Landon by a lopsided tally of 802,984 to 380,828 with the Union Party's William Lemke of North Dakota grabbing 60,297 votes and 10,626 opting for the Socialist Party's Norman Thomas.

Fondly recalling his father's independent candidacy in 1924, a campaign that many had hoped would lay the foundation for a new nationally-organized third-party and eventually a badly-needed realignment in American politics, placing conservatives and reactionaries in one camp and the nation's progressives in another, Phil La Follette hoped to finally fulfill that long-delayed dream with the founding of a new National Progressive Party a couple of years later.

Still basking in the glow of his overwhelming re-election victory in 1936, La Follette broke with the Roosevelt administration in

---

[51] La Follette and Young, ed., *Adventures in Politics*, p. 228.

a series of four radio broadcasts in the spring of 1938, during which period he launched his new party, saying that it was destined to become "the party of our times."

Speaking to a cheering crowd of 5,000 supporters at the University of Wisconsin's Stock Pavilion in Madison on April 28, the 41-year-old three-term governor charged that the Democrats and Republicans had been "fumbling the ball" for a decade. Sen. Robert M. La Follette, Jr., the governor's older brother, didn't attend the Madison rally, but sent a public endorsement from Washington where he was waging a fight against FDR's Navy appropriations bill.

In his lengthy speech, the younger La Follette said that Roosevelt, while well intentioned, was "hamstrung" by conservatives and constant bickering within his own party. The country, he insisted, was hopelessly divided "between the earners on one side and the collectors on the other" and neither major party was truly speaking for the first part of that equation. The National Progressive Party, he boldly predicted, would quickly replace one of the existing major parties.

Denouncing old-fashioned capitalism as unable to meet the needs of the depression-torn nation and dismissing socialism as an unrealistic alternative, La Follette outlined his new party's agenda — public ownership and control of the nation's money supply and credit; the right to a job; decent wages; expanded powers in the executive branch "to get things done;" and minimal government interference in the economy.

"We flatly oppose every form of coddling or spoon-feeding the American people," asserted La Follette. Such government pampering, he added, applied not only to the nation's farmers and workers and those on relief, but also to business and industry. "Whatever it may cost — so help us God — we shall use the power of the United States to restore to every American the opportunity to help himself. After that, he can sink or swim," he said.

Seen by some as an unbridled bid for national power, La Follette's announcement caught many of the nation's leading liberals by surprise. Few, if any, leading progressives, including Nebraska's George W. Norris, an old friend of the La Follette brothers, had been consulted prior to La Follette's Madison kick-off. The Nebraska lawmaker told reporters that he would be "fighting in its ranks" if the new party extended FDR's policies, but would oppose the Progressive Party if it divided the nation's liberal forces.

Like many other potential allies, Mayor Fiorello La Guardia of New York City, another close friend of the La Follettes, remained aloof from the new party, apparently hoping that the GOP would nominate a liberal for president in 1940. Sen. William E. Borah of Idaho also kept an arms distance from the new party, preferring instead to revitalize the Republican Party from within.

Montana's Burton K. Wheeler, the elder La Follette's vice-presidential running mate in 1924, said that if the Democrats nominated a liberal in 1940, "the third party will have little chance," but conceded that it could be a factor if the two major parties picked conservative nominees. Wheeler, who hadn't been approached by La Follette's sons prior to the Madison announcement, reminded reporters that he intended to remain a Democrat. That wasn't surprising. At the time, the 56-year-old Montana lawmaker was the subject of a presidential boom orchestrated by powerful labor leader John L. Lewis of the CIO.

But what was surprising was the reaction from Minnesota's neighboring Farmer-Labor Party and the once-powerful Nonpartisan League, both of which issued statements saying that they saw no immediate possibility of a merger with La Follette's National Progressives. That was certainly a blow to La Follette's prospects for the new party.

Countless other liberals also viewed the new party with skepticism, convinced that any sort of left-wing challenge in 1940 would likely result in a Republican victory.

Mainstream Republicans, on the other hand, were thrilled by the breaking news out of Madison. The chairman of the Republican National Committee said that the new La Follette movement was the result of FDR's declining prestige and lack of confidence in his leadership.

Former President Herbert Hoover, speaking to reporters while changing trains in Salt Lake City, said that La Follette's new party could be a wedge for returning the GOP to power. "If the Republicans continue to stand together as they have recently, and the liberal and conservative Democrats continue to widen the breach between them as they have recently, we should be able to regain leadership," said Hoover, who was privately contemplating a political comeback in 1940.[52]

Criticism, of course, abounded from all quarters, the sharpest coming from the Left. One observer writing in *Nation* magazine described La Follette's Madison performance as "hammy" and criticized the new party's emblem — a cross and circle symbol personally designed by La Follette — as fascist, suggesting that it had

---

[52] "Hoover Scans 'New Party,'" *New York Times*, May 2, 1938.

been borrowed from the Nazi swastika. (Curiously, more than 8,000 emblems were sold at a dollar apiece in Wisconsin in the week following La Follette's announcement.)

President Roosevelt was among those who mocked the party and its emblem. "All that remains is for some major party to adopt a new form of arm salute," wrote FDR in a letter to the U.S. ambassador to Italy. "I have suggested the raising of both arms above the head," joked Roosevelt, "followed by a bow from the waist. At least this will be good for people's figures!"[53]

Liberal Democrats were particularly suspicious, viewing La Follette's unanticipated bold and grandiose move as a possible first step in a bid for the presidency, if not in 1940, then certainly in 1944. That was also the position of New York's American Labor Party, which quickly made it clear that it was sticking with Roosevelt and the New Deal.

"We agree with Governor La Follette in his analysis that both major parties are unable to solve our national economic problems," said Alex Rose, adding that while some of La Follette's proposed program appeared to be based on sound policies, many other aspects were hazy — something that could perhaps be forgiven given the party's infancy.[54]

"One must always remember that the political program emanates from Wisconsin and reflects its characteristics," continued Rose, one of the ALP's co-founders. "Other third party movements had no opportunity to influence the formation of this program."

Rose, a leader in the Hatters' Union, then strongly emphasized that the American Labor Party had no desire to abandon Roosevelt's New Deal. "We are not prepared to concede its defeat," he said.[55]

Though taking issue with some of La Follette's comments in his Madison speech, Socialist Norman Thomas was initially encouraged by the new party, particularly the governor's "analysis of the shortcomings of the New Deal," but later had a change of heart, describing the party as a "complete flop."[56] For his part, Communist Party leader William Z. Foster, speaking to a party gathering of 22,000 in Madison Square Garden in late May, attacked the La Follette Progressives as a reactionary "political will-

---

[53] Patrick J. Maney, *Young Bob: A Biography of Robert M. La Follette, Jr.*, (Madison, WI, 2003), p. 208
[54] "Say Madison Plan Booms La Guardia," *New York Times*, Apr. 30, 1938.
[55] Ibid.
[56] "Thomas Has Praise and Criticism," *New York Times*, Apr. 30, 1938; "Socialists Ignore Progressive Party," *New York Times*, Dec. 11, 1939.

o'-wisp."⁵⁷

Even the tiny Socialist Labor Party of Wisconsin, which urged American workers to reject La Follette's "sugar-coated" fascism, had something to say, denouncing the fledgling party as an imitation of European dictatorships and accusing the La Follette brothers of seeking even greater executive authority under the guise of "modernizing the bankrupt form of capitalist democracy."⁵⁸

The old-age Townsend movement, too, found little to cheer about in the Madison announcement, describing La Follette's peculiar party as a "humorous" development and little more than a publicity stunt on the part of the Wisconsin governor.⁵⁹

Believed to be nursing national third-party plans of his own, Dr. Francis E. Townsend personally refrained from publicly commenting on La Follette's new party, but several prominent Wisconsin Townsendites — mostly conservative Republicans intimately familiar with La Follette's politics — expressed their deep displeasure at the governor's ambitious undertaking by rallying behind the protest candidacy of crusading editor and songwriter John B. Chapple, who was running as an Independent Townsend candidate in that autumn's U.S. Senate race.

One of the state's most conservative and unpredictable political figures, Chapple had unexpectedly thrown himself into that year's three-cornered Senate contest which included the Progressive Party's Herman L. Ekern, the state's aging lieutenant governor and a close associate of the late "Fighting Bob" La Follette who had defeated radical congressman Thomas R. Amlie to win his party's nomination.⁶⁰

A rabid McCarthyite and virulent critic of the La Follettes who briefly challenged President Dwight Eisenhower for his party's presidential nomination in 1956, Chapple had stunned the Wisconsin political establishment by upsetting Senator John J. Blaine, a La Follette Republican, in the state's 1932 GOP primary and was again the party's nominee for the U.S. Senate in 1934, finishing third in a three-way race won by the Progressive Party's Robert M. La Follette, Jr.⁶¹

---

⁵⁷ "22,000 Communists Open Session Here," *New York Times*, May 27, 1938.
⁵⁸ "Assail La Follette Plan; Wisconsin Socialist-Laborites Call New Party Fascist," *New York Times*, May 9, 1938.
⁵⁹ "Townsendites Hit Third Party Move," *Los Angeles Times*, May 1, 1938.
⁶⁰ A leading authority on pension legislation in the United States, Ekern had helped secure passage of the Social Security Act in 1935 in the face of strong opposition from the Townsend forces.
⁶¹ William H. Chafe, *The Achievement of American Liberalism: The New Deal and Its Legacies* (New York, 2003), p. 103; "The Primaries: Something for Everybody," *TIME*, April

Ironically, La Follette's launching of his new party took place at the very moment President Roosevelt was conducting a purge of his own party in an attempt to rid Congress of recalcitrant Democrats who weren't supportive of his New Deal programs.

Thus, it wasn't entirely surprising that a few of those targeted for defeat by FDR in the 1938 primaries welcomed La Follette's new party. "Former President Hoover recommended two bathtubs for every home, or something like that," quipped New York Democratic Rep. John O'Connor, "but I suppose three bathtubs would be better." In a country of 130 million people, the embattled congressman who subsequently lost his seat in Roosevelt's purge that year, said that he could see no reason why there shouldn't be three — or thirty — political parties.[62]

Reaction from the press was mixed. The *Washington Post*, one of the few major dailies that took a broader view of the La Follette movement, welcomed the National Progressives to the playing field. The *New York Herald Tribune* weighed in similarly, describing La Follette's call for a new party as "sane and realistic," a breath of fresh air from Madison.

The *New York Sun* was also supportive, as was the *Hartford Courant*, which described the National Progressives as a challenge to both old parties, a safeguard "against the threat of tyranny."

The *St. Paul Pioneer Press* also weighed in, describing Gov. La Follette's new party as a "clean start" for American liberalism. "If the National Progressives of America do succeed," the paper editorialized, "then in fact the Democratic Party will become what Governor La Follette says it essentially is already, a sectional party of the South."

On the flip side of the coin, the conservative *Chicago Tribune* denounced the new party as a "new popular front" consisting of Karl Marx and the Marx Brothers. The *Boston Herald* called it a "tricked up version" of Huey Long's Share-the Wealth movement and the *Los Angeles Times*, in what was probably the most astute observation of all, remarked that the Progressives were neither liberal enough nor conservative enough to attract voters on either side of the political spectrum.

Within days of his Madison declaration, La Follette's office was bombarded with more than 10,000 letters and telegrams, the vast majority in support of his new party.

The National Progressives also received a boost of sorts a few

---

16, 1956.
[62] "Three Parties May Be Like Three Bathtubs, Says O'Connor," *New York Times*, Apr. 29, 1938.

days after La Follette's announcement when the Farmer-Labor Party in neighboring Iowa indicated a willingness to join La Follette's fledgling national party. "We are fighting for the same things," said George F. Buresh of Cedar Rapids, the Farmer-Labor candidate for the U.S. Senate. While they "anticipated no difficulty" in reaching an agreement with the National Progressives of America, the Iowans nevertheless added that they weren't in any hurry to change the name of their existing party.[63]

Organized in 1934 by Wallace M. Short, a Congregational minister and former mayor of Sioux City, the Iowa Farmer-Labor Party had actively competed in Iowa's 1934 and 1936 statewide elections. A veteran of the state's so-called "Cow War" of 1931 and the Farm Holiday strike of 1932, the former Sioux City mayor and state legislator was the editor of the *Unionist and Public Forum*, a farm-labor newspaper.

One of Iowa's most colorful and controversial figures, Short, a close ally of farm leader Milo Reno, first attracted national attention in 1919 when he provided a full-throated defense of the IWW's right to free speech — a daring act that nearly resulted in his recall as mayor of Sioux City.

Arguably the state's most distinguished radical figure, Short was a veteran of virtually every progressive insurgent political movement during the first half of the twentieth century — from Teddy Roosevelt's Bull Moose campaign of 1912 to Robert La Follette's Progressive campaign of 1924 and William Lemke's bid for the White House on the Union Party ticket in 1936. In keeping with that tradition, Short later supported Henry A. Wallace's Progressive Party campaign for the presidency in 1948 and had been the Farmer-Labor Party's candidate for governor of Iowa in 1934 and 1936, polling a mildly impressive 37,032 votes, or more than four percent, in the earlier contest.

Having completely lost confidence in FDR's New Deal, novelist Upton Sinclair, a lifelong Socialist who waged a spectacular but unsuccessful campaign for governor of California as a Democrat four years earlier, was also sanguine about the prospects for La Follette's infant party.[64]

While few political pundits looked at the fledgling Wisconsin-based party as a genuine threat to the prevailing two-party establishment, FDR was somewhat troubled by the news out of Madison, fearing that a progressive third-party challenge in 1940 could wreak havoc on his third-term aspirations.

---

[63] "Farm Labor Group Plan to Join New Party," *Sarasota Herald*, May 1, 1938.
[64] "Sinclair Goes to New Party," *Los Angeles Times*, June 16, 1938.

As such, Roosevelt immediately invited Bob La Follette, whom he considered the more politically savvy and significant of the La Follette tandem, to join him on a leisurely weekend cruise down the Potomac. Roosevelt's worries, however, proved to be completely unfounded.

Any presidential hopes that Phil La Follette might have been harboring were abruptly dashed when he was unexpectedly trounced later that fall in his bid for a fourth term as governor, losing to Republican Julius P. Heil, a wealthy steel manufacturer from Milwaukee, by nearly 200,000 votes.

It was a campaign that La Follette — if truth be known — never really wanted to wage in the first place, preferring instead to devote his time and energy in building his new National Progressive Party. When his potential Progressive successors thought the waters were too cold and insisted that he stand for reelection again, La Follette reluctantly agreed to seek a fourth term, knowing full well that he would most likely be defeated. His heart really wasn't in it. But there were some things worse than defeat, he later wrote in his memoirs. "The worst crime is to run out on your cause" — something he was unwilling to do, so he reluctantly took his medicine, as painful and humiliating as it turned out to be.[65]

Severely damaged by La Follette's attempt to move the party beyond the confines of Wisconsin, the Badger State Progressives took a real beating in the 1938 mid-term elections, losing the U.S. Senate race by more than 21 percentage points while retaining only two of their seven seats in the U.S. House of Representatives.

When the dust settled, the Progressive Party also lost more than a third of its strength in the state legislature, losing five seats in the Assembly and fourteen in the Senate.

The thumping La Follette received in the governor's race was matched in the state's U.S. Senate contest where Lt. Gov. Herman Ekern, a loyal lieutenant to the late "Fighting Bob" La Follette, barely finished ahead of his Democratic opponent while losing badly to Republican Alexander Wiley.

Progressive candidates in California, Delaware, Iowa and elsewhere were also decisively defeated and La Follette's National Progressive Party collapsed shortly thereafter.

In the final analysis, La Follette's short-lived national third-party was neither a left-wing nor right-wing effort, but it did indicate a growing unrest with the duopoly — a trend that would quietly continue throughout the next decade before crystallizing itself

---

[65] La Follette and Young, *Adventures in Politics*, p. 254.

in the four-cornered 1948 presidential election.

More to the point, La Follette's short-lived national party was a middle-of-the-road attempt to bring about a much-needed political realignment at a time when both major parties were drifting toward extremes. La Follette realized that most Americans still identified themselves with the political center, believing that government had an important role to play in their lives, but with certain limits. Deep down, a majority of Americans supported parts of FDR's New Deal program, but opposed the idea of a welfare state. Similarly, they were also opposed to the idea of a *laissez-faire* corporate state, as advocated by the National Association of Manufacturers and others.

The 1944 campaign would be the Wisconsin Progressives last gasp. Sadly, the party's fate had been pretty much sealed two years earlier when death cruelly intervened and denied the party of one of its greatest electoral achievements in its spectacular twelve-year history.

While Minnesota's neighboring Farmer-Labor Party went out with barely a whimper and most of the country's other minor parties fared poorly at the ballot box that autumn, the most thrilling — and ultimately tragic — achievement by a third-party candidate in the 1942 mid-term elections occurred in Wisconsin's three-way gubernatorial campaign where 49-year-old former attorney general Orland S. Loomis unexpectedly trounced Republican incumbent Julius P. Heil and Democrat William C. Sullivan, the latter of whom campaigned as an unabashedly pro-Roosevelt candidate.

Loomis, who lost a heartbreaker to Heil two years earlier — losing to the wealthy Republican governor by 12,000 votes out of nearly 1.4 million votes cast — swamped his Republican and Democratic rivals on his second try, garnering 397,664 votes to Heil's 291,945 and 98,153 for Sullivan.[66] A young Frank P. Zeidler, who eventually served three terms as the Socialist mayor of Milwaukee and later headed his party's ticket in the 1976 presidential campaign, garnered 11,295 votes while finishing ahead of two other minor-party candidates in that race.

Emerging from the Progressive Party's five-cornered gubernatorial primary in September, "Spike" Loomis — a nickname given to him as a young boy — waged a near picture-perfect campaign in the fall of 1942, out-hustling his major-party opposition at every opportunity. Running rings around his opponents while visiting

---

[66] "Loomis Swamps Heil," *Wisconsin State Journal*, Nov. 4, 1942.

virtually every town, city and rural community in the state, the former president of the Wisconsin Senate and one-time FDR-appointed director of the state's Rural Electrification Administration ran up huge pluralities in heavily-populated Milwaukee and Dane counties while carrying 51 of the state's 71 counties.

Focusing on fiscal frugality and economic issues, Loomis hammered Heil throughout the campaign, accusing the Republican governor of establishing the most "incompetent one-man rule to be found anywhere in the nation." Asserting that Heil had been an absentee chief executive, the Progressive candidate also lambasted his Republican opponent for bringing "ridicule upon the state" as a result of some of his public utterances. Heil, he said, was an embarrassment to "Fighting Bob" La Follette's progressive tradition, a legacy that had made Wisconsin a "laboratory for democracy."

"Our present state government," declared Loomis in a radio interview in early October, "has lacked competency based upon knowledge of and experience in governmental affairs, has shown brutal disrespect for the will of the people, astonishing lack of diplomacy, judgment, dignity and integrity — in its all-out determination to replace government of, by and for the people with the will of one man!"

The voters of Wisconsin overwhelmingly agreed.

The campaign, however, had taken a devastating physical toll on Loomis. Friends and supporters noticed how exhausted he looked after the election. The dark circles and deep lines on his face revealed more than a hint of strain.

Tragically, the country lawyer from Mauston suffered a series of severe heart attacks a month later — a fifth and fatal one occurring two-and-half days after the first one — setting off a series of legal fireworks for his replacement.[67]

Many Republican leaders in the state believed that Gov. Heil, a man who had been vociferously denounced by his detractors as a "buffoon" and who had been unceremoniously rejected by Wisconsin voters only four weeks earlier, should have been allowed to continue in office — an argument repudiated by the state's highest court.

Much to the chagrin of the Wisconsin Progressives, the GOP nevertheless retained the governorship. Lieutenant Governor Walter S. Goodland, a pipe-smoking 80-year-old Racine Republican who had been reelected to a third term that autumn, was

---

[67] "Governor-Elect Loomis Succumbs," *Wisconsin Rapids Daily Tribune*, Dec. 8, 1942.

named acting governor for the full two-year term when the Wisconsin Supreme Court, in a unanimous 17-page ruling on December 29 — six days before Loomis would have been inaugurated — held that the lieutenant governor should be empowered to take over the powers and duties of acting governor.

Candidates for governor and lieutenant governor ran separately in those days, not as a "team" as they have since 1970. Goodland had little difficulty winning another term that autumn, comfortably defeating the Progressive Party's Henry J. Berquist, a three-term state legislator and ex-pacifist from Rhinelander, and Democrat John M. Brophy.

Incredibly, the opportunistic octogenarian, who looked and growled like a St. Bernard, as *TIME* magazine so indelicately described him at the time, had himself sworn in as lieutenant governor by his nephew an hour and ten minutes after he learned of Loomis' death on December 7 — nearly a full month before he should have legally taken his oath of office for another term as lieutenant governor.[68]

The aging Goodland was elected in his own right in 1944, defeating Socialist-turned-Democrat Daniel W. Hoan, the former longtime mayor of Milwaukee, the faltering Progressive Party's Alex Benz, an insurance executive from Appleton, and Socialist George A. Nelson, a former La Follette Republican state legislator who had been Norman Thomas's vice-presidential running mate in 1936.[69]

The Progressive Party — a party that held nineteen seats in the state legislature at the time of Loomis's sudden passing and still claimed young Bob La Follette's seat in the U.S. Senate, as well as two representatives in the U.S. House — never fully recovered from Loomis's untimely death in 1942.

Realizing their days were probably numbered, the Wisconsin Progressives nominated the little-known Benz for governor and chose Harry Sauthoff of Madison, the second district's Progressive congressman, as the party's nominee for the U.S. Senate.

The little-known Benz, who had the blessing of the La Follette high command, narrowly defeated Leo Vuadreuil of Kenosha, a former deputy attorney general and strong supporter of FDR's bid for a fourth term, and two other candidates to narrowly capture the Progressive nomination for governor in the state's August 15 primary. Benz polled 9,448 votes to Vaudreuil's 9,207 while Ralph

---

[68] "U.S. At War: Trouble in Wisconsin," *TIME*, Dec. 28, 1942; "Wisconsin Court Gives Governor Job to Goodland," *Chicago Tribune*, Dec. 30, 1942.
[69] "Goodland Leads GOP to Triumph," *Wisconsin State Journal*, Nov. 8, 1944.

F. Amoth, a political crackpot from Eau Claire who later became an avid supporter of Joseph R. McCarthy, the notorious red-baiter, finished third with 5,691 votes, followed by Mayor John H. Kaiser of Port Washington, who garnered 4,174 votes in the four-cornered primary contest.

Only 28,719 Progressives voted in the four-corned gubernatorial primary — down from the more than 178,000 who voted for Phil La Follette when he ran unopposed in the party's primary eight years earlier.

Progressive turnout in the primary, in fact, was so dismal that Adelaide Woelfel, the party's unopposed candidate for Secretary of State in the primary, didn't receive enough votes to be nominated and was forced to run in November as an independent Progressive while four-term U.S. Representative Harry Sauthoff, whose nomination hung in doubt for nearly two weeks following the party's primary, barely qualified as the party's nominee for the U.S. Senate.[70] "It was a humiliating experience for the party of the La Follettes," a *Milwaukee Journal* reporter later noted.[71]

In many respects, the Progressive campaign that year resembled a memorial service more than a campaign. The noisy and crowded gubernatorial primary had heartened some of the party's activists, evidence that the party still had some life, but the sounds they heard that summer were nothing more than a death rattle.

Virtually unknown in political circles prior to seeking the party's nomination, Benz, vice president of the Aid Association for Lutherans, a fraternal insurance society, spent a good part of the fall campaign denying that the Progressive Party was on the verge of disintegration.[72] Benz, whose company foreclosed on only two mortgages during the entire Great Depression — a record unmatched by virtually any other company in the financial services industry — stressed his administrative abilities throughout the autumn campaign.[73]

On the stump, the Appleton Progressive called for a state-administered full employment program to deal with post-war joblessness, expected to be in the "hundreds of thousands."[74] He also

---

[70] "Single Progressive Candidate Fails to Make Ticket," *Rhinelander Daily News*, Aug. 28, 1944.

[71] "Progressive Party Is Relegated to Minor Leagues by Voters," *Milwaukee Journal*, Nov. 8, 1944.

[72] "Progressives Fear Vote Spells End of Their Party," *Milwaukee Journal*, Aug. 20, 1944.

[73] John Wyngaard, "Benz Wins Great Tribute From Independent Press" (Political Advertisement), *Sheboygan Press*, Oct. 30, 1944.

[74] "Benz Demands Employment Program," *Wisconsin State Journal*, Oct. 12, 1944.

lambasted the Republican governor for building a surplus by cutting funding for old-age pensions and attacked Democratic nominee Daniel Hoan, the former Socialist mayor of Milwaukee, for stressing his close ties to the late Robert M. La Follette, Sr., charging that "Fighting Bob" would have never supported "the corrupt political machine that today controls the Democratic Party."[75]

The Progressives, unfortunately, were unable to stave off the grim reaper. Despite giving it a whale of an effort against extremely long odds, the little-known Benz finished a distant third in the gubernatorial race, polling 76,028 votes, or 5.8%, to Goodland's 697,740 and Hoan's 536,357.

The handwriting was on the wall. The votes were still being counted when George Hampel, Jr., a Progressive state senator who had managed the party's campaign in Milwaukee, said the Progressives should join the GOP as quickly as possible. "The people respect us and look to us for leadership," said Hampel, long regarded as one of the ablest members of the Senate, "but we're not in the right vehicle. The people like to be on the winning team and it looks like the Republican Party is the winning team in Wisconsin." Hampel, incidentally, had finished a distant third in his bid for another term that year.[76]

Worse yet, the Progressives clung to only five seats in the State Senate and claimed only six members in the Assembly — down dramatically from sixteen and forty-six, respectively, during the party's high-water mark in 1936. All that remained was the embalming process. Disappointed by their poor showing in the 1944 mid-term elections, the dejected Wisconsin Progressives — a party that briefly dominated politics in the Badger State during the darkest days of the Great Depression — voted to officially rejoin the Republican Party in March 1946.[77]

---

[75] "Goodland Denies Old Age Funds Cut," *Wisconsin State Journal*, Oct. 5, 1944; "Benz Raps Hoan's 'Link' With Senior La Follette," *Wisconsin State Journal*, Oct. 30, 1944.

[76] "Progressive Party Is Relegated to Minor Leagues by Voters," *Milwaukee Journal*, Nov. 8, 1944.

[77] "Progressives Back in G.O.P.," *Chicago Tribune*, March 18, 1946. Meeting in Portage on March 17, 284 of the 415 delegates to the party's final state convention voted to affiliate with the GOP. Seventy-seven delegates voted to retain the Wisconsin Progressive Party while 51 delegates preferred to align with the Democrats and three voted to join the Socialist Party.

Chapter XXIV

The Indispensable Man

Though largely neglected by political historians, the 1944 campaign for the White House included as much suspense and intrigue as any presidential election in American history, an election marked by a deviously shameful and concerted effort by Republicans, nefariously aligning themselves with racist Democrats in the South, to hinder and suppress the participation of more than eleven million members of the armed services who were risking their lives to make the world safe for democracy.

As with Abraham Lincoln at the height of the Civil War eighty years earlier, there were even unsubstantiated reports, spread by FDR's enemies, that the President might suspend the election for the duration of the war — rumors that Roosevelt, like Lincoln in 1864, quickly put to rest. "Well, you see," Roosevelt responded when asked about the rumors during a press conference in early 1944, "you have come to the wrong place, because — gosh, all these people haven't read the Constitution. Unfortunately, I have."[1]

There were also rumors about Roosevelt's failing health and his inability to survive another term, issues that Thomas Dewey and the Republicans were understandably reluctant to exploit, especially since Roosevelt's personal physician had given him a clean bill of health. The rumors nevertheless persisted throughout the campaign.

---

[1] James McGregor Burns, *Roosevelt: The Soldier of Freedom* (New York, 1970), p. 497.

While the wartime President limited his campaigning to two dinner appearances, three public speeches, and three radio addresses, Dewey — as if to demonstrate his own youth and vigor — waged an all-out campaign, strenuously campaigning throughout the country.

Wendell Willkie, who had been wiped out in the Wisconsin primary earlier that year while trying to win the Republican nomination for a second time and later flirted with New York's fledgling Liberal Party, was one of the few prominent Republicans who came out strongly in favor of the federal ballot for soldiers. As a practical matter, he knew that laws in some states would deny members of the armed services an opportunity to cast a ballot that year. "Whether this will be more advantageous to the Republicans than to the Democrats I do not know," said Willkie. "I do know, however, that I would not wish to be elected President of the United States without every member of the armed services having an opportunity to vote to decide whether I should be."[2]

The Republican fears weren't completely unfounded. President Lincoln had received nearly 78% of the soldier vote in the dozen states that provided for a separate tabulation of military ballots during his 1864 reelection campaign against Gen. George B. McClellan. His majority was believed to have been just as large in the seven other states that permitted military absentee voting, but commingled the results with the civilian ballots.[3] Moreover, a Gallup Poll released in December 1943 showed that 61 percent of active duty military personnel favored Roosevelt's reelection.[4]

Due to the relatively weak provisions of the Servicemen's Voting Act — severely watered-down legislation that merely *recommended* rather than mandated that states should provide absentee ballots to military personnel if requested — only about 85,000 of the 11 million armed services members actually received special federal ballots in 1944, though many other active duty personnel were able to vote using their state's traditional absentee ballots.[5]

Though most political forecasters gave a slight edge to Roosevelt — as in 1940, the Elmer Roper survey conducted for *Fortune* magazine came closest, predicting a 53.5 percent share of the popular vote for FDR — many professional pollsters hedged their bets regarding the election's outcome.

---

[2] "Willkie Urges Soldier Vote," *Pittsburgh Post-Gazette*, Jan. 20, 1944.
[3] James M. McPherson, *Battle Cry of Freedom: The Civil War Era* (New York, 1988), p. 804.
[4] "Vote of Soldiers Could Decide '44 Election, Gallup Poll Finds," *New York Times*, Dec. 5, 1943; Boyd A. Martin, "The Service Vote in the Elections of 1944," *The American Political Science Review*, Vol. 39, No. 4 (Aug. 1945), p. 720.
[5] Sean J. Savage, *Roosevelt: The Party Leader, 1932-1945* (Lexington, KY, 1991), p. 180.

An already tight race had been further complicated by the absentee military vote, the size of which couldn't possibly be predicted and the outcome of which might not be known until sometime after December 5, when Rhode Island and North Dakota would stop accepting military ballots from overseas. Several others states, including Missouri, with a deadline of 6 p.m. on Wednesday November 8 — a day after the election — California, Colorado, Nebraska, Pennsylvania and Washington also accepted absentee ballots for varying periods after Election Day. Missouri, Washington and Pennsylvania, the latter of which received 620,000 applications for absentee ballots from military personnel but wouldn't count those ballots until the third week in November, were also considered too close to call.[6]

George Gallup, whose Nov. 4 survey of the twenty-one states still in play had Roosevelt and Dewey tied in five, FDR narrowly leading in three, and Dewey clinging to a lead in thirteen others, was almost certain that the hundreds of thousands of ballots cast by soldiers scattered in combat zones around the globe would determine the election.[7]

Noting that the number of absentee ballots was expected to exceed the margin between Roosevelt and Willkie in 1940, the Associated Press reported a few days before the election that the military vote would likely determine the winner in no fewer than sixteen states with a total of 235 electoral votes.[8]

Depending on the number of absentee ballots returned and counted, particularly in the unusually large number of tossup states, the election could clearly go either way. Even Norman Thomas, who had proven to be uncannily accurate in picking the winners in the four previous presidential elections, acknowledged that he was somewhat stumped, saying that while he was "gloomy about both candidates" the outcome of the race was the most difficult to predict of "any year I've ever run."[9]

As in 1940, Gallup also predicted that support for third-party candidates would be extremely light, amounting to less than one percent of all votes cast. Based on its polling, which didn't include a sampling of military personnel because such polling was forbidden, the Gallup Poll indicated that Socialist Norman Thomas would poll a modestly larger vote than he did in 1940, when he

---

[6] Roseboom, *A History of Presidential Elections*, pp. 489-490; "The Last Days," *TIME Magazine*, Nov. 6, 1944.
[7] "Gallup Says Services' Vote May Be Decisive," *Los Angeles Times*, Nov. 5, 1944.
[8] "Soldier Vote Seen Key in 16 States," *New York Times*, Nov. 4, 1944.
[9] "Hard to Pick Winner, Norman Thomas Declares," *Chicago Tribune*, Oct. 23, 1944; "In the Stretch," *TIME*, Oct. 30, 1944.

received slightly more than 116,000 votes.[10]

President Roosevelt concluded the final weekend of campaigning with a nationally-broadcast radio address from Boston's Fenway Park on Saturday, November 4, while rival Thomas Dewey participated in a huge rally at New York's Madison Square Garden. In their final pleas for support, the President criticized his Republican challenger for demonstrating "a shocking lack of trust in America" and "faith in democracy."[11]

Gov. Dewey concluded his coast-to-coast campaign with a hard-hitting speech before an enthusiastic crowd of 20,000 at New York's Madison Square Garden on Saturday evening, November 4th (see Appendix B). In his speech, which was heard by a vast nationwide radio audience, the Republican candidate charged that Roosevelt's "improvised meddling" and "confused incompetence" had unnecessarily prolonged the war.[12]

Specifically, Dewey blamed talk of the "Morgenthau Plan" during Roosevelt's September meeting with British Prime Minister Winston Churchill at the Octagon Conference in Quebec for strengthening the resolve of the German nation to resist, asserting that public discussion of the plan stopped the headlong Nazi retreat in its tracks and was tantamount to providing ten fresh German divisions on the battlefront.[13]

Among other things, Dewey promised his national radio audience a speedy victory in the war, the establishment of an international organization to keep the peace and prevent future wars, and a pledge to direct all of the government's policies in the postwar period to create jobs and opportunity for every American. "To these ends," he said, "we shall restore honesty and integrity to our national government; we shall put an end to one man rule; we shall unite our people in teamwork and harmony behind a President and a Congress that can and will work together to realize the limitless promises of America."[14]

These were not partisan objectives, concluded Dewey, but ra-

---

[10] "Gallup Poll Foresees Small Third Party Vote," *Los Angeles Times*, Oct. 25, 1944.
[11] "Falsehood Marks Republican Pleas, President Asserts," *New York Times*, Nov. 5, 1944; "Roosevelt Errors Prolong the War, Dewey Says Here," *New York Times*, Nov. 5, 1944; "Presidential Candidates Deliver Climactic Appeals," *Billings Gazette*, Nov. 5, 1944.
[12] "'Roosevelt Prolonged War By Meddling,' Says Dewey; FDR Denies Red 'Deals,'" *Milwaukee Sentinel*, Nov. 5, 1944.
[13] "Roosevelt Errors Prolong the War, Dewey Says Here; Talk of Morgenthau 'Plan' for Germany Blamed for Stiffening of Resistance," *New York Times*, Nov. 5, 1944.
[14] "'Roosevelt Prolonged War By Meddling,' Says Dewey," *Milwaukee Sentinel*, Nov. 5, 1944.

ther the wishes of the American people. "They can never be attained," he concluded, "under the tired and quarrelsome administration that has been in office for 12 long years."[15] President Roosevelt probably choked on his regular breakfast of soft-boiled eggs when he read newspaper accounts of Dewey's speech in the Sunday papers.

FDR, of course, had already addressed Dewey's oft-repeated charge that the administration was being led by a group of bickering, "tired old men." "You know," Roosevelt told a largely Teamster audience in opening his autumn campaign at the Statler Hotel in Washington on September 23, "I am actually four years older — which is a fact that seems to annoy some people. In fact, there are millions of Americans who are more than eleven years older than when we started in to clear up the mess that was dumped in our laps in 1933."[16]

Declaring that the argument against a change in administration during a period of major crisis "comes down to the bald plea for the re-election — so long as he lives — of whoever happens to be president," Dewey made his final appeal of the campaign in a fifteen-minute radio broadcast from his study in the Executive Mansion in Albany on Monday evening, Nov. 6th. The United States, said Dewey, had lurched from one crisis to another — from "war and depression and boom and depression and war again" — for the past thirty years. "The great test," he said, "is whether, knowing we need a new administration, we will make the change necessary to speed victory and to build the peace to come."[17]

In the meantime, Norman Thomas, waging his fifth consecutive bid for the White House, concluded his campaign with an address on a national public affairs radio program that same evening while the Socialist Labor Party's Edward A. Teichert, mentioned previously, gave a national radio address on the Mutual Broadcasting Network at the party's huge Town Hall rally in New York, asserting that neither major party had a solution for the country's postwar unemployment crisis. The fact that both major-party candidates focused on expanding unemployment insurance and social security throughout the campaign was a "dead giveaway," asserted Teichert, that Democrats and Republicans alike expected mass joblessness after the war.[18]

---

[15] Ibid.
[16] Rosenman, *Working with Roosevelt*, p. 475.
[17] "Dewey Asks Votes to Rebuke 4th Term Bid, Speed War Victory," *New York Times*, Nov. 7, 1944.
[18] "Dewey, Roosevelt Will Climax Drives Tonight," *Ogden Standard-Examiner*, Nov. 4, 1944; "Two Parties Fail, Laborite Charges," *Miami Daily News*, Nov. 5, 1944.

Prohibitionist Claude A. Watson, who only seven months earlier had preposterously predicted that a union of dry voters would miraculously sweep him into the White House, wrapped up his final weekend of campaigning with a few last-minute appearances in California.[19]

Reconciled to the fact that he was locked in a nip-and-tuck battle with Norman Thomas for third-place honors, Watson threw a few barbs at President Roosevelt in one of his final campaign speeches, telling delegates to the Southern Baptists' California general convention that the United States was indeed a Christian nation. Realizing that FDR was headed for an unprecedented fourth term, the Prohibitionist ignored Dewey and directed his criticism at the Democratic president. "Whenever a politician assumes to himself to become the high priest for the nation, and offers prayer over radio, and fails to make his request in the name of Jesus Christ, he cannot expect to have his prayer answered," said Watson, referring to a prayer Roosevelt had penned for U.S. soldiers in early June as Allied troops poured onto the beaches of Normandy. Quoting from the Bible, the Prohibition candidate then reminded his Baptist audience that "rulers are not a terror to good works, but to evil." That's news today, he quipped, drawing laughter from the crowd."[20]

In the campaign's waning hours, Socialist Norman Thomas was informed by one of Dewey's supporters that the Republican candidate shared his position on the Allied demand for an unconditional surrender. Highly skeptical, Thomas immediately sent a telegram to his Republican rival on the eve of the election — literally only hours before the polls opened on Nov. 7th — asking Dewey if he believed Germany should be forced to surrender unconditionally.[21]

Professing that he didn't quite understand the flip-flopping Republican's latest stance — Dewey, after all, had repeatedly endorsed the idea of unconditional surrender throughout the campaign — Thomas asked the governor to clarify his position in a public statement. "You have denounced [the] Morgenthau plan," wrote Thomas, "but accepted unconditional surrender and other semi-official threats, which are as bad for our boys as the Morgenthau plan."[22] To nobody's surprise, least of all his own, Thomas never received a reply.

---

[19] "Union of 'Drys" Would Result in Victory, Is Claim," *Milwaukee Journal*, April 17, 1944.
[20] "Dry Candidate's Barbs Pointed at Roosevelt," *Los Angeles Times*, Nov. 4, 1944.
[21] "Thomas Queries Dewey," *New York Times*, Nov. 7, 1944.
[22] Ibid..

THE INDISPENSABLE MAN

In the campaign's final days, nationally-syndicated columnist George E. Sokolsky, the son of a Russian émigré rabbi and later a staunch defender of Wisconsin's Joe McCarthy and a key figure during the nationally-televised Army-McCarthy hearings, urged the American people to vote their conscience. There was no such thing as a wasted vote, argued Sokolsky, a man later described as "the high priest of militant U.S. anti-Communism."[23]

"I have always admired the little handful of Americans who every four years vote for Norman Thomas on the Socialist ticket," wrote the Hearst columnist, a Dewey supporter who admitted to personally casting a vote for the Prohibition Party's Roger Babson in 1940 and said that he was likely to have voted for Thomas in 1944 if the GOP had nominated Willkie again. "They know that he will never be president of the United States," Sokolsky wrote of Thomas's supporters, but they most certainly "are not wasting their votes. They are not throwing them away."[24]

Despite such sentimentality, Thomas knew instinctively that votes would be few and far between. In fact, one would probably need a magnifying glass to read his vote totals. After all, the Greatest Generation was focused exclusively on the race between FDR and Dewey. As the *Washington Post* — predicting one of the smallest third-party showings in history — observed in an election-eve editorial, "scarcely a word has been heard or a line printed in the past few weeks about the four other candidates for the presidency."[25]

As Americans headed to the polls on Nov. 7th, U.S. servicemen in Germany were bombarded with shells containing Nazi propaganda leaflets bearing the slogan, "Jews govern, suckers fight: Vote for Roosevelt's Hebrew might."[26]

Believing that it would have been too great a risk to swap horses as victory in World War II loomed on the horizon, on Election Day the American electorate returned Roosevelt to the White House for a fourth time. Despite rumors of the President's failing health and the fact that several million men and women in the armed services had been disenfranchised — thanks largely to obstinate Republicans and southern Democrats — resulting in a smaller turnout than in 1940, Roosevelt defeated Dewey by a pop-

---

[23] George E. Sokolsky, "Cast Ballots as Free Americans," *Zanesville Times Recorder*, Nov. 6, 1944; "The Press: The Man in the Middle, *TIME*, May 24, 1954.
[24] Ibid.
[25] "Long Shots," *Washington Post*, Nov. 6, 1944.
[26] "Nazi Viewpoint," *Fort Lauderdale News*, Nov. 8, 1944.

ular vote 25,612,474 to 22,017,570 while amassing an overwhelming majority of 432 to 99 in the Electoral College.

Roosevelt carried thirty-six states while polling 53.4 percent of the popular vote to Dewey's 45.9 percent. As a result of a noticeable drop in his popular vote in the South, where the outcome was never in doubt, FDR received 1,314,000 fewer popular votes than in 1940, when he polled 54.7% of the vote against Willkie.

In New York, the American Labor and Liberal parties provided Roosevelt with a combined 825,640 votes, or nearly a quarter of his total in the state. Roosevelt received 496,405 votes on the ALP line and 329,235 votes on the Liberal Party ticket — all but 23,080 on the latter ticket being cast in the five counties of Greater New York.[27] The staggering number of votes cast for FDR on third-party tickets was an amazing accomplishment in and of itself, and more than ten times the number of votes cast nationally for any of the minor-party candidates for president in that despairingly depressing year for America's alternative parties.

Though Dewey fell agonizingly short in Michigan, which had gone narrowly for Willkie in 1940, he defeated the president in Ohio, Wisconsin and Wyoming, three states that voted for Roosevelt four years earlier. He also carried all of the other states that supported Willkie: Colorado, Indiana, Iowa, Kansas, Maine, Nebraska, North and South Dakota, and Vermont. Despite FDR's lopsided margin in the Electoral College, the race was actually much closer than it appeared. According to Svend Petersen, a switch of 303,193 votes in a dozen states would have given Dewey the victory.[28]

The loosely-organized states' rights and largely racist anti-Roosevelt Democrats, led by the Texas Regulars whose electoral slate in the Lone Star State was credited with 135,439 votes, or nearly twelve percent of the statewide total, also finished comfortably ahead of the country's nationally-organized minor parties. Remarkably, the anti-Roosevelt slate in Texas actually carried one of the state's 254 counties. In addition to the votes cast for the Texas Regulars, John Breedin's slate of electors pledged to Virginia's Harry F. Byrd garnered 7,799 votes in South Carolina, and an unpledged anti-Roosevelt slate of electors in Georgia received 3,373 votes.

Like the renegade Texans, the country's nationally-organized minor parties were left in the dust. The Socialist ticket fell far short

---

[27] "Roosevelt Total Vote in State is 3,304,238," *Dunkirk Evening Observer*, Dec. 5, 1944.
[28] Svend Petersen, *A Statistical History of the American Presidential Elections* (New York, 1963), p. 99.

of the grossly inflated predictions made by Maynard Krueger and campaign manager Harry Fleischman, the party's young national secretary — serving in that capacity from 1942 to 1950 — who believed that Norman Thomas would post his strongest showing since 1932, when he received nearly a million votes.[29] They couldn't have been more inaccurate. In fact, when all the votes were counted, the country's best known Socialist was barely a footnote in the 1944 presidential campaign.

Failing to secure a place on the ballot in major states such as California, Illinois and Ohio, Thomas limped home with a dismal 79,010 popular votes in twenty-eight states — the worst showing in his half-dozen campaigns for the nation's highest office. His meager total included 2,515 write-in votes in California, a state that had given him more than 63,000 votes a dozen years earlier. Thomas's best showing occurred in Wisconsin, where he netted just a shade under one percent of the vote.

Voters in Grant County, Oregon, provided Thomas with his strongest showing at the county level. It was a delicious irony that a county named after Civil War Gen. Ulysses S. "Unconditional Surrender" Grant had given the only presidential candidate critical of the Allies demand for an unconditional surrender in World War II nearly 5.5 percent of the vote.

The Thomas-Hoopes ticket also received more than three percent of the votes cast in Taylor County, Wisconsin, which had been Thomas's strongest county four years earlier. Largely due to the party's stronghold in the working-class city of Reading, Berks County, Pennsylvania — a county that gave Thomas 21.9 percent of the vote at the height of the Great Depression in 1932 — provided Thomas with his third best showing at the county level with nearly 2.7 percent of the vote.

Sadly, the party's gubernatorial, U.S. Senate and congressional candidates didn't fare much better. Socialist candidates were trounced everywhere, including in the party's so-called strongholds. Milwaukee's Walter Bubbert, a longtime landscape architect, conservationist and history buff, was the only Socialist in the country who survived the party's 1944 shellacking when he garnered more than 30,000 votes in a partisan race to retain his post as county surveyor. Without any Democratic or Republican opposition, the 36-year-old editor of the *Wisconsin Archeologist Quarterly* easily defeated an Independent Progressive to win another term. Every other Socialist candidate in Milwaukee — the city that gave

---

[29] "U.S. Votes Today; War Ballot Count May Delay Verdict," *New York Times*, Nov. 7, 1944.

Thomas his best showing — was overwhelmingly defeated.[30]

While technically finishing in third place — the same relatively coveted position he achieved in the 1928, 1932 and 1940 campaigns — nearly twice as many protest votes had been cast for anti-Roosevelt presidential electors and for independent Democratic electoral slates pledged to Virginia's segregationist Harry Byrd in a handful of southern states than for the Socialist nominee. Those were indisputably reactionary and racist votes and said profoundly more about the country, particularly in the South, than they did about noble Norman and the herculean effort he made that year.

Prohibitionist Claude A. Watson, waging the first of two spirited bids for the presidency as the nominee of America's oldest third party, received a somewhat respectable 74,761 votes in twenty-seven states, including 12,574 votes— one-sixth of his national total — in the party's Indiana stronghold. Watson's next strongest state was Oregon, where the colorful teetotaler and his little-known vice presidential running mate, Andrew Johnson, qualified for the ballot as independents. The Prohibitionists garnered 2,362 votes, or one-half of one percent, in that state, followed closely by Watson's home state of California where the dry crusader netted 14,770 hard-earned votes, including 6,081 in Los Angeles County, or slightly more than four-tenths of one percent of the statewide total.[31]

The Socialist Labor ticket of Edward Teichert and Arla Albaugh garnered 45,189 votes in sixteen states — the party's strongest showing in a presidential election since 1932. Like Thomas, however, Teichert's little-remembered candidacy hadn't caused any sleepless nights in the White House.

Remarkably, Teichert trounced Norman Thomas in New Jersey by a margin of 6,939 to 3,358, more than doubling his rival's total in that state. The Socialist Labor aspirant also outpolled his famous Socialist rival in heavily-populated New York, garnering 14,352 votes to 10,553 for Thomas. Teichert, moreover, received a relatively impressive 11,902 votes in New York City alone, compared to only 6,117 for his much better-known Socialist rival. The *New York Herald Tribune* called Teichert's showing "a minor but unexpected incident," angering the SLP which maintained that, unlike their nominee, Thomas entered the campaign "with the

---

[30] "County Gains by Democrats," *Milwaukee Journal*, Nov. 8, 1944; "Stop 'Surplus' Giveaway," *Socialist Call*, Nov. 24, 1944.
[31] "Ballots Close; Teetotalers Under Line," *Eugene Register-Guard*, Sep. 23, 1944; "Interesting Data Found in County Vote Analysis," *Los Angeles Times*, Dec. 6, 1944.

blessing of the capitalist press and radio as the 'official' Socialist candidate, with a backlog and steady stream of free publicity that has made him a nationally known figure." The little-known Teichert, they said, enjoyed none of those advantages — and they were right.[32]

Curiously, Gerald L. K. Smith's isolationist America First Party, which shamefully received considerably more newspaper coverage than Teichert's seriously conducted candidacy on the Socialist Labor ticket, polled a negligible 1,530 votes in Michigan and 251 in Texas. Except for perhaps the few right-wingers who actually bothered to scribble in her name, it came as no surprise that there weren't any votes officially recorded for the erratic Agnes Waters. The same thing was true for Rev. Leo Donnelly, the National Greenback Party's little-remembered nominee.

With precious few exceptions, things were just as bleak for independent and third-party candidates in most state and congressional elections that fall.

Like Thomas himself, Socialist candidates generally performed terribly at the ballot box. Aside from the four percent showing by Raymond Hofses in the party's Reading stronghold and the modest two percent share of the vote garnered by Jasper McLevy in Connecticut's gubernatorial race, only seven of the party's other 32 candidates for seats in the U.S. House polled more than one percent of the vote while not a single one of the party's U.S. Senate hopefuls cracked the one-percent mark that year.

The only truly credible showing by an independent candidate for governor that autumn occurred in North Dakota where state attorney general Alvin C. Strutz, a 41-year-old ally of maverick William Langer who was supported by the state's Nonpartisan League, received 38,997 votes, or 18.8%, in a triangular contest won easily by his Republican opponent Fred G. Aandahl. Strutz, who later served as chief justice of the North Dakota Supreme Court, decided to run as an independent after being defeated in the Republican primary earlier that year.

Aside from the relatively strong showing by former American Legion national commander-turned independent U.S. Senate candidate Lynn U. Stambaugh in North Dakota, a state noted for its political complexities, and the 73,089 votes garnered by Madison congressman Harry Sauthoff on the dying Progressive Party ticket in Wisconsin, candidates running outside the two major parties were hardly a factor in the 1944 U.S. Senate contests that autumn.

---

[32] "Teichert's Vote 14,352," *New York Times*, Dec. 8, 1944; "S.L.P. Vote Shows Rise; Vote for Teichert in N.Y. Almost Doubles Thomas's," *Weekly People*, Vol. LIV, No. 34, Nov. 18, 1944.

THE LOWEST EBB

Coupled with the overwhelming defeat of longtime Rep. Hamilton Fish in New York, Stambaugh's spirited candidacy not only enabled a Democrat to capture one of North Dakota's U.S. Senate seats for the first time in more than three decades, but also contributed mightily to isolationism's final political casualty — the unseating of longtime Republican Sen. Gerald P. Nye.[33]

Nye, whose first name was pronounced with a hard "G," was but one in a galaxy of colorful politicians with roots in the state's powerful Nonpartisan League, a constellation that included Yale-educated William Lemke, independent-minded William Langer — "the last blown-in-the-bottle Populist" and one of only two members of the U.S. Senate to vote against the UN Charter in 1945 — and Usher L. Burdick, a longtime congressman who was raised among Sioux Indians.

Running as the Nonpartisan League's nominee for one of the state's three U.S. House seats, the "boy statesman" from North Dakota came within an eyelash of defeating his Republican opponent, not once — but twice — on the same day in 1924. Nye, whose Senate subcommittee later helped convince a majority of Americans that Wall Street financiers and the munitions industry were responsible for U.S. entry in World War I, was narrowly defeated by Republican Thomas Hall, losing by 1,255 votes in a special election to fill the remainder of the late George M. Young's term in the 68th Congress and by a slightly larger margin in the race for a full term beginning in December 1925.

Curiously, nearly six thousand more votes had been cast in the special election for Young's short-term seat than for the regular term. Why voters cast more votes in the short-term race than for the six-year term remains one of the lingering unsolved mysteries of North Dakota politics.[34]

Despite losing twice on the same day, the 34-year-old Nye ended up going to Washington anyway. One of the country's leading isolationists in the period prior to World War II, the fiercely independent North Dakotan, giving up his country editor's desk for the rough and tumble of the nation's capital, was appointed to fill a vacancy in the U.S. Senate caused by the death of Republican Senator Edwin F. Ladd the following year. One of the most intellectually competent men to emerge from the Great Plains during

---

[33] Widely denounced as an "obstructionist," New York's isolationist congressman was defeated in his bid for a thirteenth consecutive term, losing to Newburgh attorney Augustus W. Bennet — a Republican who captured the Democratic and American Labor Party nominations — by more than 8,000 votes. Fish had narrowly defeated Bennet in the GOP primary in early August.

[34] "Watching the Political Parade," *Bismarck Tribune*, Oct. 8, 1938.

this period, "Gerald the Giant-Killer" served in the U.S. Senate from 1925 until his defeat in 1944.

Nye was arguably the most influential isolationist in the country. "We didn't win a thing we set out for in the last war," he thundered in the years leading up to World War II. "We merely succeeded, with tremendous loss of life, to make secure the loans of private bankers to the Allies."[35] It was a sentiment shared by a majority of the American people, including the Socialist Party's Norman Thomas.

The North Dakota lawmaker was also an outspoken critic of the nation's banking system and proposed a new central bank, placing control of all money and credit in the hands of the Federal Reserve, during the acrimonious debate over the 1935 Banking Act. Dubbed the "Prosperity Bill," Nye's legislation was drafted and championed by Father Charles E. Coughlin, but was overwhelmingly rejected in the U.S. Senate in July of that year. The final vote was 59-10.[36]

Like other America First spokesmen, Nye had been roundly criticized for his role in the non-interventionist movement in the months leading up to the attack on Pearl Harbor.

The North Dakota senator, in fact, gave a speech in Pittsburgh a couple of hours after the December 7 attack in which he said the Roosevelt administration had been doing its "utmost to provoke a quarrel with Japan." He also accused Britain of "making a studied effort" to start a war between the U.S. and Japan as a way of drawing the country into the wider global conflict. "Britain," he said, "has been getting this ready since 1938." It was only at the end of his speech that he finally informed his audience of the deadly attack on Pearl Harbor, adding somewhat reluctantly that "if the facts are as presented, there is only one thing for Congress to do — declare war."[37]

The *Pittsburgh Press* vigorously denounced Nye and the other America First speakers for concealing the attack until the end of their meeting and blasted the participants for jeering and hissing an Army colonel who tried to inform the audience of the attack. "Never has there been such a disgraceful meeting in all Pittsburgh

---

[35] Manchester, *The Glory and the Dream*, p. 126.
[36] "Coughlin Bank Plan Defeated," *Wisconsin State Journal*, July 26, 1935. In addition to the North Dakota lawmaker, the nine other senators who voted for Nye's central bank plan included Democrats Hattie Caraway of Arkansas, Oklahoma's Elmer Thomas, Burton K. Wheeler of Montana, and Rush D. Holt and Matthew M. Neely, both of West Virginia, as well as Republicans Thomas D. Schall of Minnesota and Lynn Frazier of North Dakota. The Farmer-Labor Party's Henrik Shipstead also voted for Nye's banking bill.
[37] "Jap Thrusts Wipe Away Factionalism," *Minneapolis Star*, Dec. 8, 1941.

history," the paper bemoaned. "Those who participated in it should forever hang their heads in shame."[38]

Nye's popularity was clearing waning. Having amassed the largest popular vote of any North Dakotan in history in winning reelection with more than 72 percent of the vote in 1932, Nye had a somewhat tougher time holding onto his seat in 1938. Narrowly defeating Gov. Langer, his former ally-turned nemesis, in a bitter June primary, Nye again faced the mercurial Republican governor in the autumn campaign.[39] Langer's independent candidacy had the backing of the state's powerful Nonpartisan League.

The contest was a real grudge match, the culmination of a five-year feud between the two men. In a particularly nasty campaign in which Langer depicted the incumbent as a Washington nonentity and creature of wealth who had done little for North Dakota farmers while Nye tore the governor apart on issues of graft and corruption, Nye — barely polling fifty percent of the vote — prevailed in November, defeating Langer by a margin of 131,907 to 112,007, with the little-known Democratic nominee nearly polling the difference with 19,244 votes.

Things were even more difficult six years later. Having barely survived the Republican primary, the former America First spokesman was clearly in the fight of his political life. An already tough reelection bid was made even more difficult by Stambaugh's independent candidacy in the general election

The 53-year-old Stambaugh, a successful Fargo attorney, had come within 972 votes of upsetting Nye in the state's June 27 Republican primary, a four-cornered race that included an inexplicably lackluster campaign waged by Rep. Usher Burdick, William Langer's handpicked candidate who was backed by the influential Nonpartisan League, and Arthur C. Townley, the League's aging founder who polled a not inconsequential 1,300 votes, mostly at Burdick's expense. Stunningly, Nye carried only twenty-one of the state's fifty-three counties in the primary.

Nye's unapologetic isolationism had been the central focus of the primary campaign, an issue Stambaugh wasted little time aggressively exploiting, accusing the longtime senator of hating the British and holding America's allies in contempt. He also claimed that Nye wanted to "wrap the United States in a blanket" while cutting off its relationships with other nations in the world. "Had he succeeded in his efforts to defeat lend-lease, selective service,

---

[38] "Disgraceful," *Pittsburgh Press*, Dec. 8, 1941.
[39] Nye defeated Langer in the June 28th Republican primary by a margin of 91,510 to 86,359.

neutrality revision and other last-minute preparedness measures," charged Stambaugh, "German and Jap forces might be converging on Bismarck tonight."[40]

Stambaugh, who had long advocated U.S. participation in world affairs, continued to hammer away at Nye's unrepentant and rabid isolationism throughout the autumn campaign.

An ardent foe of the New Deal, Nye claimed that he had been targeted for defeat by Sidney Hillman's powerful Political Action Committee. In fact, Nye, whose candidacy was strongly supported by William Lemke, Father Coughlin's candidate for president on the short-lived Union Party ticket in 1936, was convinced that Stambaugh's primary challenge had been arranged by his one-time ally Langer at the instigation of the Democrats — a charge that likely contained more than a grain of truth.

As expected, Langer's followers in the Nonpartisan League rallied behind Stambaugh's independent candidacy, enabling the Fargo lawyer to split the Republican vote while amassing an impressive 44,596 votes, or 26.2 percent of all votes cast in the Senate race. Stambaugh's relatively strong showing as an independent made it possible for late-starting Democrat John Moses, whose campaign was delayed while he was recovering from abdominal surgery at Mayo Clinic, to defeat Nye by a relatively comfortable margin.

Moses, a three-term governor of North Dakota, never fully recovered from his surgery and died on March 3, 1945, shortly after taking his seat in the Senate. Milton R. Young, a Republican, was named to fill the vacancy and a special election was scheduled for June 1946.

Hoping for political redemption, Nye sought to regain his old seat, but was repudiated by the Republican state convention, which nominated Young on the third ballot. Nye, however, remained in the race as an independent, but ran poorly, garnering a dismal 20,848 votes while losing to Young by nearly a four-to-one margin. Nye was stunned by the magnitude of his defeat, saying that he was "thoroughly surprised by what appears to be so decisive a defeat." He never again sought public office.[41]

The courageous decision by Wisconsin's Harry Sauthoff to give up his relatively safe seat in the U.S. House to wage what was

---

[40] Wayne S. Cole, *Senator Gerald P. Nye and American Foreign Relations* (Minneapolis, 1962), p. 212.
[41] "Langer Leading in N.D.; Young Beats Nye for Senate," *Minneapolis Star-Journal*, June 26, 1946.

almost certainly going to be a doomed candidacy for the U.S. Senate left the nation's minor parties with only two members in the U.S. House: the ALP's Vito Marcantonio in New York, who ran unopposed in 1944 after capturing the American Labor, Democratic and Republican nominations, and the Progressive Party's Merlin Hull in Wisconsin, a 73-year-old newspaper publisher from Black River Falls who, remarkably, was easily reelected to a seventh term against only token Socialist opposition.

Beyond a mildly impressive showing by North Dakota's Usher L. Burdick, no other independent or third-party candidate came close to winning a seat in the 79th Congress. Burdick, a five-term congressman and former president of the Farmers' Holiday Association, filed for his seat in the U.S. House of Representatives as an independent after losing the Republican nomination for the U.S. Senate earlier that year, polling nearly 40,000 votes in the latter contest.

That's not to suggest that third parties didn't wield considerable influence in some state and congressional contests that autumn, especially in New York City, where the American Labor and Liberal parties provided the margin of victory for major-party candidates in at least eleven races, including three for Congress. The ALP and the Liberal Party also supplied the winning margins in five State Senate races and three for the Assembly.[42]

In addition to wholeheartedly supporting leftist Marcantonio, the older American Labor Party provided an additional line on the ballot for no fewer than thirty-seven Democratic congressional aspirants in the state of New York and fielded its own candidates for the U.S. House in six other districts.

Two of its most spirited campaigns took place in the fourteenth congressional district where labor leader James V. King, president of the New York district of the State, County and Municipal Workers, an affiliate of the CIO, amassed an eye-opening 28,766 votes, and in the ninth congressional district where attorney and longtime party activist Jacob A. Salzman tallied 16,521 votes.

Leo Isacson, a Bronx lawyer and member of the party since its founding in 1936, was the lone member of the American Labor Party elected to the New York legislature that year. Isacson, who later flabbergasted political experts when he routed his Democratic, Republican and Liberal opposition by capturing nearly 56 percent of the vote in a special election to win a seat in Congress on the party's ticket in February 1948 — an extraordinarily promising

---

[42] "ALP, Liberal Vote Elected 11 Here," *New York Times*, Nov. 29, 1944.

precursor to former Vice President Henry A. Wallace's Progressive Party candidacy for the White House later that year — was elected to the state assembly on an American Labor-Republican fusion ticket.

In addition to the nearly 21,000 votes cast in Brooklyn's tenth congressional district for former city councilman Louis P. Goldberg, the lone congressional candidate running exclusively on the Liberal Party ticket that fall, New York City voters gave 19,561 votes, or nearly 11 percent of the total, to John A. Devany, a conservative Democratic assemblyman running under the Constitution Party banner in the state's 25th congressional district.

The ultraconservative Devany, a 44-year-old lawyer from the Bronx who lost badly to Rep. Charles A. Buckley in the Democratic primary earlier that year, had waged something of a one-man war against alleged Communist infiltration in the state government during his fifteen years in Albany.[43] He later won a libel suit against Michael J. Quill, president of the Transport Workers Union, for slanderously describing him as "an agent for fascism" and "an agent for Hitler in America" during his 1944 congressional campaign.[44]

While candidates running outside the two-party system generally performed poorly at the polls that autumn, at least two former third-party activists captured seats in the U.S. House of Representatives as Democrats. Andrew J. Biemiller, a prominent member of the Socialist Party's militant faction who had actively campaigned for Norman Thomas in 1932, was elected in Milwaukee's traditionally Republican and heavily German fifth congressional district, defeating an isolationist former Republican congressman by nearly 10,000 votes. As mentioned previously, Socialist Edwin W. Knappe, a Milwaukee attorney and secretary of the Wisconsin party, polled 4,758 votes in that race.

Biemiller, who once taught history at Syracuse University and the University of Pennsylvania and later served on the committee that drafted the Socialist Party's controversial Declaration of Principles in 1934, carried all but the city's 15th, 18th, 19th, 22nd and 26th wards in his successful campaign. A graduate of Cornell University, the 38-year-old Biemiller had been elected to the state legislature as a Socialist in 1936 and caucused with the majority Progressive Party, serving as the latter party's floor leader from 1939-41.[45]

---

[43] "Fish Renominated; Marcantonio Wins on All 3 Tickets," *New York Times*, Aug. 2, 1944; "Slates are Filed by Minor Parties," *New York Times*, Aug. 17, 1944.
[44] "John Devany Dies; Ex-Assemblyman" *New York Times*, Sept. 11, 1966.
[45] "Wasielewski, Biemiller Win," *Milwaukee Sentinel*. Nov. 8, 1944.

THE LOWEST EBB

In Washington, Hugh DeLacy, an ex-Seattle city councilman and former president of the Washington Commonwealth Federation — a coalition of left-wing political organizations heavily influenced by the Communist Party — defeated his Republican opponent to win the seat previously held by Warren Magnuson. Magnuson had given up his seat to run for the U.S. Senate that year.

A former English instructor at the University of Washington, the 34-year-old DeLacy had long been suspected of being a member of the Communist Party and was working as a longshoreman at the time of his election. Accused of being a Communist and anti-American, the former shipyard worker was overwhelmingly defeated in a bid for a second term in 1946 — a year when the state's entire Democratic delegation in the U.S. House, except for Henry "Scoop" Jackson, was swept from office. DeLacy later worked as an organizer for Henry Wallace's 1948 presidential campaign, serving as the Progressive Party's state campaign director in Ohio.

Shortly after the election, an unusually gloomy Norman Thomas admitted that his party was virtually dead as a national entity. "While the Socialist Party will and must live as a great educational force," he said in early December, "it is never likely to be an electoral factor of great consequence in a national election."[46] His comment stunned many of the party's younger activists and he later denied that he said that the party was "dead," telling them that he had been misquoted by an AP reporter.[47]

The five-time presidential candidate also issued a dire warning, saying he believed that the United States was on the road to fascism or some variant thereof. By differing so little in policy and merely focusing on personalities, the two major parties had unwittingly created a "fertile field" for fascism to take hold in the country, he cautioned. The only thing that could prevent fascism and preserve democracy, continued Thomas, was "a spontaneous emergence of a coalition of progressive groups — from labor, the farm and from regional minority parties." The chronic joblessness that he expected to plague the country in the first few years following the war, he said, could "provide the spark for a new political realignment and possibly the rise of a new party somewhat similar to Canada's Cooperative Commonwealth Federation."[48]

Given his age — he turned sixty a few weeks earlier — Thomas said that if a coalition party emerged four years from then it was

---

[46] "Thomas Fears Fascistic U.S.," *New York Sun*, Dec. 1, 1944.
[47] Norman Thomas, "Socialist Party 'Death' Highly Exaggerated," *Socialist Call*, Dec. 15, 1944.
[48] "Thomas Favors New Coalition," *Times-Picayune*, Dec. 1, 1944.

highly unlikely that he would become its presidential candidate. "I look for a new, younger leader," he said. "I believe there will be a new crop of young leaders in all parties after the war." Those who served in the war, he added, will want to be heard, a prospect that would virtually doom Gov. Thomas Dewey's chances of gaining the Republican nomination again in 1948. "Any candidate who didn't have a uniform on will have a tough time," observed Thomas. "I think Dewey knows this."[49]

Still obviously despondent over his own bitterly disappointing showing in the 1944 presidential election — a campaign in which he not only laid bare his conscience, but valiantly expended as much time, energy, and effort as in any of his previous bids for the White House — Thomas told a reporter in the spring of 1946 that he didn't plan to run for office ever again. "There ought to be a law against a man running for president five times," he scoffed. "I wouldn't even run for dog catcher now."[50]

Too much an evangelist and far too concerned about his fellow human beings to throw in the towel when there was so much more to accomplish, it wasn't long before the silver-haired Thomas was off and running once again for the highest office in the land.

---

[49] Ibid.
[50] "Norman Thomas Won't Run Again, Even for Dog Catcher, After 5 Defeats," *Binghamton Press*, Apr. 30, 1946.

APPENDICES

Appendix A

President Franklin D. Roosevelt's State of the Union Address, Jan. 11, 1944

To the Congress of the United States:

This nation in the past two years has become an active partner in the world's greatest war against human slavery.

We have joined with like-minded people in order to defend ourselves in a world that has been gravely threatened with gangster rule.

But I do not think that any of us Americans can be content with mere survival. Sacrifices that we and our allies are making impose upon us all a sacred obligation to see to it that out of this war we and our children will gain something better than mere survival.

We are united in determination that this war shall not be followed by another interim which leads to new disaster- that we shall not repeat the tragic errors of ostrich isolationism—that we shall not repeat the excesses of the wild twenties when this Nation went for a joy ride on a roller coaster which ended in a tragic crash.

When Mr. Hull went to Moscow in October, and when I went to Cairo and Teheran in November, we knew that we were in agreement with our allies in our common determination to fight and win this war. But there were many vital questions concerning the future peace, and they were discussed in an atmosphere of complete candor and harmony.

In the last war such discussions, such meetings, did not even begin until the shooting had stopped and the delegates began to assemble at the peace table. There had been no previous opportunities for man-to-man discussions which lead to meetings of minds. The result was a peace which was not a peace.

That was a mistake which we are not repeating in this war.

And right here I want to address a word or two to some suspicious souls who are fearful that Mr. Hull or I have made "commitments" for the future which might pledge this nation to secret treaties, or to enacting the role of Santa Claus.

To such suspicious souls—using a polite terminology—I wish to say that Mr. Churchill, and Marshal Stalin, and Generalissimo Chiang Kai-shek

APPENDIX A

are all thoroughly conversant with the provisions of our Constitution. And so is Mr. Hull. And so am I.

Of course we made some commitments. We most certainly committed ourselves to very large and very specific military plans which require the use of all Allied forces to bring about the defeat of our enemies at the earliest possible time.

But there were no secret treaties or political or financial commitments.

The one supreme objective for the future, which we discussed for each Nation individually, and for all the United Nations, can be summed up in one word: Security.

And that means not only physical security which provides safety from attacks by aggressors. It means also economic security, social security, moral security—in a family of Nations.

In the plain down-to-earth talks that I had with the Generalissimo and Marshal Stalin and Prime Minister Churchill, it was abundantly clear that they are all most deeply interested in the resumption of peaceful progress by their own peoples—progress toward a better life. All our allies want freedom to develop their lands and resources, to build up industry, to increase education and individual opportunity, and to raise standards of living.

All our allies have learned by bitter experience that real development will not be possible if they are to be diverted from their purpose by repeated wars—or even threats of war.

China and Russia are truly united with Britain and America in recognition of this essential fact:

The best interests of each nation, large and small, demand that all freedom-loving nations shall join together in a just and durable system of peace. In the present world situation, evidenced by the actions of Germany, Italy, and Japan, unquestioned military control over disturbers of the peace is as necessary among nations as it is among citizens in a community. And an equally basic essential to peace is a decent standard of living for all individual men and women and children in all nations. Freedom from fear is eternally linked with freedom from want.

There are people who burrow through our nation like unseeing moles, and attempt to spread the suspicion that if other nations are encouraged to raise their standards of living, our own American standard of living must of necessity be depressed.

The fact is the very contrary. It has been shown time and again that if the standard of living of any country goes up, so does its purchasing power- and that such a rise encourages a better standard of living in neighboring countries with whom it trades. That is just plain common sense—and it is the kind of plain common sense that provided the basis for our discussions at Moscow, Cairo, and Teheran.

Returning from my journeys, I must confess to a sense of "let-down" when I found many evidences of faulty perspective here in Washington. The faulty perspective consists in overemphasizing lesser problems and thereby underemphasizing the first and greatest problem.

THE LOWEST EBB

The overwhelming majority of our people have met the demands of this war with magnificent courage and understanding. They have accepted inconveniences; they have accepted hardships; they have accepted tragic sacrifices. And they are ready and eager to make whatever further contributions are needed to win the war as quickly as possible — if only they are given the chance to know what is required of them.

However, while the majority goes on about its great work without complaint, a noisy minority maintains an uproar of demands for special favors for special groups. There are pests who swarm through the lobbies of the Congress and the cocktail bars of Washington, representing these special groups as opposed to the basic interests of the Nation as a whole. They have come to look upon the war primarily as a chance to make profits for themselves at the expense of their neighbors — profits in money or in terms of political or social preferment.

Such selfish agitation can be highly dangerous in wartime. It creates confusion. It damages morale. It hampers our national effort. It muddies the waters and therefore prolongs the war.

If we analyze American history impartially, we cannot escape the fact that in our past we have not always forgotten individual and selfish and partisan interests in time of war — we have not always been united in purpose and direction. We cannot overlook the serious dissensions and the lack of unity in our war of the Revolution, in our War of 1812, or in our War Between the States, when the survival of the Union itself was at stake.

In the First World War we came closer to national unity than in any previous war. But that war lasted only a year and a half, and increasing signs of disunity began to appear during the final months of the conflict.

In this war we have been compelled to learn how interdependent upon each other are all groups and sections of the population of America.

Increased food costs, for example, will bring new demands for wage increases from all war workers, which will in turn raise all prices of all things including those things which the farmers themselves have to buy. Increased wages or prices will each in turn produce the same results. They all have a particularly disastrous result on all fixed income groups.

And I hope you will remember that all of us in this Government represent the fixed income group just as much as we represent business owners, workers, and farmers. This group of fixed income people includes: teachers, clergy, policemen, firemen, widows and minors on fixed incomes, wives and dependents of our soldiers and sailors, and old-age pensioners. They and their families add up to one-quarter of our one hundred and thirty million people. They have few or no high pressure representatives at the Capitol. In a period of gross inflation they would be the worst sufferers.

If ever there was a time to subordinate individual or group selfishness to the national good, that time is now. Disunity at home — bickering, self-seeking partisanship, stoppages of work, inflation, business as usual, politics as usual, luxury as usual these are the influences which can undermine the morale of the brave men ready to die at the front for us here.

APPENDIX A

Those who are doing most of the complaining are not deliberately striving to sabotage the national war effort. They are laboring under the delusion that the time is past when we must make prodigious sacrifices- that the war is already won and we can begin to slacken off. But the dangerous folly of that point of view can be measured by the distance that separates our troops from their ultimate objectives in Berlin and Tokyo — and by the sum of all the perils that lie along the way.

Overconfidence and complacency are among our deadliest enemies. Last spring — after notable victories at Stalingrad and in Tunisia and against U-boats on the high seas — overconfidence became so pronounced that war production fell off. In two months, June and July, 1943, more than a thousand airplanes that could have been made and should have been made were not made. Those who failed to make them were not on strike. They were merely saying, "The war's in the bag- so let's relax."

That attitude on the part of anyone—Government or management or labor—can lengthen this war. It can kill American boys.

Let us remember the lessons of 1918. In the summer of that year the tide turned in favor of the allies. But this Government did not relax. In fact, our national effort was stepped up. In August, 1918, the draft age limits were broadened from 21-31 to 18-45. The President called for "force to the utmost," and his call was heeded. And in November, only three months later, Germany surrendered.

That is the way to fight and win a war—all out—and not with half-an-eye on the battlefronts abroad and the other eye-and-a-half on personal, selfish, or political interests here at home.

Therefore, in order to concentrate all our energies and resources on winning the war, and to maintain a fair and stable economy at home, I recommend that the Congress adopt:

(1) A realistic tax law—which will tax all unreasonable profits, both individual and corporate, and reduce the ultimate cost of the war to our sons and daughters. The tax bill now under consideration by the Congress does not begin to meet this test.

(2) A continuation of the law for the renegotiation of war contracts—which will prevent exorbitant profits and assure fair prices to the Government. For two long years I have pleaded with the Congress to take undue profits out of war.

(3) A cost of food law—which will enable the Government (a) to place a reasonable floor under the prices the farmer may expect for his production; and (b) to place a ceiling on the prices a consumer will have to pay for the food he buys. This should apply to necessities only; and will require public funds to carry out. It will cost in appropriations about one percent of the present annual cost of the war.

(4) Early reenactment of the stabilization statute of October, 1942. This expires June 30, 1944, and if it is not extended well in advance, the country might just as well expect price chaos by summer. We cannot have stabilization by wishful thinking. We must take positive action to maintain the integrity of the American dollar.

(5) A national service law- which, for the duration of the war, will prevent strikes, and, with certain appropriate exceptions, will make available for war production or for any other essential services every able-bodied adult in this nation.

These five measures together form a just and equitable whole. I would not recommend a national service law unless the other laws were passed to keep down the cost of living, to share equitably the burdens of taxation, to hold the stabilization line, and to prevent undue profits.

The federal government already has the basic power to draft capital and property of all kinds for war purposes on a basis of just compensation.

As you know, I have for three years hesitated to recommend a national service act. Today, however, I am convinced of its necessity. Although I believe that we and our allies can win the war without such a measure, I am certain that nothing less than total mobilization of all our resources of manpower and capital will guarantee an earlier victory, and reduce the toll of suffering and sorrow and blood.

I have received a joint recommendation for this law from the heads of the War Department, the Navy Department, and the Maritime Commission. These are the men who bear responsibility for the procurement of the necessary arms and equipment, and for the successful prosecution of the war in the field. They say:

"When the very life of the nation is in peril the responsibility for service is common to all men and women. In such a time there can be no discrimination between the men and women who are assigned by the government to its defense at the battlefront and the men and women assigned to producing the vital materials essential to successful military operations. A prompt enactment of a National Service Law would be merely an expression of the universality of this responsibility."

I believe the country will agree that those statements are the solemn truth.

National service is the most democratic way to wage a war. Like selective service for the armed forces, it rests on the obligation of each citizen to serve his Nation to his utmost where he is best qualified.

It does not mean reduction in wages. It does not mean loss of retirement and seniority rights and benefits. It does not mean that any substantial numbers of war workers will be disturbed in their present jobs. Let these facts be wholly clear.

Experience in other democratic nations at war — Britain, Canada, Australia, and New Zealand — has shown that the very existence of national service makes unnecessary the widespread use of compulsory power. National service has proven to be a unifying moral force based on an equal and comprehensive legal obligation of all people in a Nation at war.

There are millions of American men and women who are not in this war at all. It is not because they do not want to be in it. But they want to know where they can best do their share. National service provides that direction. It will be a means by which every man and woman can find that inner satisfaction which comes from making the fullest possible contribution to victory.

APPENDIX A

I know that all civilian war workers will be glad to be able to say many years hence to their grandchildren: "Yes, I, too, was in service in the great war. I was on duty in an airplane factory, and I helped make hundreds of fighting planes. The Government told me that in doing that I was performing my most useful work in the service of my country."

It is argued that we have passed the stage in the war where national service is necessary. But our soldiers and sailors know that this is not true. We are going forward on a long, rough road — and, in all journeys, the last miles are the hardest. And it is for that final effort—for the total defeat of our enemies — that we must mobilize our total resources. The national war program calls for the employment of more people in 1944 than in 1943.

It is my conviction that the American people will welcome this win-the-war measure which is based on the eternally just principle of "Fair for one, fair for all."

It will give our people at home the assurance that they are standing four-square behind our soldiers and sailors. And it will give our enemies demoralizing assurance that we mean business — that we, 130,000,000 Americans, are on the march to Rome, Berlin, and Tokyo.

I hope that the Congress will recognize that, although this is a political year, national service is an issue which transcends politics. Great power must be used for great purposes.

As to the machinery for this measure, the Congress itself should determine its nature — but it should be wholly non-partisan in its make-up.

Our armed forces are valiantly fulfilling their responsibilities to our country and our people. Now the Congress faces the responsibility for taking those measures which are essential to national security in this the most decisive phase of the nation's greatest war.

Several alleged reasons have prevented the enactment of legislation which would preserve for our soldiers and sailors and marines the fundamental prerogative of citizenship — the right to vote. No amount of legalistic argument can becloud this issue in the eyes of these ten million American citizens. Surely the signers of the Constitution did not intend a document which, even in wartime, would be construed to take away the franchise of any of those who are fighting to preserve the Constitution itself.

Our soldiers and sailors and marines know that the overwhelming majority of them will be deprived of the opportunity to vote, if the voting machinery is left exclusively to the States under existing State laws — and that there is no likelihood of these laws being changed in time to enable them to vote at the next election. The Army and Navy have reported that it will be impossible effectively to administer forty-eight different soldier voting laws. It is the duty of the Congress to remove this unjustifiable discrimination against the men and women in our armed forces- and to do it as quickly as possible.

It is our duty now to begin to lay the plans and determine the strategy for the winning of a lasting peace and the establishment of an American standard of living higher than ever before known. We cannot be content, no matter how high that general standard of living may be, if some fraction of our people — whether it be one-third or one-fifth or one-tenth — is ill-fed, ill-clothed, ill housed, and insecure.

This Republic had its beginning, and grew to its present strength, under the protection of certain inalienable political rights — among them the right of free speech, free press, free worship, trial by jury, freedom from unreasonable searches and seizures. They were our rights to life and liberty.

As our nation has grown in size and stature, however — as our industrial economy expanded — these political rights proved inadequate to assure us equality in the pursuit of happiness.

We have come to a clear realization of the fact that true individual freedom cannot exist without economic security and independence. "Necessitous men are not free men." People who are hungry and out of a job are the stuff of which dictatorships are made.

In our day these economic truths have become accepted as self-evident. We have accepted, so to speak, a second Bill of Rights under which a new basis of security and prosperity can be established for all regardless of station, race, or creed.

Among these are:

The right to a useful and remunerative job in the industries or shops or farms or mines of the Nation;

The right to earn enough to provide adequate food and clothing and recreation;

The right of every farmer to raise and sell his products at a return which will give him and his family a decent living;

The right of every businessman, large and small, to trade in an atmosphere of freedom from unfair competition and domination by monopolies at home or abroad;

The right of every family to a decent home;

The right to adequate medical care and the opportunity to achieve and enjoy good health;

The right to adequate protection from the economic fears of old age, sickness, accident, and unemployment;

The right to a good education.

All of these rights spell security. And after this war is won we must be prepared to move forward, in the implementation of these rights, to new goals of human happiness and well-being.

America's own rightful place in the world depends in large part upon how fully these and similar rights have been carried into practice for our citizens. For unless there is security here at home there cannot be lasting peace in the world.

One of the great American industrialists of our day — a man who has rendered yeoman service to his country in this crisis — recently emphasized the grave dangers of "rightist reaction" in this nation. All clear-thinking businessmen share his concern. Indeed, if such reaction should develop — if history were to repeat itself and we were to return to the so-called "normalcy" of the 1920's — then it is certain that even though we shall have conquered our enemies on the battlefields abroad, we shall have yielded to the spirit of fascism here at home.

APPENDIX A

I ask the Congress to explore the means for implementing this economic bill of rights- for it is definitely the responsibility of the Congress so to do. Many of these problems are already before committees of the Congress in the form of proposed legislation. I shall from time to time communicate with the Congress with respect to these and further proposals. In the event that no adequate program of progress is evolved, I am certain that the nation will be conscious of the fact.

Our fighting men abroad — and their families at home — expect such a program and have the right to insist upon it. It is to their demands that this Government should pay heed rather than to the whining demands of selfish pressure groups who seek to feather their nests while young Americans are dying.

The foreign policy that we have been following — the policy that guided us at Moscow, Cairo, and Teheran — is based on the common sense principle which was best expressed by Benjamin Franklin on July 4, 1776: "We must all hang together, or assuredly we shall all hang separately."

I have often said that there are no two fronts for America in this war. There is only one front. There is one line of unity which extends from the hearts of the people at home to the men of our attacking forces in our farthest outposts. When we speak of our total effort, we speak of the factory and the field, and the mine as well as of the battleground — we speak of the soldier and the civilian, the citizen and his government.

Each and every one of us has a solemn obligation under God to serve this nation in its most critical hour — to keep this Nation great — to make this nation greater in a better world.

Appendix B

Thomas Dewey's Speech
Madison Square Garden, Nov. 4, 1944

Senator Curran and Fellow-Americans:

All over the world tonight Americans are fighting for the right of free men to govern themselves. Here at home we are waging a political campaign to make secure the liberties for which they fight.

Openly and in plains words John Bricker and I, in the name of the Republican Party, are dedicated to these propositions:
1. To speed total victory and with it the prompt return of our fighting men by putting energy and competence in Washington behind the magnificent effort of our military command.
2. To provide American leadership in the world for an effective organization among all nations to prevent future wars.
3. To direct all government policies in the peacetime years ahead to achieving jobs and opportunity for every American.
To these ends,
We shall restore honesty and integrity to our national government;
We shall put an end to one-man rule;
We shall unite our people in teamwork and harmony behind a President and a Congress that can and will work together to realize the limitless promise of America.

There are no partisan objectives. They are in truth the objectives of the American people. They can never be attained under the tired and quarrelsome administration that has been in office for twelve long years. They can only be attained by a new, vigorous administration that comes fresh from the people. That's why all over the country the people are saying it's time for a change.

America is determined to win a speedy and overwhelming victory in this war. All of us have perfect confidence in our military and naval commanders. But this war cannot be won alone upon the battlefronts. It must also be won at home. And each of us must play his part.

As recently as September 1, General Eisenhower renewed his earlier prophecy that Germany could be beaten in 1944 if everyone at home would do his part. Yet last Thursday and again one hour ago Mr. Roosevelt decided to tell us that the war had still a long way to go.

What happened in two months to cancel General Eisenhower's prediction? Mr. Roosevelt has not told us the whole story, but part of it we know.

APPENDIX B

Mr. Roosevelt and Mr. Churchill held a conference in Quebec. Our Secretary of State was absent. Our Secretary of War was also left home. In their stead Mr. Roosevelt took with him that master of military strategy and foreign affairs, the Secretary of the Treasury, together with his private plan for disposing of the German people after the war. The plan was so clumsy that Mr. Roosevelt himself finally dropped it — but the damage was done.

The publishing of this plan while everything else was kept secret was just what the Nazi propagandists needed. That was as good as ten fresh German divisions. It put fight back into the German Army; it stiffened the will of the German nation to resist. Almost overnight the headlong retreat of the Germans stopped. They stood and fought fanatically.

Here is how the military expert of *Newsweek* described the tragic consequences of this blunder, and I quote him: "This necromancy ruins Gen. Dwight D. Eisenhower's campaign. Now he finds himself faced by resistance he never expected and which, in my opinion, would never have materialized had Allied political warfare been astute instead of idiotic."

So says the military expert.

Here's a report from the front by the United Press and I quote it: "The home-front talk about stern treatment for a defeated Germany has inspired bitter and fanatical resistance among German troops, in this sector at least, and the GI's are a little bitter about it. Sometimes the doughboys who are fighting and dying in the mud on this side of the Moselle, the report continues, wish people at home would quit announcing what they think should be done about a defeated Germany. Some soldiers said today, the report concludes, that they thought it might be better to win the war first."

What does that mean? It means that the blood of our fighting men is paying for this improvised meddling which is so much a part and parcel of the whole Roosevelt Administration. And tonight, at the very moment when his own confused incompetence has thus prolonged the war in Europe, Franklin Roosevelt went on the radio and claimed for himself the credit for everything our engineers, our war workers, our industry, our farmers and our fighting sons have done.

We are advancing and we shall reach our goals. Once rid of capricious, personal government, once we give our whole, our united thoughts to victory, we shall reach Berlin and Tokyo quicker and with less cost.

Let me make one thing clear: Your next administration will never claim credit, personal or political, from the achievements of the American people or from the sacrifices of their sons and daughters. But it will put a stop to the incompetence in Washington which is costing the lives of American men and delaying the day of final victory.

That's why it's time for a change.

The people of this country are determined that we shall not again go through the heartache and sacrifice of these past three years. This war must be the last war. We shall take the lead in the formation of a world organization to prevent future wars. And we know that effort can never be the work of one man or of one nation. It can never be the product of secret agreements worked out in secret conferences between two or three rulers.

THE LOWEST EBB

For the United States, this great effort must have the support and understanding of all our people. And it must, under our Constitution, have the support and approval of the people's representatives in Congress.

Yet Mr. Roosevelt, year after year, has systematically abused and insulted the members of Congress. Having already alienated his own leaders in Congress, he has now gratuitously insulted the Republican leadership of the Senate and the House. Those leaders joined with me in an effort to lift the program for lasting peace above partisanship. They publicly pledged themselves to support the program for lasting peace on which Secretary Hull and I had cooperated. But this harmonious non-political approach was not politically profitable to Mr. Roosevelt, so he denounced the Republican members of Congress and rewarded their high-minded action by the masterful charge of erecting "a party spite fence between us and the peace."

The time has come to bring an end to this name-calling and abuse. American participation in a world organization for peace can only be built by a President and a Congress — Republicans and Democrats alike — working together in harmony and in mutual respect. To achieve that harmony, we must have a new chief executive who believes in that fundamental principle and who practices it. That's another reason why it's time for a change.

When victory is won, eleven million Americans will return home from our fighting forces. They will be looking for jobs and opportunity.

They want to marry, go to work and get ahead. Twenty million war workers will be looking for jobs in peacetime industries. If we are not to betray those who have fought and worked for victory in this war, we must have here in America a land of opportunity, a land of full employment at high wages, with a rising standard of living.

My opponent talks once again of jobs in the future, but he offers us nothing except a repetition of the New Deal policies which failed for eight straight peacetime years. This administration took office when the worldwide depression was nearly four years old. No previous depression in the whole hundred years of our history had lasted more than five years. Yet Mr. Roosevelt contrived to make that depression last eleven years — twice as long as any depression in the whole century.

He had unlimited power; he spent 58 billion dollars; yet in March 1940 there were still ten million unemployed. Under the New Deal it took a war to get jobs.

We dare not, we must not risk the future of our country in the hands of those who never succeeded in eight peacetime years in even approaching full employment. We need to sweep away the strangling mass of rules and regulations, of petty bureaucratic interferences. We need to sweep away the old dank, wretched atmosphere of hostility and abuse. We need once more to let the American people — industry, labor and agriculture — know that their government believes with them in the American tradition of opportunity for all.

We need an administration that cares more about little business than it does about big government. We need an administration that will not be afraid of the peace — that will want to bring our fighting men home when victory is achieved — and will keep its promise to do so. And that's another reason why it's time for a change.

There are other reasons. For twelve years we have watched the shifty, slippery nature of the present national administration. It has stood for no principle except self-perpetuation in power. The result has been decay of the moral fiber of government. That decay reached its logical result when Franklin Roosevelt was compelled to admit that it was he himself who sponsored the notorious One Thousand Club. This is the scheme which offers in writing for $1,000 "special privileges" and a voice "in the formulation of administration policies."

Never in our history has corruption been so brazen. Never before has a president admitted sponsorship of such a scheme.

All this is the inevitable result of too many years in power — and the desire for perpetual office. It is exactly what every great American, beginning with George Washington and Thomas Jefferson, warned against. It is inevitable that it should have produced political leadership which today publicly defines politics as the science of "how who gets what, when and why." I say the young men of America are not fighting and dying for these corrupt and decadent practices. In the name of those men, the American people will rise up and repudiate that whole philosophy of government. The time has come to put an end to government by "who gets what, when and why." That's why it's time for a change.

Today the great Democratic Party, weakened by twelve years of one-man rule, is being leased out to men who boast that they owe no allegiance to that party or its principles. It has been put on the auction block, for sale to the highest bidder, and the highest bidders are Sidney Hillman's Political Action Committee and Earl Browder's Communists. There is only one way for the real members of the Democratic Party to win in this election. That is to join with Republicans in defeating the New Dealers, the Political Action Committee and the Communists. That's why those who believe in our system of government, Republicans and Democrats alike, agree today that it's time for a change.

In this campaign I have set forth a constructive program for the years ahead built soundly, brick by brick. It shows how we can achieve our objectives — each of them, including full employment, high, stable income for labor, agriculture and business, broader old-age benefits, tax reduction with an increased national income and freedom of both labor and business from crippling government regimentation.

My opponent has offered no program, nothing but smears and unspecified complaints, and the reason is because the New Deal has nothing to offer save more of the same quarreling and vacillation which has marked its career for twelve long years. We can no longer afford the luxury of a government which spends half its time quarreling with itself and the other half quarreling with one segment or another of our people. In the years immediately ahead we need new hands to steer the Ship of State steadily through the balance of the war, then into quiet peacetime waters where we can again make progress. We need to learn to work together, again, in unity as a nation. We need above all to renew our faith; faith in the goodwill of our fellow-men regardless of race, creed or color; faith in the limitless future of our country.

Our nation was founded and built by men of great faith and goodwill, who came here to do great things. They created our institutions in the image of their beliefs. First of all, they believed in Almighty God. That was the rock on which they built. They believed in the moral law. They believed in the dignity of man. In the Bill of Rights they consecrated and established that dignity of man without distinction of race, creed or color. They believed that man should be free — free to worship after the dictates of his own conscience, free to live in his own home, to raise a family — free to speak his own mind without fear or favor, free to get ahead in the world. They believed that government should be the servant, not the master of the people. Because they believed those things and built upon them, this nation has been richly blessed of God.

Our people have known hardship, but they have never despaired. They have faced great odds, but they have never known defeat. To them the difficult is never too difficult. With them the impossible can be brought to pass.

Let us in this election send a ringing affirmation to all the world that the love of freedom is still strong in the hearts of the American people. Let us register our faith that in America there is no indispensable man. Let us prove that free government does still live. Let us send the thrilling message round the world that America has changed administrations in order to speed victory and insure lasting peace — the thrilling message that freedom is the most vital thing in the world — that we intend to have it — to hold it forever.

Appendix C
Freedom for All!
1944 Socialist Party Platform

In their struggle for freedom, peace and plenty, the American people face four paramount and closely interrelated issues: (1) the winning of the earliest possible peace that will last; (2) the provision of economic security for every American, with the preservation and increase of liberty; (3) the establishment of fraternity among all races, with equality of rights and obligations; (4) the improvement of the techniques of democratic political action.

On this platform for dealing with these issues, the Socialist Party, confident that the development of a strong party with mas support is essential to the struggle against fascism and the winning of the kind of world we want, seeks the support of the American people.

1. WINNING OF THE PEACE

The winning of the peace cannot be the result of appeasement of Nazism or of any other aggressive imperialism.

Neither can it be the consequence of the "unconditional surrender" of the German and Japanese to the rulers of the USSR, Great Britain and the United States of America. Shouting that slogan, the Roosevelt administration is prolonging this war and inviting the next by underwriting with the lives of our sons the restoration and maintenance of the British, Dutch and French empires in the Far East, and the Balkanization of Europe between Moscow and London.

Averting New Wars

New war will not be averted by a triple alliance of the major powers — with China as a "poor relation" — even though such an alliance with its already obvious rivalries may be masked behind a plan for a vague association of nations. Yet this is the pattern for the future which most Republican, as well as Democratic leaders accept.

The alternative to an uneasy and impermanent triple alliance for policing and exploiting the world is not an America first of isolationist imperialism equally dangerous to democracy and peace. But toward one or the other of these forms of imperialism and the fascism which accompanies it the policies of both old parties inexorably lead us.

Against so dire a fate, we summon the American people and the people of our allies to demand an immediate political peace offensive based on the offer of an armistice to the people of the Axis nations on the following conditions:

Conditions for Peace

1. The peace should be organized on the acceptance of two fundamental principles: (a) the equal rights of all peoples of every race to order their lives without subjection to any race of nation; (b) the necessity that self-determination be accomplished by organized co-operation, from which no people, enemy, neutral or colonial, shall be excluded, and the establishment of political and economic arrangements for removing the causes of war, settling disputes, guaranteeing security and conquering poverty.

2. As a guarantee of good faith and a condition of armistice, the German and Japanese people must: (a) replace governments guilty of gross deceit and cruel aggression by governments in whose good faith reasonable confidence way be reposed; (b) withdraw their military forces from all occupied territory and rapidly disarm; and (c) wherever possible, restore loot and give refugees a new economic start.

3. The United Nations, on their part, must pledge themselves specially (a) to free the European nations overrun by Germany; (b) to help them guarantee their independence through a United States of Europe or strong regional federations to supplement a world federation; (c) to refrain from interference in the internal affairs of nations thus freed; (d) to extend material aid for immediate relief and reconstruction of devastated countries without using such aid as a weapon for political domination; (e) to reject all demands for Axis slave labor in the postwar world; (f) to decide boundary questions which do not yield to negotiation by plebiscite under international authority; (g) to turn away from imperialism by guaranteeing speedy self-government, not only to lands now occupied by Japan, but to colonial territories under white rule. Where guidance to such independence is necessary, it shall be under international authority.

4. As a guarantee of good faith and a condition of the success of any federation, the United Nations must pledge themselves after the establishment of peace to follow the disarmament of the enemy countries by ending their own competitive armaments and military conscription and working out international guarantees of mutual security.

These points together comprise a peace offensive capable of inspiring revolt against the Axis dictators, winning the confidence of their victims and saving thousands of American lives.

2. ECONOMIC SECURITY WITH LIBERTY

The people of America fear the joblessness and depression which they think that the great boon of peace will bring. They remember that on the eve of the war boom, 23% of them were dependent on made work or relief and 40% lived just on, or below, the level of proper subsistence in respect to food.

In spite of this fear, what can be done in war can be better and more democratically done in peace, but only if we will plan for plenty for all as we have planned for meeting the insatiable appetites of the god of war.

APPENDIX C

Poverty and joblessness cannot be conquered by private capitalism under the false alias of "free enterprise," which is extolled today, ignorantly or hypocritically, by such diverse groups as the Republicans, the Democrats, the Communists, Wall Street monopolists, little business, farmers — and even labor leaders.

Planning for plenty is wholly incompatible with a return of the control over our great productive machinery to private owners — very largely absentee owners — while the government commits itself to overcome the periodic crisis of a scarcity economy by maintaining the unemployed at subsistence levels. This has been and is the economic program of the New Deal.

Socialists pioneered in the advocacy of social insurance. We favor its extension and improvement. We endorse all possible help to returning veterans. We demand that the new public domain — the war plants now owned by the government — be used in the struggle against unemployment and not handed over to big business.

But that is not enough. Only profound social and economic reorganization will enable men to use our marvelous technological resources for the complete conquest of poverty.

Democracy — Not Bureaucracy

The commanding heights of our economic order; our system of money, banking and credit; our natural resources; our public utilities and all monopolies, semi-monopolies, and other exploitive industries, must be socially controlled. To be effective that requires social ownership, but not autocratic administration by agents of a bureaucratic state. We do not need to exchange "government of the workers, by the bosses, for the profits of absentee owners" for "government of the workers, by the bureaucrats, for the glory and power of the military state."

Two forms of administration of socialized enterprise will go far to protect us against this danger: (1) public corporations operated for the people's benefit through directors representing consumers and the various categories of workers with hand and brain in each such industry; and (2) growth of consumers' co-operatives on the Rochdale Plan.

The democratic state can further play its part by the proper control of the fiscal system and by taxation based on the two principles of the ability to pay and the encouragement of production, both of which exclude the sales tax. A postwar tax program must not be used to support the big business system and hinder the growth of social enterprise. Taxes on the rental value of land should be used to end absentee landlordism; sharply graduated inheritance taxes should prevent the perpetuation of vast estates and a carefully proportioned capital levy tax should aid socialization. Such taxation will also be found necessary to prevent enormous and growing national debt from leading us into financial disaster.

As against exploitation by private owners or the state, the right of workers to organize and to bargain collectively must be restored and protected. We oppose in war or peace the conscription of labor and the outlawry of the right to strike. Free labor is essential to a free America.

There is no more essential function of labor than the raising of food and fibre. We pledge our support to all measures looking to the conservation of our soil and the production of abundance with adequate regard to American farmers. We pledge our aid to the working farmers against exploitation by absentee landlords, bankers and middle-men. We recognize the principle of occupancy and use as the only rightful title to farm land.

Where family farming has already been replaced by great plantations and company farms, or where modern technology forces large scale farming, we demand the social ownership and cooperative operation of such land plus the use of the most modern techniques and tools. Where conditions favor family farming we encourage the security of such farmers through cooperative credit, purchasing and marketing. We reject the compulsory collectivization of family farms along Russian lines.

We advocate the extension of social insurance to farm workers and provision of social security for farmers and farm workers displaced by age or technological changes. We advocate planning for full and balanced production of food and fibre in a hungry world. We advocate the further development of government agencies essential to carrying out these proposals, including the upbuilding of a Bureau of Cooperatives in the Department of Agriculture. We oppose the subversion — often the illegal subversion — of government agencies, especially the extension service of the Department of Agriculture, and agricultural colleges, to promote the profits and power of special interest groups now so dominant in the farm bloc.

3. EQUALITY AND FRATERNITY OF RACES

Democracy requires the application of the principle that each person is to be accorded social, political and economic equality, and judged solely on the basis of his own deeds, rather than by his race, religion, or national origin.

Specifically, we pledge ourselves to work for American hospitality to war refugees and the end of the exclusion of certain Asiatic peoples. The law applying to the Chinese the general provisions concerning immigration and admitting them to citizenship, should be extended to all Asiatic countries.

We demand the complete restoration of their rights as citizens to the 70,000 Americans of Japanese origin on the West Coast who were evacuated en masse, without trial or even hearing, and confined in centers which, however humanely run, are concentration camps.

We condemn anti-Semitism, Jim-Crowism, and every form of race discrimination and segregation in the armed forces as well as civil life. We urge the passage of anti-lynching and anti-poll tax laws and the prompt enactment of legislation to set up a permanent federal Fair Employment Practice Committee.

We reaffirm our historic opposition to any doctrine or practice of a master or favored race, not only in the realm of law, but in such labor unions — fortunately a minority — churches, political parties, and other basic social organizations as today countenance it. One of the conditions that will help make permanent the end of racial prejudice is the maintenance of full employment.

4. DEMOCRATIC POLITICAL ACTION

Year after year, by law and custom, the two old parties tighten their monopoly of the ballot. They are divided by no principles, but only by tradition and desire for office. Their platforms consist of generalities which are designed to prevent intelligent discussion and clear decision of issues. In consequence, pressure groups are the principle effective agencies in legislation and a situation is created which will aid the rise of a fascist demagogue in a period of postwar reaction.

The situation cries aloud for a democratic socialist party with mass support, such as our Canadian neighbors have developed in their Cooperative Commonwealth Federation.

Labor in the United States must establish its independence of current governmental control if it is to bargain freely with employers and government. The interests of a free labor movement are going to be better served as it severs its connections with the old parties, and unites with farm and consumer groups and minority groups seeking justice, to build a new kind of political party.

The issues here discussed are basic; they affect the lives of us all and destiny of America. They cannot be solved separately.

An America disgraced by racial tensions which occasionally find expression in lynchings and race riots cannot lead the way to a peace which depends upon worldwide reconciliation of races on the basis of equality of right.

An America which cannot or will not provide useful jobs for its own people will easily be led into militarism, imperialism, and new war itself as palliatives for unemployment.

An America which cannot or will not perfect the tools of democracy will be relatively defenseless against a rising fascism.

The struggle for plenty, peace, and freedom is one and indivisible. The success of that struggle alone will prevent the continuing sacrifice of our sons and their sons to endless cycle of wars.

If you believe these things, you will throw away your vote and your chance to make it count unless you VOTE THE SOCIALIST TICKET.

But a Socialist vote is not enough. Socialism is not the winning of an election but the winning of a new life.

If you want to be effective in the long fight for these causes, JOIN THE SOCIALIST PARTY!

Appendix D

1944 Prohibition Party Platform

Preamble

We, the representatives of the Prohibition Party in National Convention at Indianapolis, Indiana, November 10, 11,12, 1943, recognizing Almighty God as the source of all just Government and with faith in the teachings of the Prince of Peace, do solemnly promise that if chosen to administer the affairs of the nation, we will use all the power placed in our hands to serve the people of the United States, and that we will hold their interest above those of ourselves and our party. To do this requires the effective carrying out of the following program of Government.

A Constitutional Party

Pledge of Loyalty:
In this time of our national crises we pledge our loyalty to the Constitutional Government of the United States, to our flag and to the Republic for which it stands. We have supreme confidence in this basic law of the United States to meet ever-changing national and world conditions. Believing this, we are utterly opposed to the violation of the Bill of Rights, and to the rapidly growing tendency toward totalitarian Government in the United States.

State Rights:
We will confine the power of the executive department of the Government within the limits provided by the Constitution, will decentralize the national administration and restore to the several states their constitutional place in Government.

The support of state government in all its constitutional rights is the current bulwark against tyranny and dictatorship. We condemn the present administration for its extreme concentration in Washington of control over minor affairs.

Abolition of Bureaucracy:
We will do away with all bureaucratic devices with overlapping functions which are causing enormous waste of public funds and man power, and will conduct Government by means of constitutional methods.

APPENDIX D

No administrative board or agency should be at the same time accuser, jury, judge and hangman. Departmental decisions ought not to be final. All decisions of administrative boards or agencies should be reviewable by our courts to preserve our liberties.

Law Enforcement:

We will maintain the integrity of democracy by enforcing the laws enacted by elected representatives of the people or by popular vote.

Money:

We believe that the Constitutional provision for the issuance of money and determination of the value thereof is a sound and feasible monetary policy.

Taxes and Government Economy:

We pledge a reduction in taxes. We condemn most vigorously the administration's extravagance and maladministration of Government funds since long before the War. We stand for radical reduction in Government expenditures.

In the states we favor the effort to limit the tax rate to one percent of full value of property, in order to prevent foreclosure and confiscation, and assist the home owner, farmer, real estate owner, and others to preserve their property. But there can be no reduction in taxes unless we abolish the present increasingly expensive paternalistic bureaucracy.

Ballot Law Reform:

We demand the repeal of the many state ballot laws which have been enacted to make the two-party system impregnable, and which now deny to independent voters and minority groups the fundamental right of free political expression.

Moral Issues Supreme:

Moral and spiritual considerations, as well as economic should determine national policies. Therefore, we pledge to give them first place. To this end we will strengthen and enforce laws against gambling, narcotics, and commercialized vice now so openly violated and nullified by inaction of the parties in power.

Preventing Juvenile Delinquency:

In the interests of the moral well-being of children, youth, and the public, we urge the necessity of higher standards of decency in the enactment and enforcement of laws concerning the radio, moving pictures, literature and the stage. Since the motion pictures and the radio have become such powerful factors in the character formation of our youth, we pledge that all public officials concerned will enforce adequate laws to prevent obscenity, profanity and education tending to crime as now current in movie and radio. As a fundamental protection for youth, we will strengthen the teaching of moral precepts in the public schools and will establish and effectively enforce in the public school system scientific education on alcohol and other narcotics.

A Party of Service, Not Spoils:

The two dominant parties are committed to the spoils system and when in office have prostituted governmental power to serve their own selfish party interests instead of the whole people. That system has led to excessive government expenditures, high taxes, and a scandalous alliance of crime with politics. We pledge ourselves to an honest, efficient and economical administration.

Social Security and Old Age Pensions:

We will extend the Social Security Act so as not to exclude any groups from its provisions, and will include a system of insurance for all aged persons, and administer it so as to preserve the incentives of initiative and thrift.

Co-operatives:

Co-operative and profit sharing enterprises are a natural outgrowth of democracy. Government under our administration will encourage such enterprises.

Labor and Capital:

We commend organized labor for its constructive contributions to the general welfare, but steps should be taken to protect labor unions from invasion and exploitation by racketeers. We would require unions to keep their records open to members and to government inspection and to file periodic financial reports, the same as corporations.

Because we stand for Industrial Peace and National Security, we believe the time has come for the Government to assume responsibility for the protection of itself and the public against the waste and terror of industrial warfare, and to that end we will enact and enforce legislation granting and defining the rights of labor to bargain individually or collectively, to negotiate, arbitrate and to establish courts of industrial relations as the final tribunal for all industrial disputes, which will seek for both labor and employing capital equal justice, and to the nation and the general public protection against the paralysis of industry due to their warfare.

Presidential Term:

American traditions will be best served by limiting the presidential office to a single term of six years.

Church and State:

The Constitutional separation of Church and State must be maintained. We will not tax church or religious activities. This, however, should not exempt individuals engaged in religious work who, as citizens, are subject to taxation.

Crime:

We seek to diminish crime, first by suppressing the traffic in alcoholic beverages and other narcotics which pervert the people; second, by bringing about a realignment of politics which shall unite the moral-minded citizens and overcome the alliance of the underworld with the political machines; third, by effective enforcement of the law; and fourth, by the general adoption of those systems of judicial procedure which have proved most efficient and progressive.

Monopoly:

Monopolies have not ceased to exist but have become an increasing public evil. Government under our administration, in order to safeguard the rights of the common citizen, will be alert to prevent combinations of trade or of wealth which would monopolize any branch of industry or our natural resources.

No Racial Discrimination:

Recognizing that God created of one blood all nations to dwell upon the face of the earth, we declare in favor of full justice and equal opportunity for all people, whatever their religion; racial or national origin.

Agriculture:

Believing that more people should be attracted to agriculture we favor an equitable, stable price structure for farm products. We will develop a sound program for the maintenance of individual ownership of farms.

Marriage and Divorce:

To maintain the sanctity of the home we favor the enactment of uniform marriage and divorce laws.

Freedom in Fact:

It is falsely said we should not criticize the administration in time of War. We do not need less criticism in time of War, but more. It is to be hoped such criticisms will be constructive, but better unfair attack than autocratic repression. HONESTY AND COMPETENCE REQUIRE NO SHIELD OF SECRECY, nor need fear criticism, dishonesty and fraud. Those who would usurp our rights while paying lip service to our ideals should not be shielded from it.

Domestic Post-War Problems:

The nation must accept responsibility for an adequate national program to provide opportunity for employment in suitable and satisfactory occupations not only for all men and women in the military service but also those civilians who have been employed in discontinued war industries. This program should provide special training for the disabled and unskilled. We plege ourselves to utilize the services of public-spirited men and women representing labor, industry, and the general public, to join in a thorough-going honest effort to work out a solution of this complex problem.

World Co-operation:
Recognizing the supreme challenge and opportunity which confronts America to help secure a more just and permanent peace following this War, we insist upon preparation for that responsibility by setting up righteous standards which will guarantee to all people more equal opportunities and the rights to life, liberty, and the pursuit of happiness. To this end we advocate constructive co-operation and collaboration with all nations in some form of world organization but military alliance with none.

True Use of the Ballot:
We pledge our support to the original purpose of the ballot, which is to register the individual voter's conviction on principle, and not merely to elect persons to office. We recognize church leaders, pastors, church officials, members and editors of Christian literature as very influential on behalf of higher standards of political action, and we urge them to recognize and teach the true use of the ballot for principle. We urge them to unite in this party, which upholds righteousness as implied in the Ten Great Commandments and the Golden Rule.

The Liquor Problem:
Right thinking people are alarmed at the rapidly growing peril of the liquor power as now manifested:

1. Inflicting the alcoholic appetite upon millions of girls and women.
2. In multiplying juvenile delinquency.
3. In increasing gambling, vice and all kinds of crime.
4. In combating the efforts of the church and other moral forces.
5. In dominating our great organs of public opinion.
6. In subjecting political leaders and parties to its control.
7. In delaying, if not endangering, the success of our war effort.

The re-legalizing of the liquor traffic has brought about the worst moral reaction of modern times. Present conditions are due directly to the action of Government in restoring the liquor power through repeal of the Eighteenth Amendment, and repeal was due directly to the platform pledges of both the old parties in the 1932 presidential campaign.

Of all the wrongs committed by Government none has been worse than the authorizing of the liquor traffic to degenerate our own citizenship.

There is no higher duty of Government than to overcome the forces of evil. This cannot be done by political parties who are subservient to liquor votes. Parties dependent upon wet support are incapable of furnishing a solution.

We urge the realignment of voters and the union of good citizens in a political party not dependent upon the liquor traffic for votes. The Prohibition Party is that party.

APPENDIX D

A political party committed to prohibition (as a party principle) is the only adequate method for marshalling the agencies of Government to overcome the liquor power.

We urge all good citizens who believe in these principles, to cast their votes for them by supporting with their ballots this progressive program of government.

Appendix E

Edward A. Teichert's Speech on the Mutual Network, Nov. 4, 1944

Friends, Fellow Workers and All Other Forward-Looking Citizens:

Suppose by some magic that you could look into the future. And that you could see this country of ours as it will be five, ten or fifteen years from now. Suppose this is what you saw:

A nation plagued, on the one hand, by mass poverty and unemployment, and, on the other hand, by stores and warehouses filled to overflowing with unsold commodities.

If this somber picture strikes a responsive chord and recalls to your mind familiar scenes of the nineteen-thirties, let me point out some possible slight differences. The millions of jobless workers may not be as desperate as they were in the thirties. Although they do not look very happy or robust, perhaps reforms have made enforced idleness less terrifying than it was in the days of the breadlines during Coolidge and Hoover. Perhaps unemployed workers who are sick receive free medical care. Maybe expectant mothers get maternity benefits. Maybe the aged manage to starve "decently" on old-age pensions. And perhaps unemployment insurance somehow enables idle workers to keep body and soul together — for a while anyway. Finally, the monotony of enforced idleness may be broken for some of the unemployed by an occasional job in public works.

Rosiest Picture Possible

Even with the reforms, this isn't a very a very pretty picture, is it? But note this: Even at the very best, it is the rosiest picture conceivable of this country five, ten or fifteen years from now *if we keep the capitalist system!*

The well-informed person knows that it is not an accurate picture. The situation in all probability will be much worse than the one I have painted.

One important thing I have left out. With mass unemployment the competition for jobs is intensified. And competition for jobs makes the social soil fertile for racial strife, for anti-Semitism, and for all the other evils spawned by the capitalist system of dog-eat-dog.

Watch Out For Booby-Traps!

Do you doubt this? Then I shall prove it. I shall show you that we can add up the score now; that it isn't necessary for us to wait for capitalism to reenact the dreadful tragedies of the past. I shall do this by exposing the promises of the politicians and capitalist spokesmen as so many booby-

APPENDIX E

traps.

But I shall do more than that; I shall show you that we can avert the calamity of postwar unemployment, and, with it, racial strife and strife between classes and nations. I shall ask you to grant *one* point, to accept *one* premise. I shall ask you to concede that we have all the material requirements, the machines, the resources, and technical "know-how" to make this land of ours a veritable paradise. If you concede this — and you can scarcely dispute it in view of our demonstrated capacity to produce for war — then I am positive that I can convince you of the imperious necessity to abolish capitalism, and to reconstruct our society along Socialist lines.

First, let's take up some of these-booby-traps.

The Produce-More-Have-More Booby Trap

There is scarcely a bankers' meeting, or a Chamber of Commerce or manufacturers' convention, at which some stuffed shirt does not get up to say that if we are to have full employment and high wage levels, we must increase our productivity. "To have more, we must have more to divide," is the way he usually puts it. In other words, we must be patient and wait for technological improvements that will increase our output per man before expecting wage increases.

Do you believe this? Then let me show you what actually happens under capitalism as technology improves.

When a worker takes a job, he is really selling his labor power. Labor power is a commodity. As Abraham Lincoln put it: "Labor is like any other commodity in the market; increase the demand for it and you increase the price of it." By the same token when you decrease the demand for labor, wages or the price of labor power, fall.

The Iron Bouncer

Now what actually happens when new and improved machines are installed? What happens is this: The iron bouncer comes in one door and workers are kicked out of another. The workers, thus displaced, join the army of unemployed.

But what about workers who are lucky enough to keep their jobs?

With the new machine their output may be doubled, or tripled. Do their wages go up proportionately? You know better. It's with labor as it is with pork chops. When there are too many hogs on the market, the price of pork chops goes down. And when there are too many workers on the labor market, wages go down.

The new machine, instead of bringing higher standards to the workers — even to those workers lucky enough to keep their jobs — only adds to the surplus of labor in the labor market, a surplus which exerts a downward pull on wages.

But fully to appreciate the fraudulence of the claim that "to have more of the good things of life, we must have more to divide," we have only to recall the thirties. If the capitalists who give us this song and dance and who now pretend to be so solicitous of our welfare, are so anxious to divide the abundance with the workers, why didn't do some dividing then?

Why, instead of dividing, did they dump food in the ocean, burn it and plow it under? Why did they deliberately curtail production? Why? *Why? WHY?*

The idea that we can enjoy a more abundant life under capitalism by increasing out output is a falsification of the economic facts. It is a booby-trap. Watch out for it.

The Low-Prices-High-Wages Booby-Trap

Then there is another booby-trap to watch out for. Our swivel-chair labor leaders in both the American Federation of Labor and the C.I.O. spend much of their time these days speaking to employer groups, and telling employers that the secret of prosperity is increased purchasing power through higher wages. They try very hard, as Mr. James Carey, of the C.I.O. did a week or two ago before the silk-stocking audience at the Herald Tribune Forum, to convinced the capitalists that raising wages is in the capitalists' own interests.

I don't know how the rest of you felt about Mr. Carey's proposal, but it struck me as very funny, and also very stupid. If there is one thing you can't accuse our employers of, it is overlooking any bet to enhance their own material interests.

Workers as Customers and as Producers

But there is at least an element of validity in the labor leaders' argument. Moreover, the employers see it. They admit that higher wages would increase consumption somewhat, raise employment, and otherwise, in some measure, help to create tolerable conditions. Their big difficulty is how to put the theory into practice.

For example: A piano manufacturer would like every worker in the country to have the money to buy a baby grand piano — *except the workers who make them!* These are the workers he exploits directly, and if he raises their wages he reduces his own profits. It's like dividing an apple — if you make one-half larger, the other half must be smaller. The result is that he, and all other capitalists, do everything they can to keep the workers' stomachs permanently in the vicinity of their backbones.

Make no mistake about it. Our own so-called labor leaders are helping to set the booby-traps in which we're supposed to let ourselves get caught. That shrewd industrialist, the late Mark Hanna, was right when he called them the "labor lieutenants of the capitalist class."

Booby-Trap Loaded with Blood and Tragedy

Now for the third booby-trap, and the most sinister of them all.

With increased frequency of late we have been told that "full employment" rests on our ability to export the surpluses into foreign markets. As Mr. Henry Wallace puts it: "I am convinced that if we are to have full employment we must have five or ten years of exports in a big way."

Now, we do not deny that if the capitalists can sell in foreign markets all the workers produce, but can't buy back, we *will* have full employment.

APPENDIX E

But they couldn't see the surplus abroad before the war; how can they possibly sell the immensely greater surplus after the war? We do not doubt that they will try. So will the capitalists of all the other nations who are in a similar predicament. And what does this mean? It means hot, bitter trade rivalry, and, ultimately, a third world war.

Watch out for the full-employment-based-on-exports booby-trap. It is loaded with blood and tragedy for the working class, and for humanity.

Dewey in the Free Enterprise Clouds

Have the politicians a solution for postwar unemployment? Mr. Dewey hasn't. Mr. Dewey has resolutely closed his eyes to the appalling consequences of capitalism. Planting both feet firmly in the "free enterprise" clouds, Mr. Dewey charms us with glowing forecasts based on the alleged backlog of peacetime business. We shall need a million homes a year, he says, six million vacuum cleaners, and so on.

The figures are exciting — at first blush. But let us examine them more closely. Let us ask: What do these figures mean when translated into actual jobs? A correspondent to the *New York Times*, of September 13, did just that. He broke Mr. Dewey's figures down into jobs. And this is what he discovered:

"Using prewar conversion figures of the average number of man-hours consumed in industry to manufacture these items, such as about five thousand man-hours per home, six hundred man-hours per automobile, fifty man-hours per vacuum cleaner, etc., the total comes to about eleven billion man-hours or five million man-years." In other words, Governor Dewey's list of immediate postwar needs will provide jobs for only five million workers for one year — less than half the number of workers now in the armed services! Of such stuff is Republican prosperity made!

Roosevelt's "Plans" for Full Employment

Then, what of the Democrats! Has Mr. Roosevelt a solution to postwar unemployment? Several days ago Mr. Roosevelt wrote a letter in which he said: "Our plans call for full employment."

What plans? Have *you* seen any plans? Has *anyone* seen any plans?

The only plans we have seen are plans to put our youth in compulsory peacetime military service for a year. Is *this* a solution to unemployment?

Another of Mr. Roosevelt's plans, which we have been vouchsafed the opportunity to see, calls for a vast road-building program. Is *this* a solution?

And still another is Senator Wagner's bill to extend so-called social security. Is *this* a solution? To us it looks less like a solution to unemployment than it does an attempt to appease the unemployed. The fact is, these plans are based on the expectation that there *will* be vast unemployment in the postwar world, and the best way to hold unrest in check is to make certain that the unemployed have at least the minimum requirements for life.

Hedging on the "Full Employment" Promise

Senator Wagner, and other politicians, in their overzealous attempts to catch votes, are making the flat promise of "full employment." But it is noteworthy that when Mr. Roosevelt's most ardent campaigner, the discarded Vice President, Henry Wallace, spoke of the subject in New York, September 30, he said:

"I don't say Roosevelt will give you full employment, but he will come a lot closer to it than the other candidate."

Suppose he can. Suppose there would be twenty million unemployed under Mr. Dewey and only fifteen million unemployed under Mr. Roosevelt. Is this a reason to support capitalism, and the candidates of capitalism?

Big Business Thinks Jobs-for-All Impractical

Now let's turn our attention to big business. Does big business have a solution to unemployment? Why, big business *anticipates* unemployment after the war. Moreover, big business regards a surplus army of jobless workers as both desirable and necessary. In a pamphlet, written for the National Manufacturers Association, Mr. Paul G. Hoffman, president of the Studebaker Corporation and chairman of the Committee for Economic Development, says:

"I don't believe it is even socially desirable to have jobs for every man or woman who may want a job."

To those who know how capitalism works it is quite obvious that what Mr. Hoffman means is that it is a good thing, for the capitalists, when there is a surplus of workers, for a surplus of workers depresses wages, and supplies a ready reserve of exploitable labor.

We repeat: Big business wants a surplus of workers. As the conservative capitalist journal, *Business Week*, coldly observes: "Ten million unemployed scarcely means the return of paralyzing depression."

And there you have it! Prosperity and mass unemployment, both at the same time!

Something to Ponder

Of course! It's childish to imagine that the leopard of capitalism can change his spots. Business just isn't run for the purpose of giving workers jobs. This is the way Mr. Sewell L. Avery, the head of Montgomery Ward & Company, put it. "A corporation's efficiency," said Mr. Avery, "is indicated by the number of men it can *release* from a job, not by the number of men hired." Anyone afflicted with utopian notions about full employment under capitalism would do well to ponder Mr. Avery's words soberly, very soberly, indeed.

The hard fact is that as long as we have the capitalist cause we shall have the capitalist effects. And whether the administration be Republican or Democratic, it must inevitably turn to public works and unemployment insurance to appease the workers and prolong the rule of private property.

Add Up the Score Now!

Why should it always be that we awaken too late? Why can't we add up the score now? The fundamental contradiction gnawing at the vitals of capitalism — the fact that the workers receive in wages only a fraction of their product — resulted in prewar surpluses, and in idle factories and idle men. That the same cause will produce the same effect is as plain as the sum of two-plus-two. Then, why should we blind ourselves to common logic?

Why not come right to the point and admit that capitalism belongs with feudalism and chattel slavery — in the ash-barrel of history. That if progress is to be the law of the future as it has been of the past, we must abolish this insane system and build a society in which the industries are owned collectively, managed democratically, and in which production is carried on for use?

The Socialist Labor Party appeals to you in this campaign to get yourself out of the vicious circle of capitalist-implanted habits of thought. Under a system of collective ownership of the socially operated industries, and production for use, there can be no such thing as unemployment. There can be no such thing as industrial stagnation, or involuntary poverty. When the workers own the industries collectively and run them democratically through Industrial Union councils, new machines, instead of kicking workers out of jobs, will kick hours out of the working day. Nor will there be racial friction in this new and infinitely better world. For when the workers receive the full product of their labor, living standards will rise until everyone will have the necessities and comforts enjoyed exclusively by the wealthy class today. There will be jobs for all under Socialism! It will be the more the merrier! Where there is no economic fear and no competition for jobs, race prejudice and anti-Semitism vanish along with the strife upon which prejudice feeds.

Goal of Socialism

The goal of the Socialist Labor Party is the Industrial Republic of Labor — a completely free and democratic system based on common ownership of the industries and industrial representation. We shall elect our foremen in the shop, our management committees in the factory, and our representatives to an Industrial Congress to take the place of the present productively useless political Congress. Its duties will be the simple ones of administering production to the end that a maximum of the good things of life are produced with a minimum of human effort — giving us leisure in which to live, laugh and learn.

How to Get There

It is up to us to bring to birth this new and happy world. No one will do it for us. Repudiate the barbarous social system that exploits the mass of useful producers for the benefit of the few We must unite politically under the banner of the Socialist Labor Party, not to demand reforms such as old-age pensions, unemployment insurance, and the like, but to demand the abolition of capitalism. The Abolitionists did not ask for reforms to alleviate slavery. They demanded its abolition. The Revolutionary Fathers did not put any immediate demands in the Declaration of Independence. They insisted on unconditional surrender of the British. The Socialist Labor Party platform likewise contains but *one* demand, the unconditional surrender of capitalism, and the ticket of the Socialist Labor Party, which I have the honor to head, represents this demand, these principles. By supporting this ticket you signify your agreement with the proposition that capitalism must go and that society must be reconstructed along Socialist lines. But you signify more. In asserting your independence from capitalist opinion, you also pledge yourself to continue the struggle beyond the election and until freedom is won. For this fight *will* go on. Make no mistake about that. It will go on until the American workers unite, as a class, politically and industrially, to consummate their historic mission — politically under the banner of the Socialist Labor Party, and industrially into one big Socialist Industrial Union.

An Invincible Power

This union must be built, for the present unions, run as they are by labor lieutenants of the capitalist class, and based on acceptance of capitalism, obviously cannot do the job. The present unions are far better suited to the role of Labor Front under the industrial feudal set-up that will surely come if we leave capitalism in control of affairs.

Organized industrially, however, we wield an invincible power, capable not only of backing up the Socialist ballot by taking possession of the industries, but also prepared to run them and avert chaos and distress while the change from capitalism to Socialism is made. Moreover — and this is the important thing — the Socialist Industrial Union provides the administrative organs and framework for the Socialist government. As the thirteen colonies became the thirteen states of the United States, the industrial unions become the units of the Industrial Republic of Labor.

Workers of America! Unite With Us to Abolish Capitalism!

Workers of America! Repudiate the barbarous social system that exploits the mass of useful producers for the benefit of the few who merely own. Unite with us to demand the termination of the social system which dooms us to a lifelong tenure of wage slavery, with unemployment, poverty and wars as inseparable and ever recurrent features. Unite with us to establish the Socialist Republic of Peace, Plenty and International Fraternity!

Appendix F

1944 Presidential Election
Tuesday, Nov. 7, 1944

	Roosevelt Dem.	Dewey Rep.	Thomas Soc.	Watson Proh.
Alabama (11)	198,918	44,540	190	1,095
Arizona (4)	80,926	56,287		421
Arkansas (9)	148,965	63,551	438	
California (25)	1,988,564	1,512,965	2,515	14,770
Colorado (6)	234,331	268,731	1,977	
Connecticut (8)	435,146	390,527	5,097	
Delaware (3)	68,166	56,747	154	294
Florida (8)	339,377	143,215		
Georgia (12)	268,187	59,879		36
Idaho (4)	107,399	100,137	282	503
Illinois (28)	2,079,479	1,939,314	180	7,411
Indiana (13)	781,403	875,891	2,223	12,574
Iowa (10)	499,876	547,267	1,511	3,752
Kansas (8)	287,458	442,096	1,613	2,609
Kentucky (11)	472,589	392,448	535	2,023
Louisiana (10)	281,564	67,750	7	55
Maine (5)	140,631	155,434		
Maryland (8)	315,490	292,949		
Massachusetts (16)	1,035,296	921,350		973
Michigan (19)	1,106,899	1,084,423	4,598	6,503
Minnesota (11)	589,864	527,416	5,073	
Mississippi (9)	168,479	11,601		
Missouri (15)	807,357	761,175	1,750	1,175
Montana (4)	112,556	93,163	1,296	340
Nebraska (6)	233,246	329,880		
Nevada (3)	29,623	24,611		
New Hampshire (4)	119,663	109,916	46	
New Jersey (16)	987,874	961,335	3,358	4,255
New Mexico (4)	81,389	70,668		148
New York (47)	3,304,238	2,987,647	10,553	
No. Carolina (14)	527,399	263,155		
North Dakota (4)	100,144	118,535	943	549
Ohio (25)	1,570,763	1,582,293		

THE LOWEST EBB

Oklahoma (10)	401,549	319,424		1,663
Oregon (6)	248,635	225,365	3,785	2,362
Pennsylvania (35)	1,940,479	1,835,048	11,721	5,750
Rhode Island (4)	175,356	123,487		433
S. Carolina (8)	90,606	4,610		365
South Dakota (4)	96,711	135,362		
Tennessee (12)	308,707	200,311	792	885
Texas (23)	821,605	191,425	594	1,017
Utah (4)	150,088	97,891	340	
Vermont (3)	53,820	71,527		
Virginia (11)	242,276	145,243	417	459
Washington (8)	486,774	361,689	3,824	2,396
West Virginia (8)	392,777	322,819		
Wisconsin (12)	650,413	674,532	13,205	
Wyoming (3)	49,419	51,921		
TOTALS	**25,612,474**	**22,017,570**	**79,017**	**74,816**

Teichert, Socialist Labor Party:
California, 180; Connecticut, 1,220; Illinois, 9,677; Iowa, 193; Kentucky, 326; Maine, 335; Massachusetts, 2,780; Michigan, 1,264; Minnesota, 3,176; Missouri, 221; New Jersey, 6,939; New York, 14,352; Pennsylvania, 1,789; Virginia, 90; Washington, 1,645; Wisconsin, 1,002. Total: 45,189.

Byrd, Southern Democrat:
South Carolina, 7,799.

Smith, America First:
Michigan, 1,530; Texas, 251. Total: 1,781.

Unpledged Anti-Roosevelt Electors:
Texas Regulars, Texas, 135,439; Independent Democrat, Georgia, 3,373.

Bibliography

Abbott, Philip. *The Exemplary Presidency: Franklin D. Roosevelt and the American Political Tradition.* Amherst, MA, 1990.
Ahamed, Liaquat. *Lords of Finance: The Bankers Who Broke the World.* New York, 2009.
Alexander, Jack. "Paul McNutt: "It Would Be Kind of Nice to Be President, Wouldn't It?," *Life Magazine,* (Jan. 29, 1940).
Anderson, Jervis. *A. Philip Randolph: A Biographical Portrait.* Berkeley, 1972, 1986.
Appelbaum, Patricia Faith. *Kingdom to Commune: Protestant Pacifist Culture Between World War I and the Vietnam Era.* Chapel Hill, 2009.
Barnard, Ellsworth. *Wendell Willkie: Fighter for Freedom.* Marquette, MI, 1966.
Beld, Gordon G. and David C. McMacken. *A History of Alma College: Where Plaid and Pride Prevail.* Charleston, S.C., 2014.
Bell, Daniel. *Marxian Socialism in the United States.* Ithaca, 1996.
Bennett, Scott H. *Radical Pacifism: The War Resisters League and Gandhian Nonviolence in America, 1915-1963.* Syracuse, 2003.
Benson, Clarence H. *Techniques of a Working Church.* Whitefish, MT, 2005.
Black, Conrad. *Franklin Delano Roosevelt: Champion of Freedom.* New York, 2003.
Bornet, Vaughn Davis. *Labor Politics in a Democratic Republic: Moderation, Division, and Disruption in the Presidential Election of 1928.* Washington, D.C., 1964.
Brinkley, Alan. *Voices of Protest: Huey Long, Father Coughlin and the Great Depression.* New York, 1982.
Buchanan, Patrick J. *Churchill, Hitler, and the Unnecessary War: How Britain Lost Its Empire and the West Lost the World.* New York, 2008.
Bucki, Cecelia. *Bridgeport's Socialist New Deal, 1915-1936.* Urbana, IL, 2001.
Buhle, Mari Jo, Paul Buhle, and Dan Georgakas, Editors. *Encyclopedia of the American Left.* Urbana and Chicago, 1992.
Burleigh, Nina. *A Very Private Woman: The Life and Unsolved Murder of Presidential Mistress Mary Meyer.* New York, 1998.
Burns, James MacGregor. *Roosevelt: The Soldier of Freedom.* New York, 1970.
Chafe, William H. *The Achievement of American Liberalism: The New Deal and Its Legacies.* New York, 2003.
Chomsky, Noam. *Deterring Democracy.* New York, 1992.
Clark, Norman H. *Deliver Us from Evil: An Interpretation of American Prohibition.* New York, 1976.
Clarke, Peter. *The Last Thousand Days of the British Empire: Churchill, Roosevelt, and the Birth of the Pax Americana.* New York, 2008.
Cole, Wayne S. *Senator Gerald P. Nye and American Foreign Relations.* Minneapolis, 1962.
_____. *Charles A. Lindbergh and the Battle Against American Intervention in*

World War II. New York, 1974.
Coleman, Stephen. *Daniel De Leon*. Manchester, United Kingdom, 1990.
Colvin, D. Leigh. *Prohibition in the United States: A History of the Prohibition Party and the Prohibition Movement*. New York, 1926.
Cort, John C. *Dreadful Conversions: The Making of a Catholic Socialist*. New York, 2003.
Coser, Lewis A. *Greedy Institutions: Patterns of Undivided Commitment*. New York, 1974.
Crawford, Bill. *Please Pass the Biscuits, Pappy: Pictures of Governor W. Lee 'Pappy' O'Daniel*. Austin, 2004.
Cross, Wilbur L. *Connecticut Yankee: An Autobiography*. New Haven, 1943.
Cunningham, Sean P. *Cowboy Conservatism: Texas and the Rise of the Modern Right*. Lexington, KY, 2010.
Dabney, Lewis M., Editor. *Edmund Wilson: Centennial Reflections*. Princeton, 2014.
Dalleck, Robert. *Lone Star Rising: Lyndon Johnson and His Times 1908-1960*. New York, 1991.
Delton, Jennifer A. *Making Minnesota Liberal: Civil Rights and the Transformation of the Democratic Party*. Minneapolis, 2002.
Dershowitz, Nathan. "The Socialist Labor Party," *Politics* [New York], Vol. 5, No. 3, (Summer 1948).
Doenecke, Justus D. *Storm on the Horizon: The Challenge to American Intervention, 1939-1941*. Lanham, MD, 2003.
_____. *In Danger Undaunted: The Anti-Interventionist Movement of 1940-1941 as Revealed in the Papers of the America First Committee*. Stanford, 1990.
Domhoff, G. William. *The Power Elite and the State: How Policy Is Made in America*. New York, 1990.
Dreier, Peter. *The 100 Greatest Americans of the 20th Century: A Social Justice Hall of Fame*. New York, 2012.
Dubin, Michael J. *United States Congressional Elections, 1788-1997: The Official Results*. Jefferson, N.C., 1998.
_____. *Party Affiliations in the State Legislatures: A Year by Year Summary, 1796-2006*. Jefferson, N.C., 2007.
_____. *United States Gubernatorial Elections, 1932-1952: The Official Results by State and County*. Jefferson, N.C., 2014.
Dubinsky, David and A. H. Raskin. *David Dubinsky: A Life with Labor*. New York, 1977.
Dubofsky, Melvyn and Warren R. Van Tine, Editors. *Labor Leaders in America*. Champaign, IL, 1987.
_____. *John L. Lewis: A Biography*. Urbana, IL 1986.
Durham, James C. *Norman Thomas*. New York, 1974.
Ely, Joseph B. *The American Dream*. Boston, 1944.
Erdel, Paul. "Great Preachers of the Missionary Church," *Reflections*, Vol. 9 (Spring and Fall 2007).
Fleischman, Harry. *Norman Thomas: A Biography*. New York, 1964.
Fleming, Thomas. *The New Dealers' War: F.D.R. and the War Within World War II*. New York, 2001.
Foster, William Z. *History of the Communist Party of the United States*. New

BIBLIOGRAPHY

York, 1952.

Fowler, Gene and Bill Crawford. *Border Radio: Quacks, Yodelers, Pitchmen, Psychics, and Other Amazing Broadcasters of the American Airwaves.* Austin, 2002.

Frederickson, Kari. *The Dixiecrat Revolt and the End of the Solid South, 1932-1968.* Chapel Hill, 2001.

Frum, David. *Dead Right.* New York, 1995.

Gibson, Donald. *Wealth, Power, and the Crisis of Laissez Faire Capitalism.* New York, 2011.

Gieske, Millard L. *Minnesota Farmer-Laborism: The Third-Party Alternative.* Minneapolis, 1979.

Girard, Frank and Ben Perry. *The Socialist Labor Party 1876-1991: A Short History.* Philadelphia, 1991.

Goldman, Ralph M. *The Future Catches Up: Selected Writings of Ralph M. Goldman,* Vol. II. Lincoln, NE, 2002.

Goodwin, Doris Kearns. *No Ordinary Time: Franklin & Eleanor Roosevelt: The Home Front in World War II.* New York, 1984.

Gorham, Charles. *Leader at Large: The Long and Fighting Life of Norman Thomas.* New York, 1970.

Gregory, Raymond F. *Norman Thomas: The Great Dissenter.* New York, 2008.

Hamm, Richard F. *Shaping the Eighteenth Amendment: Temperance, Reform, Legal Culture, and the Polity, 1880-1920.* Chapel Hill, 1995.

Hammond, Scott John, Robert North Roberts and Valerie A. Sulfaro. *Campaigning for President in America, 1788-2016.* Santa Barbara, 2016.

Harris, Benjamin. "The Perils of a Public Intellectual," *Journal of Social Issues,* Vol. 54, No. 1, 1998.

Haynes, John Earl. *Dubious Alliance: The Making of Minnesota's DFL Party.* Minneapolis, 1984.

Henderson, J. Paul. *Darlington Hoopes: The Political Biography of an American Socialist.* Glasgow, Scotland, U.K., 2005.

Henderson, Richard B. *Maury Maverick: A Political Biography.* Austin, 1970.

Hendrickson, Kenneth E. "Triumph and Disaster: The Reading Socialists in Power and Decline, 1932-1939, Part II," *Pennsylvania History,* Volume 40, Number 4 (October 1973).

Hiltzik, Michael. *The New Deal: A Modern History.* New York, 2011.

Janney, Peter. *Mary's Mosaic: The CIA Conspiracy to Murder John F. Kennedy, Mary Pinchot Meyer, and Their Vision for World Peace.* New York, 2013.

Jeansonne, Glen. "Gerald L. K. Smith: From Wisconsin Roots to National Notoriety," *The Wisconsin Magazine of History,* Vol. 86, Issue 2 (Winter 2002-2003).

_____. Gerald L. K. Smith: *Minister of Hate.* Baton Rouge, 1997.

_____. *Messiah of the Masses: Huey P. Long and the Great Depression.* New York, 1993.

_____. *Women of the Far Right: The Mothers' Movement and World War II.* Chicago, 1996.

Johnpoll, Bernard K. *Pacifist's Progress: Norman Thomas and the Decline of American Socialism.* Chicago, 1970.

Johnson, Curtiss S. *Raymond E. Baldwin: Connecticut Statesman.* Chester, CT,

1972.

Johnson, Donald Bruce. *The Republican Party and Wendell Willkie*. Urbana, IL, 1960.

Johnson, Frederick L. "From Leavenworth to Congress: The Improbable Journey of Francis H. Shoemaker," *Minnesota History*, Vol. 51, No. 5 (Spring 1989).

Jordan, David M. *FDR, Dewey, and the Election of 1944*. Bloomington, IN, 2011.

Josephson, Matthew. *Sidney Hillman: Statesman of American Labor*. Garden City, 1952.

Karsner, David. "The Passing of the Socialist Party," *Current History* (June 1924).

Kasparek, Jonathan. *Fighting Son: A Biography of Philip F. La Follette*. Madison, 2006.

Kauffman, Bill. *Ain't My America: The Long, Noble History of Antiwar Conservatism and Middle-American Anti-Imperialism*. New York, 2008.

_____. *America First! It's History, Culture, and Politics*. Amherst, N.Y., 1995.

Keillor, Steven J. *Hjalmar Petersen of Minnesota: The Politics of Provincial Independence*. St. Paul, 1987.

_____. "A Country Editor in Politics: Hjalmar Petersen, Minnesota Governor," *Minnesota History*, Vol. 48, No. 7 (Fall 1983).

Kenneally, James J. *A Compassionate Conservative: A Political Biography of Joseph W. Martin, Speaker of the U.S. House of Representatives*. New York, 2003.

Kennedy, Stetson. *Southern Exposure: Making the South Safe for Democracy*. Tuscaloosa, AL, 1991.

Kinzer, Stephen. *The Brothers: John Foster Dulles, Allen Dulles, and Their Secret World War*. New York, 2013.

Klehr, Harvey. *The Heyday of American Communism: The Depression Decade*. New York, 1984.

La Follette, Philip and Donald Young, Editor. *Adventures in Politics: The Memoirs of Philip La Follette*. New York, 1970.

Leuchtenburg, William E. *Franklin D. Roosevelt and the New Deal, 1932-1940*. New York, 1963.

_____. *The FDR Years: On Roosevelt and His Legacy*. New York, 1995.

_____. *The White House Looks South: Franklin D. Roosevelt, Harry S. Truman, Lyndon B. Johnson*. Baton Rouge, 2005.

Lipset, Seymour Martin and Gary Marks. *It Didn't Happen Here: Why Socialism Failed in the United States*. New York, 2001.

Lipsitz, George. *The Possessive Investment in Whiteness: How White People Profit from Identity Politics*. Philadelphia, 2006.

Lorence, James L. "Gerald J. Boileau and the Politics of Sectionalism: Dairy Interests and the New Deal, 1933-1938," *Wisconsin Magazine of History*, Vol. 71, Number 4 (Summer 1988).

Lotz, Philip Henry, Editor. *Distinguished American Jews*. Freeport, N.Y., 1970.

Luthin, Reinhard H. *American Demagogues*. Gloucester, MA, 1959.

Madison, James H., Editor. *Wendell Willkie: Hoosier Internationalist*. Bloomington, IN, 1992.

Mahl, Thomas E. *Desperate Deception: British Covert Operations in the United*

States, 1939-44. Washington, D.C., 1999.

Malloy, Sean Langdon. *Atomic Tragedy: Henry L. Stimson and the Decision to Use the Bomb Against Japan.* Ithaca, 2008.

Manchester, William. *The Glory and the Dream: A Narrative History of America 1932-1972.* New York, 1974.

Maney, Patrick J. *Young Bob: A Biography of Robert M. La Follette, Jr.* Madison, 2003.

Marable, Manning. *Race, Reform, and Rebellion: The Second Reconstruction and Beyond in Black America, 1945-2006.* Jackson, MS, 2007.

Martin, Boyd A. "The Service Vote in the Elections of 1944," *The American Political Science Review,* Vol. 39, No. 4 (Aug. 1945).

Maurer, James Hudson. *It Can Be Done: The Autobiography of James Hudson Maurer.* New York, 1938.

Mayer, George H. *The Political Career of Floyd B. Olson.* Minneapolis, 1951.

McArthur, Judith N. and Harold L. Smith. *Minnie Fisher Cunningham: A Suffragist's Life in Politics.* New York, 2003.

McCoy, Donald R. *Landon of Kansas.* Lincoln, NE, 1966.

McFarland, Keith D. *Harry H. Woodring: A Political Biography of FDR's Controversial Secretary of War.* Lawrence, KS, 1975.

McKay, Seth Shepard. *Texas Politics, 1906-1944.* Lubbock, 1952.

McNamara, Robert S. *In Retrospect: The Tragedy and Lessons of Vietnam.* New York, 1995.

McPherson, James M. *Battle Cry of Freedom: The Civil War Era.* New York, 1988.

Medoff, Rafael. *Militant Zionism in America: The Rise and Impact of the Jabotinsky Movement in the United States, 1926-1948.* Tuscaloosa, 2002.

Miller, Robert Moats. *How Shall They Hear Without a Preacher? The Life of Ernest Fremont Tittle.* Chapel Hill, 1971.

Moser, John E. *Right Turn: John T. Flynn and the Transformation of American Liberalism.* New York, 2005.

Morris, Sylvia Jukes. *Price of Fame: The Honorable Clare Boothe Luce.* New York, 2014.

Neal, Steve. *Dark Horse: A Biography of Wendell Willkie.* New York, 1984.

Nichols, John. *The "S" Word: A Short History of an American Tradition...Socialism.* Brooklyn, 2011.

Nordin, Dennis S. *The New Deal's Black Congressman: A Life of Arthur Wergs Mitchell.* Columbia, MO, 1997.

O'Brien, Steven G. and Paula McGuire. *American Political Leaders: From Colonial Times to the Present.* Santa Barbara, 1991.

Olmsted, Kathryn S. *Real Enemies: Conspiracy Theories and American Democracy, World War I to 9/11.* New York, 2009.

Olson, Lynne. *Those Angry Days: Roosevelt, Lindbergh, and America's Fight Over World War II, 1939-1941.* New York, 2013.

Ostrander, Gilman M. *The Prohibition Movement in California, 1848-1933.* Berkeley, 1957.

Ottanelli, Fraser M. *The Communist Party of the United States: From the Depression to World War II.* New Brunswick, 1991.

Parmet, Herbert S. and Marie B. Hecht. *Never Again: A President Runs for a*

Third Term. New York, 1968.
Peace, William J. *Leslie A. White: Evolution and Revolution in Anthropology*. Lincoln, NE, 2004.
Peel, Roy V. *The 1932 Campaign: An Analysis*. New York, 1935.
Peters, Charles. *Five Days in Philadelphia*. New York, 2005.
Petersen, Arnold. *Daniel De Leon: Internationalist*. New York, 1944.
_____. *Daniel De Leon: Social Scientist*. New York, 1945.
Phillips, Kevin. *American Dynasty: Aristocracy, Fortune, and the Politics of Deceit in the House of Bush*. New York, 2004.
Pietrusza, David. *1932: The Rise of Hitler and FDR—Two Tales of Politics, Betrayal, and Unlikely Destiny*. Guilford, CT, 2016.
Pleasants, Julian M. *Buncombe Bob: The Life and Times of Robert Rice Reynolds*. Chapel Hill, 2000.
Ribuffo, Leo P. *The Old Christian Right: The Protestant Far Right from the Great Depression to the Cold War*. Philadelphia, 1983.
Rice, Daniel F. *Reinhold Niebuhr and His Circle of Influence*. New York, 2013.
Richardson, Darcy G. *A Nation Divided: The 1968 Presidential Campaign*. Lincoln, NE, 2002.
_____. *Others: "Fighting Bob" La Follette and the Progressive Movement – Third-Party Politics in the 1920s*. New York, 2008.
Rising, George. *Clean for Gene: Eugene McCarthy's 1968 Presidential Campaign*. Westport, CT, 1997.
Robinson, Greg. *A Tragedy of Democracy: Japanese Confinement in North America*. New York, 2009.
Roosevelt, Elliott. *As He Saw It*. New York, 1946.
Roseboom, Eugene H. *A History of Presidential Elections: From George Washington to Richard M. Nixon*. New York, 1970.
Rosenman, Samuel I. *Working with Roosevelt*. New York, 1952.
Rosenof, Theodore. "The Political Education of an American Radical: Thomas R. Amlie in the 1930's," *Wisconsin Magazine of History*, Vol. 58, Number 1 (Autumn 1974).
Rosenstone, Robert A. *Crusade of the Left: The Lincoln Battalion in the Spanish Civil War*. New York, 1969.
Rosenstone, Steven J., Roy L. Behr and Edward H. Lazarus. *Third Parties in America: Citizen Response to Major Party Failure*. Princeton, 1984.
Ross, Jack. *The Socialist Party of America: A Complete History*. Lincoln, NE, 2015.
Rothbard, Murray N. *For a New Liberty: The Libertarian Manifesto*. Auburn, AL, 2006.
Ryan, James G. *Earl Browder: The Failure of American Communism*. Tuscaloosa, 1997.
Safire, William. *Safire's Political Dictionary*. New York, 2008.
Sarles, Ruth. *A Story of America First: The Men and Women Who Opposed U.S. Intervention in World War II*. Westport, CT, 2003.
Savage, Sean J. *Roosevelt: The Party Leader, 1932-1945*. Lexington, KY, 1991.
Schafer, Axel R. *Countercultural Conservatives: American Evangelicalism from the Postwar Revival to the New Christian Right*. Madison, 2011.
Schlesinger, Arthur M., Jr. *The Age of Roosevelt: The Politics of Upheaval*. New

York, 2003.

Schneider, James C. *Should America Go to War? The Debate over Foreign Policy in Chicago, 1939-1941*. Chapel Hill, 1991.

Seidler, Murray B. *Norman Thomas, Respectable Rebel*. Syracuse, 1967.

Seldes, George. *Facts and Fascism*. New York, 1943.

Severn, Bill. *Toward One World: The Life of Wendell Willkie*. New York, 1967.

Shannon, David A. *The Socialist Party of America*. Chicago, 1967.

Simon, Bryant. *A Fabric of Defeat: The Politics of South Carolina Millhands, 1910-1948*. Chapel Hill, 1998.

Slayton, Robert A. *Empire Statesman: The Rise and Redemption of Al Smith*. New York, 2001.

Smith, Jean Edward. *FDR*. New York, 2008.

Steward, Dwight. *Mr. Socialism, Norman Thomas: His Life and Times*. Secaucus, N.J., 1974.

Stolberg, Mary M. *Fighting Organized Crime: Politics, Justice, and the Legacy of Thomas E. Dewey*. Boston, 1995.

Storms, Roger C. *Partisan Prophets: A History of the Prohibition Party*. Denver, 1972.

Stuhler, Barbara. *Ten Men of Minnesota and American Foreign Policy*. St. Paul, 1973.

Sunstein, Cass R. *The Second Bill of Rights: FDR's Unfinished Revolution and Why We Need It More Than Ever*. New York, 2004.

Swanberg, W. A. *Norman Thomas: The Last Idealist*. New York, 1976.

Taylor, Jeff. *Politics on a Human Scale: The American Tradition of Decentralism*. Lanham, MD, 2013.

Thomas, Norman M. *Human Exploitation in the United States*. New York, 1934.

_____. *Socialism Re-Examined*. New York, 1963.

_____. "Reflections of an Old Campaigner: The Disabilities of a Third Party," *Commonweal*, Vol. 41, Issue 10, (Dec. 22, 1944).

Tyler, Gus. *Look for the Union Label: A History of the International Ladies' Garment Workers' Union*. Armonk, N.Y., 1995.

Valelly, Richard M. *Radicalism in the States: The Minnesota Farmer-Labor Party and the American Political Economy*. Chicago, 1989.

Waldman, Louis. *Labor Lawyer*. New York, 1944.

Watson, Claude A. *Repeal Has Succeeded*. Winona Lake, IN, 1945.

Wessel, David. *In Fed We Trust: Ben Bernanke's War on the Great Panic*. New York, 2009.

White, Graham and John Maze. *Henry A. Wallace: His Search for a New World Order*. Chapel Hill, 1995.

White, Ray B. *The False Christ of Communism and the Social Gospel*. Whitefish, MT, 2007.

Wilkie, Curtis. *Dixie: A Personal Odyssey Through Historic Events That Shaped the Modern South*. New York, 2001.

Williams, Mason B. *City of Ambition: FDR, La Guardia, and the Making of Modern New York*. New York, 2013.

Williams, Oscar Renal. *George S. Schuyler, Portrait of a Black Conservative*. Knoxville, TN, 2007.

Wolf, Thomas P., William D. Pederson, and Byron W. Daynes. *Franklin D. Roosevelt and Congress: The New Deal and Its Aftermath*. Armonk, N.Y., 2001.

Wunderlin, Clarence E., Jr. *Robert A. Taft: Ideas, Tradition, and Party in U.S. Foreign Policy*. Lanham, MD, 2005.

_____. *The Papers of Robert A. Taft, Volume 3, 1945-1948*. Kent, OH, 2003.

Yeadon, Glen and John Hawkins. *The Nazi Hydra in America: Suppressed History of a Century; Wall Street and the Rise of the Fourth Reich*. Joshua Tree, CA, 2008.

Zieger, Robert H. *John L. Lewis: Labor Leader*. Boston, 1988.

Zimmerman, Joseph F. *The Government and Politics of New York State*. Albany, N.Y., 2008.

Zinn, Howard. *The Zinn Reader: Writings on Disobedience and Democracy*. New York, 1997.

Zucker, Norman L. *George W. Norris: Gentle Knight of American Democracy*. Urbana, IL, 1966.

INDEX

A

Albaugh, Arla A., 365, 465, 467, 474, 485, 488-491, 493, 495, 498, 504-505, 507-508, 710
Alfange, Dean, 275, 277, 374-375, 377, 402
Allen, Devere, 112, 134, 148, 176, 273, 330, 341-344, 347-348, 351
Allred, James, v, 640, 642, 655
America First Committee, 251, 254-255, 257, 259-260, 262-263, 265, 271-272, 274, 513, 529, 533, 576
America First Party, 397, 513, 516-518, 624, 647, 71
American Commonwealth Party, 25, 163, 325
American Democratic National Committee (ADNC), iii, iv, 380, 524-531, 535, 536-537, 540-546, 550, 554-557, 559, 561-568, 570, 572-577, 600, 608, 613-614, 622, 628, 663-664
American Labor Party (ALP), x, 117, 188, 191-192, 196, 201, 208, 210-212, 226, 242-243, 250, 274-277, 298, 367-377, 380-382, 385, 400, 402, 404, 435, 507, 570, 593, 691, 708, 715-716
American Rock Party, 531, 534
Amlie, Thomas R., 163, 686-688, 692
Anderson, C. Elmer, 672
Anderson, Spencer, 334
Archer, Gleason L., iii, 528, 544-546, 550, 554-557, 559, 562, 564, 566, 568, 573, 576

B

Babson, Roger W., 218, 244, 406, 408, 412, 414, 425-426, 430-433, 707
Bailey, Josiah W., 588
Barr, John U., vi, 528, 572, 579-607, 609-610, 614
Bennard, George, 441
Benson, Elmer A., 671-674, 677-679, 681-683
Benz, Alex, 698-700
Biemiller, Andrew, 69, 323, 335-336, 717
Blake, Edward E., 409, 428
Blalock, Myron G., 633-634
Blomen, Henning A., 481
Boileau, Gerald J., 687
Boll, John C., 337
Boller, Paul F., 317-318
Borden, Joseph C., 351, 364-366, 484
Breedin, John K., 607, 613-618, 708
Bricker, John W., iv, 19, 23-24, 58, 392, 515-517, 524, 555-556, 560, 566, 613, 621, 626, 650, 656-658, 660, 664, 667
Browder, Earl, 111, 135, 169-171, 190-191, 196, 202, 205, 218, 225, 231-237, 239-241, 244, 290, 295-298, 360, 373, 419, 562, 564, 570,-571, 607, 647
Bubbert, Walter, 709
Buckley, William F., Jr., 86, 262
Budny, Stanley, 336-337
Burdick, Usher L., 712, 714-716
Burnham, Robert G., 443
Butler, George A., 637
Butterworth, John C., 478
Byrd, Harry F., Sr., iv-vi, 15-16, 58, 128, 337, 525-526, 528, 539, 554-555, 560, 577, 579, 582-599, 602-609, 613-614, 617-

618, 622-623, 627-628, 632-633, 639, 650, 655, 664-666, 708, 710

C

Carr, Elizabeth Stephens, 436, 438, 480
Carrier, Floyd C., 406-407
Chapple, John B., 394, 691
Cheney, Coleman B., 28, 47, 153, 274-277
Childs, John L., 375, 378, 380-381, 384, 387, 401-402, 411
Churchill, Winston, 17-18, 43, 247, 249, 284-288, 308, 355, 372, 418, 573, 618, 704
CIO Political Action Committee, 296-298, 359-360, 363, 369, 372, 379, 386, 400, 504, 552, 573, 626, 628, 639-640, 714-715
Claessens, August, 29, 97, 118, 158, 166, 183-184, 253-254, 382
Clement, Travers, 32, 252, 263
Colvin, D. Leigh, 99, 408, 430-431, 452, 457
Committee for Constitutional Government, 529, 530, 545
Commonwealth Party of America (Woodring), iii, 520, 522, 524
Communist Party, x, 68, 70, 111, 115, 124, 134-135, 139-140, 152, 156, 167, 170, 174, 181, 190, 196, 202, 205, 209, 218, 231-232, 234-241, 268, 276-277, 295=297, 360, 368, 373-374, 419, 431, 552, 558-559, 647, 687, 682, 691, 717
Communist Political Association, x, 296
Comstock, William A., 528, 565
Conner, Martin S. "Mike", 591-592, 600, 603, 607
Connors, Margaret, 357-363
Constitution Party (1952), 354
Coughlin, Charles E., .160-161, 164, 186, 190, 193-195, 197-198, 202, 212, 227, 348, 514, 527, 529, 532, 535, 566, 712-713, 715
Cox, William W., 478
Cozzini, Georgia, 479, 496-497
Counts, George S., 372, 375, 384
Creager, Renfro B., 648, 656-659
Cullen, Hugh R., 574, 653

D

Dabney, Virginius, 600-601
Darcy, Sam, 159, 296
Davenport, Russell W., 383-384, 390
Davey, Seth A., 440
Decker, Rutherford L., 422
DeLacy, Hugh, 717-718
Dershowitz, Nathan, 471-473
Detroit Declaration, 151-152, 169, 182, 253
Devany, John A., 716-717
Dewey, John, 38., 112, 118, 132-135
Dewey, Thomas, iii-vi, viii, 19-23, 25, 48, 51, 212, 221, 243, 277, 282-284, 290, 292, 294, 297-300, 307-310, 313-317, 320, 324, 328-330, 359-360, 378, 383, 388, 391-394, 396-397, 399-400, 402, 404, 424, 428-430, 440, 489, 492, 508, 511, 515-519, 524, 529, 533-534, 554, 556, 558, 560-561, 563-568, 570, 575, 601, 606, 613, 616, 618-619, 621-622, 625-626, 645, 650, 656-660, 662-669, 703-708, 718
Dies, Martin, 648-649
Dixon, Frank M., 525, 536, 538-539, 541, 557, 577-579, 611
Donnelly, Leo Charles, 517
Dubinsky, David, 242, 320, 368-373, 378, 383-385, 399-400, 402, 570, 607
Dulles, Allen, 256-257, 545
Dulles, John Foster, 71-73, 257
Dumbarton Oaks Conference, 285-285, 290, 299, 360, 402, 511

INDEX

E

Edwards, Wesley G., 450
Eisenhower, Dwight D., 23, 56, 58-60, 62, 64, 72-75, 81, 257, 300, 438, 477. 580, 582, 692
Ely, Joseph B., iii, 231, 355, 525, 527, 546-554, 566-567, 586, 602
Emerich, George A., 441
Emmerich, J. Oliver, 583

F

Farkas, William, 483, 503-504
Farley, James A., 15-16, 53, 169, 228, 243, 525, 531, 543, 550, 589, 604
Fish, Hamilton, 249, 254, 259, 359, 397, 519, 655, 680, 711-712
Fisher, Louis, 482
Fleischman, Harry, 25, 32, 41, 44, 49, 53, 55-56, 97-98, 103, 107-108, 135, 142, 145-146, 153, 157, 188, 191, 193, 202, 204, 220, 225, 271, 291-293, 302-303, 321, 506, 709
Flynn, John T., 251, 255-256, 261, 272, 274, 533-534, 564
Foster, William Z., 139-140, 232-233, 235, 239, 295-296, 691
Friedman, Samuel H., 29-30, 56-58, 60-61, 80, 266, 269, 275, 277, 371

G

Gannett, Frank, 529-530, 573, 575
Garrison, Robert H., 428, 439
Gehres, Albin Walter, 44
Germany, Eugene B., 539, 600, 632, 634, 639, 646, 650
Gesensway, Mary, 484-485
Gibson, Merritt H., 647-648
Ginsberg, Charles, 482-483
Goldberg, Louis P., 173, 183, 382, 404, 716-717
Goldwater, Barry M., 81-84, 354
Goodwin, Richard N., 76

Goodwin, William J., 531-536, 562, 574-575
Graham, Chester A., 28
Grove, Theos A., 484

H

Haight, Raymond L., 156
Hamilton, Leverne, 337
Harrington, Michael, 77, 80, 83
Harriss, Robert M., 528-529, 536, 539, 575
Hartmann, George W., 266-270
Hass, Eric, 61, 82, 139, 435, 467, 475, 477-478, 487, 498, 506, 511
Haydock, Earl H., 452
Hayek, Friedrich, 26-27, 514
Heisler, Francis, 25
Henry, Aaron, 78-79
Herder, Milton, 486-487
Herzel, Paul, 464-465
Hillman, Sidney, 18, 196, 218, 242, 297-298, 319, 360, 363, 367-374, 376, 379, 386, 504, 562, 564, 570-571, 573, 593, 604, 607, 609, 626, 628, 646-647, 715
Hinshaw, Virgil P., 451
Hoan, Daniel W., 94, 100, 129, 131, 141-142, 154, 187, 323, 338, 698, 700
Hoffman, Max, 375
Hofses, Raymond S., 28, 146, 200, 335, 337, 711
Holdridge, Herbert C., 294. 307, 316-317
Holmes, John Haynes, 100, 110-111, 205, 229, 240, 250, 272, 274, 313, 330
Holston, George G., 437, 440
Holtwick, Enoch A., 438, 452, 479
Hoopes, Darlington, vii, 27-30, 32, 56-62, 75, 80, 146, 176, 187, 191, 307, 310-313, 317, 319, 325, 330, 382, 709
Hoover, Herbert, 15, 23, 41, 81, 97, 99, 101, 107, 115-117, 120-122, 126-139, 132, 134, 138,

140-141, 157, 159, 161, 200, 221, 259, 289, 325, 400, 448, 457-460, 521, 547, 595, 605, 626, 637, 656, 664, 690, 693
Horvath, James C., 484
Huffman, Jasper A., 438
Hull, Cordell, 23, 273, 287, 525, 572
Hull, Merlin, 337, 715-716
Humphrey, Hubert H., 69, 71, 75, 82-85, 89-90, 670

I

Independent Party of Florida, 622-626
Isacson, Leo, 716

J

Jenkins, Joseph C., 590
Johansen, Herman A., 486
Johnson, Andrew N., 407
Johnson, Lyndon B., v, 559, 630

K

Keep America Out of War Congress (KAOWC), 206-208, 254-255, 260-261, 272, 334
Kellems, Vivien, 340, 352-354
Kelly, Bernard G., 439, 478
Kennedy, John F., 19, 75-79, 81, 83, 255-257, 292, 518, 577, 651
Killip, James A. W., 410, 433
King, James V., 716
Kirk, Russell, 318
Klobuchar, Walter J., 480
Knapp, Frank J., 639
Knappe, Edwin, 335-337, 716
Knotek, Frank J., 475-479
Kramer, James J., 592, 599-600, 602
Krueger, Maynard, 25-27, 30-31, 48, 56-57, 203, 213-214, 216, 220-221, 240-242, 271, 275, 325-326, 709

L

La Follette, Philip, 141, 258, 685-687, 690-696,
La Follette, Robert M., Jr., 141, 163, 207, 221, 683, 685, 687-688, 690, 692
La Guardia, Fiorello H., 21, 40, 103-110, 116-118, 152, 167, 210-211, 220, 266-270, 309, 315, 372-373, 400, 529, 532, 534, 687, 689-691
Laidler, Harry W., 35, 135, 159, 173, 184, 186, 201, 212, 368, 375, 382
Landon, Alf, 15, 188, 197, 231, 234, 390, 398, 524, 550, 688
Langer, William, 69, 291, 429, 711-712, 714-715
Laski, Harold J., 322-323
Latham, Sidney, 641-642, 644, 647, 655
League for Industrial Democracy, 35, 67, 121, 135, 143, 159, 183, 195, 206, 273, 382
Leeke, Granville B., 438
Lemke, William, 193, 195-198, 200-202, 244, 687-688, 694, 712, 715
Lewis, John L., 18, 196, 206, 218, 229, 234, 242, 258, 520, 690
Liberal Party, x-xii, 80, 91, 183, 298, 367-368, 374-387, 399-405, 435, 523, 570, 702, 708, 716-717
Lindbergh, Charles A., 249, 256-258, 260, 262-265, 268-269, 321, 515-516, 534
Long, Huey P., 16, 161-166, 194, 228, 356, 399, 446, 514-515, 556, 584, 693
Loomis, Orland S., 683, 696-698
Luce, Clare Boothe, 213, 285, 347, 349, 352-364, 519
Lucey, John F., 657-658, 664
Lundeen, Ernest, 162, 259, 675-677
Lundeen, Norma, 675-681

INDEX

M

Maassen, Adolph, 337
MacArthur, Douglas, 19, 24, 354, 392, 394, 411-413, 515
Mackay, Joseph, 483
Marcantonio, Vito, 162, 250, 275, 372, 717
Marret, Yona M., 478-479
Maurer, James H., 94, 96-97, 100, 129-130, 140, 149, 174, 177, 192
Mayhew, Stanley, 337, 351, 361, 363
McCarthy, Eugene J., 75, 82, 89-90, 93, 221, 547, 675
McCarthy, Joseph R., 58, 61, 67-68, 71-73, 314, 334, 394, 479. 536, 566, 692, 699, 707
McCloy, John J., 291-292
McCormick, Robert R., 67, 255, 359, 394, 399, 515
McDonald, James E., 531, 662
McGlue, Charles H., 546, 561, 566-567
McGregor, Temple H., 651
McLeod, Scott, 71-73
McLevy, Jasper, 50-51, 177, 181, 186, 191, 307, 312-313, 332, 338-347, 349-352, 363-366, 711
McNutt, Paul V., 16
Miller, Charles R., 442
Minnesota Farmer-Labor Party, iii, 131, 162, 530, 670-684, 688, 690, 696
Moody, Dan, v, 606-607, 632, 636-637, 642, 652
Moore, Ralph, 613
Morris, Sam, 408, 428, 647
Munn, E. Harold, 441
Murray, Elizabeth C., 337
Murray, Philip, 18, 319, 604

N

Nalle, I. Beverly, 623, 626
Nationalist Party, 515
Nelson, George A., 186, 338, 344, 698
Niebuhr, Reinhold, 51, 100, 112, 147, 173, 252, 288-289, 298, 378-379
Nielson-Lange, Johannes, 451
Nixon, Richard M., 72, 75, 90, 450, 477, 518
Nonpartisan League, 193, 429, 690, 711-712, 714-715
Nooney, Ruth, 604-606, 623
Norris, George W., 132-133, 400, 689
Nye, Gerald P., 198, 250-251, 254-255, 258, 263, 399, 515, 522, 533-534, 655, 711-715

O

Olson, Helen, 483
Olson, O. Alfred, 483
O'Brian, Robert E., 528-529, 542, 561-562, 613
O'Connor, John J., iii, 379-380, 527-528, 541, 544-545, 556, 559-561, 563-565, 570-572, 628-629, 663, 693
O'Daniel, W. Lee "Pappy," iii, v, 526, 529, 531, 540, 558-559, 562-563, 573-576, 617, 622, 630, 649-656, 659-663, 669
Orange, Aaron M., 140, 277, 489
Osburn, Charles R., 442

P

Paine, George Lyman, 338
Palmer, Charles, 438, 476
Parrish, Hollis B., 440
Parrish, Richard, 79-80
Patman, Wright, 638, 641
Petersen, Arnold, 196, 467-471, 473-474, 476, 479-480, 499
Pinchot, Amos, 255-256
Pinchot, Gifford, 386, 456
Pirincin, Joseph A., 475, 510
Prentis, Henning W., Jr., 330-331
Progressive Party of Wisconsin, iii, 163, 333, 336-337, 683-700, 711, 715-717

Prohibition Party, viii, 24, 61, 99, 306, 324, 406-408, 410-413, 415, 419-422, 424-433, 435-438, 440-443, 450-452, 456-459, 462, 476, 479-481, 490, 624, 707

Q

Quinn, John P., 475, 477, 492, 493

R

Randall, Charles Hiram, 408, 451-463
Randolph, A. Philip, 27-29, 43, 48, 65, 79, 210, 214, 314, 335, 375, 578
Rankin, Jeannette, 318
Rayburn, Sam, 545, 604, 651-652
Reed, James A., 128, 453, 528, 548
Regnery, Henry, 529, 576
Renfro, Connie C., 593, 639-640, 642-643, 646
Reynolds, Dallas McCord, 487
Reynolds, Robert R., 515-516
Rickenbacker, Eddie, 255, 515
Riger, Morris, 335
Robb, Clarke T., 337
Roberts, Ray C., 334, 437
Rockefeller, Nelson A., 76-77, 80
Romer, Henry A., 517
Roosevelt, Elliott, 18
Roosevelt, Eleanor, xi, 34, 52, 75, 383, 421, 484, 526
Roosevelt, Franklin D., ii-xi, 13-22, 25, 28, 31, 40-44, 46, 52-53, 61, 75, 82, 91, 121, 123, 125-127, 131-134, 137-141, 144-145, 155, 157-158, 160-161, 165, 167-168, 174, 179-180, 186, 188-191, 193-194, 196-202, 204, 206-207, 212-213, 217-219, 222-231, 234, 237, 240-246, 248-261, 264-269, 273-274, 276, 279, 281-294, 296-300, 307-310, 313, 315-320, 324-330, 336-337, 342, 355-357, 359-360, 362-363, 367-368, 371-372, 374-375, 377-380, 382-383, 385-386, 388, 390-391, 393, 397, 399-404, 410, 417, 422, 424, 427-428, 432, 437, 440, 448-449, 451, 456, 461, 466, 482, 486, 492, 502, 507, 510-511, 515, 517-522, 524-528, 530-532, 534, 536-551, 553-559, 561-577, 584-586, 588-591, 593-661, 664-669, 682-683, 685-708, 713
Roosevelt, Franklin D., Jr., 91, 400
Root, E. Tallmadge, 439
Rose, Alex, 242, 371, 373, 378, 381, 384, 401, 690
Rosenman, Samuel I., 17, 138, 292, 386

S

Salzman, Jacob A., 716
Sanderford, Roy, 635, 647, 649, 656
Sauthoff, Harry, 333, 698-699, 711, 715
Schnur, Frank, 478-479
Schuyler, George S., 313-316, 330
Scopes, John T., 147-148, 412
Seay, Harry L., 639, 641, 645, 663
Seldes, George, 207, 363-364
Sheldon, George L., 629
Shipstead, Henrik, 131, 259, 676-677, 713
Shuler, Robert P., 443-451
Sim, James, 483
Sinatra, Frank, 403
Sinclair, Upton, 65, 154, 163, 167
Small, Clint C., 632, 651
Smith, Al, 98-100, 102, 110, 116, 126-127, 132, 200, 231, 400, 457, 530, 547-550, 589, 595, 605, 626, 637
Smith, Ellison D. "Cotton Ed," 584, 611-613
Smith, Gerald L. K., 193-194, 197, 263, 359, 397-398, 411, 513-515, 517-518, 624, 647, 656, 711

INDEX

Smith, Tucker, P., 28, 51
Smith v. Allwright, iv, 631, 634
Socialist Industrial Union, ix, 465-466, 468, 485
Socialist Labor Party (SLP), ix-x, 61, 82-83, 139-140, 196, 202, 231, 277, 290, 307, 324, 351, 364-366, 371, 375-376, 380-381, 431, 435, 436, 439, 464-512, 692, 705, 710-711
Socialist Party, i-ii, vi, viii, 14, 24-25, 27-31, 35-36, 39-41, 46-48, 55-59, 61, 64, 71, 75, 77, 79-83, 93-94, 96-99, 101, 111, 113, 115, 119, 122, 129-130, 132-133, 135, 138, 139, 140-147, 149, 152-157, 159, 162-166, 168, 170-171, 174-175, 177-182, 184, 186-193, 196, 199-201, 203-204, 208-210, 212-216, 219, 223, 231-233, 236, 239, 241-242, 245, 252-253, 263, 265-268, 274-277, 279, 281, 291, 293, 295, 298, 303-307, 312, 314-318, 321-325, 327, 330, 332-334, 336, 338, 341, 343-346, 350, 355, 357, 361, 364-365, 367-368, 375-376, 381-382, 425, 431, 435-437, 442, 449, 473, 475, 484, 489, 494, 496, 501-504, 506, 508-510, 551-552, 688, 711, 713, 717-718
Sokolsky, George, 76, 411, 707
Southern Democratic Party, 538-539, 589, 607, 613-614, 618
Sparks, C. Nelson, 392-393
Stambaugh, Lynn U., 711, 714-715
Stassen, Harold E., 19, 51, 73, 93, 383, 393-395, 671-677, 681-683
Steiner, Herbert, 480
Steinhilber, Walter, 483
Stevenson, Adlai, 57-58, 60, 75, 438, 477, 547, 580, 582
Stevenson, Coke, 539, 634-637, 665
Stimson, Henry L., 291, 329, 422, 521

Storm, Charles E., 483
Strutz, Alvin C., 711
Stump, J. Henry, 28, 30, 332, 476
Sulston, Josephine B., 436-437
Sweeney, John E., 509
Sweeney, Martin, 564
Swope, Gerard B., 122

T

Taft, Robert A., 19, 22-23, 59-61, 69, 259, 261, 392, 397, 533, 535-536, 576
Talmadge, Eugene, 58, 559, 611, 620-621
Taylor, George S., 481-482
Teichert, Edward A., ix, x, xii, 290, 324, 365, 380, 465, 467, 474-475, 488-508, 510-513, 705-705. 710-711
Texas Regulars, iv, 539, 594, 611, 630-631, 633-634, 646-669, 708
Thomas, Evan, 270-271, 497
Thomas, Norman M., i-ii, vi-viii, xii, 14, 16, 24-32, 34-69, 71-92, 94-116, 119-124, 129-149, 151-160, 162-225, 230-232, 240-263, 265-304, 307-332, 334, 338, 342-346, 348, 365-367, 370, 375, 377-378, 380, 401, 489-490, 496, 501-504, 513, 518, 525, 545, 551,-552, 554, 558, 578, 582, 688, 691, 698, 703, 705, 707, 709-711, 713, 717-719
Thomas, Violet, 36, 48, 54, 109, 111, 156, 183, 243, 270-271, 302-303
Thompson, Carl W., 437
Thompson, Dorothy, 52, 228, 260
Thurmond, J. Strom, vi, 51, 61, 401, 489, 579-580, 582, 605, 665
Tittle, Ernest Fremont, 318-319
Tobin, Daniel J., 53-54, 321
Tomsich, Mario B., 332-333
Townley, Arthur C., 197, 714
Townsend, Francis, 163, 193-195, 197, 675, 692

Truman, Harry S., 16, 18, 44, 46, 49, 51, 68-70, 81, 221, 243, 310, 379-380, 382, 400, 402-403, 489, 554, 559, 565, 573, 580, 604, 608, 611, 617, 622, 626, 628-629, 633, 637-638, 644, 654, 660, 666
Tugwell, Rexford G., 386-387
Tyler, Gus, 208, 252, 385

U

Union for Democratic Socialism, 64-67
Uphoff, Walter H., 32, 333
Upshaw, William, 408, 430
Upton, Upton A., 479

V

Van Essen, William J., 148-149, 181, 187
Varney, William F., 408-409, 458
Viereck, George, 678-679
Villard, Oswald Garrison, 37, 101. 112, 133, 207, 255, 272

W

Waldman, Louis, 94, 100, 110, 113, 135, 149, 153, 169, 171-184, 187-190, 252-253
Wallace, Henry A., 16-18, 46-51, 53-54, 135, 160, 179, 205, 226-229, 297, 319, 362, 378-380, 401-403, 420, 489, 530, 561, 591, 602, 604, 606, 681, 687, 694, 716, 718
Waters, Agnes, 446, 449, 517-519, 710

Watson, Claude A., viii-ix, xii, 24, 307, 324, 406, 408-409, 412-432, 439-441, 490, 513, 620, 706, 710
Waybright, Edgar W., 605, 622, 625
Weber, Henry P., 470
Weiner, Max, 239
Wells, John Mason, 441
Wettstein, Louis P., 480, 509
Wheeler, Burton K., 219, 230, 250, 255, 258, 263, 397, 456, 515, 520, 533-534, 690, 713
Wheeler, Eva C., 462
White, Leslie A., 487
Whitehead, Carle, 334
Wiggert, Adolf, 478, 495-496
Willkie, Wendell L., xi, 13, 15, 19, 23, 54, 217, 221-230, 237, 240-245, 248-249, 259, 276, 308, 314, 324, 363, 367, 383-402, 420, 480, 513, 515, 523, 529, 532, 545, 550, 564-565, 593, 602, 619-620, 626, 632, 667, 702-703, 707-708
Wilson, Edmund, 319
Wilson, Willis R., 438
Wolf, Nathan, 270
Woodring, Harry H., iii, 520-530, 536-544, 546, 550, 577, 579, 585-586, 612-613, 664

Y

Yeater, Waldo E., 437

Z

Zahnd, John, 438, 517
Zeidler, Frank P., 77, 336, 382, 696

www.ingramcontent.com/pod-product-compliance
Lightning Source LLC
Chambersburg PA
CBHW071054230426
43666CB00009B/1710